Rise to Greatness

RISE TO
GREATNESS

*The History of Canada
from the Vikings to the Present*

CONRAD
BLACK

McCLELLAND & STEWART

LIBRARY AND ARCHIVES CANADA CATALOGUING IN PUBLICATION

Black, Conrad, author
Rise to greatness : the history of Canada from the Vikings to the present / Conrad Black.

Includes bibliographical references and index.
Issued in print and electronic formats.

ISBN 978-0-7710-1354-6 (bound). – ISBN 978-0-7710-1355-3 (html)

1. Canada – History. I. Title.

FC165.B53 2014   971   C2014-904644-8
C2014-904645-6

Published simultaneously in the United States of America by
McClelland & Stewart, a division of Random House of Canada Limited

Library of Congress Control Number: 2014944153

Every effort has been made to trace copyright holders and to obtain their permission
for use of copyrighted material.

The excerpt from "Canada: Case History: 1945" by Earle Birney is taken
from One Muddy Hand: Selected Poems, Harbour Publishing, 2006,
www.harbourpublishing.com. Reprinted by permission.

The poem "W.L.M.K." by F.R. Scott has been reprinted with the permission
of William Toye, literary executor for the estate of F.R. Scott.

Typeset in Electra by M&S, Toronto

Cover and text design by CS Richardson

Printed and bound in the United States of America

McClelland & Stewart,
a division of Random House of Canada Limited,
a Penguin Random House Company
www.randomhouse.ca

1 2 3 4 5   18 17 16 15 14

To these dear friends, by agreement in each case,
all of whom assisted me in different ways with this book:

Paul G. Desmarais (1927–2013)
Paul Johnson
George Jonas
M. Brian Mulroney
John N. Turner
George (Lord) Weidenfeld

Contents

Acknowledgements

THANKS IN PARTICULAR, and for the sixth consecutive publication, to Barbara for her customary forbearance and to my close associate, Joan Maida, for her patient and efficient help, and thanks also to Doug Pepper and Jenny Bradshaw and their colleagues at Penguin Random House Canada. Others who have been helpful are very numerous, including those to whom the book is dedicated. Many can be deduced from the text as it has been my privilege to know a large number of the personalities prominent in the last fifty years of the narrative. I am deeply grateful to all who have assisted me.

Foreword

WHEN I SUGGESTED TO CONRAD BLACK that he should write a history of Canada, I knew that, if he accepted the idea, he would do it well. I had no idea that he would do it so quickly. I should have known better. Black is a man of decision. Once he has decided to do a thing, nothing is allowed to stand in his way. Having agreed with me that a history of Canada was needed, he set to. He was well, indeed superbly, qualified for the job. He has been a successful businessman. He has been an outstanding newspaper owner. He has been involved in politics at local, national and international levels. He is wonderfully articulate, and a man who sees things with remarkable clarity. Not least he is subtle.

I stress subtlety because the history of Canada is a study in understatement. It is an enormous country, like the United States. But whereas, in America, everything that happens is proclaimed from the house-tops, printed in capital letters, painted in technicolour and reverberates with blood and thunder, Canadian history rarely rises above a whisper. Its story is fascinating but it is written in lower case. It has produced many remarkable men and, increasingly, women. But in the theatre of the world they seldom take centre stage. Its very size underlines its character. Amid its huge prairies and limitless tundra, its boundless wastes of ice-floes and frozen seas, the outstanding characteristic is silence. One must listen, and listen hard. And what emerges is paradox.

Canada is like one of those banks said to be too big to go bust. Its sheer enormity saved it from outright conquest by any one state. Wrested from its native population by Samuel de Champlain – whose extraordinary life is an epic in itself – its very size in the eighteenth century proved too much for France to hold during a period of British naval supremacy. Yet equally the British were obliged to compromise with its French-speaking inhabitants to keep it against the "manifest destiny" of the United States. This bargain, the first in the history of colonialism – and the most enduring – was the prototype of many such in Canada's two centuries of trade-offs and peaceful adjustments. Under a British flag Canada was able to avoid absorption in America until the aggressive moment had passed, and experiments in federation had taken root. The history of Canada during the nineteenth century and even the twentieth contains many anxious periods, and moments of near disaster, but catastrophe was always avoided, and the prevailing language of her march through the decades is one of concession and yielding, conciliation, rapprochement, mending and mediation, patching, healing and setting right. Studied closely, Canadian history reveals much heroism in detail, but a heroism enacted quietly and with the minimum of histrionics.

Black recounts this progress with a lively satisfaction and often with humour, but he also narrates an accompanying saga of Canada's emergence in the world as a model of calm common sense, good government and quiet rectitude. Canada, like all countries, has made mistakes – and Black points them out – but she has seldom persisted in foolishness, and her record of learning from error, and not making the same mistake twice, is exemplary. Amid the deafening clamour of strident voices on the world scene, Canada's has somehow contrived to make its own calm contribution listened to and even heeded. In recent years, indeed, Canada's influence in the world has grown steadily, and with justice.

Canada, as the saying goes, always punches above her weight, as the experience of two world wars plainly shows, though the metaphor ill pertains to a country always anxious to avoid the language of conflict. It is perhaps lucky that Canada, unlike Australia, never took up the English national game, cricket, a pastime characterized by long soporific spells punctuated by periods of raucous bellicosity. Canada chose, instead, to excel uncontroversially at ice-hockey.

When I was a boy, the great thing I knew about Canada – all English boys in the 1930s knew it, and rejoiced in it – was the existence of the Royal Canadian Mounted Police, the "Mounties." It may now seem archaic, for it is "Royal" and horse-bound. But it did, and still does, conjure up an image of security and manliness, of bringing order in a wild country and doing it with a touch of romance. "The Mounties always get their man" is a splendid phrase Canada has given the world, and the Mounties add a touch of colour to a country whose history is, as a rule, reassuringly monochrome.

Black's book certainly does not omit such rare but striking moments of glamour in the story he tells. But his chief task, and he does it with aplomb, is to concentrate on the way in which Canada has continued to avoid the pitfalls which beset nations – often only by a hair's breadth – and to show how a physically vast portion of the world, which could so easily become unmanageable, has contrived to conduct its affairs with reason, justice and moderation, and to set its neighbours, big and small, near and distant, a good example. It is, on the whole, a noble story, and Black has told it well.

PAUL JOHNSON

Jacques Cartier (1491–1557), whose missions to Canada (as he called it) on behalf of the French king Francis I in 1534, 1535–1536, and 1541–1542 established him as the first European explorer of the St. Lawrence, which he also named, and the discoverer of Montreal (at the site of the bridge that now bears his name there). The painting, in 1844, is mere surmise, as no contemporary depictions of Cartier survive.

Introduction

CANADA HAS OFTEN HAD A PERILOUS EXISTENCE, but not for a long time has the threat been ravenously belligerent neighbours or exploitive colonizers. In order even to be conceived, Canada had to be, first, French so as not to be easily assimilated by the American colonists and revolutionaries, and then British, to have a protector to avoid being subsumed later into the great American project. For one hundred years prior to the First World War, Canada had gradually to wrest autonomy and then sovereignty from its distant Imperial protector while being important enough to Britain's position in the world balance of power opposite Germany and America to merit the Empire's protection from the United States. And it had to be resistant, but not offensive, to the inexorably rising power of America. It had to balance the strength of the British Empire against the appetites of the United States. These were large worldly forces for an underpopulated and tentative country to try to manage. Canada has often had to reformulate its natural

purposes to avoid succumbing to the spontaneous temptations of annexation to its mighty and relentlessly successful neighbour; it has also had
to be enough of a bulwark against an Anglo-Saxon tide to retain the
federalist adherence of the French Canadians, however unenthusiasti-
cally at times. It has been a protracted and intricate, unheroic, but often
almost artistic survival process. Canada was never threatened with a
tragic or pitiable fate but has faced a constant threat to its will to nationality for more than two centuries.

Though Britain's eviction of France from Canada in the Seven Years
War is generally referred to, especially in French Canada, as "the
Conquest," it was just the replacement of one European colonial power
by another. French Canada has never been conquered; its triumph over
demography and acculturation and climate has been astounding. Neither
has English Canada been conquered. And Canada is, with the other three
largest national land masses, Russia, China, and the United States, almost
the only country that has been extant for more than four hundred years
as a jurisdiction that has never been conquered. By contrast, in the lifetimes of many readers, almost every continental European country except
Sweden, Portugal, Switzerland, and European Turkey has been militarily
assaulted and wholly or partially overrun.

The consequences of what Charles de Gaulle and William Lyon
Mackenzie King called in 1944 the "overwhelming contiguity" of the
United States to Canada were to promote a more fervent adherence to
the British Empire and Commonwealth than would otherwise have
been attractive to Canadians, tempered largely by the need not to seem
to the French third of Canadians obsessed by maternal adoration at the
expense of the (achingly slowly) emerging national interest of Canada.
When the decline of Britain in the world made the British connection
too threadbare to sustain Canadian nationality, Canada officially
embraced its fortuitous status as a bicultural country, the home and beneficiary of two of the world's most distinguished languages and cultural
traditions within the same broad land. It was a commendable effort and
it is genuinely embraced by many, including a very talented elite that
has exercised an influence that many regard as disproportionate.

But the fickle mood swings of Quebec – from cynical aspirations to
creeping independence to genuine enthusiasm for an association of official equals – are far from the effervescent celebration of biculturalism

that the initial promoters of this vision espoused. Generally Quebec's default position has been a sullen and lethargic addiction to transfer payments from English Canada that enable Quebec to have an almost entirely white-collar, largely service economy where its non-French compatriots discreetly pick up much of the bill while the official Quebec apparat gambols in the trappings of subsidized nationhood. What has happened is that Canada has survived what was a severe federal crisis, almost without violence or excessive uncertainty. While doing this it has attained a scale of activity in most fields, including cultural and commercial activities, that make it interesting enough to itself to reduce the formerly insatiable preoccupation with American influence in every sphere.

For 150 years, Canada's lot was the honourable but unglamorous one of tugging at the trouser leg of the British and Americans and even, in the most unpromising circumstances, the French, trying to navigate between the ambitions and aversions of those countries, aligning now with one and now another, but almost never against any of them, while avoiding the extreme inflammation of Quebec nationalism. The skills acquired and practised were remarkable and sophisticated, but not the stuff of legends and anthems. As will be recounted in this book, Canada did, in its intuitive but nearly flawless calculations, move in parallel behind, but not too far behind, the United States as its survival and growth as a distinct jurisdiction required. So subtle, and often ingenious, has this progress been, half feline precision, half the plucky earnestness of the eagle scout, that Canadians have generally failed to notice their own virtuosity. And certainly the world has.

As the American colonists moved, with world-historic strategic brilliance, to encourage the British to expel the French from America, and then persuaded the French, contrary to their own interests and overburdening their own capacities, to assist them in evicting the British from America, the French Canadians made their pact and peace with the prudently magnanimous British that enabled Quebec to resist the temptations of the American Revolution and salvaged the northern half of the continent, at least temporarily, for the British Crown. The American colonists' manipulation of the world's two greatest powers (France and Britain) was a work of genius. But the French-Canadian elicitation from Britain of generous guaranties of its language, law, and religion just before the American Revolution, founded Canada, a haven for the French and for the American Loyalist resisters who quickly came. Canada was almost all French at the start of the American Revolution but almost half English in the aftermath of it, and had only one-twentieth of the population of the new Republic of Liberty (including its several hundred thousand indentured slaves). By a narrow margin, the French and English Canadians and their British garrison held the borders against the Americans in the War of 1812, and after the Napoleonic Wars the power of the British Empire enabled Canada to shelter under the Imperial wing for fifty years. While the United States descended toward civil war over issues related to slavery, Canada worked out Responsible Government, squaring the squabbling interests of its French and English, and the often exasperated British, with only minor incidences of violence.

The agony of the American Civil War inflicted 750,000 dead on a population of thirty-one million, and reduced almost half the secessionist states to rubble and ashes. But America, at last, was unbound and united, with the greatest army in the world and an unlimited horizon. At just this point, and just in time, an improbable congeries of provincial Canadian statesmen persuaded a largely skeptical Mother Country to underwrite the world's first transcontinental, officially bilingual, parliamentary confederation. A new country was launched, on a fantastically novel basis, to the bemused incredulity of the leaders of the triumphant American Union. But it grew quickly on steel rails and immigration borne by steamships and held its status as an autonomous democratic dominion within the British Empire. Despite the astounding economic and demographic growth in the United States that almost tripled its population between the Civil War and the First World War, Canada maintained its population generally at about 10 per cent of that of the United States and its level of prosperity quite close to that of America.

The attraction and retention of immigration, and the development and binding together of half a continent that was for most of Canadian history really just a ribbon between patches of territory that happened not to be American, was an arduous task without the national identity complex that accompanied it for two hundred years. Movements to continental and to Imperial free trade were generally resisted, and Canada advanced, unexceptionably, but almost imperceptibly, and certainly unflamboyantly, through and around the shoals of strengthening nationhood, from colony to dominion to junior ally and then to a rather important ally, as world wars and then a worldwide Cold War came, and ended victoriously. They were won by alliances distinguishedly led by the British and French, then the British, French, and Americans, then the Americans and the British, and then the Americans alone, at the summit of the world's nations.

After the First World War, when Canada was a valued junior ally of its traditional senior kindred states, there was no question of hostility between any of these powers anymore, but the self-consciousness of subordinancy gave way to a Canadian self-doubt about its raison d'être as an independent country in an era when regions were coalescing, especially in the move to a federal Europe. The distinctions between Americans from the northern states and English-speaking Canadians were much subtler than those between the people from different regions of the United States itself, such as New England and Texas. Canadians often found it difficult to explain why their country should not unite with the United States, voluntarily, as there was no longer any question of it being swallowed by its neighbour in an act of aggression. After the British connection and biculturalism faded as plausible answers, there was recourse to platitudes about Canada being kinder and gentler (originally an expression of President George H.W. Bush about his own country, not Canada), and about more generous social programs.

Canada was gentler than the United States, but partly because it was less dynamic and motivated: its social programs were more generous, but its taxes were also higher. As a rallying cry, such feeble exhortations were never going to stir the population to demonstrativeness. Canadians had developed a very original and effective way of managing through their unique and amorphous problems: endless good-faith discussion and the massaging around of the country's ample resources, like a liniment to heal the lesions, done gradually and with such sincere verbosity that wounds healed and attention moved on to new problems susceptible to the same sort of treatment. There was almost never the sudden clash nor even long-drawn trials of vigilance, just earnest altruism, solicitous but firming up when necessary, and backed by adequate tangible resources, the surest cure to most grievances. It was so implicit, colourless, and gradual, those who were in dissent were partly appeased, partly rebuffed, but mainly simply exhausted by endless and bountiful goodwill.

And then at the end of the twentieth century, after four hundred years of continuous Western history, as the United States completed a two-hundred-year rise from ambitious colonists to a national supremacy in the world without the slightest precedent or parallel in all history, American quality of governance suddenly declined. The country inexplicably wallowed in the debt of instant gratification and became distracted by military adventurism that was benignly intended but terribly costly for any possible benefit that it might bring to America. The United States ceased, for the first time since its earliest days, to seem strong in the world, or to have a mystique that dazzled, or even impressed, the world. It was almost dysfunctional, and rather inept and even corrupt and uncompetitive, in many fields. It was a convenient time for a great power to enter a period of sluggishness that is neither dangerous to the world nor irreversible, and it has assisted Canada to assume a confidence born not just of its own attainments but of the evidence of the ordinariness, in many ways, of what had always seemed a demiurgic and omnipotent adjoining nationality.

Canada's hour, not of celebrity, much less of dominance, but of confidence and world significance, has struck, whether Canadians, so long accustomed to an almost furtive and tentative political distinctiveness, yet hear the peal of the summons or not. Most of Canada's leadership elites cling to the attitudes of a dominion, a middle power. They have been so long waiting for their time, watching, like the rest of the world but from a ringside seat, the engrossing spectacle of America that they are slower than the Canadian people to answer the call of Canada's status as one of the world's ten or twelve most important countries.

"The Land God Gave to Cain":*
Original Inhabitants and
Early Explorers, 874–1603

1. Canada's Original Inhabitants

When European explorers began to settle Canada, at the end of the fifteenth century, there were probably about two hundred thousand (so-called) Indians in what became Canada, though scholars bandy about a range of numbers. The Algonquin – including the Abenaki and Montagnais on the Lower North Shore of the St. Lawrence River (as Jacques Cartier named it), the Micmac and Maliseet in what became Acadia and Nova Scotia, and the Ottawa, and Huron, and Chippewa (or Ojibwa) north of the Great Lakes – were directly or indirectly threatened by the more bellicose and fierce Iroquois south of the Great Lakes. The Iroquois were divided into the Seneca, Cayuga, Oneida, Onondaga,

---

* As described by Jacques Cartier on first seeing it (the north shore of the Gulf of St. Lawrence), 1534.

and Mohawk. On the Great Plains were the Cree and the Blackfoot, north of them were the Athabascans, and on the west coast were the Salish on the mainland and the Haida on Haida Gwaii (the Queen Charlotte Islands). The Indians were splendid woodsmen and crafts-men, but they were a Stone Age culture and economy that had not discovered the wheel. Their religion was largely superstitious. A few of the Algonquin and Iroquois tribes engaged in conventional agricul-ture in southwestern Ontario and along the St. Lawrence valley, and some fairly substantial settlements were erected south of the Great Lakes. The far western Indians had plank houses and more compli-cated social structures, with nobles and slaves, which were already the subject of a good deal of abuse when the Europeans reached the Pacific in the eighteenth century. But most Indians were nomadic, moving on after they had hunted down, fished out, or chased off most of the game and fish.

The women of the tribes, with the approval of the elders, coupled physically with many young braves before selecting one and mating for life. There were some impressive native ceremonies, and remarkable skills, but it was, despite much subsequent romanticization, a very prim-itive form of society. The life expectancy was twenty-five to thirty years, about the same as for Europeans at the time, and the North American natives proved very susceptible to contagious European diseases such as smallpox. The main groups quarrelled with one another and almost all considered war a natural and desirable state. Prisoners, including women, were almost always tortured to death, and then scalped, and those who were captured usually awaited their fate with unimaginable and majestic stoicism, completely resigned to a horrible death. It was an interesting sociological divertissement for arriving Europeans, but not an attractive life, and problems were compounded by an Indian tendency to define a treaty or pledge in temporary and flexible terms, subject to change according to circumstances. This was a legitimate cultural difference, but it led to great animosity, as the Europeans accused the natives of treachery and were accused in return of hypo-critical sanctimony. Both charges were often accurate.

European firearms, especially cannon, and superior military tactics generally conferred a huge advantage on them in any recourse to vio-lence, and for a time Indians were susceptible to the idea that Europeans were supernatural, but the Europeans' conduct soon disabused the natives of any such flattering concept. It soon emerged that native people had a great propensity to alcoholic consumption but a congenitally reduced capacity for it. In general, the French, British, and Dutch colonists, who were effectively the only nationalities that tried to set up permanently in what became the United States and Canada, except for a slight Spanish presence along what is now the Mexican border and the Gulf Coast, divided between those who despised the Indians and made little effort to develop any cooperative relationship with them and those, like the founder of Quebec and of Canada, Samuel de Champlain, who saw them as interesting and talented candidates for religious conversion, education, and stable and useful alliances. The attitude of Champlain was entirely justified and vindicated, but not always emulated, though the French, because they were more interested in religious conversions and were soon less populous than the British colonists and less threatening to the Indians demographically, and were the pioneers in the fur trade, got on better with the Indians than the British did. It is fair to say that the Indians were capable people of much promise but that their civilization, though exceptional in some arts, crafts, and in physical prowess, was uncompetitive with much of Europe for the preceding two thousand years.

There remains the issue of the moral and legal justification for the occupation of the Americas by the Europeans. It was a rich and underpopulated area and the occupants were, from the standpoint of the potential of the human species, underutilizing it. Despite the sentimentality of Longfellow, James Fenimore Cooper, Chateaubriand (with his bunk about *le beau sauvage*), Indian society was not in itself worthy of integral conservation, nor was its dilution a suitable subject for great lamentations. To the extent that the Americas were underdeveloped, the arrival of the Europeans was a positive thing. Unfortunately, the conduct of the exploratory and colonial visitors was very uneven and frequently utterly reprehensible. The claim of a spiritual eminent domain grounded in the holy mission of Christianization is harder to sustain on sectarian grounds. But it must be said that the Christian missions were generally extremely humane, disapproved of feeding the native people's addiction to alcohol, and tried to spread literacy and civility and to temper the exploitive abuses of the European commercial interests. The Jesuits, in particular, were astonishingly dedicated, venturing for years on end into the wilderness, sometimes forfeiting their lives to the savagery of their hosts or the elements, in pursuit of a civilized reconciliation of the best of both cultures, including the adaptation of native religious rites to Christianity. The Jesuits, Sulpicians, and Récollets (Franciscans) had a much more commendable record with the Indians than did the Puritans, who regarded them as almost irretrievable savages.

Where the Indians were essentially hunters and fishermen, exposure to the Europeans moved them swiftly from the Stone Age to the Iron Age, and copper pots and metal hatchets and knives and needles replaced the previous articles of stone and bone. Woollen clothing was much more comfortable and efficient than the costumes of animal hides the Indians had been using. Muskets assisted in the hunt and in internecine combat, but alcohol became a terrible problem and the Indians became more commercialized than they were qualified to be, which made them vulnerable to being manipulated corruptly, and in this sense the decline of the integrity and simplicity of their previous life was regrettable. The fur trade was ultimately tragic for the Indians and the French. It transformed the Indians into avaricious agents for the French, and it substituted for a real civilizing mission or durable colonial and nation-building objective for the French. While the British colonists (and Britain evicted the Dutch from North America in the 1660s) came in large numbers to build a new life and found a new country, the French came sparsely and sought only profit. There was constant strain between the French government attempting to counter the British in the New World and the commercial interests that directed the economic life of the French settlements and cared only for the profits generated by the fur trade.

2. The Early Explorers and Colonists, 874–1603

Centuries before any Western European dared to cross the North Atlantic, Vikings, Norsemen from Denmark and Norway, who had been in the habit of terrorizing the northern British Isles, moved steadily westward, stopping at the islands in the far northern Atlantic, the Hebrides, Iceland in 874, and Greenland in 986. The first individual name in

Canadian history was Leif Ericsson, who landed in Newfoundland, Vinland it was called, apparently on the north coast near L'Anse aux Meadows in 1000, having taken as his mission in life the establishment of Christianity in Greenland. Leif, who was Erik the Red's son, was from Greenland, and was converted to Christianity in Denmark before returning to his native island, where he won over his mother to the faith, but not his resistantly impious father. Leif's brother, Thorvald, also travelled to Vinland and tangled repeatedly and with uncertain results with the Dorset Eskimos, whom the Vikings called Skraelings. While these voyages were shorter than those of Columbus and others to the south, where the world is wider, and were possible by island-hopping, they were astonishingly bold, in largely open boats with crews that did not exceed thirty-five men.

There is a good deal of evidence that fishermen from the Basque coast of Spain, the French coast of the Bay of Biscay, Portugal, and the west coast of England had been fishing off the Grand Banks of Newfoundland for at least a century prior to Columbus's much celebrated discovery of America in 1492. Columbus alleged that he had visited Iceland in 1477. There was great demand for fish in Western Europe, and the astounding fecundity of the Newfoundland fisheries were a magnet, as fish could be salted and preserved for the return journey.

By the late fifteenth century, nation-states were starting to grow out of the Christian world that survived the collapse of the western Roman Empire and the assimilation of the barbarian tribes and clans and the repulse of the Arab Moors from France and Spain. The first great powers were Britain, France, the alliance in the Holy Roman Empire of Austria and Spain and most of the Netherlands, and the Turks, who periodically showed up at the gates of Vienna, capital of the far-flung Holy Roman Empire.

The English, French, Spanish, and Portuguese were all fascinated by tales of the wealth of the Orient, silk, spices, gems, and precious metals, and the theory that the earth was round was well-established by the late fifteenth century, so all of those countries sponsored missions across the western ocean in search of China and the East Indies. Ferdinand Magellan set out in 1519 for the Pacific, as he named it, and reached it through what became known as the Straits of Magellan, at the southern end of South America. His ship, the *Trinidad*, with four accompanying vessels, was commissioned by the king of Spain, the Holy Roman emperor Charles v (Magellan was Portuguese). It completed the first circumnavigation of the globe, though Magellan himself was killed in the Philippines.

Before this mission, a group of largely Italian navigators had sailed directly west, Columbus to the Caribbean, and in 1497 John Cabot, a Genoese of Venetian citizenship, to Newfoundland. He raised the funds in Bristol, Britain's chief Atlantic port, and sailed from that port in a single ship with a crew of only eighteen. Cabot reached Newfoundland and Cape Breton and followed the coastline south for a while, convinced he had reached the outer approaches to Asia, before returning home. King Henry VII, founder of the Tudor dynasty, was sufficiently impressed to give Cabot an annuity and encouraged his financial supporters in Bristol to fund a voyage of five ships in 1498. It was another remarkable feat of navigation and seamanship but generated nothing of economic interest, and Cabot did not return to North America. King Manuel of Portugal sent the Florentine navigator Amerigo Vespucci to the Caribbean and Brazilian coasts. Vespucci played a role in securing Brazil for Portugal, and his Christian name was the origin of the word *America*, but his principal message was that the Americas could not be part of Asia.

John Cabot's son, Sebastian Cabot, conducted several expeditions, including the first known effort, in 1508, to reach China via a northern route through the Arctic. In 1526 he led a four-year expedition that explored the shores and rivers of Brazil, following which he carried on with expeditions to the New World for decades and received the titles of captain general and grand pilot of England and great navigator of Spain. The ambitious king of France, Francis I, got into the act by sending the Florentine mariner Giovanni da Verrazano to North American waters in 1524, where he explored the shore from Narragansett Bay to the Carolinas and carefully examined what became New York Harbor (though he failed to identify the Hudson River as significant), whose entrance and the gigantic and graceful suspension bridge across it bear his name today. Verrazano did claim to have glimpsed the Pacific but likely saw Chesapeake Bay instead. By this time, the European monarchs were getting a little bored with fish, however much they enhanced the dining pleasure of their subjects. In order to secure royal or private commercial support, these sea captains, when they returned, made the most extravagant and spuriously corroborated claims for what they had seen and tended to be listened to with considerable skepticism by those who had underwritten their voyages and were hoping for the return of ships loaded to the gunwales with gold, silver, and the treasures of the exotic East.

The success of the Spanish in finding gold and silver in South and Central America had aroused the acute jealousy of the British and French. The strength of these national monarchies rose as they became defined national kingdoms with coextensive cultural identities, as the power of the papacy declined after the Western Schism from 1378 to 1417 – when there were two popes, one in Rome and one in Avignon – and with the Protestant Reformation. This began in 1517 with Martin Luther's Ninety-Five Theses, nailed to the church door at Wittenberg, and it was followed by Calvinist and other outbreaks of dissent and by the apostasy of Britain's King Henry VIII in 1529, following his failure to obtain a divorce from Pope Clement VII, who was heavily dependent on Emperor Charles V, the nephew of the queen Henry was seeking to divorce. (Luther was especially incensed that the popes, who were wealthier than "Crassus," set out to build the most opulent edifice in the history of the world, St. Peter's Basilica, with "the money of the poor rather than their own.") St. Ignatius Loyola and St. Francis Xavier founded the Society of Jesus (the Jesuits) to lead the counterattack on the Protestants in 1534, and the Roman Catholic Church launched the Counter-Reformation with the Council of Trent from 1545 to 1563.

The national governments of the major powers profited from the discomfort of the Holy See, and Charles V even had the papal domains sacked by one of his generals in 1527 when he considered Clement VII guilty of ingratitude. This, not the theological niceties, which the Holy See would customarily overlook if the petitioner was one of the most powerful kings in Christendom, was the background to Henry VIII quitting the Church of Rome and establishing himself as supreme governor of the national Church of England. As he had previously enjoyed the title of Defender of the Faith, accorded him by the pope because of a learned paper the ecclesiastic Erasmus had written for him, Henry caused the British Parliament to confer on him the same title, and the monarch of the United Kingdom (and Canada) bears it yet.

The Western world's four most powerful leaders were Henry VIII, Francis I, Charles V, and the Turkish potentate, Suleiman the Magnificent. When the Turks pressed the Holy Roman Empire very hard, the French and British would support it. Otherwise, the French were constantly nibbling at the Empire and effecting divisions between the constituent Austrians, Spanish, and Dutch, distinct nationalities which had little in common except the consequences of dynastic coincidence.

Two of the most decisive naval engagements in history came later in the sixteenth century: the Venetian and Imperial defeat of the Turks at the Battle of Lepanto in 1571, which announced the failure of the Turks to seize dominance of the Mediterranean; and the British defeat of the Spanish Armada in 1588, which signalled the beginning of Spanish decline. Francis Drake, the British deputy commander against the Spanish Armada, and long a dangerous adversary of the Spanish empire on both sides of the Atlantic, completed Britain's first circumnavigation of the world, from 1577 to 1580 (and the first of any country where the same person commanded the entire journey).

Well before these epochal events, the scramble to find a way through northern waters to the Orient had been very ambitiously pursued. Francis I had not been pleased with the meagre results of Verrazano's mission in 1524, and sent his own countryman Jacques Cartier, who had already been to Brazil and Newfoundland, on a return voyage across the North Atlantic. Cartier was sponsored by his bishop, of Saint-Malo in Normandy, the abbot of Mont Saint-Michel, and Francis charged him with discovering the most direct route to the Far East across the western ocean. Cartier had seen the mouth of the St. Lawrence, and probably thousands of European fishermen had also, but no European, as far as is known, had ventured into the river (which Cartier named after St. Lawrence). Cartier set forth in the spring of 1534 and reached Newfoundland in the astonishingly short time of only twenty days (a steady speed of almost five knots). He went through the Strait of Belle Isle and along the north shore of the Gulf of St. Lawrence, which he found so rugged and barren he called it "the land God gave to Cain." He was more positive about the Magdalen Islands, Prince Edward Island, the Baie des Chaleurs (which, as the name implies, he found reassuringly warm), but in August he returned to France in respect for autumn storms on the North Atlantic not having got farther upstream than Anticosti Island in the mouth of the St. Lawrence River.

While this was not all Francis had hoped for, Indians that Cartier met on the Gaspé Peninsula (where he erected a large cross and claimed all of North America for his king) gave him some furs, and told him of the vastness of the waterways into the interior up the St. Lawrence. It did not appear to presage the approaches to China, but it did appear to be an immense and rich country. The gigantic scale of the mouth of the St. Lawrence, far greater than any other river mouth in the world, inspired great hope of something rivalling or surpassing Mexico and Brazil.

Cartier brought back two Indians whom he wished to train as translators, and the king was sufficiently interested to send him back the following year. He sailed upriver past his former limit to Tadoussac, where the Saguenay River rushes, six hundred feet deep, into the St. Lawrence, and on to Stadacona, the imposing site of present-day Quebec City, and then to Hochelaga, site of Montreal. The Lachine Rapids west of Mont Royal, as Cartier christened the mountain at Hochelaga, were so named by him in the hope that beyond them was China (*la Chine*). Cartier spent the winter at Stadacona, where 25 of his 110 men suffered from scurvy until a liquid derived from spruce proved to be a remedy. The Indians continued to talk of the vast riches up the Saguenay and the Ottawa and beyond Lachine, but declined to assist in any way any French liaison with the natives they might encounter. Cartier took the local chief, Donnacona, with him back to France, where the chief, emboldened by the splendours of Paris and the outlying royal precincts, gave voice to his burgeoning imagination as he waxed lyrical on the boundless wealth of his homeland to King Francis and all within earshot.

Francis authorized a return by five ships commanded by Cartier in 1541, followed by three more ships under the corsair Jean-François Roberval. The Spanish were concerned at any other power seeking to establish itself in the New World, but the Portuguese monarch assured Charles v that Francis would not find anything of the slightest interest in the area Cartier would be exploring. (On the basis of this information, Charles assured visitors that the land along and up the St. Lawrence was "of no value, and if the French take it, necessity will compel them to abandon it."[1]) Francis instructed Cartier to establish a permanent settlement and carry his explorations as far as he could, including investigating what Donnacona assured the king were the abundant gold, silver, and "cloves, nutmeg, and pepper" of the Saguenay, preposterous claims given the northern clime.[2] (Donnacona died in France, and would never be held accountable for his outrageous liberties with the truth.) Cartier's colonists were largely composed of prisoners who had been released for the occasion, but he also had three hundred soldiers. He wintered at Cap Rouge, upriver from Quebec. Roberval had detoured to raise money for the mission by seizing British ships as prizes, though the countries were at peace, and arrived in mid-summer of 1542 at Newfoundland. By this time, Cartier had lost confidence in the colonizing mission but had what he thought to be diamonds and gold to inspire the king with the riches of the new country, and he returned to France, disobeying Roberval's instruction to go back up the St. Lawrence. (The riches proved to be quartz and iron pyrite. The phrase "not worth a Canadian diamond" was long a dismissal of worthlessness in Paris.) Cartier remained at or near Saint-Malo after 1542, in reasonable comfort, until he died there on September 1, 1557, aged sixty-six. His modest home survives, almost unchanged.

This first effort at establishing a colony was a fiasco. More successful was the fur trade, which caught a fashion in France and started to respond to sharply rising demand for fur coats and hats. Private sector French traders made direct contact with the Indians and forged alliances with the Algonquin and Huron (from *huré*, meaning "bristly," after their Mohawk hairstyles, as they are now known), forming what became known as the Laurentian Coalition, which continued through the seventeenth century and all of the eighteenth. The profits from the fashionable French fur trade and what the profits could buy for the recently savage and isolated Indians drove them to hunt down the fur-bearing animals of the Canadian interior, as the depredations of the world's fishing countries would ultimately strain even the fisheries of Newfoundland's Grand Banks. (Canada was so-called because *kanata* was the Indian word for a meeting place, but Cartier had initially thought the natives used the word in reference to the specific place Stadacona.) Eventually, after the death of Francis in 1547 (two months after Henry VIII), France dissolved in conflict between the Catholics and Protestants (Huguenots), as the Reformation and Counter-Reformation got into high gear.

In 1588, the year of the Spanish Armada, Étienne Chaton and a nephew of Jacques Cartier, Jacques Noël, gained a monopoly on the fur and copper (more an ambition than a fact at this point) industries for twelve years, which was quickly reduced to copper only when competing Breton merchants agitated at court. Chaton and Noël brought in sixty convicts a year, but the project gained no traction. From 1576 to 1578, Sir Martin Frobisher made three voyages in search of the Northwest Passage, landing at Baffin Island and what is now Frobisher Bay, and returning with 1,400 tons of, as he imagined, gold ore, which eventually proved, after being assayed in London, to be as worthless as Cartier's "gold" and diamonds turned out to be twenty-five years before. There was a half-hearted effort by the inept Marquis de la Roche in 1578 to bring some convicts to Canada to begin to colonize, but the convicts mutinied and were deposited on Sable Island, where they lived off cattle left there years before by the Portuguese and, as there was no wood or stone, "lived like foxes underground."[3] They were returned by fishermen to France in 1603. That any of them survived was an eloquent testament to man's capacities of survival. A new effort, by Pierre Chauvin, a Huguenot, accompanied by the accomplished fur trader François Gravé Du Pont and the Sieur de Mons, gained a new monopoly on the fur trade for ten years from King Henry IV in 1594, conditional on a serious effort at colonization, a project that France had been ineffectually making gestures toward for fifty years. Chauvin put down fifty settlers at Tadoussac, where the Saguenay flows into the St. Lawrence, but the weather was so inhospitable through the first winter that only sixteen survived to the spring. Again, the agitation of competing merchants, Norman and Breton, challenged this monopoly, and Chauvin died in 1602.

British commercial interests sent the adventurer and half-brother of Sir Walter Raleigh, Sir Humphrey Gilbert, to Newfoundland in 1583 to establish a colony from which to explore for the Northwest Passage, and to establish British authority over the fishing rights and fish processing there. He brought a motley group of misfits, convicts, and declared lunatics and is generally credited with founding the British Empire when he proclaimed British sovereignty over Newfoundland, but the colony was not a success as there were no follow-up supplies. On the way home, Gilbert travelled on the smallest ship of his squadron, sitting on the fan deck reading St. Thomas More's *Utopia*. His last known words as he declined to transfer to the *Golden Hind* from his little ship the *Squirrel*, which foundered with all hands, were that "We are as close to heaven by sea as by land."

France was able, after the Reformation, and over nearly two hundred years, from the time of Richelieu in the 1620s to the departure of Napoleon in 1815, to consolidate its position in Europe, assure the division of the German-speaking centre of the continent, and aggravate the strains in the Holy Roman Empire to its profit, dealing separately and successfully with the Austrians, Spanish, and Dutch. But France was never really able to determine whether it wished to direct its ambitions across the Rhine or the English Channel, the Alps and Pyrenees being less tempting goals.

Britain's great minister Thomas Cardinal Wolsey (lord chancellor from 1515 to 1529) had perfected the technique of exploiting Britain's insular status, without adversaries that could invade it on land, to manipulate the balance of power and assist now one country and now another on the continent. He aided the French and the Spanish and Habsburgs as required to prevent one side attaining superiority over the others and to make the Spanish-American empire vulnerable and keep the French empire, ultimately, to Britain's leavings. Under Henry VIII and his second daughter, Elizabeth I, who between them reigned almost a century (from 1509 to 1547, and from 1558 to 1603), England entrenched its national church with the monarch at the head of it; developed the world's most powerful navy; detached itself from European loyalties, as opposed to mere interests; united with Scotland; and perfected Wolsey's balance of power strategy that served it through the pre-eminence of Spain (until the rise of Richelieu), of France (to the end of Napoleon), of Bismarck's united Germany (to the defeat of Hitler in 1945), and of the Russian-dominated Soviet Union until its implosion at the end of the twentieth century. By then, the sceptre of world influence and the power to manipulate local correlations of forces had passed in peaceful alliance from Great Britain and its Empire to the United States. From the early sixteenth to the middle of the nineteenth century, the ebb and flow of power in Europe would depend on Britain's ability to prevent any power, France for most of that time, from becoming so predominant in Europe that it could threaten the British in their home islands. France was the richest and most populous of the European powers until Bismarck united the Germans and, seventy-five years later, Russia had been industrialized and somewhat efficiently organized under the Communists.

This system of continental alliances and overseas imperialism was just starting to emerge, and would take some decades to be thoroughly imposed, as Britain and France sent explorers to the east coast of North America, soon landed settlers, and fanned out into the new continent, claiming it for the home country. With a treaty of solidarity with Suleiman, Francis began the tactic, frequently invoked in the future, of reaching outside Western and Central Europe to try to balance intra-European conflicts, as Richelieu would, a century later, more successfully, with King Gustavus Adolphus of Sweden. Both were controversial moves for Catholic France, and would presage the impulses for startling modern *volte-faces*, such as the Nazi-Soviet Pact of 1939 and President Richard Nixon's visit to China's Mao Tse-tung and Chou En-lai in 1972. Canada would eventually evolve from being a pawn to a player in this long-running great power chess game.

PART I

Colony:

1603–1867

Samuel de Champlain (c. 1570–1635), successively exploration leader, lieutenant to
governors and viceroys of New France, and captain general and commander "in
the absence of my Lord the Cardinal de Richelieu" of New France, 1603–1635;
founder of Quebec. Champlain was a soldier, navigator, cartographer, colonial
administrator and builder, writer, and courtier of astonishing versatility, courage,
and determination. He crossed the Atlantic more than thirty times and went over
many dangerous rapids but never learned to swim. He was one of history's great
propagators of European civilization.

Champlain, the French Monarchy, New France, and the Maritime Colonies, 1603–1754

1. The Rise of the French Bourbons: Henry IV

Francis I's son, Henry II, had died in 1559 when he shattered an opponent's lance in a joust, causing a splinter to strike him in the eye. Henry was succeeded by a sickly fifteen-year-old, Francis II, who was dominated by his mother, Mary Queen of Scots. The Valois dynasty was clearly unstable, and there were contentious factions among the great nobles. The Catholic House of Guise in eastern France, the Protestant House of Condé in the west, and the less exalted, more moderate and uniformly sectarian Catholic southern houses of Bourbon and Montmorency all aspired to take over the kingdom. Under the zealous impulsion of Queen Mary, Protestants were persecuted, tried as heretics, and, if they refused to recant, tortured to death. Francis II died in 1560, just a year after his succession, and was nominally replaced by his ten-year-old brother, Charles IX, but the head of the state was his mother, Catherine de' Medici, who tried to impart moderation from her splendid chateau at Chenonceau. Her policy failed to appease the Protestants but outraged the papists, and after the personal guard of the Duke of Guise killed more than a hundred Protestant worshippers and burned down a prominent church in March 1562, France erupted in denominational civil war of extreme brutality. The Condés raised a Protestant army and sought assistance from the English and German Protestants. The Catholic factions imported Swiss and Spanish soldiers to assist them, and there were terrible atrocities and assassinations, including of the Duke of Guise, and twenty-five thousand people died in the clash of contending armies at Dreux, followed by more than a thousand civilians in the sack of Rouen. The truce of the Edict of Amboise of 1563 lasted uneasily for four years, and then a second war broke out from 1567 to 1568, which was tamped down by the Peace of Longjumeau. This too collapsed as the most violent phase of the religious wars engulfed France.

It was into this atmosphere of almost constant and general violence that Samuel de Champlain was born, in 1570, and baptized a Protestant. The young king's mother, Catherine de' Medici, conceived a plan to end the strife through the time-honoured method of dynastic alliance by marriage, and the king's sister, Marguerite de Valois, was given in marriage to the Protestant Prince Henry of Navarre. The wedding, in Paris, on August 17, 1572, was a great occasion, but four days later a leading Huguenot, Admiral de Coligny, was seriously wounded in an assassination attempt, and the following day Charles IX, twenty-two years of age, and with the full authority of a king, approved closing the city gates and chaining the boats in the Seine to their moorings. Prince Henry and the current Duke of Guise were arrested, Coligny was murdered in his convalescent bed, and the king ordered a bloodbath of the Huguenots. In what became known as the St. Bartholomew's Day Massacre, about two thousand Protestants, including many prominent nobles, were murdered. The able future prime minister Maximilien de Béthune, Duke of Sully, just twelve years old and a Protestant boarding school student in Paris, only escaped with his life by walking back to his residence with a Catholic liturgical book under his arm. Prince Henry, less than a week after his wedding, was informed by his brother-in-law the king that he could convert to Roman

Catholicism or be put to death at once. This was the swift demise of his mother-in-law's policy of toleration. He made the life-saving choice and spent three years as a thorough debauchee in luxurious captivity in the Louvre Palace.

Charles IX died in 1574 of tuberculosis, only twenty-three years old, and was succeeded by his brother, Henry III, who had just been elected king of Poland. (In a novel arrangement, Poland, which was being gradually reduced by its more powerful neighbours, had its always-fractious nobles elect an outsider king.) Henry returned to Paris, pursued a conciliatory policy, and allowed his brother-in-law Prince Henry of Navarre to depart. The Huguenots had been shattered by the massacre of their leaders who had come to Paris for the wedding of national unity and religious peace, but they retrenched into strongholds, such as La Rochelle. Prince Henry went to La Rochelle and renounced Catholicism, but was coolly received by the Huguenot leaders and trusted by no one. But he raised an army of moderates, both Catholic and Protestant, and famously wrote a Catholic officer that all who "unswervingly follow their conscience are of my religion, as I am of all who are brave and virtuous."[1] He was widely, and perhaps not unjustly, suspected of opportunism, but he believed that atrocities committed for religious reasons were unchristian crimes as well as political mistakes. And he had judged accurately, as some of his more talented successors did, the point at which the French become alarmed at chaos and violence and require the restoration of security. He became a unifying figure. He also proved a very competent military organizer and a brave and inspiring commander.

This growing moral and martial success aroused the envy and suspicion of the king and the Catholic factional leader, Henry, Duke of Guise. War erupted yet again, as the king and Guise tried to repress Henry of Navarre in what became known as the War of the Three Henrys. Henry of Navarre defeated both his rivals, separately, in the field. The king and the Duke of Guise were assassinated, and in 1589 Henry of Navarre, the friend and patron of the Champlain family, was the genealogical successor to Henry III, as a distant cousin and a brother-in-law, and founded the Bourbon dynasty. In 1593, Henry of Navarre became a Roman Catholic for the third time, while assuring tolerance of Protestantism. He would be one of France's greatest monarchs as

Henry IV (from 1589 to 1610). He allegedly said, "Paris is worth a mass," one of the most famous utterances in French history.*

Samuel de Champlain was a man of exceptional talent and interest for any time or place. He was a master seaman, experienced at both naval and commercial navigation, a soldier, a colonial administrator and entrepreneur, a courtier and adventurer, a cartographer, explorer, gifted and prolific writer, scientist, and agronomist; born a Protestant, he became a robust but very tolerant Roman Catholic, and he was a sociologist and anthropologist. He was a Cartesian man of reason, but also a dreamer and visionary – grandiose but not absurd in his plans and practical in his methods. And it must be said that he was successful and will rank forever as one of the very greatest Europeanizers of North America. He crossed the Atlantic approximately thirty times, from 1599 to 1633, and never lost a ship, other than once when he replaced an incapable captain in a tempest and deliberately grounded the ship and saved the entire complement. Yet he never learned to swim.

Champlain was born and raised in Brouage, a fortress town near the sea in the southwest of France, thirty miles south of La Rochelle and fifteen miles north of the mouth of the Gironde estuary. In the religious wars that wracked France after the middle of the sixteenth century, Champlain's family was loyal throughout to the local Protestant faction head, Henry of Navarre.

Champlain's father received a commission as a navy captain from the king, and his cousin was the "chief whipper-in of the royal dogs," a serious position in those fervent hunting times. Samuel himself received a pension from an early age and was so evidently favoured by the king that there were persistent rumours, never in the slightest substantiated, that he was the king's illegitimate son. Certainly, Henry's swashbuckling romantic life would make such an event possible (he had nearly sixty women who were durable enough to qualify

---

* Along with his grandson's *"L'état c'est moi,"* his great-great-grandson's *"Après moi le deluge"* (Louis XIV and XV), Napoleon's "From the sublime to the ridiculous is a single step" as he left Moscow and started the retreat, and Charles de Gaulle's "France has lost a battle; France has not lost the war." (Only the comments of Napoleon and de Gaulle are certain to have been uttered by them, but the others are possible, appropriate, and in character.)

as mistresses, and countless more hurried liaisons, and was often in the Champlains' area during what he always called his "peasant youth," a reflection on his free-wheeling conduct rather than the modesty of his circumstances.)

Champlain emulated his monarch, who lived well but not with the grandiosity of subsequent French rulers, from Louis XIV to Napoleon, nor with the distant austerity of Robespierre or de Gaulle. He was informal and popular and frequently travelled around the country incognito acquainting himself with common opinion.

Henry IV's best efforts to bury the religious factionalism in a patriotic quest for unity and prosperity did not immediately bear fruit. The worst of all the religious wars of the time broke out, unleashed by the Catholic extremists known as the Catholic League. Again, the Spanish and Italians were invited to intervene. Henry became a rallying figure for all France against invaders and domestic fanatics. In a bitter campaign of five years, from 1594 to 1598, Henry led in the field and defeated his enemies in one region after another, starting in the south. Samuel de Champlain joined the king's forces and quickly graduated from a trooper to a logistics officer and aide to one of the king's regional commanders. At Crozon in Brittany, Britain's redoubtable Queen Elizabeth sent a force to assist Henry in expelling the Spanish from the fort they had seized there. The Spanish fought to the last man, and the only prisoners taken, when returned with honours, were hanged by their commander.[2] Champlain's bravery in fierce and close combat was conspicuous. Among the British whom he met and with whom he became friendly was the explorer-adventurer Martin Frobisher. Henry won the war of the Catholic League and then, in April 1598, promulgated the Edict of Nantes, establishing Roman Catholicism as the established religion of France, but guarantying toleration of Protestant worship. In May, the Peace of Vervins with Spain equitably ended forty years of violent religious conflict. It also opened increased possibilities for all the maritime powers to focus again on the New World. For their own convenience, the British and French professed amicable competition north and east of the Azores, but acknowledged their rivalry beyond and to the south, declaring their non-acceptance of the Spanish and Portuguese effort to proclaim a monopoly of legitimate interest in what became Latin America.

The king took up the Catholic rites, visited the sick, touched the afflicted, and once a year washed the feet of paupers. Henry used his treasury to reward those who rallied, while crushing those who resisted and pardoning the defeated, provided they then adhered. He was a populist king who spoke of assuring that even the poorest in the very rich country of France would "have a chicken in his pot," a phrase that would ricochet through the centuries even unto American president Herbert Hoover on the eve of the Great Depression of the 1930s. He embarked on major public works, including the beginnings of the great parks and quais and boulevards of Paris and a vast improvement in roads and canals to pull the country physically together. It had been a terrible sequence of religious violence; only in the German states in the Thirty Years War would sectarian violence be more sanguinary, and there it was more powerfully assisted by marauding foreign armies.

In Britain, while there were perturbations, they were relatively easily endured. Henry VIII was succeeded by his underage and sickly son, Edward VI, who died at age fifteen after a reign of six years in which a regency council presided. He was succeeded by his half-sister, Henry's eldest daughter, Queen Mary, who was a Roman Catholic, daughter of Catherine of Aragon, whom Henry had divorced in the controversy that led to the apostasy from Rome of the Church of England. She burned the archbishop of Canterbury, Thomas Cranmer, at the stake after wringing recantations from him and conducted a vengeful sectarian persecution. At the suggestion of the ubiquitous Charles V, she married his son Philip, who on his father's abdication in 1556 would become King Philip II of Spain and lord of the united Netherlands, while Charles's brother, Ferdinand, succeeded him as Holy Roman emperor in Austria, Germany, and Italy. (This was a victory for the rival powers, as the Empire, like Diocletian's, was too unwieldy and too subject to competing local national ambitions to continue. Britain and France rose in relative strength.) Mary's Spanish marriage was unpopular in England, and her religious policies divisive, but she died childless in 1558, and was succeeded by Elizabeth I, a Protestant, who reaffirmed her father's religious independence but ruled with firmness and intelligence for forty-five years and was a great English nationalist. (In the perversity of these times, Henry VIII had executed Anne Boleyn, the wife he broke up the Roman Church in England to marry, on a trumped-up charge of adultery and because she could not bear him a male heir, and the heir she did produce, Elizabeth, would be the greatest monarch in British history.)

Henry IV quickly evinced the interest Francis I had had in exploration and foreign trade and empire. He set up companies to lay claim to the North Pole and the presumed Northwest Passage, sponsored voyages down the coast of Africa, and reasserted the French interest in New France, as Canada was called, and in Acadia and Newfoundland, where several countries were drying and salting their fishing catches on land before shipping them back to Europe. Norman and Breton merchant seamen went as far afield as Archangel in the Russian Arctic and Madagascar in the Indian Ocean. But his particular emphasis was on New France, where he hoped to found a prosperous new colony, feudal but rich and generously governed. His minister, the capable Maximilien de Sully, disapproved of all colonial activities as a waste of resources from which France would never derive the slightest benefit. France was never entirely to rise above this ambiguity in overseas policy, which particularly asserted itself whenever, which was often, there were pressures or temptations on France's frontiers.

Imbued with the Breton spirit of the sea and exploration, and with the patriotic fervour and catholicizing passion of the convert, Champlain considered how to make himself useful and important to King Henry IV's overseas designs. He determined that the first step was to sign on to a Spanish ship and get a glimpse of how communications with its American empire was organized. Foreigners were generally banned from making this passage by the Spanish, and unauthorized entry to New Spain was punishable by death. Champlain's uncle, Guillaume Allène, was a remarkable shipowner and captain from Marseilles who was a captain in the French navy and a pilot-general in the Spanish navy, held himself out at different times as Catholic and Protestant, and was a wealthy landowner in Spain and France. He was engaged after the War of the Catholic League to evacuate a Spanish garrison back to Spain from Brittany, and at his nephew's request invited Champlain to join the expedition to Cadiz, where it remained for some time, and where Allène and Champlain hoped it would be assigned to one of the great treasure fleets sent to New Spain to collect booty. Champlain "reconnoitred" Cadiz and Seville and recorded his impressions. This was not exactly espionage, as he did not unearth secrets, but it was intelligence. Allène's ship (he was a part-owner of it) was hired by the Spanish to join a treasure fleet; he was unable to make the trip himself but successfully requested that his nephew be permitted to do so.

The fleet was to clear the British freebooter the Duke of Cumberland out of Puerto Rico, where he had done much damage with a squadron of twenty ships. Champlain was interested at first sight in the natives they encountered at island stops on the way, and was very impressed at the prosperity and extent of Spanish operations in Puerto Rico, which the British had departed by the time the fleet arrived there, in 1599. Champlain took the unusual step of chatting at length with natives and African slaves, and was appalled at the severity and frequency with which they were whipped by their Spanish masters, to the point that the slaves sometimes were forced to wear wooden gags to stifle their cries of pain as the lash was laid on them. Champlain's trip lasted for two years and took him to Venezuela, Mexico, and Cuba. He was everywhere disgusted by the brutal Spanish use of forced labour to pillage the native lands of their subjects, and after observation, and an unusual amount of socializing with the locals, believed that they were of "a very quick intelligence," not at all inferior to that of Europeans, a revolutionary opinion at that time. He was particularly unimpressed by the priests who beat the natives with sticks on the steps of the churches for trivial offences, especially for non-attendance at religious services. Champlain was barred from visiting the Mexican silver mines, and so could not advise the French government exactly where they were, but he was a very observant informant, and combined his talents at affability with great natural skill as a writer, sketcher, and cartographer. Champlain saw the potential for an isthmian canal, and much admired the fortifications and harbour of Havana.

He returned to Cadiz in 1601, and finding his uncle in poor health, he helped him clean up his tangled affairs and obtain proper medical attention. Allène died in July 1601, leaving his thirty-year-old nephew as heir to his considerable, if complicated, assets. Champlain lingered in Cadiz and wrote what he titled an intelligence report for the personal attention of the king of France, then he returned directly to the French court, was granted an immediate audience with the king, and submitted his findings, replete with sketches and maps. Henry was much pleased and augmented Champlain's pension and directed him to remain at court.

Henry built an impressive gallery attached to the Louvre along the Seine, and in the ground floor of it he created offices for his overseas activities. The court astronomers, surveyors, cartographers, navigators, and geographers were installed there. Champlain became one of the king's geographers. His particular field was the study of the failure of past French efforts at colonization in North America, those of Cartier, Chauvin, and the Marquis de la Roche, which have been mentioned, and also the unsuccessful efforts of Jean Ribault and René de Laudonnière in Florida in the 1560s. Champlain considered that the Spanish had written the book on how not to colonize, treat the natives, manage the resources discovered, or impart the benefits of Christianity. Champlain was effectively the king's supreme colonial planner, and carefully developed, as none of his predecessors had, the outline of how to proceed. He recognized the need for meticulous preparation and careful exploration before choosing the place to settle (Sable Island, barren, perpetually wet, a hundred miles off the Grand Banks, treeless, and sandy – hence its name – was the quintessence of where not to start). The natives had to be approached with respect and induced to cooperate in their own constructive interests, and always transacted with honourably. Champlain was convinced that part of the problem had been disorganization and dispersed authority, and he required that henceforth such missions had to have a virtually military structure and discipline. He recognized that supplies of all kinds had to be assured and that a generous food supply was essential. And he saw that only a tolerant religious policy would succeed, as in Henry's France, and that Christianity would have to be imparted by example and not by sword and lash.[3]

There was a constant debate in Henry's time over any overseas effort, prompted by Sully. The king generally overruled him, as he felt a spirit of adventure and believed that the world was a vast canvas on which France had to project itself as a matter of national security as well as prestige. This was a little like the debates between the British imperialists and Little Englanders or continentalists, such as Disraeli and Gladstone, or, in the United States, expansionists and isolationists, such as Theodore Roosevelt and Grover Cleveland, nearly three hundred years later. The king gave Vice Admiral Aymar de Chaste, a venerable and distinguished officer and former governor of the port city of Dieppe, a commission to establish a colony in New France. Champlain gave de Chaste a copy of his "Brief Discourse on the West Indies and New Spain," and de Chaste invited Champlain to accompany him to New France as his deputy commander, an appointment the king happily endorsed. This was how things stood when Samuel de Champlain sailed on a return mission with the colourful Breton François Gravé Du Pont in 1603. Champlain would conceive, energize, and execute a new and continental French strategy. Here, at last, was the founder of New France, of Quebec, and of Canada. The history of Canada, tenuous and tangled, but gradually flooding into the story of a great nation, was about to begin.

2. Samuel de Champlain, the First Canadian and Founder of Quebec, 1603–1616

Champlain went to Honfleur at the mouth of the Seine and hired the well-travelled old ship of about 140 tons *Bonne-Renommée* (Good Renown). He had hired Gravé Du Pont as captain for the voyage and rounded up two Montagnais Indians as interpreters. The expedition was financed by groups of merchants from Saint-Malo and Rouen, who provided two smaller ships. The French kings rarely paid more than a modest part of the cost of these missions, which put intense commercial pressure on the colonists. The little flotilla departed on the Ides of March, and after a stormy crossing and close encounters with towering icebergs, and after almost grounding on the Grand Banks, it traversed the hundred-mile mouth of the St. Lawrence, cruised along the Gaspé coast, and then returned into the Gulf of St. Lawrence and dropped anchor at Tadoussac, at the mouth of the Saguenay, on May 26, 1603. They arrived in the midst of a Montagnais celebration of one of their rare victories over the Iroquois. The Indians were displaying more than one hundred scalps and torturing prisoners, who accepted their gruesome fate resignedly and apparently without reproach. Champlain had one of his Montagnais give an uplifting speech of solidarity on behalf of the great French king and recount the kindness with which he and his colleague had been treated in France. The leading native, who was styled a sagamore, responded in very welcoming words. Champlain was particularly impressed with the Indian birchbark canoes, so light a single man could carry one and yet able to carry a cargo, human or otherwise, of a thousand pounds. Champlain showed his customary interest in and courtesy toward the Indians, and opened what proved a solid alliance with the Montagnais that would continue (and good relations with the French Canadians endure yet).

Champlain went up the Saguenay, a mighty river, but which flows from and through rather sparse country. He noted the profitable fur trade that the Montagnais conducted as middlemen between European buyers, who came for that purpose but had no interest in settling, and tribes to the north such as the Mistassini and Peribonka, and learned of Hudson Bay. On June 22, the exploratory party moved up the St. Lawrence from Tadoussac and came to the fertile and picturesque (then as now) Île d'Orléans, as Cartier had named it, near Stadacona. This became Quebec, after the Indian word *kebec*, meaning a narrowing of the river, and Champlain realized at once that this was the appropriate place for the settlement to be launched. He carried on to the southwest and was advised by his Indian companions of a river that flowed toward "Florida," by which they meant Lake Champlain, Lake George, and the Hudson River. He continued on to Montreal, and ascertained from the local natives the approximate distance to and proportions of the Great Lakes and Niagara Falls before returning to Tadoussac. The party spent the next month exploring and mapping and sketching the Atlantic coast along the Gaspé. They returned from the Grand Banks to Le Havre in the astounding time of fifteen days, not even four times as long as the crossings between Europe and New York of the great Blue Riband liners of three centuries later – *Mauretania, Europa, Rex, Normandie,* and *Queen Mary.* This implied a steady speed of about seven knots.

The voyage was judged a complete success, as it opened good relations with the natives and generated a very accurate series of maps and accounts, published by Champlain in the book *The Savages,* which in the early seventeenth century meant something like "In the Wild" and did not connote anything sinister, or even primitive, but rather a state that was natural and promising. Champlain and his party had seen what F. Scott Fitzgerald imagined, a third of a millennium later, the first Dutch sailors had seen: "A fresh green breast of the new world . . . [that] had once pandered in whispers to the last and greatest of all human dreams; for a transitory enchanted moment man must have held his breath in the presence of this continent, compelled into an aesthetic contemplation he neither understood nor desired, face to face for the last time in history with something commensurate to his capacity to wonder."[4] This was, from all accounts, especially Champlain's own, a fine expression of the exhilaration and suspense Champlain felt at the prospects for New France and his possible role in the development of it. Champlain and the other humanists of that contemporary French school led by Descartes and Montaigne "transformed the purpose of the Renaissance into the program of the Enlightenment." Champlain "planted the seed of New France, and bent the sapling to the pattern of its growth. Their history bears witness to the importance of small beginnings in the history of great nations."[5]

Champlain was distressed to find on his return to France that Vice Admiral de Chaste had died. He recruited to replace him the Sieur de Mons, a wealthy Protestant nobleman (with a Catholic wife), who was also a loyalist of the king and influential with the merchants in the Norman and Breton ports who were looked to for financing. De Mons had survived the Chauvin debacle in New France of 1601 to 1602. The two men attended upon the king and revived the notion of a passable route to China through the Great Lakes. Henry was unconvinced of that but wished to continue the project and encouraged them. De Mons, after the disaster of wintering in Tadoussac, wanted to settle in Acadia, in what is now Nova Scotia. Champlain was intoxicated by the scale and might of the St. Lawrence and wished to anchor New France there. De Mons sold the king the idea that a colony could be successfully established in Acadia at no cost if the colonizers were granted a monopoly on the fur trade of New France. The king agreed and issued the commission, commanding the colonizers also to propagate the Roman religion, while, as in France, permitting freedom of religion. De Mons raised the necessary capital from merchants in Rouen, Saint-Malo, La Rochelle, and Saint-Jean-de-Luz, and as the treasury was not paying anything, Sully could raise no objection.

These policies raised two of the main problems of the French, compared with the British, in colonization efforts. The king of France gave away commercial rights in exchange for private sector support of missions to settle and colonize, which resulted in a conflict of motive inherent to each colonial operation. Those representing the commercial backers resented anything spent on colonization and were at odds with the settlers themselves. But only a growing and ever more self-sufficient settlement would make the colonial presence secure. Second, the presence of Catholics and Protestants diluted the evangelizing mission of the colonial settlements, confused the Indians, and made the purposes of the effort relatively ambiguous. A third comparative problem was that the French did not like to emigrate at all; France was, as it remains, a rich and temperate country, and inducing the French permanently to leave has always been much more difficult than it has been to persuade the British or most other European nationalities to emigrate. The final problem in this series was about to emerge: the sale of alcoholic beverages to the Indians. The French soon discovered the Indian love of and weakness for brandy. The fur traders and other commercial interests were strenuously in favour of this traffic, because it conferred great comparative advantage in negotiating with the Indians when brandy could become part of the consideration. But the Roman Catholic clergy objected, as it was held to be unchristian to exploit that weakness and to promote drunkenness generally.

De Mons and Champlain rounded up 120 "workers," who were a higher sociological cut of settler than the derelicts and convicts who had generally been thrown into the breach up to then, and there were also a number of noblemen, a few surgeons, three priests (including one Protestant), and the apothecary Louis Hébert, who went on to immortality in the history of what became Quebec. Three vessels sailed on April 7, 1604, and anchored in an Acadian cove on May 8. They explored what is now the Nova Scotia, New Brunswick, and Maine coast and eventually decided upon Saint Croix Island, about fifty miles west of the present Saint John, New Brunswick, as the place to establish themselves, and settled in for the winter. It was a disaster. About thirty-five of their party died of scurvy and related ailments, and many others were desperately ill. For many years afterward, the Indians called it "the island of bones." Only eleven of seventy-nine settlers were in good physical condition in the spring of 1605. De Mons and Champlain had jointly chosen the site and jointly accepted responsibility for the mistake. Champlain had taken the opportunity to explore the Maine coast in the summer of 1604, and again in 1605, and made very accurate maps of it.

The beleaguered settlement moved from Saint Croix Island to Port-Royal, now Annapolis Royal, Nova Scotia, in 1605, and there was a further mapping expedition along the Maine and Massachusetts coast in 1606. De Mons returned to France in 1605 to find the king impatient and contemplating a project to carve territory out of Portuguese Brazil. De Mons had brought with him a thirty-foot Indian canoe, which put on an impressive passage down the Seine under the king's appreciative gaze, as well as a moose, a caribou, a muskrat, a hummingbird, antlers, and collections of bows and arrows, dead birds, and Indian portraits. A fort was commissioned at Port-Royal, measuring sixty feet by forty-eight feet, whose construction Champlain supervised, having passed on the opportunity to return to France with de Mons.

There had until recently been no women among the French settlers, and Jean de Biencourt de Poutrincourt brought fifty more settlers, all male, to Port-Royal in July of 1606. Champlain had encountered some violent hostility from Cape Cod Indians that autumn, but he and Poutrincourt, bringing three wounded men with them, were welcomed back to Port-Royal with an elaborate theatrical entertainment on the beach in November. For the 1606–1607 winter, Champlain instituted the "Order of Good Times," a weekly feast that raised morale with an abundance of wine and game. When the winter ended, the first vessel to arrive from France, on May 24, brought letters from de Mons that advised that the enterprise had failed. Some of the merchants had been taking graft, and some also claimed that the colonists had failed to honour their obligations to amplify the fur trade. A subsequent vessel arrived with orders for the return of the colonists, and reluctantly, given that the colony was somewhat successful and the crops that had been planted were being harvested, the entire settlement left in August for the return to France. This mission was a success also in the excellent relations that had been fostered with the local Indians, but it had been betrayed at home. Champlain and others were determined to try again, and to make sure that the enabling authority from France was not subject to such capricious revocation. It would be on to Quebec.

Champlain and Poutrincourt returned to France in August and September of 1607 in a crowded old ship with what Champlain's biographer called "a fragrant cargo of 100,000 codfish."[6] Poutrincourt presented the young Indian they had brought with them to the king, who also received the five Canada geese his subjects had brought back, which found a comfortable home in the fountains of Fontainebleau. But "once again, after so much effort, no French settlement survived in North America . . . [and] the honk of Canada geese made a mocking chorus on the fate of New France."[7] Sully, acting on behalf of, and well paid by, some of Paris's leading hatters, persuaded the king to revoke the ten-year monopoly he had granted four years earlier to de Mons. Champlain reckoned that there were already eighty ships, many French, operating out of the St. Lawrence and ignoring the royal grant of the trade, but no colonization could be undertaken without either that revenue or direct assistance from the French government, so Sully was deliberately strangling an effort that he did not believe was in France's interest, and when doing so substantially profited him. The British had set up a colony in Virginia in 1607 (named after the late queen, Elizabeth, whose claims to virginity were not above dispute). The crowns of Britain and Scotland had been united in a distant Stuart cousin of the Tudors, James I of England and VI of Scotland, when Elizabeth died after a brilliant reign, much and justly glorified by Shakespeare, in 1603.

The British were also putting settlers in Maine, which France, as the name implies, claimed. If the French colonization effort, which since Cartier's arrival had been stillborn for more than seventy years, did not get going soon, Britain, with its superior navy, would take over everything north of the Rio Grande, including the entire fur trade. The short-sightedness of the Paris hatters, and even the otherwise gifted Sully, dismayed Champlain, who commented acerbically on the narrow greed of these grasping businessmen. ("These envious folk were clamouring not for their own advantage, but for their own ruin."[8] The self-destructive greed of businessmen was already and would remain a recurring theme, and would include such lapidary formulations of it as Lenin's comment that the "capitalists will sell us the rope we will hang them with.") De Mons and Champlain succeeded in persuading Henry to overrule Sully and the monopoly was reinstated for one year. De Mons bustled from port to port along the entire Atlantic littoral of France and raised the money needed to mount another expedition. It was agreed after vigorous but learned debate between

Champlain and de Mons that they would found a colony at Quebec – which Champlain championed as easier to defend than Acadia, closer to the fur trade, and in the midst of already friendly Indians – and that a smaller party would re-establish the settlement in Acadia. The colonists recruited were a more promising group than the mixed bag of Acadia and the riffraff of previous missions. There were skilled carpenters, masons, and other artisans, a surgeon, but no clergy. Two young men who would become historic figures in Canada, Étienne Brûlé and Nicolas Marsolet, came along.

Champlain arrived at Tadoussac on June 3, 1608, and after facing down trespassers installed at Tadoussac who were buying furs from the Indians without a licence, by reminding them of the likely response of the king if his commission was ignored, Champlain proceeded on to Quebec, assiduously mapping and sounding as he went. He chose the height of land as the place for a fort and the present lower town beneath it as the location of a trading settlement. This was the founding of Quebec. Racing the inexorable approach of winter, he drove the artisans to build an ample storehouse to be sure of food for the season, and what was called the *habitation* to assure more commodious shelter from the elements than previous settlements had had. Champlain pushed his party so vigorously, though without the sadistic flourishes of the Spanish, that a minor mutiny occurred. Champlain had an objective tribunal at Tadoussac adjudicate, then pardoned the lesser conspirators but hanged and beheaded the ringleader and had his severed head mounted on a pike on the ramparts in Quebec.

Despite Champlain's best efforts, twenty Frenchmen died over the winter, seven of scurvy, including the surgeon, and thirteen of dysentery. In June 1609, new and ample supplies arrived from France, but the monopoly (which Champlain did not have the means to enforce), had again lapsed, and the investors had provided funds for only sixteen settlers, a corporal's guard with which to enter the second year of what grandiloquently styled itself "La Nouvelle France." A few soldiers were also sent to assist in maintaining order. De Mons, who had not come to Quebec, also ordered Champlain to return to France for the winter. Before doing so, Champlain executed his plan to strengthen Indian alliances by emboldening the Algonquin of the St. Lawrence valley opposite the more ferocious Mohawk Iroquois to the south, who threatened and intimidated them. Champlain could muster only twenty men, but they were backed by some hundreds of Montagnais and armed with the arquebus, an early firearm that discharged up to four metal balls fairly accurately for a greater range than that of an arrow. Champlain proceeded upriver and had a very convivial meeting with two of the leading Algonquin chiefs, whom he invited, with a large contingent of their braves, to come to Quebec and enjoy the hospitality of the king of France. A week of dancing and festivities ensued, and then Champlain gathered twelve of his countrymen and sixty of the more courageous Montagnais and executed his plan to enter the territory of the Iroquois, proceeding up what is now the Richelieu River. (Richelieu was now twenty-four and edging forward in the royal entourage, but it would be another fifteen years before the future cardinal disposed such power as to cause Champlain to rename Canadian geography after him. Champlain did not scruple, however, and nor should he have, as the first European to see it, to name Lake Champlain.)

On July 30, 1609, at what in the following two centuries would become fabled in the history of both Canada and the United States as Ticonderoga, Champlain's formations encountered a larger Mohawk war party, which was amazed at the impudence of the intruders, whose confidence was shored up exclusively by the presence of the twelve Frenchmen with three arquebuses. The Algonquin had warned the Iroquois that the French had weapons such as the Iroquois had not seen, and when the two formations were only fifty yards apart, Champlain stepped forward resplendent in gleaming armour and a cuirass, as well as his arquebus. The Mohawk looked upon him in some amazement, and at a range of thirty yards, as the elite braves beside the Mohawk chiefs drew their bows at him, Champlain discharged his arquebus, killing the two chiefs and the lead bowman. His arquebusier colleagues, whom he had ordered to enfilade the Mohawks on his right, then fired their weapons, killing the last of the chiefs and a number of other senior warriors as the Montagnais raised a mighty ululation of triumph. The Mohawk formation "shuddered in a strange way and then came apart."[9] The Mohawk broke and fled. Champlain and his allies withdrew, and the French were horrified at the vicious torture the Montagnais perpetrated on their prisoners, scorching their fingers and penises, tearing out their nails and entrails, and forcing some to eat the sliced-up heart of another. Champlain remonstrated, to no effect, that this was evil and subhuman behaviour.

Champlain had changed the balance of power among the Indians and earned the goodwill of the northeastern tribes in a manner the French and French Canadians have never lost. He departed almost at once for France and went at once to Fontainebleau, where he was cordially received by the king, who was naturally delighted at this bizarre triumph of French arms in the wilderness. The king was entirely favourable but declined to restore the fur monopoly. The financial backing was still in place, however, and Champlain returned to New France, arriving at Tadoussac on May 26, 1610, and going quickly on to Quebec. The winter had been mild and the extensive stores had seen the garrison through with minimal illness. Champlain was successfully implored by the Montagnais to lead them again against the Iroquois, who were assumed to be contemplating revenge. On the journey, he was severely assaulted by mosquitoes "so thick that we could hardly draw breath," and then, when he and his party came upon an improvised Mohawk fort about three miles inland from the St. Lawrence, near the mouth of the Iroquois (Richelieu) River, he was almost killed by an arrow that struck him in the neck close to the carotid artery. The Mohawk made a better fist of it this time, and the arrows were "flying on all sides as thick as hail."[10] Champlain ordered the Montagnais to provide a shield for axmen to fell trees onto the improvised Mohawk stockade, opening up a space for his arquebusiers to pepper the enemy inside. Again, the Mohawk tried to flee, but most were massacred or captured and taken home for ritualistic torture. Champlain was given one prisoner, whom he did not mistreat and tried to turn into a peace agent, but the prisoner escaped and fled at the first opportunity. For the rest of his life, Champlain bore the scar of the Mohawk arrow on his neck and ear, and Indians would touch it fetishistically, as a "talisman."[11] These great French victories created a peace of respect with the Iroquois that lasted for about twenty-five years.

Tragedy struck France and New France when Henry IV was assassinated on May 14, 1610, while Champlain was at sea, which news overtook him when he returned victorious to Quebec. The king was murdered by a Catholic fanatic, François Ravaillac, who stabbed him in his carriage because he disapproved his policy of religious toleration.

Champlain returned at once to a capital where all had changed. The new king was Henry's nine-year-old son, Louis XIII, and power would be exercised by the much-wronged widow of Henry and mother of Louis, Marie de' Medici. Marie was an intelligent woman, had the confidence and culture of her family, and was also very beautiful, as a series of paintings she commissioned from the Belgian artist Peter Paul Rubens attests. She had an Austrian mother and, of course, an Italian father, and did not grasp the virtue or maintain the popularity of her late husband's nationalist policy, in Europe or overseas. She dispensed with Sully (a continuing Protestant) in 1611 and replaced him with Concino Concini, the husband of her foster sister, Leonora. Concini was a devious Italian manoeuvrer of high cunning in narrow circles but inaccessible to the affections or even respect of the French. The court became a teeming infestation of claimants, faction heads, and courtiers, and Champlain could make no headway in such an intense and fetid political atmosphere, where all that counted was what was immediate, tangible, and opportunistic, and there was no time or constituency for the long-term strategic interest of France.

In his extraordinary versatility, Champlain had a try at ardent court politicking, working on previous contacts, and, at the age of forty, taking a well-connected wife, Hélène Boullé. It was not one of French history's many riveting romances, but they got on well enough for some years, and Champlain, both by the nature of his person and of his avocation, was quite faithful, if not, perforce, very attentive. (Madame had little ambition for the rugged challenges of early seventeenth-century Quebec.) Champlain also tried to emphasize the Christianizing mission of his project and generate support among the leaders of the clergy, but they were as complicated and politically factionalized as the secular court entourage, and Champlain was not altogether believable in this role. Much of his adult life was a scramble for favour from the court; merchants and other commercial interests; the bishops and religious congregations; the military and navy; and the imagination of the literati. With uncertainty rampant on both sides of the great western ocean, he returned to New France in the spring of 1611.

For some years from this point, New France survived only because of the will and ingenuity of Samuel de Champlain. He worked tirelessly to promote the vision in France and to broaden the base of the colony and expand its population and ambit. He was fighting an uphill battle on both sides of the Atlantic. On his exploratory visit in the summer of 1611, he shot the Lachine Rapids in the company of the Indians, an exercise this fearless man found terrifying (bearing in mind that, despite his immense talents as a mariner, he could not swim). In Paris, he lobbied all his contacts and finally got to the young king. Marie de' Medici was hopeless, from Champlain's standpoint, but Louis XIII would be able to assert himself in a few years. De Mons retired as the chief backer of New France, as he was now old and tired, in body, soul, and pocket book. De Mons also felt that as a Protestant he would have little chance of making it work with the queen regent. Champlain recruited the Count of Soissons, Bourbon governor of Normandy, as governor of New France, but a month after the count's formal installation, he abruptly died. Undaunted, Champlain moved on and recruited the Prince of Condé, one of France's greatest nobles, who insisted on being viceroy of New France, which Champlain eagerly promoted in the hope that Condé would secure the colony the return of the fur trade monopoly. He did, and the monopoly was restored for twelve years.

Triumphant again, Champlain returned to New France in the spring of 1613. It had been a mild winter and the colony was healthy, but still painfully small. Champlain's project this spring was to go up the Ottawa River to, as he imagined to be at the end of it, Hudson Bay. (This was named after the Englishman Henry Hudson, who between 1607 and 1611 was engaged by the English to find a passage to China in the north, did discover Hudson Bay, and then tried to thread his way to China through North America on behalf of the Dutch and discovered the Hudson River. He was back in the Arctic in 1611 on behalf the English, but conditions became so difficult, there was a mutiny and he and his son were put in an open boat and never seen again.) Champlain and his party got about fifty miles upriver from the present city of Ottawa, more than a hundred miles from the St. Lawrence, before Champlain's misinformant confessed under pressure from the local Indians that his claims of a temperate passage to the East were false. Champlain released the scoundrel, who walked into the woods. His fate is unknown.

Champlain returned to France and quickly formed a new

investment company, the Compagnie du Canada. Champlain published another well-written book, accompanied by excellent maps, *The Voyages of the Sieur de Champlain*, dedicated to the king and the queen regent. Champlain was more successful than ever in drumming up support for his project from commercial interests, but his marriage wobbled badly and his wife tentatively left him.

For his 1615 return to Quebec, Champlain brought a group of Récollet fathers (Franciscans) to get the Christianizing mission going and broaden his support for New France at home. His motive was not entirely cynical and avaricious. He was disgusted by the barbarity of the Indians, even as a veteran of the terrible religious strife in France in the previous century, and believed in the need for and value of the civilizing mission of France. He also hoped that at least some of the Indians could eventually become bona fide citizens of New France, that there could be some intermarriage, and that the population might, accordingly, grow more quickly than it would from the meagre propensity of the French to emigrate. Once returned to the colony, Champlain gave the friendly Indians a tutorial in the strategy and tactics of war: that it should only be conducted for a defined and attainable objective, not from boredom or habit, and that it should depart the formalism of Indian war-making and be based on surprise and the application of overwhelming force at the decisive point, not just a general melee. He also warned against violation of civilians and enunciated the objective of defeating the warriors and war-making capacity of hostile tribes but encouraging their civilians to be comfortable, unthreatened, and quiescent in the arrangements France's Indian allies established.

This time he undertook an ambitious and strenuous exploration up the Ottawa River, west past Lake Nipissing to Georgian Bay, southeast to Lake Ontario, and then south to what is now the site of Syracuse, New York. He was impressed at Huron towns of thousands of people, with palisades thirty-five feet high, wooden buildings, and relatively sophisticated agriculture based on the harvesting of corn. The plan was to penetrate to the heart of Iroquois country, defeat them decisively in a surprise engagement, and then withdraw. He had thirteen arquebusiers and several hundred Indian braves for this foray, but battle was joined by an advance party ahead of him and he had to discharge his sinister and astounding weapons to prevent his allies from being defeated and missed the chance to massacre the main Onondaga (Iroquois) force, which quickly retired within its fort. The Indians accompanying him declined to follow Champlain's advice about how to seize the fort and, after an unsuccessful attempt to set fire to it, withdrew. Champlain considered it a defeat, but the effect was useful: it was not such an outrage that the whole Iroquois coalition of tribes felt compelled to retaliate, but it put them on warning that the Algonquin, reinforced by the French, were not to be trifled with. Champlain ended up spending the winter with the Huron, which enhanced his knowledge of them and strengthened his hopes that they could be civilized to Christianity, a gentler life, and the benefits of citizenship in New France. He returned in August 1616 to a France that was soon to come under the sway of one of the greatest and most powerful statesmen in the history of Europe.

3. Canada under Richelieu and Champlain, 1616–1635

Champlain and the faithful Gravé Du Pont returned to Paris in September 1616 to discover that Marie de' Medici was fighting for her political life. He learned on landing at Honfleur that the viceroy of New France, the Prince de Condé (father of the illustrious army commander), was in the Bastille, charged with treason, rebellion, and *lèse-majesté*. The Marquis de Cadillac had replaced him as viceroy and governor, and Champlain's position as lieutenant-governor was purportedly awarded to someone else. The great nobles, led by Condé, disliked the Spanish and Italian influence at the court and over the queen regent, and the Estates General presumed to meet to express discontent. The twenty-nine-year-old bishop of Luçon, Armand Jean du Plessis, who would soon enough become known to the world as the Cardinal and Duke de Richelieu, had distinguished himself at the Estates General as a champion of the Church and supporter of the queen regent, and was asked to give the address there summarizing the findings of the assembly, and then was appointed chaplain to the queen. He attached himself to the flickering star of the queen's favourite, Concini, but when the queen proposed to marry her son, Louis XIII, and daughter off to the daughter and son of the king of Spain, there was such unrest in official French circles it led to factional skirmishing verging on civil war. And when Condé arrived in Paris to attend the Royal Council, where he was next in line to the throne after the adolescent king, Queen Marie had him arrested. Condé's wife insisted on sharing his imprisonment and in the Bastille gave birth to a stillborn child. Like many of Marie's late husband's senior advisers, Nicolas Brulart de Sillery, a patron of Champlain and chancellor of France, was banished from court, and on taking leave of the fifteen-year-old Louis, he suggested that the king could assert his majority. This theme was taken up by the grand falconer, the king's friend Charles d'Albert, Duke of Luynes. Louis did so and had Luynes seize Concini on the bridge of the Louvre. When Concini supposedly resisted, he was impaled, and his wife was imprisoned, tried, and convicted (in a spurious proceeding) of witchcraft and summarily executed by fire. The queen regent was banished to Blois, and Richelieu departed with her. But conditions were unstable, and the outcome of the acute tension in the royal family and upper nobility was not clear. It was a rough-and-tumble climate of intrigue, where the fortunes of all the participants fluctuated wildly and any misstep could be fatal.

Champlain was reinstated, as was Sillery, and Champlain returned to Quebec in the summer of 1617 for only about ten days before rushing back to the teeming conspiratorial atmosphere of the French court. He did bring to New France with him and install there the apothecary Louis Hébert, Poutrincourt's brother-in-law and a member of the expedition to Acadia in 1606. He is reckoned the first settler of New France, and is a folk figure and an honoured name in Quebec to this day. Champlain directed that his work crew build Hébert and his family a solid stone house. By now, there were about seventy Frenchmen living at Quebec, but few of them had any intention of remaining there. In France, Champlain conducted his usual hustling and selling job on the merchants of the coastal cities, emphasizing fisheries, furs, aspirant Christian souls among the natives, even the possibilities of forestry and lumber for shipbuilding and residential construction, whatever seemed to work. The king approved his efforts and renewed his commission, but with an instruction not to interfere with the fur trade. The unpromisingly divided nature of the French enterprise in Canada continued: the fur-seekers would ignore Champlain, who would not benefit from this principal source of revenue in the New World, and colonization alone would not lure many from the temperate and cultivated glories of France to the stern winters of this transoceanic extremity. Louis Hébert and others were soon complaining, with good reason, that the commercial interests were exploiting the settlers. The clergy were soon also raising very vocal objections to the tactics of the fur traders, especially in bartering brandy for furs and swindling and degrading the native people.

In 1619, the queen escaped from Blois and began promoting a rebellion against her son, whose adviser, the falconer Luynes, advised the recall of Richelieu with a mandate to try to settle down the dowager queen. Richelieu did so, in an early sequel to his success at the Estates General in 1614 and in what would become a long and astonishing sequence of diplomatic master strokes. And he produced the Treaty of Angoulême, which ended the internecine hostilities and gave the queen freedom of movement and a seat of honour on the Royal Council, but confirmed the absolute power of the king. There was some continuing armed dissent from this, but it was suppressed without unusual difficulty. Condé was released and restored to all his offices and properties, including the ultimate authority over New France, but he had lost interest during his sojourn in prison and sold that office to his brother-in-law, the Duke of Montmorency.

Richelieu was now a figure of relentlessly increasing power, the master of intrigue as well as of national strategy. He believed that the greatness of France depended on an absolute monarchy that would be too powerful for any faction to depose or ignore or for sectarian or regional squabbling, and that only an omnipotent royal dictatorship could organize France successfully and make it the greatest power in the world. To this end, he naturally enjoyed the increasing support and even gratitude of the king. Louis was nineteen in 1620 and not a physically strong or well-adjusted young man. His father had been disappointed in his puny physique and respiratory ailments and diffident nature, and to impart toughness and manliness to him, his parents directed governesses and tutors to whip him as often and harshly as practical. This was in accord with pedagogical concepts of the time, in France and elsewhere. Montaigne decried the education of boys that generally involved "horror and cruelty . . . violence and compulsion . . . until classes be strewn with bloody stumps of birch-rods."[12] The results of this policy were mixed. Louis was morose and was thought to be bisexual, as he was regularly surrounded with pretty girls and boys, but he was also cunning, calculatedly unpredictable, and extremely conscious and protective of his own authority, and proved a competent commander of troops.

In these ever-shifting circumstances, Richelieu was insuperable. He transferred his loyalty from the queen mother to the king, but used his influence with the queen to calm spirits. He became the indispensable person for the avoidance of civil strife, and when Luynes died of scarlet fever in 1621 he became the king's most influential adviser. For Louis, Richelieu was a providential source of wise and imaginative advice and its ruthless execution, and for Richelieu the king was a reasonably permissive master who embodied the state that Richelieu wished to create for every patriotic and personal reason. Louis XIII successfully commended Richelieu to Pope Gregory XV as a cardinal in 1622, and Richelieu joined the Royal Council in 1624 and replaced Charles de La Vieuville as the head of it in that year. At thirty-nine, he became history's first prime minister, and would retain the position until he died in 1642. Many subsequent relationships, such as Joseph II and Metternich, Frederick William II and Bismarck, and even Richard Nixon and Henry Kissinger, bore some resemblance to this one.

Champlain returned to Quebec in 1620 with an enhanced mandate, some officials to assist him in the administration, and the beginnings of royal enthusiasm for a durable colony that would be commercially self-sustaining and a centre of missionary proselytizing. On his arrival at Tadoussac, he had to dodge illegal traders in larger and more heavily armed ships than his. He found Quebec "in a desolate and ruinous condition."[13] He ordered a complete reconstruction of Quebec, starting with a serious fort, and the replacement of the tumbledown buildings and tenements that the settlement had become. The king had restored the pension that his father had granted Champlain, and Montmorency, as reports poured in from the senior officials in Quebec of the reconstruction being effected, doubled his salary as lieutenant-viceroy and commandant. The king and his advisers did discourage the dispatch of Protestants to New France, which, although it reduced the sectarian ambiguity of the colony, also probably deprived it of many highly motivated settlers, as flight from religious persecution of both puritans and Roman Catholics spurred much colonial activity in the British colonies to the south. Champlain had largely completed his ambitious building plans by the autumn of 1624, and had detained his purposeful wife for four uninterrupted years in the colony. They returned to France so he could renew his agitation for more generous patronage from the monarch he served, aware that almost unlimited power now rested in the hands of the Cardinal and Duke de Richelieu, who had completed the transfer of his flag to the king from the queen mother, whose former affection had turned to hatred, embittered, it was widely alleged, by unrequited passion.

Montmorency also tired of this responsibility and sold on the viceregal office of New France to his nephew, the Duke of Ventadour, for one hundred thousand livres. (It need hardly be emphasized that the fact that such positions were virtually articles of commerce denominated for their potential profitability to the incumbent did not augur well for the prospects of good government.) The new viceroy was only twenty-eight, a fervent Roman Catholic, and a believer in the colonizing and civilizing mission of a French empire. This conformed neatly to the views of the king and his cardinal prime minister, and Ventadour confirmed Champlain as lieutenant-viceroy and commandant of New France and asked him to remain a year with him in Paris to advise him of Canadian affairs and help him sort out his affairs generally. Champlain and his wife were happy to do this, as he lumbered determinedly into his third decade as France's M. Canada.

Ventadour gave the businessmen of Caen a monopoly on the fur trade provided they hired only Roman Catholics as captains of their ships, and fishing remained open to all. Living conditions and relations with the Indians had deteriorated since Champlain left in 1624, and by 1626 there were only forty-three French residents of New France. Champlain returned in the spring of 1626 and took the colony in hand yet again. He founded a farm at Cap Tourmente, about thirty miles from Quebec, and put in train the beginnings of Quebec's agricultural self-sufficiency.

Despite the small numbers of people in New France, religious squabbling descended even to complaints at noisy psalm-singing by

Protestant ship crews on the St. Lawrence, and Champlain had to impose reduced decibel levels on such moments of sectarian exultation.

In 1627, Richelieu decreed a new regime for the colony in an attempt to resolve the endless backbiting that reverberated even in Paris. He retired Ventadour, abrogated existing arrangements, and gave a commercial monopoly and a composite colonial and commercial and ecclesiastical mission to the Compagnie de la Nouvelle France, also known as the Canada Company and as the Company of One Hundred Associates. The cardinal himself subscribed as Associate Number 1, and Champlain was Associate Number 52. Everyone invested three thousand livres. The company claimed all of North America from Florida to the Arctic Circle, which was preposterous given the activities of the British from Maine into what are now the Carolinas, and the Dutch in what is now New York. In early 1628, there were just 55 French in Quebec, whereas in 1630 there were 270 Dutch in the New Netherlands (New York), 300 Pilgrims at Plymouth, and 1,275 English settlers with 22 African slaves in Virginia.

The French and British attempted a reconciliation in 1625 with the marriage of Louis XIII's sister, Henrietta Maria, to the incoming king of England, Charles I, so that both countries could concentrate on besting the Spanish and the Habsburgs. Unfortunately, the English king and his new wife got off to a bad start and quarrelled rather fiercely, and Louis left half of the promised 2.4-million-livre dowry owed to Charles unpaid. At the same time, the Huguenots, with British connivance, were making rebellious noises, and Richelieu famously described them as "a state within a state." Louis and Richelieu attacked the Huguenot stronghold at La Rochelle, which Charles sought to assist, and after closing the port by building a breakwater across its channel of access, Richelieu, in his new capacity as a grand admiral (he had already had himself proclaimed director of navigation and commerce), sealed off the besieged town and starved the Huguenots into submission. The population was reduced from twenty-seven thousand to about five thousand, by famine, disease, and inflicted casualties, when La Rochelle finally surrendered in 1628, after being starved and bombarded for fourteen months. In revenge, Charles and his advisers determined to seize the French colonies in North America and the fisheries of Newfoundland. Money was so tight that Charles privatized this part of the war, and English buccaneers and freebooters proved to be very effective. The Alexanders and Stewarts seized Acadia, and in 1628 the swashbuckling Kirke family, Englishmen who lived in France, began intercepting French shipping on the St. Lawrence. Richelieu ignored the concerns of some of his partners in the Company of One Hundred Associates and had the king order the resupply of New France as if there were no naval war in progress. The mission got to Anticosti Island, where its leader, Admiral Claude Roquemont de Brison, "erected a cross among the seals and polar bears."[14] The Kirkes burned down Champlain's farm and its crops at Cap Tourmente and blocked all traffic on the river at Tadoussac. Champlain beat off their attempted assault on Quebec, but he was obliged to go through another winter without being resupplied with food, gunpowder, or stores of any kind. Kirke's squadron was larger and more heavily armed than Roquemont's, which attempted to come upriver hugging the south shore. Kirke was too alert for that. Both sides fought valiantly in a fifteen-hour firefight, but Kirke overpowered Roquemont eventually, killing the French admiral and about a hundred others, including many prominent settlers. Every vessel in the French fleet was annihilated gallantly or compelled to strike its colours and surrender. The Kirkes returned the survivors to France.

It was a desperate winter for Champlain and his fellow Quebecois, and he led them with his customary courage, sharing to the least crumb the uniform rations of all. They struggled through to the spring, managed to barter some food from the Montagnais, and replanted their gardens. The Kirkes returned in overwhelming force on July 20, 1629, and after extensive negotiation skilfully conducted by Champlain, with both he and Lewis Kirke addressing each other with exquisite courtesy, Champlain salvaged what he could but had no choice but to surrender Quebec. The Kirkes brought everyone back to Britain on the way to France, and the French were well-treated, though dysentery swept the ships and even eleven of Kirke's men died of it. To Champlain's considerable irritation, Étienne Brûlé and Nicolas Marsolet, now skilled interpreters of the Indian languages and astute traders, changed sides to the British. Champlain had heard that peace had been negotiated between the home governments, but Kirke assured him that there was no truth to this. Champlain reminded him that if the report was correct, the seizure of Quebec by the British was illegal. Once in London,

Champlain ascertained from the French ambassador that the war had indeed been ended and that the British takeover of New France was illegal. Champlain waited in London on the assumption that he could return almost immediately to Quebec if the weather did not close in, but nothing happened and finally he departed for Paris on November 30. He was unaware that Louis had still not paid the second half of the promised dowry for his sister as King Charles's bride. Champlain arrived in Paris without a position and with nothing to govern, having lost his investment in Richelieu's Company of One Hundred Associates, and was informed by his wife that she no longer wished to live with him or be his wife. In Catholic France of that era, a divorce or annulment was out of the question, but it was a heavy blow to Champlain, now in his sixtieth year.

Undaunted by this avalanche of bad news and improvident events, Champlain attended upon the king and the cardinal and gave them one of his eloquent sketches of the brilliant future of New France and the vocation of France to span the ocean, be a power in world commerce, lead Europe in the exploration of the whole world, spread Catholic Christianity, and demonstrate its capacity to build and create. Everything from the route to China to the "infinite number of savages who could be brought to Christ" was trotted out in Champlain's torrential sales pitch.[15] His principals were pretty jaded, but they generally subscribed to the nationalistic aspects of his vision and assured Champlain they would push matters with the British king, who was Louis's brother-in-law, after all. But they became distracted by a successfully conducted war in Italy and were in no hurry to pay another 1.2 million livres to the grumpy newlywed king of England, and the matter languished, despite Champlain's perfervid lobbying, for three years. Champlain was his usual energetic self and wrote his ambitious and most successful book, *Voyages of New France*, dedicated to "Monseigneur le Cardinal Duc de Richelieu." It was a mighty tract of promotional puffery for the potential of North America and the virtues of the American Indian, and in a master stroke of lobbying, Champlain published a lengthy and effusive summary of the merits of New France as a national French project in an influential magazine, *Le Mercure Français*, which he entrusted for its editing and final presentation to the original éminence grise, Father Joseph du Tremblay, the Capuchin friar who was Richelieu's closest (in fact, only) confidant and had already entered the history and folklore of France with his chief. The book and article were accompanied by Champlain's greatest feat of cartography.

The Treaty of Saint-Germain-en-Laye in 1632 ratified the peace, paid off the dowry, and restored French overseas possessions. The Company of One Hundred Associates sent the prominent and successful transatlantic merchant Émery de Caën to Quebec to regain possession of New France, and he boldly did so, as the British handed over and departed in July 1632. Richelieu appointed his cousin, Isaac de Razilly, to command in Quebec with a commission in which the name was left blank, but his cousin filled in the name Samuel de Champlain instead of his own, explaining to his illustrious relative that Champlain was the obvious person to resume command. And this was done; Razilly took over the restoration of Acadia.

Champlain returned to New France in March and April 1633, bringing two hundred people with him, including some women and children and four Jesuit priests. The Jesuit superior of France blessed the ships of Champlain's flotilla. It was ninety-nine years since the first arrival of Jacques Cartier, and the French were finally taking steps to generate a permanent colonial community. Quebec had become a frontier town of roustabout French and British traders and adventurers, and the Kirkes had burned down Champlain's *habitation* and fort. Once again, Champlain set his men to work building the sinews of what he intended to raise up, as he had promised the king: a grand capital, Ludovica, of a great French empire in the New World. He started with a new chapel that he named Notre-Dame-de-la-Recouvrance (Our Lady of Recovery).

The dispute over alcohol was now raging. The British had made the chief introduction of alcohol to the Indians, and as they were less preoccupied with Christianizing them, and as the reverent clergy played a more secondary role in the British colonies than in New France, the British had fewer qualms about this form of inducement, to which the Indians continued to show themselves very susceptible. It gave the British a trade advantage that aroused much resentment in French commercial quarters, though at this point Champlain was sentencing French violators of the prohibition on selling alcohol to the Indians to flogging.

The greatest problem was the deterioration in relations between the pro-French Algonquin and the Iroquois in Champlain's absence from New France. The Algonquin were not naturally inclined to peace with their ancient foe, and the Iroquois were much less inclined to leave them in peace in the absence of Champlain or a strong French replacement for him. Champlain outlined these issues in lengthy letters to Richelieu and sought the cardinal's authorization to conduct an aggressive war against the Iroquois. Richelieu was apparently unconvinced, as he did not, so far as is known, reply. Richelieu did not like wars anyway, though he was prepared to subsidize others to make war in the common cause, as he was already doing in the Thirty Years War, which was raging in Central Europe. Champlain waxed rhapsodic over his plans for New France in these letters to Richelieu, who was in favour of the empire and was promoting French colonization in the Caribbean and south and west Africa, and in India as well. But the cardinal was preoccupied with more pressing business than Canada. In 1635, Richelieu finally intervened directly in the Thirty Years War, and thus had only very modest resources available for New France or other colonial undertakings. The long struggle for control of Germany between the Habsburgs and the Bourbons was reaching a climax. Richelieu recognized, as did all astute European statesmen for the next several centuries, that the key to maintaining France as the greatest European power was to assure the division of the German-speaking areas. Richelieu's objective was to leave Germany divided into dozens of small principalities, with France as the guardian of the independent German states, to prevent the Habsburgs from combining all of them under the direction of Vienna in what Richelieu (more or less accurately) considered the confidence trick of the Holy Roman Empire. Richelieu had built a great French state and founded the French Academy to direct the country's cultural initiatives, and his *chef-d'oeuvre* would be the consolidation of French power with an overlordship protecting the fragmentation of the German states whose unity all Europe had feared since Roman times.

Richelieu was more forthcoming on the matter of peopling the New World. Champlain found seventy-seven French in Quebec, whom he supplemented with his shiploads. Louis Hébert had died from a fall on the ice in 1627, but his widow married a ship's carpenter and they had started the first French family of the New World. The next family was that of Abraham Martin, a Scot married to a French woman, who became a master pilot and fishing captain on the St. Lawrence and a farmer on what are known to history as the Plains of Abraham. In 1634, in accord with Richelieu's policy as prime minister and director of navigation and commerce, as well as founder and premier shareholder in the Company of One Hundred Associates, two hundred more settlers of both sexes arrived, and the following year three hundred more. A thousand more immigrants would arrive between 1636 and 1640; 3,500 between 1640 and 1659; and 9,000 between 1660 and 1699. Champlain laid out the seigneurial domains in elongated strips of land abutting the St. Lawrence and the other great rivers of the colony, especially the Richelieu and the Ottawa.

More than two-thirds of the present eight million French Canadians are descended from the eleven hundred French women who came to New France between 1630 and 1680. The largest share of immigrants, perhaps a quarter, came from Normandy.[16] The nasalized form of speaking that became familiar in Quebec, with flattened vowels and a profusion of religious words as curses, arose from western and central-western France in the early seventeenth century. Since 1950, as contact with metropolitan France was reopened, the gap that developed between France and Quebec in the previous three centuries has substantially narrowed, and is now not too much greater than the corresponding differences between English as spoken in the British Isles and North America.

Richelieu's nephew, Isaac de Razilly, was as ambitious for the Acadian colony that he repossessed from the British as Champlain was for New France. Sir William Alexander had tried to set up a British colony in what was called Nova Scotia in 1621, and made a profit centre from selling local baronetcies to Scots, but the project failed after a year. Razilly brought in fifteen French families to relaunch the colony in 1632. (They were astounded to find "lobsters as big as little children," with claws that could "hold a pint of wine."[17]) Richelieu funded this project through the Company of One Hundred Associates also, and in 1633 Razilly brought in more than one hundred settlers. The same astounding demographic fecundity as in Quebec obtained in Acadia. Razilly built several fortifications, but this very capable and principled man, who had many of the best qualities of his illustrious uncle but was not the devious master of intrigue that Richelieu was, died of natural causes aged forty-eight. He was widely mourned, including by his uncle, whom he had motivated to set up a French fort in Morocco, where it was the beginning of the French takeover of that country finally completed nearly three hundred years later. The death of Razilly brought on a rending struggle for Acadia between two robust adventurers, Charles de La Tour and Charles de Menou d'Aulnay, which was only resolved after d'Aulnay seized La Tour's headquarters in his absence and hanged his followers (La Tour's wife died slightly more decorously as d'Aulnay's prisoner), whereupon La Tour fought back, outlasted d'Aulnay, consolidated his position by marrying d'Aulnay's widow in 1653, and soldiered on to 1665.

In 1634, Champlain began the chain of fortified posts at intervals westward and south and northwest from Quebec that would eventually connect New France to the Gulf of Mexico and to Hudson Bay and the Great Plains. The first of these was at Trois-Rivières, where the Saint-Maurice River flows into the St. Lawrence.

The two interpreters that Champlain had brought from France in 1610, Étienne Brûlé and Nicolas Marsolet, who defected to the English during the Kirke era, had very different fates. Brûlé had to take refuge with the Indians but eventually quarrelled with them, allegedly because of his womanizing, and the Huron executed him, relatively humanely by their standards. This was thought to be the only Frenchman the Huron killed, and Champlain did not reproach them for it. Brûlé was forty-one. Marsolet eventually made his peace with the French and conducted a very profitable trade with the Montagnais. He married a French woman, they had ten children at Tadoussac, where he was known as "the little king," and he lived to the age of ninety, a seigneur several times over, dying in 1677 prosperous, a legend to French, English, and Indian, and full of years and honours.

Other noteworthy graduates of Champlain's interpretation service were Olivier Letardif, Champlain's principal interpreter on his major explorations and reconnaissances in the 1620s, who lived on to 1665 and became a seigneur and eminence of the Company of One Hundred Associates, and Jean Nicollet, who became an explorer in his own right and discovered Wisconsin, imagining the present site of Green Bay, a meatpacking and football centre, to be the gateway to China. He narrowly missed the discovery of the upper Mississippi. He drowned in the

St. Lawrence in 1642 while racing to rescue an Iroquois brave from being tortured to death by the Huron. Both Letardif and Nicollet married daughters of Louis Hébert's wife and her second husband and became rather gentrified by the rustic standards of New France.

A word should also be added about Champlain's policy of encouraging intermarriage with Indians, creating the Métis section of the population, which eventually numbered, officially, about three hundred thousand people by the beginning of the twenty-first century, but probably, if all such melanges are taken into account, must really stand at one to several million Canadians. Tragically, the susceptibility of Indians to Western illnesses sharply reduced their life expectancy, and as the French population of New France rose, that of the Indians declined.

Samuel de Champlain died on Christmas Day 1635, aged sixty-five, in his *habitation* at Quebec. He left most of his considerable means to the inhabitants of Quebec, stipulating various endowments and works he wished constructed, and his French assets to his wife, who lived on for many years in a convent (though the will was contested by avaricious relatives in France). He had been largely immobilized by a stroke in October 1635, and gave a prolonged general confession, going through his entire life, to the senior Jesuit in the colony. He again sketched out to secretaries and clergy at his bedside in grand detail his brilliant vision for New France, all of which and much more came to pass, except that, while remaining French, New France eventually ceased to be associated with France. He grasped early and entirely the grandeur of the new continent and the permanence of a French community on the St. Lawrence. Every man, woman, and ambulatory child in Quebec – Stadacona as it had been when he first saw it more than thirty years before – attended Champlain's funeral. His grave, under the Quebec basilica, was burned in a fire in 1640 and has not been exactly rediscovered.

Champlain was a man of astonishing determination, intelligence, imagination, and integrity, a founder of Canada who well-earned the pride and the gratitude of all his future countrymen of every ethnicity, including the natives, whom he loved and esteemed with unfeigned respect. As a founder of a country and nationality, he bears comparison with the very most distinguished, not excluding the illustrious father, 140 years later, of the American republic.

4. The Great Intendant and the First Bishop, 1635–1672

The missions to the Indians were slowly taking root and confirm again the power of the Christian message and the determination of the messenger. The "black robes," as the Jesuits were known, vanished for a year or more into the bowels of the continental wilderness with the Algonquin tribes that had agreed to accept them, and endured the smokehouses, lack of hygiene, constant noise and loneliness. Their hosts, though suspicious of them, did not harm them. Among the most interesting documentary records of the time were *The Jesuit Relations*, which were collected, edited, and published. Initially, they only gave the sacrament of the dying as a supplement to the indigenous rites, but, as was the Jesuits' experience with the heathen in other places, even in China, eventually some of the adult natives converted and despite the censure of their fellow tribesmen accepted the Christian yoke. The objective continued to be to rally the Indians to the faith and then to the Crown and the laws of France, and – in addressing these lamentable absences summarized by Champlain in the phrase *"ni foi, ni roi, ni loi"* (neither faith nor king nor law) – to make New France one community of two peoples united in the same faith. It was always a very optimistic scenario.

Marie de l'Incarnation (1599–1672) and some Ursuline sisters arrived in 1639 to build and staff a convent and provide for the education of the girls of the colony, including Indians. Richelieu's niece, the Duchesse d'Aiguillon, sent three Augustinian sisters, who founded the Hôtel-Dieu de Québec, a hospital which has been in continuous operation in Quebec City ever since. The bishop and theologian Jacques-Bénigne Bossuet called Marie de l'Incarnation the Saint Teresa of New France. Jeanne Mance (1606–1673) was the founder of nursing services in Montreal, and worked closely with Marie de l'Incarnation, and with Marguerite Bourgeoys (1620–1700), founder of the Congrégation de Notre-Dame, who arrived in Montreal in 1653. (Marie de l'Incarnation was beatified in 1980, and Marguerite Bourgeoys was canonized in 1982, both by Pope John Paul II.)

The governor replacing Champlain was Charles Jacques Huault de Montmagny, who had an extensive military background on the fringes of civilization. He was a veteran of the Turkish Wars, and like John

Smith in Virginia, he saw the North American Indian in the same light as primitive outlaws to advanced Christian civilization. His appointment did not augur well for New France's relations with the Indians that Champlain had gone to such lengths to placate. By 1641, the depredations of the Iroquois were causing serious inroads in the free movement of furs into and along the Great Lakes and down the St. Lawrence. Richelieu himself sent funds for the construction of a fort where the Richelieu River flowed into the St. Lawrence, as the Iroquois attacked ever more aggressively, apparently targeting the Huron but also the French. Undeterred by this challenge, France sent Paul de Chomedey, Sieur de Maisonneuve, a straightforward soldier, to enact Champlain's plan for a fort at what is now Montreal. He was accompanied by Jérôme Le Royer de La Dauversière, a wealthy and pious man of commerce, and by the Abbé Jean-Jacques Olier de Verneuil, who founded the Sulpician Seminary, and by Jeanne Mance, who for twenty years was, with Maisonneuve, Marie de l'Incarnation, and Marguerite Bourgeoys, the guiding inspiration of Montreal, which for most of that time was severely endangered by the Iroquois. These were people of immense courage and virtue; few cities can have had such exemplary founders.

Cardinal Richelieu died on December 4, 1642, aged fifty-seven, after eighteen years as first minister and twenty-one years as the leading counsellor to Louis XIII, who died five months later, in May 1643, aged forty-two. The two men had greatly strengthened the French state internally and opposite other European powers. Pope Urban VIII commented that "if there is a God, Cardinal Richelieu will have much to answer for. If not, then he was a great man." He is rivalled only by Bismarck, and possibly de Gaulle, as the greatest statesman in the history of the nations of continental Europe. France remained the greatest power in Europe until the end of the Napoleonic Wars, two hundred years after Richelieu first rose to prominence by dismissing the Estates General. Richelieu was succeeded by his selected disciple, the Italian (but well-acculturated to France) Jules Cardinal Mazarin. Louis XIII was succeeded by his infant son Louis XIV, only five, who would rule for seventy-two years, and in his own right, from 1661 to 1715.

In 1648, the Thirty Years War finally concluded with the Treaty of Westphalia, which Richelieu had largely drafted and left for Mazarin, and which splintered Germany into three hundred principalities and

states. This weakening of the Holy Roman Empire in Germany was complimented by the establishment of the independence of the Portuguese
and the Dutch Republic from Spain. This terrible war inflicted an estimated eight million casualties in Central Europe, but France dodged
most of it, emerged as Europe's greatest power, and it was the culmination of Richelieu's work.

Unfortunately, as soon as that war ended, and before the French
army could regain the frontiers of France, the wars of the Fronde broke
out, unleashed by great nobles who resented the centralization of power
under Richelieu and the cardinal's taxation of them to support the
central government and his wars of expansion in Europe. They would
not have attempted such a rebellion against Richelieu, but did chase
Mazarin out of the country twice. These wars were on behalf of feudal
noble rights and were mounted by an odd coalition of dissentient noble
traditionalists and overtaxed bourgeois. The toing and froing of the
combat had as much the character of *opéra bouffe* as of real warfare, but
the great marshals Turenne and Condé were for a time in opposition
to the young king and his chief minister. The royalists prevailed eventually, though they made some concessions. Naturally, the French government was seriously distracted from colonial affairs.

In Britain, Charles I's high-handed treatment of Parliament and his
erratic conduct led to the English Civil War, the king's trial and execution, and the Puritanical Commonwealth, set up and governed in very
authoritarian manner by Oliver Cromwell, a talented and courageous,
but strident and inflexible, man. Britain, too, had things other than
colonial adventures to consider, until the return of Charles II, who had
been given asylum and assistance by his cousin Louis XIV, in 1660.
Under Charles II (reigned 1660–1685) and his brother, James II (reigned
1685–1688), relations were excellent with Louis XIV, and peace reigned
between France and Great Britain in all spheres (apart from a brief and
inconclusive scuffle in the Netherlands from 1665 to 1667).

In New France, the chief concern was the Iroquois, whose aggres-
sivity was strangely assisted by the diseases that had been imported by
the French, Dutch, and British, and had reduced their population by
almost half. The leaders of the five Iroquois tribes determined that they
had to replenish themselves demographically as increasing numbers of
Europeans arrived, and the logical way to do so was to overwhelm and

enslave neighbouring tribes (that had been similarly decimated by illness) and add them to their population. From 1648 to 1650, the Iroquois
attacked the Huron with relentless persistence, going far beyond the
traditional punitive raid.

The Iroquois effectively stopped the fur trade on the Ottawa. The
French were able to keep it open on the St. Lawrence, but the Iroquois
starved it farther back toward its sources in the north and west. Huronia,
near what is now Midland on Georgian Bay, was ravaged on March 16,
1649, and after killing the Jesuits in the most gruesome manner – most
infamously Jean Brébeuf and Gabriel Lalemant – by scalping, mock
baptisms with scalding water, and assault with red-hot hatchets, the
Iroquois marched the Huron off to captivity, where they were integrated
into subordinate roles among the Iroquois. (Brébeuf and Lalemant
died, with perfect calm and bravery, in silence, and were canonized in
1930, and Pope John Paul II conducted a very heavily attended service
at the site of their deaths in 1984.) Brébeuf had made serious inroads
with the Huron, and there is room for conjecture about what the impact
would have been if he had substantially succeeded and the Huron had
come en masse to Catholicism. It could have vastly increased the viability of New France. As it was, with the parent country seriously distracted,
the colony was not able to enjoy peace with the British and had to fight
for its life against the Iroquois.

The French set up refuges for the Huron and other victims
from friendly tribes at L'Ancienne-Lorette, site of the present Quebec
City airport, just west of the city, and at Caughnawaga, across the
St. Lawrence and slightly west of Montreal. But the Iroquois were
prowling around Montreal and Trois-Rivières, and although they
could not frontally attack strong French emplacements, they almost
completely stopped the fur trade for more than a year and threatened
the strangulation of the raison d'être of New France. Part of the problem had been that Montmagny had not known how to overawe the
Iroquois as Champlain had, nor how to inspirit France's Indian allies
against their more ferocious Indian rivals by displays of bold military
intrusion and decisive use of firepower.

In 1648, after twelve years, Montmagny handed over the governorship of New France to the acting governor of Montreal in the absence
of Maisonneuve, Louis d'Ailleboust de Coulonges. But d'Ailleboust had

no particular plan to deal with the crisis, and much of the responsibility for protecting New France devolved on Maisonneuve, governor of Montreal from 1642 to 1665. In 1652, Maisonneuve returned to France to raise, on his own authority, and in the absence of any coherent government policy, one hundred volunteers to help defend Ville-Marie, as Montreal was still known, whose population had dwindled to fifty frightened souls. Maisonneuve raised his rescue party and returned, and Ville-Marie gradually recovered its population. By this time, d'Ailleboust had retired as governor and been replaced by a career colonial service official, Jean de Lauzon, who held the post from 1651 to 1657. He owned Montreal Island and the Île d'Orléans and was the greatest landowner in New France. Lauzon was learned and distinguished, but was not effective at dealing with the Iroquois.

It is now generally believed that the turning point in the fortunes of the struggle of New France with the Iroquois came in May 1660, when the twenty-four-year-old soldier-adventurer Adam Dollard des Ormeaux, with the approval of Maisonneuve, led a group of sixteen volunteers on a ten-day canoe trip up the Ottawa River for a raid on the Iroquois. At an abandoned stockade at Long Sault, his party was surrounded by seven hundred Iroquois and attacked. Dollard and his companions, assisted by about forty Huron, conducted a fierce three-day fight against overwhelming odds and eventually all were killed, but after killing or wounding perhaps twenty times their number of the enemy. The engagement, known as the Battle of Long Sault, has achieved a folkloric status in Quebec, largely thanks to the historical treatment of it by the twentieth-century Quebec nationalist leader Canon Lionel Groulx. He portrayed it as like the Battle of the Alamo at San Antonio, Texas, in February and March 1836, when 189 Texans were finally overwhelmed by 1,800 Mexicans under the seven-times president of that country, General Antonio L. Santa Ana. The resisters, led by Davy Crockett, Jim Bowie, and William Travis, all perished, but killed four to six hundred of their opponents. Dollard's stand inspired his countrymen and was a caution to the Iroquois of what aroused and well-armed Frenchmen could do.

This was the era when enthusiasm for the fur trade caused young Frenchmen in New France to venture determinedly into the back country as what became known as coureurs de bois, spending years on end with the natives and becoming themselves the middlemen in the fur trade, and the Algonquin took the place of the Huron. The coureurs de bois tended to be lawless, disorderly people, rough and ready and brave men who did not take direction from the civil government or the ecclesiastical authorities, but performed an essential service in reviving the fur trade, the commercial lifeline of New France. Because of the intervention of the Iroquois, it became much more difficult for the French to get their hands on furs – the Huron could not get them to the docks of Trois-Rivières or Quebec, and the coureurs de bois had to open new routes or organize their suppliers to approach more circuitously, where the Iroquois did not penetrate. For the perilous history of New France through the first half of the seventeenth century, under Champlain's inspired and clever example, the French, minimal though their numbers were, could work with the Indians, favouring some against others and being indispensable to their allies. For the last half of that century, there was a war for the survival of the colony, although the colony gradually got the upper hand and strengthened. While the Iroquois could intimidate, kill, scatter, and subsume the Huron, they could not replace them in the fur trade. They were not as efficient canoers, nor as adept at growing corn, which the Huron bartered for fur, and did not have the commercial aptitude of the Huron. This was also the time when the issue of selling brandy to the Indians became particularly heated. The French needed it as an inducement, especially as the British were selling rum, but the religious character of the colony was also becoming more pronounced; the spirit of Protestantism, so useful in commercial matters, was sorely missed.

The principal agent of this intensification of religious zeal and organization was François de Laval de Montmorency, appointed apostolic vicar by order of the pope (Alexander VII) in a compromise between the Sulpicians, who wanted a loyalist of the king of France, and the Jesuits, who wanted someone who would be more independent of the crass secular interest of the French crown. Laval had been educated by the Jesuits, but he was a secular deacon, and, as a relative of the Montmorency family, one of the greatest in France, was an abbé and a nobleman. Laval gave up his considerable fortune to his family to pursue missionary work and was going to embark for Tonkin, in China and Indochina, when that mission was stopped by the Portuguese government, which had been inconvenienced by the agitation of missionaries, especially Jesuits, for more humane treatment of natives in the Portuguese and Spanish territories in Latin America.

Lauzon was followed as governor by Pierre Voyer d'Argenson de Mouzay, governor from 1658 to 1661, and then by Pierre d'Avaugour, governor from 1661 to 1663, and Laval quarrelled with all of them over the sale of liquor and the primacy of authority between Church and state. Under cardinals Richelieu and Mazarin, the French state and Church worked closely together and the French Church was Gallican, essentially a national church that obeyed the pope in doctrinal matters but tried not to disagree with the French state – that is, the king – in secular affairs. The Jesuits tended, though Laval because of his worldly background finessed this, to report directly to the pope through the Society of Jesus, and were thus ultramontane (taking their direction from across the mountains, i.e., Rome) and sought complete independence from secular rulers, whose material interests they had often felt – as in the appalling exploitation of the natives of South and Central America – differed sharply from Christian spiritual values.

Laval would remain a mighty force in the colony for fifty years, and he plunged into controversy at the outset, rejecting the claimed authority of the archbishop of Rouen, who regarded New France as part of his see and who already had a vicar general in the colony, as did the Jesuits and Sulpicians. Laval had the inside track with both the pope and the king and would not hear of it. He began his episcopate (he was technically the bishop of Petraea) by visiting every family in the See in its home.[18] Laval's passion for his faithful was matched by the fervour he displayed in enforcing his will on the secular community. He returned to France in 1662 to demand the recall of the governor, d'Avaugour, for authorizing the sale of brandy to the Indians, and Louis xiv obliged him. Laval returned to Quebec in 1663 with the new governor, Augustin de Saffray de Mézy. He immediately set up a seminary, where he lived, and this became the nucleus for Laval University, which grew into one of the premier institutions of higher learning in the French-speaking world.

By the time Laval arrived in Quebec, New France, under the original planning of the Company of One Hundred Associates led by Richelieu and Champlain, was supposed to have a population of thirty thousand, be flourishing in agriculture, fisheries, fur, lumber, and a variety of precious and base metals, and a reliable profit centre and source of gains for the company's investors. But in fact it had only three thousand inhabitants, compared with fifty thousand English in New England, thirty thousand in Virginia, and ten thousand Dutch in the New Netherlands (New York), including some families that went on to very great renown, such as Roosevelt, Rockefeller, and Vanderbilt. Charles II founded new colonies in Pennsylvania (allotted to the evangelical Christian William Penn) and in North and South Carolina (named, of course, after his indecorously deceased father and himself). Thus, even 350 years ago, the European populations of what became, more than a century later, the United States and Canada, were at a ratio of thirty to one. This demographic correlation would not only tilt the scales between the British and the French in North America, but, in subsequent centuries, between the sovereign countries themselves.

By this time, Cardinal Mazarin had died and been succeeded as chief minister (but only as director of finance, as Louis XIV would govern personally) by the very capable secular administrator Jean-Baptiste Colbert, who later assumed all the other posts to do with trade, economics, and shipping. Louis XIV was now twenty-three and determined to exercise power directly, and without so powerful a minister as his father had had with Richelieu, or even Mazarin, who commended Colbert to the king. Louis had been much shaken as a child by the violence and mob disorder in the wars of the Fronde, with Paris itself twice in the hands of unruly insurgents and hordes of mere vandals. He was set at the head of Europe's and the world's most powerful country with the engine of Richelieu's unprecedentedly centralized state under him, and the strategic fruit of the Thirty Years War to harvest. Louis was ambitious as monarch and Frenchman, and was determined to change the world and start by asserting his authority everywhere. It was part of his concept of France's role in the world that it should strengthen its presence in North America and redefine its civilizing mission well beyond and above conducting desperate canoe sorties among the swarms of insolent, savage bushwhackers that terrorized his overseas subjects right up to the walls of their fortified towns.

Colbert exposed the extravagance and embezzlement of his rival, Nicolas Fouquet, thus enhancing his own prospects. Fouquet had built himself the opulent house Vaux-le-Vicomte, as well as a fortified island to which he could retire if out of favour. Louis manoeuvred him into selling his office as attorney general and then prosecuted him and sentenced him to life imprisonment, where he was comfortable, and stoical, but lonely and accompanied by his servant, whom Alexandre Dumas made famous as the title character in *The Man in the Iron Mask*. Once installed in Fouquet's official place, Colbert raised tariffs, promoted the production in France of sophisticated glass and mirrors, on which Venice had enjoyed a virtual monopoly, fostered textile manufacturing that competed with that in the Netherlands, and founded the Gobelins tapestry works. He founded the French merchant marine and tried to reduce the ranks of the clergy by raising the eligible age for seeking holy orders. He also tried to reduce the exemptions and privileges enjoyed by nobles and the clergy in the tax system, and impressed upon the king the fact that half of the taxes assessed in the country either were not paid or were embezzled. He was able to make a good deal of progress here, and to reapportion tax more efficiently and equitably. Colbert famously stated that "the art of taxation consists in pulling the quills out of the goose so as to get as many feathers with as little hissing as possible."

Louis and Colbert soon recognized that part of the problem in New France was the greed and intractability of the commercial interests that effectively ran the colony. Louis abolished the charter of the Company of One Hundred Associates, which had operated somewhat reasonably while Richelieu watched it from France and Champlain supervised its operations, but had become an irresponsible siphoning operation. In 1664, he gave full authority to the French West India Company, which proved an insane idea, though the company never had the time or lack of oversight to permit it to become as steeped in lassitude as the predecessor enterprise. In 1663, New France had become a royal province and was to be governed by a Sovereign Council composed of the governor, the bishop (vicar general until Laval was elevated to bishop in 1674), and five other councillors who were chosen by the king, in practice on the recommendation of the governor and bishop. The council could hear petitions from the syndics representing various groups of inhabitants. (It replaced and had rather greater powers than the Council of Quebec of 1647.) .

The metropolitan government was also emulated by the creation of the position of intendant (*superintendent* may be the closest equivalent in English, in the sense of superintending public policy, not a mundane jurisdiction like a residential building). The first occupant of this position in New France was Colbert's protégé, Talon (and Colbert held this title in the French state). Talon joined Laval and Governor Saffray de Mézy on the Sovereign Council. The first intendant, the Sieur Robert, had been appointed in 1663 but never arrived to take up his post. Talon arrived on September 12, 1665, with the new governor to replace de Mézy, Daniel de Rémy de Courcelle. Talon accepted the post of intendant from Colbert on the understanding that it would be for a defined term and he would be able to trade in the fur business on the side for his own account.[19] Louis had sent three hundred skilled labourers the year before to get cracking on the buildings and roads a serious settlement would require, and they had already accomplished much. (Depictions of these personalities show that the king, Colbert, Talon, and Laval all looked almost the same: dark curly hair in ringlets – except for Laval's, which in keeping with his tonsure was less luxuriant – and somewhat raffish moustaches.)

In 1665, Louis sent the Marquis de Tracy, a battle-scarred veteran of many campaigns, including the Turkish Wars, to Canada with the Carignan-Salières regiment of one thousand trained and combat-proven troops. (They had an astoundingly top-heavy 117 officers, thirty-five of whom were over sixty, and the regiment rioted when informed of their destination, but they were dispatched with the authority the French state now habitually exercised.[20]) The Iroquois had never faced anything like this, and Tracy's first effort, an insouciant plunge through the snows of the Quebec winter, did not achieve anything, but it built forts at Sorel, Chambly, and the outlet to Lake Champlain, and in 1666 Tracy and the regiment, supplemented by six hundred semi-trained militiamen, marched into the heart of Iroquois territory, frightened the Mohawks out of their homes, burned to ashes all five of their villages and all their crops and stores, and returned with minimal casualties. The Indians quickly sent peace envoys to Quebec, and a satisfactory peace was agreed in 1667. His mission largely fulfilled, Tracy moved on to other trouble spots in the French empire, but the combination of Courcelle, Laval, and Talon invigorated administration and life in New France. Talon wrote Colbert letters that demonstrated that he was the first person since Champlain to grasp what Canada could become, but Colbert replied that this would require much accelerated emigration and that neither he nor the king wished "to unpeople France to people New France." This was rubbish of course, as the provision of five hundred immigrants a year, with the astounding birthrate that French Canadians achieved and maintained, would have given the colony a population of half a million by about 1700, and that level of immigration was not 10 per cent of the casualties France incurred in Louis's wars. But this response from Colbert indicated that although the will to make something of Canada was greater and more practically executed than before, limits to the scale of the mission persisted.[21]

Talon set to work organizing an armada of fifty vessels conveying workers, tools, and building materials back and forth to the sites where forts were being built. He founded three towns around what is now Charlesbourg (now Lower Town Quebec), and obtained settler status for many of the Carignan-Salières soldiers; this endowed the colony with a very solid militia, on the model of the Roman military colonies, which Talon invoked. He increased cultivated acreage by 50 per cent a year and harvests accordingly. He founded a successful ship-building industry and launched a commercial maritime exchange with the French West Indies. Copper and iron ore were discovered and developed on the upper Ottawa and at Baie-Saint-Paul. He built a brewery in Lower Town Quebec, which soon produced four thousand hogsheads of beer annually, half for export to the West Indies, and provided a strong market for local grain. Between 1667 and 1671, 1,828 people immigrated, a large number young women, almost all of whom were married within a year. Talon gave away fifty livres in household supplies to every girl or woman getting married, and there was a "king's gift of 20 livres for every young man marrying by the age of 20 and a penalty for any father who had an unmarried son above the age of 20 or unmarried daughter above the age of 16." Talon specified that the girls must be "without physical flaws and had nothing about them that might provoke distaste."[22] Colbert encouraged this, and in one letter to Talon suggested "the mark of shame" for those who willfully refused to marry (apart from clergy, of course). From 1665 to 1668, the population increased from 3,215 to 6,282. It was not only people who were prolific. In 1664, there was only one horse in New France; in 1698, there were 684. There were similar patterns with cattle, sheep, and even mules. (There were concerns that too many horses would make the population too social and even alcohol-dependent, and cause it to lose its proficiency with snowshoes.)[23]

In 1654, the British, in an expedition of four ships from New England, had overwhelmed the small Acadian settlements at Port-Royal and along the Penobscot and Saint John rivers. They seized Acadia as a consolation prize for being insufficiently strong to take New Amsterdam from the Dutch. But in the friendly atmosphere between Louis XIV and his cousin Charles II, Acadia was returned to the French in 1670. Comparatively heavy immigration tapered off after 1673, as Louis and Colbert became heavily engaged in wars on the frontiers of France and manpower and fiscal resources were concentrated there, on Louis's ambition to advance into Flanders and to the Rhine. Petty criminals continued to be sent (161 smugglers and poachers were received in Canada between 1723 and 1749).[24] Talon encouraged the production of tar and potash and hemp, though these products were only moderately successful commercially.

Laval departed for France from 1672 to 1675 for the purpose of elevating his domain to a bishopric after his intense battle with the archbishop of Rouen, who persisted in treating Canada as a far-flung group of his parishes. Laval returned with a fine episcopal ring to present for obedient veneration by all, as the bishop of New France in 1675, victorious again, as he almost always was in this sort of infighting, which was as constant on the Sovereign Council in Quebec as it was with the Sulpicians in Quebec and the secular orders of France. Laval's success with the king was more remarkable as he was seeking an ultramontane status, reporting directly to Rome and not to bishops of the Gallican Church whose elevation had been approved by the king.

In 1674, Louis and Colbert wearied of the effort to charge money-grubbing merchants with a mission of national expansion and Christian and cultural edification and finally declared New France a colony where France paid the bills and reaped the rewards and made all the decisions.

Despite Talon's efforts to diversify the economy of New France, the relentless economic reality, heightened by the turn of fashion in Paris to emphasize fur coats for women and fur hats for both sexes, was that the fur trade was more important than ever. The Iroquois threat had been beaten back by the mid-1670s and renewed interest arose in the question of whether there was a passage to China through or around Hudson Bay. The scale of competition between France and Britain in the fur trade was fairly civil while the Stuarts reigned in London, up to 1687, but both sides were putting outposts and trading stations farther and farther away from points of export (Quebec, Boston, and later New York). The expansion of the fur trade was facilitated by the relative quiescence of the Iroquois. When they contemplated an attack on the Ottawas, the partner of the French in the fur business, they were advised by the effective governor, Courcelle, that that would bring full-fledged war with France and they desisted. By this time, the first serious efforts to expand the hinterland of fur production and exportation were being focused on the west and south.

René-Robert Cavalier de La Salle, a Norman Jesuit who left the Society for the temptations of exploration, teamed up with Louis Jolliet, a Quebec native, and the French Jesuit Jacques Marquette, and from 1669 to 1672 they explored south to the Ohio River and as far as the present Louisville, Kentucky. In 1673, Jolliet and Marquette went down Lake Michigan and struck west up the Fox River, discovered the northern Mississippi and followed it down to about 430 miles from the Gulf of Mexico, at the mouth of the Arkansas River, where they started to run into Indians with Spanish goods. They were the first people to engage in serious mapping of the middle and upper Mississippi, and they beat a path for ambitious French fur traders. Jolliet and Marquette returned and wintered near the present Chicago. Jolliet would later explore the northern Labrador coast and vanished in 1700 while sailing to take possession of Anticosti Island, which had been granted to him in recognition of his services. Marquette struck farther west but died in 1675 of the effects of dysentery in what is now Michigan. All this while, two vintage swashbucklers, Pierre-Esprit Radisson (1636–1710) and his brother-in-law Médard des Groseilliers (1618–1696), were active fur traders, sometimes for the French and sometimes for the English, depending on the identity of the highest bidder. (Radisson married the daughter of "Admiral" Sir John Kirke, who had seized Quebec in 1629.)

Jean Talon departed Quebec in November 1672 and was graciously received by the king and his finance director, Colbert. Talon became premier valet to the king and premier secretary of the king's cabinet, and served in these influential capacities to his master's entire satisfaction until he died in 1694, aged sixty-nine.

5. Governor Frontenac, 1672–1689

The new governor who replaced Courcelle in 1672 was Louis de Buade, Comte de Frontenac, one of the epic personalities of New France. If Champlain's father had been friendly with Henry IV, Frontenac's father was a childhood friend of Louis XIII, and Governor Frontenac was allegedly named after him. Frontenac was eighteen years older than Louis XIV and knew him, cordially but respectfully, most of his life. He joined the army at age fifteen, in 1635, became a colonel at twenty-three and a brigadier general at twenty-six, and fought continuously in Flanders, the Netherlands, and Italy, until France, under the great marshals Condé and Turenne, got to the Rhine, to the gates of Munich, and humbled the Spanish, and in 1648 the Peace of Westphalia was signed.

Frontenac's gallantry was conspicuous, and he was wounded many times. He was cunning and fierce and a proven soldier, but was effectively unemployed after peace broke out, and he returned to his estate and abruptly married the beautiful and socially prominent Anne de La Grange, contrary to her parents' wishes. Frontenac's wife was very friendly with one of the great diarists and court figures of the second half of the seventeenth century, Anne Marie Louise d'Orléans, Duchess of Montpensier, niece of Louis XIII, god-daughter of Richelieu, daughter of Gaston d'Orléans, whom Richelieu had exiled because of his attempted coup against him, and the grandest and wealthiest heiress in Europe at the time. Louis XIII had given her the title "granddaughter of France," and as her father was known as "Monsieur," she became universally known as "la Grande Mademoiselle." She rejected marital overtures from England's King Charles II (her cousin), Portugal's Alfonso VI (whom she dismissed rather severely as "alcoholic, impotent, and paralytic"), and Duke Charles Emmanuel of Savoy. Frontenac's marriage was unhappy, and his wife influenced the princess to disparage him acerbically in her sulphurous diaries. (Vita Sackville-West, in her biography of la Grande Mademoiselle, remarked that "M. de Frontenac seems to have got on better with red Indians than with his wife."[25])

Frontenac lolled on his estate in a condition of some dissolution and racked up heavy debts in the fifteen years after Westphalia, and was glad to go back to war, first against the Turks in Hungary, and then, by the intervention of Turenne, on loan to the Venetians in the French mission to assist that fading city state in its forlorn attempt to keep the island of Crete from the Turks. Frontenac put up a tremendous fight in an impossible cause and was rewarded with the governorship of New France at the age of fifty-two. He was an erratic administrator, extravagant and somewhat financially corrupt, showy, boastful and impetuous, but a strong leader and a capable general, a flamboyant personality who had little of the administrative judgment of Talon, who departed as Frontenac arrived, or of the principles and self-discipline of Laval, with whom he quarrelled constantly for decades, usually over utterly trivial matters. Canada was an appointment for Frontenac that promised to erase his financial problems, because of the salary and the opportunity for self-enrichment, and got him away from his wife and her friends, who found his presence anywhere near the court annoying. The king gave him a special grant of fifteen thousand livres for expenses and a personal guard of twenty men.

The Quebec habitant of this time was a rugged but independent-minded man. His life was not gentle, but the seigneurs depended on the tenant farmers to clear their land, and the habitant was far from a serf. He had a respectable, handmade home, plenty to eat as long as he could shoot, grow, or trap it himself, and he was more prosperous, more optimistic, and healthier than the distant cousins he had left behind in France, and was less likely to be overtaxed, conscripted to war, or uneducated. And the seigneurs had nothing like the material or social incumbency of the French nobility, steeped for centuries in the wealth of *la douce France*.

"For young and daring souls the forest meant the excitement of discovery, the licence of life among the Indians, and the hope of making more than could be gained by the habitant from his farm. Large profits meant large risks, and the *coureur de bois* took his life in his hands. Even if he escaped the rapid and the tomahawk, there was an even chance that he would become a reprobate."[26] The coureur, however (who numbered about four hundred at the time of Frontenac's arrival), was valuable in keeping the fur trade moving, and worth his weight in gold in wartime, when he knew the country and the wood-crafts as well as the Indians did, and was as technically sophisticated as the best-trained French or British soldiers. But the coureurs were insubordinate and self-interested and often fell afoul of the governors and the clergy.

The Quebec Church, Jesuits, Sulpicians, and Récollets were mission-aries, and their original principal activity was ministering to and trying to convert the natives. By the time Frontenac arrived, the policy of Talon to increase the European population by immigration and encour-agement of procreation had created a demand for a more pastoral church, which gave Frontenac all the pretext he needed to begin a lengthy tug-of-war with Laval. Frontenac's other opening gambit was to summon the various leaders of social and corporate elements in the colony in a miniature Estates General, for which he was as sharply slapped down by the king and Colbert as the several months required for back-and-forth communication allowed. Louis and those in his entourage were absolutists, and they did not want any such popular consultations anywhere in the kingdom.

Frontenac's next endeavour was a summit meeting with the Iroquois at Cataraqui, where Kingston now is, in July 1673. Here in 1674, La Salle built the first of many forts that were strung out along the fur-trading routes over the next fifty years, but Frontenac arranged that he would profit substantially from it. Frontenac brought as many soldiers as possi-ble and arrived at Cataraqui in a large flotilla of canoes and barges with cannons mounted on them, the governor and his entourage in rich fin-ery. It was an effective show of strength, and Frontenac was always theatrical. This opening encounter was a success, and the new governor was clearly the heir to Champlain at the subtleties of dealing with the Indians, firm but respectful and honourable and well-served by his desire always to present a powerful facade. Less successful was Frontenac's dis-pute with Maisonneuve's successor as governor of Montreal (and Talon's nephew-in-law), François Perrot, whom Frontenac imprisoned for ten months over the status of coureurs de bois, whom Perrot favoured and subsidized. For good measure, Frontenac hanged a coureur within sight of Perrot's prison cell. Finally, the matter was pleaded before the king himself by Perrot (after whom Île Perrot, adjacent to Montreal, is named).

The king found for Frontenac and sent Perrot for a symbolic three weeks in the Bastille, but told Frontenac not to be quite so heavy-handed with local governors again.

The ambiance began to heat up again in September 1675 when the newly installed Bishop Laval returned after an absence of four years. Rarely has authority in a small place been shared by two personalities as strong and certain to disagree as these two men. Frontenac had not been in Quebec three months when he began sending messages back to France, of which Laval, still in France, was quickly apprised, reporting that the Jesuits were over-profiting from the fur trade and were more interested in pelts than souls, were unreasonably blocking the sale of brandy, and in the guise of missionary work were ignoring pastoral duties. There was only one resident priest and Laval did handle the money the Church collected from all sources, which Frontenac judged avaricious and the cause of injustices. Laval responded that the governance of the Church was no legitimate concern of the secular leaders of the colony. The bishop and the governor even quarrelled over the extent of deference to be shown to the governor during religious services, and finally Louis XIV had to resolve this also, imposing the example of the honours shown the governor of the French province of Poitou. Frontenac didn't care for the Sulpicians either, but conciliated the Récollets and was an observant Roman Catholic himself. At bottom, Frontenac was a Gallican who thought the king and his representatives should control civil matters and that the king should influence the choice of bishops and abbots, and Laval was an ultramontanist who believed that the Pope and his bishops were autonomous and had a right to interfere in secular issues with moral implications. This discord would continue in Quebec for nearly three hundred years, to the time of Richelieu's namesake and distant relative, Premier Maurice Duplessis in the 1950s.

The brandy issue was very divisive. Laval believed that it reduced the Indians to the level of beasts and was wicked, and he punished vendors of alcohol to the Indians with excommunication. Frontenac and the traders pointed out that the colony would die without the fur trade, which would go entirely to the British if the French did not barter with brandy (which was called the King of France's "milk" and which the Indians preferred to English rum and whisky). The king finally had to choose between Laval, the Jesuits and Sulpicians, the Sorbonne, the archbishop of Paris and his own chaplain, Père La Chaise (after whom the famous Paris cemetery is named), on the one side, and Frontenac, Colbert, the University of Toulouse, and a wide range of commercial interests on the other. Frontenac also battled with Talon's successor as intendant, Jacques Duchesneau, starting with Frontenac's rather puerile objection to the intendant chairing the meetings of the Sovereign Council. This absurd dispute dragged on for five years, in which there were terrible scenes at the meetings (every Monday morning), and Frontenac countered the numerical predominance of the Laval-Duchesneau faction by regularly ordering the physical removal of several of the councillors, which, as governor and commander of the military and the police, he could do. The intendant and governor quarrelled over almost everything, including reciprocal allegations of skimming the fur trade for their own benefit (charges that were probably not unfounded in either case). Frontenac even imprisoned Duchesneau's son for composing an impudent couplet about him. These issues too were referred to France, and finally Colbert became so exasperated that in 1682 he recalled both Frontenac and Duchesneau. As historian Charles W. Colby wrote of Frontenac when he sailed for home in 1682, "He had guarded his people from the tomahawk and the scalping knife. With prescient eye he had foreseen the imperial greatness of the West. Whatever his shortcomings, they had not been those of meanness or timidity."[27]

Laval was almost as impossible a character as Frontenac, but less hot-tempered and vain, and Marie de l'Incarnation described him as "saintly and apostolic."[28] Many of these disputes were the result of Frontenac's simply unreasonable personality, but they do not, and ultimately did not, obscure the fact that at his most important task, keeping the colony safe and keeping marauding Indians well away, Frontenac was entirely successful. There were no skirmishes with the Iroquois throughout these ten years, and New France was free to prosper and grow, which it did. Along with this was Frontenac's great success in extending trading posts and sending explorers out to the north, west, and south. He was also an ambitious builder of public works, including a sewage system and the conversion of Quebec's market into a royal square, with a bronze bust of Louis XIV. He laid out a plan for Quebec to become a majestic capital, which was largely followed.[29] The explorer René-Robert Cavalier de La Salle proved a powerful ally of Frontenac.

Accompanied by Frontenac's influential wife, he carried a letter from Frontenac to the king and came back with a patent to explore the entire continent between the Great Lakes and the Gulf of Mexico, and did so, not with a great organization or a blank cheque from the French government, but with the slender resources he was able to muster privately, and by his own superhuman determination and courage, with his valiant friend, Henri de Tonty.* Unfortunately, without guidance from Frontenac, La Salle took progressive leave of his senses and pursued a private scheme for the fortification of the Mississippi delta. He lost control of his men, some of whom murdered him in March 1687, stripping his corpse and leaving "him to the mercy of the wolves and other wild animals." It was a cruel fate for any authentic hero.³⁰

Another great figure of the era was the leader of the coureurs de bois, Daniel Greysolon Dulhut. He was the explorer of the Sioux country and the guardian of the French interest at Michilimackinac, near the coming together of lakes Huron, Michigan, and Superior. The coureurs were an immense asset for the French, unlike any comparable group of wilderness and Indian experts available to the English, and the intendant Duchesneau was trying to ban them from the woods, largely because he considered them agents of Frontenac. The governor successfully resisted this, but it was another argument that went to the king for adjudication. Frontenac had seen at once the merits of Dulhut and was his champion throughout. Where Frontenac saw the forts and trading posts along the rivers and lakes in the interior as essential to establishing the French claim to much of North America, the Jesuits saw these posts as centres of debauchery and exploitation of the Indians. Both were correct, and this conflict, closely connected to the dispute over the issue of trading brandy to the Indians, exposed the severe division between the French objectives in the New World and the clerical and secular elements that pursued them.

In the War of Devolution (1667–1668), Louis had secretly secured British and Dutch neutrality and struck the Spanish Netherlands

---

* Henri de Tonty (1649–1704) was a Sicilian-born explorer whose family fled Sicily for France shortly after he was born because of his father's involvement in an unsuccessful revolt against the Spanish occupation of Sicily. His brother, Alphonse de Tonty, was co-founder of Detroit.

when Spain was distracted in war with Portugal, and gained appreciably in annexed territory. In the Third Dutch War (1672–1674), he had secretly bribed Sweden to remain neutral and Charles II to support him. Unfortunately for this design, Charles took this occasion to issue a Declaration of Indulgence relieving Roman Catholics and non-Anglican Protestants of many restrictions, and Parliament rebelled, passed the Test Act against Catholics in 1673, and withheld funding for the war effort alongside France in 1674. But Louis's armies under marshals Condé and Turenne, and his navy under Admiral Abraham Duquesne, prevailed and it was a very successful war, though a costly one. The war with Holland distracted France and reduced assistance to New France. But the Peace of Nijmegen, a series of treaties signed in 1678 and 1679, ended, satisfactorily from the French perspective, the wars between France, the Dutch Republic, Spain, Brandenburg, Sweden, Denmark, Munster, and the Holy Roman Empire, and pushed the northeastern French frontier almost to its present extent. Thereafter, Louis did not make equivalent diplomatic efforts to reinforce his military initiatives, and the balance of his wars (which never abated for long) were not overly successful.

England had seized New Amsterdam in 1664 and began to populate the Hudson Valley from Manhattan to Albany. The English governor, Sir Edmund Andros, sought to build an alliance with the Iroquois, although good relations persisted between the cousins Louis XIV and Charles II and James II. The Iroquois were too wily not to see the potential of playing the European powers against one another, and the English were soon visibly much more formidable than the Dutch, and, of course, were already well-established in New England, Virginia, and the Carolinas. The new governor of New France succeeding Frontenac, Joseph-Antoine Le Febvre de La Barre, shortly showed himself to be personally avaricious and incompetent at dealing with the Iroquois. The Iroquois attacked the Illinois Indians, with considerable effect, in 1680, but were careful to steer clear of the French and the Indian allies of the French. Frontenac, seeing the danger, had asked the king for another six hundred troops, but did not receive them. The blandishments and encouragements of the English steadily raised the ambitions and provocations of the Iroquois. As Governor La Barre saw himself as an entrepreneur in the fur trade, he saw La Salle and Tonty as competitors, and schemed to sabotage their efforts, which were under-taken altogether for the greater glory of the king of France.

In July 1684, La Barre made the disastrous error of trying to overawe the Iroquois with a force of only two hundred Frenchmen and several hundred more Indian allies at a council with the Iroquois at the southeastern corner of Lake Ontario. It was "a ghastly joke."[31] La Barre threatened the Iroquois with war against a united front of French and English, a challenge which the Indians knew to be pure conjuration. La Barre was replied to by Grangula – "Big Mouth," as the French aptly called him – who, in keeping with the Indian custom of formal orations at such encounters, noted the weakness of the French and was dismissive of La Barre virtually as an interloper and a mendicant, and as a poseur. These not completely inaccurate characterizations heaped before the ranks of both sides on the French governor, who had come a great distance to parlay, was an unprecedented fiasco in the 150-year history of the French presence in Canada going back to Jacques Cartier. The new intendant, Jacques de Meulles, reported it caustically to the French court, and Louis recalled La Barre in mid-1685, replacing him with the Marquis de Denonville, a fervently Catholic soldier and an honest man, but completely ineffectual. There were only ten thousand French in New France, many of them women and children, and as the Iroquois swarmed and massed, the colony was consistently more endangered. The new governor of New York in 1683, Thomas Dongan, though a Roman Catholic himself, was a nationalist of the British Empire and redoubled Andros's efforts to manipulate the Iroquois. Denonville became especially irritated by Dongan's plan to build a fort at Niagara Falls.

New France was so delicate and vulnerable, even eighty years after Champlain founded the colony, that its fortunes could darken suddenly, and did. Champlain possessed the genius of diplomacy and tactical military acuity, and the advantage of European arms opposite a relatively easily mystified Stone Age array of bitterly divided Indians. Frontenac was a fierce, cunning, and battle-hardened general, and if he lacked Champlain's finesse and Cartesian culture, he knew how to conduct a military campaign and had the theatrical panache to present a plausible facade of great apparent strength. And after the Stuart restoration following the death of Cromwell, the British kings Charles II and James II owed much to the French king and avoided serious conflict with him.

Louis XIV, for his part, in his frontier wars from the Peace of Westphalia in 1648 to the Treaty of Utrecht in 1713, added Alsace, Lorraine, Franche-Comté (the free county of Burgundy, adjacent to the ancient duchy, between Dijon and Basel), Artois, Verdun, Metz, Saarlouis, Thionville, Montmédy, Lille, and Valenciennes to his eastern and northeastern borders, and Perpignan in the southeast. The Battle of Rocroi in the first days of Louis XIV's reign in 1643 under Condé had established that the French had Europe's finest soldiers, and in general they continued to be so for 180 years, until the end of the Napoleonic era. Every one of those towns added more people to the kingdom than there were Europeans in New France at the corresponding time, and it is not clear that Louis's strategic priorities were mistaken. France was never going to be strong enough to secure all its borders against its continental rivals and defeat the British on the oceans of the world, so the wealth of Canada, which ultimately vastly exceeded the hopes of a mere gateway to China, were always going to be difficult to hold, first against the British, and then against the local forces of independence. The additions to France's frontier territory added greatly to its permanent strength and security. While the logic may have been clear, this did little for the isolated and beleaguered colony.

Where Britain needed a ruler of the political astuteness and inspiring and conciliatory leadership qualities of Henry IV, who would minimize religious quarrels and emphasize the national interest, and to some degree had that in the stylish and clever Charles II, the succession of his brother on Charles's death in 1685 opened the gravest dangers in the opposite direction. James II was a rather belligerent Roman Catholic in a country that was now largely Protestant. He had, against his brother's wishes, converted to Rome in 1668, but Charles forbade the Roman Catholic baptism of James's daughters Mary and Anne. (Charles had no legitimate heir.) James produced a Toleration Act for the benefit of Roman Catholics, Protestants who were not Anglicans, Jews, and non-believers, but this was seen by the Anglican and noble and Parliamentary establishments (which were fairly co-extensive) as an assault on the rights of Parliament (which it wasn't, but James had the sort of authoritarian and erratic personality that invited such concerns). When James II's Italian second wife, Mary of Modena, gave birth to a male heir (though it was falsely charged that he was a changeling produced to the maternal bed in a warming pan), Parliament asked James's son-in-law, William III of Orange, the Dutch leader, to invade England. He did so, successfully, setting up a joint monarchy with his wife, James's daughter, Queen Mary II, as she became. (By coincidence, William was William III of the Dutch and the English.)

This brought the final defeat of Catholicism in England and ended the era of tranquil relations between England and France until the rise of a united Germany as a threat to both countries two hundred years later. James resumed his life in exile, attempting only one serious return, which William defeated at the Battle of the Boyne in 1690. This engagement was part of the Nine Years War (1688–1697), following Louis's Revocation of Henry IV's tolerant Edict of Nantes and various manoeuvres of Louis to expand his influence in the Rhineland. He should never have incited the antagonism of the grand coalition of England, the Netherlands, Spain, the Holy Roman Empire, and Savoy and Piedmont, when assisted only by the Scottish and Irish Jacobites. This conflict was known as King William's War in Britain and America, and as the War of the Grand Alliance to France's other enemies.

6. The Return of Frontenac, 1689–1701

As this war began, New France was very vulnerable. The effective banning of French Protestants from the colony by the Jesuit (Bishop Laval) influence had stopped the one natural source of large-scale French immigration, as the Catholic majority was very comfortable in temperate and commodious France. The antagonism of the English and their maritime supremacy assured that they could threaten the delicate lifeline to New France and could arm and motivate the Iroquois, whom Champlain had wheedled and Frontenac overawed. And the withdrawal of Frontenac and his replacement by two successive incompetents reduced New France to a state of acute weakness.

In an initiative that can only be described as insane, Governor Denonville decided to ship off as galley slaves to France the Iroquois men in two of that tribe's villages on the north shore of Lake Ontario who had been baptized Christians by the Sulpicians. In July 1688,

Denonville plunged into Iroquois country but withdrew after a skirmish with the Seneca, in which the French took only about ten dead to more than a hundred Seneca. This led to another French disaster: the Huron chief Kondiaronk betrayed the French to the Iroquois and provoked an Iroquois attack on the French at Lachine, in August 1689, and at La Chesnay a couple of months later, killing more than sixty French. This was too much for the French government, and as New France hovered perilously near the jaws of the numerous and blood-curdling Iroquois, incited and well-armed by the English, Frontenac was dispatched back to Quebec in October 1689 to resume the governorship from Denonville. He was sixty-nine, but ready for a brilliant climax to his remarkable career. "The universal mood was one of terror and despair. If ever Canada needed a Moses, this was the hour."[32]

Louis-Hector de Callière, governor of Montreal, had worked out a plan of attack that was approved by Louis and his senior advisers, including Frontenac before he departed France, and he was charged with carrying it out. Two French warships were to harass New York, while a raiding party was to descend on the upper Hudson from Quebec. The returning Frontenac arrived too late to execute the plan as formulated but refined it to an even bolder thrust by three overland groups on snowshoes in January 1690, when complete surprise could be reasonably assumed. The three thrusts were: 210 men, mainly French, from Montreal against Schenectady, led by Nicolas d'Ailleboust de Manthet and Jacques Le Moyne de Sainte-Hélène; 26 French and 29 Indians led by François Hertel from Trois-Rivières against Dover, Permaquid, and other Maine settlements down into New Hampshire; and 50 French and 60 Indians led by René Robineau de Portneuf against what is now Portland, Maine.

All three achieved surprise, devastated English settlements, and all the commanders effectively turned a blind eye to Indian outrages against the civil populations. War at this time was not usually overly chivalrous even in Europe (as in the sack of Magdeburg in 1631, with twenty-thousand civilians killed, and the storming of Drogheda in 1649 by Cromwell, with perhaps five thousand killed), but where Indians were allowed free rein, extreme and indiscriminate violence was likely. In the three raids, about two hundred people were killed, about three-fifths men and one-fifth each women and children. Perhaps two hundred able-bodied adults were marched back as prisoners, and about a hundred elderly people, women, and children were unharmed and not physically displaced. François Hertel (who commanded the expedition into New Hampshire) had been tortured by the Iroquois as a youth, having had a thumb chopped off and a finger burned off, but he was a brave commander who, as the eminent historian Francis Parkman remarked, was unjustly decried after these raids as "the abhorred chief of Popish malignants and murdering savages."[33]

It seems odd that Callière and Frontenac attacked English-American civilians rather than the Iroquois, and they can have been in no doubt that the English would soon retaliate, but Frontenac was trying to win back the Indians, which he had a chance to do by impressing them and demonstrating the fallibility of the English Americans. He had a chance to win the Iroquois over, but no possibility of winning the English over. The English struck back in the summer of 1690 with John Schuyler leading a land force along what in the next 125 years would become the well-travelled route on or beside Lake Champlain against Montreal while a naval squadron from Boston under Sir William Phips invested Quebec. Schuyler's initiative, like most that would follow the same path, of all nationalities and in both directions, was a fiasco. It burned some crops around La Prairie but never really threatened Montreal.

The American colonists had been encouraged by the bloodless surrender of the tiny French garrison at Port-Royal, and Massachusetts subscribed the onerous sum of fifty thousand pounds and sent thirty-four ships on the expedition to Quebec. They only arrived on October 16, very late in the season to do more than bluster, a tactic Phips tried against Frontenac, a singularly unsuitable subject of such attentions. Under a white flag, Phips sent a messenger demanding surrender. Frontenac received the messenger in his citadel surrounded by his officers and officials, all in the most extravagant regalia of their offices, with Frontenac in full livery impersonating the entire dignity of the mighty and opulent monarch he represented. Phips's envoy read his ineffably pompous ultimatum, demanding compete surrender, following which "you may expect mercy from me, as a Christian," but failing which he would "make you wish you had accepted of the favours tendered." Better was Frontenac's immediate promise, before the hour allotted for consideration of the ultimatum had even begun, that "you will receive my answer from the mouths of my cannon."

Frontenac had summoned Callière from Montreal with seven hundred soldiers, and when Phips landed thirteen hundred men on the Beauport Flats below Quebec, the French shot them up, retired across the Saint-Charles River, but prevented the Americans from coming across and easily won the artillery duel with their big guns on the cliffs of Upper Town. The British couldn't supply the troops they had landed, and Phips wasted his ammunition on unfocused bombardments. "Harassed by the Canadians, wet, cold, and starving, [the Americans] took to the boats, leaving behind them five cannon."[34] The Canadians, commanded by a Frenchman, decisively defeated an all-American force, which slunk back to Boston to retire the heavy debt the colony had assumed to finance this hare-brained assault. The Canadians even got the flag on Phips's flagship, which had been torn off its mast and dumped in the river by fire from the ramparts. "In the shouts of rejoicing which followed Phips's withdrawal we hear the cry of a people reborn."[35]

The defeat of the Americans at Quebec did not go unnoticed by the Iroquois, who in any case knew what to expect from Frontenac, a cunning and indomitable fighter whom they could not treat as Big Mouth had dared to treat Governor La Barre. Unfortunately, the feeble Denonville had burned down Fort Frontenac at Cataraqui, near the present Kingston, just before its namesake returned to resume the governorship in 1689. Frontenac tried to arrange a new peace with the Iroquois, based on assertions of French strength by some Indians that he brought back with him from France, who were happy to attest to the might of France and the determination of the returned governor. A council took place where the insidious English (or Americans – the distinction was becoming relevant) were invited. The council heard a feisty case for the French from a Christian Iroquois but rejected the overture and formed an alliance between the English Americans, the Iroquois, and representatives of the tribes of the West, the Michilimackinac (Ottawa and Huron), in a coalition to destroy New France. The western tribes were in fact just wavering, and Frontenac moved quickly to shore them up. He sent 150 men to reinforce his garrison at Michilimackinac, and they defeated an Iroquois band on the way and scalped some of them to impress the Ottawa. The raids on Schenectady and the other targets had impressed some of the waverers, and at a great council with Frontenac in Montreal in August

1690, Frontenac, in a diplomatic tour de force, showed few of his sixty-eight years as he danced the Ottawa rites and won the western Indians into coalition against the Iroquois. They knew the Iroquois were a mortal threat and that if the French were dispensed with they would be massacred by their more numerous and ferocious kinsmen.

Three years of intense war between the Iroquois and the western Indians with their French allies ensued as New France gasped for sustenance through the tenuous supply line from France intermittently ruptured by the Royal Navy as the Nine Years War dragged on. In order to be sure of fur revenues, Frontenac had to assure a safe path for furs from the north and west down the Ottawa, and his first priority was to deal with the Iroquois. There were incessant skirmishes in which the habitants were heroes defending their farms against Iroquois raiders, with no quarter given or asked on either side. In 1692, Madeleine de Verchères rebuffed an Iroquois attack on her family home though she was only fourteen, assisted only by an eighty-year-old man, one younger man, and two children. In 1691, a return attack by Peter Schuyler, a relative of the unsuccessful John Schuyler of the year before, was beaten off quite crisply by the French, killing about forty American militiamen. From 1692 to 1694, the French Acadians and their Abenaki allies, under Baron Jean-Vincent de Saint-Castin, carried havoc all along the Maine shore, scorching English homesteads. But Frontenac's great stroke was his expedition against the Onondagas of 1696. Undeterred by his seventy-four years, he drove into the heart of Iroquois country with two thousand men and cannon and mortars that his indefatigable soldiers and their Indian allies dragged over portages and floated on barges, moving south from Lake Ontario. He compelled the Onondaga and then the Oneida to burn their camps and flee with only what they could carry, leaving it to the French to burn the crops and anything they had left behind. Frontenac judged it imprudent to proceed too much farther, as he would be vulnerable to English-American main forces, but he had given the haughty Iroquois a thrashing sufficient for them to seek peace after the Nine Years War came to an end with the Peace of Ryswick in 1697.

In Europe, Louis was outnumbered and wrong-footed and eventually lost a few outposts on or near the Rhine while affirming control of Alsace, lost Catalonia back to Spain, but regained Pondicherry in India,

Nova Scotia, and gained the present Haiti. The British Parliament thanked King William III for having "given England the balance of Europe," but Louis, in his mad egotism, had gone to war with almost the whole continent plus Britain and had just about drawn the contest. With a little diplomatic finesse to procure some allies, France could generally prevail against its continental neighbours. In North America, hostilities sputtered on sporadically with the Indians, but New France was no longer threatened by the English Americans and the Royal Navy.

While Frontenac was defeating the Iroquois and rallying the more moderate tribes, he was also demonstrating his strategic gifts by pursuing an ambitious plan to compensate for the growing British American strength on the Eastern Seaboard: he organized an offensive to regain control of Hudson Bay and to descend the length of the Mississippi and fortify its mouth by a maritime expedition. His goal was to develop a linear network of posts and forts through the Great Lakes and down the Ohio and Mississippi to its mouth and bypass the English possession of the Atlantic coast from Maine to the Carolinas. Despite its slender resources, New France would control the interior of the continent and its main outlets to the western ocean: Hudson Bay, the St. Lawrence, and the vast river system that debouches through the mouth of the Mississippi into the Gulf of Mexico. It was a plan of genius, and it was largely executed by a Canadian, Pierre Le Moyne d'Iberville, one of the greatest soldiers and sailors in Canadian history. He was born in Ville-Marie (Montreal) in 1661, one of twelve brothers, who included Jacques Le Moyne de Sainte-Hélène, the leader of Frontenac's expedition against Schenectady in 1690; Charles Le Moyne de Longueuil, governor of Montreal; and Jean-Baptiste Le Moyne de Bienville, founder of New Orleans (in 1719). D'Iberville started his career as an adventurer as a cabin boy in his French uncle's ship trading to Port-Royal in 1673. The Hudson's Bay Company had been founded in 1670 by Charles II. The competing French Compagnie du Nord was founded by Louis XIV in 1682. D'Iberville had been in the fur trade in the western Great Lakes for several years, and became the second-in-command in the French expedition to seize the English forts on James Bay and Hudson Bay in 1686. Three of the four forts were captured (Moose Factory, Fort Rupert, and Fort Albany). D'Iberville returned to France in 1687 to seek support and came back the following year as commander of a naval expedition that captured three Hudson's Bay Company ships. He was a cunning and courageous fighter on land and sea and in all climates; was successful in Hudson Bay in 1690, 1694, and 1697; and was an effective coastal raider against New England in 1692, 1695, and 1696. In 1696, he also rescued the French outpost at Placentia, Newfoundland, from a British siege and then devastated most of the English settlements on that island and captured St. John's. (Placentia Bay would be made world famous 245 years later by a shipboard meeting between the Second World War Grand Alliance leaders Winston S. Churchill and Franklin D. Roosevelt – Chapter 7.)

The French minister of the navy and colonies, Count Pontchartrain and Maurepas, entrusted d'Iberville with the task of establishing a fort at the mouth of the Mississippi in 1698. D'Iberville sailed directly from Brest and the following year founded Biloxi, and in 1701 he built a fort at what is now Mobile, Alabama. La Salle's old sidekick, Henri de Tonty, was still active and joined up with d'Iberville in transacting with the Gulf Coast Indians. D'Iberville sold nine thousand furs in New York that the coureurs de bois had brought down the Mississippi. While Frontenac seduced the western Indians, subdued the Iroquois, and secured Quebec, he and d'Iberville, building on the great work of La Salle and Tonty and with the four hundred or so coureurs de bois, had built up a vast internal American empire of the fur trade that was, as historian W.L. Morton wrote, as "endlessly expansive and fragile as a spider's web." (He also aptly described d'Iberville as "that hybrid of d'Artagnan and Pierre Radisson."[36]) There has been some dispute ever since over the relative weight in the motives of Frontenac and d'Iberville of patriotism, strategic enterprise, and personal avarice, but these bold and brilliant swashbucklers fashioned an astonishingly durable and far-flung colonial and commercial entity out of very sparse materials and inconstant support from the home country. Never again would Canada have such influence in North America, and probably not one Canadian in a thousand, two hundred years later, has any idea that Canadians founded the great American cities of Chicago, Detroit, St. Louis, New Orleans, Saint Paul, Louisville, Des Moines, Mobile, Baton Rouge, and Biloxi, which today have a combined metropolitan population of more than twenty million.

Frontenac died at Quebec on November 28, 1698. He was seventy-six years old. Next to Champlain, he had been the greatest figure in the history of New France, now 164 years since the first arrival of Jacques Cartier. Frontenac was quarrelsome, a braggart, and somewhat corrupt, traits that Champlain did not possess, but he was an inspiring leader in desperate times and he provided for the survival of New France, well-launched into the eighteenth century. The able Callière succeeded him as governor. (He was the brother of François de Callières, Louis XIV's assistant, who wrote out the king's letters and often signed them for him. It was often alleged that the royal amanuensis exercised his great but surreptitious power in the interests of his brother.) Frontenac's greatest victory was posthumous, like Richelieu's at Westphalia, as, in 1701, under Callière's aegis, a council at Montreal of the French, the Iroquois, and Michilimackinac tribes agreed a durable peace and smoked the calumet all round. The other great figure of New France in the second half of the seventeenth century, Bishop François de Laval, had given way under the strains of his long episcopate and retired in 1688. But after a brief sojourn in France, he returned to his beloved Quebec, where he continued to be a great moral influence as the emeritus bishop right up to his death in 1708, aged eighty-five.

New France was ostensibly delivered, a remarkable feat of survival largely wrought by the inhabitants themselves. But the weaknesses that had been inherent in New France remained. There was only a trickle of immigration from France, while people poured into the English-American colonies from all parts of the British Isles. The French government barely maintained the colony, while it insisted on being paid for its efforts by renting out the fur trade, and an irreconcilable conflict resulted and was constantly being fought out between the practitioners of the fur trade and the colonial government that was trying to build a balanced and civil society. As we have seen, the Jesuits, Sulpicians, and Récollets came as missionaries and performed admirably and often heroically, but they were constantly at war with the commercial interests, and often the official secular authorities, over the trade of alcohol to the Indians, which reduced the natives to a pitiable state but was essential to the conduct of the fur trade that was all that kept the colony economically alive. The French religious regime, as we have also seen, discouraged immigration from France even prior to Louis XIV's revocation of the Edict of Nantes. As Henry IV and then Richelieu, and then Louis XIV, expanded France, they concentrated overwhelmingly on surpassing their continental neighbours which were always a direct threat. The English steadily built upon their insular strength and ability to surpass all other countries in the sea power necessary to take and hold an overseas empire.

The blunder of Louis in ending the era of French religious tolera-tion, followed at once by the ineptitude of James II fumbling the crown of England into the hands of avaricious Dutch Protestants, ended the brief era of French-English cordiality in which New France could flour-ish. The habitant was more of a rough and ready frontiersman than his more numerous New England neighbours. He was not much more prolific, if at all, as the Puritans had large families also, but he had none of the New Englanders' democratic practices and institutions. There were syndics among occupations, but no town meetings, and no sense of ability to petition the authorities. The English had executed their king, albeit at the behest of someone (Cromwell) who, once he had died, they exhumed and beheaded and then displayed his decom-posing head on a pike. Parliament, despite many problems and "Remonstrances," had sat for centuries. Its powers fluctuated, but it could not just be ignored, as Cromwell had demonstrated. The Estates General of France were hardly of comparable authority, and Richelieu, as it turned out, had shut them down for 175 years in 1614.

7. Queen Anne's War (the War of the Spanish Succession), 1701–1715

Louis XIV's policy of almost continuous war had been a departure from Richelieu's practice of incentivizing others to do the fighting, and had brought France substantial expansion on its eastern frontiers, though not as quickly or cost-efficiently as Richelieu's subtler and more patient and manipulative methods. But it had severely strained the country's finances, and, with acts of conspicuous extravagance such as the con-struction of the Palace of Versailles, the most opulent residence in the world, had incited serious resentment among the majority of the French population of high taxes and overindulgence of the nobility and clergy. There were too many poor peasants in a naturally rich country.

Louis had also become complacent about the diplomatic strategy to accompany his wars of aggrandizement; France was the strongest country in Europe, including Britain, but it couldn't get to the British Isles and wasn't strong enough to prevail over all the continental powers that would naturally be ranged against it, especially with the tangible encouragement of the British. But France went through the Nine Years War (1688–1697) and entered the eighteenth century with no serious allies. Richelieu's successors had grasped the virtues of his absolutism and central authority, but not his genius for acquiring allies, especially allies who would actually do most of the fighting. And unlike Richelieu's wars, these recent conflicts were largely fought on French soil, on the backs of the French, the foreseeable result of Louis having dispensed with serious allies.

In England, James II's daughter, Mary II, died in 1694, leaving William III, the deposed and exiled king's son-in-law and the joint monarch, to govern alone until his death in 1702, when James II's other daughter, Anne, became queen. She had had seventeen pregnancies with her persevering Danish husband, resulting in three children who did not live longer than eleven years, two who died within two hours, six who were stillborn, and six miscarriages. In the Act of Settlement of 1701, Anne's heir presumptive was named as the elector of Hanover, grandson of King Charles I's sister (Anne's great aunt).

When King Charles II of Spain died in 1700, he left his crown to the grandson of Louis XIV, Philip, Duke of Anjou, including all Spain's possessions in the New World. In his mad egotism, Louis declared, "The Pyrenees are no more."[37] Louis had ample opportunity to prepare for this event, and instead of detaching the Dutch and the Austrians from the English, when he purported to accept the crown of Spain for his grandson, he found himself fighting the War of the Spanish Succession (1701–1714), supported only by the Philippian Spanish and for a time the Bavarians, against the Holy Roman Empire, Britain (in 1707, the Acts of Union joined Britain and Scotland in the Kingdom of Great Britain), Prussia, Hanover, Savoy, the Dutch Republic, Portugal, and Carlist Spain. There were about 250,000 soldiers on each side, and the Grand Alliance forces led by the Duke of Marlborough and Prince Eugene of Savoy faced the French under the Duke of Villars, marshal general of France (in the first year and last five years of the war). All three were very capable commanders. It was a long war, closely fought.

In North America, there had been no respite in the previous wars, as the Iroquois made peace, if they did, when it suited them and not the chancelleries of Europe. So the War of the Spanish Succession did not immediately have an impact in America and Canada. The exhaustion of the combatants in the late continental struggle was compounded in New France by the buffetings of the fur trade. The opening up of Hudson Bay and the Mississippi created a degree of competition that affronted the mercantilist controlled markets of Colbert and Talon on which the trade had been built. And fashion abruptly changed in Paris, as it has been wont to do since, and the use of beaver fur in hats and as trim on outerwear abruptly declined. New France had had recourse in 1685, under Intendant Jacques de Meulles, to the issuance of card money (playing cards, torn in pieces and signed to a certain value). Frontenac reverted to this in the 1690s, and under the pressure of the War of Spanish Succession, with irregular resupply from France and the burdens of preparing for even technical skirmishing with England, recourse was had to it again. It eased liquidity concerns, but as always, including at time of writing, when the money supply is simply increased without a corresponding increase in productivity or wealth-generation other than simply by the velocity of money transfers, inflation results. (Much of the cause of the American Revolution seventy-five years later, and the American banking crisis sixty years after that, was the result of intense political dispute over similar issues. The less formulaic French of the New World managed it relatively effortlessly with a temporary debasement of the currency that was less foreign to their national experience and culture.)

In the New World, the only early stirrings of this new war were in Acadia, where the Massachusetts militia crept continually up the coast, closing the river mouths to the Abenaki tribe, who owed their loyalty to the French priests and the redoubtable Saint-Castin, scourge of the New Englanders. Pontchartrain and Callière, veterans of protracted Indian combat, urged and supplied the Abenaki, chiefly to keep the English Americans away from the French colonies. Callière also concerted with his successor as governor of Montreal, Philippe de Rigaud de Vaudreuil, a plan to provide preveniently for English-American advances by building forts and posts to which friendly Indians could repair in times of military pressure instead of being scattered and slaughtered by the Iroquois whenever the dark aboriginal spirits or

English money and rum motivated them to flex their muscles. To this end, in 1704 the coureurs de bois, so frequently the *bêtes noires* of the authorities of New France, were amnestied (as was also the custom in conflict, when their bold indiscipline could be deployed to advantage). These preparations were quite successful, and New France soldiered into the new conflict in good condition. Despite a smallpox outburst in 1703 and a crop failure in 1705, in 1706 the resident French population was more than sixteen thousand, with a slight female majority. With the population increase, the value of land went up, and seigneurs began to try to exact a price for the land the habitant was supposed to earn by clearing it. In 1711, decrees were issued forcing the cession of cleared land to the habitants for reasonable fees. There would be forfeiture by the tenant if he didn't maintain the land, and by the seigneur if he didn't transfer title. Cultivated land sharply increased, and after 1705 New France was self-sufficient in agriculture, other than in years of severe crop failures.

The War of the Spanish Succession was inconclusive for the first three years, but the Duke of Marlborough and Eugene of Savoy's victory over the French at Blenheim in 1704 blocked the way of the French army to Vienna and knocked Bavaria out of the war, where it had been a French ally. In the same year, the British took Gibraltar. After Blenheim, Marlborough returned to the command in the Netherlands and Eugene to the command in Italy, where he was generally successful in preventing the French from advancing, especially in his defeat of them at Turin, and eventually evicted them from that country. Marlborough, leading the British, Dutch, Danes, and some Germans, pushed France out of the Netherlands. Fighting was indecisive in 1705 and 1706, until Marlborough's decisive victory at Ramillies (near Maastricht), in May 1706, which enabled him to occupy Brussels, Bruges, and Antwerp.

While this was happening, there were intermittent but prolonged negotiations between Callière and the British governor of Massachusetts, Joseph Dudley, over a possible treaty of peace between their colonies. French privateers from Port-Royal continued to beset the New England ports, and the Abenaki were unleashed from time to time to annoy the British while retaining official but implausible deniability for the French against accusations that the Abenaki had acted with French encouragement. These provocations finally sunk the local peace negotiations, but the New Englanders did not get organized to attack Quebec until 1711, fully justifying Champlain's view that Quebec was so remote and loftily situated that it would be impregnable to attack other than by a massive amphibious assault.

France held its frontiers through 1707, and the attempted allied assault on Madrid was defeated by the French and pro-French Spanish at Almansa, where the French commander, the Duke of Berwick, was James II's illegitimate son and the Duke of Marlborough's nephew, as Berwick's mother was the duke's wife's sister, Arabella. The Duchess of Marlborough was Queen Anne's closest friend and was instrumental in each phase of Marlborough's political and military career. Marlborough came south with his armies and Eugene north with his in 1708 and severely defeated the French at Oudenaarde. Louis felt compelled to open talks for peace. He was prepared to cede Spain and even to allow the allies to dispose of his grandson, Philip, as king of Spain, and to make a financial contribution to that end, but the allies, against the advice of Marlborough and Eugene, demanded that Louis defeat and expel his own grandson, for whose right to govern France and Spain Louis had gone to war. (Dynasties ruled, but kinship did not ensure loyalty in any of them.) This was too much for the Sun King, and in what was in some respects his finest hour, he appealed to the entire French nation for more volunteers for the army and for endurance of a special surtax. France responded, and the Duke of Villars, who had resigned because noble fellow officers had resisted his request for a lightning strike against Vienna in 1703, was recalled to lead the defence of the country.

In the bloody Battle of Malplaquet, which was effectively Villars's defence of Paris against the again-combined forces of Marlborough and Eugene, the French technically lost, as they retired from the field, but only because Villars was wounded, with a cannonball shattering his knee. The allies took twenty thousand casualties, twice the number suffered by the French, and Villars really defeated the combined allies led by their two greatest generals. In the following year, the allies were defeated in Spain, and France regained Barcelona. Villars successfully led his army through 1711 to the reconquest of a good deal of lost ground. To make his life easier, Queen Anne quarrelled violently with Marlborough's duchess, sacked her from her place of influence, and the death of the king of Spain opened up the prospect of reunion of the crowns of Spain and the Holy Roman Empire (Austria). The British and Dutch had not slogged through ten years of heavy combat for any such prospect. The pro-peace Tories defeated the pro-war Whigs, and the queen and the royal majority in the House of Lords swung over to the peace party. Marlborough remained loyal to his departing Whig allies and to the presumptive future king, the elector of Hanover (who would in three years become King George I of Great Britain on the death of Anne). The queen recalled Marlborough, and Villars routed the allies, now led by Eugene, at Denain on the French frontier and continued his advance.

In North America, where the War of Spanish Succession was known as Queen Anne's War, as the Nine Years War had been known as King William's War, nothing involving direct combat between the English Americans and French Canadians, as opposed to Indian surrogates, had really happened until a Massachusetts contingent led by Colonel Francis Nicholson, captured Port-Royal in 1710, shut down the French privateers, and renamed it Annapolis Royal. There was another farcical advance overland on Montreal, which withered and gave up without firing a shot after disease thinned its active ranks en route. An assault upriver against Quebec was attempted, but the expedition, commanded by Sir Hovenden Walker, had navigational problems and grounded, losing eight ships and the mission, in emulation of the 1690 fiasco that Frontenac had seen off, limped back to Boston. The French exterminated a large Fox band of Indians in a clash near Detroit, and unsuccessfully attempted to seize the British Fort Albany in Hudson Bay, and repulsed other attacks on some of its forts.

Peace finally broke out again, in the treaties of Utrecht in 1713 and of Rastatt and Baden in 1714. France retained its borders, and Philip remained as king of Spain, but renounced the crown of France. France conceded much of Acadia to Britain, but with vague boundaries that were bound to lead to further friction, and ceded half of the Caribbean island of Saint Kitts and recognized British possession of Rupert's Land and Newfoundland. This gave the Hudson Bay forts back to Britain, and thus left Great Britain that access to North America and left it athwart the Gulf of the St. Lawrence, though France retained Cape Breton Island and Île Saint-Jean (Prince Edward Island). The British had sovereignty over the Iroquois, a mixed blessing, but potentially dangerous for

France, and the right of both countries to trade with all the Indians effectively divided eastern North America close to the main waterways through to Lake Superior. This would prove a lasting division. Spain ceded its position in the Netherlands, Naples, Milan, and Sardinia, all to the Habsburgs (Austria), and Gibraltar and Minorca, as well as a thirty-year monopoly on the non-Spanish slave trade in the Americas, to Britain. Spain lost; the Holy Roman Empire, Great Britain, and the Dutch won; and France again drew the issue with almost all the other European powers against it. These were unwise wars to no purpose for those who began them, and every peace left so many shaggy edges that it was almost certain to generate another war, and this one did.

France was becoming enervated by these endless wars – twenty-seven years of war in forty-one years, from 1672 to 1713 – like having two Thirty Years Wars plus the civil war of the Fronde and several lesser conflicts in less than a century. And there was no point to the costs in blood and treasure of constant war if it was only to break even, which was all France did after 1678, only to show that La Belle France could, unto herself, hold a coalition at bay. This was inferior strategic direction.

While the French were forgetting some of Cardinal Richelieu's lessons, the British were steadily perfecting the techniques of Cardinal Wolsey's game: divide and prevent conquerors in Europe, seize and hold the sceptre of the seas, and take the best of the non-European world for the home islands in the name of civilization, meaning commerce and public administration. Christianity was only a flourish to the British. To the extent foreign policy was a crusade, it must be for the national interest, not the extension of a sectarian province in the kingdom of God.

In the New World, France had retained its access to Newfoundland fisheries, and this was the traditional training ground of French mariners and seamen, and while the British were encroaching on the edges of New France and the trend was disturbing, the colony itself was intact and growing. In 1714, the governor, Vaudreuil, sent Pontchartrain a series of urgent recommendations: to increase the military garrison, reintroduce trading licences to keep the Indians from being commercially seduced by the English, and, for the same motive, re-establish the sale of brandy at Frontenac, Detroit, Michilimackinac, and other trading forts; to provide a special incentive to the Abenaki to keep their alliance;

and to fortify Île Royale (Cape Breton). It was an intelligent, but a necessarily defensive, strategy to maintain the tenuous French hold on the northeastern and central parts of the continent. Pontchartrain agreed.

Canada's greatest soldier and fighting sailor, Pierre Le Moyne d'Iberville, had captured the British island of Nevis in the Caribbean and announced that the entire population were prisoners of France, but died of yellow fever at Havana a few months later, in 1706, while planning an attack on the Carolinas. He was forty-five. The Duke of Villars became Louis's minister of defence and one of only six men in French history to enjoy the sonorous title marshal general of France. He played an important role in the regency of the 1720s, and returned to active service, aged eighty, in the War of the Polish Succession. But after leading his armies successfully, he died peacefully in his campaign billeting, aged eighty-one. This war was the last throw for Louis XIV, who had reigned seventy-two years when he died in 1715, fifty-four of them by direct dictatorship since the death of Richelieu's assiduous disciple, Mazarin, in 1661. Louis was a talented man, cultured, patriotic, a genuine Roman Catholic, and a dutiful if very autocratic and profligately extravagant monarch. He was the personification of the grandeur of France in many fields, and a monarch who inspired pride among many French and respect among most foreigners, even Eugene of Savoy. He had expanded the country and, to a small degree, its empire, but he had not really raised France's relative importance from where he had found it, as France's rivals, except for Spain, had gained at least as much. And he had done nothing to endow the country with flexible political institutions that would enable it to weather the ages without terrible internal conflicts. He was the greatest figure of his age in Europe, but not the greatest ruler, an honour that would probably go to Peter the Great, of the now emerging Russia. Louis XIV would come to be seen as illustrative of the dangers, as well as the grandeur, of absolutism.

The absence of any democratic institutions or traditions in France made their colonial regime less effective and spontaneous than that of the English, though they did better under inspired leaders such as Champlain and Talon and Frontenac. Under Richelieu, the die was cast for absolute royal dictatorship. This produced capable but unrestrained government under very able leaders, but irremediable incompetence under poor leaders, and ultimately even talented absolute monarchs at the head of such a rich country and intelligent nationality overreached (Louis XIV and Napoleon). In the end, the British model of constitutional rights and civil responsibility, for all its absurd frictions and political vapidity, was a superior system that encouraged less public cynicism, a more motivated population, and greater probity in government than French absolute monarchy. Britain never had a revolution or civil war after 1660, while France has had a total of twelve violent changes of regime (though several were almost bloodless) after the Bourbon dictatorship finally exploded in 1789, and, as has been referred to, domestic conditions were far from peaceful through most of the seventeenth century, despite Richelieu's authoritarian genius.

8. La Vérendrye, Westward Expansion in North America, and King George's War (the War of Austrian Succession), 1715–1754

Governor Vaudreuil revived the sluggish fur trade by folding the Company of the Colony, a Montreal enterprise that had been undercapitalized, unable to enforce its position opposite the Indian fur trappers and suppliers, resistless against the fickleness of fashion, and a victim of the erratic wartime communications with France across a North Atlantic dominated by Britain's Royal Navy. Vaudreuil delivered the colonial fur monopoly to the Company of the West in 1718, a mainly French concern, more amply financed by merchants of the French port cities. While peace reigned with the British and Americans, the massacre of the Fox band at Detroit in 1712 was just the opening shot in the Fox Wars, in which that stubborn and fierce tribe fought for their historic right to be the middleman between the Sioux who trapped the beavers and provided the fur and the French who sent the fur to market overseas. It was the nastiest and most violent permutation of a grubby commercial argument.

New France perversely resented the expanding reach of its adventurers, as commercial opinion in Montreal and Quebec saw Louisiana, founded at this time, and posts along the Mississippi and Ohio systems that fed it and exported furs through New Orleans, as a competitor and a drain and distraction. The first Fox War lasted only from

1714 to 1716, but the Fox won a skirmish in 1715, killing the son of Claude de Ramezay, who was at the time the acting governor of New France, and d'Iberville's nephew. The French pushed them back into Wisconsin, and there was a peace from 1716 to 1727, though one punctuated by frequent skirmishing. The Fox earned their name by their cunning and obduracy and nipped at the French spider web of trading posts and forts whenever they saw an opportunity. The French empire in North America was built on French élan and imagination and had tensile strength but no mass of reserves of people or resources. To the British Americans, who had no strategy at this point but were a string of communities of homogeneous British seeking a better life as colonists, the French and French Canadians were a distant annoyance, but to the Indians they were a mortal threat to their territory and livelihood.

The fortification of Île Royale (Cape Breton Island) began in 1720, as construction of the powerful fort of Louisbourg was put in hand at English Harbour. As it turned out, there was a good deal of corruption in the contracting, and the fortifications and plans were not all they appeared. Louisbourg was portrayed, in France and in Canada, as the Dunkirk of the New World, and Louis XV eventually said that it was so expensive he should be able to see it on the horizon from Brittany, but it was not as formidable a bastion as it was billed. The fort did assist Vaudreuil in promoting Abenaki harassment of the British colonists inching up the New England coast, and the Abenaki War, in which France spuriously claimed to be neutral, began in 1722. The New York traders were also moving north from what is now Albany, and established Fort Oswego on the south shore of Lake Ontario in 1726. The French answered with their fort at Niagara the following year. To protect the fur trade, brandy flowed from the French to the Indians in ambitious emulation of the thundering waters of the Niagara River; the forces of lucre (not exceptionally) had won the long battle with the pieties of the Catholic missionaries.

As the British approached from New York, they also encroached from Hudson Bay. All of their forts and posts in James and Hudson bays were operating vigorously, though the British usually awaited the arrival of Indians bearing and selling furs, rather than seeking them out. Between 1688 and 1721, Henry Kelsey (immortalized in the Stan

Rogers song "Northwest Passage" as "brave Kelso"), William Stuart, and James Knight ventured up the Churchill, to Great Slave Lake and inside the Arctic Circle, Knight perishing from famine and illness at Rankin Inlet in 1721 at the age of eighty-one. They were still looking for the route to China, more than two hundred years after the search began, as well as the copper deposits that various Indians had described in terms that caused credulous British and French to imagine another El Dorado in the North. Kelsey also went out onto the Great Plains and was apparently the first European to see huge herds of buffalo and to encounter large numbers of grizzly bears. But the British were hereafter unchallenged in the North, and the Indians were happy to bring their wares to them. This pincers movement from the north and up from south of the Great Lakes forced the French to move west and push through Wisconsin and down the Mississippi to continue to be Europe's main supplier of furs. This produced the Second Fox War, from 1727 to 1733, in which France won most of the engagements but the Fox only retreated before permanent insurmountable force. They defended their commercial and territorial prerogatives with what the French considered, hardly disinterestedly, to be perverse ferocity and guile.

The man for this hour, and, as it turned out, the last of the great French explorers of North America, was the Canadian Pierre Gaultier de Varennes, Sieur de La Vérendrye, like d'Iberville a native of Trois-Rivières. He had gone as a youth to France to enlist in the French army and served with gallantry under Villars against Marlborough and Eugene at Malplaquet, where thirty thousand men were killed or wounded and Paris was successfully defended. He was invalided out of the army and exchanged as a prisoner of war and returned to Canada, where he married and settled down to farming and part-time fur trading for fifteen years. In 1726, when he was forty-one, his brother was made commander of the French posts and forts on the north shore of Lake Superior, and he replaced his brother as commandant when he took a command position in the Second Fox War. La Vérendrye worked out a plan with Vaudreuil's successor, Governor Charles de Beauharnois, starting with La Vérendrye's construction of a fort on Lake Winnipeg, which would be used to project a comprehensive exploration to the west. This project was paid for by Quebec merchants, and the division of ambitions in La Vérendrye's conception of his mission between fur trading and profit and exploration, the making of history and the extension of the glory of France and of Canada, has never been remotely clear. In Versailles, Pontchartrain had been succeeded as navy and colonies minister by his son, the precocious (he was only twenty-six) Count of Maurepas, who was an imperial expansionist, as long as the French government didn't have to pay for it, and he favoured La Vérendrye's plan.

In 1731, La Vérendrye and fifty followers, including three of his sons, struck out for the west. In the ensuing three years, they built forts on Rainy Lake, Lake of the Woods, and Lake Winnipeg. In 1734, La Vérendrye returned to Quebec to refinance his business, and by 1735 he was supplying more than half the fur exported from Quebec. In 1736, one of La Vérendrye's sons and eighteen comrades in the expedition were killed by the Sioux at what became known as Massacre Island on Lake of the Woods. La Vérendrye intervened with the Cree to prevent a general melee among the Indians that would imperil the supply of furs to the export market, so precarious, even two hundred years after the arrival of Jacques Cartier, was the economy of New France.

Choosing between the Saskatchewan River, which flowed west from Lake Winnipeg, and the Missouri River, which flowed southeast into the Mississippi, having come through what is now North Dakota, as the likeliest to be the fabled River of the West that would finally take Europeans to the Pacific Coast, La Vérendrye inexplicably chose the southeastern- rather than the western-flowing candidate, and in 1738 got to a point about seventy miles east of what is now the Montana–North Dakota border. He was again in Quebec in 1740, and in 1741 embarked on his fourth western expedition and built more forts on lakes Winnipeg and Manitoba and sent his son, Louis-Joseph de La Vérendrye, as far west as the Bighorn Mountains of Wyoming. Maurepas, apparently oblivious to the fact that La Vérendrye had to sell furs to pay for his expeditions, criticized him for spending too much time on commerce and not enough on exploration, and La Vérendrye retired in 1743. This episode illustrated again the dangers of running a shoestring operation to try to subdue hundreds of thousands of natives, end-run the British and their colonists, who were more than thirty times as numerous as the French of New France, and maintain control of the fur industry over nearly five million square miles. Maurepas eventually realized his error and reappointed La Vérendrye, who was now a prosperous and much admired Canadien, and La Vérendrye was preparing to go west and explore the Saskatchewan (which would eventually have brought him to the Rocky Mountains), when this implacable veteran of Malplaquet, forty years on, died in Montreal in 1749, aged sixty-four.

The governor and general court of the Hudson's Bay Company had assumed that the only competitive threat they would face would be French naval attacks on their northern forts and posts, and, in what proved a considerably whiter elephant than Louisbourg, built a formidable fortification called Prince of Wales Fort at the mouth of the Churchill River, under the supervision of the talented but obstreperous surveyor and mason Joseph Robson. After five years in Hudson Bay, Robson was sent home almost accused of mutiny, and testified before a parliamentary committee that the management of the Hudson's Bay Company had "slept for eighty years by the frozen sea," an excessive critique.[38] But what the company management had reckoned without was the intrepid French and French-Canadian traders and explorers outpacing them on land and advancing well to the west, making workable arrangements with all the Indians except the Fox. The Fox remained very difficult, and had to be dealt with as a military challenge, until Paul Marin de La Malgue, a capable colonial soldier, took command in 1736 and managed with a conciliatory policy to achieve a peace, where suppression at musket-point had failed, based on retention of their role as middlemen by the Fox. Thus ended the Second Fox War, in 1733 (though there would be further frictions). Farther south, in Louisiana, the French had to conduct a war with the Chickasaw and Natchez, who were encouraged by the South Carolinians. These tribes did not appreciate being bypassed by the French and cut out of the commercial loop, and the second Baron de Longueuil was sent to assist his uncle Pierre Le Moyne d'Iberville, founder and governor of Louisiana.

New France continued to be a tenuous proposition, but the French population of what is now the Province of Quebec had grown from eighteen thousand in 1713, to thirty-four thousand in 1730, to forty-three thousand in 1739. A nationality was developing, and the cultivated agricultural area had multiplied five-fold in the first third of the eighteenth century, to 163,000 arpents, from which more than a million bushels of cereal were harvested. New France was no longer on constant life-support from France, other than in military terms opposite a sophisticated threat from the British and British Americans. Sawmills, shipbuilding, pitch, hemp, brewing, iron-making, weaving and elemental textiles were all carrying forward the modest beginnings provided by Jean Talon. By 1744, New France was a net exporter. Unfortunately, the isolation which had challenged but protected it could not be continued much longer.

In the twenty-five years after the War of the Spanish Succession, the techniques of the transatlantic fishing industry evolved, and the processing of the fish, which had been done on the ships, was largely transferred to the shore, and settlement began in earnest. There were women in the processing crews, and as these provided a number of the settlers, "their presence made the 'residence' over winter something more than a bachelors' doss-house."[39] The French informally retained part of the Newfoundland shore, and processed fish very competitively also at Gaspé, Canso, Île Saint-Jean (Prince Edward Island), and Louisbourg. The Acadians, cut off from the shore by the northern movement of the New Englanders, and cut off also from New France, drifted into an ambiguous status, by which they took no oath of allegiance to the British Crown, and retained their language and religion and were effectively a neutral element in a small buffer zone between the British and French empires. Their status was implicitly tolerated by the British, and they "again became a people without a history,"[40] but they remained loyal to their neutrality pledge.

The War of the Austrian Succession (1739–1748), like anything having to do with Austria in its capacity as the continuator of the Holy Roman Empire, was very complicated. It was a series of conflicts overlapping in geography and time and was, even more than the Nine Years War and the War of the Spanish Succession, a world war. It was known as King George's War in North America. The Anglo-Spanish aspect of it was known as the War of Jenkins' Ear (so described by Thomas Carlyle, 119 years after it began, after the ear of a British merchant seaman – which was severed by the Spanish in a dispute arising from the concession of the non-Spanish slave trade to Great Britain in the War of the Spanish Succession – was produced as evidence in Parliament); the

First Carnatic War in India; and the First and Second Silesian Wars in Central Europe. Apart from the imbroglio over Robert Jenkins's ear, which started as a bilateral Anglo-Spanish dispute in 1739, the war ostensibly began because the daughter of the emperor of Austria Charles VI, Maria Theresa, was his heir, but under Salic law because women were not eligible to hold all the thrones that had been accumulated by the head of the Habsburgs, other powers professed to have an interest in defending this absurd relic of male self-exaltation that flew in the face of such great monarchs as Elizabeth I of England. In fact, every power in Europe wanted to nip away at the polyglot, ramshackle empire centred in Vienna that grouped German, Slavic, Italian, Spanish, Hungarian, Bohemian, Polish, Romanian, and Dutch chunks and oddments of Europe. Charles VI had foreseen this problem with the Pragmatic Sanction of 1713 and had gained the adherence of most of Europe to that acceptance of a female heir to his titles. The Holy Roman Empire could not have a female monarch, but the plan was for Maria Theresa's husband, Francis Stephen, to succeed as Holy Roman Emperor and Maria Theresa would succeed to her father's status as queen of Hungary, Croatia, and Bohemia, archduchess of Austria, duchess of Parma, and a passel of lesser thrones, crowns, and tiaras, suzerainties and protectorates that had been accumulated in the Habsburgs' five hundred years of military, diplomatic, and matrimonial aggrandizement.

The real start of the war and the most important result of it was the ambition of Prussia's King Frederick II, generally known as Frederick the Great, to challenge Austria for the headship of the Germanic world and join the ranks of the great powers. To this end, seizing an obscure pretext furnished by the Treaty of Brieg of 1537, Frederick claimed the right to dissent from the previously agreed Pragmatic Sanction, and invaded Silesia in December, 1740. Because Frederick, inaugurating a long and sanguinary era in international warfare, had trained his professional Prussian army more intensively than any army since the elite legions of the late Roman Republic, he was able simply to seize Silesia almost unopposed. The stately European habit had been an elaborate quadrille of warnings and ultimata accompanied by a mobilization conducted with as much deliberateness and fanfare as possible as part of an antique ceremony of affected grandiosity and intimidation. Frederick had a standing army, not one that had to be recruited after the exchange of war messages, and Prussian infantry could reload and fire at three times the speed of Austrian infantry. As the world would learn, Prussians tended also to be more militaristic by nature than the more convivial Austrians (and most other nationalities). Frederick ruled a scattered group of non-contiguous units and splinters created by Richelieu and Mazarin's Treaty of Westphalia almost a century before, with precisely the aim of assuring the dispersing of German Europe among many entities all of which were to be encouraged jealously to guard their autonomy. Frederick had doubled the population of Prussia in one stroke. The beginning of the unification of Germany and of an authentic German great power endowed with an exceptionally formidable army, were the principal outcomes of this war. And though very few people recognized it at the time, the combination of the rise of a militarily powerful German kingdom and the continued perfection of the British technique of assisting fluid coalitions in Europe designed to perpetuate a stalemate among rival countries while overwhelming all competitors on the high seas and in the sweepstakes for desirable colonization, were radically to alter France's long pre-eminence among the powers of Europe.

This is not the place for the history of this intricate and far-flung war, and it is only summarized to the extent of its impact on Canada and its history. The French and Bavarians led the countries joining Prussia in trying to take chunks out of the beleaguered Holy Roman Empire, but Maria Theresa, whose reign (from 1740 to 1780) was almost coextensive with Frederick's (from 1740 to 1786) and overlapped with that of Catherine the Great in Russia (from 1762 to 1796), soon showed her mettle and doubly made nonsense of the objection to one of her sex wielding her position. Her husband was forced out of Prague by the French in 1741 and the Bavarians and the elector of Bavaria, had himself crowned king of Bohemia, and claimed also to be the grand duke of Austria and Holy Roman Emperor Charles VII. Maria Theresa called for the support of the people of Hungary, and tens of thousands volunteered; she mobilized relatively quickly, and on the day of Charles VII's trumped-up coronation occupied the Bavarian capital of Munich, and then regained Prague. Frederick, who was only seeking Silesia, made a secret truce with Maria Theresa, but with her successes she revealed the arrangement to detach some of Frederick's allies because of his treachery, as she hoped to regain Silesia. Great Britain, in keeping with its traditional policy of supporting the underdog, came to the aid of Austria, and in an unprecedented and subsequently unattempted feat for the House of Hanover once enthroned in London, King George II defeated the French in 1743 and forced them back across the Rhine.

The French were only interested in picking up what was easily had and thereafter focused on encroaching on the part of the Netherlands that Austria had seized from the Spanish after the war for the succession in that country thirty years before. For this task, France had the services of another of its greatest military commanders, Maurice, Comte de Saxe, like Turenne and Villars a marshal general of France. (He was the illegitimate son of August the Strong, king of Poland and elector of Saxony. European rulers and nobles at this time had an astonishing number of illegitimate children.) Saxe defeated the British and Dutch at Tournai and Fontenoy in 1745. Bavaria, thoroughly chastened, made peace with Austria after the pretender Charles VII conveniently died. Maria Theresa gave them back what she had taken from Bavaria, which thus overcame its objections to a female ruler of the Holy Roman Empire, though Francis Stephen would hold the title. Frederick had become alarmed at Maria Theresa's progress and re-entered the war in 1744, but was now the only opponent of Austria on its actual borders, as the War of the Austrian Succession, apart from a final slugging match between Frederick and Maria Theresa, was henceforth fought out in the Netherlands, Italy, and in colonial operations. Frederick won four battles with the Austrians in Silesia in 1745, and they made peace at the end of 1745 – the Prussian king confirmed the annexation of Silesia but accepted the Austrian grand duchess and her husband as emperor. Austria generally held its position against the French and Spanish in Italy, but Saxe defeated all comers in the Netherlands, and it was fortunate, even for so talented and victorious a general, that a Russian army – peace having been made between Russia and Sweden, and after Russia had chosen to assist Austria – marching from Moscow to the Rhine arrived only a few days too late to join the fray in what were now the Austrian Netherlands.

The war in India (First Carnatic War), had gone well for France under Joseph François Dupleix, who captured Madras. The British had won the naval engagements in the Atlantic and West Indies, though not in the Mediterranean. France had not been able to lend any support to the planned Jacobite invasion of England, because its fleet was unable to find a window of superiority in the Channel. (The invasion, planned to come from Dunkirk, would have encountered a very frosty reception from the apostate English.) And in Canada, Louisbourg, touted as the Dunkirk or Gibraltar of North America, was known by the British from the observations of their fishermen and agents to be vulnerable to attack by land, and the great fort was captured easily by a contingent of Massachusetts militia transported by the Royal Navy and commanded by William Pepperrell. Cape Breton was also overrun without undue effort, in 1745. No effort was made to assault Quebec, and the war that raged in various parts of Europe and India and across many seas did not much affect events in the interior of North America. The French were stunned and humiliated by the fall of Louisbourg and mounted two expeditions to regain it, but they were prevented from being carried out by the weather, in 1746, and by a British naval interception, in 1747, in which the French commander, the Marquis de La Jonquière, was captured. Halifax harbour was surveyed for future use by the Royal Navy in 1749. The Acadians remained faithful to their collective pledge of neutrality in the indecisive fighting of that sector,[41] but the British would not guaranty that they would never be required to take up arms against France. The British (Americans) did mobilize the Mohawks to attack the French, and they got close to Montreal. The French replied with a raiding party led by Rigaud de Vaudreuil, son of the former governor, which razed the town of Northfield, Massachusetts. Both sides were employing Indians and not restraining their native allies from indulging their extreme notions of the rules of war with civilians, women, and children. Again, New France held its own against a more powerful neighbour, but these tactics stoked American anger and belligerence. The strong-minded governor of Massachusetts, William Shirley, took to emulating Cato about Carthage: "Delenda est Canada" (Canada must be destroyed).

The Treaty of Aix-la-Chapelle, which ended the War of the Austrian Succession, was the ultimate confirmation of the absurdity of the entire exercise, except for the party that started it. Frederick the Great was recognized as ruler of Silesia, a brilliant coup that pushed Prussia forward as a great power, alongside Russia, Austria, France, and Great Britain. Maria Theresa lost Silesia of course, but certainly made her point that she ruled the empire, and her husband possessed the euphonious and honorific title of Holy Roman Emperor. She had to concede back Parma and Piacenza to Spain, but kept Genoa and Modena, which the French and Spanish had tried to take. Maria Theresa also regained everything France had taken in the Austrian Netherlands, because the British graciously agreed to return Louisbourg and Cape Breton to France if France would give back Madras to Great Britain and the Austrian Netherlands to Maria Theresa. It was not a sensible arrangement for France, and French statesmanship must be faulted. France had won what is now Belgium and could have held it; it had no more ability to fight the British in India than it did in Canada, and unless French policy were turned on its ear (Jenkins got full vengeance for his severed ear, as Spain conceded the continuation of British control of the slave trade) and it was prepared to buy off European rivals, which now included the frightening Prussian garrison state and the numerous Slavonic masses of Russia, France would never be able to rival Britain on the high seas while protecting its land frontiers. The offended vanity of the French caused them to trade hard-won and important towns on their borders, including Brussels, for the return of Louisbourg and Cape Breton, which had little strategic value and could not possibly be held if the British were serious about taking them back. Handing over Madras was acceptable, though it was a marvellous victory for Dupleix, because the French could not retain it either and could not possibly supply troops in combat in India across thousands of miles in two oceans dominated by the British.

The disparity in strategic judgment of the main powers was becoming clear: Britain was generally able to assure the avoidance of continental dominance by any power, and welcomed the rise of both Prussia and Russia as adding further complexity to the power equations of Europe, making it more difficult for France or Austria to be preeminent. It had demonstrated again its naval superiority other than in French home waters in the Mediterranean, and even there the French had had to combine with the Spanish.

Several events of this war would resonate ominously through the next two centuries, including the march of a Russian army to the Rhine, the sudden Germanic unleashing of unanticipated and undeclared war on a tight timetable of a pre-mobilized and highly trained military, and recourse by the French to an unjustified nostalgia for defensive installations. In failing to choose between continental and overseas objectives, France would be unable to maintain both. Austria was holding her position, Britain consolidating and expanding hers, and Russia and Prussia were ambitious newcomers adding to their stature. The rise of those countries added further bulwarks against the incursions of the Turks, who had been beaten back from the gates of Vienna in 1683 with the help of over fifty thousand Polish and German troops who came to the assistance of the Austrians at the request of Pope Innocent XI, who then organized an alliance with the Russians, Poles, Austrians, and Venetians that cleared the Turks out of Hungary. The Turks would be in steady retreat out of Europe all the way into the twentieth century.

France sent the Marquis de La Galissonière to New France even before King George's War was over, as deputy governor to the less energetic La Jonquière. He was a very capable man, the highest grade of noble French colonial statesman, and he convinced himself, and passionately advocated, counterbalancing events in Europe by maintaining a French presence in North America. This was heartfelt and eloquently argued in his letters back to his government from Quebec,[42] but he was mistaken. The way to succeed was to seek and maintain peace with Britain. That was the only country that could deprive France of its empire, and if France were not at war with Britain, it could not be threatened by any land power. It could have conceded Britain a modest superiority in the colonial arena, but a much less one-sided balance than ultimately emerged, and in exchange extracted British approval of some French gains in Belgium, the Rhineland, and Italy, and the two countries between them and together could have operated some sort of balance between the Central and Eastern European powers and taken what they wanted from the empires of Spain and Portugal. They did get to this point about one hundred years later, jointly supporting the Turks against the Russians in Crimea and at the Congress of Berlin in 1878, but France so misjudged the strength of Prussia that it virtually midwifed the unification of Germany more than a century after these events.

In fact, La Galissonière's government did more than it should have to strengthen his *beau geste* romantic notions of the future of New France. La Galissonière sought a French naval buildup and reinforcement of its position in Acadia and on the Ohio. He thought that the French presence in the interior could be strengthened to the point where it effectively blocked the growth of the British seaboard colonies across the Appalachians. The British sent three thousand military settlers to Nova Scotia as soon as the late war ended and surveyed and created the port of Halifax, named after the president of the Board of Trade, the Earl of Halifax. Both sides increased their presence in the Ohio Valley, and in 1752, the pro-French Ottawa burned down a British fort, sent the British traders back unharmed, but tortured their Miami Indian allies and literally ate their leader. In 1753, La Galissonière sent a mission of 2,200 marines, militia, and Indian allies to make a portage from Lake Erie to the Ohio and build Fort Le Boeuf on the Ohio almost midway between its formation by the joining of the Allegheny and Monongahela rivers, and where it flows into the Mississippi.

It was clear that this was just another ceasefire, and a brief one at that, especially in North America. The British Americans were outraged that Louisbourg, which they had taken for king and country, had been given back for a fortress city in India and concessions to the Austrians. Shirley's call to arms against the French and their Indian allies was taken up in America and resonated strongly in London too. For New France, as a French colony, the omens were sombre, but there was an alternative perspective. By the end of King George's War in 1748, New France had fifty thousand French-speaking inhabitants and was a self-sustaining entity. If it came into the hands of the British, they would have no interest or ability to impose deracination of the population by inundating them with English-speaking people or deporting them. And Great Britain was the only power that could ultimately protect New France from being swamped by the Americans. Quebec was now a viable and permanent entity, and while it could not determine its own destiny, it could play a role in choosing it.

The English colonies had a steady demographic lead of between twenty and thirty to one over New France. The prospects of the French colony were always in doubt and were now, in the mid-eighteenth century, precarious. However, if the objective is not seen as a permanent French possession in North America, but rather as a largely French country in North America separate to that which would arise from the English colonies, then the omens were not entirely unfavourable. For such a largely French country to exist, it could not be based initially on British immigration, as any such entity would ultimately cohere with the English colonies, if not as colonies then as components of an independent successor to them. But the French population that was growing on the St. Lawrence would have to have British protection to survive. A French entity governed by France would ultimately be overwhelmed by the British, or by the Americans themselves, as the British would be unwilling to assist the French in the retention of their American possessions, and the Americans would eventually be too powerful for France to deter it from swallowing New France. And as Quebecers have always recognized, any association with the United States, however agreeable in other ways, would spell the end of Quebec as a French-speaking society. Britain, with the world's most powerful navy, would be too strong for the Americans to make war on it in North America, other than briefly and for narrowly defined objectives, for at least another two centuries. (At which point it could have been hoped, with good reason, that there would be no serious differences between Great Britain and what became the United States. Of course, this was what happened.)

Whoever lived in the northern part of North America, despite an often severe climate, was bound to do well, as it is a rich place. But if those people wished to have their own country, the components of it would have to be diverse and would have to come through a protracted and difficult minuet.

Quebec would have to be culturally French to resist the temptations of American union, from fear of cultural assimilation, and would have to be British politically, to deter the Americans from simply seizing it. So to survive, New France would have to become British-governed, and America would have to cease to be British-governed. And then a loyal English component would have to be found to add to the French Canadians to make them all adequately numerous to populate a transcontinental country and to attract the sponsorship of the British Empire, while retaining a will not to be subsumed into the English-speaking American state to the south.

The odds against all this happening in the right sequence and such a country being born and surviving were long, but there was a chance of it. No one thought of it at this time, as far as is known, but conditions changed more quickly in the New World than in Europe. Frontenac had died in Quebec just eight years before the birth in Philadelphia of one of the principal founders of the American Republic, Benjamin Franklin. For the idea of Canada, all would depend on this intricate and precise sequence of associations and disengagements. There was probably no one in the world who realized, at the start of the eighteenth century, that there had at least been a conception of the Canada that has arisen in the subsequent three hundred years. That national soul was embryonic, but it was healthy and would prove tenacious of life.

Sir Guy Carleton, Lord Dorchester (1724–1808), acting governor and governor of
Quebec 1766–1778, commander and co-chief negotiator of British forces in North
America 1782–1783 (where he more than held his own with George Washington);
governor general of The Canadas 1786–1796, chief author of the Quebec Act.
Though dour and grim and disappointed in much of his career, Carleton was a
capable soldier, governor, and statesman whose relatively generous policy to the
French Canadians was essential to the survival of Canada in the American
Revolution and the subsequent success of Canada, and a model that distinguished
the British from other empires.

CHAPTER 2

Carleton, American Wars, and the Birth of Canada and the United States

The British defeat the French, the Americans and French defeat
the British, and the British and Canadians draw
with the Americans, 1754–1830

1. New France Becomes French Canada:
The Seven Years (French and Indian) War, 1754–1763

Always before, wars between European powers had been triggered in Europe, but in 1754 to 1756, the opening shot in what became the Seven Years War* was fired in the wilderness of America, and on the authority of a subaltern who in the ensuing forty years would become one of the titans of world history, a young plantation owner from Virginia, George Washington. Washington, twenty-one in 1753, was already a substantial acquirer of land when he volunteered to take two hundred men assigned by Virginia governor Robert Dinwiddie and deliver a letter to the French commander at the Forks of the Ohio asking him to "desist" and

---

* The French and Indian Wars in North America, the Third Silesian War in Prussia and Austria, the Pomeranian War in Sweden and Russia, and the Third Carnatic War in India.

withdraw. Showing an impetuosity he did not much exhibit at the height of his career, Washington determined on an assault on the French, who had just evicted by force and with casualties the British from the site of the present Pittsburgh (named after the eminent contemporary British statesman William Pitt, later Earl of Chatham). Coming upon a thirty-five-man French and Indian scouting party, the Americans attacked the French and killed their commander, a M. Jumonville, and nine others. Washington's own account of this is a bowdlerized and self-serving description of a defensive response to a French attack. The French and some of Washington's followers claim that Washington's party initiated fire, allegedly in fidelity to Dinwiddie's instructions, although the Virginia governor had no authority to urge an attack on the military of a foreign power. One of Washington's Indian allies sank a tomahawk into Jumonville's skull preparatory to relieving him of his scalp.

Washington quickly repaired to a stockade he constructed and named Fort Necessity, but was soon invested by a much larger French siege force that poured fire into the fort, causing his men to panic and crack open the rum supply. He accepted an offer of honourable withdrawal, leaving two hostages (including the soon-to-be-famous Captain Robert Stobo) and pledging on his honour that none of his men would return to the Ohio country within a year. He had taken thirty dead and seventy wounded to fewer than ten French casualties. His men carried off the corpses, assisted the wounded, and made for home, though many deserted as soon as they were clear of the French. Washington remained calm, brave, and collected, but it was a fiasco that has been somewhat obscured, and his men did fire the first shots in what would be one of history's more important wars.

The British government was led by the Duke of Newcastle as prime minister, who had been over thirty years in government, first with the great Whig leader Robert Walpole and then with Newcastle's brother, Henry Pelham. Newcastle was a crafty political manoeuvrer in domestic and foreign matters. He appeased his monarch with generous grants to George II's native Hanover (which George, who spoke German even in London, still ruled) and maintained an alliance with Austria, Spain, Denmark, and Hanover. He worked up a plan with George II's favourite son, the Duke of Cumberland, who had a mixed military record, to

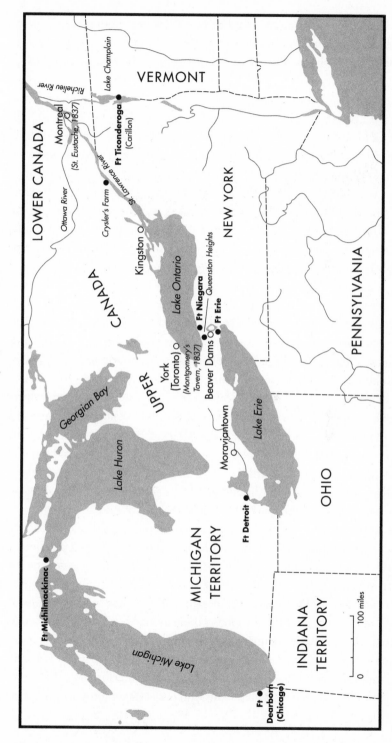

Sites of the Revolutionary War and the War of 1812

send two Irish regiments to America under the command of General Edward Braddock, a spit-and-polish professional with no knowledge at all of warfare in the interior of North America. Braddock was to uproot the entire network of forts Duquesne (the French commander who succeeded Jonquière as governor of New France) had built from the Great Lakes to and down the Ohio to the Mississippi. Newcastle had no military aptitude: "Annapolis must be defended, to be sure Annapolis must be defended . . . where is Annapolis?"[1] (Duquesne had built this network with a force of eleven thousand French, Quebec militia, and Indians, and had lost four hundred of his men in skirmishes and spent four million livres on this project, which grew from the Marquis de La Galissonière's plan.) Braddock arrived in America in February 1755 and immediately aroused great discontent by his haughty dismissal of the local militia as a band of roughnecks.

Braddock and Cumberland had devised a wildly ambitious plan to blockade the Gulf of St. Lawrence; Governor Shirley of Massachusetts would lead his militia against the French fort at Niagara; and Braddock himself would mop up the French forts south of the Great Lakes and join Shirley for an attack into Canada at the west end of Lake Ontario and then east and north to Montreal, Trois-Rivières, and Quebec. On July 10, 1755, Braddock's "flying column" of fifteen hundred, which managed five miles a day and included hundreds of civilian workers and a number of the officers' whores, was attacked by eight hundred French and Indian forest war veterans, who sniped at them from all sides while the Indians emitted their blood-curdling screams. Braddock was mortally wounded, and Washington, who was along as an aide, though suffering from dysentery and hemorrhoids, gallantly organized a retreat. It was a disaster: the British redcoats suffered a thousand dead and wounded, to twenty-three dead and sixteen wounded among the French and their Indian allies. "The Indians and Canadians stepped out among the wounded and the killed to pick up such plunder as they had never known, and to lift for the wigwams of the up-country such strings of scalps as Canadian winds had never dried."[2] The wreckage of Braddock's force plodded back to Philadelphia in July and announced it was taking quarters for the winter, which would only begin in five months. The 1755 campaign was over. Shirley never did advance on Niagara, which was the only part of the plan that made any sense, as that was the bottleneck for the flow of men and supplies and furs between Quebec and the web of French forts and posts down the spine of America. Shirley, who had been sputtering "Delenda est Canada" for over ten years, was made a scapegoat for the debacle, sacked a year later, and returned to Britain for a time.

The British did better in Acadia, seizing the French fort at the narrow isthmus connecting Cape Breton and Nova Scotia and deporting fourteen thousand French and French-speaking Indians from Cape Breton, and what are now Nova Scotia, New Brunswick, and Prince Edward Island. The deportees went in approximately equal numbers to France, Louisiana (where they became the basis of the Cajuns), and were assimilated into the population of New England or resumed residence in Acadia when conditions improved. It was a forerunner of ethnic cleansing and a shabby episode for which there was not the least excuse. There was also the usual ineffectual feint toward Montreal, and the Royal Navy stopped a couple of French ships in the St. Lawrence, but most men and supplies came through.

In London, Pitt accused the Whigs, led by Newcastle, of promoting the interests of the monarch's native Hanover over those of Great Britain. To complicate matters, Frederick the Great was George II's brother-in-law, but they viewed each other with no great warmth of affection, and George suspected Frederick of coveting Hanover. Newcastle played a typically devious game, negotiating and renewing Britain's defensive treaty with Russia in 1755. Frederick feared Russia even more than George, thinking of Hanover, feared Prussia. Frederick and Newcastle negotiated a non-aggression pact in 1756, which automatically became a pact of mutual assistance should anyone "disturb the tranquility of Germany," which was interpreted as meaning in particular an attack on Hanover or Prussia. Newcastle had outsmarted himself. Maria Theresa of Austria so hated Frederick for stealing her province of Silesia that she terminated her alliance with Britain, and Russia then declined to ratify the non-aggression agreement with Britain, and France renounced its alliance with Prussia and formed a new alliance with Austria – its rival of 250 years, since the time of Charles v and Francis i – and Russia. These gyrations were known as the Diplomatic Revolution of 1756.

In 1755, there were 15 million people in France, 6 million in Great Britain, excluding a somewhat disaffected Ireland, 3.5 million in Prussia, 2 million in the Netherlands, 1.5 million in the American colonies, and 60,000 in New France. Quebec's population, with one to every twenty-five Americans, was still just the population of one of the smaller German principalities. But America and New France had the highest standard of living of any of these places, as well as the fastest population growth. The American colonies were receiving most of the absolute population growth of Great Britain as immigration.

In an act reminiscent of his lightning strike against Silesia in 1740, Frederick, without a word of warning, invaded the Austrian province of Saxony in July 1756, and Austria, France, and Russia declared war on Prussia. Newcastle was still trying to bribe countries into an alliance against France that would restrain that country from going to war over provocations in North America, while Pitt accused him of pusillanimity and paranoia about the status of Hanover, which was now threatened by both France and Austria. Newcastle, finally, reluctantly, declared war on France on May 18, 1756, in response to provocations in the New World, including the falsified British version of the Washington-Jumonville encounter of almost two years before.

As war broke out, a new French commander arrived in New France, the distinguished career soldier Louis-Joseph de Montcalm. Braddock was replaced by the Earl of Loudoun, a pompous, ineffectual buffer who had little experience at serious combat and was no match as a field commander or theatre strategist for Montcalm, who invested and captured Fort Oswego at the southeastern corner of Lake Ontario, taking sixteen hundred British prisoners. Loudoun had formulated a plan to take Louisbourg and left New York in a hundred-ship force carrying six thousand troops bound for that destination on June 20, 1757. It took to late July to join forces with a Royal Navy escorting and bombardment fleet and for fog to abate, and the naval commander, Admiral Francis Holburne, declared it too late and impractical to proceed, as the French now had a large naval squadron at Louisbourg.

At the same time, Montcalm, with three thousand French, three thousand militia, and two thousand Indians (who had come from up to fifteen hundred miles away and from thirty-three different tribes and nations), invested Fort William Henry on Lake George, the entrance to the Hudson Valley from Quebec. Montcalm arrived on August 3, his forces spearheaded by fifteen hundred Indians, naked, gliding swiftly and silently up the lake in their canoes. Montcalm had brought artillery, and within six days had partly smashed the fort, which, after a respectable fight, surrendered. Montcalm allowed the British to retire, leaving an officer behind as a prisoner for security, and with a guaranty not to return to the area for eighteen months. Montcalm took all the stores and artillery and arms, and promised to return the wounded as they recovered the ability to travel. This did not conform to the Indian notion of how to treat defeated enemies, especially the notion of it they entertained after getting well into the spirit issue, both authorized and looted. The Indians chased after the retreating British, killing two hundred and capturing five hundred. Montcalm personally led the parties of retribution to compel the Indians to honour his promises, and he got back all but about two hundred prisoners, who were killed or dragged off by the Indians, including the boiling and eating of an English soldier in a public ceremony near Montreal.

Montcalm and the new governor of New France, Pierre de Rigaud de Vaudreuil, son of Philippe, knew that the Indians would now be impossible allies, as they didn't really care which side they were on and were concerned with taking or scalping prisoners and seizing their possessions. They also realized that this outrage would be represented in America as deliberate French policy, in keeping with the worst caricatures of French popishness, treachery, and barbarity. The relatively large basic population of the British colonies, angered by this atrocity and frightened by Montcalm's proximity at the head of eleven thousand battle-proven men, would now be much easier to mobilize than it had been. In the ten days following this massacre, the formerly sluggish Connecticut and Massachusetts mobilized and sent to Loudoun twelve thousand militiamen. The general alarm was unnecessary, as Montcalm had to withdraw, as he had run out of supplies, and his Indians, upon whom he relied for reconnaissance, deserted, resentful of their treatment, which they judged much inferior to that accorded their supposed enemies.

In Europe, the French, Swedes, Austrians, and Russians were not cooperating well on the development of a strategy to deal with Frederick, but Frederick's invasion of Bohemia in 1757 was unsuccessful, as the Austrians prevented him from taking Prague and largely reoccupied the imperishable Silesia. In the gloom that descended with this news, Newcastle and Pitt made a joint government, and Pitt managed to reverse Hanover's proposed withdrawal from the war following Cumberland's defeat there, though it required a large bribe to the Hanoverians of the kind Pitt had always opposed. Frederick bounced back and defeated the French and the Austrians in the last months of 1757.

One of the most important events of that year in the war was the arrival in London of Benjamin Franklin as representative of Pennsylvania and several other American colonies. Franklin was already a famous inventor, intellectual, scientist, printer, and statesman, and he was very respected in the most influential British circles. He began at once to propose a new arrangement between Britain and America that would reflect what he was convinced would soon become the larger population of America compared with the home islands of Great Britain. There was some discussion in Britain of whether Canada, if successfully occupied, should be taken permanently as a prize of war, rather than the French islands in the Caribbean, which produced large quantities of sugar, rum, molasses, and even tobacco and cotton. Franklin's views, though not determining, would be influential, and he articulated an emerging strategy for the English population of America.

Pitt sent nine thousand troops to help defend Hanover, and they briefly managed to cross the Rhine into France, which in this war had no general comparable to Condé, Turenne, Villars, or Saxe, the heroes of the French wars of the last ninety years. (Montcalm would have done better on the Rhine than the commanders the French had there.) Pitt seized the French slave trading operation at what is now Dakar, Senegal, and arranged an immense grant (£670,000) for Prussia. The war in Europe began with Frederick's unsuccessful invasion of Moravia, and he had constantly to bustle around the edges of his diminutive kingdom repulsing Swedes, French, Austrians, and Russians, who took an unpardonable amount of time to agree simultaneous attacks toward Berlin on all fronts. There had been little progress by either side anywhere in the far-flung war as 1758 opened.

* * *

It was at this point that the genius of William Pitt was first brought to bear on the 150-year Anglo-French contest in North America. Loudoun had just revealed his war plan for the new year to the New England governors, and they were being garrulously discussed in the Massachusetts Assembly, doubtless to the delectation of the French, when Pitt responded to a letter to him from Loudoun, in which the commander-in-chief virtually accused the colonial governors of insurrection, by sacking Loudoun and replacing him with General James Abercromby "to repair the losses and disappointments of the last inactive and unhappy campaign."[3] Pitt settled long-standing grievances by ordering that colonial officers have the same rank in the British Army and that they be equipped to a serious standard. (The Americans were greatly annoyed that a lowly British lieutenant was able to command a senior American colonial officer, as Washington had become, and that American units, even if their uniforms were appropriate, were under-armed ragamuffins in military terms.) The Massachusetts legislators had balkily rejected Loudoun's request for 2,128 men, but were now so uplifted that they voted to raise 7,000 men for the war, and within a month the colonies had raised 23,000. The combination of the Indian outrages the previous summer following the rout at Fort William Henry, and Pitt's enlightened policy, mobilized the colonies' pool of manpower of 1.5 million (including 150,000 slaves). The predominance of the Royal Navy assured that France would not be able to counteract the correlation of forces in Britain's favour in North America.

Under the stolid Abercromby, Pitt had promoted strong officers who were not politically influential or close to the royal family so that Pitt's control of the armed forces would be uncontested. Lord Ligonier, aged seventy-seven, and the greatest British general between Marlborough and Wellington (not counting Washington), became the army commander, and Admiral Lord Anson the chief of staff of the navy. The forty-one-year-old Colonel Jeffery Amherst and the thirty-one-year-old Colonel James Wolfe were put in charge of the attack on Louisbourg with fourteen thousand men; Fort Duquesne (Pittsburgh) became the target for a force of seven thousand headed by Dr. and Brigadier John Forbes; and Fort Carillon (Fort Ticonderoga) and Fort Frontenac were to be taken by forces of twenty-five thousand led nominally by Abercromby but in fact by Viscount Howe. Montcalm could not have produced more than twenty thousand able-bodied men between sixteen and sixty in his entire population. He was also suffering from food shortages because of a poor harvest and a shortage of munitions because of the British blockade, and was hampered by the separation between civic and military authority, and especially by the avarice of the intendant, François Bigot. (Bigot was eventually tried and exiled with confiscation of property for his corruption. This might partly have been a scapegoating, but in the lore of Quebec he is regarded as a monstrous crook. He would die in Switzerland, an outcast, in 1778.)

Amherst and Wolfe invested Louisbourg on June 8, 1758, and it fell on July 26, after the French garrison of 5,000 had taken 1,700 casualties. Amherst took everyone prisoner and completed the ethnic cleansing of the Acadians by deporting the entire civil population of 8,000 to France. Montcalm routed Abercromby's inept assault at Fort Carillon (as Howe was killed by a French sniper as the British approached). Though he had only 3,600 men to the British force of 16,000, he drew Abercromby into a charge against entrenched and fortified positions and enfiladed him with sharpshooters, inflicting more than 2,000 casualties to trivial losses of his own. On the other hand, Fort Frontenac was captured by the British on August 26, as 4,000 men attacked a fort defended by only 110 Frenchmen, and the British seized all the French lake craft and a large supply of stores. The French blew up Fort Duquesne and withdrew at the approach of Forbes.

At the end of 1758, the British controlled the Gulf of the St. Lawrence and had severed the connection between New France and the ambitious network of forts and posts along the Ohio and Mississippi it had taken more than a century to build. The St. Lawrence from Tadoussac to Montreal was all that was left. Over the winter, Pitt's forces captured the sugar-rich French Caribbean island of Guadeloupe.

As Horace Walpole, the long-serving prime minister's belletrist son, wrote grudgingly of the Tory Pitt: "Our bells are worn threadbare with ringing for victories."[4] For 1759, Pitt ordered Amherst to proceed up Lake Champlain yet again and take Montreal, while Wolfe was to make an amphibious landing near Quebec and capture and occupy that city. In an odd diversion, Amherst proceeded to the south of Lake Ontario and captured Niagara, at the opposite end of that lake to Fort Frontenac. Wolfe landed 8,500 men on Île d'Orléans, just east of Quebec. Montcalm fought with his customary agility, skill, and courage, and Wolfe was afflicted by influenza, indigestion, and depressive attacks. Although Wolfe's relations were not good with his brigade commanders, Robert Monckton, George Townshend, and James Murray, he asked them their advice and they recommended that he move his forces on the river past Quebec and resume the attack from the west, as the skirmishing below Quebec had yielded no advantage to the British and Montcalm had inflicted much worse casualties than he had suffered. This would separate Montcalm from reinforcements that might come from Montreal and was presumed to be a less fortified and strongly defensible side of Quebec than the ramparts of the Citadel.

Wolfe's planning was importantly assisted by Captain Robert Stobo, originally of the Virginia militia, who had accompanied George Washington on the ill-fated trip to Fort Necessity, where Washington left him as an agreed prisoner as security to his promise to withdraw from the area around the sources of the Ohio River. Stobo had been sent back to Quebec as a prisoner and circulated easily there until he was discovered to be a spy and was imprisoned, a death sentence not having been confirmed by Paris. He escaped from prison, caught up with Wolfe, and told him minute details of the French defences, and possibly even of the access to the Plains of Abraham, west of Quebec from the landing point known since as Wolfe's Cove. Wolfe moved 4,500 men upriver on the tide and then came back with the current on the night of September 12, 1759. He followed Stobo's guidance in threading up the steep path to the Plains, while his forces left behind to the east of Quebec conducted a skilful ruse. Montcalm only arrived at the Plains at 9:30 a.m. on September 13, and became concerned that Wolfe would succeed in bringing up artillery from his ships and determined to attack, though he expected the arrival of two thousand of his best men from Montreal led by his capable subordinate General François de Lévis. Wolfe had entertained doubts about the British plan, which Brigadier Murray had dismissed as insane, but held to it, and Montcalm ran out of patience waiting for Lévis and attacked frontally, supported by Indians and other skirmishers on the northern flank of the British. The British repulsed the French with artillery fire and disciplined musketry and the defenders fell back toward Quebec.

As the British advance began, Wolfe was mortally wounded by snipers but was advised by his staff while still conscious that the French were withdrawing and that the battle was certainly a victory. Montcalm too had been severely wounded, and was carried from the field, dying in a delirium at four o'clock the next morning. The column from the west arrived about thirty minutes too late to be decisive in the battle, and Montcalm was succeeded as commander by the governor, the able Vaudreuil.* All the French forces were concentrated northwest of the city and retired to Montreal. Lévis quickly shaped them up and marched them crisply back to Quebec, where they arrived one day after that city, which had only a skeleton garrison, accepted the generous terms of Townshend, who had succeeded Wolfe in command of the British. Lévis and Vaudreuil retired to Montreal as the winter descended. New France was reduced to one city. Townshend took the last ship out of Quebec before ice made the St. Lawrence impassable and bequeathed command to Brigadier Murray, who bunked his seven thousand men in with seven thousand regular inhabitants of the city, which had rations for only that number. Murray became the governor of Quebec and was considerate of the French, sharing rations equally, and quickly developed an affection for the French Canadians, which was reciprocated. It was an auspicious start to new arrangements, and the British were not really a presence at all in the seigneuries along the St. Lawrence and the rivers that flowed into it.

In Britain, a thousand bonfires celebrated the fall of Quebec, and Pitt, a florid orator, told Parliament, "Ancient history may be ransacked and ostentatious philosophy thrown into the account before an episode can be found to rank with Wolfe's."[5] The French were not as perturbed as

---

* This was Pierre de Rigaud, Marquis de Vaudreuil-Cavagnial (1698–1778), governor of Louisiana from 1743 to 1753, and of New France from 1755 to 1760. He was born in Quebec, where his father, Philippe de Rigaud de Vaudreuil (c. 1643–1725), had been the governor of New France from 1703 to 1725. Philippe's grandson and Pierre's nephew, Admiral Louis-Philippe de Vaudreuil (1724–1802), would be deputy commander of the French navy during the American Revolutionary War, in which he scored some important victories. It was a very distinguished Franco-Canadian family.

the British were jubilant. Louis xv's prime minister, the Duke of Choiseul, had assembled an army of one hundred thousand men near the Channel ports and ordered the navy to come to transport it to Britain. The French leadership convinced itself that it was a clever ploy to indulge Pitt's preoccupation with colonies and lure the British navy to distant places while France struck at the British home islands. This was hardly an unfamiliar concept to the British, who barricaded the French fleet into Toulon in the Mediterranean and then pursued it to the Bay of Biscay and into Brest. Admiral Sir Edward Hawke, one of Britain's greatest seamen, came to grips with the French fleet in nasty weather in Quiberon Bay on November 20, 1759, and eliminated seventeen French ships for only two losses of his own. This was the effective end of the Choiseul plan, and the Anglo-French part of the Seven Years War was henceforth an unfeasible struggle between an invincible sea power and an unconquerable land power, between a shark and a lion, or a whale and an elephant. Britain was doing well in India also.

In Europe, the war had gone poorly for the Anglo-Prussian alliance in 1759, as the Prussians had lost ground to the Russians and Austrians, and Frederick had contemplated abdication and even suicide. Hanover was safe, and the British didn't care what happened in Central and Eastern Europe, as long as no individual power became preeminent among Austria, Prussia, and Russia. Maria Theresa's armies regained Saxony and again pushed into Silesia. The Russian empress, Elizabeth, Peter the Great's daughter, even briefly took Berlin until Frederick rushed back from the frontier to evict her army, but she remains more than 250 years later the only Russian leader except Stalin to take Berlin.

In the spring of 1760, Lévis suddenly arrived at the western approaches to Quebec and defeated Murray at the Battle of Sainte-Foy and drove him back into the walled city of Quebec, but he had no artillery with which to reduce the ramparts and had to withdraw. Murray had begun a grand tradition of important implications by fostering cordial relations with the French through the winter and not interfering at all with their law and customs and local officials. Amherst arrived at Montreal in the summer. The city had no fortifications and had had no supplies from France for several years, and on generous and respectful conditions from Amherst, Vaudreuil surrendered it. The war in North America was over and New France ended with it.

The war in Europe dragged on a little longer. France couldn't invade Britain, had no interest in intervening in Central or Eastern Europe, and couldn't even bring itself to a full-hearted attack on Hanover, especially after George II died in 1760 and was succeeded by his grandson, the very headstrong George III, who disliked his grandfather and had no interest at all in Hanover. He was the first Hanoverian British king to speak English properly, or even as a first language. Choiseul succeeded, inexplicably, in dragging Spain into the war on France's side, in 1762, claiming that Britain would next be attacking Spanish possessions in the New World. The British, who had almost run out of French imperial extremities to attack, responded by seizing Havana. Pitt and then Newcastle were sacked by George III, who distrusted Pitt's brilliance and force and considered Newcastle, after thirty-six years in cabinet, and with some reason, a slippery politician. The king put in as prime minister his tutor, the Earl of Bute, who was completely unqualified to take their place.

Czarina Elizabeth died in 1762, and the throne of Russia was held briefly by her dull-witted German nephew, Peter III, who worshipped Frederick the Great, withdrew from the war, and was promptly murdered with the presumed complicity of his wife (in one of the most unevenly talented marriages in history), the formidable Catherine the Great, as she became. (Frederick, a cultured man and friend, as Catherine was, of Voltaire, wrote a couplet about Elizabeth when she died: "The Russian Messalina, the Cossacks' whore, / Gone to service lovers on the Stygian shore."[6] The death of Elizabeth was the salvation of the hard-pressed Frederick, and in 1945 the Nazi leaders hopefully compared the death of Roosevelt with it.[7])

British debt had risen through the war from 74.5 million pounds to about 133 million pounds, and bonds to cover the deficit had to be issued at punitive rates of interest. Both France and Britain faced financial problems and peace beckoned, as it did to war-weary Austria, and certainly Frederick's beleaguered Prussia as well. Spain was not prepared to cede Havana, and Choiseul worked out a compromise whereby he gave Louisiana, which France clearly could not hold and which the British were capable of seizing at any moment, to Spain in exchange for Spain ceding to Britain the Gulf Coast from the Mississippi to the eastern border of Alabama, and Britain gave Havana back to Spain in exchange.

Benjamin Franklin had been the agent of Pennsylvania and some other American colonies in London since 1757, and had never ceased to lobby and agitate for the permanent expulsion of France from Canada. There was a considerable body of opinion in Britain that wanted to keep France's rich Caribbean islands, and leave France with Canada, which Voltaire described, in a phrase that rankles yet in Quebec, as "a few acres of snow." All Franklin's voluminous correspondence at this time, including his widely circulated "Canada Pamphlet," fervently advocated the British takeover of Canada. As long as a great European power was bordering the American colonies, they were not safe. It worked out as Franklin had hoped and advocated. France regained its Caribbean islands, the African slave-trading station at Gorée, and the Indian port city of Pondicherry, and kept the Gulf of St. Lawrence islands of Saint-Pierre and Miquelon, with which to service its fishing fleet and continue to train seamen for France's navy. Britain ruled North America and India. There is no evidence that Franklin thought explicitly of American independence, but he made it clear that he anticipated the Americans would outnumber the people of the Mother Country about the time it happened (eighty years later) and saw the balance of power within the British world shifting steadily across the Atlantic. But if New France were governed by the British and by home rule, and not by the Americans, the Americans could not claim to be threatened, but neither could they lay claim to Quebec. Franklin had a vision of the greatness of America, but no one had any idea what to do with French Canada. It was a self-sufficient entity with a national identity and a heroic tradition. It had a reasonable framework of laws and was devoutly Roman Catholic, an ultramontanist outpost that, but for geographic inconvenience, could virtually merge with the Papal States.

The Treaty of Paris was signed on February 10, 1763, and the Peace of Hubertusburg five days later between the Eastern European powers. Maria Theresa regained Saxony, but Frederick retained Silesia. The

Seven Years War had been utterly stupid for everyone except the British and Americans. The other countries made war almost continuously, at great cost in lives, treasure, and physical damage, for marginal gains and losses of territory; the royal dynasts amused themselves with inter-dynastic marriages and quarrels for which the people paid. Talented autocrats like Richelieu and Frederick the Great, and for a time Louis XIV, could make the system work for them and their nations' interests, up to a point, but ordinary despots just squandered what they blowzily believed to be their divine right to rule capriciously. France had lost prestige, and lost an empire. Prussia did not gain an inch, but was confirmed in the fraternity of the great powers, with Britain, France, Austria, and Russia. Britain had a debt bomb it would soon wish to share with America. Pitt had been the great war statesman (starting a tradition that would be followed after successful British wars with other great powers, he was ousted as the trumpets of victory were sounded), Frederick was the great commander, and Franklin was the great strategic prophet.

New France had been a bold and a brave experiment. It was never going to be able to compete with the colonies to the south, peopled by the British, a seafaring nation around all their island perimeter, a nationality that liked to explore and resettle and possessed a great navy. But New France was now, in peacetime, serene and untroublesome. All the French establishment in Quebec except the clergy departed. (Lévis became a marshal of France and died in 1787. His son fled to Britain during the French Revolution, but with the civilizing gentleness of the Reign of Terror, Lévis's widow and three daughters were executed on the guillotine for the crime of nobility.) French Canada was self-sufficient in food and trade, and was accustomed to a prodigious birthrate that was certain to provide a natural population increase. Deportation was out of the question, as the population was much greater than that of the Acadians, and the French Canadians had not had unlimited affection for the French, who hastily deserted them, but liked what they saw of the British, who provided a security against the Americans the colony had never had and governed without the unappealable authoritarianism and corruption the French often brought with them. The achievements of the early Canadians, such as d'Iberville, Joliet, and La Vérendrye, had been astounding. The tenacity and national integrity of the French Canadians were impressive, and impressed all who came in touch with them.

As long as the British protected the French Canadians, they would flourish. The British were already looking to the Americans, who had the most prosperous 20 per cent of the world's British, to help them pay for the cost of the late war, and without the French threat on their northern border, the Americans could be much feistier, as was their nature, with the home country than before. The French Canadians were pliant clay for a new nationality and the conditions for Canadian nationhood were starting, imperceptibly, to fall into place. The embryo of Canada of half a century before was now a fetus.

2. Toward Conciliation in Canada and Schism in America, the Quebec Act, 1763–1774

The British Army ruled with exemplary tact and fairness in the quiet interregnum in Quebec from 1760 to the end of the Seven Years War in Europe in 1763, when it was not clear whether Canada would be retained by Britain or returned to France. Franklin lobbied perfervidly in London for the former course. Amherst, who was officially the chief authority as theatre military commander in New York, posted a "placard" throughout Montreal and Trois-Rivières advising the inhabitants that they could keep those firearms necessary for hunting, that the Canadian militia would be replenished, and that all requisitions by the British Army were to be paid for at a fair price and in cash, which caused a mutiny in Quebec, as the soldiers were accustomed to these things being provided for them by the British government. Murray put down the mutiny, which was a salutary lesson to everyone, including the inhabitants, who had not been accustomed to such discouragement of official rapine under the French. Civil adjudication was to be by captains of militia, with appeals, under Murray in the Quebec district, to the existing courts of what had been New France. Murray spoke French well and liked, and was liked by, the French and French Canadians, and he was confirmed as governor of Quebec after the Treaty of Paris allocated it to Britain. Murray took a dim view of the first few hundred British arrivals, mainly opportunistic American sharpers and swindlers claiming to be the merchant class of the new British colony with the conqueror's pride of place.

When it came in 1763, the Treaty of Paris only allowed the Québécois to practise their "religion according to the rites of the Romish church as far as the laws of Great Britain permit," which was not very far. But there was little change, and the position of the Catholic Church was undisturbed. The fifth bishop of Quebec,* Henri-Marie Dubreil de Pontbriand, had died in 1760, and the British were not prepared to allow a nominee of the king of France or the pope until matters were settled. The diocese (which technically extended to New Orleans) was directed by the vicars general of Quebec and Montreal, with conspicuous concern for the wishes of the governors, and the Jesuit, Sulpician, and Récollet parish priests were not interfered with, but were closely watched by the British for any subversive tendencies. There were few incidents. Jean-Olivier Briand was chosen by the Holy See, consecrated in France, and informally advised in England to go to Quebec and assume his role without fanfare. He did this and was eventually recognized, in the terms of the occupiers, as "Superintendent of the Romish Church" (in other words, bishop). The playing-card money resorted to in Quebec was rejected by the British as of no value, and the colonial administration was bankrupt. Bigot and his friends took with them everything that was left except the copper roofs of the main buildings. The outrages inflicted by the British on the Acadians served as a cautionary warning to the people of New France. The seigneurial land and tenancy arrangements were respected, as was the French civil law, but the harsh French criminal law was replaced with the British version of criminal justice, draconian by contemporary standards, but a soft impeachment and penalization of the wrongdoer by the standards of France. Amherst gave those residents unable to accept the change eighteen months to pack up and leave Quebec. Most of the secular leadership of New France departed.

The native people who had been allied with the French were less quiescent. The individual American colonies all had territorial ambitions

---

* After Laval, from 1674 to 1688, and Jean-Baptiste de La Croix de Chevrières de Saint-Vallier, from 1688 to 1727, Louis-François Duplessis de Mornay, from 1727 to 1733, and Pierre-Herman Dosquet, from 1733 to 1739.

to the west, if there were not another colony separating them from the politically unorganized interior. And those colonies that did not adjoin the Indians, such as most of New England, had classes of settlers and speculators who invoked the patronage of their colonies of origin, unofficially setting up colonies of colonies in the interior. The relations with the Indians were conducted as much in the private sector as by governments and were replete with the most dubious practices, most frequently the plying of Indians with alcohol and then purporting to buy tracts of their land at risible prices. When, as inevitably happened, the Indians rebelled at this trickery, hostilities broke out and the western frontier developers who had despised and evaded the control of the colonial governments screamed like banshees for their protection as ambassadors of civilization and progress beset by the lowly savages and heathen, and the colonists, full of complaints though they habitually were toward the Mother Country, echoed the concerns of the frontiersmen in demanding Imperial protection for their depredations on the Indians.

The Cherokee War of 1758 to 1761 was the first such problem, and was doubtless instigated by the French traders and soldiers who worked with the Cherokee. The British stabilized this and other dissatisfied Indian groups. Amherst, while respectful of Britain's ancient and majestic foe across the English Channel, regarded the North American Indian with complete disdain aggravated by a total lack of curiosity. He assumed that with the end of their ability to play the French and British off against each other, the Indians would roll over like poodles and confine their savagery to internecine squabbles. More knowledgeable and successful were a Swiss brigadier in the British frontier forces, Henry Bouquet (a soldier of fortune who had also served in the Dutch and Sardinian armies), and the supreme British expert in relations with the North American Indians, Sir William Johnson. (Johnson was British superintendent of Indian affairs from 1756 to his death in 1774. He carried his interest in the natives to rather energetic intimacy with Indian women, siring between twenty and one hundred illegitimate children with many women of a number of tribes and bands. He may have exploited not only his position but the tribally approved promiscuity of young Indian women until they found their mate.) Between them, by an artistic combination of tact and force, Bouquet (who founded and named Pittsburgh) and Johnson stabilized the outer frontier edges of the British-American colonies.

Pontiac's War, named after the Ottawa leader who was the most prominent of the many chiefs involved, began in May 1763 after Amherst stopped the practice of presenting gifts to the Indian leaders, which was a matter of prestige in the eyes of their tribes and nations, and the end of the policy was considered humiliating and insulting. Amherst also cut the supply of gunpowder, which the Indians saw as a sinister and unfriendly act (and which had been the effective cause of the Cherokee War). The Indians were all concerned about the incessant westward pressure of the British, where the French had been content just to send agents, missionaries, and armed parties among them but did not constitute the demographic threat of an occupier as the British (Americans) did. Pontiac grouped together the Ottawa, Ojibwa, Potawatomi, Huron, Miami, Wea, Kickapoo, Mascouten, Piankashaw, Delaware, Shawnee, and Wyandot. They seized a number of the smaller French forts and laid siege to Pittsburgh and Fort Detroit but did not capture them. Johnson successfully negotiated some of the tribes out of the war. Bouquet beat the Indians off at Pittsburgh, but not before he and Amherst had discussed in writing trying to infect the Indians with chicken pox from blankets the British distributed. There was the Royal Proclamation of October 7, 1763, which recognized the Indians as having some rights to their territory. Amherst was withdrawn to Britain in 1764 and replaced with General Thomas Gage, and Johnson and others produced a negotiated end to all phases of the war by 1766. Amherst's policies were reversed and the proclamation was interpreted as giving the Indians "reserved" territory (the origin of that word in that context) west of a line along the peaks of the Alleghenies. The British and Americans lost 450 soldiers dead, 2,000 civilians killed or injured, and 4,000 moved to avoid Indian marauding. The Indians lost about 400 dead and an unknown number wounded and afflicted by combat-related illnesses, perhaps 2,000 or so. Pontiac's war is generally reckoned a draw.

The Royal Proclamation also established the boundaries of a new British province of Quebec. In accepting reserved Indian territory beyond the Alleghenies, it tried to force further British settlement north into Quebec and south into the Floridas (as they then were).

There was some hope of swamping and assimilating the French, but no thought of culturally suppressing or deporting them. But the flow of homesteaders continued to move steadily west and to exacerbate problems with the Indians, who saw with resentment the white man's advance in a demographic tidal wave, which the vanguard of Euro-American civilization made little attempt to palliate. In 1768, the southern border of Iroquois lands was moved to the west, to the Ohio, by the Treaty of Fort Stanwix.

Murray proved a durably enlightened and popular governor. As the Royal Proclamation foresaw an assembly, and British law excluded any Roman Catholic elector or member of such an assembly, the five hundred or so English-speaking merchants in Quebec agitated for the selection and convening of just such a body. Murray construed his authority, as civil governor starting in 1764, to include determining when the assembly would be established, and he did not choose to establish one in these circumstances. Instead, his council was, in so far as there was one at all, the legislature. He packed it with protégés, the like-minded, and sympathizers with the French. He also intervened to vacate the nomination of Vicar General Étienne Montgolfier of Montreal as the next bishop, supporting instead Vicar General Briand of Quebec, who was confirmed by the British Crown and the French Church and the pope.

The greedy American merchants of Montreal and Quebec had enough influence with the Board of Trade in London (a cabinet office) to have Murray recalled in 1766 for his pro-French attitudes. They complained of their inability to monopolize legislative authority to their own less than 1 per cent of the population, and even complained that Murray was an insufficiently regular (Protestant, of course) church attender. The French seigneurs responded in Murray's favour, but he was further compromised by a peculiar episode in which one of the most bigoted and authoritarian magistrates, Thomas Walker, was assaulted in his home while having dinner with his wife and part of his ear was severed, which caused acute concern in the colony. Despite these perturbations, which affected almost exclusively the English, Murray's sage and tolerant decisions, unvaried by his successor, provided the thin thread which connected the French Canadians and the British Crown that alone could protect them from the Americans.

The British government, for obvious reasons, favoured the older British colonies over the French-Canadian foundling. Seal hunting and hunting on the north shore of the Gulf of the St. Lawrence had been cut off by the 1763 Royal Proclamation, in favour of Newfoundland and, supposedly, to prevent the smuggling of French goods to Quebec. (Neither side of that fantasized transaction had any interest.) With the French masters of the interior in the fur trade cut off from their former buyers in Montreal, they did the best they could with the Hudson's Bay Company and whatever American competition could be found, until Montreal merchants, and especially the Nor'Westers (North West Company), returned to the fray. The Hudson's Bay Company had sent Anthony Henday to the Blackfoot country in 1754, and Samuel Hearne followed with mining exploration trips to the shore of the Arctic Ocean in 1769 and 1772. After examining how the Newfoundland fishing industry had evolved to the benefit of New Englanders over the fishermen who came from Britain, the British government appointed Captain Sir Hugh Palliser governor of Newfoundland in 1764, with a mandate supported by the Royal Navy to reserve fishing on and near the Grand Banks to the British at the expense of the Americans, who were compensated by being able to take the place of the French in the Nova Scotia fisheries. By 1775, there were approximately eighteen thousand people in Nova Scotia, mainly New Englanders attracted by the rich agriculture.

In 1765, the law officers of the British government, showing a sagacity that had temporarily deserted them in American matters, concluded that the Roman Catholics of Quebec were not subject to the restrictions imposed on their co-religionists in the United Kingdom. The British still had no real idea of what to do with Quebec, but as London's relations worsened with the Americans and warmed with the French Canadians, the Board of Trade, which had some authority in colonial matters, recommended in 1769 an assembly in Quebec that would be "complete" by allowing Roman Catholics to vote and to sit in the legislature. This legislature should deal with the matter of Quebec's courts, laws, and religious matters. On his recall at the insistence of the parvenu English merchant community, Murray reported to the secretary of state (Southern Department), his direct superior, that the English Quebeckers were scoundrels: "All have their fortunes to make and I hear few of them are solicitous about the means whereby the end can be obtained; in general, the most immoral collection of men I ever knew and of course little calculated to make the new subjects enamoured with our laws, religion, and customs." The French of Quebec he described as "a frugal, industrious, moral race of men who from the mild treatment they received from the king's officers . . . had greatly got the better of the natural antipathy they had to their conquerors."[8] Murray went on to distinguish himself in the (unsuccessful) defence of Minorca, and remains a respected and benign figure, in war and peace, at a decisive point in Canadian history.

Benjamin Franklin, already a world-famous inventor, printer, and writer, and in Britain a member of the Royal Society and honorary doctor of Oxford, as was his illustrious contemporary Samuel Johnson, returned to London in 1764 as debate began on the Stamp Act. The near-doubling of British public debt, largely incurred to evict the French from North America, caused the British king, government, and Parliament to believe that the wealthiest fifth of Englishmen, the Americans, must equitably, and as a practical fiscal necessity, pay down some of the debt incurred to disembark France from North America. Franklin soon discovered the extent of the gulf that was opening between British and American opinion. As relations warmed between Britain and French Canadians, and deteriorated between Britain and British Americans, the implications of these shifts would soon be evident, and would ultimately be earth-shaking.

The removal of the French from North America made Britain dispensable to the American colonists, and the heavy costs of the British victory in the Seven Years War, and the increased cohesion the colonies achieved in the war, altered the correlation of forces between Britain and America. The British did not notice this, but the more astute Americans did. Franklin had advocated the union of the American colonies at a congress in 1754 in Albany, and in the same year had written to a British scientific friend, the distinguished naturalist Peter Collinson, that "Britain and her Colonies should be considered as one whole, and not different states with separate interests."[9] He made a proposal that was considered by the Board of Trade and passed on to Newcastle, who ignored it, for what amounted to a tighter format of the eventual

Commonwealth. This was before the British Empire extended far into populations that were not Caucasian (India was a joint national and private sector operation).

Most emigration from Britain continued to come to the American colonies, and significant numbers of Germans and Dutch were also arriving. If the Irish, a very large number of whom were fractious and discontented, are not included in the British population, the shift of demographic weight from Britain to America would come earlier, and if the French Canadians were included with the Americans – and Franklin assumed, then and later, that they would join the Americans when the connection with France was severed, and would be quickly assimilated to the English-speaking world, even if they were bilingual (he took no account of religious differences) – America would, within about fifty years be set at the head, in all respects except perhaps ceremoniously (that is, it would not be the residence of the constitutional monarch), of a very powerful, transatlantic, and globe-girdling British-American entity. It was a grand vision.

Franklin was the most politically far-sighted of the American leadership, and the first inkling of what he was facing came to him in London in 1760, the year of the final fall of New France to Amherst, when he met Lord Granville, president of the Privy Council and one of the most influential members of the government, who listened to his suggestions but responded that "the king is the Legislator of the Colonies," and his will "is the law of the land."[10] By 1770, the American colonies had more than 25 per cent of the British Isles' population and a substantially larger share of wealth and income, far greater resources, and a fraction of the indigenous debt.

The Stamp Act imposed a tax on printed and paper goods in the colonies, including even newspapers and playing cards, and was so called because the assessment of the tax was signified by a stamp. Britain already had such a tax, and it was not obvious to the British, after their expensive exertions on behalf of the Americans, why those colonies should not share the tax burden of the wars that cleared their horizon. The Stamp Act was presented by Pitt's brother-in-law, George Grenville (not to be confused with Lord Granville), who asserted Parliament's right to impose taxes anywhere in the British Empire, a right that was not challenged in Parliament. Grenville did allow one year for the tax to be applied to the American colonies to give them the opportunity to devise a substitute method of raising revenue and retiring debt. The only alternative proposed was by Franklin himself, who suggested establishment of a colonial credit office in America to issue bills of credit and collect interest for their renewal. It was a disguised paper currency and public finance scheme that would have addressed the British insistence that all payments be in cash, and gold and silver was scarce in America. It would have been somewhat inflationary, but America was growing quickly, and it would have been infinitely more tolerable to the taxpayers than the Stamp Act. Franklin, as disappointed as he was in the blasé indifference to the emerging problem that he found in London, was just as astounded by the depth and ferocity of feeling on the issue in America.

The Pennsylvania and Virginia and other houses of assembly adopted inflammatory resolutions of objection, the florid Virginia orator Patrick Henry taking it upon himself to warn George III of the fate of Julius Caesar and Charles I (as if their fates were similar or had any relevance to these circumstances – assassination and pseudo-judicial murder, swiftly followed by the elevation of their heirs in each case). Franklin appeared before Parliament on February 13, 1766, to answer for America, and did so brilliantly, and with persuasive fluency. He was well-received, and partly because of him, Parliament repealed the Stamp Act, but at the same time it passed the Declaratory Act, which asserted its absolute right to legislate on any subject for the colonies, America no less than Gibraltar or the Falkland Islands (or Quebec). Franklin was optimistic and wrote home of the prospects of "imperial reform." But the atmosphere thickened and prospects darkened, and there were references to the imposition and collection of taxes in America by force. Franklin knew that the British, almost none of whom had been in America, had no idea of what they would be undertaking. The British were coming perilously close to one of the supreme errors of government: the imposition of a tax that is not collectible. It would take scores of thousands of soldiers milling about among their own countrymen, where desertions would be heavy and the chances of being punished for it would be slight. The average American artisan and farmer had a better income and easier life than a British soldier on an active mission, and the British could not strand most of their army indefinitely overseas.

Franklin wrote that America was "an immense territory favoured by nature with all advantages of climate, soil, great navigable rivers and lakes, etc.," and that it "must become a great country, populous and mighty; and will in a less time than is generally conceived be able to shake off any shackles that may be imposed on her and perhaps place them on the imposers."[11] Unmoved by such verities, and by the cooler and wiser heads of the greatest British statesmen of the time, William Pitt, Edmund Burke, and Charles James Fox, Parliament, dominated as it could be by the system of controlled elections in under-populated boroughs and the prevailing influence of the House of Lords, adopted the Townshend taxes (named after the chancellor of the exchequer, Charles Townshend) in 1767, which were excise taxes on a range of English manufactures, including paper, glass, paint, and eventually tea. The tax could have been collected in England, but in a rubbing of the American nose in what was fancied to be Parliamentary authority, Townshend set up a board of customs commissioners in America to collect the tax. American reaction was predictably pyrotechnic, and the foremost American, George Washington, who was not only its leading military officer but one of the largest landowners in the Ohio Valley, called in 1769 for an outright boycott of British goods and moved some of the production of his own plantation at Mount Vernon, Virginia, from cotton and tobacco to arts and crafts. In the same year, for the first time in writing, he envisioned a possible recourse to armed rebellion.[12]

Franklin warned parliamentarians in London that to avert disaster the Townshend taxes would have to be repealed entirely in America, even if replaced with something else. The issue was no longer raising revenue, however, but one of authority and jurisdiction, and for no logical reason the British dug their heels in on tea; they were prepared to repeal the excise taxes on everything else. In 1773, the thirty-year-old Virginia plantation owner, polymath, and legislator Thomas Jefferson proposed a committee of correspondence to coordinate acts of resistance of all the colonies. Washington, Franklin, and Jefferson would be the three key players on the American side in the drama that was to come. Matters came to a head and began their steep descent toward violence when, on December 16, 1773, members of the Sons of Liberty, a Boston autonomist organization led by Samuel Adams, a militant opponent of any official American inferiority to Britain, disguised themselves as American Indians, stormed the tea ships, and threw 342 chests of tea into Boston Harbor. The perpetrators went to great lengths to show they were not an unruly mob, repairing locks on the ships and punishing one of their members who pocketed tea leaves for his own use. This virtual college prank, the Boston Tea Party, shattered the Anglo-American relationship.

Murray had been replaced as governor of Canada in 1766 by an underestimated man, then and subsequently, an ascetic Ulsterman, Colonel Guy Carleton. Carleton was forty-two and had been a close friend of General James Wolfe since they were junior officers together. Carleton had been the military tutor to the young Duke of Richmond, which caused King George II's resentment, and the king refused to allow Carleton to accompany Wolfe in Amherst's mission against Louisbourg. After strenuous lobbying from Wolfe, reinforced by the venerable Field Marshal Ligonier, the king permitted Carleton to accompany Wolfe on the attack on Quebec in 1759 as quartermaster general. Carleton played a key logistical role at the Plains of Abraham and was wounded slightly. He also distinguished himself, and was again wounded, in the taking of Havana in 1762, and was promoted to full colonel.

Carleton took over the headship of a colony that was in most respects serene. There were no more concerns about attacks from the British and Americans, nor about supply from Europe, as the Royal Navy delivered what it wished on all the world's oceans. The government was more consultative and much less overbearingly authoritarian. Religious practice was unchanged, and the local bishop, who had often in the past had his differences with the French governor, went out of his way to accommodate the British successor, who was, in the case of both Murray and Carleton, careful to avoid frictions. There was none of the childish argument that occurred in the time of Frontenac and Laval about the ceremonial precedence of Church and state. There was, however, a pettifogging and priggish British magistracy which "passed severe sentences on the little frolics of exuberant privates, and this with an unctuous malevolence that was doubtless galling to the men whose devotion alone had made a career in Canada possible for these eighteenth century Bumbles."[13]

As conditions deteriorated in America, Carleton quickly came to share his predecessor's high regard for the French Canadians and began to see them as allies rather than as sullen former enemies. Unworldly and castaway though the French of Quebec were, it was impossible for them not to divine in these swiftly moving events a comparative empowerment coming so quickly on the heels of the nightmare of British conquest that had haunted the colony for over 150 years. Unlike the Americans, the French Canadians endured the Stamp Act with equanimity. Carleton perceptively saw that the French Canadians were chiefly concerned to conserve their religion and language and legal system, and that in exchange for the protection by the British of those national characteristics, they could be very loyal British subjects. In barely a wink of the eye of history, the French Canadians went from being in terror of British overlordship, to a grateful bulwark of it, at least as a stopgap. Carleton started by renouncing any pay and perquisites for his office, which astounded the Québécois, still reeling from the plundering of Bigot and his light-fingered coterie.

In one of his early acts, Carleton had to deal with the allegation of a discharged soldier, George McGovock, against the alleged intruders and despoilers of Magistrate Walker's ear two years before. In a spectacular trial, it appeared that McGovock was not just a perjurer – earning a conviction for perjury after the accused were acquitted – but that he had colluded with Walker, his former landlord. The trial was a partial French-English, Catholic-Protestant contest, as one of the defendants was a French officer and all were friendly with senior French militia. Public opinion was against Walker, and he was severely embarrassed by the result. He became a local proponent of all American grievances and was eventually jailed by Carleton, rescued by Americans, and returned to his native Boston for the balance of his tempestuous career.

Carleton had to deal with the problem of the law: the French liked the swiftness and low cost of court access under the French system, but it was a different law, governed by French precedent, which was irritating in itself and practically incomprehensible to the administration in Quebec and difficult to obtain. The substitution of English criminal law had been popular with the public, as it instituted habeas corpus and put an end to the rack and interrogation under torture. London sent legal officers to Quebec to make a recommendation, and this issue dragged on for a few years, but Carleton became convinced that Quebec needed to devise its own civil code, to keep what was familiar, incite pride, and emancipate the province from recourse to French precedents. In 1767, Carleton also sent London a descriptive letter about his new domain in response to inquiries on legal matters. He accurately described the demographic impossibility of redressing the preponderance of French over English, as all British emigration would be to "the more cheerful climate and more fruitful soil of His Majesty's southern provinces."

Carleton presciently saw that it could come to war in America, and that France could support the Americans and try to raise an insurrection in Quebec to regain the province as a platform for assisting American rebellion. He proposed construction of a proper citadel and constructive steps to appease the French-Canadian leadership, whom he found preferable in every way to the American commercial sharpers who were most of Quebec's English population. Carleton also proposed a military integration with the French Canadians, to build an allegiance of Quebec's militia to the British Crown, and generally showed great foresight. His recommendations were popular with Lord Hillsborough, secretary of state for the colonies, and with the king himself. Carleton also recommended that the Indian lands handed over by France in the Treaty of Paris continue to be governed from Quebec, to flatter the province, retain British control in what was now its most reliable North American outpost, and to assist a commercial revival in Montreal. It was understood that an act of Parliament would have to be passed to resolve the ambiguities in Quebec and strengthen the British hand there as matters became more tenuous in the American colonies, and Carleton returned to London in 1770 to pursue his role as governor by intensive lobbying for constructive and conciliatory legislation. It was a fateful decision.

It was a lengthy and tortuous process, and Carleton appeared repeatedly before committees of both houses of Parliament to be interrogated by the prime minister, Lord North, and others. He made a powerful impression. The Quebec Act was presented in the House of Lords on May 17, 1774. It declared that Canada included territory that was inhabited by significant numbers of Virginians and Pennsylvanians and was coveted by more, and was certain to add to American grievances. Everything to the west, an almost uncharted vastness, was assigned to Canada. This part of the act was a manifestation of the heavy-handed insensitivity that had contributed so much already to the rancour of the Americans. The Roman Catholic Church was accorded full freedom, including in its ability to collect money from the faithful, not with the weight of taxation but with all moral and social suasion short of that. English criminal law was confirmed and Quebec civil law was maintained, with full rights of practice and evidence in French. The knotty issue of an assembly, which Quebec had never had and was not clamouring for, was ducked, and authority was vested in a governor with an executive and legislative council of from seventeen to twenty-three members. The Quebec Act was adopted by both houses, though Pitt, now Earl of Chatham, voted against, as he considered it provoking to the Americans.

The Quebec Act did elicit some entertaining responses from the Americans. The liberality accorded the Roman Catholic Church was furiously attacked by the dissident Americans, who reviled Roman Catholicism as "a religion which had flooded England with blood, and had spread hypocrisy, murder, persecution, and revolt into all parts of the world."[14] The nascent Continental Congress heard without notable dissent the characterization of Roman Catholicism as a "bloodthirsty, idolatrous, and hypocritical creed."[15] The American malcontents in their polemical zeal became almost febrile in their simultaneous abhorrence of French Canada's religion and their solicitude for the French Canadians, and in their rage against the seigneurial system – unaware that it was retained, with liberal modifications, at the request of all the French, landholders and tenants – and the general withholding of juries – which was again at the request of the Québécois, because of the expense of the system and doubtful judicious qualifications of the likely jurors. In a general address of the American congressional delegates to the French Canadians, Quebec was told "in elaborate and bombastic periods what they ought to do, and what they ought to want, in order to become good Englishmen, and [that] they ought to be profoundly miserable, and that their brethren of the other provinces (who had never before in history had a good word for them) were grievously moved at their degradation."[16] This address also reminded the French of their small numbers and told them to choose whether they would be considered by the rest of the continent as friends or "inveterate enemies."

This incendiary but somewhat incoherent document was translated, printed, and posted throughout the former New France by American agitators among the English-speaking population of Quebec, including the discountenanced Magistrate Walker of the brutalized ear. There is no evidence of what impact it had on the public, and there was little visible unrest, but the clergy almost unanimously condemned the agitation as xenophobic sectarian hate-mongering and a self-serving American call to bloodshed for no possible satisfactory end for Quebec. Whatever the merits of American complaints against the British, this was a fair description of their attempted seduction of the French Canadians. The ecclesiastical leadership sarcastically referred to the implausibility of any solicitude from the Americans, French Canada's most relentless enemy for 150 years. Within two years, the Americans would be holding themselves out as the beacon of liberty and toleration for the whole world, and never, in fact, countenanced official religious discrimination. Had they been able to assume more quickly that ideal in their overture to Quebec, it would have been more acceptable. The French Canadians, as long as the British were treating them well, were unlikely to succumb to any American blandishments, out of fear of cultural assimilation. But they owed entirely to the Roman Catholic Church the provision of education and health care, and, accordingly, the survival of the race on the rugged shore of the St. Lawrence. Quebec was wholly and fervently Roman Catholic; the diocese was sufficiently small, sixty-five thousand or so, that the bishop was able, in the course of a year, to visit every parish, and almost the entire population of adult communicants annually knelt individually before him and kissed his ring in symbolic submission. Such a bond had been earned and not much abused, and would not be sundered overnight by American pamphleteers denouncing Rome as a prostitute and a bloodsucker.

The British, who had so mismanaged their relations with their American relatives, had handled the much less comprehensible, if infinitely less demonstrative, French Canadians with civility and even genius, though, as has become the Canadian custom, Carleton's achievement has been largely underestimated.[17] North America was on the brink of a volcanic eruption, but the chances of a distinct entity in the northern part of the continent had taken another turn for the better; the French character of Canada would be preserved, but instead of being under mortal threat from the British, it enjoyed that country's determined protection against Quebec's old enemies in New England and New York. It was not clear what could be made of Quebec and the maritime colonies, but as Governor Guy Carleton returned to Quebec in the summer of 1774, the chances were good that something novel and durable and interesting could come of them. Nothing seemed certain, so all was possible.

3. The American Revolutionary War, 1774–1783

Events in America deteriorated swiftly after the Boston Tea Party. The British Parliament revoked the Charter of Massachusetts Bay, substituted a military government, and purported to shut down Boston Harbor until the value of the tea that had been destroyed was repaid. Thomas Jefferson drafted a resolution condemning the Intolerable Acts, as the Americans have called them ever since (even the British called them the Coercive Acts), but the awkward governor of Virginia, Lord Dunmore, vetoed it, and when Jefferson (although at his most pious a deist) adopted another resolution calling for a day of "fasting and prayer" for the Boston protesters, Dunmore dissolved the Virginia legislature, the House of Burgesses. The legislators repaired to the Apollo Room of the Raleigh Tavern in Williamsburg, and adopted a resolution calling for, in an early manifestation of the American genius for grandiose labelling, a "continental congress" to meet at Philadelphia and organize resistance to British rule. At this point, Jefferson was a raving pamphleteer. He wrote guidelines for the Virginia delegation at the congress that were rejected as too incendiary but were published, including in London, as "A Summary View of the Rights of British America." Jefferson reasonably claimed for the colonists all the rights of free-born Englishmen, but started to veer off from realities with the claims that the colonists had been "unaided" by the Mother Country and were treated by Britain as conquered people, and he ignored entirely discussion of whether the British were entitled to any compensation from the Americans for expelling the French[18] from Canada for them. Jefferson even devised a pure fiction about pre–Norman Conquest, Anglo-Saxon respect for human rights to which Americans were entitled. It was almost entirely moonshine, but it showed how far things had deteriorated in just eleven years since the end of the Seven Years War if even an apostle of the Age of Reason such as the Sage of Monticello could be the author of such a turgid and contorted fairy tale.

The Continental Congress met in the autumn of 1774, called for a complete boycott of British goods, and adjourned until May 1775. Franklin, in London right to the end, did his best with the British government, with the overt assistance of Chatham. Chatham spoke in the House of Lords on January 20, 1775, supporting the Continental Congress's resolutions and praising Franklin. Nine days later, he presented a bill that would recognize the Continental Congress, restrict Parliament's right to legislate for American trade, repeal most of the legislation of the last ten years pertaining to America, and require that any tax imposed in America be with American consent through their legislators. If adopted, this measure would have salvaged the relationship, but the ministry, representing the king and led by his most obsequious supporters, vituperatively rejected Chatham's bill. This was the end; the die was cast, and Franklin left London a few weeks later, arriving in Philadelphia on May 5, 1775.

The war had already begun, on April 19, when the governor of Massachusetts, General Sir Thomas Gage, sent British redcoats to seize guns and munitions stored by the militia at Concord. Minutemen (Americans ready to fight at a minute's notice) exchanged fire with them at Lexington and at Concord Bridge, outside Boston, and the British retreated back into that city without accomplishing their mission, which was designed to prevent an armed rebellion. (There has been an immense mythologization of these events. No one knows who fired the first "shot heard round the world," and Paul Revere did not ride alone and never got to Concord, having been captured mid-ride by the British.)[19]

The Continental Congress reconvened shortly after Franklin's return and professed to establish the Continental Army, composed of the Massachusetts militia and six other companies the representatives of the dissident colonies thought could be dispatched. On the motion of John Adams, a prominent Massachusetts lawyer, Colonel George Washington was drafted as commander of the new army (and endowed with the rank of general). The two sides met at Bunker Hill, adjacent to Boston, on June 17, 1775. The British held the field at the end, but lost half their force and three times as many casualties as the Americans (about 1,100 killed and wounded British) and retired into Boston, where

Washington arrived after a month and imposed a professionally executed siege. The British withdrew by sea to Halifax, on March 17, 1776.
On July 5, 1775, the Continental Congress sent King George III a final
appeal, asking for his impartial adjudication of the differences between
his British and American subjects. It was a reasonable document (which
Washington, Franklin, and Jefferson all signed). On August 23, the
king responded, condemning "the traitorous correspondence [and]
counsels . . . of diverse wicked and desperate persons within this realm."

In May 1775, Ethan Allen and his Green Mountain Boys (from
Vermont) had seized Ticonderoga and Crown Point (having commanded the former to "surrender in the name of the Great Jehovah
and the Continental Congress"), and Benedict Arnold briefly occupied Saint-Jean, near Montreal. Arnold marched to Quebec, as the
Royal Navy would make an amphibious assault impossible. It was a
remarkable achievement, but Arnold had substantially underestimated
the length of the march. Governor Guy Carleton was left to defend
the colony with very puny forces. He had hoped to rally the Québécois
with the Quebec Act to active support against the Americans and was
disappointed. "The most ungratefullest wretches," he ungenerously
called them in a letter home,[20] but at least they were benignly neutral,
a feat his Quebec Act accomplished. Only a few hundred of them
answered Washington or Franklin or Jefferson's siren calls. Carleton
had only the French-Canadian militia and the Indians, volunteers,
and a corporal's guard of British soldiers to work with. The militia, in
emulation of the colonists to the south, elected their own officers, and
Carleton, stiff Ulsterman though he was, rolled with the waves in
order to have some sort of force with which to repel the Americans.
Carleton remained in Montreal to supervise the defence of the most
vulnerable point, but hurried to Quebec on the news of Arnold's
siege of that city in November, narrowly avoiding capture by the
Americans by disguising himself as a civilian. He and the Americans
under Arnold and General Richard Montgomery each had about
1,800 men, but the Americans had no artillery and were almost
defenseless against the enclosing winter.

Arnold suffered many more desertions of Canadians than Carleton
did, and when he attempted an assault on Quebec on December 31, he
was beaten off. Montgomery was killed, and a quarter of the invading

force was captured. Carleton treated the captured French Canadians generously, which further tilted the balance of local opinion. Arnold tried to maintain the siege through the winter in the hope of reinforcements, but these did not arrive before the relieving British ships came up the St. Lawrence to Quebec, arriving on May 5. Carleton had played a weak hand with great skill.

The American force collapsed and retreated, debilitated by famine and illness and soundly beaten in the field, but Carleton avoided trying to wipe them out. He knew they would not be back, did not want to embitter the families of 150 or so *congressistes* (followers of the Continental Congress) still with the Americans, and still hoped that the solidarity of the revolutionaries would shatter. It was, again, almost certainly the correct command decision, as a full-blooded chase would not have influenced the outcome in the main theatre and would only have envenomed the Americans against the Canadians. The players and allegiances had changed, but it was another brilliant defence of Canada, worthy of Champlain or Frontenac or Montcalm.

The Americans were also repulsed in Nova Scotia, in November 1776, and never generated the strength to overcome the ability of the Royal Navy operating from Halifax to deliver amphibious attacks in the rear and flanks of the modest forces available for the invasion. By retaining military rule, and then government by a "privy council" derived from the legislative council, Carleton retained former governor Murray's pro-French administration, which was made more explicable by the questionable loyalties of some of the English Montreal merchants recently arrived from the now disaffected southern colonies. Carleton continued to prove as judicious a governor as he was resourceful a soldier.

It has suited the convenience of both sides to consider the Americans to have been a tiny knot of rustic malcontents, the British in their snobbery and the Americans in pursuit of the heroic stature of their national founders as underdogs. In fact, the Americans were now almost 30 per cent of the population of the home islands, and the richest British population in the world. America had 60 per cent of the population of Frederick the Great's Prussia, and was more populous than the Netherlands or Sweden. The British did not have a large army and were facing the suppression of an overseas revolt by a population that could easily attract the sympathy of the underpaid British soldiers in what was, in a sense, a civil war. It is generally estimated that about a third of the Americans were not in favour of the revolt, but an approximately equal percentage of British public opinion did not favour the king's policy either, and that dissident minority was more likely to grow than were the anti-revolutionary Americans. As is well known now, suppression of guerrilla wars that have general popular support requires almost as many soldiers as the adult civil population it is desired to suppress, unless the asserting power is prepared to slaughter civilians in blood-baths of the innocent. In this case, both the manpower required and the only tactic for mitigating the requirement were completely out of the question. Franklin knew Britain well and was confident that the British were dependent on an utterly delusional confidence in the loyalty of the American population, apart from, as they imagined, a few trouble-makers, and that they had no idea of what could really be involved in defeating the rebels. He thought Britain's enthusiasm for the conflict would erode fairly quickly. Washington had known well the military and civil authorities the British had sent out to America in the preceding twenty years, and except for the leaders of Pitt's great offensives of 1758 to 1760, they were almost uniformly hopeless. Washington also knew that the present British government would not be remotely as competent as Pitt had been in choosing and equipping their commanders. The third key leader of the American Revolution was Jefferson, who knew nothing of war and not much at this point of diplomacy, but recognized the possibility of uplifting colonial opinion, demoralizing and confusing British opinion, and electrifying the world by claiming that what was afoot, far from being the unseemly dispute over taxes that it largely was, was the dawn of human liberty.

The Continental Congress narrowly passed a resolution requiring the colonies to suppress British government within their borders and struck a committee headed by Jefferson to write a declaration of independence. He did so over three weeks in the Philadelphia boarding house he lived in during the session of the Congress, and accepted light amendments from Franklin and John Adams. Jefferson presented his draft on June 28, and it was adopted and signed on July 4 (though at first only by John Hancock and Charles Thomson, president and secretary

1. A nineteenth-century Norwegian artist's conception of Leif Ericsson's landfall at Labrador c. 1000 A.D. It accurately portrays the modest size and primitive nature of his open vessels.

2. The usual fantasized portrayal of Champlain's arrival among the native people. Despite the Stone Age, pre-wheel, and incessantly barbarous nature of indigenous society, Champlain really respected the native people and was the last Canadian leader to do so until John Diefenbaker 350 years later. The commercial antics of his countrymen (and the British, and Dutch) soon disabused the natives of over-reverent attitudes to the newcomers.

3. Another imaginative rendering of Champlain, in Georgian Bay in 1615. He rarely entrusted his transport to the natives and the place of the clergy was generally somewhat less prominent than is depicted here.

4. Armand Jean Duplessis, Cardinal and Duke de Richelieu (1585–1642), Louis XIII's cunning, cultured, and omnipotent prime minister. He dismissed the Estates General and made the fateful decision that France should be an absolute monarchy and avoid any notions of democracy or power-sharing. He extended France's borders by war and diplomacy and orchestrated the Thirty Years War to fragment Germany. Richelieu was a patron of Champlain and supported New France.

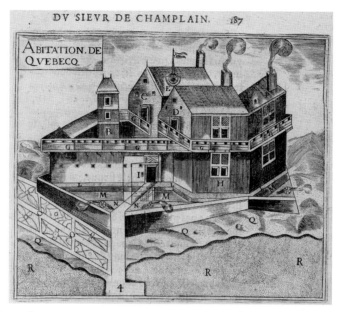

ABITATION.DE
QVEBECQ

5. Champlain's Habitation, the first European effort at residential construction in Canada, built in 1608–1610. B is a bird-house; C and D are barracks; H is Champlain's own quarters; 4 leads to a quay.

6. The building of Quebec, which began in 1608, but this looks more like Champlain's revisions and stone enhancements of 1620.

7, 8, 9, 10. Seventeenth-century French officialdom were look-alikes: clockwise from top left, Louis XIV (1638–1715); his capable and innovative finance minister Jean-Baptiste Colbert (1619–1683); New France's Great Intendant Jean Talon (1626–1694), who vastly increased the population, agricultural production, and industrial base of the colony and was the forerunner of later successful public-private sector cooperation under such strong ministers as Francis Hincks, Clifford Sifton, and C.D. Howe; and Quebec's formidable first bishop, Saint (as of 2014) François-Xavier de Laval-Montmorency (1623–1708).

11, 12, 13, 14. Clockwise from top left: Pierre de La Vérendrye (1685–1749) (at Lake of the Woods), born in Trois-Rivières, he shipped overseas to join the French army and was wounded at Malplaquet, and returned to explore and trade from Lake Superior to Hudson's Bay, the Dakotas, and almost to the Rocky Mountains; Major General Sir Isaac Brock (1769–1812), a brilliant and farsighted commander who forced the surrender of a larger American force at Detroit and saved Upper Canada at Queenston Heights, where he died in the tradition of Wolfe and Nelson; Louis-Joseph Papineau (1786–1871), legislator, tractarian and seigneurial rebel, he lost his following with his agnosticism and annexationism; William Lyon Mackenzie (1795–1861), "a bristling terrier," editor, rebel, first mayor of Toronto, the pugnacious grandfather of Canada's most cautious prime minister.

15. Lord Elgin (1811–1863), personally selected by Victoria to introduce responsible government as governor general (1847–1854); had been governor of Jamaica and went on to be representative to China, Palmerston's postmaster general, and viceroy of India.

16. Sir Francis Hincks (1807–1885), Irish immigrant, merchant, banker, editor, railway promoter, principal collaborator of Baldwin and LaFontaine, premier of Canada 1851–1854, won a public exchange in the British press with Disraeli and Gladstone over responsible government, governor of Barbados and British Guiana, and Macdonald's Dominion Finance minister.

17. George Brown (1818–1880), founder of the Toronto *Globe*, a founder of the Canadian Liberal Party and the Anti-Slavery League, "shuffled" out of the premiership by Macdonald after four days in 1858. Very hostile to French Canadians and to Roman Catholic "priestcraft," he joined with Cartier and Macdonald to design and promote Confederation.

18. George-Étienne Cartier (1814–1873), railway lawyer and promoter, Conservative leader in French Canada, co-premier of Canada (1856–1862) and Macdonald's Defence minister (1867–1873), put through the Civil Code and moved creation of the Canadian Pacific Railway.

19. English mobs burned down the Parliament buildings in Montreal in 1849 to protest the Rebellion Losses Bill, disqualifying Montreal thereafter as the capital of Canada.

20. The Battle of Batoche in the Métis Revolt, 1885; twenty-four were killed and about seventy-five wounded. This was one of the supreme crises of Macdonald's career as there was talk of annexation to the U.S., and Canadian Pacific was almost bankrupt. Macdonald brilliantly refinanced CP as a national security measure, sent forces west by rail, crushed the revolt, completed the railway which was profitable at once, and he was reelected twice again.

21. The trial of Louis Riel, 1885. Riel declined to plead insanity, though he almost certainly was, and was found guilty of treason. The judge ignored the jury's recommendation of mercy and imposed the death sentence. This was backed by Macdonald, in one of his few serious political errors, as there was no need for such a draconian penalty and it aroused French sentiment, including even Laurier. Riel seemed to wish martyrdom, though he may have changed his mind later, and he was hanged on November 15, 1885, aged forty-one. He was mad, heretical, and corrupt, but the Métis had some legitimate grievances.

of the Congress). The Declaration of Independence had three elements: the new regime in America was portrayed as the vanguard of the Age of Reason of Locke and Rousseau and Voltaire. George III was demonized as a Caligulan tyrant, and the American native people were subjected to a blood libel as barbarous and irredeemable savages, conferring on Americans the civilizing duty to dispossess them of the vast continent. Poor old George III was arraigned for having "plundered our seas, ravaged our Coasts, burnt our towns and destroyed the lives of our people" and for "Cruelty and perfidy scarcely paralleled in the most barbarous ages." Even allowing for the contentious times, Goebbels would scarcely have chinned himself on this orgy of hyperbole.

The first purpose, and the only one that has long survived, was bannered at the beginning and the end: "We hold these truths to be self-evident, that all men are created equal, that they are endowed by their Creator with certain unalienable rights, that among these are Life, Liberty, and the pursuit of Happiness.—That to secure these rights, Governments are instituted among Men, deriving their just powers from the consent of the governed,—That whenever any Form of Government becomes destructive of these ends, it is the Right of the People to alter or to abolish it." These words, and the conclusion, pledging everything including "our sacred Honor" to fight for the achievement of independence, have enjoyed an immense historical resonance, both for their eloquence and their historical significance. But they are a bit rich considering that this was not a conflict that significantly changed the civil rights of those in revolt or raised them above the British people from whom they were separating themselves, and that the revolution was largely carried out by slaveholders (including Washington and Jefferson). There were almost no slaves in Britain, and only about three thousand in Canada, and the debates on these American issues in the British Parliament, where the opposition was led by Chatham, Edmund Burke, and Charles James Fox, were considerably more rigorous and just as free-wheeling as those in the fledgling American Congress.

From the Canadian perspective, the interesting reference in the Declaration was the complaint against the king "for abolishing the free System of English laws in a neighbouring Province, establishing therein an Arbitrary government, and enlarging its Boundaries so as to render it at once an example and fit instrument for introducing the same absolute rule into these Colonies." Of course, this was an outrageous allegation, even from a revolutionary trying to enflame opinion and recruit support. The British had removed the French threat over which the Americans had made themselves hoarse in alarm for more than a century, had dispensed with the barbarism of French criminal law, and had liberally accorded the French Canadians the civil law they wished, which was not in the least uncivilized, and the notion that the British proposed to expand this regime into the British colonies was fatuous. The complaint was not really the imposition of arbitrary rule in Quebec but the failure to hand the subjugation and assimilation of the French population over to the Americans. This is hypocrisy well beyond the acceptable licence of the civilized propagandist, a realm where Jefferson normally resided, and with distinction. Naturally, this was not a tocsin that enthused the Québécois, who, fifteen years after the so-called conquest, were seriously beginning to enjoy themselves. Having their English governors exchanging fire with their long-antagonistic English-speaking neighbours was not in itself a distressing event for Quebec. And at this point, for obvious reasons, the French Canadians preferred the British to the British Americans (though of course they were not then, and have not been since, over-brimming with affection for either).

The principal editorial change to Jefferson's draft had been the removal of his claim that George III had been responsible for the importation of slavery into America, an untrue charge, and a monstrous one coming from Jefferson, who had seven children with a comely slave and (unlike Washington) did not even bring himself to emancipate his slaves in his will, which didn't take effect until fifty years later. The British regarded the Americans as ingrates and have never, to this day, understood what they were so upset about. And they were ingrates. The Americans regarded the British as overbearing and presumptuous meddlers, and they were certainly that. Jefferson masterminded the public relations effort, with the assistance of Thomas Paine and some other propagandists, and scored an epochal propaganda knockout victory over poor old Farmer George III and his lackeys, but it was a struggle between two almost equally advanced and conditionalized democracies. It was decided by the evolving correlation of forces and leadership abilities of the two sides. Given the complexities of suppressing such widespread irritation in the colonies, as long as Washington could keep the war going long enough, the Americans were almost sure to win, as Washington and Franklin clear-headedly saw. As the Declaration of Independence was solicited by the Continental Congress in June 1776, so the Congress also called for "articles of confederation" between the colonies and an effort to recruit European allies, which was entrusted to Franklin, as the dean of the very modest American diplomatic fraternity (and he had only been an information officer in London).

This is not the place for anything but the sketchiest history of the Revolutionary War, apart from its impact on Canada. The British took the offensive, recaptured Boston, and compelled the withdrawal of Washington and his army to New York. Washington rashly projected his forces across the East River from Manhattan into Brooklyn, where they were roughly handled in the Battle of Long Island, and he was fortunate not to have his retreat interdicted by the Royal Navy back across the river, an evacuation he conducted with skill (9,500 men and their artillery on the night of August 30, 1776). Washington now adopted the tactics he would employ for the next several years, retreating inland to White Plains and then New Jersey, staying well back from the coast and compelling the British to deploy much of their forces protecting supply lines from the ports, which also required extensive occupation manpower. American irregulars were agile at harassment and British desertion rates were often high, as Franklin and Washington had predicted, as they plodded endlessly around in the interior of America, being sniped at and having their supplies burned and stolen but rarely encountering a serious enemy.

The British took 2,700 prisoners at Fort Washington at the northern end of Manhattan on November 16, and there was much premature celebrating in Britain at this news, as in Pitt's time. Washington conducted a scorched-earth retreat to Trenton, New Jersey, and then across the Delaware into Pennsylvania, leaving nothing but ashes, rubble, and snipers behind, and then, in an act of military genius, he recrossed the Delaware on Christmas and Boxing Day with six thousand men, attacked the unsuspecting British and their Hessian mercenaries at three points, exploiting the heavily hungover (post-Christmas and prematurely triumphant) condition of the Germans, and rolled on to Princeton and

Morristown, just ten miles west of Manhattan. The Congress, whom Washington detested as composed mainly of cowards and meddlers and crooks (a fair assessment), had already decamped from Philadelphia to Baltimore in fright prior to Washington's counterattack. The opposing armies sat at Morristown and New York until the spring of 1777. Washington's men only enlisted for six months at a time, regardless of when their six months were up, and by March he was down to three thousand men, though he carefully concealed this from his opponent, General William Howe, who had eighteen thousand. Howe partially crossed the Hudson in June, but Washington outmanoeuvred him, and Howe retired to Staten Island, then as now an improbable jumping-off point for the conquest of America.

In July, Howe embarked fifteen thousand men by ship, and Washington marched to and fro on the shore for a month until Howe landed near Philadelphia. Washington almost drew the Battle of Brandywine with Howe on September 11, 1777, and remained between the British Army and the revolutionary capital, but when Howe drew his remaining forces south from New York, Washington had to abandon the capital (the second largest English-speaking city in the world, with 35,000 people compared with London's 750,000). Howe stationed eighteen thousand redcoats in Philadelphia in September, but it was not really a militarily useful objective. At this point, after two years of war, the British held New York and Philadelphia and almost nothing else in all of the thirteen colonies (as they had again vacated Boston). Washington almost defeated Howe again, on October 4, at Germantown, near Philadelphia, but his battle plan was too sophisticated for his rough militiamen, who were brave and were good shots, but were somewhat undisciplined and under-drilled in their field formation.

In a serious error, the British gave command of the northern force not to the able Carleton, but to General John Burgoyne, for an advance down the now well-travelled route from Montreal by Lake Champlain and Fort Ticonderoga (Carillon). It was proposed to come all the way to New York, meeting the Royal Navy at Albany, and thus to sever the colonies in two, separating all of New England from most of New York, New Jersey, Pennsylvania, and the south. The plan was well-conceived, but Burgoyne was not the man to execute it. After the Americans vacated Ticonderoga, they narrowly defeated Burgoyne at Bennington, and then smashed him at Saratoga on September 19, 1777, capturing him and much of his army, which was then deported. The victor was the treacherous General Horatio Gates, who then sought to displace Washington as commander. But Washington, despite his demeanour of austere disinterest, was a very astute politician and scotched the Conway Conspiracy, as it was known, and Gates was chastened. This was the first clear appearance of Washington the adroit politician; his third and greatest career (after soldiering and land management and accumulation) was underway. Carleton had watched impassively as Burgoyne's badly planned mission set out to rupture the rebellion and instead squandered itself and expanded the ranks of Britain's enemies in America. For the balance of the war, the chief Canadian activities were raiding parties into New York and Pennsylvania to destroy food and other supplies being assembled for Washington, and raids down the Mississippi, which remained entirely in Canadian hands. Carleton returned to Britain in 1778 and was replaced as governor by the Swiss adventurer Sir Frederick Haldimand (François-Louis-Frédéric Haldimand). He had been in Quebec before, under Abercromby in the Seven Years War, and had been governor of Trois-Rivières in 1762, in which capacity he had supervised the expansion of the ironworks, the famous Forges du Saint-Maurice.

Washington went into cramped, cold winter quarters at Valley Forge, near Philadelphia, and lost a quarter of his ten thousand men to malnutrition and frostbite, but improved training with the help of German soldier of fortune Baron Friedrich von Steuben and maintained morale by his selfless example and visibly full participation with the men in rations and discomfort. As the combat had unfolded, Benjamin Franklin had carried out to perfection his mandate to seek allies, arriving in Paris on December 4, 1776, dressed in plain black and wearing a fur hat, and at once impressing the French with his puckish humour, sly wit, worldliness, familiarity with the works of the leading thinkers, and, not least, his talents at seduction around the court of the young king Louis XVI. The moralistic and oppressively worthy John Adams was sent with him, but he was so scandalized at some of Franklin's techniques that Franklin had him sent on to negotiate a loan from the straitlaced Dutch Protestants, to whose company he was better suited. Franklin, a printer, among his many other vocations, installed a printing press in the basement of his residence in Paris and cranked out a wildly propagandistic newspaper claiming British atrocities and American victories almost every day. The American victory at Saratoga and the strong stands at Brandywine and Germantown, tempted France – despite the warnings of the king's talented treasurer, A.R.J. Turgot, of the precarious state of the country's finances – to seek revenge for the severe defeats it had suffered at the hands of the British in the Seven Years War. In one of the greatest feats in the history of diplomacy, Franklin persuaded the absolute monarchy of France, which had never even convened a legislature since Richelieu had dismissed the Estates General in 1614, to enter the war on the side of republicanism, democracy, and secessionism, and France did so, on March 13, 1778. It was a stunning and world-changing triumph for the seventy-two-year-old Franklin.

Following the crushing defeat at Saratoga and the entrance into the war of France (which would have done much better demanding some concessions back from Britain in exchange for staying out of the war), the British surrendered entirely to their fantasies and persuaded themselves they could win the Revolutionary War by de-escalating their participation. Howe asked for ten thousand more men and was sacked and replaced by General Henry Clinton, and Clinton was ordered to defend the West Indies. He abandoned Philadelphia and Rhode Island and repaired back to New York while disposing forces to Florida, a militarily worthless and almost unpopulated place, to defend the West Indies against the anticipated French attack. Washington engaged Clinton as he retired from Philadelphia and almost defeated the British again at Monmouth Courthouse in June 1778. The British abandoned the north except for New York and focused on South Carolina and Georgia, having reinforced their false conviction that the great majority of Americans were loyal to the British Crown and were just being coerced or swindled into neutrality, or even complicity in rebellion, by the malcontents with their wild Jeffersonian allegations. Not 10 per cent of the Americans had seen anything of the British in the three years the war had been going on. Washington made camp at West Point, on the Hudson north of New York, where he could move into New England or New Jersey, or block an approach from the north, while the action on the ground shifted to the south. Washington gave the Marquis de Lafayette a command, to encourage active French participation in the war.

Clinton had a distinct success in an amphibious attack by 3,500 men on Savannah, Georgia, but was repulsed when he marched on Charleston by the obese and narcoleptic, but yet formidable, American general Benjamin Lincoln. The French navy put in its first appearance in this war with a badly misconceived attempt to recapture Savannah. In an astounding plan, Clinton determined on an amphibious attack on Charleston from New York in late 1779. He and his naval commander, Admiral Mariot Arbuthnot, hated each other, the armada was broken up in storms and there was great discomfort aboard. There was no such concentration of loyalist support as the British imagined, as the coastal areas of South Carolina had only nineteen thousand whites and sixty-nine thousand slaves, but the landing was a success, and Charleston was taken and occupied. Clinton treated the civilians generously, but one of his cavalry commanders ran down a retreating column of Virginians, ignored a white flag and massacred 350 Americans. Washington had another grim winter at Morristown, and with the customary attrition of winter, his force of fifteen thousand was again reduced by two-thirds. The dishonesty and incompetence of the Continental Congress filled Washington with a clear vision of the need for a strong but non-monarchical government.

The devious Horatio Gates, over Washington's objections, was appointed southern commander (Washington favoured the very able Nathanael Greene) and suffered a terrible defeat at Camden, South Carolina, in August 1780, losing more than half his army, which was twice as large as that of his British opponent, who suffered a fifth of Gates's casualties. Gates fled the battlefield and galloped two hundred miles before stopping, when he was relieved by Greene as head of what was now "a naked and dispirited" army. Greene faced the competent British commander who had routed Gates, Sir Robert Walpole's nephew, Lord Cornwallis. The two duelled and skirmished with the advantage to Greene and his capable understudies, Daniel Morgan and Francis Marion.

At West Point, the able General Benedict Arnold, disappointed at having been passed over too often, deserted to the British in September 1780 (escaping capture by the Americans by only a few minutes). He was placed in command of the loyalist forces and was redeployed to the south, where Cornwallis elected to make the bold move of marching north to Virginia to try to destroy the centre of the rebellion. The British held only New York, Wilmington, North Carolina, and Charleston and Savannah, and were suffering steady attrition chasing around after Greene and Marion and Morgan. Cornwallis arrived at Petersburg, Virginia, on May 20, 1781. The British couldn't win the war, and fatigue with the war was much greater in Britain than in America. Nor could the British indefinitely keep most of their navy in American waters while they were at war with France, because of the danger of invasion of the British Isles, and they could never provide enough troops to quell the rebellion. There was a danger that at some point, Washington and Greene, who had come close already, would win a decisive battle and the entire British effort would collapse. France proposed a ceasefire with each side keeping what it held. This would have left the British with something and detached the French from the war. But George III would not hear of it. (If the Americans had accepted it, it would have been a very temporary arrangement, swiftly followed by the second bite of the cherry.)

Cornwallis was concentrated at Yorktown, Virginia, when Washington saw the chance to end the war. He persuaded the French to join him in the north for a quick march to the south, and to disembark 3,300 men by sea near Yorktown. Washington and the Comte de Rochambeau, commander-in-chief of the French forces, descended from north of New York to Yorktown by forced marches, leaving only 3,500 men facing Clinton in New York (they agitated and moved around and created the impression of being much more numerous). Cornwallis, with 8,500 men, was soon encircled by 15,000 Americans and French, and although Clinton had promised him reinforcements, and the British admiral Samuel Graves had promised to bring him out, neither did so, and Cornwallis was forced to surrender on October 19, 1781. It was now hopeless; the British were finished and everyone knew it. Parliament finally rebelled and refused to authorize any more offensive action in America; Lord North was sent packing after twelve disastrous years as prime minister. The Marquess of Rockingham, a close collaborator of Chatham (who had died in 1778), became prime minister, and Charles James Fox was placed in charge of negotiations. He sent Thomas Grenville to deal with Franklin in Paris.

The French wanted something for their trouble and their essential contribution, and the Americans demanded unconditional independence and the handing over of Canada, which they had failed to take for themselves. The British would give away no more than they had to, and preferred to make concessions to their grumpy American cousins than to their foe of centuries, the French. Franklin ignored French claims, which evaporated after the great British admiral Sir George Rodney caught a French and Spanish fleet in the Caribbean and gave it the customary decisive thrashing meted out by the Royal Navy, which settled down French demands considerably. (Rodney captured the French admiral, De Grasse, who had been decisive in keeping British reinforcements away from Yorktown.) As the war ended, Governor Haldimand had been conducting extensive negotiations with the brothers Ethan and Ira Allen, who had led Vermont's secession from New York and whom Haldimand believed were on the verge of granting free passage to British armies through Vermont into New York and New England when the end of the war became likely after the British surrender at Yorktown. The French, under the great seaman and explorer the Comte de Lapérouse, captured two of the main forts in Hudson Bay in 1782, and with them the explorer Samuel Hearne, whom Lapérouse treated very courteously. This event didn't alter the course of the war, and Lapérouse resumed his career, taking him to all the oceans and continents of the world except Antarctica. The Americans had a number of naval successes with swashbuckling privateers, especially John Paul Jones.

The Treaty of Paris ended the American Revolutionary War on September 3, 1783. The British dropped their claims of debts for the services rendered in the Seven Years War and the Americans – Franklin, suffering from kidney stones at the age of seventy-seven, aided by the very capable John Jay – promised compensation for the confiscated Loyalist property on behalf of the thirteen individual colonies, but subject to their agreement and they were not going to pay a cent, as the British knew. There were side deals about joint navigation rights on the Mississippi, and the British encouraged the Americans to evict Spain from the Gulf Coast, including Florida. (Not much encouragement would be required on this subject.) Britain retained all of Canada and all it started with in the West Indies, and broke the siege of Gibraltar after four years. Britain returned Minorca to Spain, but the French had been swindled by Franklin, and the Spanish by the French, and neither power gained anything for its efforts, which, in the case of France, were decisive in the outcome. Carleton, who had finally been appointed commander in North America but for the task of handing over New York, ignored Washington at the final ceremonies there and refused to give back three thousand fugitive slaves, who were evacuated to the West Indies as free men.

Washington had won the war and Franklin the diplomatic battle, and Jefferson had composed the founding documents and polemical rationale, but the articles of confederation that were written up were clearly inadequate. Independent America was a rudderless and incoherent country, until Washington, and one last time Franklin, led it to the adoption of a new dispensation. Thus began the great American experiment that would astound the world through all the intervening years. It would be a powerful challenge and an opportunity for Canada, the long unnoticed spectator in the American drama, made more gripping by the American genius at promotion and dramatization of events. Canada had had a brilliant war, and next to America itself it was the big winner. Approximately fifty thousand Loyalists had fled the American colonies and settled in Quebec or on the north shore of Lake Ontario and in Nova Scotia. With the Nova Scotians, the combined population in the colonies north of the new American country was about 150,000 people, almost 60 per cent of them French. Developing and maintaining a raison d'être for Canada would be a difficult task in the ensuing two centuries and more, and one which Canadians, because of their natural reticence and ambiguity, would not always be well-equipped to address. The Americans made it clear that they did not accept the permanence of any foreign presence to their north, but they could not seduce the French Canadians nor easily entice back the tens of thousands of Americans who had just fled, having been mistreated and had their property expropriated in the new post-colonial America. And while they could outlast British patience and commitment in a guerrilla war among those in revolt, the Americans certainly could not successfully challenge British power where it rested on popular approval, as Carleton had shown with a handful of French Canadians and Indians. Canada was the "more obscure progeny of the American Revolution . . . the offshoot of the losing side of a great racial upheaval,"[21] and with an unpredictable and exotic French wild card. The British had no idea what to do with the Canadians, such as they were, but they were now more than just the (French) speck on the map they had been for 250 years, and had demonstrated some level of distinctness, as well as an aptitude for political and cultural and martial survival. They might eventually prove to be strong, if not very pliable, clay for a new nationality.

4. The Beginnings of a Bicultural Canada, 1783–1793

At this time, Canada, to Britain, was the naval harbour of Halifax; the fortress city of Quebec; a refuge for the Loyalists who had fled America; the fur trade; and this inexplicable community of stoical French castaways. The tentative frontier was through the Great Lakes, leaving all Lake Michigan to the Americans, and from Lake Superior northwest to Lake of the Woods and then due west. Pressure and protests in London from the fur trading community of Montreal caused a great British reticence to withdraw from the forts along the Ohio and the northern Mississippi. Because the British weren't much interested in North America apart from the American colonies, they did not take as hard a line as they might have about the section of the continent between the Great Lakes and the Ohio River, or along the south shore of the St. Lawrence River for the first 150 miles after it debouched from Lake Ontario. In the earliest notions of a role for the components of Canada, New York's chief justice, William Smith, a Whig who initially favoured the revolution but was eventually repelled by it and departed at war's end to Canada as a Loyalist, touted, and his friend Carleton agreed with him, the possible role of Canada as a bulwark against eventual American aggression toward Britain itself. The British government did respond with reasonable promptness and generosity to the claims of Loyalists, thus solidifying their resolution as citizens of the Empire, subjects of the British Crown, and fugitives from what soon became the United States.

By the end of the Revolutionary War, three-quarters of the sixteen thousand people of northern Nova Scotia were Loyalist arrivals, and New Brunswick was set up as a colony, with a governor, a council, and a legislature. Sir Guy Carleton's brother, Thomas Carleton, was appointed governor. Newfoundland inched toward colonial status when, in 1791, disorder in the winter months reached such a level in the absence of the naval governor, that a full-time, year-round chief justice was named. The fisheries of the Grand Banks continued to attract the fleets of Europe and America, but Newfoundland had not made hasty jurisdictional progress: it was three hundred years since John Cabot had claimed the island for King Henry VII. These maritime colonies were given greater preferences in trade with the British West Indies than they could at first fulfill, but it was an encouraging gesture by the home government.

A number of whole regiments of Loyalists had moved from upstate New York and Pennsylvania and New England, and though an effort was made to send them to the Atlantic colonies and maintain the almost entirely French character of Quebec, and five hundred were settled in the Gaspé, these were farmers, and they wanted the richer farmland adjacent to the St. Lawrence, the Richelieu, and the northern side of the Great Lakes. These military families, like those that Talon and Frontenac had imported to New France, proved to be staunch and resourceful defenders of their farms. In addition to Loyalists of the most explicit kind, there were also Germans, Scottish Highlanders, Mennonites, Dutch, and Quakers, who were either monarchists who feared republicanism as disorderly or were simply tired of the strife and violence of the revolution, which, though it left large parts of the country unscarred, did severely tear up parts of New York, New Jersey, Pennsylvania, and Virginia.

In the circumstances, the Quebec Act was going to be a difficult regime for the increasing numbers of non-French. The seigneurial system implied avoidance of the sort of freehold the Loyalists and British immigrants were accustomed to, and as years passed after the American Revolution, it became clear that some thought would have to be given to the structure of government in remaining British territory in North America, however uncertain were the ideas of the ultimate disposition of those colonies. The English in Quebec, their numbers now heavily reinforced, wanted jury trials, normal civil rights, starting with rights of habeas corpus, an elected assembly, as long as it wasn't entirely packed out by the French advocates of Bourbon autocracy. The problem was that the English had a right to more and different rights than what had been given to the French, and the French were entitled to retain the system they favoured, and reconciling the two positions in the same jurisdiction was a challenge. Haldimand had continued Carleton's policy of supporting the French Canadians over the British Montreal merchants, and in 1784 successfully sued a government agent, John Cochrane, whom Haldimand thought unethical. The British merchants considered this oppressive, and they petitioned London for the governor's recall. Haldimand took home leave, and was not sent back to Canada after 1784. He was replaced, first by his deputy governor, Henry Hamilton – who had a civilian background (he had been the governor of Detroit) and expanded the use of jury trials – but after a year, on the urging of Haldimand and the French, Hamilton was replaced in turn by another who cleaved to the Carleton-Haldimand tradition of favouring the French: Henry Hope. Hope did not try to roll back the progress of jury trials and habeas corpus, but kept the colony under the tight control of the governor, backed by the pro-French majority on the council. William Pitt the Younger was now prime minister (he took office in 1783 at the remarkable age of twenty-four, and would govern a total of twenty years). Pitt sent Sir Guy Carleton, now Lord Dorchester, back to Canada as governor in 1786 with a mandate to propose reforms to the colony's governing statutes.

Dorchester by this time was taking a good deal of counsel from former New York chief justice William Smith, the dean of the Loyalists. Smith sought a replication of the government of the United Kingdom, in the hope that it would attract back into the Empire at least a larger harvest of Loyalist waverers and possibly even some of the former American colonies who were now floundering in disunion and virtual bankruptcy under the Articles of Confederation, which conferred no authority at all on the Continental Congress. Smith believed that the American Revolution had been caused by an excess of democracy and proposed to Carleton a system in which monarchical and aristocratic elements balanced the democratic ones. The problem with this vision was two-fold. Washington and Franklin convened the Constitutional Convention in Philadelphia in 1787 and, with the younger James Madison and Alexander Hamilton doing most of the drafting, produced a brilliant and practical Constitution for the new republic. Second, the Smith vision flew directly in the face of the French preference for the civil law, the seigneurial system, and relatively authoritarian government. Dorchester and Smith tugged at the problem until their efforts were authoritatively supplemented by those of the foreign secretary, Lord Grenville (Pitt the Younger's cousin), who subscribed to Smith's vision of copying British government in Canada and converting the French Canadians to its virtues.

Grenville's plan included a strengthening of the position of governor, the separation of the executive and the legislative council, an elected assembly, and, most importantly, the division of Quebec in two parts, one overwhelmingly French and the other almost entirely English-speaking. They were Lower and Upper Canada, depending on how far along the St. Lawrence River they were. He proposed a colonial nobility and an established Anglican Church in the English-speaking colonies, and sent his plan to Dorchester for his comments. Dorchester persuaded Grenville that a Canadian nobility would be unsuitable to the rugged egalitarian sense of the frontier, and Smith, a Presbyterian, objected to anything smacking of an established church, but Grenville retained that feature. The Constitutional Act, as it was styled, was adopted in 1791. The King, Privy Council, House of Lords, and House of Commons were replicated in the governor, Executive Council, Legislative Council, and Legislative Assembly. An eighth of Crown land was set aside for the Protestant clergy, and money was set aside for the construction of Protestant rectories. The exact borders could not be specified, because the British had not vacated the posts and forts trading with the Indians down to the Ohio. The Quebec Act's protection for the Roman Catholic Church, French civil law, and French language continued entirely in the French section of Canada. The implicit ambition of the Royal Proclamation of 1763 to assimilate the French had not been retrieved; and the 1774 to 1791 elevation of the French had only been varied to allow for an elected legislature and to confine it to the area of French majority.

The Constitutional Act was another great step forward in the laying of a cornerstone for a new eventual country. Though it was Grenville's bill and not Dorchester's, Dorchester helped to modify it and implemented it and it is another ingredient in his seminal role in Canadian history. He would retire as governor in 1796 after a total of twenty years (serving as governor of Quebec from 1768 to 1778 and of Canada from 1786 to 1796), and had held high military commands intermittently, from being Wolfe's quartermaster general starting in 1758, to negotiating the transfer of New York to George Washington in 1783 (and securing the safe passage of the Empire Loyalists and fugitive slaves to British territory). His leadership in producing the Quebec Act and the Constitutional Act and in launching Canada as an Anglo-French entity gives him a status in Canada's history roughly as distinguished and important as Champlain's. He would die in his country home in southern England in 1808, aged eighty-four.

There was now a group of remnants of the French and British empires, invested with a will to survival and possibly to survive together, based on fear of the Americans, in the case of the French, of cultural assimilation, and of the English, of the potential for chaos of American republican government. The debates prior to parliamentary enactment at Westminster were famous only for the exchange of acerbities between Edmund Burke and Charles James Fox, who had agreed about the American Revolution, over the significance of the French Revolution, which had begun to unfold in 1789.

France had gained nothing from its endless wars in the eighteenth century. It had held its own for the first half of the century, been soundly beaten by the British in the Seven Years War, and swindled by the Americans in their Revolutionary War, and the extravagance of Louis XIV had left France, as Turgot had warned Louis XVI before he was politically seduced by Franklin, in an acutely over-taxed and financially precarious condition. In May 1789, to raise revenues, Louis XVI summoned the Estates General for the first time since Richelieu dismissed them in 1614. The Estates General had twelve hundred delegates. Three hundred were from the first estate, the clergy, which owned 10 per cent of France's land and paid no tax, and three hundred were from the second estate, the nobility, which owned about 30 per cent of the territory of France. About half of these delegates were somewhat reform-minded. The remaining six hundred delegates represented 97 per cent of the population, but most of them were professionals, businessmen, and the bourgeoisie. There was no direct representation at all of the 60 per cent of the French who were rural peasants or the urban poor. The French Revolution gathered strength slowly, and though one of the defining moments in the history of the Western world, it was a rather farcical sequence of events until it took on a violent character and then became a nightmarish national horror story. After a few weeks, the first two estates tried to exclude the third, which repaired to a covered tennis court and, joined by forty-seven of the nobles, pledged to continue their demands for reform. They called themselves the National Assembly, and the king unwisely tried to dissolve them on June 27, 1789. Riots ensued that rippled around the country, especially in Paris, and culminated in the seizure and destruction of the famous Bastille prison on July 14. It contained only five counterfeiters and two lunatics (the half-mad dissolute the Marquis de Sade had been released just a week before). The governor of the Bastille was lynched and decapitated and his head carried around on a pike through a number of Paris's less salubrious neighbourhoods by tens of thousands of demonstrators.

On August 4, the National Assembly voted to abolish almost all aristocratic and clerical privileges, and on August 26 adopted a Declaration of the Rights of Man based largely on the American Declaration of Independence. (Jefferson was now the American minister in Paris.) On October 5, a mob of five thousand women and men dressed as women marched to Versailles and compelled the return of the royal family with them to the Tuileries Palace (the Louvre), where they were more or less detained. (They reasoned that the king's guards would not fire on women.) Count Mirabeau was the principal figure of the National Assembly and a constitutional monarchist adept at isolating and outwitting the extremes that were always present and agitating. It was one of the misfortunes of French history that he died suddenly in March 1791, following a particularly frolicsome evening with two dancers that he brought home with him for an afterpiece of *tableau vivant* following a night at the opera. A new constitution largely written by Mirabeau retaining but limiting the powers of the monarchy was proclaimed on May 3, 1791.

In another misfortune, Queen Marie Antoinette (daughter of Maria Theresa, who had died in 1780) persuaded the king that they should flee Paris, which they did on June 20, disguised as servants. They crowded everyone into one slow carriage and foolishly stopped for the night at Varennes, close to the frontier of the Austrian Netherlands, and were recognized, arrested, and ignominiously returned to Paris as prisoners. The moderates felt betrayed by the king and the extremists claimed to be vindicated. The queen's brother, Austrian emperor

Leopold II, asked for all Europe to help restore the French monarchy. On August 27, Leopold and the Prussian king, Frederick William II (Frederick the Great had died in 1786), along with Louis's brother the Count of Artois, met at Pillnitz and urged all Europe to restore Louis to power. This accomplished nothing except a paroxysm of patriotic rage in the National Assembly, which declared war on Austria in April 1792. Except for one year, war would now continue until 1815, taking the lives of probably 750,000 French and five million or more Europeans of other nationalities. Conflict would engulf Europe from Cadiz to Moscow and from Copenhagen to Naples, and even to Egypt and Palestine (where the British commander, the flamboyant Sidney Smith, would grandiloquently announce, rather prematurely as it turned out, that Napoleon Bonaparte's "extraordinary career has come to an end on the Plains of Nazareth"). The revolution now careered to the left in sanguinary lurches, massacring innocents and factions in horrifying circumstances and feeding a primordial bloodlust that stupefied the world, even those who initially wished the revolution well, like Jefferson and Fox. There were mass executions and drownings in the provinces, and the committee of Public Safety produced the Terror in Paris and elsewhere from 1793 to 1794, until Maximilien de Robespierre, its leader, set out to execute the sinister Joseph Fouché, subsequently police minister under successive regimes, and was overthrown and, with almost all the committee, was sent to the guillotine also, to the delirious joy of the fickle, bloodthirsty mob.

If the king had had the remotest notion of how to govern, he would not have had to call the Estates General. If he'd had any political acumen, he could easily have set himself at the head of the Reformers as the indispensable man. If he had even managed his flight sensibly, he would have survived, rather than being publicly executed on the guillotine, as was his wife, and could have returned to Paris and to office, as his brothers did, in the baggage train of the Duke of Wellington's army. France would delight, awe, and inspire the world in many fields in the centuries to come, but after the supreme climax of its war-making in the conflict that that had now started, it would oscillate between claiming the torch of egalitarian liberty and the holy sepulchre of Gallican Catholicism and authoritarian monarchy. It would never be altogether plausible in either role. And despite the defection of the Americans, the British strategy of naval and Imperial paramountcy while gaming the alliance system in Europe would outdistance the French rival. In its enervation and instability, France would, within the lifetimes of people born as the French Revolution began, lose the ability to keep Germany divided and eventually be overshadowed and on two occasions militarily defeated by Germany, which in the twentieth century would become so powerful and aggressive it would unite the French, British, Russians, and Americans in successful opposition to it.

The American and French revolutions opened an era of intensified intercontinental great power rivalry, ideological fermentation, and Anglo-Saxon pre-eminence, with allies, and at intervals subject to rending struggles. Quebec would emerge as the second most important French population in the world, and after the French Revolution would be little subject to French influence for the next 175 years. French Canada was now increasingly alone but imperishably robust, as it and its accidental English-speaking compatriots struggled to make enough out of Canada to justify British protection of it from the ravening Americans, who installed General George Washington as their first president in 1789, an office he would discharge with great integrity and foresight. If the pieces of Canada could follow a path between the British and Americans, while maintaining a community of interest between the French and British within, a country could take hold and play a role in the mature phase of the world drama that opened both ominously and hopefully in the revolutions of the last quarter of the eighteenth century.

The retention of the forts along and near the Great Lakes rankled with the Americans, as did the British and Canadian incitements to the Indians to maintain relations with them while avoiding serious provocations of the Americans. The Indians had grown accustomed to and adept at playing the Americans, British, and French against one another, and viewed with concern the narrowing of their options and the inexorable approach of the American civil population, which was starting to come across the Appalachian Mountains in significant numbers, preceded by astute land speculators, in particular George Washington (who became one of the wealthiest people in the new republic thereby, though he declined a salary as president; his out-of-pocket expenses only were paid). The British, with considerable dexterity, claimed they were holding the forts they had promised to hand over to the Americans, because the Americans had failed to compensate the Loyalists they had persecuted, financially and otherwise, who had removed largely to Canada. This was somewhat spurious, as the British perfectly well knew that the American side in the peace negotiations had only promised best efforts with the several states, and there was no agreed sanction for the expected outcome of no tangible compensation for the Loyalists, apart from what the British chose to provide.

With this encouragement, the Indians tentatively subscribed to the British line that they had not sold out their Indian allies, and the pro-British faction of Indians along the Ohio River, led by Joseph Brant (a relatively worldly native who visited Britain in 1785–1786), set itself up with tacit British support, as a buffer zone between Canada and the United States, and tried to hold the area between the Ohio and the Great Lakes. They even defeated American general Arthur St. Clair when he led a force across the Ohio in 1791. In 1768, in the Treaty of Fort Stanwix, the British had conceded the native people the land between the Ohio River and the Great Lakes, and in the Treaty of Paris in 1783 they conceded the same territory to the Americans. They probably could not have achieved "Indian" approval of their settlement with the American revolutionaries, but "they might have done better than the surrender of land that was not theirs."[22] It somewhat prefigured Palestine 140 years later, when the British promised the same territory to the Jews and the Arabs, except that the correlation of forces was not so one-sided as it was on the Ohio, and sorting it out has been an even longer and bloodier process.

The fur trade directed from Montreal prospered, as the Americans had unsophisticated operators in this field for a time (it had been occupied by French and British and Canadians), and because explorers financed by the Montreal merchants, led by Peter Pond and Alexander Mackenzie, had explored due west, building on the work of La Vérendrye, well in advance of American exploration to the south. Mackenzie (1764–1820), had emigrated with his family to New York from Scotland in 1774, and escaped the Revolutionary War, which his father fought through in the British Army, by accompanying two aunts to Montreal in 1778. He was a member of Pond's western exploration in 1787, discovered the great river now named after him in 1789 and followed it to the Arctic, and discovered the Peace and Fraser Rivers and went overland to the Pacific in 1793, ten years ahead of the comparable exploits of Lewis and Clark in the United States (and famously painted on the rocks "Alexander Mackenzie, from Canada by land, July 22, 1793.") There was contemporary exploration of the Pacific coast by sea, by American Robert Gray, who discovered the mouth of the Columbia River in 1792, and by British captain George Vancouver, who charted along the coast of what are now the state of Washington and the province of British Columbia, from 1792 to 1794. Mackenzie had been bankrolled by the North West Company, which was much more adventurous than the Hudson's Bay Company, still largely preoccupied with trading through the bay that gave the company its name. "In the fur trade, as later in lumbering and other activities, the Scottish and French, as masters and men, formed an irresistible combination."[23] Mackenzie set up his own exploration venture, with independent backers, as did others, and the competition was fierce, and sometimes violent. This caused the passage in London of the Canada Jurisdiction Act of 1803, allocating jurisdiction over these disputes to Canadian courts. The North West Company's David Thompson would explore and set up trading posts through the Rockies and to the mouth of the Columbia River from 1806 to 1811.

5. The French Revolutionary and Napoleonic Wars, 1793–1812

Issue was joined between Great Britain and the revolutionary government of France in 1793, in what would prove the last and greatest war between them. It was a war in which Napoleon would electrify the world and lead France to its highest point of influence and official glory and genius, before the combined forces of almost all of Europe drove him out. And after immense devastation and carnage, Pax Britannica would be established and maintained by British naval and financial power and cunning diplomacy, and confer a century of comparative peace on the world. The British stopped and detained American ships on the high seas but dutifully paid for confiscated cargo. They did not want another war with Washington's America while Britain was in a death struggle with France. Washington had adopted the policy of maintaining an army of twenty thousand veterans in order to deter Britain from outrages on the high seas with the implicit threat of a takeover of Canada, and this policy was retained by his successor as president, the first vice president, John Adams of Boston. This policy successfully deterred the British from overplaying its oceanic supremacy through the three terms of the first two presidents, from 1789 to 1801. The British were sufficiently concerned to avoid another conflict with the Americans that they received constructively a mission from the talented diplomat and first (and then current) chief justice of the United States, Benjamin Franklin's former understudy, John Jay. (Franklin had died in 1790, aged eighty-four, having helped produce the Constitution under his chairmanship of the Constitutional Convention. Though Franklin was not a conventionally religious man, every clergyman in Philadelphia of every denomination, and almost all the adult population of the city, followed him to his burial place.) Jay's mission signalled in advance the end of non-compliance by Britain with the peace treaty of 1783. There has been some criticism of the British for not holding out for a more southerly border for the independent colonies, but given that the St. Lawrence and the Great Lakes were the boundary established by the Treaty of Utrecht in 1713, and considering the narrow margin of survival of any non-American jurisdiction in the northern part of the continent, and the correlation of demographic and other forces that was almost certain to emerge, the British reserved as much as they could possibly defend.[24]

The treaty that resulted from the conversations between Jay and Britain's foreign secretary, Lord Grenville, known as Jay's Treaty, was signed on November 19, 1794, and was ratified by both countries. The British vacated the posts and forts in the northwest up to the Great Lakes and Lake of the Woods, by June 1796. Indian grievances were not directly addressed, leaving the Americans a free hand to deal with the Indians as heavy-handedly as they wished, with little doubt or concern over the result. An American force under General Anthony Wayne defeated the incumbent western Indians at the Battle of Fallen Timbers in 1794, and in 1795 the Indians signed the Treaty of Greenville, by which the territory that in 1803 became the state of Ohio was evacuated by the Indians and yielded up to "the weight of the American frontier, swarming, restless, and ruthless."[25] The British had ended the practice of seizing American sailors as alleged deserters, but compensation for this practice was waived by the Americans in exchange for formal acceptance that the United States would not pay anything for the displaced Loyalists. The dispute about access to the British East and West Indian trade was resolved in a compromise: unrestricted access in the East and inward traffic in the West Indies up to seventy tons per vessel, but no American export from the British West Indies of cotton, molasses, sugar, or other staples. Trade was upgraded to a most-favoured-nation reciprocal basis, and joint commissions would deal with a Maine–New Brunswick border dispute, pre-revolutionary debts, and compensation for illegal British seizures of American vessels.

By this time, Thomas Jefferson had retired as the country's first secretary of state (foreign minister), and although he avoided criticism of Washington personally, he was in a bitter battle with the Federalists (the political party led by treasury secretary Alexander Hamilton and Vice President John Adams). Jefferson and his chief associate, James Madison, denounced Jay's Treaty over treatment of debts, inadequate concessions in access to the West Indies, and the British refusal to discuss return of fugitive slaves (this request from the chief authors of the Declaration of Independence and the Constitution, widely accepted, including by the bloodthirsty hordes of France now in revolt, as beacons of human liberty). The treaty was a good deal for both sides: it assured peace between them, freed Britain to face the French challenge without having to worry about Canada, and the commercial arrangements provided the United States an immense fiscal bonanza in tariff revenue that enabled it to reduce debt and maintain the army necessary to deter Britain from recourse to abuse of its naval supremacy at American expense. For Canada, it was the removal of the perpetual American threat (whether Canada had been governed by the French or the British), though, as it turned out, less durably than had been hoped.

The hostilities between England and France during the French Revolutionary Wars had few consequences in Canada. The Maritime colonies were quite somnolent through the 1790s. Île Saint-Jean became Prince Edward Island in 1799. There was fairly steady immigration from the Scottish Highlands and Ireland, usually Roman Catholics, and the newcomers were generally relieved to be away from sectarian discrimination and on more fertile soil, and were not initially very active politically. In Lower and Upper Canada, political life was less serene. In the mid-1790s, there were about 150,000 people in Lower Canada, only about 10 per cent of them English, and perhaps 50,000, almost all English, in Upper Canada. There continued to be immigration from the United States to Upper Canada, and also immigration from the British Isles to this first inland British colony in the world.

In Lower Canada (Quebec), there was naturally more interest in the French Revolutionary Wars than there was among English Canadians. One of Quebec's secondary adventurers, Henry-Antoine Mézières (1771–1846), who had emigrated from France with his family and published some nationalist reflections in the Montreal *Gazette* (founded by Fleury Mesplet, who was always closely watched by the British governors as a loyalty risk), travelled to the United States and met with and fell at once under the influence of the minister of the French revolutionary government in Philadelphia, the bumptious "Citizen" Edmond-Charles Genêt (1763–1834). Genêt had arrived as minister in 1793 at Charleston and immediately began paying for French privateers to be serviced and refitted there and to prey from American ports on British shipping, despite American neutrality arrangements. He ignored warnings from Washington and Jefferson, threatened to go over their heads to the country, and his accreditation was revoked. The French government under Robespierre requested his return for trial and almost certain execution, but Washington granted him asylum. Genêt moved to New York and eventually married the daughter of the nine-term governor of that state and future vice president, George Clinton. Mézières published in 1793 the pamphlet "Les Français libres à leurs frères les Canadiens," which assured the habitants that France had emancipated herself and would do the same for them. It did not resonate strongly, as most opinion in ultra-papist Quebec was outraged at the seizure of Church property in France and the extreme violence of the revolution under the Gironde, Georges Danton, and ultimately Robespierre.

Following the Constitutional Act of 1791, Lower Canada elected a majority of French-Canadian legislators to that colony's first Assembly. There were riots in 1794 against the colony's Militia Act, and again in 1796 against the *corvée*, a seigneurial tax. The government was vigilant, and in the 1796 episode found and charged some of the agents the now Americanized Genêt had sent to Quebec. One, David McLane, was convicted of treason and hanged, drawn, and quartered in traditional French (and earlier English) manner. This had the desired effect of settling the atmosphere. Opinion stirred again at the appearance of a French squadron off Nova Scotia in 1797, but there was no real engagement and the squadron soon withdrew. Mézières moved between France and Quebec for the balance of his life, trying to popularize French views in the French-Canadian media, but he was generally more careful about incitements to rebellion than he had been when he published a few inflammatory pamphlets under Genêt's influence.

In the mid-1790s, forty-five émigré Roman Catholic priests arrived from France at Quebec, and the episcopal and secular leadership of the colony assured that they would fan out across French Canada and proselytize on the evils of the French Revolution. The French Canadians were certainly not enthused about being governed by the English, but nor did they have much nostalgia for the French. When it appeared that the revolution might raise the power and prestige of all the French in the world, they were happy to imagine themselves the beneficiaries of that. But the French Canadians knew they could not culturally survive American absorption without British protection, and generally made the best of it.

After 1791, the Eastern Townships, immediately east of Montreal and north of the border of Vermont, were set aside from Crown land reserved for the Protestant clergy and generally used as country estates for the pleasure of the leaders of the English commercial and professional community in Lower Canada, and for small farm holdings for Loyalist settlers from the United States. An Anglican bishopric of Quebec was established in 1793, and the first occupant of it was Bishop Jacob Mountain. The last local member of the Society of Jesus (the Jesuits) died in 1800, and the land reserved by the French crown for the Jesuits was consigned in 1801 to the Royal Society for the Advancement of Learning. This was in fact an effort to Anglicize the French population through its children, but it foundered in the face of implacable French opposition and the intelligent refusal of the British to squander the one card that maintained the French Canadians voluntarily in the British Empire: that it protected them from cultural assimilation by the Americans. The Peace of Amiens in

1802, though it only lasted a year, cooled out whatever heat had been generated by the French Revolution. By this time, the First Republic had given way to the Directory, which had proved one of the most corrupt and licentious governments in world history, and the directors had been sent packing in 1799 by the thirty-year-old general who cleared the Austrians out of Italy and conquered Egypt, Napoleon Bonaparte, leader of the Consulate. Napoleon would soon prove one of the most compelling and talented leaders, as well as probably the greatest military commander in the history of the world, but the cult of Napoleon lacked both the exaltation of soul and idealistic promise of the early and unsullied revolution, and the legitimacy, of the latter Bourbons inflated though it was by false grandiosity and disserved as it was by pandemic incompetence and pig-headedness.

Altogether of a different order were the challenges of Upper Canada. Colonel John Graves Simcoe (1752–1806), who was commander of the Loyalist regiment the Queen's Rangers in the American Revolutionary War, was appointed lieutenant-governor of Upper Canada in 1791 and arrived in 1792. He was chosen by Grenville over Dorchester's recommendation of Sir John Johnson, a veteran of relations with the native people and of the commerce and the politics of the fur trade. Simcoe was impetuous and favoured another war with the United States to push the frontier of the Empire as far south as the Ohio. Both he and Dorchester were outspoken hawks toward the United States, and Dorchester was officially rebuked for his polemical belligerency.

While Simcoe's ambitions for his colony were not immediately realistic, his constructive energy was useful. Initially, his capital was Newark (Niagara-on-the-Lake), but he proposed to move it southwest to a new site safer from American attack, which he named London, situated on what Simcoe christened the Thames River (formerly the La Tranche River). Dorchester did not approve that move, though the Canadian city of London was founded. Simcoe's second choice was Toronto, which he renamed York, after King George III's second son, the Duke of York. Simcoe had expansive ambitions to create a model of British rule and government in the heartland of America, as a magnet and advertisement for the virtues of British rule. The idea that the United States would discern the error of its ways at this point was very far-fetched, but the consequence of the policy was a consistent and rather successful effort to attract American settlers to the rich farmland of what is now Ontario. Simcoe founded a military pioneer corps, which he named after his old regiment, the Queen's Rangers, which was entrusted with the task of clearing and building roads that would pull the colony together. He laid out what are still Dundas Street, from Toronto to Burlington to London; Yonge Street, from the waterfront in Toronto into the interior; and the Danforth Road, from Toronto eastward to Kingston (all named after colonial officials). It was a microscopic replication of the colonizing methods of ancient Rome (which aroused as much respect from the British as an empire as it had hostility as a church).

Simcoe spent a good deal of attention on the legislators, haranguing them with his ideal of British government in the American wilderness. His policy of advertising for settlers in the United States was rather visionary, and did bear fruit, but the arrivals were attracted by the quality of the land and virtual gift of it, not by British government and the Crown, and many retained republican sympathies. But the combination of British institutions and a blend of Loyalist and American attitudes did give Upper Canada the character that much of the future country of Canada still somewhat retains, of a creative melange of British and American sources for the nature of government and society. Less successful was Simcoe's championship of the Church of England, and he favoured the establishment of both the Church of England and the Church of Scotland.

This was not practical, although the Roman Catholics were not an obstacle in Upper Canada at this early date. Most of the population were non-episcopal Protestants: Methodists, Presbyterians, Baptists, Quakers, and Mennonites, and they were strenuously opposed to an established church. Their will prevailed. Simcoe was only the resident chief of the colony for four years, as he had to return to Britain for health reasons in 1796 and resigned in 1798. He returned to active military service in the Napoleonic Wars in 1798 and was nominated military commander in India in 1806 but died before he could take up the post. Simcoe was a man of more energy than judgment in some respects, but also a far-sighted and a galvanizing leader, and he left a permanent and constructive imprint on what became within a few decades the largest province of the slowly emerging country that he had, in large measure, prophesied.

As the nineteenth century began, Upper and Lower Canada and Nova Scotia were all in the hands of self-sustaining and self-promoting elites, the Family Compact in York, the Château Clique in Quebec, and the Halifax Ring. The Loyalists predominated in the English-speaking colonies, and in all three the factor that facilitated their unbreakable incumbency was their power over the sale and granting of public lands. The Iroquois had driven the other tribes out of most of Upper Canada, and there were vast acreages of arable land and farming and forest products that were available to be dispersed. Similar opportunities existed to the comparable ruling circles in the other colonies, and they enriched themselves and their friends. The steady inflow of American settlers to Upper Canada, which Simcoe assumed was inspired by monarchist anglophilia, was seen by his successors, Peter Russell and General Peter Hunter, to be a potential threat after the war with France resumed in 1803.

Historians have disagreed ever since over who was responsible for the resumption of hostilities in Europe, and a case certainly can be made for Napoleon's claim that he was provoked by British non-compliance with all terms of the Peace of Amiens. But he shortly declared himself holder of the new position of emperor of the French and arranged for a patina of referendary legitimacy for the putsch. His navy succeeded in luring the Royal Navy under Admiral Horatio Viscount Nelson to the Caribbean, but he could not embark his army quickly enough for England before Nelson returned and defeated the combined French and Spanish fleets at Trafalgar on October 21, 1805. The standoff between the invincibility of Britain at sea and the pre-eminence of France on land was accentuated by Napoleon's stunning defeat of the Austrians and Russians at Austerlitz on December 2, 1805, shattering the first of many coalitions and allegedly causing the death from demoralization and alcoholism of William Pitt the Younger, one of Britain's greatest leaders, after a total of twenty years as prime minister and chancellor of the exchequer, on January 23, 1806. Pitt was succeeded by his cousin, Grenville, in what would be known as the "ministry of all the talents," as it began the British practice of coalition government in serious wars with other great powers. (Pitt's foremost rival, Charles James Fox, was foreign secretary. The government's principal achievement was the abolition in the British Empire of the slave trade in 1807.)

Napoleon had already concluded that he would not be able to hold the interior of North America along the Mississippi that he had extorted from Spain in the Treaty of San Ildefonso of 1800, and in 1803 he sold it to the United States. Since 1801, Thomas Jefferson had been the president and James Madison the secretary of state, and James Monroe was special emissary to France to negotiate the purchase of what was now called Louisiana, 828,000 square miles bounded by the Gulf of Mexico and to the east the Mississippi, and extending to the Canadian border and west to what would become Montana and east to Lake Huron. Much of this territory was discovered and originally organized by French and French Canadians, especially La Salle and d'Iberville, as well as Jolliet and Marquette. Napoleon was undoubtedly correct that France could not maintain the whole Louisiana territory, and had lost the oceanic and colonial competition to the British at the Plains of Abraham, at the latest. He was also correct that in selling it at a bargain price to the United States he was accelerating the rise of that country to challenge Britain for leadership in the English-speaking world and the great world beyond Europe and across the seas. What he could not foresee was that as the Anglo-American balance shifted toward the Americans, the British would acquiesce in this and tuck themselves in under the Americans' wing; instead of fragmenting the English-speaking world, Napoleon was making it stronger. The United States paid only fifteen million dollars virtually to double the size of the country.

The implications of this for Canada were that the United States would grow more quickly even than had been anticipated, and would be more aggressive along the Great Lakes and to the west of them than had been feared. However, the correlation of forces on the continent changed in an unexpected way also: Jefferson, who believed in small and decentralized government, virtually disbanded the army that Washington and Adams had maintained. This removed a potential threat to the Canadian colonies, but it also removed the deterrence of Britain from resorting to her usual high-handed methods on the high seas. The removal of this deterrence could prove too great a temptation for the Royal Navy and the government that controlled it, and provocations on the customary scale could bring the countries to war, in which, once again, for the third time in the lifetimes of people in their mid-fifties in 1810, invading armies would come again to the shores of Lake Champlain and the Niagara and St. Clair Rivers. Jefferson and Madison, extremely intelligent men who made an immense contribution to the founding and early development of their country, were possessed of the mad illusion that they could substitute economic warfare for a standing army on their northern border. Jefferson would famously say that the conquest of Canada was "a mere matter of marching."[26] So it was, but he deprived the United States of the forces to do the marching. (On a more positive note, he did found the military academy at West Point, upriver from New York City, which would provide the country with more than two hundred years of a non-political officer corps.)

The British could not now resist the temptations of simple assertion of their unchallengeable naval might and routinely stopped and searched American ships, confiscated cargo, removed alleged deserters from the Royal Navy, and impressed American seamen into British service. In addition, the British reimposed strict rules on third parties removing cargo from the British West Indies. Napoleon imposed a European-wide boycott of Britain in 1806 from Berlin, having occupied the Prussian capital after another of his breathtakingly victorious campaigns, and Fox responded with a naval blockade of the entire Mediterranean and Atlantic coast of Europe from Gibraltar to Naples and to Copenhagen. A very galling incident occurred in 1807 off Virginia, when the British *Leopard* stopped the American *Chesapeake*, and, when the U.S. frigate resisted, subdued her with four broadsides that killed three and wounded eighteen Americans. The British ignored the resulting American demand for an apology and compensation, and Jefferson secured a complete trade embargo against all foreign countries (since Britain now controlled all sea commerce on the North Atlantic). His policy was a disastrous failure. The Northeast became a hotbed of British- and Canadian-encouraged smuggling. The embargo had almost no effect on Britain, which then imported from Latin America the foodstuffs it had previously bought from the United States, and none on France, which controlled almost all Europe and did not buy much from America anyway. American ships that were at sea when the embargo was imposed just ignored the

American law, did not return to home port, and continued as international traders with the full support of the Royal Navy. The British benefited from the absence of American competition. Napoleon joined in the mirth at America's expense by seizing ten million dollars' worth of American shipping in European ports, saying that any such ships were obviously British, as no American flag vessels would ignore the laws of their country. Jefferson ignored the requirement of warrants for searches in enforcement of his embargo, declared the Lake Champlain area in a state of insurrection, and American exports and the resulting tax revenues plummeted by 75 per cent, as did living standards throughout New England and the main Atlantic ports. Jefferson himself was almost immobilized by migraines in his last year in office and signed the repeal of his embargo three days before the inauguration of Madison as his successor, on March 1, 1809. Peace in North America was more secure for a time.

In Quebec, Napoleon's spectacular and brilliantly engineered campaign victories naturally earned some pan-French enthusiasm, but it was fairly muted. There were periodic inflammations, however, as when Bishop Mountain in 1805 questioned the established status of the Roman Catholic Church in the colony. More vexing was the dispute in the Assembly and in the press between the English-Canadian argument for land taxes and the French-Canadian preference for customs duties to pay for the expansion of necessary services such as courts and other public works. To combat the English propaganda of the Quebec *Mercury* and the Montreal *Gazette*, three French-Canadian lawyers, including Jean-Thomas Taschereau, founder of one of French Canada's greatest families (a cardinal, a premier, and chief justice of Canada and of Quebec), founded *Le Canadien*. The latter newspaper cleverly attacked the regime on exemplary British grounds of insufficient responsibility of government, especially in the unanswerability of the government's advisers to the Assembly for the actions they proposed. In 1807, the new governor of British North America, Sir James Craig, badly botched the delicate political balance by overreacting to the French objection to the seating of the Jewish Ezekiel Hart of Trois-Rivières because they did not think he could properly take the oath, and by overruling their objection to the preposterous idea of judges sitting in the Assembly. Craig prorogued the Assembly in 1806, and again in 1809, when it presumed to expel Hart and a judge, and he dissolved the Assembly in 1810, when it prepared to vote on the issues of seating Jews and judges. He then seized the presses of *Le Canadien*, suspended the mails, virtually declared martial law, and arrested and detained without trial Taschereau and his associates. When the 1810 elections essentially replicated the previous Assembly, Craig reacted irrationally and sent his secretary, H.W. Ryland, to England to urge revocation of the Constitutional Act. The British made the much wiser choice of recalling Craig and replacing him with another in the numerous and colourful school of Swiss adventurers, Sir George Prevost. Prevost proved a perceptive governor on the political side, and accurately concluded that the greatest problem politically was not the attractions of Napoleonic France but the lack of responsible government: the accountability to the Assembly of the governor and his advisers in the Executive Council.

The wartime economy, as is often the case, was booming. Wheat production and the fur trade expanded (and the Montreal merchants did not find the competition of either the Hudson's Bay Company or John Jacob Astor's American Fur Company intimidating). And in the Eastern Townships, a potash industry arose. With the closing of the Baltic to Britain by Napoleon's Berlin Decrees of 1806, Canada became the favoured supplier of British shipyards, filled to capacity with war construction. The white pines of the St. Lawrence and the Ottawa River proved to be ideal masts for the Royal Navy. The great trees were cut in the winter and floated on rafts to the ports downriver.

With steadily increasing immigration, both from the United States and the crofters and tenant farmers of Scotland and Ireland, the agitation steadily rose for government responsible to the local people and not only upward to the British government. Two notable colonizers, Lord Selkirk (1771–1820) and Colonel Thomas Talbot (1771–1853), were bold pioneers who brought substantial numbers of British colonists to settle on territory they had assembled. The real loyalty of the American settlers in Nova Scotia, the Eastern Townships, and Upper Canada was a matter of acute official concern, but as events developed it seemed that most of them were non-political and not the American agents that some had feared.

Despite letdowns, most of the native people near Canada still favoured the British and Canadians over the Americans, as they were less numerous and had more integrity in upholding agreements. An offensive by General William Henry Harrison in 1811 against the Shawnee at Tippecanoe was claimed as a great victory by the Americans, but was in fact a drawn contest with the talented Indian leader Tecumseh. These endless advances of the Americans tended to push more native people into Canada as an informal but very talented militia. This was the condition of the continent as war with the United States again hove into view as a prospect, because America had failed to deter, and Britain could not resist, provocations on the high seas.

In fact, Canada now needed a war, provided it was not overrun: it was time to start knitting together the fragments left over by the American Revolution, and to test loyalty to, and the viability of, a non-American entity to the north of the United States. As Jefferson had disbanded almost the entire U.S. Army, the prospects of surviving such a war were promising, provided assistance from Great Britain was adequate.

6. The War of 1812, 1812–1815

The War of 1812 was a response by the Americans to Britain's high-handed exercise of her control over the world's oceans, especially the North Atlantic and the Caribbean. The unsubtle British and Canadian assistance to Tecumseh and his coalition in 1811 had naturally rankled with the Americans, and there were incidences of Indian raids from Canada into the United States that the Americans could hardly have been expected to tolerate in silence. It was also practically impossible for the authorities in Lower or Upper Canada to determine if the steady flows of immigrant settlers from the United States were Loyalists or merely opportunists taking advantage of the incentives provided for people who would populate and develop the Eastern Townships near Montreal and the fertile land along and just north of the St. Lawrence and Lake Ontario and Lake Erie. There were fears in more apprehensive quarters that much of this immigration was effectively a guerrilla movement orchestrated by American authorities, whose annexationist appetites for Canada had neither abated nor ceased to enjoy public expression. In fact, most of these people were fairly apolitical, came with or soon started families, and were legitimate homesteaders who weren't a fifth column for the Yankees, but nor were they thirsting for the opportunity to take up arms for the timeless (if intermittently mad) George III, now lumbering determinedly through his sixth decade on the British throne.

James Madison, one of history's greatest law-givers, as chief author of the Constitution of the United States, effectively inherited the presidency from his mentor, Thomas Jefferson. He had earned high prestige but was not a particularly authoritative figure (as is illustrated by the fact that his vice president, George Clinton, simultaneously ran for president, a unique occurrence in the country's history). Though Jefferson had cancelled his trade embargo on Britain and France in his last days as president, there were still trade restrictions in effect that were rather sketchily enforced. The inability of the United States to have the British and French take its sovereignty seriously was demonstrated in Madison's amateurish floundering over these issues in his first months. The British minister in Washington, David Erskine, announced that the British would on June 10, 1809, revoke the orders-in-council that authorized seizure and search of foreign vessels and impressment of their sailors. Madison responded with a proclamation on April 19 of that year announcing the end of any trade restrictions with Great Britain. The British foreign secretary, George Canning, disavowed Erskine on May 30, and recalled him. Madison restored the embargo on August 9.

In early 1810, prominent congressmen put through a measure authorizing the president to ban all trade with Britain or France if the other had relaxed its offensive measures. (These were the only players, as France controlled all Europe as far east as Russia and Britain controlled all the oceans and seas.) The French foreign minister, the Duke of Cadore,* informed the American minister in Paris, John Armstrong, that France was ending its trade blockade, and Madison, undaunted by the fiasco with the British the year before, announced on November 2, 1810, that all restraints on trade with France had been removed and an absolute embargo would be reimposed on Britain. (This was nonsense in itself, as the British could intercept all shipping between France and

---

* Cadore had replaced Maurice, Count de Talleyrand, who had retired because he was concerned that Napoleon's judgment had become too erratic. Talleyrand would be back.

the United States if they so wished.) Britain then completely blockaded New York as a port, redoubled the impressment of American sailors, and let it be known that the French foreign minister had swindled the American government. France did not, in fact, end the American trade exclusion at all, as became clear in the ensuing months.

Astonishingly, Madison had made no effort to regroup the well-trained and equipped army of twenty thousand that Washington and Adams had maintained as a threat to Canada and a restraint on Britain's tendency to exploit its mastery of the seas. Neither Jefferson nor Madison, highly intelligent men and statesmen though they both were, seemed to grasp the missing element in their failed plans. It was on August 4, 1812, that Jefferson wrote that taking Canada was "a mere matter of marching."[27] This would have been true if there had been sufficient numbers of trained and armed personnel to make the march. There were not. Neither Jefferson nor Madison had played a significant military role in the Revolutionary War or had any idea of how to conduct a war. On November 5, 1811, Madison publicly accused the British of "hostile inflexibility in trampling on rights which no independent nation can relinquish," and on April 1, 1812, he asked Congress for a complete embargo for sixty days, and was empowered three days later to call up one hundred thousand militiamen for up to six months. (The Americans still had the idea that a citizens' untrained force could leave home for six months and settle any serious dispute.)

By this time, in one of the most fateful decisions in the history of Europe, Napoleon had determined to resolve differences with Russia by invading that country. His mighty Grand Army of more than five hundred thousand, about half of them French, invaded Russia, starting on June 24, and the world was little preoccupied with the cavils of America. Britain had been, in fact, on the verge of finally easing its policy on American shipping when, on May 11, 1812, for the only time in British history, the prime minister (Spencer Percival) was assassinated, by a madman. The delay, as Lord Liverpool was installed as Percival's successor, held up the repeal of the obnoxious trade and search and impressment decrees until June 23. On June 18, Congress had passed the declaration of war Madison requested on June 1, with more than a third of the congress, including most senators and congressmen from New England, New York, New Jersey, and Delaware, voting against. Madison had violated the first rule of taking a democracy to war: the requirement of massive public support for the costs and sacrifices to be endured.

Canada, by contrast, had the benefit of having at the head of both the civil and military government a prescient and courageous soldier-statesman, General Isaac Brock, who had foreseen war and been preparing for it for six years. Born in 1769 (the same year as Napoleon and the Duke of Wellington), Brock served with distinction in the Netherlands and was ordered to Canada in 1802 as a regimental commander. He was principally occupied at first with subduing a mutiny, following which seven of his men were executed, and in 1806 he became the army commander for all of Canada. Brock strengthened the fortifications at Quebec and created a naval force on the eastern Great Lakes that gave the British superiority on Lake Erie and Lake Ontario. In 1811, he was promoted major general and civil administrator for Upper Canada as well. He declined his long-sought home leave because he feared that war was imminent. He emphasized intensive training of the militia, strengthened Upper Canada's fortifications, and engaged personally in detailed contingency planning with the leaders of the native people, especially Tecumseh, with whom he established a warm rapport. Brock learned of the outbreak of war before some of the American frontier units did, and managed a post-outbreak sneak attack on an almost slumbering garrison at Fort Mackinac (on Mackinac Island in Lake Huron) with a mixed force of militiamen, fur traders, natives, and a few British regulars, on July 17. This emboldened Upper Canada and the neighbouring native people.

When Revolutionary War commander William Hull attacked across the St. Clair River from Detroit to what is now Windsor, Brock was able to disregard the over-cautious orders of the theatre commander, General Sir George Prevost, who wished to cling to the defence. Brock coordinated strategy with Tecumseh and, although outnumbered two to one by Hull, intimidated the American commander by dressing his militia in worn-out British uniforms and marching them about while returning them out of sight to their original stepping-off point so they could again strut across the landscape, creating the impression of a much larger and better trained force than he really had: a classic *ruse de guerre*. He had Tecumseh's forces utter blood-curdling ululations of lethal intent and sent into Hull a message saying, "It is far from my inclination to join in a war of extermination, but you must be aware that the numerous body of Indians who have attached themselves to my troops will be beyond my control the moment the contest commences."[28] Hull was afraid that his daughter and grandson, in the fort at Detroit, would be massacred, and after a day's artillery barrage he abruptly surrendered on August 16. His fears were somewhat validated by the seizure of Fort Dearborn (Chicago) by Tecumseh's allies on August 15 and the gruesome murder of the entire garrison. Hull's entire force of two thousand was taken into captivity and he was court-martialled and sentenced to death for cowardice, though, in deference to his Revolutionary War record, the sentence was commuted to a dishonourable discharge.

The balance of the American campaign plan for 1812 were the other usual attacks along Lake Champlain to Montreal and the penetration at Niagara and around Lake Ontario to seize York (Toronto), as in the Seven Years and Revolutionary Wars, although the British had demonstrated more than fifty years before that the only way to subdue Canada was to advance up the St. Lawrence and stage an amphibious assault on Quebec. (And, as was recounted in Chapter 1, this was rebuffed twice before, by Champlain and by Frontenac, and, given the naval balance of forces, was completely out of the question now.) Next off was the attack at Niagara, led by political appointee and reserve general Stephen van Rensselaer, whose attempt to cross the Niagara River on October 13 led to the Battle of Queenston Heights. Brock quickly arrived at the crossing site and led his men, as was his custom, in counterattack. He repulsed the American force but was mortally wounded, his last words allegedly being "Push on, brave York Volunteers!" Although Brock's replacement, Colonel John Macdonell, was killed an hour later as he pressed home the attack on the Americans, reinforcements arrived and the action ended in an entire British and Canadian victory, facilitated by the decision, adopted in mid-battle, by many of the New York reservists that they had no obligation to put themselves in harm's way outside the borders of New York State. Van Rensselaer was sacked and replaced by General Alexander Smyth, whose half-hearted effort to recross the Niagara on November 28 was easily routed. He too was sacked, and the third initiative, north to

Montreal on the well-travelled route past Ticonderoga (Carillon), was led by General Henry Dearborn. But his troops, also reservists, found the virtue of their defensive vocation within New York as timely and persuasive as had van Rensselaer's charges, and they refused to enter Quebec. Dearborn returned to Plattsburgh without having fired a shot, and joined the senior ranks of fired commanders. Madison also fired the war secretary, William Eustis, and replaced him with the former minister to France, John Armstrong. (It was following Queenston Heights that Laura Secord, 1775–1868, learned of an imminent attack by American invaders and walked twenty miles through the night to warn the British Army, contributing to the victory of the defenders at the Battle of Beaver Dams. Her service went unrecognized until the Prince of Wales and future King Edward VII, travelling in Canada in 1860, learned of it and personally awarded her a pension at the age of eighty-five. She has since become celebrated by a popular brand of chocolate confections.)

The Americans did rather better in single combat at sea, but they couldn't really challenge the British navy when it appeared in strength. Madison, though a former secretary of state who might have been expected to have a better sense of the correlation of forces, had the chargé he maintained in London, despite the state of war between the two countries, ask the British foreign secretary, Lord Castlereagh, if Britain would negotiate peace on the basis of an end to impressment of American sailors, the end of the blockade of American ports, and the payment of compensation for damage to American shipping and shore facilities. Castlereagh declined to open discussions on any such basis.

It had been an utterly ludicrous opening to Madison's righteous war, but he was re-elected in November over DeWitt Clinton, the nephew of his former vice president (who had died in office). The younger Clinton began an honourable American tradition of the party out of office in wartime, presenting a responsible anti-war candidate. Despite the catastrophic start to the war, and the terrible divisions with which the war began and which it had already exacerbated, Madison won, with 128 electoral votes to 89, although Clinton carried all the states from the Canadian border to Pennsylvania except Vermont. The South, the West, and Pennsylvania put the president across.

* * *

The world balance of power had changed while the series of fiascos unfolded on the American-Canadian border: Napoleon lost most of his army in Russia, and although he defeated the Russians in direct combat, even on his retreat when he was heavily outnumbered, and the ancient Russian capital of Moscow had been burned to the ground, Napoleon's allies deserted him, and the mighty French exertions would no longer be adequate. Napoleon's military genius perhaps reached its highest point as he fought his way out of Russia against more numerous and surrounding armies accustomed to winter war, but his vastly extended empire could not sustain such a blow. The hour of Britain was opening; that of France ending. In one of the demiurgic emperor's many lapidary utterances, Napoleon said, with a shrug as he departed Moscow and began the famous retreat after the Russians burned their capital under him, "From the sublime to the ridiculous is a single step." There was nothing sublime about the War of 1812, but it had begun well for the British and Canadians – though Brock was a grievous loss who would not be fully replaced – and there had been almost no evidence of disaffection from the recent American arrivals in Upper Canada and the Eastern Townships of Quebec.

Brock had had two thousand British troops and almost as many Canadian regulars, particularly the Glengarry Highlanders and Colonel Charles de Salaberry's Lower Canada Voltigeurs. There began what would be the almost unbroken Canadian tradition of avoiding conscription but soliciting volunteers and quickly assimilating them into the regular forces. This separated the loyal from the indifferent. The Americans, including Hull in his briefly rampant state at Detroit before his surrender, claimed to be liberating their separated countrymen from the British tyranny (that they had voluntarily sought), and they did gain a small number of recruits, but most of the recent arrivals from the United States just kept their heads down and stuck with their peacetime occupations until the outcome was clear. The British did not blockade the New England ports or New York through 1813, in order to encourage American objectors to the war. The American privateers did some damage to British commercial shipping in the Caribbean and the North Sea and forced the British merchantmen into convoys; and, conversely, the British wrought havoc all along the Atlantic coast with raiding parties.

The performance of the United States in 1813 was a considerable improvement, and the war settled into a race between the Americans shaping up into a serious national military effort and the British getting clear of the fading Napoleonic menace and into a position to apply irresistible force against their former countrymen across the sea. A group of Kentuckians led by the Speaker of the House of Representatives and leader of the so-called war hawks, Henry Clay, recruited General (of militia) William Henry Harrison, the alleged victor of Tippecanoe, as head of the Kentucky militia, and Madison confirmed him as a general in the regular army. At the head of a mixed force of ten thousand, Harrison was entrusted with the mission to retake Detroit and invade Upper Canada. He regained Detroit but was defeated by the British and Canadians at Frenchtown and took a thousand casualties. He persevered and was successful at Fort Meigs (on the Maumee River in Ohio) in May and Fort Stephenson (Fremont, Ohio) in August. In September, Tecumseh was killed by Colonel Richard Johnson at the Battle of Moraviantown (near present-day Chatham, Ontario). (Johnson would be elected vice president in 1836 on the slogan "Rumpsey, dumpsey, who killed Tecumseh?" and Harrison would make it all the way to the White House in 1840 on the inflated memory of Tippecanoe.) In October, Captain Oliver Hazard Perry scored a heavy naval victory on Fort Erie, fighting with trained sailors against hastily recruited Canadian sailors. He sent to Harrison the famous message "We have met the enemy and he is ours." (Perry's flagship, the *Lawrence*, was named after the captain of the *Chesapeake*, a frigate that engaged in an unsuccessful gunnery duel with the British *Shannon* a few months before in which Lawrence's last words were "Don't give up the ship!" which became the motto of the United States Navy.)

The Americans also did markedly better at the Niagara crossing point than had van Rensselaer the year before. General Dearborn and Colonel Winfield Scott (who would become one of the most durable and competent commanders in American military history over the next fifty-five years) successfully crossed the river, wheeled eastward, and occupied York (Toronto), burning down the buildings of the Legislative Assembly and the governor's residence (against Dearborn's orders). It was a contested operation and the Americans took significant casualties, including the western explorer Zebulon Montgomery Pike, after whom Pike's Peak in Colorado is named. This was a stinging defeat for the British and Canadians, but Dearborn was inexplicably replaced by one of the egregious scoundrels of American history, General James Wilkinson. Wilkinson had allegedly joined the famous Conway Cabal conspiracy against Washington after the Battle of Saratoga, had been fired as clothier general of the U.S. Army for his involvement in a system of corrupt kickbacks, had been accused of conspiring with former vice president Aaron Burr in the events that led to Burr's famous prosecution for treason, and Madison had just unsuccessfully attempted to court-martial him. He had been released from custody on Christmas Day 1811, and was now to attack along the St. Lawrence eastward to Montreal while General Wade Hampton approached north beside Lake Champlain to converge with him on that frequent but rarely attained target Montreal. The British and Canadians had fifteen thousand defenders well dug in at Montreal and their perimeter forces defeated Hampton at Chateauguay. Wilkinson's advance units were defeated by a smaller force at Crysler's Farm on July 13 and 14, west of Montreal.

Both American forces withdrew and neither got within fifty miles of their target. The British and Canadians pushed the Americans back out of Upper Canada at Niagara, and after the Americans burned a village near Niagara Falls and retreated across the river, their pursuers seized Fort Niagara, killing, wounding, or capturing more than five hundred Americans. In the last days of 1813, the Indian allies of the Anglo-Canadians, with their presumed approval, burned down Buffalo, New York.

It had become a nasty little war, but after nearly two years, Canada was holding, and the likelihood of British reinforcements was sharply rising as the very long sequence of revolutionary and Napoleonic wars seemed to be entering its final phase, with Britain and Russia as the winning powers. Napoleon suffered his first defeat, after scores of victories over all comers, in the Battle of Nations at Leipzig, where the combined Russian, Prussian, Austrian, and Swedish armies outnumbered him three to two and more than five hundred thousand men were engaged. He continued his westward retreat to the Rhine as the British, under Wellington, pushed his peninsular army out of Spain after eight years of fierce combat.

Czar Alexander I had always favoured America and ignored Napoleon's blockade in respect of it. Now that he was in close alliance with the British, he offered America's able minister to Russia, John Quincy Adams (son of the former president and himself a future holder of that office), his good offices as mediator of the War of 1812, and Adams gratefully accepted. Castlereagh could not brush off the czar as he had Madison the year before, and while he declined mediation, he sent the secretary of state, James Monroe, an offer of direct negotiations in November 1813. He had had secret negotiations in mind, but Madison sought congressional approval for such talks, to alleviate some of the opposition to the war, and sent an eminent delegation (including Adams, Clay, and the able treasury secretary Albert Gallatin) to talks with the British at Ghent, in what is now Belgium. The Americans outranked their British analogues, but Napoleon abdicated in April 1814 and removed to the island of Elba in the Mediterranean, and Castlereagh and Wellington joined the immense Congress of Vienna, where they were the principal co-protagonists in the reordering of much of the world, with the Austrian foreign minister, Klemens von Metternich (who would be known in the coming decades as the "coachman of Europe"); the cunning secretary of state of the Holy See, Ercole Cardinal Consalvi; and the ineffable survivor and schemer French foreign minister Charles Maurice de Talleyrand, back now with the Bourbons, as he had been many years before, prior to his dalliances with the First Republic, the Directory, the Consulate, and Napoleon's empire, and his service still had decades to run (with whomever ruled). Talleyrand accomplished the remarkable feat of convincing the British, Austrians, Russians, and Prussians that France was an ally against and victim of the stateless mountebank Napoleon (whom he had served with great assiduity as foreign minister for ten years). The British always wanted as many great powers in Europe as possible, the better to balance the scales, and the Austrian emperor was loyal to his French Bourbon in-laws. (Marie Antoinette was the current emperor's aunt.) America was not invited, and the affairs of the Americas were not official subjects of discussion, but there was extensive talk of sending Wellington with his large and battle-hardened army to Canada, where the Royal Navy could certainly transport them easily.

The British did send another fourteen thousand men from the Duke of Wellington's peninsular army to America in June 1814, and as peace discussions began, Castlereagh employed the classic negotiating tactic of escalating hostilities. He tightened the blockade even on New England and New York, and ignored Madison's olive branch of lifting the embargo. After the experiences in Europe, the British were now vastly more competent than they had been in the Seven Years and Revolutionary Wars. Both sides adopted the usual three-pronged attack plan: at Detroit and Niagara, and along the shores of Lake Champlain. The British added the ravages of shore parties landing at Chesapeake Bay and moving inland, and this time the British ability to conduct amphibious warfare would pay off. For the 1814 campaign, the Americans had thirty-four thousand men in their regular army, and they were now pretty good troops. The commanders, Harrison, Scott, and the rising General Andrew Jackson, were also capable. The British and Canadians had almost as many soldiers with now imminent prospects of reinforcements. The Americans had more militiamen, about one hundred thousand, but they were useless outside their own states and a mixed bag there. The Americans controlled Lake Erie; the Canadians controlled Lake Ontario; the Anglo-Canadians held all the St. Lawrence; and the Royal Navy could roam and maraud at will along the Atlantic and Gulf coasts of the United States. It was becoming a standoff pretty close to where it began, but there was some hard fighting left.

Winfield Scott led the Americans to a fine victory at Chippawa, near Niagara, in July. Three weeks later, there was a drawn engagement at Lundy's Lane, near Niagara Falls, with both sides taking about 850 casualties, but the Americans withdrew and then ceded Fort Erie to the British. Sir George Prevost, the cautious British commander in Lower Canada who had so hampered the much lamented Brock, mishandled his expedition south to Ticonderoga with eleven thousand men and was defeated by a smaller force. He was deservedly sacked. More successful was the main landing on Chesapeake Bay on August 19 of four thousand veterans of the British Army in Spain embarked directly from France with only a short stopover in Bermuda. With Madison and his cabinet looking on, the bumbling American commander failed with seven thousand reservists to stop the shore party at Bladensburg, nine miles from Washington. The government fled, Madison on foot because of problems with his horse, and the British entered Washington unopposed on August 24. In revenge for the burning of York, the British burned all the government buildings except the patent office. The executive mansion was gutted inside and the walls scorched; it was later whitewashed, earning it the name it has held ever since. Mrs. Dolley Madison coolly removed what she could and left with the official portrait of George Washington under her arm (she was refused lodging by an irate woman in the Virginia countryside who resented the recent conscription of her husband). The British observed correct discipline and there was no looting or abuse of the civil population. They re-embarked, unmolested, by sea on August 25, and after two days the itinerant American government returned to an unenthusiastic welcome from the populace. The British moved unsuccessfully against Baltimore three weeks later, where Francis Scott Key wrote what became "The Star-Spangled Banner," which would become the national anthem, following the attack on Fort McHenry. The Washington foray was not important strategically, but it was a stunning propaganda victory and was seen throughout and well beyond the British world as a well-administered and much deserved whipping of the upstart republic by the great empire from which it had seceded but was now emerging as unambiguously the greatest power in the world. The British occupied Maine, but apart from that the frontiers remained pretty much as they had been.

Madison dismissed the war secretary, Armstrong, and took the step, unique to this day in the country's history, of calling upon James Monroe, the secretary of state, to be simultaneously the war secretary, with a mandate to bring the war to an end by whatever combination of fighting and negotiating would achieve that end. This made Monroe a virtual co-president and, if he could end the war satisfactorily, almost certainly the fifth president, and the fourth to come from Virginia. When the news of the burning of Washington was received in London and Vienna, British terms in the continuing peace conference stiffened, but they moderated again with news of the defeat of Prevost at Lake Champlain. The Duke of Wellington was offered the command in Canada, but he enjoyed his position in Vienna and having fought many hard battles in Spain, and before that in India, he was not eager for the position. There is no doubt that under his command his army would have defeated any American army it encountered, but the entire British Army was only ninety thousand men and the United States now had eight million people, and not much that would be permanent would be accomplished except perhaps a southern adjustment of the frontier west of the Appalachians. The British, once again, would have to withdraw eventually, though as a result of attrition, not a disaster like Yorktown. Europe was at peace, so there was no need for any blockade, search and seizure of ships, or impressment of sailors. The British would not pay reparations, and neither side would make any concessions of borders. Wellington advised that the facts on the ground did not justify any changes of borders, and if Britain wanted to establish an Indian buffer zone or regain any other territory conceded in 1783, it would have to send Wellington's army to take it by force and hold it against a country that would be steadily increasing in strength and numbers. This was not judged worthwhile and the British negotiating position was modified to conform with these realities on November 26, 1814, at Ghent, and peace was signed there on December 24.

The war was not quite over, as, before word of the peace had reached North America, Wellington's brother-in-law, General Sir Edward Pakenham, landed forty miles east of New Orleans on December 13 with 7,500 men. The U.S. commander of the southern military district was General Andrew Jackson, a drummer boy in the Revolutionary War and veteran of successful operations against the southern Indians. He was a violent man who had survived much personal combat and many duels, and he was a fierce and anglophobic nationalist. Ignoring his orders from Monroe not to disturb Spanish Florida, he had already occupied Pensacola, and he bustled back to New Orleans on December 15 to be in position to attack the British expeditionary force on December 23. He spent the next two weeks building fortifications and obstacles around New Orleans and was heavily entrenched with artillery and sharpshooters deployed on the flanks of all likely approaches to the town when Pakenham attacked with 5,300 of his regulars on January 8, 1815. The British redcoats walked upright and in tight formation straight into the trap ringed with Jackson's artillery and his long-rifled Tennessee and Kentucky sharpshooters, deadly shots. It was an insanely unimaginative plan of attack, but the

British tried it bravely twice. Pakenham was killed and the British took more than two thousand casualties, compared with eight American dead and thirteen wounded. The British withdrew, decisively beaten for the first time in the war in a relatively large action. News of the New Orleans victory arrived in the still-scarred rubble of official Washington a few days later, and news of the Treaty of Ghent arrived there on February 11. Jackson was well on his way to being America's leading political figure over the next thirty years (though Monroe was now assured of the succession, in the Virginia dynasty, to Madison, having saved the administration's chestnuts in both the War and State departments).

It was, in its origins – as the Americans could have avoided it by building an army capable of occupying Canada, and the British by being less high-handed at sea – a silly war, and, as has been recorded, was declared by the Americans after the British had announced a readiness to remove the *casus belli*, and was apparently won by the Americans, at least on balance, after it had ended. The economic cost to America had been huge and the strain on national unity very great. The opportunity to take Canada had been lost and would only come again, fleetingly and at considerably greater risk, much later. Though an inept war leader, Madison had redeemed his standing by his modesty and preparedness to admit error, and in the end the Americans made their point that they could not simply be treated as a complete geopolitical irrelevancy at the ends of the earth. Next to the five great European powers – Britain, Russia, France, Austria, and Prussia – the United States was in the second rank of the world's nations, and rocketing upward to become their peer. Spain, Turkey, even China, were in descent, and others, such as the Dutch and Swedes, stood still. Overcoming such a terrible division in the country, holding its own in the New World with the British, and forcing Britain's merchant shipping into convoys, with no help from the French, was an achievement for the United States, even allowing for the distraction of the British in Europe. Britain had not won the war, though it certainly was, with Russia, the big and (more durable) winner of the Great War in Europe. But the Americans, if they had been wiser, could have taken Canada and didn't, so Britain, like America, won something and lost nothing.

Largely unappreciated, the victor of the war was Canada. For the first time since Champlain founded Quebec in 1608, Canada was not in imminent danger. New France had been threatened by the British until the Quebec Act in 1774, when it responded to Carleton's blandishments and jumped to the British side in the opening Anglo-American schism, and the French and new British Canadians had been under threat from the Americans for the following forty years. Now, with peace reigning in Europe, the Americans would not dare tangle with Britain, and the Canadians, who were an enigma of centrifugated fragments before the War of 1812 in the eyes of their colonial captors and inheritors, bulked more distinctively in the eyes of the British, with whom they had shown a will to associate that tickled both the self-interest and the bewitching mystique of the colonial vocation that was to take hold of British public policy over the next century. In accepting and honouring the informal agreement of 1774, the French Canadians showed a political acuity at dealing with the British and with English Canadians that they have never lost. The doughty French habitant and coureur de bois, and the rugged Loyalist or simply transplanted American who had defended his land against the Yankees, all of whom made first-class militiamen, had earned the paternal goodwill of their transoceanic king-protector. With the ingenious and fierce natives, they were the forerunners of the vast Kiplingesque gallery of the local pillars of empire, from Gunga Din to Shaka to the bushmen of Africa, the Maori of Australasia, and the gentle cannibals of Tonga, and most of all the rugged British and Irish who, whether from a love of adventure or the force of desperation, carried the British flag and civilization to the farthest corners of the world. Canada, though only half-formed and with limited relations between its main parts, had demonstrated a collective will to live, and even a preliminary community of interest between its principal components. "The essence of the War of 1812 is that it built the first storey of the Canadian national edifice."[29] Champlain and Carleton had laid the foundations.

7. The Early Struggle for Responsible Government, 1815–1830

Even before the War of 1812 ended, the Canadian settlements were pushing west. The Earl of Selkirk (1771–1820), who had evacuated some poor Scots to Prince Edward Island in the early years of the century, established, as a shareholder of the Hudson's Bay Company, a settlement of Scots and Irish in the Red River Valley, near the modern Winnipeg, which he called Assiniboia, with the idea of blocking the access to the west of the competing North West Company. The Nor'Westers stirred up the Métis (of mixed European and Indian descent) against Selkirk's settlers, objecting to the export of pemmican (Indian beef), which the Nor'Westers needed to feed their canoers to the west and north. The settlers were driven out in 1814 and came back in 1815, but were broken up again after the Battle of Seven Oaks in 1816. Selkirk himself re-established the settlement in 1817, but a British government commission was established and litigation proceeded through Canadian courts until the two competing companies were merged under British government auspices in 1821, with, between them, 173 posts. The governor of the Hudson's Bay Company and de facto viceroy of Western Canada from 1820 to 1860 was the redoubtable Sir George Simpson, who in the course of his long career negotiated with the U.S. government and with British prime minister Sir Robert Peel over the Oregon boundary, with the kings of France and Belgium and British prime minister Lord Aberdeen over the sovereignty of Hawaii, and with the Russian government over rights along the Alaska coast. He ruled his vast but underpopulated domain from a large house in Lachine, west of Montreal, a community so named (Chapter 1) because the Indians represented it as being near the gateway to China.

The Treaty of Ghent was rounded out by the Rush-Bagot Agreement of 1817, which demilitarized the Great Lakes except for police vessels, and, in parallel agreement, extended the northern boundary of the United States along the forty-ninth parallel from Lake of the Woods to the Rocky Mountains. The Americans made some concessions on fisheries, and it was agreed to govern jointly the Oregon territory between the Russian- and Spanish-administered areas (Alaska and California). Rush-Bagot drew out representatives of the very highest ability for both countries.* Their agreement demarcated the approximate spheres of influence between Great Britain and the United States in North

---

* Richard Rush (1780–1859), the minister to Great Britain, former attorney general, and future candidate for vice president and secretary of the treasury, was an extremely capable public official, as was his analogue, Sir Charles Bagot (1781–1843), husband of the Duke of Wellington's niece, minister to Washington, and future ambassador to Russia and to the Netherlands, and he will re-enter this narrative as governor general of Canada.

America and has been a complete success these nearly two centuries. The United States had about eight million people and the Canadas and maritime colonies about seven hundred thousand, so the ratio of about eleven to one was a reduction of the previous imbalance of about thirty to one faced by New France opposite the Americans.

Nova Scotia had about eighty thousand people and had enjoyed representative government for nearly sixty years. The governor controlled a large Crown revenue and appointed his council, which was executive, legislative, and judicial. It was a strange little fiefdom, but it worked well, having neither the Anglo-French frictions of Lower Canada nor the rough and ready boisterousness of Upper Canada. Newfoundland was as wild and woolly as Prince Edward Island was bucolic and tranquil. Nova Scotia shipping and shipbuilding flourished between 1815 and 1830, when the British advocates of free trade opened up the West Indies to greater penetration by the Americans.

Only in Lower Canada was there the separation of political power from racial majority, as the English effectively controlled the province through the British governor and his appointed council, and through the commercial dominance of Montreal's English merchants. Democracy and nationality were conjoined, as in Ireland, though the oppressions of the majority by the minority would prove much gentler and easier to overturn than they were in Ireland. In Quebec, the French majority would chafe at their exclusion from political and commercial power, exemplified by the fact that their most formidable political leader, Louis-Joseph Papineau, would be the speaker of the Legislative Assembly from 1815 to 1837 but was never in government.

In Upper Canada, the population was growing quickly, but resentment would grow, because the Family Compact perpetuated its power by doling out to relatives and protégés large quantities of disposable Crown land. One of the early agitators against this oligarchy was the Scottish social and political reformer Robert Gourlay (1778–1863), who advocated universal suffrage to literate men in Scotland and fair wages for workers in England. He came to Canada in 1817 and campaigned from the start for a fair distribution of Crown land, and in 1819 was imprisoned and deported for his trouble, only returning in 1856. Gourlay fell right in with the spirit of the Reformers, and especially with their gift for polemical hyperbole, claiming, typically, that "corruption, indeed, has reached such a height in this province that . . . no part of the British empire witnesses the like."[30] (It was a good thing for everyone that he didn't visit Ireland, much less India.) The rest of British North America, from Labrador to Lake Superior and then west between the Rush-Bagot forty-ninth parallel and the North-West Territory to the Rockies, was Rupert's Land. Both Rupert's Land and the North-West Territory were governed by the Hudson's Bay Company after its merger with the North West Company in 1821.

Shortly after the War of 1812, the Canadian agricultural areas began producing ever-larger surpluses, initiating a pattern of growth that continued to world-significant heights when the western prairies yielded to general and efficient cultivation later in the century. Upper Canadian lumbering and farming were greatly facilitated by postwar canal-building: the Lachine Canal to go round the rapids west of Montreal, begun in 1821; and the Rideau and connecting canals between 1826 and 1834, which opened an alternate route between the St. Lawrence and the Great Lakes, with military defence in mind. (The same thought inspired the even more ambitious Erie Canal in New York State, which connected the Hudson above New York to the Great Lakes but proceeded about twenty miles south of Lake Ontario to steer clear of British and Canadian navy vessels on Lake Ontario. Since there would never be serious animosity along that frontier again, neither country need have bothered. The Canadian Welland Canal, to bypass Niagara Falls and try to rival the Erie Canal for traffic into the western Great Lakes, was also built in the 1820s.

American immigration into the Canadas dried up after the war, but immigration from Britain and Ireland became more evenly divided between the United States and the Canadas, after the American colonies had for more than fifty years siphoned off almost all the natural population expansion of the British Isles. The early years of crop failures and chronic food shortages in Ireland sharply increased the volume of immigration, Protestant and Roman Catholic, from that province of the United Kingdom, and substantial numbers of Scots continued to flow into Nova Scotia. The growth of the British population of Lower Canada was more than balanced by the continuing heavy French-Canadian birthrate, but it aroused renewed fears among the French that there was a movement afoot to assimilate them and wash them out among the rising tide of English-speaking people in North America.

The Roman Catholic Church of Quebec, having been guaranteed by the Quebec Act in 1774, though not exactly an established church in Lower Canada, had a special status but played its role as a national church with great comprehensiveness and ingenuity. The bishop of Quebec sat on the Executive Council and drew a councillor's salary, and the Church had the right to tithe its members. It could not enforce and collect the tax through the powers of the state, though it effectively formed a pillar of the established power in the colony. But despite the steady rise of an Irish Catholic population in Quebec, the Roman Catholic Church was also the ark of the national ambitions of, and the conservator of the national distinctiveness of, the French Canadians. It provided most of the education and medical care the French population received, and although it ruled the faithful with unyielding authority, it did so with minimal corruption, moral or financial, with great social compassion, and with a burning sense of mission. In the other provinces, it was a minority church, largely representing the oppressed in the New World, as it often had in the Old.

Among Protestants, the substantial majority in Upper Canada and Nova Scotia, there was agitation for an established church (the Church of England), but this was stiffly resisted by the non-episcopal or congregational churches, as well as by the Roman Catholics and Lutherans (the other churches that have bishops; there were few Eastern Orthodox in Canada at that time). The real public debate was over whether there should be state-supported non-denominational or multi-denominational schools. This debate played heavily into the growing controversy over the pursuit of liberal constitutional democracy, a movement that was advancing along parallel lines in Great Britain and the United States, although, of course, both were sovereign countries in which the issue of where authority resided had been determined, apart from the breadth of the franchise and the powers of the non-elected upper house. (The United States Senate was chosen by the legislatures of the states until early in the twentieth century.)

In Lower Canada, there had already been great controversy, starting in 1806, over whether judges could sit as legislators in the councils and Assembly, and there were several rending controversies over the right of the Assembly to impeach a judge or the chief justice. Where the powers of elected versus appointed officials became more competitive was in 1818 and 1819, when the Governor of Lower Canada, Sir John Sherbrooke, and then the Duke of Richmond (who, as mentioned earlier in this chapter, had been tutored by Guy Carleton) followed by Lord Dalhousie, did not have enough to pay their governments' expenses from discretionary sources, and were reduced to asking the Assembly to fund them. Sherbrooke did so successfully in 1818, but thereafter gridlock developed. The Legislative Council, dominated by the English commercial class, supported the governor and voted against the Assembly's effort to restrict the salaries of members of the Executive Council and oversee the expenses of the government. In 1823, the governor was one hundred thousand pounds short, and there were widespread allegations of official corruption as well as incompetence. In the Assembly, Speaker Papineau was able to lead a powerful and often theatrical popular opposition.

Louis-Joseph Papineau (1786–1871) was the first of a formidable sequence of popular tribunes who mobilized and expressed the collective will and ambition of the French Canadians. His father, Joseph Papineau, a successful notary, had carried messages to Carleton between Montreal and Quebec, at considerable risk to himself, in the American Revolutionary War, and Louis-Joseph, the future national leader, volunteered as a militiaman to assist in the successful defence of Lower Canada from the Americans in the War of 1812. It was in 1812 that he was first elected to the Legislative Assembly, and in 1815 he was elected its Speaker.

He was no enemy of Britain or of monarchical institutions, but an impassioned advocate of popular rights. Papineau had been a prodigy at the Petit Séminaire of Quebec (though he was expelled from his previous college) and was moved to enter political life by the reactionary regime of Governor Sir James Craig, in office from 1807 to 1811, who was a racist and a very authoritarian soldier who had spent much of his life in the British Army fighting the French. Craig considered a legislative demand for the right to approve government expenditures to be verging on treason in wartime, and was unable to see the French Canadians otherwise than as a conquered people. The French Canadians referred to Craig's term as the "Reign of Terror." Sir George

Prevost (1811–1816), who followed Craig, was a Swiss American by birth and much less hostile to the French. His term was dominated by the War of 1812, when a general truce between factions prevailed, which largely continued under his successors Drummond, Sherbrooke, and the Duke of Richmond.

In the first year of Dalhousie's term, 1820, the governor took the side of the appointed Legislative Council against the claims advanced by the Assembly, led by Papineau, that the popular house had the right to review and approve, or not, every item of the government's budget. Papineau unearthed many instances of glaring, if rather trivial, corruption: absentee office-holders on the official payroll, judges demanding direct payments from litigants appearing before them, and so on. But what really raised the ante was the movement for a united province of Lower and Upper Canada, to water down the French, and the revival of the prohibition of the French language in debates in Lower Canada's legislative houses. Papineau sailed to Britain from New York in January 1822 to lobby against these anti-French measures, and made a very good impression in London. By his culture, charm, felicity of expression, and imposing and patrician bearing, he belied the aspersions that had been made, and somewhat accepted, of French Canadians as virtually savages and at best serfs. Papineau won the argument, and the union of the provinces was not pursued, but he returned to spend the next five years in deadly embrace with Dalhousie over fiscal prerogatives. Papineau had the best of the argument, made his argument well, and may be said to have won, as the succeeding governors, Sir Francis Burton (Lower Canada) and Sir James Kempt (Canada), made compromises that Dalhousie opposed, and Dalhousie was effectively repudiated by the British government. But Papineau also often spoke in terms of unnecessary violence, and while he stirred popular opinion, he roused great concern among more influential groups and tended, as firebrands do, to quarrel needlessly and protractedly with his colleagues in what became the Patriote movement. For a time, he was able to cooperate with the English-Canadian moderate Reformer John Neilson, but as Papineau became more militant, all bridges to moderate English-speaking Reformers were blown up.

This controversy continued all through the 1820s and was aggravated by the demand by the English leadership of Lower Canada to reunite the two Canadas, ostensibly to end the arguments over the division of revenue between Upper and Lower Canada under the Quebec Revenue Act of 1774, but really to try to bring the English toward a cultural majority in a united province. A bill to that effect was in preparation in committee in Westminster, with the approval of the colonial secretary, Lord Bathurst, when the protests of the French majority in Lower Canada and most of the English of Upper Canada caused it to be set aside. Bathurst was a rigorous supporter of Dalhousie's efforts to sideline the attempt to achieve popular legislative control over supply (in other words, funding the government). Despite the terrible defeat in the thirteen American colonies, and all the lessons of the benign Carleton, the British authorities still tended to lapse back into authoritarian mode. Tensions built and tinder piled up throughout the 1820s in both Canadas.

In Upper Canada, the Reform movement began in the early 1820s with a controversy over the right of Americans who had not formally been naturalized to be considered citizens of the province. This grey area was exploited to disqualify Barnabas Bidwell from taking his seat in the Assembly, and to attack his son, one of the leading Reformers, Marshall Spring Bidwell. The greatest impact of this question was on the eligibility of such contested people to hold land in Upper Canada, and it was finally resolved in 1828 with a bill naturalizing everyone who had come to the province prior to 1821 and had remained there.

An even greater dispute arose over the Clergy Reserves. The Anglican leader, Archdeacon John Strachan, subsequently the bishop of Toronto, wished the entire vast reserve of land set aside for the churches to be consigned to the Church of England, which claimed to be an established church in Canada. This was not going to be successful, because of the size and status of the Roman Catholic Church and the alliance between the British governors and the Catholic bishops. The senior legal officials of the colony determined in 1819 that the Church of Scotland had an equal right. The issue took off in 1824, when it was determined to begin distributing the land for development, and the other religious denominations protested the pre-eminence of the local Churches of England and Scotland. The low church opposition was led by the leader of the Methodists, Egerton Ryerson. He caught Strachan red-handed submitting a grossly inflated

Anglican share of the population to the colonial secretary. Ryerson's campaign was instrumental in obtaining a Reform majority in the Assembly in 1828.

The secular opposition was led by the Scottish immigrant William Lyon Mackenzie, "a shrill-toned, bristling terrier of a man."[30] Mackenzie was born in Forfarshire in 1795 and moved to Canada in 1820, setting up in Dundas a store that sold drugs, hardware, jewellery, toys, dyestuffs, and paints, as well as being a circulating library. He started his newspaper, the *Colonial Advocate*, in 1824. He styled himself "the westernmost journalist in the British dominions on the continent of America" and assumed on his own authority, as he put it, "the office of a public censor."[31] He helped the Reform opposition to crystallize, and they won the Assembly elections in 1824, which only served to demonstrate the impotence of the popular end of the political system, as the Family Compact carried obliviously on. In the words of Stephen Leacock, "Like the clansmen of his native land, [Mackenzie] tried to storm an entrenched and strongly fortified position by a frontal attack in which defects in equipment and in tactics were to be made good by a glorious charge whose driving force was the red blood of passion, whose reserve was the fury of hate." He "lacked that sobriety of purpose which rescues [Reform movements] from the violence of uncharted agitation."[32] One of Mackenzie's particularly outrageous and provoking editorial onslaughts caused a mob (including a member of the lieutenant-governor's household) to sack his printing plant, smash his press, and scatter his type. He received a generous damages award from the courts and assumed the status of a semi-martyr.* Of course, Mackenzie and his cohorts exaggerated the evils of their opponents in the governing class in Upper Canada. They were stuffy, pompous, authoritarian, and lacking in imagination and liberality, were even hypocrites, but they weren't overly corrupt beyond normal patronage and nepotism, nor very repressive. But they were terribly self-satisfied, resistant to change, and lacking in any panache or accessibility to popular affection; more or less what one would expect from distant British provincial officials who fancied themselves to be

---

* Readers should note Mackenzie's character to contrast it with that of his grandson and namesake, W.L. Mackenzie King, not born for another fifty years, who would exercise an immense influence in Canada in the subsequent century. King was almost supernaturally cautious.

important, a genre that lingers yet in Southern Ontario and even lurks in the shadows in some of the mustier institutions of Toronto.

The Atlantic provinces progressed much more calmly, even the unruly Newfoundlanders. A mixed Assembly, partly elected and partly appointed, was established there in 1832. In New Brunswick, a more civilized tug-of-war than in Quebec occurred in the 1820s over the power to raise and spend money, with the Assembly gradually gaining ground, but that debate was subsumed in the question of the right to exploit timber lands. A commissioner of Crown lands, Thomas Baillie (1796–1863), a forceful veteran of the Battle of Waterloo, was installed, and he created a force of forest rangers and instituted a policy of licensing and charging for cutting rights, a policy that impressed the Colonial Office and eased the government's financial problems. Baillie became a member of the Executive Council and the surveyor general, but incited such antagonism that he was eventually stripped of his powers, and authority over Crown lands was conceded to the Assembly. Baillie had turned down the fallback position of postmaster general of Jamaica in 1833, and continued for a time as surveyor general of New Brunswick.

In Prince Edward Island, the principal political issue, and the main public entertainment, was Governor Charles Douglass Smith, who quarrelled with everyone, including the militia, which, in his determination to subdue, he called in the army to surround and then fire upon. The army naturally refused, and Smith's effort to have the officers involved court-martialled and executed was also unsuccessful. He was soon at daggers drawn with the Assembly, and smashed the windows in the provincial Parliament in January to force them out physically. He was successful in this, but they petitioned London so vehemently that Smith was recalled in 1824, and in the ensuing comparative calm relations between the governor and the legislators unfolded relatively serenely.

In 1828, the colonial secretary, William Huskisson, received herniating masses of petitions from aggrieved supporters of the Patriotes in Lower Canada and the Reformers in Upper Canada. The principal issues were Dalhousie's refusal to accept the re-election of Papineau as Speaker of the Assembly, a dangerous issue, as the French of the province, apart from the bishop, were excluded from the Executive Council and were only represented in the Assembly, and the speakership was the only office within their gift and choice. Questions of democratic reform were becoming poisonously combined with issues of race, language, and, to some degree, sectarianism, with the Roman Catholic Church forcefully advocating the French-Canadian interest in public and in the highest council of the province. It was seventy years since the Plains of Abraham, and the French Canadians couldn't be treated as enemies in their own country anymore.

The leaders of the Church advised peaceful remonstrance and action, but too reactionary a stance by the governors could undo all the good work of the enlightened agents of British rule back to Carleton and Murray. In Lower Canada, the battle for control of revenue and spending was at least as advanced as it was in Upper Canada, and the additional explosive ingredient of race greatly exacerbated it. There was also a growing demand for more complete local government in the Eastern Townships, especially courts, where the objection was largely the reverse of the province as a whole: the English-speaking population claimed it was not being adequately served in its own language, a phenomenon which in Europe in the following century would become known as irredentism: a minority within a minority. The English Lower Canadians continued to call for one big province, to increase their numbers as a percentage within the jurisdiction.

In Upper Canada, apart from the control of the revenues and spending of the government, the battle over the effort to promote an established church where the sectarian numbers did not justify it, and the fight between Strachan and Ryerson for control of the Clergy Reserves chunk of Crown lands and of public education through the charter of King's College, had inflamed the province's fissiparous tendencies. An election in Upper Canada was necessitated in 1830 by the antique practice of dissolving Parliament on the death of the monarch, the stylish but profligate George IV. By this time, Mackenzie had already squandered much of the goodwill that would ordinarily accrue to the Reformers by provoking legislative battles over the post office and the chaplaincy of the house, the first an Imperial matter and the second irrelevant to any serious policy question. And by this time the tide had turned at the Imperial level. Lord Liverpool, who had succeeded as prime minister following the assassination of Spencer Percival in 1812, took a stroke after fifteen years as premier and retired in 1827. George Canning, Viscount Goderich, and the Duke of Wellington had succeeded as prime minister in the following three years.

The repeal of the Test and Corporation Acts and Catholic Emancipation in 1828 and 1829 indicated the drift of public events, and in this atmosphere a select committee of the House of Commons was struck to consider the mountainous petitions that had come in to Huskisson. The committee accepted all but the request for the reunification of the Province of Canada, moved yet by Edmund Burke's comment that "to attempt to amalgamate two populations composed of races of men diverse in language, laws, and customs was a complete absurdity." The committee recommended full control over funding by the Assembly, except for a civil list to cover the cost of the governor, the executive councillors, and judges, the amount voted for the life of the monarch. It recommended that the Executive and Legislative Councils be separated and that judges belong to neither. All public accounts should be audited, the Jesuits' estates should be dedicated to public education, and while it could not form a recommendation about the Clergy Reserves, it did oppose the unidenominational use of the practical consequences of King's College. Dalhousie was censured for his treatment of Papineau, and "an impartial, conciliatory and constitutional system of government" was commended to and recommended for both the Canadas. This was a pretty radical, and certainly a progressive view from the British Parliament, and Sir James Kempt was instructed by the Colonial Office to implement the entire report in Lower Canada and to assure the admission of French and pro-French members of the Executive and Legislative Councils of Quebec. Once again, the British system had distinguished itself by a show of liberality that was prescient and disinterested and broadly justified, a liberality that distinguished itself among the world's methods of self-government and seemed to continue British competitiveness with the United States in the struggle for world leadership in the most intelligent and advanced political systems among major countries. It greatly alleviated tensions in Lower Canada for a time.

Kempt (1765–1854) had been all through the American Revolutionary and Napoleonic Wars, served in the Netherlands and Egypt, was quartermaster general of British North America (from 1807 to 1811), was a major general on the staff of the Duke of Wellington in Spain, and became a close friend of the duke, was a brigade commander in Upper Canada during the War of 1812, fought at Waterloo, and was a well-regarded and diplomatic lieutenant-governor of Nova Scotia from 1820 to 1828. He was tapped by Wellington, then prime minister, and Huskisson for the very delicate task in Canada, after the Earl of Dalhousie (1770–1838), Kempt's friend and mentor in colonial matters, was kicked upstairs to the military command in India. Kempt accepted the appointment with reluctance, as he liked Nova Scotia, and said that he would serve only two years. The Colonial Office was promoting, in all the Canadian colonies in the 1820s, the notion of control of the province's money by the elected Assembly and appointed Legislative Council jointly, as long as the governors had civil lists which would assure the salaries and expenses of the executive officials for years in advance. Kempt and Dalhousie both warned that this would soon lead to the popular assemblies reaching for complete control over all finances and that the Crown would be resistless against such pressures. Dalhousie, in a larger and more difficult role, over both Canadas, made his point bluntly and engaged in an outright struggle with the Patriote party of Papineau in Lower Canada and the compulsively belligerent Mackenzie's Reformers in Upper Canada. It had started to go horribly wrong when Dalhousie returned in 1826 after a year's home leave in which his acting successor, Sir Francis Burton, had agreed a bill that put all official revenues, Crown and otherwise, in one public fund and voted a sum for the executive expenses of the government for a year. This was an accretion of legislative power in which Westminster reluctantly acquiesced and which Dalhousie tried to roll back when he returned. He vetoed a similar bill in 1826 and funded the government by an illegal appropriation of the province's money.

Kempt recognized much more clearly than had Dalhousie that some concessions were going to have to be made by the Crown or the example of the dissentient Americans would become fashionable. He did not show his hand and met patiently and courteously with all factions and avoided controversial utterances, hoping that the select committee's recommendations, which included empowering him to enact all the conclusions, would be approved by Parliament, or at least that he would receive straightforward direction from the home government. No such guidance was forthcoming, as Wellington's Tories clung to office against the rising reform tide. When the Assembly of Lower Canada convened in November 1828, eighteen months after Dalhousie had uproariously prorogued it, Kempt devised a formula for confirming Papineau as Speaker without actually re-electing him, a proposal that had been vetoed by Dalhousie. It was an elegant and necessary climbdown, and on the strength of it Kempt accepted a measure similar to that of 1825, which did implicitly yield discretionary fiscal ground to the Assembly. (The chief justice, in his capacity as Speaker, had to cast a tie-breaking vote to get it through.) There was consternation in Westminster and a threat of disavowal, but more sensible views prevailed and Kempt's suave compromise was accepted and repeated in 1830. In the meantime, Kempt had helped guide through both legislative houses of Lower Canada an expansion and redistribution of seats in the Assembly that gave representation to the English of the Eastern Townships but left them under-represented. A mixed criterion of population and geographic extent was used to produce the boundaries of the constituencies.

There was again a considerable flutter in London, but the cabinet, under Wellington's direction, ratified the measure. Kempt allowed that "my Legislative Bodies are composed of such inflammable materials that I feel myself seated on a Barrel of Gunpowder not knowing from one moment to another how soon an explosion may take place."[33] He was relieved, when his promised retirement was accepted, to hand over his position to Lord Aylmer in October 1830. Kempt had only palliated matters in Lower Canada and had little impact on Upper Canada, and the British government continued to dither and failed to enact the recommendations of the select committee. Kempt went on to a successful term as master general of the ordnance, with a seat on the Privy Council and the rank of full general, and lived to see the start of the Crimean War but not the embarrassment of Wellington's old army, dying at eighty-nine in 1854. His were the best days Canada would know politically for another fifteen years.

There were two essential problems. The first was that the government and the Legislative Council in Lower Canada were British, or dominated by the British, and the Assembly, like the majority of the population, was French, and though the Constitutional Act of 1791 had tried to replicate the British system of government, it could not adapt to that ethnic and cultural divide, which was also economic and sectarian. The second difficulty was that the governors in Canada had little patronage, and so they had only slight ability to influence the political tides and currents, unlike the royal party and the king's friends in London. As Papineau stated, "The British had an aristocratic hierarchy that could not be replicated in the Canadas, "when everyone without exception lives and dies a democrat; because everyone owns property; because no one is more than a small property-owner."[34]

Though Great Britain was fifteen years into its Pax Britannica, the home islands were convulsed in controversy over Catholic emancipation, an expansion of the franchise, and democratization of constituency sizes; Ireland was about to suffer a terrible famine; India was not stable; and Canada, the premier colonial effort that survived the American debacle, was almost in tumult over the failure to deliver democracy in a society that had a great many small farmers and petty bourgeois, but no peasants, compounded by the grievances of the well-treated but not equal French and the temptations posed by the rising power to the south.

Yet the future was hopeful. The Age of Reform was upon the West. The progressive Whigs and liberal Tories under prime ministers Grey, Peel, Russell, and eventually Disraeli were replacing the entrenched and sometimes reactionary Tories of the Liverpool and Wellington stripe. On the heels of the severities of twenty years of war, Britain endured the rigours of economic sluggishness followed by very swift and profound transition as the Industrial Revolution took hold, produced astounding productivity increases, and dislocated large numbers of workers and farmers as industry was mechanized and modernized. The sacrifices of war gave way to a demand for progress and prosperity. A crowd of about seventy-five thousand gathered at Manchester on August 16, 1819, to hear Henry "Orator" Hunt, a leading radical advocate of electoral reform, and local magistrates sent in the municipal yeomanry, supplemented by mounted hussars, causing the death of eleven civilians and the injury of hundreds in what became known, mockingly, as the Peterloo Massacre, after the exploits of the British cavalry at Waterloo. Great controversies and incidents arose, through to the transportation to Australia in 1834 of six trade unionists from the Dorset town of Tolpuddle imprisoned for administering "illegal oaths" for "seditious" purposes. They became known as the Tolpuddle Martyrs and were pardoned after two years.

With Britain wracked by such problems, it is little wonder that they were replicated to some degree in British North America, where industrial evolution was less advanced, and accumulated poverty less widespread and embittered, but racial and and cultural divisions were much more serious even than the perennial Irish problems, and the influence of the surly, vast, and intimate neighbour America greatly exceeded any concerns the British had about the disposition of the continental powers. In France, the Bourbons, who had returned to Paris in the wake of Wellington's army – having, as Talleyrand remarked, "learned nothing and forgotten nothing" (which did not prevent him from serving them as foreign minister, as he had preceding regimes) – were sent packing once and for all in a comparatively bloodless revolution and replaced by France's first constitutional monarchy, apart from a few months on the slippery slope to the guillotine of Louis XVI. King Louis Philippe, a supposedly egalitarian king, would rule for the house of Orleans. (Talleyrand served as his ambassador to London.)*

Louis Philippe (1773–1850), a good and unpretentious man who had loyally fought in the revolutionary armies and been a Jacobin, but fled the Terror, in which his father was guillotined, was an adequate constitutional monarch, but he was not legitimate and not galvanizing, and was ground between the monarchists, the revenant Bonapartists, and the republicans, and departed after eighteen years, succeeded by a Bonapartist republic (a self-limiting transition that quickly became the Second Empire). France's chronic instability and its oscillations between political systems and extraordinary personalities reduced its

---

* The last Bourbon, Charles X, decreed the death penalty for profaning the sacraments of the Roman Catholic Church and a draconian law of restitution for property seized and other grievances arising from the previous forty years of tumult, completing the emollient trifecta with the imposition of severe censorship. The rather timid legislative houses rebelled, bringing the various Paris militia and constabulary units with them and pulling the masses of the riot-prone and tested Parisians out in huge numbers, whereupon Charles decamped from Saint-Cloud to Britain and the curtain came down with an indifferent thud on a quarter-millennium of Bourbon rule.

comparative influence and accentuated the corresponding inexorable rise of the Anglo-Saxon powers.

In the United States, a rough and ready self-made frontiersman, General Andrew Jackson, rode a popular wave in a broadening electorate and an ever westward-expanding country and became the seventh president, and the first who was neither a prosperous Boston lawyer nor a wealthy Virginia plantation owner. Jackson had killed many men, in war and in duels, and in summary executions, including two unoffending Englishmen (the unhappy Messrs. Arbuthnot and Ambrister) whom he apprehended in Florida in 1818 and accused of aiding America's Cree and Seminole opponents. Jackson was tempestuous, an enthusiastic slave owner, and a warmonger, but also an important president and statesman. The Constitution of the United States attributed, for purposes of calculating the number of members of the Electoral College, which chose the president and vice president, and the membership of the House of Representatives, three-fifths of the slave population (about 15 per cent of the total American population). Thus the slave state voters, since slaves could not vote, had a larger relative influence than free state voters. This, and the fundamental moral problem of people owning other people, caused increasing difficulties in America, as the notion of slavery did in the advanced countries of Europe. Slavery was declared illegal in England in 1772, the slave trade was outlawed in the British Empire in 1807, and slavery was abolished throughout the British Empire in 1833. Slavery was abolished in France by the First Republic in 1794, restored partially by Napoleon in 1802, in one of his less felicitous initiatives, and was altered and restricted and finally abolished completely throughout the French empire in 1848.

But in the United States, it was a "fire bell in the night," said Thomas Jefferson, author of the lapidary phrases about all men being created equal and such truths being self-evident. The South insisted on having the same number of states as there were in the North so that slave states would have equal representation in the United States Senate (where each state has two senators), even as the northern states expanded their populations more quickly. The northern states received most immigration, and there was only an economic reason for slavery in the South, where African and Caribbean workers were more productive in agriculture than Caucasians, being more adapted to tropical weather. The Missouri Compromise of 1820 restricted new slave states to south of the parallel 36°30' (the Missouri–Arkansas border). But the problems of rounding up fugitive slaves and the demands for the protection of slavery by the South steadily rankled in the North, and by 1830 Jackson had had to threaten the military suppression of South Carolina and the trial and execution for treason of anyone (including his vice president, John C. Calhoun) who voted for a measure that would authorize the nullification of federal law within the state or prevent the collection of federal customs duties in that state. (When the governor of South Carolina, Robert Hayne, asked Senator Thomas Hart Benton if the president were not exaggerating, the senator replied, "I have known General Jackson a great many years and when he speaks of hanging, it is time to look for rope.") In these circumstances, the United States was doubly unfit to challenge the British presence in Canada; it did not want its shoreline bombarded, did not wish the cost of the size of army that would be needed to prevail, and the South would no longer accept territorial acquisitions that added to the number of free states and people. For nearly a century, from the War of 1812 to the Spanish-American War, the only war the United States attempted that would add population and territory was the Mexican War, from 1846 to 1848, where the resulting additional states were equally divided between slave and free states. Canada would acquire a distinguished record accepting fugitive slaves.

While the American slavery crisis festered and Britain remained master of the seas, Canada was safe from the Americans as it had not been since Champlain founded Quebec more than two centuries before. Canada was not as isolated as it had been and was not immune to the same forces that affected these larger jurisdictions. British colonial governors were starting to be recruited among men of some administrative experience and not just stern and often francophobic veterans of the long struggle against Napoleon. To the extent that Britain could coherently embrace orderly reform and impart the same message through its colonial proconsuls, Canada's prospects were good. The embryo of a Canadian identity was just discernible in retrospect in New France, a foundling after the Seven Years War, but it was the runner-up winner of the American Revolution because it acquired

Britain as a defender against the Americans and a powerful infusion of Loyalist compatriots, and Canada came closest to winning the War of 1812. Canada was moving, even through these difficulties, to a more mature stage. Conditions were as Kempt described in his reference to a keg of gunpowder, but there was a chance of useful and not overly destructive combustion.

The War of 1812 had kindled in Whitehall the suspicion that something could be made of what was already Britain's principal colony (India being a patchwork of alliances, arrangements, and suzerainties). The indecisive conclusion of the War of 1812 in fact made it decisive: the British would defend Canada, but did not wish to; the Americans couldn't take the risk of attacking Canada; and no one wanted war. So, for the first time in their history, the inhabitants of what became Canada were quite secure. North America was no longer an individual player in the European minuet of the great powers, and the well-trampled invasion routes at Detroit, Niagara, and up and down Lake Champlain would henceforth be trod only by armies of tourists. As the Americans had manipulated the British against the French and the French against the British in order to gain their independence, the Canadians would have to be sufficiently desirable as a colony to assure that Great Britain deterred the Americans from their unquenched appetite to annex the northern half of their continent while they developed their own institutions and sought greater autonomy from the country on which they relied for protection. The scattered colonies had already endured sterner challenges.

People in Nova Scotia and Lower and Upper Canada were all doing well economically and thinking of what was to become of them politically. Few of them wanted to shelter as dependent colonies of the British Empire indefinitely, but most were not impressed with the jingo and swaggering temper of the Americans either. Independence was not at this stage an option: military protection could not be dispensed with, and the different colonies didn't have an unlimited community of interest, not even a fully shared language.

There was no talk yet of bundling these Canadian colonies together in a single sovereign jurisdiction. But people were coming of age who would think in such terms. There was growth and fermentation in the

Canadian colonies; they were increasingly valuable and self-sufficient. The embryo left by the French was an active subject of expectancy, straining to emerge. The magic thread stretching back over two hundred years from earliest Canadian times would not be severed, even by long odds, spasms of indifference, and rude events. Great trials, and opportunities, were almost at hand.

Robert Baldwin (1804–1858) and Louis Hippolyte LaFontaine (1807–1864), effectively co-leaders of the opposition in the United Province of Canada, 1840–1842 and 1843–1848, and co-premiers 1842–1843, 1848–1851, and the fathers of responsible government and democratic home rule in Ontario and Quebec. LaFontaine was chief justice of Lower Canada (Quebec) 1853–1864. Baldwin and LaFontaine began official political cooperation between French and English Canadians and steered the disparate colonies with great perseverance and liberality toward bi-cultural nationhood.

Baldwin, LaFontaine, and the Difficult Quest for Autonomy from Britain While Retaining British Protection from the United States, 1830–1867

1. Crisis, Rebellion, and Reaction, 1830–1839

The Canadas and Atlantic colonies had come through the wars well, and were the subject of modest imperial optimism. But there was no consensus about their political future locally or in London and minimal contact between the units of British North America. They presented almost a blank political canvas and complete uncertainty about the policies and personalities to steer the way forward. Beyond a general desire for a more autonomous status of their public administration, the inhabitants persevered like milling sheep, seeking everything: more independence but continued military solidarity from the British, and liberty and prosperity equivalent to that of the Americans but without political absorption. Every consensus was fragmentary and all political leadership was factional.

These communities were still evolving from the simple organizations and mores of the pioneers, which provided plenty of food and fuel but generated little export income. "In such a society, it was the poor man's homespun virtues that met with approval. Things were simple and ostentation frowned upon. Everybody was religious." (Meaning either Catholic or Protestant, as almost everyone was one or the other.) "Wit and Wisdom were close to the soil. . . . In contrast with the United States, there was little imaginative conception of the future. But . . . men were striking their roots into deep soil and slow growth makes the hardest wood."[1]

While less complicated than Lower Canada because of its smaller scale, shorter history, and the absence of the ethnic frictions and the legacy of conquest, Upper Canada was a turbulent cauldron also. In the 1830 elections in Upper Canada, the Reformers were routed. William Lyon Mackenzie and Barnabas Bidwell held their districts, but many of their colleagues were defeated. The victory of the royalist conservatives in the 1830 election in Upper Canada left the ministry in the incapable and reactionary hands of Attorney General Henry Boulton and the solicitor general, Christopher Hagerman. The government was prepared to concede control of the purse to the Legislature and wanted only a minor concession to British usage, but Mackenzie worked this up to a usurpation of immense proportions, and he abused his parliamentary immunity from allegations of defamation with a torrent of the most sulphurous libels and slanders in the *Colonial Advocate* and in the Assembly. He fell, in Stephen Leacock's words, to "irresponsible vanity."[2] In this contest of extremists, Mackenzie, though his tactical judgment was no better than that of his opponents, was closer to the right and the future, and he was, in his slightly demented fashion, an authentic popular spokesman, as Louis-Joseph Papineau was among the French, though more eloquently, and with greater moderation (though moderation was not Papineau's strong suit either). The government picked a quarrel by accusing Mackenzie of a breach of privilege by publishing the journal of debates without appendices, an absurd complaint that failed, as did the subsequent claim of publishing libels. Mackenzie replied with a frenzied onslaught in the *Colonial Advocate* that included the denunciation of the Assembly as a "sycophantic office for registering the decrees of a mean and mercenary executive." The Assembly responded with the charge against Mackenzie of "gross, scandalous, and malicious libels," and it expelled him, describing him (with zoological confusion) as a "dog" and a "reptile," on December 12, 1830. In the resulting by-election, Mackenzie ran as a popular hero and martyr. The governing party did not present a candidate, and the Reform leader won a landslide and brushed aside efforts to prevent him taking his seat. His newspaper office was attacked again, and he was roughed up at a political meeting in Hamilton. Mackenzie determined to emulate Papineau, and in May 1832 embarked for England bearing petitions from supporters in the cause of what was known as responsible government (wherein the ministry was answerable to the democratically elected House). He was met by a blizzard of counter-protests, but the political tide in Britain was running in his favour, and although his own written submissions were not especially well-crafted, Mackenzie did have a successful interview with William Huskisson's replacement at the Colonial Office, Lord Goderich (who had had a brief tour as prime minister between Canning, who followed Liverpool, and Wellington). Goderich sent the Upper Canada government a message asserting that he would not be informing himself entirely on the basis of their account of these events. This was seen by the authorities in York (Toronto) as "an elegant piece of fiddle faddle."[3]

A really monstrous farce ensued, as Mackenzie was denied the right to sit by Boulton and Hagerman's outrageous conception that Mackenzie had forfeited that right, having twice been expelled, a finding for which there was no support in law or in fact. Mackenzie again won a by-election, unopposed, and was again denied his right to sit, and the new colonial secretary, Lord Stanley, sacked Boulton and Hagerman, though Hagerman pleaded so intensely to Stanley, he was allowed to remain. (Boulton was sent to Newfoundland and was so shaken by the rough-and-tumble of that unruly province that he returned to Upper Canada a convert to the virtues of responsible government.) Mackenzie was again expelled on an old claim of libel, and on the advice of the lieutenant-governor, Sir John Colborne, he went to the clerk of the Executive Council, who administered the oath, but even after all this, and having been sponsored by the governor and sworn under his auspices, the Assembly would not allow him to sit and ordered his arrest by the sergeant-at-arms. He was released after a very ferocious debate but was still denied his seat. Mackenzie was elected the first mayor of Toronto, as York was now renamed. New elections for the Legislative Assembly were held in October 1834, and Mackenzie did win, both personally and as head of the Reform movement. But he would have done better, and brought a stronger group of candidates in with him, if he had not published an inflammatory letter from his friend the English radical Joseph Hume. Mackenzie had himself appointed chairman of a select committee to inquire into the many neuralgic grievances of Mackenzie himself and his followers. The "Seventh Report on Grievances" was sent to the new colonial secretary (the job was a hot potato), Lord Glenelg, in the first government of liberal Tory Sir Robert Peel. The "Seventh Report" vented the now traditional concerns of Mackenzie and his cohort: patronage abuses, official compensation, the war between the churches, land grants, pensions, public accounts, and the long-drawn-out struggle over jurisdiction in revenue collection and spending.

It was at this time that Colborne inexplicably chose to carve fifty-seven Anglican rectories out of the Clergy Reserves and make this very large donation to the church striving to be recognized as established. Although Colborne had the right to do this, it was an insanely mistimed venture, and Colborne was abruptly sacked as lieutenant-governor of Upper Canada. Colborne (1778–1863) was another old soldier and bearer of an astonishingly varied career. He was a hero of the Battle of Corunna (1809), where Napoleon drove the British out of Spain and into the sea, and served with distinction in the Peninsular War and at Waterloo, where he led the attack that broke the Imperial Guard, the only time in history that such an event occurred. He was lieutenant-governor of Guernsey from 1821 to 1828, and of Upper Canada from 1828 to 1836. His promotion of public works and immigration schemes produced a 50 per cent increase in the province's population during his term, but his preferential treatment of recent British immigrants and his diversion of public lands to the Church of England and his favourites in the Family Compact not only led to his recall but seriously compromised the loyalty to the Crown of more people than should have been susceptible to Mackenzie's ravings. On his recall as governor, he was confirmed as commander of the armed forces in the Canadas, in which role, and briefly as governor general, he would play an important part in the events to come. He became a peer, a field marshal, and rounded out his remarkable career as lord high commissioner of the Ionian Islands from

1843 to 1849 and commander of the armed forces in Ireland from 1855 to 1860. With a more civilized and subtle opponent than Mackenzie, Colborne's imperious bigotry would have been even more damaging than it was, and Canada in the 1830s was not the place for a governor who, like Sir James Craig thirty years before, had spent all his adult life at war, generally with the kinsmen of the French Canadians. He is best remembered in Canada now as the founder of Upper Canada College, a well-known private school in Toronto modelled on Elizabeth College in Guernsey.* Showing again how erratic British colonial management could be, Colborne was replaced by the catastrophically ill-suited Sir Francis Bond Head.

In Lower Canada, the government offered the olive branch of surrendering its control of customs duties in 1831, but Papineau and his followers refused a permanent civil list and demanded the abolition of the appointed upper house. In the Montreal municipal elections of 1832, demonstrations and riots became so robust that three people were killed by the military garrison in the restoration of order, and Papineau and his followers in the press called the governor, Lord Aylmer, a murderer in consequence (though he did not leave Quebec during the disturbances). There would be times in the next few years when Papineau and his closest comrades seemed to be torn between a fear of being executed for treason and a desire to achieve that fate. In fact, British despotism was not so severe or inflexible as to justify going to such extremes, and most of the aggrieved acted accordingly, but many were tempted by the allure of mounting the scaffold before a large and sullenly sympathetic crowd and being dispatched by the executioner for the cause.

Stanley, the War and Colonial secretary, in 1833 (1799–1969, better known as the 14th Earl of Derby, three times prime minister, and, with Disraeli, the leader of the Conservatives between Peel and Salisbury, from 1846 to 1881), hinted darkly that it might be necessary to curtail the rights of some colonists, and Papineau, after two years

---

* It has been a well-respected school with many eminent people as old boys, but it carried some of the snobbery, severity, and philistinism of its founder forward more than 125 years to the time there of the author.

of pyrotechnics, produced with his collaborators the Ninety-Two Resolutions of February 21, 1834. This was a flammable forensic effort even by Papineau's standards, and he was a much more urbane and artful composer of such farragos than Mackenzie. Papineau attempted to follow the uplifting lead of Jefferson in his Declaration of 1776 and of the authors of the Declaration of the Rights of Man in France in 1789. The assembler and composer of the Ninety-Two Resolutions was Augustin-Norbert Morin, the province's ablest political writer. Papineau contributed the more vitriolic passages in this marathon of protest ("One recognizes here and there the lion's claws"[4]).

Papineau presented the Ninety-Two Resolutions to the Legislative Assembly on February 28, 1834. They were approved by the Assembly and sent to London. The principal demands were for an elected Legislative Council and an executive responsible to the Assembly, and Assembly control of money bills, both in the collection and application of revenue. This could have been formulated in tolerably grandilo-quent terms and effectively conformed to what progressive elements in Great Britain were seeking, and the new king (since 1830), William IV, was not particularly hostile. The petitioners stated their loyalty to the British Crown but expressed anger and frustration at the failure of most of the governors sent to Canada to confer these rightful benefits of British political citizenship. Unfortunately, just as Papineau wobbled between rebellion and agitation for reform, he could not resist impos-ing threats and almost seditious utterances upon his naturally more temperate amanuensis, Morin. As Canada had already experienced, it was in these matters in a grey zone between the precedents offered by the British and the Americans. The British were moving too slowly and absent-mindedly not to lose some Imperial support in the Canadas, but English and French Canadians had to immerse themselves in delusion to imagine that they had either the depth of grievance that drove the Americans to revolt or the slightest prospect of emerging from a revolt with a viable sovereign country: either the British would crush them or the Americans would swallow them whole, or both in succession and by arrangement between the Anglo-Americans, after Washington had calmed the slave states with parallel adventures in Cuba or elsewhere in Latin America. (There would be intermittent agitation in the United States for the balance of the century to seize Cuba, Mexico, and Central

America, both before and after the resolution of the slavery crisis.)

It would unnecessarily tax the patience of readers to recite all the Ninety-Two Resolutions, but these excerpts faithfully convey the flavour of them.

> It was [Aylmer, the governor] who refused to shut down [an epidemic of Asiatic cholera in 1832] by closing the gate of the St. Lawrence; he it was who enticed the sick immigrants into the country, in order to decimate the ranks of the French Canadians.

This surpassed even Jefferson's distribe against George III as a blood-stained tyrant and his blood libel on the American Indian. Papineau and Morin (the young and promising Louis-Hippolyte LaFontaine had a small hand in it also), continued:

> We are in no wise disposed to admit the excellence of the present Constitution of Canada. . . . Your Majesty cannot fail to observe that the political world in Europe is at this moment agitated by two great parties, who in different countries appear under the several names of Serviles, Royalists, Tories, and Conservatives, on the one side, and of Liberals, Constitutionalists, Republicans, Whigs, Reformers, Radicals, and similar appellations on the other; that the former is, on the American Continent without any weight or influence except what it derives from its European supporters, and from a trifling number of persons who become their dependents for the sake of personal gain, and of others who from age or habit cling to opinions which are not partaken by any numerous class, while the second party overspreads all America. . . . Your Majesty's Secretary of State is mistaken if he believes that the exclusion of a few salaried officers would suffice to make that body harmonize with the wants, wishes, and opinions of the People, as long as the Colonial Governors retain the power of preserving in it a majority of Members rendered servile by their antipathy to every liberal idea.

It was inexorable:

> In less than twenty years the population of the United
> States of America will be greater than that of Great
> Britain, and that of British America will be greater than
> that of the former English colonies, when the latter
> deemed that the time was come to decide that the in-
> appreciable advantage of being self-governed, ought to
> engage them to repudiate a system of Colonial govern-
> ment which was, generally speaking, much better than
> that of British America now is.

After renouncing any threat, Papineau concluded this Resolution:
"Your Majesty's faithful Canadian subjects are not sufficiently protected
in their lives, their property, and their honour."

Even allowing for the florid standards of public documents of the
time, and even more among French- than English-speakers, it was little wonder that this interminable, prolix, and pompous torrent of
hints and incitements of revolution and miscellaneous insults was
ignored by its addressee and his secretaries of state. Indeed, it is a
credit to the indulgence of the British government, Crown, ministers,
and Parliament, that it elicited no acknowledgement at all until Lord
Russell dismissed it, rather impetuously, in his own Ten Resolutions
three years later. (Russell, then the home secretary, mockingly adopted
the formula of resolutions that authorized the Canadian colonial governments to spend money on reasonable ends without any approval of
the Legislature. This was unnecessarily provocative, and no colonial
initiative should have come from the Home Office, but by this time the
British had mismanaged the whole matter out of control, thus finally
creating the opportunity for real progress.)

Papineau's problem was that he was not only ambivalent about
whether he wanted a negotiated and civilized resolution of problems or
a violent uprising, although he must have known that the consequences
of armed revolt could be hazardous to his physical longevity, either in
action or by subsequent prosecution. He further grossly exaggerated
the importance of the issues, as Mackenzie did. Of course, it was
becoming obsolete and discordant to the times in the English-speaking

countries and some others for somewhat broadly elected representatives not to control the finances of the state, at least by oversight, and to require governments to be answerable to them. But it wasn't an impingement on freedom of speech or legal due process, or relevant to generally rising levels of prosperity, at least in the Canadas. It was a cause that could bring out demonstrators in temperate months in appreciable numbers, but no sane people were really prepared to die for something just to accelerate the timetable of what seemed likely to happen anyway.

The 1834 elections in Lower Canada were "attended with riots and tumultuous gatherings [and] Revolutionary committees." (French-Canadian politicians have long been among the world champions in instant recourse to polemical hyperbole.) Votes of supply (funding the government) had failed from 1832 to 1835, and Colborne paid his government's bills only by borrowing from the war chest. Both of the Canadas were now descending steeply down the slope to civil strife. All they wanted was reform as was occurring in what Canadians could ambitiously call peer jurisdictions, to be granted by a country that was on the verge of a clear victory for liberal reform, and the agitators in the Canadas, in their frustration, had bridged the cultural gap, and the Mackenzie-Papineau factions were in comradely touch with each other, as were some of the less radical and promising members of both political communities.[5]

But Papineau committed the cardinal error of easing up to annexation. He completely overlooked the hypocrisies and enfeeblements of American republicanism, and like a credulous yokel (an attitude that would often afflict future French-Canadian nationalists) he was dazzled by America and drank the chalice of its mythos to the lees. "The period makes it easy to understand where Charles Dickens got the nonsense he put into the American chapters of *Martin Chuzzlewit*."[6] America was a great and rising force that compelled the world's attention, but it was a slaveholding country headed toward civil war, and as a policy assimilated culturally all arrivals who spoke any language except English. The United States was just twenty years from an election in which a party headed by Millard Fillmore, a former president, would take 22 per cent of the vote on a platform that would have effectively stopped immigration, banned Roman Catholics from public office, and required any newcomer to the country to wait twenty-one years before becoming a citizen.

Papineau saw what he wanted to see, in Canada and elsewhere, and did not have a reliable compass of tactical judgment to see him through the storms that he was trying to intensify. Mackenzie was no better, but he did not possess the culture of Papineau, nor the responsibility of leading so distinctive and particular a people as the French Canadians. Papineau had passed through the Legislature a bill providing for popular participation in the selection of Roman Catholic Church wardens and in the review of parish accounts, and the clergy deserted him, almost en bloc. French-Canadian Catholicism was patriotic but authoritarian. And, in coming to the edge of armed revolt and annexationism, Papineau was bringing down on himself the Church's implacable disapproval. The Church had never ceased to advance the French-Canadian interest, through the bishop of Quebec in the Executive Council and by providing practically all the social services the people of Quebec would have for over 250 years after Champlain raised the flag of France in the New World. Papineau was rushing into a personal cul-de-sac, yet could be an unwitting agent for precisely the moderate change that he had innocently begun by espousing. Mackenzie, in comparison, was a hothead; he had his uses but not the grandeur to bring down on himself as a public leader a personal tragedy in the manner of Papineau.

Fortunately, more moderate and serviceable Reform leaders were starting to appear in both Canadas. Robert Baldwin, the son of an immigrant from Ulster, who became both a lawyer and a doctor, having started professional life as a schoolteacher, was born in York on May 12, 1804. He was taught by Archdeacon John Strachan at the latter's Home District Grammar School. (This was succeeded by Colborne's Upper Canada College as the city's leading boys' school, and the leading girls' school, named after Bishop Strachan, was eventually set up just two blocks west of Upper Canada College.) Baldwin's father, William Warren, had prospered, and his commodious house Spadina stood on the street of that name, on heights overlooking the town. (The preserved nineteenth-century house there now was substantially rebuilt on the Baldwin House.) Robert Baldwin was elected to the Upper Canada Legislature with the assistance of Mackenzie and the Reformers in 1829 and took the place vacated by John Beverley Robinson, the august head of the Family Compact, when he retired as attorney general to become chief justice of the Court of King's Bench. Baldwin's almost entire preoccupation was the attainment of responsible government. As a child, he had witnessed the American destruction of York, and while not anti-American, he was in favour of the British association, as long as Canada progressed as quickly as practical toward self-government, and his vision came to include close cooperation with democratic and culturally tolerant elements in Quebec.

As the political climate thickened through the 1830s, Baldwin's closest ally in the pursuit of responsible government was Francis Hincks, a southern Irish Protestant born in 1807, who came to Canada in 1830 after visiting Barbados and being persuaded by a visiting Montrealer of the merits of Canada. He travelled on from Montreal to York "by stage and schooner," a voyage of ten days.[7] After returning to Belfast to marry, Hincks came back to York and was one of the founders in 1832 of the Farmers' Joint Stock Banking Company, but soon left it because of the involvement in it of the Family Compact, and was one of the founders of the Bank of the People. He became a close friend of Baldwin while a tenant of the elder Baldwin, and he became active in Reform politics while branching into the Mutual Assurance Company and setting up a warehousing business adjacent to his bank. He was appointed an official examiner of the Welland Canal in 1833 after budgetary overruns.

Baldwin and Hincks and others were pursuing reform by moderate means, keeping civilized relations with the Tory royalists and Mackenzie and his followers, when one of the British Colonial Office's more seriously infelicitous appointees, Francis Bond Head – a retired major and South American mine manager whose only public sector administrative experience had been as an assistant Poor Law commissioner – to his own "utter astonishment"[8] took up his post as the lieutenant-governor of Upper Canada in January 1836. Even those who sent him told Head to conciliate the malcontents, and Joseph Hume assured Mackenzie that the new governor would be a reformer.[9] Head took an immediate dislike to Mackenzie, whom he considered a "raving . . . madman"[10] (an ungenerous but understandable impression), but offered positions on the Executive Council to Robert Baldwin, who impressed him, to Mackenzie's ally Dr. John Rolph, and to the former receiver general

John Henry Dunn. The Reformers at first declined, but then accepted. But when Head made it clear that he would not accept or compromise with what he called "the smooth-faced, insidious doctrine" of responsible government,[11] the entire Executive Council resigned (even though Baldwin had made it clear that he did not share Papineau's enthusiasm for an elected Legislative Council, only an Executive Council answerable and responsible to the Legislative Assembly). This was an inauspicious start to the term of someone who described himself as a "political physician"[12] coming to heal the wounds of the province by his own skill.

Two days after the resignation of the Executive Council, the Assembly overwhelmingly approved a motion calling for a responsible Executive Council and expressing no confidence in Head's replacement of those who had resigned. Head publicly denounced the Reformers, including those whom he had just invested, as "disloyal Republicans who were bent on encouraging a foreign invasion"[13] – that is, annexationists – which was untrue and unfounded. The Assembly voted the cessation of all funding for the government, and Head dissolved the House. Head plunged into the election campaign that followed, advising the secretary of war and colonies, Lord Glenelg (1778–1866), secretary from 1835 to 1839, that he was fighting "low-bred, antagonist democracy." As Baldwin sailed to Britain to lobby the British government, Head wrote Glenelg that Baldwin was a revolutionary agent. As often happens, the forces of reaction were initially successful at spooking moderate opinion. The Methodists were afraid of being tarred with the brush of extremism, and kept their distance from the Reformers, while the Anglican establishment went all out for the governor's supporters, with an eye on the Clergy Reserves. Glenelg, having heard from Head, refused even to see Baldwin, and on July 13, 1836, Baldwin wrote Glenelg a seminal letter that ranks as one of the great state papers in Canadian history. Baldwin unhistrionically outlined the condition of the province and wrote that the only, but full and sufficient, remedy was responsible government over all the internal affairs of the province.

In Baldwin's absence, the Reform movement organized the Constitutional Reform Society of Upper Canada with Baldwin's father, Dr. William Baldwin, as its chief, Francis Hincks as its secretary, and a program of responsible government and the abolition of the Anglican rectories accorded by Colborne. (Colborne had been sacked, though retained as military commander, but his creation of the Anglican rectories with the Clergy Reserves had not been repealed.) Head and his partisans engaged in wholesale electoral "intimidation, violence, and fraud,"[14] exploited the disposition of most people in a British colony to respond when the governor warns of revolution, republicanism and mayhem, and won the election. He was unable to form a government that commanded the respect of the province or to get anything useful through the Assembly, and it became clear to those who had sent him that he was a bad choice. The Methodists defected from the governor, as he did nothing about Colborne's favouritism to the Anglicans in the disposal of the Clergy Reserves, and Lord Russell's belated Ten Resolutions (mad, and surprising from a distinguished liberal statesman and later a successful prime minister) discouraged and alienated the moderate Reformers, (though they showed admirable economy of words and rhetoric as a response to Papineau's ninety-two turgid declamations). Russell proposed that the appointive Legislative Council represent all interests and that some members of the Assembly be included in the Executive Council, and that provincial patronage be more generally distributed.

By this time, matters had reached the verge of combat in Lower Canada, and Head, in his mad overconfidence, sent all the regular troops in Toronto to Kingston to be able to intervene on Colborne's orders against Papineau's now apprehended uprising. Once Papineau understood that all he could expect was scornful silence from London, he raised the temperature again, with a session in the Assembly, on February 23 and 24, 1835, that rivalled the most wildly extreme tirades of the National Convention and National Assembly in France in 1792 to 1794. As Alfred De Celles remarked – though, unlike in the earlier debates in Paris, the lives of the speakers were not at stake – "The tragic side [of speakers being guillotined if they did not prevail among their colleagues] is lacking in the case of the [Lower Canada] Assembly, but in the perspective of the future, we have a glimpse of the executions of 1838."[15] Papineau completely shed the required impartiality of the Speaker of the House and accused Lord Aylmer (a rather inoffensive, if also ineffective, lieutenant-governor) of "slaughter" of the three people killed following the Montreal municipal election. Almost the only member of the Assembly who contradicted Papineau was Colonel Conrad Augustus Gugy, a bilingual Tory and a fearless, if somewhat unsubtle, man, who yet, speaking in his second language opposite a consummate orator, exasperated Papineau and drove the Speaker to even more stratospheric extremes than were already his custom. Gugy said, "After all is said and done, the whole thing is a mere hunt for offices, which positions are claimed without any attempt to inquire whether there are to be found a sufficient number of educated Canadians to fill them," and likened Papineau to Danton and Robespierre.[16] Aylmer rebuked the Assembly, and Papineau had his remarks expunged from the record and uttered a diatribe of his own. It was all getting beyond words; there was no legislation nor any point to the unceasing torrent of incivilities. Conditions were aggravated by a poor crop and depressed commerce.

The Colonial Office, acting late, recalled Aylmer and replaced him with the conciliatory Lord Gosford (1776–1849), as both governor general and lieutenant-governor of Lower Canada, and as high commissioner (with Sir Charles Grey and Sir George Gipps) to inquire into the state of Lower Canada and recommend constructive solutions. Gosford conducted himself with exquisite and much appreciated tact and convened the provincial Parliament in October 1835 by prophetically touching on the pre-nascent raison d'être of the Canada of the future as "sprung from the two leading nations of the world." Gosford was making some headway, and was very attentive and affable, but was suspected of tokenism. But in early 1836, perceptions were soured by the publication, in London, of his instructions to make no concessions on anything apart from the British American Land Company, which had seized a million acres of non-arable land for the benefit of doubtful friends of the regime deserving of patronage for reasons having nothing to do with the public interest.

The prevarications of the British government were legitimately irritating to all Canadians. The Irish Nationalist leader, Daniel O'Connell, said, "If this is what you mean by justice, Canada will soon have no reason to be jealous of Ireland. . . . With a population three-fourths French Canadian, only one-fourth of the public offices is awarded to that element." He also decried the presence of judges and other public officials on the Legislative Council.[17] Gosford convened

Lower Canada's Parliament in October 1836 and said that the revelation of his instructions had been incomplete, that he had a broader and more constructive mission than just stonewalling calls for reform, and that his sole reason for bringing the legislators together was to vote supply (fund the government). Papineau declined to be moved, though in polite terms, and Gosford ended the session. At this point, Papineau undoubtedly represented most French Canadians, most of the Catholic Irish, and even some under-enfranchised English-speaking residents of the Eastern Townships.

In Upper Canada, Francis Bond Head had grossly exceeded his office, been flagrantly partisan, led the achievement of an unjust election result, had delivered nothing to those he had cajoled, dragooned, or bribed with promises of official preferment for their support, and presided through a government that had little popular approval, over a discontented population, but one that had no thoughts of revolt against a constitutional British monarch. In Lower Canada, there was equivalent discontent, aggravated by offended ethnic sensibilities, but Papineau was on an express, self-issued, one-way ticket to oblivion. He was on the verge of taking up arms against the British Army, still led by the racist snob but fierce general and Waterloo veteran Colborne; the Roman Catholic Church, to which almost all French Canadians owed and proffered unswerving ultramontanist obedience; the English interests that dominated the commerce of Lower Canada; and the ragged but deep ranks of sensible, tenacious, French-Canadian petits bourgeois and farmers, who didn't particularly care how Parliament was organized as long as their uncomplicated lives were not disturbed by state intrusion or over-burdensome taxation, and they had no complaints with the British government in those respects.

The insolence of the British government in ignoring petitions, even Papineau's abrasive screed; and in refusing to consider what they had, by 1837, effectively conceded to the British of the home islands; and which the Americans had taken by force more than fifty years before; and in sending to Canada more authoritarian military officers of no political aptitude rather than agents of constructive collaboration was annoying, but it reflected the inability of the British government to take Canada seriously. They were only there at all because the Americans had complained so noisily about France being in Quebec. That caused them to

develop Halifax, begin the Maritime colonies, and evict the French.
They had not given much thought to what to do with any of it when the
Americans seized their independence, deluging Upper Canada with
Loyalists to whom the British felt a commendable duty of help and protection. Between them all, they had resisted President Madison's assault
in 1812, a law-giver's blundering simulation of a conqueror. And now,
the Americans, for reasons of their own internal divisions and British
power, were not a threat. The Canadians had nowhere to go and no
ability to do much except complain, and dire threats of rebellion, and
even, from the rabble-rousing French demagogue Papineau, to join the
Americans, who were not interested, did not resonate in Whitehall or
Westminster. Russell's further curtailment of the powers of democratic
government, because of the Assembly's refusal to fund the government,
was so galling, it could, eventually, have raised annexationist sentiment
in Upper Canada, to which the Americans would respond.

Canadian frustration was understandable and justified; so was
British skepticism, but not British obstinacy and misplaced authoritarianism. As with the War of 1812, which Canada needed – to pull itself
together, engender some collective pride and pan-Canadian interest, as
long as Canada was not overrun – so an uprising was now needed. It
would not and should not succeed, but it was necessary to establish
Canada's credentials as something more than a place of passive colonists subsisting on the American border, and to send London a message
that Empire could not indefinitely be imposed as imperious arrogance
alone, with no synchronization with the political rights of the people of
Great Britain. Once again, luck was with the gestating Canadian project, and once again, after so much foreboding and concern, the reality
of rebellion was trivial, but adequate for the larger purpose of raising a
national consciousness where there had been little of one, and in getting the more effective attention of the colonial power.

Papineau responded to Russell on May 14, 1837, at Saint-Laurent:
"The people should not and will not submit to them [Russell's reactionary resolutions]. The people must transmit their just rights to their
posterity even though it cost them their property and their lives to do
so." Not 1 per cent of Québécois would act on such a call, or risk anything to attain Papineau's objectives, but it was enough to rouse the
1 per cent who would. The distinguished journalist Étienne Parent

deserted Papineau and counselled moderation. Monsignor Lartigue, bishop of Montreal, urged caution in circulated notices read in all churches, in July and again in October, as did the bishops of Quebec and Trois-Rivières. At Saint-Charles, in October, a public meeting endorsed a boycott of British goods (as insane an enterprise as Jefferson's and Madison's efforts in the same direction earlier in the century, as Quebec had a trade surplus with Britain, but Papineau had no commercial aptitudes at all, Quebec's commerce was largely in the hands of the English Quebeckers, and his call to boycott was ignored by almost everyone). There was now frequent street combat between the Doric Club (loyalist and moderate, though seekers of reform) and the Fils de la Liberté, modelled on Samuel Adams's Sons of Liberty, who had perpetrated the Boston Tea Party sixty-four years before.

Like many long-apprehended events, the revolts, when they came, were an absurd anticlimax, despite 175 years of unstinting effort since to recreate them as high drama and patriotic heroism. Papineau and his fellow Patriote, Dr. Edmund Bailey O'Callaghan (1797–1880), leader of the Irish malcontents and editor of the *Vindicator,* on the advice of a priest who told Papineau his continued presence in Montreal was "a cause of disorder,"[18] departed to Saint-Hyacinthe. This was reported to the authorities, who were aware that Papineau and Mackenzie had been setting up secret groups around both colonies, Papineau borrowing some of the terminology of the French Revolution, and Mackenzie from Jefferson's correspondence committees and the American militiamen. Papineau and O'Callaghan striking out for the Maskoutain country was too much for Sir John Colborne, still smarting from having been fired as civil governor for his bigoted high-handedness, and he effectively took charge as commander of the armed forces of Canada, such as they were, and issued warrants for the arrest of the two wayfarers and several of their more prominent collaborators. A company of the Montreal Volunteer Cavalry was conducting two arrested Patriotes, Dr. Joseph-François Davignon (1807–1867) and Pierre-Paul Démaray (1798–1854), a notary, back from Chambly to Longueuil when they were overwhelmed by a detachment of the Fils de la Liberté led by Bonaventure Viger (1804–1877). Wolfred Nelson (1791–1863) and Thomas Storrow Brown (1803–1888), the co-generals of the Patriotes, gathered several hundred Patriotes at Saint-Denis and Saint-Charles to begin resistance. Civil order was becoming tenuous in various parts of the province, but the execution of arrest warrants was the first sign of a response from the British and Canadian authorities, and, once roused, Colborne showed a commendable aptitude for the reimposition of order. Colonel Charles Gore, another Waterloo veteran, was instructed by Colborne to arrest the leaders of the rebellion and disperse the malcontents. He was to proceed to Sorel and then along the bank of the Richelieu River to Saint-Denis with five companies and a howitzer. Saint-Denis would be approached from the opposite direction via Saint-Charles by six infantry companies with a couple of field pieces led by Colonel (later General) George Augustus Wetherall (1788–1868), another well-travelled colonial officer (who had served in Africa and India). The soldiers floundered through mud and torrential rain that turned to heavy snow, and Gore was forced to withdraw from Saint-Denis. The Patriotes signalled one another with church bells and did a creditable job of blowing up bridges on the British route of march, though the British officers were familiar with this kind of harassment and made their way fairly well, given the weather and terrain. The British only withdrew a few hundred yards, but had to spike their howitzer after it became mired in the mud. Weatherall's force fared better, and he arrived at Saint-Charles on November 25, shelled the palisade there that sheltered the approximately 110 Patriotes, and then assaulted the position. The Patriotes fought respectably for an improvised force but were put to flight by the British and Canadian regulars. "General" Storrow Brown, accused of deserting his men before the action began, claimed, fourteen years later, that he had gone forward to reconnoitre, was forced to retreat with his men, whom he tried unsuccessfully to control, but, "finding after a long trial, my strength and authority insufficient, I considered my command gone, turned my horse and rode" to Saint-Denis.[19] The truth was never established, but was unheroic and is not entirely material. Gore arrived at Saint-Denis on December 1, where his men found the mangled corpse of one of their comrades, murdered by the Patriotes, and defied Gore's orders for professional discipline and torched the town.

The scene of action moved to Saint-Eustache. Here, Amury Girod (1800–1837), another Swiss adventurer and veteran of wars in Mexico, and, according to Alfred De Celles, a self-styled general, "headed a band of excited and misguided peasants."[20] On the approach of Colborne himself, with artillery and cavalry, Girod fled and committed suicide. Colborne encountered the Patriotes holed up in the local church, set fire to the house beside the church to cover their investiture of it, and the Patriotes fired down form the choir. But when Colborne's men fired the church as well, they fled out of it and surrendered. Colborne ordered that the Patriotes be treated honourably as prisoners of war, but some of his militiamen, still outraged at the apparent murder of one of their comrades at Saint-Denis, massacred a number of the rebels who had thrown down their arms. On December 5, the governor general, Lord Gosford, proclaimed martial law in Montreal and declared a reward for the capture of Papineau and a few of the other Patriotes. Papineau made good his escape to the United States. Colborne had the pleasure of a final mopping-up operation at Lacolle and Odelltown, and Wolfred Nelson, who had retired to and sallied forth from Vermont, in De Celles's words, "returned to Vermont after the collapse of his unfortunate invasion, covered with the ridicule he had richly earned by his proclamation of a Canadian Republic and his own election as president, and loaded with the awful responsibility of having caused the loss of many lives, besides helping to hurry to the scaffold or into exile men who had been duped by his fallacious representations."[21]

Colborne, still aroused by the outrage, as he considered it to be, of his dismissal from the gubernatorial chair of Upper Canada, and by the impudence of the ungrateful papist French rebels, marched about the countryside for some days burning down villages on slender pretexts and rounding up insurgents, of whom ninety-nine of the hundreds that were detained in Montreal were court-martialled and sentenced to death. Of these, only twelve were executed and the remainder transported to Australia. This was severe enough, but Colborne was denigrated as a virtual pantywaist and weakling by some of the outraged Montreal English merchant class. The *Montreal Herald* called for the summary execution of all the prisoners: "Why winter them over, why fatten them for the gibbet?" It was a revolt which in some ways presaged and prefigured the comedies of Gilbert and Sullivan (though there were certainly dark moments and the execution of a dozen men, and in those days the transportation of scores of others were not a risible consummation). None of this hyperbole, on one side or the other, prevented Nelson from returning from exile and becoming mayor of Montreal. Nor did any of it prevent Bonaventure Viger – after being exiled to Bermuda, returning, being imprisoned and escaping, and being pardoned – from becoming the proprietor of Montreal's leading cheese shop; nor Storrow Brown, one of Quebec's first Unitarians, after a stint in exile as a journalist in Florida, from returning to Quebec and entering the hardware business, in which he had previously gone bankrupt in one of the many personal dramas that led to his alienation from the colonial regime. Edmund O'Callaghan remained in New York and was for many years the state secretary and archivist. He served in this capacity through the latter stages of the Albany Regency (founded by eventual president Martin Van Buren, 1782–1862, and secretary of state William L. Marcy, 1786–1857) and through the succeeding ascendance of Lincoln's early rival and secretary of state, William H. Seward, and New York governors and unsuccessful presidential candidates Horatio Seymour and Samuel Tilden. It was a well-deserved rout for Papineau and his coterie of scoundrels, gullible camp-followers, and misfits, and an unjust triumph for the racist swaggerer Colborne, but the consequences, as usual in the developing annals of Canadian fortune, were benign.

French Canada was not to endure unaccompanied the humiliation of its rebels. William Lyon Mackenzie, not to be denied his moment of demonstrative futility, and undeterred by the shambles in Lower Canada, strove fearlessly, not to say mindlessly, on into the thickets of revolt. Mackenzie realized that Head's overconfident movement of the forces in Upper Canada to Kingston left Toronto unguarded by the regime, and he received a comradely message from Papineau inviting him to join the Patriotes in revolt. (The fact that Papineau was now an annexationist wasn't mentioned, and to the extent that there was any real solidarity between the malcontents in the two provinces, it was minimal.) Mackenzie met with his senior collaborators, and it was agreed to issue a call for supporters, stopping just short of a call to arms, and a summons to Toronto, where it was hoped that the arms of the absent forces and militia could be seized and used by the rebels. There was doubt and hesitation, and Mackenzie set out on a tour of inspection of his partisans. He returned to Toronto in a very purposeful condition after about ten days and scheduled an uprising in Toronto for December 7, although the kindred uprising in Quebec was already in serious difficulty. Mackenzie decreed the start, then departed to coordinate again in the rural districts, and the generalissimo of the rebels, one Anthony Van Egmond (1778–1838), who claimed to have been a Dutch officer in Napoleon's forces, was ordered by Mackenzie's skittish colleague Dr. Rolph to bring the date of the rebellion forward to December 4. The rebel forces gathered at Montgomery's Tavern, three miles north of Toronto, and awaited the accumulation of numbers adequate to a serious assault on the government.

Toronto was in an alarmed state, but sixty men led by Colonel Allan MacNab arrived from Hamilton, followed by more reinforcements, and the volunteer militia formed up and marched north on December 7, in quite passable field formation, with drums beating and a couple of field pieces and chased the rebels out of Montgomery's Tavern and scattered them in all directions. This was the end of it. Governor Head had asked to see Baldwin, who, like Hincks, had had nothing to do with the rebellion, and Rolph, who had. Baldwin and Rolph carried a message to Mackenzie, now back at Montgomery's Tavern, and were informed that if the governor wished to deal with Mackenzie he would have to do it in writing. Baldwin dutifully carried Mackenzie's message back to Head and then returned to Mackenzie to tell him that the governor refused. Mackenzie fled to the United States and for a time occupied Navy Island in the Niagara River and organized several unsuccessful expeditions into Canada. Commodore Andrew Drew and Colonel MacNab cut loose Mackenzie's supply ship, the *Caroline*, and towed her away and burned her, and the British government successfully urged the government of the United States to desist from tolerating the aggressive supply of Mackenzie' fugitives and sympathizers.

Mackenzie returned to Canada on an amnesty Baldwin and LaFontaine promulgated in 1849, but found that he no longer commanded any support, and died, grumpily as he had lived, in 1861, aged sixty-six. Rolph returned in 1843, founded a medical school, and became a member of the Legislature and commissioner of Crown lands and died in 1870, aged seventy-three. Papineau was sheltered by friends along the route he furtively followed toward the U.S. border, which he crossed on November 25, 1837, going on to France, where he failed to rouse much support for his cause and published a rather bowdlerized version of the insurrection. He returned to Canada and to his splendid seigneurial house at Montebello in 1845, where he lived on, a subject of quaint and generally respectful curiosity, until his death in 1871, two weeks short of his eighty-fifth birthday.

Louis-Hippolyte LaFontaine had been close to Papineau but had always eschewed violence and rebellion; LaFontaine had importuned the governor, Lord Gosford, to call the Legislature when violence impended, and on his refusal had embarked for England, moved on to France, and returned to Canada in May 1838. He was briefly arrested in November 1838 as the rampaging Colborne lay about him in a nirvana of suspended habeas corpus and filled the places of confinement in Lower Canada with anyone he took against, but was released after a few weeks without any charges having been laid.

It had been a perfect episode for the Canadian idea, as the War of 1812 had been a perfect war. The revolutionaries had alarmed and got the attention of the colonial power, but their failure and the performance of Baldwin, Hincks, and LaFontaine, and the population as a whole, had impressed the British that they were appreciated and had reasonable moderates to work with.

The United States was relatively immobilized and couldn't exploit conditions. It had surmounted the Nullification Crisis (as described in Chapter 2), but there continued a delicate balance between the slave and free states, and the country wanted no part of a quarrel with the mighty British Empire, especially over Canada, which, French and English, had spurned American blandishments and successfully resisted its military advances at every opportunity from 1774 on. When the dust settled, the British recognized that reform was necessary. They were inexplicably, excruciatingly, slow, as in Ireland (where the Great Famine was just beginning, which would starve to death or force out half the population), and as they had been in America, India, and later Africa and the Middle East, and even in Britain itself. But at their own stately tempo, the British began to be more confident that Canada was viable, worthy of effort, and a doughty offspring. And Canada, in its manner, soon celebrated its rebels, while reaping the benefit of the placatory policy they induced, after the brief interregnum of overreaction. Papineau and Mackenzie had begun the process of Anglo-French political cooperation in Canada, had accelerated the stalled march to responsible government, and have become modest heroes in the thin canon of Canadian revolt. The Canadian pattern of inexorable progress along a path of rarely perturbed moderation, almost noiseless and always tortuous, and always navigating between and well within extremes, was steadily emerging.

2. The Beginning of Canadian Unity and Democracy, 1839–1846

The failed rebellions and the effective official response eventually produced the logical and almost inexorable compromise: the elevation in the eyes of the disconcerted population, and legitimacy in the eyes of the colonial authorities, of those who had called for reform but had eschewed violence. Both sides stepped back, and the hour of Robert Baldwin, Louis-Hippolyte LaFontaine, and Francis Hincks impended. But there was an elaborate and often exasperating ritual still to come as the British political class sorted out its Imperial policy.

The phrase "responsible government" arose from a letter written by Dr. William W. Baldwin, Robert Baldwin's father, to the prime minister, the Duke of Wellington, in 1828 in which Baldwin urged "a provincial ministry . . . responsible to the provincial Parliament, and removable from office by His Majesty's representatives at his pleasure and especially when they lose the confidence of the people as expressed by the voice of their representatives in the Assembly; and that all acts of the King's representative should have the character of local responsibility."[22] This was not only an English-Canadian ambition. In 1833, Étienne Parent (1802–1874), editor of Le Canadien, spoke of "the formation of a provincial ministry on the model of the imperial ministry which might give unity, coherence, consistency and finish to our legislation."[23] The middle way that would be the key to the identity and survival and development of Canada was emerging: subordinate in international matters to Britain to retain its protection and avoid the assimilation of the French and annexation of all Canada to the United States; and democratic parliamentary government in all local affairs to assure, other than in national sovereignty for the practical reasons mentioned, Canadians civil rights equivalent to those enjoyed by the citizens of Great Britain and the United States. (France, lurching syncopatedly from regime to regime, was no longer a presentable constitutional model for emulation, and would not be until the founding of the Fifth Republic 120 years later.) The practical problem was the reflex in official British circles that cabinet government responsible to an elected parliament would immediately bring sovereignty, as governmental authority was assumed to be indivisible, a nonsensical view in fact, and doubly so because Canadian self-interest required the British connection to protect the country from the Americans, who by this time were trying to distract themselves from the fissure of slavery by waving about the intermittently bloody shirt of "manifest destiny"* (that is, the ordained mission of America to rule the whole continent).

The Maritime colonies navigated toward responsible government less convulsively than did the Canadas. The cause in Nova Scotia was led by Joseph Howe (1804–1873), editor of the *Novascotian* from 1827 and member of the Legislature from 1836. He secured his acquittal on a charge of seditious libel in 1835 with a six-hour address to the jury substantiating his claims of official corruption in a landmark case in the history of the legal protection of a free press. He was a passionate Nova Scotian and Briton, and the cause of responsible government in his hands in that province could never be mistaken for republicanism. The Newfoundland House of Assembly asked for a responsible system in 1838, though it did not immediately achieve it, and in New Brunswick the concept became identified with control of Crown land and the attribution of timber rights, and the appetite for democracy was temporarily sated by the removal of Thomas Baillie in 1837.

In London, the well-travelled cynic Prime Minister Melbourne (1835–1841, following Peel's first ministry) and Glenelg concluded that reform was necessary and justified; Gosford and Colborne were recalled and Head's resignation tendered and accepted before he could be uprooted, and a very substantial politician, John George Lambton, Earl of Durham (1792–1840), was appointed with practically unlimited powers to recommend a resolution of Canadian difficulties. Durham was immensely

---

* The phrase was coined by John O'Sullivan (1813–1895) in the *Democratic Review* but was made famous by the *New York Morning News* on December 27, 1845.

wealthy, from inherited coal-mining interests, very liberal (he was widely known as "Radical Jack"), and very influential, as the son-in-law of former prime minister Earl Grey, whom he had served as lord privy seal, in which capacity he had helped write the seminal First Reform Act of 1832. He served Melbourne in the important office of ambassador to Russia (then the world's second greatest power after Great Britain) from 1835 to 1837, and his nomination to Canada showed the success of the Canadian rebels in getting the attention of the British and their preparedness to be more flexible. But if the rebellions had had their farcical aspects, the Imperial response would not be entirely above that either.

Durham arrived in May 1838, lordly and distinguished, neither military spit and polish nor bush-league colonial routine, a viceroy of energy, style, and a liberal mind. He was high commissioner and governor-in-chief of the Canadas, as well as lieutenant-governor of Lower Canada. He reigned with greater grandeur and ceremony even than Frontenac nearly 150 years before, and through the British minister in Washington, Durham entered into direct discussions with the government of the United States. Durham visited the United States at Lewiston, near Niagara Falls, where he was well-received by a miscellaneous group of locals and vacationers. Durham dismissed the existing Executive Council and replaced it largely with members of his own entourage, which included the controversial Sir Thomas Turton (1790–1854) and the even more tempestuous Edward Gibbon Wakefield (1796–1862). Wakefield had been a maximum-security messenger between kings, prime ministers, and military commanders during and just after the later Napoleonic Wars and a prominent supporter of colonization schemes in South Australia and New Zealand. He had spent three years in Newgate Prison for abducting an underage daughter of a wealthy man from her boarding school, and had been suspected of, though not charged with, perjury and forgery in the alleged alteration of his father-in-law's will. Because of his checkered past, his appointment was informal, but gave explosive ammunition to the government's opponents.

Durham, in his excessive self-assurance, dealt with dispatch with the leftovers of the rebellion but went beyond his jurisdiction and ignited partisan rivalry in the British Parliament. It was impossible to try the French-Canadian accused, because no jury in Lower Canada, nor probably any judge either, would convict, so he wrung confessions from nine of the prominent rebels, banished them to Bermuda, and pardoned everyone else. He declared Papineau and several of his co-rebels to be exiles for life, subject to execution if they returned. He had no authority to do anything of the kind, nor any right to require Bermuda to accept the banished rebels. The effect was benign in French Canada, where there was relief that there would be no general severity toward the colony, and where there was not unlimited sympathy for those who had led such a hare-brained and ill-starred revolt. The departure of Colborne was also greeted with general relief. When controversy arose in the British Parliament over Durham's banishment of the nine confessed Lower Canada rebels to Bermuda, the former lord chancellor in Grey's cabinet, Lord Brougham (1778–1868) – a famous maverick reformer who had been one of the leaders of the fight against slavery and had successfully defended Queen Caroline, the long-estranged and much-wronged wife of King George IV – turned against Melbourne and selected Durham as a vulnerable target. Melbourne, unwilling to condone the presence or require the dismissal of Edward Gibbon Wakefield, rather cravenly abandoned his high commissioner, conspicuously failed to accept the exiled rebels on behalf of the colony of Bermuda or approve Durham's proclamation, and revoked his ordinance of pardon of most of the rebels. Durham, on October 9, 1838, issued a further proclamation stating that "if the peace of Lower Canada is to be again menaced, it is necessary that its government should be able to reckon on a more cordial and vigorous support at home than has been accorded to me."[24] The *Times* of London wrote that the high commissioner had become the "High Seditioner," and the government recalled him. Durham had already felt that he had no option but to resign his commission (which he had technically exceeded), and did so, sailing for home before he was sacked and arriving in December 1838. Thus, the portentous incumbency of the "vain, sulky, and egocentric"[25] Durham lasted less than six months and ended ludicrously, but it would long resonate. While at sea, Durham, Wakefield, Turton, and a couple of others wrote most of the Durham Report, which was to be one of the most important state papers in the history of Canada.

Also while Durham was at sea, a few hundred exiles and American sympathizers invaded Canada, proclaimed a republic in French Canada, and held out for five days of fairly heavy combat with British soldiers and Canadian militia at the Battle of the Windmill, near Prescott, Ontario, from November 12 to 16, though outnumbered seven to one by the British-Canadian attacking force. The leader of the invaders was a Finnish-Polish adventurer, Nils von Schoultz (1807–1838), and the defence of the colony was led by Henry Dundas (1801–1876), another globe-girdling British colonial soldier and grandson of Pitt the Younger's home and war secretary and first lord of the Admiralty, Henry Dundas, the first Lord Melville (1742–1811). Von Schoultz was tried at Kingston and pleaded guilty, though he was advised against doing so by the legal adviser accorded him, the twenty-three-year-old Scottish-born Kingston lawyer John Alexander Macdonald, making his first appearance in this narrative, who would go on to be the greatest personality in nearly five centuries of Canadian history. Von Schoultz made an excellent impression on everyone, declared his guilt, and said that he had been misled into believing that Canada was being mistreated by the British, as his native Poland was by the Russians, and effectively stated that he deserved to be executed. He was duly convicted and hanged, an interesting and sympathetic but short-lived man of action and courage.

Durham had grasped a great deal during six months in the Canadas and was a perceptive observer and trenchant writer and editor (of the efforts of his collaborators). He ascribed the problems of the Canadian colonies to animosity between the English and French of the two Canadas, and the absence of responsible government, which Canadians rightfully considered to be as much owing to them as it had been owed to the citizens of Great Britain and the United States. He exposed, accurately and mercilessly, the racist pretentions and exploitive practices of much of Lower Canada's English community. Durham proposed to cure both problems with a single stroke: a united Province of Canada governed on the principle of responsible government. "Without a change in our system of government, the discontent which now prevails will spread and advance. . . . It is difficult to understand how any British statesman could have imagined that representative and irresponsible government could be successfully combined" (that is, that legislators could be elected but not direct the administration of the government). Durham pointed out, somewhat laboriously, but no more than the circumstances warranted, that it needs no change in the principles of government, no invention of a new constitutional theory, to supply the remedy which would, in my opinion, completely remove the existing political disorders. It needs but to follow out consistently the principles of the British constitution, and introduce into the government of these great colonies those wise provisions by which alone the working of the representative system can in any country be rendered harmonious and efficient. . . . The responsibility to the united legislature of all officers of the government, except the governor and his secretary, should be secured by every means known to the British constitution.[26]

Durham gave great impetus to the cause of responsible government and was correct, but hardly original, in recognizing the importance of it to stabilize Canadian opinion and assure the development of both Canadas, and this was the great merit of his report.

Less felicitous was his stated belief that the union of the Canadas would inevitably lead to the assimilation of the French Canadians into the English, liberating them from the heavy burdens of being stranded and centrifugated French speakers on an overwhelmingly English-speaking northern two-thirds of the North American continent. He wrote, "I have little doubt that the French, when once placed, by the legitimate course of events and the working of natural causes, in a minority, would abandon their vain hopes of nationality."[27] He excoriated the English community of Lower Canada (which had fawned over him) and held their arrogance and sharp commercial practice responsible for the failure to acculturate the castaway French Canadians to the virtues and allure of the English culture. (Durham mercifully stayed fairly clear of sectarian disparagements.) "From a majority emanating from so much more extended a source, I do not think they would have any oppression or injustice to fear," he wrote.[28] To paraphrase Durham himself, it is difficult to understand how any British statesman could so completely misread the tenacity of the French Canadians, who had persevered for nearly a quarter of a millennium and now numbered about 650,000 (well-baptized and regularly confessed Roman Catholic) souls (compared with an English-Canadian population in the Canadas of about

500,000). So even with a united Canadian province, the English were not getting all the way clear to leadership of the whole colony without some further fiddling. It was astounding that Durham so misread the effect of the implementation of his recommendations. Durham had relied heavily for his conclusions on the two people who most impressed him in Canada: Robert Baldwin, with his single-minded insistence on responsible government, and Adam Thom, a Scottish-Canadian Lower Canada lawyer, who despised the French Canadians but was not part of the English-Quebec establishment, though with his *Anti-Gallic Letters* he did take the lead of the English political faction in the province (and was a subsequent editor of the *Montreal Herald*). Durham essentially amplified the sensible preoccupations of Baldwin and the articulate bigotry of Thom. He took on board that the Atlantic colonies did not wish to merge with the Canadas but that some sort of affiliation between all the British North American entities that conserved a fair degree of autonomy would work, and that Lower Canada could not now live in a system ruled by a French majority with the powers that responsible government would confer. A united Province of Canada thus had a certain logic, especially to a Benthamite utilitarian like Durham; this was the Age of Reason, torqued up by the precise engineering and efficiency of the Industrial Revolution. This was the perspective that caused him to write, "If the Lower Canadians had been . . . taught to subject themselves to a much greater amount of taxation, they would probably at this time have been a much wealthier, a much better governed, a much more civilized, and a much more contented people."[29] Then, as now, such liberal nostrums are hazardous; Quebec finally put that theory to the test 120 years later, and it hasn't worked. The liberal Durham cared for the oppressed, and his protest to the czar on behalf of the Poles when he was the ambassador in St. Petersburg was sincere (which made von Schoultz's likening of Canadians to oppressed Poles piquant). As W.L. Morton wrote, Durham's "complacency was the complacency of Macaulay, his zeal the zeal of governor general William Bentinck abolishing suttee in India."[30]

Of course, union would only make the French Canadians indispensable and unprecedentedly powerful in a larger jurisdiction than the one where the implications of their majority status had been denied them. "The Act of Union, as passed, represented not Durham's victory, but his defeat."[31] And the exercise would be a training session for running an autonomous country by French-English cooperation, a concept that had never been attempted anywhere, except to a slight degree, and on a miniature scale, in New Brunswick. Those whom the departed governor left behind, or at least the politically cleverer people among them, were not slow to realize this. Durham's flippant assumption of inexorable assimilation of the French, though simplistic and unjust and asinine, demonstrated again the difficulty even the British, the most successful colonists in world history, had in managing overseas populations, including those composed of kindred (Upper Canada) or at least long-familiar (Lower Canada) groups.

Durham was an intelligent but stormy character, a bright meteor that flared across the British political sky and passed prematurely. He died of tuberculosis at Cowes, on the Isle of Wight, on July 28, 1840, aged only forty-eight. He is little remembered in Britain but is vividly remembered in French Canada as the active voice of English assimilationist ambitions, and is honourably recalled in English Canada as a principal agent of democracy in Canada. The most memorable phrase in his generally well-written report was that English and French Canadians were "two nations warring in the bosom of a single state."

Like a magic football of irregular shape that always bounces in the preferable direction, Canada took what was useful in Durham's report and effectively ignored the rest. Durham provided the next rung on the political ladder to a novel form of Canadian sovereign state, renovated the relationship with Great Britain, and opened the opportunity, which the ablest statesmen of the Canadas rushed to exploit, of building bridges between the French- and English-Canadian communities and creating a political consensus to prepare British North America for statehood. The thread from Champlain and Carleton of a Canadian country, which came through the wars, was grasped by able hands.

The British government and Parliament were generally minded to adopt Durham's recommendation of a union of Upper and Lower Canada, in the bipartisan, shared hope that it would tranquilize the Canadians. Few people in Westminster or Whitehall had any interest in Canada, although it continued to reconfirm its status as the premier colonial entity (India continuing to be a patchwork of alliances, commercial concessions, and colonial and military conquests).

The British wanted union to be at the request of the Canadians, and were ambivalent about responsible government despite Durham. But Upper Canada's legislators were very fractious, the Tories still opposed to responsible government and the subordination of the executive to the legislative, and most members of all groups wary of saddling Upper Canada with all the sorrows and complexities of Lower Canada. Lord John Russell was now the colonial secretary, succeeding Glenelg, and he continued to oppose the devolution implicit in responsible government. He received a sharp rejoinder from Joseph Howe, in his "Four Letters to Lord John Russell." Howe was approximately as eloquent as Durham in his advocacy of responsible government and his rebuttal of Russell's incongruous (for another relatively enlightened liberal) view that a colony could not enjoy such latitude was very well-formulated. (The inevitable end of that argument had been decisively demonstrated by the Americans seventy-five years before, and the Canadians had already given more than a hint of it.) New Brunswick and Prince Edward Island were indifferent to the Durham Report, but the genie was now out of the bottle, and responsible government was not just the subject of factional or even rebellious agitation but the recommended route of a special high commissioner and governor general sent to recommend a solution to British North American problems.

The Melbourne government, bobbing and weaving as was its nature, tentatively decided to enact union of the Canadas and duck responsible government, but decided to wait for the results of the efforts of the next governor to stabilize Canada. He would be the capable businessman and authority on trade and tariffs Charles Poulett Thomson, who had been vice president of the Board of Trade in Grey's government, serving with Durham and Brougham, and president of the Board of Trade under Melbourne. His new post was now an unpromising one: the last governor general of Canada to have left in good standing and voluntarily at the end of a full term was Sir Robert Milnes in 1805, thirteen governors before.* The British had not sent over a governor

---

* Before Dunn, Craig, Prevost, Drummond, Sherbrooke, Kempt, Richmond, Dalhousie, Aylmer, Gosford, Colborne, and Durham.

remotely of the stature of Guy Carleton, who departed in 1796 after a total of twenty years in the office. Obviously, something had to change, if not in an orderly fashion, then otherwise. The new governor arrived in Quebec in October 1839. Shortly after his arrival, Thomson – who, though a clever and efficient businessman and very contemporary industrial revolutionary, was no instinctive politician (unlike Kempt and Gosford) – wrote Russell that "the large majority [of those whom he consulted, French and English] advocate warmly the establishment of the union."[32] This impression was entirely conjured from his hopeful imagination.

In Upper Canada, Thomson got a genuinely positive reception, because the Reformers were the emergent majority and they had been misled by British official insinuations to believe that union would bring responsible government, which was practically their only public policy concern. As always, Chief Justice John Beverley Robinson (1791–1863), the leader of what was left of the Family Compact, undaunted by any traditional restraints on political advocacy from the bench, gave contrary advice, but Thomson correctly read that opinion in Upper Canada was of another mind. (Robinson was now more than halfway through his fifty-year tenure as one of the leading political and public figures of Upper Canada.) On October 16, 1839, Russell, by directive, empowered colonial governors to remove executive councillors when they determined that such a step accorded with the public service. This greatly strengthened Thomson's hand as he set about being, as a friend put it "the Castlereagh of the Canadian Union."[33]

The English-dominated Special Council of Lower Canada (Legislative and Executive Councillors) was happy to give the governor a civil list and to accede to the Act of Union, which they saw as delivering them from the jaws of the local French majority. Thomson led the Upper Canada Reformers down the garden path of equating union with responsible government (government "in accord with the well-understood wishes of the people" was his phrase.)[34] By this ruse, and by a constructive compromise settlement of the Clergy Reserves issue that respected the non-Anglican denominations while still giving a fine share to the Church of England, Thomson secured Upper Canada's approval of the union. It was a smooth political operation, but it was achieved at the expense of ignoring the French majority in Lower Canada and swindling the Reform majority in Upper Canada.

Thomson tried to conciliate all substantial factions, offering La-Fontaine the post of solicitor general of Lower Canada right after LaFontaine, now the indisputable political leader of the French Canadians, had addressed a large public meeting at Montreal and denounced union in vitriolic but not seditious terms. LaFontaine declined the offer. Thomson went on to Nova Scotia, where the lieutenant-governor, Sir Colin Campbell, disputed Howe's interpretation of Russell's Delphic utterances to imply official support of responsible government. Thomson damped down that fire by persuading Campbell to offer, and the Reformers to accept, three places on the Executive Council (though Howe declined). This, it eventually emerged, was the definition in practice of Russell and Thomson's flim-flam about governing in accord with the public's wishes, putting responsible government Reformers on a council that wasn't responsible to the voters. The Empire and its agents were holding the line, but by recourse to methods that were clearly going to snap under the strain of their disingenuousness.

To complicate matters, there was skirmishing along the northeast border with the United States in the lumbering region known as Aroostook. The British were again fearful of American infiltration, and relations were aggravated by the arrest in New York State of Alexander McLeod, one of the unit that had cut loose and burned Mackenzie's supply vessel on Navy Island in the Niagara River after the failure of his uprising. The United States was preparing to annex Texas and absolutely did not want a dispute with Great Britain, which, with France, was encouraging Mexico to hang on to Texas. Lord Palmerston, Melbourne's more purposeful brother-in-law, now settling into his second decade as foreign secretary, resolved the McLeod affair and sent Lord Ashburton (Alexander Baring, 1774–1848, of the banking family and another president of the Board of Trade, under Peel) to Washington as a special emissary. He and the U.S. secretary of state, the eminent orator and frequent senator and leading politician of New England, Daniel Webster, would resolve the Aroostook border dispute and other matters in the Webster-Ashburton Treaty of 1842.

Thomson got the Act of Union through in the Canadas and it thus rather easily cleared the British Parliament in the spring of 1840. He was rewarded with elevation to the peerage as Lord Sydenham and Toronto. The Act of Union that was adopted was a more modest affair than had originally been proposed; it was modelled on the union of Scotland and England of 1707 rather than that between Ireland and Britain in 1801. There was only one Legislature and one government, but the civil law of Lower Canada, seigneurial rights, and the pride of place of the Roman Catholic Church were all preserved from Carleton's original brainstorms of 1774 and 1791. There were two attorneys general and two school systems in the united Province of Canada, but only English as a language of record and legislative debate, a deprival of a status French had enjoyed in the Lower Canada legislatures. The demographic preponderance of the French was gerrymandered away by the artificial imposition of equal representation between the two components, at forty-two members each from Upper and Lower Canada. This was outrageous, but the practical impact was that it would be impossible to govern without some French representation. Eighty years after the Plains of Abraham, the French, although a feeble and fatuous official effort was being made to demote their language, were being admitted to a share of self-government, though the authority of the elected Legislature was still being restrained by a thread of viceregal autocracy disguised in a fog of official obfuscation. There was a high property qualification for legislators of at least five hundred pounds, and a life-appointed Legislative Council of at least twenty members, with no provision for representation of both races. Municipal legislation was left to the united province to address. (John Graves Simcoe, as lieutenant-governor of Upper Canada, had in 1792 established a county system there imitative of the British, though it was directed by the province and not locally. But in Lower Canada there was no local government at all outside the cities, apart from the rickety seigneurial and Roman Catholic parish systems.)

In close emulation of Britain, henceforth, all money bills had to be introduced by the government, which eliminated the largely scandalous recourse to log-rolling and back-scratching by private members introducing their preferred causes and subjects of patronage. Sydenham's Clergy Reserves measure had been found inadmissible by the law officers of the U.K. government, and to preserve his plural establishment he secured a new treatment of the subject that was not really a solution but at least cooled the issue and punted it forward for some years.

There were no political parties, just the Château Clique, the Family Compact, the amorphous Reform movements, and special interests such as Egerton Ryerson's militant Methodists. Sydenham called for elections on the new basis in 1840, rigged the French out of four members by a preposterous demarcation of electoral districts, and toured about Upper Canada ostensibly on a viceregal tour to show the flag and encourage the reign of normalcy but in fact to promote moderate candidates who were neither minions of the Compact nor unacceptable radicals. He was not partisan between Tories and Reformers, as long as they were moderate, and was much subtler and in all respects more capable than the unlamented Francis Bond Head had been in the previous election of 1836. He had appointed Baldwin attorney general of Upper Canada in February 1840, and a member of the Executive Council in 1841, but ministers continued to be responsible to the king and not to Parliament. Baldwin and LaFontaine had been in close touch and had far-sightedly gone some distance to working out a joint approach to adapting the new arrangements to the successful conclusion of the long march to responsible government.

In the 1841 election, in Canada West, as Upper Canada was now called, there were six or seven Compact supporters and an equal number of extreme Reformers, and about thirty Baldwinite Reformers. Baldwin himself was elected in two districts. In Canada East, twenty French Reformers were elected and the rest were the English or non-reform French, though Sydenham's partisan districting and violence by English elements at a number of polls undoubtedly influenced the result undemocratically. LaFontaine was among those defeated, almost certainly by an infelicitous combination of official and English skulduggery. A gigantic step forward for reform, and for French-English relations with it, was taken by Baldwin when he had LaFontaine returned for York North, the constituency he chose not to hold of the two that had elected him. Baldwin's gesture, and LaFontaine's acceptance of it in preference to leading an embittered Quebec bloc manipulating the balance of power in the Legislative Assembly, set Canada on the course to a federal, bicultural country.

Sydenham had chosen Kingston as capital of the united Province of Canada, and at a pre-session caucus of the Reformers, Baldwin gained approval of his insistence that Sydenham replace the three Tory members of the Executive Council with Tory or Reform moderates, though in other respects there was reluctance to confront the governor directly at this early point. Baldwin had insisted that LaFontaine be brought onto the Executive Council or he would resign from it. The three cleared that hurdle, at least in concept, and Baldwin declined to stand for Speaker of the Assembly, as Reformers, such as Papineau, had previously done, and Sydenham showed great finesse in causing the election of a moderate Reform candidate for that position. But Baldwin resigned from the Executive Council on June 14, 1841, at Sydenham's refusal to sack the old-guard Tory members. Sydenham continued his almost artistic tightrope act as the session opened with the government in the hands of Toronto lawyer and legislator "Sweet William" Draper, so called because of his oratorical suavity and persuasiveness.

Sydenham put through a loan to be guaranteed imperially for 1.5 million pounds to refinance debt and engage in important public works, including taking over the Welland Canal from private interests, canalizing the St. Lawrence above Montreal to facilitate travel between the Canadas, and an ambitious road-building program in Canada East, the Eastern Townships, and the Gaspé. He also put through a system of locally governed counties throughout the Province of Canada and an act for public elementary education. The only important measure he had to defer was the establishment of a currency-issuing bank. But Sydenham and Draper had retained public and Assembly confidence with a very adroit and clever evasion of the burning issue that commanded the interest of all. Draper, confirming his entitlement to his nickname, spoke in the Assembly on June 15. He declared that he would not cling to his office, as attorney general for Canada East and effectively the premier, "one day longer than he held the confidence of the Assembly"; that he construed the governor's role as a combination of representing the monarch [as of 1837, Queen Victoria], and as participating as a minister of the government, responsible to the Mother Country, and Draper referred piously to an (imprecise) "degree of responsibility to public opinion." He had emulated but improved upon the placations of Kempt and Gosford and talked all around the edges of the issue without saying whether the ministers had to resign if they lacked the confidence of the Assembly. Sydenham and Draper were agile, but this charade couldn't go on indefinitely. If responsible government didn't come reasonably soon, there would be another revolt, and it would be less risible than those of 1837, with the United States the chief beneficiary of it.

Baldwin replied immediately after Draper and forced the issue of responsible government to a determination. Sydenham's program was so imaginative and popular that he was still one full step ahead of the ravening popular dragon of responsible government. Hincks spoke after Baldwin and decried the failure to proclaim legislative control of government, the voting of a civil list (emoluments of the governor and his ministers) by the Imperial government, and Sydenham's gerrymandering, which in Canada East alone had twenty-six legislators representing "350,000 souls" and sixteen representing only 63,000. He described the suppression of the French language in the Assembly as "an unjust and cruel measure."[35]

Sydenham showed himself a legislator and administrator of remarkable energy, and in the same session he reduced the severity of the penal system, abolishing the pillory and reducing the number of capital offences. He put through an increased protective tariff and struck a commission for the reform of the seigneurial system. As an administrator, he reorganized the departments, and, with Durham, and with Russell's support, installed a coherent national administration in place of antiquated colonial fussing and compulsive systematic irresolution.

On September 3, 1841, Baldwin made another of his major interventions and moved a resolution endorsing responsible government. Draper had these tabled and replaced by what are known as the Sydenham–Harrison Resolutions (Samuel Bealey Harrison was Draper's co-leader of the government). These held that the people's most important political right is "having a provincial Parliament for the protection of their liberties," the "exercise of a constitutional influence over the executive departments," and that the head of the executive government is responsible" to the Imperial government alone, but that, nevertheless, this can only be done "by and with the assistance, counsel, and information of subordinate officers in the province." The Sydenham–Harrison Resolutions held that the government must have the confidence of the representatives of the people, who "have a right to expect that the Imperial authority shall be . . . exercised in the manner most consistent with their wishes and interests." This was a threadbare effort to finesse the question one more time, and this was where matters stood when Sydenham died, on September 19, fifteen days after being thrown from and dragged by his horse, causing multiple fractures and a mortal infection. He was just forty-two and was undoubtedly a man of great talent. He would not have been able to waffle and straddle much longer, but while he lasted he was a remarkably effective governor, and probably the ablest, and in some respects one of the most successful, since Dorchester.

To replace Sydenham, the returned prime minister Sir Robert Peel (Melbourne having retired), a reform Conservative, and his colonial secretary, Lord Stanley, sent another governor of very high ability, Sir Charles Bagot (1781–1843). Bagot was an intimate of Thomas Grenville, (son and brother of prime ministers), of future foreign secretary Clarendon, and of Russell, and was married to the niece of the Duke of Wellington. He was a naturally talented and confident man who took easily to diplomacy. He had negotiated the Rush-Bagot Agreement after the War of 1812, which demilitarized the Great Lakes and extended the frontier west from Lake of the Woods to the Rocky Mountains. He was minister to Russia and to the Netherlands, where, in 1831, under Palmerston's guidance, he had helped bring Belgium into existence as a country. He had counselled kings, emperors, prime ministers, and future presidents of the United States for twenty-five years. Bagot saw as soon as he arrived that Sydenham's effort to sweep every contentious issue under the rug of energetic legislative activity could not continue, and even less could his effort to govern without the French in a united province whose population was in majority French. Sydenham's ample works projects had induced general prosperity in Canada West, the Eastern Townships, and in Nova Scotia, where the Bank of Nova Scotia, founded in 1832, and the British and North American Royal Mail Steam Packet Company, founded by Samuel Cunard of Halifax in the 1830s, were leading the greatest boom in that province's history, prior or subsequent.*

---

* Cunard, 1787–1865, was a pioneer in the age of steam, which at sea and in the development of railroads was revolutionizing all transport. There was already much talk of a railroad from Halifax to Montreal. Cunard Line ships would be among the most famous passenger vessels and war-time troop carriers in all history, including the *Mauretania*, *Aquitania*, *Queen Mary*, and *Queen Elizabeth*. He was an early opponent of any racial discrimination and reprimanded his own officials for conveying the African-American leader Frederick Douglass to Britain in segregated accommodation.

Stanley's instructions of October 8, 1841, though he was a very intelligent man, were the sort of mindless, dictatorial piffle that British Imperial officials often inflicted on those who had to deal with radically different realities on the ground. He was much influenced by the francophobic, fire-breathing, Imperial zealot Allan MacNab (1798–1862), a talented lawyer, militiaman, politician, industrialist, and co-owner of the Great Western Railway. Stanley "was a moderate conservative who could not believe that there were real parties in Canada – nothing but parish politics and disloyal factions. If anyone was to have power he preferred that it should be the old reactionary group headed by Sir Allan Napier MacNab." Stanley lumbered the departing Bagot with a lot of boathouse twaddle: "If the stream be still against you, bend your back to your oar like a man and, above all, take none into your crew who will not bend their backs too. . . . MacNab is to dine with me on Thursday."[36]

Bagot well knew that this was no crew party on the Cam on an English summer Sunday, and fortunately for everyone, not least Stanley, ignored this bunk. Draper and Harrison both told Bagot that he would have to broaden the government and bring in some French. The whole responsible government issue obviously could not be fumbled and dissembled through another session. Bagot did succeed in attracting to the ministry the talented and courageous Francis Hincks as inspector general of public accounts, forerunner to the minister of finance. When he approached LaFontaine, the member for York North said that no French-Canadian Reformer would join the Executive Council without Baldwin. Baldwin would not enter if even pensions were paid to two particular officials from the old pre-Durham regime. (Baldwin was completely preoccupied with responsible government, but that meant absolutely every aspect of it, down to the last grievance, perquisite, and farthing.) There was nothing for it: Draper, a conscientious and moderate Tory, who did not believe in democratic government as it was emerging, though he was a passionate supporter of civil rights and due process, resigned from the Executive Council, taking the like-minded Henry Sherwood with him. Two other conservative Tories followed. They were effectively replaced by Robert Baldwin and Louis-Hippolyte LaFontaine, in September 1842, in what is generally known as the first Baldwin–LaFontaine ministry. Jean-Joseph Girouard did not feel he could accept the post of Crown land commissioner but recommended his friend Augustin-Norbert Morin (1803–1865), Papineau's co-author of the inflammatory Ninety-Two Resolutions. The urbane Bagot wrote to both Girouard and Morin in impeccable French accepting Girouard's suggestion, and Morin joined the ministry. Hincks and Harrison remained in what was now a very talented group to be leading such a jurisdiction of only about 1.3 million people.

This was an earth-shaking event in Canadian terms. Though it was far from the official acceptance of what Baldwin and LaFontaine had been demanding, it effectively recognized that the civic values that almost all Canadians – as well as prevailing opinion in the United Kingdom and the United States (apart from the moral and social cancer of slavery) – favoured could not be assured without control of government by popularly elected representatives. British North America's leading advocates of responsible government were now at the head of the ministry in a manner that Sydenham, a comparative liberal scarcely dead a year, had considered "inadmissible," and the political leader of French Canada was effectively the co-premier of 80 per cent of British North America and dealing with a very suave and reasonable governor who had ambiguous instructions from a progressive Tory home government. It was just five years since the fizzled rebellions, but the rebels had been crushed with such dispatch that insurrection was durably deterred, and those who shared most of the rebels' aims but eschewed their support of violence were now in partial control. Canada had been loyal enough to retain British protection, with which there could be no American attempt at annexation.

The Canadian leaders were not playing the British and Americans against each other as artfully or deliberately as Benjamin Franklin and George Washington, sixty to eighty-five years before, had encouraged the British to evict the French from Canada and the French to help the Americans evict the British from America. They were operating on a smaller scale and in a lesser place, but the principle of a small group of colonists – by a combination of sincere conviction and tactical adroitness – navigating between larger powers, being closer now to one and now to another, and emerging by increments as an autonomous entity with little to fear from either, was similar, though America had essentially run the British gauntlet after thirty years and Canada would have to walk on eggshells for almost a century before it could be a little more spontaneous. But the combination of courage, vision, and tactical artistry to achieve such an ambitious and complicated end was similar in concept, if Canada's reprise of it was less bold in execution and less dramatic in its contemporary impact on the world. America seized the attention of the whole world, which it has never lost, and Canada advanced subtly, imperceptibly, and largely unnoticed. Both countries retained these traits even as well-established nations, sometimes to a fault, in both cases.

Unfortunately, Sir Charles Bagot died as events crested, as tragically, though not as prematurely, as Sydenham. He suffered an excruciating decline induced by heart disease, starting in the fall of 1842, but not before he had the pleasure of writing Stanley (Bagot's dispatches were perhaps the most elegantly written of any Canadian colonial governor, French or English),

> I have united the voice of seven-eighths of the House of Assembly . . . [and] met the wishes of a large majority of the population of Upper Canada and of the British inhabitants of Lower Canada. I have removed the main ground of discontent and distrust among the French-Canadian population. I have satisfied them that the Union is capable of being administered for their happiness and advantage and have consequently disarmed their opposition to it. I have excited among them the strongest feeling of gratitude to the provincial government, and if my policy be approved by H.M.'s government, I shall have removed their chief cause of hostility to British institutions, and have added another security for their devotion to the British crown. . . . The present crisis has offered the occasion; I have seized it.[37]

Bagot was under no illusions that he was scandalizing the Blimpish Imperialist humbug of Stanley and MacNab and their co-reactionaries, but he was largely correct in his claim: he had broken the logjam, though some obstructions remained, and had made it possible for Canada to take another giant step toward permanence and nationhood.

Baldwin, speaking in the Assembly on September 17, 1842, spoke the truth (as this righteous man always did): "The great principle of responsibility is formally and solemnly recognized. . . . From this period dates a revolution effected without blood or slaughter; but none the less glorious. . . . The connection between this country and the mother country . . . [is] not a union of parchment, but a union of hearts and of free-born men."[38] Above all, Bagot recognized that "You cannot govern Canada without the French."[39]

Stanley was shaken and considered recalling Bagot, a step for which, of course, there was already much precedent. But the governor had already indicated he was unwell, and Stanley was concerned with the effect of his actions on Parliament and the other major powers, in Europe and the United States; he had no interest in what the Canadians thought of anything. As Bagot had hoped and suspected, Stanley recognized that the die was now cast and there could be no turning all the way back, even under a new governor, after what Durham the Whig and Bagot the enlightened Tory had done. The British could not cope with another rebellion undertaken in pursuit of the policies enunciated by liberal British governors, and if British military guarantees of its North American colonies were ended, those colonies would be snaffled in double-quick time by the United States, whatever the southern slave-holders thought of it. The army of the United States could not be held again on the well-travelled approaches along Lake Champlain and at the Niagara and St. Clair Rivers by Canadian militiamen alone.

Stanley, with some elegance in the circumstances, replied to Bagot, "We are prepared to support [your policy], and defend you for having pursued it. Only we must rest your defence on the impossibility of your carrying on the government without having recourse to the men whom you have called to your councils."[40] Bagot's achievement was crowned at the polls. LaFontaine and Baldwin were required to seek re-election after joining the ministry. York North easily returned LaFontaine, but violence and intimidation by the Orange Lodge caused Baldwin to be defeated in his home district of Hastings by forty-nine votes, and his favour to LaFontaine was immediately returned by one of LaFontaine's followers retiring as member for Rimouski, which district easily returned the unilingual Torontonian Robert Baldwin on January 30, 1843. The complete segregation of French and English Canadians, which had obtained since the arrival of the Loyalists from America sixty years before, could not be more decisively terminated than by the installation of a joint ministry with the leaders representing each other's co-nationals and co-religionists (though neither, and especially LaFontaine, was a very energetic communicant). Sir Charles Bagot died in his residence in Kingston on May 18, 1843, although he had already resigned and his replacement had just taken up his post. Bagot sadly made it fifteen governors general in a row who did not complete full terms in good official condition, but he must rank as one of the great statesmen in Canada's history.

Stanley chose Sir Charles Metcalfe as the next governor general of Canada: a distinguished colonial official in India and Jamaica, a rather stern and inflexible traditionalist unaccustomed to give-and-take with colonial leaders, though a good-natured and liberal-minded man. Unfortunately, Stanley could not help himself and gave Metcalfe the secret mission to prevent the inclusion of the French and the triumph of the Reformers from leading to the full-blown installation of responsible government as irreversible orthodoxy. It was an impossible task. A coolness soon arose between the ministers and the governor over the issue of patronage, which LaFontaine made it clear to Metcalfe's secretary, Captain James Higginson, should be approved by the ministers and not just arbitrarily determined by the governor. In the 1843 session, the main ingredients of the Baldwin–LaFontaine agenda were Baldwin's bill to curb the Orange Lodge, especially in its tendency to intervene violently in elections (including his own late defeat in Hastings), with the Secret Societies Bill, and his University Bill, designed to wrench King's College out of the bejewelled episcopal hand of John Strachan and create a secular and multi-denominational University of Toronto. Metcalfe, with no warning, reserved the Secret Societies Bill after it had passed, for review by the Imperial government (and after he had had a clandestine meeting with the head of the Orange Lodge, Ogle Robert Gowan, in which the grand master of the Grand Orange Lodge later said Metcalfe had predicted the early departure of Baldwin, Hincks, and Harrison[41]). The University Bill was so beset that the ministry suspended pursuit of it pending review and possible amendment. The agitation was led by Strachan (who subscribed himself "John, by Divine Permission, First Bishop of Toronto"[42]) and petitioned that (his former student) Baldwin's bill "is in its nature atheistical, and so monstrous in its consequences that if successfully carried out . . . it would utterly destroy all that is pure and holy in morals and religion, and lead to greater corruption than anything adopted during the madness of the French Revolution. . . . Such a fatal departure from all that is good is without a parallel in the history of the world."[43] It was a feisty session, with all the French- and English-speaking legislators mixed together. Baldwin described the French-Canadian members as "sitting at the feet of the honourable Knight [Metcalfe] as a political Gamaliel."[44]

The ministers then pushed the patronage issue and demanded Metcalfe's approval that the ministry be consulted on all appointments to public office. Metcalfe refused, and the entire ministry resigned, except for Dominick Daly (1798–1868), a likeable veteran placeman who was provincial secretary for Canada East. Metcalfe eventually prorogued and reconstituted the ministry under the returning Draper, with Denis-Benjamin Viger (1774–1861), an old Patriote who had been a member of the Quebec Assembly from 1810 to 1838, when he was briefly imprisoned, as co-premier with Draper. They also recruited Papineau's somewhat less excitable brother, Denis-Benjamin Papineau. Durham's old sidekick Edward Gibbon Wakefield made a cameo reappearance in Canada, well-paid by the North American Colonial Association of Ireland, and got himself elected to the Assembly, but he resigned after a few months, following the death of his brother in England, and departed Canada forever. He was a strong supporter, and even confidant, of Metcalfe while he was present, and was regarded as a traitor by the Durhamite Reformers. Wakefield and Francis Hincks engaged in a fierce and entertaining exchange about Canadian matters in the London press for some months, as Hincks submitted columns to the *Morning Chronicle* and Wakefield moved around the Tory press like a pollinating bee. Wakefield grossly misrepresented the state of opinion in Canada, and Hincks, a greatly more substantial character, won the exchange, but it enlivened the subject and raised interest in it in the Imperial capital.

Nothing more occurred legislatively, and Metcalfe dissolved the Assembly for new elections in September 1844. They were the most violent in Canadian history. The Irish navvies who were working on the canals that Sydenham had laid down intimidated voters in many constituencies but were bipartisan, depending on which side paid them.

Metcalfe and his followers pushed loyalty and the avoidance of a French takeover in Canada West, while the followers in Canada East tried to exploit Patriote resentment of the rise of LaFontaine. It was in some respects an unholy alliance between old Upper Canada Tories and old Lower Canada quasi-rebels. William Draper himself took a high road oratorically and stuck with Sydenham's old benignities and prevarications, but without Sydenham's disdain for the French Canadians. The ministry won a paper-thin victory in the Assembly, after a very doubtful exercise of a free franchise. Baldwin and LaFontaine were returned, but Hincks was defeated. There were too many contradictory factions supporting the ministry for it to accomplish much, and Draper and Viger essentially kept a caretaker regime going with some dexterity until 1847. Draper tried a university bill almost identical to Baldwin's, but the Tories would not let it come to a vote. Overtures were made to LaFontaine by the agile Draper, cunning in tactics but a principled Tory, but LaFontaine would only return to office on his terms. Baldwin was not approached but would have had nothing to do with it if he had been. He wrote LaFontaine after the talks, conducted through the Speaker of the Assembly, René-Édouard Caron (1800–1876), of which Baldwin was kept fully advised, that Draper's design to unite a Tory majority in Upper Canada with a Reform majority in Lower Canada would ultimately facilitate "the schemes of those who looked forward to the union as a means of crushing the French-Canadians." Baldwin believed that a coalition of ethnic majorities would inevitably lead to the suppression of the French by the English and the collapse of any notion of a viable Canada, and that Tories and Reformers must both seek support among both groups. An English Party and a French Party, in initial cooperation, he wrote, "will not be injurious to the French Canadian portion of our population alone. It appears to me equally clear that it will be most calamitous to the country in general. It will perpetuate distinctions, initiate animosities, sever the bonds of political sympathy and sap the foundation of public morality."[45] In taking the position that the English and French Canadians had to collaborate in governing Canada, and that Canadian political parties had to have representation among both French and English Canadians, Baldwin and LaFontaine made Canada possible. If there were an English-Canadian party and a French-Canadian party, nothing but perfunctory or superficial collaboration between the two Canadas would be possible, and French Canada, if union were perpetuated on a reformed basis, would always be subject to the imposition of the tyranny of the majority. Only a country and political movements based on a fusion of legitimate English and French interests would be able to function durably. Baldwin showed himself not only to be a seeker of colonial rights and autonomy, but a statesman whose vision of the Canada of the future was extraordinarily clear and accurate, presciently arrived at and courageously pursued. He awaited confidently the collapse of this final stand by the flat-earth imperialists.

3. Reform at Last, 1846–1851

It was an illogically protracted debate, and the central fact of it was that almost nobody in the British Parliament, government, or Opposition, knew anything about conditions in Canada. In general, they waffled between such indifference to the castaway colonists that they were prepared to abandon them to the Americans and, on the other hand, a generally stronger and more frequent apprehension that the Americans not seize British North America by infiltration and border skirmishing by irregulars. (It continued to be generally recognized that the United States had even less enthusiasm for war than the British government did, reflecting the might and prestige of the British Empire and the growing American preoccupation with slavery.) On February 2, 1844, Stanley declared in the House of Commons, "Place the governor of Canada in a state of absolute dependence on his council, and they at once would make Canada an independent and republican colony." The colonial secretary, in his effervescent imperialism, overlooked that a republican colony is practically impossible. Responsible government, as Baldwin, LaFontaine, Hincks, Durham, and Bagot understood it, overlooked "altogether the distinction which must subsist between an independent country and a colony subject to the domination of the mother country," Stanley said.[46] It was hard to believe that the holder of such obtuse opinions would, in the next twenty-five years, be the prime minister three times, albeit briefly. In domestic matters, he was a sensible (if often flustered) ally of Disraeli.

What Stephen Leacock describes as the "magnificent stupidity" of Stanley's view was captured in his rhetorical Manichaean division of Canadians between "rebels" and "honest men," and his assertion that the Crown must dispense patronage only to those "who, in the hour of peril, had come forward to manifest their loyalty and to maintain the union of Canada with the Crown of England."[47] Of course, this was simply nonsense, and formulating the issue like this assured that there would be no possibility of a successful resolution of Canadian problems. Stanley concluded by referring to Baldwin and LaFontaine, specifically, as "unprincipled demagogues and mischievous advisers." They were leaders of the opposition in a kindred, if less sovereign, Parliament, and this was a shocking breach of parliamentary etiquette, as well as a complete misreading of the individuals. Stanley effectively repeated Russell's Ten Resolutions of reply to Papineau. To avoid another severe defeat in North America, the British Empire would have to be protected locally from the stupidity, on these issues, of its leaders in both major parties. They had learned little in the seventy years since the American troubles began, and there had been few Americans then to warn them except Benjamin Franklin, and his advice was rejected, despite the support of Chatham, Burke, and Fox. Now, there was no such eminent support in Westminster, but Baldwin, LaFontaine, and Hincks, and some younger men such as John A. Macdonald and George-Étienne Cartier, could deliver popular support for sane policy if the British would listen to it. As Baldwin had told a large gathering of supporters at Toronto on May 12, 1844, "This is not a mere party struggle. This is Canada against her oppressors. The people of Canada claiming the British Constitution against those who withhold it: the might of public opinion against faction and corruption," and, though he deemed it inadvisable to say so, against the antediluvian stupidity of those overseas protectors who alone assured, by their positions and not their qualities as statesmen, the comparative passivity of the ravening, but unabashedly democratic, Americans.[48] The debate continued in Canada through the mid-1840s in all the florid hyperbole of Victorian prolixity.

The radicals who opposed Stanley, such as Mackenzie's friends Joseph Hume and John Roebuck, did so to harass a Tory minister and from a visceral liberality that required greater local autonomy, not from any knowledge of the facts. Only Baldwin and LaFontaine and Hincks and their supporters had a realistic alternative to the choice between either continued complete subordination to the lofty and often pretentious whims of British governors or instant assimilation into the sprawling American republic. The French Canadians generally liked American republicanism but knew that joining the United States would be the end of the French language other than as an historic relic. The English Canadians had no problem with the Americans culturally, as an English-speaking country, but they did not like what they generally regarded as chaotic, corrupt, and boastful American republicanism, tainted by the evil of slavery. The smart Canadians were effectively playing a game of chicken, using revolutionary agitation to push Britain into realistic concessions of autonomy without it becoming so exasperated that it withdrew the protection that kept British North America from being swallowed whole by the Americans.

As the 1845 Canadian session ended in March, having achieved nothing except new heights of acrimony, it was announced that Sir Charles Metcalfe would be elevated to the peerage. Thomas Cushing Aylwin (1806–1871), a Reform member from Quebec City, though a Harvard University graduate and former solicitor general for Canada East, infelicitously declared in the Assembly that "it would be more fitting that Metcalfe should be recalled and put on trial."[49] These sentiments, which were expressed by an unseemly number of Reformers, were particularly inappropriate in the light of Metcalfe's deteriorating physical condition. He had had a bout of cancer before taking up his post in Canada, and by the summer of 1845 he was in agonies compounded by near blindness, and requested his recall. He departed Canada in November 1845, the sixteenth consecutive governor general of Canada not to finish his term at its normal end in good political and physical condition. Lord Metcalfe of Fern Hill died on September 5, 1846, a brave and dedicated man who had been sent on an impossible mission.

The acting governor general was Charles Murray Cathcart (1783–1859), the director of military forces, a doughty general who had slogged all the way through the Napoleonic Wars, had three horses shot out from under him at Waterloo, and had been the governor of Edinburgh Castle before coming to Canada. Lord Cathcart was sent to deal with an anticipated crisis in relations with the United States. The Rush–Bagot Agreement of 1818 had extended the Canadian–American frontier to the Rocky Mountains. Beyond was the Oregon Territory, which stretched from California to Alaska (then a Russian territory) and it was agreed that it should be subject to joint government by Britain and the United States. By 1844, this had become an issue in America. The British had proposed extending the Rush–Bagot line to the Pacific coast and Canada receiving all of Vancouver Island, but they also wanted navigation rights to the mouth of the Columbia River in the United States. In the piping days of manifest destiny, this became a political issue for the Democrats, who adopted in the 1844 election the slogan "Fifty-Four Forty or Fight!" meaning that the United States would take the whole territory right to Alaska and shut Canada off from the Pacific Ocean. The winning candidate in the election, James Knox Polk, America's first "dark horse," who had not been a contestant at the start of his party's convention, was a colourless but very astute former Speaker of the House and governor of Tennessee. The convention was hung between former president Martin Van Buren and General (his military career was mainly spent fighting the native people) Lewis Cass (1782–1866), and so historian George Bancroft suggested Polk, who very narrowly defeated the Whig candidate, former Speaker, secretary of state, and giant of the U.S. Senate, Henry Clay, who had been seeking the presidency for the third time. (Polk rewarded Bancroft with the posts of secretary of the navy and minister to Great Britain.) Polk was a protégé of the fierce and still influential former president General Andrew Jackson, and campaigned on a platform that also included the annexation of Texas. This implied the admission of Texas as a slave state, although Mexico had abolished slavery, including in Texas, some years before. Admitting Oregon as a free state would balance new admissions of states to the union between slave and free states. In fact, Polk had no intention whatever of going to war with Britain; exactly the reverse. He used the sabre-rattling of his campaign to win a compromise close to what Britain had been proposing over Oregon with the additional ingredient that Britain would cease to support Mexico in resisting the American annexation of Texas. Britain and France had both been trying to contain American expansion southward, and the Americans were not prepared to tolerate their interference.

* * *

While this issue heated up, the Irish famine caused the Peel government to revoke the Corn Laws that restricted the import of foodstuffs. The rural Tories professed not to believe that that law, which benefited British farmers, had anything to do with conditions in Ireland, and Lord Henry Bentinck led a revolt of the agrarian faction of the governing party, but the real engineer of the split in the party was Benjamin Disraeli, embittered at what he considered the role of anti-Semitism and both patrician snobbery and bourgeois bigotry in his exclusion from Sir Robert Peel's government. Disraeli (who was a baptized Anglican but an ethnic Jew) cracked the party wide open and began the task of reconstructing it on progressive lines, which he pursued with conspicuous ultimate success over thirty-three years as leader of the Conservative Party in the House of Commons or overall, including three partial terms as chancellor of the exchequer and two stints, totalling seven years, as a very capable, as well as legendarily witty, prime minister. The fall of the Peel government brought in Lord John Russell, who had succeeded Melbourne as Liberal leader, with Palmerston back in the Foreign Office, and, as colonial secretary, Earl Grey, son of the prime minister who had passed the First Reform Act and Catholic Emancipation and the abolition of slavery in the British Empire. Grey had studied the Canadian problem and knew that the repeal of the Corn Laws was the end of the official rationale of the colonies as suppliers of raw materials for Britain and a market for British manufactures. He substituted a new basis of the relationship: shared interest and the political advantages of Imperial solidarity but with the blessings of liberty for all kindred (that is, Caucasian) people in the Empire. Grey said, "The nation has incurred a responsibility of the highest kind which it is not at liberty to throw off," by which he meant, in the Canadian context, that Britain should hang on to all it could in North America by steering between the local "rebels" and the aggressively watchful Americans.[50] "To English Tories, the outer Empire meant dominance and a chance of jobs for younger sons, to English Whigs and radicals it meant trade and if trade could be done with other countries to better advantage, the Empire became a nuisance. . . . Colonists having repudiated the Tory political view of Empire and the metropolis having repudiated the traditional mercantile conception, it was not surprising that the home government was willing to concede both fiscal and political autonomy."[51]

Out of the personal tragedy of Metcalfe, the agitation of Baldwin, Lafontaine, and Hincks, the tectonic shifts in Britain and Ireland and the tensions over Oregon and Mexico, the innate genius of the British, Canadian, and American political systems suddenly asserted themselves. Like a kaleidoscope where everything suddenly comes into focus, all the variables aligned swiftly: Palmerston was happy to accept the arrangement that Peel's foreign secretary, Lord Aberdeen, sent to Polk just as the Peel government left office in June 1846, and under Palmerston's instructions, the British minister completed an Oregon agreement with Polk, which the president had the U.S. Senate ratify. This cleared away the danger of a two-front war and Polk then focused on Mexico, which blundered into a war in which the Americans over the next eighteen months almost effortlessly relieved Mexico of nearly 1.2 million square miles which provided the future states of Texas, Oklahoma, Utah, Colorado, New Mexico, Arizona, Nevada, and California.

As this was happening along the Mexican border, Grey persuaded Russell and Palmerston that there was no practical alternative to setting up the advanced British North American colonies (including Nova Scotia, where Joseph Howe was leading the agitation for responsible government, against the governor, Viscount Falkland, whom Howe threatened to horsewhip), along semi-autonomous, democratic, and cooperative lines. The twenty-seven-year-old monarch Queen Victoria had already come to this conclusion and had proposed to Stanley the appointment of Lord Elgin (1811–1863), a very successful and enlightened governor of Jamaica in the wake of disturbances there, as Metcalfe's successor, as there was no need for Cathcart after the resolution of the Oregon issue with the United States. She reiterated the suggestion to Grey, who spontaneously concurred, and Elgin arrived with instructions to scrap the tightrope and deliver what Durham had recommended and Bagot had promised. Victoria was probably influenced in her views by her intelligently liberal husband Prince Albert of Saxe-Coburg and Gotha, and Elgin in his by the fact of being Durham's son-in-law. The Liberal hour had struck in Britain and the dawn of Reform in Canada was at hand.

* * *

British embrace of free trade and the decline of Imperial preference started a tug of war between economic orientation to the United States and the rest of the world, especially, at the outset, Britain and the Empire. One of the preliminary ingredients of responsible government was a Canadian-originated tariff policy, and protection asserted itself quickly, but the first consequence was economic recession, and the population of Montreal declined in the late 1840s from 65,000 to 58,000.[52]

Lord Elgin arrived in Montreal on January 29, 1847. Expectations were high for an end to the constitutional impasse. William Draper's government had reached, in Leacock's words, "its last stage of decrepitude."[53] "Sweet William," the "artful dodger," couldn't keep the balls in the air any longer and retired and went to the Court of Queen's Bench (and remained a jurist for the rest of his life, as chief justice of the Court of Common Pleas from 1856 to 1869, and of the Court of Appeal from 1869 to his death, aged seventy-six, in 1877). Draper was a talented and generally admirable transitional figure from the abusive parochialism of the Family Compact to the responsible government enacted by those who would bring Canada to nationhood. Henry Sherwood became the attorney general (premier in fact) in a joint government with the timeless Dominick Daley, but only to play out the string of the outgoing Assembly: a caretaker operation in which Denis-Benjamin Papineau was the only French Canadian, the ambiguous bearer of a famous name. The new regime survived by only two votes a bruising confidence battle on its opening address led by Baldwin and LaFontaine. The session did incorporate enterprises for the "magnetic telegraph," as its predecessors had for railways (which will be summarized in Chapter 4), and emergency relief for the victims of the Irish famine who were arriving, in pitiable and desperate condition, in Canada. Baldwin was the co-founder of the Emigration Association of Toronto, which gave great assistance to these destitute people, who would yet make a great contribution to the new country on whose abundant shores they had fetched up.

There was little suspense of the result when Governor General Elgin dissolved the Assembly for new elections on December 6, 1847, and on January 24 Baldwin and LaFontaine and the returning Hincks swept the Canadas, Baldwin's Liberals taking twenty-six of the forty-two constituencies in West Canada, while LaFontaine carried thirty-six of the forty-two in East Canada. Baldwin would sit for Toronto and LaFontaine for Montreal, and the former districts of both returned partisans who better spoke the language of the voters, but their terms as representatives of the others' provinces and ethnic and cultural groups remain a distinguished link in the political progress of Canada. On election night, Baldwin said, "We shall have no more representatives of the sovereign making the doctrine of the Charleses and Jameses the standard by which to govern British subjects in the nineteenth century. . . . [They] will be distinguished by adherence to the constitutional principles acknowledged by all parties in England, which will relieve Her Majesty's representative from the invidious position of head of a party and will render him . . . a living spirit and the connecting link which binds this great colony to the parent state in affectionate and prosperous union."[54] Thus began what became known, not undeservedly, as the Great Ministry.

The Assembly met on February 28, and Baldwin's motion to put Augustin-Norbert Morin in as Speaker in place of Sir Allan MacNab passed 56–19. (Papineau's chief collaborator in the Ninety-Two Resolutions thus replaced the chief of the militia that routed the Upper Canada rebels.) Apart from the co-leaders and Francis Hincks, the new ministry included René-Édouard Caron, Thomas Aylwin, Étienne-Paschal Taché, and William Hume Blake. A program of comprehensive electoral, judicial, and university reform, public works, an interprovincial railroad from Quebec to Halifax, and the takeover of the postal service from the Imperial government were all announced. Elgin also announced on behalf of the Imperial government that the non-acceptance of French as an official language of the Legislature was repealed – news he imparted in very comprehensible French – and that, subject to the legislators' approval, the Queen proposed to pardon all those still serving any form of penalty in respect of the upheavals of 1837 and 1838. Louis-Joseph Papineau had already received a non-prosecution decree from Metcalfe on LaFontaine's request, and had been elected in 1847 as member for Saint-Maurice. His return was not a success: he raged against the prorogation while those elevated to the ministries had to go through a further election, and when the session reconvened in 1849, he unwisely and ungratefully attacked LaFontaine for a "constitution of the country" that was "false, tyrannical, and calculated to demoralize the people, conceived by statesmen of a narrow and malevolent genius" who would lead French Canada to "results that are ruinous and disastrous." LaFontaine, to whom Papineau owed his right of return and election and the French Canadians owed their full emergence from inferior political status to full partnership in a voluntary union, and who had declined office from Metcalfe and Draper, eviscerated his former chief: "Behold now this man obeying his ancient instinct of pouring forth insult and outrage, and daring . . . to accuse me and my colleagues of venality, of a sordid love of office, and of servility to those in power . . . [were it not for whom, Papineau] would be in Paris, fraternizing, I suppose with the red republicans, the white republicans, or the black republicans and approving, one after the other, the fluctuating constitutions of France."[55]

In fact, for the French Canadians, all had changed utterly. Their isolation was, at least conceptually, over, and they were invited to participate in full equality with English Canadians in an entity that enjoyed the freedom of British citizens, the protection of the British Empire, and the rising prosperity of the New World, in a harmony with the great American republic that British statesmen had suavely negotiated at the expense of the distant Mexicans (who had no more possibility of holding what they had just lost to the United States than Canada would have of retaining its independence if the British withdrew their protection of it). LaFontaine had referred to Papineau's love of republicanism and revolutionary posturing. Papineau was intoxicated by the lengthy and ever-changing political menu of France, while most Canadians and most others preferred, at least for themselves, if not as spectators, the political continuity with gradual reform of Great Britain.

Following the debacles of the French Revolution, and the Bourbon Restoration, Louis-Philippe, the egalitarian king, though one of the wealthiest men in France, was installed on behalf of the House of Orléans and ran a constitutional monarchy that favoured the bankers and industrialists and gradually lost the bourgeoisie and was never popular with the working class. The franchise was gradually whittled down to about 1 per cent of the people by 1848, and the opposition, which included large numbers of republicans, socialists, and supporters of other potential monarchs, was clearly an immense challenge to any chance of continuity of the regime. Very large dissident elements arose around competing newspapers and held banquets in their own honour as a way of avoiding the politically restrictive laws against the opposition. The French bourgeoisie noted the First Reform Act in Britain. Opposition grew, and instead of appeasing the moderate elements and gently closing the gate on the rest, Louis-Philippe outlawed these political banquets, eliciting a general revolt (as only the French would mount against a banning of good dinners). Mobs forced the resignation of the prime minister, the historian François Pierre Guizot, and then marched on the Quai d'Orsay (the Ministry of Foreign Affairs). By accident, a musket was discharged, volleys followed, and fifty-two people were killed, mayhem followed, and Louis-Philippe fled to London in the footsteps of Charles X (who had died twelve years before). The Second Republic was founded, and the poet Alphonse de Lamartine, an absurd choice to lead such a complicated country, became provisional president. The electorate was multiplied thirty-fold with universal adult male suffrage, to nine million, and the chronic problem of unemployment (about a third of the workforce in Paris) was tackled by the National Workshops, an advanced workfare program. There was the predictable flight of capital and polarization of political opinion, and the Lamartine government was soon forced to impose new land taxes that aggravated the sharpest divisions of French society. A well-known trajectory, to be followed frequently in the future, was followed. The radicals called for international revolution (and Poland, which had been divided between Austria, Prussia, and Russia, was the first to heed the call). By this time, Klemens von Metternich, who had been foreign minister of the Holy Roman Empire since 1809 and chancellor of the Austrian Empire since 1821, was sent packing by angry mobs, even in placid Vienna (to London, of course). Richard Wagner had been among the more energetic demonstrators in Vienna, as Friedrich Engels had been among the more prolific pamphleteers and polemicists in Paris, harbingers of German militarist nationalism and of the Communist movement, which would henceforth lurk in Europe's future.

Everything in the old and unsettled continental Europe, everything between gradually reforming Britain and glacially immoveable Russia, was coming loose. The working class of Paris, fearing they were

losing out again, seized the National Assembly and proclaimed a provisional government, but were chased out by the National Guard as the
forces of reaction gained the upper hand. The National Workshops
were shut down in June, hundreds of thousands of working-class rioters
erected barricades, and General Louis-Eugène Cavaignac was recalled
from Algeria to quell the disorder. He did this brusquely and crushed
the uprisings with 125,000 troops and special militia. In the election for
president of the Second Republic on December 10, 1848, Cavaignac
ran as the candidate of the reactionary right, Alexandre-Auguste Ledru-
Rollin ("I must follow the mob, for I am their leader") as candidate
of the moderate reformers, François-Vincent Raspail as candidate of the
far left, and Napoleon's nephew, Louis-Napoleon Bonaparte, as enigmatic candidate of French greatness and the satisfaction of everyone.
Raspail received around 50,000 votes, Ledru-Rollin 370,000, Cavaignac
1,475,000, and the smooth-talking charlatan Bonaparte 5.58 million,
and so this was the devolution of all these events that so entranced the
returned Papineau.

In the world, the dynamism of America was sapped by the agony
of slavery; France was a shambles of riots, revolutionaries, poseurs, and
men on horseback; Central Europe was in complete disorder as Prussia
gained, Austria slipped, the patchwork of nationalities seethed and
agitated, and Russia was little advanced from the Middle Ages. Great
Britain led the world in political reform, in the Industrial Revolution,
and in its serene, sea-borne strength, and diplomatic cunning and ability to manipulate the permutations of the world's powers to its own gain.
Pax Britannica was entering its most brilliant phase, over the next
twenty years, until the resolution of America's slavery schism and the
rise of Bismarckian Germany would present a benign American rivalry,
and a mortal German challenge.

In Canada, now sheltering happily in the British orbit, but not so distant
from or impervious to the great events of the Western world as it had
been, the entire reform program of Baldwin and LaFontaine was passed.
This may be taken as Canada's entirely positive and peaceful contribution to the epochal year of 1848 that convulsed Europe from Paris to
Warsaw. Under the Great Ministry of Baldwin and LaFontaine, a protective tariff in response to Peel's move to free trade, the queen's amnesty, a

well-crafted reorganization of the judiciary, a radical and well-designed reorganization of municipal government, Baldwin's university initiative, and railway legislation, were all intelligently debated, constructively amended, and adopted. It was a model of self-government such as few other national or quasi-national jurisdictions could claim. Francis Hincks proved a virtual Alexander Hamilton of Canada. A railway connecting the St. Lawrence at La Prairie to Lake Champlain and the Hudson at Saint-Jean had already been built, as had part of the Grand Trunk Railway from Montreal to Portland, Maine, and parts of the Great Western and Northern Railways. Hincks as inspector general began the Canadian practice (which would crest a century later with C.D. Howe) of government aid to private sector works of national economic interest by promising 6 per cent assistance by the government on half the cost of any railway of more than seventy-five miles in length. Hincks's effort at freer trade reciprocity with the United States required five years to bear fruit, but was the forerunner of the unsuccessful effort of Sir Wilfrid Laurier sixty years later, and of the Free Trade Agreement successfully pursued by Brian Mulroney eighty years after that.

Much the most controversial measure was the Rebellion Losses Bill, which was well-accepted as it applied to victims of the events of 1837 and 1838 but evoked extreme controversy over what the Tory English claimed in the most violent terms was a craven and corrupt reward to "aliens and rebels," as Allan MacNab rather loosely described large numbers of his French-speaking compatriots. MacNab and the Upper Canada solicitor general, William Blake, almost came to blows in the Assembly. The act excluded from benefit anyone convicted of an act of rebellion. Upper Canadian losses were paid from a fund collected in Upper Canada; it was proposed that Lower Canadian losses be paid from a general fund of the Province of Canada. This naturally enflamed the sensibilities of the susceptible (though here again, this was just the modest opening ripple of a pelagic wave of transfer payments that would flow from English to French Canada more than a century later). In fact, as the arithmetic worked out, it was not especially favourable to French Canadians, as LaFontaine laboriously explained, but this was a bold step in internecine Canadian relations.

Conditions were aggravated by the return of William Lyon Mackenzie, and the international press took note of the agitation. The

New York Herald predicted the imminent secession of Canada from the British Empire (which in fact no one anywhere in the Canadas was seeking), and the *Times* of London, the most influential newspaper in the world, reported a tense struggle between "Royalists" and the sympathizers with "rebellion" and declared that Canada "hangs by a thread." Elgin gave assent to the Rebellion Losses Bill on April 25, 1849. The governor's carriage was stoned, with him in it, and fire bells in Montreal called out the mobs in emulation of the only larger French-speaking city in the world, where they had shown their explosive potential in driving out Louis-Philippe the year before. And in the highest Parisian tradition, the House of Assembly was stormed and sacked and burned to the ground, including the parliamentary library of twenty thousand books, as the mobs stoned firemen who came to extinguish the blaze. MacNab saved the portrait of the queen, but in the following three days the homes of Hincks and LaFontaine and the boarding house where Baldwin stayed were attacked and partially destroyed, and the governor's carriage was again attacked, pursued by an assortment of vehicles, and Elgin's brother was seriously injured.

The only incongruity in the comparison with Paris is that the mobs in this case were angry English Montrealers who resented liberality to the French majority of Lower Canada. These frictions, the product of ancient racial hatreds and the isolation of the two Canadas from each other, would be a long time passing. Montreal forfeited its right to continue as the country's capital (which would then alternate in four-year terms between Toronto and Quebec), and to this day the city has its English-speaking population to thank for that. Both houses of the British Parliament debated the issue of the Rebellion Losses Bill in June 1849. The strongest critic, in force of argument, not ferocity, was William Ewart Gladstone, then forty and a rising former colonial secretary. Benjamin Disraeli spoke in support of the measure and of Grey's conduct, but the principal substantive reply to Gladstone, who despite his thoroughness was afflicted by misunderstandings, came in a lengthy letter from Francis Hincks in the *Times*. Hincks was in London to arrange financing for his public works program, but also as a special envoy on the Rebellion Losses issue, and he met with Russell, Grey, Gladstone, and others. Hincks pointed out Gladstone's errors in accusing Baldwin and LaFontaine of being ex-rebels, and Disraeli's in surmising that there was an issue of French domination of English Canadians. Both British future prime ministers thought there had been no rebels in Upper Canada. Hincks, a capable editor himself (of the Montreal *Pilot*), wrote with exactly the appropriate combination of factual rigour and wry humour that "I should imagine that the author of *Coningsby* [one of Disraeli's slightly racy novels] understands the meaning of getting up a 'good cry' to serve party purposes," and generally reflected that "it is very unsafe for parties at a distance of three thousand miles to interfere in our affairs. . . . I claim for myself and my colleagues [in Upper and Lower Canada] that we have as much true British feeling as any member of that party which seems to wish to monopolize it."[56]

Hincks supported his economic mission with a pamphlet entitled "Canada and Its Financial Resources," and recorded that from 1824 to 1848 Upper Canada's population had risen by 400 per cent and Lower Canada's by 50 per cent (they were now both around 750,000) and that similar figures of growth were attained in every sector of the economy. The Canadas were the most prosperous part of the British world, and the ratios of public revenues to debt were very favourable. His mission to London was an overwhelming success on all fronts. Elgin and his ministers had all played difficult roles with great firmness and steadiness; the crisis passed and Canada moved a giant step closer to autonomous statehood under the sponsorship of the majestic British Empire.

Britain repealed the last of the protectionist Navigation Acts in 1849, which greatly opened up the harbours of Quebec and Montreal and the canalization of the St. Lawrence, and the expanded access to the lower Great Lakes accelerated rising prosperity. There were further reforms in 1850, including a reduction in postal rates, the establishment of separate school systems for Roman Catholics – a world-leading advance in religious toleration – and further judicial reforms. The radicals were now gaining strength, as English Canada started on what would long prove its vocation of being at the vanguard of reform. Clear Grits, as the left wing of the Liberals were called, demanded universal (adult male) suffrage, election even of the governor, secret ballots, no property qualifications for MPs, fixed term elections, a gentler judicial and usury regime for the poor, the end of primogeniture, and secularization of the Clergy Reserves. A group of followers of Papineau led by Antoine-Aimé

Dorion (1818–1891) called itself the Parti Rouge and adopted a platform similar to that of the Upper Canada radicals and demanded the dissolution of the union of Upper and Lower Canada to boot.

Baldwin and LaFontaine attacked the Clergy Reserves issue in 1850, proposing the abolition of the Anglican privilege, but this would require repeal of the Imperial statute of 1840. The goal was to open up this vast Crown land holding to national development after wrenching it free of the inflexible grip of the Anglican (or any other) church. Hincks was for secularization but thought it impractical; LaFontaine was not in favour of secularization, as he thought the land should be dedicated to educational purposes; and Baldwin straddled the issue, elegantly enough but not convincingly. The fissures within the Great Ministry were obvious. On June 26, 1851, to open the divisions in the ministry, the radical factions pushed a cleverly designed bill in favour of abolishing the court of chancery. Baldwin lost the vote among his Upper Canadian colleagues because of the avarice of the elected members of the bar, and only was able to defeat the measure by reliance on LaFontaine. Robert Baldwin, ever the conscientious man, tired and sated by the victory of his long quest for responsible government, resigned on June 30, 1851. All sides graciously praised his achievements and his character, and LaFontaine announced that he would retire at the end of the session.

The Great Ministry passed into history, where its benign influence has been indelible. In the election that followed, Baldwin felt it his duty to stand for re-election but did not campaign and was uninterested in the outcome; he only felt it his duty to give his constituents the ability to vote for or against him. (He lost narrowly.) LaFontaine withdrew, but in 1853 was appointed chief justice of Lower Canada and exercised that role with great distinction until he died, a baronet, on February 26, 1864, aged fifty-six. Robert Baldwin retired completely to his comfortable Toronto home (Spadina), and declined, for reasons of health, his former protégé John A. Macdonald's offer of the post of chief justice of common pleas in 1855 and a seat on the Legislative Council in 1858. He died on December 9 of that year, aged just fifty-four. Both men sacrificed their health and longevity to build a bridge between the solitudes of English and French Canada, entrench democratic rule in both, and end any formal advantage of one group over the other. They were pioneers in building an officially bicultural parliamentary democracy and steered successfully through fierce gales on a middle course of democracy without mob rule, property without oligarchic privilege, and retention of the backing of the British Empire to deter the intrusion of the United States, while attaining the same rights for Canadians that British (and American) citizens enjoyed. They managed by the logic and irresistible merit of their goals as by the patience, moderation, and suavity of their methods. "Baldwin retained his Anglicanism, his colonial aristocratic attitude (he owned fifty thousand acres), and his attachment to the Crown. . . . He was too cold, too correct, too consistent, and like Aristides, too just, for popularity, but it is to him more than to any other one man that Canada owes self-government. . . . LaFontaine committed his people . . . to constitutionalism. Lower Canada, thanks to him, was not to become a precedent for Ireland. No aspirations towards the widest possible future for the race were to be abandoned, but in the future, these were to be realized at the polls and through debate, not through gunpowder."[57] They were unswervingly principled, tolerant of any reasonable opposition, and had no interest in office for the mere sake of holding it. They came into public life with a purpose and left it when the purpose was accomplished, like Cincinnatus, or Washington. The debt of all Canadians to them, 170 years later, is very great.

4. The Hincks–Morin Government, 1851–1854

The opposition to the Reform government was divided between the anti-conservative *rouges* of Canada East, who were somewhat anti-clerical and well to the left of the Reformers in social and constitutional policy, and the Clear Grits in Canada East, who were rabidly anti-French and anti-Roman Catholic, but also rather populist and anti-establishment. The leader of the *rouges* was Antoine-Aimé Dorion, and of the Clear Grits George Brown, the founder and editor of the Toronto *Globe*. Brown opposed aid to separate schools, distrusted the French influence in the government, was opposed to any state favoritism to any church, and suspected the regime of not wishing to secularize the Clergy Reserves. These issues were aggravated by what was called "the papal aggression question," imported from Britain, because the Roman Catholic Church in Great Britain had reconstituted itself on a diocesan basis after a lapse of three hundred years since it was shattered and suppressed by the apostate Henry VIII. This was what the great theologian, Roman convert, former vicar of Oxford, and future cardinal John Henry Newman in one of his most famous addresses called the Second Spring. Such was the fragility of religious tolerance even in advanced corners of the British world that so innocuous an event could be widely construed as aggression.

In a by-election in Ontario in the spring of 1851, Brown had stood and Hincks did not give him the Reform endorsement. Brown was defeated, it was believed, especially by him, by the influence of Irish and German Roman Catholic immigrants. Baldwin resigned from office that June, and Brown withdrew from the Reform party and ended all connection with it in July. On the retirement of Baldwin and LaFontaine, a new government was formed headed by Francis Hincks, the financier and former tenant of the Baldwin family, newspaper editor, and capable public administrator, who had earned widespread respect as inspector general in the Great Ministry, and Augustin-Norbert Morin, co-author with Louis-Joseph Papineau of the now rather quaint Ninety-Two Resolutions of 1834 and Speaker of the Legislative Assembly through the profound debates of the Baldwin–LaFontaine era. He consented to serve as co-leader with Hincks, and they had an agreed division of work. Hincks, the man of commerce, was chiefly concerned with railways, public works, and trade and tariffs, and Morin, as provincial secretary and commissioner of Crown lands, pursued the old bugbears of the abolition of the seigneurial regime, separate schools in Canada West, where they were a good deal more contested a concept, for obvious reasons, than in French Canada, and the transformation of the Legislative Council into an elected House. The seigneurial and Legislative Council issues were the last hangovers from Morin's days as a sidekick of Papineau, and he was concerned to clear away the detritus of revolutionary disaffection in Lower Canada, which he had sloughed off personally more than a decade before.

Hincks and Morin advised Governor General Elgin to dissolve the Assembly for new elections, which were held in December 1851, and returned the Reform majority pretty much as it had been. The new industrial passion was railroads, and they did offer astounding prospects of moving people and freight with unimagined rapidity and in undreamed-of volume. There was naturally a competition between Canada and the United States, as there had been in the fur trade, to develop rail lines to the west and from the interior of North America to the Atlantic, or to water that connected to it. Hincks had been the champion of the Guarantee Act in the previous government, which had opened the era of Canadian public and private sector cooperation in great projects with assurances of a government guaranty of 6 per cent interest for the debt of railways of more than seventy-five miles once they had been half built. Once installed as co-leader of the government, Hincks got back to work on a plan for joint financing by Canada, Nova Scotia, and New Brunswick of a railway from Halifax to Windsor or Sarnia, on what was then the western boundary of Canada and a point of entry into the United States. Hincks was dealing with the premiers of the two Atlantic provinces: Edward Chandler of New Brunswick and Joseph Howe of Nova Scotia. The two provinces wanted separate routes to the sea, as Howe was opposed to Saint John, New Brunswick, being given direct access to such a railway, as it would increase its ability to compete with Halifax. Hincks went to Halifax and gave such a powerful speech in favour of his plan (which Chandler supported and made both cities an ocean terminus of the line) that Howe was persuaded and graciously changed his position. The only remaining roadblock was the professed reluctance of the Imperial government to assist a plan that would be vulnerable to American attack in the event of hostilities. Hincks returned to Britain to persuade Westminster to assist the railway and to repeal its 1841 Clergy Reserve Act and enable the Canadas to legislate their own solution. He was also seeking a reciprocity trade agreement with the United States. (Derby, the former Lord Stanley, and Disraeli were now in office, with Disraeli as chancellor of the exchequer and leader of the House of Commons.)

Hincks found the new colonial secretary, Sir John Somerset Pakington, very unsympathetic, and Hincks, with an agility at moving between the public and private sectors shared by few others in Canadian history, concluded that British government support, if available at all, would be very late and heavily conditionalized. He negotiated financing in the City of London for a main rail route from Montreal to Toronto and Hamilton as a private sector undertaking. Pakington fully justified Hincks's foreboding by ignoring him and informing Elgin directly that the Clergy Reserve Act would not be modified or repealed, and he rejected Hincks's proposal to enhance the possibilities for a trade reciprocity arrangement with the United States by granting American vessels free navigation of the St. Lawrence River. Hincks called upon Pakington again and told him that "there will be no end of agitation in Canada if the attempt be made to settle this question permanently according to public opinion in England instead of that of the province itself."[58] Despite the desperately slow progress toward responsible government that had finally achieved its object, and all the unsatisfactory superannuated generals and humdrum careerists that the British generally inflicted on the Canadas as governors, and the reactionary reflexes of even otherwise rather liberal colonial secretaries such as Russell, this was a surprising disappointment to descend on the visiting chief minister of a colony that now had over 10 per cent of Britain's population and formidable prospects and was considerably more prosperous per capita than the Mother Country.

This was the worst decade of the Irish famine, and emigration to Canada from the British Isles increased from 25,000 per year in the early part of the 1840s to almost 50,000 per year near the end of the decade. It peaked in 1847 with 90,000 arrivals at Quebec City, 40,000 of whom eventually reached Toronto, a city of only 20,000 at the start of the year. (The Roman Catholic and Anglican churches cooperated admirably in settling these people.) From 1841 to 1851, the population of Canada West increased from 452,000 to 952,000, while that of Canada East grew in the same period from 697,000 to 890,000. The force of English-speaking immigration seeking an English-speaking but British destination thus enabled this inland colony to outstrip Lower Canada despite the mighty Quebec birthrate. There were at this point about 550,000 people in Nova Scotia, New Brunswick, and Prince Edward Island, so these colonies together had almost as many citizens as had the Thirteen Colonies at the start of the American Revolution seventy-five years before (this excludes the Americans' 500,000 slaves at that time). Only the need for British protection from the American appetite for national expansion condemned Canadians to the patient rote of petitions and importunity to which the British, for a while longer, subjected them, *de haut en bas*, though more from indifference than from disdain. In his hostility to the French and to Roman Catholics, George Brown quickly became the leading opposition figure from Canada West, and that province, which had been quite happy with parliamentary representation equal to Canada East's when Canada East was more populous, now railed vituperatively against under-representation opposite the French papists.

Hincks, though a life-long supporter of representation by population, sagely told the Assembly, "The truth was that the people occupying Upper and Lower Canada were not homogeneous. . . . They differed in feelings, language, laws, religion, and institutions, and therefore the Union must be considered as one between two distinct peoples, each returning an equal number of representatives."[59] Baldwin, LaFontaine, and Hincks, and not at this point Brown, grasped what was essential for Canada to be viable: the French Canadians had to be numerous and tenacious enough to be durable; they had to be joined by an at least equal number of English-speaking non-Americans; the two groups had to work out their own arrangements, as they were doing in what was set up just a decade earlier by Durham and Sydenham with the impossible and discreditable ambition of assimilating and acculturating the French; and the whole would need the protection of the British, however patronizingly furnished, until Canada was strong enough no longer to be irresistible bait to the expansionist ambitions of the United States.

Hincks continued his tussle with the Imperial Protector to the 1852 session, where he gained adoption of his resolution that the Parliament of the Province of Canada had the authority to settle the Clergy Reserves question without reference to Westminster, and the British Parliament did, in fact, repeal the 1841 Clergy Reserves Act, leaving the Province a free hand to deal with secularization of the reserves and reform the seigneurial system. Hincks also gained approval of his expanded plan to build the Grand Trunk Railway from the year-round port of Portland, Maine, to Quebec and Montreal and west to Toronto and on to the U.S. border at Sarnia. This brought Hincks into productive contact with another eminent straddler of the public and private sectors, Alexander Tilloch Galt. Hincks sponsored discussions between Galt and William M. Jackson, a London financier who had returned from Britain with Hincks, and Jackson and Galt, with Hincks's backing, packaged together a lot of projects, rights-of-way, real estate, and uncompleted road beds and unfinished lines, which formed the base of this spinal railroad of 12,100 miles and financed by an underwriting from Baring Brothers in London. The Government of the Canadas was to guaranty three thousand pounds of bonds for every mile completed, and these measures were passed without significant opposition in bills of 1852, 1853, and 1854.

Another rather inspired measure that Hincks presented and which was adopted was the Municipal Loan Fund Bill, which facilitated municipal participation in railway construction by pledging the issuance of bonds of the Province of Canada on its credit in international financial markets, backed by municipal railway bonds that would not ordinarily have access to those markets. This led to some controversy, as Hincks and the mayor of Toronto, John George Bowes, at Bowes's suggestion, bought some Toronto debentures from the contractors of the Ontario, Simcoe and Huron Railway at a 20 per cent discount. Hincks arranged their resale as sterling debentures, enabling Hincks and Bowes to trouser an almost ten-thousand-pound profit in quick time on an investment of forty thousand pounds. They did not reveal their interest as the City of Toronto and the government of the Province of Canada consolidated debt under Hincks's Municipal Loan Fund provisions. Bowes's municipal opponents got wind of the mayor's windfall, the City sued him, and Hincks's participation emerged in the ensuing proceedings.

Hincks vehemently denied wrongdoing, but Brown and others were handed an open goal and were able to generate tremendous suspicion and hostility over other episodes where the public interest and that of Hincks himself appeared to have been infelicitously commingled. Brown wrongly accused him of buying St. Lawrence and Atlantic Railroad shares on insider information, and he was also wrongly accused of profiting from a bond issue by the City of Montreal on the London market that Hincks had tried to help negotiate. There was a great flurry of other allegations, including one of profiteering from land acquisitions adjacent to the canal at Sault Ste. Marie. But the most damaging charge, and the only one that may have had some merit, apart from the non-disclosure of the Bowes arrangement, was that a thousand founders' shares of the Grand Trunk Railway had been issued in Hincks's name and the deposit for payment had been made by the contractor. The explanation was that Hincks was holding the stock in trust for distribution to ordinary Canadians, but it had the appearance of a bribe. When Hincks returned in June 1854 from a visit to London and to Washington, where he had led negotiations on a reciprocity treaty, he was met by a hostile Assembly, and he and Morin advised Elgin to dissolve Parliament for new elections. (Elgin sponsored the Reciprocity Treaty of 1854, between all of British North America and the United States, as he believed, correctly, "that nothing but entrance to the American markets could save Canada for the Empire."[60]) Given the falsity of almost all the allegations against Hincks and the unjust charge that he was deliberately dragging his heels about secularization of the Clergy Reserves and reform of the seigneurial system, Hincks and Morin did well to be returned with the largest parliamentary group, but they were without a majority and tendered their resignations on September 8.

Hincks feared that Brown and John Sandfield Macdonald (leader of the Canada West English Catholics and solicitor general) would, if they got control of it, sever the link between the Reform party of Canada East and its French-Canadian allies and destabilize the union, French-English relations, and the entire status of the Canadas as a prospering entity worthy of British protection, and he tried to put together alternative coalitions. He did not directly succeed, but the imperishable Sir Allan MacNab reappeared as a conciliatory figure and proposed a coalition with Morin in which the followers of Hincks would play a prominent role, Hincks himself having determined to withdraw from public life. Hincks endorsed this plan and the program of the new government in waiting, which included secularization of the Clergy Reserves (eliminating Brown's endlessly and loudly repeated fear that the Province's various religious denominations would stultify its development by holding vast acreages in permanent mortmain, the cold terror that could only grip a disestablished Protestant); abolition of seigneurial tenure (it was now largely exercised by English-Canadian proprietors to exploit cheap farm labour); and the transition to an elected Legislative Council.

The traditional Tory view of Hincks was recorded a century later by conservative historian and authoritative John A. Macdonald biographer Donald Creighton: "A clever little man – a typical sharp-eyed child of that unpleasantly prolific marriage between railways and responsible government, Hincks had gone about the business of furthering his own personal interests with the direct, uncomplicated ingenuity of a precocious infant. He had presented the public with a scandal so simple, so instantly comprehensible, so wholly malodorous that it brought unmitigated damage to the government."[61] This was an absurdly biased and unjust account, but a faithful echo of the vitriolic partisanship of the era of which Creighton wrote, though Macdonald himself was not overly censorious about it (and did worse himself). A select committee of the Assembly sat for two years looking into Hincks's conduct and concluded that there were no grounds to accuse him of corruption. Whatever his intentions with the thousand shares of Grand Trunk that he didn't pay for, he never took possession of them and the only indiscretion was his failure to reveal the deal with Bowes, which the laws and regulations of the time did not require. Bowes had to return his share of the profit but Hincks did not. Francis Hincks retired from the Assembly on November 16, 1855. He had intended to take up the presidency of the Grand Trunk Railway, but while he was in England on a business holiday, Queen Victoria herself offered him the post of governor of Barbados and the Windward Islands. This was a complete vindication of his probity, and he accepted it and served as a progressive and well-regarded governor until moving on to the larger posting of governor of British Guiana (Guyana) in 1861. Francis Hincks did not evidently possess the insight into monetary policy of Alexander Hamilton, but he did possess in full measure Hamilton's grasp of economics and the likely course of industry. He stands as probably the greatest unifier of the public and private sectors for the greater national good that there was in North America between Hamilton and C.D. Howe, the American-born Canadian economic czar of the Second World War and the postwar boom, a century after Hincks. Hincks had rendered great service, not only as an economic minister, but also as Baldwin's chief adjutant in the pursuit of responsible government and as a brilliant diplomatic envoy to the Imperial government on several occasions and thorny issues. His service to Canada, when defamatory cant and emotionalism subsided, would be long and gratefully remembered, and he would be back and in a great office in a matured country after his sojourn in the Caribbean.

The first Canadian railway was the sixteen-mile Champlain and Saint Lawrence Railroad line to go round the rapids on the Richelieu River and improve the link from the St. Lawrence to the Hudson. It was a horse-drawn railway for its first year until a locomotive could be imported in 1837. A series of what were called portage lines, linking inland harbours, were built in the following decade: Buffalo to Goderich (on Lake Huron); Toronto to Collingwood (on Georgian Bay); and Sir Allan MacNab's Great Western Railway from Buffalo through southwestern Ontario to Detroit. These lines undercut the economic viability of Montreal, which accordingly sought a rail link to an all-season Atlantic port; this was the origin of the interest in Portland, Maine, after the British government dragged its feet on the proposed line to Halifax and Saint John, because that line would have to go down the Saint John River valley and would be too close to the United States to meet British requirements for military security (which were hardly going to be met by a railway whose terminus was in Portland, Maine). Portland was closer to Montreal than was Boston, but both cities sought to rival New York as gateways to and from the interior by a state-assisted and shorter route through Canada and the Great Lakes. This brought Alexander Galt into the equation, as the leading industrialist of the Eastern Townships. Galt was the commissioner of the British American Land Company, of which his father had been one of the founders, from 1843, when he was only twenty-six, to 1855. In this role, he laid out communities, planned and shaped the emerging city of Sherbrooke, and assembled land and assets for a railway. Galt would have an important political career, and then be a successful diplomat, but always seemed more interested in the commercial implications of what he was doing than anything else. (After the burning of the Parliament Building in Montreal in 1849 by English opponents of the Rebellion Losses Bill, he even signed the reactionary petition for annexation by the United States, along with such implausible signatories as the *rouge* nationalist leader, Antoine-Aimé Dorion.) Galt worked with all comers, including the sponsors of the grandiloquently styled European and North American Railway, and organized the St. Lawrence and Atlantic Railroad to go to the U.S. border and connect there with the Atlantic and St. Lawrence Railroad, being laid northwest from Portland.

The Intercolonial Railway had been much bandied about as a project to link Quebec and Halifax, but it failed to gain the official tangible support required, and was followed as the chief project by the Grand Trunk. This was founded by vote of Parliament on the motion of its counsel, George-Étienne Cartier, leader of the French-Canadian *bleus* (as opposed to Dorion's Liberal *rouges*), long-serving chairman of the Parliamentary Railway Committee, and, next to John A. Macdonald, the most important Canadian politician of the next twenty years. As this was a project which linked Montreal with the U.S. border at Sarnia and Detroit, as well as Buffalo, it satisfied the leading Canadian centres but did nothing for the Atlantic provinces. Galt had already built his line to Portland from Montreal and had a permit to extend to Kingston, and further additions to Toronto, and from Toronto to Guelph, with a group led by the Polish-Canadian financier Casimir Gzowski. The young and thinly populated provinces were in danger of being overbuilt with railways. Hincks put through legislation that would effectively combine the Grand Trunk and St. Lawrence and Atlantic, as well as encouraging the rationalization of other lines. Galt was a more efficient builder, and the Grand Trunk was extravagantly built by British contractors who went bankrupt in the mid-1850s, requiring further substantial infusions of provincial and municipal grants, thirty-five million dollars by 1867. Francis Hincks was better off governing the placid and temperate Barbados than presiding over the railway he had vitally helped to conceive. All that can be said is that there was even greater financial chaos in the railways of the United States, where there was less government involvement and no regulation of the securities issues floated to lay the track and buy the rolling stock. This led to some severe turbulence in the financial markets intermittently through the rest of the nineteenth century in the United States.

5. The MacNab–Morin Government and the Rise of John A. Macdonald and George-Étienne Cartier, 1854–1858

Sir Allan Napier MacNab was one of the great swashbucklers of Canadian history. He was born at Niagara-on-the-Lake in 1798, the son of a lieutenant in John Graves Simcoe's Queen's Rangers, and his first career was as a soldier. He enlisted on the outbreak of the War of 1812, aged only fourteen (surpassed as the youngest soldier in this narrative only by Andrew Jackson, who enlisted in the American Revolutionary army at the age of twelve). MacNab fought at Sackets Harbor,

Plattsburgh, Black Rock, and Fort Niagara, and was mustered out of service as a sixteen-year-old ensign. He became a lawyer and moved to Hamilton, where he thought the opportunity greater and more egalitarian than at York (Toronto). His first prominent case came in 1827 when he defended the men accused of tarring and feathering George Rolph (a brother of Mackenzie's close associate Dr. John Rolph, who had been exiled for five years but returned and was in the Hincks–Morin government as commissioner of Crown lands). George Rolph had been accused of adultery and was represented as counsel by William W. Baldwin, Robert Baldwin's father. MacNab made himself a Tory and Imperialist hero by refusing to testify in 1829 before an Assembly committee chaired by the elder Baldwin investigating the hanging in effigy of Sir John Colborne at Hamilton by a mob of Tories. On the basis of Mackenzie's insistence that MacNab be sent to prison for ten days for his refusal, which he was, MacNab was elected to the Assembly in 1830, where he remained for twenty-seven years. He succeeded in returning the favour to Mackenzie by having him banned on spurious grounds from the Assembly's proceedings a total of five times. Through the 1830s, MacNab became one of the greatest and most prescient landowners in the province of Upper Canada, and was generally very successful as a developer and land speculator. He was widely thought guilty of unscrupulous practices, and while many of the allegations made against him were politically motivated, it seems likely that his ethics, even by the rumbustious standards of the place and times, were not unimpeachable. By 1837, he was a successful local banker (the Gore Bank), railway owner (the Hamilton and Port Dover and the Great Western Railways), steamship owner, builder, and even tavern owner, as well as land speculator. He built a formidable seventy-two-room house, called Dundurn Castle, that survives preserved in its original state on Burlington Heights.

MacNab, though a loyal Imperial Tory, was also pro-American and operated businesses there, conducted financings in New York, and sought closer commercial relations with the United States. He was ostensibly an Anglican, but as there was no Anglican church in Hamilton for many years he attended a Presbyterian church. His second wife (his first wife died) was a Roman Catholic, and MacNab ended his life as a convert to that faith and long opposed the leader of the Orange Lodge, Ogle Gowan, the arch-foe of MacNab's adversary Robert Baldwin. Upper Canada was young and underpopulated, but it still had a very contentious political atmosphere. MacNab was elected Speaker of the Assembly in 1837, but the rebellion of that year was the occasion for his most energetic military activity. As was touched upon earlier in this chapter, he "hastily collected" approximately sixty men and sped on one of his boats to Toronto, where a shaken Governor Francis Bond Head, who had sent all his regular forces to Kingston to be able to assist Colborne in seeing off Papineau, invited MacNab to take over the defence of York. Under the nominal command of a retired colonel, MacNab led a thousand men on December 7 to Montgomery's Tavern and put the rebels to flight. Head then entrusted MacNab with the command of a force to subdue rebels in the village of London, which MacNab did in rather disorganized fashion with, as he later acknowledged, "six times as many men" as he needed. MacNab was generous with the rebel prisoners, and wound up this derring-do by helping to organize and command the seizure and burning of Mackenzie's supply ship, the *Caroline*, at Mackenzie's base on Navy Island in the Niagara River, from which he was conducting raids on Upper Canada. Despite criticism from General Colborne, Conservative leader William Draper, and the still formidable John Beverly Robinson, MacNab received a knighthood. He had in fact, by his loyalty, spontaneous leadership, and courage, earned it.

MacNab opposed responsible government, as it would, he claimed to fear, sever ties with Britain, and he didn't much like the look of union of Upper and Lower Canada, though the reason was that he feared excessive French influence in the regime designed by its creators to subsume and anglicise the French. MacNab tangled with Sydenham (though they could have had a lot in common as businessmen), and when the governor persuaded Draper's associate Samuel Bealey Harrison to run for the Assembly in Hamilton, MacNab ran against Harrison and defeated him. MacNab had been a pioneer in the technique of rushing to London with his coattails trailing out behind him to lobby the susceptible British overlords, but he eventually found that they were less responsive to his blandishments and importunings, and he imposed the customary course correction to reopen civilized discourse with Baldwin and Draper and discovered the demographic (that is, political) virtue of the French Canadians. MacNab, in the mid-1840s to early 1850s, was also very distracted by the railway industry, which he was determined would not depart the station without him; with typical and commendable forthrightness, he said, after downing "one or two bottles of good port . . . [that] all my politics are railroads." He chaired the Assembly's railway committee seven times between 1848 and 1857, and Brown, predictably, accused him of gross improprieties in the same scattergun and unsubstantiated manner that he and the *Globe* levelled allegations at Hincks. MacNab promoted his Great Western Railway by denigrating the competition as an American Trojan Horse in one case and an heirloom from the avaricious stuffed shirts of Old York on the other, while rather shamelessly, but not as corruptly as Brown claimed, using his influence in the Assembly for his own gain. MacNab's slippery hyper-selling of watered stock, as well as his slipshod administrative methods and egregious use of his political position, reduced his standing, and he was removed as president of the Great Western in 1849, though he continued as a director. He was ousted by Baldwin and LaFontaine as Speaker of the Assembly in 1848, though not without a generous resolution of thanks, in favour of Morin, at the start of the Great Ministry.

MacNab was beset by creditors, having lived at the outer edge of his means, and was also intermittently gouty, but he went into defensive mode, recalibrated his guns, and soldiered on under new rules of engagement yet again. He was scandalized by the Rebellion Losses Bill, and he gasconaded as a hero of the burning down of Parliament, having carried out the portrait of Her Britannic Majesty as flames licked at it, but he was careful to avoid the annexation petition. He hastened back to London waving the union flag, but was rebuffed, largely by Hincks's victory in the exchange of editorial opinions with Gladstone. MacNab, needing a new repertoire, returned defeated but unbowed. He eased out Sherwood as leader of the Tories in 1850, spoke always with moderation of the French, kept the High Church, imperialist lackeys at arm's-length, and criticized the Great Ministry only on sensible grounds. It was a compelling performance that did not come naturally to him, and he carried it into the leadership of the opposition against Hincks. He engaged in frequent constructive discussion with Morin's entourage, and when Hincks was suddenly vulnerable to charges of impropriety (stopping well short of behaviour of which MacNab was in fact guilty), in an unusually clear illustration of the fluidity of political fortunes, the music stopped and MacNab's turn had come.

Allan MacNab suddenly had a brief shining moment at the forefront of reform; his government enacted its (and Hincks's) program: the militia was restructured, an issue where MacNab himself was knowledgeable; the Clergy Reserves were finally secularized and this perennial issue was drained of its venom; the seigneurial system, which had become an absurd anomaly exploited by sharpers rather than being, as it was intended, the cradle of a legitimate and conscientious and deserving French-Canadian nobility, was abolished; and the Legislative Council became elective. These were the swift and important attainments of the government headed by the most energetic and visible enemy of the 1837 rebels, in league with Morin, the chief author of the Ninety-Two Resolutions and the chief henchman of the great Patriote Louis-Joseph Papineau. Canada's genius for compromise and adaptation while retaining what it needed to survive and grow and define itself advanced another notch. Allan MacNab had a brilliant moment as dean of the vanguard of reform; Baldwin and LaFontaine must have watched in gape-mouthed disbelief.

For Allan MacNab, fortune fled suddenly and on winged feet, as often happens to people who have kept their world's attention as a juggler for too long. He was the subject of new rumours of self-directed financial largesse. He was taking money from the Great Western Railway as a payoff to withdraw while negotiating with the Grand Trunk he had so long opposed, and was premier of the province all the time though rarely present in the Assembly because of his advancing gout (the habit of two bottles of port at a sitting would not have helped that condition). For Allan MacNab, it all gradually slipped away. MacNab retired as premier and sailed for England in 1856. (Elgin, having successfully completed his work, departed to take up his new post as high commissioner to China, then in the midst of the Opium Wars. He had been one of the most effective and well-regarded governors any part of the Canadas had seen, and remains so.) Allan MacNab returned to Canada to retire from the Assembly in 1857, re-embarked to Britain and unsuccessfully sought election in Brighton to the British House of Commons in 1859, came back to Canada and was elected to the Legislative Council he had made an elective body in 1860, and was elected the Speaker of that House in 1862. He was adroitly trying to balance his accounts to the end. He died at his imposing Dundurn Castle on August 8, 1862, aged sixty-four, leaving an estate of no value but able to acquit its debts, his conversion to Roman Catholicism assuring him of controversy to the end and beyond.

"Inept at planning and organization but a promoter and enthusiast in many commercial, military, and political schemes, MacNab cultivated an image at the expense of substance. . . . But because he was not completely of the feudal world or a member of its ruling class, or completely of the world of steam and entrepreneurial activities, he was able to serve as an unsteady link between both."[62] Withal, he was a patriotic Canadian, a brave soldier, an important figure in the suppression of the rebellion, an influential guide of the old Tories to the harbour of Baldwinian reform, and, at the last, the agent of profound and benign change that had long been sought by crusaders more zealous and virtuous and consistent than himself.

The long, tumultuous, brilliant, and seminal hour of John Alexander Macdonald had come, not by chance but by his own enlightened merit, augmented by his talent for almost artistic chicanery. Macdonald had been born in Scotland in 1815, came to Canada at age five with his family, who settled in Kingston, and became a lawyer and was elected an alderman in 1843, and a member of the Assembly as a Conservative in 1844. Macdonald remained a member of Parliament for fourteen consecutive terms, forty-seven years, until he died. He was made receiver general and a cabinet member by Sweet William Draper in 1847, but the government was defeated in 1848. Brown's *Globe* editorialized, on Macdonald's elevation, that he was "a harmless man . . . a third class lawyer," but the more perceptive Lord Elgin, showing the new minister unusual as well as insightful attention, wrote his boss, Grey: "The prospects of the administration are brighter – a certain Mr. Macdonald, a person of consideration among the moderate Conservative, anti-Compact party has consented to accept the office of Receiver General."[63] He was back again in 1854 as organizer of the Liberal-Conservative coalition headed by MacNab and Morin, in which government Macdonald served as attorney general and was the real strength of the regime as MacNab, gouty and irascible, scrambled to salvage his fortune in preference to his public office. As MacNab ceased to be presentable as leader of the government, and three Reform ministers retired, Macdonald waited patiently a little longer and then also resigned with his Conservative colleague in the government, and then orchestrated MacNab's departure in 1856, becoming the strong man of the new government, but with Étienne-Paschal Taché as premier and Macdonald as attorney general and co-leader. Macdonald was absent in Britain promoting government projects there, and returned in the autumn to find himself leading the post-MacNab Conservatives in a coalition in which his co-leader, Taché, had retired and been replaced by George-Étienne Cartier. The government was narrowly re-elected on the heels of a landslide in Canada East, but Macdonald defeated his opponent in Kingston, John Shaw, by the almost totalitarian margin of 1,189 to 9, and Shaw was burned in effigy.

The Assembly had voted in 1856 to move the government permanently to Quebec, but in 1857 Macdonald persuaded the Assembly to reconsider and to ask Queen Victoria to choose the site of the permanent capital of the united Province of Canada, which had been bouncing around since the inhospitable English Montrealers had torched the Parliament in Montreal to the ground in 1849. Macdonald privately asked the Colonial Office to invite Her Britannic Majesty to defer her decision for ten months, until after the election, but in February 1858 she revealed her selection of the small but conveniently located Bytown, on the Ottawa River, and in gratitude for this distinction the slightly remote lumbering town, named after Colonel John By, renamed itself Ottawa. On July 28, 1858, an opposition Canada East member proposed a motion declaring Bytown an unsuitable place and asking the queen to reconsider her decision. A number of Macdonald's caucus supported the motion, the government was defeated, and Macdonald resigned. Elgin's successor as governor general, Sir Edmund Walker Head, invited George Brown to try to form a government. The law of the time required incoming ministers to resign their seats in Parliament and seek confirmation by the electors of their status as ministers. Those who had held office in the previous thirty days could return to those offices without an election. Pending the by-elections for Brown and his ministers-designate, Macdonald held a majority in the Assembly, and he defeated the government. Head declined Brown's request for a dissolution and Macdonald resumed office with a majority, as fewer than thirty days had passed since his government's defeat on the Bytown vote. Macdonald's ministry was restored, its majority intact, and what became known as the "double shuffle" entered into the lore of the country. Head insisted that the flim-flam be alleviated somewhat by making Cartier the premier and Macdonald the deputy. This was acceptable, but Macdonald ran the government, as everyone, including Cartier, a capable businessman but not remotely as adept a political operator as his chief, knew.

Macdonald was a man whose political aptitudes developed more quickly than his policy positions. He was never anti-American, but seems from his earliest political days to have considered the nature of American government unstable and prone to corruption, oppression, demagogy, and righteous outbursts of national aggression. And he was always wary of the American ambition to subsume Canada. He regarded slavery as inhuman barbarity overlaid by hypocrisy (a reasonable view, after all) and considered constitutional monarchy a superior system to republicanism, of which the United States was the only durable example in a serious country until the French Third Republic, unlike its predecessors, put down roots after 1871. A Scot, though not a notably religious man, Macdonald favoured an official treatment for the Church of Scotland as established as the Church of England, but he knew that the position of the Roman Catholics made such consideration of established Protestant churches impractical. Macdonald was a fair-minded man, without religious or racial prejudice, in the tradition of the Scottish Enlightenment. He feared American annexationism and considered the Reformers too prone to speak loosely of annexation whenever they were unable to sweep the country. (His political suspicions of the United States did not inhibit his respect for it as a fellow democracy and his admiration for many American contemporaries.) These suspicions conformed to his preference for constitutional monarchy where the sovereign was prominent enough to prevent the accumulation of too much power in the hands of officials without exercising much power personally, which seemed to him a better system of checks and balances than the American system, where one man was chief of state, head of government, commander-in-chief of the armed forces, and likely to control the Congress sufficiently to immunize himself against the judiciary (as was the case with Jackson in particular).

From Macdonald's wariness of America came his genius for staying close enough with Great Britain to deter American hegemonists, and he developed to a fine art the necessary steering of a path between the two powers, enjoying American meritocratic prosperity and liberty and optimism with British forms of government. He was rarely overly impressed with the aptitudes of the British to judge Canadian events and political personalities, or to negotiate with the Americans, who he thought usually swindled the British. But pro forma deference to the shared Mother Country was a small price to pay for the deterrent power of being under the umbrella of the British Empire opposite the Americans. Macdonald early developed the idea that Canada could develop a distinctive and even superior form of government, but knew that it depended on the pillars of taking the best of American positivism and British political moderation; the subtle and not overly cynical invocation of the two countries against each other for properly Canadian ends while being faithful and inoffensive to both; and frank and full collaboration with the French Canadians. These views developed in tandem with the acquisition of the political skills and arts necessary to shape events. His ability to achieve and hold power progressed at about the same speed as his notion of what to do with political power in the general good, of course, through the agency of his own fiercely defended incumbency. Even in the era of Lincoln, Bismarck, Palmerston, Disraeli, Gladstone, and such figures of lesser great powers as Cavour and Andrássy, John Macdonald was a noteworthy statesman who would leave a durable and entirely positive influence in the world.

6. Toward a United Canada, 1858–1862

In the United States, the long agony of slavery was now perilously approaching its climax. The supreme effort to resolve the issue had been made in the Compromise of 1850, led by three of the greatest figures in the history of the United States Senate, Henry Clay, Daniel Webster, and Stephen Douglas. It finished the tortuous process of assimilating the winnings of the Mexican–American War to early statehood, and abolished the slave trade in Washington, D.C. But it left two ticking time bombs: squatter sovereignty by which territories, as they became eligible for statehood, would determine by referendum whether they wished to be admitted as free or slave states; and a harsh tightening of the fugitive slave laws that grossly discriminated against anyone accused of being a fugitive slave in a free state, over-rewarding bounty hunters and denying the alleged fugitive any practical right of self-defence. It disgusted all moderate opinion in the North and incited the South to believe that slavery could spread to northern states (where there was no economic rationale for the importation of slaves, as they were not more productive agricultural workers in cooler climates than whites were). This assured that there would be miniature civil wars in each territory in the run-up to the determination of whether it would seek admission as a free or slave state. This is exactly what happened in Kansas in 1854, where there were competing vote totals and a great deal of violence between the two armed camps. There were terrible scenes in the attempted rounding up of fugitive slaves, and in 1857 the Supreme Court determined in the Dred Scott decision that the Missouri Compromise boundary for the admissibility of slavery of 36.30 (the Missouri–Arkansas border), was an unconstitutional confinement of slavery and that even fugitive slaves who were apparently free by operation of the law were not free and had no rights unless they were specifically emancipated by their owners. The old Whig Party had disintegrated and a new party, the Republicans, had been founded by the Whig leaders in the major states and held to the platform that slavery could not spread beyond its existing borders. The South let it be known that it would consider the election of a Republican as president to be cause for secession, and the principal Republican leaders, including the senator and former governor of New York William Henry Seward, and the talented Illinois lawyer and former congressman Abraham Lincoln, who ran against Douglas for the Senate in 1858, made it clear that any attempt to secede would be resisted by force. The great American Union was sleepwalking toward the precipice.

Canada had had an excellent record of receiving fugitive slaves. Approximately forty thousand fugitive slaves made their away along the Underground Railroad to Canada, where they were generally provided for generously and were free to move about without any segregation or restriction, though most lived in Black communities that were assisted by anti-slavery organizations in Canada, Great Britain, and the United States. The leading American anti-slavery advocates Harriet Tubman and John Brown lived in Canada at times. Tubman, one of the great heroines of American history, regarded herself as a Canadian and resided in St. Catharines, near the Niagara River, in the late 1850s. John Brown attempted to recruit white volunteers in Canada for his plan to seize the armoury at Harper's Ferry, Virginia, in 1859, an action that was suppressed by General Robert E. Lee, then of the Union Army, and for which Brown was hanged, though no one had been killed. There were at least eleven black Canadian doctors who were fugitive slaves or sons of fugitive slaves who served in the Union Army in the Civil War, and the white Canadian doctor Alexander Ross, an anti-slavery activist who had many fugitive slaves as patients, at the request of President Lincoln himself, assisted in breaking up a Confederate spy ring in Montreal. Josiah Henson, the model for Uncle Tom, the chief character in Harriet Beecher Stowe's novel *Uncle Tom's Cabin*, which sold an unheard-of total of more than two million copies in the first decade after its publication in 1852, lived in Canada for many years.

An escaped slave, Joseph Taper, settled near St. Catharines in 1839 and wrote this letter back to his former and still putative owner:

> I now take this opportunity to inform you that I am in a land of liberty, in good health. . . . Since I have been in the Queens dominions, I have been well-contented . . . man is as God intended he should be. That is, all are born free and equal . . . not like the Southern laws which puts man made in the image of God, on level with brutes. . . .
>
> We have good schools, and all the colored population [are] supplied with schools. My boy Edward who will be six years next January, is now reading, and I intend keeping him at school until he becomes a good scholar. . . .
>
> My wife and self are sitting by a good comfortable fire happy, knowing that there are none to molest [us] or make [us] afraid. God save Queen Victoria.[64]

The high point of the Cartier–Macdonald government of 1858 to 1862 was the visit to Canada of Prince Albert Edward in 1860, more than forty years later King Edward VII. He came in place of his mother, to whom the invitation was originally directed. Queen Victoria did not like sea travel. The Prince arrived at Gaspé on August 12, 1860, was met by Governor

General Edmund Walker Head and George-Étienne Cartier and a welcoming delegation, and proceeded up the St. Lawrence to Quebec. This was the first visit to the New World by an heir to the throne of Britain, and was conceived and choreographed by the prince consort, Albert, who was often very innovative. Edward was accompanied by the Duke of Newcastle, the colonial secretary and a crony of Gladstone's tainted by scandal because of the adultery and divorce of his wife and the recent elopement of his daughter with the mad and alcoholic son of the Marquess of Londonderry, who was soon committed for drunkenly assaulting her and died violently in an insane asylum. In the complicated British manner, Newcastle's daughter was eventually one of the future Edward VII's many mistresses, and she ultimately died prematurely of syphilis. The royal tour began in St. John's, Newfoundland, where, according to the New York Herald, the prince appeared to "have a very susceptible nature and has already [while dancing with the young ladies of Newfoundland] yielded to several twinges in the region of his midriff."[65]

Cartier was apparently very convivial, even singing French-Canadian songs and performing dances for the future king. The party went on to Montreal by ship, and Edward officially opened the Victoria Bridge across the St. Lawrence, then the longest in the world. The next day, the dignitaries attended an extravagant luncheon at the home of Sir George Simpson on Dorval Island, three miles west of Lachine. Simpson, in effect, as the governor of the Hudson's Bay Company, the viceroy for forty years of nearly two million square miles, was an admirable host, but it was the end of his career, albeit a fitting one: he died of a stroke a few days later. The prince laid the cornerstone for the Parliament Buildings in Ottawa on September 1 and, calling himself Baron Renfrew, visited the United States as the guest of President Buchanan, who was well-known to the royal family as a former minister to Great Britain. In Parliament, the clever and eloquent MP Thomas D'Arcy McGee called Cartier a "primo boffo," and Cartier, a spirited partygoer despite his generally austere public aspect, responded that McGee was a "baboon." Cartier was sometimes fierce in debate as well as loquacious. Joseph Howe called him a "seagull screaming in the wind . . . [with] a harsh, bad, dictatorial manner."[66] The royal visit was a huge success, although the Orange Lodge was so strong in Kingston (it was banned in Great Britain), it was agreed not to land the prince there, and Macdonald was left to explain this to his constituents.

Sir Edward Walker Head, the second consecutive clearly success-ful governor general (though he was something of a crony of Macdonald and Cartier), departed in 1861 (he had enjoyed Canada despite having lost a son by drowning at Shawinigan on the St. Maurice River in 1859), but his association with Canada would continue, as he would become the governor of the Hudson's Bay Company in 1863. He was succeeded as governor general by Charles Viscount Monck, a sensible and equa-ble diplomat, whose task was to urge upon the British North Americans the virtues of federation and of shouldering a greater burden for their own defence.

Southern states began seceding from the American Union after the election victory of Abraham Lincoln in November 1860 and Lincoln made it clear that he considered secession to be insurrection, which he was legally empowered to suppress. The American Civil War, or the War Between the States, began in earnest with the Confederate victory at the first Battle of Manassas, or Bull Run, on July 21, 1861. Both sides called for a maximum effort, and it was soon clear that the war could be long and sanguinary. Viscount Palmerston had been prime minister of Great Britain for five of the past six years, having previously been foreign secretary for fifteen years and before that the secretary at war for twelve years. He was a very powerful and astute statesman, the ne plus ultra of gunboat diplomacy, who had been one of the creators of the Kingdom of Belgium and of the authors of the resolution of the status of Schleswig and Holstein (between Denmark and Germany, which resolution, he later said, only two people other than him had understood: "One is dead, one is mad, and I've forgotten"). He had suc-cessfully ended the Crimean War, had no love for America, and, like Russell and Gladstone, would have preferred a Confederate victory to cut America down to size. The comparative outsiders, Disraeli and Prince Albert, warned of the dangers of provoking even a war-wracked America, because however the war ended, British colonies and interests in the Americas would then be indefensible against the Union, and mor-ally Britain could not take up a stance in favour of slaveholding and secession. Palmerston was a feared and forceful man who threatened war on Greece over the status of a single British citizen, Don Pacifico, a

Portuguese born in Gibraltar. Palmerston sired an illegitimate child in his seventies (Disraeli said that making this fact public would only increase Palmerston's majority at the next election), and served as prime minister into his eighties.

The British were concerned that American belligerency, in this atmosphere, was an increased possibility and they sent fourteen thousand trained soldiers and sizeable grants to mobilize, train, and equip an enlarged Canadian militia. Palmerston's colonial secretary, the Prince of Wales's friend Newcastle (only a distant relative of the prime minister of a century before), encountered New York Senator William H. Seward in the autumn of 1860, while accompanying the prince, just after Seward had lost the Republican presidential nomination to Lincoln. Seward would soon become secretary of state, and he told Newcastle that he knew Britain would not dare go to war with the United States. Newcastle replied, "There is no people under Heaven from whom we should endure so much as from yours; to whom we shall make such concessions. . . . But once touch us in our honour and you will very soon see the bricks of New York and Boston falling about your heads." This was the reason Canadian leaders endured so much intermittent condescension and obtuseness from the home government: these sentiments were all that kept American hands off Canada for the 130 years from the American Revolution to the First World War.[67] Yet Macdonald was able to say "in 1861 that the province was becoming an ally rather than a dependency of Great Britain."[68]

In November 1861, an American warship stopped the British steamer *Trent* near the Bahamas and removed two Confederate diplomats bound for Britain and France. The British demanded their release, which Lincoln eventually granted, and sent eleven more brigades of soldiers to Canada. John A. Macdonald was created minister of militia affairs and mobilized thirty-eight thousand men, and was gratified that the French Canadians responded with as much enthusiasm as English Canadians. (This supports the traditional French-Canadian argument that they will yield to no one in their determination to defend Canada itself. European and Middle Eastern wars were another matter.) The atmosphere between the Americans, British, and Canadians was fragile. A new verse was added to the American patriotic marching ditty "Yankee Doodle":

Secession first he would put down,
Wholly and forever;
And afterwards from Britain's crown,
He Canada would sever.

Yet Canadian volunteers for the Union Army were considerable, some as an act of immigration. The total is disputed but may have been as great as forty thousand.[69] In these taut circumstances, the British and British North Americans saw the virtues of federation, both on its increasingly clear intrinsic merits and to strengthen Canada against postwar America, whether a sullen hornet of a North shorn of the southern states, or a rampaging Union bull, armed to the teeth and flush with victory.

Alexander Galt had an extensive interview with President Lincoln on the evening of December 4, 1861. "He is very tall, thin, and of marked features, appears fond of anecdote, of which he has a fund. I liked him for his straight-forward, strong common sense." Lincoln assured Galt that the press in neither the United States nor in England, "as he had the best reason to know, reflected the real views of either government." He had accepted the private assurances of Earl Russell to his minister in London (Charles Francis Adams, son and grandson of presidents), about outstanding issues, and "had implicit faith in the steady conduct of the American people," and the current war would not place "success-ful generals in positions of arbitrary power. . . . He pledged himself as a man of honour that neither he nor his cabinet entertained the slightest aggressive designs upon Canada, nor had any desire to disturb the rights of Great Britain on this continent." Galt and the British and Canadians to whom he reported were reassured, and he was much impressed by the president, but not altogether reassured of what might happen as a great war was clearly just beginning with the Confederate rebels. Galt told Lord Lyons, the British minister in Washington, that Lincoln had said that the North would lose the war if it lost Virginia, Kentucky, Missouri and Maryland. (It held all but Viriginia.) Lyons gave Galt a letter for Monck, urging Canadian defence and providing for a special code for an emergency without rousing American suspicions.[70]

* * *

There were the usual claims, far from unfounded, of irregularities in the relations between government and the Grand Trunk Railway. Fortunately for Cartier and Macdonald, as the 1862 election approached, George Brown's deputy as Opposition (Clear Grit) leader, William McDougall, immolated himself by arguing in Parliament that "Upper Canada is oppressed by a foreign race." And if the Anglo-Saxon race were not given relief from the injustices of the Union . . . [and] "there were a bad harvest and consequently great distress, they would have no alternative but to look to Washington."[71] Cartier and Macdonald saw at once the potential advantage to them of this tactical lunacy of casting racist slurs on the French and raising the spectre of annexation for the Loyalist English Canadians; and annexation, at that, to a neighbour in the midst of a terrible civil war. It was one of the great political gaffes in Canadian political history, and in favour of political leaders who knew how to pull out the stops. Macdonald called the election a choice between "constitutional monarchy or the Yankees." Cartier tried the assimilationist bugbear in Quebec and defeated the *rouge* radical leader Dorion in the constituency they contested in Montreal, but he lost members of Parliament in French Canada because of the fear that even Macdonald's Conservatives had assimilationist tendencies and would take advantage of Canada West's now greater numbers over their French-speaking compatriots. Canada West now had 285,000 more people than Canada East, and the agitation for representation by population, which the French had not sought when they were the majority, was an easy vote-winner among the English. This necessitated blunders like McDougall's for Macdonald to be able to navigate around it. Macdonald won a solid victory and Brown went down to personal defeat.

Apart from anything else, Canada certainly had a population, between Halifax and Sarnia, that crossed the threshold for statehood: 3.1 million people, about a third of them French. This compared with 31.4 million in the United States, 29 million in the United Kingdom, 36 million in France, 38 million in Germany, but 3.3 million in the Netherlands, 2.5 million in Switzerland, a little more than 4 million in Portugal and Romania, 3.9 million in Sweden, and only 1.6 million in Denmark and 1.2 million each in Argentina and Australia.[72] Canada was ready to take the next giant step in her ineluctable destiny. English-Canadian desire for representation by population and French-Canadian opposition to it were going to make government unmanageable until some new formula was arrived at. The outline, if not the details, of that formula were now, finally, obvious: federation, protecting regional interests and merging what would become national interests, just as the British began to urge that course to make British North America more capable of self-defence.

From the mid-1840s on, politics in Canada and other advanced countries became intricately mixed up with the progress of the railway industry, and for most of the rest of the nineteenth-century politicians and railway owners and operators had complicated relations, to the point that they were, in some cases, the same people. Along with Viscount Monck, the Duke of Newcastle sent to the Canadas in 1861 one of the most talented railway operators in the world and one of the very greatest and most intelligent active in Canada (where some truly noteworthy railroading personalities are about to appear, to keep Alexander Galt company). Sir Edward William Watkin (1819–1901) was given an informal mandate by Newcastle to clean up the Grand Trunk and also to prepare the way for a transcontinental railway north of the United States, which Newcastle correctly foresaw was all that would keep Canada out of the hands of the Americans whatever the outcome of the American Civil War. Watkin became a partner in his father's Manchester cotton business in his mid-twenties, founded the *Manchester Examiner* in 1845, and in the same year became the secretary of the Trent Valley Railway. This line was sold to another, which merged with more lines as the nascent industry steadily consolidated, and in his late twenties Watkin became assistant manager of the resulting London and North Western Railway. He visited the American and Canadian railways when he was in his early thirties and published a book about railway management in 1852 that became a manual for the industry internationally. Unlike most people in his position, his specialty was the construction and management of railways and not just the financing and stock market promotion of them, though he was conversant with that aspect of the industry also. He became the general manager of the Manchester, Sheffield and Lincolnshire Railway in 1854, held this position until 1862, and was the chairman of that road from 1864 to 1894.

Watkin cleaned up the Grand Trunk by re-equipping it, suspending interest payments, and moving the headquarters to London. But he fulfilled his remit from Newcastle by advocating the Canadian Pacific Railway. He did this while building the railway from Athens to its port of Piraeus, reorganizing the railways of India, building a railway in the Belgian Congo to serve the mining industry in Katanga, and gradually took over a combination of ten British railways, as well as the New York, Lake Erie and Western Railroad. At the summit of his career in the 1890s, he was chairman of the South Eastern Railway in England, the Metropolitan Railway, and with his Manchester, Sheffield, and Lincolnshire and related lines, which were amalgamated into the Great Central Railway, controlled most of the railways from the south coast of England through London and into the Midlands and to the industrial cities of the North. He was also chairman of the Chemin de Fer du Nord, which owned the railway from Calais to Paris, and he controlled most of the traffic between the British and French capitals. He started, but for political and financial reasons did not proceed with, an English Channel tunnel, and a resort and deepwater port at Dungeness, Kent. Watkin was the last person before 2007 to build a mainline into London, and he was a Liberal member of Parliament from 1857 to 1858, 1864 to 1868, and 1874 to 1895, under Palmerston, Gladstone, and Rosebery. Though other, and very able, men actually founded the Canadian Pacific Railway, Watkin's role in starting the serious consideration of the transcontinental railway was seminal.

7. Toward Confederation, 1862–1864

The virtue of Confederation was that it not only made a stronger entity opposite both the Americans and the British (practically the only nationalities that were of any concern to British North Americans at the time) by fusing together all the disparate elements of British North America, but that in having a federal Parliament where representation was by population, enough powers could be ascribed to the provinces to safeguard regional and minority concerns and to protect civil rights, while empowering a national government, even if gradually, given British sensibilities and the state of American expansionist virility. The organizing confederal principle was strength of the whole at the level of defence, international relations, interprovincial transport, currency, and fiscal and monetary policy, but retention of all the particular pre-occupations of the different colonies including both Canadas. The logic of the idea was now obvious, and it was the logical coruscation of the will to distinctive survival that first flickered up under Champlain and proved, against all odds, an inextinguishable flame after Jean Talon brought in enough (especially female) immigrants to make New France demographically, and then economically, self-sustaining. The French had to achieve a critical mass, which they had before France was ejected by Britain from North America, and then America had to secede from Britain and drive or spill enough English Loyalists into Canada to attract British protection against the Americans and give the Canadians the opportunity to control, populate, and develop all of the northern part of the continent (except Alaska), and the English and French Canadians had to learn to cooperate, which they did after Durham threw them together, in his obtuse English superiority, imagining that the English Canadians would then assimilate the French majority. Of such misjudgments was Canada born. This process had arrived at the point where the parts of British North America had to group together with the blessing and support of the British Empire. It had been a tortuous and implacable process, and even Confederation would not protect Canada from the power of America's ability to dazzle and dominate by its overpowering success and panache. But it would give British North Americans a platform, and the only possible platform, from which they could fight to develop an identity, a national confidence, and international respect.

In 1778, the chief British Army engineer in North America, Colonel Robert Morse, had written to Guy Carleton about the state of fortifications in New Brunswick and Nova Scotia, and added his strong suggestion of federation between these provinces and Lower Canada.[73] According to D'Arcy McGee, who was emerging as one of the most brilliant Canadian politicians and the chief spokesman for Irish Catholics in Canada, the idea of Confederation originated with Richard John Uniacke, the attorney general of Nova Scotia in the early nineteenth century, who submitted a scheme for colonial union to the British government in 1800. McGee also credited Jonathan Sewell, chief justice of

Lower Canada from 1808 to 1838; Upper Canada Chief Justice John Beverley Robinson, Lord Durham; Peter Stevens Hamilton, a Nova Scotia writer; and Alexander Morris, member of Parliament for Lanark South at mid-century, who advocated the measure in a pamphlet entitled "Nova Britannia."

George Brown, "a huge, earnest, clumsily vital man,"[74] without initially desiring to do so, pushed Canada West toward Confederation by stirring up the hustings with the theory that English Canadians were being short-changed by the French. The French would not accept representation by population, as it would place too much power over them in the hands of crypto-francophobes and anti-papists like Brown. Brown considered the complete breakup of the Canadas as reactionary and a backward step, and he was an expansionist and advocate of extending Canada West beyond the Great Lakes and toward the Pacific. He wrote in January 1858 that the present arrangement was clearly inadequate and there were only three alternatives: legislative union with proportionate representation ensuring full powers to the cultural majority; federal union with some powers disposed by representation by population and others reserved to provinces; and dissolution of the union.[75] He was pessimistic that the terms could be worked out adequately and thought it would be extremely difficult to bring in the Atlantic colonies, but he did not oppose it conceptually.

Cartier's assistant, Joseph Taché (Étienne Taché's nephew), had, under Cartier's supervision, prepared thirty-three articles that he published in Hector-Louis Langevin's *Courrier du Canada*, which proposed a central government in charge of criminal justice, commerce, trade, public works, navigation, and militia. Cartier, even before Macdonald, believed in the desirability of Confederation as the way to give French Canadians back their legislature, reduce the possibility of absorption by the United States, and confer on his people the political balance of power in an enlarged Canada. Galt favoured Confederation with a strong central government for economic and nationalistic reasons. Edmund Walker Head, on behalf of the Imperial government, encouraged all of this. Cartier declared in the throne speech of August 1858 that his government would pursue federation, and he went to London to put this view to the government and the queen herself in October of that year. The Earl of Derby and Disraeli were then in office and their colonial secretary, Sir Edward Bulwer-Lytton (1803–1873, author of

The Last Days of Pompeii and many other novels, books of verse, operas, and the famous opening "It was a dark and stormy night," and a friend of Disraeli's through literary connections) was skeptical and suspected Cartier of trying to assert an advantage over the Maritime provinces. Cartier returned to Quebec chastened but dazzled after a very respectful reception, including three days with Queen Victoria in the bracing atmosphere of Windsor Castle.

In 1859, the Liberal legislators of Upper Canada had called for a Liberal convention to consider all options to improve the functioning of government and specifically mentioned the federal, dissolution, and representation by population alternatives. Later in that year, the Lower Canadian members of the Opposition met and called for a federal union in which the federal government would deal with tariffs, the post office, patents, and the currency; and the provincial legislatures would deal with education, property, justice, and the militia. When the Liberal convention occurred, it was recognized by everyone that legislative union with the clear predominance of English-speaking people would never be accepted by the French. The leading spokesman for the federal option was future Ontario premier Oliver Mowat, who stressed free access via the St. Lawrence to the oceans of the world, and free trade between provinces. The dissolution alternative was championed by George Sheppard, one of Brown's editorial writers at the *Globe* (which had become a daily in 1853). Brown himself favoured a federal option but with very strong provincial rights. He also said, in his peroration at the 1859 convention, "I hope there is not one Canadian in this assembly who does not look forward with high hope to the day when these northern countries shall stand out among the nations of the world as one great confederation. . . . Who does not feel that to us rightfully belong the right and the duty of carrying the blessings of civilization throughout these boundless regions, and making our own country the highway of traffic to the Pacific." The convention called in the end for a central authority of very limited powers as well as the separation of the provinces. This was the condition of opinion in the Canadas, and the Upper Canada Conservatives were more federalist than the Liberals, when the American Civil War erupted. With the Americans in a state of total bellicosity and the British demanding and incentivizing Canadian self-help by adopting the structures suitable to self-defence, federalism became an idea whose time had come, from all angles, upon the nervous and fractious Canadians.

Macdonald, whether deliberately, by instinct, or by accident, whether with Cartier's concurrence or not, produced the circumstances that would force movement to a solution. In May 1862, he proposed a bill calling for the training and equipping of a militia of fifty thousand men, which would cost a million dollars a year to finance. He rambled intoxicatedly through the first reading of the bill and was absent for the second reading, it was assumed for the same reason. In the midst of consideration of the Militia Bill, the able if mercurial finance minister, Alexander Galt, introduced a budget that revealed expenses of $12.5 million and a deficit of nearly $4 million after a substantial tax increase. The Opposition railed against fiscal ineptitude and strongly suggested that the Militia Bill was really a sinkhole for the satiation of Macdonald's and Cartier's alleged addiction to the joys of patronage. Macdonald gave his bill third reading in an apparently hungover condition, and no one uttered a word. It went to a vote and the government lost, almost certainly by design, though Cartier became quite histrionic about being defeated for trying to defend the country. The sobered Macdonald (he had had serious illnesses in his family that naturally affected his mood and powers of concentration) was completely philosophical. The government had to resign, and as Brown could not possibly win a vote of confidence, the governor general was left with no alternative but to call upon the bland and rather ineffectual duo of the Scottish Roman Catholic from Cornwall John Sandfield Macdonald and Louis-Victor Sicotte, a moderate opponent of Cartier without being a soulmate of Dorion, to try to govern. This created a vacuum, which Macdonald and Cartier surely knew would put immense pressure on Brown to try to compromise with them and move toward a grand coalition and a consensus for Confederation.

The Sandfield Macdonald–Sicotte coalition was a temporary catchment for all the sundry forces of those fatigued and irritated by the contestation of the last few years, including John Macdonald's skulduggery with the double shuffle. Thus, D'Arcy McGee, the unseated Dorion, and the blunderbuss McDougall sheltered there while they caught their breath and collected their thoughts. Brown wrote, "A greater set of jackasses . . . was never got by accident into the government of any country."[76] Even the generally rather temperate Governor General Monck described them to Newcastle, who on Palmerston's behalf was monitoring Canada very closely, as "a wretched lot [incapable of] rising above the level of a parish politician."[77] Both Brown and Monck were being a bit ungenerous, but it was clearly a stopgap regime while the main players prepared for the concluding rounds in Canada's long march to statehood.

On August 21, 1862, Newcastle wrote Sandfield Macdonald demanding a militia of fifty thousand, precisely the issue on which Macdonald and Cartier were defeated. At the same time, via Watkin, the premier was informed that the British government would guaranty a three-million-pound loan to build the Intercolonial Railway linking the Canadas and the Maritimes as long as the line was built well back from the U.S. border. In September, the able premiers of Nova Scotia and New Brunswick, Joseph Howe and Samuel Leonard Tilley, came to Quebec with large entourages to discuss with Sandfield Macdonald how to take up the British government offer. They were all happy to accept the proposal, but when this was conveyed to Newcastle via Monck, Newcastle came back that the offer was entirely conditional on the acceptance and creation of the required militia. As this government was only installed on the rejection of such a project, the whole issue went temporarily dormant. For the first time in many years, the Imperial government was well ahead of the Canadians in thinking and providing for the future security and good government of the Canadas.

The government started to disintegrate, as had been foreseen. McGee, one of the most talented and intelligent politicians in British North America, defected to John A. Macdonald and Cartier, and Sandfield Macdonald, in order to hold his Quebec support, had to give the relatively radical *rouge* Dorion a blank cheque, which caused Sicotte to decamp in 1863, and he soon went to the bench. Cartier and John A. knew that they could push over the Sandfield Macdonald–Dorion house of cards when they chose, but there was no point to it until George Brown was prepared to work with them.

In January 1863, Cartier went to Washington to probe the U.S.

government. At this point, the fortunes of war were very uncertain. The Union had won at Antietam, on September 17, 1862 – one of the bloodiest days of the war, with twenty-three thousand casualties on the two sides combined – when Lee invaded the North and tried to envelop Washington, but Lincoln fired his commander, General George McClellan, for not following up on his victory. Lincoln had purported to emancipate the slaves on New Year's Day 1863, but the proclamation only applied to Confederate territory, little of which had been occupied by the Union at this point. The Union was concerned to have stable relations with the British at this changeable point in the war, and both William H. Seward, now secretary of state, and Lincoln himself received Cartier with great cordiality and respect. Cartier, though leader of the Opposition, was treated like a head of state, and ten thousand Washingtonians turned out to hear him speak at an out-door banquet arranged in his honour by the British minister, Lord Lyons.[78] Never before or since has the United States been so seriously *in extremis*, and not for 125 years would a Canadian visitor be received so respectfully.

There was a new Canadian election in July 1863, and the Conservatives effectively gave Brown a pass in his district and he returned to Parliament. Cartier and McGee defeated Dorion in Quebec, but Brown's Liberals gained against John A.'s Conservatives in Canada West. Cartier was eagerly entreating Brown, and they had a number of private meetings, with some sponsorship from Monck. Brown wished to displace John A., who didn't mind being sidestepped but was not prepared to be eliminated. On March 14, Brown moved in Parliament for the creation of a parliamentary committee to consider the problems of the union and a memorandum Cartier had written about federation in 1858. In the ensuing debate, Macdonald spoke for a stronger federal government than Cartier favoured, covering his position in English Canada opposite Brown, but somewhat straining his popularity with Cartier's followers in Canada East. Brown was very strong in Canada West but hated by the French; Macdonald held much of Canada West and was fairly well regarded in French Canada, and Cartier was thought the lesser of French evils in Upper Canada but was always forced to manoeuvre and dodge to retain adequate support in Lower Canada against Dorion and the more radical French.

By this time, the war in the American states was reaching a climax. Lincoln had changed commanders after Fredericksburg and Chancellorsville, the bloody sequels to Antietam and the last two Confederate victories of Robert E. Lee. On July 4, 1863, the eighty-seventh anniversary of the Declaration of Independence, Lee was defeated at Gettysburg, Pennsylvania, northwest of Washington; and the great fort of Vicksburg, Mississippi, surrendered after a fierce siege to Union general Ulysses S. Grant. The two battles cost a total of dead, injured, and prisoners of more than one hundred thousand men, 60 per cent of them southern.

Grant was appointed commander of all the Union armies, later known as the Grand Army of the Republic, and William Tecumseh Sherman was appointed commander of the Union armies of the West; the Union proceeded down the Mississippi to New Orleans, cutting off Texas, Arkansas, and Louisiana from the Confederacy, and in the spring of 1864 Sherman began an advance through Tennessee and Georgia that would sever those states, as well as Mississippi, Alabama, and Florida, from the Confederacy, while Grant's army (whose name and size and quality of troops and officers evoked Napoleon's Grand Army of sixty years before) moved directly against the Confederate capital of Richmond with overwhelming force. The last chance of the Confederacy was to defeat President Lincoln in the November 1864 elections. These developments, and contemplation of a triumphant and united America with a vast army, a prospect that had never existed before, motivated Newcastle, on behalf of Palmerston, to intensify pressure, via Monck and Watkin, who were plying the Canadian leaders, on Cartier, Brown, and the other players to compose their differences and get back to nation-building.

John A. Macdonald and Cartier pretended there was a division between themselves to assist in the recruitment of Brown to a pro-federal common front, Macdonald continuing to profess a much more centralized and English-dominated federation than the French Canadians could possibly endorse. This had the desired effect of pulling the rug from under Sandfield Macdonald, who invited Étienne Taché to join him in government in March 1864, but excluding Cartier in order to keep Dorion in the tent. Taché declined, but someone from the Macdonald–Cartier camp leaked the overture, Dorion and his followers, who were never content with Sandfield anyway, walked out and the government collapsed. Sandfield had one more try, with Taché, who was standing in for Cartier, as Cartier and Macdonald waited for Brown to join them in a federal coalition. Brown met with Galt and John A. Macdonald at the St. Louis Hotel in Quebec on June 17, 1864. The next day, Cartier joined the discussion and it was agreed to join forces and ratify the previous day's agreement to pursue "a federative system, applied either to Canada alone, or to the whole British American provinces."[79] Macdonald had stuck to his preference as long as it was an academic and tactical issue, but was prepared to compromise and have representation by population in the federal Parliament, and the protection of local and minority interests, under a new division of powers, by the provincial Parliaments; so was Brown, and so were all the factions except the Quebec quasi-separatists and the detritus of the English rednecks.

The deal was struck quickly and cordially. Rumours were rife, and when Parliament met on June 22, Macdonald and Cartier, each in his own language, referred to the emergence of a consensus. Brown rose and told a silent House, haltingly at first, but with rising fluency, volume, and emotion, that all should work for Confederation "as a great national issue," and he very graciously praised Cartier and Taché for working with him. He resumed his place, and the Speaker of the House stood, and the whole chamber exploded in applause and joyous relief, only Dorion and his followers feeling excluded. A bottleneck of a decade had been cleared, and the strongest government in the history of Canada emerged, led by Taché, John A. Macdonald, Cartier, Brown, Galt, McGee, Mowat, Langevin, and McDougall. Monck wrote, later that day, to the governors of Nova Scotia, New Brunswick, and Prince Edward Island, asking that a delegation from the Canadas be permitted to attend the conference that was about to take place to discuss the federation of the Maritime provinces. The request was cheerfully agreed to, and Cartier, Macdonald, Brown, Galt, Langevin, and McDougall all sailed to the Charlottetown Conference on placid waters under clear skies at the end of August.

8. The Road to Confederation, 1864–1867

There was a visiting circus in the pleasant, white-painted Prince Edward
Island capital of Charlottetown, which attracted large crowds from
around the province while the delegates met. The Maritimers agreed to
defer their own discussion of union and invited the Canadians to join
them to discuss an agenda of full union. Cartier opened with a magisterial address on the virtues of federation. He said French-Canadian
nationality would be preserved, as would other regional concerns in
the other jurisdictions, by provincial legislatures. But a federal union
was the manifestly best way to exploit the vast potential of the whole
country, including all the territories between the United States and
the Arctic (except Alaska). Cartier and Galt in particular, and the other
Canadians, made an impassioned plea for the necessity of federation to
defend against the United States, achieve a financial settlement that the
Imperial government would assist, and that would cause it to supervise
and facilitate railway construction. Macdonald, Brown, Cartier, and
McGee all dazzled the Maritimers with their different but effective
and persuasive styles of oratory, particularly at a sumptuous banquet
that stretched from mid-afternoon to midnight on the Canadian vessel
that conveyed its delegates, the *Queen Victoria*. An itinerant celebration
now unfolded, in Halifax, Saint John, and Fredericton.

The delegates adjourned to Quebec in October, where in seventeen days of intensive discussion they hammered out details and
achieved a high degree of agreement. Macdonald gave the key address
on October 11, the second day of the Quebec Conference. "It was the
speech for which he had been consciously preparing for the last five
years, for which indeed, his entire career had been an unconscious
preparation."[80] His basic points were that a strong central government
was necessary to assure success, avoid the sort of terrible fragmentation
that had occurred in the United States, and that British and not
American institutions had to be emulated. He held the residual powers clause giving unallocated jurisdiction to the States and people to
be the severest flaw in the U.S. Constitution, but he thought in terms
of one level of government versus another, not the citizens versus government in general. He favoured equality of regions and not provinces.
Macdonald was the leading figure of the Quebec Conference and

carried the entire issue, with some compromises, and the federal government would control all interprovincial matters including foreign and defence policy, money, and banking and the criminal law, and the provinces would control property, civil rights, and education. The federal government could tax as it wished, but direct taxes were a concurrent jurisdiction. It was all summarized in seventy-two resolutions. George Brown, as fierce a combatant as any against much of what had been approved, wrote his wife at the end of it of what had been agreed: "On the whole, it is wonderful – really wonderful. When one thinks of all the fighting we have had for fifteen years and find the very men who fought us every inch now going far beyond what we asked, I am amazed, and sometimes alarmed lest it all goes to pieces yet."[81]

At the end of the conference, Edward Cardwell (1813–1886), Palmerston's colonial secretary, who would be best known as Gladstone's reforming war secretary almost a decade later, sent the conference a warm assurance of the complete agreement and support of the British government. The government in London had warmly debated Canadian policy after the dispatch to Canada and report of Colonel Sir William Jervois the previous autumn. Jervois found Canadian defences lacking and called for an increased local effort. Cardwell supported this and Gladstone suggested, as he would from time to time over his public career of over sixty years, that the colonies were more trouble than they were worth. Palmerston closed the debate with the statement that "There may be much to be said for the theory put forward by some, that our colonies are an encumbrance and an expense, and that we should be better without them, but that is not the opinion of England and it is not mine."[82]

All parts of what was striving to become a united, federal, Canada were pursuing the common goal, as the U.S. Civil War moved toward a bone-crushing Union victory, an eventuality that would require maximum Canadian preparedness, the avoidance of even the slightest provocation of the United States, and the lock-step support of Great Britain. Cartier had had a rather worrisome visit to Washington in 1864, now much more confident of the Union cause than on the occasion of his visit a year earlier, and 1864 proved a year of unbroken northern victory. The purpose of his visit was to urge the renewal of the Reciprocity agreement, which would otherwise expire in 1866. He found the Senate foreign relations committee chairman, Charles Sumner, an abolitionist firebrand who admired Canada's reception of fugitive slaves, quite pleasant, but William H. Seward was protectionist and prickly about the various abrasions that had occurred. Cartier did not meet the president on this visit.

On October 20, 1864, a party of twenty-five Confederates living in Canada crossed into Vermont, robbed a bank of $210,000 and killed someone, injured twenty other people, and burned down much of the town of St. Albans, Vermont. Cartier attended upon Monck who ordered the militia to arrest the raiders, who had retired back to Canada, and they were rounded up just before an American posse caught up with them ten miles inside the border with Lower Canada. Cartier and some of his colleagues met with the American consul in Montreal and pledged absolute Canadian neutrality and made placatory noises in all directions, which the British amplified. Cartier handled the settling down of the affair with vintage Canadian genius for cooling things out through endless palaver and intricate formalities. He had the American demand for extradition brought before Taché's son-in-law, police magistrate Charles-Joseph Coursol, and assigned three prominent defence counsel to the defendants, who were led by a theology student at the University of Toronto from Kentucky, Bennett Young. The defence counsel were the future prime minister of Canada. J.J.C. Abbott, William Kerr, and Rodolphe Laflamme (who assigned some of the work to his law clerk, Louis Riel, who will reappear prominently in the next chapter). Abbott endlessly and monotonously cross-examined the defendants and called for delays for various formalities, and finally challenged Coursol's jurisdiction to hear an extradition matter, an impeachment which Coursol swiftly conceded. Cartier made another visit to Washington, was cordially received by President Lincoln, and even Seward commended him and the Canadians as exemplary neighbours, and the whole issue just faded away after the Canadian Parliament voted restitution to the violated Vermont bank and a strict alien law, and Cartier had the perpetrators imprisoned for a time for common assault. Lincoln was reelected, General Sherman burned Atlanta to the ground the day after the election and cut across Georgia to the sea at Savannah, scorching everything to ashes on a path more than a hundred miles wide, before turning into the Carolinas. Few could have imagined that the great American experiment could come to such a terrible, noble combat.

The Canadian federalists, many of them of recent persuasion but with the fervour of conversion, were trying to race the Union armies. Grant and Sherman were now unstoppable, and rolled up what was left of the Confederacy from both ends. Lincoln was reinaugurated on March 4, 1865 and famously promised to abolish slavery "even if God wills that all the treasure piled up by the bondsman's 250 years of unrequited toil shall be sunk and that every drop of blood drawn by the lash shall be repaid by . . . the sword." And he promised "to do all which may achieve and cherish a just and a lasting peace, among ourselves and with all nations." Lee surrendered to Grant at Appomattox Court House, Virginia, on April 9 in a very gracious and dignified meeting with his former subordinate, and Sherman, like Grant as magnanimous in victory as he was relentless in combat, received the surrender of the southern Confederate forces eight days later.

In the meantime, Lincoln was assassinated. An untried Tennessean auto-didact, Andrew Johnson, chosen for vice president because he was the only southern senator who remained loyal to the Union, became president. Power passed to the leaders of the Congress, who were, fortunately for Canada, more interested in a Carthaginian Peace with the South than in tangling with the British Empire. While the Union Army occupied the South, the pressures to demobilize the mighty armies of Grant and Sherman and restore the integrity of the diluted currency, prevailed over thoughts of plunging into a new war with Britain over Canada, though the prospect excited some orators and editorialists. It had been a horrible war, in which 750,000 had died and nearly 500,000 were wounded in an American population of 32 million. Canada and Britain pressed noiselessly on toward a new era in Canada while the Americans settled scores in a manner that bore no resemblance to the peace of reconciled brothers that the great Lincoln favoured and would have pursued.

There was prolonged debate in the Canadian and other colonial Parliaments on the Quebec Resolutions, and all the members of the Coalition shared the burden of the discussion. Sandfield Macdonald and Dorion led the only knots of outright resistance but there were endless demands for clarification and reassurance, especially on the Intercolonial Railway, without which New Brunswick would rescind its adherence. Cardwell laid the burden of defence on the Canadians; Jervois had recommended 200,000 pounds for the fortification of Quebec but London only provided 50,000, and Palmerston found Gladstone "troublesome and wrong-headed" on the whole issue of supporting Canada.[83] On March 4, 1865, Tilley, the capable and firmly federalist premier of New Brunswick, was defeated in his election and that province effectively withdrew from the Quebec arrangements, and a fluish Macdonald yet carried the argument in Parliament with his contention that union was not the only issue in that election and that, in any case, the result was not permanent and was a cause to accelerate union and not postpone, amend, or reconsider it. The leaders of the coalition, Macdonald, Cartier, Brown, Galt, and McGee, repaired to London to lobby Westminster and were splendidly feted and warmly received, even by the querulous Gladstone. They straggled back to Canada in the early summer, after, in Macdonald's case, he had received an honorary doctorate from Oxford, and amid "the saturnalia of under-graduate Oxford. . . the well-known melodrama of grave ceremony and uproarious fun was once more re-enacted" at the Sheldonian Theatre.[84]

Sir Étienne Taché died on July 30, 1865, and Monck asked Macdonald to become the formal head of the government, as he was the de facto head of it. Brown threatened to break up the government if the trium-viral equality of Macdonald, Cartier, and Brown were altered, and the comparatively unexceptional Sir Narcisse Belleau, an understudy of Taché's on the Legislative Council, was selected as a compromise nominal premier. Once again, as before the Great Coalition was formed, the move to Confederation stalled; the British did nothing and the government had nothing to say or do to advance defence or railway construction. Bafflement and suspense reigned as the Assembly rose for the late summer. New pressures arose from the United States, as the Irish recruits and draftees demobilized from the U.S. Army flocked in large numbers to militant Irish Fenian organizations along the border and began conducting raids into Canada.

Palmerston died on October 18, 1865, two days short of his eighty-first birthday, after a public career of more than fifty years. His last words were alleged, perhaps apocryphally, to have been, to his doctor:

"Die, my dear doctor? That is the last thing I shall do." He was the first statesman and only the fourth commoner (after Isaac Newton, Lord Nelson, and the Duke of Wellington) to receive a state funeral in Britain. Russell replaced him as an interim leader, but the fifteen-year era of Gladstone and Disraeli was about to open.

Tilley's chief colleague in New Brunswick, Charles Fisher, was returned to his provincial house in a by-election in November, and federalist hopes in that province improved. Macdonald had largely financed Fisher's campaign with private funds from Canada West. Repeated Fenian raids, including in New Brunswick, were practically ineffectual, but stirred opinion in Canada and embarrassed the United States; not even the most jingoistic American expansionist wished the mighty American Union to advance on the coat-tails of this rag-tag of Irish bigots and hooligans, much less to be dragged into war with the British Empire over their antics. George Brown did resign from the government in December 1865, but did not withdraw his support for the Quebec Resolutions or take out against the ministry; he was dissatisfied on the single issue of the attempt to renew the Reciprocity Agreement with the United States which he felt was being mismanaged, and which did expire.

On May 31, 1866, the Fenians led their main attack across the border at Niagara Falls, and killed nine Canadian militiamen and wounded thirty before being repulsed and chased back across the border. There was a tremendous firming up of Canadian opinion, and large votes of defence estimates by Parliament that pleased the British and even attracted the notice of the Americans. It was a purposeful reaction to an outrageous provocation. On June 12, Tilley and Fisher were returned to office in New Brunswick bringing that province back onside the Quebec Resolutions. Despite a febrile atmosphere in Canada in the aftermath of the Fenian incursion, and a governmental crisis in Britain which caused the downfall of Russell and the return for the third time, of the Earl of Derby as prime minister and Benjamin Disraeli as chancellor of the Exchequer and leader of the House of Commons, Maritime delegates embarked for London, hoping to get approval and enactment of the Quebec Resolutions. Russell and Cardwell pledged their support on this to Derby, Disraeli, and the new colonial secretary, the very capable and well informed Earl of Carnarvon. But Macdonald and the other Canadians declined to make the trip, seeing no prospect of ratification in that session. In the midst of all this toing and froing, and as Britain sent military reinforcements to Canada, and the government of Canada moved to its new quarters in Ottawa, Brown launched an attack in the *Globe* against Macdonald's intemperance, that is, drunkenness. In the circumstances, it was an amusing divertissement in a tense time, as the Maritime leaders fumed and carped in London. Joseph Howe, the Nova Scotia opposition leader, was at this point a strenuous opponent of Confederation, and he had some currency in London, because of his rebuttal of Russell's Ten Resolutions twenty years before.

It was finally agreed that the Canadian delegates would depart for London in November, and they arrived and started the final conference for the preparation of the British enabling legislation at the Westminster Palace Hotel, facing Westminster Abbey, St. Margaret's Church, Parliament Square and the Parliament buildings and Big Ben, on December 4, 1866. Macdonald was elected conference chairman. It proceeded well until Macdonald fell asleep with his candle still burning on the night of December 12, and was badly burned by a fire in his bedroom that he and Cartier and Galt put out with the water from the jugs in their rooms. They were working against the deadline of a Nova Scotia election that would come in the spring and that Howe would likely win. Macdonald sent Carnarvon the refined agreement for transmission into a legislative bill on Christmas Day. The only problem the British had, as they prepared for the tense consideration and debate of what would be the Second Reform Bill, another great expansion of the franchise, was the fixing of the size of the Senate, unlike the flexible numbers of the British House of Lords. It was agreed that a small number of additional senators could be appointed. Another problem arose over Macdonald's reference to the Kingdom of Canada, which fussed Derby, whom his chief colleague for over twenty years, Disraeli, described as always "in a region of perpetual funk." (Certainly this had been his approach to Canada as colonial secretary when he was Lord Stanley.) Derby was concerned because this terminology had raised a question in the U.S. House of Representatives by Congressman H.J. Raymond. "Dominion of Canada" was devised as a compromise. The British North America Bill was quickly finalized and introduced for first reading in the House of Lords on February 12, 1867. Four days later, John A. Macdonald, whose first wife had died some years before, remarried, Susan Agnes

Bernard, daughter of a Privy Councillor, at St. George's Church, Hanover Square. The bishop of Montreal officiated, daughters of the members of the Canadian delegation (Misses McDougall, McGee, Tupper, and Archibald) were bridesmaids, and the toast to the bride at the banquet at the Westminster Palace Hotel was given by the bridegroom's old but friendly adversary, Francis Hincks, now governor of British Guiana, but a friend of the bride's family from when he was governor of Jamaica. As distinguished historian Richard Gwyn remarked, it was the end of solitude and thereafter, as some of his wife's relatives lived with them, "Macdonald had in-laws the way other people had mice."[85]

Joseph Howe was in London and agitating, with a petition signed by thirty thousand Nova Scotians against Confederation, but Carnarvon spoke powerfully in the House of Lords in favour of the bill, and was very effectively supported by Monck, speaking as a viscount and as sitting governor general of the United Province of Canada. It went through committee without difficulty and little notice was taken of Howe's petition. The passage through the House of Commons was in gaps between intense and contestatious discussion of Disraeli's generous expansion of the franchise, the Second Reform Bill, which, he good humouredly acknowledged, was designed "to dish the Whigs." Carnarvon's minister in the Commons, Sir Charles Adderley, did a workmanlike job, and was strongly supported by Cardwell, as Carnarvon and Monck had been in the Lords by Russell. The Radical leader, John Bright, spoke against the bill, and advanced the Joseph Howe argument, but received little support. Macdonald and the other senior delegates had a private audience with Queen Victoria, who welcomed them warmly and expressed strong support for the legislation and the new status of the emergent Dominion. The British North America Act was adopted on March 4, 1867, to be formally enacted in Canada on July 1 (by royal proclamation of May 22). The future Marquess of Salisbury resigned in protest against Disraeli's Second Reform Bill, as did Carnarvon, a week later, but the Canadians were clear of the imbroglio, and the British Parliament, with even Gladstone speaking in favour, endorsed the promised guaranty for the Intercolonial Railway that Watkin had created and connected to the Grand Trunk, represented with unfailing agility by Cartier. It had all been a superb piece of management and statesmanship, chiefly by Macdonald and secondly by Cartier, but with the help of many others.

Carnarvon called upon his colleagues in the proverbial Mother of Parliaments to "rejoice that we have shown neither indifference to (the Canadians') wishes nor jealousy of their aspirations, but that we . . . fostered their growth, recognizing in it the conditions of our own greatness."[86] He predicted that Canada would grow to be one of the great nations of the world. It was the greatest birth of a new nation in the world since the American Revolution, though that honour would soon pass to the reunified Italy and the newly united Germany.

The birth of a new nation, the consummation of the genius of Champlain and Carleton, of Baldwin and LaFontaine, and of those who would actually create it, was at hand. The embryo that existed in New France a century after Champlain founded Quebec, which had become a mysterious conception a century later at the time of the War of 1812, was now, obviously, an autonomous country of novel composition and immense proportions, about to be born.

PART II

Dominion:

1867–1949

John A. Macdonald (1815-1891), effectively co-leader of the opposition in the
United Province of Canada 1862–1864 (when this photograph was taken), and
sole leader in the Dominion of Canada 1873–1878, and co-leader of the United
Province 1856–1862 and 1864–1867, and prime minister of Canada 1867–1873
and 1878–1891, principal father of Canadian Confederation and founder of the
Conservative Party of Canada, and the preeminent figure in Canadian public
life for nearly forty years. Sly, imaginative, bold, and colourful, only Canada's
comparatively modest size kept him from general acceptance in the company
of the world's greatest statesmen in the second half of the nineteenth century
with Lincoln, Palmerston, Disraeli, Gladstone, Salisbury, Cavour, and Bismarck.

Macdonald and the World's First Transcontinental, Bicultural, Parliamentary Confederation

The Pacific Railway, the National Policy,
and the Riel Rebellion, 1867–1896

1. The Launch of the Great Dominion, 1867–1871

Viscount Charles Monck asked John A. Macdonald, the only possible choice, to be the first prime minister of Canada. To remain in the government, William McDougall, though he and his colleague William Pearce Howland had been all but tarred and feathered at Brown's Reform convention in June, insisted on three cabinet seats for his faction, and that left Macdonald with only one other Ontario cabinet place, which he filled with his old law partner, Alexander Campbell, leaving the old Tories of the MacNab stripe unrepresented. McDougall and his colleagues also insisted on the "rep by pop" (representation by population) gesture of Quebec having one member of cabinet fewer than Ontario. George-Étienne Cartier had no problem with that, as long as three of the Quebeckers were French, and he, Hector-Louis Langevin, and Jean-Charles Chapais had all staked their claim. That left only one place for the English and Irish of Quebec, and Macdonald had planned to name both Alexander Galt and Thomas D'Arcy McGee. Charles Tupper, a future party leader and prime minister of Canada, had agreed to represent Nova Scotia, and New Brunswick would be represented by Samuel L. Tilley and one other. Tupper generously broke the impasse by standing down and recommending the appointment of a Roman Catholic Irishman, Edward Kenny. In the same spirit, McGee, Confederation's greatest prophet, stood aside. This was the composition of the government. Macdonald had asked that the governor general become a viceroy, but this did not happen, for the same reason that the country was not a kingdom, because of the Earl of Derby's fear of American republican sensibilities. This really was nonsense, as even Champlain and his successors had had that title.

For many decades Canadians tended to compensate for their own self-doubts and for British deference to the United States with "superior airs – an attempt to ascribe undesirable characteristics to the successful neighbour and to oneself indefinable qualities of refinement, breeding, and moral excellence – the habitual escapist refuge of the weak in the presence of the strong. At bottom it was mainly a simple human lust for the luxuriant fruits just over the garden wall. . . . After 1865 there was a whole catalogue of reasons for fear."[1]

The first election of the new Parliament was in August 1867, and Macdonald won easily. George Brown was defeated in the South Ontario constituency where he stood and would never sit in the Canadian House of Commons, though he did resurface as a senator. John Sandfield Macdonald led the opposition, though he would not stay long and had just been elected premier of Ontario when the new Parliament convened on November 7, 1867. The rising figure in the opposition was Edward Blake of Toronto, whose father, William Hume Blake, had served in the Great Ministry of Baldwin and LaFontaine, and whom Macdonald had challenged to a duel twenty years before. The other opposition notables were the comparative misfit Antoine-Aimé Dorion, the dour and phlegmatic Alexander Mackenzie, and the aging tribune of Nova Scotian separatism Joseph Howe ("that pestilent man," Macdonald called him), who led all but two of the MPs from his province in opposing Confederation yet was sitting there participating in debates. (This would be a scarcely recognized precedent for

Quebec separatists 120 years later.) They claimed to be opponents to the new Constitution and their province's adherence to it, but "they never relapsed into sullen eccentricity or deliberate obstructionism."[2] Macdonald's Conservatives won one hundred seats to sixty-two Liberals and eighteen others, and 50 per cent of the vote to 49 per cent Liberal (excluding the anti-Confederation vote).

Early in 1868, Macdonald was advised that the British government would hand over to the Dominion the vast expanses of Rupert's Land and the North-West Territory, as had been agreed in the enabling legislation, only if Canada compensated the Hudson's Bay Company or secured a judicial decision that it was not bound to do so. At the same time, the Nova Scotia Assembly empowered Howe and three others to go to London and demand Nova Scotia's release from Confederation. Galt, a temperamental man, had churlishly resigned as finance minister in the first days of the government (over treatment of the Commercial Bank of Canada), and Macdonald now offered him and the selfless Tupper the mission to go to London and counter Howe's performance there. Galt declined, and there was some criticism of the choice of Tupper, as sending such a loyal and distinguished representative of the government might appear to legitimize the separatists.

On the evening of April 7, 1868, the equally public-spirited McGee spoke at length and eloquently in support of Galt, and was assassinated after the debate for his trouble. Macdonald rushed to McGee's house and helped to carry out the body of his slain comrade, who was six days short of his forty-third birthday. Tupper handled his mission to London effectively, and the new colonial secretary, the Duke of Buckingham and Chandos, rejected Howe's advocacy, and the great radical reformer John Bright's (1811–1889) motion for a royal commission of inquiry was ignominiously voted down. Just before a convention that Howe had organized to take the Nova Scotian repeal movement forward, Macdonald himself went to Halifax to offer to meet privately with Howe and discuss with flexibility and openness Howe's reservations about Confederation, as he was holding public meetings to arm himself with an enhanced mandate. Tilley had told Macdonald that privately Howe would settle for some financial concessions. Macdonald was accompanied by Tupper, Cartier, and, in a generous gesture, Howe's friend John Sandfield Macdonald, who was now a convinced federalist.

Macdonald met privately with Howe in the office of the lieutenant-governor after church services on Sunday, August 2. It was clear to Macdonald that Howe's "big head with its rather coarse features and grey, untidy hair, was heavy with the dull, stupefying realization of final defeat."[3] Howe could not make a third appeal to Westminster and had no way to lead Nova Scotia out of Confederation. His convention orated and fussed and appointed a committee chaired by him to determine a course of action. After a few days, and after his colleagues batted down Howe's effort to pretend that Macdonald was in Halifax because the Imperial government had asked him to go there, and by casting a tie-breaking vote on his committee, Howe got the authority to negotiate with Macdonald. They agreed that they would wait for prorogation of the Nova Scotia Legislature and then Macdonald would send Howe a letter with minor concessions in it that Howe could use to persuade his repeal-zealous followers that they had won the match and should stand down and one of them (Howe in fact) would join Macdonald's government.

Macdonald sent Cartier and McDougall to London to negotiate the acquisition of the Hudson's Bay charter rights and prepared his legislation to establish a Supreme Court of Canada. He got the signal from Howe and sent him a letter that seemed to succeed, but Howe still needed coaxing, as he could not bring the provincial government. Macdonald, as only he could do, flattered Howe's considerable ego and said that his "will will be law," because of his stature in his native province. Viscount Monck departed after a very successful term, the third successive full and satisfactory governorship (after Elgin and Edmund Walker Head), and was followed by Sir John Young. The London picture clouded with Gladstone's defeat of Disraeli, who had finally succeeded Derby. Gladstone was skeptical of the Canadian enterprise, and Bright, who was anti-Empire and very impressed with the American political system and national aspirations, was in his government. Macdonald arranged for the British government to reject repeal by Nova Scotia while he gave Howe, who came to visit him in mid-January 1869, a letter approving increased fiscal subsidies for Nova Scotia and had him sworn to the cabinet as president of the council. It was a complete victory, but Howe had a plausible claim to success also. The negotiations with the Hudson's Bay Company had proceeded satisfactorily, and Macdonald announced at the opening of Parliament in April that the government would be presenting legislation acquiring for Canada all the territory to the Arctic and the Pacific. (Russia had sold Alaska in 1867 to William H. Seward, as U.S. secretary of state, for $7.2 million, 2.5 cents per acre. The treaty of cession cleared the U.S. Senate by one vote after the Russian government bribed a number of senators, so eager were they to be rid of the territory.) Macdonald nominated the rather difficult William McDougall (who had handed him and Cartier the 1862 election with his attack on the French Canadians and his flirtation with annexation) to be the governor of Rupert's Land. To replace McDougall as minister of finance, Macdonald chose his wife's family's friend Sir Francis Hincks, the old Baldwinian Reformer, now technically a Liberal, continuing what Macdonald, for his own political convenience, persisted in calling a coalition. The arrival of Hincks caused Richard Cartwright, previously a supporter of Macdonald, to decamp abruptly to the Liberals, but Macdonald got the better of that exchange; the arrival in the ministry of Hincks and Howe provided heavy reinforcements.

Macdonald became a father again at age fifty-four (of a girl, who proved soon to be significantly mentally handicapped), and the pressures of his life were further sharply increased when in January 1869 he was advised by Sir Hugh Allan, the prominent ship owner, in his capacity as chairman of the Merchants' Bank, that Macdonald owed the bank $79,590.11.[4] Macdonald managed to scrape together all his savings, put a mortgage on his main asset, a residential land development in Guelph, Ontario, and stabilized his finances, but now, after having held high political office for over eleven years, he had a net worth of approximately zero. Having almost stopped drinking in the first two years of his second marriage, he started again under the pressures of these personal events (he assumed he could manage the political vagaries all right). Macdonald was working to induce both Prince Edward Island and Newfoundland into Confederation, and was planning to offer provincial status to British Columbia. But in November 1869, as McDougall went to take up his new post, Macdonald learned from American newspapers that Métis rioters and squatters were preventing his new governor from being installed, and had captured the Hudson's Bay Company post at Fort Garry (now Winnipeg), and had taken control of the Red River settlement. It came to light that some Canadian settlers had sorely provoked the Métis, who had overreacted, under, it was feared, the influence of missionary priests from France and large American commercial interests. Jay Cooke, the promoter of the Northern Pacific Railway, seemed to be subsidizing unrest as a pre-emptive harassment of a competing Canadian transcontinental railway. The role of the Hudson's Bay Company in stirring up the Métis was also questionable. The American newspapers were playing these problems as a tremendous humiliation for the young country, and the truth is that it was a serious embarrassment. Macdonald adopted the cunning tactic of refusing to hand over the agreed three hundred thousand pounds and taking over the territory until Canada could be promised peaceful possession. It was up to the vendor to clear the area, and Macdonald represented the McDougall fiasco as an embarrassment to the British government, not Canada. The British would have more success at deterring the Americans and placating the natives than he could.

Macdonald had a sharp exchange with Gladstone's colonial secretary, Lord Granville, and explained that a military expedition was impossible in the winter, and that open disorder "would . . . completely throw the game into the hands of the insurgents and the Yankee wire-pullers." Direct American interference could not then be ruled out.

At this point, another of the remarkable builders and pioneers of Canadian history puts in his first appearance: Donald Smith, later Lord Strathcona and Mount Royal (1820–1914), who was a veteran of about twenty-five years as a factor in Hudson's Bay and Labrador, who was Hudson's Bay Company's principal representative in Canada, and who called upon Macdonald and pledged support for whatever he chose to do. He was given a joint mandate by the government of Canada and the company to go to the scene of the problems and try to sort them out. Unfortunately, McDougall had not lost his capacity for extreme impetuosity, and without cooler minds to supervise him, he flew off half-cocked, unaware of the delay in the handover which had been scheduled for December 1, 1869, and issued a proclamation of his own authority in the queen's name. He pronounced himself lieutenant-governor of Rupert's Land and commissioned the former surveyor Colonel John Stoughton Dennis to raise and outfit a force to subdue and discipline the Métis rebels. Dennis began what Macdonald later called "a series of inglorious intrigues," and a number of incidents occurred, culminating in the surrender of McDougall and Dennis's force to a much larger group of armed Métis. The Métis leader, Louis Riel (last seen here as a law junior to Rodolphe Laflamme in the St. Alban's Vermont incident), then proclaimed a provisional government at Red River, precisely what Macdonald had feared and what he thought might be a prearranged pretext for American interference. (General Ulysses S. Grant was now president of the United States, on a rather nationalistic platform, though he was a man of moderate conduct, and he made no secret of how agreeable it would be to subsume Canada into the United States as a sorbet after victory in the Civil War.) Smith and two other co-emissaries, Grand Vicar Jean-Baptiste Thibault and Colonel Charles de Salaberry, would just be reaching Fort Garry as the year ended.

In January 1870, the American minister in London, John Lothrop Motley, closely interrogated officials of the Hudson's Bay Company and evinced what was reported as an unseemly interest in the Red River. (Motley had been a student in Germany with the young Otto von Bismarck, and he remained the closest personal friend of the Prussian minister-president, who was soon to become the chancellor of the German empire he was about to create. Motley was an unusually worldly diplomat.) Macdonald was now considering a military expedition as soon as the weather would permit one, probably in April. He wrote to his former minister of finance, Sir John Rose, now resident in England and well-connected there, on January 26, 1870, that it was "a fixed idea in Washington that England wants to get rid of the colonies, indeed, Mr. Fish [President Grant's secretary of state, Hamilton Fish] has not hesitated to say so." Fish had made inquiries of the British minister in Washington, Sir Edward Thornton, about a free vote in Canada on the question of annexation.[5] Archbishop Alexandre-Antonin Taché of St. Boniface (1821–1894), who had long been a moderate champion of the Métis, was recalled by Macdonald from Rome, where he was attending the First Vatican Council. After extensive discussion with the prime minister, Taché hurried west to join Smith, Thibault, and Salaberry as emissaries to the disaffected followers of Riel. McDougall, "very chopfallen and at the same time very sulky," wrote Macdonald, returned to Ottawa, unemployed.[6]

The 1870 parliamentary session opened with much ceremony attending the presence of Prince Arthur, Victoria's third son (who would become Duke of Connaught and governor general of Canada in the First World War). There was debate about the tense condition of Rupert's Land, and by this time McDougall, with infinite predictability, had worked out an elaborately falsified version of events that imputed to the incompetence and malice of others every aspect of the shambles for which he was, himself, chiefly responsible. Alexander Galt, a restlessly talented man but an impulsive politician, was now confecting policy initiatives like a hyperactive child, and inflicted on Parliament a discussion about the assumption of full treaty-making powers for Canada and a complete economic union with the United States. The first idea would be timely before too long, but complete independence from Britain in foreign policy while awaiting that country's military assistance to assure Canadian control of the vast centre of the country before American intervention under a president who recently was the victorious commander of the greatest army in the world was not the optimal occasion for Galt's latest hobby horse. And economic union with the potential defiler of the emerging dream of Canada was a perversely untimely nostrum. Like an indulgent uncle, Macdonald ignored McDougall and Galt as he worried about the gnawing vulnerability of his new country stretched between the caprices and whims of its two larger and not wholly cordial national relatives. Though suffering the distress of sadness in his family and of an acute personal financial crisis that could conceivably end his career, he kept his nerve and his judgment and did not allow alcohol to affect his perceptions or serviceability.

Smith had made great inroads with the Métis and had addressed a large assembly to explain his mandate and offer reassurances on behalf of Macdonald. The English Métis now came forward, and they considerably diluted the anger and venom of the French, as they had no cultural or religious grievances. The whole group informally chose Riel as their leader, which limited the licence he would have to unleash a revolution, but it also gave him a higher degree of legitimacy. A committee of forty people, representing twenty French and twenty English parishes, was struck, which produced a list of concerns and grievances that Smith could bring back to Ottawa, and Taché, Thibault, and Salaberry were all working to settle things down. The local Hudson's Bay operative well beneath Smith and outside his authority, John MacTavish, resented the change and threw his lot in with the Métis, and was a fifth column for Riel, who was also being encouraged by one of the Fenian leaders, William Bernard O'Donoghue, who became the treasurer in Riel's provisional government. Unfortunately, the governor of the Hudson's Bay Company, an apparently unrelated William MacTavish, foolishly took the word of John MacTavish, his namesake, and, believing that the transfer to Canada was deferred, he conferred some level of recognition on Riel. If Grant had been as aggressive as Andrew Jackson or Theodore Roosevelt, lesser military commanders but more astute politicians, he would have snaffled the Red River up, paid off the Hudson's Bay Company, and made sufficient placatory noises to hose down the British, who would have gone to war if Quebec and Ontario had been invaded, but not over a shadowy frontier Gilbert-and-Sullivan farce like this. Jackson had less firm legal ground to seize Florida in 1818, and Roosevelt would have less legal cause to seize Panama in 1903.

As usual with Gladstone, there was great uncertainty about deploying force in faraway places for fuzzy causes (this was the tamest prelude to the Siege of Khartoum, from 1884 to 1885), but Granville prevailed with his opinion that there was "no alternative to standing by the Canadians. . . . The prompt assertion of authority is probably the safest." As long as the British and Canadians could get their forces there before the Americans got down to serious infiltration or the powder keg blew up, the situation could still be managed. Smith, Taché, and the others had to keep Riel talking for another month. The British pledged military assistance on March 6, conditional only on completing the transfer from the Hudson's Bay Company and generous treatment for the aggrieved minority; neither was a derogation from what Macdonald intended. Granville saw, even if his chief needed a little tutorial on geostrategy, that the occupation of all North America west as well as south of the Great Lakes would make the United States an even more overpoweringly strong country than the Union victory in the Civil War had assured it would soon become.

On March 4, Riel summarily executed Thomas Scott, who had taken up arms against Riel's provisional government, was captured, and struck one of his guards. This created an immense clamour in Canada, and English Canadians were now screaming for suppression of the insolent Métis while French Canadians still had some sympathy for their original grievances. One Gilbert McMicken, who had access to Fenian information but was opposed to their tendency to violent attacks on Canada, warned the Canadian government that a large Fenian assault on Canada could be expected for April 15. The day before that, Macdonald wrote the colonial secretary, the Earl of Carnarvon, out of office, and reproached the Gladstone government for taking this moment to pull all British garrisons out of Canada in an economy measure. "We greatly distrust the men at the helm in England," he wrote, and added that American officials "connived at" Fenian outrages and "yet this is the time [Gladstone and his colleagues] choose to withdraw every soldier from us, and we are left to be the unaided victims of Irish discontent and American hostility." It was implicit that the Irish discontent had been entirely created by the British.[7]

Macdonald had mobilized the entire militia, which bristled at every possible crossing point and effectively faced down the Fenians. More complicated was the turmoil in intra-Métis politics, where Riel was a clever but dictatorial personality. He sent his representatives to Ottawa, though two (Father Ritchot and Alfred Scott) were immediately jailed and charged with complicity in the murder of Thomas Scott. Macdonald had them released after a few days, and conversed extensively with the third delegate, "Judge" John Black, recorder of Rupert's Land. Black was fairly sensible, but Riel wanted to rule absolutely and sent the delegates with a list of demands that far exceeded what the convention, half composed of English-speaking, mainly Protestant Métis, had approved. One of the demands was admission of Assiniboia as a province, and in this Riel was joined by the Roman Catholic leadership, including Macdonald's emissary, Bishop Taché. The French and Catholics wanted another French province to bracket Ontario and assure that their language and religion shared in the growth of the West. By demanding a province, Riel had dampened the possibility of American intervention and given Macdonald the opportunity to start to ease tensions by the already traditional Canadian formula of patient and more-or-less good faith negotiations. The English provinces were demanding military suppression of Riel, and Cartier's followers were restive and hostile to such a recourse, as they too wanted a French province around Lake Manitoba and the Red and Assiniboine rivers. Macdonald could carry the country by crushing the Riel uprising, but he would shatter his party and split the country entirely on English-French lines, which would be the negation of his entire central ambition to build a transcontinental, bicultural, parliamentary federation.

Macdonald was concerned at the foot-dragging of the British and worried that the Americans might prevent him using the jointly operated canal at Sault Ste. Marie for the passage of the expeditionary force he was going to send to the Red River, whether the British participated or not (although Canada had never disturbed the movement of soldiers or munitions through its canals during the late Civil War). The British sent Sir Stafford Northcote (1818–1887), Disraeli's closest associate in the House of Commons but now the governor of the Hudson's Bay Company (as the British Conservatives were out of office), to Ottawa to conduct reconnaissance for the government and the company. The Americans sent special State Department officer J.W. Taylor to Ottawa to assess the temper of men and events in Canada's capital. Macdonald met with the three delegates from Riel's regime on April 24, and Ritchot, their chairman, was adamant about Riel's post-convention escalated list of demands, and about being treated as officially recognized representatives of an established jurisdiction. Macdonald, detesting every minute of it, slogged through the negotiations, resigned to giving them their province and happy enough to entrench French rights as long as the English and Protestants were protected too, while the military mission, to be led by the rising star of the British Army, Colonel (future Field Marshal) Garnet Wolseley, prepared to embark for the Red River. Macdonald was almost through on April 27, and then "broke out," as his entourage put it. He became too affected by liquor to function rigorously and from April 29 to May 1 was subject to the process thus described by Northcote to Disraeli: "His habit is to retire to bed, to exclude everybody, and to drink bottle after bottle of port. All the papers are sent to him and he reads them, but he is conscious of his inability to do any important business and he does none."[8] The Conservatives in the House of Commons became fractious, as Brown's *Globe* proclaimed the prime minister's shameful drunkenness and the Tory press said he was indisposed. He returned to the House on May 2, pale and not in the best voice, but master of the facts and of Parliament and gave the agreed Manitoba Bill first reading. Except for an adjustment to the new province's borders to include the home of the pro-Canadians at Portage La

Prairie that Riel had tried to redistrict out, the bill went through easily and was about to be adopted on May 6 when the prime minister, waiting in his parliamentary office, was laid low by an acute attack of gallstones. Macdonald was incapacitated for two months, and departed in July for a convalescence in Prince Edward Island, where he was kept informed but also much badgered for decisions. By mid-September, when he left Charlottetown, he was almost completely recovered.

Events had moved benignly in his absence, with Cartier as acting prime minister. Wolseley's mission occupied Assiniboia without incident and Manitoba became the fifth province (Prince Edward Island was still aloof, with Newfoundland), and Macdonald's terms for British Columbia had been accepted and all had been agreed except by the federal and B.C. parliaments. Under these arrangements, Macdonald had taken another mighty step of nation-building by pledging to start a railway to the Pacific within two years and finish it within ten. As 1870 ebbed away, there was restored domestic tranquility, though the question of amnesty for Riel and his henchmen had the potential for trouble, and the Americans were still capable of being difficult, though they had missed the opportunity to strike with maximum effect during the Red River crisis.

In his annual address to the Congress, Grant, in remarks presumably composed by Fish, opined that "the Imperial government is understood to have delegated . . . [much] jurisdiction . . . to the colonial authority known as the Dominion of Canada, and this semi-independent but irresponsible agent has exercised its delegated power in an unfriendly way. . . . It is hoped that the government of Great Britain will see the justice of abandoning the narrow and inconsistent claim to which her Canadian provinces have urged her adherence."[9] This was chiefly, though not exclusively, a reference to fisheries. Grant, who was less belligerent than his secretary of state, wrote, in respect of Canada's law providing for the seizure of American vessels "preparing to fish" in Canadian waters, that "should the authorities of Canada attempt to enforce [this law], it will become my duty to take such steps as may be necessary to protect the rights of the citizens of the United States."[10] He had already stated how altruistic it would have been for the United States to have done the people of the Dominican Republic ("San Domingo") the favour of annexing that country. It would have been, but the Senate balked, and he didn't push it, and didn't really push the Canada issue too far either. (Conditions in Canada and the Dominican Republic were hardly comparable, other than in their ability to tickle America's ravening territorial appetite.) Collision was avoidable, but the tenor of the relevant parts of his message was a completely unacceptable semi-non-recognition of Canada, as Britain prepared to propose a joint commission designed to compose all differences between the British Empire and the United States. This commission was established, as the rise of Germany motivated Britain to compose its differences with other great powers, and especially the United States, which, though it eschewed any interest in European affairs in the Monroe Doctrine forty-five years before, was now rivalled only by Great Britain and Germany as the greatest power in the world.

In 1870, the Prussian army had captured the French emperor, Napoleon III, who followed Charles X, Metternich, and Louis-Philippe into exile in London. France was defeated by a vast coalition in 1814 and 1815, after Napoleon I had defeated every power of Europe singly and in groups and occupied the whole continent from Lisbon to Moscow. But in the end Paris was occupied, and now France had been defeated by Prussia, which was about to occupy Paris again by itself and had surpassed France as continental Europe's greatest nation. The bloodbath of the Paris Commune, and the showdown between the forces of radical and moderate change that followed all abrupt French institutional changes, finally produced a close division between the monarchists and the republicans that was only resolved when the imbecilic Bourbon pretender, the Duke of Chambord, rejected the compromise proposal of a constitutional monarchy with a national flag that had the *bleu-blanc-rouge* tricolour of republicanism on one side and the Bourbon fleur-de-lys on a white field on the other. It was out of the question for the lily to be inserted in the middle white bar of the republican flag, and the absurdity of a flag with different designs and colours on each side was rejected by Chambord as conferring too much legitimacy on the republicans. And thus did republicanism prevail in France. The failure of the absolute monarchy of Champlain's patron, Richelieu, in less capable hands than his, weighed oppressively on the French 250 years later. Yet the Third Republic would preside over an implacable spirit of revenge and recovery, and the greatest cultural flowering in French history. France lost two provinces, Alsace and Lorraine, to Germany, and in its desire for a favourable rematch with the Germans would celebrate republicanism with the other great republic and revolutionary country, America, prefabricating and sending the Statue of Liberty to New York, and would even rediscover its long-lost brethren in New France.

The leading Western powers all went through immense changes between 1865 and 1871. The United States suppressed its insurrection, abolished slavery and ended the special constitutional and electoral status of slave-holding states, and emerged from its ordeal unbound before a limitless horizon. The numerous German principalities, duchies, city states, and mini-kingdoms created by Richelieu and Mazarin at Westphalia in 1648 were united into Bismarck's German empire at the Palace of Versailles, over the prostrate French. The kingdom of Italy was welded together from constituent kingdoms and provinces in Cavour and Garibaldi's Risorgimento. France returned to republicanism with a burning national purpose. Japan, traumatized by the American opening of its ports in 1853, restored the absolute Meiji monarchy on the Chrysanthemum Throne and began a massive modernization and aggressive naval and colonial program that soon spread into Siberia and across the western Pacific. Not the least significant and durable of these events would prove to be the Confederation of Canada, which even as that fledgling lineal patchwork of regions laid out a transcontinental railway and began to populate a half-continent, was still, for a little longer, disdained by an American president as a quasi-colonial upstart. Of the late twentieth century's G7 countries, only Great Britain did not have a profound political metamorphosis, as a succession of talented moderate reformers that we have glimpsed (Peel, Russell, Palmerston, Disraeli, Gladstone, Salisbury) moved the country and its mighty Empire steadily forward through social and franchise reform for most of the nineteenth century, in the name of a strong-minded, constitutional queen-empress (as Disraeli would make Victoria). Radical institutional change was in vogue, Canada's was bloodless and effective, and eventually made a difference to the world.

But the greatest immediate difference in this contemporaneous series of national reawakenings was caused by the sudden emergence of

Germany as the continent's greatest power. Disraeli, whose sublime cunning was sometimes obscured by the raw cynicism of his wit, made a prophetic warning speech from his place as leader of the Opposition on February 2, 1871, that would resonate across the next three generations: "The [Franco-Prussian] war represents the German revolution, a greater political event than the French revolution. I don't say a greater, or as great a social event," which was unknowable. "Not a single principle in the management of our foreign affairs, accepted by all statesmen for guidance up to six months ago, any longer exists. There is not a diplomatic tradition that has not been swept away. You have a new world, new influences at work, new and unknown dangers and objects with which to cope. . . . The balance of power has been utterly destroyed, and the country that suffers most, and feels the effect of this great change most, is England."[11] Gladstone did not think in these terms, but Disraeli and his foreign affairs critic and successor, the Marquess of Salisbury, who between them would rule for twenty of the next thirty-one years, did. When the *furor Teutonicus* Bismarck unwittingly created would finally be subdued, seventy-five years later, tens of millions of Europeans would have been slaughtered, America would rule the world, and Canada would be perhaps its most reliable ally.

Secretary of State Fish proposed to Lord Granville a joint commission to resolve the fisheries issues that arose after the lapse of the 1854 Reciprocity Treaty with Canada, continuing the pretense that Canada was just a delegate of the British. Granville proposed that the scope be broadened to embrace all outstanding issues between the countries, including the American grievance that the British had allowed the Confederate raider *Alabama* to sail. Fish accepted that concept, and Granville covered the problem of Britain representing Canada by inviting Macdonald to be one of the five British commissioners on the ten-man panel. The talks opened in Washington in early March 1871. Hamilton Fish led and dominated the American delegation and opened with a proposal to buy the Canadian fishing rights. Macdonald declined this, and held his corner well with the British, but it was obvious that the British wanted to settle any difficulties with the United States, as they had with Jay's Treaty in 1794 after the French Revolutionary War broke out in Europe. The German victory in the Franco-Prussian War was now clear, and it was equally clear that British notions of how to maintain and manipulate the balance of power in Europe would have to be recalibrated, as Disraeli had been the first to note. But under any scenario, Britain could not carry any baggage of American ill will. Macdonald was seeking a less grudging recognition from the United States and a revival of as much as possible of the trade relaxation of the lapsed Reciprocity Treaty. The British commissioner, Earl de Grey and Ripon, wrote to Granville that he expected a great deal of difficulty with Macdonald.[12]

Much horse-trading went on, and slowly shifting incentives were offered as Macdonald struggled to retain British solidarity for a much tougher line than Fish had any intention of accepting. Fish made it clear to the British that he could not, for political reasons, resuscitate reciprocity. Starting on March 9, he did sweeten his cash-for-fisheries offer with some tariff concessions. The British immediately claimed the Americans could not be moved farther, but Macdonald disagreed. Macdonald and the British commissioners both waved about telegrams of support they had elicited from Granville and one of his officials, and Macdonald, with great skill, managed to keep the British more or less onside for a more aggressive game of poker, though their instructions were to make a deal, and no one in their delegation or in Whitehall was much concerned with the consequences to Canada. The Americans raised the ante to free entry into the United States of Canadian fish, coal, salt, and lumber. It was significant movement, and the British again lobbied Macdonald intensively to accept, but he did not. Macdonald sent a lengthy message to London that captured Gladstone's sense of fair play, and the prime minister told Granville on behalf of the whole cabinet "to hold a little with Macdonald."*[13] Macdonald sometimes used the governor general of Canada as a conduit, and Young, who was now Lord Lisgar, was very cooperative in assisting Macdonald in the battle for the hearts and minds of the Foreign Office with the appeasers on the British delegation to the talks.

On April 15, Fish said that he had to retract and water down his previous offer, and the British all very knowingly reproached Macdonald for pushing the Americans too far. Macdonald still would not be

---

* Gladstone wrote that, if pushed, Canada would say "If gifts are to be made to the United States, surely we are better to make them ourselves and have the credit of them."

moved, and the British then offered him the inducement that Britain would pay compensation for the damage done by the Fenian raids. This was a personal flourish of Gladstone's. Macdonald still did not budge, and Gladstone declared him to be "rampantly unreasonable."[14] Finally, it was agreed that the *Alabama* claims would be settled by international arbitration, the emperor of Germany would be arbiter of the boundaries in the Juan de Fuca Strait between Vancouver Island and the American mainland, catches of Canadian fish would enter freely into the U.S., and American fishermen would have full access to Canadian waters. Freedom of navigation of the St. Lawrence was granted in exchange for freedom of navigation on the Yukon, Porcupine, and Stikine Rivers and for ten years to Canada on Lake Michigan, and Canada would receive a substantial cash payment to be determined by a commission. The Treaty of Washington was signed on May 8, 1871. The British did compensate Canada for the Fenian raids, and guaranteed the first 2.5 million pounds for the Pacific railway.

John A. Macdonald had done as well as anyone could, and had made his point. Historian W.L. Morton may slightly, but only slightly, exaggerate by writing that there was

> indirectly, grudgingly, and ungraciously, American acceptance of the fact that the republic was faced from sea to sea by an independent American nation as free, as well-organized and as stable as itself, but founded on an explicit and final rejection of American institutions and of American manifest destiny. A superficial victory for Grant and Fish, the Treaty of Washington was in fact the greatest diplomatic check the United States had accepted since its foundation. It had agreed to share the continent with a self-governing Canada; the continental imperialism of the past was ended with the ending of British imperial power in America.[15]

This was not clear to all the parties, though Macdonald had made his point that he was not a puppet of the British, that Canada was obviously setting up a real country bound by an ambitious railway, and that improved relations between Britain and America were of greater benefit as a deterrent to American appetites for Canada than whatever had been lost by straining the Canadian relationship with Britain, aggravated by Gladstone's skepticism about the Empire generally.

The government had an impressive record to take to the voters, but hanging fire were continuing Nova Scotian discontent, aggravated by the failure to restore reciprocity; Cartier's problems in Quebec arising from the Red River, even though Wolseley had sent Riel packing without any casualties; and it was recognized from the outset that the transcontinental railway was going to be very expensive. Macdonald did a swift pivot and represented the fishing exportation agreement to the United States as a great triumph and the failure to achieve full reciprocity as the blessing of tariff-protected industry and soaring employment just ahead. John A. Macdonald had led Canada, at least tentatively, to another milestone in the long, steep, treacherous path to nationhood.

2. Fall and Resurrection, the Pacific Scandal, and the Wilderness Years, 1871–1878

The Treaty of Washington, as Jay's Treaty was in the United States in 1794, was severely criticized by the Canadian nationalists, who accused Macdonald of selling out, oblivious, as the critics of Jay's Treaty in that young country were, of the unbalanced correlation of forces between the new country and the old. This was an imbalance in this case made more lopsided by the fact that Macdonald was trying to deal with two greater and senior powers, one of which threatened Canada's independence, and the other the country on whose strength and goodwill Canada's independence opposite the Americans depended. There was much criticism of the fisheries exchange, though this was eventually addressed by the $5.5 million Canada won in arbitration. It was, at the time, a handsome award, and it says something for Macdonald's judgment that he achieved it, and something for the United States that, despite flag-waving senators and congressmen empurpling the air with bellicose polemics, it paid the award. To opposition claims that Macdonald had been steamrollered, his colleagues, especially Joseph Howe, denounced "England's recent diplomatic efforts to buy her own peace at the sacrifice of our interests."[16]

Macdonald, in the ratification debate in the House and in the following general election campaign, took the high road and said that the entire agreement, including the resolution of the *Alabama* claims, had resolved all the serious differences between the English-speaking countries, that they had between them established a procedure of negotiation and arbitration and were setting a new and benign precedent for the world, and that it would have been a horrible mistake, a tragedy, and a suicidal error for Canada to block that process. He said that in this process, Canada had gained a new and unambiguously independent status for itself:

> I believe that this treaty is an epoch in the history of civilization . . . and with the growth of the great Anglo-Saxon family and with the development of that mighty nation to the south of us I believe that the principle of arbitration will be advocated as the sole principle of settlement of differences between the English-speaking peoples, and that it will have a moral influence in the world. And . . . it will spread itself over all the civilized world. It is not too much to say that it is a great advance in the history of mankind, and I should be sorry if it were recorded that it was stopped for a moment by a selfish consideration of the interests of Canada.[17]

This proved, of course, optimistic, but he was correct in the extremely important point that it marked the end of any serious threat of recourse to war between the British, Americans, and Canadians (though not entirely to peevish sabre-rattling) and that this would prove a decisive turn in world history. It was also a distinguished beginning of Canada's capacity and determination to negotiate foreign arrangements for itself.

As the autumn of 1871 elapsed, the U.S. Senate had not taken up the Washington Treaty, and the British government had not produced its 2.5-million-pound guaranty for the Pacific railroad. Most worrying, the settlement of the final numbers for the *Alabama* claims seemed almost impossible to agree. Time was slipping by, and Macdonald wanted to clear the current agenda and go to the people in 1872 with a new and imaginative program. The Toronto *Mail* was founded in 1872 as a

Conservative voice in competition with Brown's *Globe*, and Macdonald, in preparation for the general election, had its editor, T.C. Patterson, unfurl what he called the National Policy. It was an almost visionary program that emphasized increased tariffs to protect industry and counter continentalism and the swiftest practical construction of the transcontinental railway, and was broadened to include rapid development of the West and the promotion of heavy European immigration for that purpose, and the admission of all the adjacent territories as provinces as soon as practical (Newfoundland, Prince Edward Island, Saskatchewan, and Alberta). The parliamentary session carried over into 1872, but the Washington Treaty finally passed easily, largely because of Macdonald's suave handling of it, and Ontario was accorded a further six constituencies because of the last census. A rather liberal Trades Union Act was passed and there were no problems with the routine housekeeping matters, and Parliament was dissolved for new elections in the late summer. It was a stormy campaign.

Railway politics had raised their hoary head in a way that would prove immensely controversial. Two companies had been chartered by the Dominion government to build the railway that was committed to in the admission of British Columbia as a province: the Canadian Pacific Railway, led by Sir Hugh Allan (1810–1882) of Montreal, owner of the world's largest private steamship line (thirty-two ocean-going vessels) and founder and president of the Merchants' Bank of Canada, which had a number of prominent American investors; and the Inter-Oceanic Railway, headed by Senator David Lewis Macpherson (1818–1896) of Toronto. Macdonald attempted to negotiate a merger, and negotiations to this end were conducted by his friend Sir Alexander Campbell, but they foundered on the issue of which man would be the president. Allan kept raising the pressure and threatening dire consequences, and the strain on Macdonald was such that he uncharacteristically lost his temper in an election meeting with his opponent in Kingston, John Carruthers. The prime minister had to stay in Kingston, where there was a very close battle, even after eight consecutive terms and with all the prerogatives and prestige of the head of the government. Macdonald himself finally effected a corporate coalition headed by Allan, telegraphing Cartier with instructions to assure Allan of that and leaving other considerations until after the election. He had held the line long enough to bring Macpherson on board as a participant under Allan and so had not simply put him over the side. An immense mystique had built up about Allan, as they would from time to time about other Canadian industrialists over the next 140 years. Allan amassed great political influence by the liberal distribution of money among the small constituency electorates of the time, and in central Montreal there were many jobs that were effectively dependent on the leaders of the banking and shipping industries. He was also prepared to finance whole parties with very large contributions.

In the 1872 election, the government's ability to prevail in Quebec, as throughout the last twenty years, would depend on the political strength and acuity of Sir George-Étienne Cartier. (He was a baronet, a senior position to Macdonald's knighthood, and he was named George by his French-Canadian parents after King George III.) And Cartier was infirm, physically and politically. As it turned out, he was suffering from Bright's disease, a kidney malfunction, and was losing vigour and mobility, and as he was leading the charge against American investors in the national railway, he was not well seen by Allan. On July 30, 1872, in high campaign, Allan told Cartier and telegraphed Macdonald that the presidency of the railway was not sufficient; he must also have the majority of directors and the assurance of government support. It was an outrageous ultimatum to an incumbent government in mid-election campaign, but he was a heavy-handed opportunist. He referred to the government's wish to be assisted with funds in the pending elections, including "immediate requirements" for Cartier, Langevin, and Macdonald himself, totalling sixty thousand dollars. This was an outright bribe, of course, and Cartier, in his unfit and politically desperate state, urged accepting. Macdonald read Allan's telegram with, as his biographer Donald Creighton wrote, "amazement and apprehension." He considered going at once to Montreal, but the voting began the next day, August 1, and he felt he could not leave Kingston. He telegraphed a rejection of Allan's demands. Allan backed down, and Macdonald won his personal election safely enough by the standards of the times, 735 to 604. This was all a good break for the prime minister, but Allan had not withdrawn his financial offer, and Macdonald distributed the twenty-five thousand dollars Allan had deposited to his account in his own name in the Merchants' Bank in Montreal among needy Conservative candidates in Ontario.

Macdonald asked Allan's lawyer, John Abbott, for more and more money, wiring on August 26, "I must have another $10,000. Will be the last time of calling. Do not fail me. Answer today."

So capable and wily a veteran as Macdonald must have been in a terribly distracted condition to write such an indiscreet message. When the election was over, Macdonald had taken $45,000, though nothing for himself, and Cartier and Langevin had taken the utterly outrageous total of $117,000 from Allan. The government was re-elected with a reduced majority, and was put across, ironically, by the efforts of Howe and the able young Tupper in Nova Scotia, where four years before, the province, led by Howe, was seething with anti-federal sentiment. The only greater factor in the government's success was Allan's money. Cartier lost his own district and held only a bare majority of the Quebec MPs, but without the cash infusion from Allan the government would have been defeated. The result was very close: one hundred Conservative MPs and 49.9 per cent of the vote to ninety-five Liberals and 49.1 per cent. There were five other MPs. The government lost a number of districts in Ontario, and Francis Hincks was defeated personally. This was the end of the political careers of Cartier and Hincks, two of the greatest founders of Canada as a federal state. The country owed them a great deal, including a more dignified end to their political careers. Cartier soon departed for medical treatment in England under Dr. Bright's professional successor. He and Macdonald, close partners for seventeen years, fifteen at the head of the government, were not to meet again.

Macdonald turned at once to trying to settle the railway dispute, but Macpherson's position had hardened. He declined to join with Allan and demanded a greater public revelation of Allan's accounts. Strong foreign participation in the national railway was an issue of great emotional strength in Canada at the time, especially where the foreigners were Americans. Macpherson's research made it clear that Allan had not removed but merely disguised the presence of the Americans in his group, and the whole arrangement between the two railroad companies had unravelled amid mutual recriminations.

Macdonald must have known that any revelation of the Allan campaign contributions and the conditions for them would blow his government apart. The matter appeared to be settling down as 1872 ended, but on New Year's Eve Macdonald received an unscheduled visit from George W. McMullen, who owned the *Chicago Evening Post* and was the leader of Allan's American associates in the railway project. He came heavy-laden with correspondence from Allan that made it clear Allan had, in Donald Creighton's words, been "transformed [from] a sober, inhibited, Scottish merchant into a Roman emperor, free of restraint and drunk with power. Ambition, cunning, vanity, incredible indiscretion and duplicity . . . without reserve" were revealed in the two-hour conversation. Allan had even had "the sublime impertinence" to try to collect from McMullen the $343,000 he had spent to buy himself the presidency of the railway.[18] Allan had barely begun to stand down the Americans, contrary to his pledges to Macdonald. The prime minister tried to fob off on his unannounced visitor the theory that McMullen's grievance and recourse were against Allan, but McMullen wasn't having it and said that either the government must now, re-elected, enforce the original agreement, with a full American presence, or dispose of Allan entirely, and that any attempt to allow Allan to get away with the eviction of the Americans would oblige him to ensure that "the Canadian public . . . be promptly put in possession of all the facts."[19] Macdonald, outwardly composed but shaken, played for time and professed a need to get to the bottom of Allan's skullduggery.

Lisgar had departed – a well-regarded, successful, if unflamboyant governor general – and been replaced by the grander and more florid and colourful Lord Dufferin, with whom Macdonald quickly developed an excellent rapport. Truncated terms and seriously unpopular or erratic viceroys were now almost as unimaginable as flexible and politically worldly sympathizers with Canadian ambitions had been in the pre-Elgin years. The opposition was now in the hands of the stolid Alexander Mackenzie and the more intelligent and articulate, but somewhat erratic, Edward Blake, as well as the perennial Antoine-Aimé Dorion, an anomalous quasi-separatist in a federal House, a formula to which Quebec would have recourse again from time to time. At least the fierce and pugnacious George Brown, though still a spirited editor, had not returned to public life. As this volcano silently heated up, Macdonald scored another victory and enlisted Canada's seventh province, Prince Edward Island. The status of the Dominion was good, if the railway could be settled, even if the condition of the government was being undermined, invisibly to the public.

At the end of February 1873, Charles M. Smith, an associate of McMullen in Chicago, wrote Macdonald that his group effectively saw no distinction between Allan and the government and demanded satisfaction. Allan was about to go to London to try to raise money from the British to replace the Americans, and Macdonald sent the just involuntarily retired Hincks to prevent him from leaving and try to broker a deal with McMullen, who was prepared to come to Montreal. It was becoming clear that Allan, so successful a ship owner and banker, had made an unspeakable shambles of the national railway and behaved completely dishonestly. Macdonald now regarded him as "selfish, unskilful, and unreliable," and he was correct.[20] Allan assured Hincks that all was being composed, but Macdonald didn't believe it, with good reason.

The next blow fell on April 2, when the Opposition member for Shefford (Granby, Quebec), Lucius S. Huntington, rose in the House and proposed the creation of a select investigative committee of seven MPs to inquire into the circumstances of the granting of the railway charter to Allan's company. Huntington asserted that Allan was in fact fronting Americans whose existence in the consortium had been falsely concealed and denied, and that Allan had made very large donations, some of them of American-sourced funds, to government ministers and candidates in exchange for improper preferments, including the granting of the charter. He did not elaborate, and Macdonald improvised the strategy of simply ignoring him and imposed silence on his benches. Huntington's motion, technically a confidence vote, was defeated comfortably. To quell concerns, on April 8 Macdonald moved appointment of a committee of five, three of his men and Blake and Dorion, with John Hillyard Cameron, fractious Conservative, as chair. An Oaths Bill was then hastily passed, empowering this committee to take evidence under oath. Macdonald doubted the constitutionality of this measure, since the Imperial Parliament had not granted such rights, and as usual in such matters he was correct, as the colonial secretary, Earl Kimberley, confirmed on May 8. (Kimberley's chief interest at this point was a discovery of large diamond reserves in South Africa, and the site was named after him.) Macdonald had outsmarted his foes, and his proposal of a committee of inquiry had to be accepted. He was still playing for time and planned to adjourn or prorogue for an extended holiday, while making all sorts of compassionate noises about allowing Cartier and Allan's counsel, Abbott, time to come back from overseas to testify. The railway at this point, with an elaborate board of directors, no capital, and under siege from its principal candidate shareholder, was "a pompous fraud."[21] The publicity of the controversy in London, and the bandying about of the phrase "Pacific Scandal," which sounded to British ears like Robert Walpole's South Sea Bubble, coupled to Allan's blustery and inept negotiating tactics, sank the proposed financing in the City of London, as Barings and Rothschilds and the other houses refused unequivocally to consider it.

On May 20, 1873, Sir George-Étienne Cartier died in London, aged fifty-nine. He was widely eulogized on both sides of the Atlantic as co-father of the country with Macdonald, who profoundly mourned the passing of his forceful and brilliant comrade through a tremendous chapter of the country's history over nearly thirty years. Cartier received an immense funeral in Montreal on June 13.

Macdonald was intermittently drinking to serious excess, sometimes at unadvisedly public places and occasions. His committee on the Pacific Scandal began sitting on July 2. Macdonald personally cross-examined the witnesses on behalf of the government and with his customary skill. All Lucius Huntington seemed to have was the McMullen-Allan correspondence, and Huntington, Blake, and Dorion failed to produce Allan's letters to McMullen purporting to break off relations with the Americans. Allan's reputation was in tatters and his career as an aspiring railway baron was over, but his financial condition was solid. His brief dazzling moment as Canada's great political kingmaker ended in abrupt disgrace. Macdonald felt confident and unwell enough to take a holiday at his modest farm near Rivière-du-Loup in mid-July, and was just settling in when McMullen, with the connivance of the opposition, opened the kimono wide in the Toronto *Globe*, the Montreal *Gazette*, and the Quebec *L'Événement*. Macdonald and Cartier's desperate requests for money at the end of the election campaign a year before were jubilantly trotted out. Macdonald said to Dufferin, in whom he confided quite wholeheartedly, "It is one of those overwhelming misfortunes that they say every man must meet once in his life." The prime minister again wallowed in alcohol for a couple of weeks while Parliament was adjourned. In such times, as Sir Stafford Northcote (Disraeli's close associate and a

Macdonald-watcher) said, Macdonald "excludes everyone." He rallied sufficiently to go privately from Rivière-du-Loup to Lévis, and after a few days the opposition began circulating word that he had committed suicide,[22] a rumour that only ceased and was instantly forgotten when he returned to Ottawa on August 10.

Macdonald put on a very spirited and persuasive performance at the committee hearings that opened on September 10. And he exposed the fact that Huntington had gained his material by a break and enter and theft at Abbott's office, though the identity of the felon was not established. Lord Dufferin began the late summer by assuming that he could simply abide by the vote of Parliament on the issue of Macdonald's ability to continue in office, and asked the prime minister for a personal defence that he could use to placate the Imperial authorities. This, in practice, meant Gladstone, who was no friend of Macdonald or of Canada. Macdonald gave Dufferin a lengthy and solid chronology and explanation on October 9, but on October 19, having met with the commissioners, Dufferin told Macdonald in writing that it was "an indisputable and patent fact that you and some of your colleagues have been the channels through which extravagant sums of money, derived from a person with whom you were negotiating an arrangement on the part of the Dominion, were distributed throughout the constituencies of Ontario and Quebec, and have been applied to purposes forbidden by the statutes." He acknowledged that Macdonald's opponents had done as much and paid great homage to Macdonald's services and qualities, and wrote, "Your personal connection with what has passed cannot but fatally affect your position as minister."[23] Dufferin had come to this conclusion with reluctance, as he had great admiration and liking for Macdonald, which he frequently expressed to Kimberley (and which Macdonald did not entirely requite). However, Macdonald was heartened on October 21 when Dufferin told him that Kimberley had effectively instructed him to be governed by Parliament.

Debate on confidence in the government began on October 27, 1873, and the ministerial benches were still confident. Macdonald adopted the policy of waiting for Blake, whom he assumed, from his silence, had something up his sleeve, and he wanted to see it. Macdonald's majority declined as the debate wore on, and Donald Smith was one of the late defectors, as Macdonald was frequently drink-taken and appeared pale, hesitant, trembling, and of quavering voice. Suddenly, on the evening of November 3, Macdonald concluded that Blake was bluffing, that he had no more ammunition, and he signalled that he wished to speak. There was a brief adjournment to permit members to return and the galleries to fill. The prime minister began at 9 p.m., and it was clear from the start that he was entirely in control of himself and at the top of his form. He had no notes, did not pause, and did not repeat himself, and held the Commons chamber spellbound for five hours as everyone recognized they were witnessing a superb historic performance. Without bluster or anything verging on the maudlin, he defended his actions and evoked the national interest without descending to, or even toward, the rascality of false patriotism. "I leave it to this House with every confidence. I am equal to either fortune. I can see past the decision of this House . . . but whether it be for or against me, I know – and it is no mean boast for me to say so, for even my enemies will admit that I am no boaster – that there does not exist in this country a man who has given more of his time, more of his heart, more of his wealth, or more of his intellect and power, such as they may be, for the good of this Dominion of Canada." All knew that this was nothing but the truth. There was thunderous applause and a visibly composed and respectful Opposition. After a pandemonium of congratulations and an emotional scene among the government members and much of the gallery, which included Lady Dufferin, Blake began a reply, and the House rose at 2:30 a.m. No one present that night and early morning would ever forget it.

It had been a mighty tour de force, and Macdonald had certainly salvaged his career. He met his cabinet on November 5, and they agreed that the issue was lost but the character of the Opposition and composition of opinion had changed from scandal-ridden revulsion at moral turpitude to a civilized view that a change, but not a permanent banishment, was called for. The Pacific Scandal was a very shabby business, and Macdonald's achievement in downgrading it from a career-ending debacle to a faux pas, punishable in full by an electoral rap on the knuckles, was a greater accomplishment than would have been a slippery survival by a hair's breadth in a permanently uproarious Parliament. Macdonald was hopeful that he could regain his health and vigour, hold his party, and exploit what he was confident would soon be exposed as the ineptitude of the Liberals. He announced to the House on

November 5 that he had tendered the resignation of the government to the governor general and recommended to him that Alexander Mackenzie be invited to form a government. The Liberals would have to clean up the railway mess. Theirs was a hollow victory; Macdonald had suffered a setback distinguished by his heroic mastery of his departure. The only victors were a few not overly distinguished American businessmen who had humiliated Canada and made their point, but in a way that so artistic a political chief as Macdonald could turn to the country's, and his party's, and his own, advantage.

Macdonald met his caucus on November 6 and urged them to choose a younger leader. It will never be known if he was serious or was just playing possum. There was no denying that he had made some serious errors, and errors that reflected unflatteringly on his ethical judgment. But there was also no denying that he was by far the greatest political leader in the country, who had been a party leader for seventeen years, and leader or co-leader of the government of Canada or of the provinces that held 80 per cent of Canada's people for fifteen of those years. He was the principal founder and builder of the country. Dufferin wrote Disraeli's returned colonial secretary, the well-disposed Carnarvon, on December 8, "Sir John Macdonald and his party are entirely routed, and nobody expects them to rally during the present Parliament."[24]

There was no need to hurry to replace him, and whatever disappointment there was at the Pacific Scandal, and there was widespread distaste for such a tawdry episode, his party was not at all sure it wished to dispense with him. As time passed, and not much time, his pause on the Opposition benches would look less like the tapering down of a great career than an *entr'acte* between two halves of a mighty public life, the second possibly even more spectacular and accomplished than the first. A new election was called by Mackenzie and Blake for late January 1874, and they predictably won a clear-cut victory. The Liberals emerged with 129 MPs and 53.8 per cent of the vote to 65 Conservatives with 45.4 per cent of the vote. There were 12 independents. Macdonald, though determinedly contested again by Carruthers, won, after recounts, by a paper-thin margin. He could relax, begin rebuilding his party, enjoy the spectacle opposite, and restore his physical and psychological vitality. Neither he nor his caucus members were in any hurry for him to go, and although he was only a year younger than Cartier, he had been much more robust and was not yet sixty. The redoubtable Benjamin Disraeli was about to sweep Gladstone out of office and form one of Britain's greatest and most successful governments at the age of seventy, after leading his party in the House of Commons and overall out of a deep wilderness it had languished in for over twenty-five years.

Macdonald observed an almost total silence while his own wounds healed and strength returned, and the Liberal honeymoon passed. The first initiative of the new government was to reopen the trade negotiations with the United States arising from the Treaty of Washington, which required them to test their fervently advanced complaint that Macdonald had negotiated incompetently. George Brown, now a senator, was sent to Washington to "transmute this give-away sale into a profitable commercial arrangement. Fish . . . could hardly have been more uninterested, uncooperative, and unenthusiastic."[25] Brown was assisted in Washington by the fact that he was well-known as a newspaper editor and publisher, and well-regarded by the Republicans for his fierce opposition to slavery. He did achieve a considerable breakthrough: duties on a wide variety of manufactures and raw materials were to be gradually reduced over years. But both countries were now dipping into serious economic recession, and Canadian interests were becoming steadily more receptive to Macdonald's National Policy of protective tariffs. Macdonald told Tupper, who was effectively his deputy leader, as Cartier had not been replaced in Quebec, that, with time, our motto "country first, party afterward . . . sown upon the waters would come back to us, and not, I think, after many days."[26] Yet Macdonald did not press the point publicly, as he thought the country did not yet want to hear from him, and time was on his side as the economy declined and the country got a look at its new leader and his team.

Macdonald had one more indignity to suffer in this sequence. It was finally determined that he had been returned in a vitiated election, and a by-election was called in Kingston. He won, again over Carruthers, but by only seventeen votes, at the very end of 1874.

As 1875 progressed, the carapace of the Liberal government started to crack revealingly. Mackenzie was honest and steady, and not fanatical like Brown or moody like Blake. He "was good, stout, serviceable,

Scotch tweed."[27] But as Dufferin wrote to Carnarvon, "My prime minister is not strong enough for the place. He is honest, industrious, and sensible, but he has very little talent. He possesses neither initiative nor ascendancy."[28] Mackenzie had been a stonemason and was very proud of his working-class background, but he had none of the flair that usually makes a good political leader. Dorion, who was never really very enthused as a federal minister and was a thoroughly ambivalent man about Confederation itself, left after a few months to become chief justice of Quebec. Edward Blake, the apparent strongman of the regime, also resigned after a few months and gave a controversial speech at Aurora, Ontario, shortly after he resigned. It was a pastiche of the faddish Liberal views of the time: Senate reform, proportional representation, a very chippy attitude toward Great Britain, and an abrupt reduction in the inducements already contractually promised to British Columbia. It was a prudish, slightly left, little Canada, humbug speech that opened divisions in the government. Blake helped found the *Liberal* newspaper as a rival to the *Globe* and encouraged the Canada First movement. It was a serious schism. Macdonald, though the beleaguered leader of a beaten party, was not the sort of opponent that could be given such an opportunity without his exploiting it. The Reform sector of the political spectrum had never been pulled together, and Mackenzie was not the man to stop its accelerating dishevelment. Macdonald still bided his time, increasingly confident that the government would not succeed and that the country would become nostalgic for him, especially as economic depression settled on it.

Macdonald had presented or proposed bills for creation of a Supreme Court of Canada in 1869 and 1870 and 1873 and considered it another important step in nation-building. He generally supported the government's Supreme Court Bill of 1875, but violently attacked an amendment abolishing appeals to the Judicial Committee of the Privy Council of Great Britain; though this was not ultimately the effect of the bill, as it was composed in contemplation of changes in British judicature that had been announced but did not occur. Macdonald's game was to keep the British connection warm so that he could accuse the Liberals of being deliberate or inadvertent annexationists. On July 9, 1877, he would utter the famous line "I am British born . . . and a British subject I hope to die." Now that the Confederacy had been crushed in the United States, he overtly stated, Britain and its power of deterrence was the only protection Canada had against the Americans. And he imputed to the entire American public a fervent belief in the manifest destiny of the United States to occupy all of North America. This was a slight exaggeration, but it played well with susceptible Canadian voters.[29] Of greater interest was Mackenzie's sweetening the terms for British Columbia, Blake having accused Macdonald of a sellout to that province. The date for completion of the transcontinental railway was extended to 1890, but Ottawa was to pay the province two million dollars a year for the building of internal railways within British Columbia. This bill passed, with Blake voting against the government, but Mackenzie made further concessions to Blake, who rejoined the government. The *Liberal* newspaper and the Canada First movement folded. The Liberals had driven a stake (almost a last spike) through the heart of Macdonald's railway, to the point that they were having trouble resuscitating it; no one in the private sector would touch it financially. This gave Macdonald plenty of room to claim that if he had not been overturned the railway would be largely finished by now and at reasonable cost. As the economic depression worsened, Macdonald hammered his tariff protection plan harder, to the appreciative agreement of the manufacturing and farm communities.

Following the unification of Italy that deprived the Holy See of the secular government of Rome and the Papal States, the Vatican Council gave Pope Pius IX the status of infallibility, but only in matters where papal authority had always been exercised consistently. It was a symbolic elevation of his authority, but it horrified the Protestant and secular worlds, and there was a scaled-down re-enactment of the Reformation and Counter-Reformation, as ultramontanism, the declared superiority of religious over secular authority, asserted itself in the most Catholic places, including Quebec and such parts of the Roman Catholic world as Poland, Ireland, Spain, Portugal, and parts of France, Germany, and the Austro-Hungarian Empire. Bismarck then unleashed his *Kulturkampf* and restricted Catholic education and other liberties, and Pius IX denounced him as "Attila in a helmet" and in similarly graphic strictures. In Quebec, the bishops raised their voices in criticism of anything they judged secularizing, and bedevilled the government of Quebec. The problems with the conservative Roman Catholic clergy were vividly illustrated by the absurd Guibord affair, in which an unrepentant but dying member of the Church-condemned (but not very subversive) Institut Canadien was denied the sacrament, as well as the convenience, of burial. He remained unburied for six years while the matter was litigated to the Privy Council in London, then needed a military escort to get him past rioting mobs to the cemetery, where he was interred in a steel and concrete vandal-proof tomb, in ground which his bishop then deconsecrated. The anti-papists, who would soon be led by D'Alton McCarthy, were just as extreme.

The excitable Alexander Galt lashed out at ultramontanism and expressed impatience with Macdonald for not doing the same. But Macdonald, no devotee of theology, correctly judged that "ultramontanism in Canada depends on two old men, the Pope and Bishop [Ignace] Bourget [of Montreal]. . . . There can be no doubt that there is an agreement between the Catholic powers that the next pope shall not be ultramontane. In fact, it is absolutely necessary for Europe that he should be a liberal Catholic who will cure the split in the Church." The next pope, elected in 1878 after Pius IX's thirty-two-year pontificate, was the suavely liberal and conciliatory Leo XIII, who though sixty-eight on election, reigned for twenty-five years.[30] Macdonald also told Galt, "Use the priests in the election, but be ready to fight them in the Dominion Parliament."[31] As usual, Macdonald's instinct, even in ecclesiastical politics, was exact. Lucius Huntington, who had first lifted the rock on the Pacific Scandal, attacked the ultramontanists quite gratuitously in a by-election campaign speech in Argenteuil, which was bound to cost his party dearly in French Canada and with other Roman Catholics as well, especially the Irish.

By the spring of 1877, as Dufferin wrote Carnarvon, as "he wrinkled his nose in fastidious disgust: 'The two parties [are] bespattering each other with mud'" (in view of the coming election).[32] The Liberals unearthed the fact that Macdonald had kept control of a substantial part of the Pacific Scandal money for two years after he resigned as prime minister, and some had to be returned. As the session ended in May, Dufferin again wrote Carnarvon: "Blake is ill, thoroughly broken down with overwork and excitement and irritability of the brain. . . . Mackenzie looks like a washed-out rag and limp enough to hang upon a clothes line."[33] Four years before, Dufferin regretfully assumed Macdonald's political career was through; now, he foresaw his return.

Through the summer, Macdonald barnstormed Quebec and Ontario in full cry as in olden times, accompanied in Quebec by the rising star Joseph-Adolphe Chapleau and the fading eminence Hector-Louis Langevin. On July 9, fifty thousand people cheered Macdonald loudly and at length in Dominion Square in Montreal.

In 1878, Macdonald found and pushed another hot button, created by the Eastern Crisis between Russia and the Turks, which caused Disraeli to go to the Congress of Berlin and face down Bismarck, forcing the Russians to ease pressure on Turkey and emerging with Britain in possession of Cyprus. It was a triumph for Disraeli, but it aroused concerns in Canada because of the scare of war, for the first time, between the British Empire and Russia, the only European country relatively close to Canada. Macdonald threw into the pre-electoral hopper a proposal for a permanent army. With tariffs Macdonald seized the nationalist standard "Canada for the Canadians," and with his Imperial enthusiasm he was trying to bag the loyalists at the same time as he explained with impeccable national feeling that only the Empire could deter an American takeover of Canada. He explained his proposal for a standing army to Stafford Northcote: "Without this, Canada will never add to the strength of the Empire, but must remain a source of anxiety and weakness."[34] With his National Policy of tariffs to revive industry and agriculture and create the revenue needed to finish the great railway, he had armed himself with a full quiver of political arrows. The third Parliament of Canada came to a close amid furious argument, as Macdonald had never forgiven Donald Smith for deserting him in his time of need in 1873, and accused him now of using his position in Parliament to promote a railway scheme of the Saint Paul and Pacific Railroad, in which he was an undisclosed participant. For good measure, Macdonald seized on the dismissal of the Conservative premier of Quebec, Charles Boucher de Boucherville, by the Liberal lieutenant-governor, Luc Letellier de Saint-Just (who accused the premier of "contemptuous neglect" of his gubernatorial dignity), which the Opposition leader represented as tantamount to the repeal of responsible government. The very last words of the session were Macdonald's allegation against Smith of being "the biggest liar I ever met."[35]

Canada voted on September 17, 1878, and Sir John A. Macdonald ("The weevil came in with the Grits and prosperity with John A."[36]) was returned to office as prime minister with a landslide about as great as Mackenzie's had been four years before. He was defeated in his home district of Kingston after ten consecutive terms, but was elected on the night for Marquette, Manitoba, and Victoria, British Columbia, and chose to sit for Victoria to boost his placation of British Columbia and help finish the railway. The Conservatives had 134 MPs with 53.2 per cent of the vote to 63 Liberals with 45.1 per cent of the vote and 9 independent MPs. It was a great and a sweet victory, and Macdonald attended upon Lord Dufferin, whose reception of him was "gushing."[37] The governor general told the returning leader that "on personal grounds the warmest wish of his heart was granted."[38] (It was ever thus.)

3. The National Policy, the Railway Crisis, and the Riel Rebellion, 1878–1886

Alexander Mackenzie had been, in effect, a caretaker. In addition to founding the Supreme Court, he introduced the secret ballot, set up the Royal Military College (where a large building is rightly named after him), and created the post of auditor general. This and Brown's tariff reductions with the United States were the product of five years of his leadership, a thin but not distasteful gruel, but he was ineffective at stopping or alleviating the depression that accompanied the demobilization in the United States and the deflation of the currency as Grant retired the paper "greenbacks" that Lincoln had issued to pay for the war and he almost killed Macdonald's railway. Mackenzie remained in Parliament until he died in 1892, aged seventy, and three times declined a knighthood out of loyalty to his working-class origins. He was a thoroughly decent, thoroughly unexciting leader. Macdonald bustled back into office as a new MP from British Columbia with a full agenda, first of all to bind his new province to the old. Of the senior members of his original government, only Tupper (who soon became minister of railways and canals), Sir Samuel Leonard Tilley of New Brunswick (minister of finance), Langevin (minister of public works), and Alexander Campbell (receiver general and then postmaster general) remained. Macdonald would be considerably more dominating than he had been when Cartier, Howe, and Hincks, not to mention Brown, Galt, and

Taché, had served with him. He assumed the new post of minister of the interior, which had been established to oversee the development and populating of the West. Tupper would lead the construction of the Canadian Pacific Railway, Tilley would bring in the new tariffs. Alexander Galt had been appointed by the British government to the Fisheries Commission, where his performance was much appreciated, and Macdonald gave him a special mission to develop increased trade links with the principal countries of Western Europe, a task which flustered the British as smacking of too much independent-mindedness by Canadians.

Dufferin returned to Britain a very successful and respected governor general, to be replaced by the Marquess of Lorne, son of the Duke of Argyll, and son-in-law of Her Imperial Britannic Majesty Victoria, Queen and Empress. To have a royal princess (Louise) as consort to the governor was a signal recognition of Canada's rising status in the Empire. There was a new move by Dufferin and Sir Michael Hicks Beach, Disraeli's latest colonial secretary, that Canada's governor general become a viceroy. But the prime minister (now the Earl of Beaconsfield, Disraeli having departed the House of Commons for an easier life in the Lords in 1876, after thirty-nine years as an MP) declined out of the same concern for American sensibilities about monarchical incursions in their hemisphere that in 1867 prevented Canada from becoming a kingdom and a viceregal post. (It was allegedly Tilley who first proposed the status of Dominion.) Macdonald, Tupper, and Sir Hugh Allan went together to Halifax to greet the arriving governor. Macdonald confined himself to his room in the lieutenant-governor's residence and drank himself almost into a stupor, telling his secretary, when the new governor general's ship approached and he was urged to pull himself together, to "vamoose from this ranch!"[39] Macdonald rallied quickly and greeted the viceregal and royal arrivals appropriately.

To deal with the government's National Policy on tariffs, Lorne was enlisted as a go-between with the Imperial government, which could be assumed to disapprove of protectionist measures at Britain's expense. Macdonald and Tilley offered concessions, but could not grant outright *ex gratia* preferments. The new parliamentary session opened on February 13, 1879, and the tariff was the core of the Throne Speech. The British government was pained by the measure but acknowledged that it was within the authority of the Dominion to enact. As the tariff debate dragged on interminably, the fracas with Letellier de Saint-Just and Boucherville came to a climax and the cabinet reluctantly voted to ask Lorne to dismiss the lieutenant-governor of Quebec for his arbitrary treatment of the premier. Macdonald privately told Lorne that it "was impossible to make Frenchmen understand constitutional government."[40] They agreed to send the whole issue to London, and Langevin and John Abbott were sent to make the federal government's case, not that Macdonald much liked it.

The tariff was finally adopted. Macdonald beat off an attack of cholera and went with his wife on a semi-working holiday in Britain, arriving in London in early August. Macdonald sought a British guaranty for the financing of the transcontinental railway, but as Hicks Beach told him, the Canadian tariff was not popular in London and getting a railway loan guaranty through would not be simple. He also wanted to establish Galt as resident minister in London, another step into foreign affairs. He made headway on both issues, was inducted into the Imperial Privy Council, had an audience with the queen, and had a very satisfactory dinner with Beaconsfield at his country house, Hughenden Manor. Beaconsfield pronounced him "gentlemanlike, agreeable, and very intelligent, a considerable man."*[41] This was high praise from Bismarck's only contemporary rival and one of the greatest and wittiest leaders in British history. Despite the balkiness of Hicks Beach, the City was very receptive of Tilley's overtures, and there appeared to be enough capital available for construction to begin anew in earnest. (The Union Pacific Railroad was a huge project for the United States, which had a population of forty million people; the Canadian Pacific was more costly and ambitious, over more difficult terrain, in a country one-tenth the size with not one-twentieth of the credit as the United States. It was a brilliantly bold ambition.) As Macdonald had told Sir Stafford Northcote, "Until this great work is completed, our Dominion is little more than a 'geographical expression.' The railway completed, we become one great united country with a large interprovincial trade and a common interest."[42] He was back in Ottawa in late September.

---

* Disraeli added that "I think there is a resemblance" (between Macdonald and himself). Disraeli was relieved that Macdonald had "No Yankeeisms except a little sing-song occasionally at the end of a sentence."

Canada was prospering; the depression was lifting across the continent, but the imposition of the National Policy program was fortuitous and was widely credited with the recovery, to which it had doubtless contributed. It took almost to the end of November for the British government to respond to Macdonald's proposal of a resident minister, which they could not accept because of the clear implication of an independent foreign policy. As the foreign secretary, and soon to be Beaconsfield's successor as party leader, the Marquess of Salisbury wrote to Lorne, "The solid and palpable fact [is] that if they [the Canadians] are attacked, England must defend them . . . England must decide what their foreign policy shall be."[43] Hicks Beach added that the British would be very solicitous for Canadian views on matters of interest to Canada.

The converging lines of Canadian interest had finally collided: in pursuing greater autonomy, Canada had got to the point of seeking a degree of sovereignty that made the British uncomfortable as guarantors of Canadian borders and security. Canada could have either British protection or an autonomous foreign policy, but not a blank cheque from Britain to assure Canada's security whatever it chose as a foreign policy. This was a strained, by the British government, interpretation of the role and significance of a resident minister, but Macdonald would do the necessary to retain an unambiguous British guaranty. After a good deal of toing and froing, the title "high commissioner" was agreed upon in early February 1880, and Galt would be the first occupant of the post. It was one of the last acts of the Disraeli-Beaconsfield government, as the Conservatives were defeated by Gladstone in April 1880, and Beaconsfield soon retired in favour of Salisbury and died in 1881, aged seventy-seven, after twenty-two years as Conservative Party co-leader, followed by thirteen years as sole leader.

Macdonald, now sixty-five, had fainted in a regular service in his church in Ottawa on March 26 and considered retiring, as he had from time to time, but his cabinet beseeched him to put any such thought out of his mind, and he did. George Brown was murdered by a discharged employee of the Toronto *Globe* on May 9, 1880. He was sixty-one. He had been a talented and forceful man and a capable editor who had rendered inestimable service joining the Great Coalition to bring about Confederation. He was a bigot and too inflexible to be a good politician, but he was a Father of Confederation and a formidable reform politician and newspaperman. It would be ninety years before another prominent politician was murdered in Canada (Pierre Laporte in 1970).

Macdonald, Tupper, and John Henry Pope had been appointed by the cabinet as a committee to go to London to recruit financing for the Canadian Pacific Railway (CPR) project. There had already been a domestic overture from George Stephen, president of the Bank of Montreal; Donald Smith, who was Stephen's cousin; and James Jerome Hill, the Canadian president of the Great Northern Railway. They controlled what was now called the Saint Paul, Minneapolis, and Manitoba Railway, the subject of the furious debate at the end of the pre-electoral session of Parliament in 1878 when Macdonald shouted, as the Black Rod announced the ceremony of dissolution of Parliament, that Smith was the greatest liar he had known. Their relations, though hardly cordial, were better now. The British and continental expressions of interest in CPR financing gradually fell away as Macdonald and his colleagues toiled through August in London on a challenging regime of commercial negotiations. The Canadian prime minister knew that he would never make a more important decision and that he would have to be a good deal more meticulous than he had been a decade before dealing with Sir Hugh Allan. The Stephen-Smith offer was to build the railway if given $26.5 million and 35 million acres. Macdonald conducted negotiations with his usual skill and was close to agreement with an Anglo-French-German group represented by financier J.A. Puleston and backed by Société Générale of Paris, for $19 million and 32 million acres. It was down to Puleston and Stephen, and the Puleston offer started to soften and wobble as Stephen came firm at $25 million cash and 25 million acres. Macdonald was a good deal more impressed by George Stephen than by his cousin Donald Smith, and he took the offer, ostensibly as a winning competitive bid, but in fact as winner of a one-horse race. Some British and continental firms joined Stephen's group, including Société Générale, and agreement was signed on October 21. The parliamentary session to deal with the Canadian Pacific opened on December 9, and Macdonald, fluey and fatigued, attended the opening session, but the government was led in the ensuing spirited debate by Tupper. The agreement included a number of controversial concessions apart from cash and land. The railway was given a substantial tax holiday and an almost unlimited right to build branch lines. It was allowed to import what it needed duty-free, and no permits would be given to railways in direct competition at close proximity for twenty years.

The Anglo-Canadian alliance had failed financially, though it held politically (rather limply while Gladstone was at the other end of it, but sufficiently to maintain Imperial solidarity). The only non-railway matter Macdonald had dealt with in London was his views of contributing to Imperial defence, which were that Canada could be relied on if Britain were under direct threat, as Britain would be if Canada were, but anything less urgent would have to be assessed on a case-by-case basis. Canada was having to make its own way, and its national railway was largely financed in Canada, or at least by Canadians with their own developed financial relationships. The Liberals attacked on straight, continentalist, anti-national lines and said that building a railway to the north of Lake Superior was a scandalous waste of resources. Macdonald's policy was the only one consistent with Canadian independence of the United States and with the notion of Canada as a functioning and coherent national entity. The debate was intense and often vituperative, with frequent all-night sessions. Macdonald's health started to give way, but he roused himself to a great effort when, on January 17, 1881, the Liberals presented an alternative scheme which on its face contained none of the controversial aspects of the government's bill and carried much smaller incentives in cash and land. Macdonald rose as soon as the Opposition bill was presented to the House by Tupper (as the responsible minister) and said, "We have had tragedy, comedy, and farce from the other side."[44] He exposed the new offer as one to build a prairie section only, connected at both ends to the United States, which would run the trade of Western Canada into that country, and not to build a transcontinental railway at all. "The whole thing is an attempt to destroy the Pacific Railway. I can trust to the intelligence of this House and to the patriotism . . . and common sense of this country . . . which will give us a great, a united, a rich . . . a developing Canada, instead of making us tributary to American laws, to American railways, to American bondage, tolls, freights, to all the . . . tricks that American railways are addicted to for the purpose of destroying our railroad."[45] Once more, a mighty intervention by John A. Macdonald had quelled near pandemonium in the House of Commons and in business circles, and it silenced the New York and London media which, for their own purposes, had been conditioning their readers to discount the Canadian government's project. A business associate in Toronto wrote the prime minister that because of his address, "the champagne corks have been flying a humming fire of artillery."[46] The Canadian Pacific Bill was passed by the House of Commons on a division of 128 to 49 on February 1 and was enacted by Lord Lorne on February 27, 1881. Macdonald had taken the country another giant step forward, and was again the indispensable man.

Macdonald now turned his full attention to the next phase of the National Policy: the systematic encouragement of immigration to settle the West and assist in the financial development of the railway. He had left the colonial secretary a lengthy memorandum on the subject, and Alexander Galt's principal mission in his new and much-discussed post in London was to push such a scheme. But, as usual, Gladstone had no interest in Canadian matters and nothing happened. George Stephen had had a try also, with no success. Macdonald determined to return to Britain in the summer of 1881 to try to get this plan rolling, as well as to seek more sophisticated medical advice, as he had been very fatigued after the parliamentary session. He arrived in Britain on May 29, 1881, after what was now down to an eight-day sea voyage from Quebec. Macdonald was diagnosed with a pre-gouty condition and recovered well over the summer, with a regime of sedate country life and a strict diet, coupled with an ample evening social life, including private dinners with Gladstone and the Conservative leader, Salisbury. He was able to lobby for his immigration plan, and Gladstone, who was personally fairly agreeable, accepted to fund a modest program for Irish emigrants, but not on the basis of any favouritism for the British colonies. Macdonald met with the powerful Roman Catholic primate of England and Wales, Henry E. Cardinal Manning, and made some headway in urging support for what he billed as a humane and promising scheme for organized emigration to a friendly destination. He returned, in excellent health and spirits, to Quebec on September 17.

The following year, he would arrange for Toronto's archbishop, John Joseph Lynch, to visit Britain and Ireland and try to generate enthusiasm for a New Ireland in Northwest Canada. The issue would be further complicated in 1882 when the Irish Roman Catholic Conservative MP John Costigan put through a bill calling for Home Rule in Ireland

and the restoration of civil rights in that province of the United Kingdom. This was no business of Canada's, but Macdonald did not want to interfere with a private member's bill on the eve of an election, and it passed on April 21. On May 6, 1882, the new chief secretary for Ireland, Lord Frederick Cavendish, and his undersecretary, Thomas Henry Burke, were murdered in Phoenix Park in Dublin, near the viceroy's residence. The reaction in Britain and Scotland was predictably outraged, and the colonial secretary, Earl Kimberley, wrote to Lorne that "the people of this country . . . are not in a temper to be trifled with by anglers for Irish votes at elections for colonial legislatures."[47] The whole subject of Irish immigration was swamped in recriminations over the Cavendish murder, and Galt again resigned over Gladstone's slights (which were, for once, not just conjured by the hyper-sensitive Galt). Macdonald had written to his mercurial high commissioner that "Gladstone . . . is governed by his hates, and is as spiteful as a monkey. In a fit of rage he might denounce Canada and its future, and show the danger continually hanging over England by Canada's proximity to the United States, and the necessity of her fighting our battles. In fact, there is no knowing what he might do."[48] Macdonald also objected to Britain's likely acquiescence in American assertion of a sole right over an isthmian canal connecting the Atlantic and Pacific in Central America, and felt strongly that Canada now had a greater population than that of the United States at the time of the Monroe Doctrine nearly sixty years before, and had the same interest in traffic between the oceans, and that Britain was an American power, despite the loss of the Thirteen Colonies. In the circumstances, he did not judge it appropriate to lobby Westminster on the issue, but the Anglo-Canadian alliance was reaching the point of diminishing returns, as Gladstone resented the burdens of the defence of Canada and Macdonald didn't think Britain was doing a very thorough job of protecting the Anglo-Canadian interest against the Americans.[49] (In fact, Canada's population was only about three-fifths of that of the United States at the time of the Monroe Doctrine.)

The plans for the Canadian Pacific Railway were altered to go just north of Lake Superior, rather than farther north into the interior, and through the Rockies on a more southerly route, from what is now Calgary rather than Edmonton. Further economies and advances on the construction timetable were achieved by George Stephen's engagement of

William Cornelius Van Horne (1843–1915) as general manager of the railway, who knew all aspects of railroading (including how to operate a locomotive). He added a telegraph line, a freight delivery service, and eventually a steamship company at the terminals of the rail line to connect across the Atlantic and Pacific, and a trans-Canada chain of luxury hotels. These changes in the plan of the railroad reduced the costs and protected the anticipated Canadian markets better from the Americans' Northern Pacific Railway, but carried the transcontinental competition directly to the Americans in a way that had not been foreseen on either side of the border. The equation was complicated by the desire of Joseph-Adolphe Chapleau's Quebec government to sell its Quebec, Montreal, Ottawa and Occidental Railway, which the Northern Pacific was expressing an interest in buying, and by Northern Pacific's effort to buy some small branch lines in Manitoba. Such arrangements would put the Northern Pacific Railway on a path intercepting the Canadian transcontinental line at two points, and would enable it to buy the goodwill of the government of Quebec and even of Macdonald's Quebec federal caucus, and Macdonald moved pre-emptively to stop the threat. Tupper reported against the Northern Pacific initiative in Manitoba in November, and early in 1882 the application of the company that would bring the Northern Pacific into Manitoba, the Manitoba and Southeastern Railway, was disallowed. Macdonald was going to face off against the forces of decentralization in railways, as he had over distribution of powers when the British North America Act was being debated and hammered out.

The provinces were instantly addicted to steam, and the most pugnacious was Ontario, led by Macdonald's old law clerk, Oliver Mowat, now finishing the first decade of his twenty-five-year term as premier of the province. They had crossed jurisdictional swords already, with the northern boundary of Ontario, which Macdonald had referred to the Judicial Committee of the Privy Council in London, and over liquor sales, where they had competing bills. Macdonald contended that Mowat was taking on too many powers with the provincial licensing of establishments and abusing the concurrent jurisdiction over direct taxes, and the federal government was upheld as acting within its rights. But the greatest confrontation was arising as 1881 ended, over Ontario's Rivers and Streams Bill, which was debated in the federal Parliament in the context of whether the federal government would exercise its right of disavowal of this Ontario measure as ultra vires to the province. The bill was overturned by Ottawa in 1882. Macdonald was for a strong federal government in all matters.

The pre-electoral jockeying reached its most abrasive with Macdonald's Representation Bill, which translated the decennial census into one extra MP for Manitoba and five for Ontario. In his usual bare-knuckled manner, Macdonald made as much of a gerrymander as he could of the new electoral map, squeezing Liberal votes into as few districts as possible.* There was a broad policy difference between the main parties: Edward Blake attacked Macdonald's transcontinental railway and proposed a north-south rail integration with the United States and virtual free trade with that country, though his opposition to Macdonald's tariffs had softened in the light of economic and political realities. Mowat wanted greater provincial prerogatives than had been agreed, and he threatened Macdonald's entire idea of a Great Dominion. It was a bruising election campaign, but Macdonald won his twelfth consecutive term in Parliament, sitting for Lennox, Ontario, near Kingston. In his ninth election as party leader or co-leader, he was victorious for the seventh time, bringing in 134 MPs to 73 Liberals and 4 others. The popular vote was 53.4 per cent Conservative to 46.6 per cent Liberal. Macdonald won in Ontario, though he lost a few MPs, and carried all provinces except Manitoba. It was the clear-cut victory he had sought. Joseph-Adolphe Chapleau (1840–1898), the able premier of Quebec, was elected in a federal by-election a month later and became the leader of the French-Canadian members of the government as secretary of state of Canada. Macdonald met the 1883 parliamentary session in good spirits and continued his tussle with Mowat, who in February 1883 was narrowly re-elected in Ontario; the federal government introduced and passed the Intoxicating Liquors Bill, to establish a uniform regime for the sale of alcoholic beverages.

Galt was an incorrigible controversialist, giving speeches around Britain commenting on domestic British affairs. When he was rebuked in the British press and again offered his resignation to Macdonald in 1883, the prime minister accepted it and appointed Tupper to replace

---

* The term "gerrymander" was named after the fifth U.S. vice president, Elbridge Gerry, who redistricted sometimes in the shape of a salamander to achieve his ends.

him. On May 11, Stephen, who had been in London drumming up support for a public offering of Canadian Pacific stock and lobbying the British government on the immigration question, telegraphed Macdonald that Gladstone had finally agreed to invest a million pounds in the company Stephen proposed setting up to coordinate the immigration efforts of Canadian Pacific and the Hudson's Bay Company. The British government's change of heart was undoubtedly due to increasing levels of violence in Ireland, and Macdonald had some misgivings about accepting support for Stephen's immigration company if it meant that the government of Canada would be construed as guarantying all Stephen's railway loans and stock issues. The issue was still being considered when the Marquess of Lorne and Princess Louisa departed, successful and well-regarded, and Lorne was replaced as governor general by Lord Lansdowne, a prominent Anglo-Irish peer and landowner.

The combination of the onset of a recession in 1883 and the breakneck pace with which Van Horne was thrusting the railroad out across the country was running Stephen out of money, and he called on Macdonald on October 24, 1883. Stephen believed he could go back to the capital markets and obtain the working capital he needed if the Canadian government would provide 3 of the 5 per cent he was paying on the railway's stock, a guaranty for which he would pay twenty-five million dollars, fifteen million of it at once. It was an imaginative proposal that was immediately accepted, and Macdonald also determined to end the Grand Trunk Railway's ceaseless and insidious campaign of media disparagement of Canadian Pacific in New York and London by threatening to call the federal government's loans to that company, which he had the legal right to do.

Stephen was not successful in raising the money he sought in New York to pay the federal government for its support, and modified his plan downward, but, as happens in corporate financial crises, the company came under great pressure, and he told Macdonald that if Canadian Pacific was not refinanced with government assistance, the government would have to take over its operations or shut it down and allow its assets to rust. Macdonald regarded Canadian Pacific as symbolically intertwined with Canada and an essential enterprise to salvage for the credibility of the country as a whole, as well as of his government and himself. He summoned Charles Tupper back from London, where, although he was the high commissioner now, he continued as minister of railways and canals. Tupper signed a comfort letter to the Bank of Montreal at the very end of 1883, and this stabilized the railway briefly, but Stephen was back in the middle of January asking for a loan of $22.5 million secured by a first mortgage on the railway and all its unencumbered assets. Here, again, suddenly, Macdonald faced a supreme crisis that challenged the viability of Canada itself. As Donald Creighton wrote,

> Blake, the Grits, the Grand Trunk 'scribblers,' the specu-
> lators in New York, the correspondents of Reuters and the
> great American press associations – the whole great
> watching ring of [Macdonald's] enemies – would do
> everything in their power to misrepresent, belittle, and
> defame the plan which he would have to sponsor. Every
> trumpery, criticism, every local protest, every sign of pro-
> vincial or regional discontent – anything and everything
> which could be used to injure his scheme through the
> very destruction of Canada's credit – would be picked up,
> magnified, exaggerated, twisted out of all recognition of
> the truth.[50]

Everything John A. Macdonald had worked for, hoped for, and believed in throughout his public career of forty years was now at stake, and the complexity of managing the problem was aggravated by a crisis among the native people and Métis of the North-West Territories. Their crop had failed, and they were being moved by treaty onto new reserva-tions, in part to make way for the railway. In one sense, the collapse of the railway would alleviate the condition of the Métis, but in fact the whole Confederation project was now on the line, and Macdonald steeled himself, in his seventieth year, to address the greatest crisis of his life. In December, a large convention in Winnipeg had created the Manitoba and North-West Farmers' Union to protest high freight rates and demand relief. The settlers were not only angry and economically strapped themselves, but also their increasing, surging numbers had irritated the always volatile condition of the Métis. Already, the dis-contented settlers and Métis were making the familiar reflexive noises about looking to Washington, and while Gladstone was moved to comparative amicability toward Canada as a receptacle for violent and impoverished Irish peasants, there was no reason to believe that he would do much to deter American responses to widespread annexationist noises in Western Canada, were they to arise. Macdonald would address the problems in the order of their imminence, and on February 1, 1884, Tupper rose in the House of Commons and introduced a comprehensive eleven-clause bill for the relief of the Canadian Pacific Railway.

The ensuing debate was predictably acrimonious and protracted, and the atmosphere further confused by the government of Quebec asking for financial relief with the approval of almost all of Macdonald's Quebec caucus, which, if it defected en bloc, would bring down the government. The fractious John Costigan, who had brought the wrath of Gladstone down on Canada with his resolution supporting Home Rule two years before, purported to resign, and rumours were rife and fanned by the media, which panicked London and New York investors, and even Canadian lenders. The Bank of Montreal declined Tupper's request for a short bridge loan for Canadian Pacific, and Stephen wrote Macdonald on February 17 that he was seeking in New York "$300,000 which we think will keep us out of the sheriff's hands until Tuesday or Wednesday."[51] The railway and the government, and in many respects the country, had all abruptly reached the final extremity. Macdonald talked Costigan out of resigning, personally stabilized the Québécois, who, he told Lansdowne, were "guilty of a rather ignoble plot" which he had stopped with promises of "large pecuniary aid . . . but this combination of the French to force the hand of the government of the day is a standing menace to Confederation."[52] So it was.

Putting first things first, Macdonald rammed through the Canadian Pacific legislation 136 to 63. The House gave final approval on February 28, and it was approved by the Senate on March 5 and received immediate royal assent, not more than one whole day before the national and transcontinental railway would be insolvent. The financial crisis abated quickly, but the future of the railway was still cloudy, and beyond that was the question of whether Canada itself, now in an economic recession with no end in sight, could endure this sudden doubling of its commitment to this very ambitious project. Macdonald thought so, but there was no precedent for such an ambitious cobbling together of so vast a territory, and, as always, the American behemoth loomed, aggrandizing and grudging, though not so much hostile to Canadians, who had been inoffensive, as skeptical about Canada as a concept.

On March 7, the Judicial Committee of the Privy Council found for Ontario in the Rivers and Streams Bill, thinking that lumbering was the chief industry of the country, so ignorant of the country from which the case was evoked were their lordships. The "comically disreputable controversy"[53] over the sale of alcoholic beverages couldn't go on forever. The Manitoba and North-West Farmers' Union met again later in March and warned incoming settlers to stay away, threatening revolt and secession. Macdonald was at first not too concerned, as the premier of Manitoba, John Norquay, was a federalist. Norquay came to Ottawa, and Macdonald made some palliative concessions, but Norquay took the concessions back to Manitoba, reneged, and led a bipartisan attack on the federal government in his Legislature. Macdonald kept cool and withdrew his offer without any suggestion that anything would replace it. Finance Minister Tilley, in London in June, warned Macdonald that there was a widespread media campaign in progress to discredit Canada, and the financial markets there were not receptive to any Canadian securities, public or private sector. It was agreed to take just a small bond issue, and that at a higher rate than was expected or objectively justifiable. Macdonald, again strained physically, took his holiday near Rivière-du-Loup in late June, just before the completely unforeseen return to the Saskatchewan River country, after an absence of over ten years, of Louis Riel.

Rumours persisted of armed revolt, but Macdonald was quite collected, as always, and told the lieutenant-governor of Manitoba that "the Fenian business has taught me that one should never disbelieve the evidence of plots or intended raids merely because they are foolish and certain to fail."[54] The substantive claim of the Métis was that they shared fully in the rights of the native people and that this had been implicitly recognized in the Manitoba Act. It was not clear whether the Métis were seeking grants of land, alternative compensation, or a second round of compensation, having, in many cases, squandered the first. They had been accorded a settlement, and their concerns were taken very seriously, but it was suspected that the ranks of the agitators were swollen with scoundrels coming back for a double dip. At least, in the early months of his return, Riel was counselling moderation and behaving cautiously. Macdonald returned from a rainy holiday not greatly refreshed or invigorated, and to be greeted with the unwelcome news that Mowat had been upheld again by the Judicial Committee of the Privy Council in the question of the northern border of Ontario and that the federal government had to yield a large part of what had been Rupert's Land. Macdonald departed for England on October 8, taking George Stephen with him, for what proved an immensely satisfying trip. The weather was good, and Macdonald was treated with extravagant respect; Gladstone had Macdonald awarded the Grand Cross of the Bath, and he dined privately with Queen Victoria and was feted with all the flattery and pomp the British can lay on. As Germany became more powerful, even the somewhat pacifistic Gladstone began to reconsider Britain's strategic assets, and the Canadian association was certainly one. And Macdonald himself, after nearly thirty years in frequent government in Canada, was becoming a personal institution.

Uplifting and salubrious though London was, Macdonald's problems pursued him. Riel had met with Bishop Grandin and Amédée-Emmanuel Forget, clerk of the North-West Territories, who went to Riel as emissaries of Macdonald and Lansdowne, and had given them his demands, which included two million acres for Métis schools and hospitals, special land grants which would be renewed in favour of newborn Métis as they came of age, and interest on the entire value of the western lands on the division of forty cents an acre, twenty-five to the Métis and fifteen to the entirely native people. Of course, this was nonsense, but Riel also hinted that he could scale back his demands if well taken care of personally. After 1875, Macdonald publicly claimed to want to bring Riel to justice in Canada, but in fact bribed him to stay away. Riel indicated that for a few thousand dollars he would de-escalate the crisis and stay away at least for a while. But Macdonald, who generally had no problem deferring issues, did nothing as demands became more shrill and violence loomed.[55]

In addition, as Macdonald's travelling companion, Stephen told him Canadian Pacific was at the end of its resources again. The government support it was receiving could keep the construction of the railroad going, but the commitments to interest on loans and dividends could not be funded much longer. Stephen and Donald Smith showed the way with a personal loan to the railway of fifty thousand pounds, and Macdonald promised that he would try to do it one more time with the Canadian Parliament, though Tupper could not desert his high commissioner post again and would have to remain in London.

Macdonald was back in Canada at the start of 1885, just in time for his seventieth birthday, which was an authentic national celebration. The United States exercised its right, at the first opportunity, to abrogate the Treaty of Washington, because of its irritation at the $5.5 million it was forced to pay Canada for access to its fisheries, but also so outgoing President Chester A. Arthur could hand an embarrassment to his successor, Grover Cleveland (the first Democratic president elected since James Buchanan seven presidents and twenty-eight years before).

All through January, the condition of the CPR became more precarious, as workers struck because of delays in pay, small creditors complained, and the usual voices of doom poisoned the wells in the London and New York markets. Stephen again besieged Macdonald, but the prime minister was advised by his cabinet, backbenchers, and influential friends that it could not be done again. He waited for the implications of the failure of the project to drag grumbling politicians to their senses. Stephen and Smith again advanced their own money, $650,000, to pay the January dividend. Blake congratulated Macdonald for not mentioning the railway in the Throne Speech. Macdonald declined to show his hand on the railway, as he declined British urging to outline a fisheries policy opposite the United States – the Americans had cancelled the treaty, and they could propose what would replace it – but he did announce that it was no longer acceptable for the federal electorate to be determined by provincial officials. Macdonald also abstained from the war hysteria that afflicted the country and the whole Empire after word arrived on February 6, 1885, of the massacre of General Gordon and his men by the Mahdi at Khartoum. The reluctant Gladstone had already sent the versatile Imperial enforcer Wolseley to Khartoum, where he arrived two days late and withdrew. (Wolseley was then immortalized by Gilbert and Sullivan as "the very model of a modern major general." Gordon was not avenged until General H. H. Kitchener defeated the Mahdist army at Omdurman in 1898 and occupied most of the Sudan and imprisoned the surviving murderers of Gordon.) Macdonald played this coolly also, taking the position that Canada would participate if the entire Empire was under threat, but not in local disturbances. He wrote to Tupper, "Why should we waste money and men on this wretched business? Our men and money would be sacrificed to get Gladstone & Co. out of the hole they have plunged themselves into by their own imbecility."[56] If the North-West flared up again in Canada as it had fifteen years before, Canada would deal with it and not ask for relief from Britain as Macdonald had on the earlier occasion.

The tempo of the North-West crisis was swifter: a petition arrived on January 5 which appeared not to be from Riel but enumerated the familiar demands. The cabinet concluded that it would establish the number of Métis and distribute to them the land and paper money they had requested, though Macdonald told the House, "Well for God's sake let them have the scrip; they will either drink it or waste it or sell it; but let us have peace." The payments were made, but peace was not so easily had. The Métis regarded this step as a delaying tactic. Riel met with the local priest, Father Alexis André, and a member of the North-West Council, who represented in a summary of the four-hour meeting to Macdonald that Riel offered to fold the unrest in exchange for a sizeable payoff for himself. Macdonald declined this overture. The fact is that Riel was by now suffering from intermittent dementia and had a delusionally messianic view of his own religious significance. He had lapsed into what the Roman Catholic hierarchy considered to be heresy, including his assertion that Montreal's Bishop Bourget should immediately be recognized as pope. By mid-March, the atmosphere was becoming very fraught, with a good many local threats of recourse to violence. And Riel put out feelers to Cree chiefs Poundmaker and Big Bear for a solid front. (It was only nine years since Sitting Bull had defeated the 7th Cavalry and killed General Custer and his men at the Little Bighorn in Montana.) On March 23, Macdonald sent General Frederick Middleton, commander of the Canadian militia, to Winnipeg, and the next day Leif Crozier of the North-West Mounted Police and a force of one hundred of his men were attacked at Fort Carlton. (The same day, George Stephen was advised that negotiations were over and concluded that Canadian Pacific would have to declare bankruptcy.) On March 27, Macdonald rose in the House to reveal that there had been a military encounter with armed rebels at Duck Lake, in the District of Saskatchewan, and that an insurrection was in progress.

He seized on the brilliant improvisation of tying the North-West and Canadian Pacific crises together. Macdonald explained with some apology what he called his "crude" strategy to General Middleton: he would accelerate consideration of the Métis land claims and make placatory overtures to the Indian leaders, starting with enlisting the locally trusted Father Albert Lacombe (1827–1916), a missionary who persuaded the Blackfoot chief Crowfoot to stay clear of the Métis disturbance. Orders were given at once to increase provisions for the native people throughout the West in an *ex gratia* goodwill gesture. The other side of his pincer movement from this goodwill offensive was to dispatch forces at once and utilize the railway. Instead of asking for Imperial troops and waiting three months, as he had with Wolseley's military mission in 1870, while the breakup of the ice in the St. Lawrence occurred and the endless portages of the route west of Lake Superior were undertaken, large numbers of trained volunteers came forward at once and the Canadian Pacific Railway transported them swiftly across most of the route to the Saskatchewan country. Volunteer units marched through the main streets of eastern cities on March 29 and 30 and entrained. Van Horne saw to their arrival at Winnipeg starting on April 4, and on April 9 Middleton led the advance guard in an attack on Riel's headquarters, where he claimed to have established another provisional government, at Batoche. Riel had not counted at all on the ability of the Canadian militia and railway system, and assumed that he could dither and negotiate for three months, as he had before. Nor had Riel had the tactical sense to try to entice the United States to do some of his bidding and frighten the British, which the Americans were now very capable of doing. The American media dutifully reported, and the London newspapers credulously repeated, that Canada was facing a full-scale Indian uprising. The Americans became neurotically sensitive at the thought that Canada could manage through its problems with the native people without the bloodshed and setbacks that even battle-seasoned U.S. forces had endured, from Fallen Timbers in 1794 to the Little Bighorn in 1876.

In fact, Macdonald's standing force and the still-abuilding national railway effectively snuffed out the rebellion before it could take hold. On April 16, Van Horne informed Stephen, who told Macdonald, that Canadian Pacific could no longer pay its employees and the entire operation could collapse at any moment. Still Macdonald waited, eight more days, and then, on April 24, telegraphed the Bank of Montreal that legislation to assist Canadian Pacific would be presented to Parliament imminently. The prime minister was advised that that would not do, unless the legislation was actually presented. This was nervy treatment of the head of the government, and on April 25 came news from the North-West of the arrival of a column of troops at Battleford and also of an indecisive engagement at Fish Creek. The Canadian public was aroused, an insurrection was in progress, and the national railway, on the verge of completion, was also about to collapse and shut down. The perils of the birth of Canada were undiminished nearly twenty years after the launch of the country. On May 1, Macdonald gave parliamentary notice of a rescue plan for the railway that consisted of cancelling the entire mortgage on its assets and the thirty-five million new shares and replacing them with thirty-five million dollars of new mortgage bonds which would secure an immediate further cash advance of five million dollars. On May 2, there had been another sharp and close engagement at Cut Knife Hill, but on May 13 Adolphe-Philippe Caron (1843–1908), the minister of militia and defence, read the House of Commons a telegram from Middleton recording the capture of Batoche and the collapse of the Métis uprising.

Macdonald, alone of the senior ministers, retained the stamina for what he called the most difficult and fierce debate of his forty-two years of parliamentary activity, and on June 16 he got through his franchise bill, taking the composition of the federal electorate into federal hands, and then jammed through the railway relief bills over the next several weeks. A terribly bitter and exhausting session ended on July 27, but it was one of John A. Macdonald's greatest triumphs: the crushing of revolt by domestic forces and assurance of the completion of one of the engineering marvels of the world in the transcontinental railroad, while, with infinite reluctance, the government of the United States hinted that it would have to deal with Canada to satisfy the New England fishermen. Macdonald's dream was taking shape in tangible form at last. It had been the genius of using two terrible crises as the justification for, and method of, resolution of each other – one of the most difficult and stylish techniques of crisis management – and if Macdonald had misjudged the timing, or the appropriate level of determination, or lost the stamina to manage and control it all himself, including in a parliamentary session that lasted two and a half days without interruption, it all would have collapsed, and the young country would have gone down with it.

The Métis had very substantive grievances, but Riel's movement was a fraud, and Riel was of doubtful sanity and probity. He was chiefly preoccupied with a messianic mission he generally believed he possessed, and was apart from that preoccupied with feathering his nest. Of the 779 Métis petitioners, it emerged that 586 of them were ineligible, either as settlers who had no ethnic claim, as Métis who had already been paid and were coming back to the well, or as Americans who were just grazing in Canada with cupped hands in a false cause. Macdonald managed a partial reorganization of cabinet, as Tilley departed (to become again the lieutenant-governor of New Brunswick), by securing the nomination of John David Thompson of Halifax as minister of justice. Thompson was very highly regarded but had the political disadvantage of being a Roman Catholic convert and was, at more than 225 pounds, significantly overweight for his height of five feet seven inches, which affected his cardiological condition.

The trial of Louis Riel ended in Regina on August 1. The jury of six Protestant men found him guilty and recommended mercy, but the judge sentenced him to be hanged. A sharp division developed not so much along sectarian lines, as Riel's claim to being a Roman Catholic was now tenuous and the Church was not altogether enthused about him, but along French-English ones. There was not as much sympathy for the Métis as there should have been, given the generally shabby treatment of them. The French Canadians wished for clemency; the English Canadians, including most Roman Catholics among them, wanted him hanged without delay or mercy. Riel had the benefit of excellent counsel, and when Macdonald granted the necessary reprieve, they pressed Riel's appeal to the Judicial Committee of the Privy Council, which did not normally hear criminal cases. The petition was dismissed on October 22. At the trial, Riel's counsel had argued that he was not guilty by reason of insanity, but Riel had confounded their efforts by proclaiming his sanity and acting accordingly. Three prominent doctors were invited to opine on Riel's present mental condition, as they had no perspective on his mental state at the time of the offence.

The Riel and Canadian Pacific dramas went right to the wire together, as the railway was rushing to drive the last spike in the Rocky Mountain passes before the weather became too difficult, and the Riel commission was working to a similar deadline, though because of the political weather only. Donald Smith drove the last spike of the Canadian Pacific Railway on November 7, 1885. The medical evidence on Riel was in by November 10: two of the doctors found Riel accountable, and the other felt he was sensible in political matters but not religious subjects, but did not allow for the two to be confused in Riel's mind. There are indications that Riel ardently wished to be executed, and if his goal was fame and martyrdom, that was the correct decision. One of the jurors said Riel was really condemned for the murder of Thomas Scott in 1869, and Macdonald, when the medical opinions were in, allegedly said, rather coarsely, "Riel will hang though every dog in Quebec barks." Louis Riel was given the comforts of the Roman Catholic Church in his last days, and immediately after reciting that Church's version of the Lord's Prayer with Father André on the morning of November 16, 1885, was precipitated through the trapdoor of the gallows to his destiny. His pulse required four minutes to stop and he died of strangulation, but he probably lost consciousness at once. Macdonald seems to have realized that Riel's execution could be a problem for his party in Quebec; there is little doubt that by contemporary standards there was real doubt about Riel's lucidity, and Macdonald could easily have guided the case in that direction. If Riel was determined to die for his cause, Macdonald may have been equally determined that he do so, to emphasize Canada's seriousness and for his own gratification at the end of one of his and Canada's most eventful years, and of a crisis that had shadowed most of the brief history of Confederation.

4. The Last Victories of the Old Chieftain, 1886–1891

Macdonald travelled to Britain a week after the execution of Riel, and even in the crisp and dark humidity of December he found London and its environs invigorating. He rejoiced in the electoral victory of Lord Salisbury, but it was very precarious, and the Irish nationalist leader Charles Stuart Parnell held the balance of power. Macdonald met with

The Territorial Evolution of Canada and the Building of the Railways

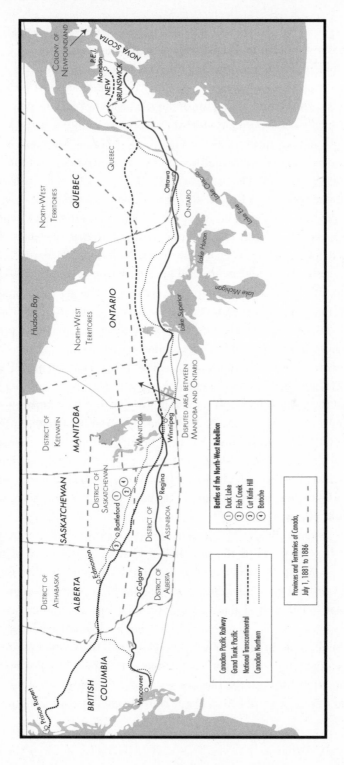

Battles of the North-West Rebellion
1. Duck Lake
2. Fish Creek
3. Cut Knife Hill
4. Batoche

Canadian Pacific Railway
Grand Trunk Pacific
National Transcontinental
Canadian Northern

Provinces and Territories of Canada,
July 1, 1881 to 1886

Salisbury at the Foreign Office on January 4, 1886. As he made the rounds in London, he received reports of the conversion of the Quebec Liberal Party, which had held the government of that province for only one year since Confederation, to the Parti National, led by Honoré Mercier, who was breathing fire about the death of Riel. His new party, purportedly a Liberal-Conservative, all-French coalition party, kicked off with a mass meeting at the Champ de Mars in Montreal, where thirty-seven orators succeeded each other in panegyrics about the "government of hangmen" in Ottawa. Even Wilfrid Laurier, the rising federal Liberal star, who had briefly been Alexander Mackenzie's revenue minister and had been in Parliament since 1874, after three years in the Quebec Legislature, allowed that if he had lived on the banks of the Saskatchewan, he would have taken up a rifle too. Macdonald came down with a nasty cold and missed the Riel debate, where Hector-Louis Langevin's grasp of tactics and Thompson's of the legal issues, and his powerful summing-up address in his first test as justice minister, carried the House and caused the rejection of a Quebec Conservative private member's bill censoring Riel's execution by 146 to 52. The successful end of the North-West affair and the completion of the Canadian Pacific Railway, and its efficient performance in putting down the uprising, had ended the commercial death watch in London and New York and shut down the railway's critics. As Tilley had become lieutenant-governor of New Brunswick (again), the new finance minister was Archibald Woodbury McLelan, who had the pleasure of announcing that Barings had refinanced the CPR's bonds and that the entire debt of the company to the Canadian government had been paid off in the six months since the last spike was driven.

In foreign affairs, Macdonald, now in a position of comparative strength, had declined the proposal of Cleveland's secretary of state, Thomas Bayard, that Canada allow the Americans into Canadian fishing waters without the United States relaxing tariffs against Canadian fish. As Macdonald said of Bayard to Governor General Lansdowne, "He appeals to us as good neighbours to do what he does not offer as a good neighbour to do to us."[57] So Macdonald ordered that Canadian authorities enforce the Rush-Bagot Convention of 1818 and prevent American vessels from fishing in Canadian waters. The American fishing ship *David J. Adams* was seized in Digby Harbour in May 1886. This quickly aroused American outrage, and the U.S. government, as was its wont, ignored Ottawa and demanded that the British rein in their bumptious colonial minions and yokels. Gladstone, briefly back in office for the third time, and his colonial secretary, Granville, telegraphed Lansdowne to reserve Macdonald's Fisheries Bill as soon as it was passed by the House. Once again, Canada was facing the opposition of both great Anglo-Saxon powers. This was a distinct and humiliating defeat, though Macdonald undoubtedly had domestic opinion with him on the issue. However, Mercier was looking more and more like the winner of the next Quebec election, and in Nova Scotia the Liberal William Stevens Fielding swept the spring elections on a platform of seceding from Confederation; Nova Scotia had been hard hit by the decline of the West Indies trade.

Macdonald took his summer holiday in 1886 on a transcontinental train trip, departing for the West on July 10. He went through the Rocky Mountain passes seated high on the engine with his wife in front of the smoke stack, with an astonishing view of the breathtaking scenery and marvels of engineering by which the road had been laid. Macdonald had a very agreeable meeting with his old ally Crowfoot, who had helped rally the native people against the Métis insurrection. On July 24, they arrived at Port Moody, and Macdonald simulated Sir Alexander Mackenzie nearly a century before and said, "From Canada by rail."[58] The Canadian Pacific steamer *Princess Louisa* took the party on to Victoria.

They returned to Ottawa on August 30. Macdonald's chief concern was to have Britain lift the reserve of his Fisheries Bill and secure Royal Navy support in policing the enforcement of the Rush-Bagot Agreement so he could get the attention of the United States, and he sent Lansdowne on this mission, pleased that Salisbury had turned the tables on Gladstone and now appeared to be in office for a full term. On October 14, Mercier almost won the Quebec election; there was no clear winner, but the Conservative regime in that province was tottering. Mercier emerged as head of a Liberal–Parti National coalition and was sworn in as premier on January 30, 1887. He was soon calling for a federal-provincial conference to agree a redistribution of powers. Undeterred by this and by the rigours of the Canadian winter, Macdonald called an election, campaigned with all his old energy, and on February 23 was re-elected to a fifth term as prime minister of the Dominion after three terms as co-leader of the

Province of Canada (and back again for the twelfth time as MP for Kingston). It was close enough: 124 constituencies to 80 for the Liberals, and 50.7 per cent of the vote to 48.9 per cent.

The election result was the last straw for Edward Blake, a brilliant but inconsistent man, who had neither the personal charm to develop a warm rapport with his close colleagues nor the flamboyant personality that would make him accessible to a broad public. Macdonald always appeared more companionable to his partisans, as well as more human and yet more substantial to the public, which had grown accustomed to his presence and his quick wit, and even his amiable rascality. Blake was a successful advocate of the provincial interest in cases before the Judicial Committee of the Privy Council after his retirement from Canadian politics, and was chancellor of the University of Toronto from 1876 to 1900. He served as an Irish nationalist member of the British House of Commons from 1892 to 1907. He returned to Canada after retiring from that role and died in Toronto in 1912, aged seventy-eight. A committee under Sir Richard Cartwright (1835–1912) of eight prominent Liberals was struck to choose a new leader. (Cartwright had been a follower of Macdonald but quit the Conservatives to join the Liberals in 1869 when Macdonald brought back Sir Francis Hincks. Cartwright had been Mackenzie's finance minister.) Blake ignored the recommendations of Cartwright's committee and, in his most important contribution to Canadian history, proposed Wilfrid Laurier as leader of the Opposition. Laurier, born in Saint-Lin, in the Laurentians, thirty miles north of Montreal, was a lawyer and the founder of a *rouge* newspaper called *Le Défricheur* (the deforester, or woodsman) in Arthabaska on the south shore of the St. Lawrence, which was effectively closed by a prohibition on buying, advertising in, or reading it from Trois-Rivières authoritarian ultramontane bishop Louis-François Laflèche (who allegedly said of his episcopal method, "Rule them with a rod of iron, and break them like a vase of clay," and prior to one election allegedly reminded his diocesans that "Heaven is *bleu* [Conservative], and Hell is *rouge* [Liberal]"). Laurier, after his term in the Quebec Legislative Assembly from 1871 to 1874, was a member of the federal Parliament continuously from 1874 to 1919. He was not overly prepossessing in his early parliamentary years, and he was outraged by the hanging of Riel, but he had impressed Blake, and would soon be recognized as a political leader of unusual talent and qualities, and would rival Sir John himself, in Parliament, on the hustings, and in his stature in the history of Canada. But the selection of a French-Canadian and Roman Catholic leader of a national party two years after the execution of Riel was a bold move, the first sign of the genius of the Liberal Party that would chiefly guide the country for a century.

Mercier started what would be a durable tradition by convening an interprovincial conference to share grievances with Ottawa, so Quebec's secessionist ambitions could skulk forward behind the skirts of English Canadians who only wanted some degree of decentralization. Then, and for at least the next 125 years, such unholy alliances would be announced and sustained with a great bellowing of *bonne ententiste* platitudes and claptrap.

Tupper's forceful performance in London as high commissioner helped produce Anglo-American agreement to hold a joint commission for the settlement of all abrasive issues between the United States and Canada. Tupper was rewarded by being appointed the Canadian delegate at the joint commission in Washington, where the British would be represented by the redoubtable and strenuous Joseph Chamberlain. Macdonald managed to generate some optimism about the meeting, but when it convened it was soon clear that the Americans were not serious and that the Cleveland administration was so intimidated by the Republicans in the Senate that they would not discuss tariffs at all. The thin agenda that remained was not worth the trouble of attendance even of Tupper and Thompson (who again made a good impression), much less Chamberlain. Tupper and Thompson suggested a vastly scaled-down proposal of licensing American ships to be serviced in Canadian ports in exchange for agreed fees or reciprocal rights to bring Canadian fish into the United States duty-free, but the conference adjourned without this proposal being taken up. More important and even less promising was Mercier's interprovincial conference, which swiftly descended into a contest over who could demand a more systematic dismemberment of the prerogatives of the federal government. Macdonald completely ignored the provincial bloviation and had a pleasant sojourn with Chamberlain, who spent the holiday in Toronto and Ottawa and gave a strong address at the Toronto Board of Trade on December 30, 1887, warning darkly that free trade and commercial union, which the Canadian Liberal Party was embracing, was interchangeable with annexation. Macdonald found Salisbury and Chamberlain infinitely preferable to Gladstone and Granville.

On March 14, 1888, Cartwright introduced a motion calling for complete commercial reciprocity with the United States, which obliged Macdonald to lean more heavily than he would have liked on the Anglo-Canadian alliance, as any such course as Cartwright proposed would almost certainly lead eventually to the absorption of Canada into the United States. Cartwright argued that one of every four native-born Canadians had had to emigrate to the United States, and that three of every four immigrants to Canada had moved on to the United States. His figures were probably exaggerated (Cartwright was an over-whiskered one-trick pony about commercial union with the Americans), but the panache of America was overwhelming, and its ability to draw the "wretched refuse of the teeming shore" of Europe produced aston-ishing figures of population and economic growth in the 1880s.[59] In comparison, Canada seemed a plodding country, clinging to the bor-der of surging America like a hobo trying to board a passing express train. Canada had almost completely surpassed the danger of American military assault, only to be threatened by the irresistible suction of the swift rise of post–Civil War America.

Macdonald did agree to a further guaranty of Canadian Pacific along with Stephen's ultimate acquiescence to the ban of new rail charters in Manitoba, which somewhat appeased sentiment in that province. The desultory discussions in Washington were not proceeding anywhere. A very soft agreement was rejected by the U.S. Senate on August 21, and two days later the normally very pacific President Cleveland (who would not even authorize the takeover of the Hawaiian Islands), asked for congressional authority to sever all commercial contact with Canada. Macdonald hoped for Cleveland's re-election in 1888, as he believed that if Benjamin Harrison won, James G. Blaine "will be, as secretary of state, the actual government."[60] The British minister in Washington, Sir Lionel Sackville-West, incautiously wrote a British resident in America that Cleveland would be a better president for British interests. This was made public, and Sackville-West immediately resigned. Harrison won the election, though Cleveland led in the popular vote, and Blaine was back as secretary of state. He had been the secretary under presidents Garfield and Arthur, and the presidential candidate in 1884, and was a Maine nationalist. As 1888 ended, the Canadian harvests had been good and some of the formerly widespread rural discontent was clearly subsiding.

Honoré Mercier, whose attempt to promote a provincial common front for the dismemberment of the authority of the federal government had also subsided, was by now on to a new controversy. The Jesuits' estates in Quebec, going back to French rule, had been frozen when the Spanish and French kings prevailed on Pope Clement XIV in 1773 to repress the Society of Jesus (the Jesuits), apart from in Prussia and Russia. The extensive Jesuit properties in Quebec were taken over by the British Crown in 1800 when the last Quebec Jesuit died, and handed on from Britain to the Legislature of Lower Canada in 1831 for use for educational purposes. The Jesuits were re-established by Pius VII in 1814 and by the 1860s were agitating for a restoration of their position in Quebec. The Roman Catholic bishops in Quebec claimed that the property reverted to them, in their diocesan authority, not to the Society of Jesus. Mercier, a comparative secularist, asked the pope, Leo XIII, to decide between the Jesuits and the bishops and said the government of Quebec would abide by that decision. His Jesuits' Estates Bill providing for that solution was adopted by the Assembly. The pope's decision, which Mercier proposed to execute, was for the distribution of four hundred thousand dollars to be divided among the Jesuits and bishops, and sixty thousand dollars was allocated to the Protestant Committee of Public Instruction. Opposition gradually rose to this measure, based on the supposed outrage of a papal decision causing the distribution of property in a country within the British Empire. The correspondence between Leo XIII and Mercier was largely reprinted in the preamble to the bill. Protestant opinion was very vexed (and even Donald Creighton referred to it as "this most iniquitous law"[61]), but Macdonald declined to be drawn and was able to tell Tupper he could reassure the Duke of Norfolk (the traditional lay leader of Britain's Roman Catholics, and the premier duke and earl marshal of England) that Mercier's law would not be revoked. In fact, the government of Quebec had every right to consider that it had only been a trustee and take the pope's guidance on the merit of the different claims from among the Roman

Catholic authorities, and the Protestants were provided for propor-
tionately. D'Alton McCarthy, an arch Imperialist (and the Protestant
parliamentary equivalent of the unfortunate Joseph Guibord's bishop),
had supported a bill calling for revocation of Mercier's measure, but
Macdonald spoke against it on March 29, 1889, referring to the religious and racial strife of bygone years, and the revocation motion was
defeated 188 to 13. Unfortunately, McCarthy had already launched a
public movement against the bill in English Canada, though the
authority of Mercier's government to act as it did was not seriously
at issue.

McCarthy's agitations led to a demand for the end of the protection
of French and Catholic rights in Manitoba and the North-West
Territories. In the parliamentary session that opened in January 1890,
McCarthy proposed abrogation of French rights in the (very small)
school system of the North-West Territories, and on February 12
Macdonald adopted the expedient of allowing a proposal to go forward
that left the matter for local determination. This would not work for the
French, who, in the person of one of Laurier's Quebec members,
Cléophas Beausoleil, moved an amendment stating that the pursuit of
racial harmony was the reason for the protections and nothing had
changed to reduce the desirability of that end. This split the House
and the Conservative caucus, whose French-speaking members
endorsed the Liberal motion. Macdonald and Laurier crossed swords
when Laurier effectively described the Conservatives as a party of bigotry. Macdonald replied very effectively that the Conservatives had
repealed the Act of Union's provision for English-only parliamentary
debates; that he had prevailed over Liberal George Brown's vehement
opposition to a co-equal status for French in the country; Macdonald
forcefully said: "There is no paramount race in this country; there is no
conquered race in this country."[62] But he pointed out that the sensibilities of Quebec were not the only point at issue and the wishes of the
local majority had to be considered, as Quebec, in other contexts, was
never slow to assert. Macdonald made his point, and was still, at
seventy-four, and after forty-six years in Parliament, twenty-six of them
in power, the master of the scene. But it was then, as it would be in
the future, an unbridgeable gap. Finally, on February 18, the vote on
the Beausoleil motion confirmed the nightmare of both Macdonald

and Laurier: every French-speaking member of the House except Joseph-Adolphe Chapleau (next to Thompson, Macdonald's most talented minister) voted for the motion, but both caucuses split, and the English-Canadian MPs, who were almost twice as numerous, including the prime minister and friends of Laurier, voted against or abstained. Macdonald and Thompson proposed a final compromise which assured government publications and court proceedings in the North-West Territories in both languages and reiterated the official status of French in the country, and left it to the Legislature of the territory to determine the language of its proceedings. This peeled back a number of the French MPs and increased the majority to 149 against 50 opponents, a mixed bag of McCarthyites and die-hard *rouges*. Macdonald had reassembled the centre again, one more time, and Laurier had not opposed him.

On February 26, 1890, Tupper's son, Charles H. Tupper, the new minister of marine and fisheries, arrived in Washington for a resumption of the endless discussion of fishing and sealing, specifically fur-seal hunting in the Bering Strait. The American secretary of state, the inevitable James G. Blaine (known to his followers from his presidential campaign of 1884 as the "plumed knight"), made Tupper feel very unwelcome. The British minister, the third party in the negotiations, Sir Julian Pauncefote, engaged in the now customary British practice of urging acceptance of everything the Americans wanted or offered. Blaine (only the second person twice to be the secretary of state, Daniel Webster being the first) made it clear that he was surprised and not pleased to see a Canadian representative at all. Pauncefote wrote up a draft agreement which Tupper brought back to Ottawa and Macdonald and the cabinet examined. The Canadians demanded the inclusion of the American Pribilof Islands in the agreement, and not just regulation of the high seas, and had to threaten the British with acceptance of the draft only under protest if Canadian wishes were not complied with. This threat carried the point, and the draft agreement was given to the Americans on behalf of Great Britain and Canada on April 29. They learned on May 22 by the cavalier means of a State Department press release that it had been rejected by the Americans, who were sending a coastguard cutter to seize vessels sealing in the

Bering Sea. A Royal Navy squadron then took station at Esquimalt, British Columbia, as Salisbury was a good deal more purposeful than his minister in Washington.

Relations with the Americans were further clouded by the impending McKinley Tariff, which threatened a severe reduction in Canadian exports to the United States. Macdonald conducted a speaking tour in the eastern provinces in the summer of 1890, and stated in Halifax that the United States still aimed at the annexation of Canada, either straightforwardly or indirectly through commercial union. The immediate crisis lifted with the Democratic victory in the congressional elections of November 1890, which sank Senator (and future president) William McKinley's tariff. But the United States entered into direct tariff reduction negotiations with Newfoundland, and Macdonald demanded of the British that they not allow British North American interests to be divided and exploited by the Americans. He suspected the Americans of preparing to pour money into the next Canadian election to support the Liberals as the party of reciprocity, which he assimilated to annexation. On Macdonald's forceful insistence with the British, the Newfoundland discussions were delayed, and Britain sponsored direct Canadian negotiations with Washington through Canadian plenipotentiaries and not as delegates on a British mission. Blaine dragged his heels on this but on January 28, 1891, had an extensive interview with an editor of the Liberal Toronto *Globe* on which the secretary of state tried to stampede Canadian voters from under the prime minister in what was assumed to be an election year. Blaine had betrayed Macdonald with an offer of informal talks to be held secretly, in preparation for which Macdonald sent out comprehensive proposals, and then Blaine revealed the American desire for talks to a Canadian opposition newspaper with assurances that no talks were in progress.

Blaine was a veteran of bruising American political wars going back to Lincoln's time, but he was not as experienced as or cannier than Macdonald, who responded to this challenge by dissolving Parliament at once and returning to the people for a fourteenth term and for the eleventh time as party leader. He campaigned vigorously, though seventy-six and struggling with bronchial problems and, toward the end of the campaign, acute fatigue. The United States and Great

Britain were closely watching the election. The Conservatives had had problems with financial indiscretions in Langevin's public works department, though the minister himself was not directly implicated. But such matters were obscured in the Conservative campaign for Canadian independence behind their slogan "the old flag, the old policy, the old leader." The Liberal editor who had interviewed Blaine, Edward Farrer, had printed up a rabidly pro-American pamphlet for very private circulation, but the Conservatives got hold of it and accused the Liberals of being a virtual annexationist front and, in a recurring Canadian theme, a Trojan Horse for the United Sates. All assumed that this would be Sir John A.'s last campaign, and as long as his stamina held, he put all he had into it, and was everywhere received as a legendary, folkloric figure. Any man nearly fifty years of age (Laurier was forty-nine) had been in his cradle when Macdonald was first elected to Parliament, and it was twenty-seven years since he had formed the Grand Coalition with Brown, Taché, Cartier, Galt, Mowat, and McGee to bring on Confederation. On March 5, 1891, the old chief did it again, winning 118 constituencies to 90 for Laurier, or 52 per cent of the vote to 46.4 for the Liberals. Macdonald made the race all the way, and it was a sweet victory, not so much over Laurier, who ran a very respectable and civilized race and gained ten MPs, but against the Ontario commercial unionists and the overbearing government of the United States. There was little sign of American financial assistance to the Liberals. Congratulations flowed in to Macdonald, including from Salisbury and, via Stanley, Victoria herself, queen and empress.[63]

Macdonald met the House and seemed in good form on several days, though rather tired on others, and he suffered a series of strokes and was confined to his home after May 29. The entire country conducted a vigil, and in the evening of June 6, 1891, the prime minister died. Langevin, his faithful follower of thirty-three years, and Laurier gave parliamentary eulogies on June 9, French Canadians both, though each spoke in English and French. Langevin broke down and had to resume his chair, saying, "My heart is full of tears." Laurier, as was his custom on serious occasions, was tasteful and eloquent and sonorous, and he spoke for all. The place of the deceased in Canadian life, he said, "was so large and so absorbing that it is almost impossible to conceive that the political life of this country – the fate of this country – can continue without him. His loss overwhelms us. . . . [It] overwhelms me and it also overwhelms this parliament as if indeed one of the institutions of the land had given way."[64] It had.

Macdonald lay in state in the Senate chamber and thousands came to pay tribute to him. Sir Casimir Gzowski laid a wreath of roses from Queen Victoria on his chest. There was a simple service in St. Alban's Church, where the Macdonalds had been frequent worshippers. Most of Ottawa's population watched the progression of the funeral cortege from Parliament to the church and then to the railway station. Historian Arthur Lower was moved to invoke Wordsworth: "Thou linnet in thy green array, Presiding spirit here today, Dost lead the revels of the May, and this is thy Dominion."[65] So it was. Every engine on his transcontinental railway was draped in black and purple, including the one that pulled the funeral train to Kingston. Thousands more conducted him to City Hall and the next day to join his family in Cataraqui Cemetery, near the site of the fort built by Frontenac more than two centuries before, in ground overlooking where the Great Lakes funnel into the St. Lawrence for the mighty, broadening surge to the Atlantic Ocean.

Canada was alone, without the great man who had assembled it, bound it together with immense diplomacy and cunning between all the regional and factional pressures inherent to the country, and between the foibles and sinister traits of appetite and indifference of which the American and British governments were always capable. He had consummated the long struggle for national life with a successful start, and had guided the new and gangling country along the path of early nationhood. John Alexander Macdonald had been brilliant and unerring at critical moments: Confederation, completing the railway, avoiding commercial union with the United States, preserving relations between the founding races. He had dominated the public life of his country for nearly two whole generations, since the Great Ministry of Baldwin and LaFontaine. Even in the era of Lincoln, Bismarck, Disraeli, and Gladstone, he was a great statesman. His work was far from over, but now someone would have to take his place.

5. The Confused Succession and the Liberal Hour, 1891–1896

The country, the Conservative Party, the governor general, were all completely unprepared for the death of Sir John A. Macdonald. The only person who wasn't was the Opposition leader, Wilfrid Laurier, who would have to wait almost four and a half years for the end of one of Canada's great anticlimaxes.

The logical successor to Sir John A. Macdonald was John Sparrow David Thompson, the very capable minister of justice. Thompson himself had misgivings about accepting such a call, because he was a convert to Roman Catholicism, which he thought might not be acceptable to Conservative voters. He was not a theologically complicated convert like Cardinal Newman and the other leaders of the Anglican Oxford Movement who rallied to Rome in the middle of the nineteenth century; he had adopted the faith of his wife at the time of their wedding, and was a strenuous communicant. This could be assumed to alienate a substantial number of Protestants, and he had not endeared himself to the Roman Catholics by his vigorous defence of the execution of Louis Riel, heretic though Riel was. Governor General Stanley (son of the former, often misguided colonial secretary and prime minister) hoped that Macdonald would have left some hint of whom he favoured as his successor, but he did not. Stanley canvassed the senior cabinet members and Thompson declined the post, because of his religion and because, at forty-eight, he believed he was not ready.

Apart from Thompson, the outstanding younger man of the cabinet was Joseph-Adolphe Chapleau, the former premier of Quebec. But he was a tempestuous character who had almost quit over the hanging of Riel and had little feel for English Canada. Macdonald's contemporaries were led by Langevin, who was already severely damaged by scandals in his public works department, and was tired and far from uplifting; Tupper, who had the stamina and intelligence, but was enjoying himself in London and did not want the position; and the leader of the Senate, Sir John Abbott. Abbott had had a varied career, originally famous as the defender of the St. Albans (Vermont) raiders, and then as Sir Hugh Allan's lawyer from whose office the damaging leaks of the Pacific Scandal were stolen. Abbott had signed the annexation petition after the Parliament Buildings in Montreal were burned down in 1849, but repented that; had one term as mayor of Montreal; and had an indifferent electoral career and held several secondary positions. Thompson advised Stanley to invest Abbott with the position of prime minister as an interim choice, and he became the first native-born Canadian and the first senator to hold that office. He made it clear that he was a caretaker.

The public works scandal forced Langevin's departure in the autumn of 1891, as Langevin's former fixer, the inconstant and shadowy Joseph-Israël Tarte, ferreted out too much damaging information for him to continue. Tarte (1848–1907) had begun as a mainline Macdonald-Cartier-Langevin Conservative and editor of several newspapers, including *Le Canadien* and *L'Événement*; drifted over to be an ultramontanist and first a supporter and then an opponent of Chapleau; drifted back toward Chapleau and Langevin; and then veered over to Laurier. Abbott tried to tidy things up, and instituted some civil-service reforms and revisions to the Criminal Code, but had no ideas about what to do to alleviate deepening economic problems that swept much of the Western World. He had no impact at all on the public consciousness and made no effort to settle in as a serious incumbent with the ambition to remain. He was only six years younger than Macdonald and there was no hint of renovation to him. The weaknesses of a government that had won six of seven general elections since Confederation were temporarily disguised by the Baie des Chaleurs Scandal in Quebec, which ended Honoré Mercier's meteoric career, and by another of Edward Blake's self-detonating grenades, in which he announced what became known as the West Durham Letter, in which he expressed the probability of annexation to the United States. (Baie des Chaleurs was a miniature Pacific Scandal, as the government of Quebec issued a contract to finish a railway from Matapédia to Gaspé, which had suffered severe delays and cost overruns, and it came to light that much of the payoff to the former contractor was kicked back to the Quebec Liberal treasurer, Ernest Pacaud, and some of that went to pay for a luxurious holiday for Mercier in France. Lieutenant-Governor Auguste-Réal Angers, a partisan Conservative, dismissed Mercier, who was indicted with Pacaud, but both were quickly acquitted. Mercier became a much admired figure of Quebec history, but died just two years later of diabetes, aged fifty-four.)

Abbott, too, was afflicted (by brain cancer), retired in November 1892, and died eleven months later, aged seventy-two. (Some of his descendants were prominent, including his great-grandson, the film actor Christopher Plummer.) The government and governor general did the only sensible thing and called on Sir John Sparrow David Thompson, former premier of Nova Scotia, judge, and federal justice minister. Thompson's stoutness (he was still overweight for his five feet seven inches), at forty-eight, must have impaired his health. He had a great foreign policy success when he argued Canada's case personally in Paris in March 1893 at the arbitration of the Bering Sea dispute over seal hunting, in which the United States claimed effectively a sole right to the hunt. Thompson led the argument for other countries and was upheld. (Again it must be said that if the Americans had just done what they wished by *force majeure*, while it would have ruffled some important feathers, the Royal Navy would not have challenged the United States, and it is unlikely at this point that the Russians or Japanese, the only other countries with serious naval units in the area, would have either.)

By the time of Thompson's accession, the Manitoba Schools Question, a return of an issue which Macdonald had hosed down with the utmost difficulty in the North-West Territories, had flared up, fanned by local Protestant elements led by Clifford Sifton (1861–1929), a formidable lawyer and publisher who became attorney general of Manitoba when he was just thirty. Sifton was immensely energetic and competent, and possessed a powerful and imaginative vision for Canada. The core of the Manitoba problem was that the province was set up in 1870 in haste, under the pressures of Riel's initial agitation at the head of the Métis, and reflecting a thoroughly bicultural (if far from sophisticated) society, and had then been inundated with settlers who spoke English or were continental European immigrants who assimilated to the local English-speaking community. The Manitoba Legislature's abolition of state aid to Roman Catholic schools, which had been provided for in the Manitoba Act, was contested by the Manitoba Catholics, successfully at the Supreme Court of Canada, which spared the federal government the political difficulty of entering the controversy, but in 1892, in a perversely meddlesome misreading of the basic spirit and texts of Canadian federalism, the Judicial Committee of the

Privy Council overturned the Canadian Supreme Court decision. Thompson was Abbott's minister of justice at this point and litigated over whether the federal government had the right to legislate directly in such matters. As if to complicate Canadian public life as much as possible, the Imperial Privy Council now determined that Ottawa could do so. Thompson was considering how best to juggle this hot potato when he visited Great Britain in the late autumn of 1894. He got on exceptionally well with Queen Victoria and stayed with her at Windsor for three days. Thompson was urbane and witty, and might have been a great prime minister, but he died of a coronary at lunch at Windsor in the queen's presence. She gave him a state Roman Catholic funeral (a unique occasion) at St. James's Church, Spanish Place, Manchester Square, London, attended by Cecil Rhodes, Alfred, Lord Tennyson, Dr. Leander Starr Jameson (a year before his famous raid in South Africa), Lord Mount Stephen (as George Stephen had become in 1891), Sir Charles Tupper, and, representing Lord Rosebery's government as the senior Roman Catholic in British public life, the Marquess of Ripon, former viceroy of India, first lord of the admiralty, and colonial secretary. At Ripon's urging, Thompson was returned to Canada on the cruiser *Blenheim*, painted black for the occasion, for a state funeral in Halifax on January 3, 1895, attended by the governor general, most of the government, and five lieutenant-governors (including, from Quebec, the newly installed Chapleau). Thompson was respected by all, and his premature death was seen, even by Laurier and the opposition, as a great personal and official loss.

The new governor general, the Earl of Aberdeen (grandson of the prime minister replaced by Palmerston in the Crimean War), had only one choice, to bring back Tupper from London. But inexplicably,* except for his dislike of Tupper and the fragmentation of the government, Aberdeen called upon one of the most improbable figures ever to head the Canadian government, Mackenzie Bowell, former head of the Imperial Triennial Council (i.e., the world council) of the Orange Lodge. He was Sir John A.'s emissary to the lunatic papophobic vote, though his views had softened somewhat, and he was a prominent figure in Belleville, Ontario, having been an MP there for twenty-five of his sixty-nine years before becoming a senator. He owned the Belleville newspaper the *Intelligencer.* Bowell was minister of customs from 1878 to 1892, and then minister of militia (he was a reserves colonel and had taken part in the repulse of the Fenians), and minister of trade and commerce and leader of the Senate under Thompson. His most important public service had been the mission that Thompson entrusted to him to Australia in 1893, which led to an intercolonial trade conference he organized in Ottawa in 1894 attended by six Australian provinces, Fiji, the Cape Colony of South Africa, and Hawaii (which the newly re-elected President Cleveland refused to annex to the United States). It was a considerable success and aroused British concerns about creeping autonomy within the Empire. Bowell was not a bad or completely incompetent man, but he was an utterly insane selection for the office of prime minister, especially in the midst of the Manitoba schools controversy. He was a small, bald, heavily white-bearded man who looked like "a bitter Santa Claus with crafty eyes."[66]

Bowell was a doubly unlikely person to grapple with the Manitoba schools problem, but he groped his way toward a strategy: on the recommendation of Charles H. Tupper (son of Sir Charles), he would propose remedial legislation which was issued as an order-in-council on March 21, 1895, requiring restoration of the provincial government's aid to separate schools. The plan was to represent that the Privy Council decision enabling such a remedy effectively made it obligatory, to conform with the promises entrenched in the British North America Act and the Manitoba Act. The plan was to defend Catholic rights and hang on to enough of the French vote in Quebec and elsewhere (Acadia, the Ottawa Valley in Ontario, and pockets of Manitoba), and the Irish and German Catholic vote, while retaining the Protestant base of the Conservative Party's support by professing merely to be obeying the law, upholding the spirit of Confederation, and keeping faith with Sir John A. It wasn't a bad plan for a very difficult problem, if Bowell had had the stature and credibility to hold the line in his cabinet and caucus. Sir Joseph Pope, Macdonald's long-time secretary, recalled, "a weak and incompetent administration . . . a ministry without unity or cohesion of any kind, a prey to internal dissensions until they became a spectacle to the world, to angels and to men."[67] More generously, Arthur Lower wrote: "The ex-grandmaster of the Orange Order prepared to coerce the Protestants of Manitoba in the interests of French Catholicism. . . . It is to [Bowell's] honour that he decided to follow the arduous path of duty."[68] Laurier was waffling and obfuscating, and drowning the issue in platitudes about his "sunny ways" with the implication that the whole matter could be smoothed over with a little goodwill and soft soap. This was moonshine, not only in fact, but also because Laurier did not believe a word of it himself. He was carefully considering his position, and exploiting his advantage in being able to await the government, which had to make the first move. Tupper had wanted to issue the executive order and then go to the country at once, but Bowell allowed himself to be persuaded to await another session in 1896, hoping that the issue would subside. Tupper, who must to some degree be assumed to have been representing the interest of his father in taking his rightful place as prime minister, was only dissuaded from resigning by the interventions of Aberdeen, the ubiquitous Sir Donald Smith, and Senator George Drummond (1828–1910), the principal director of the Bank of Montreal. The minister of agriculture, Senator Auguste-Réal Angers, resigned in irritation at the delay in July 1895, and Bowell was unable to replace him with a French Canadian. At the other end of the ethno-sectarian spectrum, Nathaniel Clarke Wallace, one of Bowell's successors as grand master of the Orange Lodge, resigned in December. Instead of recognizing that he was losing his tenuous hold on the government, Bowell hung grimly on into 1896.

Joseph-Israël Tarte was the supreme calculator of Quebec opinion, who had been on every side of the main issues in that province from flirtation with the *rouges* and the English Tories to being a potential candidate as a papal Zouave to defend ultramontanism and the Papal States from Italian nationalism and the insolent independence of the secularists.* Tarte had fetched up in the entourage of Wilfrid Laurier, and gave the Liberal leader the undoubted benefit of his considered opinion that Laurier could vote against the imposition of federal remedial legislation and hold the Liberals' Protestant and English-speaking vote. He even thought Laurier could pick up some votes from the bigots if Bowell opted for remedial legislation and that he would be able to

---

* The only foreign war for which French Canada has ever had any general enthusiasm was the Italian Risorgimento, to which Quebec contributed corps of "Papal Zouaves" to help defend the Papal States against the secular Italian unificationists. The cause was not successful, and the Zouaves' contribution to it, though they received a delirious public send-off, was not noteworthy.

defend himself in Quebec because he was the only French-Canadian party leader in the electoral race, that blood was thicker than water, and he could hold the line on the necessity, when running for national office, to put country ahead of religion and sell the greater vision of a French-Canadian head of the country rather than Catholic schools for a small knot of people in a remote frontier province. Laurier was persuaded, though he continued to keep his own counsel, even expressing a readiness, at one point, to stand aside for Sir Oliver Mowat if the twenty-five-year premier of Ontario wished to take the federal leadership. (This offer was undoubtedly insincere, and was not pushed with any vigour, but it was very disarming. Here was a party leader who manoeuvred cunningly to hold his opinion and translate it into the headship of the government while professing readiness to hand over to another. It was subtle tenacity wreathed in modesty and team spirit.)

Once his plan was in place, Laurier advanced it very assiduously; he maintained the smokescreen of indecision and enigmatic vagueness, but concerted with Sifton and Thomas Greenway, the Manitoba premier, that they would call a snap provincial election on the issue, which they did. They were overwhelmingly re-elected (thirty-one constituencies to seven Conservative) on January 15, 1896, after a campaign that consisted entirely of hammering the Roman Catholics and thumbing the province's nose at Ottawa. Bowell could not imagine that Laurier was prevaricating for any reason than to disguise his helpless shackling by the French Catholic faction of the country, but he had to act, as he had been challenged by Manitoba and was pledged to deal with it in the 1896 parliamentary session, or call an election without indicating what the government's position was on what the country now considered the main issue of public policy. And the election had to be held before May. Bowell's cabinet revolted, led by the finance minister, George Foster, and Charles H. Tupper, who was, in his own right, a respected veteran of the battles with Washington. Bowell falsely told Aberdeen that the disenchanted ministers balked at the remedial legislation, in contravention of well-established Conservative and government policy, and offered his resignation, which Aberdeen rejected, out of respect for the principle Bowell claimed to be defending, and out of dislike of Tupper. The resigning ministers canvassed enough colleagues to ensure that they could not be replaced; no one would accept to stand in the place of those who purported to resign, and the governor general was advised that the revolt was not caused by policy differences but by lack of confidence in Bowell, whose resignation Aberdeen then accepted at once. Bowell was facing removal by his own caucus and loss of a confidence vote. Snarling that his government was "a nest of traitors," he folded his hand: the elder Tupper, who should have been called when Thompson declined after the death of Macdonald, and certainly after Thompson died, was summoned back from the sumptuous consolations of London, and Bowell would hold the fort while he returned and won a by-election and remedial legislation was brought forward.

The Conservatives still thought they had Laurier on the horns of a dilemma and their stupefaction was considerable in all areas of their party when Laurier crossed the Rubicon on March 3, 1896, and proposed that the remedial bill that Bowell had introduced be tabled and allowed to die with the parliamentary session. The Liberals obstructed the bill, dragging it to the end of the session, despite a strong effort by the returned seventy-year-old Tupper, and the bill was withdrawn on April 16, the House was dissolved on April 26, and Bowell resigned as prime minister and party leader the following day, to be replaced by Tupper. Bowell continued as an active member of the Senate right up to his death on December 10, 1917, seventeen days short of his ninety-third birthday. He had made a strenuous trip to the Yukon the year before he died.

The campaign was already well underway, and was a shabby fraud on both sides, replicating and surpassing the most inelegant chicanery of Macdonald; it was as if the old chief had not really died. The Conservatives told Quebec they were the only defenders of the Catholics and the French, and told the other provinces they were only doing what the supreme judicial authorities and the governing legislation required. The Liberals pitched directly to the bigoted voters of English Canada and told Quebec they were upholding the dearly embraced Quebec totem of provincial rights, and that Laurier would resolve it all with his now terribly tired pieties about his "sunny ways," and if necessary would punish an inflexibly narrow-minded province. The more conservative Roman Catholic bishops were in full cry throughout Quebec, and their influence was not negligible.

The Liberal cardinal Elzéar-Alexandre Taschereau's successor as cardinal-archbishop of Quebec and primate of Canada, Louis-Nazaire Bégin, verged on publicly accusing Laurier of heresy. Monsignor Louis-François Laflèche of Trois-Rivières, who had shut down Laurier's newspaper Le Défricheur twenty years before, was, predictably, the most outspoken and vehement of Laurier's episcopal opponents. In English Canada, where the Roman Catholic Church had historically been less influential, the episcopate was more restrained. Canada voted on June 23. Tupper's gallant fight and the cynicism of Tarte's playbook that Laurier had followed were discernible in the close popular vote: 46 per cent Liberal to 45 per cent Conservative, but Laurier carried Quebec, forty-nine MPs to sixteen, which provided his margin of victory. Blood and language counted more than uncompromising piety, and Laurier and Tarte's calculation that even rigorous Roman Catholics would vote for the only co-religionist in the race was accurate. Laurier won the country 117 to 86 Conservative MPs, with 10 independents. Oddly, Manitoba returned four Conservatives to three Liberals. Laurier was invested as prime minister on July 10, 1896.

It was a strong ministry, led by William Fielding as minister of finance, after twelve years as premier of Nova Scotia (he had won his first election as premier on an overtly secessionist platform); Sir Oliver Mowat as minister of justice, after twenty-five years as premier of Ontario; Sir Henri-Gustave Joly de Lotbinière at Inland Revenue, the former (Protestant) premier of Quebec and future lieutenant-governor of British Columbia, an authentic Frenchman, descendant of the Vaudreuils, pioneer scientific forester, and son of a professional daguerreotypist (who was the first person to photograph the Acropolis); William Mulock as postmaster general; Sydney Fisher at agriculture; the uncommonly abrasive and even querulous Sir Richard J. Cartwright at trade and commerce (he had wanted finance, but his fervour for commercial union with the United States made that politically unfeasible); Israël Tarte at public works; Charles Fitzpatrick in the semi-cabinet post of solicitor general; and, soon, Clifford Sifton as minister of the interior and superintendent of Indian affairs.

Thus ended, for over a century, the Conservative era in federal affairs. Five leaders of that party would be elected prime minister in the next century, but only one would win a second full term for his own party. Macdonald and his squabbling heirs had dominated the public life of Canada since Macdonald became attorney general in Sir Allan MacNab's government with Augustin-Norbert Morin in 1854. The improbable country was well-launched, though still attached to Britain's apron strings and terribly overshadowed by its neighbour. But it was a testimony to the country's quickening maturation that it handed itself over to a French-Canadian Roman Catholic despite all the frictions that had followed the colonial combat in North America and that trick-led through the land yet.

It shortly emerged that in Laurier, Canada's luck had held. It had, without suspecting it, set at its head a very talented statesman. These two prime ministers, Macdonald and Laurier, led their parties for a total of sixty-seven years, overlapping only for four, and governed forty-three years, thirty-four of the first forty-four years of Confederation. Between them, they dealt with all ten of the U.S. presidents between Abraham Lincoln and Woodrow Wilson, and were undoubtedly more talented political leaders than all of them except Theodore Roosevelt. Apart from all their other talents, the suavity and finesse of John A. Macdonald and Wilfrid Laurier contributed indispensably to Canada's navigation of the last years in its three-hundred-year history of vulnerability to the Americans. The country's passage to nationhood would not be untroubled, but its very life would never be threatened with sudden extinction by foreign *force majeure* again.

Laurier's presence at the head of this cautiously emerging country demonstrated the uniqueness of its ambition and tentative achievement as the world's first transcontinental, bicultural, parliamentary Confederation. Astonishingly, Wilfrid Laurier would prove a statesman of approximately equivalent stature to the country's principal founder, the ultimate proof of a new country's strength and raison d'être.

Canada's progress since the Seven Years War had been in some ways more surprising than that of the United States, but it was comparatively modest, subtle, and under-celebrated; and it was, even more than 130 years later, suspensive and dependent on hoped-for events and outcomes. After one long lifetime from the achievement of American independence, the former thirteen colonies rivalled the British and pre-nascent German empires as the greatest nation in the world. The great United States had emerged from the horrible and noble agony of its Civil War a mighty force in the world and one unchallengeable in its hemisphere, and destined in fifty years to grow, demographically and economically and by all the indices of the power of a country, on a scale the world had never seen. Canada's task, as its new leader saw, was to keep pace quietly with that growth, and simultaneously reduce its vulnerability to America and its consequent dependence on Great Britain to counterbalance that diminishing vulnerability. It was not a heroic task, or one easily rendered in anthems and slogans to rouse a people, but it was, for that, no less a desirable and, when attained, brilliant achievement. The emergence of a magnificent country was the more remarkable for being unsuspected. Unlike the United States, Canada was never predestined to greatness.

Wilfrid Laurier (1841–1919), federal leader of the opposition 1887–1896 and
1911–1919 and prime minister of Canada 1896–1911; a permanent symbol of
French–English conciliation, largely responsible for getting the country through
World War I without immense domestic strife, and chief ultimate architect of
the rapid development of Western Canada. Laurier was suave, mellifluous, and
very bicultural. British statesman Joseph Chamberlain called him, unflatteringly,
"the dancing master," but he was a consummate politician of great principle
and durability.

CHAPTER 5

Laurier, the Dawn of "Canada's Century,"* and the Great War, 1896–1919

1. Internal and External Stresses, Manitoba Schools, and Relations with the United States and Great Britain, 1896–1897

With the election over, and given Charles Tupper's victory in Manitoba, the government of that province was interested in settling what it could with the federal government over the province's separate schools. Wilfrid Laurier had said he would do what he could for the French and Roman Catholics of Manitoba, and he asked Oliver Mowat as justice minister to deal with Manitoba's attorney general, Clifford Sifton, when the Manitobans arrived in August 1896 in Ottawa to try to settle the issues. Laurier sent his local pastor from Saint-Lin in the Laurentians and another mid-level clergyman to open up a back channel with the senior curial officials in Rome, and sent Israël Tarte and the young

---

* Phrase of Laurier's in the 1904 election and after.

Henri Bourassa to Manitoba to conduct research there. Bourassa wrote up a report on the positions of the various parties that so impressed Laurier he sent it to Rome under his own signature and with the approval of the cabinet. What had emerged by November as a settlement was retention of the blending of schools rather than separate boards, but a restoration of Catholic and French-language teaching where parents wished it and their numbers were adequate to justify it. Otherwise, no distinction was made between French and other languages apart from English, but instruction was available in the other language and in the Catholic religion where a workable threshold of numbers was attained. Reasonable influence was to be accorded Roman Catholics on school boards and in the determination of curricula and school texts. Laurier released the outline of the agreement on November 19. The Orange Lodge attacked the settlement as a sellout to priestly influences, and Archbishop Adélard Langevin of St. Boniface denounced it as a "farce," saying, "The fight has only begun."[1] But most Catholics and Protestants in English Canada thought it a reasonable compromise. At the end of the year, Laurier organized a more powerful delegation to go to Rome to hose down the still-squawking Canadian bishops: Solicitor General Charles Fitzpatrick (1853–1942); Edward Blake, who had acted for the Manitoba Catholics at the Judicial Committee of the Privy Council; and, thanks to the intervention of Governor General Aberdeen, Charles Russell, son of Lord Russell and an influential figure in Rome. Russell quickly obtained for Fitzpatrick and Blake an audience with Pope Leo XIII's thirty-two-year-old assistant, Rafael Cardinal Merry del Val (1865–1930), who conducted them to a meeting with the genial and much admired eighty-seven-year-old pontiff. Laurier made steady progress assuring and building moderate opinion; implementation of the settlement began.

Cardinal del Val would arrive in Canada for a very thorough and strenuous visit in May, and met and intensively interviewed everyone with an interest in Manitoba schools, including Premier Greenway, whom the cardinal tracked down in rural Ontario. Laurier pronounced him "the most prince-like man I have met,"[2] and the cardinal returned to Rome having made a splendid impression on everyone but without giving a hint of the advice he would give to the pope. The nod from the Holy See would completely disarm Laurier's local episcopal critics, and would have a halcyon effect on the whole sectarian climate of the country.

Laurier departed for Britain and the immense festivities around Victoria's diamond jubilee on June 5. Laurier was suspicious of Joseph Chamberlain's role in the occasion, as one who had leapt upon the Imperial bandwagon and was calling for a united Empire in war and peace. The Boer War was almost under way, and few of the colonial leaders were much interested at this early stage in following Great Britain into that morass. Laurier was eloquent and sociably adroit and made a good impression on everyone, including the monarch and the vast crowds that came out for all parts of the ceremony. And he was happy to receive a knighthood. At the end of the splendid British state parliamentary session, Chamberlain convened the eleven colonial premiers present, with Laurier their undisputed leader, and pushed his notions of an Imperial Parliament, an Imperial defence plan, and Imperial free trade. Laurier was admirably prepared from all the ambiguities about his sunny ways that he had employed to obfuscate and finesse his way through the more treacherous domestic issues, to defer and postpone any such ambitions, and he did so. On Imperial free trade, he stuck amiably to his guns that Canada was ready but would not make exception for Germany and Belgium as Chamberlain wished, and if Britain did not put the Empire ahead of her chief rival in trade, she should not expect startling progress in the other areas; the Dominions were not, for instance, going to give an unlimited military commitment to a Great Britain that put German commercial relations ahead of Imperial ones. Even the London newspapers supported the colonial/Dominion position. Lord Northcliffe's mass circulation *Daily Mail* pompously announced, "For the first time on record, a politician of our new world has been recognized as the equal of the great men of the old country."[3] Laurier withdrew and went on to France, much decorated and celebrated, something of an oddity as the French-speaking (bilingual) head of the premier (and still the only) British dominion, a reassurance to the British of the general success of their own *mission civilisatrice*. In France, where, after a couple of his impeccably inflected and affectingly respectful speeches, Laurier's reception was very positive, and with a good deal less condescension than in London – and then he went to Rome for a pleasant reunion with Merry del Val and a very cordial audience with Pope Leo XIII, who was still looked to expectantly to help de-escalate Canadian sectarian tensions. All Canada welcomed the prime minister home at the end of August. Thirty years after Confederation, Laurier had added a large cubit to the stature of Canada in the world. He followed this success with a visit to Washington in November, where he was well-received by the new president, William McKinley. They agreed to establish a joint high commission to negotiate all outstanding trade issues, and Laurier selected Joseph-Adolphe Chapleau, who was about to retire as lieutenant-governor of Quebec, to head the Canadian side, an able Conservative and former Quebec premier, who would be a unifying figure.

On December 18, 1897, Leo XIII was heard from at last. His encyclical, *Affari vos*, addressed the Manitoba Schools Question. The pope noted the rights guaranteed to Roman Catholic children and parents in the British North America Act, and that these rights had been violated by the Manitoba Legislature and that the Roman Catholic episcopate of Canada had correctly objected to these violations. The pope described the Laurier compromise with Premier Greenway, without mentioning the individuals, as providing improvements that were "defective, unsuitable, insufficient," and assured that bishops who sought further enhancements of Catholic rights "have our concurrence and approbation." However, moderation should be maintained, he wrote, and if "anything is granted by law, or custom, or the goodwill of men which will render the evil more tolerable and the dangers more remote, it is expedient and useful to make use of such concessions. . . . There is no kind of knowledge, no perfection of learning, which cannot be fully harmonized with Catholic doctrine."[4] The pope had given Laurier enough to work with to end the acute schism between the Quebec clergy and much of the Liberal Party.

The controversy still rippled the waters in the French Roman Catholic clergy that aspired to a strong French presence in the West. St. Boniface's archbishop, Adélard Langevin, never ceased to declaim publicly against the iniquities of Laurier's betrayal, and at two meetings organized in Ottawa between Langevin and Laurier by Montreal's archbishop, Paul Bruchési, the prime minister warned the archbishop that if the issue were reopened it would do great damage to the French fact throughout Canada and divide the country unfavourably along sectarian lines, with most of the Roman Catholics and all of the Protestants seriously irritated by this continuing agitation. In all of the circumstances, he had done his best – the pope himself had said as much – and whatever improvements could be made to the status of the French in Manitoba would now have to come with time (and were unlikely, given the demographic trends; this was the last throw in the French attempt to challenge the English-speaking population and settlers in the West, and it was unpromising). Laurier was at the head of a country where many "were more British than the queen and many were more Catholic than the pope."[5]

Comparatively composed and civil though America was becoming, an example of its proclivity for belligerent juvenilism and jingoism arose over the absurd issue of the border between British Guiana and Venezuela. Britain snatched most of Guyana from the Dutch in 1814, as it facilitated and its army largely accomplished the liberation of the Netherlands from Napoleon. Britain surveyed the border with Venezuela and produced a demarcation in 1840 that Venezuela did not accept, but as it was trackless jungle unpopulated by any civilized people, no interested party considered it worth arguing about until there were discoveries of gold along the border in 1887. At this point, the British withdrew their 1840 suggestion and pressed a new one well to the west of it, miraculously including rich gold-producing areas. Venezuela rejected this, severed relations with Britain, and asked for American support. The issue finally bubbled up to American notice in 1895, when Venezuela asked for American mediation, which Britain rejected. President Cleveland's last secretary of state, Richard Olney, produced an astoundingly expansive notion of the Monroe Doctrine (which conceded established European positions in the Americas, including Canada, forswore any interest in Europe, and only objected to new initiatives for extra-hemispheric conquest in the Americas). Olney informed the British prime minister, Lord Salisbury, that "the United States is practically sovereign on this continent and its fiat is law upon the subjects to which it confines its interposition. Why?" – as if he were conducting a primary school tutorial and not addressing Victoria's first minister, head of the world's greatest Empire, and, with the death of Disraeli and the impetuous dismissal by German emperor Wilhelm II of Bismarck in 1890 after twenty-eight years as minister-president of Prussia and seventeen as chancellor of the German empire which Bismarck founded, the most accomplished international statesman in the world –

"It is because, in addition to all other grounds, its infinite resources combined with its isolated position render it master of the situation and practically invulnerable as against any or all other powers."[6]

In addition to all his other attainments, Salisbury was head of Britain's greatest family, the Cecils, who were elevated by Elizabeth I in the sixteenth century to a position they had never yielded through four dynasties (Tudor, Stuart, Orange, and Hanover) and the Cromwell interregnum. He replied to this bumptious and transitory official with the suavity of his standing and the eminence of his position that the Monroe Doctrine was scarcely relevant, as the border in question had antedated that event and Her Imperial Britannic Majesty's government had no need of American arbitration. It was magnificent, but Britain could not win this argument. It was facing a challenge from Germany, which, as Salisbury's late chief had predicted twenty-four years before, upended the balance of power in Europe and could move the fulcrum for control of that balance from the hands of Britain to those of America. Olney would not have understood any of this, and probably neither would the president he served, the very scrupulous quasi-pacifist Grover Cleveland, former mayor of Buffalo, New York. But Salisbury judged it appropriate to de-escalate this exchange. After Cleveland released the correspondence and told Congress that the United States would regard any attempt to alter the Venezuela–British Guiana border by force as an act of war, Salisbury handed the over-heated question to Joseph Chamberlain. Chamberlain, who sought a triple alliance between Great Britain, the United States, and Germany, declared that war between Britain and America "would be an absurdity as well as a crime. The two nations are more closely allied in interest than any other nations on the face of the earth."[7] It all settled down, went to international arbitration by an agreement of 1897, and that process eventually approved the British position of 1840 but not of 1887, and everyone was satisfied.

What was noteworthy was the propensity of the Americans to rise to instantaneous bellicosity without an apparent thought to where it might lead. Again, the young Theodore Roosevelt, the thirty-seven-year-old president of the New York City Police board of commissioners, wrote, "Let the fight come if it must. I don't care whether our seacoast cities are bombarded or not. We would take Canada. . . . It seems to me that if England were wise, she would fight now. We couldn't get at Canada until May, and meanwhile, she could play havoc with our coast cities and shipping. Personally, I rather hope that the fight will come soon. The clamor of the peace faction has convinced me that this country needs a war."[8] Of course, this was objectively nonsense. The British could defend Canada quite well unless the Americans remobilized a force at least half the size of the Union Army. The British could reduce every American Atlantic, Gulf, and Pacific coast city to rubble for as long as they pleased. The British chose to wind it down because they did not want their relations with the United States compromised over such a tertiary issue. But it showed that a man who would soon be a very effective architect of America's assumption of a front-rank place among the world powers was still a blustering schoolyard bully. In 1890, Joseph Pulitzer's *New York World* reported that in Canada "five or six million dollars judiciously expended . . . would secure the return to Parliament of a majority pledged to the annexation of Canada to the United States,"[9] because "Canadians have always been looking over their neighbour's fence . . . they have been small-town people giving themselves big city airs."[10] The vagaries of the American personality had always, then and for nearly a century to come, to be taken very seriously by Canadian leaders.

2. The Great Development of the West, 1897–1899

Laurier, who had founded his career as a national figure on his affectation of unimpoverishable optimism, ushered in good times. The western farmers had developed earlier-maturing wheat to surmount or avoid frost and had improved yields and could generally afford better implements. The industrialization of Western Europe and the eastern United States had raised the demand for wheat, and the American farmlands, after thirty years of massive immigration, were filling up, raising interest in the potential of Canada. The senior vice president of Canadian Pacific, Thomas G. Shaughnessy, wrote to Laurier, as he had to Tupper, proposing a railway from Lethbridge through the Crowsnest Pass to Nelson, British Columbia, to keep in Canada the transport business of the gold, copper, and coal mines that were being developed in Western

Canada.* The new spurt in business activity and increasing immigration drove railway promoters William Mackenzie and Donald Mann to propose a new railway in Central Canada and spurred the Grand Trunk Railway to bid for another transcontinental route north of the CPR. Van Horne and Shaughnessy warned Laurier of the dangers of overbuilding, but the temptations to encourage such construction were almost irresistible.

Early in 1897, Sifton arrived from Manitoba to take up his position as minister of the interior with an open mandate to increase assimilable immigration. Canada had 5.4 million people, more than Sweden, Denmark, the Netherlands, Switzerland, Portugal, Greece, Bulgaria, Scotland, Ireland, Argentina, or South Africa, but it was only one-thirteenth the population of the United States. Since 1867, Canada's population had increased from 3.3 million while that of the United States had increased from 40 million to 75 million. Sifton found his department tired and unfocused and vowed to change it. It was time to reinvigorate the pace of Canada's growth and development. Clifford Sifton, a man whose natural ferocity was heightened by advancing premature deafness (he was only thirty-six), had arrived in Ottawa as an MP and minister of the interior in late November 1896 having signed off on the Manitoba schools settlement. He had a practically unlimited mandate from Laurier to develop the West and take real possession of the vast centre of the country from Winnipeg to the Rocky Mountains that La Vérendrye had originally explored 160 years before. The CPR and lesser railways had been granted twenty-four million acres but had only taken up two million, in order not to pay taxes on the rest. Sifton decreed that the railways had to choose what they wanted and take possession and pay taxes on it and yield the rest. Thus cleared of the railway grants, the unclaimed land was made available in 160-acre homesteads, free, to settlers who undertook to develop and occupy them. All accumulated regulations were cleared away, and Sifton ordered his officials to do everything possible to make it easier for sincere applicants to take

---

* Shaughnessy (1853–1923), a meticulously efficient administrator, had worked with Van Horne in the United States and complemented his imaginative and visionary qualities. The son of Irish immigrants to Milwaukee, he would follow George Stephen (Lord Mount Stephen) and Donald Smith (Lord Strathcona) to the House of Lords, and was considered for the position of head of the Irish Free State when it was set up in 1922.

up the land. He began an advertising campaign in thousands of American newspapers and in Britain and continental Europe, opened offices all over Europe and some in the United States, set up fairs and exhibitions abroad, hired publicists in those countries, and exploited the newspapermen's notorious weakness for free travel by bringing publicists to Canada and showing them the "amber waves of grain . . . [upon] the fruited plain," to quote a celebrated American anthem, to inspire the penurious, downtrodden masses of Europe with a vision of land, food, freedom, abundance, and opportunity.

None of it was a mirage. It was a brilliant and visionary campaign that made Sifton, within a couple of years, one of the great builders of Canada, with Jean Talon, John Graves Simcoe, Francis Hincks, George Stephen, and a select few others. The Allan line ships (which Shaughnessy was about to buy for Canadian Pacific) and the CPR and Grand Trunk were lumbered by Sifton with the task of providing practically free passage for settlers to the West. (Shaughnessy simultaneously commissioned the largest and fastest passenger liners on the Pacific, an honour Canadian Pacific would hold through the Second World War.) As Laurier biographer Joseph Schull wrote, "Wherever a restless man looked up Sifton intended him to see the great sheaf of wheat and the beckoning gateway to the golden west. . . . This ruthless close-mouthed man was asking for all but absolute control over four hundred million acres of land. He was asking for the power and the money to exploit them and he was going to take what he could get in the way of humankind. One looked at those unyielding agate eyes, burning resentfully as deafness closed round him, and wondered for the future. But Sifton got what he wanted."[11]

By 1903, the Laurier-Sifton immigration policy would be bearing fruit and Canada was again beginning to track toward the less lopsided one-to-ten population ratio with the United States. Immigration totals to Canada had bumped along at 15,000 to 20,000 per year apart from the balloon of the Irish famine, when they peaked at about 80,000 in 1847. There were (rounding to the nearest thousand), 17,000 in 1896; 24,000 in 1897; 32,000 in 1898; 45,000 in 1899; 43,000 in 1900; 56,000 in 1901; 89,000 in 1902; 139,000 in 1903; lateral movement until 212,000 in 1906; 272,000 in 1907; a 40 per cent dip through 1908 and 1909; and then a rebound to 287,000 in 1910; 332,000 in 1911; 376,000 in 1912; and a staggering 401,000 in 1913. The population of the United States almost tripled between the Civil War and the First World War, from 33 million to about 95 million, but in that period annual immigration increased from 319,000 in 1866 (the highest annual figure before that had been 428,000 in 1854, the only time American immigration surpassed 400,000 prior to 1872) to 1,218,000 in 1914. This was the second highest total in all of American history to the present, surpassed only in 1907 with 1,285,000. Annual immigration to the United States was greater than 1,000,000 six times in the ten years from 1905 and 1914, and never exceeded 400,000 after that (apart from uncertain but high numbers of tolerated illegal immigrants from Mexico in the last third of the twentieth century). These peak million-plus immigration years represented annual increments of 1.1 to 1.3 per cent of the overall population. Once Laurier's program was fully cranked up by Sifton, between 1903 and 1913, immigration was at the rate of between 2.5 per cent and the 5.5 per cent of 1913.[12]

From 1901 to 1911, the population of Canada rose, according to the decennial census, from 5.37 million to 7.21 million, an increase of 34 per cent. This was a growth percentage the United States had at times approximately equalled, and in four decades (the 1790s, 1800s, 1840s, and 1850s) very narrowly exceeded, but after the mid-nineteenth century only approached again once, in the 1880s (with 30.1 per cent). Between 1820 and 1900, the grievous total of 1,051,000 Canadians and Newfoundlanders emigrated to the United States, a total of immigrants to that country exceeded only by newcomers from Germany, Great Britain, Ireland, and Austria-Hungary, and about equal to immigrants from Italy. In the Laurier decade of 1900 to 1910, this number of Canadian emigrants to the United States contracted to 179,000 (and both these totals would have been partially countered by immigration into Canada from the United States), while Italy and Russia surged ahead of Canada in overall numbers, and in that decade Sweden, Norway, and Greece also exceeded Canada as a net source of immigrants to the United States. Sifton set up the North Atlantic Trading Company in Hamburg to transport "the stalwart peasant in a sheepskin coat," and between 1897 and 1912 Canada received 784,000 people from the United States, perhaps half of them returning Canadians, 961,000 from Great Britain, and 594,000 from continental Europe.

The Laurier-Sifton immigration and western settlement policy was a grandiose design, on the scale, in ambition, imagination, and determined execution, of the Canadian Pacific Railway. It was very productive immigration, and all economic indices, agricultural and industrial, reflected, and in some ways amplified, the population growth. Most of the immigrants assumed they were coming to an English-speaking continent and assimilated to the English-language communities, but the French Canadians essentially held their share of the total population with their formidable birthrate, spurred on by the moral and material incentives of church and state in Quebec.

Richard Cartwright, who had so enthusiastically called for free trade with the United States, was sent by Laurier to London to talk matters over with Joseph Chamberlain, now colonial secretary, whose latest preferred cause was Imperial free trade. This rival commercial union got Cartwright's attention, and he returned no less convinced a tariff-cutter but less precisely focused than he had been. Israël Tarte won respect as an ambitious, and not just patronage-obsessed, minister of public works. He worked closely with Sifton and with Andrew Blair at Railways and Canals to build the terminals and grain-handling and other port facilities to feed and service the settlers and the growing economy. He wrote Laurier that he would "assure the solid friendship of the Grand Trunk and the Canadian Pacific at the same time. With these two great railway companies behind us we could stand up to the fury of the clergy."[13] William Mulock was an imaginative head of the post office and pushed for faster deliveries in-country and overseas. Sydney Fisher at Agriculture and Sir Louis Davies at Fisheries also toiled fruitfully to get the products of their spheres out to the world as cheaply and profitably as possible. It was an energetic and dynamic ministry and illustrated how run down the Conservatives had been, renewed only by John Thompson and kept going only by the overarching national strategy, tactical genius, and immense prestige of Macdonald, who could always rip the patriotic flag out of the hands of any opponent, but had spent himself building and defending Canada and its national railway.

As minister of finance, William Fielding reinforced the dynamic tenor and appearance of the government with his first budget, on April 22, 1897, the most important such occasion since Samuel Tilley had unveiled his chief's National Policy nineteen years before. He introduced a regime of selective tariffs, promising reciprocity to those who offered it themselves and starting out with Chamberlain's idea of Imperial solidarity, which bulletproofed the government against Tupper's Tory opposition. Fielding explained that the tariff was for revenue and not protection, but in fact it provided as much protection as the previous government had done. Fielding put Britain on the spot: Chamberlain, to take up Fielding's proposal, would have to sever Britain's preferential trade relations with her great German rival and some other European countries. That was for Salisbury's government to sort out.

The meetings of the joint high commission with the United States were delayed because of the Spanish-American War, in which Spain had resisted an ultimatum from the Americans to end its oppressions in Cuba and declared war on the United States, and had been pulverized on land and sea within a few weeks, losing Puerto Rico and the Philippines as well as Cuba. This was the last of the *Boys' Own Annual* fun wars in which the United States had excelled. Henceforth, it would be waging war with deadly and determined enemies. Joseph-Adolphe Chapleau had died and was replaced as head of the Canadian side at the joint commission by Laurier himself. The opening session was at Quebec on August 23, 1898. The other Canadians were Cartwright, Davies, and a Liberal MP who owned a lumber business, John Charlton. There was only one British representative, the emollient Lord Herschell. The Canadian secretaries were Macdonald's old assistant, Joseph Pope, and the bright young man of Quebec public life, Henri Bourassa.

It was another feather in Laurier's cap that it was an almost entirely Canadian delegation and that the meetings moved between Quebec and Washington. Of such details is sovereignty gathered, when it has to be negotiated gradually and without alienating the power from which it is obtained. There was good progress on fisheries and all tariffs, but the Alaska boundary was stickier, and this had attained heightened importance because of the discovery of rich quantities of gold in the Yukon, with the usual inrush of prospectors, panhandlers, adventurers, and hucksters, and the demand for a railway to the goldfields. (This discovery made Seward's purchase of Alaska in 1867 seem especially opportune.) The redoubtable Sifton had led an exploratory trip there in the autumn of 1897. After a month's holiday, the joint commission resumed its sessions in Washington in December 1898, and proceeded into the New Year in a much more congenial atmosphere than had obtained when the Canuck-baiting man of Maine, James Blaine, had been in the chair. McKinley's first secretary of state had been Senator John Sherman, brother of the general, and, after a year, William Day, who had been assistant secretary of state under Sherman and who then moved on to the Supreme Court. Day was about to be replaced by the urbane and very capable former minister to Great Britain and Spain, and one-time secretary to Abraham Lincoln, John Milton Hay.

The economy was reviving in Canada as elsewhere, very conveniently, and it was accompanied and propelled by the gold strike in the Yukon and a fever of railway building. A new era of expansion was beginning, and Laurier had no less ardent a concept of what Canada could become than had Macdonald. Canada had established itself as a country with extensive powers of autonomy, and had run the gauntlet successfully between American aggression and British hauteur and indifference, but the challenge remained of earning the esteem of those powers and of maintaining a raison d'être for an independent nationality opposite the immense United States contiguity. Illustrative of residual American skepticism was the opinion of the young Theodore Roosevelt written in the latter years of the Macdonald era:

> Not only the Columbia but also the Red River of the North – and the Saskatchewan and Frazer [sic] as well – should lie wholly within our limit, less for our own sake than for the sake of the men who dwell along their banks. Columbia, Saskatchewan and Manitoba would, as States of the American Union, hold positions incomparably more important, grander, and more dignified than they can ever hope to reach either as independent communities or as provincial dependencies of a foreign power. As long as the Canadian remains a colonist, he remains in a position which is distinctly inferior to that of his cousins, both in England and in the United States. The Englishman at bottom looks down on the Canadian, as he does on anyone who admits his inferiority, and quite properly, too. The American on the other hand, with equal propriety,

regards the Canadian with the good-natured condescension always felt by the freeman for the land that is not free.[14]

What Roosevelt could not be expected to understand, and which
few Canadians could articulate, but what real or adoptive Canadian
leaders – from Champlain and Frontenac through d'Iberville and La
Vérendrye, Dorchester, Brock, Baldwin, LaFontaine, Macdonald,
Cartier, and Laurier – grasped with a romantic intuition that crystal-
lized gradually over the centuries into a full national ambition replete
with a sophisticated tactical playbook, was that, to avoid being subsumed into the United States, Canada had to accept the status Roosevelt
and his countrymen cordially disparaged, because there was, at the end
of the long rainbow, the possibility of creating a society more civilized
than America's in a country that, while smaller, would yet eventually
enjoy the instances of mass and distinction that would fully sustain an
independent but never chauvinistic national spirit.

3. The South African War, 1899–1901

By the late 1890s, Britain, and gradually the whole Empire, had become
thoroughly distracted by South Africa. The British held the Cape
Colony and Natal (Cape Town and Durban), and the original Dutch,
the Boers, had largely migrated to the Orange Free State and the
Transvaal with their slaves, to get away from the British, who had abolished slavery and ran a gentler society. Gold and diamonds attracted the
British and a disparate retinue of fortune-seekers steadily into Boer
territory, where they were eligible for citizenship only if they were at
least forty years old and had been resident for fourteen years. The Boers
were a hard, hostile, inaccessible, and profoundly isolated people. This
was largely Chamberlain's gig, and he was not only carrying out the colonial dreams of Cecil Rhodes and aiming at a Cape-Cairo railway to provide a British spine to the entire African continent, but also aspiring to
bring the whole Empire in a campaign of solidarity to subdue the Boers.
He saw it as a civilizing mission and an occasion to awe the world with
the power of the British Empire, which had not engaged in even slightly
serious combat since the Crimea, and before that since the Napoleonic

Wars. He saw it also as a means to pursue his goal of a unitary Empire, the better to face down the German empire, now led by Victoria's hyperactive and impetuous grandson Emperor Wilhelm II, who was becoming more unstable every year. (Bismarck died in 1898, aged eighty-three, as had Gladstone, aged eighty-nine.) Laurier, as was his nature, regarded all this Imperial bellicosity with cool suspicion, further stirring the antagonism of Chamberlain, as he balanced the aloofness of the French Canadians to Imperial concerns against the Colonel Blimp, Queen-and-Empire pugnacity of the Orange English, personified by his MP for North Victoria, Sam Hughes. Hughes had been a volunteer in some of the actions against the Fenians and was a man of unlimited military affectations. It was as if the British and their Imperial camp followers wanted to emulate the derring-do of the Americans with the Spanish. But the Americans came to the aid of disaffected colonial populations whom the Spanish could not govern and could not suppress. The Boers were primitive, but they were unanimous and they were fierce.

The Aberdeens, as friendly with Laurier and his wife, Zoé, as they had been frosty with Tupper, departed, and would be much missed, after giving the Lauriers a silver loving cup inscribed with *"Oublier, nous ne le pouvons"* ("We cannot forget"). They were replaced by Earl Minto, an old Conservative, a veteran of military action in many parts of the Empire, including as Frederick Middleton's chief of staff in suppressing the Riel Rebellion of 1885, following which he declined Macdonald's offer of the leadership of the North-West Mounted Police. He would prove an energetic and enthusiastic governor, but never developed much rapport with Laurier.

Importunings from Westminster to Laurier for indications of solidarity and preparedness to contribute troops to a South African war began in earnest in February 1899 and grew in frequency and urgency. Chamberlain put Minto up to inquiring in March if Canada would be sending a contingent to anticipated military actions. In April, Rhodes's South African League Congress cabled the Canadian branch of the British Empire League asking for a resolution in support of the British against the Boers. The English-Canadian press, including in Montreal, was almost unanimous in whipping up Imperial sentiment, but French Quebec was glacially unmoved and uninterested. The Liberal caucus and Laurier's cabinet meetings became tense and sharply divided. Israël

Tarte, who knew Quebec sentiment better than anyone and knew all the shadings of opinion, having been an espouser of a full kaleidoscope of them himself at different times, warned Laurier not to touch the issue. On July 31, Laurier tried to put himself at the head of a bipartisan effort to tame surging events with a resolution, seconded by Conservative George Foster, expressing sympathy for the British government's efforts to obtain justice for the British in the Transvaal. Laurier stated that his resolution was intended to assure the British South Africans that Canada agreed with them and thought that right was on their side, and to express the hope that this mark "of universal sympathy extending from continent to continent and encircling the globe, might cause wiser and more humane counsels to prevail in the Transvaal and possibly avert the awful arbitrament of war."[15] The resolution was unanimously adopted and followed by a stirring rendition of "God Save the Queen." Minto took the bull by the horns on instructions from Chamberlain, who saw his vengeance on Laurier for what he considered his filibustering of his Imperial solidarity conference in 1897. The governor general informed Laurier in the presence of an unappreciative Tarte and others that once the shooting started, loyal opinion would surge and carry Laurier with it, whatever the prime minister's personal pusillanimity. For good measure, Minto dismissed Sam Hughes as quite unfit for service as he had not had the benefit of three years' proper military training.[16]

Laurier was quoted in the *Canadian Military Gazette* on October 3, 1899, as being prepared to assure the dispatch of a Canadian military contingent, and was anxiously questioned on his return from a speaking tour in Ontario by Tarte and the now thirty-one-year-old protégé of Laurier and Tarte, Henri Bourassa. Laurier gave the Toronto *Globe* an interview (something he very rarely accorded) in which he referred to the assertion in the *Military Gazette* as a complete falsehood. He punted the issue forward again by saying that no contingent could be promised without a vote of Parliament, which, of course, had not been consulted.

Laurier went to what had been envisioned as a congenial pan-American occasion with McKinley and the timeless Mexican president, Porfirio Díaz, on October 7, 1899, but it didn't accomplish anything and America was rife with pro-Boer sentiment, especially in Chicago, a largely Irish and German city. On October 9, the Boer government of Transvaal, led by President Paul Kruger, gave the British an ultimatum to withdraw their armed forces from the borders of Transvaal and the Orange Free State. They had been deployed there to back British demands that the British within those states be granted the rights of citizens (which might confer a majority power to the British newcomers, mainly seekers of gold and diamonds). The British government rejected the ultimatum, and the South African, or Boer, War began on October 12.

Chamberlain had been misled by the *Canadian Military Gazette* article and sent Minto a cable and letter accepting the Canadian contingent, which had not in fact been offered and which the prime minister denied had even been officially considered, and Chamberlain sent accompanying instructions that the approximately five hundred men he was expecting should be armed by Canada and embark directly for Cape Town by October 31. There should be no colonial officer higher than a major, and Hughes was specifically told that the Empire did not wish to employ the regiment or brigade he had promised to raise and that he personally would not be welcome. Chamberlain, like the British generally, were massively overconfident, and before they finished with this very messy affair, they would pour 450,000 troops into South Africa and would be a great deal more appreciative of any assistance they could get, even from "that parched glory-hunter" Hughes.[17]

Laurier felt his way to the compromise that would keep the country together, as he had over the Manitoba Schools Question. He would not call Parliament after all; after several very agitated cabinet sessions, in which Tarte, sick and troubled by a speech impediment and by poor English, made the case that Quebec would have none of it, and the English-Canadian ministers made it clear that although they were not as peppy as Chamberlain seemed to think Canada was, they felt that something had to be done. Laurier authorized, with cabinet approval, the outfitting and dispatch of up to one thousand volunteers. Tarte was not seeking to prevent volunteers from going, and the cost of such a small force would not require any special taxation. Laurier met with the Quebec caucus, summoned to Ottawa by Tarte, and showed them the order-in-council which would be promulgated the following day, October 14, and left no doubt that the die was cast. To Bourassa, who asked if he had taken account of Quebec opinion, Laurier replied, with his customary sagacity, "My dear Henri, the province of Quebec does not have opinions; it has only sentiments." Bourassa peppered him rather irritatingly with questions, which Laurier answered with some patience, until he put his hand on Bourassa's shoulder and said, "My dear young friend, you do not have a practical mind." Bourassa said that authorizing this intervention would cause him to resign as an MP or to become an outspoken opponent of the ministry.[18] He did resign, contrary to Tarte's advice, though he was soon re-elected as an independent and was a Laurier opponent thereafter. Bourassa (1868–1952) was Louis-Joseph Papineau's grandson, and was less violent but not greatly more practical, though he was an ardent Roman Catholic and was never remotely an annexationist, both unlike Papineau. The contrast in personality and career could scarcely have been greater between this grandson of Papineau and William Lyon Mackenzie's grandson and namesake, William Lyon Mackenzie King, who will soon make his debut, in a very prolonged appearance, in this narrative.

The Canadian contingent, as it became known after all, sailed on October 30, 1899, one day before Chamberlain's peremptory deadline. It was already becoming clear that the British had taken on a great deal more than they had bargained for, as the initial Boer attacks were successful, and Mafeking, Ladysmith, and Kimberley were subjected to prolonged sieges. The British commander, Sir Redvers Buller, soon proved incompetent, as British generals at the beginning of wars usually did, and was replaced by Minto's old chief, Field Marshal Lord Roberts, as reinforcements were sent and solicited. Chamberlain's tune changed very quickly and perceptibly as the whole Salisbury government realized they had plunged into war with a very doughty opponent which had the gold to pay for sophisticated arms and munitions and, as an underdog against the world's greatest empire, attracted very widespread moral support, despite the Afrikaners' porcine habits and attachment to slavery. Instead of the Empire joining in Britain's cavalier and spirited parade march to Pretoria, Chamberlain found himself earnestly soliciting solidarity in the Imperial cause in, to take a phrase from the satirical *Punch* magazine of the time in another context, "a voice grown mighty small."

The whole world, except for the loyal parts of the Empire, applauded as the Boers gave Chamberlain and Salisbury a very bloody nose. In January 1900, a second Canadian contingent shipped out, and Lord Strathcona and Mount Royal, as Donald Smith now was, financed a cavalry regiment.* Hughes finally bulled his way into combat, shouldering aside Chamberlain and Minto and the British commander in Canada, the ludicrous poltroon Major General Edward Hutton, who was so imperious and disdainful and meddlesome that Laurier told Minto if Hutton were not recalled, Laurier would resign and run an election on the backs of the arrogance and stupidity of the British.

As the trade discussions with the Americans proceeded into 1899, it became clear that Pacific Coast interests in the United States would prevent American acceptance of any sea access to the Yukon by ships from Vancouver. This revelation came as Laurier concluded that a railway to the Yukon would be too expensive to be economical. If no agreement could be found on the Yukon, Laurier adhered to Macdonald's policy of always taking to a strong line in negotiations with the United States, and there would be no agreement on anything. Traditional Liberal optimism about free trade with the United States gradually wilted, as did notions of Senate reform, which the Liberals had promised. After a good deal of analysis, Laurier considered a method of combining the Senate and House of Commons for some votes, thus diluting the Senate's capabilities as a legislative retardant. Joseph Chamberlain, from the lofty chair of the Colonial Office, implied that this would be a violation of the guaranty of provincial rights implicit in the federal formula of the British North America Act (a well-founded concern, in fact), and another Liberal pipe dream, so easily embraced and advocated from the Opposition benches, faded.

An unbidden development that more or less blindsided Laurier was the sudden enthusiasm for prohibition of alcoholic beverages. In Canada, as in the United States, a movement – led by housewives tired en masse

---

* Strathcona was into the prolonged final phase of his astonishing career, having accepted the position of high commissioner in London following Tupper. He was governor and principal shareholder of the Hudson's Bay Company, president of the Bank of Montreal, still a very prominent director of Canadian Pacific, chairman of the Burmah and the Anglo-Persian oil companies, chancellor of McGill University, and would continue in the high commission, very effective and influential, to his death in 1914, aged ninety-three, just before the end of the pre-war world in which he had flourished, from his start as a poor Scottish immigrant, through twenty-five years as a factor in the far north, through Parliament, the Riel Rebellion, the desperate birth of the Canadian Pacific Railway, for which he drove the last spike, to the culmination of his career as one of the great industrial barons and philanthropists of the Golden Age.

of drink-sodden husbands, and the churches militant of congregational and evangelical Protestantism – had suddenly arisen to ban drinking. Laurier, worldly Catholic as he was, could not take the issue seriously, but a Prohibition referendum was held, with one-third of eligible voters casting a ballot, and the prohibitionists carried the country by just thirteen thousand votes. Ontario and Quebec, not for the last time in plebiscitary matters, showed the difference in the cultural and sociological nature of their majorities, as Ontario prohibitionists won 154,000 to 113,000, but in Quebec the prohibitionists were drubbed 122,000 to 28,000. It wasn't a racially defining issue, but the tipplers of English Canada were grateful for the solidity of their French, Irish, and German-Catholic countrymen, while, to the Low Church Protestants, the evils of Rome were more evident and sinister than ever.

In December 1899, Sir John A. Macdonald's capable and well-liked son, Hugh John Macdonald, had defeated Laurier's fellow Liberal and schools co-contractant, Thomas Greenway, to become the premier of Manitoba. Henri Bourassa, having resigned as a member of Parliament, stood again as an independent in Labelle, and Laurier ensured that there was no official Liberal against him. He was acclaimed and returned to the House of Commons, sponsored by Tarte. Bourassa demanded the relevant correspondence between Chamberlain and Laurier, which the prime minister graciously produced and which caused him no embarrassment. Bourassa opposed raising the pay-scale of the Canadian contingents from Imperial to Canadian rates on the grounds that they were Imperial troops. This raised the hackles of the House, and Bourassa assured in February and March that the parliamentary debates of the new (Canadian, according to Laurier) century were quite acrimonious. The Liberal Quebec bloc held firm behind its leader, and Ontario, though it was more participationist, appreciated that Laurier, in the circumstances, was doing his best, and all regions were very prosperous and disinclined to take an undue interest in Africa. Eastern European immigrants were now responding to Sifton's inducements and flooded into the West.

The war issue came to a head on March 13 when Laurier, after careful consideration, declined to move or support the motion Bourassa had conceived of declaring that the dispatch of troops to South Africa did not constitute a precedent, and declaring that there could be no change in the official relationship between Canada and Great Britain without an election and parliamentary approval. Laurier told Bourassa that such a measure would be both superfluous and inflammatory. This was a master stroke by Laurier, as he considered presenting the motion carefully enough to avoid Bourassa's personal animosity, and Bourassa could be relied upon to present his case forcefully enough for English Canadians to grasp the fervour and even the rigour of the Quebec nationalist position, which they would never have heard so forcefully and clearly formulated as Bourassa would now make it. Bourassa spoke for three hours, mainly in his impeccable English (he was an alumnus of the College of the Holy Cross in Worcester, Massachusetts), and on this occasion was not at all reminiscent of his grandfather. He accepted the Conquest, was an admirer of the British, proclaimed himself a follower of Burke, Fox, Bright, and Gladstone, and said that he only sought the genuine equality of the founding races and strict adherence to the British North America Act. Canada should not be an adjunct to a discreditable, repressive, and avariciously motivated attack on the free Boer people, and should not be supporting that action in the indirect, slippery, sophistical way that it was. He told a hushed and respectful, though not an approving, House, "Mr. Chamberlain and his frantic disciples, and his unconscious followers both English and Canadian [i.e., English and French Canadian], are leading us toward a constitutional revolution the consequences of which no man can calculate. . . . It is our duty as a free parliament representing the free opinion of the people to say what is going to be the policy of the people."[19]

Laurier rose as soon as Bourassa finished. It was the most dramatic moment in the House of Commons since Macdonald's defence of his conduct in the Pacific Scandal in 1873. The Liberal benches were ready for their leader to assert himself, and Wilfrid Laurier was fully prepared to show his mettle. He referred with exquisite courtesy and without condescension or scorn to Bourassa and won the match cleanly with "I put this question to my honourable friend: What would be the condition of this country today if we had refused to obey the voice of public opinion?" The French Canadians recognized that English Canada demanded that volunteers be allowed to participate and that discouraging that level of support for the Empire would have put an unsustainable strain on Confederation and caused the rejection of the government in English

Canada; and the English Canadians recognized, with unaccustomed vividness and disquietude, how strongly dissentient was the French-Canadian nationalist position. The English could see that going much further would stampede Laurier's Quebec support out from under him, and the French Canadians could hardly complain if people wished to volunteer for such a cause. The division was a solid endorsement for the prime minister, and Tupper's ultra-loyalist message as Opposition leader did not resonate well.

That night, Tarte, unwell, and a dangerous source of unpredictable political coaching for Bourassa, left to take up his post as Canadian high commissioner to the Paris International Exposition (chiefly remembered for the Eiffel Tower), but really for Laurier to get him out of the way and to enable him to try to restore Tarte's fragile health. By now, British arms were making greater progress, which continued as forces, under more purposeful command, poured into South Africa and overwhelmed the Boer capacity for direct resistance. On June 7, 1900, Laurier moved a resolution of congratulations to Her Imperial Britannic Majesty on the recapture by her armies of the Boer capital at Pretoria. Tupper spoke strongly in support, but Bourassa could not resist even this ill-chosen window of opportunity: "I admire the might of England, I admire many of the deeds that England has done throughout the world, but this war will not add an ounce to the glory of the English flag." Bourassa was drowned out in cries of "shame," followed by a bellowed, scarcely sonorous rendition of "God Save the Queen." Of course, Bourassa was correct that it was nothing to celebrate to subdue such a stubborn people, but it was a step forward for civilization, the enemies of slavery in particular, and the spirit of the moment was one of relief at the victory of a great and kindred power. Having done Laurier the favour of showing English Canadians what the prime minister had to contend with in French-Canadian nationalism, Bourassa had now discountenanced his fellow Québécois with a motion that was nasty, provoking, and insolent; and he had given Laurier the opportunity to rise again, as he seemed almost effortlessly to do, to the task of providing the voice of reason for the balanced continuity of Canadian national progress and understanding. Apart from anything else, Canada, contrary to Bourassa's woolly and premature aspirations, was in no position to part company altogether from Britain, and especially not in the hour of her victory, given continuing, if declining, vulnerability to the United States, which was about to be governed by the most belligerent president in its history, Theodore Roosevelt, with the sole possible exception of Andrew Jackson.

The South African War was now passing into the guerrilla phase, where scores of thousands of civilians were rounded up into detention camps in which conditions could and should have been better and over twenty thousand women and children perished from illness and malnutrition. Ultimately, over four hundred thousand British and Empire soldiers were required to burn the crops of the Boers and starve them into surrender. It was not an image-building initiative by the country that celebrated itself in Elgar's stirring "Land of Hope and Glory" as the "Mother of the Free." Chamberlain asked Laurier via Minto if Canada wished to be invited to the peace conference and if it wished to attend a colonial council, of the kind Chamberlain had been championing since the jubilee year of 1897. Laurier distantly replied that Canada did not ask for an invitation to the peace conference but would attend if asked, and that if the purpose of a colonial council was to discuss Imperial defence, he thought it premature. A total of seventy-three hundred Canadians had participated on the British side in the South African War (89 were killed, 135 died of disease, and 252 were wounded).

On June 19, 1900, Laurier sacked Thomas McInnes, the lieutenant-governor of British Columbia, whom he had appointed from the Senate, for apparently ignoring the results of the recent election in that province. It was a useful and somewhat dramatic precedent, reinforcing responsible government, which had supposedly reigned in Canada for over fifty years. After a summer of holidays and preparation, Laurier dissolved the House of Commons on October 9 for an election on November 7. Sifton returned from Vienna after unsuccessful attempts by specialists to cure his deafness, but took to the hustings with his usual energy and vehemence undimmed by his conspicuous ear trumpet. Tarte was also back; he had not liked the Parisians, nor they him, and he had made a number of rather provocative speeches complaining about a wide range of French national traits, British government policies, and assorted Canadian shortcomings. His most noteworthy hour in Paris was when the president of the republic, Émile Loubet, was about to enter the Canadian pavilion at the Paris Exposition by the side door, having been in the neighbouring Australian pavilion. Tarte had the door closed and let it be known that he was not "in the habit of receiving by my kitchen door." He was noisily resentful of not being treated by the French or the British, and certainly not anyone else, as the representative of a self-governing country.

Laurier had an unbeatable formula and had earned the respect of the whole country. Good times were rolling, and Laurier had given Imperial Preference to the Imperialists and rebuffed Chamberlain for the nationalists, French and other. He had threaded the needle on South Africa, with enough solidarity and enough independence, with Canadians free to choose for themselves and no one coerced to anything. Even the pope had endorsed his schools efforts, and he had not gone to war against the Protestant majority. He had held his ground against the Americans and gained considerable recognition and prestige, for himself and for Canada, from the British, Americans, the papacy, and the French (even if Tarte did not share in the esteem of the French). On November 7, the government was re-elected safely enough, with 139 Liberal MPs to 75 Conservative, compared with 132 and 81 four years before, and the spread in the popular vote also widened slightly, from 52 per cent to 47.4 in 1896, to 52.5 per cent to 46.9 in 1900. Sir Charles Tupper was defeated in his own constituency, and the "Ram of Cumberland," as he was known in his lusty younger days, was retired at last after a distinguished public career of forty-five years. The first head of the Canadian Medical Association, and a Father of Confederation, he tried to run an ultra-Imperial campaign, but Laurier crowded him onto the political shoulder. Tupper returned to London and lived happily in retirement for another fifteen years, dying at ninety-four on October 30, 1915. Borden and Laurier eulogized him in Parliament on February 7, 1916, Borden, a classicist, closing with the famous charge "*Si monumentum requiris, circumspice*" ("If you wish a monument, look about you"). After so long and distinguished a career, Tupper deserved no less.[20]

Queen Victoria died on January 22, 1901, after a reign of sixty-three years and seven months. After a suitably mighty funeral attended by her offspring the king-emperors of Britain and India, Germany and Russia, the entire post-Waterloo era of three generations was laid in the grave with her. The stylish and flamboyant Edward VII, sixty-one, and his ever-youthful (despite her husband's countless infidelities) consort, Alexandra, ascended the thrones. The death of the venerable grandmother of Europe could only exacerbate the rivalry between Britain and Germany; already, the insouciant Kaiser Wilhelm had allowed Bismarck's League of the Three Emperors, between Germany, Austria-Hungary, and Russia, to lapse, casting aside the late chancellor's device for separating an avenging France from alliance with Russia. Wilhelm had openly favoured and helped supply the Boers, and was always chippily criticizing his British relatives, overawed though he was in the presence of Victoria and even Edward. Such was the power of Germany that Great Britain was, at the very end of the long Salisbury era (Salisbury retired in 1902 after fourteen years as prime minister, having served Disraeli as foreign minister before that), drawing close to France and Russia to preserve the balance of power. The British and their Empire were preparing to depart splendid isolation and concede that they could no longer hold the fulcrum between contending continental blocs and had to throw themselves into the balance. This was what Disraeli had warned of after the unification of Germany in 1871, and was the reason that Richelieu and Napoleon and even Metternich had gone to such lengths to keep Germany divided. It was also the reason that underlay Chamberlain's perfervid promotion of a unitary Empire (as well as an alliance with Germany and the United States, the three greatest powers). The Gladstonian era of questioning the utility of the Empire now seemed as distant as the Middle Ages, though Gladstone had retired from his fourth term as prime minister only seven years before Victoria died ("Not that bore again," Victoria had said when told that she had to send for him as he formed his last government at the age of eighty-three). Ominous though these events were for the world, they were useful for Canada, as it was now more highly prized by Britain and therefore more certain of British, and even French, support than ever; and as there was no power left in Europe capable of tilting the balance between the arrayed nations of the old continent, this sceptre was passing, unsought, to the United States, which would soon have to construe its national interest in more sober terms than promenading as the suzerain of the Americas and occasionally perplexing its neighbours. The world, and Canada's place in it, were becoming unaccountably complicated.

4. Imperial Relations, 1901–1903

In March 1901, Bourassa, as Laurier had confidently foreseen, went completely overboard with his parochial histrionics and moved a parliamentary resolution asking Britain to conclude an honourable peace that would recognize the independence of the Boers. Britain had poured four-fifths as great a force into South Africa as that which constituted the Grand Armies of Napoleon and Grant and Sherman, and had not done so to re-establish the status quo. In fact, it was a generous peace when it came, and created, in 1910, the Union of South Africa, with full and equal rights for the Boers, and though slavery was ended, white supremacy continued for almost all of the new century. As Laurier's biographer Joseph Schull writes, Bourassa's "speech was merely another exercise in irritation and the speaker's accumulating rancours carried him on to the verge of imbecility."[21] He averred that the South African War had shortened the late queen's life (to eighty-two years) and he would not be "an accomplice of murderers of the queen." Like his grandfather, though without the violent afterpiece, he had gone too far, and Laurier dispensed with him in the brief but deflating reflection that it was extraordinary that someone who would not approve offering any assistance to Britain was so generous with his advice to that country.[22]

Robert Laird Borden, a Halifax lawyer and MP, was formally elected leader of the federal Conservatives. He was a less volcanic and energetic figure than Tupper, and seemed a rather pallid alternative to the elegant, refined, worldly, and bilingually mellifluous prime minister now in his fifteenth year as Liberal leader, though only just turning sixty. Laurier greeted the Duke and Duchess of York (the future King George V, son of Edward VII, and Queen Mary) at Quebec in September 1901, as the Alaska boundary dispute flared up again. The Americans would not accept Laurier's approach to a Canadian-American agreement that might make ocean access in the southern "panhandle" of Alaska available to British Columbia and the Yukon. Sensing the British urge to conciliate America, as European conditions became steadily more tense and difficult, the Americans summoned a conference in Washington and invited the British and Canadians to send a joint delegation. It was as if nothing had changed in Canada's status and

America's attitude to Canada since Macdonald's heroics at the Washington Conference on trade in 1871.

Laurier conducted Their Royal Highnesses across the country on the Empire's greatest railroad in September, and the tour stopped respectfully on September 19 to observe the death by assassination of President William McKinley while he attended an exposition in Buffalo, New York, just a few miles from the Canadian border. With the accession of the forty-two-year-old vice president, Theodore Roosevelt, former rancher, New York City Police commissioner, Rough Rider colonel of volunteers in Cuba in the Spanish-American War, learned historian, former assistant secretary of the navy and governor of New York, it seemed that America had its own Kaiser Wilhelm. They were almost exact contemporaries, and full of energy and bravado, but fortunately Roosevelt proved a serious and intelligent, if very nationalistic president, and a man of integrity, courage, and even judgment, though he continued to be impulsive. None of these compliments could be applied to the German kaiser, except his energy, and occasionally his flare. Laurier accompanied the royals back from Vancouver and saw them off, a very pleasant and successful cameo appearance and another gesture of Britain's swiftly appreciating judgment of Canada's increasing utility in the strategic chess game unfolding in the chancelleries of Europe and ramifying over the whole world.

Bourassa returned from a tour of Europe and began what would be his practice over the next forty-five years of addressing large crowds in public places with very carefully prepared texts that would be lapidary reflections on history and national and international affairs, think pieces for the edification of the French-Canadian race. It was a rather portentous role to be taken up by a thirty-three-year-old, even a grandson of Papineau and former protégé of Laurier. Bourassa's address on October 20, 1901, at the Théâtre National in Montreal praised the British as creators of liberty, dissented from Imperial union because British and Canadian interests were at odds, warned against pan-Americanism, and evinced little solidarity with the Americans. Bourassa felt English and French Canadians had too many differences in goals and outlook to concert usefully in one country, and warned that the British were not the champions of liberty of olden times but were now Chamberlains and Rhodeses and were grasping hegemons. He evinced no love of the

French and didn't much emphasize his incandescent Catholicism, and so his magisterial speech, which was certainly erudite, recondite, and pedantically formulated, criticized everyone and everything but was neither nihilistic nor at all enlightening about the way forward. No one really knew what to make of it, except that Bourassa was likely to be around with a following to dispose for a long time.[23]

Laurier had a very challenging and prolonged showdown with Chamberlain in London in the spring and summer of 1902. He went initially for Edward VII's coronation, but it had to be deferred for six weeks because the king had to have his appendix removed on the original coronation day. Chamberlain gathered the constituent Empire leaders and pressured them as aggressively as he could on the virtues of Imperial intimacy in foreign and defence policy. He was still not prepared to countenance interrupting trade relations with Germany for the benefit of kith and kin, though it was the inexorable rise of Germany that drove Chamberlain and his colleagues to such paroxysms of Imperial affection. And in Canada the game of loyalist hosannas in English Canada tempered by cautious prevarication in Quebec reached new depths of opportunism and evasion. For once, Bourassa captured it: "The only point in real dispute between both parties is which will eat the biggest piece of the jingo pie. All this, of course, does not prevent them from selling Canada wholesale to American railway magnates."[24] Laurier was a human barometer, moving ahead of opinion or reacting deftly to it, shifting weight from one foot to the other. But whatever the criticisms from Bourassa and Tarte on one side and the Conservatives and ultra-loyal English on the other, and some French *"vendus"* ("sell-outs") as Bourassa called Laurier unjustly, Laurier kept a plausible version of the emergent Canadian national interest alive. He declared before he departed Canada in May 1902 for London that he was always open on trade matters but saw no reason for an adjustment of political or defence relationships, and told Parliament that he flatly refused to join the transatlantic movement to bring Canada "into the vortex of militarism which is now the curse and the blight of Europe."[25]

    Chamberlain had a much-refined argument from that of the jubilee of 1897, sustained as it had been by the august and tranquil glories of Victoria and her time. Now the kaiser was churning out battleships, sabre-rattling in Europe and Africa, and the new American kaiser was furiously building ships and an isthmian canal in Panama to facilitate movement of the expanded American fleet between the Atlantic and Pacific. Even the pacifistic Cleveland had been pugilistically assertive in the absurd sideshow of the Venezuela-Guiana border, and Canada in particular should beware of where the Americans might cast their covetous, greedy eyes next. They had all seen in South Africa – where gold, diamonds, and the rights of overseas Britons were at stake – how the whole world had cheered on the gross, brutal, Afrikaner Trekboer peasants, who had trudged by foot and in ox cart five hundred miles more than sixty years before to escape a regime whose offence had been that it had abolished slavery.

Chamberlain's pursuit of an Imperial Council with powers to tax and regulate the whole Empire received no support, and would not have had any in the United Kingdom itself if there had been any notion of it not being simply a method for the British to pick the pockets of the related jurisdictions. Nor was any country present any more prepared than was Great Britain itself to barricade itself into an Imperial protectionist fortress. These overseas units and outposts of the Empire were largely resources-based economies and had to have access to the great industrial importers of raw materials, especially the United States, Japan, and parts of Western Europe apart from Britain. Chamberlain was selling moonshine, and only the fervour with which he was able to torque himself up to a cause, and the urgency of the German challenge, prevented him from seeing it himself. (He broke both major parties in half in his career and was about to split the Conservatives, who passed to the leadership of Salisbury's nephew, Arthur James Balfour, in 1902.)

In any case, he had no takers. Defence was the real kernel of the discussion. Britain was assuring the security of its Empire, and had rallied most of the time when necessary, though there would never have been the American threat to Canada from 1812 to 1815 if Britain had not grossly overplayed its hand and committed acts of war against the Americans on the high seas. Australia continued to make a contribution to the Royal Navy, and others pledged modest sums, but none of them was under any direct threat. Canada's condition was different because of its immense and unpredictable American neighbour. Laurier said that Canada would remain loyal in the event of a great and common emergency, would soon set up her own modest navy for the defence of both coasts, and would not otherwise pre-pledge anything or anyone to a central Imperial force. Chamberlain and Laurier exchanged expressions of surprise at each other's position. Chamberlain was outraged, though he could scarcely have feigned surprise, and called Laurier privately "the dancing master" and expressed a preference for "a cad who knows his own mind."[26] As always, British statesmen had almost no grasp of the distinctiveness and wariness of the French Canadian, and certainly Chamberlain, and even Minto, who should have known better, little realized the forces Laurier had always to master in Quebec. Laurier sagely declined a peerage and departed and made the now customary calls in Paris and Rome, where he was much more graciously received than by His Majesty's government, but he was unwell and tried, without success, to rest in Switzerland and the Channel Islands, and to get a proper medical diagnosis. Rumours abounded, and he returned to Canada in October 1902 amid great perplexity over his health.

At this point, the ineffable Israël Tarte – infirm, semi-unilingual victim of a speech impediment and bearer of an unenviable but well-earned reputation for irascible and unstable judgment, high in chicanery at all times – made his play, imagining that he might be able to take Laurier's place. Two days after his return, on October 20, Laurier abruptly fired Tarte, "having expressed to you my well-settled opinion upon the consequences of your recent attitude."[27] Laurier's doctors finally diagnosed asthma, not the cancer he and his wife had feared, and he departed in mid-November for a convalescent holiday at Hot Springs, Virginia, interrupting it only for an unproductive and cool, though perfectly civilized, meeting with Roosevelt and his secretary of state, John Hay, in Washington. He went on to Florida, one of the early trailblazers in what would become a passionate French-Canadian love affair with that state, and returned to Canada in January in good health and spirits, having even placated Bourassa by sending him the record of his dealings with Chamberlain, eliciting the reply "Now that the procession of boot-lickers has passed . . . I become again your firm and sincere supporter."[28]

In his navigation of the vagaries of Anglo-French relations in Canada, Laurier was both calculated and intuitive, and his performance both masterly and artistic. In the high and mysterious tradition of Champlain,

Frontenac, Carleton, Brock, Baldwin and LaFontaine, and Macdonald, Wilfrid Laurier was the indispensable man who protected the magic golden thread of Canadian sovereign nationhood that had been spun out imperceptibly from the founding of Quebec nearly three centuries before. His greatest test and contribution were to come, but he was already an eminent figure in Canadian history.

5. Railways, Anglo-American Relations, and the 1904 Election, 1903–1905

The gigantic grain harvests in the western provinces and territories overloaded the capacity of the Canadian Pacific and forced consideration of new railway construction. From 1900 to 1905, Manitoba's grain production doubled from fifty million to one hundred million bushels, and approximately equal harvests were coming or were very foreseeable from the territories between Manitoba and the Rocky Mountains. (Between 1901 and 1911, Calgary and Edmonton both increased in population from four thousand to forty thousand.[29]) The intrepid railwaymen Donald Mann and William Mackenzie (both knighted in 1911) had bought and built and extended some western spur lines and announced plans for the Canadian Northern Railway. Mann (1853–1934) was from Acton, Ontario, and studied to be a Methodist minister before becoming a lumberman and then working on the construction of the Canadian Pacific followed by railways in China and Latin America. Mackenzie (1849–1923) was a local politician and sawmill operator from near Peterborough, Ontario, who also worked on the CPR for many years, and then became a co-founder of the Toronto transit system and of the Brazilian Traction Company in São Paulo. These adventurous and able men were eager to fill the need for greater railway trackage.

Laurier had come to regard the Americans with as much suspicion as Macdonald had. They had tariff walls against most Canadian manufactures and foodstuffs (though the remains of the National Policy reciprocated to some, but to a lesser, degree. The Americans maintained constant tariff pressure toward continental assimilation as a matter of policy). The Americans made the most dire threats against any Canadian adherence to Imperial preference, and to some extent held the Canadian railway system hostage, as Canadian Pacific now had fifteen hundred miles of track inside the United States, the terminus of the Grand Trunk Railway was at Portland, Maine, and even Mackenzie and Mann's Canadian Northern ran through Minnesota. Only the indifferently managed and unprofitable Intercolonial Railway was entirely within Canada, running from Montreal to Halifax. Laurier settled on the new ambition to rationalize the rail system, ran a rail line across the country to the north, giving width and depth to the ribbon of the CPR and to increase the strategic mass and strength of the country thereby. This would assure that there were no bottlenecks in fully exploiting the work of the millions of immigrants who would arrive in the first decade of the new century. There were vast tracts of timber, hydro-electric resources, and promising indications of mining prospects all across Central and Northern Canada, and it was time to access and populate and exploit these areas. It was a rational sequel to the government's ambitious immigration policy.

Laurier's preferred plan was to link the Grand Trunk, which came out of the east as far as North Bay, Ontario, with the Canadian Northern, which came as far east from Edmonton as Thunder Bay, at the head of Lake Superior. Laurier was determined to handle the key stages of the railway arrangements himself to be sure of avoiding any replication of Macdonald's debacle with the Pacific Scandal. He would accede to the long-standing demand for an impartial railway commission to set rates and schedules, and he planned a commission of inquiry generally into the country's transport needs. The fissiparous politics and self-interested antics of some of his ministers frayed even Laurier's strength and patience, but it was tentatively agreed that a new company, Grand Trunk Pacific, would be set up, jointly owned by Grand Trunk and the Canadian government, to lay track west from North Bay, and the government would build a line east from North Bay through northern Quebec to the Atlantic, call it the National Transcontinental, and lease it to Grand Trunk when it was finished.

The project started on this basis, though there were obviously a great many contentious loose ends left to be resolved. Laurier acknowledged that the government would be building track that the private sector (the Grand Trunk) thought uneconomic, but in the tradition of Simcoe and Hincks and Sir Charles Tupper (as railways minister), he was justifying a mixed public-private sector approach as essential to the national interest, which he broadened in this case to include facilitating the development of northern Quebec. On the assumption that the government would never be called on its guaranty of Grand Trunk Pacific bonds, and that the lease of National Transcontinental would amortize its cost, Laurier could claim the government wasn't really spending much. The reliability of those assumptions was another matter. Canadian Pacific, which because of its market position and preferments from the government could take no part, let it be known privately that it thought Laurier was overbuilding for the country, though everyone conceded that only the politicians could judge the politics. As plans developed, the line would not extend as far northwest of Quebec as had been hoped, and the narrow projection of Canada to the west seemed unlikely to be much broadened.

The plan arrived at was for an eastern terminus at Moncton, New Brunswick, because it was politically impossible to choose between Saint John and Halifax, and it would plunge through northern Quebec, join up in the approaches to North Bay with the Grand Trunk, run north of Lake Superior to Winnipeg, and proceed somewhat north of the Canadian Pacific the rest of the way, making as much use as possible out of the Canadian Northern. Laurier was suspicious of his railways minister, Andrew Blair, and considered him too friendly with Mackenzie and Mann, and a few days before Laurier proposed to table his Railway Bill, Blair resigned and tabled to the House of Commons his correspondence with the prime minister, declaring that the government's proposal was "one of the most indefensible railway transactions that has ever taken place in this country." Van Horne, whom Laurier had hoped would head his transportation commission, declined to do so, but Laurier pressed on with his bill and presented it himself on July 30, 1903, on such a forced legislative march that he was unable to furnish Robert Borden, the Opposition leader, with whom he enjoyed very cordial relations, with a copy. It was a tremendous gamble, but Laurier was determined and led the debate with all flags flying:

> We cannot wait because at this moment there is a trans-
> formation going on in our national life which it would be
> folly to ignore and a crime to overlook; we cannot wait

because the prairies of the Northwest, which for countless ages have been roamed over by the wild herds of the bison or by the scarcely less wild tribes of red men, are now invaded from all sides by the white race. They came last year one hundred thousand strong and still they come in greater numbers. . . . Heaven grant that while we tarry and dispute an ever-vigilant competitor does not take to himself the trade that properly belongs to Canada.[30]

It took him until September 29 to get his bill through, and Laurier then pronounced, with what his biographer Schull called "the same nervous shrillness" he had employed in presenting the bill, that "a new star has risen upon the horizon, a star not in the orbit of the American constellation but a star standing by itself resplendent in the western sky, and it is toward that star that every immigrant, every traveler, every man who leaves the land of his ancestors to come and seek a home for himself now turns his gaze."[31] The prime minister's prognosis was to prove optimistic, but it was an interesting vision. It possessed the grandeur appropriate to his optimism and necessary to lift the Canadians out of the slough of demeaning comparisons with their neighbour. And although the United States was not going to provoke the newly maternally protective British, it did not, in the person of its assertive young president, favour or even accept the durability of the Canadian effort at nation-building.

Canadians played a role in international railway-building; Sir Edouard Percy Girouard (1867–1932) was engaged by Lord Kitchener to build a railway 235 miles across the Nubian Desert in 1897, which facilitated the British victory at Omdurman in 1898. He became the president of the Egyptian State Railways, the director of Imperial Military Railways in South Africa, which greatly aided the Empire in the South African War, and was appointed by Winston Churchill, then colonial secretary, as governor of Northern Nigeria, where he built more railways and was an efficient economic planner. He was recalled from his position as a managing director at armaments maker Armstrong-Whitworth to be Director General of Munitions in the "Shell Crisis" of 1916.

While the railway debate raged, any prospect of a satisfactory outcome of the Alaska boundary issue evaporated. The treaty the Americans wrote up left everything to a commission of arbiters, composed of three Americans, two Canadians, and one British, all of whom would take an oath "impartially [to] consider the arguments and evidence."[32] No informed person, and certainly not Laurier, could doubt what a rigged outcome that procedure would produce. Chamberlain, despite his Imperial effusions, gave the store away in advance by accepting all this without consulting Laurier, and the outcome was sealed when the Americans revealed that their arbiters would be Elihu Root (1845–1937), who was Roosevelt's secretary of war; Henry Cabot Lodge (1850–1924), a strident Rooseveltian expansionist, six-term U.S. senator, and critic of the British Empire and of Canada in particular; and Senator George Turner (1850–1932) from Washington, whose constituents would not tolerate, and he would not entertain, any concessions to Canada. The British delegate, the chief justice of England, Lord Alverstone, could be assumed to be under orders from Chamberlain to throw in with the Americans. Chamberlain had even suggested that there be two British and just one Canadian, but Laurier brusquely rejected that and named Sir Louis-Amable Jetté (1836–1920), the lieutenant-governor and former chief justice of Quebec, and Allen B. Aylesworth (1854–1952), who would soon join Laurier's cabinet and be the minister of justice of Canada, and would be a senator from 1923 until his death at age ninety-seven. These were capable men, as were Alverstone and Root; Lodge was a belligerent and rather treacherous patrician; and Turner was a journeyman one-term senator and lawyer from Spokane.

The discussions were learned and mannerly, but Roosevelt made it clear that the matter would be resolved as he wished or he would have Congress authorize him to resolve the matter by force. The British were not going to go to war over such a trivial matter, and Canada was cooked. Alverstone, on orders, effectively defected to the American side, and Jetté and Aylesworth wished to walk out and return home rather than be a party to the charade that was developing. Laurier told them to remain and to tell Alverstone that while Laurier understood realities, the Americans were cranking up simply to seize the territory necessary for their interoceanic canal in Central America, and that while no one could stop that either, the approval of the British would be desired by the Americans. Jetté and Aylesworth were to tell their British colleague, in Laurier's own words, that "if we are thrown over by [the] chief justice, he will give the last blow to British diplomacy in Canada. He should be plainly told this."[33] He was, but it had no effect, and on October 20, 1903, the commissioners came down four to two for the United States on all points. The Alaska boundary would follow a line between the peaks of the mountains nearest to the ocean, excluding any sea access for Canada. Three days later, in a vigorous debate in the Canadian House of Commons, all sides were in agreement. Borden was infuriated by the British, and Bourassa, for once, spoke for many of his anglophone colleagues when he said that nothing was to be expected from the British connection. Laurier, disappointed but realistic as always, spoke for the country and all parties when he said, "We are only a small colony, a growing colony but still a colony. . . . We have not in our own hands the treaty-making power which would enable us to dispose of our own affairs. . . . So long as Canada remains a dependency of the British Crown, the present powers that we have are not sufficient for the maintenance of our rights."

This was ground-breaking and important, a piercing recognition of the truth (the significance of which was noticed publicly in Britain only by the *Manchester Guardian*).[34] Of course, underlying it was the greater truth that Canada, if completely independent, would have to absorb worse outrages from the Americans. Canada had finally almost run out the string; it was still not able to protect itself from the Americans, and the British were barely able to make up enough of the difference in the correlation of forces. Canada had to get greater support from Britain while making itself a less tempting target for the bullying tendencies of the Americans. The problem was not as daunting as others Canada had faced throughout its history, but it was not easily tractable and in one way and another would grate on the country for most of the century. Canada was on a treadmill of world politics, running faster and faster but gaining only slowly in its ability to assure its own security, because as quickly as it grew in importance to the British, the power of the United States grew also and Britain's dependence on the goodwill of the Americans grew with it. The solution was conceptually simple: the development of Canada into a fully self-reliant country. But Canada still inhabited a bipolar political world, and of the two poles, the United States still coveted Canada, its appetite only reduced to dismissive extortion and unequal treaties by the deterrent power of the British, whose will to deter was now barely greater than their need to appease the Americans, and was only sustained by their ambition to retain Canada as a source of natural and human resources to be put to use in the event of war with Germany.

No one cared about the Canadians *qua Canadians* except the Canadians, and they were riven by Imperial, annexationist, and French-autonomist factions. Fashioning and pursuing a national interest out of these domestic and foreign ingredients was unusually challenging. Macdonald and Laurier had brought the country along as quickly and astutely as anyone could, but a great power, as the Americans had discovered in the previous century, could not be raised up quickly out of a rugged wilderness, and a great power was the only country the other great powers weren't always trying to pluck like a chicken.

Laurier thought better of his promise to table his correspondence with Chamberlain. If he revealed publicly the extent of his anger with the British sellout to the Americans over the rather secondary issue of the Yukon's access to the ocean, it could alter the delicate and already very imperfect balance in relations with the United States and the United Kingdom. Roosevelt had not scrupled to sever the province of Panama from Colombia by inciting a farcical banana-republic secessionist coup and then buying the rights to an isthmian canal for less than the Colombians had had the impudence to request, all in November 1903. Laurier could not be certain that if he had had a public bust-up with the British government over the Alaska boundary, Roosevelt would not have offered Balfour and Chamberlain an alliance against Germany in exchange for a free hand in Canada with respect for British commercial interests, and that the British would not have taken it. Roosevelt was so strong politically and so popular with his countrymen, with such a rich prize as Canada to collect he would probably have got a British alliance through the Senate. (It would not have been a bad deal for anyone except, assumedly, the Canadians, as Germany would not have got into war with a British Empire shorn of Canada but backed by a United States that held all North America above the Rio Grande and was allied also to France and Russia. Strong though Germany was, she could not have taken on those four powers at once. The United States would have doubled its natural resources in one stroke, and if world war ever occurred it would be on more favourable terms for the West than was ultimately the case.)

It is unlikely that any such precise conjecture was in Laurier's mind, but his duty and purpose were the advancement of Canadian interests, and this sometimes required the observation of more discretion than came naturally, even to such an equable and gracious statesman. Chamberlain's pre-emptive capitulation to the Americans over the Alaska boundary made his previous advocacy of Imperial solidarity all the more hollow.

The wheels started to come off the train car of Laurier's new railway almost at once. By early 1904, the British financial houses that were supposed to underwrite the Grand Trunk bond issue, which the government was guarantying, pointed out that the peg of the guaranty to the cost of driving the railroad through the mountains was impractical because, as the experiences of Canadian Pacific and the American transcontinental railroads had shown, it was impossible to see what rock slides, washouts, and other obstacles would arise. Laurier approved what amounted to an open-ended guaranty of the cost of the mountain section of the railway and jammed the revised bill through the House in April 1904, over Borden's prudent but unexciting proposals to trim, wait, and study, and to build up the Intercolonial Railway, which ran to his native Halifax, dispense with the National Transcontinental, which would serve Laurier's Quebec, and distribute a few plums to the ubiquitous Mackenzie and Mann. The Grand Trunk and Intercolonial Railways eventually proved invaluable in moving Canada's war effort in munitions, food, and supply during the two world wars, but for a time they seemed to be questionable political projects.

The 1904 session opened with the introduction of twenty-four-year-old Bourassa protégé Armand Lavergne (1880–1935) as the MP from Montmagny, sponsored by Laurier. He was widely alleged to be Laurier's illegitimate son, as his mother, Émilie, was a Laurier intimate from Arthabaska. Lavergne's father, Joseph, Laurier's law partner, had been named a judge by Laurier, and the senior Lavergnes and Laurier, though they did not deign to refer to the rumours publicly, privately denied them. When the young Lavergne, who did have a physical resemblance to Laurier, was taunted on the hustings with the allegation that he was a bastard, he replied that he obviously could not be certain who his biological father was, that he had always been told that it was Joseph Lavergne, but that he had cause for pride whether it was Mr. Justice Lavergne or Sir Wilfrid Laurier and he was proud of his close relationship with both. This generally shut down the snickerers.

Less remarked on at the time, but of greater importance to the future of Canada and the Liberal Party, was the acclamation the same month of Ernest Lapointe (1876–1941) as MP for Kamouraska for the first of eleven consecutive terms, which would raise him to a position analogous to George-Étienne Cartier's as a virtual co-prime minister for most of the twenty years between 1921 and 1941. The session ended with minor confected acrimony over Laurier's reference to the British commander of the Canadian militia, the Earl of Dundonald, as a "foreigner," which he immediately amended to "stranger" (the French word *étranger* means either), after he had fired him by order-in-council following heel-dragging by Minto when Dundonald condemned agriculture and acting militia minister Sydney Fisher's rejection of some of Dundonald's recommendation, for the militia. Dundonald accused Fisher of scurrilous interference, and Fisher replied that the local militia regiment in his Eastern Townships constituency was being transformed into a "Tory political organization."[35] The brief uproar passed quickly and after the summer holiday, Laurier requested dissolution for new elections on November 3.

It was in this election that Laurier warmed up the theme that "the twentieth century belongs to Canada." He told audiences that some of them would live to see Canada achieve a population of sixty million. If the rate of growth of the first decade, 34 per cent, had been sustained, the population would have passed that target. Even if the decades in which there were to be world wars are put at increases of half that percentage, Canada would have reached one hundred million people at the end of the first decade of the twenty-first century, but its actual population in 2010 was one-third of that figure. Of course, Laurier could not foresee the collapse of the French-Canadian birthrate, nor the sharply rising prosperity of Central Europe in the last half of the twentieth century. His optimism was necessary to the imposition of his aggressive program and to inspirit his countrymen with a vision of a much stronger and more self-reliant nation than the one in which they lived, but it was bound to lead to some disappointments.

On October 18, Andrew Blair, the former railways minister, resigned as chairman of the railways commission, a position Laurier had given him as a sinecure and placebo, and repeated his opposition to the Grand Trunk extension plan and his entry into the election campaign in opposition to the government. There were briefly wild rumours that

Mackenzie and Mann had bought the newspaper *La Presse* from the ailing Trefflé Berthiaume to turn it against Laurier, and that secret arrangements had been made, should the Conservatives unseat the Liberals, for Blair to become Opposition leader Robert Borden's railways minister and make a sweetheart deal with Mackenzie and Mann over the corpse of Laurier's plan.

Borden, a man universally conceded to be honourable and upright, publicly warned anyone who had contributed to his party in expectation of special favours that his money would be refunded. Laurier warned Berthiaume that if *La Presse* were sold to Mackenzie and Mann, he would expose the affair as a betrayal of French Canada and an attempted sleazy purchase of a federal election, and he had Blair explicitly warned that he was flirting with his own ruination if he got into any of this. There was no sale of *La Presse*, Blair returned to his native New Brunswick and said nothing, and on November 3 the country re-elected Laurier with an increased majority. He won 137 MPs (up from 128) to 75 Conservatives. It was a loss to the Conservatives of four seats, including Borden's own constituency; he returned the next year in a by-election. The Liberals gained 0.6 per cent to take almost 51 per cent, and with 45.9 per cent the Conservatives lost 1.65 per cent.

On January 18, 1905, Hugh Graham, owner of the *Montreal Star*, who had patched together the arrangements between Berthiaume and Mackenzie and Mann, brought the parties back together at the Saint James Club in Montreal and the sale of *La Presse* was completed with a rider that the paper would continue to be a "generous" supporter of Sir Wilfrid Laurier.[36]

Five days after the Canadian election, Theodore Roosevelt won the most lopsided American presidential election since James Monroe ran unopposed for re-election in 1820. Roosevelt won 56 per cent of the vote to 38 per cent for his Democratic opponent, Judge Alton B. Parker, and his eighty-one-year-old running mate, Henry Gassaway Davis, and 336 Electoral College votes to 140. But on election night Roosevelt made an ill-advised statement he would soon regret, that he would not seek another term. At the end of 1904, Minto departed, not entirely lamented, and was replaced as governor general by Earl Grey, grandson of the reforming prime minister who passed the First Reform Act and abolished slavery and was a leading proponent of Catholic Emancipation, and nephew of the

Earl Grey who as colonial secretary from 1846 to 1852 was one of the decisive champions of responsible government. This was a promising pedigree.

6. Challenges to the Laurier Ascendancy, 1905–1910

The main work of the next session was the admission of Saskatchewan and Alberta as provinces, and the principal issue in this activity had to do with the schools. This had been a shabby tale since the original very fair agreement made by George-Étienne Cartier and George Brown to launch Confederation. In that arrangement, in the four founding provinces, Roman Catholics and Protestants, whether in a majority or minority, had the right to their own schools, supported by a school tax levied on the whole population. The original Manitoba compromise, in response to the first Riel uprising, closely followed that pattern, as did Mackenzie and Blake's statute for the North-West Territories in 1875. This last was effectively revoked by the Ordinances of the North-West Territories of 1890, as the Manitoba arrangements had been revoked by Sifton and Greenway in the mid-1890s. All that could be done for these two new provinces in their current capacities as territories was that, where the numbers of French-speaking students made it practical, French instruction was provided in the last hour of the school day, and the priest could take the last half of that hour for religious instruction, although such schools were provided for by a supplementary tax on parents who wished it, who were also obliged to pay the school tax for the Protestant system. With Clifford Sifton taking treatment for arthritis in a thermal spa at Mudlavia in Indiana, Laurier re-enlisted Henri Bourassa and set him to work with the apostolic visitor Monsignor Donato Sbaretti, former bishop of Havana. On February 21, Laurier introduced his bill, and when interrupted by a question from Dr. Thomas Sproule,* a Conservative Ontario MP and grand master and sovereign, and later

---

* Sproule (1843–1917) was an MP from 1878 to 1915 and then a senator. He opposed any non-British immigration and any toleration of Roman Catholic schools. He made Mackenzie Bowell, a former occupant of the same position in the Orange Order, seem an angelic champion of ecumenism. Canada was not as worldly a place as its two first re-elected prime ministers would indicate; Sproule would be Speaker of the House of Commons from 1911 to 1915.

world leader, of the Orange Order, Laurier put down his notes and confirmed that the bill addressed the issue of schools not as a matter of state and separate schools, but as a matter of national policy and Canadian patriotism: "Are we to tell [the French and the Catholics], now that Confederation is established, that the principle on which they consented to this arrangement is to be laid aside and that we are to ride roughshod over them? . . . I have never understood what objection there could be to a system of schools wherein, after secular matters have been attended to, the tenets of the religion of Christ, even with the divisions which exist among his followers, are allowed to be taught."[37]

It was a cathartic moment. Sir Wilfrid Laurier – who had fought many of the bishops over Manitoba and lobbied Pope Leo XIII directly and via his friend Cardinal Merry del Val to approve the climb-down in Manitoba so that he could accommodate Sifton and win the 1896 election; who was certainly a Roman Catholic but not at all a fervent, pious, or overly obedient one, and no slave to the episcopate – as the thrice-chosen head of the whole country, would not indulge the bigotry and debasement of Confederation again. The Roman Catholics among the nearly five hundred thousand people of Saskatchewan and Alberta were not numerous, but Laurier would not again disappoint sentiment in Quebec, which, as he had told Bourassa, ruled that province, not opinion. (Leo XIII had died in 1903 after a pontificate as distinguished as his predecessor Pius IX's had been tumultuous. Pius X was now pope and was on his way to sainthood.) Laurier effectively proposed a return to the original policy of Confederation in the schools of the new provinces.

Sifton returned from Mudlavia five days later and resigned from the ministry. An intense internecine struggle ensued in the government and the Liberal caucus. Laurier allowed others to carry the debate as he tested the waters to ascertain what was possible. William Fielding, the powerful and respected finance minister, returned from abroad and told Laurier he would resign too if the bill was not altered. Eventually, by mid-March, Sbaretti acknowledged that Laurier could not be asked to sacrifice his government and lose everything, and that some compromise was necessary. Sifton would not return to the government, and Laurier did not want him back, but Sifton and Solicitor General Charles Fitzpatrick, through intermediaries, worked out a compromise that was quite close to what Laurier and Sifton had worked out for Manitoba nine years before.

Sifton and even Fielding were not happy taking a backward step, any more than Laurier was from his initial position, but Laurier understood that he could go with this or face the disintegration of his government, and he presented the amended clause to the House on March 22, 1905. The balance of the debate was grim but civilized. Bourassa was relatively restrained but indicated, then and thereafter, that Quebeckers had only their own province as a country, "because we have no liberty elsewhere."[38] Unfortunately, he was not entirely inaccurate, and eventually Canada would pay a heavy price for this shabby and bigoted dismemberment of the rights assured in 1867 to the French and the Roman Catholics (which with massive immigration were decreasingly coextensive designations). Once again, Sir Wilfrid Laurier had done his best for his co-religionists and fellow francophones, but above all for the adherents to the original spirit of Canada, the continuators of Carleton and Baldwin and LaFontaine and Macdonald and Cartier, and even, in the supreme moment of his public life, of George Brown, of the double French and English majority. And once again, Laurier had pushed it as far as he could but made the compromise he had to make to preserve as much as possible of the ideal he was defending. Laurier lost Bourassa and Armand Lavergne, but held the rest of his bloc. The enlistment of Bourassa as an author of the original bill, and then his disembarkation, was a dangerous trajectory, and Laurier knew it. With Sifton and Bourassa, he had lost large chunks off both sides of his governing coalition, on a very secondary issue. It was more, not less, difficult than it had been to hold the ultramontanists and the Orangemen in one country in the times of Baldwin and LaFontaine and Macdonald and Cartier. And with such internal strains, it was no time to have a confrontation with either the British or the Americans, both of whom had substantial blocs of loyalists and emulators within Canada. Laurier had committed one of the few serious errors of his long career.

In 1906, Laurier had to cope with a great many challenges to the probity and decorum of his ministers. After ten years of government, his administration was less distinguished than it had been. Not only Mowat, Tarte, and Sifton, but Mulock and Fitzpatrick had gone, the last two to the bench. The able Alaska boundary commissioner, Allen

Aylesworth, initially replaced Mulock as postmaster general, but then replaced Fitzpatrick at justice, and the capable Rodolphe Lemieux took over the Post Office. Fielding, having been found responsible for some improper electoral practices, resigned but was immediately re-elected in a by-election and continued as minister of finance. Richard Cartwright, less obstreperous than in the past, continued at trade and commerce, but from the Senate. The railways minister, Henry Emmerson, was such a chronic alcoholic, he kept incapacitating himself with pratfalls and finally signed a pledge to Laurier that he would abstain completely, which carried him through the year. Robert Borden's cousin Frederick Borden, the luxuriantly moustachioed militia minister, was the subject of constant and intense rumours of a scandalous degree of philandering. Henri Bourassa found it all too tempting to resist and made an unctuous speech about moral decay in the House on March 26, 1907, but Laurier dismissed him as one who "gropes in the gutter . . . after insinuations and tittle-tattle."[39] Bourassa called for an initial inquiry, but "without submitting himself to the drudgery of obtaining evidence."[40] Emmerson fell off the wagon, and Laurier informed the governor general, Earl Grey, that he had to be removed, which he was, solemnly declaring to the House as he resigned, in response to an innuendo of Bourassa's, "I have never been in a hotel in Montreal with a woman of ill repute."[41] The effect of these problems was to put an increasingly heavy workload on the prime minister.[42] Laurier exercised his usual finesse in passing a Lord's Day Act that pleased Protestant Ontario but was actually written with the collaboration of Montreal's Roman Catholic archbishop, Paul Bruchési, who was concerned about the profanation of Sunday; and with the working class in mind, as, in the name of religiosity, it assured everyone a holiday. Laurier touched all the bases.

Laurier went to London in April 1907 for his third Colonial Conference. Much had changed. Chamberlain had split the Conservatives with his impassioned advocacy of an Imperial trade bloc that would not be stunted or inhibited by deferences to Germany and Belgium, and in 1905 Balfour had led the divided party to defeat at the hands of the Liberals, led by Sir Henry Campbell-Bannerman. The ministry was divided between converts to the virtues of Chamberlain's claims for Imperial preference and Gladstonian advocates of an ad hoc foreign policy and skepticism about the Empire. Chamberlain himself had suffered a severe stroke in 1906 and had gone from public life. The colonial secretary was Earl Elgin, son of the distinguished governor general who had been selected personally by Queen Victoria and who installed the Great Ministry of Baldwin, LaFontaine, and Hincks. His undersecretary was the thirty-one-year-old, three-term MP Winston Churchill, who was much in evidence and already clearly a coming figure. Churchill and Herbert Henry Asquith, chancellor of the exchequer, and David Lloyd George, the president of the Board of Trade, both also future prime ministers, were the strong men of the government. It was bound not to be as contentious as previous councils, not least because of Chamberlain's absence. The former leader of the Boer army and once the most wanted man in the British Empire, Louis Botha, absolved and knighted, attended as president of the new dominion the Union of South Africa, but the dean of all the government leaders present was the august prime minister of Canada. Laurier opened with the assertion that all the delegation heads were His Imperial Britannic Majesty's prime ministers and all should be of equal status and the meeting, effective at once, and that hereafter these meetings should be renamed the Imperial Conference, and this motion was adopted unanimously.

Laurier was impressed by the presence and cooperative participation of Botha, and thought it reflected generously on both sides in the late South African War; it was a reassuring demonstration of the liberality of the British practice of government. He and all the dominion leaders made the point that they could not subscribe to an Imperial parliament that would override the local parliaments, most of which, including Canada's, had not come quickly or easily to an exercise of any sovereign authority. Not much emphasized, but in the minds of the delegates, was the realization that the British plan was more of an extension of British control over autonomous dominions than a submission of all the participants to an international legislature. On Imperial preference, Laurier led discussion by saying that all the natural forces in North America were for trade on a north-south axis, and that successive Canadian governments for nearly a century had poured resources into canals and railways to superimpose an east-west trade route, that Canada was already largely excluded from the immensely rich market of the United States and could not go an inch or a farthing deeper into the abstention from non-Imperial markets. Sifton happened to be in England, and he collaborated closely with Laurier in the presentation of the trans-Canada connection between Great Britain and the Atlantic parts of the Empire and Australia and the Pacific. Obviously, the Suez Canal served as the link from Great Britain to India, but Laurier insisted on increased use of Canadian ports and railways for shipments between the south and far Pacific and the British Isles, the Caribbean, and West Africa.

The inevitable advocacy of a defence union, energetically advanced by Churchill (whose bumptious precocity annoyed the dominion leaders), did not meet with favour from any of the other countries, and the Australians, led by Prime Minister Alfred Deakin (1856–1919), were no longer quiescent in the British design effectively to subsume the military personnel and resources of the whole Empire into the forces of the United Kingdom to be disposed around the world according to the overall strategic desires of the British government. It must be said that given how incompetent and insensitive British colonial personnel often were, it is equally astonishing that they still had the effrontery to press such proposals and that they retained any loyalty at all from the dominions and colonies. The standards of British colonial administration were unlikely to have been more exalted and enlightened in other parts of the Empire than they were in Canada, where the Carletons, Bagots, and Elgins were outnumbered two or three to one by the Bond Heads, Colbornes, and Dalhousies. The council was a personal and policy success for Laurier, and there was progress, if it fell well short of the magic wand of Imperial solidarity behind the Mother Country that the new government was pursuing less single-mindedly than had its Conservative predecessor. Britain had recognized the rise of Japan as a potential useful counterweight to the Russians, who intermittently threatened them in India, and to the United States, and had concluded the Anglo-Japanese Alliance in 1902. This caused Japan to be seen throughout the Empire in a friendly light during the Russo-Japanese War of 1904 and 1905, which the Japanese won. Not so popular were the rising numbers of Japanese immigrants to Canada, and in Canada's absolutely first autonomous diplomatic act, Laurier sent his labour minister, Rodolphe Lemieux (who was also postmaster general), to Tokyo, where he negotiated "a gentlemen's agreement" limiting Japanese immigration to Canada of unskilled labour to four hundred people per year. It was a good but modest start on sovereignty.

Laurier spent a month on holiday in Italy and Switzerland and returned refreshed to Canada. Bourassa retired from the federal Parliament, resigned to barricading himself into Quebec, not a separatist exactly, but an isolationist. He was going to run against the Liberal government of Quebec, now and for many years to come in the strong and capable hands of Laurier's provincial ally and Honoré Mercier's son-in-law, Sir Lomer Gouin. Laurier told Bourassa, "I regret your going. We need a man in Ottawa like you, though I should not want two."[43] Bourassa stood for the Quebec Legislative Assembly in the Lower St. Lawrence district of Bellechasse, where he was mown down by the Gouin Liberal machine. This was not unexpected by Bourassa, but he declined offers from both Laurier and Borden to run unopposed for re-election to the federal Parliament. He would remain a prominent figure in Quebec for forty years, but would rarely be seen in Ottawa again. Lavergne followed Bourassa out of Ottawa and they were elected in the Quebec general election of 1908, Bourassa having the pleasure of personally defeating Gouin, who was, however, simultaneously elected in another district and easily re-elected province-wide as premier.

Bourassa began a campaign for a moral and intellectual awakening of Quebec, and returned from a visit to France appalled by the secularism of the republic and redoubled in his ardour as a Catholic intellectual. Israël Tarte had died on December 18, 1907, three weeks short of his sixtieth birthday. He had been one of the most unevenly talented political operators in Canadian history, of extremely high intelligence and acuity but of erratic judgment, always fragile integrity, and generally poor health.

Bourassa was absent for the tercentenary celebrations, from July 20 to August 1, 1908, of Champlain's founding of Quebec. The Prince of Wales was back in Canada, and the French sent the Marquis de Lévis and the Comte de Montcalm, both ostensibly good republicans now. Both Britain and France sent naval squadrons. They were now close allies in the Entente Cordiale, and with Russia, locking arms against the ever-rising Germany. The British speakers over-celebrated Wolfe; the French *tricouleurs* were a bit conspicuous for the pleasure of the British; and the French were too ostentatiously secular for the liking of the Roman Catholic primate of Canada, Quebec's archbishop, Cardinal Begin. The United States was distinguishedly represented by Roosevelt's vice president, Charles W. Fairbanks, the highest ranking incumbent American official ever to set foot in Canada. Laurier enjoyed it and was very generously received by the populace, and it was possible on those fine summer days to believe that he had secured enhanced international recognition for Canada and for French Canada.

It was time for another election, though there was no burning issue. Sifton ran again as a loyal supporter of Laurier. The prime minister launched his campaign at Sorel, Quebec, on September 5. His improvised theme was that he be allowed to finish his work, without much specificity about what that was. The gist of it became clear in Laurier's assertion at Montreal on September 23: "In 1896 Canada was hardly known in the United States or Europe. In 1908 Canada has become a star to which is directed the gaze of the civilized world. That is what we have done."[44] This was surely more than a century ahead of the facts and as endearingly egregious a piece of self-serving flim-flam and claptrap as anything Sir John Macdonald ever inflicted on a cheering audience, but it drew heavy applause and was not without a vigorous kernel of truth.

On October 26, 1908, Sir Wilfrid won his fourth consecutive term, tying Macdonald's record for consecutive victories (though Sir John had won two previous non-consecutive terms after Confederation and three times in the Province of Canada). It came out well in the breakdown of the constituencies, but there was clearly, as is inevitable in a democracy, a sense that it was time for a change. Borden was no spellbinder, but he was solid and impressive in his unpretentious way, and the government was getting tired and was carried exclusively by Laurier's prestige, suavity, and eloquence. The Liberals dropped four seats for a total of 133, the Conservatives gained ten with 85; the Liberals dropped two percentage points in the popular vote, to 48.9, and the Conservatives held their position at 45.9. It was a clear mandate, but far from a landslide, and at times there were signs that Laurier was starting to lose his touch. He had produced his education proposals for Alberta and Saskatchewan knowing that they would be explosive, as if he was seeking Sifton's resignation, but he must also have known he could not get them through. He seemed happy enough without Sifton, with his bigotry and humourless zeal and distracting ear trumpet, but then tried to seduce him into returning to cabinet when they were working together at the Colonial Conference trying to put over the "All Red Route" of Imperial communication across Canada between the Atlantic and Pacific. Sifton did not return to cabinet but stayed in the fold as a candidate, and it was clear when the election results were in that he was now an electoral liability in the West.

Time would prove that the most important of the many new faces elected in 1908 was that of William Lyon Mackenzie King, thirty-four, in York North, industrial consultant, and specialist in labour and welfare questions. Cautious and unprepossessing, his shadow would be long over the land and he would be much seen in the world the next forty years, most of them as the unlikely but craftily inexorable successor to Macdonald and Laurier. Laurier was disappointed in the election result and decided that it was time to retire. He made an appointment to see Grey and recommend that Fielding be invested as prime minister, but Fielding talked him out of it.[45]

Roosevelt had honoured his word and declined renomination, though he would certainly have been re-elected easily. He designated as his successor the capable Cincinnati lawyer, former federal judge, very successful governor of the Philippines, and war secretary William Howard Taft. Taft made it clear from the outset that he would pursue a more placid foreign policy than had Roosevelt (who had, however, won the Nobel Peace Prize by brokering the end of the Russo-Japanese War) and that he was interested in freeing trade with all the substantial trading partners of the United States. Taft and his family had a summer home at Murray Bay (La Malbaie), Quebec, and he knew Canada well and liked it. (Many years later, he laid the cornerstone of the Murray Bay Golf Club, on which he is referred to as "William Howard Taft, President, the Murray Bay Golf Club, President and Chief Justice, the United States of America.") A distinct uptick in Canadian-American relations seemed to impend.

The great issue in the first session of the new Parliament was the question of a Canadian navy, brought to the floor of the House by George Eulas Foster (1847–1931), a redoubtable Conservative veteran who would serve forty-five years in Parliament and in the cabinets of seven prime ministers. He was from New Brunswick, a professor of classics and an arch-Imperialist, who was only prevented from making a serious bid for the headship of his party by a questionable American marriage to his divorced housekeeper and an awkward role in the failure of a trust company. He is generally credited with originating the phrase, in reference to Salisbury's Great Britain, "splendid isolation." On March 29, 1909, Foster introduced a bill for a Canadian navy, the role of which was couched in moderate terms of protection of Canada's ocean shorelines and as appropriate to "the spirit of self-help and self-respect which alone befits a strong and growing people."[46] The Bourassa Québécois were strenuously opposed to any program of armaments, especially one that would project military forces as a navy could, as likely to involve Canada in European wars. The French Canadians had an even greater horror of such involvements than did the recent immigrants to Canada from Europe who had fled the oppression, poverty, and constant wars of the old continent. The French Canadians had no sense whatever of loyalty to France, now Britain's most intimate ally, as they felt that the French had simply abandoned them 150 years before and treated them as habitant *paysans* and *colons* ever since. Whatever condescensions English Canadians felt they had endured from the British were only slight and subtle compared to the vertiginous hauteur with which the French generally peered down their noses and directed their pretentiously inflected barbs at their long-lost cousins in Quebec. And Foster, who raised the issue, and the Imperialists who filled the ranks of the Conservative Party and were not unheard among the Liberals either, essentially wanted Canada to do its part and leaned to an outright contribution to Imperial defence as conceived and directed by the British without serious consideration of the wishes of the dominions.

Earlier in March, the British first lord of the admiralty, Reginald McKenna, had said that Germany was closing the gap on Britain in the pre-eminent warship the *Dreadnought* (named after the first such ship, which was a battleship with almost all its armament large guns of twelve-inch barrel diameter or more). McKenna said that if Britain's naval construction program was not stepped up, the two countries would be of equal strength in these capital ships and that Great Britain could not then assure its mastery of the sea lanes. This challenge to Britain's maritime supremacy was the first since that posed by the seventeenth-century

Dutch, if not the sixteenth-century Spanish, with a German program of battleship construction that aroused the entire British nation to demand immense budgets for their navy with rallying cries of "Two keels for one" (the demanded ratio of battleship construction) and "We want eight, and we won't wait!" This was the usual alarmism of defence ministers and nationalist public opinion, but there certainly was now a very serious challenge. Traditional battleships were around thirteen thousand to fifteen thousand tons and had four big guns, usually eleven- to thirteen-inch. The British built up a commanding lead in these ships with forty of them, to twelve German, twenty-five American, and fifteen French. *Dreadnought*, the brain-child of Admiral of the Fleet Lord (Jackie) Fisher, first sea lord from 1904 to 1910, was built in 1906 with ten twelve-inch guns and eighteen thousand tons, and immediately rendered other capital ships obsolete. Fisher (1841–1920) is generally reckoned one of the most important figures in the history of the Royal Navy, and his career in the navy spanned the era of wooden-hulled vessels with muzzle-loading cannon, to the aircraft carrier. When McKenna warned of a possible loss of British leadership, France had no dreadnoughts but projected twelve by 1914, and the United States had six and projected eight more by 1914. Germany had eight, to Great Britain's thirteen, and projected eleven by 1914. Spurred on by a national and Imperial determination to retain the sceptre of the seas, the British projected and built eighteen more. They grew larger, to between twenty-five thousand and thirty thousand tons, and the later ones had fourteen- and fifteen-inch guns. The British had also developed the battle cruiser, which had a dreadnought's size and guns but less armour and correspondingly greater speed. In 1909, the Germans had three such ships and projected three more, and the British had seven and projected two more. These vessels could make from twenty-five to over thirty knots and could run down smaller ships, but could not, because of their vulnerabilities, exchange fire with modern battleships, as would be demonstrated at the Battle of Jutland in 1915, when the British lost three of them to German gunnery (which was always very accurate), and again in 1941, when the great forty-two-thousand-ton battle cruiser *Hood* was blown up by the German battleship *Bismarck* at a range of sixteen thousand yards, leaving only three survivors in a crew of fifteen hundred. (The Japanese, Italians, Russians, and Austro-Hungarians also had sizeable fleets, but

Britain had alliances with France, Russia, and Japan; war was now unthinkable with the United States; and the French and British between them could assure the Mediterranean. The challenge was Germany in the North Sea and in the North Atlantic.) In sum, it was a serious threat, but the British were responding to it, and the diplomatic incompetence of the German emperor had confronted Germany with the threat of a two-front war with Russia and France on land (as neither was capable of challenging Germany alone) at the same time as fighting an uphill battle to gain parity or superiority at sea with Great Britain, which could be counted on to send heavy land reinforcements to France in the event of war on that front. The Triple Entente was apparently stronger than the Central Powers (Germany and Austria-Hungary), but it was tenuous and worrisome and the world was almost on a hair-trigger, as these alliances could bring one country into war after the other and plunge all Europe into conflict within a few days. Canada had had no experience of thinking in such terms, and no prominent native-born Canadian had had anything to do directly with combat in Europe since La Vérendrye fought at Malplaquet two hundred years before.

Laurier received Foster's resolution very cordially and said that he still fervently held that if Britain should be directly challenged, Canada must wholeheartedly support it, and in such event it would be his duty to "stump the country and endeavour to impress upon my fellow countrymen, especially my compatriots in the Province of Quebec, the conviction that the salvation of England is the salvation of our own country."[47] Laurier agreed with Foster and Borden on an amended resolution approving the "organization of a Canadian naval service in cooperation with and in close relation to the Imperial navy."[48] The resolution passed unanimously and all seemed settled in consensus. Laurier sent the minister of marine, Louis-Philippe Brodeur, and the minister of militia, Borden's cousin Frederick Borden, to London for the Imperial Defence Conference, where they fended off the inevitable British agitation for the construction of warships that could be instantly conscripted into the Royal Navy. They rejected this but asked for British Admiralty advice on the launch of the Canadian navy with an opening annual budget of three million dollars. The British, with no great grace, said they would think about it. Montreal's Archbishop Bruchési wrote Governor General Grey, "When the bell rings, we shall all go."[49] But it was not long before the consensus of the House of Commons began to fragment. There were denunciations of a "tin-pot navy" and demands for an outright grant of ships and money to Britain, as Borden's party rippled and wavered under him.

Even less satisfactory was the slow and costly progress of the Grand Trunk, which needed a further ten-million-dollar infusion in this session. Borden claimed that the whole enterprise would cost the country about $250 million in cash and in guaranties of bonds, which Laurier denied, and added that guaranties didn't particularly matter as long as they weren't called and didn't strain the country's credit. It would get worse.

In June, Laurier founded a Department of External Affairs, though of sub-cabinet rank, and entrusted the Ministry of Labour to the thirty-five-year-old William Lyon Mackenzie King. King was a pioneer in the field of labour relations, had written the Industrial Disputes Investigation Act of 1907, and had proved an extremely effective arbiter. He was an efficient civil servant and armed the Canadian government with one of the world's most advanced labour statistical services. He was a bleeding heart up to the point of never losing respect for the leading incumbent capitalists. Enigmatic, cold, and efficient, he was never likeable but never to be underestimated. King was a bachelor who was adored by his mother, William Lyon Mackenzie's daughter, and more than requited the regard; he was a talented, highly intelligent, but colourless idealist, distinctly moulded by calculation and opportunism.

King's ostensible analogue, Papineau's grandson Bourassa, was following exactly the opposite course, one at odds with the political establishment around the great and long-serving prime minister, to whom King was constantly trying to come closer and more helpfully. Bourassa's effort to destabilize Gouin had failed; Gouin denounced Bourassa and Lavergne in a powerful speech to the Legislative Assembly as men "who all their lives have thought only to hate and destroy. At Ottawa they worked only to destroy the men who undertook something for the country – Laurier, Brodeur, Lemieux, Fielding, Sifton." (The latter two were not popular in Quebec.[50]) Lavergne, always unpredictable, joined the militia and became a captain, even as he continued as Bourassa's sidekick; and Bourassa, frustrated at leading a political movement of his own and now forty-one, founded a nationalist newspaper, *Le Devoir*, on January 10, 1910. The descendants of the unsuccessful revolutionaries of 1837 would be the ultimate insider and the ultimate outsider of Canadian public life in the first half of what their venerable sponsor had announced as Canada's century.

Le Devoir, after the predictable launching pieties, opened fire on Laurier as the man who had sent troops to South Africa, abandoned the French and the Roman Catholics in the schools of Alberta and Saskatchewan, and now wished to create a navy, while he "veiled in golden clouds the betrayals, weaknesses, and dangers of his policy."[51] The day following this churlish tirade, January 12, Laurier presented his naval bill; a naval college and naval board were to be set up, and an entirely voluntary force in all circumstances was to be established. A fleet of five cruisers and six destroyers, a respectable opening force, would be created and would be entirely under the control of the Canadian government. It could be put at the disposal of His Majesty (that is, Great Britain), but only by act of the Canadian Parliament. The naval question reigned for several months, despite Grey's agitations, on orders from London, for Laurier to agree to American trade offers even before they were formally made. The British government was now incapable of thinking of any foreign policy issue but the great-power equation with Germany, and the United States was the only nation left that could really shift the balance. The British doubted that Italy would throw in with the Central Powers, who had so little to offer Italy; the Japanese couldn't influence the balance in Europe, important though they were in the far Pacific; and the Turks had faded. But, if it came to it, the Americans could be determining (as it did, and they were).

Laurier could not have been more clear that there was no open-ended commitment to Britain's wars, as there had not been in South Africa. The Quebec Conservative leader, Frederick Debartzch Monk (grandson of Louis Gugy, debunker of Papineau; it seemed everyone except Laurier in Canadian politics in this era was the grandson of some politician), echoed Bourassa's comments, which were that the bill was "a national capitulation . . . the gravest blow our autonomy has suffered since the origin of responsible government. . . . Let the notion occur to a Chamberlain [completely incapacitated], a Rhodes [dead], a Beers [a reference to the de Beers brothers, two Boer farmers who sold their land to Cecil Rhodes and never did anything that could have offended even Bourassa], to gold-seekers or opium merchants, of causing a conflict in South Africa or India, in the Mediterranean or the Persian Gulf, on the shores of the Baltic or the banks of the Black Sea, on the coasts of Japan or in the China Seas, we are involved, always and regardless, with our money and our blood."[52] This was rank demagogy, rabble-rousing rubbish that was an excavation in irresponsibility even for Bourassa.

Borden was wobbling under threat of his own imperialists and stuck to supporting Laurier's navy, but he expressed a preference for simply giving to the British Admiralty the cash that creating a navy would require. No war was imminent, Laurier was not in the slightest enfeebling the national interest, but Laurier was beset from both sides by fantastic imputations of an ambition to transform Canadian youth into British cannon fodder on one side, and of treacherous betrayal of the motherland on the other. This was Bourassa's refrain; the following year he harangued a large audience with his theory that Laurier and Borden were "only cowards and traitors. . . . I say that when a man [Laurier], whatever his personal qualities, so despises the confidence and love which a people has given him – such a man is more dangerous to his religion, his country, even to the British Crown than the worst of Orangemen."[53] It was hard to imagine that the mass of decent, sensible Canadians could be much swayed by such venomously bankrupt arguments. The naval bill passed on April 20, but the controversy was not over. And Bourassa could still be dangerous to Laurier, who was more dependent than ever on Quebec to provide him a majority in the country's Parliament.

7. Reciprocity, 1910–1911

Given the delicacy of relations with London, Laurier was especially sensitive to a possible improvement in relations with the United States. President Taft made very amicable noises, and a giant of three hundred pounds and a moderate jurist by background, he was a good deal less ferocious and opinionated than his predecessor. Fielding visited him in Washington in March 1910, and Taft explained that he disapproved of the tariff his Republican colleagues in Congress had recently legislated which imposed a 25 per cent duty on anything coming from a country that gave any other country a preferable tariff treatment to what it gave the United States. Canada did that under Imperial preference. Taft sought a plausible escape hatch, and after consultation Fielding proposed that a group of thirteen obscure items, such as prunes, on which Canada gave a preference to Britain and British possessions, be subject to preferential entry from the United States also. Taft happily and cordially agreed, and the super tariff was waived for Canada. Canada went a step further and made the thirteen items subject to free entry from all countries, and the U.S. secretary of state, Philander C. Knox, who had been Roosevelt's trust-busting attorney general, wrote Laurier expressing a desire for a broader tariff reduction between the countries. Taft and Knox coined the term "dollar diplomacy" and were, in foreign affairs, chiefly concerned with American commercial and trade interests.

King Edward VII, a talented and popular monarch, died on May 6, 1910, and was of course succeeded by the Duke York and Cornwall, who had twice visited Canada and who became King George V.

Mackenzie King deftly settled a Grand Trunk strike that threatened to delay or interrupt the prime minister's extensive tour in the West in the summer of 1910. King's meticulous report of his mediation spared no opportunity for self-praise, but Laurier had come to appreciate King's cunning and thoroughness, though "he still was not wholly sure of his tiresome little minister."[54] Laurier returned from the West to Montreal on September 9 to speak to the Eucharistic Congress, a great event in official Roman Catholic circles, where he and Bourassa would be rival attractions. There were a cardinal legate from Rome, large episcopal delegations from the United States and Europe, and five hundred thousand pilgrims. The Irish Roman Catholics, now quite numerous and stronger in Ontario than the French, led by Bishop Michael Francis Fallon of London, Ontario, advocated curtailing French-language rights and divided Catholic opinion in Canada. In Montreal, the Irish met in St. Patrick's Church and the French in Notre-Dame Church. Laurier arrived for lunch at the opulent home of Thomas Shaughnessy, president of Canadian Pacific, with the most senior foreign clergy who attended the congress. He went on to a reception at the Windsor Hotel given by the New York Catholic Society and then spoke at Notre-Dame in Place d'Armes. He was presented very respectfully by Bruchési and gave a cautious address that gave no offence to Protestants but no inspiration to Catholics either.

He was followed the next day by Archbishop Francis Bourne of Westminster, who rivalled in his blundering insensitivity the most inept of his secular countrymen who had intervened in Canada and said that Canadian Catholicism must not be linked to the French language, but as English-speaking co-religionists multiplied, by immigration and assimilation, it must rather be identified with the English language. What possessed him to say such a thing in the second largest and most Catholic French city in the world defies imagining. Two innocuous addresses followed, and then Bourassa had the chance of a lifetime. He both rose and stooped to it, delivering a paean to French Canada's service to Catholicism and its heroic history of defying the numbers and being the leading carrier of the flame of Roman Catholicism in all of North America: "We are only a handful, it is true; but in the school of Christ I did not learn to estimate right and moral forces by numbers and wealth. We are only a handful, but we count for what we are and we have the right to live. . . . Let us go to Calvary, and there on that little hill in Judea which was not very high in the world let us learn the lesson of tolerance and of true Christian charity."[55] That of course was almost the last cause that Bourassa was promoting, but it was a powerful address that electrified the masses of Quebec and seriously overshadowed Laurier's bland performance.

Laurier saw the dangers of Bourassa, but still had deep support in Quebec, unlike Conservative leader Borden, who could not control Monk (a disciple of Bourassa) and could not control his servile Britannophiles like Foster either. With the foreign bishops and the fervent pilgrims gone, Laurier returned to Montreal on October 10. He spoke to a large and admiring crowd and denounced the "Pharisee . . . defenders of a religion that no one attacks; who wield the holy water dispenser like a club, arrogate to themselves the monopoly of orthodoxy, who excommunicate those whose stature is greater than theirs; who have only hatred and envy as their motive and instinct, who insulted Cardinal Taschereau and made Chapleau's life bitter; those whom the people with their picturesque language described as 'Castors.'" These were fighting words, forcefully delivered and almost deliriously received.

Bourassa, a formidable intellectual snob, would be particularly outraged to be called a *Castor*, or beaver, the popular description of ignorant and reactionary Catholic bigots and know-nothings.[56]

Fielding's negotiations in Washington went better than he or Laurier
had dared, or had any reason, to hope. Taft proved completely congenial and full of genuine goodwill. The Americans were prepared to
allow free entry for Canadian agriculture and forest products, minerals,
and fish; tariffs on Canadian manufactures would be lowered appreciably; and all the United States asked was that Canadian tariffs be lowered
on American imports to the levels enjoyed by other countries. Fielding
broke new ground in what eventually became the widespread concept
of "anti-dumping" provisions. Taft was interested in giving American
consumers lower prices; he was not overly concerned with protection of
American agriculture and industry, which were both booming and
didn't need protection. On January 26, 1911, Fielding announced the
astonishing trade agreement to a House of Commons that was mainly
pleased and, for the rest, stunned. But as debate wore on, opposition
arose and gathered strength. Sifton, though he had accepted the chair
of Laurier's commission on natural resources, was against the agreement
and went over to the Opposition on the issue. Borden, though silent at
first, received the demurral of his Imperialist base, though Imperial preference was not affected. Such was the suspicion of the United States in
these circles that it was assumed something reprehensible must be
behind the Americans' sudden rush of apparent reasonableness. It was
claimed that this was starting down the slippery slope to commercial
union and annexation. The railways, led by Van Horne, were opposed,
and behind them the principal banking and financial interests. Sifton
attacked the reciprocity agreement in the House on February 28; he
even lamented that there would be a decline in the entry of U.S. capital
to build branch plants, as they would no longer be necessary, though
Canadian manufacturing tariffs were scarcely being adjusted at all.
Laurier spoke with great power and authority on March 7 and dismissed
all opposition as based on narrow self-interest or unjustified fear. That
analysis was almost certainly accurate, but unfortunately it affected a
very large and susceptible share of the population.

Laurier sailed for Britain on May 12 to attend the coronation of

George V and the attendant Imperial Conference. All went well, and more even than at Victoria's jubilee and Edward's coronation and the previous conference, Laurier was the eminent statesman of the British Empire. He was graciously received everywhere, and Asquith himself, now prime minister, agreed with him that it was time to bury Chamberlain's apparently almost imperishable notion of an Imperial legislative council. The countries were affiliated by the Crown but they were autonomous and were not puppets of Westminster. The Canadian prime minister returned to Quebec on July 10.

On the next day, he told a very large crowd on the Champ de Mars in Montreal, as Henry IV told his young followers at the Battle of Ivry, "Follow my white plume and you will find it always in the forefront of honour." Laurier believed that he could rout the unholy alliance of the foes and slanderers of his government and of his reciprocity agreement, and on July 29 he dissolved Parliament for an election on September 21. To get his side of the arrangement adopted, Taft had had to resort to the American manifest destiny infelicities of old about Canada becoming "only an adjunct to the United States." In a letter to Theodore Roosevelt published on April 25, Taft continued that reciprocity "would transfer all [of Canada's] important business to Chicago and New York, with their bank credits and everything else, and it would increase greatly the demand of Canada for our manufactures. I see this as an argument made against Reciprocity in Canada, and I think it is a good one."[57] And the Democratic Speaker of the House of Representatives, Beauchamp "Champ" Clark, of St. Louis, Missouri, announced that "We are preparing to annex Canada." Laurier's opponents naturally made great hay of this, but Laurier fought hard and energetically, and slathered his opponents as cowards and hypocrites. In Trois-Rivières on August 17, he recounted all that he had been accused of in English and French Canada, always opposite failings, over a public career of forty years since his first election campaign. In Ontario, he said that John A. Macdonald was the Moses of reciprocity who showed the country the Promised Land. "I am the Joshua who will lead the people to their goal."[58]

On September 19 in Montreal, Laurier's automobile was caught by a crowd dispersing from one of Bourassa's meetings. The young militants rocked and kicked the car and insulted the prime minister. Tory money was pouring in to support Bourassa, including a miraculous payment for tens of thousands of subscriptions to *Le Devoir*, thus reducing Bourassa to the indignity of paid hack of reactionary and protectionist English-Canadian finance. "O Canada" was reworded in a version that began "O Bourassa," and in a very brief foray to Ontario, Bourassa even spoke to the French Canadians at Sudbury. It had been an inexplicable tactical error for Laurier to arouse the hopes of Bourassa on Catholic schools in Alberta and Saskatchewan, losing Sifton and his like-minded followers, and then to reverse field and lose Bourassa and his large following. He seems briefly to have wearied of the inevitable Canadian compromise, and only rediscovered a taste for it after he had taken a lethal dose of the poison of sectarian strife. It was preposterous that Bourassa would be making common cause with the francophobic, ultra-Imperialist Orangemen of Ontario and the Anglo fat cats of English Montreal, but Laurier had suddenly allowed the Siftonian bigots to grasp hands with the ultramontanist crypto-separatist Zouaves.

On September 21, the Liberals lost 48 MPs, dropping from 133 seats to 85, and the Conservatives gained 47, rising from 85 to 132. The Liberals lost 3.1 per cent of the popular vote, descending to 45.8, and the Conservatives gained 2.3 to bring in 48.6 per cent. Laurier lost seven ministers in their own districts, including Fielding, Fisher, and King. The prime minister had not really renewed his government, had been reckless about the damage that Sifton and Bourassa could do at the fringes, had been overconfident after four consecutive victories and the negotiation of such a brilliant trade arrangement with the United States, and had gone to the country prematurely, as he could have waited up to two years before promulgating reciprocity, an issue that did require popular endorsement but could have been better prepared and presented. He should not have allowed his opponents to represent it as commercial union and the slippery slope to annexation when in fact Canadian tariffs were almost unaltered and Imperial preference was unaffected. He had had a winning issue with the navy but let it slip. For all his talent and suavity and courage, Laurier proved not to have entirely consistent political judgment. And he should have reflected on the fact that no democratic leader had ever won five consecutive terms as head of a national government (and none has since).

Although he lost control of the radical centre at the end, Laurier had held the country together through fifteen difficult years and vitally strengthened it with immense immigration and development. The population had grown by 40 per cent under his government, and the economic indices had advanced even more. Even in this election, he had won as many English-speaking votes outside Ontario, Manitoba, and British Columbia as had Borden. He had shown English Canada that a French and Roman Catholic leader could serve their interests well, and shown French Canadians that one of theirs could be accepted in English Canada. He had popularized a national interest of progress, goodwill, and confidence, embodied it in his own universally respected person, and greatly enhanced the standing of Canada in London, Washington, Paris, and Rome. He had been a leader of very high distinction. Although Laurier would surrender the government almost on the eve of his seventieth birthday, Gladstone and Disraeli had shown that great things could be done by democratic leaders in their seventies. His service to his country was, in some respects, still to achieve its greatest and noblest height.

8. Robert L. Borden and the Coming of the Great War, 1911–1914

Borden personally could not have been more gracious. He would not have his victory procession, on his return to Ottawa on September 24, in which a hundred men pulled his carriage with a network of ropes, go down Laurier Avenue, and he told Sir Wilfrid to take all the time he wanted before handing over. Laurier was magnificently dignified and unbowed in defeat and won, yet again, the admiration of all for his human qualities. Borden wrote admiringly in his memoirs of "Sir Wilfrid's . . . chivalrous and high-minded outlook and attitude."[59]

Borden's cabinet was, of necessity, unexciting. Bourassa had declined a place, and Lavergne declined without having been asked. George Foster was not acceptable to the monied Toronto interests as minister of finance, and he had to settle for trade and commerce, as Cartwright had before him. Thomas White took finance. Sam Hughes, at militia, was a human grenade with the pin pulled, and Frederick Monk at public works was scarcely less highly explosive. Borden would write of Hughes that he had "earned a promotion but I hesitated for some time because of his erratic temperament and his immense vanity. . . . [Hughes] frankly admitted his faults and told me that he realized his impulsiveness but that he would be more discreet in the future. However, discretion did not thereafter prove to be a prominent characteristic."[60] The young, at thirty-seven, Arthur Meighen of Manitoba was soon named solicitor general, while Laurier managed to find employment for his protégé Mackenzie King as head of the Liberal Party Information Office, a position well-suited to his talents as an inside fixer and schemer, as Meighen would prove a talented and articulate holder of his position. Meighen and King would be at each other's throats intermittently for more than thirty years. Monk was the senior party figure in Quebec, who had been the link with Bourassa and Lavergne. Bourassa had helped to elect most of the twenty-seven Quebec Conservatives, and Monk had to be given the customary French-Canadian patronage playpen of public works, but Borden was under no illusion that he was really in control of his Quebec colleagues. The grand leader of the Orange Lodge, Dr. Thomas Sproule, took his place as Speaker of the House of Commons (in which capacity his performance would be exemplarily gentlemanly).

In April 1912, Borden holidayed in New York City and Hot Springs, Virginia, from which place, in an illustration of the latest progress in communications, he spoke, as did President Taft from Washington, to a meeting of the American Press news cooperative at the Waldorf Astoria Hotel by telephone, and their remarks were conveyed with perfect clarity to all those attending by individual telephone receivers. Among those present were former Canadian resident Alexander Graham Bell (1847–1922), inventor of the telephone, and Thomas Edison (1847–1931), inventor of the electric light.[61] This was a subtle but profound change from forty years earlier, when James G. Blaine professed to find the presence of even one Canadian commissioner at the Washington Conference to be distasteful. Borden had an intense visit to London and Paris in July and August and made a good impression in both capitals. He was unaffected, forthright, and knew his mind, a respectful Empire man but clearly a patriotic Canadian, and never an overawed toady. He spoke at numerous banquets and weathered the sumptuous, liver-busting London circuit fatigued but unbowed, neither giddy, bumptious, or unnatural, a gracious, solid, colonial statesman, though there was little of the sly and entertaining Macdonald fox or the elegant Laurier showman about him. The French, including the premier, Raymond Poincaré (who would only relinquish that post to become president of the republic the following year), were pleasantly surprised that Borden could give an address in French, as he did at the Société France-Amérique, and Poincaré complimented him that his French was more comprehensible than that of his colleague, the postmaster general, Louis-Philippe Pelletier, who accompanied Borden in place of Monk.[62] This cultural gap was long a problem in France-Quebec relations, though it abated eventually as the quality of spoken French improved in Quebec and the French became more appreciative of French Canada's accomplishments and status as the second French entity in the world by most measurements.

Borden was impressed by Churchill as first lord of the admiralty, both by his energy and his high and quick intelligence. He found the prime minister, Asquith, urbane and convivial (Campbell-Bannerman had died in 1908), but was especially impressed by Lloyd George, now the chancellor, and Balfour, the Opposition leader, as gracious, charming, and very witty men. Of course, these four were all prime ministers at some point, and all would play important roles in the great dramas about to unfold. Churchill waxed very enthusiastic about the plan for a Canadian payment for three capital ships for the Royal Navy, and explained to Borden that this was a win-double, because it would not only make an important addition to the British battle fleet, but would not technically be British construction and might therefore avoid an escalation in the tensions with Germany. Borden records this in his memoirs without comment, but it is inconceivable that either man could have believed Germany would not consider any such step as the straightforward escalation of the naval arms race between the two empires that it would be.

This constituted a change in the British position of 1909, which had been to encourage Canada and Australia to build their own forces (even if in British shipyards) and use them to see off enemy surface commerce raiders, and if necessary merge them as required into the Royal Navy. The change reflected the increasing severity of the German challenge. Borden asked for both a private memorandum on the naval crisis and a publicly usable one that would smooth matters for diplomatic purposes but convey enough urgency to be useful to him in his own Parliament. Churchill complied, but allowed to close colleagues that it was challenging to run the gauntlet between admission that Britain was underprotected, or that Canada would be underprotected, all the while avoiding an outright imputation of impending treachery to Germany (though Churchill considered all three to be the case and told Borden that Germany could attack Great Britain at any time.)[63] Borden called it "the most irritating document from authority in Britain since the days of Lord North."[64]

While this issue raged in Canada, the United States had a tumultuous election, between three presidents. Theodore Roosevelt had been scandalized by what he thought were reprehensibly primitive measures in support of monopoly capitalism undertaken by his successor, President Taft, and was particularly outraged at Taft's comparative lack of interest in conservation. He entered the presidential primaries against his successor, and was generally successful, but was sandbagged by the old guard conservative members of the Republican Party, who assured the renomination of Taft. Roosevelt stalked out of the party, announcing, "We are at Armageddon and I fight for the Lord." He announced his candidacy at the head of the Progressive Party, and the governor of California, Hiram Johnson, ran with him as vice president. The Democrats had had a rending battle between three-time unsuccessful nominee and leader of the bimetallists (the broadening of the gold standard to include silver), the silver-tongued orator William Jennings Bryan of Nebraska; the Speaker of the House, Champ Clark of Missouri; and the reformist governor of New Jersey and distinguished former president of Princeton University, one of America's foremost educators and public intellectuals, Thomas Woodrow Wilson. Bryan, thrice previously denied the highest office by the voters, running third, withdrew and gave his support to Wilson, thus, given the Republican split, effectively anointing him to the great office that had so tenaciously escaped Bryan. Wilson won, Roosevelt came second, Taft eventually became the only person in the country's history to be both president and chief justice, and Bryan became secretary of state. Wilson was an anti-militarist and anti-imperialist, an intellectual anglophile, an expert on comparative government, and an admirer of the parliamentary system. A very promising era in trans-border relations seemed to be opening.

Robert Borden unveiled his naval program to the House of Commons on December 5, 1912. There would be thirty-five million dollars to pay for three British dreadnoughts, and the Canadian navy was scaled back to practically nothing. When he finished his presentation, he sat down abruptly, missed his chair, and sat heavily on the floor, breaking his spectacles, an awkward moment and unpromising augury.

"Oh, ye Tory jingoes," taunted Laurier. "You are ready to furnish admirals, rear admirals, commodores, captains, officers of all grades, plumes, feathers, and gold lace; but you leave it to England to supply the bone and sinews on board those ships. You say that these ships shall bear Canadian names. That will be the only thing Canadian about them. . . . You are ready to do anything except the fighting."[65] The program was the work of Winston Churchill, now thirty-eight. He promised "the largest and strongest ships of war which science can build or money supply," and was feted around Whitehall for a golden egg from the yokels in the great Dominion, which would employ thousands of British shipbuilders and fulfill the dreams of storybook Imperialism: overseas cash for British industry, defence, and deployment in the great European game. The gloating was premature.

The satanic alliance with Bourassa came apart with Ontario's Regulation 17 in 1912, which rolled the teaching of French back to the first years of public education and in heavily French districts only. Monk resigned from the cabinet in September, dissatisfied with the indifference of the government to the French Canadians and alarmed at what was shaping up as the government's naval policy. Monk had sought a plebiscite on the issue of a contribution to the Royal Navy of thirty-five million dollars, but the English-Canadian ministers, representing staunchly the parliamentary rather than the referendary tradition, declined. It was not a bad idea of Monk's, as the government would have carried the plebiscite; it would have lost the plebiscite in Quebec, where both Laurier and Bourassa would have opposed it, but Quebec having made its statement, and the country overall having voted for the government, Laurier would have found it difficult to use the Liberal majority in the Senate to block it. This, as Borden had tried to explain to the British on his visit, was a distinct possibility. Monk retired from the House in March and died in May 1913, aged only fifty-eight. He had been a fairly able man but had been completely overshadowed by Laurier and Bourassa, and even by Lavergne and Tarte.

Borden made a good argument, technically, that Britain was seriously challenged and that the British Empire was not a great land power and that the entire defence of it rested on the naval forces. The British, and thus the whole Empire, were severely challenged, and according to Borden, Canada would squander precious time and resources building a department of the navy from the ground up with the personnel and physical plant of a new ministry; it was better to inject money directly for maximum and swiftest possible assistance to the common effort. The problem with this was that it completely ignored the national aspect. Borden, no less than Laurier and Macdonald, proclaimed at every opportunity the growth, predestined greatness, and rising strength of Canada, yet his idea of defence, for a country that was not itself under any possible threat from anyone, as long as the Americans did not become neurotic (which was almost unthinkable under Woodrow Wilson), was simply to pay a form of filial tribute for Britain's use against Germany. It was a course of action that lacked grandeur in itself, and which directly assaulted ingrained French-Canadian dislike for what Quebec considered needless involvement in Europe's quarrels. And it did nothing for Canada, no navy, no sailors, no employment. Canada was going to have to have a navy, a serious shipbuilding industry (at which it had made a promising start nearly 250 years before in Jean Talon's time), and a defence ministry eventually; why not now? Borden told the House of Commons, "Almost unaided, the Motherland, not for herself alone, but for us as well, is sustaining the burden of a vital imperial duty and confronting an overmastering necessity of national existence. Bringing the best assistance that we may in the urgency of the moment, we come thus to her aid, in token of our determination to . . . defend on sea as well as on land our flag, our honour, and our heritage."[66]

This was pretty heavy going; no one could doubt that Britain was not reciprocally quite so committed to the interests of Canada. There were and had always been, as has often been recorded in this narrative, distinct differences in the interests of Canada and Great Britain, and Borden was proposing a course that would pretend that there were no such differences. At least if Canada built her own navy, as the British had asked until recently and Laurier had proposed, it would be a card in Canada's hand and not anyone else's. Once the thirty-five million dollars were paid out to the British Exchequer, British shipyards would get the orders, the British Admiralty would deploy the ships, and Canada would have nothing beyond the lighthouses on her shores. It was a conceptually vulnerable position that in some ways replicated Laurier's error with the Alberta and Saskatchewan schools: Borden was completely writing off Quebec. But Laurier had blundered into the schools question of the new provinces in his fourth term as head of the government; Borden had been prime minister for only eighteen months. He had never had the Quebec nationalists in his camp other than for reasons of their rank opportunism, and he would never get them back now. He could have assuaged the imperialists in Canada by modifying Laurier's bill a little, and produced the ships almost as quickly. Churchill and Asquith and Balfour had no votes in Canada, and on this issue Britain did not have much bargaining power; the British were in a challenged position and they should be grateful for any assistance Canada furnished them. Borden was advised by the new governor general, the Duke of Connaught (third son of Queen Victoria, brother of Edward VII, and uncle of King George V), that the king was highly pleased with his bill and his supporting address.[67] This was fine, but how did the king, the duke, and the prime minister propose to get this divisive measure through the Senate? Laurier, in his reply to Borden, was clearly aiming at forcing a dissolution, confident that he would take everything in Quebec on this issue and convince English Canadians that it was no betrayal of Britain for Canada to build her own navy.

The debate dragged on, and Borden, who habitually suffered from carbuncles on his neck in stressful times, finally enforced closure in the House of Commons. But on April 29, 1913, Laurier had his Senate leader, Sir George Ross, advise the government leader in the Senate, James Lougheed, that the Liberals would not allow the Navy Bill to pass the Senate unless either it was simply added to Laurier's Navy Act so that the thirty-five million dollars would be contributed to a Canadian navy, or, in addition to the contribution to the Royal Navy, twenty million dollars was voted to the Canadian navy. This was reasonable, as well as good politics. Borden and Laurier could both have what they wanted. In his memoirs, Borden claims that Laurier would not support either of these compromises,[68] but that cannot be accurate. It had, as great questions often do in Canada when they are not carefully managed in a way that builds the centre of the controversy to adequate strength to prevail over the opposite ends of the issue, degenerated into a farcical impasse. Borden claimed an unlimited international emergency but floor-managed a divisive bill in a way that assured he could not win in Parliament and could not win if he took the issue to the country. He told the House of Commons on June 6, 1913, a year after his formative trip to London, that Canada "expected to take over and pay for the three ships which Great Britain proposed to lay down in substitution for those which Canada would have provided under our Bill."[69] This too was moonshine, a dream, though not a bad improvisation in response to Laurier on the day of prorogation. The Canadian Parliament adjourned to January 15, 1914, as Europe sleepwalked toward the most terrible war in human history (though not 1 per cent of it would be fought at sea).

In the debate on the speech from the throne, Borden quoted the German newspaper *Hamburger Nachrichten* rejoicing at the decision of the Canadian Senate, and then Parliament debated what Borden described in his memoirs as "the importation of Hindus into Canada," and all seemed oppressively normal as the House adjourned for the summer.

The prime minister went to Muskoka for a month's holiday on July 23, but was induced by an increasingly urgent series of messages from Ottawa to return to the capital as war clouds suddenly darkened in Europe. Crown Prince Franz Ferdinand of Austria was assassinated in Sarajevo, Bosnia, on June 28, 1914, by an anarchist, Gavrilo Princip, who was acting for the Pan-Slavic group Black Hand. The Serbian government seemed to have been slightly aware of the conspiracy, though it was not directly involved in it. The German emperor gave Austria-Hungary, under their alliance, what he called "a blank cheque" to deal with Serbia as it wished. The world was generally sympathetic to the Habsburg dynasty on the tragedy it had suffered, as Vienna prepared its stance toward Serbia, which was a state sponsored by Russia in the Romanov ambition to lead the Slavic world opposite its ancient Austrian and Turkish enemies. The French president, Poincaré, and premier, René Viviani, visited St. Petersburg from July 20 to 23 and urged the Russian government not to yield to excessive Austro-Hungarian bullying of Serbia. As soon as the French leaders had left the Russian capital, Austria served an ultimatum on Serbia demanding suppression of anti-Austrian organizations and publications, dismissal of officials hostile to Austria, prosecution of accessories to the plot, sanitization of school curricula, and abject apologies. Serbia responded in conciliatory terms but was fuzzy in some areas and declined the requirement of prosecutions without suitable evidence.

The British foreign secretary, Sir Edward Grey, proposed an international conference on Austrian-Serbian problems, which France and Russia accepted but Vienna, with German support, declined as unsuitable in the circumstances of the affront to the Austro-Hungarian Empire's honour. Vienna and Berlin believed the czar was bluffing in his support of the Serbs, and Austria-Hungary declared war on Serbia on July 28. France urged a strong response on Russia, and Germany offered non-violation of France and Belgium if Britain remained neutral. Britain declined, as Germany was effectively seeking to pummel Russia to its own unlimited satisfaction. Between July 29 and August 3, all five of the great European powers (excepting Italy), were ratcheting up toward general mobilization while tossing out conditional offers of de-escalation. It was a game of chicken between governments in varying states of gross irresponsibility.

The bellicose and juvenile German emperor, Kaiser Wilhelm II, pushed Austria. France, unshakeably bent on recovering Alsace and Lorraine, encouraged Russian resistance as long as it was confident of British support, and Britain refused to be finessed or intimidated by Germany but urged caution on everyone. Russia ordered general mobilization and then reduced it to mobilization against Austria-Hungary only. Germany demanded cessation of preparations for war on the Russo-German frontier, and the czar rejected his cousin, the German emperor's intervention and reverted to full mobilization. Germany declared war on Russia on August 1. Belgium declined to give Germany free passage through its territory, and Germany invaded Belgium and declared war on France on August 3. Britain declared war on Germany on August 4 in fidelity both to its Entente Cordiale with France and its guaranty of Belgium, which went back to Palmerston's co-establishment of that country in 1830. Austria-Hungary declared war on Russia on August 6. Italy announced her neutrality, and a few weeks later Turkey joined the Central Powers against the Allies. Almost all the leaders of the five great powers were like children playing with dynamite, with no idea of what they were starting. It would be as complete a state of war as had existed in Napoleon's time, but with mass armies and a new concept, developed in the American Civil War, of total war, engaging the whole population.

The German and Russian emperors, Victoria's grandsons and absolute monarchs, exchanged telegrams in English threatening war and signed "Willie" and "Nicky." Wilhelm pushed the eighty-four-year-old Franz Joseph of Austria ahead of him, and the czar manipulated the Serbs. The French would take war to recover Alsace and Lorraine and their place as the greatest power in Europe, but knew they could not do it without the Russians and British. The British did not want war but could not tolerate Germany overrunning France again, or even Belgium. Wilhelm allowed war to break out in the east, dragging Germany into war with Russia. He had second thoughts at one point about assaulting the French and provoking the British, and told Helmuth von Moltke, nephew of the victor of the Franco-Prussian War and chief of the German general staff, to suspend mobilization, and Moltke responded that it was too late. The emperor replied, "That is not the answer your uncle would have given me." That was undoubtedly true, but nor would the kaiser's father or grandfather have accepted any such answer. Wilhelm had great energy and ambition, reasonable intelligence, but erratic judgment and was not brave. The combination was catastrophic in the most powerful national leader in Europe. Nicholas II was better natured but even less intelligent and was an unperceptive vacillator. Franz Joseph was the ancient, semi-comatose nursemaid for the last chapter of the seven-hundred-year Habsburg dynasty in Vienna. The British and French, as democracies, had more responsive and alert leaders, but Asquith and Viviani, though worthy liberal statesmen, were not of the metal to deal with the earth-shaking crisis that was coming and would eventually be replaced by war leaders in the highest traditions of both of Canada's storied founding nations. Sir Edward Grey, sober and detached, said, as lamps were lit around Whitehall in the last hours of the British ultimatum to Germany, "The lights are going out all over Europe; we shall not see it again in our lifetime."

In Ottawa, censorship and export controls were imposed, bank notes were declared full tender to prevent gold hoarding, and expansion of the money supply and detention of foreign ships were permitted. Borden, in the name of the governor general, who was on a summer tour in the West, exchanged peppy messages with the British government and confirmed, on his own authority, that if Britain was at war, so was Canada. The apocalypse had come.

* * *

Parliament opened on August 18. The governor general (like his staff) was in khaki as he delivered the speech from the throne. The Duke of Connaught initially imagined that he really was the commander of Canadian forces, and Borden had to apprise him gently of the constitutional fact that he was no more the commander in Canada than his nephew the king was in Great Britain. As Borden graciously allowed in his memoirs,

> Sir Wilfrid was as eloquent as usual. . . . He said: "There is in Canada but one mind and one heart . . . all Canadians stand behind the Mother Country, conscious and proud that she has engaged in this war, not from any selfish motive, for any purpose of aggrandisement, but to maintain untarnished the honour of her name, to fulfil her obligations to her allies, to maintain her treaty obligations, and to save civilization from the unbridled lust of conquest and domination. . . .
>
> "It is an additional source of pride to us that Britain did not seek this war. . . . It is one of the noblest pages of the history of England that she never drew the sword until every means had been exhausted to secure and to keep an honourable peace.
>
> "If my words can be heard beyond the walls of this House in the province from which I come, among the men whose blood flows in my own veins, I should like them to remember that in taking their place today in the ranks of the Canadian army to fight for the cause of the allied nations, a double honour rests upon them. The very cause for which they are called upon to fight is to them doubly sacred."[70]

Borden responded and thanked the leader of the Opposition for his eloquent words and the spirit which prompted them. In a quintessentially Canadian touch that was also typical of Borden, profoundly decent and thoughtful man that he was, he went out of his way to praise the German people: "They are not naturally a warlike people, although unfortunately they are dominated at this time by a military autocracy. No one can overestimate what civilization and the world owe to Germany. In literature, science, art and philosophy, in almost every department of human knowledge and activity, they have stood in the very forefront of the world's advancement." He praised the half-million German Canadians: "No one would . . . desire to utter one word . . . which would wound the self-respect or hurt the feelings of any of our fellow citizens of German descent." Borden continued, "While we are now upborne by the exaltation and enthusiasm which comes in the first days of a national crisis, so great that it moves the hearts of all men, we must not forget that days may come when our patience, our endurance and our fortitude will be tried to the utmost. In those days, let us see to it that no heart grows faint and that no courage be found wanting."[71]

These were the statesmanlike utterances of decent, realistic, and strong men, leaders of a mature country in a world crisis of unprecedented gravity, easily comparable, in the quality of their reflections and the clarity with which they were expressed, with analogous personalities in the ancient great powers of Europe.

9. Canada and the Great War, 1914–1917

The German war plan, devised by Field Marshal Alfred von Schlieffen, the former chief of the German general staff, was to advance in overwhelming strength along the Channel coast of Belgium and France ("Let the last man on the right touch the Channel with his sleeve") and encircle Paris from the north and the west, severing Britain from France and France from its capital. Von Schlieffen was an authority on the Punic Wars and wrote a treatise on Hannibal's encirclement of the Romans at Cannae, which was emulated in his plan for France and was somewhat revived in the great German blitzkrieg in France a generation later. The French plan, Plan XVII, devised by their commander, (future) Marshal Joseph Joffre, was to advance into the former provinces of Alsace and Lorraine, which had been lost in 1871, and then into Germany. The Germans aimed at a quick knockout of France while holding the Russians in the east with relatively light forces. Although von Schlieffen's last words allegedly were "Keep the right wing strong," his successor,

Moltke, weakened the right wing and revised the German plan to move south before Paris and cut it off from the main French armies by moving to the east of Paris. After about two weeks of the war it was clear that the Germans were moving to the west of the French and the French attack in Alsace and Lorraine was repulsed. Recognizing the great danger in which France now was, Joffre imperturbably discarded the plan he had worked on for twenty years and made a hasty but orderly retreat toward Paris, which would be defended to the last man. Moltke considered a French recovery impossible by the first week in September, and even detached a few divisions to be sent to Russia. The Germans arrived on the Marne, just thirty miles north and east of Paris and were suddenly attacked by French armies totalling over a million men from the north, west, and south on September 5, and though the Germans had nearly one and a half million men, they were caught off balance, and in six days of very heavy fighting, in which nearly five hundred thousand casualties were taken by the two sides combined, and the French were reinforced by one hundred thousand British and by the Paris militia sent forward in six hundred requisitioned Paris taxis, the Germans were forced to fall back forty miles. The armies then extended their fronts to the English Channel and the Swiss border and settled into more than four years of horribly bloody trench warfare where the advantage was with the defence and attacks were in the face of massed machine gun and artillery fire on both sides. There would be decisive fighting on the Russian and Turkish fronts, but in the greatest theatre, France, bloodletting would be without precedent and beyond imagination. The first Battle of the Marne was a ghastly prefiguring of the courage and sacrifice to come.

The initial Canadian Expeditionary Force of twenty thousand was organized by Sam Hughes, who was, as Borden informed him, "beset by two unceasing enemies. Expecting a revelation, he was intensely disappointed when I told him that they were his tongue and his pen."[72] The Canadian division sailed from the Gaspé on October 3 in a heavily escorted convoy and made a safe passage to Plymouth. "Hughes delivered [and later published] a flamboyant and magniloquent address to the troops, based apparently on Napoleon's famous address to the Army of Italy. It did not enhance his prestige and indeed excited no little mirth in various quarters."[73] Rumours shortly arose and persisted that cronies of Hughes were milking defence procurement contracts and Borden set Solicitor General Arthur Meighen to look into it. Two more of Borden's French-Canadian ministers resigned, Louis-Philippe Pelletier and W.B. Nantel. Pelletier, who had replaced Monk, blamed his departure on "a swelling of the feet."[74]

On April 22, 1915, the Germans attacked the Canadians at Ypres and introduced their latest weapon, chlorine gas. Two battalions were virtually wiped out, and three-quarters of the Princess Patricia's Canadian Light Infantry were killed, but the Canadians fought on in the most unbearable conditions and held until British and French reinforcements relieved them. The action cost the lives of over six thousand men and brought universal commendations, including from King George V, and great recognition for Canada in the media of the world and from all the allied governments.

Canadian war production steadily stoked up, and recruitment continued to be good, although it was clear by mid-1915 that it was likely to be a long war and that it was a relentless struggle with very heavy casualties on a narrow front. In June 1915, Borden sailed for Britain from New York, though on a Canadian ship. The great British liner *Lusitania* had been torpedoed and sunk by a German submarine on May 7 off the coast of Ireland with the loss of 1,198 lives, including 124 Americans. President Wilson demanded an apology, reparations, and an assurance from the Germans that they would desist from unrestricted submarine warfare. The Germans tried to justify the sinking by claiming that the *Lusitania* was armed (it wasn't) and that it carried contraband. There was a small number of rifles on board, but that was not a significant purpose for the voyage of one of the world's greatest ships, and Wilson made further demands on the Germans that evidently carried the implicit threat of war. The Germans backed down and renounced unrestricted submarine warfare, but Wilson's secretary of state, William Jennings Bryan, considered the German policy not greatly more provoking than the British practice of searching ships on the high seas and blockading German ports and resigned. On a more positive note for the Allies, Italy accepted Anglo-French promises of a generous carve-out of Austro-Hungarian territory and entered the war on the side of the Allies on May 22, 1915. Borden was naturally received with great respect and sincere gratitude in Britain, especially by the king, on July 13 and again on July 28. Borden had set himself the goal of seeing every single wounded Canadian serviceman in British and French hospitals. He did not quite succeed in that but visited fifty-two hospitals, almost entirely unpublicized, and his solicitude was warmly appreciated. He met with the ninety-four-year-old Sir Charles Tupper, still very sensible, and with two influential Canadians who were British MPs, Max Aitken (later Lord Beaverbrook) and the future British prime minister Andrew Bonar Law. He agreed with the former British ambassador in Washington, the well-respected Lord Bryce, that after the war there would either be a common foreign policy in which the dominions would be seriously consulted, or each would have its own foreign policy.

In the horrible stresses of war, it was becoming clear that Canada, in particular, was a fully sovereign state that could no longer be a subject of British tutelage or considered by the United States a tentative or derivative British suzerainty. Borden met with Lloyd George, now the minister of munitions, who outlined to Borden his plans for an Imperial Munitions Board which coordinated all production of ordinance in the Empire, and to which Canada made a very sizeable contribution. The chairman of the Bank of Commerce, the National Trust Company, and the Simpsons department store chain, Joseph Flavelle (1858–1939) proved an exceptionally efficient director of munitions production in Canada.

Borden returned to Canada in September, and after extensive discussion and correspondence with Laurier, it was agreed to extend the term of Parliament from September 1916 by a year, subject to further deferral. Borden was always careful to speak in both official languages wherever it was appropriate; his French was accented but comprehensible and reasonably fluent, and he always referred to "our two great founding races." He didn't know much about Quebec politically, but was not at all offensive to French sensibilities in his own personality. Connaught, who had considerably less understanding of the French Canadians than Borden did, had urged him to censure Le Devoir at one point earlier in the year, but Borden pointed out that that was exactly what Bourassa would wish and that the British press had been much more obstreperous during the South African War.

In his address to the country on New Year's Eve 1915, Borden expressed the intention of increasing the Canadian forces – which had sent a second contingent and now had about 60,000 men overseas – to

500,000. Between September 1914 and October 1915, 171 new infantry battalions were formed, as well as many other units, including naval forces. In Canada's population of eight million, it was astonishing that about 500,000 did volunteer, including 234,000 infantry – though from July 1916 to October 1917, fewer than 3,000 men went overseas as volunteer infantry. But there was a great variety of other forces, including forestry, signals, and medical units, navy, and the new flying corps. Unemployment had dried up by 1915, and defence industries employed ever-larger numbers of people. Federal government expenses tripled to almost $600 million from 1913 to 1917, and Thomas White, the rather unimaginative finance minister, was running deficits of up to half the spending budgets, though he did, starting in 1916, retroactively tax supplementary war profits. The London financial markets were absorbed by British needs and New York was usurious, so, almost by accident, Canada started to finance itself and backed into Victory bond drives. It was hoped that $150 million would be raised, but more than $500 million came in on the first try, and then twice as much again as the war continued. Canada was suddenly a sophisticated and self-sufficient financial market.

In January 1916, an eight-month campaign by 570,000 British, French, Australian, New Zealand, Newfoundland, and Indian troops to crack open the Dardanelles and knock Turkey out of the war had been repulsed by 315,000 Turks led by their future reforming president Mustafa Kemal Atatürk. Each side took about 250,000 casualties, and it temporarily derailed the career of Winston Churchill, who was demoted from the Admiralty to the non-portfolio of chancellor of the Duchy of Lancaster. It was, in retrospect, a poor idea, poorly executed, and the thirty divisions involved could have been better used in France. Fortunately, no Canadians were involved, but it did not raise dominion confidence in the British high command. From February 17 to 20, the Australian prime minister, William "Billy" Hughes, visited Ottawa and had very cordial discussions with Borden and Laurier and Connaught. He agreed with the Canadian political leaders, and said so in subsequent weeks when he went on to London, that the dominions must have their own foreign policy. Any thought of the dominions as colonies had already been buried with their valorous volunteers who had died in France and elsewhere.

For most of 1916, from February 21 almost to Christmas, the supreme battle of the Western Front raged at Verdun in northeastern France. German armies totalling 1,250,000 men attacked the military centre of Verdun, surrounded and honeycombed with forts, including Douaumont, allegedly the greatest single fortress in the world. It was entirely a French-German contest, and each side lost approximately 350,000 dead and about 200,000 wounded, the greatest battle in the history of the world. The French were cut down to a single supply road, and there were some desertions, but the defence was stabilized by General Henri-Philippe Pétain and at the end of the year the Germans disengaged. Whole villages were destroyed, a vast acreage was deforested and pockmarked with a lunar devastation of artillery craters. The ground was covered with the dead for miles around, and when the scene was cleaned up after the battle, the remains of 180,000 French soldiers were consolidated in one eerily majestic site, the Douaumont ossuary, on the height of land over the battlefield.

While the Battle of Verdun was raging, as a diversion the British and Canadians and Australians, and then the French as well, launched an offensive on the Somme. It lasted from July 1 until November 18 and was fought by 1,200,000 Allied soldiers against 1,375,000 Germans, and although fewer men were killed than at Verdun, the total casualties were higher, about 624,000 Allied soldiers and 450,000 Germans. The British took 60,000 casualties on July 1 alone, and the overall result was, like everything on this front, inconclusive. By early 1917, Canada had endured 25,000 dead and 45,000 wounded.

Canada sent a third division to France in 1915, and in January 1916 announced the imminent departure of a fourth. These were not large numbers by German or French standards, but Canada was not a large or close country, and these were volunteers who had acquired and would retain a reputation as first class soldiers, and in this increasingly desperate struggle every increment of military strength helped.

On February 3, 1916, the Parliament Buildings in Ottawa very inconveniently burned down, killing two visitors (who had dined with Sir Wilfrid and Lady Laurier the night before) and three staff members. The prime minister and most of the ministers and MPs had to flee for their lives. Apparently, the fire was started by a lighted cigar butt igniting waste paper in a basket, which spread to curtains and to the

Canadian Involvement in the First World War

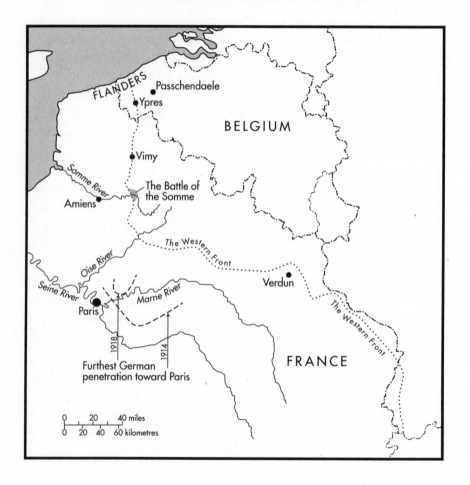

often-varnished panelled walls, which took like tinder. Parliament sat for a time in the Victoria Memorial Museum (now the Canadian Museum of Nature).

The greatest naval battle in the history of the world, up to that time, occurred on May 31 and June 1, 1916, at Jutland, off the coasts of Norway and Denmark, when the German High Seas Fleet, seeking to draw out and destroy a large part of the British Home Fleet, and thus to eliminate the British numerical advantage, found itself facing the main units of the British Grand Fleet. The German navy, commanded by Grand Admiral Reinhard Scheer, consisting of sixteen battleships, five battle cruisers, six pre-dreadnoughts, eleven cruisers, and sixty-one torpedo boats, encountered the main battle fleet of the Royal Navy, commanded by Admiral Sir John Jellicoe, consisting of twenty-eight battleships, nine battle cruisers, eight armoured cruisers, twenty-six cruisers, and seventy-eight destroyers. The weaknesses of the battle cruiser design where the enemy's gunfire was accurate, as it was with both navies, was demonstrated with the loss of three of these ships by the British and one by the Germans. (The British battle cruiser commander, Admiral Sir David Beatty, famously said as he watched one of the battle cruisers blow up, "Something is wrong with our bloody ships today.") The British also lost three armoured cruisers and eight destroyers, and the Germans one pre-dreadnought battleship, four cruisers, and five torpedo boats. The British suffered 113,000 tons sunk, 6,094 men killed, and 851 men wounded or captured, to 62,300 tons sunk for the Germans, 2,551 men killed, and 507 wounded. Germany had apparently won on the day, but they retired and escaped from the British through minefields and their navy did not put to sea again. The British blockade continued. This was the exposé of the strategic idiocy of the German emperor. It was the construction of the German navy that had driven Britain out of isolation and a friendly disposition to Germany and into the arms of the French and Russians. Two indecisive days, a few hours in fact, of exchanging fire with the British navy was the upshot of this vast naval competition and the hair-trigger alliance that led to this terrible hecatomb of a war. Rarely has human folly been so vividly and tragically depicted as in the history of the kaiser's naval enthusiasm and its consequences.

The controversy over Sir Sam Hughes's handling of defence contracts, and his erratic nature generally, agitated him to wild outbursts, including an unacceptably impudent letter to Borden, who fired him on November 9, 1916, to the relief of almost every affected party on both sides of the Atlantic and all political parties. Borden, accompanied by one of his Alberta MPs, Richard B. Bennett, set out on a tour to encourage recruiting, starting in Quebec. Calls for conscription, nearly two and a half years into the war, were starting to be heard, and the implications of such a step were bound to be extremely serious. In his memoirs, Borden kindly opines, "The Canadian of French descent is essentially a most desirable and useful citizen. He is devout, industrious, hard-working and frugal," and so forth. The lack of any great desire to help the metropolitan French was partly ascribed to Borden's belief that "the Quebec peasant was sometimes told that the sufferings of the French people were just retribution for the unholy spoliation and humiliation of the [Roman Catholic] Church in France."[75] It is a wonder that a government leader who wrote even after the fact of one-third of his countrymen as if they resided on the far side of the moon was so successful labouring under such unselfconscious delusions. Borden was playing with political high explosives.

In November, Woodrow Wilson, on the slogan "He kept us out of war," was narrowly re-elected president of the United States over the Republican nominee, former New York governor, and Supreme Court justice Charles Evans Hughes. In December 1916, the British cabinet concluded that the direction of the war was inadequately efficient and Asquith was pushed out as leader of the Liberal-Conservative coalition. David Lloyd George took his place with the support of the Conservative and Labour parties, but with most Liberals leaving government with Asquith. A war cabinet was set up composed of Lloyd George, Lord Curzon as leader of the House of Lords, Arthur Henderson as head of the Labour Party, Lord Milner as a troubleshooter, and Bonar Law as chancellor of the exchequer. The Conservative colonial secretary, Walter Long, wrote Borden, assuring him that he should not be disconcerted at his own absence from the war cabinet, as it implied no non-recognition of the vital role of the dominions, and so on. An emergency Imperial War Conference was called by the new prime minister in London for late February 1917.

On February 1, Wilhelm II made the most catastrophic strategic error of anyone in the world between the invasion of Russia in 1812 and the Japanese attack on the United States in 1941 when he announced unrestricted submarine warfare. German submarines would attack and sink neutral shipping on the high seas. In practice, this meant the merchant flag vessels of the United States and was tantamount to a declaration of war on that country. At last, the finely calibrated balance of the Triple Entente and the Central Powers was about to be disrupted in the Western Allies' favour by the suicidal misjudgment of the German emperor. His blunder is even more noteworthy because it preceded by only six weeks the collapse of the czarist government and the end of the three hundred years of the Romanov dynasty. A moderate and reforming provisional government headed by Alexander Kerensky was set up in Russia, with the Bolsheviks under Vladimir Ilyich Lenin in sinister opposition, and the country continued unsteadily in the war, but its continued participation was doubtful. There was initial rejoicing in the West that the often heavy-handed autocracy of the czars had been replaced by a democratic system, but the intolerable strain and blood-shed of the terrible world conflict was clearly winding up to a climax. If Germany had not provoked the United States it could certainly have got a favourable peace. Even without having to combat the Russians, who could not and did not continue in the war much longer, Germany might not have been able to win decisively in the West. The French, British, and Germans were all exhausted, though France had borne the greatest burden of all, both as a percentage of casualties among its population and in the extent of its territory that had been pulverized by the violence of war.

By late February 1917, Lloyd George had wrought a revolution in Empire relations. Britain was *primus inter pares* at the meetings, but the dominions were of equal stature, as Laurier had proposed in 1897, and India was represented by the Maharajah of Bikaner. Borden was very impressed with Lloyd George and even more by the South African representative, Field Marshal Jan Smuts, who fifteen years before had been on the other side and led the Boer militia. Borden's friend Billy Hughes, of Australia, was present, and Borden, with Smuts, Hughes, and the New Zealand and Newfoundland premiers, and the Indian representative and the secretary of state for India, Austen Chamberlain, son of the late Imperial firebrand, agreed a resolution, which Lloyd George and his government approved, confirming the autonomous status of the dominions.* On Borden's motion and Smuts's second, their rather pro-lix resolution was unanimously adopted at the first meeting of the Imperial War Cabinet, on March 2.

The deterioration in German-American relations proceeded apace while Lloyd George was holding his meetings, and the imminence of American entry into the war greatly cheered the group. To add to the Germans' misjudgments, the foreign minister, Alfred Zimmerman, had sent a telegram to the German minister in Mexico suggesting that he propose to the Mexican government that if Germany and the United States went to war against each other, Germany would assist Mexico in regaining the territory lost to the Americans in the Mexican-American War. Wilson had intervened ineffectually in Mexico after faction heads in the Mexican Civil War, especially Pancho Villa, had raided across the border into New Mexico. The British intercepted Zimmerman's message and happily gave it to the United States, and Wilson made it public.† President Wilson delivered his war message on April 2 at the Capitol, and it remains one of the great state papers of U.S. history. He galvanized the nation and electrified the whole world by his vision, elo-quence, and erudition: "The world must be made safe for democracy . . . the right is more precious than peace. . . . To such a task we can dedicate our lives and our fortunes, everything that we are and everything that we have, with the pride of those who know that the day has come when America is privileged to spend her blood and her might for the principles that gave her birth and happiness and the peace which she has trea-sured. God helping her, she can do no other." Life and meaning and purpose were imparted, at this very late date, to the unspeakable carnage in which tens of thousands died every few days, on all sides, for years, to move an army commander's headquarters a few thousand metres closer to the opposing army's capital.

In other respects, 1917 would be a difficult year for the Allies, even compared to those that had preceded it. The Germans sank 881,000 tons

---

* There had been periodic revivals of discussion of Newfoundland joining Canada; it came close in 1895 and was back as an idea just before the war. The time would come, but not until after another war.

† Some discussions to settle some of the Mexican violence had taken place at Niagara Falls, Ontario, but the Canadian government was only involved as a facilitator.

of Allied shipping in March. The French offensive in Champagne in April, the British and Canadian offensive in Flanders from June to November, and the Russian offensive of July had all failed, and the Austro-Hungarians, reinforced by the Germans, almost knocked the Italians out of the war at Caporetto, north of Venice, in the late autumn, where the Italians lost 650,000 men in two weeks. The British and French had to send reinforcements to the Italians, cutting short the Passchendaele campaign, which between August and November occupied about fifty divisions on each side and claimed at least 250,000 casualties on each side, including nearly 17,000 Canadians. The Canadians, in another much admired battlefield performance, ultimately captured the western part of the town of Passchendaele itself. But by late 1917, American soldiers, raw but healthy and high-spirited, were arriving in France at the rate of 200,000 a month. Germany would have to defeat the French in their anticipated offensive of the spring of 1918 or they would be overwhelmed by the end of the year. Wilson raised the U.S. Army from 200,000 to over four million men in eighteen months, and built the navy up to over 500,000 men.

From April 9 to 12, 1917, all four Canadian divisions, with the British on their left and the French on their right, attacked the main German position overlooking the Douai plain, next to Vimy Ridge. General Sir Julian Byng knew how to prepare for the offensive; a large model of Vimy Ridge had been built and the Canadian soldiers made familiar with its topography. Captured German artillery was used to train Canadians how to operate captured German field pieces, as it would be impossible to drag up Canadian artillery. A chemistry professor from McGill University, Colonel Andrew McNaughton, developed a system of counter-fire based on location of German guns from their flash and sound. The Canadian divisions moved in unison right behind a sweep of artillery fire that had continued for several days and cleared the ridge after four days of intensive combat. It was a great Canadian victory that brought warm congratulations from senior officials of all the Western Allies. At this point, Canada had graduated to a new level of successful nationhood scarcely recognizable from the condescensions of James G. Blaine twenty-six years before, or even the threat of force on the Alaska boundary fourteen years before. Canada was deputy leader of the Empire, Great Britain's premier ally and respected associate in the Great War of the United Kingdom, the United States, and France. There could be no further question of the legitimacy or permanence of the country opposite the great world; its struggles now would be within itself. The Imperial War Cabinet and Imperial Conference wound up on May 2, and when Borden returned to Canada on May 14, he wrote in his diary, on seeing again the vast St. Lawrence, "Northern lights . . . were most beautiful. The majestic river seemed to typify my country's future, strong, deep, wide, and mighty."[76] Perhaps, but not at once or without further incident.

10. Unlimited Emergency, 1917–1918

Borden returned convinced that conscription was necessary and announced this to Parliament. The core of his position was in the excerpt from his statement to the House of Commons: "All citizens are liable to military service for the defence of their country, and I conceive that the battle for Canadian liberty and autonomy is being fought today on the plains of France and Belgium. . . . If this war should end in defeat, Canada, in all the years to come, would be under the shadow of German military domination." This, objectively, was not true. There was certainly an argument to be made for conscription, but the very virtue and unique heroism of the dominion efforts in the Great War were that volunteers went overseas for a cause that was one of principle and affiliation and was not based on any threat to their own countries. Whatever happened in Europe, German domination of Canada was not in the offing. In times easily and not so distantly recalled, the domination of Canada by the United States was quite conceivable, but no one was fighting against that in Europe, such threat as there had ever been of that had passed, and no matter how gallant the Canadian forces, and they were very brave and very professional, they could not have stopped a serious American military assault at any time since the end of the American Civil War (and still could not). A large number of Canadians, including the great majority of French Canadians, had never seen Canadian participation in the war as a defence of Canada itself, though certainly of values Canada shared and favoured.

The Military Service Bill, which aimed to raise between fifty thousand and one hundred thousand more members of the armed forces, was introduced on June 11, 1917. Borden pre-emptively denied in the most vehement terms that it was prompted by the British, or that the matter had ever been discussed with the British government. ("No more absolute falsehood was ever uttered by human lips. If there had been any suggestion from them, I . . . would not have tolerated it."[77]) He told Parliament, "It has been said of this Bill that it will induce disunion, discord, and strife and that it will paralyze the national effort. . . . Why should strife be induced by the application of a principle which was adopted at the very inception of Confederation? . . . I am not so much concerned for the day when this Bill becomes law, as for the day when these men [overseas] return if it is rejected." The debate continued from June 18 to July 6. Laurier disputed that the Militia Act authorized conscription for any reason except the defence of Canada itself (which was almost undoubtedly accurate). "Naturally [Laurier] used, with his accustomed adroitness and eloquence, the statements made by me in the earlier parts of the war that the government had no intention of enforcing compulsory military service," Borden later wrote.[78] The second reading of the bill was voted on at 5 a.m. on July 6. Borden gained slightly more English-speaking Liberals than Laurier gained Quebec Conservatives, but the division in the country was stark.

Laurier's position was that the government could impose conscription but only after a referendum on the issue, or a general election, and that imposing it without either was morally and legally ultra vires to Parliament. Borden had offered, and continued to offer, coalition government with equal numbers of ministers from both parties, apart from the post of prime minister. Laurier declined to join a coalition for the purpose of facilitating conscription, said that this was not what he had subscribed to when he approved extending the life of the existing Parliament, and made it clear he would not extend it again. He also made it clear in private conversations with Borden (and these were eminently courteous throughout, both leaders being gentlemen in all matters) that he expected the Conservatives would win an election on the issue of conscription; they would carry English Canada but lose Quebec and the French districts in New Brunswick, Ontario, and Manitoba, but Laurier would keep Bourassa at bay. Laurier thought conscription a mistake on all counts, but if it was going to come, Borden would have to put it across for his own political account and the party of opposition would at least be an unambiguously federalist party and not Bourassa and his crypto-separatist seducers.

In Borden's respectful words,

> Sir Wilfrid Laurier arose, indomitable as ever, with his back against the wall: "I find myself . . . estranged from friends who were just as near and dear to me as my own brothers. . . . Every one of my honourable friends knows that I have not tried to impose my views upon any of my followers. . . . I have my conscience and they have theirs; but the situation shows that we are face to face with a cleavage which, unless it is checked, may rend and tear Canada down to its root." He said that he had been invited to join a coalition with no statement that conscription was intended, and accused the government of deceiving the House. "They did not consult me [on conscription] then they were kind enough to ask me to carry on what they had [secretly] devised. As in the play of children, they asked me: 'Close your eyes and open your mouth and swallow.' I refused. . . . I oppose this Bill because . . . it is an obstacle and a bar to that union of heart and soul without which it is impossible to hope that this Confederation will attain the aims and ends that were had in view when Confederation was effected. All my life I have fought coercion; all my life I have promoted union; and the inspiration that led me to that course shall be my guide at all times, so long as there is a breath left in me."[79]

Arthur Meighen, now Borden's chief lieutenant (as Ernest Lapointe was now Laurier's), gave a rather pettifogging reply, and Borden excused himself from giving Laurier notice of it because "in the stress of Parliamentary activities and under the strain of our war labours, there was no opportunity to discuss it with him."[80] Borden could not have imagined that posterity would accept that he was too busy to discuss conscription with the leader of the Liberal Party for the last thirty years, half of them as prime minister. There were further measures to assure the right of servicemen at the front to vote (who could be assumed to support the conscriptionist party, though it would be unfair to impute that motive to the government for going to such lengths, and Laurier refrained from doing so). Laurier did oppose a ragged voting act that gave some women, especially the wives of members of the armed forces, the right to vote, but denied it to the descendants of nationalities with which Canada was at war. In a fine flourish, the leader of the Opposition called it "a retrograde and German measure." Cloture was imposed, and clear and very courteous and not overly lengthy letters were exchanged, for publication, by the leaders and released at once. Laurier was consistent that he could not join a coalition that would then propose conscription, and could not join one after the imposition of conscription, but that as long as an election was held on the issue, which he said as early as May 25 the government would win, he believed that Quebec would obey the law, and he would urge that course.

Borden wrote of Laurier, then seventy-seven, that "if he had been ten or fifteen years younger, I am confident that he would have entered the proposed coalition. . . . I am convinced that he underrated his influence and that Quebec would have followed him."[81] He credited Laurier with a patriotic distrust of Bourassa but thought Laurier exaggerated Bourassa's influence. That was a bit rich considering that if it were not for Bourassa's ability to stir up Quebec, Borden would probably not have been elected in 1911. Borden, in his memoirs, published twenty years later, apparently thought that he had had the better of the argument, but he had not, other than in the short term that Laurier had foreseen. He got his conscription, but it did not influence the outcome of the war; the Americans were providing all the fresh troops the Allies would need. With best will, but an almost Wilhelmine disregard for the political consequences, Borden put great strain on the country and handed Quebec to the Liberals, and with it thirteen of the next seventeen elections after the vote about to be held, not counting one that produced an unclear result: there would be fifty-one years of Liberal government between 1921 and 1984.

All through July and August, Borden engaged in intensive discussion to form a union (coalition) government, to the point that from September 4 to 9, he "was confined to the house by nervous prostration."[82] It was mid-October before Borden was able to organize a coalition with nine Liberals led by Newton Rowell of Ontario as president of the Privy Council. Parliament was dissolved (Connaught had left in 1916 and been replaced by the Duke of Devonshire, but the governor general's role in these matters was diminishing), and the election took place on December 17, with little suspense about the result. The campaign had not been overly tumultuous; conscription was almost the only issue, though the Liberals criticized some of Hughes's blunders and liberties in defence procurement.

Borden graciously almost failed to refer to the accuracy of his predictions that the Grand Trunk Railway would be a difficult financial proposition. The government had agreed to pick up six hundred thousand treasury shares for a price to be settled by arbitration, but after taking account of a government cleanup of twenty-five million dollars' worth of loans and debts. In wartime, the accounts did not look so disquieting. On December 17, for a Parliament expanded from 221 to 235 constituencies, the Conservative-Liberal coalition raised their numbers from 132 conservatives in 1911 to 153, and their vote from 48.5 per cent for the Conservatives in 1911 to 56.9 per cent for the coalition candidates. Sir Wilfrid Laurier's Liberals lost only 3 seats to emerge with 82, and won 38.8 per cent of the vote, down from 45.8 per cent. It was certainly a clear mandate for Borden, but Laurier had taken every predominantly French district in Quebec and held a respectable number of constituencies elsewhere, actually winning in Prince Edward Island and running well in the prime minister's home province of Nova Scotia, though Sir Robert Borden was returned safely enough in his home district. The nationalist opposition had not tried to sideswipe Laurier, and when the conscription issue passed and normalcy returned, the Liberals seemed likely to regain their previous competitive position in English Canada, and also to retain Quebec for a long time, as they did. The issues of Catholic school funding in Ontario, the navy, and conscription sank the Conservative Party in Quebec for two whole generations. Borden did produce legislation giving full suffrage to women (though this would not apply to Quebec until 1940). Canada was relatively advanced in these matters, and there was no significant resistance to women's rights. There had been municipal voting rights for women and Married Women's

Property acts from the 1880s. "In Canada no such feminist movement as later developed in England [and the United States] could get under way, simply because there was not the requisite resistance to it."[83]

The Bolshevik Revolution led by Lenin chased out Kerensky on November 8, 1917, wound down the war effort, and Trotsky negotiated a Carthaginian peace with Germany at Brest Litovsk on March 3, 1918. France, as the ultimate trial approached, installed its greatest and fiercest political leader, Georges Clemenceau, on November 24, 1917. Clemenceau was a physician, a former schoolteacher in the United States when a fugitive from Napoleon III (his first wife was an American), a veteran of the upheavals after the Paris Commune, a mayor of Montmartre, the editor who published Émile Zola's defence of Captain Dreyfus, a cultural eminence, and a former prime minister and member of the National Assembly and Senate for more than thirty years before he was invested with practically unlimited authority to win the war. He was seventy-six and universally known as "the Tiger." The advantage was with the Allies unless the Germans could score a quick knockout before the Americans were very numerous in France. The French general, soon marshal, Ferdinand Foch, was named supreme Allied commander on the Western Front. He was a soldier intellectual of Bergsonian élan and immoveable determination, and was equal to the task of matching wits and wills with the German commanders, Field Marshals Paul von Hindenburg and Erich Ludendorff. As a cadet writing his graduating examinations at the military school in Metz in 1871, Foch learned from the celebratory booming of German guns that Metz had become a city of the German empire. It had been his dream for forty-seven years to restore Metz to France, and now that was his formal, and in his view, his sacred, mission. And with the sly and efficient Welsh shaman Lloyd George, the gigantic intellect and forceful executive Wilson, and now the ferocious Clemenceau, the leadership gap in favour of the Western Allies over the often hare-brained kaiser would be decisive, if the imminent German lunge could be contained even for a few months.

Woodrow Wilson presented to Congress on January 8, 1918, what became known as the Fourteen Points. It was a world-shaking charter for a new postwar order: open and openly negotiated covenants of peace;

absolute freedom of the seas; tariff reductions and equality of trade; reduction of national armaments to the point required for domestic security; impartial adjustment of all colonial claims with equal weight to the native people and colonizing powers; evacuation of Russia by foreign forces and her self-determination;* evacuation of Belgium, Serbia, Romania, and Montenegro by foreign forces; restoration of Alsace-Lorraine to France; access to the sea for Serbia and the opening of the Dardanelles; self-determination for the peoples governed by Turkey, but a secure and sovereign Turkey; an independent Poland with access to the sea; and a general association of nations on the basis of an equality of rights for all nations regardless of size and strength.

Borden had a very satisfactory visit to Washington at the end of February, where he was graciously received by President Wilson, Secretary of the Treasury William G. McAdoo (who was Wilson's son-in-law), Secretary of State Robert Lansing, Secretary of War Newton Baker, and the War Industries Board chairman, financier Bernard Baruch, as well as the British ambassador, Lord Reading. A good deal was achieved in integrating defence production arrangements and assuring conservation of some of Canada's $500 million annual wartime balance-of-payments deficit with the United States. The bilateral and trilateral relations between the countries were now, in the light of the common cause, on a completely new footing, and the patronization of Canada as a virtual foundling was over at last.

There was severe anti-conscription rioting in Quebec City starting on March 29, which the municipal police ignored, and which included the destruction of the registrar's office. Four thousand troops were dispatched, although only one thousand were deployed, but on April 1 fire was exchanged and several soldiers were seriously wounded and four rioters killed. What amounted to martial law was imposed by order-in-council. There were some anti-French reflections by private members in Parliament (by Conservatives Colonel John Allister Currie and Henry Herbert Stevens), and Laurier replied judiciously, supporting the imposition of the law but strenuously rebutting what amounted to ethnic slurs from Currie

---

* Russia had been invaded in the Far East and through the White Sea by a variety of foreigners for a variety of motives, as the civil war between the Bolsheviks and White Russians proceeded.

and Stevens. Borden followed and rebuked his own caucus members in unambiguous strictures. It is generally believed that there were about thirty-five thousand French-Canadian volunteers in the armed forces. There was a perceptible gap in war enthusiasm between French and English Canadians, but that is neither surprising nor discreditable.[84]

The Germans launched their supreme play on March 21, 1918, with an attack in great strength toward Amiens, at the hinge of the British and French armies, with the goal of wheeling northward and forcing the British into the sea. Foch reinforced the British, who held, although the force of the attack pushed them back up to forty miles. The Germans renewed their offensive with another very heavy blow on April 9, west of Lille, but still aiming to crack open the Allied line, and wheel north to the sea. The British commander, Field Marshal Sir Douglas Haig, had prepared a deeper defensive position and held the German advance to seventeen miles, and those at heavy cost. The Germans renewed the offensive on May 27, to the south of Amiens, now at last marching on Paris, from whose gates they had been beaten back nearly four years before. They captured Soissons and closed to within forty miles of the French capital, but the French lines did not break at any point, and every inch of ground was contested with extreme tenacity. The German offensive resumed with intense attacks of massed infantry, heavily supported by artillery, from June 9 to 15, east and north of Paris, against fanatical French resistance. Paris, as the symbol of freedom and of the great alliance of the French and English-speaking peoples, and at the hour of the historic coruscation of French culture and civilization and martial bravery, had become in the minds of much of the world almost a holy city of light. The Germans reached the Marne again, less than thirty-five miles from the Arc de Triomphe, at the end of June, as Foch declared, "We will fight before Paris, within Paris, and beyond Paris,"* and demanded of all units to hold their ground at any cost; that is, to the last man. The supreme climax of the Great War had come at last.

The Second Battle of the Marne was fought between July 15 and August 6 by fifty-eight Allied divisions (forty-four of them French, eight

---

* Clemenceau is sometimes credited with originating the statement, but it expressed the views of both men, and by now, of almost all their countrymen.

American, four British, two Italian) and fifty-two German divisions, about one million soldiers and over a thousand heavy guns on each side. The Allies had several hundred tanks, and both sides had hundreds of primitive warplanes. The Allied lines held, and Foch counterattacked; the Germans had no more reserves and gradually gave way. The main salient that had threatened Paris between Soissons and Rheims was eliminated by August 6. Paris was safe; the tide was turned. The Allies had taken 133,000 casualties (95,000 French, 17,000 British, 12,000 American, and 9,000 Italians from only two divisions), but had inflicted 160,000 German casualties. The German offensive was broken, and Foch became marshal of France. The British, Canadian, and Belgian armies, supported by 50,000 Americans, surged forward on August 8 and pushed the Germans back from Amiens, and Foch ordered a series of offensives along the entire front, from the English Channel to the Swiss border, to win the war.

11. Victory, 1918

From late May to mid-August, Borden was in London and Paris. He was feted by all the leading figures of the British government from the king down, and met Clemenceau twice. He did forcefully object, supported by some of the other dominion figures, to incompetent British commanders, an opinion to which Lloyd George was generally receptive, but Borden seemed almost oblivious to the Second Battle of the Marne, apart from being up until midnight on the evening of July 14 with Lloyd George, Smuts, Milner, and Field Marshal Sir Henry Wilson, and agreeing to tell Haig that if Foch's order to place four divisions at the disposition of the French army near Rheims put the British Army in jeopardy, he didn't have to obey the order. The order was not pressed by Foch and was overtaken by events. Borden undoubtedly gave a good account of himself by the simple display of the qualities which came naturally to him: intelligent, good-humoured, articulate, and consistent support of the collective goal. But the Imperial War Cabinet obviously was more of a sop to the dominions than a decision-making group. The British talent for marshalling their Imperial flock had evolved from the peremptory to the collegially discursive, progress certainly, but the dominion leaders were still to a large degree being snowed with an illusion of collective authority. The outcome of one of the decisive battles of world history Borden records in his memoirs, drawing from his diary, thus: "In the morning [of August 4, 1918] we received confirmation of the German retreat to the Aisne."[85] Admittedly, Canadian units were not engaged in the battle, and Canada was providing about 6 per cent of the forces under Foch's command as generalissimo of the Allied armies.

Borden spent a great deal of time in commendable visits to troops and military hospitals and giving undoubtedly well-formulated speeches at overpowering banquets and luncheons in historic places, but seems to have had minimal contact with those who were actually running the war. Canada had at least graduated to the point where it was received with courtesy and measured gratitude, but it was not at the top table. The one useful agreement for Canada to come from these sessions was the agreement that postwar emigration from the United Kingdom would be encouraged to go to Empire destinations. (Macdonald had agitated for that in visits to London thirty-five years before and been ignored by Gladstone.) After a last visit to 10 Downing Street and a luncheon given by the mighty press proprietor Lord Northcliffe, owner of the *Times* and the *Daily Mail*, Borden embarked on August 17 on the *Mauretania*, the illustrious holder of the Blue Riband for fastest transatlantic passage and sister of the tragic *Lusitania*, escorted by five destroyers. On board, he made the cordial acquaintance of aid administrator and future president of the United States Herbert C. Hoover.

In an address to twelve thousand people at the Canadian National Exhibition in Toronto on September 2, Sir Robert Borden certainly spoke for most of the country when he spoke of his pride at the dispatch of 414,000 Canadian soldiers to Europe to fight "the Huns," as he called them for the first time publicly. He concluded,

> Fiends incarnate would shrink from the nameless outrages by which [Germany] has deliberately degraded the name of humanity; they would blush for the barbarous and brutal cynicism with which she has scorned and broken every decent convention of public law and international usage. . . . There is no desire to crush or humiliate the German people but they have stamped themselves as

brutal, uncivilized, and barbarous; and they must prove themselves regenerate before they can be received again on equal terms within the world's commonwealth of decent nations. And this is the message I bring you from the Canadian army. Stand fast to your purpose; abide the issue and vindicate the cause of justice and humanity.[86]

As wartime oratory goes, this was well above average and was well-received.

Foch's great offensive was irresistible. By early November, the Allies were at a ragged line from Brussels to Namur, Luxembourg, Metz, and Strasbourg, and the Germans had been cleared from Alsace and half of Lorraine. The Italians, reinforced by eleven French and British divisions, had decisively defeated the Austro-Hungarians at Vittorio Veneto in late October. The Central Powers disintegrated. Bulgaria surrendered on September 30, and on October 2, a new German government, through the Swiss, asked President Wilson, as did Austria on October 7, for an armistice based on his Fourteen Points. The French and the British explained that they had not been consulted about the Fourteen Points and did not agree with all of them, and Wilson declined to deal with the kaiser, who he believed did not represent the German people. The German navy, ungrateful although most of its surface ships had in the last four years spent only two days at war, mutinied at Kiel on November 3; Austria-Hungary surrendered on November 4; a revolt broke out in Bavaria on November 7; the kaiser abdicated and fled to the Netherlands on November 9; and a German republic was declared on November 11. It was only twenty years since the death of Bismarck.

After Wilson threatened Lloyd George, Clemenceau, and the Italian premier, Vittorio Orlando, with a separate peace, they accepted on November 5 the Fourteen Points as a basis of negotiation, provided that they would determine what "freedom of the seas" meant and that Germany would be required to pay reparations. Wilson accepted this and communicated these conditions via the Swiss to the Germans, whose government was in a state of chaos. The Germans requested an armistice, and Marshal Foch was authorized by the Allied powers to receive German peace representatives. Foch, who now commanded the greatest host in human history, over six million battle-hardened soldiers, did this in his mobile command headquarters, his famous *wagon-lits* train on a siding in the Compiègne Forest on November 8, and an armistice was signed by which all hostilities would end at 11 a.m. on the eleventh day of the eleventh month of 1918.

Germany would evacuate all occupied territory, the left bank of the Rhine, and the bridgeheads of Mainz, Coblenz, and Cologne; the Allies retained a full right to claim war damages; the entire German fleet would be interned in British ports; the treaties of Brest Litovsk and Bucharest (which Germany had dictated to Romania when it occupied it in 1915[*]) were abrogated; all German tanks, aircraft, and heavy artillery were to be destroyed; all prisoners of war and deportees were to be returned; and Germany was to hand over 150,000 railway cars, 5,000 locomotives, and 5,000 trucks.

12. The End of the Laurier-Borden Era, 1918–1919

The day before the armistice, Sir Robert Borden arrived in a Great Britain where Lloyd George had just prevailed upon King George V to dissolve Parliament for new elections. Although the parties remained distinct, the government stood for re-election as a coalition, and the Asquith Liberals ran as anti-coalition candidates and the Lloyd George coalitionists also ran as Liberals. The Liberal-Conservative coalition won 526 constituencies to barely a hundred opponents, between the Asquith Liberals and the Labour Party, but Bonar Law and Walter Long and Arthur Balfour's Conservatives outnumbered the Lloyd George Liberals by almost three to one. Asquith was defeated personally, and it was a testimony to Lloyd George's acuity and footwork that he was retained as prime minister. Lloyd George offered Borden the position of representing all the dominions at the Paris Peace Conference, which was soon to convene. Borden, with commendable but entirely typical selflessness, declined and said that the Australian, South African, and New Zealand prime ministers should all attend as well. Lloyd George and Lord Curzon, leader of the House of Lords but soon to be foreign secretary, favoured a

---

[*] This was after Romania was persuaded by the British and the French to declare war on Germany, an act of national suicide.

trial of the kaiser, but the king, speaking of his first cousin, said he should be left to his "present condition of contempt and humiliation."[87] Unfortunately, George V was not as generous with his other recently dis-employed imperial cousin, the czar, and denied him entry to Great Britain, which if granted might have spared the slaughter of the entire Russian royal family in a grim foretaste of the nature of communist rule.

Borden dissented from an Imperial War Cabinet vote to prosecute Wilhelm II and urged that the United States be entreated to shed its iso-lation and join in close alliance with the British Empire, whether in the context of the League of Nations that President Wilson wished to estab-lish or otherwise. Borden had a number of his ministers with him, and they met as the cabinet at home would and considered papers that had been cabled from Canada, and then Borden met with the Imperial War Cabinet and War Committee, and subcommittees of those groups, and with individual British and Empire officials. Because of his even person-ality, he became something of a go-between, joining intensely with Lord Reading and Balfour and others to try to defray anticipated problems between Wilson and Lloyd George. For a Canadian government leader, it was a position of heady proximity to the world's most powerful states-men. Macdonald, Laurier, and Borden had all moved quickly up the ladder in the international status of their office. Borden took equably in his stride the fact that he was suddenly being listened to apparently atten-tively by people (such as Curzon) who had the power, with a very few others, to decide the disposition of German colonies and the division of territories in Arabia and the Holy Land, and the frontiers of the emerging national states being carved out of the collapsed or subdued empires of the Romanovs, Habsburgs, and Hohenzollerns. Borden became a confi-dant of many of the conferring personalities, including the South African leader, Louis Botha, and faithfully recorded Botha's high admi-ration for Sir Wilfrid Laurier, and did not demur in any way from it. Borden was a man of limited imagination but very high qualities of integrity and fairness and good sense, almost to a fault in a country so complicated internally and delicately placed internationally. For a Canadian prime minister, a talent for a ruse or occasional evasion was very useful, a quality possessed in abundance by Borden's two illustrious predecessors, not to mention the man who would soon follow and length-ily hold the premier office of the state.

On December 28, Borden agreed with Botha to make common cause for governors general representing the British monarch in any country to be of the nationality of that country rather than British. (Lloyd George purported to agree, but slippery as he was, neither he nor anyone else did anything about it for more than thirty years.) Borden sat at the grand occasion to welcome President Wilson to London with Haig, who denounced the French and preferred the Germans, testimony to the difficulties of intimate alliance. (Foch famously said at about this time, "I have less respect for Napoleon now that I know what a coalition is.") Wilson claimed that the American public favoured his League of Nations, though the British were not convinced. Wilson was very impressive in speeches in London, where he had just arrived, but most who met with him found him rather desiccated, though extremely intelligent. Borden spoke cogently of the utter impracticality of some of the ideas for German reparations and said that even with the burden reduced to scale, Canada could not sustain 10 per cent of what they were planning to lay on Germany.[88] Lloyd George outlined to the war cabinet on December 29 the gist of his first very extensive conversation with Woodrow Wilson. It had gone quite well, as they had agreed on the League, on not returning German colonies, and on the imposition of armament limits on Germany. Wilson opposed armed intervention in Russia, sided with the Yugoslavs over the Italians, whom he regarded as tantamount to pickpockets (although they had just taken over two million casualties in the common cause), and did not want the peace conference to be a farce, its participants called to attendance to rubber-stamp pre-agreed deals cooked up between the Big Three. The British bore some resentment of the power and confidence of the American latecomers to the war, and Borden sagely warned them that no one knew better than Canadians the foibles of the United States and its statesmen but that the greatest success that could come from the peace conference was a close and solid relationship between the United States and the British Empire.[89] Borden was instrumental in assuring that while the five convening powers – the four chief Western Allies and Japan – would have five delegates each at the peace conference, the dominions, including India, would each have two, as would smaller participants such as Romania, and New Zealand, because of its small population, would have one. Borden had made it clear that if Britain did not support the dominions in this requirement of suitable direct representation, the consequences to the Empire would be extremely grave. He declined to take an occupation zone in Germany for more than a short period.

The entire British delegation went en bloc to Paris on January 11 and stayed in the Majestic Hotel, where the British, suspecting the regular Majestic staff to be packed with French government informants, brought in London hotel staff. Starting on January 20, 1919, Borden began taking daily French lessons from a Mlle. Perret to brush up his conversational French. Australia's Billy Hughes proved very cantankerous in demanding Australian annexation of German islands in the Pacific. Wilson was opposed to annexation and wanted League of Nations mandates, as he regarded all these arrangements as being of questionable legality. Lloyd George heatedly told Hughes that Britain would not go to war with the United States in pursuit of Australia's right to the Solomon Islands. Wilson was undiplomatic, but his intellect and articulation, as well as the power of his country, gave him great influence. Clemenceau was suspected by Lloyd George of intending to drag his feet until Wilson returned to the United States, while Borden became friendly with Wilson's grey eminence, the powerful and mysterious (honorary) Colonel Edward Mandell House. At one point, Lloyd George, who was a tricky negotiator, dangled the colonial government of the British West Indies before Borden, but unfortunately Borden was "deeply imbued with the Americans' prejudice against the government of extraneous possessions and peoples."[90] It would have been a good way of bulking up Canada's population, saving foreign exchange spent during Canadian winters in Florida, and rationalizing a navy.

In early February, Lloyd George offered Borden the position of British ambassador in Washington, and Borden, astonishingly, said he would accept it if his colleagues could spare him; it could not, at this stage, have been anything but a demotion, though potentially a very important position for a year or so. Apart from the hierarchical implications, the notion that a British prime minister would invite a Canadian prime minister to represent British interests in Washington is very odd, but, imperialist as Borden was, he does not seem to have been anything but flattered by it.

* * *

On February 17, 1919, in Ottawa, Sir Wilfrid Laurier fainted in his office but recovered quickly and by himself and determined that he should go home. Rather than call for his chauffeur and possibly cause concern, he left unobtrusively and took a streetcar home to his comfortable house on Laurier Avenue. He went to bed for the night, and was dressing in the morning when he again fainted. He recovered consciousness to find himself back in bed, being ministered to by Sister Marcelline, who had cared for him before when he was unwell. He smiled and said, "It is the bride of the Divine Husband who comes to help a great sinner." Though he declared himself to be "only a little weak," he received the sacrament of the dying. Amid "a murmurous hush," he felt another constriction, tightened his hand on that of Zoé, his wife of fifty-one years, impassively uttered his valedictory "C'est fini," and passed on.[91] He was seventy-seven. Borden sent a generous cable to Lady Laurier and ordered a state funeral that would render maximum homage to one who, as Borden said in a statement from Paris, "was from the first a commanding figure, and during a long period the chief figure in our public life" (in fact from the death of Macdonald to the moment he died, nearly twenty-eight years). After a laborious testimony to his grasp of public issues and political "dexterity," Borden came closer to the essence of the deceased: "His personality was singularly attractive and magnetic; and with this he combined an inspiring eloquence, an unfailing grace of diction in both languages and a charm of manner which gave him a supreme place in the affection and respect of . . . all Canada."[92] He lay in state in the improvised Parliament at the Victoria Memorial Museum, where all the desks and chairs were cleared except the place for one, symbolic both of the position of prime minister and of leader of the Opposition, positions he had occupied for a total of thirty-two years. A suitably grand but tasteful funeral ensued, and he was buried in Ottawa.

Apart from what he achieved as prime minister, and especially the rapid growth of the country and its population, Laurier, by the power and integrity of his own personality, alone preserved the character and potential of Canada as a bicultural confederation. It was illustrative of his tolerance that when the Salvation Army began marching through Quebec cities and there were demonstrations and attempts to ban them, he said, "If need be, I will march at the head of their processions with them."[93] He had fought the largely symbolic school issue as it moved west from the Ottawa River to the North-West Territories and through Manitoba, Saskatchewan, and Alberta, and did what he could to preserve the nature of the original arrangements respecting both founding cultures, even though the inexorable march of events between France and Britain, and the difference in scale of the accretions of the English- and French-speaking peoples, made French schools in such chronically minority conditions a difficult proposition. But he had kept alive and had strengthened – as only a statesman of his felicity and comprehension of the cultures and psychology of both founding races which he possessed, by inheritance, intuition, and study, could do – the spirit of mutual respect, and even of reciprocal need, that alone could be the basis of the great nationality he foresaw in rich imagination, and pursued with unwavering idealism and faith, for fifty years.

Laurier's stance in reluctantly accepting conscription if it was the subject of a referendum or election and accepting to go down to defeat, while the country divided sharply along French and English (by ancestry or assimilation) lines, is all that saved a party that could serve as an ark for the conservation and safe maturation of the original bicultural spirit of Confederation until the virtue of the original vision was generally appreciated and Canada was free to fulfill its potential. Laurier could have been a virtual co-prime minister in a grand coalition, as he could, years before, have become a member of the House of Lords. He knew what he had to do to preserve himself as a force of national legitimacy, to preserve his party as the continuator of the Great Ministry of Baldwin and LaFontaine and of the Great Coalition of Macdonald, Brown, Cartier, and the others, and to prevent French Canadians from being hijacked by Bourassa in permanently embittered separation, longing and scheming for actual independence.

Without Laurier, there would have been two parties, one French and one English, with a permanent English majority, a climate of permanent hostility between the two communities, and a completely dysfunctional country. Because of him, there was either a Quebec prime minister of Canada or a de facto Quebec co-prime minister for French-Canadian affairs for seventy of the eighty-five years following the next election after his death, in 1921. As leader of the government, he always struck the right compromise in education as in the navy, and as he did in opposition over participation in the war.

Robert Borden was the best of the well-disposed, rather righteous, always upright English gentlemen who contributed so much to Canada. He took French lessons in Paris, and thought the French Canadians were likeable and simple people who were shortchanged by not being English but were welcome fellow citizens. But he had little realistic notion of what would be necessary to impress the French Canadians sufficiently with Canada for them actually to believe in it; or to convince English Canadians adequately of the uniqueness of Canada for them to think of themselves as completely independent of the British; or to make all Canadians adequately self-confident to deal with the United States evenly, with neither reactive chippiness nor fawning submission. If invited to resign the headship of the government of Canada for the British embassy in Washington, Laurier, unlike Borden, would have had no interest in it. Less politically cynical than Macdonald but armed with the flair and romantic inspiration of a Latin statesman, as opposed to a canny Scottish realist, he was a providential successor to Macdonald. Between them, they had brought Canada from the craving for autonomy in local affairs of the responsible government debates in the 1850s, to honoured, if not overly influential, participation in an epochal international conference that sixty-five years later would remake the world. Their thoroughly unlikely successor, who claimed Sir Wilfrid had wished him to be his successor as soon as his mentor was interred, was visible, but not prominent, in the wings, like the nanny in an Edwardian family photograph.

Robert Borden was a very solid figure of the second rank, and he soldiered on in the country's interest at Paris, with which, like all visitors, he was very impressed as a splendid capital of great boulevards and elegant facades, beautiful women, and high culture, a world where he was not completely at ease but which he recognized for its gracious wit and style. He became the vice chairman, to Clemenceau, of the Greek Committee, and took the chair for a time following an assassination attempt on the French leader. Though seventy-eight and with a bullet in his lung, Clemenceau survived and returned, completely unfazed, after a few weeks. Borden met and was impressed by Marshal Foch on March 1, 1919.

On March 8, there were riots among Canadian troops impatient to return home, and twelve were killed and twenty-one wounded.* Borden recorded in his diary that "this is very distressing and sad" and demanded "an exact report of these serious and unfortunate events,"[94] but does not otherwise refer to them in his memoirs. Apparently, it was routine grousing of infantrymen that was incompetently managed and allowed to get seriously out of hand, and not indicative of the morale of the army, which, though the men were impatient to return home, was quite strong.

Borden remained in Paris for most of the time until May 14, when he departed for London and then for Canada. A great range of questions had been wrestled with, and Borden was clearly a popular and emollient figure. His performance presaged the international lot of Canada for the whole interwar period and into the era that followed: he was courteous, sensible, could be taken anywhere and sat next to anyone, and would not rock the boat (unlike the Australian Hughes, who at one point in a discussion of the rights of colonial natives expressed preparedness to seat cannibals in the Australian parliament). There was vigorous and unsuccessful debate on a Japanese motion for a rule of racial equality. Borden offered equality between nations; Smuts diluted it to open, equal, and honourable relations between nations and just treatment of their nationals within the territories of other nations. Lord Robert Cecil, undersecretary of foreign affairs and chairman of an Imperical Committee on the League of Nations, diluted it further to equal treatment to all foreign residents being nationals of other members of the League of Nations, within their territories.[95] This, of course, was not what the Japanese sought at all, and it was impossible to get the kind of declaration that would have distinguished the lead conferenciers as racial egalitarians. (Wilson, for all his pacific idealism and intellectual love of freedom, was a Virginian Presbyterian who had little regard for non-whites, especially African Americans.) The Paris Peace Conference did agree on the covenant and basic arrangements for the League of Nations before adjourning in May to permit the national leaders to go back to their jobs. There was no spirit of

---

* On March 5, Sir Arthur Currie gave Borden his history of the last hundred days of the war. Borden recorded that he was "extremely proud of it. During that time, the Canadians fought against forty-seven divisions of the German Army; all these divisions were defeated, and fifteen were destroyed." This was slightly misleading, as Canada only had four divisions, but their record was a splendid one.

euphoria, but at least a sensation of having achieved something, when they broke up. Europe had seven new states: Latvia, Lithuania, Estonia, Poland, Hungary, Czechoslovakia, and Yugoslavia.

Borden sailed on RMS *Aquitania*, a hundred feet longer, ten thousand tons heavier, a deck taller, but four knots slower than the *Mauretania*, on May 19 for New York and arrived in Ottawa on May 27, after an absence of six months and three weeks. The Treaty of Versailles was signed, with Canada signing with the other dominions, with the United Kingdom under the heading "British Empire," Canada was thus assured a place in the League of Nations. Canada had sought to profit nothing from the peace, and did not, apart from a token payment of German reparations.

So ended the greatest war in history. Sixteen million people had perished and twenty-one million were wounded, including, among the major combatants: 3,300,000 Russians killed and 4,950,000 wounded; 2,920,000 Turks killed and 400,000 wounded; 2,470,000 Germans killed and 4,250,000 wounded; 1,700,000 French killed and 4,270,000 wounded (in a population of a little over 40,000,000); 1,570,000 Austro-Hungarians killed and 3,600,000 wounded; 1,240,000 Italians killed and 950,000 wounded; 1,000,000 British killed and 1,660,000 wounded; 117,000 Americans killed and 206,000 wounded (but about half the dead from the influenza pandemic at the end of the war); and 67,000 Canadians dead and 150,000 wounded. (The Australians had 90 per cent as many casualties as Canada with only 60 per cent of Canada's population, both amazing figures for countries not under direct threat and almost all of whose casualties were volunteers.)

The world had been remade, but not very durably. Foch called it when he said, as the terms were revealed, "This is not peace; it is a twenty-year ceasefire." He was out only by four months and probably assumed the United States would ratify the Treaty of Versailles, and this was already in doubt. Despite the sorrows and exertions and internal strains, Canada had earned the respect of all in terrible combat and had come as close as a serious participant in such a horrible massacre could come to having a good war, an astonishing progress from the rickety Confederation of just fifty years before. Much of the Western World was now a charnel house, crowded with destitute, mutilated, and trauma-tized survivors. In every sense, to the victors now went the spoils.

William Lyon Mackenzie King (1874–1950), leader of the federal opposition 1919–1921, 1926, 1930–1935, and prime minister of Canada 1921–1926, 1926–1930, 1935–1948. Eccentric and over-cautious but a very astute and skilled navigator of decades of economic and international crises, he held the country together through the conscription debates and plebiscite of 1942–1944, and led a war effort that impressed the world.

CHAPTER 6

King and the Art of Cunning Caution Between the Wars, 1919–1940

1. The Retirement of Borden and the King-Meighen Rivalry, 1919–1921

When Sir Wilfrid Laurier died, William Lyon Mackenzie King (1874–1950) was a resident of the United States, a close friend and adviser to John D. Rockefeller Jr., and under offer from Andrew Carnegie to take over his philanthropies at the then high salary of twenty-five thousand dollars a year and likely to write his biography also, for one hundred thousand dollars. Rockefeller was miffed at this effort to raid his industrial adviser and friend and matched Carnegie's salary offer. Though diffident, devious, and unprepossessing, King, at forty-four, had been extremely successful. Laurier's biographer Joseph Schull wrote of King, a bit tartly, "That chubby Joan of Arc, with the voices of destiny and duty always harping at one ear and the voice of the Rockefellers at the other, was hardly the stuff of heroes. His bank account grew and he watched it with anxious eyes. He still yearned for a soul-mate and shied like a wary faun from each prospective woman."[1] Laurier had written him, "No man in Canada has your chances, today. The thing is for me to bring you forward all I can."[2] King was a very hard-working, completely humourless, deeply and mystically religious man whose faith was accentuated by extreme ancestor veneration (his mother and grandfather), a social Christian who yet admired honourably earned wealth and disdained socialism. He was in some respects the man of the new era, an expert in industrial relations who had (largely) written a turgid and ponderous volume on the way forward in postwar industrial relations, *Industry and Humanity*. He could hold himself out as something of an intellectual, not only as an industrial relations expert, but as a five-time university graduate (in law and arts, from the University of Toronto, Osgoode Hall Law School in Toronto, the University of Chicago, where he worked in Jane Addams's settlement home Hull House, and Harvard, where his doctoral thesis was on oriental immigration to Canada, which he opposed, as "Canada should remain a white man's country.") Ever the politician, at Toronto, as an undergraduate, he fomented a students' strike in 1895 whose real object was to secure him a teaching position. In this he was unsuccessful, but he worked closely with William Mulock, the vice chancellor, who was trying to undermine the chancellor, former Liberal leader Edward Blake. (Mulock rewarded King by making him a deputy minister in Ottawa just five years later.) He possessed great, focused ambition and a talent at devious self-insinuation, all thoroughly disguised and accentuated by his perpetual affectation of the utmost sanctimony.

He was, in his caution, his lack of spontaneity, and his endless manoeuvring and obscurantism, the anti-hero. But as time would prove, he possessed the ingredients for astonishing political success: he knew only a little of French and not much of Quebec, except that it was necessary as a whole-hearted participant to make Canada work and assure the country a sufficiently interesting future to lift it to complete independence from the British and the Americans. In this, he was a true federalist, a true nationalist, whose head would never be turned by the attentions of Canada's senior allies, and he would be vastly more subjected to them than any past or future Canadian leader, except perhaps Brian Mulroney in his close relations with President Reagan and the senior President Bush. And he was a true Liberal; he came back to

Canada and loyally ran in the 1917 election in a hopeless cause in York North for Sir Wilfrid. He was acceptable to Quebec because he had remained absolutely loyal to Laurier and opposed conscription, and to English Canada he was just adequately plausible as the postwar man who would work for industrial peace and progress and would be a modernizer, a technocrat, and even, in his very odd way, a visionary. William Fielding was his natural rival and in some respects the logical successor to Laurier, but he had deserted Sir Wilfrid on the issue of Alberta and Saskatchewan schools and on conscription and stood as a Liberal Unionist candidate in 1917, though he did not join the government when he was elected. But Fielding was seventy-one, was completely unacceptable to Quebec, and if the country and the Liberal Party did not know King well enough, they knew Fielding too well. It had been such a terrible war, even for Canada, there was a natural desire to turn the page and reach for the leaders of tomorrow rather than those who had distinguished themselves in the recent past. This was unlike the Second World War, which, even though it lasted longer, was a war of movement, led and won by dynamic men who acted decisively, and never seemed simply mired in slaughter for years on end. King was unexciting, but he appeared to be the best available, and he claimed, with stentorian fervour, from the moment of Sir Wilfrid's last breath if not before, to be his indisputable heir and chosen successor. Lady Laurier inconveniently confirmed to King that, on the eve of his death, her husband had said that Fielding was the man to unite the Liberals, so King rested his claim to the succession on his own uncorroborated recollections of conversations with the late leader.

King's chief backers were Peter Charles Larkin (1855–1930), the fantastically successful son of a Montreal bricklayer, who founded and built the Salada Tea Company, one of the greatest tea suppliers and marketers in the world; and the publisher of the *Toronto Star*, Joseph Atkinson (1865–1948). These were the days of discreet campaigns, and King went to England to maintain the appearance of indifference as he worked up comparative labour and related studies, but he returned in time for the first Liberal convention in August 1919, where he participated effectively in platform committees about labour and social issues and gave a strong keynote speech projecting the Liberal commitment to people of modest means. King's opponents called him a busboy of the Rockefellers and a shirker and absentee during the Great War, but his supporters made much of the fact that he had stuck with Laurier and come back from the comfortable fold of the Rockefellers to run in a lost cause in 1917.

The piously idiosyncratic King spent the day of the leadership vote, August 7, meditating and praying as delegates chose between him; William Fielding; former railroads and canals minister George Perry Graham (1859–1943); and the acting party leader, Daniel Duncan McKenzie (1859–1927) of Nova Scotia. King was put across by Quebec, and by Ernest Lapointe in particular, and the combination of the two men would dominate the public life of the country for the next twenty-two years. King won on the fourth ballot, with 476 to Fielding's 438. On achieving the victory, he thought of his parents and grandparents and of Sir Wilfrid: "I thought: it is right, it is the call of duty. . . . I have sought nothing." (His selection was far from a draft.) "It has come from God. The dear loved ones know and are about. . . . It is to His work I am called, and to it I dedicate my life. . . . The people want clean and honest government; ideals in politics, a larger measure of social reform. I am unknown to the people as yet, but they will soon know and will recognize. The Liberal Party will yet rejoice in its entirety at the confidence they have placed in me. They have chosen better than they knew." (This at least was probably accurate.) "May God keep me ever near His side and guide me aright."[3] This was to prove a formidable intellectual and psychological armament: King was always convinced of his proximity to God and of his virtue, and to his task he brought a relentless cunning, never compromised by overconfidence and in difficult times made desperately imaginative by the conviction that he was fighting for his life and for God's will.

Prime Minister Robert Borden was very aware of the dangers of having no French Canadians in his government and toured about Quebec in July and August conferring with dignitaries and trying to recruit some, especially Sir Lomer Gouin, who doubted that he could be elected as a Unionist.[4] He proceeded to Saint John, New Brunswick, to greet the arriving Prince of Wales and accompanied him on the battle cruiser *Renown* to Quebec. Borden's car was stoned by angry crowds at Chaudière Junction, but otherwise he was indifferently received by the population in Quebec. Mackenzie King's elevation as Liberal leader is referred to in Borden's memoirs with the reflection that in the summer of 1917 King "was ready to join the proposed Union government." Borden didn't identify the source of that intelligence, and it was very unlikely, as King was not in Parliament and knew that his political future lay in clinging to Laurier like a limpet. He first enters the prime minister's memoirs in his new role when, "as usual, he spoke eloquently and well" in thanking the Prince of Wales for his speech in Ottawa on August 29. The chief subject of discussion at this time, much considered by the cabinet, was whether it would affront the sensibilities of the conservative Christians of Canada if the Prince of Wales played a private game of golf for his own exercise on a Sunday.

All remaining unallocated land within fifteen miles of any railway was reserved for returning servicemen, and the Soldier Settlement Board was established to acquire land for entitled veterans and assist them financially in setting up farms. Forty-three thousand servicemen took advantage of the opportunity.[5]

The government accepted independent recommendations that were only enacted in 1923 to unify and refinance and nationalize the Grand Trunk, Grand Trunk Pacific, Canadian Northern, National Transcontinental, and Intercolonial railways into the twenty-two-thousand-mile Canadian National Railway. The consolidation left a good deal of grumbling in British financial circles.

The Great War had radically altered the balance of British and American economic and commercial power in Canada. In 1914, 22 per cent of foreign investment in Canada was British and 23 per cent was American. By 1922, the majority was American. Imports by Canada from the United States were 250 per cent of British in 1901; in 1918, they were ten times as great. Canadian exports to the United States increased from less than half the total in Britain in 1901 to 80 per cent of exports in Britain in 1918.[6]

In the autumn of 1919 and through to the spring of 1920, there was back and forth between Ottawa and London about the establishment of a Canadian minister in Washington. The British approved this from the beginning but also stipulated the need for what the colonial secretary Lord Milner called, in a cable to Borden on October 28, 1919, "well-balanced protection of Imperial and Canadian interests." This would require having the Canadian minister operate out of the British embassy.

Borden went along with this, but the line between Canada as an Imperial entity and as a completely sovereign country was clearly becoming blurred. No one could accuse the Canadians, especially with Borden at their head, of rushing the fences of sovereignty, but they were drawing close to them.[7] Yet the Washington appointment was only filled in 1927.

Borden spent much of October and November convalescing in Virginia from acute fatigue. By November, the whole issue of American ratification of the Peace Treaty, and specifically of the League of Nations, had bubbled up, and on the urgent request of Lord Grey, former foreign secretary and now British ambassador in Washington, Borden agreed that in the event of a dispute between a member country and any of the dominions, India, or Great Britain, the British Empire bloc of six would abstain from voting in the League. This addressed a specific concern raised by some of the isolationists in the U.S. Senate. It was part of the energetic effort the British and their Imperial confreres made to ease the United States into the world and into the collective security system. President Wilson had not taken Senate opinion into account. The Senate has to ratify foreign treaties with a majority of two-thirds, and the opposition Republicans held the majority of Senate seats. Wilson realized very late that he could have a substantial problem, and on September 4 he set out on a speaking tour to rally opinion. His health collapsed in late September and he returned to Washington, where he suffered a massive stroke on October 2. Wilson refused to compromise, the Republicans had the votes, and the Treaty of Versailles was not ratified.

On December 10, 1919, on medical advice, Borden told his senior colleagues that he believed he had to retire for health reasons, failing which "I would become a nervous wreck."[8] Borden announced his impending retirement and departed on January 4, 1920, with Admiral of the Fleet Earl Jellicoe, victor, in so far as the British were victorious, of the epochal Battle of Jutland, for a trip to South Africa to discuss Imperial naval solidarity. (In fact, they went to Havana, Jamaica, and Trinidad, and then Jan Smuts, now South African prime minister, disinvited them because he was holding an election, and they returned to Britain, all on the battle cruiser *New Zealand*.) Borden had a month of London society, from the king and Lloyd George down, and returned to Halifax on February 28, and then went to New York and descended into the Carolinas by train, where he stayed until

May. Borden recorded that in his absence, "extraordinary ideas akin to anarchy and insanity manifested themselves among some electors,"[9] and was somewhat aggrieved at his inability to have "a year's uninterrupted holiday," an unheard of concept for the head of government of any jurisdiction. He returned to Ottawa on May 12, 1920.

The U.S. Senate returned to the Treaty of Versailles, in light of its importance, in February 1920, but opinions had not softened on either side. Wilson was now too infirm to concentrate for more than a few minutes a day, and his wife, Edith, ran the government. If the vice president, Thomas R. Marshall, had declared Wilson incapacitated, the president would have attracted general sympathy, and Marshall and the secretary of state, Robert Lansing, would have got something through, and would have got the United States into the League, even with reservations. But Wilson forbade any public reference to his illness and seemed determined either to be sustained or to die for the cause. He was denied even this, and his career ended in tragedy and rejection.

Without official American continuance as a British and French ally, the peace would be very precarious. Britain and France, exhausted by their recent ordeal, were not fundamentally stronger than Germany and Russia, if the latter two were governed purposefully. Germany and Russia were even more dilapidated than their victorious enemies now, but in a few years it would be impossible to resurrect a balance of power in the world if Germany was in revanchist mode and at peace with Russia and the United States was disconnected from Europe.

The Allies had deployed 195,000 soldiers to Russia from 1918 to 1920, led by 70,000 Japanese, ostensibly to protect their interests, but really to seize an eastern chunk of Russia. The second largest contingent was Czechs, Austro-Hungarian prisoners of war whom the Bolshevik leaders released to return to the Western Front via Vladivostok to join the Western Allies against the Central Powers. Most of them did not embark and instead engaged in the Russian Civil War against the Bolsheviks. The British landed 40,000 men at Archangel and Murmansk to secure vast supplies that had been deposited there, and to assist the anti-communist White Russians in their struggle with the Bolsheviks. The United States sent 24,000 men, and there were French and Canadians and Greeks in the Caucasus as well. But the interventions were an uncoordinated shambles. The Western Powers left in 1920, having achieved nothing, and after the war the combination of Soviet military success and U.S. diplomatic pressure forced the Japanese back to their original frontiers in 1924.

Borden finally announced his retirement to his caucus on July 1 with a constructive and dignified address that was not in the least partisan or acerbic. He departed office as he had exercised it, a good, thorough, honest, and capable man, though somewhat unexciting and without the genius of national leadership of the complicated country he governed, though very amply endowed with executive competence and courage and patriotic sprit. He must be judged a successful and rather distinguished, but not a great or inspiring, prime minister. After consulting his cabinet colleagues quite intensively, as was necessary to extract a consensus, it was agreed that Arthur Meighen should succeed him, and he did, on July 10, 1920.

Arthur Meighen had just turned forty-six when he was installed as prime minister. He was five months older than Mackenzie King, and they had been at the University of Toronto together, where their relations were poor, as they remained. While they were both Presbyterians, Meighen was decisive and bold, and not subtle, either in his judgment or in his techniques as a leader. He tended to lay about him with a broadaxe, and was an effective debater and speaker, but he saw problems in essentially administrative rather than political terms. King had been returned to Parliament in a by-election in Prince Edward Island and congratulated Meighen on his election as party leader of the governing coalition (most of whose Liberal members withdrew, pointing to the end of the war and the retirement of Borden). King told his incredulous fellow members of Parliament that for him, personally, it was "a source both of pride and of pleasure" that Meighen had been elevated, a man "whose friendship [with King], through a quarter of a century, had survived the vicissitudes of time, not excepting the differences of party warfare and acrimonies of political debate."[10] This was bunk; they intensely disliked each other throughout those twenty-five years, and their mutual dislike would become much more intense in the nearly thirty years to come.

Meighen, as the leading parliamentarian after the death of Sir Wilfrid, and the chief parliamentary manager of Borden's government, was indelibly identified in Quebec with conscription, and he was generally assumed to have little chance in the sixty-two mainly French-speaking constituencies of that province. While Henri Bourassa could hardly be said to speak for the whole province, his authenticity as a nationalist spokesman was notorious, and on Meighen's elevation he wrote in *Le Devoir*, "Mr. Meighen typifies, in his person and temper, as may be gathered from the positions he took in the past and from his speeches, whatever Anglo-Saxon jingoism contains that is most brutal, exclusive, and anti-Canadian. His name is coupled to the most arbitrary and hateful measures passed by the Tory-Unionist government during the War."[11] The interplay between King and Meighen in debate was memorable, with King sanctimoniously speaking for a constituency to which Meighen was not easily accessible, and Meighen replying with savage causticity which entertained the legislators but did not win him any votes: "I am sure if any improvement of character or conduct on my part could be looked for as a result of the scolding from the Leader of the Opposition . . . I rise very much chastened and purified by it. I recognize the privilege of being given lessons in candour and honesty and frankness at the hands of my honourable friend."[12] (Meighen regarded King throughout their fifty-year acquaintance as an unmitigated scoundrel and hypocrite, an opinion which is not completely unjust, though the adjective is excessive.) Meighen delighted in exquisite denigrations of his opponent, such as "circuitous sinuosity."[13]

Despite his forensic talents and parliamentary dexterity, Meighen was not very efficient at moving pending matters along, and he generally had a cloth ear for public opinion. He dithered on the matter of consolidating the Grand Trunk with other non–Canadian Pacific lines, and dithered on naming a Canadian minister in Washington, although two-thirds of the business of the British embassy in Washington was now conducted on behalf of Canada. At the London Empire Prime Ministers' Conference that began on June 20, 1921, he was junior in years, and to some extent in prestige, to Lloyd George, Jan Smuts, Australia's Billy Hughes, and even New Zealand's William Massey (1856–1925, prime minister 1912–1925), but he spoke well and was adequately convivial. The chief issue was the Anglo-Japanese Treaty, which the British had negotiated when they had presciently seen the rise of Japan and moved to assure that Japan did not threaten British interests in the Far East. Australia and New Zealand, as Pacific countries, had the same interest, but Meighen saw it as a matter that threatened relations between the British Empire and the United States, which regarded Japan as a rival in the Pacific. Meighen faced off with Hughes, a bantam rooster, a former cow- and sheep-herder, farmer, cook, sailor, prospector, trapper, teacher, and labour organizer, and a powerful speaker.

Lord Curzon was now the British foreign secretary, and his compromise – to seek a conference with the United States, Japan, and China – was reckoned something of a victory for Meighen, as the Empire had acted in unison as Lloyd George and Smuts had proposed, and the Anglo-Japanese Treaty, a potential vexation to the United States, lapsed. Canada was always America's most reliable advocate in Imperial circles. Out of this grew the Washington Naval Disarmament Conference. The net effect of that conference was to deprive the Western Allies (the British, French, and Americans) of twenty capital ships that would have been useful in future conflicts such as in convoy protection and support for amphibious landings in the next world war. Since the German navy had scuttled itself in Scapa Flow under the gaze of the British in 1919, and the Russians weren't invited and didn't have much of a navy anyway, it was an orgy of self-enfeeblement by the victorious Allied powers, compounded by the fact that the Japanese ignored the agreement's limits, and all the powers eventually cheated on the tonnages of battleships, as even the British, Americans, and French exceeded the thirty-five-thousand-ton limit for new battleships when the time came to build them (the King George v, Washington, and Richelieu classes, as well as the German Bismarck and Italian Vittorio Veneto ships). It was impossible even to verify the tonnages of huge ships that required years to construct, and arms control would become steadily more complicated as the delivery systems became smaller, and easier to hide, in the missile age. The Americans, in the Washington Naval Treaty, submersed themselves in the euphoric nonsense that they were contributing importantly to world peace without surrendering sovereignty as they would have had they subscribed to the League of Nations. Meighen was ultimately correct: it was better to stay close to the United States than to rely on the good faith of Japan.

The American Republican leaders – including the new president, Warren G. Harding; the secretary of state and previous Republican presidential candidate, Charles Evans Hughes; and influential anti-League senators such as William Edgar Borah and Henry Cabot Lodge – thought that with such gestures they could keep faith with the isolationists while usurping the clothes of the Wilson Democrats as peacemakers and internationalists. (Theodore Roosevelt had died in 1919, aged sixty. Had he lived, he would have been nominated and elected, and it would have been a different and better world with him leading the United States through the early 1920s.) Meighen returned to Canada on August 6, and greeted the new governor general, Lord Byng of Vimy, the popular former commander of the Canadian Corps in France, on August 10.

By their imposition of conscription, the Conservatives had almost made Canada a one-party state for the next two generations; the new Liberal leader – though very eccentric, not very companionable, and strangely inaccessible to public affection – would, as decades succeeded each other, and to say the least, make the most of the Conservatives' grievous political miscalculation over conscription.

2. Mackenzie King I: A Canadian Phenomenon, 1921–1926

The political omens for the Conservatives were unpromising not only in Quebec. Meighen was a very vulnerable leader politically, as he was known in Quebec as the legislator who drafted and managed the Conscription Bill, and to the working people of the country as the man who had prosecuted and imprisoned the leaders of the general strike that had been briefly unleashed in Winnipeg in 1919, while Westerners disliked him for his support for high tariffs to favour the Eastern manufacturing industries. He was oblivious to the currents of popular opinion and imagined that the winning point in a debate before a learned forum would carry the country. He thought he could embarrass King with his inelegant straddle on tariffs, from hints of opposition to the tariff in the West, where lower prices on manufactured goods were sought, and measured support for retention of the tariff in Ontario and Quebec, which sought protection for their manufacturing jobs. King was easy to offend but almost impossible to embarrass. He waffled about a tariff for revenue, using that as a smokescreen to disguise his meaning (which wasn't clear even after scrutiny of his laborious diary).

When the election campaign came, since Meighen had already lost Quebec and the West, the chief contest was in Ontario, where there were eighty-two constituencies. On election day, December 6, 1921, King voted early, spent much of the day praying on his knees before the portrait of his mother which he employed for idolatrous as well as decorative purposes (a light shone on it every minute of every day), and calculated the result, which came in early. The Conservatives elected only 49 MPs, most in Ontario, and Meighen was defeated in his own Manitoba constituency of Portage la Prairie. The farmers' Progressive Party, was, if it wished it, the official Opposition with 58 MPs, and King was the prime minister-elect with 118 seats, including all 65 in Quebec and his own restored constituency of York North. From the Conservative–Liberal Unionist total of 1917, the Conservatives lost two-thirds of their seats, or 104 MPs, and almost half their popular support, which declined from 57 per cent to 30 per cent. The Liberals gained 2.3 per cent and 36 MPs, 33 of them outside Quebec, so most of the Liberals' gains were the return of the Liberal Unionists. Most of Meighen's losses were to the angry Progressives, who came from nowhere to take 21 per cent of the vote. Fortunes had reversed themselves dramatically: where four years before the Liberals had been split, largely on English-French lines over conscription, now the traditional Conservatives were split between agrarian reformers and free-traders, and Eastern industrial middle-class voters and protectionists. Ernest Lapointe was a deft Quebec strategist for King, and Meighen was alone and adrift in terms of political support, apart from the ancient commercial Tories of Ontario. To some degree, it must be said, Meighen was taking the bullet for Borden on the conscription issue, except that Meighen had been an even more fervent supporter of the measure than Borden had.

Three weeks before the election, Lady Laurier had died and had left her husband's home, the three-storey yellow-brick Laurier House in Ottawa's Sandy Hill district on Laurier Avenue East, to King. The property was in disrepair and needed about thirty thousand dollars' worth of restoration. King's "fairy godfather," as he called him, the tea executive Peter Larkin, set up a forty-thousand-dollar fund for King – as he had a hundred-thousand-dollar fund for Laurier – from which King could renovate and decorate and re-furnish Sir Wilfrid's house. King did this, including the installation of an elevator, and took up residence in January 1923. Lady Laurier's motive in leaving the house to him was not any great affection for King, but a desire to return it to the Liberal Party which had (at the urging of Clifford Sifton in 1897) bought it for Laurier for $9,500. Larkin was rewarded for his largesse on this and other occasions with the high commission in London (succeeding Galt, Tupper, Strathcona, and Sir George Perley). Larkin went on a few years later, with Sir Herbert Holt, president of the Royal Bank of Canada and of the Montreal Light, Heat and Power Company, and others, to set up a fund of $225,000 for King, and $100,000 for Lapointe. (Such arrangements in modern times would have been political suicide.)

Once in office, King did not surprise. "There was nothing of Henry V about [him]; no one can imagine him leading his dear friends once more into the breach or closing the wall up with his Liberal dead."[14] He perfected his techniques of gradualism and compromise, and concentrated on consolidating what he held and pitching to the Progressives and other elements, always trying to strengthen the centre and add elements to his coalition. The Progressive Party leader, Thomas Crerar (1876–1975), had become a farmers' leader through his prominence in the Manitoba Grain Growers' Association, and was appointed to Borden's cabinet in 1917 as a Unionist minister of agriculture and then elected to Parliament. He quit the government in 1919 in protest against Meighen's protectionist policies. King foretold that Crerar would have no interest in being leader of the Opposition, and Crerar's large bloc of MPs was completely unorganized and had just grown suddenly like a mushroom, with no unifying or organizing force except militant agrarian discontent. King tried hard to attract Crerar and the United Farmers premier of Ontario, Ernest Drury, to join his government, but was not quite successful on this occasion. The strong men of King's government, apart from the deceptive and enigmatic King himself and Ernest Lapointe, were Sir Lomer Gouin, the almost Napoleonic apogee of confidence as premier of Quebec from 1905 to 1920, and William S. Fielding, back in 1921 as minister of finance, as he had been from 1896 to 1911. Given Gouin's power in Quebec, King reluctantly prevailed on Lapointe to allow Gouin to take justice while Lapointe settled for marine and fisheries. King and Lapointe had already opened an intimate political relationship that included going together to Sir Wilfrid's grave in Ottawa to pledge loyalty to their late chief. Gouin was a Montreal area politician. He was closely allied to Montreal's big business interests, including Holt's power company, while Lapointe was a Quebec City and eastern Quebec representative, where there was much more sympathy with tariff reduction and other measures that King judged necessary to win over the Progressives and solidify his countrywide majority.

King stretched his coalition by opposing an amendment that would have prevented cabinet members from being company directors, a sacrifice that would have been intolerable to Gouin in 1922. (When he retired after fifteen years as premier of Quebec in 1920, Gouin said he would rather have been president of the Bank of Montreal, of which he had been a director while premier.) King began espousing and enacting a relatively independent foreign policy opposite Great Britain, and produced a stream of small concessions to the Western farmers. Rumours were rife that there was a serious rift between King and Gouin at the summit of the party. Gouin and Fielding opposed any softening of the tariff, any concession of federal control of their natural resources to the Western provinces, and they opposed King's proposal to bury Sir Wilfrid's ill-considered Grand Trunk Railway inside the newly nationalized Canadian National Railways. King showed great political acumen and infinite patience in appearing, and it was more than a semblance, the voice of executive moderation and conciliation in advocating these measures while gradually backing Gouin and Fielding into a reactionary corner. (Fielding opposed Canadian independence from Great Britain, composed his own Imperial solidarity wording for "O Canada," and objected to the Red Ensign as a naval flag that appeared to be a communist banner. He was not really presentable in the postwar political climate.) Difficult though it is to think of Mackenzie King in these terms, it was providential that he took the Liberal leadership. Canada entering the 1920s and choosing either Meighen's brand of reaction or Fielding's would have made it a terminally sober country, and given it a government without much place for the French Canadians.

Another splendid opportunity was handed to King by Meighen in September 1922, when a dispute arose between Turkey and Great Britain at Chanak (Çanakkale), near the Dardanelles, where the Turkish army threatened what was designated by end-of-war arrangements as temporarily neutral territory under British control. King learned from a reporter on September 16, 1922, that the British government was publicly calling for troops from the dominions to help Britain subdue Turkey. The next day, the colonial secretary, Winston Churchill, cabled King a request for the immediate dispatch of Canadian forces for deployment to Turkey for possible combat. King was understandably annoyed at this peremptory requisition from the British for the commitment of combat forces in a matter that did not really threaten Britain and the cause of which was unknown to Canada. (It was in fact traceable to ham-fisted British excess in trying to bully a proud and still formidable former adversary, now led by Mustafa Kemal Atatürk, probably the world's premier statesman in the early 1920s.) There was in this British backsliding into thinking of the dominions, including India, as just a ready reserve for the satisfaction of British manpower needs, with no consultation or community of interest or policy development at all, an eerie echo of the tenacious and devious resistance to responsible government in Canada seventy-five to ninety years before. All of this had been settled. King instantly improvised a method of dealing with it that typified his genius for instinctively laying his hands on the way to reassure his followers, avoid inflaming his enemies, and sweep up the moderate centre: Canada would not go to war, in this instance or any other, without the approval of Parliament. This wasn't betrayal of the Mother Country, was completely consistent with Canadian independence, and imposed a cooling-off period of whatever duration King selected, since only he could decide when Parliament could determine any issue. King lamented in his diary that "the fate of the Empire is . . . in the hands of a man like Churchill." (Ten years later, Churchill, on a visit to Canada, acknowledged that he should not have made a public declaration without ministerial consultation.[15] Ten years after that, they would be amicably shouldering mighty burdens together.)

Most sentiment in the country sided with King, favouring support for Britain if it needed it and it was justified, but by Canada's decision, not Britain's summons. But Meighen flung himself into the trap laid by events and told a Toronto audience, "Canada should have said: 'Ready, aye, ready; we stand by you.'"[16] (This was originally a Great War phrase of Laurier's.) This was a divergence even from Borden's view that Canada had "nearly" become autonomous and was not subject to unconditional demands for combat forces in this cavalier way. King was on firm and precedented ground and could invoke statements made by Macdonald, Laurier's stance on South Africa, and both Laurier and Borden's positions on the Great War. The Chanak crisis settled down quickly, and thus both Churchill and Meighen were shown to have shot from the hip with thoughtless and misguided reflexes, and Meighen's lack of political judgment was again on display. What some of King's supporters called the "kindergarten school diplomacy" had to end. The next step in this process was King's direct negotiation with the United States of the Halibut Treaty. It was absurd that the British would, as they did, strenuously object to a first Canadian treaty on straight sovereign terms over such an improbable and apparently pedestrian issue. In fact, Pacific halibut fishing was a considerable commerce, and Canadian nationalists could jubilate that the country was finally negotiating its own treaties and was not hobbled by British appeasers trying to buy American goodwill at Canada's expense, as Macdonald had endured at Washington in 1871 and Laurier over the Alaska boundary in 1903. Mackenzie King had swum to national independence holding the tail of a halibut, and not even Meighen could get too jingoistically exercised on behalf of an affronted Empire about that.

In the autumn of 1923, Mackenzie King carried his muted crusade for greater Canadian autonomy to the Imperial Conference. It was outrageous that there should be any ambiguity at this late date about Canada's standing as an independent country; and it was doubly outrageous that the British government could imagine, given that country's impecunious postwar condition and the wealth of Canada – now a nation of nearly ten million under no possible threat from the United States and certainly not anyone else – that it had any automatic authority over anything Canada did. Canada had repaid the paternity and avuncular sponsorship of both founding countries in the First World War, and only the phenomenon of public psychology responding slowly to geopolitical realities explains why Canadian leaders had to put up with any of this, though perhaps the reticence of the leaders themselves may have prolonged this artificial state of subordinacy somewhat.

The Canadian Conservatives had regressed from their founder, Macdonald, who was a realist about the workings of Whitehall and only indulged the Imperial government as much as necessary to be sure of being plausibly under its protection while the American bull intermittently rampaged in the polemical blathering and bloviation of its public men. Borden ascribed French-Canadian lack of enthusiasm for the Imperial framework to Quebec's isolation, superstition, and unworldliness, and even he made a fairly vigorous stance for recognition of Canada as a consultative partner in a more collegial Empire. He seems never to have taken on board that the Imperial War Cabinet was a sham and a talking shop manipulated by the Welsh trickster Lloyd George while he milked the Empire of men and resources in Britain's hour of need. Meighen, a Manitoban and twenty years younger than the Atlanticist Nova Scotian Borden, was at this point an unsubtle, heel-clicking servant of the overseas Imperial king-protector. He hadn't thought it through. King had, but his natural caution and desire always to find the radical and cozy centre, to find the route to his goal that offered the least resistance, no matter how circuitous, like a heat-seeking missile, forfeited the admiration of those who liked firm and crisp leadership. That is a quality that is almost always in short supply in the federal government of Canada, because Canada is a country that spans sharply different cultures that have never been homogenized. The French segregationists, the nostalgic unitary Imperialists, the American-oriented continentalists, and the outright Canadian nationalists, are always hard, but not impossible, to coordinate, so King pursued his own mysterious course with mind-numbing tortuosity, making placatory gestures to almost all electorally identifiable groups as he made his noiseless way. It was deft, and even artistic at times, but so singular, so imperceptible, that the gallery that cheered him was confined to a few sycophants and spiritualist cranks through whom he communicated with those who had gone ahead to the "Great Beyond," in particular his mother and Sir Wilfrid Laurier, as well as some people he had never known, such as William Ewart Gladstone. It was bizarre, but it was oddly successful, and it is not for others to mock the achievements of one who accomplished so much, for so long, no matter his frequent humbug and obscurantism.

King departed for London accompanied by Professor Oscar (O.D.) Skelton of Queen's University, who had favourably reviewed King's *Industry and Humanity* and had publicly commended him on his handling of the Chanak incident. The prime minister also took with him

John Dafoe, the acidulous but perceptive editor of Sifton's *Manitoba Free Press*, who had been critical of King's diffident and indecipherable leadership techniques but had warmed somewhat to him in office, though he had reservations about accompanying him and only did so at Sifton's request. Skelton would join King's government as deputy minister of external affairs, found the Canadian foreign service, and exercise greater influence on the personnel and formulation of Canadian foreign policy than anyone in the country's history. He was an authentic Canadian nationalist, a respecter of both the British Empire and the United States, but an advocate and, in so far as he could be, a propagator of an independent course for Canada. He suffered the disadvantage of most Canadians who would seek to be pathfinders, or at least of most between Laurier and Pierre Trudeau: he had no flamboyance or panache, a necessary ingredient in raising the heavy dough of Canadian excitement, overlaid as it always is by caution and doubt, often including a generous portion of self-doubt.

At the conference, and as King had anticipated, there was a renaissance of enthusiasm for a unified Imperial foreign policy. Stanley Bruce, the Australian leader succeeding the unfeasible Hughes, favoured it, as Australia feared Japanese expansion; Smuts of South Africa also favoured it, because he had so mesmerized the British political leadership, Liberal and Conservative, that he expected to be the most eminent figure in an Imperial council or ministry. King, in a vintage formulation, said, "Our attitude is not one of unconditional isolation; nor is it one of unconditional intervention."[17] Smuts, not altogether in jest, called him "a very terrible person." The Australian Richard Casey (a future governor general of that country) compared him and his nationalism to "a vandal who pulls down a castle in order to build a cottage."[18] Lord Curzon (1859–1925), the foreign secretary – who had been sent as the brightest of the Souls (an elite British group of talented and stylish aristocrats that included Tennants, Wyndhams, Lyttletons, Asquiths, Coopers, and Balfour) to be, at forty, the youngest viceroy of India ever – had just been passed over by King George V as prime minister (to succeed the terminally ill Andrew Bonar Law) for Stanley Baldwin, whom Curzon described, with some reason, but typically, as of "the most profound insignificance." He was more acerbic even than usual when he described Mackenzie King as "obstinate, tiresome, and stupid, and nervously afraid of being turned out of his own Parliament when he gets back."[19] The description was fair, except that King was anything but stupid; his *passes d'armes* with the legendarily exalted ("I am George Nathaniel Curzon, / A very superior person" began a popular current sendup) yet tragic Curzon left them with no reciprocal regard or understanding. Curzon's brilliant career faded and he died in 1925. Winston Churchill later said that Curzon's "morning had been golden, the noontide was bronze, and the evening lead."[20] Mackenzie King was like a shadow, who remained for a very long time, was unprepossessing or even irritating when animated, but who left his mark, when he finally departed, with a greater imprint than many apparently weightier people.

King stood his ground well in London, and he gave and intended no offence to Canadian Imperialists, but gratified Canadian nationalists and isolationists, French and English. He did what he had come to do, and as a bonus he had impressed Dafoe, the most influential opinion leader in the Western provinces. In November 1922, King had pounced on Gouin and others for trying to reopen discussion of what had been agreed about tariffs and control of natural resources and stormed uncharacteristically that he would not be humiliated nor have his position usurped. There were further disagreements over King's plan to resurrect the subsidized railway rate instituted with the 1897 Crow's Nest Pass Agreement, which would reduce shipping costs for the Western farmer. With infinite and almost sadistic patience, King held to his position and appeared endlessly indulgent, and even Job-like, in his toleration of recalcitrant and dissentient members of the team. Finally, William Fielding's health deteriorated, and in 1923 he handed over most of his duties as finance minister to an associate minister, James A. Robb, and in 1925 retired altogether, aged seventy-five. By then, and a few months later, partly for health reasons and partly because he had been hemmed in by King and Lapointe and couldn't do anything, feeling himself like Gulliver in Lilliput, Gouin too resigned, in January 1924. King wrote in his diary that Gouin had "served only interests."[21] This shortchanges Gouin for his vital role in isolating Bourassa politically and strangling his effort at political success, but it is true that Gouin regarded Quebec's interest, the interest of the Montreal financial community, and his own political and pecuniary interest as being almost identical. He had been succeeded as premier of Quebec by the patrician and capable

Louis-Alexandre Taschereau, nephew of the cardinal and son, cousin, and father of justices of the Supreme Court of Canada (chief justices in two cases), and as federal justice minister by Ernest Lapointe, who, as King's Quebec lieutenant, was virtual co-leader of the government and de facto co-leader of the federal Liberal Party.

King's patient, devious, systematic removal of rivals and dissidents was a bloodless and ultra-moralistic replication of some of the methods of his almost exact contemporary and analogue in shadowy communist manoeuvring, Stalin. They were both party leaders for twenty-nine years, though King started five years earlier. Both claimed the legitimate succession to illustrious predecessors (in Stalin's case, Lenin) and were enigmatic and uncharismatic, but endlessly calculating and possessed the genius of survival. Of course, the parallels are superficial; Stalin was a bloodstained monster while King was a fidgeting turbopious Christian mystic and a mark for spiritualist quacks and charlatans. But to a degree they followed similar methods of leaving the flamboyance and the spectacle to others while endlessly negotiating around and manipulating the susceptibilities and frailties of small numbers of insider party functionaries.

With Fielding and Gouin gone, King did reduce the tariff on items of greatest concern to the Western farmers. As he had expected, Crerar had departed public life not having been able to square joining King's government with his duty to his supporters, and as the Progressives had never seriously put down the roots of a party, they were burning out like prairie wildfire in the rain and King expected to reap the political benefit. The area where the government had a vulnerability greater than King had appreciated was in financial irregularities in the Customs Department, presided over for many years by Jacques Bureau, six-term MP and now senator, from Trois-Rivières. The department, especially in Quebec, had been heavily undermined by the vast bootlegging and smuggling interests that took over the alcoholic beverage business in the United States when the Americans officially imposed Prohibition in 1919. It was one of the most insane legislative initiatives in American history, as it simply handed one of the country's greatest industries over to what quickly became organized crime, including some individuals whose folkloric renown (such as Chicago's Al Capone) would surpass the fame of many of the current politicians. The smugglers of liquor into the

United States, past bribed border officials of both nationalities, brought cheap American manufactures back with them. It was estimated that this traffic was costing the federal government about fifty million dollars a year in lost customs revenue, and an appreciable amount of this was going into the pockets of Bureau and his officials. The chief customs enforcement officer of Montreal, Joseph Bisaillon, was sending stocks of whisky to Bureau, and the minister's own chauffeur was moonlighting as a driver of a car used for smuggling, a car which had itself been smuggled into Canada. At a meeting with Lapointe and Arthur Cardin, an influential Quebec MP and Lapointe's successor as minister of marine and fisheries, at Laurier House on September 1, 1925, Bureau turned up drunk. This did not endear him to his leader (who rarely drank, and never to excess), and Bureau was sacked as minister and replaced by Georges Boivin, who removed Bisaillon but did not seriously address the problem.

King dissolved Parliament for an election at the end of October and believed that his tariff for revenue would be a workable cover for the distinctly different views on tariff matters he was propounding in the East and West, and that he would reap credit for his constructive but somewhat nationalistic stance in the Empire and as the only candidate who could keep English and French Canadians happily together. The crowds on the campaign trail were thin but not hostile, and King seemed to do well on the radio, the first election where this medium figured, as about one hundred thousand Canadian homes had radio receivers. King's radio voice was reedy and his syntax was always complicated, and he never departed from a very flat monotone. His spiritual media assured him the omens and auguries were good. On October 28, election eve, King had another stirring seance and was convinced that his own father (whom he took at first for Sir Wilfrid) assured him that he would win the election.

The spirits were mistaken, or were misunderstood. The Conservatives made the greatest gains of any party in one election in Canadian history up to that time, picking up 36 of the constituencies that had been held by the Progressive Party in 1921, as well as 30 others, including 18 from the Liberals. The Conservatives would have 115 MPs, up from 49, on 46.1 per cent of the popular vote, up from just under 30 per cent. Liberal members of Parliament were reduced to 100 from 118, representing 39.7 per cent of the vote, down from 41 per cent in 1921. The Progressives won 22 seats on 8.5 per cent of the vote, compared to 21.2 per cent in 1921 and 58 MPs. The Conservatives had 68 of 82 Ontario MPs, and where they had been whitewashed in six of the nine provinces in 1921, in 1925 Meighen had 10 of 14 British Columbia MPs, 10 of 11 from New Brunswick, and 11 of 14 from Nova Scotia. Two Labour candidates were elected, including the eminent socialist James Shaver Woodsworth, and two independents, including Henri Bourassa, returning to Ottawa, inexplicably, after an absence of nearly twenty years. There were two United Farmers of Alberta MPs, an independent farmer and official Socialist. The Conservatives elected four Quebec MPs, all from predominantly English districts. Mackenzie King was defeated in his own riding of York North, as he had been in 1911, and seven of his ministers also lost. Though full of moral reproaches at Conservative dishonesty and vote-buying with oceanic contributions allegedly provided by Montreal and Toronto business interests, King was philosophical and not panicked or deprived of his inextinguishable sense of self-preservation.

The unexpected result seems to have been attributable in part to skepticism about King's tariff evasions, in part to anger at corruption in the Customs Department – though Canadians, who did not adopt countrywide Prohibition, had no moral problem with selling liquor to the Americans, though they were less enthused by gangsters like Capone – and in part to a backlash against the claim that the Conservatives would divide the country, and except in Quebec no credence at all was attached to the suggestion that Meighen would blunder into war, a charge based on the Chanak episode. In Quebec, the Liberals pulled out all the stops, as Taschereau declared, "Meighen . . . has sent our boys to Flanders Fields. It is he, who, with his conscription law, has filled the cemeteries of Flanders with 60,000 Canadians."[22] Taschereau was finally reduced to claiming he had been misquoted, but it was a very shabby campaign of smear and fear, and in Quebec it worked; but not elsewhere. Grim shock though the result was for the government, there was no reason to doubt that the Progressives would continue to vote with the Liberal Party, and that would give King 122 MPs in a house of 245, even if he was not among them himself. He was almost certain to be sustained in the House of Commons, if he chose to meet it, although Meighen was clearly at the head of the largest party. King determined to convene Parliament.

When he met the governor general, Lord Byng, on October 30,

Byng's opening gambit was, "Well I can't tell you, my dear friend, how sorry I feel for you," as he cranked up to receive the prime minister's resignation. Byng said that King had the option of asking for dissolution – which the governor general said he could not grant in good conscience – of resigning, or of remaining. Byng would accept whichever was King's choice, but told him, "As a friend of yours, may I say that I hope you will consider very carefully the wisdom of" resigning.[23] He prattled on a bit about how undesirable it would be to rely on the Progressives and J.S. Woodsworth. King said he was inclined to remain but would think about it. Lapointe urged him to continue, as did most of his entourage, but Vincent Massey, the urbane but unsuccessful Liberal candidate in Durham, Ontario, and scion of a family that was roughly the English-Canadian equivalent of the Taschereaus, though commercially more experienced, urged him to hand over to Meighen. Naturally, King took his cue from the spirits, who had moved quickly, via his principal current medium, Mrs. Rachel Bleaney, to interpret the election in a way entirely consistent with their pre-electoral predictions of victory. "I cannot do other than regard all Mrs. Bleaney tells me as revelation."[24] Doubtless, King was sincere in this, but it was an interpretation that certainly suited his convenience. On November 2, King returned to Government House and told Byng he intended to remain. The governor general told him he thought Meighen had earned the right to try to govern and asked him to continue to think about it overnight. King took a few hours, conferred with his cabinet again, and confirmed his decision to Byng.

Byng would later claim that it was at least agreed between them that if King lost a confidence vote he would not dispute that Meighen could have a chance at forming a government. By this time, Meighen was becoming impatient for a call from Byng to do just that. He continued in that angry condition through to the opening of the new Parliament on January 26, 1926. In the meantime, on November 16, in a speech in Hamilton, Meighen did an apparent U-turn on Chanak and implied that Canada should not go to war without a general election. He assured the numerous outraged commentators after this bomb burst that allowance would of course be made for matters of urgency, but no one now imagined that it would be possible to hold up a war decision for two months while the people were consulted, nor that it would be appropriate not to have Parliament sitting for two months prior to such a decision. King largely ignored Meighen to allow him to stew in his own juice with his angry partisans, who were almost ready (aye, ready) to muzzle their leader as they hovered on the brink of office. There was a faction among Liberals that thought of trying to depose King in favour of Saskatchewan premier Charles Dunning, who was about to join the federal government and dreamt of little else but thought better of trying to make such a move. Lapointe and most of the senior party leadership and organization had been well massaged by King and were solid, and King was now leading them in an intricate sequence of steps to retain power; this was no time to challenge a leader who was beleaguered but on top of his game and manoeuvring with cool-headed shrewdness to defeat an accident-prone opponent he had bested before.

There were a number of social encounters between King and Byng and his wife. The governor general had stopped the repetitive assurances that King was his "friend" (always a suspect practice, but especially from a British viscount and field marshal), but he was quite civil. Lady Byng (although she donated a trophy to the National Hockey League for sportsmanlike conduct) was vituperative and barely able to bring herself to speak with King. More piquant is the claim from Lady Byng's lady-in-waiting, Eva Sandford, that the prime minister, seated next to her at dinner at Government House, had twice pinched her thigh. This made the rounds, to some titillation, even from those Rockliffe doyennes who thought King unlikely to be so bold or even motivated. (As his secret history posthumously revealed, King was not lacking in sex drive, but his very restrained manner and status as a bachelor incited the much laboured inference that he was asexual.) In the Throne Speech of January 1926, Byng read King's very tactical political program: farm loans; completion of the Hudson Bay Railway from The Pas, Manitoba, all the way to Churchill; a neutral Tariff Advisory Board; and a concession of control of Alberta's natural resources to the provincial government. King shortly discovered the virtues of a national pension scheme also. The pension was only twenty dollars a month, was means-tested, and was dependent on agreement with the individual provinces, but it bought the government the support of Woodsworth and his Labour colleague Abraham Heaps. The pension bill passed the House in March, but then the Conservative senators killed it, in another act of political suicide in the highest traditions of Meighen's promise of a general election to determine if the country could go to war.

In mid-February, King had returned to the House of Commons representing Prince Albert, Saskatchewan. Lapointe was the House leader and deftly floor-managed the government's rather opportunistic program until, in June, a special parliamentary committee unearthed the fact that Jacques Bureau's replacement as customs minister (after Bureau removed nine full cabinets of ministerial files), Georges Boivin, while he was minister, had employed bootleggers and smugglers, and had sprung one of them from prison to assist a local Liberal candidate. Lapointe and Cardin refused to hear of Boivin resigning and locked arms with their colleague. King, who by now knew something about the mind of French-Canadian politicians, wrote in his diary that this sense of chivalry was commendable but that he felt such loyalty was "open to question" in moral terms, or, more to the point, in considering the practicalities of holding on to one's – that is, his – position. On June 22, 1926, Henry Herbert Stevens (1878–1973), the hyperactively aggressive Conservative Vancouver MP from 1911 to 1940, moved a motion of censure against Boivin and of no confidence in the government. Woodsworth tried to derail it with an amendment deferring everything to a Royal Commission, but it failed. King concluded that he would not wait for such a dispute to be resolved but would seek dissolution for new elections, which he did on June 26. He sought to avoid the vote of censure proposed by Stevens that was now likely to pass. This led to one of the great political controversies in Canadian history.

Byng felt King had no right to expect dissolution without losing a confidence vote or equivalent; he thought it the "negation of Parliament's authority."[25] The counter-theory, that King had every right to request dissolution and that, as King had been sustained by Parliament many times in six months, the governor general had to grant it, also has many adherents. In general, a prime minister who has retained the confidence of the house, and especially who still ostensibly retains it, has the right to dissolution when he requests it. It cannot be within the governor general's prerogatives to impute and judge the motive of the prime minister in requesting dissolution and to determine, if a confidence motion is before the House that is apt to be lost, that the prime minister must suffer the ignominy of defeat before requesting dissolution. King momentarily took leave of his political senses and asked Byng to seek advice from the British government. This, Byng naturally refused to do; King should never have asked, and Byng was right to refuse. King resigned himself to his fate, which he still expected to be a benign one, and on June 28, 1926, tendered his resignation and that of the government to the governor general. Lady Byng wrote Lord Tweedsmuir, the famous novelist John Buchan (and future governor general), that King was "a scurvy cad" wallowing in "his own despicable depths of moral degradation,"[26] a hilariously severe censure for such a self-righteous man as King.

Byng called upon Meighen to form a government, and John Dafoe and many others professed to believe King's career was about to end ignominiously. To deal with the requirement to resign and seek personal re-election of an incoming minister, Meighan himself resigned and named his other ministers as ministers without portfolio and provisional heads of other ministries, thus avoiding a sure minority position in Parliament and a fiasco that would replicate Macdonald's famous "double shuffle" defeat of George Brown in 1858 (Chapter 3). King raised an immense outcry at this mockery of Parliament and the public will. The Progressives joined him in this, and even Byng, who had brought this farce down upon the country, when he saw Meighen's cabinet, called them "the worst looking lot he had ever seen assembled around Parliament."[27] Meighen was defeated in the House and called on Byng, who had to grant dissolution, for a new election on September 14, 1926.

Incredibly, the other players had fumbled directly into King's hands. Meighen, who had effectively defeated King in all but the arts of survival in the 1925 election, had been completely outmanoeuvred for six months, starting with his insane call for electoral approval before the country could engage in foreign combat. Byng had opened with King on a note of patronizing treacle about "my dear friend" and with poor advice he had no business pressing, and then in some funk composed of egoistic pique and profound stupidity declined King's request for dissolution, pushed government on Meighen, who should have declined it so that at least the ensuing electoral gambit of King's would just be an attack on a foolish governor general, of which Canada had had plenty, though none recently. Instead, Meighen tried to form a government, which he should have known to be impossible, attempted a silly ruse, an activity to which he was morally as well as intellectually unsuited, and it all came down and hung around their necks like toilet seats, as if Byng and Meighen were puppets in a children's farce, controlled by the Liberal leader. And King now buried the customs scandal which brought him down in Parliament and could have killed him electorally, and distracted the country with a bogus campaign for popular sovereignty over an arrogant, meddlesome British governor who had been colluding, if not conspiring, with a shifty, saturnine, and medieval Tory – unfair caricatures of Byng and Meighen of course, but somewhat plausible on these events. For good measure, Meighen campaigned for a high tariff again, and against old-age pensions.

Again and again in his long career at the summit of Canadian public life, King would snatch a dazzling deliverance from apparently hopeless circumstances. The night of dissolution, July 4, King strolled in his garden at Kingsmere, in the Gatineau Hills – where he had more than two hundred acres of rolling hills and a comfortable country house, and installed ruins that he acquired from various sites in Europe – and sang one of his mother's favourite hymns, "O God of Bethel," to himself. As he thought of his mother's "beautiful flight to heaven," a "beautiful bird" with "a scarlet head" descended on one of his bird baths, which confirmed him in the predestined and benign trajectory of events.[28] It was all so fantastic that the utility of King's much-mocked practice of communing with those in the Great Beyond should not be ruled out entirely in an attempted explanation of this sequence of events and subsequent similarly astounding ones.

On September 14, the Liberals gained 16 MPs to win a total of 116 seats, on 42.9 per cent of the vote, an increase of 3.1 per cent. The Conservatives elected 91 candidates, 24 fewer than before, though it was on 45.4 per cent of the vote, a drop of only 1 per cent and still 2.5 per cent more than the Liberals and a substantial lead in English-speaking Canada. The Progressives lost half of their 22 MPs, retaining 11, and lost a majority of their votes, dropping from 8.4 per cent to 3.9 per cent. And the United Farmers of Alberta, who had only had one-third of 1 per cent of the overall vote in the 1925 election, gained by almost 500 per cent to win 1.9 per cent of the countrywide vote, but jumped from 2 MPs to 11. The Progressives were not opposed by the Liberals, and their leader, succeeding Crerar, Robert Forke, joined King's government, making the combined Liberal-Progressive total of MPs a comfortable 127. The United Farmers of Alberta were also a good deal closer to the Liberals in policy terms than they were to the Conservatives.

King was elected with a margin of more than four thousand in his adoptive district of Prince Albert, over a determined thirty-one-year-old candidate whom King referred to in his voluminous diary with the words "We have seen the last of this young man Diefenbaker." This would be the only occasion in Canadian history when two candidates who would be prime ministers ran against each other. (It was far from being the last of John Diefenbaker. He would ultimately hold the all-time Canadian record for general election victories as MP, thirteen terms.) Meighen again lost his own constituency of Portage la Prairie, and soon announced his retirement from politics. King and Meighen were both fifty-two in 1926. Meighen was a powerful and talented politician but needed the guidance of a senior figure to direct his fire; he was a brilliant second-in-command, an Anthony Eden, or in military terms a Stonewall Jackson, but not a successful commander. He would be heard from again, as Diefenbaker would, and Meighen's subsequent career would have its rewards, not least in amassing a substantial fortune and seeing the success of his sons in the law and finance and a much-respected (and bilingual) grandson who would become a successful Quebec and Ontario lawyer, political candidate, and eminent senator.

King encountered the Byngs a few more times before they left in October 1926, and after. When Their Excellencies departed Ottawa, Byng was cordial, but Lady Byng "looked at me like someone from the Chamber of Horrors." They were back on a private visit in 1932, when King was in opposition. Byng was again cordial, but his consort was an ice queen and said nothing. The men reminisced and agreed to disagree on their recollections. King wept with mellow satisfaction at this civilized end of it, and even Lady Byng was a little more forthcoming, but she remained, wrote King to himself, "a viper." Lord Byng died in June 1935, aged seventy-two, and King had a seance with intimates in which Byng appeared and allegedly asked for forgiveness, which King was happy to grant. A few weeks later, Lady Byng wrote to King's opponent and the incumbent prime minister, R.B. Bennett, and referred to "that fat horror King . . . little beast. How I hate him for the way he treated Julian [her husband, known to friends as Bungo]. He is the one person in the whole world to whom I would do whatever harm I could. . . . I loathe liars and traitors. He is both."[29] He was more of a fabulist, responding to wishes that took the shape of revelations and visitations, than he was a liar. And he was certainly not a traitor; Byng was the chief author of the shambles of 1925 and 1926. But in all his apparent diffidence, King moved with preternatural, if amoral, and sometimes even ignoble, cunning, and while his virtuosity was little appreciated, the fallout of his agile manoeuvring left many incoherent with rage.

3. Mackenzie King II: Toward the Great Depression, 1926–1930

King embarked on another trip to an Imperial Conference on October 6, 1926, accompanied by Lapointe, Massey (whom King was naming as minister to Washington, finally filling the post created in 1920, as Canadian sovereignty creaked forward at less than a snail's pace), O.D. Skelton, and lesser officials. Though he was better established and more confident than in 1923 on the same mission, King was perceived by at least one participant as having "gone fat and American and self-complacent."[30] There was the usual schism among the participants on the issue of unity of foreign policy. The Australians and New Zealanders, not wanting to be left alone in the far Pacific between the isolationist and America-centric United States and the aggressive Japanese, wanted a tight relationship with the British, whose navy could still provide some deterrence against Japan. The South Africans and the Irish, both of whom had conducted prolonged rebellions against the British, were opposed with a ferocity that few other nationalities could approach. Sitting in the centre was the ultimate man in the middle, the increasingly familiar and endlessly enigmatic figure of Mackenzie King. He imagined Imperial conspiracies everywhere, but there were not many. The rather pedestrian and crisis-averse Stanley Baldwin was the British prime minister; Lloyd George had gone, with the old Liberal Party, into the unofficial opposition, where he would remain for another twenty years. Curzon was dead; Balfour was lord president of the council and near the end of his very long career. Churchill was busy in the exchequer and the foreign secretary was Austen Chamberlain, and neither was much in evidence at this meeting. Leo Amery was secretary for war and colonies and was present, but not with any fervently held agenda to push forward. It was a great deal less lively than in the days of Joseph Chamberlain's crusades and Lloyd George's devious orchestrations.

Europe was drowsy, as Germany and Russia were still pariahs; the trauma of the Great War was receding, prosperity was reviving, and there did not seem to be much need to do anything. The British were happy now with Canada opening its legation in Washington as long as the minister kept their ambassador informed, which only highlighted the absurdity of having delayed this step for seven years. King's main objective at the conference was to alter the role of Canada's governor general after the disagreement he had had with Byng. He proposed that the British government open high commissions in the dominion capitals and that governors general represent only the Crown. There was easy and general agreement on this point, and it was a useful step. It fell to King to be the leading conciliator with General Barry Hertzog, since 1924 the South African leader, and from all the debate about the organization of the Empire it was agreed that the dominions and the United Kingdom had equal powers and that the autonomous countries, including the United Kingdom, would together form the British Commonwealth of Nations. Everyone was happy with this formula except the king, who lamented that "poor old Balfour has given away my Empire."[31]

Mackenzie King was naturally delighted with the outcome of the London conference and was happy to carry the small nationalist torch in Canada, but also covered his right flank with ringing assurances of the centrality of the monarchy in Canadian national life. It was the now familiar King formula: he was taking jurisdiction and status for Canada from the British and pleasing the nationalists while singing "God Save the King" in more stentorian voice even than the Canadian Tories, who were reduced to complaining of King's decision to compound the heresy of the legation in Washington with the appointment of ministers to France and Japan.

There were impressive ceremonies on July 1, 1927, to celebrate the sixtieth anniversary of Confederation. The Prince of Wales and the Duke of York – the future kings Edward VIII and George VI – visited, as did Prime Minister Stanley Baldwin, and most impressively the world's greatest newsmaker in the 1920s, American aviator Charles Lindbergh.

Mackenzie King inserted himself heavily into proceedings in ornate gold-braided swallow-tail coat. His addresses were broadcast internationally, and he announced in his diary that he had reached audiences over a greater surface of the world than had ever been reached before (which was untrue, both King George v and Pope Benedict xv had exceeded him). He also engaged in his customary hyperbole in his diary in matters involving himself when he wrote that the day "was the beginning of Canada's place in the world, as a world power." Inevitably, King regarded the laying of wreaths at the foot of the new statue of Laurier (facing the Chateau Laurier hotel in Ottawa) as "a proud moment, almost a great spiritual triumph."[32]

The following day, by the intervention of Vincent Massey, Charles Lindbergh arrived. Lindbergh had electrified the world with his solo flight across the Atlantic from New York to Paris, and King found him "a more beautiful character" than he had ever seen; "like a young God who had appeared from the skies in human form – all that could be desired in youthful appearance, in manner, in charm, in character, as noble a type of the highest manhood as I have ever seen." There was a series of tremendous entertainments for Lindbergh, and he came to Laurier House for the night. Exceptionally, the prime minister allowed himself a few glasses of champagne. Lindbergh completely won over his host by claiming kinship and demonstrating considerable knowledge of King's grandfather and namesake. A pilot who had accompanied Lindbergh from the United States, a Lieutenant Thad Johnson, had crashed in an air show manoeuvre over Ottawa, and King ordered a state funeral for him on Parliament Hill, with the parliamentary flag lowered. An honour guard of the Royal Canadian Mounted Police conducted the casket to Union Station, across from Parliament Hill, as Lindbergh himself flew low overhead and threw down flowers on the funeral train.

Even allowing for Kingsian exaggeration, Canada was adding a cubit to its stature, and Mackenzie King was showing himself very adept at playing a mediating role in the Commonwealth and tastefully calling attention to Canada in ways that his predecessors had not attempted. This was a mighty celebration of the diamond jubilee of a confederation which, when launched in 1867, was greeted with indifference or skepticism by most foreign observers, including most of those in the British and American governments.

Canadians were by now turning up as military, scientific, and ideological adventurers in unsuspected places. General Gordon Guggisberg (1869–1930) of Galt, Ontario, served as a military surveyor in Singapore and Nigeria and was a very progressive governor of the Gold Coast (Ghana), and was ahead of his time in believing in racial equality and governing accordingly, in Ghana and in 1928–1929, British Guiana, and is publicly revered in Ghana still. Dr. Norman Bethune (1890–1939) of Gravenhurst, Ontario, was a surgeon in the Royal Navy in World War I, and provided free medical care to poor people in Montreal before becoming a communist and serving with the Republicans in the Spanish Civil War and then the Chinese Communists in China. He was the medical chief for the Chinese Eighth Route Army in the Sino-Japanese War, but he died of blood poisoning, having cut his finger performing an emergency operation in the field and was gratefully eulogized by Communist leader Mao Tse-tung, and is still well remembered in China. Frederick Grant Banting (1891–1941)of Alliston, Ontario, served in the Canadian Army Medical Corps in World War I and then in hospitals and laboratories in Toronto, and with Charles Best and J.J.R. MacLeod, pioneered in the development and general application of insulin, and, with MacLeod, won the Nobel Prize for Medicine in 1923. He and Best pursued valuable medical research at the Banting and Best Institute in Toronto, and he died in an air crash in 1941 on his way to England to work on improved pressurization for military aircrews.

In policy matters, King passed the pension he had promised Woodsworth as part of his survival plan after the 1925 election, and none of the provincial premiers dared to fail to pay their share of the modest pension. The third Dominion-Provincial Conference was held in 1927 (Laurier and Borden had each hosted one), and the alliance between Quebec and Ontario – which became a feature of federal-provincial affairs and in fact the principal opposition to the federal government in place of the official federal Opposition – was much in evidence. It was an unlikely match between the Low Church Protestant Orangeman Howard Ferguson and the patrician nephew of a cardinal, Louis-Alexandre Taschereau. While this tandem irritated King and strained relations with the federal Liberal Party in Quebec, it effectively ended systematic discrimination against Roman Catholic and French-language education in Ontario. Ferguson had been the minister of education when Regulation 17, which curtailed French education in Ontario far beneath what the British North America Act had promised, had been introduced in 1912. Ferguson now softened the official stance, and French and Catholic education were henceforth more generously facilitated. King left it to Lapointe to lead in jurisdictional matters, as he wanted no part of an argument with Taschereau (though he couldn't abide Ferguson and in his diary in 1930 called him "a skunk"[33]). King was pleased that the conference avoided spectacular fireworks and didn't really accomplish much. The latter feature would often be replicated in such conferences in the future, but the first precedent of a placid session would frequently not be followed.

In 1927, Lapointe had visited Geneva and demonstrated the wide serviceability of his organizational and parliamentary talents by arranging the election of Canada to a three-year term on the Council of the League of Nations. This was a considerable feather in Canada's cap (and certainly in Lapointe's), but King was uneasy about being dragged into European quarrels, even in these halcyon days. They had one of their rare arguments, and it became so heated that Lapointe threatened to resign, a thought so doom-laden for King's political future that he conceded the point at once to his chief associate. (Canadian interveners at the League of Nations "were inclined to confine themselves to sonorous sentiments about the duties of man, the excellent way in which the two Canadian races got along with each other, and the blessings of peace, so much so that 'the Canadian speech' came to be received each year with a certain amused boredom."[34]) King quickly became slightly intoxicated with the international circuit, however, an enthusiasm mitigated only by the "sacrifice" of giving up his farm at Kingsmere for the summer of 1928 to attend at Geneva as one of the six vice chairmen of the session. He and Lapointe travelled in style on the splendid new *Île de France*, the first of the great postwar liners, and King went to Paris to sign the asinine Kellogg-Briand Pact, which purported to "outlaw war as an instrument of national policy," a move enforced exclusively by moral suasion. It was another example of the United States prevailing on the nations of the world to join it in substituting psychology and theology for foreign policy, as the successor gesture to the Washington Naval Treaty, so the Americans, or at least the Republicans, could prove to themselves that they could advance the cause of peace outside the

League of Nations as well as they could inside it, a self-serving fiction, as the next fifteen years would tragically prove. To be fair to King, he never attached much credence to the Kellogg-Briand Pact (between the U.S. secretary of state and the French foreign minister), but he liked it because it required nothing of Canada and might result in the United States becoming more active in the world, which he sensibly realized was absolutely necessary to the security of the democracies.

The highlight of this trip to Europe was King's cordial visit with the Italian leader, Benito Mussolini, who only six years into his dictatorship was behaving responsibly and showing none of the Ruritanian absurdity and imitative bellicosity that he would inflict on the world in the 1930s and early 1940s. King found Mussolini somewhat sad, but decisive, well-informed, courteous, solicitous, and with a certain likeable softness of manner. He did not like the manifestations of dictatorial authority observable in the arbitrary power of the Italian police (who stopped his car), but Mussolini had cleaned "up the government and House of Representatives filled with communists . . . cleaned the streets of beggars and the houses of harlots . . . [which caused King to be] filled with admiration."[35]

Just out of government after five years as chancellor of the exchequer, Winston Churchill crossed Canada in the summer of 1929 on a speaking and book-promoting tour and was much impressed with the scale of activity and the beauty of the country. From the glories of Banff and Lake Louise, with the majestic mountains and emerald lakes, he wrote his wife, on August 27, on the stationery of the Banff Springs Hotel,

> I am greatly attracted to this country. Immense developments are going forward. There are fortunes to be made in many directions. The tide is flowing strongly. I have made up my mind that if Neville [Chamberlain] is made leader of the Conservative Party, or anyone else of that kind, I clear out of politics and see if I cannot make you and the kittens a little more comfortable before I die. Only one goal still attracts me and if that were barred I should quit the dreary field for pastures new. . . . "There's mighty lands beyond the seas." However the time to take decisions is not yet.[36]

Of course, that is not how it worked out, but it indicates how inspiring Canada was in the golden summer of 1929.

Canada, like the rest of the world, sleepwalked over the financial cliff and into the grim depression of the 1930s, which would only end with the resumption of the world struggle begun in the Great War, with armed forces in greater numbers, more fanatical combatant regimes, and more destructive weapons. There is no evidence that any serious person in the prosperous summer of 1929 foresaw what was coming in the next decade, though some had misgivings about the fact that the boom in equities (the stock market) vastly exceeded other economic indicators and was largely financed by debt. People bought shares, but most of the purchase price was a balance of sale secured by the stock that had been purchased; if a downturn began, the shares would be sold to liquidate the debt and the expanding cascade of stock being dumped would broaden, deepen, and accelerate the stock market plunge. This was what happened starting on October 29, 1929. This was the famous Wall Street Crash, and the pattern emerged of terrible market collapses followed by plateaus, and of political and financial leaders, who knew nothing about the complicated interaction of arithmetic and public psychology that determined supply and demand, solemnly announcing that the worst was over. The new American president, Herbert Hoover – who had been commerce secretary for eight years under the good-time Charlie Warren Harding and the reassuringly silent and inert Calvin Coolidge, who succeeded Harding on his death from a coronary in 1923 – kicked off this sequence of falsely optimistic pep rallies with the assurance that "the economy is fundamentally sound." It wasn't, and his policy prescription was the worst that could have been found, in an era when economics was a much less understood and academically examined subject than it has become. Hoover championed higher taxes, higher tariffs, and a smaller money supply, a perfect equivalent to pouring gasoline on the fire of economic contraction.

In 1920, the United States had wished for something entirely different from the mighty intellect and burning idealist Woodrow Wilson, and that is what it got in the amiable philistine Harding. The 1920s were a decade of boisterous dances, the speakeasy (to circumvent the gangster-tainted lunacy of Prohibition), the burgeoning talking-film and radio industries, the stock ticker, and the retrospectively mocking

spectacle of statesmen bustling to conferences about German war reparations and Allied war loans that would never be paid or repaid, and
collective security that would crumble and be contemptuously tram-
pled in the dust. The whole world would be aflame with war and ancient
centres of civilization given over to genocidal atrocities on an unheard
of scale and smashed to rubble. The pulsating optimism of 1929 became
what the British writer W.H. Auden, expressing the guilt of a generation
for the squandering of the postwar opportunity, welcomed a decade
later, in 1939, as the end of "a low, dishonest decade." Auden then almost
welcomed the purifying punishment of the terrible war just getting
under way, to chastise the world for its venality and cowardice and bring
the stern peace and disillusioned stability of the Old Testament and an
end to the narcissistic frivolity and systematic evil that had hijacked the
world and threatened every traditional notion of civilization.

The era of the pariah states, Germany and Russia, formidable geopolitical countries and distinguished cultures absenting themselves meekly
from the senior councils of the world and leaving them to the grey and
weak men of France and Britain – while America worshipped the golden
calf and the stock ticker, guzzled illegal liquor, and shrank foreign policy
to pretentious charades like the naval disarmament treaty and Kellogg-
Briand – all of it was coming to a prolonged and horrible end. As always,
Canada was not important enough in the world to be responsible for the
colossal policy failures that doomed the world, and had abstained from
the more deranged practices whose reckoning was at hand, but was
much influenced by the terrible Samsonian thrashings and lurchings of
the great powers and would try conscientiously to take care of itself and
do what was sensible. And, as always, it would do a good job of that. The
magnetic pull of the United States continued to be heavy through the
1920s: about 1,160,000 Canadians, most of them new arrivals from
Europe, moved on to the United States, though Canadian population
growth had been substantial, rising to about 10.4 million. Canada was
progressing, but it was a swim upriver when the United States remained
more attractive to immigrants.[37]

There were very few national leaders who had come through the
1920s and would make it through the 1930s, and none in the democratic world who, having managed that remarkable feat, would then
have a good war and a good peace in the 1940s; none except William

Lyon Mackenzie King. There would be painful setbacks and not a moment of panache or flair, but King would come through, and his generally unappreciative country would come through with him. Since he did not foresee what was coming any better than those who would not survive it, even with the collaboration of his seers and conjurers, he would intuit and manoeuvre his way through instinctively. A terrible era was upon the world when the premium would be on survival. By that criterion, Canada had exactly the right man.

In the early days of the economic decline, King did not understand the extent of it and completely misjudged the political implications. He concluded that it was better to go for an election in 1930 than to stretch his term to 1931, as matters might get worse. But uncharacteristically, especially for the author of *Industry and Humanity*, who passionately (in so far as that adverb could ever be applied to his activities) admired and wished to help people of modest means, he did nothing to appear sympathetic to the early victims of the economic depression. He considered a visit from Winnipeg's mayor, Ralph Webb, who asked for federal help with the rising cost of unemployment relief, to be "clearly a Tory device to stir up propaganda against the government [and put it in] an embarrassing position."[38] Some opposition MPs had the effrontery to quote in Parliament from *Industry and Humanity* (which was rivalled only by Hitler's *Mein Kampf* and Stalin's *The Foundations of Leninism* as the most densely written work of any of the world's political leaders of the 1930s, though King's tenor and content were certainly a good deal more peaceable and benign). His first line of defence was a typical recourse to constitutional niceties, akin to "Parliament will decide": that unemployment was a provincial and municipal responsibility. He was slow to grasp that the crisis was quickly getting beyond the utility of such evasions. In Parliament on April 3, 1930, he said he did not think conditions were sufficiently serious to require direct federal assistance, that furthermore, "we have other uses for our money," and, most insouciantly, that he "would not give a single cent to any Tory [provincial] government." These were inexplicable lapses and completely out of character for such a cautious leader and one so genuinely interested in the working and agrarian classes and the lower middle class. While he himself had fairly rich (and good) taste in art and wardrobe, he had the demeanour and consistency of a bourgeois, and extended intellectual and professional sympathy for and interest in the economically vulnerable.

At an election meeting in Edmonton in May, when heckled by some people claiming to be unemployed, he said that "some people are unemployed because they don't want to work," and accused one of his tormentors of being "a slacker."[39] He eventually realized he had made some oratorical mistakes, but typically claimed he had been taken out of context and eventually explained to John Diefenbaker and to his future assistant and prominent Liberal cabinet minister in the 1950s and 1960s, J.W. Pickersgill, that he made the comment on the advice of his Ontario provincial adversary, Premier Howard Ferguson, given at a luncheon where King had several drinks just before his speech (this was unusual and these are lame excuses; he certainly was not intoxicated, did not have a high regard for Ferguson, and must simply not have been thinking).*[40]

King still did not realize the gravity of the economic problems and devised the tactic of proposing Imperial preference. President Hoover and the Republican leaders in Congress were calling for tariff increases, and King thought he had discovered an alternate market to the United States with the bonus that "we will take the flag once more out of the Tory hands."[41] He thought he could replicate Macdonald's folkloric campaign of 1891 for the "old flag, the old policy, the old leader." But the policy was new, the leader wasn't old – and even when he was old, he was not a galvanizing figure like Sir John A. – and the flag had nothing to do with it. There were four hundred thousand unemployed, and there was no interference in the politics of Canada in 1930 as there had been forty years before to provoke Macdonald.† King's political genius was never an intuition of popular taste; it was to steer between contrary buffeting trends while holding to the centre and always adding personnel and voting blocs to his centrist-liberal core. He had brought Saskatchewan's premier, Charles Dunning, in as minister of finance, though he disliked him personally, and both leaders of the Progressives, Thomas Crerar as

---

* In his diary of June 17, 1930, King recounts a dream of being rudely asked for money by two naked beggars, the next two federal Conservative leaders, R.B. Bennett and R.J. Manion. He was boarding a ship for England, but gave them some clothes, but they were ungrateful and vanished into a club. King interpreted the sea voyage as the election campaign. It is not that far-fetched a dream but his very sober determination of it, as if it had clear and important meaning, is rather bizarre.

† Secretary of State James G. Blaine had effectively proposed federal union to a Liberal Toronto reporter (Chapter 4).

minister of railways and canals in 1929 (after eight years of cajolery) and Robert Forke as minister of immigration and colonization from 1926 to 1929, when King put him in the Senate. He thought the Prairies were secure, not because he had any piercing insight into the views of the inhabitants, but because he had recruited their most talented and popular politicians to his team, as Lapointe was for Quebec. King's mastery was one of cautious pursuit of the sensible course buttressed by recruitment of the strongest local faction and fiefdom heads; it didn't have much to do with his own vision of the country and the world, though his perceptions in these areas were often astute.

In mid-April 1930, King took a holiday in Bermuda and New York with his supporters long-time Liberal organizer Senator Andrew Haydon and the financier Senator Wilfrid Laurier McDougald. McDougald picked up King's hotel bill in Bermuda of four hundred dollars, and King enjoyed the lovely island, though he was slightly disconcerted by the "women, and girls, who were bathing in abbreviated suits," though some were "rather pretty to look at." King seems never to have had the least idea of why McDougald lavished such attention on him. McDougald had a holding company called Sterling Industrial Corporation which, after Beauharnois Light, Heat and Power Company had invested in it, had recycled that money and extensive borrowings into the stock of Beauharnois. But the Beauharnois acquisition of its interest in Sterling was conditional on federal government approval of Beauharnois's plan for extensive hydroelectric development of the St. Lawrence River about twenty miles southwest of Montreal. On the announcement of the proposal, the stock of Beauharnois soared, and Haydon's law partner, John Ebbs, was a business partner of McDougald, and Haydon's firm did almost all Beauharnois's legal work and received a fifty-thousand-dollar annual lobbying fee. A close friend of Premier Taschereau's and of King's, Senator Donat Raymond, was also a member of the promoting group, and King was careful enough to ensure that consideration of the project was meticulous and disinterested. There is no indication of a financial impropriety by King personally, but he was unusually careless in being quite so intimate with men who were close partisans, and in the case of McDougald had contributed to Peter Larkin's fund of $225,000 to provide the prime minister financial independence. It appears to have been King's naïveté about commercial matters rather than a failing generated by his avarice (which was considerable) that created this compromising condition. There were no immediate repercussions, but Beauharnois was a time bomb as King returned to Ottawa in May 1930 and had Parliament dissolved on May 30 for elections on July 28.

Richard Bedford Bennett (1870–1947), a wealthy and successful Calgary lawyer and investor, originally from New Brunswick, and a Conservative MP from 1911 to 1917 and again from 1925, was elected leader of the Conservative Party and of the official Opposition in October 1927. He was a very confident and forceful man, who always seemed on the knife-edge between being an extremely effective leader and a blowhard and a bully. Bennett was a bachelor, a Wesleyan crusader for good causes, and a humourless, driven man. King expected him to be a difficult opponent, as destructive and aggressive as Meighen, but less intellectual and probably with better political judgment. He had a good deal of business support and injected a substantial amount of his own money into his campaign.

Bennett embarked in early June on a fourteen-thousand-mile rail campaign tour and at every stop hammered the economic depression and promised to deliver the country from it and from King. He opened his campaign in Winnipeg, where he promised to use tariffs "to blast a way into the markets of the world." It was nonsense of course, and much of Bennett's technique was just bluster, but to a frightened country that was suddenly very concerned about rising unemployment and crashing commodity prices and tired of King's mealy-mouthed equivocations, Bennett had an appeal that caught the moment. He engaged in whole-sale fear-mongering with a sighting of a tidal wave of economic disaster if current incompetence and dithering and cynicism were not replaced by Bennett's can-do, roll up the sleeves, Western vigour. King tried to be more forceful and declarative, but he was a known and not overly exciting quantity, and there were large numbers of hecklers at most of his meetings. Ferguson declared that "King is the issue," which was not an elevation he meant kindly. Although King was startled by the ad hominem attacks, which seemed to be better directed to the public mood and a lower intelligence than had Meighen's polysyllabic barbs, he was philosophical, always playing the long game, and still thought on election eve that he would win. With Quebec and most of the Prairies, as he thought, firm, the Liberal formula would enable him to win with just bits and pieces from Ontario, British Columbia, and the Maritime provinces. He was supported in his optimistic opinion by the spirits, which, according to his diary, never seemed to stray far from his desires.

On July 28, 1930, King suffered the only real defeat he sustained in seven elections as federal Liberal leader. Bennett's Conservatives won 134 constituencies, a gain of 43; the Liberals won 90, a loss of 26. The Conservative popular vote rose from 44.7 per cent to 47.8 per cent; the Liberals' share of the total vote also increased, from 44.2 per cent to 45.5. The United Farmers of Alberta lost two of their MPs and retained nine, on a reduction in the popular vote from 2.1 per cent of the countrywide total to 1.5 per cent. The Progressives had now largely folded into the Liberals, vindicating in some measure King's tactics; they declined from 11 to 3 MPs as their overall percentage of the vote declined from 4.2 per cent to 1.8 per cent. The prime minister had at least hung on to his own constituency, but the shocking development was the election of twenty-five Conservatives in Quebec, a clear response to economic conditions and to a Conservative leader who, though he was opposed even to a Unionist government in 1917 and was a conscriptionist, was not particularly identified with conscription, as Meighen had been. Lapointe may have lost some prestige in the province in minor jurisdictional differences with Taschereau, who remained the master of the province, though two rising opposition figures would bear watching: Camillien Houde, mayor of Montreal, starting in 1928, and Maurice Duplessis, member of the Legislative Assembly for Trois-Rivières, starting in 1927.

King, though he frequently wallowed in self-pity and fear for his health and endurance, and for conditions that he could not control, such as the antics of antagonistic provincial premiers or world conditions, was rarely overly rattled by reversals. They were always part of the divine plan and were bound to be temporary, because of his virtue, repentance of his shortcomings, and methodical thoroughness. Election night 1930 was such an occasion. "I will be glad to throw onto Bennett's shoulders . . . finding a solution for unemployment," King said. "My guess is that he will go to pieces under the strain."[42] He knew that Bennett was a shoot-from-the-hip Westerner who had no idea what he was getting into, and that conditions were now more likely to deteriorate than improve. Bennett had made such brash claims, and disillusionment would not be long in coming. From 1911 to 1919, King had patiently waited (in the House of Rockefeller) for his hour to come. Now, he would wait again, but with a historic and comfortable home and a country property, a solid fund provided by his partisans, and an interesting task as leader of the Opposition with much to oppose as Bennett lost his swagger fighting heavy economic headwinds. The country, which became bored and impatient with King, could soon rediscover his reassuringly unflamboyant qualities. He had held almost even with the Conservatives in the popular vote, and while his political reasoning about holding Quebec and the Prairies had not entirely been successful, that reasoning would keep him in the party leadership, as those regions were, within the Liberal Party, solidly loyal. After a few months, King summoned Rachel Bleaney, his principal spiritualist, and invited her to explain her mistaken interpretations and prognostications, but he saw the new era as an opportunity to be more rested, enjoy the spectacle of Bennett's discomfort, and, he certainly emphasized in his diary, "reconstruct my own thought and life."[43] Involutional, generally cynical, and self-obsessed though King was, he did not hesitate to blame himself, never lacked humility before God, and saw any setback as a deserved humiliation resulting from his own errors, but also an opportunity graciously presented by his creator to regroup, pull himself together, and be worthy to come back stronger than ever. One of the many aspects of King's odd personality that his opponents – who all, except Borden, underestimated him – never understood was that he was more dangerous in his relentless and unshakeable perseverance than in his shameless and sometimes breathtaking unscrupulousness. The new man of government prepared to govern; the old leader of opposition prepared to oppose. In these tumultuous times, both were assured of challenging days ahead.

4. Richard Bedford Bennett: Man of Thunder, 1930–1935

R.B. Bennett was sworn in as Canada's eleventh prime minister on August 7, 1930, and also as minister of finance and receiver general, president of the Privy Council, and secretary of state for external affairs. Sir George Perley became deputy prime minister and minister without portfolio. The postmaster general would be the former and long-serving leader of the provincial Conservative Party of Quebec Arthur Sauvé (a gentlemanly doormat for the unstoppable Taschereau regime). The minister of marine, traditionally a French-Canadian position, would be Alfred Duranleau; Charles H. Cahan would be the secretary of state; Robert J. Manion would be minister of railways and canals; and Henry Herbert Stevens would be secretary of trade and commerce. It was a passably purposeful but not an especially memorable group to begin with, and did not become one. Ontario premier Howard Ferguson became high commissioner in London, succeeding Larkin and Perley. In taking so much direct responsibility on himself, Bennett was making himself the lightning rod for any reversals and disappointments that would come, and there were bound to be some. Domineering from the start, Bennett frequently fielded questions that were not directed to him; he set out to provide a new level of personal, comprehensive government. This impression was furthered when Bennett called a special session of Parliament for September 8, 1930, and opened it with a twenty-line Throne Speech, in which he presented a stimulus package to generate jobs and upwardly revised protective tariffs.

Bennett departed for London on September 22. The Statute of Westminster had been adopted, which provided that no law of any commonwealth country should become law in any other of the countries unless they wished it so, and it was given royal assent in December. This was not a popular measure with the provincial governments, which tended to like Westminster better than Ottawa, as it was less meddlesome and partisan. To achieve favour with the provinces, Bennett prevailed upon the British to accept an amendment for the Canadians that assured that changes to minority rights in the Canadian provinces since 1867 would not be altered. His other chief function was to plump for Commonwealth and Imperial preference in trade, which was the cornerstone of his plan to blast Canada's way into markets. Bennett, who travelled with his sister, visited battlefields in France and toured around Britain and Ireland before returning to Canada.

In accord with the Statute of Westminster, the 1865 Colonial Laws Validity Act was abrogated. The doctrine of "repugnancy" to British legislation was stricken. Shortly after this achievement, for which he was generally felt responsible, especially in Canada, Bennett gave a large hint of where his government was going when he advised the provinces that Ottawa would have to cut back its contribution to unemployment benefits, as he announced 10 per cent cuts in the pay of federal employees. But he launched public works programs to try to soak up the unemployed. In March 1931, he had offered price supplements for wheat, whose price had plunged to thirty-nine cents a bushel, subsistence levels and less than a quarter of what it had been in 1929. He improved and made more generous and accessible the pension King had passed for Woodsworth, and as one province after another ran into funding problems, he raised the federal government's contribution to the pensions from 50 to 75 per cent.

The controversial aspects of the Beauharnois scandal percolated to the surface in early 1931, after Robert Gardiner, the head of the United Farmers of Alberta, got hold of Beauharnois documents that were, to say the least, suggestive of impropriety. Bennett struck a five-man committee to look into it. The committee, of which Gardiner was a member, quickly unearthed a web of shady transactions and controversial links with senators Haydon, McDougald, and Raymond. All were called to testify before the committee. Raymond, who was a wealthy man to begin with, didn't know much, and Haydon suffered a coronary attack and was unable to testify. McDougald did appear, and it emerged that Beauharnois had been billed by McDougald $852.32 for the trip to Bermuda and New York, so it appeared that King's travel had been paid for by the company. King met with Bennett and asked that the reference to the payment of his travel expenses not be made public, as he had known nothing about them. Bennett was offended that King had recently called him a "dictator," and King alleged that he had only done so in response to some rudeness of Bennett's; it was a pretty childish and churlish business, and over small sums. There was a reference to this payment in the committee's report, and King made a statement in the House denying that he had known anything about the bill being paid by Beauharnois or that he had ever discussed any aspect of Beauharnois with McDougald or Haydon. As McDougald's July 20 date with the committee approached, King filled his diary with recitations of horrible dreams he was having, in which his mother was trying to help him through the crisis.[44] His particular concern was that McDougald would mention the Larkin fund of $225,000 amassed for him, to which McDougald had contributed $25,000. But

McDougald did not; he responded effectively to all questions and said the paper trail showing that Beauharnois had paid for the then prime minister's travels was a clerical error. The committee report sharply criticized McDougald and Haydon but did not mention King at all, and King tried to bury the matter with a maudlin speech in the House of Commons of over three hours. He said that the Liberal Party was passing through "the valley of humiliation" but promised to lead his party back to "higher and stronger . . . ground than it has ever occupied in the past."[45] King was immensely relieved and even considered that his Irish terrier, "little Pat," who had been unwell, in licking King's hand when he recovered, had "so reminded me of mother . . . like her spirit sent to comfort."

McDougald was forced to relinquish some of his stock and retire as Beauharnois's non-executive chairman, but the greatest problem he faced was from Arthur Meighen, now the government leader in the Senate, and as strident as always. Meighen demanded that McDougald, Haydon, and Raymond all be expelled from the Senate. King met McDougald at Laurier House and, instead of showing any gratitude for McDougald's discretion over the Larkin fund and his fine improvisation over the secretarial error, he firmly pressed McDougald to resign from the Senate. Several weeks later, King visited McDougald at his home in Montreal and gave back fifteen thousand of the twenty-five thousand dollars that the senator had given to the Larkin fund. He had even presumed to draft a letter of resignation for McDougald. The following night, King had further complicated dreams, which he recorded in his diary, and concluded that "it is true that spirits are guiding me. This is as real as anything in my life – it is worth everything."[46] Much has been made of King's interest in the spirits, but he is probably more the victim of his apparently unsuspecting openness in leaving such candid diaries than of aberrantly exotic religious and spiritual views. No other statesman, apart perhaps from Gladstone, has left quite such detailed and apparently complete summaries of his mood and thoughts. (Surely he wasn't holding anything back.) And one of his diaries, on physical matters, with excruciating detail on bowel movements and the like, is even more startling. No one knows what other statesmen have thought; it was just that King wrote such things out and left them, deliberately, for his literary executors, with the same naïveté with which he failed to insist on repaying McDougald when he picked up his hotel bill in

Bermuda and wrote in his diary that the act was "mighty gracious."[47] As devious and calculating as King was in political matters, including his manipulation of colleagues, he was strangely vulnerable and trusting in unfamiliar situations, such as commerce. McDougald eventually did resign from the Senate to end the investigations, and Meighen only laid off Haydon when he received a doctor's attestation to Haydon's infirm condition. Haydon never recovered; he died on November 10, 1932, aged sixty-five. King was a pallbearer, but at the funeral he avoided McDougald. The balance of McDougald's career was an anticlimax, and when he died on June 19, 1942, aged sixty, King declined to be a pallbearer, having gone to some lengths to keep his distance from McDougald in the intervening years. King wrote in his diary that McDougald "lacked principle and understanding. It is well that he is at rest." He had completely air-brushed from memory his own errors, and even ten years after these events self-righteously exonerated himself from any trace of possible misconduct or even simple error.

The episode determined King to clean up Liberal organization and fundraising, and he turned to Vincent Massey, whom he disliked as an arrogant snob wallowing in inherited wealth and pretense to cultural distinction. Massey had been offered the post of governor of Western Australia by James Thomas, the British secretary of dominion affairs. King enticed Massey to the position he had in mind for him by suggesting the highly valued commission in London when he returned to office. Massey pompously declared his desire to "help" King, and the party leader sharply pointed out that he didn't need help, the Liberal Party did, and he was tired of condescending expressions of a desire to help him from people who were no use to him at all. Massey, who was a vain and greedy careerist, asked if he would still be eligible for the London post if he accepted the Australian position while awaiting King's return to office. King took pleasure in assuring him that he would not. Massey eventually became head of the National Liberal Federation and engaged Norman Lambert as the general secretary, while King prevailed on his former secretary, Norman Rogers, to be a senior policy adviser.

The depression put great pressure on the Canadian Pacific and Canadian National and other railways. Bennett and the railways and canals minister, Robert Manion, set up the Committee on Railways and Shipping, with Robert Hanson as chairman (both subsequent leaders of the Conservative Party), and the committee took evidence, satisfied itself that Sir Henry Thornton, the chairman of the CNR, was extravagant, self-indulgent, and inefficient, and forced him out. (He died, of cancer, penniless, in New York eleven months later.) Bennett established the Royal Commission to Inquire into Railways and Transportation, chaired by the chief justice of Canada, Sir Lyman P. Duff. This commission reported in September 1932 that the two railways should remain separate and maintain competitive pricing but cooperate in all respects to reduce operating costs. Duff, like Bennett, feared a monopoly and its abuses. King attacked all this as a putsch against Thornton and a partisan move to pack the management of Canadian National with Conservative hacks and placate the Montreal financial community. Liberal opposition caused Bennett to introduce his railways legislation establishing a joint supervisory committee for both railways in the Senate, and Meighen put it through and sent it on to the House of Commons, where it passed after a lively debate. It was a creative measure, with representatives of both railways and of the railway workers on the committee.

In response to growing interest in radio broadcasting, Mackenzie King had set up the Aird Commission (John Aird was a retired bank chairman) to make recommendations about this new industry, prompted in part by complaints from the Roman Catholic Church in Quebec about Jehovah's Witnesses taking to the airwaves to denounce Quebec's principal religious denomination. This commission urged that seven publicly owned stations be set up in different major cities to compliment the sixty-two private broadcasters already operating. King ignored the report, but Bennett, a more decisive and often more innovative personality than King, was interested in the concept and took it up, encouraged by the Canadian Radio League, a vast umbrella organization of governments and interest groups whose national council included future prime minister Louis St. Laurent and commander of the Canadian army in the First World War General Sir Arthur Currie, now principal of McGill University. There was hostile lobbying from the newspaper industry, which apparently helped motivate Mackenzie King to continue to counsel caution, but Bennett drove on, until interrupted for a whole year by a challenge from the government of Quebec that claimed that granting radio licences was a provincial matter.

Bennett had the better of the argument, and he and the minister of marine and fisheries, Alfred Duranleau, who was inexplicably in charge of radio matters, won at the Supreme Court of Canada and successfully resisted Quebec's appeal to the Judicial Committee of the Privy Council. Bennett appointed a parliamentary committee chaired by Raymond Morand to advise on how to implement the ambition to enter public broadcasting, and that committee's report was tabled in the House of Commons on May 9, 1932, and embodied in legislation establishing the Canadian Radio Broadcasting Commission that was signed into law on May 26, 1932. The legislsation also set up 5,000-watt stations at Montreal, Toronto, Winnipeg, and Red Deer (to reach Calgary and Edmonton), and planned thirty-two more stations. Whatever one may think of the successor publicly owned radio and television networks in French and English, Bennett deserves great credit for this bold step that put Canada at the forefront of international public broadcasting.

The Ottawa Imperial Economic Conference, originally scheduled for 1931, took place from July 21 to August 20, 1932. It is a sign of Bennett's forceful personality that he was invited both to host the conference in Canada and to chair it. He pushed his favoured plan of Imperial trade preference as the principal objective, and received general acclaim from the Canadian press and public for the competent and efficient way in which he directed the proceedings. The British government delegates attending dissented from this, as both Stanley Baldwin, the lord president, and Neville Chamberlain, the chancellor of the exchequer, found Bennett stubborn, egotistical, and often rude. At this point, the British government was a ramshackle coalition patched together by King George v himself, whereby the battle-weary Labour prime minister, Ramsay MacDonald, was propped up by a much larger group of Conservatives led by Baldwin, frequently the acting prime minister, and Chamberlain. Chamberlain had proposed tariff increases early in 1932 but agreed to defer them until after the Ottawa conference. As the conference approached, Bennett relinquished the post of minister of finance and handed it over to former Nova Scotia premier Edgar Rhodes.

Bennett commissioned a good deal of economic research prior to the conference, and one of the documents that emerged described the history of American branch plants in Canada, the number of which had increased from 259 in 1922 to 964 in 1932, with the investment that accompanied them standing at $540.6 million. Nearly 25 per cent of all manufacturing wages earned in Canada was earned by employees in these American-owned plants. While this raised questions about sovereignty, Canada's gross domestic product declined from $6.1 billion in 1929 to $3.5 billion in 1933. Per capita income fell in the same period by 48 per cent (44 per cent in Ontario, but 72 per cent in Saskatchewan[48]), and the unemployment rate rose from 3 per cent in 1929 to 30 per cent in 1931. In the United States, the industrial sector of stock market averages had declined by more than 90 per cent. Bennett got a lot of bilateral tariff reductions at Ottawa, but was unable to "blast [his] way" into a comprehensive plan of Imperial preferences. Stevens proved an energetic and often effective promoter of foreign trade in these very difficult times.

In November 1932, the United States elected Governor Franklin D. Roosevelt of New York – a sixth cousin, but by marriage a nephew, of Theodore Roosevelt – as president. He defeated President Hoover by seven million votes and 57 to 40 per cent of the vote, and installed a regime that he styled the New Deal. Roosevelt deftly reorganized the collapsed banking system, guaranteed bank deposits, reopened the commodities and stock exchanges, organized vast workfare programs in infrastructure and conservation projects, introduced unemployment insurance and state pensions through the social security system, promoted both cartels and collective bargaining to raise wages and prices, shortened the work week, refinanced the public's failed residential mortgages, and generally began to bite heavily into unemployment, reducing it from 33 per cent in 1933 to under 10 per cent in 1940, to practically zero at the end of 1941. Roosevelt rolled the gold standard back to international transactions. The world, led by Great Britain's abandonment of the domestic gold standard, had abandoned its main currencies to the certainty of inflation, but also embraced a steady policy for softening economic slumps by increasing the money supply (printing money, in conventional parlance). This policy would ramify widely and for many decades, and the end of it has not come yet.

Bennett had done what he could with Empire and Commonwealth trade preference, which, in sum, apart from atmospherics, wasn't much. The promise to "blast" Canada's way into the world's markets was now hollow and even mocking, as the world's tailspin continued. It was time for an abrupt change, and the opportunity for such a shift was provided by the new administration in Washington. Roosevelt was a comparative free-trader and was prepared to experiment and change to pull his country out of the downward spiral. The Bennett plan for Canada of substituting Empire trade for continental trade was always illusory and was only embraced after the United States plunged into the dark world of protectionism. Bennett had the gift of not being dogmatic about solutions, and could alter a proposed a course of action by 180 degrees from what he had long advocated, without a pause or the least slackening in his confident, almost bombastically assertive, manner. The new American president had changed the Western world's psychology, almost as had his former chief, Woodrow Wilson, with his transformation of the unheard of bloodbath of the First World War into a crusade for democracy in 1917. Roosevelt declared that "the only thing we have to fear is fear itself," and that "our problems, thank God, concern only material things. . . . There is plenty, but a generous use of it languishes at the very source of the supply." He laid down an activist, interventionist, partially inflationary attack on the depression. Roosevelt was skeptical of economists, but recognized that the so-called dismal science was half psychology and half Grade 3 arithmetic. He expanded the money supply and deployed his formidable oratorical powers to uplift the country, and he succeeded. Hoarding ended, millions worked in Roosevelt's ambitious workfare programs, and confidence began to return to the naturally high level it usually seeks and attains in America. It did not require preternatural powers of observation for Bennett to realize that if his mandate could be salvaged and extended, three-fifths of the way through his term, it would have to be by tucking into the American economic upturn and related revival of confidence.

In 1933, Vincent Massey held a policy conference in Trinity College School in Port Hope, near his considerable house, Batterwood, to which he enticed the British Liberal leader, Sir Herbert Samuel; Roosevelt brain trust member Raymond Moley; railway owner, investment banker, New Deal workfare director, and future ambassador to Moscow and London, secretary of commerce, governor of New York, and ambassador at large, Averell Harriman; and others. King was entirely opposed and wanted Massey to stick to fundraising, and while he attended, and found some of the participants interesting, he complained lengthily in his diary of (his own) constipation and reproached Massey yet again as a pretentious snob.[49] He continually reminded Massey that if he wanted the London high commission, he should work harder and more effectively for the Liberal Party, and Massey did prove an efficient organizer. King found Massey's enthusiasm for the new Roosevelt administration distressing, as he regarded the New Deal as far too interventionist. (Once he met Roosevelt and fell thoroughly under the domination of his power and personality, his views would evolve radically.)

Bennett visited Roosevelt on April 27, 1933. (At one point, he was in the White House at the same time as British prime minister Ramsay MacDonald and Premier Édouard Herriot of France; all were seeking the silver bullet of the Roosevelt magic.) After the drear and drudge of the unsmiling Hoover, reduced as he was to reedy assurances that prosperity was "just around the corner" and that "grass will grow in the streets of a hundred cities and a thousand towns" if Roosevelt was elected, Roosevelt was the golden, smiling, bonhomous, and silver-tongued apostle of returning prosperity. Roosevelt signed the Reciprocal Trade Agreements Act in June 1934, but trade wasn't really the key to prosperity; all the industrialized democracies were in similar condition, and what was needed was stimulation of economic activity in all of them. By moving public expenses from indirect relief to minimum wages for useful work, including flood control and reforestation, Roosevelt increased consumer spending, and the steady shutdown of the economy – which had affected, first, consumer goods and retail, then manufacturing and raw materials – started to rewind upwards, spurred on by Roosevelt's secular gospel of returning plenty, recited in his extremely artful and persuasive "fireside chats" on the radio explaining the administration's course.

Bennett's latest biographer, John Boyko,[50] claims that Roosevelt deliberately dragged the trade talks out to sandbag Bennett and assist King. There is no evidence of any such thing, and no effort is made to prove it in the biography. The author's citation of a diary entry by King on June 4, 1935, makes no such case. An obscure Harvard professor, William Elliott, was visiting the U.S. legation in Ottawa, asked to meet King, and told the Opposition leader that a trade treaty to reduce tariffs was likely. King said he had assumed this and that he thought Bennett would try to use it as his last fling at re-election. It was agreed that the treaty could have been concluded two years before, but it was not clear from this conversation who was judged responsible for the delay, and there is certainly no suggestion by King or Elliott that Roosevelt, as Boyko writes, had delayed passage to assist King politically. That, and the companion assertion that Elliott, on behalf of the U.S. government, promised King that the United States would reward Canada in tariff matters if Canada adopted at the next Imperial Economic Conference positions to which the United States was amenable, is not what King wrote and is wildly improbable. King wrote that it was not clear that Elliott spoke with any authority, but that he, and he believed the American government, hoped Canada would promote not only greater trade between Canada and the United Kingdom, but between both those countries and the United States.

Roosevelt had strongly emphasized what he called "the policy of the good neighbor" in the hemisphere, and had acted accordingly, relaxing restrictions on the sovereignty of Cuba and withdrawing the Marines from countries where they had been deployed by Republican presidents. There is not one shred of evidence in the Roosevelt archives or those of his foreign policy officials that he favoured any party in Canada or ever sought to influence Canadian politics. This is a wild sky-ride by a sympathetic Bennett biographer driven to outright fabrication, presumably to help explain the impending political demise of his subject. (Boyko's is an interesting and generally a good biography, but this aspect is anti-historical.)

In August 1933, Bennett had chaired the World Wheat Conference; Canada, the United States, Argentina, and Australia all agreed to try to strengthen prices by reducing production. Bennett was doing his best, but conditions were continuing to deteriorate. In July 1933, a committee Bennett had set up headed by Britain's Lord Macmillan, who had performed a similar function in Britain, went on tour across Canada, seeking opinions on the virtue of establishing a central bank. The Canadian chartered banks opposed the step, for obvious reasons of resistance to regulation, but in its report made public in May 1934, the committee favoured a central bank for reasons other serious countries had judged sufficient, and enabling legislation was adopted in July 1934. In September of that year, Bennett installed the very intelligent and successful choice of Graham Ford Towers (1897–1975), the thirty-seven-year-old general manager of the Royal Bank, as governor, a post he occupied with distinction for twenty years. Again, Bennett showed himself a decisive and pioneering leader, though in this case he had no significant opposition from King, or even Gardiner's angry farmers or Woodsworth's discontented workers and their academic champions. Bennett also did his best with the advancement of the project for the canalization of the St. Lawrence and the Great Lakes to permit large ocean vessels to sail to the heart of the continent. But after very skillful negotiation with Ontario, Quebec, and the United States, the project stalled in the tenebrous thickets of competing American interests, and particularly squabbling between New York, Philadelphia, and Boston against Chicago, Detroit, and Cleveland. Even Roosevelt was unable to break it loose before the next Canadian elections. Again, Bennett had demonstrated great tactical skill as a negotiator and vision as a builder, and deserves credit for the effort, which he generally did not receive when the St. Lawrence Seaway was finally opened twenty-five years later.

Bennett had begun to be impressed with Franklin D. Roosevelt about the day he was inaugurated and turned the current of public affairs with his inaugural address. But Bennett presaged (and did not emulate) the president's Civilian Conservation Corps by opening camps for single unemployed men, ninety-eight camps initially, in British Columbia, but for only two thousand young men, in the autumn of 1932. Within two years, the number of people engaged at any one time surpassed 11,000, and by 1936 more than 170,000 people had lived and worked in these camps. They were in wholesome natural surroundings, but a significant number soon objected to what they regarded as unduly Spartan quarters. A widespread movement of objectors started to agitate in April 1935 for better living and working conditions, and the program was compromised by infiltration by communists and radical worker organizations, although the camps had always been represented as emergency facilities to move hardship cases to salubrious surroundings where they were safe and cared for, but paid below the minimum wage. The camps also were victimized by the division of powers in Canada, and this was a concurrent jurisdiction. It became a truism that the provincial camps were preferable to those run by the Department of National Defence. The inhabitants ignored the government ban and founded the Relief Camp Workers Union. One of Bennett's officials, General Andrew McNaughton, got ahead of his leader, rounding up all sorts of chronically unemployed and sending them to what were redesignated as camps of detention. Despite the benign and even generous character of the camps, Bennett's enemies were winning the public relations battles and convinced the people that the camps were for the inconvenient victims of Bennett's economic policy and run with inhuman severity. The Relief Camp Workers Union flourished.

The long-time labour agitator Arthur "Slim" Evans, formerly of the notorious International Workers of the World, most recently of the Drumheller, Alberta, correctional facility after being convicted of embezzling union funds, was the principal leader of the unrest.

On release, he was engaged by the Communist Party of Canada in its front organization, the National Unemployed Workers Association, and on December 7, 1934, he organized a demonstration of five hundred unemployed at the provincial Parliament building in Victoria. The premier of British Columbia, Thomas Dufferin Pattullo, was almost panicked by this agitation and became a rather limp lightning rod between the extreme unemployed organizations and the federal prime minister.

The Canadian media tended to be either gullibly submissive to this sort of agitprop or maliciously biased against the Bennett government, and the federal government had no idea how to parry this sort of insidious smear campaign without seeming to smash the most disadvantaged and meritorious petitioners for a better break. It was a snowballing, no-win, public relations disaster for Bennett. In August 1931, Bennett had had Tim Buck and seven other leaders of the Communist Party of Canada arrested and charged with unlawful association and seditious conspiracy, offences that were practically impossible to prove, and Bennett, with his booming voice and swallow-tail coats and striped trousers, staring unsmilingly at the country, became a sitting duck for his opponents, not only on the far left, but even for the followers and image-makers of that comfortable old shoe Mackenzie King. The Liberal leader may have been odd and ungalvanizing, but he could not be refashioned into a fright figure by the mothers of Canada to terrorize their children into eating their porridge and taking their castor oil. Buck was finally released in November 1934, and his liberation was celebrated by seventeen thousand people in Toronto's new and impressive Maple Leaf Gardens. Seated on the stage during Buck's powerful address was the new premier of Ontario, populist Liberal Mitchell Hepburn.

There was a long sequence of violent strikes around the country that contributed to the deterioration of the public discourse: coal miners in Estevan, Saskatchewan, in September 1931 (three miners killed by gun-shot wounds); miners in Corbin, British Columbia, in June 1934 (many injured); rioting farmers at Innisfail, Alberta, in November 1934 (the strike leader, George Palmer, beaten and tarred and feathered and abandoned in a field by the RCMP); Toronto Garment Workers; Halifax Sewer Workers; the Vancouver general strike of April and May 1935, where Slim Evans ran an illegal tag day, then attacked a police station in New Westminster, forced the release of union members who had been arrested, and then loudly boasted across the country of having intimidated the police. With this, the tide of public opinion began to turn.

In the last act of the Bennett administration, a leading role was played by Bennett's brother-in-law William Duncan Herridge, who had been Bennett's principal speechwriter in 1930 and who Bennett appointed to succeed Vincent Massey as minister to Washington. (Herridge was married to Bennett's sister Mildred.) From this vantage point, Herridge wrote Bennett lengthy summaries of the latter Hoover and early Roosevelt years, and is generally credited with persuading Bennett to launch his own New Deal, rather imitative of Roosevelt's in its radicalism and the use of radio broadcasts to launch it, and designed to inspirit the country as Roosevelt had done in America, but apparently more psychological than substantive. John Boyko and others have made a commendable effort to improvise an explanation that contradicts Mackenzie King's rather humorous and persuasive charges that Bennett had undergone "a death-bed conversion." The argument that Bennett acted spontaneously and that the logical time for the call to radical change, which the prime minister made in five radio addresses, starting on January 2, 1935, is based on the theory that the time had come then, and not for any coherently explained reason earlier, for radical change. Herridge did recommend a call to a radical program without specifics, to emphasize that Bennett was the person to promulgate such a program, and that the time for it had come then and not before. And he did write that to Bennett,[51] but it is inconceivable that either of them believed a word of it, or indeed that any serious historian would. Roosevelt was the only democratic leader in the world who had been successful in rolling back the depression; he was overwhelmingly well-known and popular in Canada, and everything else Bennett had tried had failed. He didn't "blast [his] way into" anything except a stone wall of deepening depression. Urban unemployment afflicted almost half the wage earners of Canada from 1933 to 1935.[52] Even after the United States had begun to recover under Roosevelt, there was little sign of it in Canada. Bennett's term was almost at an end, and how Herridge imagined that his brother-in-law could persuade anyone that he was the man to do a 180-degree turn and produce a dramatic legislative program based on the theory that capitalism was broken and big business had failed the country, and be believed without providing any specifics, escapes comprehension.

The new program was revealed in a series of five half-hour speeches called "The Premier Speaks," in which Bennett claimed to be laying out his election program and giving the country time to discuss it. He staked out the logical tactical position: he was saving capitalism, not assaulting it, and thus tried to steal the clothes of the left to shelter the right from the political and economic tempest, as Roosevelt was rather artfully doing. Stephen Leacock, head of McGill's department of political economy and a frequent critic of Bennett, wrote approving of the first speech in the series. King wrote in his diary of Bennett's "nauseating egotism." In his second address, on January 9, Bennett proposed unemployment insurance and comprehensive pensions. The third speech laboriously exalted the virtues of fairness and spun certain recent and pending legislation and declared, completely implausibly, that it would have been a mistake to think in such comprehensive terms earlier in his term when the need of the improvident and the dispossessed was so dire that direct relief was what was necessary (which he had not, in general, provided). The fourth speech was about finance, and Bennett referred to his Bank of Canada as "an instrument of social justice." And he denounced "selfish men, and this country is not without them," whose greed "looms larger than your happiness."

Bennett charged out of the political gate with the last of his speeches resplendent in the shining armour of the reformer and the man of benign action, while the Liberals were the party of inertia, the status quo, and the depression: "If you are satisfied with conditions as they are, support Liberalism." It was so audacious, it was magnificent, in a way, but he cannot have imagined that it would work. The legislative product of the series of speeches was the Employment and Social Insurance Act, which applied only for those who were already working and hardly justified the stentorian fanfare Bennett had given it. When it was presented in the House of Commons, Lapointe and King zeroed in on its constitutionality very quickly: Lapointe elicited that Bennett had broached it with the provinces but then broken off discussions because of lack of likely agreement. King asked if the prime minister had considered asking the Supreme Court for a constitutional opinion. Bennett said that he had not, because he was confident of his bill's constitutionality. As on so many other matters, it was difficult to imagine the source of Bennett's confidence.

After this one, King wrote in his diary that he "felt humiliated to think of the country being in the hands of such a man. . . . I uttered spontaneously the words 'What a buffoon.' It was really pathetic, the absolute rot and gush as he talked – platitudes – unction and what not, a mountebank and hypocrite, full of bombast and egotism . . . sickening and disgusting."[53] Even allowing for King's inevitable partisanship, it was a very strange initiative that had all the characteristics of a desperation play by a government almost out of time and a leader at the last extremity of his endurance. Bennett suffered a heart attack on March 7, but he fought uncompromisingly on from his hospital bed. He roused himself from it to go to Britain in April to observe George v's silver jubilee (taking Mildred Bennett Herridge and the young foreign policy adviser Lester Pearson with him). Bennett vastly enjoyed himself, especially his visits with the royal family. The continuing good health of Canadian fealty to the British (and Canadian) Crown was well-expressed in Bennett's letter to the king after his private audience. The terms of it are hard to comprehend from a perspective three generations later, but it illustrates the difficulty that remained in instilling a suitable sense of nationality even in the most highly placed Canadians: "I state the simple truth when I state that I came away from the Castle with even deeper feeling of affection and devotion for my king and queen, and I shall continue to aspire more earnestly to serve the Crown to the best of my ability, sustained by the conviction that my Royal Master expects His servants to do the best within them."[54]

On April 26, 1935, Evans's Vancouver militants sacked the city's main Hudson's Bay Company store and Vancouver mayor Gerry McGeer read the Riot Act from the war memorial in Victory Square: "Our Sovereign Lord the King enjoins and commands to all who are here present to disperse immediately and return peacefully to their homes and legitimate occupations under threat of being found guilty of an infraction that may be punished by life imprisonment. God Save the King." The next day, the strikers divided into three columns, befuddled the police (whose crowd control tactics were amateurish), and occupied the Vancouver City Museum. McGeer offered to give them three days' worth of food rations if they left the museum undamaged, and this was agreed. The unions and demonstrators lost many sympathizers, but Bennett didn't play his cards as well as he might have. Instead of bargaining earnestly and allowing the extremism of Evans and others to be obvious and thus alienate moderate opinion, or remaining silent and waiting for bourgeois concern to escalate, he tried at every stage to face down and overpower his opponents as the personification of authority. In the desperate economic times, he alienated as many people as he impressed. But he fought his corner in the only way he knew, and with a singular, if somewhat misguided, integrity. On May 20, Bennett replied to Mayor McGeer – who had cracked and was beseeching the prime minister to buy off the rioters and demonstrators – that those who left the camps were a provincial responsibility and that he was paying no Danegeld; it was McGeer's and Premier Pattullo's responsibility to maintain order. On May 30, Evans convened a public meeting where 70 per cent of his now shrinking following voted to leave Vancouver and entrain for Ottawa.

A progress followed across the country, where Evans's officials showed a deft hand at advance work. The star advance man, Matt Shaw, had even arranged to encounter Governor General Lord Bessborough on a railway platform in Vancouver; he politely expressed his grievances for ten minutes and then moved on amicably after a hearty handshake with His Excellency. At each stop on the way east, there were large receptions and groups to assist the strikers and feed and shelter them, while Bennett gamely returned to the House of Commons from hospital and lamented that so much of Canada's youth had been misled by communists.[55] In June, the cabinet decided to stop the On to Ottawa Trek, as it was now known, presumably in imitation of the South African Boer objectors to the abolition of slavery of a century before. To the irritation of Saskatchewan's tough and capable Liberal premier, James Gardiner, it was determined to stop the trek at Regina, headquarters of the RCMP. Just as the showdown was at hand, Bennett sent railways and canals minister Robert Manion and well-respected local MP and agriculture minister Robert Weir to meet the trek leaders. They met at length on June 17, and the complainants had six demands: fifty cents an hour, specified hours, accessible first aid in the camps, workers' committees in the camps, removal of the camps from the jurisdiction of the Department of National Defence, and a national system of unemployment insurance, and they wanted to speak directly with Bennett. Bennett approved first-class fares for the leaders to come to meet him, good treatment for the rest who waited, and free passage home for those who wished it. Manion had negotiated well and Bennett responded sensibly.

The two groups met in the Cabinet Room in the Parliament Buildings on June 22, 1935. Evans and Bennett faced each other. Bennett allowed Evans to speak at length and then ascertained that of his eleven visitors only one was a Canadian and he accused them of being lawbreakers. He particularly focused on Evans for his embezzlement conviction, and Evans exploded and called Bennett a liar. Bennett showed his barristerial talents as he outwitted and infuriated several of the visitors while remaining glacially calm himself. He made the now customary offers about the return to the camps or to the homes of the strikers, and warned the group that continued illegalities would not be tolerated. Evans accused him of raising "the red bogey," and Bennett arranged for their return to Regina for the showdown. He explained the entire proceedings in the House on June 24 and said that the RCMP had been ordered to stop the trek.

The reckoning came at last on July 1 in Regina. After about five hundred trekkers and sympathizers gathered in Market Square and Evans was well-launched in an address to his faithful, bat- and club-swinging police debouched from Mountie vans and dispersed the crowd in gratuitously bloody fashion. Attempts to regroup were overridden by mounted police. Some store windows were smashed and cars overturned, but the federal police ran down the scattered demonstrators, who improvised barricades and pelted the police with rocks and bottles. The police replied with tear gas and then gunfire. One policeman was killed, thirty people were hospitalized, and a hundred trekkers were arrested, including Evans and Shaw. The trekkers' campgrounds were surrounded by machine-gun emplacements and Premier James "Jimmy" Garfield Gardiner arranged for rail transport out of Saskatchewan east and west. On the westward train, an effigy of the prime minister was hanged and the "body" hung off the side of the train for passers-by to see. In the following days, King and Woodsworth attacked Bennett, who again, as he had so often, made a good legal defence of the government, pointing out that conditions in the camps were better than in lumber camps and that continuing education through Frontier College was available. Bennett overlooked the fact that the latest violence had been entirely initiated by the RCMP and compared himself, with his usual cloth ear in public and political relations matters, with President Grover Cleveland and his suppression of the Pullman Strike in 1894, an incident few Canadians would recall and very few with favour.

Evans continued to be an active communist and raised money for the communist side in the Spanish Civil War, which began the next year. Two of the eleven with whom Bennett met in the Cabinet Room in Ottawa died on the communist side in that war. King and Lapointe elected to allow Woodsworth to lead the debate in the House of Commons and not to run any risk of seeming to be mollycoddlers of communists. Two commissions were established to inquire into these events, one in British Columbia and one in Saskatchewan. Though the B.C. commission criticized Bennett for not paying adequately for the campers' work, both sustained his version of events, said the camps functioned well and as advertised, and held that the residents had been exploited by communist agitators. Few people agreed with the trek organizers, but most Canadians found all these incidents embarrassing and un-Canadian and thought Bennett responsible for an unjustified and regrettably public use of force.

On July 2, 1935, the day after the riot in Regina, Bennett's former close colleague Henry Herbert Stevens had risen in the House and said that Bennett, while being technically correct in his handling of events, had become, by his pigheaded severity, the greatest promoter of communism in Canada. Stevens and Bennett had been close friends going back to their first election to Parliament in 1911, but on January 15, 1934, when at Bennett's request Stevens took his place as the main speaker at the National Shoe Retailers' Association convention, Stevens had condemned predatory pricing in the retail industry and especially blamed the big department stores. Then he went a step further and announced that the government would attack on this front. Response to the speech was quite positive, but Bennett was outraged that Stevens had spoken for the government in enunciating policy and told him so, whereupon Stevens resigned. Bennett moved to prevent a party schism, and had Manion speak with Stevens and propose a parliamentary committee with Stevens as chairman to look into it. Stevens was happy with this, but the working of his Price Spreads Committee split the cabinet between the friends of big business, especially the large retailers Eaton's and Simpson's, and the more populist of the cabinet members. Stevens asked that his committee be converted into a Royal Commission to survive the current Parliament, and so popular were its hearings and findings that Bennett agreed, and Stevens continued as chair of the Royal Commission on Price Spreads and Mass Buying. Stevens next launched a vituperative attack on Sir Joseph Flavelle for price gouging in his capacity as proprietor of Simpson's and produced a pamphlet that accused Flavelle of criminal practices. These were fighting words.

Bennett was in Britain during the summer of 1934, but at the October 25, 1934, cabinet meeting, he disapproved the attack on Flavelle and concluded that Stevens's remarks were defamatory. This quickly degenerated over the next couple of days to Stevens's resignation and a blinding public dispute between the two men. The Royal Commission continued with William Kennedy of Winnipeg as chairman, and Richard Hanson of New Brunswick became the new minister of trade and commerce. Stevens stormed out of the Conservative caucus, and Bennett had a full-scale schism to add to his other problems. The schism yawned further when Sir Herbert Holt and Sir Edward Beatty, probably Canada's two most prominent businessmen, offered Stevens three million dollars to set up his own party and split the Conservatives at the polls. It is hard not to imagine Mackenzie King playing a role in this. On May 23, the government proposed Criminal Code amendments to enact some of the Price Spreads Commission recommendations. On June 10, 1935, Bennett and Stevens had a full exchange in Parliament, slugging it out over the differences between them. They were both powerful speakers, their fluency reinforced by righteousness. Bennett liked the hard-hitting report eventually produced by the Price Spreads Commission under Kennedy, but his party was tainted by the general sense of severity over the On to Ottawa trekkers, and split between the Conservatives and Progressives. Mackenzie King quietly rubbed his hands in anticipation of the election. It would not be long now.

5. Mackenzie King III: The False Paradise of Appeasement, 1935–1938

Despite their lack of rapport, King and Bennett had some similar qualities: they were abstemious bachelors, lonely men, and had developed elaborate methods of reliance on themselves alone. They liked and sought female companionship and even aspired to marriage, but nothing ever worked. The fact that they were both bachelors was occasionally raised in Parliament. In the midst of a boring debate in the mid-1930s, questions were raised about Doukhobor women walking around their farms naked on hot days, and King was jocularly asked what he would do if such people interrupted a summer day by dancing on his lawn. His immediate response, which drew great laughter, was that he would send for the prime minister.[56] From 1932 to 1934, Bennett had a romantic relationship with Mrs. Hazel Beatrice Colville, a twice-divorced Roman Catholic and daughter of Sir Albert Kemp, who had served with Bennett in the cabinet of Sir Robert Borden. Bennett imposed as a condition of marriage that Mrs. Colville give up alcohol, cigarettes, and Montreal's nightlife, but she gave up Bennett instead. King had had his share of rebuffs also.

The election was finally called for October 14. King announced a strategy of extreme caution even by his standards. He was the leader of the party of straight capitalism, a balanced budget, and fiscal integrity, but also compassion and social welfare for the needy, with the usual gaps in that endlessly tedious and almost uniform affectation of being a "social liberal and a fiscal conservative." The Liberals would run explicitly against Bennett as a one-man government that was as incompetent as it was authoritarian. King's spirits were working overtime as the advice flooded in from mother, grandfather, Sir Wilfrid, Gladstone, and

22. Donald Smith, Lord Strathcona (1820–1914), co-founder of the
Canadian Pacific Railway, drives the last spike to complete it, November 7,
1885, nine days before the hanging of Louis Riel. A Scottish immigrant,
he served nearly twenty-five years as a Hudson's Bay factor in Labrador,
and twenty years as a provincial and federal legislator, became head of the
CPR, the Bank of Montreal, Hudson's Bay Company, chancellor of
McGill University, and Canadian high commissioner in London until he
died at ninety-three. Edward VII, in respect for his philanthropy, called
him "Uncle Donald."

23. Robert Laird Borden (1854–1937),
prime minister of Canada 1911–1920,
here walking with Winston Churchill,
first lord of the Admiralty, in London
in 1912. Borden had opposed Laurier's
plan for a Canadian navy, and
accepted Churchill's proposal that
Canada simply give Britain the money
to build British ships in British yards
and man them with British sailors, and
defer a Canadian navy. Borden was a
competent prime minister, but was
lumbered with an obsolete deference
to Britain, and ignorance of, but not
hostility to, French Canadians.

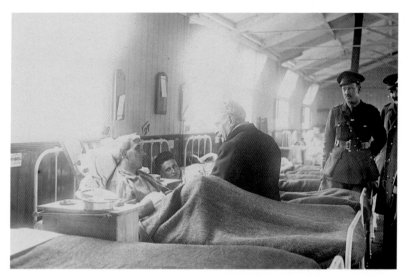

24. Prime Minister Borden visiting convalescing Canadian soldiers in a military hospital in Britain in 1915. He almost succeeded in his ambition to visit with every single wounded Canadian in the military hospitals of France and Great Britain, and was a very conscientious war leader, and a sensible and moderate voice in Allied councils, getting along well with President Wilson, Prime Minister Lloyd George, and Premier Clemenceau.

25. Mackenzie King and his beloved dog, Pat, to whose gestures King attributed vast insights and spiritual motivations, walking in front of Laurier House, on Laurier Avenue, where Laurier and then King lived for nearly fifty years. Lady Laurier left the house to King but disputed that Sir Wilfrid had named King his successor.

26. The successors to Robert Borden as Conservative leaders, Arthur Meighen (1874–1960) and R.B. Bennett (1870–1947). Both were briefly prime minister, but though very capable men in some ways, were considered by the public to be bombastic, and impulsively belligerent, and were tactically no match for King.

27. Regina riots, July 1, 1935: A "trek" eastwards by disgruntled residents of conservation work camps for the unemployed, organized by the Canadian Communist Party, was deemed to be an insurrection by Prime Minister Bennett, and stopped in this fracas at Regina by the RCMP. Two people were killed and it was a political debacle for Bennett, who was defeated a few months later by the returning Mackenzie King.

28. Ernest Lapointe (1876–1941), King's Quebec lieutenant and Justice minister, King, future governor general Vincent Massey (1887–1967), and Peter Larkin (1855–1930), founder of the Salada Tea Company, whom King called "my (financial) angel" and appointed high commissioner in London. King was irrationally hostile to Massey. This is the Imperial Conference of 1926.

29. King's Library in Laurier House. He governed Canada from here for more than twenty years. The painting is of King's mother (reading a life of Gladstone) – a light shone upon it at all times. Here he received Churchill, Roosevelt, de Gaulle, Eisenhower, Truman, George VI, and in an adjacent room, he communicated with the spirits of those he revered.

30. The governor general, Lord Tweedsmuir (novelist John Buchan, 1875–1940), Mackenzie King, President Franklin D. Roosevelt (holding, because of his polio, his son James's arm). Tweedsmuir was a capable governor general but exaggerated his knowledge of the United States and the possibilities for effective action of his position. Though Roosevelt's great power and dazzling personality cast their spell on King, he was not overawed and the agreements he made with Roosevelt were always valuable for Canada.

31. King George VI and Queen Elizabeth arrive in Canada at Wolfe's Cove in Quebec, May 17, 1939, on the Canadian Pacific liner *Empress of Australia*, formerly Kaiser Wilhelm II's yacht *Tirpitz*, to be greeted by King and Lapointe in their most formal attire. Ten weeks after the king and queen departed, Britain and Canada were at war with Germany. The visit of Roosevelt, above, and of George VI were the first official trips of incumbent holders of their offices to Canada.

32. Charles Gavan (Chubby) Power (1888–1968), about to be associate minister of National Defence, Ernest Lapointe, King, and the Defence minister (and King's biographer) Norman Rogers (1894–1940) announce to the country Canada's entry into the war in September 1939. King and Lapointe had already proclaimed the formula to avoid a reenactment of the crisis of 1917: full participation by the country, but voluntary overseas service.

33. King and Louis St. Laurent announcing victory in Europe, May 8, 1945: Power had retired, and Lapointe and Rogers had died, but King had recruited St. Laurent as successor to Lapointe and Laurier, and he, King, soldiered on through and out of the war. "After World War I, 'business as usual'; after World War II 'orderly decontrol'; always he led us back to where we were before."

34. De Gaulle and King in 1944; they both railed against the authority of the Big Three and got on well together. Neither really spoke the other's language so the source of King's mirth here must remain a mystery.

35. Churchill graciously attended a Quebec cabinet meeting in September 1944, with the just reelected Maurice Duplessis, now on his best war-time behaviour as a Gaullist sympathizer and head of Quebec's Victory Bond Drive.

36. Louis S. St. Laurent and his wife, Jeanne, with Mackenzie King at the trumped-up convention where St. Laurent was chosen to succeed King. Recruiting St. Laurent when Lapointe was incurably ill was one of King's many brilliant strokes. Despite his apparent joviality, King was sick at the thought of retiring after twenty-nine years as Liberal leader.

37. Four prime ministers: Louis St. Laurent, Winston Churchill, Anthony Eden, and Lester Pearson at Ottawa airport in 1954. St. Laurent and Pearson were well respected by foreign leaders.

St. Luke and St. John; they were unanimous, in their table-rapping knocks as interpreted by King's well-compensated inter-life interpreters, that King's hour of political resurrection was at hand. King endlessly announced that the country needed "not the fist of a pugilist, but the hand of a physician." No one could divine or excavate any precise meaning in King's speeches, though they were fortified by the republication of *Industry and Humanity*, now almost as hardy a perennial as *Anne of Green Gables*, and the republication of a biography of himself by John Lewis from 1925, a rather bland and, to say the least, supportive volume that King and his assistant, Norman Rogers, heavily rewrote until, as King modestly allowed, it was "far from being a political pamphlet. It comes pretty nearly being a first class biography." (That is not the general opinion of informed posterity.)

Bennett had ignored his party organization for five years and done little fundraising, and there was not much to fall back on as the election approached. "Vote for Bennett" was not a spell-binding exhortation, though they did have some clever radio advertisements in which professional actor Rupert Lucas, who played Mr. Sage, an average and sensible Canadian, gave brief, clear, withering dismissals of Mackenzie King as a cowardly, self-important, blundering, cowering nincompoop. Almost as amusing as these Conservative plugs was King's dismissal of them as "scurrilous, insidious, and libelous." (He meant *slanderous*, but was so overwrought he misspoke.) They were somewhat as he described, especially as they were not billed as Conservative advertisements, but, like all good caricatures, there was a kernel of truth in them. Vincent Massey scrambled aboard King's private train car in Toronto in the last week of the campaign to receive a fierce dressing down for meddling, giving poor advice to Liberal candidates, and wearing down everyone's patience with his sanctimonious claptrap about service and duty to the party and so forth, when, said King, Massey was only interested in "helping himself" and only the prospect of the high commission in London "kept him to the party." It was a contest between two frightfully self-important and introverted men, and the clash of their histrionics is entertaining in diaries and correspondence, but there were no witnesses to it, and their association of convenience continued for a long time. King wound up his campaign at Maple Leaf Gardens before more than seventeen thousand people, where he appeared with many of his candidates and shadow ministers and was connected by radio with eight Liberal provincial premiers, from Prince Edward Island to British Columbia, all piped in live to the Gardens in an impressive political and technical tour de force. King gave a good and vigorous speech despite a collar that, he confided to his diary, was uncomfortably tight.

On the evening of October 14, William Lyon Mackenzie King enjoyed one of the greatest triumphs of his career. The Liberal Party came out of the election with 173 MPs in a Parliament of 245, up from 90 in 1930, and the Conservatives were down to 39 from 134. There were 17 members for the new Social Credit Party led by John Horne Blackmore (which replaced the United Farmers of Alberta), and 7 members for what was now J.S. Woodsworth's Co-operative Commonwealth Federation (CCF), running on the "Regina Manifesto" of 1932, a blueprint for a social democratic state. H.H. Stevens's Reconstruction Party, running 174 candidates, elected only Stevens but took 8.7 per cent of the vote. The other percentages of the popular vote were 44.7 for the Liberals, up from 44; 29.8 for the Conservatives, down from 48.3; 4 for Social Credit; and 9.3 for the CCF. (The United Farmers and Progressives had had 3.3 per cent between them in 1930.) Social Credit had just won the Alberta elections, and their leader, William Aberhart, was now the premier of that province. Blackmore (1890–1971) was the first Mormon elected to Parliament in Canada and sought the repeal of the anti-polygamy law and was a militant anti-Semite who distributed the *Protocols of the Elders of Zion* from his parliamentary office. Twelve of the eighteen government ministers were defeated in their own constituencies, although Bennett and all the other party leaders were personally re-elected. It was not only a crushing victory; it fragmented the opposition and vindicated King's unelectrifying but mortally astute strategy of pitching the Liberals – playing simultaneously on Canadian suspicion of radicalism and sympathy for the unfortunate – as the party that would keep Canada safe for the comfortable while making it more comfortable for the poor, would make Canada work for the French, and could assure the English Canadians that they would prevent the French from becoming too uncooperative or restless. King passed his hands, so accustomed to the spiritualist's table (in the little room adjoining his commodious and well-stocked library upstairs in Laurier

House), over the entire political topography of the country and always knew where to smooth out, where to knead up, where gently to level, all the depressed or inflamed points. It had not been a difficult election to win, but it was a great achievement to have won it so convincingly, with all the elements of opposition (including Stevens's Reconstruction Party) reduced to uncoordinated regional or dogmatic clans and cliques. About a quarter of all votes were cast for a motley collection of third parties; the politics of Canada were fissiparous, but the great Liberal ark of national continuity, launched by Laurier and refloated by King, and captained, between them, for over sixty years, remained seaworthy and on course. Before retiring on election night, King knelt before the illuminated picture of his mother and prayed, as was his custom on great personally emotional occasions, thanking God for His "mercy and guidance," and "kissed the photos of all the loved ones" (all long dead of course, and not all even known to him in life, such as Gladstone).[57]

King's new government was not greatly different in composition to his previous one: Ernest Lapointe in justice and Charles Dunning in finance, but also James L. Ilsley of Nova Scotia (1894–1967) in revenue, Thomas Crerar in mines and resources, Norman Rogers in labour, Jimmy Gardiner, the just-departed premier of Saskatchewan, in agriculture, Charles Gavan Power of Quebec City in pensions and national health, and, most important, Clarence Decatur Howe, an American-born civil engineer, as minister of transport. If King enjoyed the greatest majority any prime minister of Canada had ever had, it was also true that the country was entering a lengthy era when the chief opposition to the Liberal federal government was not the blurred succession of Conservative leaders who sparred briefly with Mackenzie King and his successor, but the premiers of Quebec, Ontario, and Alberta.

The much-battered Quebec Conservative Party, out of office since 1897 and reduced to a handful of members of the Legislative Assembly, several of them English, was relieved to be done with Arthur Sauvé when he departed in 1930 to be Bennett's postmaster general. He was replaced by the rollicking, garrulous, rotund Camillien Houde, who would serve eight terms as mayor of Montreal and in both the provincial and federal parliaments, and enjoy immense popularity as representative of the respectable and law-abiding working class and petit bourgeois of Montreal. Houde replaced Sauvé in 1930 as Quebec Opposition leader, but was defeated by the mighty Taschereau Liberal machine in the election of 1931, and was pushed aside by the figure who would dominate the public life of Quebec for nearly thirty years, Maurice Le Noblet Duplessis (1890–1959), member of the Legislative Assembly for Trois-Rivières from 1927 to 1959. Duplessis was acting leader of the Opposition from 1931 to 1933, leader of the Quebec Conservative Party from 1933 to 1935,* and leader of an amalgamation of the Conservatives and a dissident faction of Taschereau's Liberals called Action Libérale Nationale, which he cobbled together as the Union Nationale in the midst of the 1935 election campaign and led from its inception until his death, in 1959, during his unprecedented and unequalled fifth term as premier of Quebec. Duplessis's genius was to manage to persuade the conservatives and nationalists to vote together, an artistic feat only one of his successors has managed. Duplessis severely shook Taschereau's government in 1935, coming within a few seats of victory, and in 1936 convened the Public Accounts Committee, which he held in session for many weeks while he trotted out evidence of financial abuses on a serious and widespread scale across the Liberals' thirty-nine-year term. The most damaging revelations were that the premier's brother had been pocketing the interest on the bank account of the Legislative Assembly and, demonstrating the danger of the ridiculous in politics, the fact that the minister of colonization, Irénée Vautrin, had charged to the province approximately twenty dollars to buy himself a pair of short trousers for use when he was visiting colonization sites. "Les Culottes de Vautrin" became a lethal rallying cry for the opposition in the 1936 elections, which Duplessis won in a huge landslide, following which, he put his more radical coalition partners, who had been promising "bigger prisons and taller gallows" for the Liberals, over the side in his cabinet. "I said they could all be ministers; I didn't say they would be ministers without portfolio."[59] Duplessis was far from an extremist, but he was

---

* Duplessis was nominated as permanent leader of the Quebec Conservatives at their convention in Sherbrooke on October 5, 1933, by Laurier and Bourassa's old protégé, Armand Lavergne, now deputy Speaker of the House of Commons, in a fiery speech ending, "The gates of glory shall be opened to him; he is deserving."[58]

an autonomist who sought the full measure of Quebec's powers under the British North America Act. He struck the formula, which has proved durable in Quebec, of always demanding more jurisdiction but not proposing or attempting to secede.

In Ontario, Liberal Mitchell Frederick Hepburn (1896–1953), an onion farmer who left school after being falsely accused of throwing an apple at Sir Adam Beck, the head of Ontario Hydro, and knocking off his top hat, and former member of the United Farmers of Ontario, had served in the federal Liberal caucus with King from 1926 to 1930 and was elected the province's youngest premier in 1934 (aged thirty-seven) on a populist and anti-Prohibition platform. He sold the lieutenant-governor's residence, auctioned off the former premier's official automobile, and courted the goodwill of the less well off, though he soon proved himself a conspicuous drinker and womanizer (faults that would also hamper Duplessis's career, until, confined to an oxygen tent in 1942, Duplessis renounced alcohol and lived more sedately thereafter). Hepburn would be a serious thorn in the flesh for King, especially as he was a Liberal.

And in Alberta, William Aberhart (1878–1943), a long-serving school principal and evangelical Christian won the election of 1935, just ahead of the federal election. He had discovered the virtues of monetarist Major C.H. Douglas's Social Credit movement, which sought to pay workers and farmers more to align their income more closely with the value of their production. Aberhart founded the Social Credit Party when the United Farmers of Alberta declined to support such a platform. Though without legal qualifications, he became attorney general as well. He would seek to confer greater authority on his provincial government than the British North America Act allowed, in order to give "prosperity certificates" to those of modest means. These three premiers, especially, would more than compensate for King's ability to treat the official federal Opposition with a good deal more cavalier a disregard than he had been able to show Borden, Meighen, and Bennett in the 1920s.

Bennett retired as Conservative leader in 1937 and moved to Great Britain, where he became a viscount with the help of his childhood friend Lord Beaverbrook, owner of the London *Daily Express*, and he died at his home there on June 26, 1947, just short of his seventy-seventh birthday. He was the chief owner of the Eddy Match Company and was a wealthy and generally very successful man, and a generous one, who gave away more than two million dollars of his own money in his last ten years in Canada, including a good deal to poor and unemployed people who wrote him while he was prime minister. He exaggerated his ability to master an unprecedented international economic emergency, and the applicability generally of executive determination to the government of a federal state like Canada. His autocracy and forcefulness and apparent certitude were reassuring at first, but soon disappointed and then annoyed Canadians, and his changes of course seemed opportunistic and probably were, rather than, as he represented them, parts of a master plan for introducing new policies at stages of a gradually improving crisis (which was bunk), or at least flexibility before unbidden events (also a generous interpretation most of the time). Yet Bennett was far from ineffective and was certainly not lacking in good intentions. He had a number of successes and left the country some important institutions, boldly conceived, especially the CBC and the Bank of Canada. When he left office, the wholesale price index was rising and exports had increased by about 75 per cent since 1932, but the Great Depression continued.

But though intelligent and dynamic and well-motivated, Bennett didn't really understand the nature of the country or the conditions in which it developed. He was too dazzled by the trappings of the British monarchy and Empire, knew little of the United States, and neither knew about Quebec nor was on a first-name basis with anybody who did. Canada was so complicated because of the Anglo-French relationship, competing regional interests, and its delicate relations with both the British and Americans that a high and complicated insight and intuition were necessary to govern it successfully.

Robert Borden had understood most of the international part of this, and was aware that Quebec required special handling, though he did not actually try to provide it himself and only gained office because of an unholy alliance with Bourassa that Borden himself never fully understood and held it because of the war emergency. But Bennett, though not identified with francophobic acts and policies as Meighen was, knew absolutely nothing of any of this. King, an alumnus of Chicago and Harvard and intimate of the Rockefellers, a former society tutor (of French and German) at Newport, Rhode Island, knew a great deal about the United States, and for all his shortcomings, absurdities, and quirks had an almost demiurgically acute political sensitivity, both intellectual and intuitive, which conveniently fused in a genius for political survival. He would now be put to the test of very stern times, and would pass the test in his ineffably complicated way.

In the world, the horizon had darkened unrecognizably since King left office in 1930. In Germany, the National Socialist leader, Adolf Hitler, foaming anti-Semitic blood libels and swearing revenge on the victorious allies of the Great War, was installed as chancellor on January 30, 1933, and consolidated his position as führer, or dictator, on the death of the aged president, Field Marshal Paul von Hindenburg, in 1934. By 1935, Hitler had already begun the rearmament of Germany and had only narrowly been denied the annexation of Austria by the intervention of Mussolini in 1934. The Japanese had invaded Manchuria in 1931 and were steadily expanding their aggressions against China. In January 1932, the American secretary of state, Henry L. Stimson, had sent identical notes to China and to Japan saying that the United States would not recognize any territorial adjustments achieved by force, and specifically any which narrowed what American secretaries of state had been referring to since John Hay thirty years before as the Open Door Policy to China. Of course, there had been no open door to China for decades as most of the huge country was carved up into spheres of foreign influence, and this was just another figment of the roseate imagination of American diplomats. Stimson's position became known, rather portentously, as the Stimson Doctrine, and four days after it was proclaimed, the British announced their full faith in the word of Japan that the Open Door Policy would not be threatened. This began the bifurcation between the Western European appeasement of aggressive dictatorships and the more purposeful American approach that generally continued into the twenty-first century.

At the end of January 1932, Japan responded to the public expression of British confidence in their pacific intent by bombarding and seizing Shanghai. Stimson proposed to the British foreign secretary, Sir John Simon, a joint protest to Japan, but Simon chose to act through the League of Nations. In October, the League adopted the Stimson Doctrine, and in May 1933 Japan withdrew from Shanghai, a League victory obtained by the non-League United States. In October 1932, the League's Lytton Commission condemned Japanese aggression in China, but in a foretaste of the feeble quaverings of the appeasers, it recognized Japan's rights in Manchuria, the status of which was immersed in the League sophistry of being an "autonomous" state under Chinese "sovereignty" but Japanese "control." Words had already lost their meaning in the placation of aggression even before things began seriously stirring in Europe. But despite this undignified and pusillanimous accommodation, Japan abruptly withdrew from the League in March 1933. Germany followed in October 1933. The disintegration of the world had begun.

Mussolini, impressed with the success of Hitler's bellicosity, attacked the completely unoffending kingdom of Ethiopia in 1935, and instead of responding with a risk-free reply of force, the British and French, either of which could have given Mussolini a good thrashing on land or sea, rolled over like poodles and agreed the Hoare-Laval Pact, which would have given Italy most of Ethiopia, in a gesture designed to win Italian adherence to the Anglo-French alliance. Mussolini was disposed to accept it, but he waited a few days, news of the pact leaked, and the revulsion in both Britain and France at the craven sacrifice of Ethiopia was so great that both foreign ministers, Sir Samuel Hoare and Pierre Laval, were sacked.* Mussolini continued with his war, the British and French did nothing, and the League of Nations proved itself completely ineffectual, as was foreseeable once the Americans, whose creation it was, had declined to join. The Abyssinian War came up for debate while the government was changing in Ottawa back from Bennett to King, and the permanent Canadian advisory officer in Geneva, Walter Alexander Riddell, unable to get clarification from External Affairs, assumed the Bennett policy of (theoretical) adherence to collective security continued and declared Canada to be in favour of oil sanctions on Italy. This led to great controversy in Canada, as the Imperialists and the left were anti-Italian, but appeasement was strong in isolationist areas and the French favoured a triumph of catholicizing Italy against the Protestant missions and native heathen of Ethiopia. Lapointe withdrew Canada's

---

* King George v, not particularly known as a wit, said privately, "You don't send coals to Newcastle and you don't send Hoares to Paris."

support of a robust position on December 2, 1935, and Canada got in line behind the British appeasers. The Italians, who employed a form of deadly defoliant dropped from the air and did not hesitate to bomb civilians, occupied Addis Ababa in May 1936, although they never really controlled the entire country.

Ethiopia's Emperor Haile Selassie addressed the League of Nations on May 16, 1936, and movingly pointed out that his country was under occupation because he had had unlimited faith in the League, and that the great powers that were Ethiopia's guarantors now withheld from it arms and credit and even non-military assistance. He was jeered disgracefully and interrupted by lesser officials blowing whistles distributed to them by Italy's foreign minister, Mussolini's son-in-law, Galeazzo Ciano. It was a disgusting, shaming spectacle. The Kellogg-Briand renunciation of war as an instrument of national policy seemed not to be working. Germany, Russia, and the United States all had leaders for the times; the vacuum was in the enfeebled leadership in London and Paris. Stronger men were already audible in both countries and would emerge, and King would work with them, as he was already with Roosevelt. The greatest drama of modern times was starting to unfold, and Canada was predestined to play a greater role in it than it had ever performed in the world before.

Mackenzie King was an appeaser by nature, a Fabian, in tactical terms, not social policy: allow the other side to commit itself, dodge, prevaricate, feint, and entice an enemy ever deeper into uncertainty, disenthralled and unengaged, before siding with allies or, at the least, allowing Parliament to decide, preferably after a Royal Commission had plumbed the depths of the issue. To a degree, it came naturally and was the vintage Canadian tactic of good-faith deliberation and negotiation, playing out the clock until the disagreeable force at issue had spent itself. King's Senate leader from 1919 to 1942, Raoul Dandurand (1861–1942), told the League of Nations in 1925 that Canada lived "in a fireproof house far from inflammable materials." The only country that had any capacity to threaten Canada physically was the United States, and the era when that was a possibility was long past. In his Good Neighbor policy, Franklin D. Roosevelt said that Canada got a complete pass as a friendly and successful state and as a close affiliate of the United Kingdom, as he dismantled much of American overlordship of Latin America. He sent the foreign policy official he trusted most (not a numerous group), Sumner Welles, to Cuba and repealed the Platt Amendment, which had constrained Cuban finances and authorized American intervention at any time for almost any reason. He withdrew the Marines from Haiti, and renounced many of the uneven provisions of the Hay–Bunau-Varilla Treaty with Panama. The United States subscribed to a non-intervention pledge at the Hemispheric Conference of 1933, and Roosevelt pledged that the Marines would not be back as long as the rest of the hemisphere resisted outside influences. Roosevelt was concerned about pro-German and pro-Italian activity in Argentina and Brazil, and effectively made this exchange with those governments when he visited Buenos Aires, Montevideo, and Rio de Janeiro in 1937: no heavy-handed American intervention but no penetration of the Americas by overseas powers. Roosevelt knew Canada well. He had had a summer residence at Campobello Island, New Brunswick, all his life (where he came down with polio in 1921), and was as well-disposed to Canada as his presidential cousin Theodore had been skeptical.

The problem with King's isolationist pacifism was that if Great Britain engaged in a war with a great European power in which the future of the United Kingdom and the whole Commonwealth were threatened, English-Canadian opinion would stampede into war from under King, trying to drag the sluggish French Canadians with it. It was assumed, by King and everyone else, that in a major war, Canada would follow Britain, and Canada had practically no hand in the diplomatic niceties leading up to the European climax at the end of the 1930s, nor any military strength or strategic influence that could be deployed in the crises that marked the descent to war. All that could be said of Canada at the top table of the world's nations, though it was not an unenviable or insignificant encomium, was that, in the event of war, it would supply about a million first-class servicemen, a prodigious volume of natural resources, and a not inconsiderable defence production to the Allied side (that is, the side that Britain was allied to). King knew nothing about the Far East, though he had an able minister, Herbert M. Marler (1876–1940), in Tokyo from 1929 to 1936. He did know the major European countries well, but had no idea what to make of Hitler and an even less clear concept of him after his visit to the German leader in 1937, in which Hitler went through his soft-spoken masquerade as a man of peace working with a small and misunderstood country to achieve fair treatment for itself. King, unlike many others, had never entertained the slightest hope that the League of Nations would prevent war after the United States declined to join it, stating in May 1936, "Collective bluffing cannot bring collective security." (U.S. defence secretary Donald Rumsfeld quoted this in reference to the United Nations' attitude to Saddam Hussein in 2003.)

Hitler's first overt move to overturn the Versailles arrangements was his reoccupation of the Rhineland in March 1936. Roosevelt warned the French not to tolerate it, and Hitler's move was very tentative, as his move on Austria had been two years before, which Mussolini had frustrated by advancing forces to the Brenner Pass. Roosevelt's private view was that if France did not evict Hitler and occupy Germany up to the Rhine, in a year Germany would be stronger than France and the die would be cast in Europe.[60] On his trip to the League of Nations in the summer of 1936, King urged on the General Assembly the virtues of "mediation and conciliation" rather than "punishment." He was reflecting domestic opinion – and not only in French Canada – more than his own views, though since he considered the League incapable of effective action against an important country, even Italy, much less Germany or Japan, he saw no chance of much that was useful being accomplished.

He was reinforced in his (always) cautious optimism by his meetings with Stanley Baldwin and Neville Chamberlain in London on his way home. They shared to some degree with him their plan for accommodating the dictators, whom at this point they thought they could deflect into secondary places like Ethiopia, and confining Germany simply to repossessing what was rightfully German, if the punitive clauses of Versailles were ignored, as they would now have to be, as no one had any will to enforce them except those, like the Poles, who had no power to do so. King returned satiated with the deferences that the leaders of the British government had shown him; he equated Canada's progress in the world with its standing with the Imperial government, as in Laurier's time, rather than the standing it could enjoy in the world as a fully autonomous state. (Even this was an illusion, as, while Baldwin and Chamberlain were happy enough to take King partly into their confidence, they were not prepared to entertain the thought that Canada would do anything other than what they wished if the heat really came up in Europe.)

The main foreign issue, though its implications for Canada were also important, was the status of the new king, Edward VIII. George V had died on January 20, 1936, and was widely mourned in the Empire as a solid, unpretentious, and dutiful man, neither as august as his grandmother nor as stylish as his father, but steady and dignified through very difficult times. The new king was popular as a well-travelled, elegant bachelor, but he intended to propose to an American double-divorcee, Wallis Warfield Simpson, who had two ex-husbands living. This would put the king at odds with his role as supreme governor of the Church of England, which at that time did not approve remarriage for people whose former spouses were alive, and King joined Baldwin and other Commonwealth premiers in opposing the marriage. Baldwin let it be known that if the king went ahead, he would resign and there would be an election on the issue, which would be deeply divisive. Instead of finessing it, keeping Simpson somewhat out of sight and postponing thoughts of marriage while things settled down and public and political opinion evolved, as it would have, the king abdicated, on December 11, 1936, in favour of his brother, Albert, Duke of York, who ascended the throne as King George VI. Mackenzie King supported Baldwin's position quietly, and his only public statement, issued against the advice of Lapointe and O.D. Skelton, was so ambiguous it was incomprehensible and could not have influenced events at all. Typically, King congratulated himself in his diary on the seminal role he had played in the front rank in resolving the problem, a complete fantasy.[61]

By this time, the next great crisis in Europe had erupted: the Spanish Civil War, between the Republicans, who included most of the democratic groups and all of the left, who dominated the legitimist coalition (in the sense of a legitimate republic and the continued exclusion of the monarchy in a secular state), and the Nationalists, who included the armed forces, the monarchists, and all the right. It was a horrible war, as civil wars particularly are, and continued from July 1936 to April 1939. Mussolini injected tens of thousands of (not overly effective) soldiers in support of the Nationalists, and Hitler contributed air forces and supplies. Officially, there was an arms embargo, but it was extremely porous, and the Soviet Union and Mexico did not have great difficulty shipping supplies to the Republicans, and certainly no one interfered with the Germans or Italians. Even France allowed some support for both sides to go through. Portugal was mainly a conduit for the Nationalists, and both sides attracted volunteers, especially the Republicans, for whom the Canadian Mackenzie-Papineau Battalion fought. This group of leftist volunteers numbered 1,546 members, of whom 721 were killed, and Canada was surpassed only by France as the foreign power with the largest number of volunteers per capita. The Nationalists eventually won, as they contained almost all the Spanish armed forces and were more amply supported by their German and Italian sponsors than were the Republicans by theirs. This installed a thirty-six-year dictatorship by quasi-fascist General Francisco Franco y Bahamonde, but was succeeded in an orderly manner by a constitutional monarchy that has brought Spain fully into the modern world and served it well. Mackenzie King, like Roosevelt, ducked the war, or any hint of partisanship in the war, completely. Both men doubted that there was naturally much to choose between the fascist- and communist-led protagonists, and while the majority of Canadians and Americans sympathized with the Republicans, King and Roosevelt both pulled a large majority of their countries' Roman Catholic voters, and the great majority of Roman Catholics strongly supported the Nationalists over the violently anti-clerical Republicans. Approximately five hundred thousand people died in the Spanish Civil War, and almost as many fled the country.

King was back in London in May 1937 for a Commonwealth Conference and the coronation of George VI. The British conference hosts made the usual plea for one Commonwealth foreign policy, namely theirs, and King responded that the autonomy of Canada was not negotiable but that Britain could count on Canada in a crisis and that he wanted his and the other Commonwealth leaders' voices to be listened to in averting a crisis. He purported to be speaking for Roosevelt as well as himself in urging "economic appeasement," which was taking a considerable liberty with what Roosevelt actually said. Roosevelt had suggested economic concessions, which would in fact redound to the benefit of all, and avoidance of any suggestion that Hitler was being appeased, but the president, who spoke German fluently and knew the country well, had said from the start of the Hitler regime (five weeks before he was inaugurated himself) that it would be impossible to coexist with the Nazis. He had a radically different view of the developing crisis than did Baldwin and Chamberlain (who became prime minister in May 1937), both of whom he considered to be hopeless in dealing with such a compulsively belligerent and psychotic personality as Hitler. But they did not have much regard for Roosevelt either – whom Chamberlain described as "a cad," in a political sense – and thought they would do better with Mussolini and Hitler than trying to coordinate policy with Roosevelt and Stalin, who were in fact, in their different ways, the only leaders of the great powers, apart from Hitler, who knew what they were doing. All of this swirled over King's head, and his antennae were fully occupied and twitching wildly as he grasped at ways to urge war-avoidance on the British as the only way to keep Canada out of war. (The British hardly needed persuasion on the point.) From the position he had, and with the objectives he pursued, King cannot be faulted for not urging a strong line backed by the implicit threat of war, in as much collaboration with Stalin and Roosevelt as was available. This was the only course which had any chance of avoiding war, and Canada was not prepared to take the Commonwealth or North American lead in rearming, nor to initiate any substantive talks with Stalin, who would have been astounded by and skeptical of any such overture, so there was not much King could do. The Commonwealth Conference of 1937 was even less productive than they usually were, but King, always family-minded, celebrated the centennial of his grandfather William Lyon Mackenzie's and Papineau's rebellions with reflections on what he considered to be the coruscation of Canadian autonomy. For his own purposes, this is how he viewed the Commonwealth Conference, a process which, in addition, he had convinced himself, his ancestor had initiated.

King enjoyed the coronation and went on to Germany after he had a lengthy and very cordial discussion with the German ambassador in London, Joachim von Ribbentrop. Mackenzie King, ever a source of surprises, seems to be the only person in history who actually liked Ribbentrop, perhaps because of the ambassador's reminiscences about his time in Canada before the war as a champagne salesman and agent in Montreal and Ottawa. It was an amazing exchange of diplomatic whoppers: Ribbentrop claimed he might have emigrated had the Great War not broken out, and King emphasized that he was born in Berlin, Ontario, and knew the "German character at first hand." Ribbentrop explained his führer's sympathy for the workers, and King started spouting excerpts of *Industry and Humanity*. The upshot was that Ribbentrop, who became the German foreign minister the following year, arranged for an invitation for King to visit the Reich chancellor in Berlin, and this occurred on June 29, 1937. The interviews that followed with Hermann Göring, commander of the German air force and minister of economics, and with the German führer, Adolf Hitler, must rank as the most astonishing exchanges any Canadian prime minister has ever had with any foreign leaders. King had been on a carefully guided tour for two days, sitting in Hitler's chair at the Olympic stadium and at the opera and touring the zoo, to which Canada had donated some of the animals. King gave Göring a summary of the good relations Canada enjoyed with Britain but naturally explained Canada's independence from Britain, and Göring asked what Canada's reaction would be to a German takeover of Austria. King gave his usual answer to everything more complicated than the time of day: "We would wish to examine all the circumstances surrounding the matter," etc. King assured him that this had been his third Commonwealth Conference and that he had never seen such a will to friendly relations with Germany.

King went on to an almost ninety-minute interview with Hitler and began by putting the biography of himself written by his assistant, Norman Rogers, in front of the German leader. He showed Hitler the picture in the book of the house in which he was born in Berlin, now Kitchener, Ontario, and then told him of his previous visits to Berlin, Germany. Hitler, speaking softly, explained that Germany was arming only to get some respect from the world and gently objected to what he considered Britain's attempt to control Germany through the League of Nations. King reassuringly defended the British and gave Hitler a summary of the English temperament, saying that even in the midst of a house fire, an Englishman would betray no emotion and only concern for decorum and his own unflappability. Hitler explained that he could not control Germany as Stalin controlled Russia, by simply shooting people, and that he could only act if public opinion supported him. King was at pains to tell Hitler how much he would enjoy Chamberlain (this would be correct, but not for the right reasons), and how he and his ministers had opposed Chamberlain but now thought highly of him.

King's conclusions on Hitler, for his diary, were that he was "really one who truly loves his fellowmen, and his country, and would make any sacrifice for their good. . . . He feels himself a deliverer of his people from tyranny." King made allowance for Hitler's disadvantaged youth and imprisonment: "It is truly marvelous what he has attained unto himself through his self-education. He reminded me quite a little of Cardin in his quiet way." Hitler had "the face of a calm passive man, deeply and thoughtfully in earnest. . . . There is a liquid quality about [Hitler's eyes] which indicate keen perception and profound sympathy." After the end of the interview and Hitler's presentation to King of a framed and autographed photograph of himself, one of Hitler's aides told King how many Germans regarded Hitler as a god, but that Hitler discouraged that and only wished to be thought a humble and ordinary man.[62]

Mackenzie King was an intelligent and, up to a point, a worldly man, but he was completely deceived and hoodwinked by the German leader, who must, with his entourage, have reflected on the conversation – King's book about himself and pretense to knowing Germany and so forth – with considerable mirth. King did not know his limitations; fortunately, the West had more exalted office-holders in larger and more powerful countries who would eventually handle relations with Germany. Hitler and his coterie must have been deeply gratified by the success of the snow job they conducted on a fairly close associate, if not confidant, of the American and British leaders. For an embarrassingly long time, King cherished not only this idolatrous image of the German dictator, but professed to find in him a fellow spiritualist and a kindred follower of "the worship of the highest purity in a mother. . . . I believe the world will yet come to see a very great man in Hitler."[63] Not even Chamberlain and his entourage were much overpowered by Hitler as an individual. Sir Horace Wilson, Chamberlain's special representative, thought him "a draper's assistant," and recalled, "I didn't like his eyes; I didn't like his mouth. In fact, there wasn't very much I did like about him." The foreign secretary, Lord Halifax, at first meeting, almost handed him his hat.[64] It was in this beatific, almost gelatinous, haze of unfounded optimism that Mackenzie King somnambulated into the year of Munich, the apotheosis of appeasement.

6. Mackenzie King IV: The Descent to War, 1938–1940

In Canada, as the shattered official Opposition staggered back to its feet and dusted itself off and took stock of the political rubble about it, the opposition to the federal government from the largest and most activist provinces increased. The conventional Liberal wisdom holds that Hepburn, Aberhart, and Duplessis were birds of a feather, wild men, opportunists, quacks, or degenerates, demagogues all, assaulting in their bumptious and barbarous ways the citadel of Liberal federal good government. This is inaccurate, and the three were far from identical apart from their reservations about King's attitude to the federal-provincial distribution of powers. Hepburn and Duplessis and their predecessors going back twenty years had chafed under the federal government's refusal to authorize exports of hydroelectric power. King had seriously irritated Duplessis by refusing authority for the sale of electricity from a Quebec power company to the Aluminum Company of America in Pittsburgh. Hepburn had had similar problems, and in 1937 had legislated a provincial right to sell power to the United States from the provincially owned Hydro-Electric Power Commission of Ontario. In a different category was William Aberhart's attempt to regulate and direct, by provincial executive order, the conduct of banking in Alberta, to enact the Social Credit redirection of the earnings of lending and deposit-taking institutions to people of modest incomes. It was clearly a trespass in the British North America Act jurisdiction of federally chartered banking. And in yet another category was Duplessis's response to considerable anti-communist agitation following the revelation of the massacre of priests and nuns in the Spanish Civil War, which was to pass a law authorizing the provincial attorney general, who was Duplessis himself, to close ("padlock") a building used for the dissemination of (undefined) communist propaganda. The act, generally known as the Padlock Law, did not authorize the detention of anyone or the seizure of real property, just the closure of buildings and confiscation of designated communist propaganda. It was a gesture, a play to the ultra-Catholic gallery, and was not acted on for four months, until November 9, 1937, when the offices of the communist newspaper *Clarté* were locked, as was the home of the communist leader in Quebec, Jean Peron, and some allegedly subversive literature was trundled away, all to popping flashbulbs. It was a shabby business, to be sure, though no one was prosecuted and nothing of value was seized. But it led to immense agitation for the federal government to exercise its right of disavowal of the Padlock Law, as there was consideration of the same drastic measure in respect of Hepburn's electricity and Aberhart's banking legislation.

King and Lapointe had no difficulty striking down Aberhart's foray into banking as ultra vires to the provincial Legislature. They let Hepburn's legislation go without comment. With Duplessis, the Saint-Jean-Baptiste Society and other Quebec Catholic organizations crowded the federal justice minister's anterooms as insistently as did the Canadian Civil Liberties Union, headed by McGill law dean Frank R. Scott (co-author of the 1932 Regina Manifesto advocating nationalization of banks and transport and strict regulation of the private sector), and a long queue of reform and labour groups. Left and right awaited Lapointe and King's decision, which had to be made by July 8, 1938. The draconian measure of disavowal was not resorted to; Lapointe sagely noted that the majority of those demanding disavowal were from outside Quebec. The government had one MP in Alberta, fifty-six in Ontario, and sixty in Quebec; slapping Aberhart around was fun, especially when his measure was clearly unconstitutional, but overruling Hepburn could be dangerous, and attacking Duplessis on an issue like this in the middle of the Spanish Civil War could be a mortal error. Electoralism has its rights. Aberhart had a following in rural Alberta before it was a rich province. Hepburn was a fuse burning at both ends. But Duplessis was replacing Bourassa as Quebec's principal spokesman, and he would be in power fifteen years after Aberhart and Hepburn were gone. He would redefine federalism, and King and Lapointe saw him coming and were wary of what he could do in years that they would not live to see.

At a Congrès de la Langue Française in Quebec City in June 1937, the very capable and bilingual governor general, Lord Tweedsmuir, extolled the virtues of French, and nationalist academic clergyman Lionel Groulx gave a virtually separatist speech that greatly irritated Cardinal Villeneuve, but Tweedsmuir credited Duplessis in a letter to King with a "very courageous speech" attacking separatism.[65]

In response to the financial embarrassment of several of the provinces staggering under the weight of depression welfare and support payments and programs, King set up in 1937 the Royal Commission on Dominion-Provincial Relations, better known as the Rowell-Sirois Commission (after Ontario Supreme Court justice and former Liberal Unionist cabinet member Newton Rowell and prominent Quebec notary Joseph Sirois), to investigate fiscal and spending reforms to modernize Confederation. It would report in 1940.

In March 1938, as Göring had presaged to King, Hitler annexed his native Austria. There had been a contentious meeting between Hitler and the Austrian chancellor, Kurt Schuschnigg, an irresolute, pious little mouse of a man who was terrorized almost into insensibility by the Hitler King did not see, one who irrigated his chin screaming threats at his Austrian analogue while shaking his fist over Schuschnigg's head. When the Austrian escaped Hitler's presence and announced a referendum, this was seen by Hitler as an intolerable provocation, and Germany invaded Austria in overwhelming strength, to no resistance and a delirious welcome, which left little doubt that the majority wished Austria to be subsumed seamlessly into Hitler's absolute Teutonic and martial dictatorship. Hitler gave a fiery speech from a balcony of the Imperial Hotel (where, twenty-five years before, he had swept the steps and floors for the comings and goings of the grandees of the Habsburg capital) to delirious cries of Nazi fidelity from the crowd packed beneath him. Britain and France declined even to protest. Mussolini, who had prevented Hitler's annexation of Austria in 1934, approved it in 1938. Germany was on the march.

Mackenzie King, like much of the rest of the world, lived through the Czech and Sudeten crisis in extreme tension. Franklin D. Roosevelt had started his subtle campaign to stiffen resistance to the dictators in Chicago in October 1937, when he told a huge audience that aggressive states should be "quarantined," which he only loosely defined. He followed up when receiving an honorary degree at Queen's University in Kingston, Ontario, on August 18, 1938, saying that "the Dominion of Canada is part of the sisterhood of the British empire. I give to you assurance that the people of the United States will not stand idly by if domination of Canadian soil is threatened by any other empire." It had been unthinkable that the United States would tolerate a foreign attack upon Canada, but it was a welcome formalization, and a fine turn of the historic wheel when an American takeover threat had once been a frequent and justified fear, requiring steady massaging of the British to encourage their deterrence of the Americans. King replied a few days later that Canada would assure that "our country is made as immune from attack or possible invasion as . . . can reasonably be expected . . . and that enemy forces should not be able to pursue their way by land, sea, or air to the United States across Canadian territory."[66]

King was one of those who took up Roosevelt's phrase about "not standing idly by" and began to apply it a bit randomly. Thus, when Hitler raised a mighty war cry about restoring the Sudeten Germans in Czechoslovakia to the Reich and breaking up the state of Czechoslovakia, King, who was suffering an attack of sciatica as the Sudeten crisis reached its peak in late September 1938, wanted to issue a statement that "Canada will not stand idly by and see modern civilization ruthlessly destroyed." King thought that "the issue [of a Canadian commitment] is one of the great moral issues of the world."[67] This was his usual rather narcissistic perspective on world affairs, as his proposed declaration would not have much enlightened anyone, and it is not obvious what possessed him to attach such world-shaking moral significance to what Canada did, but it was unusual for him to wish to get out in front on such an issue, especially so grandiloquently. It was a difficult problem even morally, because the British and French and Canadians could not go to war to prevent Sudetenlanders from becoming German if that was what they wished to do (as they apparently did). But Hitler had no business giving ultimatums, seeking to crush the rather successful and thoroughly democratic state of Czechoslovakia and threatening to plunge all Europe into war.

Chamberlain made three visits to Germany in September 1938, the last announced as he was bringing the House of Commons and the world, by special radio connection, up to date on Hitler's threat to mobilize, with the parliamentary galleries full, including the dowager Queen Mary and the son of the U.S. ambassador, the twenty-one-year-old John F. Kennedy. (The world would not hold its breath again in a war crisis until Kennedy ably led the United States through the Cuban missile crisis twenty-four years later.) As Chamberlain was reaching the end of his summary on September 28, 1938, Hitler's reply to his latest message came in and was handed down the treasury bench to him. The prime minister paused to read it; there was absolute silence for almost five minutes of nearly unendurable tension, and then Chamberlain told the

House that Hitler had postponed his order of mobilization and had invited him, French premier Édouard Daladier, and Mussolini to confer with him the following day at Munich. He said, "I will go to see what I can do as a last resort." An emotional scene ensued as even Queen Mary, who was far from a tactile person, clutched the hands and forearms of those around her in relief. Czechoslovakia was dismembered, and Chamberlain returned to London from Munich quoting Disraeli's "peace with honour" after his great victory at Bismarck's Congress of Berlin in 1878, which Chamberlain remembered as a child. Chamberlain should not have raised hopes so high and been so triumphalist, and should not have acquiesced in the subsequent assaults on the stricken Czechs by Poland and Hungary. Winston Churchill led a small parliamentary opposition, claiming, "You had to choose between war and shame. You chose shame and you will get war." (At Chamberlain's first visit to Hitler, at Berchtesgaden on September 14, King was a little swift out of the starting blocks to praise Chamberlain: "It is well . . . for the world that [Chamberlain] was born in to it. His name will go down in history as one of the greatest men that ever lived – a great conciliator."[68]) Hitler soon turned on Poland, singling it out like a lion selecting an antelope and then making blood-curdling speeches threatening war and terrorizing the target country. Roosevelt privately doubted that the Munich Agreement would hold; Stalin gave up on the British and French and began thinking of composing his differences with Hitler, who, even as he took aim at Poland, also set his gaze on the rump state of Bohemia and Moravia, the Czechs he had promised not to assault further.

In the meantime, on November 7, 1938, a Polish Jew in Paris, Herschel Grynszpan, shot and killed the third secretary of the German embassy in Paris, and under the incitements of German propaganda minister Joseph Goebbels and Gestapo chiefs Heinrich Himmler and Reinhard Heydrich, the infamous Kristallnacht, the night of shattered glass, occurred, in which scores of Jews were killed, thousands injured, and two hundred synagogues burned. Exactly forty years later, the distinguished Social Democratic chancellor of West Germany, Helmut Schmidt, said at the Cologne synagogue, "We meet at the place and on the anniversary of the beginning of our national descent into hell." Germany would take almost all Europe and much of the world with it into hell. Roosevelt withdrew his ambassador from Berlin, and Hitler withdrew his from Washington before he could be expelled. (The ambassador, the very capable Hans-Heinrich Dieckhoff, competent despite being Ribbentrop's brother-in-law, warned Hitler that Roosevelt would take a third term as president and use his position as commander-in-chief to provoke a naval war with Germany.) A few days later, Roosevelt gave a filmed and internationally broadcast address which included the passage "There can be no peace if the reign of law is to be replaced by the recurrent sanctification of sheer force. There can be no peace if national policy adopts as a deliberate instrument the threat of war. There can be no peace if national policy adopts as a deliberate instrument the dispersion all over the world of millions of helpless wanderers with no place to lay their heads."[69]

King was no philo-Semite; he was concerned lest Jews become his neighbours at his country home at Kingsmere, Quebec. He referred to black-skinned people as "darkies," was no torchbearer for complete social integration or explicit notions of racial equality, and was not initially much concerned at Nazi anti-Semitism. But he was a sincere Christian, and he was jolted out of moral complacency by the pogroms of Kristallnacht. He wrote, "The sorrows which the Jews have to bear at this time are almost beyond comprehension. . . . Something will have to be done by our country."[70] He was no swifter than usual determining what would be done, but the thought was there. Quebec especially, including Lapointe more than Duplessis, opposed Jewish immigration, and King declined to accept any, even though the Canadian Jewish community undertook to provide entirely for up to ten thousand immigrants. Roosevelt called for a conference on Jewish immigration on March 25, 1938, which led to the Évian Conference, where a number of Latin American countries and the Danes, Dutch, and Australians responded quite generously, but the rest of the Western democracies, including Canada and the United States, did not. The same night Roosevelt spoke, Hitler addressed a large crowd in Königsberg and, as usual, quickly exposed the flabby underside of Western democratic posturing. He hoped that "those who have such deep sympathy for these criminals [Jews] will be generous enough to convert this sympathy to practical aid." He was prepared to evacuate the Jews to these solicitous countries "on luxury liners." In the end, Roosevelt did fairly well for the

Jews, taking over 120,000 refugees despite political unpopularity; he did much of it after war had begun but before the United States was involved. King, like most Canadians (and Americans), sympathized but didn't feel moved or able to do much, although his conscience stirred him at the end of November 1938 to urge the cabinet to see the issue "from the way in which this nation will be judged in years to come." He expressed his faith in "the fatherhood of God and the brotherhood of men" and the moral requirement to be "the conscience of the nation" and not just do what was "politically most expedient."[71] Lapointe and the other Quebec ministers would not be moved, and King declined to force the issue. It was a shameful response, but at least King had the decency to know it and repent it, and Hitler performed a minor service in exposing the cowardice and hypocrisy of many Western liberals.

A particularly contemptible and heart-rending example of the problem, in which Canada played a discreditable cameo role, was furnished by the unhappy episode of the *St. Louis*, a German ship that sailed from Hamburg in May 1939 with 937 passengers, mainly Jews who had bought visas for landing in Cuba. When the ship arrived in Cuba, it was discovered that the Cubans had retroactively revoked the visas to enter their country. The captain, Gustav Schröder, was a heroic champion of his passengers. He even allowed them to put a bed sheet over a statue of Hitler in the dining room while they performed Friday religious services. The problem apparently was that the American Jewish Joint Distribution Committee in New York refused to pay the customary bribes to the Cuban admission authorities. The *St. Louis* cruised northwards, and Canada, because of the fierce agitation of King's French-Canadian ministers, followed the American lead in not letting it in. The Americans at least lobbied others to admit them. Captain Schröder refused to bring his ship home until he had found a port for his passengers. (He was eventually declared a righteous gentile and is remembered at Yad Vashem in Jerusalem.) Finally, he disembarked his passengers at Antwerp, from where some were accepted into Belgium, some into the Netherlands, some into France, and 288 into Britain. Of the 937, 22 were accepted into Cuba, and subsequently about 250 perished in the Holocaust, but the rest survived. The United States at least admitted almost a quarter of Germany's Jews. Canada's record was contemptible. The time was at hand for Mackenzie King not to "stand idly by" and to highlight the "great moral issue of the world" of Canada's proposed action to prevent "modern civilization" from being "ruthlessly destroyed," but he was not over-prompt to recognize it. That was what all the world's leaders had to contemplate as 1938 limped to an end.

It is easy to mock the swift evolution of the Canadian leader's views, from rhapsodizing about Hitler's "profound sympathy" to seeing him as one who would "ruthlessly crush" civilization, in just fifteen months. If he was not as clear-sighted as Roosevelt and Churchill, he was well ahead of Chamberlain and even Lord Halifax. With a little perspective, it is easy to see the deadly roller coaster the world was on. Even so decent and moderate a man as Robert Borden spoke of the Germans as "barbarous" in 1918, and almost all the hard-liners of 1918 in Britain and France and Canada craved peace at any affordable price in the mid-1930s. And within a few months of Munich and its disappointments, most were resigned to the inevitability and the practical and moral need for war: a Manichaean finishing of the terrible task begun in 1914. It was impossible to negotiate or compromise with the enemies of civilization; they had to be destroyed or they would destroy civilization and impose a new Dark Age. Incredibly, and almost instantly, the culture of Goethe and Beethoven had been completely seduced by the severe, crisply uniformed discipline, the mighty pagan festivals, the Wagnerian folk mythos, and the uncontradicted demagogy of a satanic leader. The German people consented to a complete surrender of free will and the gift of the life of all Germany to their führer's disposition in the cause of the Fatherland; and the West was dividing between Hitler's sympathizers and those who were grimly prepared to die to prevent his triumph. King was not the most astute judge of onrushing events or supreme personalities, but he was in a class of his own as a survivor, an epochal chameleon, fitting in and holding his position no matter how the world turned and what upheavals beset and uprooted others. Like a magic visitor from another world, he looked impassively and expressed his astonishment in his diary, his prayers, and his exchanges with the spirits in his upstairs room. His methods are susceptible to skepticism or even derision, but his almost uninterrupted objective success is not.

On January 16, 1939, King abruptly declared, to the chagrin of Lapointe and his own entourage, including Skelton and his chief secretary, Jack Pickersgill, that "if England is at war we are at war and liable to attack. . . . I do not say that we will always be attacked, [or] that we would take part in all the wars of England." This time, King was right and his collaborators mistaken; it was time to prepare the country for the impending facts and to close the book on Raoul Dandurand's outworn parable about a fireproof house far from danger. On January 19, King wrote a rather obsequious letter to Hitler, fancying that he might influence the course of world history, but also, very sensibly, urging, "regardless of what others may wish, or say, or do, you will . . . see the resolve not to let anything imperil or destroy what you have already accomplished." It was a prophetic exhortation.

On March 15, the elephantine vice chancellor Göring chased the Czechoslovak president, Emil Hácha, around a desk in his Berlin office whence Hácha had been summoned, demanding he sign a request for the military occupation by Germany of Bohemia. Hácha fainted, but when he was revived, he semi-consciously signed the paper and the German army occupied Bohemia and Moravia at once, encountering no resistance but a clearly frigid reception from the Czechs. This was the turning point. Ernest Lapointe now recognized that war was inevitable and that King had been correct in what he had said on January 19. King, however, was more concerned about being taken for granted by Chamberlain, and on March 30 he gave one of his monotonous monologues about how Parliament would decide and each set of circumstances would be examined on its facts; all conscient Canadians could recite the formula like a catechism by now, having heard it for almost twenty years. Lapointe followed King with his own speech stating that King was correct of course, that in a war with a belligerent Germany, Canada would have, as a moral duty of a sovereign state and not by being dragged by Imperial apron strings, to join the fight for humanity, but that he would not be associated with a government that tried to impose conscription. This was intended, and taken, as a pledge by the King-Lapointe government that there would not be conscription. Between them, six months in advance of events, King and Lapointe had found the formula for national unity in a war that suddenly seemed imminent. Roosevelt was improvising with genius to assist the democracies and break a tradition as old as the republic and seek a third term. Stalin was craftily preparing for a change of direction that would astound the world. But apart from Hitler, whose course was clear and being pursued relentlessly, the leader who had now most carefully prepared for the gathering crisis was King.

The next day, Chamberlain made the most fatal and unnecessary of all his many tragic errors: he unilaterally guaranteed the borders of Poland and Romania, dragging France, and, as he assumed, the Commonwealth, with him, to audible groans of irritation and demurral from Laurier House and muffled sounds of incredulity from the White House. It was obvious that Britain and France were not strong enough to contain Germany in Europe. Britain could probably defend its home islands, as it had by far the most powerful navy in the world except for the United States (whose parity it had accepted at the Washington Conference, quite unnecessarily), and it had a serious air force. But no reputable military analyst could imagine that a Germany now fortified by snapping up Austria and the Czechs, and led by a mad but brilliant warlord instead of the neurotic and erratic kaiser, if it was not at war in the east, could be held on the Rhine by France, however effective the heavily fortified Maginot Line, along France's eastern frontier (an engineering marvel but a misconceived dedication of resources in the emerging era of air and mechanized war). The only powers who could resurrect the balance in Europe were the United States and the U.S.S.R. Roosevelt would do what he could, but the United States had not repudiated Wilson and ducked out of the League of Nations in order to go back to war in Europe. Stalin was all that was left, and the way to entice him was not to guaranty Poland, a shabby anti-Semitic dictatorship that had no call on the loyalty of the British, much less the Canadians, or even the French, despite the role France played in protecting Poland from the Bolsheviks (including the gallant Verdun veteran Captain Charles de Gaulle) in 1920 and 1921.

On May 17, 1939, at Wolfe's Cove in Quebec, Their Imperial Britannic Majesties King George VI and Queen Elizabeth descended the gangplank of the Canadian Pacific liner *Empress of Australia* (built originally as the Hamburg America Line *Tirpitz* and requisitioned in 1916 as a royal yacht by Kaiser Wilhelm II to receive the surrender of Allied navies that never happened). They were starting a one-month tour of Canada with a side trip of a few days to the United States. It was the first time a reigning British monarch had visited either country and was generally seen as a visit to raise morale and Commonwealth solidarity in Canada on the eve of war, and, in the United States, to make the most important try at British royal diplomacy since Edward VII's 1903 visit to Paris to seal the Entente Cordiale. Roosevelt had invited the king and queen when informed by Mackenzie King that they were coming to Canada, because he was trying to outmanoeuvre the isolationists in his country and promote closer Anglo-American relations. Roosevelt had been rebuffed by Chamberlain, who declined an invitation to visit the United States and responded so brusquely to the president's invitation to a summit conference of the great powers on the twentieth anniversary of the end of the First World War (rewriting the permanent undersecretary's draft to make it haughtier) that his reply, along with his determination to make further overtures to Mussolini to draw him away from Hitler, provoked Anthony Eden's abrupt resignation as foreign secretary in February 1938.

There had been fears that the monarchs might not be well-received in Quebec, but Lapointe, Duplessis, and Camillien Houde, in his fourth term as mayor of Montreal, were united in their wish that the king and queen be treated with respect. Quebec's primate and archbishop, the formidable Cardinal Villeneuve, called upon the Roman Catholic population to receive the exalted visitors with "respect and rejoicing."[72] The mystique of the British Crown was immense, and nowhere more so than in Quebec, given the battles fought there in its name. Mackenzie King and Lapointe met the king and queen in their Windsor uniforms with ostrich-plumed hats. Duplessis, in his address of greeting at the Legislative Assembly, said that "never shall we cease to consider the Throne as the bulwark of our democratic institutions and our constitutional liberties."[73] King claimed that Duplessis "had nothing intelligent to say all day." That was a bit rich, given some of King's gems, such as his parting "God, I believe, has chosen you for a work which no other persons in the world can perform, and I believe you can."[74] Houde helped arrange a mighty welcome in Montreal, and the entire visit to Canada and the United States, nowhere more than in Quebec, was an immense success. King even surpassed Duplessis in his deference to the monarchs. He had them to lunch at Laurier House, and the queen and King's Irish terrier, Pat, took to each other. King showed his guests his library and the portrait of his mother reading John Morley's *The Life of*

William Ewart Gladstone, a light always on her, and recorded in his diary that he "was prepared to lay my life at their feet in helping to further great causes which they had at heart."[75] King accompanied them on the rest of their trip. He was convinced that when the King's Plate, Canada's premier horse race, was won by George McCullagh, the owner of the anti–Mackenzie King Toronto *Globe and Mail*, the race had been fixed by the Jockey Club.[76]

King was delighted that Roosevelt had requested that he, and not the British foreign secretary, Lord Halifax, be the king and queen's accompanying minister in the United States. They went to Washington and New York and to the president's home at Hyde Park, about eighty miles north of New York City. They were received everywhere very generously and made an excellent impression on Americans, who saw them as a completely unpretentious and attractive young couple and infinitely closer to American notions of government and society than the goose-stepping, precisely drilled, and uniformed masses of the Nazi dictatorship of Germany. It was, as Roosevelt had intended, an eye-opener for the American people, steeped in the mythology of the excesses of George III. Roosevelt took the king and queen on his yacht to George Washington's home and grave at Mount Vernon (the first time the British royal standard and U.S. presidential standard had flown on the same vessel), and to a picnic at Hyde Park, where they ate hot dogs. FDR drove them himself to the little railway station near his home in the automobile made specially (by Henry Ford) for him with all the controls on the steering column to accommodate the fact that his legs were incapacitated by polio. Crowds on both banks of the Hudson sang "Auld Lang Syne," and as the king and queen (and Mackenzie King) departed, the president called out, "Good luck; all the luck in the world." George VI and Elizabeth returned to Britain on the magnificent forty-three-thousand-ton Canadian Pacific flagship *Empress of Britain*, one of the world's great liners (and the greatest international bearer of Canada's presence there has ever been), and ten weeks later Britain was at war.

Germany and the Soviet Union concluded a non-aggression pact on August 25, and the photograph of King's friend Ribbentrop shaking hands with Stalin and his foreign minister, Vyacheslav Molotov, startled the world. The British delegation that Chamberlain had finally sent to Moscow to try to improve relations with the Kremlin was still cooling its heels in the British embassy, having made little progress. On September 1, Germany invaded Poland in overwhelming strength on land and in the air. Great Britain and France honoured their guaranty to Poland and declared war on Germany on September 3, Chamberlain telling the world that "everything that I have worked for, hoped for, [and] believed in during my public life has crashed into ruins," not an altogether uplifting call to arms. Winston Churchill, after ten years out of office, returned to government as first lord of the admiralty, the position he had held twenty-five years before at the outbreak of the First World War. King had known him well in the 1920s, and their relations were not cordial.

The United States recognized Canada as a neutral power as King summoned Parliament to decide Canada's response to the European crisis, with no suspense about the outcome, but emphasizing that Canada would decide for itself whether it was at war or peace. On September 4, as King recorded in his diary, his shaving lather curled up like the swan in Wagner's *Siegfried*, putting King in mind of Hitler, whom, he wrote, "like Siegfried has gone out to court death – hoping for the·Valhalla – an immortality to be joined by death."[77] There were times, and this was one of them, when King's culture, and his other-worldly speculations, produced analyses that would have eluded less esoterically romantic statesmen. No one will ever know what exactly were Hitler's motivations, but King's Wagnerian idea is as believable as any. Later that day, King was driven to Kingsmere where, with his friend Joan Patterson, he attended upon the spirits, who revealed that King's father advised that Hitler had been shot dead by a Pole. When this turned out not to be the case, King concluded that he had been the victim of a "lying spirit," a concept that must have made such consultations doubly hazardous.[78]

Parliament convened in special session on September 7, and that evening King met his cabinet and promised that there would be no conscription for overseas service, that he would resign first. He addressed Parliament the next day and was quite eloquent: "We stand for the defence of Canada; we stand for the cooperation of this country at the side of Great Britain." He suggested that a Nazi attack was likely, since no other territory could possibly be as tempting to the German desire for natural resources and *Lebensraum* (room to live): "No . . . the ambition of this dictator is not Poland. . . . Where is he creeping to? . . . There is no other portion of the earth's surface that contains such wealth as is buried here."[79] He neglected to hint how he thought Hitler would convey his invading army to Canadian shores (especially as the path across the ocean would be blocked by the world's two greatest navies, deployed by Churchill and Roosevelt). Lapointe spoke immediately after King, as was customary, and said that "by doing nothing, by being neutral, we actually would be taking the side of Adolf Hitler."[80] He said that as most Canadians wanted to go to war to assist Britain, failure to do so to please a small group of (he implied) crypto-fascist isolationists would subvert democracy and incite civil, as opposed to foreign, war. Lapointe promised that there would be no conscription for overseas service, though there would be a voluntary expeditionary force. Canada declared war on Germany on September 10, with only a few Quebec MPs and J.S. Woodsworth, a pacifist, who retired as leader of the CCF on casting his negative vote, voting against. That night, King wrote of the faithful Pat, who abandoned his own bed to sleep with his master, after sharing some Ovaltine with him, "He seems completely conscious of what is going on."[81]

Germany overran Poland, and the last resistance ended with the surrender of heroic Warsaw on September 27. The Soviet Union attacked, in accord with secret clauses in the non-aggression pact, in mid-month and occupied the eastern third of Poland almost without opposition, and seized Latvia and Lithuania and Estonia as well. These four countries had enjoyed just twenty years of self-government in many generations.

It was a smooth entry into war for Canada, but an unsuspected challenge arose on September 24 when Maurice Duplessis abruptly dissolved the Quebec Legislative Assembly for new elections on October 25. He was overwrought and generally intoxicated and was certainly drunk when he made the announcement at the LaSalle Academy in Trois-Rivières, where he imputed to King not only the intention to impose conscription but to subsume the government of Quebec into English Canada and to assimilate all French Canadians. It was, without naming the Durham Report, a Brobdingnagian leap backwards toward it. American neutrality legislation barred the American financial market to

Quebec, which had just been denied a forty-million-dollar loan by the Bank of Canada (somewhat capriciously). The War Measures Act severely restricted Duplessis's executive authority, and censors would now edit what was in the newspapers and on radio. Instead of adjusting to an immense international emergency and radically new conditions, and speaking in the higher interest of Quebec and Canada, as he should have, and as a later version of him would do, Duplessis suffered an explosion of infantile rage, lost his judgment, acted under the influence of alcohol, and made the one terrible mistake of his career.

His imputation of motives to King was outrageous. Lapointe, Cardin, and Charles Gavan ("Chubby") Power, the three elected Quebec federal ministers (along with Senator Dandurand), conferred and agreed on both the need to act and the opportunity. They took the position that they unconditionally guaranteed that there would not be conscription for overseas service, and that although the previous world war had led to conscription for overseas service, that was under the Conservatives and the injustice would not be repeated. They said that if Duplessis were re-elected on the defamatory and almost treasonable basis that he was seeking a renewal of Quebec's confidence, they would all resign (including the venerable Dandurand, then seventy-nine) and leave Quebec defenceless against those who would impose conscription on the country and dispatch the sons of Quebec to foreign war. The full resources of the federal Liberal Party were thrown into the battle; Duplessis's sources of funds evaporated; monied elements from across Canada contributed to the campaign of the provincial Liberal leaders, Joseph-Adélard Godbout and Télesphore-Damien Bouchard, powerful and progressive orators, and bankrolled a massive election tour by Lapointe, Cardin, Power, and many of the federal Liberal MPs. Potential financial supporters of Duplessis's Union Nationale were warned of being blacklisted by the federal government with all its emergency powers. Duplessis's conservative base was frightened off, and his former nationalist allies whom he had disembarked after the 1936 election did not rally to him. The only newspaper in the province that supported him was Henri Bourassa's Le Devoir, which assured its readers that King would impose conscription. The bifurcation between the grandsons of William Lyon Mackenzie and Louis-Joseph Papineau, comrades in rebellion of a century before, could not be more radical. Le Devoir wrote, "With

Godbout, Quebec would be a branch-plant of Ottawa; Quebec couldn't live, think, or breathe." The Liberal *Le Soleil* wrote, "What a satisfaction it would be for Hitler if a Nazi party triumphed in French Canada." Lapointe, Cardin, Power, Godbout, Bouchard, and the other Liberals endlessly incanted that a vote for Duplessis was a vote for conscription and for Hitler. Maurice Duplessis was crushed by an insupportable weight of men and events that he had unwittingly brought down on himself.

On election night, the Liberals won seventy members to fourteen Union Nationale, and won the popular vote 54 per cent to 39, a complete reversal of three years before. Among the popular vote of French-speaking Quebeckers, Godbout and Bouchard only won 38 per cent to 34, with about 5 per cent going to a splintering of extreme nationalists and the non-French voting virtually en bloc for the Liberals. Duplessis told his Trois-Rivières constituents, who re-elected him personally, "I predict that those who have manipulated the popular vote tonight will not have long to wait before tasting the disapprobation of the public of Quebec." He told his weeping sister that she "need not worry. We shall have conscription. I will be back and next time I will stay for fifteen years." King's public statement said that a "victory for M. Duplessis would have been received with rejoicing in Nazi Germany." Cardinal Villeneuve, a cunning and unsentimental observer, who would play a very important secular role throughout the war and was entirely support-ive of the war effort, wrote Duplessis, "I presume that friends are today more scarce for you than they have been. . . . The scales of fortune and success have tipped suddenly. That changes nothing of what you were before, a man with faults but also with remarkable qualities of mind and heart, a font of intelligent ideas and aptitudes for government, a states-man. . . . Who knows that the future does not reserve for you a return to power? And you would regain it with the wisdom that adversity alone can give."[82] The Liberals had won, and deserved, a great victory, though it is unlikely that Hitler took much notice of it. For once, King's diarized self-laudations were largely justified. But in time, Duplessis and Villeneuve would prove to be the prophets.

King was preparing his position for a long war with great skill reinforced by transient good fortune. A reckoning with Ontario's Mitchell Hepburn was next. The Ontario Opposition leader, Colonel George Drew, prodded Hepburn into criticism of his federal leader. On January 18, 1940, Hepburn, with Drew's vastly amused support, proposed a resolution "regretting that the federal government . . . has made so little effort to prosecute Canada's duty in the war in the vigorous manner the people of Canada desire to see." This was untrue and was completely beyond Hepburn's jurisdictional competence as a provincial premier. King learned of the resolution, which passed easily with little dissent, as he was preparing to spend the evening at the cinema (Greta Garbo in *Ninotchka*, a comedy). When King returned to Laurier House, he couldn't reach any of his close collaborators on the telephone and finally a young male stenographer arrived and worked with the prime minister on a statement. King determined to call an election and to get round his pledge to the new federal Conservative leader, Robert Manion, that an election would only be called at the end of a session by converting the upcoming Throne Speech into an announcement that Parliament had been dissolved. It was as bold a move as the federal invasion of the Quebec election campaign. He advised the governor general, Lord Tweedsmuir, that this was his plan on January 23, and, except for telling the war cabinet, did not mention his plans to his full cabinet until January 24, the day before the opening of Parliament. (Charles Dunning had retired from finance and been replaced by James Layton Ralston, and Norman Rogers had become defence minister, as King found Ian Mackenzie, the former defence minister, like Power, drank too much, which he considered an unforgiveable gaucherie.) As King prayed on the eve of his surprise announcement, a star appeared to him that inspired him with beatific visions of his mother, and he was confident that all would be well.[83] Manion and Woodsworth were angry and flabbergasted, but the Liberals were uplifted by their chief's astuteness as he moved determinedly into his third decade as Liberal leader. Election day would be on March 26. "The premier of Ontario says King must go, and King will go – to the people." It was a good line, and King ran as the only leader capable of preserving national unity and maximizing Canada's influence in the world. The war had completed the economic recovery from the depression, and Manion's only argument was for a coalition, even renaming the Conservatives the National Government party. The Liberals were well organized, and the Conservatives had not recovered from the terrible beating

King had given them in 1935. (Tweedsmuir died of a coronary in his bath on February 11, and would be replaced as governor general by the Earl of Athlone.)

It was Mackenzie King's greatest victory of all of his seven elections as Liberal leader, a mighty sweep and a very personal triumph. The Liberals won 179 MPs on 51.3 per cent of the vote, up even from the 1935 total of 173 MPs and 44.7 per cent. The Conservatives won 36 MPs, a loss of 3, including Manion himself, and 29.2 per cent of the vote, down marginally from 29.8 in 1935. Woodsworth's CCF (he had resumed the leadership) gained 1 MP to hold 9, but, with 8.4 per cent of the total vote, had lost a whole percentage point. John H. Blackmore's Social Credit Party lost 10 MPs to hold just 7, and declined from 2.5 per cent of the vote to just 1 per cent. William Herridge, R.B. Bennett's brother-in-law, had founded the New Democracy party, and won 3 MPs and 1.6 per cent of the vote but lost in his own district. The rest of the MPs and votes were scattered, and a couple of the independents were really Liberals. Quebec delivered almost all it had for Lapointe, Cardin, Godbout, and Bouchard; Duplessis played no role at all, and the province elected only one Conservative. King had now set himself up admirably for a long war, with a new and heavy majority and an overwhelming mandate, and the severe humiliation of all his opponents, federal and provincial.

King had ridden the boom and bust between the wars very craftily, seizing on Governor General Byng's parliamentary inexperience to confound Meighen and awaiting macroeconomic conditions to expose Bennett's bluster and bravura. He had moved, as was his wont, just ahead of events as he consorted with the appeasers before abruptly changing to a more purposeful course. And before the war had affected Canada at all, he had bolted down the problems that had riven the country in the Great War: there would be no conscription for overseas service, and the government had crushed all opposition in securing an overwhelming mandate to mount a maximum voluntary war effort.

Unfortunately, Neville Chamberlain, whom King had so much admired as an appeasing prime minister, and had commended to Hitler so warmly less than three years before, was not having as good a war. The sands had almost run out for Chamberlain; unimaginable fates impended for France, Roosevelt was navigating inscrutably toward a third term, Stalin was an unfathomable enigma, Hitler was a mortal threat to civilization, Mussolini was strutting and posturing an absurd mime, and anything could happen in the western Pacific.

But in Laurier House, all was in readiness for any eventuality. Just seventy-three years after it was set up as a semi-autonomous state, and having exchanged ministers with only a handful of countries, Canada and its leader had had a remarkable rise. It was an important country, and its strength would be felt in the world. As King moved into his third decade as Liberal leader, all his skill, deviousness, and determination would be required and tested, but great days were imminent, for him and for Canada.

King with U.S. president Franklin Delano Roosevelt (1882–1945) and British prime minister Winston S. Churchill (1874–1965) at the Quebec Conference of 1943 (to which King was not really invited). Roosevelt and Churchill, probably the two greatest statesmen of the twentieth century, never knew exactly what to make of King, but he got on well and enjoyed lengthily cordial relations with both, and raised Canada's status in the world from struggling to negotiate its own fisheries agreements to founding membership in the United Nations and the Western Alliance.

King and the Art of Cunning Caution in War and Cold War, 1940–1949. From "Premier Dominion of the Crown,"* to Indispensable Anglo-American Ally

1. Mackenzie King v: The Supreme Crisis of Civilization, 1940–1941

King's luck had held, as his re-election preceded the opening of the real war by barely two weeks. After six months of what was called in the three main combatant countries the "phony war," the "*drôle de guerre*," and the "*Sitzkrieg*," in April 1940 Hitler seized Denmark in one day and defied the Royal Navy by landing at a number of points along the Norwegian coast. An Anglo-French relief force landed in Norway in mid-April but was forced to evacuate after ten days. The British returned to the northern port of Narvik in late May but had to quit that toehold also after ten days. It was another snappy, professional German military operation that was an inauspicious augury for direct British land

---

* Winston Churchill, Parliament of Canada, December 30, 1941.

combat with Germany. It precipitated a confidence debate in the British House of Commons from May 7 to 10. This was not at first expected to be a major problem for the government, but it suddenly became clear that Parliament and the country wanted a much more vigorous prosecution of the war. The debate was heartfelt, often extremely eloquent, and sometimes very nasty. Sir Roger Keyes, MP, a hero of the First World War, appeared in his admiral's uniform. Winston Churchill supporter Leo Amery, who was offered chancellor or foreign secretary but refused to be bought into the regime, quoted Cromwell: "You have sat here too long for any good you have been doing. Depart. . . . In the name of God, go!" Lloyd George, the last wartime prime minister and now dean of the House after fifty-two years, urged Neville Chamberlain to follow his own counsel of sacrifice by sacrificing his office. Churchill gamely closed for the government and did his best for Chamberlain and Lord Halifax, but the division, while it sustained the government, revealed too much disaffection for it to continue as constituted: forty-one Conservative MPs voted against their own party and fifty abstained. A national government was called for, and the Labour and Liberal Party opposition leaders made it clear that they would not serve under Chamberlain, who tendered his resignation to the king on May 10 as the long-awaited German offensive on the Western Front stormed into and over the Netherlands, Luxembourg, Belgium, and France. Chamberlain recommended Halifax, who was the king's preference, and the Labour leaders, Clement Attlee, Arthur Greenwood, and Ernest Bevin, said they would serve under Halifax or Churchill, whose views had been heavily validated by recent events. Halifax felt that there would be difficulties trying to govern from the House of Lords, which no one had done since the retirement of Salisbury in 1902. Also, his policy of appeasement and diplomacy had failed. Churchill might be impulsive, but he knew a lot about war, had predicted much of what had broken upon Europe since Munich, and was an inspiring and romantic figure and a great orator, none of which could be claimed for Halifax. And Churchill, by his personality, was going to dominate the government, and Halifax probably did not want to play Asquith to Churchill's Lloyd George.

The choice was clear, and on May 10 King George VI invested Winston Leonard Spencer Churchill, sixty-five – a veteran of thirty-nine years in Parliament and nine different cabinet positions, including the exchequer, home office, war, the air force, munitions, trade, colonies, and the navy in both world wars – with practically unlimited powers as head of a national unity government. No one had assumed the great office of prime minister in more difficult circumstances, but Churchill did so serenely. As he later wrote, "All my past life had been but a preparation for this hour and for this trial."[1] It was the custom in British history to reach for the decisive man when wars with other great powers went badly: the elder Pitt in the Seven Years War and his son in the Napoleonic Wars, Palmerston in the Crimean War, Lloyd George in 1916. Churchill's first address to the House of Commons and to the world as prime minister was on May 13, and he made it clear that everything had changed utterly: "You ask, what is our policy? I can say: It is to wage war, by sea, land and air, with all our might . . . against a monstrous tyranny, never surpassed in the dark, lamentable catalogue of human crime. . . . You ask, what is our aim? I can answer in one word: It is victory, victory at all costs, victory in spite of all terror, victory, however long and hard the road may be." The British people were relieved to have a strenuous war leader. The rising figure in France as the German onslaught broke over it, General Charles de Gaulle, now the associate war minister, said of his first meeting with Churchill – who called de Gaulle at first sight "the man of destiny" – that "Mr. Churchill seemed equal to the rudest task, provided it also had grandeur. [He] confirmed me in my conviction that Great Britain, led by such a fighter, would certainly never flinch."[2] And Franklin D. Roosevelt, who had not enjoyed their meeting in 1919 (which Churchill did not remember) and considered that Churchill had been an unregenerate Tory chancellor under Stanley Baldwin, rejoiced that the pusillanimous shilly-shallying of Ramsay MacDonald, Baldwin, and Chamberlain was over and that finally there was a fiercely motivated and experienced war leader he could work with in Downing Street.

The principal players in the greatest drama in modern times were all in place: Stalin, Hitler, Roosevelt, and now Churchill. And the second echelon was also now in view: de Gaulle, Mussolini, Chiang Kai-shek, Mao Tse-tung, Chou En-lai, Mahatma Gandhi, and, still and already there, an unlikely but inevitable warrior, Mackenzie King.

The Battle of France quickly became a debacle. The German campaign plan, called "Sickle-sweep," devised chiefly by Field Marshal Erich von Manstein, but with direct input from Hitler himself (who had won two Iron Crosses and served with distinction in the trenches throughout the First World War and was wounded and gassed), was brilliantly conceived and executed. German armour struck through the Ardennes Forest, which had been thought to be impassable to tanks, just north of the massive fortification in depth of the Maginot Line, and, contrary to the Schlieffen Plan of the First World War, turned north and separated the Belgian, northern French, and British armies, including a Canadian division, from the main French army. Churchill had now to conduct a delicate balancing act, advising Roosevelt in the most urgent terms of Britain's need to continue even if, as was increasingly conceivable after about May 20, France were flattened, and strengthening his argument with dire conjurations of how vulnerable even the United States would be if Britain were conquered, all the while proclaiming Britain to be unconquerable.

Roosevelt had his own balancing act to conduct, confecting a draft of renomination to a third presidential term, which none of the thirty men who had preceded him in his office had sought, and promising to keep America out of war, while doing everything possible to encourage the French while they lasted and the British Commonwealth to fight on. Thus, on May 20, Churchill wrote Roosevelt, "In no conceivable circumstances will we consent to surrender. If members of the present administration were finished and others came in to parley amid the ruins, you must not be blind to the fact that the sole remaining bargaining counter with Germany would be the fleet, and if this country was left by the United States to its fate no one would have the right to blame those then responsible if they made the best terms they could for the surviving inhabitants. . . . Excuse me, Mr. President, for putting this nightmare bluntly. . . . There is happily no need at present to dwell upon such ideas."[3] That of course is precisely what he wanted Roosevelt to do.

On May 24, U.S. Secretary of State Cordell Hull telephoned Mackenzie King and asked that King send at once a confidential special envoy to receive important information from the president that Roosevelt and Hull did not wish to commit to writing or utter over the telephone. Hull asked for "someone you can trust as much as yourself," and King thoroughly briefed Hugh Keenleyside (1898–1992), secretary of the War Committee of the cabinet, and sent him by air. After he had attended upon President Roosevelt and Secretary Hull, Keenleyside returned on May 26 and went directly to King's country house at Kingsmere, where he reported to King and O.D. Skelton. Roosevelt's message was that the French were doomed and the Germans would probably attack Britain quickly and with an air advantage of about five to one. Roosevelt had serious doubts about Britain's ability to withstand such an assault. His information was that Hitler would offer a relatively generous peace, seeking only some concessions from the colonial part of the Empire, and he thought Hitler might demand part or even all of the British fleet as well. Roosevelt asked King, via Keenleyside, to mobilize Commonwealth opinion against any such peace by Britain and to let Churchill know that the United States would, if asked, maintain the British fleet and protect the king and royal family and any other prominent evacuees to Bermuda or elsewhere, and would defend Greenland and the central Atlantic from German incursions.

Conditions were now so desperate that it was almost every man for himself among the three national leaders. Churchill was asking King to impress upon Roosevelt the need to help Britain be the first line of American defence. Roosevelt was asking King to rouse the dominions to demand that Britain fight to the finish and then send its navy to the United States, and King was happy to be a go-between for two great men at the head of great powers at a supreme moment of history, but refused to be the bearer of Roosevelt's initial message. King wrote in his diary on May 26 that "I would rather die than do aught to save ourselves or any part of this continent at the expense of Britain." Compromiser though he was by nature, in this immense crisis King was no less determined than Churchill, though he was not as eloquent. He refused to try to influence the dominions, who would immediately impute to him the role of American lackey, and he reluctantly entertained the thought that Roosevelt was just trying to prop up a potentially indefensible Britain as an obstacle to Hitler and inherit the Royal Navy if British resistance were overcome. He sent Keenleyside back to clarify whether Roosevelt wanted his message conveyed to Churchill directly or via the other dominions. Keenleyside returned, after conveying to Roosevelt King's suggestion that recommendations of this gravity should be made by the president to the British ambassador in Washington. He also told Roosevelt that if the president did not wish to communicate directly with the British, King would do it, but either for Roosevelt or on his own behalf, but not as part of any plan to mobilize the Commonwealth, which would be dismissed at once as the American scheme that it was. He was the junior member of the trio, but King was much too intelligent to play such an unseemly role as Roosevelt tried to give him.[4]

The Belgians surrendered to Germany without notice on May 28, leaving the continuing Allied combatants even more exposed. The British, French, and Canadians struggled with great courage and tenacity to make an orderly retreat to Dunkirk and to build that port into a redoubt. The seas were calm and the Royal Navy was historically unchallengeable in these waters. Churchill ordered heavy reinforcements on sea and in the air, and the Royal Air Force more than held its own with the Luftwaffe, though it was outnumbered, and about a thousand craft of all sizes and descriptions, yachts, tugs, ferries, and passenger ships, were mobilized, and these moved the stranded soldiers out constantly from May 28 to June 4, evacuating an astounding 338,000 men, including 100,000 French. The Germans took 40,000 prisoners and all the heavy equipment had to be left behind, but it was an inspiriting delivery of the cream of the British Army. The British had knocked out about four German aircraft for every loss of their own, though a significant number of the German planes were relatively vulnerable bombers. As this drama unfolded before the entire world, Churchill, sustained by the now-dying Chamberlain in the war cabinet, prevailed over the cautious Halifax, swayed the Labour Party members Attlee and Greenwood, and won official, open-ended approval, supported by Parliament, the king, and national opinion, for a policy of total and permanent resistance.

Keenleyside came back again from Washington on May 29 – with the evacuations from northern France to Britain already underway – with Roosevelt's request that King send as much of the U.S. message as he could justify sending to Churchill on King's own account, and that Roosevelt would follow himself in a few days if Churchill did not flare up uncontrollably. On May 31, King, in perhaps the most important missive of his very long and eventful career, sent Churchill his own formulation as the motley evacuation fleet, protected by large contingents of the Royal Navy and Air Force, continued to take off the expeditionary forces and their French comrades at Dunkirk. He wrote that

Roosevelt felt the fall of France a distinct possibility and an early attack on Britain by Germany from the air in heavy strength also a possibility. In those circumstances, while there was every reason to hope for British success, there was a possibility that Britain would not be able to carry on, and that this condition might be arrived at before the United States was able to intervene directly at Britain's side as a belligerent, in which case that victory would still be attained if the fleet and merchant navy were then sent to the overseas Empire, where the United States would assist to maintain them. "As soon as grounds could be found to justify direct and active American participation (and neither Mr. Roosevelt nor Mr. Hull believes that this would be more than a very few weeks), the United States would participate in a stringent blockade of the continent of Europe. . . . And interference [by Germany] would mean instant war."[5] It wasn't exactly what Roosevelt said, and what Roosevelt did say was both uncharacteristically clumsy, not so uncharacteristically self-serving, and was part of a shabby effort to make King the bearer of a message that would have damaged Anglo-American relations at a decisive moment if Roosevelt had delivered it himself. King handled his task brilliantly, reformulated it very skilfully, and did Canada and himself honour.

On June 4, Churchill cautioned, in a world broadcast, that "wars are not won by evacuations," but also stated as a united national resolve, and as if speaking personally to Roosevelt and King,

> We shall go on to the end. We shall fight in France. We shall fight in the seas and oceans, we shall fight with grow-ing confidence and growing stregnth in the air, we shall defend our island whatever the cost may be. We shall fight on the beaches, we shall fight on the landing grounds, we shall fight in the fields and in the streets, we shall fight in the hills. We shall never surrender, and if, which I do not for one moment believe, this island or a large part of it were subjugated and starving, then our Empire beyond the seas, armed and guarded by the British Fleet, would carry on the struggle until, in God's good time, the New World, with all its power and might, steps forth to the res-cue and liberation of the Old.[6]

Mackenzie King was as inspired by this tocsin as were the scores of millions of others who heard it, but imagined and wrote in his diary that he had incited the last flourish about the Royal Navy, by passing on, after artful editing, the message from Roosevelt. King wrote, "I am quite sure that Churchill prepared that part of his speech, which was the climax, in the light of what I sent him and that I shall receive an appreciative word of thanks from him."[7] In fact, on June 5, Churchill warned King "not to let Americans view too complacently prospects of a British collapse, out of which they would get the British Fleet and the guardianship of the British Empire, minus Great Britain," though he did thank King for his efforts.[8] This cold douche of great power ingratitude from Churchill following a very inappropriate initiative from Roosevelt was quite a letdown in Laurier House. King's role was still many cubits taller than that enjoyed by any previous Canadian leader opposite the leader of either the United States or Britain. Civilization was at stake, and Canada's voice was being heard and listened to by the American and British governments, and was better attuned to them than, temporarily, their own leaders were to each other.

The Dunkirk escape and Churchill's mighty philippics had the desired effect on Roosevelt, who abandoned his role as a devious and defeatist schemer and without consulting Congress, and despite the reservations of his own service chiefs, dispatched to Britain at once 500,000 rifles, 900 artillery pieces, 50,000 machine guns, 130 million rounds of ammunition, 1 million artillery shells, and large quantities of high explosives and bombs. The restrictive U.S. neutrality laws, which Roosevelt was in the act of repealing, were circumvented by selling this materiel to private corporations, which by prearrangement sold them on at once to the British government. There was dawdling in the War Department until officials were óverwhelmed by direct instructions from the president, even as he orchestrated his staged renomination to the presidency, and this resupply of the British Army was sent on fast American flag vessels, which the Germans would not dare to try to intercept.

The German army outnumbered and outgunned the remaining French by more than two to one, and on June 5 Germany launched a general offensive to the south to sweep France out of the war. Italy declared war on France on June 10, "flying to the aid," as de Gaulle put it, "of the German victory," and in Roosevelt's words, "The hand that has for so long held the dagger, has struck it into the back of its neigh-bour." In the same speech, at Thomas Jefferson's University of Virginia, in Charlottesville, which was broadcast to the world, Roosevelt said that if the French and British were defeated, "The United States . . . would become a lone island . . . in a world dominated by the philosophy of force," and would be in a prison "handcuffed, hungry, and fed through the bars by the contemptuous, unpitying masters of other continents."[9] Churchill and the French premier, Paul Reynaud – who had finally succeeded Édouard Daladier, and who had long advocated policies that might have avoided the horrible crisis in which he was now sub-merged – made increasingly urgent appeals to Roosevelt to announce that the United States would enter the war (which Churchill knew to be completely out of the question). Reynaud was now wrestling with a defeatist faction which wished peace at any price. His government evac-uated to Bordeaux, and Paris, declared an open city, was occupied by the German army on June 14.

Churchill did his best to energize the battered French and to shore up Reynaud and reinforce de Gaulle. He wrote Roosevelt on June 12, hav-ing just returned from the itinerant French headquarters, "The aged Marshal Pétain, who was none too good in April or July 1918, is, I fear, ready to lend his name and prestige to" capitulation. "If there is any-thing you can say, publicly or privately, to the French, now is the time."[10] Churchill made a similar appeal to King, who wrote Reynaud on June 14 on behalf of Roosevelt and himself and read his letter in Parliament: "In this hour of the agony of France . . . the resources of the whole of the North American continent will be thrown into the struggle for liberty at the side of the European democracies ere this continent will see democ-racy itself trodden under the iron heel of Nazism."[11] Roosevelt wrote to Reynaud and copied Churchill, urging on Reynaud the merits of fight-ing on, if necessary, with the French fleet (the fourth in the world and greater than Germany's or Italy's) and the French empire. He quoted his countryman and late acquaintance Admiral Alfred Mahan (the world's leading naval historian and academic strategist), and pitched directly to the French navy commander, Admiral Jean-François Darlan, whom he knew to be even more politicized than most senior French officers. Churchill was back the next day asking that this letter to Reynaud and himself be made public. Roosevelt fired his isolationist war secretary, Harry Woodring, on June 17 for opposing the shipment of arms to Britain after Dunkirk and the dispatch of a dozen B-17 bombers with them, and replaced him and the outgoing navy secretary, in a brilliant coup a few days before the Republican convention, with former Republican secretary of state Henry Stimson and former Republican vice presidential candidate (in 1936) Frank Knox. In the correspondence getting rid of Woodring, Roosevelt confirmed his "pronounced non-intervention policy." Both the spirit and the letter of this missive were at stark variance with what he had just written Reynaud and Churchill, so he could not agree to the publication of either letter. Roosevelt's artistic effort to hold the centre in American politics as he prepared to break all electoral precedents, while defending the national interest abroad, required him to exchange pledges of non-intervention with Woodring and send intimations of early intervention in the war to Reynaud. This was a long and unstable bridge between irreconcilable views, but its existence was a monument to Roosevelt's strategic insight and tactical dexterity.

Roosevelt and Churchill both knew that France was finished, and both were concerned with stretching out the resistance, such as it was, detaining as many Germans as possible in France for as long as possible, and with keeping the French navy out of the hands of the Germans. Reynaud sent de Gaulle and Jean Monnet, chairman of the Franco-British committee for the purchase of war material, and later the founder of the European Common Market, to London in mid-June to try to negotiate federal union with the United Kingdom. Churchill and his cabinet accepted, but Reynaud's government collapsed. The eighty-four-year-old Marshal Philippe Pétain, the hero of Verdun, succeeded Reynaud as premier on June 17 and asked for German peace terms. France surrendered in Marshal Foch's railway car, where the 1918 Armistice was signed, at Compiègne on June 22. The long battle between the French and the Germans was apparently over, as Germany crushed and humiliated and disarmed France, and occupied more than half of it, including Paris. The Third Republic, the most successful French regime of any durability since Richelieu, which had presided over the greatest cultural flowering in French history and had seen the country through the ordeal of the First World War, ignominiously voted itself out of existence at the

Grand Casino at Vichy on July 10, just two months after the beginning of the great German offensive. The greasy fascist collaborator Pierre Laval (of Hoare-Laval Pact infamy) would govern in the German interest in the French unoccupied zone in the name of the senescent marshal. Virtually all France meekly submitted to the Teutonic conquerors as they marched in perfect precision down the fine principal boulevards of the occupied French cities, resplendent in their shiny boots, full breeches, and shortish tunics, tightly belted at the waist and subtly emphasizing the stallion-like haunches and buttocks of Hitler's brave, drilled, and obedient legions. Not since Napoleon decisively defeated Prussia in 1806 had one great European power so swiftly and overwhelmingly crushed another. And in this case, the occupier intended to stay, and most of France, including Paris, was annexed to Germany.

Appearances were deceiving, however. Charles de Gaulle had been a pioneering advocate of mechanized and air warfare, and though only a junior minister in Reynaud's government, in the absence of anyone senior to do it he refused to accept defeat and flew to London on June 18. As Churchill later wrote, "De Gaulle carried with him, in this small aeroplane, the honour of France"[12] (so little of it now remained). He had almost no support at first, and represented only the vestiges of France's national spirit and interests, but he personified France's imperishable pride and valour and intelligence (and possessed some of its less attractive traits as well). Churchill recognized his legitimacy and gave him the BBC to use to address his countrymen. In words that would long resonate, de Gaulle said, "France has lost a battle; France has not lost the war." As he later wrote, "By the light of the thunderbolt, the [French] regime was revealed in its ghastly infirmity as having no proportion and no relation to the defence, honour, and independence of France." And of the last president of the Third Republic, Albert Lebrun, he wrote that while amiable and well-intentioned, "As chief of state, two things were lacking, he was not a chief and there was no state."[13]

Churchill bade farewell to France, a country he loved; he had been one of the founders of the Entente Cordiale thirty-five years before. He spoke in his heavily accented but comprehensible version of French: "People of France, it is I, Churchill. . . . Good night, then. Sleep to gather strength for the morning, for the morning will come. Brightly will it shine on the brave and true, kindly upon all who suffer for the cause, gloriously upon the tombs of the heroes. Thus will shine the dawn. *Vive la France!*"[14]

Few would realize it at first, but in his conduct de Gaulle joined the front ranks of the great protagonists of the mighty struggle, leaving Mackenzie King in the vanguard of the second group, and though King was not, by his position, force, or personality, a candidate for the historic stature of Churchill, Roosevelt, or de Gaulle, or for the historic significance of Hitler or Stalin, he was not found wanting, and his comment on the shocking turn of fortunes in Europe was original and intelligent: "The tragic fate of France delegates to French Canada the duty of carrying high the traditions of French culture and civilization, and its burning love of liberty."[15] Though not immediately accurate, it was a brilliant insight into the potential vocation of Quebec. The surge of support for the war in English Canada in the face of the mortal threat that had suddenly arisen imposed a respectful silence even on the traditional fascist sympathizers of French Canada. The isolationist and non-participationist Leopold Richer wrote in *Le Devoir*, "Our English language compatriots are living through these events in Europe as if they were unfolding on our own borders. Danger weighs heavily on an Empire, a mother-country, on political institutions and on a commercial and industrial system which are dear to their hearts."[16]

Though Quebec was opposed to conscription for overseas service, it was certainly in favour of defending Canada and was, except for a mere handful of woolly-minded Pétainists, emphatically on the Allied side in the war. On June 10, as Canada declared war on Italy, the defence minister, Norman Rogers, King's former assistant and biographer, was killed in an air crash near Toronto. He was only forty-five, and had been widely considered a potential successor to King. The Quebec Legislative Assembly voted a resolution of condolence to King and the federal government, moved by Adélard Godbout and seconded by Maurice Duplessis and passed without dissent, and expressed Quebec's determination "as an integral part of Canada to persist in the pursuit of this war for the defence of the liberty of conscience and the maintenance of honour among nations, to the last extremity, to ultimate victory."[17] Colonel J.L. Ralston became minister of national defence, and James Ilsley replaced Ralston as minister of finance, both capable appointees.

On June 18, the day after the French sued for peace, Churchill, in one of a series of mighty Demosthenean orations he delivered to the world by radio, concluded, "Let us therefore brace ourselves to our duties and so bear ourselves that if the British Empire and its Commonwealth should last for a thousand years, men will still say, 'This was their finest hour.'"[18] They did, and it was. The same day, King presented a measure of conscription for domestic service only, entitled the National Resources Mobilization Act. It passed easily, and the Quebec Assembly overwhelmingly defeated a resolution of dissent, but the tempestuous mayor of Montreal, Camillien Houde, precipitated a farcical controversy on August 2 when he described to a group of journalists his opposition to the inscription procedure as a deceitful preparation for conscription. When the Montreal *Gazette* reporter who had been present handed in his story, the newspaper's city editor, Tracy S. Ludington, who moonlighted as English-language public relations director of Duplessis's Union Nationale, wrote it up as a statement of advice not to register and sent it back with the reporter to ask Houde to sign it, which the mayor did. Ludington bannered it in the *Gazette* of August 5. As it was a recommendation to the population to join him in not registering, it was a violation of the War Measures Act, and the censor stopped the *Gazette*'s presses after about a quarter of its circulation had been printed and distributed. This generated an immediate agitation by the Opposition in Ottawa, now led by Richard Hanson, and in Quebec led by the vice premier, Télesphore-Damien Bouchard, to charge Houde with sedition. Ernest Lapointe returned hastily from the vacation King had ordered him to take when he had declared himself on the verge of breaking down from exhaustion, and Lapointe personally signed the warrant for the arrest of the mayor of Montreal, who was apprehended while leaving City Hall on the evening of August 5. The federal government did not announce the arrest for two days, and then did not allow Houde access to his wife, children, and counsel, federal MP Ligouri Lacombe. He would be interned in Ontario for four years, receiving letters from his wife addressed to "Camillien Houde, Hero."

More important by far than Houde's bumptious antics was the rock-solid support of the Quebec Roman Catholic Church, directed with dominating authority by the primate of Canada, Quebec's Cardinal Villeneuve, who was now the most politically influential person in the province, was recognized to be so, and was even favoured with an invitation to meet with President Roosevelt, with whom, the cardinal allowed, he had "a delicious visit."[19] He ordered all clergy to assist in the registration of the faithful under the act Houde had urged them to ignore, and made a series of righteously bellicose declarations: "French Canada will solemnly swear never to set down arms or relax efforts on the internal front until the triumph of the democratic ideal over the Axis powers is secure." He proclaimed days of consecration of the war and gave powerful addresses that were broadcast throughout Canada and to Europe and South America. Films were made promoting the war effort and featuring the cardinal, and conservative Action Française historian, French émigré, and Pétain admirer Robert Rumilly, wrote, "Cardinal Villeneuve assumed before the microphone the pose indicated by a technician, no doubt Anglo-Protestant. The transformation of the cardinal into an agent of British propaganda shocked not only the nationalists but a large number of French Canadians. The prelate's habitual attention to the presence of photographers became an object of derision."[20]

Villeneuve ignored his critics, who were, in any case, muted and overwhelmed, and he silenced and removed from public exposure any clergy that vocally dissented from his views. In one film at this time, he said, "The victory of Great Britain will be that of our country also, and of the whole Christian universe. It will be the victory of right over violence, of justice over iniquity, of charity over egotism, of divine right over sacrilegious usurpations . . . that we may be delivered from the fury of the enemies of God and humanity, that the peoples of the world may again know days of peace, charity and justice." He delighted English Canada and won thunderous applause from the Canadian and Empire clubs of Toronto when he acclaimed Great Britain as a "valorous, untarnishable defender and propagator of civilization," and quoted from Admiral Lord Nelson in evocation of the heroism of the British warrior. As he opened a large air base at what later became Quebec City's municipal airport, he exclaimed, "Damned be war, but let us yet praise the Lord for calling forth from us the heroism of combat on the ground, on the high seas, and in the air, that we may rebuild justice and make goodness the victor in the triumph of God and of our country." And he forced the publication in every parish in Canada of extracts of Pope Pius XI's encyclical *Mit brennender Sorge* ("With Burning Sorrow") of 1938, which condemned Nazi racism.[21]

There was a brief interregnum after the fall of France while everyone caught their breath. Hitler prepared to attack Britain, which prepared to defend itself as never before, not having seen the campfires of a serious invader for nearly nine hundred years, and Roosevelt prepared to overturn tradition and take the headship of his country for four more years. His opponent, the enlightened liberal Republican Wendell Willkie of Indiana and New York, supported Roosevelt's aid to the democracies but accused the president of pushing the country into war and headed a divided party whose congressional leaders were inflexibly isolationist. All would depend on Britain surviving the German air assault, as Hitler would have to clear the skies if he was to have any chance of getting an invasion force past the Royal Navy. Churchill moved most of the British capital ships to southern ports to be ready to intervene in the Channel, and as the British had fifteen battleships and battle cruisers to two German and six Italian (which were in the Mediterranean and were very gun-shy when British heavy units were about), and had six aircraft carriers to none for its enemies, an invasion without complete German air superiority would have been an immense disaster at sea. No one, and certainly not Hitler, doubted that the British would fight to the last able-bodied adult in defence of their island home. If Britain could face the air onslaught and Roosevelt was re-elected, it was possible to envision the English-speaking world responding in increasing unity to what Churchill was already calling "the common cause," in somewhat hopeful anticipation of events.

On June 20, a private bill was introduced in Congress without initial backing from the White House to bring in peacetime conscription for the first time in the nation's history. On July 3, the British attacked the French fleet at Oran, Algeria, sinking or heavily damaging three French capital ships. The only operational battleship the French retained (as others were demobilized at Alexandria) was the just and incompletely finished *Richelieu*, a powerful ship that had barely escaped from the builder's yard to the open sea as the Germans entered Saint-Nazaire. She sailed to Dakar, and would remain there for three years, the subject of Gaullist and Pétainist plots and counterplots among her officers reminiscent in complexity, if not in scale, of the activities of the ship's namesake. At the start of the Dunkirk operation, Roosevelt reckoned the British chances at one in three, but he moved it to fifty-fifty after the evacuation succeeded, and the attack on the French and the huge ovation Churchill received in Parliament made that three to two or better in favour. On July 10, Roosevelt quadrupled the already augmented American defence budget and laid down eight battleships and twenty-four aircraft carriers (there were only twenty-four carriers in the world in all navies, including the United States) and ordered fifty thousand warplanes, five times the annual aircraft production of Germany. Roosevelt was renominated in Chicago on July 19 (by prearrangement with the Democratic machine in that city, which stampeded the convention after a letter from Roosevelt had been read by the keynote speaker, Senator Alben W. Barkley, telling the delegates to vote for whomever they wished; that is, the incumbent. The same day, a long row of fanioned automobiles conducted Hitler to the Kroll Opera House in Berlin (which he preferred as a speaking venue to the Reichstag), and he made a spurious offer of peace, according to which Germany and Britain would both keep everything they now had. Churchill listened to the speech on the radio but dismissed it at once as just another act of treachery, containing no worthwhile elements and emanating from an unappeasable psychopath.

Air activity over southern England greatly increased after the middle of July, and the British continued to shoot down more German planes than they were losing, as even American journalists could verify, albeit unscientifically, just by watching the intense dogfights with binoculars in the clear summer skies. The British and German fighters were approximately equal in quality of machine and skill and courage of pilot, but the German bombers were sitting ducks when the RAF fighters broke through and attacked them. The British could recycle four-fifths of their aircrews shot down over England, as they landed on home ground if they parachuted safely, where almost all German aircrews which were shot down were killed or captured. The sinister Stukas, with their hornet-like appearance and sirens, which had so terrorized civilians in Poland, Belgium, and France, were decimated by British Spitfires and Hurricanes and after a couple of disastrous days never returned to British airspace.

Roosevelt's re-election posture was that the war emergency was so serious that he could not attend the convention that renominated him in Chicago, and could not campaign. But he went on tours of military and defence production installations, which had the same public relations value as a campaign, and he reserved the right to intervene to "correct campaign falsifications," with little doubt that he would profess to find some in need of being addressed. He asked Mackenzie King to meet him on his private train at Ogdensburg, New York, on the St. Lawrence near Kingston, on August 16 to discuss North American defence. King refused to allow American military bases in Canada, but the Ogdensburg Agreement, as it was called, led to the setting up of the Permanent Joint Board on Defence and to a high level of cooperation. Arthur Meighen spoke for the most militant Canadian imperialists when he claimed to have "lost his breakfast" reading about the agreement,[22] but most Canadians recognized that in these circumstances, the tighter and more formal the U.S. guaranty of Canada the better. Typically, King, who imputed divine intervention to his dog's indispositions and his own bowel movements, saw "the Hand of Destiny . . . as clearly . . . as anything in this world could possibly be . . . a converging of the streams of influence over a hundred years ago as to place and time and of life purpose in the case of Roosevelt and myself," he wrote in his diary on August 22.[23]

Churchill had misgivings about creeping American influence and wanted Roosevelt to confine himself to assisting Britain to survive and then join it against Germany without encroaching on what he still regarded as a British domain in Canada. The British high commissioner in Ottawa, Sir Gerald Campbell, was an astute observer of King and reported to Whitehall that the Canadian prime minister was "very complex. . . . He goes far beyond the average Canadian in his mystical and idealistic talk of a crusade or holy war against the enemies of civilization and democracy. On the other hand, he is the narrowest of narrow Canadian nationalists [who will always] consider [how] the common cause can be made to help Canada."[24] This was, after all, King's task and duty, to fight barbarism on the scale of threat Nazism had now achieved, and in doing so and in all ways to advance the Canadian national interest. From the Plains of Abraham approximately to the First World War, the British connection was almost constantly invoked by Canada as its insurance against being overrun by the United States. Now, British mismanagement of the peace in Europe had put the old country in mortal peril, and Britain was asking for Canadian help and not the other way around. The British did not seem to realize that Canada was in the war not because it was a British territory but because it disapproved of Nazi aggression and wished to support Britain when it was under threat as an independent act of solidarity, and that if, in doing that, it could add the formal military guaranty of the mighty United Sates of America, which had for so long been a threat to Canada and a rival to Great Britain, this was a thing to be done and was no legitimate cause of perplexity to Britain.

When Campbell told Churchill that King was upset by his cable, following King's message that had been prompted by Roosevelt's message to him, the British prime minister, who by this time had many more urgent concerns, dispatched a message to his sensitive Canadian analogue in which he thanked King for "all you have done" for the now proverbial "common cause and especially in promoting a harmony of sentiment throughout the New World" (a slight embellishment on what had been achieved at Ogdensburg). King carried this message around in his pocket for weeks and happily found occasion to show it to colleagues, friendly acquaintances, and reporters (and possibly even passers-by).[25] Complicated though he was in some ways, in dealings with Churchill and Roosevelt, immense world historic personalities as they were, King was quite predictable. The Permanent Joint Board on Defence had its first meeting on August 26 in Ottawa. The Canadian co-chairman was Oliver Mowat Biggar, a former member of Canada's delegation at the Paris Peace Conference and judge advocate general of Canada, and the American co-chairman was the ebullient reform mayor of New York City, Fiorello H. La Guardia, who could not be more different to King, but the two men got on well. ("He grows on one," as King wrote.[26])

Throughout August and September 1940, as the Battle of Britain flared in the English skies, the British were losing about twelve aircraft a day but recovering most of the aircrews, and the Germans were losing about thirty aircraft a day and practically all the aircrews. The British estimated German front-line air strength at the beginning of August at 6,000 and that annual German production had been increased to 24,000. The real figures for 1940 were 3,000 and 10,247. By mid-August, the air forces were swarming in the skies of southern England all day, and the British committed their final reserves; every airworthy machine they had was engaged. From August 25 to 29, Churchill sent forty bombers over Berlin, where the damage they caused was not great, but the effect on the population and on Göring and Hitler was considerable. These raids, and the unsustainable losses the British were inflicting, caused the Germans to change to massive nighttime bombing indiscriminately over populated areas. German intelligence also underestimated the strength of the RAF. The Germans thought that when they went to nighttime bombing, the British were down to 177 fighters and a production of 250 a month. The real figures were 1,084 and monthly production of 428, under the fine administrative hand of Canadian Lord Beaverbrook as minister of aircraft production. The British were free to buy what they wished from the United States (though American-built fighter aircraft were not as fast or manoeuvrable as the British and German types), and the Germans could not import aircraft from any worthwhile foreign supplier.

Roosevelt wrote Churchill on August 13 that he believed he could send him fifty First World War destroyers, which, though inferior to recent craft, could still hunt and sink submarines. Roosevelt proposed to trade the destroyers for the right to open American bases in British Caribbean islands and in Newfoundland. Roosevelt also began redefining U.S. territorial waters outwards from three miles in two-hundred-mile increments, ultimately to eighteen hundred miles, and ordered heavy patrolling of the coastal waters as redefined with any detection of German or Italian vessels to be communicated at once, *en clair*, to the British and Canadians. He had expanded this so-called neutrality zone to one thousand miles by late September. This was, to say the least, an idiosyncratic definition of neutrality, and a bold series of moves to undertake in the midst of a campaign for an unprecedented third presidential term. The Selective Training and Service Act, the first peacetime draft in U.S. history, was passed on September 20, and Roosevelt signed it at once, calling it, in Revolutionary War terms, "a muster."

Between July 10 and October 31, the RAF lost 915 aircraft and the Luftwaffe 1,733. The kill ratio came down from three or four to one in favour of the British to two to one for the whole period when the Germans shifted to night raids and the kills were about equal. Changing over to night bombing brought German losses down to within their production and training additions but made precise bombing impossible and grossly alienated international, especially American, opinion. The attacks strained but did not break British morale, and it was clear by mid-October that Britain had won the war in her own skies and that henceforth both sides would essentially control their own airspaces. On August 20, slightly in advance of events, but not unwarrantedly, Churchill had said of the Fighter Command of the Royal Air Force, "Never in the field of human conflict was so much owed by so many to so few." On October 21, he said in another of his great broadcast speeches, "We are waiting for the long-promised invasion. So are the fishes."[27] Churchill, whose mother was American, knew American politics well enough to know that in giving these inspiriting addresses and announcing a resurrection of his country's military fortunes, he was helping Roosevelt and making the president, in the midst of his re-election campaign, appear both generous and prescient in the eyes of his own voters. Military success sired diplomatic and political success.

Wendell Willkie ran a tremendously spirited campaign, which came down to the war scare "Our sons are already almost at the boats!" Roosevelt replied that he would "repeat again and again and again: your sons will not be sent into any foreign wars." The president entered the campaign in the last two weeks, and it was a spectacular windup. He hung the Great Depression on Willkie's party and strongly implied that it was infested with isolationists who were fascist sympathizers and virtual fifth columnists. Unemployment was coming down by five hundred thousand a month through the campaign, and the president ran as a reluctant candidate who had saved the nation from the Republicans' economic disaster and would save the peace for America by arming the democracies fighting America's battle on freedom's front lines. It was a believable message, and he was an invincible political operator and forensic virtuoso. On November 5, 1940, he was returned as president by a margin of five million votes, almost 10 per cent of the vote. Nearly 80 per cent of eligible voters cast ballots, and the incumbent carried 449 electoral votes to 82 for Willkie. The next day, Winston Churchill wrote him, "I did not think it right for me as a foreigner to express any opinion on American policies while the election was on but now I feel you will not mind my saying that that I prayed for your success and that I am truly thankful for it. . . . In expressing the comfort that I feel that the people of the United States have once again cast these great burdens upon you, I must avow my sure faith that the lights by which we steer will bring us all safely to anchor."[28] King telephoned Roosevelt the day after the election, and the two men had a jovial chat, as appropriate between two recently re-elected leaders on the most cordial terms.[29]

The second half of 1940 was thus almost as successful for the Allies as the first half had been disastrous. France was gone and Italy was arrayed against the British Commonwealth, but it was soon clear that the Italians were not really interested in risking all for Mussolini's superfluous supporting role beside Hitler. On November 11, the Royal Navy Fleet Air Arm attacked the Italian navy in its home base of Taranto and, with a loss of only two aircraft, permanently destroyed one Italian battleship and forced two others to ground to avoid sinking, eliminating for over six months half of Italy's battle fleet, in which time two new British battleships and several aircraft carriers would be commissioned. The implications of a torpedo attack in a shallow anchorage, as executed at Taranto, were written up in British summaries of the action and sent by Churchill to Roosevelt, who passed them on to his own senior naval officers, but the attack was more closely studied by the Japanese than by the Americans, with grievous consequences a year later.[30] The West was pleased and heartened by Finland having given Stalin a bloody nose in late 1939 and early 1940, although the Russians eventually forced the issue by sheer numbers. Stalin was cooperating with Hitler but showing no disposition to come farther into the war. The British (with the whole-hearted collaboration of the Commonwealth) and the United States (providing "all aid short of war") had firmed up the concept of the English-speaking peoples – a concept that suddenly and for obvious reasons became popular in Britain and Canada – and had together produced a stasis in Western Europe. There was no longer any immediate danger of the British Isles being overrun.

It was disappointing to King that he wasn't really on an equal footing with Churchill and Roosevelt, but all three men had been in government prior to the First World War, when the Canadians were still somewhat fearful of the United States and were generally treated

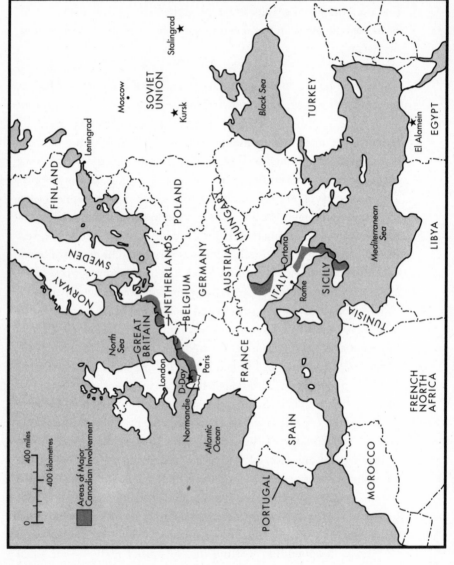

Canadian Involvement in the Second World War

by the British as a colony where foreign and defence matters were involved. Where Robert Borden had been trying to get the Liberal Senate to give the British the money to build British battleships in British yards, King negotiated in late 1939 the British Commonwealth Air Training Plan, which would prepare 130,000 Canadian, British, Australian, and New Zealand airmen. It provided initially for 64 training centres, 20,000 Canadian, British, Australian, and New Zealand air personnel per year, and a budget of $600 million, of which Canada would contribute $350 million and up to 80 per cent of the candidates. It was a very ambitious program and would prove completely successful.

In purely domestic matters, the Rowell-Sirois Commission summarized very well the fiscal and spending evolution of the different layers of government since Confederation, and concluded that the federal government should assume provincial debts, take over sole responsibility for unemployment insurance, and have sole power to collect income and corporate taxes and succession duties, and that a new system of adjustment grants should be established that would enable a uniform standard of social services to be provided across the country. Since Ontario, Alberta, and British Columbia, the wealthiest provinces, would be paying and not receiving these grants, they objected, and Quebec opposed the transfer of jurisdiction that was proposed. There was a good deal of unfortunate comment in Ontario about not wishing to pay for French Roman Catholic education in Quebec. (In fact, since the Church paid a reduced and not a secular pay scale to the clerical personnel in schools and hospitals, this would not occur, but bigotry rarely dwells long on the facts.) The Canadian federal government had already secured the right to a constitutional amendment to deal with unemployment insurance, a change resulting from the depression which now had passed, and there really was no longer any unemployment. Agreements were made for the rental of tax fields by the federal government in exchange for the assumption by it of expanded spending responsibilities, though Ontario refused to have anything to do with such an arrangement.

Canada was not a great power, of course – it was a recent colony – and Churchill was still trying to reinvent a version of Lloyd George's placebo Imperial War Cabinet, and even suggested that King might like to play a prominent role in it by moving to England. This was an insane idea on every score: the domestic Canadian political scene required very careful watching, and the Canadian war effort could not be directed from outside. King declined Churchill's increasingly urgent invitations to come to Britain for over a year, and while he was not taken fully into the confidence of his senior colleagues, he at least denied Roosevelt's request for military bases in Canada and refused Churchill's timeless efforts to subsume Canadian manpower into the British services. King had two problems, apart from the fact that Canada had less than 10 per cent of the population of the United States and 25 per cent of that of the United Kingdom, without counting any of the vast Empire that remained under direct British rule. The first was that he was directing all his efforts to becoming more intimate with Churchill and Roosevelt – and inciting the inference among his own countrymen that they regarded him as a serious confidant, if not altogether an equal – and this prevented him from making common cause with the Australians and prominent third states, especially the Free French of de Gaulle, who would be increasingly important as the French empire switched over to him, the French Resistance gained strength, and the liberation of France approached. King's second problem was that he was not an inspirational leader. He was occasionally capable of a tolerably good speech in its content, but had no presentational flare and did not have a galvanizing voice, unlike either Churchill or Roosevelt, who were both mighty orators in different ways, Churchill the erudite, fierce, fighting leader, and Roosevelt the mellifluous, almost apostolic, patrician. One of King's strengths was his indistinctness, his uncanny ability, half calculation and half intuition, to place himself at the radical centre, between poles, not to lead boldly. His strengths were essential to govern Canada through such a crisis but were a handicap in comparison to his illustrious wartime contemporaries. Canadians had learned decades before that when they wanted inspiration, it was not W.L. Mackenzie King who would give it to them.

The year ended with one of Roosevelt's most famous of all his fireside chats, on December 29, 1940. Public places across America emptied as the hour of his address approached, and 75 per cent of Americans of comprehending age listened. He said there was no hope of a negotiated peace. "If Britain goes down . . . an unholy alliance" would continue to pursue world conquest, "and all of us in the Americas would be living at the point of a gun. There can be no ultimate peace with this gang of outlaws." The "pious frauds" offered by the dupes of the dictators within America would not distract the American people. "No dictator, no combination of dictators," Roosevelt told the world, would divert the American people and government from pursuing their moral duty and national interest. "We must be the great arsenal of democracy." His address received overwhelming public approval. On June 25, the Gallup organization had reported that 64 per cent of Americans believed it was more important to stay out of war than to help Britain. On October 20, the same organization found the division of opinion on that issue exactly even; on November 19, it was 60 per cent in favour of aid to Britain whatever the consequences; and after Roosevelt's year-end address it was about 70 per cent. The eloquence of Churchill and Roosevelt, the martial bravery and stoicism of the British, and the savagery of Hitler, had turned American opinion and altered the balance of world power. But where the balance was so narrow – given the ambiguity of Italy's war commitment and the continuing, if tenuous, neutrality of the United States, the Soviet Union, and Japan – Canada was perhaps now the third most important combatant, and made a vital difference.

2. Mackenzie King VI: The Turning Point, 1941–1943

If 1940 had been the year of maximum crisis, 1941 would be the year where the road to victory became visible. King, from his own curiosity, cultivated the Japanese minister in Canada, Baron Tomii. Their conversations were relatively candid, and King assured the Japanese envoy that if Japan had "troubles," as Tomii called them, with Malaya or India, Canada would certainly support Britain. He also tried to sound a deterrent note on behalf of the United States.[31] On March 26, 1941, Tomii told King that if Germany invaded Britain, Japan would attack British Empire outposts in the Far East. (It had done the same with French Indochina, where even the communist nationalists were already nostalgic for the gentler hegemony of France.) Tomii said that Japan would ultimately emulate the political configuration of the winning side, totalitarian or democratic, in the current war. That proved to be accurate, but not, presumably, in the way that Tomii foresaw. King told him that if Japan became embroiled in war with Britain, the United States would come to the aid of the British. Tomii expressed confidence that Japan would not be at war with Britain or America anytime soon, but King did not believe him.[32]

At this point, Japan's energetic foreign minister, Yosuke Matsuoka, was bustling around Europe trying to add the Soviet Union to the Berlin-Rome-Tokyo Axis. To this end, Matsuoka negotiated a non-aggression pact with Stalin and Vyacheslav Molotov. Matsuoka was a Christian who spent much of his youth in Portland, Oregon, and in Oakland, California. He had a cordial visit with Hitler in March, but instead of aligning with Japan in the event of a conflict with Russia, the Germans said nothing of any possible disagreement with the Soviet Union. Hitler's strategic concern by early 1941 was that he was obviously not going to be able to invade Britain and was now almost at war with a United States led by the implacable, reinaugurated Roosevelt. On February 13, the U.S. Senate adopted the Lend-Lease bill, by which the United States would essentially give the British and Commonwealth countries anything they asked, and they would repay by returning it when the war was over, or, if that was impossible, by equivalent consideration when it could be done. To the press, Roosevelt compared it to lending your neighbour your garden hose if his house was on fire. It was a brilliant initiative, and it effectively meant that Hitler was facing the full weight of the United States in all but manpower, and by now Roosevelt had ordered the U.S. Navy to attack any German ship on detection within eighteen hundred miles of the Atlantic coast of the United States. Churchill described Lend-Lease in Parliament a few days later as "the most unsordid act in the history of any nation," and on March 12 the Parliament of the United Kingdom unanimously approved Churchill's resolution, expressing "our deep and respectful appreciation of this monument of generous and farseeing statesmanship. . . . In the name of all freedom-loving peoples we offer to the United States our gratitude for her inspiring act of faith."[33]

Godsend and act of genius though it was, Lend-Lease caused the transfer of some war supply from Canada to the United States, and King and Ilsley and C.D. Howe (now minister of munitions and supply) were concerned that Canada would lose exports and production, as well as foreign reserves to finance its own imports from the United States. King and his officials visited FDR at his Hudson River estate at Hyde Park, and the president rounded out Lend-Lease with the Hyde Park Declaration of April 1941, which increased American purchases from Canada by $200 million to $300 million per year and permitted American components to be fabricated in Canada and shipped on to Britain. Officials of all three countries were becoming much better known to each other. Thus, Howe became well acquainted with Roosevelt's treasury secretary, Henry Morgenthau, and with his chief troubleshooter, and, insofar as he had one, confidant, Harry Hopkins.

King was always on the lookout for talent to add to his cabinet and always sought ministers of higher quality. He tried to entice Canada's greatest financier, John Wilson McConnell, proprietor of the *Montreal Star*, and farm equipment executive James S. Duncan, of Massey-Harris, to his government, and had an informal try for Adélard Godbout. King was always pleased, and never envious or threatened, by talented people he met, and was very impressed with the young industrialist Edward P. Taylor, now working with Howe in the munitions department: "A fine-looking and really splendid fellow," wrote King.[34]

Harry Hopkins, Roosevelt's close adviser in domestic matters, and his electoral opponent Wendell Willkie, with whom his relations were cordial, both visited Britain in January and February 1941 and made a very favourable impression on the British. And Willkie delivered to Churchill Roosevelt's handwritten excerpt from Longfellow's poem "O Ship of State," which the British leader read over the airwaves: "Sail on, O ship of State! / Sail on, O Union, strong and great! / Humanity, with all its fears, / With all the hopes of future years, / Is hanging breathless on thy fate!" It was an electrifying citation, and one that reminded the whole English-speaking world how fortunate it was that its defence was being led by two men whose culture and high-mindedness largely personified the civilization whose official champions they were.

This was a scale of activity and importance that was not accessible to Mackenzie King. Canada was not adequately important, though it certainly was rather important, and King himself had no such call on the attention of the world, nor any such flare for mass leadership. He had, in the French expression, the fault of his qualities, and these were the compromise, the course adjustment, the calculated manoeuvre, not the epochal or astounding or brilliant gesture or even apercu. He had his strengths, but as usual with Canada, flamboyance, or even exceptional and evident virtuosity, was not among them.

In these circumstances, Hitler reasoned that if he did nothing Roosevelt would keep Britain afloat and eventually, when he was ready, attack Germany, and might at the same time be able to bribe Stalin into knifing Germany in the back. Hitler concluded that if he attacked Stalin now and knocked Russia out as a major power, or at least pushed it back toward the Urals, he would be immune from the danger of a two-front war, and the British and Americans would have to assemble a prohibitively immense force to land successfully in Western Europe and dislodge Germany from occupation of most of the continent and suzerainty over subordinate dictatorships in the rest (Italy, Hungary, Romania, Spain, Portugal, et cetera). It would be an immense gamble, but he had built his career on such gambles and had always won. It had a certain logic.

What is not clear is why he did not coordinate with Japan. By this time, Japan was under what was in practice an oil embargo from the United States, from which it imported 80 per cent of its oil, as Roosevelt considered the Japanese invasions of China and Indochina to be (as they were) a moral outrage. Japan would have to attack the Dutch East Indies (Indonesia) to obtain oil if the American boycott wasn't loosened. But if Hitler had attacked the Soviet Union in coordination with the Japanese, he could have promised Japan access to the Caucasian oil fields of Russia, and the British would not have dared to intercept Japanese tankers that came to fetch the oil. This would have enabled Japan to seize territory from the Russians in the east and contributed importantly to an attack on that country. In the alternative, Hitler could have made a major effort in North Africa – rather than the mere four divisions he gave Erwin Rommel, with seven ill-assured Italian divisions – to try to seize the Suez Canal and advance into the Middle East. This would have freed up oil for Japan and facilitated a combined attack on the Soviet Union in 1942.

Hitler – spurred by a fear that, if he did not move quickly, both Stalin and Roosevelt were capable of a sudden strike at him, with the connivance of the British – had the German General Staff prepare a plan for the invasion and conquest of the western Soviet Union by 180 or more German and allied divisions, starting in early May. Mussolini had foolishly attacked Greece from Albania and been given a good thrashing by the Greeks, as he was when he attempted the invasion of Egypt from Libya, which caused Hitler to send Rommel to prevent the complete sweep of the Axis from North Africa. These fiascos, and repeated British naval victories over the Italians in the Mediterranean, demonstrated how misguided the Chamberlain-Halifax policy of appeasement of Mussolini had been. (Lord Halifax had been banished by Churchill to Washington as ambassador.) When on March 27, 1941, under the influence of British and American intelligence, the Yugoslavs overthrew their prince regent, Paul, who had, under pressure, aligned Yugoslavia with Germany, and replaced him with the seventeen-year-old king and military regents, Hitler reacted with even more than his usual ferocity when challenged in Europe. By April 6, a plan was developed and execution of it began for the crushing of Yugoslavia and Greece by twenty-five German divisions and some further units contributed by the Hungarians, Romanians, and Italians. Belgrade was occupied after a week, Yugoslavia surrendered on April 17, and Germany pressed on into Greece, where the British had diverted four divisions from the defence of Egypt. The Greeks surrendered on April 20 and the British forces lost ten thousand dead or taken prisoner, and the remaining forty-five thousand men were forced into another indecorous maritime evacuation by the Royal Navy, a miniature Dunkirk. This was finished with a German paratroop invasion of Crete overcoming the defending garrison of twenty-four thousand British between May 20 and June 3, when the British again took to the boats. It was another remarkable German tour de force, but it delayed the main operation against Russia by over six weeks.

Germany launched that immense invasion, Operation Barbarossa, on June 22, with a seriously shortened campaign season before the Russian winter would close in on operations in November. If Hitler had made the main push in Africa, he could have enlisted the Japanese to his cause with Russia without the Japanese being forced to commit acts of aggression in the far and South Pacific that were certain to drag the United States into the war. Hitler was now sure to find himself fighting the Americans and Soviets as well as the British Commonwealth, unless he could knock Stalin out of the war promptly. Neither Churchill, who later lamented "the failure to strangle Bolshevism in its cradle" in 1919, nor Roosevelt had any political affection for Stalin (though they all found each other quite convivial personalities when they met), but both realized at once that if Hitler crushed the Russians it would take generations and an unimaginable military effort to dislodge him from control of Western and Central Europe. Roosevelt and Churchill both announced programs of assistance to the Soviet Union, and Roosevelt sent Hopkins to Moscow in July, where he met with Stalin and began the coordination of an immense program of assistance. The Russians fell back under the German onslaught and lost about one and a half million prisoners and about a million casualties in the first six weeks or so, but it did not become a disorganized retreat, and Stalin was able to replace practically any amount of attrition. Stalin was not a great or comfortable public speaker like Hitler, Churchill, and Roosevelt, but he set aside communist dogma, retrieved the Russian Orthodox Church leadership to call for the defence of Mother Russia, and took to the airwaves, a very rare occurrence, and told the Slavonic masses that Germans were "swarming over our country like a plague of grey-green slugs" and that "We will kill them, kill them all, and plough them under the sod." It was total war on an unheard-of scale, and all conventions of war and of humane treatment of civilians were ignored. More than twenty-five million people would perish in circumstances of unspeakable barbarism on the Eastern Front.

On August 9, 1941, Winston Churchill and Franklin Roosevelt met for the first time in twenty-two years (Roosevelt had found Churchill obnoxious at their previous meeting, which, as has been mentioned, Churchill did not remember.) They came by ship to Placentia Bay, Newfoundland, Churchill and his military chiefs on the battleship *Prince of Wales*, just repaired from its bruising encounter with the powerful German battleship *Bismarck* (which blew the bridge off *Prince of Wales* and shut down two of its three main turrets, after which *Bismarck* was sent to the bottom by a variety of other British vessels), and Roosevelt with his military chiefs on the heavy cruiser *Augusta*. The relations between the two leaders developed very well, and Roosevelt wrote his cousin from shipboard that Churchill "reminds me of a British Mayor La Guardia."[35] The Americans were impressed with Churchill's strength and determination, as they expected to be, but did not believe his war plan of relying on a naval embargo, aerial bombing, guerrilla resistance, and amphibious coastal harassments had any chance of bringing down Hitler's Reich within a hundred years, or that Churchill believed it himself, only that he was trying to ensure that Americans didn't become too fearful about entering the war. Hopkins came on board Churchill's ship, having come back from Russia, and he gave a fairly upbeat account of his meeting with Stalin, who, he said, was composed and purposeful despite the fury of the German assault.

The British found the American account of relations with the Japanese quite informative and suddenly quite promising. Roosevelt declined to stop all oil shipments to Japan, as there was still the possibility of individual tanker-loads of oil under individual export permits. Churchill began agitating for a complete shutdown of all such exports, as he was prepared to advocate anything that got the United States into the war, no matter in which ocean or under what *casus belli*. Only when Roosevelt returned to Washington did he discover that his under-secretary of state for economic affairs, Dean Acheson, had taken it upon himself to deny all such applications, determining a "practice" in the absence of a policy.

There was one of the great photo opportunities of the war as the two leaders attended a divine service on the fan deck of the *Prince of Wales* with their service chiefs standing behind them. The news film depicted them and the splendid anchorage and sleek ships, and recorded the stirring hymns ("Onward, Christian Soldiers" and "For Those in Peril on the Sea") and showed the crews of the two fleets cordially intermingled. (Roosevelt brought packages of fruit and cigarettes for all the British sailors, and the British opened their ships to give the American sailors the spirit issue, as liquor had been banned from American ships since the First World War, when Roosevelt was the assistant secretary of the navy, though he always waived the rule for himself and his official party, then and subsequently. The U.S. Navy did distribute alcohol generously for supposedly quasi-medical reasons.)

The leaders agreed on what became known as the Atlantic Charter, which renounced and opposed territorial changes other than by the authentic wish of the inhabitants; respected the right of all peoples to self-government (requiring a little fancy footwork over the

British Empire); relaxed trade; and favoured freedom of movement, international cooperation, improved standards of living for the whole world, disarmament, collective security, and unspecified international organizations. It was a distant descendant of Wilson's Fourteen Points, but it was a good manifesto, resonated well in the world, and was a jangling contrast with Nazi brutality, which it pledged to extinguish. It was another step forward for Britain and the Commonwealth to achieve such intimacy with the United States and give such form to the "common cause." Roosevelt said that he would "make war without declaring it." This was a heady turn for Churchill, who, fourteen months before, was receiving Roosevelt's request, via Mackenzie King, to send his navy and merchant ships to America when Britain came under the hobnailed Nazi jackboot. It was a great propaganda victory, and Hitler forbade his propaganda minster, Joseph Goebbels, to publish the charter at all. With the Russian armies in the field contesting fiercely with the Germans, and such unity between the British and American leaders, and Britain now unassailable in its home islands, it was a remarkable leap forward for the British from the desperate solitude of the year before.

Mackenzie King was miffed not to be asked to the Atlantic Conference, and especially not to have been given any hint of the contents of the Atlantic Charter, which outlined war aims and was composed largely by the Americans, who were not even in the war, however tenuous their neutrality had become. King inflicted on Churchill an endless series of excuses for not coming to London, covering, said the young Charles Ritchie on Vincent Massey's diplomatic staff in London, everything except a claim that "he is having the front parlour papered and is needed to choose the design."[36]

The Atlantic Conference finally smoked King out, and he did go to London at the end of August 1941, travelling for the first time in his life on an airplane, which "he found exhilarating and spiritual."[37] The main point of the visit was for King to be adequately informed of war conditions, and specifically to be reassured, as he was, that there was no indication that Canadian conscription would be necessary. He could not leave these matters to his high commissioner, Vincent Massey, whom King despised as much as ever as a scheming and pretentious careerist, though he did like and respect his understudy, Lester B. Pearson. Churchill was advised by the new British high commissioner to Canada, Malcolm MacDonald (son of the former British prime minister), that King "admires Churchill enormously, but doesn't like him very much."[38] Churchill turned on the charm and dazzled King, as he could easily do with his overpowering personality, and as Roosevelt had done with King for the last six years. Churchill publicly praised King, put him on the radio, had him to Chequers, his official country house, closeted himself with him for hours, and explained that he could not have him to the Atlantic Conference because he had to meet Roosevelt alone and that there would have been terrible jealousy on the part of the other Commonwealth leaders. King was mollified, and seduced. He visited the Canadian troops under General Andrew McNaughton, where he was lightly given the raspberry by some of the men, an incident that was rather cruelly overplayed by some in the Canadian press, a wounding experience for one so sensitive as King.

Following the Atlantic Conference, there were two transformative events during the balance of 1941. First was the steady stiffening of Soviet resistance as the German armies approached Moscow and Leningrad in a race with the oncoming winter. By mid-autumn, it was clear that this was a much different war to the one Germany had become accustomed to; it started out like Poland and France, but the scale of the territory and the manpower available to the Russians gave them, with the flow of supplies from the Western Allies, an ability to regroup. It became a very tense contest, made even more sanguinary by the heinous antics of the Gestapo in the occupied territories, where the Wehrmacht was initially well-received by Ukrainians and Belarusians unappreciative of the Russian communist efforts among them at the perfection of man since 1917. The second event was Roosevelt's decision not just to confirm an absolute oil embargo on Japan, but also to withdraw his initial verbal proposal to the special Japanese envoy to Washington of a "modus operandi" in which both sides would step back and there would be a loosening of the embargo and a de-escalation of Japanese military activity in China and Indochina. Roosevelt concluded that there was a danger of Stalin making a separate peace with Hitler, as he had in 1939, and as Trotsky and Lenin had with Germany in 1918, if Stalin did not see a prospect of victory, and that to prevent it the United States would have to enter the war. By reimposing the embargo and withdrawing the modus operandi, Roosevelt made it inevitable that Japan would attack somewhere to the south, and troop movements by the Japanese away from Siberia confirmed that. Roosevelt gave Stalin this intelligence, and Stalin withdrew his twenty divisions in the Far East and transported them on special trains of the Trans-Siberian Railway for the final defence of Moscow and Leningrad. The course of human history changed in December 1941, as the German assault on Russia stalled and fell back, and the Japanese, surpassing even Kaiser Wilhelm II's monumental blunder in 1917 of submarine warfare against American merchant shipping, attacked the United States.

It was hard to imagine that only eighteen months earlier Britain had seemed to hang by a thread. As Churchill wrote, "So, we had won after all! . . . After seventeen months of lonely fighting and nineteen months of my own responsibility in dire stress, we had won the war." There would be hard fighting, but the "British Empire [he meant Commonwealth, but old habits die hard], the Soviet Union, and now the United States . . . were twice or even thrice the force of their antag- onists."[39] Both Stalin and de Gaulle were of the same view. De Gaulle wrote, "Of course there are years of fighting ahead but the Germans are beaten. . . . The colossal war effort [that would be] mustered . . . ren- dered victory a certainty."[40] From Stalin's perspective in the Kremlin, the Germans were receding, the Americans were coming fully into the war, and the door of the cage that had kept the Russian bear out of Central and Western Europe for centuries was opening.

Mackenzie King heard of the Japanese attack on Pearl Harbor while lying down for a nap at Kingsmere, and it was an "immense relief . . . to know that their attack had been upon the U.S. in the first instance, and that the opening shots were not between Japan and Great Britain."[41] Certainly, Roosevelt was entirely confident – though he was furious that the war and navy departments' repeated warnings had not been heeded and that there were not torpedo nets around the battle fleet and air patrols out around Oahu in all daylight hours, and he dis- guised the extent of the damage, with two old battleships lost perma- nently and three out of action for many months. He was also pleased that for the first time in American history, his statesmanship and

Japanese stupidity had produced unanimous American public support for the war effort.

In two addresses to Congress at the beginning and end of 1941, he had enunciated the principles that would guide American foreign policy, and Western security policy, for at least seventy years. In January, in his State of the Union message, Roosevelt said, "We must always be wary of those who with sounding brass and a tinkling cymbal preach the 'ism' of appeasement." And in his war message of December 8, he said, "We will make very certain that this form of treachery never again endangers us." Since then, the United States has not been an appeasement power and has retained the military force to deter direct aggression by any country.* It was not generally known at the time, but isolationism was also finished in the United States, at least for a long time. Roosevelt had learned all that he needed to from his cousin Theodore and from his Great War chief, Woodrow Wilson, and he would not allow the United States again to change the world and then abruptly retreat within itself, slamming a trapdoor behind it like a retiring cuckoo-bird, as it had a generation before after the First World War.

King had been shaken by the death of his undersecretary of external affairs, O.D. Skelton, in January, so soon after that of Norman Rogers, and even more by the laboriously recorded death of his dog, Pat, also in January, at the age of seventeen. On Pat's last night, King held him and sang "Safe in the Arms of Jesus," and described every detail of his declining hours in his diary. "He had bounded in one long leap across the chasm that men call death. My little friend, the truest friend I have had – or man ever had – had gone to be with . . . other loved ones. I had given messages of love to take father, mother, Bell, Max, Sir Wilfrid and Lady Laurier, Mr. and Mrs. Larkin and the grandparents."[42] But King received the grimmest news of the war on November 14, 1941, when he was informed that his closest colleague, Ernest Lapointe, was dying of pancreatic and lung cancer. He visited Lapointe the next day, and they discussed politics as normal, including

---

* Its enemies imagined sixty years later that they could attack the United States in terrorist assaults not connected to any sovereign country and hatched in failed states where there was no functioning government, but that is less threatening than an assault by a great nation vested with the sinews of war like Germany or Japan, and cannot ultimately succeed.

a possible invitation to Quebec premier Godbout to join the federal government. King returned to see Lapointe in hospital on November 19 as he was on his way to the centennial observances for Sir Wilfrid at Saint-Lin, in the Laurentians. Lapointe asked King to secure Godbout as his successor, and to call Cardinal Villeneuve, thank him for his help, and ask the cardinal to pray for him. "He then turned to me and said we had been great associates, and reached out his hand toward mine. I said to him no man had ever had a truer friend. But for him, I would never have been prime minister, nor have been able to hold the office, as I had held it through the years. That there was never a deeper love between brothers than existed between us. That we had never had a difference all the years that we had been associated together, in thought and work alike." They kissed each other on the cheek. King called the next day and they reminisced about visiting Sir Wilfrid's grave together when their government was installed twenty years before, and King had said that Laurier "is right here with us." That afternoon, King huddled with Godbout in the kitchen of Wilfrid Laurier's house and dismissed Godbout's concerns about his English. The next day, King was back at the hospital and said, "Ernest we will see each other again." Lapointe replied, "There is nothing truer than that." King held his hand, kissed him again, and withdrew. They were not to meet again, at least not in this world.[43] Ernest Lapointe died on November 26, 1941, aged sixty-five. Cardinal Villeneuve presided over a mighty funeral in the Quebec City cathedral-basilica, and King, as he led the funeral cortège, which included almost every prominent public person in the country except the incarcerated Camillien Houde, as well as the senior diplomatic corps, thought, "How much one owes to be true to the people."[44]

There was a good deal of discussion of the succession to Lapointe. Godbout was reluctant. Cardinal Villeneuve thought Godbout would be acceptable, and Arthur Cardin urged the distinguished fifty-nine-year-old lawyer Louis Stephen St. Laurent. Godbout lost King's confidence when he urged that Télesphore-Damien Bouchard be brought into the government (he was a tempestuous man), but the telling argument was that the departure of Godbout might lead to a return by Duplessis, "a fatal thing if Duplessis ever again got hold of the government there," wrote King.[45] King telephoned St. Laurent at home as St. Laurent was sitting down to a family dinner, and they met in Ottawa on December 5. St. Laurent said that the hope that he might modestly help in winning the war was the only reason he would consider public life on the verge of his sixtieth birthday. As King wrote in his diary, "He spoke of the subject of conscription incidentally as likely to arise when the U.S. went into the war; 'if they conscripted their men for overseas, it might be necessary to do the same.'"[46]

Two days later, the Japanese attack on Pearl Harbor, Hawaii, plunged the United States into a war which covered and bled the whole world. Two days after that, St. Laurent telephoned King to accept his invitation. Everyone he had consulted had approved, including Villeneuve and Godbout (who declined a fine opportunity to be the next prime minister of Canada to retain an excellent opportunity to be the next leader of the Opposition in Quebec). Ernest Lapointe had been a Quebec leader of almost peerless character and astuteness. He was worthy in every respect of the succession to Sir Wilfrid Laurier. That Mackenzie King managed to replace him in less than three weeks with a man of about equivalent stature was a providential development for Canada.

In January 1942, in the most disreputable form of imitation of poor examples of American public policy, twenty-seven thousand Japanese Canadians in British Columbia were subjected to seizure of their assets and forced removal to internment camps at least one hundred miles inland from the Pacific coast, with grating restrictions on movement and activities. It was an exceedingly shabby measure, and the war emergency and attendant fears (and wartime racism) do not justify the complete abandonment of due process. The trustee of alien assets, who was supposed to conserve and restore them, instead sold them in 1943 at knockdown prices. Some restitution was made shortly after the war, but not until Prime Minister Brian Mulroney in 1993 was the matter put to rights, with $21,000 for each surviving detainee, restoration of citizenship to anyone deprived of it, and $36 million for Japanese-Canadian institutions.

A more edifying, and even amusing, *beau geste* occurred over the tiny French islands off Newfoundland of Saint-Pierre and Miquelon, population five thousand, which had been left with France at the end of the Seven Years War to enable France to service her fishing fleet and continue to train mariners (see Chapter 2). Vichy controlled the islands, which had a powerful radio transmitter that broadcasted pro-Axis propaganda. It was also suspected that the main Western Union telegraph cable from North America to Europe was being intercepted from the islands by the Germans. Charles de Gaulle advised British foreign secretary Anthony Eden that he wished to take the islands and put a stop to these problems, and Eden agreed with him but said the Americans and Canadians should be consulted. The Americans did not want Vichy disturbed, for some inexplicable reason (Roosevelt still had his old navy crony Admiral William Leahy, who used to drive him back from his cottage in New Brunswick during the First World War on his destroyer, as an accredited ambassador to Pétain at Vichy), and the Canadians preferred to evict Vichy themselves. De Gaulle took the initiative, and his own modest naval forces seized the islands on December 24, 1941. De Gaulle's naval commander, Admiral Émile Muselier, assured the American consul on the islands that the Allies now had complete access to them, and on Christmas Day a bona fide referendum gave 98 per cent support to de Gaulle. The U.S., Canadian, and British media, and the Canadian and British governments, were all very supportive, but Secretary of State Cordell Hull was in a febrile state of agitation and spent much time over New Year's and into 1942 fiercely lobbying Roosevelt, Churchill, and King (who through most of the war clung to Roosevelt like a treed cat and was certainly not going to fail to be in Washington when Churchill was there, as he then was) to evict de Gaulle from Saint-Pierre and Miquelon. When all the leaders, including his own president, ignored Hull, he issued a press statement calling the takeover by the "so-called Free French ships . . . arbitrary." It blew over in a few weeks, but even in his memoirs, written after de Gaulle had established himself as the authentic spokesman for France, Hull still wrote of the incident with comically exaggerated anger.[47]

Churchill, at this coruscation of his ambitions, insisted on visiting Roosevelt at once, and despite Roosevelt's efforts to defer the trip, Churchill arrived at Hampton Roads on December 22, 1941, on the battleship *Duke of York* (sister of *Prince of Wales*), and flew to Washington, where Roosevelt met him at the air terminal. On that day, just as King was worrying whether he would be cold-shouldered as he had been at the Atlantic Conference, enabling his opponents to dismiss his pretensions to being a confidant of both Western leaders as a fraud, Roosevelt called him and invited him to bring his armed forces ministers with him to Washington on December 26. King was so chuffed that he took the extremely rare liberty, though Roosevelt had urged it upon him, of closing out the call "Good bye, Franklin." (When he was president, no one except Churchill, his predecessor as governor of New York and presidential candidate, Alfred E. Smith, his mother, his wife, and a couple of relatives and old school chums, called FDR by his Christian name.) On December 26, Churchill gave a memorable address to a joint session of the U.S. Congress and received a very warm welcome, even from former isolationist leaders of Congress. The British prime minister had not left his oratorical prowess at home, and frequently drew great applause, especially when he said, of the Japanese, "They have embarked upon a very considerable undertaking; what kind of a people do they think we are?" This was one of Churchill's gambits: to claim the most intimate ethnic kinship, and not just a common language, with the United States, a novel concept to the country's tens of millions of citizens of German, Irish, African, and Italian descent. "Do they not realize that we shall never cease to persevere against them until they have been taught a lesson which they and the world will never forget?" He came on to Canada for several days on December 28 before returning to the United States. Hong Kong was taken by the Japanese in overwhelming strength on Christmas Day, and two poorly equipped Canadian battalions, which had been recently sent there, surrendered with the rest of the insufficient garrison. Of the 1,975 Canadian soldiers there, 557 died, either in action or from mistreatment as prisoners of war by the Japanese.

Churchill was naturally extremely well-received in Ottawa, and he gently told King that, as King had raised domestic Canadian political questions with him, Churchill could report that he had heard from several plausible sources that King would be invincibly strong if he allowed about three Conservatives "a look in" in his government; that is, a coalition. (Churchill did not understand the complexity of French-English issues in Canada, and the danger of a coalition government becoming conscriptionist, as in 1917, and putting intolerable strain on the country.) Churchill emphasized that he was just transmitting information, not presuming to advise. In his visit, he was at pains to emphasize King's valued and respected status with Roosevelt and himself, and King's participation in the discussion of all major issues. He was also clear that every Allied country would have to decide for itself the nature of its war participation, lest anyone imagine Britain was asking for conscription for overseas service from Canada. He spoke to Parliament on December 30 and called Canada "the premier dominion of the Crown," and told the Canadian legislators, and the world, of the French general who had predicted to the French premier in 1940, that "in three weeks, England will have her neck wrung like a chicken. Some chicken! Some neck!" His timing was perfect, and the effect was splendid, and the visit to Canada was a complete success. Churchill did his magic with King, as Roosevelt usually did, and King wrote of his guest, "I found his nature wonderfully kind, sympathetic and understanding" – this of the man who, barely two years before, King had considered too "dangerous" for high office.

The American visit, which continued for some weeks, was also a success. Roosevelt eventually left Churchill as the host in the White House, convening American generals, admirals, and officials, and removed to his home at Hyde Park. The two countries were already in disagreement about the likely timing of a full-fledged effort to liberate Western Europe. The British wanted to concentrate on the Mediterranean and leave the Germans largely to the Russians. The Americans were afraid of a separate peace between Hitler and Stalin still, and Roosevelt did not wish to face his electors again in 1944 without having made serious progress toward the expulsion of Hitler from occupied Europe. (Churchill, of course, could defer elections *sine die*, and there had not been a general election in Britain since 1935.) Roosevelt and his advisers concluded that the issue could not be forced until the United States had the preponderance of forces in the theatre. The United States and United Kingdom had been holding joint staff talks since the end of 1940, and confirmed their agreement of the Atlantic Conference that Germany should receive priority over Japan as the principal enemy. Roosevelt had already ascertained that King agreed with the Americans on the need for the earliest possible direct assault on Hitler's Europe, although the British would try for a time to represent themselves opposite the Americans as the head of a unitary Commonwealth. Roosevelt, who had known Canada all his life, knew better.

* * *

Robert Manion, defeated in 1940 at the polls personally, and comprehensively as leader of the Conservative Party, and replaced as acting leader by the inadequate Richard Hanson, was now to be succeeded by a surprising, not-so-new face, nor a very welcome one to King, Arthur Meighen. Senator Meighen would retire from the upper house to contest York South, the constituency neighbouring King's original riding of York North. The by-election would be held on February 9, the same day as by-elections in Quebec East, to replace Lapointe with St. Laurent as member of Parliament, and in Welland, to bring in labour ministry official and former trade union organizer Humphrey Mitchell (1894–1950) as minister of labour. There was also a fourth by-election in a safe Liberal district. It was convenient that Louis St. Laurent lived in the district where he stood.

On December 17, 1941, the Manitoba Legislature passed a resolution urging conscription for overseas service, a timely issue now that the United States would be sending conscript armies across both oceans. In November 1941, a Gallup poll had shown that 61 per cent of Canadians were satisfied with the federal government's management of the war, but that 60 per cent wanted conscription for overseas service.[48] Yet King somehow had it in mind that a referendum would be a good idea to settle the issue down. This was a mistake, something he rarely committed in political matters, but it was contemporaneous with another vintage lesson in Kingsian political chicanery.

In Quebec East, the candidate against St. Laurent was a Quebec political gadfly who had become almost the mascot of the nationalists: fascist, separatist, anti-participationist Paul Bouchard (1908–1997). When Bouchard ran against prominent Liberal Joseph-Napoléon Francoeur in 1937, Francoeur had promised "no participation in foreign wars." In the federal election in 1940, when Bouchard ran against Lapointe, the minister of justice said, "Participation but not conscription for overseas service." Now, St. Laurent was saying, "No conscription without consulting the people." The trajectory was clear. In York South, in the 1940 election, Conservative Alan Cockeram had won 15,300 votes to 12,800 Liberal and 5,300 for the Co-operative Commonwealth Federation (CCF) candidate, Joseph Noseworthy. Now, the local Liberal organization did not run a candidate, supposedly out of respect for the former prime minister, Arthur Meighen, but in fact, and informally, in the hope of making Noseworthy a fusion stop-Meighen candidate. Even Quebec East had to be watched closely; Bouchard had only lost by 5,000 out of about 31,000 votes cast, running against Lapointe in 1940, although Lapointe had held the district since the death of Sir Wilfrid in 1919 and had often won 80 per cent or more of the vote, and had carpeted the district for decades with tangible reminders of his official influence. As these elections were stoking up, King, weaving with agility and urgency, was still the spider at the centre of the national web he had been spinning for decades. He prorogued the longest parliamentary session in Canadian history, fourteen months, on January 21, 1942, and opened the next session the following day with the promise of a plebiscite on relief of the government from its 1939 pledge against conscription, which would be held on April 27. King thought the vote would be 65 per cent negative in Quebec but about 70 per cent positive in the country. The English-Canadian conscriptionists were opposed to a referendum, believing that as the national interest required conscription it should simply be imposed, as in 1917, but without an election as there had been in 1917. But this time, it was not so much from conformity with Great Britain alone in a European war, but to get in step with our two senior allies in a wider war. They were both conscripting for world-wide service in a war which had less heavy casualties than in the Great War, and where the issue was clearer. Hitler was much more odious than Kaiser Wilhelm II, and the rout of the great French army brought North America much closer to the front lines. The anti-conscriptionists – mainly, but not exclusively, French Canadian (there were many English-Canadian employers who were none too keen to lose their workforces to the military) – disputed that a pledge given essentially to Quebec in 1939 and repeated the following year when there was still only a "phony war" could now be reopened in a consultation of the whole country.

There was great stress on the Liberal Party, and it took the cabinet ten hours to agree on this formula of arming King with the same power Churchill and Roosevelt wielded without committing to use it, but King put it through. Arthur Cardin, the senior Quebec minister in the vortex between Lapointe and St. Laurent, was wary. In Quebec itself, both Church and state were taking a holiday on this proposition; Cardinal

Villeneuve and Premier Godbout wouldn't touch it. Godbout repeated his confidence in King, but was prone to be more deferential than was politically healthy in Quebec, restating his hostility to conscription but declaring that "if tomorrow Mr. King told me to go to Europe to shine the boots of the soldiers, I would go happily."[49] Quebec, especially in wartime, expects a less self-effacing view of federalism than that. In late April, Godbout gave a platitudinous semi-endorsement of a "yes" vote, at the very urgent request of the prime minister. The Roman Catholic episcopate maintained an absolute silence, calling it a secular matter and repeating its support of the war effort generally. In Quebec, it was hard not to see it as a double-cross, though King engaged in his usual flim-flam. In English Canada, the government was doing the honourable thing before departing from its previous pledges, and in Quebec it was merely asking for the standby authority Canada's allies already possessed, and the whole device was eventually covered in the Kingsian classic "Conscription if necessary but not necessarily conscription" (a straight lift from the Toronto Star of April 28, 1942, but it was effectively King's line throughout). His expectation was that St. Laurent and Mitchell would win, though it could be close, the fourth by-election, in a safe Liberal district without a prominent candidate would be all right, but that Meighen would probably win. King did not admit even to his diary how far the local Liberal organization had pitched in to help the CCF's Noseworthy, as he presumably wanted plausible deniability even to himself, but there is no question that, although it was not overt, the Liberals favoured the CCF, in funding and organization. The Globe and Mail and the Committee for Total War – headed and funded by prominent businessmen J.Y. Murdoch of Noranda Mines, C.L. Burton of Simpson's department stores, and James S. Duncan of Massey-Harris, whom King had considered for a cabinet position – all supported Meighen. So did Ontario premier Mitchell Hepburn, whose hatred for King had not declined and was fully requited.

The first round of the test went well for the government. In Quebec East, St. Laurent defeated Bouchard 16,700 to 12,700, only about a thousand fewer votes than Lapointe's majority of two years before, running for his seventh term (and following ten consecutive terms in the same district for Laurier). Mitchell was safe enough in Welland; the fourth contest was an easy Liberal win; and in York South, the long uneven battle between King and Meighen ended with the unprepossessing socialist Noseworthy, who had garnered only 5,000 votes two years before, defeating the former prime minister, Arthur Meighen, 16,400 to 11,900. The tortoise had disposed of the hare at last. Meighen, without a seat in either house of Parliament, had been defeated too often and was politically finished, though he lived on for nearly twenty years and made a substantial fortune.

J.S. Woodsworth had died on March 21, 1942, aged sixty-seven. King's irritating opponents seemed to be dropping like flies, as the Conservatives prepared to bring on the seventh leader he had faced (counting Meighen twice). The referendum campaign intensified. On February 11, an organization calling itself La Ligue pour la Défense du Canada gathered twenty thousand people at the Marché Saint-Jacques in Montreal, where there was a sequence of fiery speakers, including future mayor Jean Drapeau for the youth, future publisher of Le Devoir Gérard Filion for the farmers, and the pièce de résistance was the seventy-four-year-old Henri Bourassa. Though Bourassa spoke moderately as he predicted the imposition of conscription, a window-smashing riot erupted along Boulevard Saint-Laurent, the traditional point of division between English and French Montreal. There was a good deal of anglophobic and anti-Semitic sloganeering. All the newspapers except Le Devoir denounced the rioters and their affiliations, and Godbout spoke darkly about incitements to treason. Bourassa was becoming rather bizarre by this time; in October 1941, he had given a much-publicized address not only praising Pétain, Franco (of Spain), and Salazar (of Portugal), but also Mussolini, on whose crumbling regime Canada and its allies were, with conspicuous success, making war. The young Pierre Trudeau, twenty-three in 1942, strayed into the same areas, illustrating how unworldly Quebec nationalist circles were. Mussolini was now well and regularly described by Churchill as "a whipped jackal."

On April 27, 71.3 per cent of eligible Canadians cast ballots, 2,946,000 voting "yes" and 1,543,000 voting "no" – 65.6 per cent to 34.4 per cent. Quebec voted about 72 per cent "no" to 28 per cent "yes," which meant that French Canadians were 90 per cent opposed to releasing the government from its pledge and English Canadians were 80 per cent in favour. For once, King had been too cunning for his own good. The question wasn't a straight referendum on conscription, but everyone knew that was what it was, despite King's obfuscations. King was shaken by the results, but he ploughed ahead, claiming to have secured the mandate he sought, but giving no hint if he would actually impose conscription. Conscriptionists were infuriated by his evasiveness, and anti-conscriptionists were not impressed by his waffling but were reduced to supporting him as the closest they had to an anti-conscriptionist who could influence events. He had a clearer anti-conscription record than St. Laurent. With his now very divided cabinet, King said he thought conscription would be necessary, but that it wasn't yet. He was, in fact, correct. It was not necessary. There were some Canadians in Egypt, and the navy and air force were very active, but there was no shortage of manpower for any envisioned combat needs at this point. This fact enabled King to move to the next chapter of his playbook and simply ignore the issue.

Bill 80, revoking Clause 3 of the National Resources Mobilization Act and permitting conscription, was presented in Parliament and endlessly debated. J.L. Ralston offered his resignation as minister of national defence, but King declined it. Arthur Cardin resigned on May 9, but not from the Liberal Party. This somewhat slaked the thirst of the conscriptionists, as it implied they were winning. There were very difficult cabinet meetings through June where King's conscriptionist colleagues tried to elicit a definite statement, but he declined to be drawn beyond the usual bunk about "conscription if necessary" and "Parliament will decide." It was tedious and ungalvanizing and far from courageous, but King was right, and he was all that was standing in the way of a terrible national schism. If the Liberals had followed the Borden-Meighen Conservatives into a uni-cultural, Anglo-conscriptionist cul de sac, federalism would have become durably and possibly terminally unworkable. There was no need for conscription; the consequences of imposing it would have been drastic, and there was no rational reason to do it. King vividly saw the danger that if Ralston and navy minister Angus L. Macdonald succeeded in splitting the government, another unholy alliance between the Quebec Liberals and nationalists and the CCF would hold the balance of power and break up the country.

Even his great mentor Roosevelt, though he knew Canada fairly well, did not understand exactly what King was facing; he wrote on April 27, congratulating King on winning the referendum and telling him not to be too concerned about the reticence of his French-speaking compatriots. He reminisced that there had once been a good many French-speaking people in New England but that they had been assimilated eventually. He wrote that he would soon be speaking to "our planning people" about the excessive concentrations in certain cities of people of Italian, German, and Jewish origins. It was odd that he missed the Irish and the Poles and the African Americans, and he was certainly not disparaging any of these groups, but the thought that he considered he might have the authority to influence demographic flows on the basis of ethnic origin is disturbing.[50] It also shows that despite his familiarity with Canada as a cottager, a neighbouring governor, and for nine years as president, he had no notion of the official equality of two founding nations and official languages. King repeated in his diary of June 11 his belief in the role of "the Liberal Party as against extremes of Toryism and immature radicalism."[51]

Angus Lewis Macdonald, once and future premier of Nova Scotia, navy minister (minister of national defence for naval services), thought King "a twister and a wobbler."[52] Of course, he was, but that was precisely what conditions required. On June 11, Cardin gave a monumental *ex tempore* parliamentary address. He was the greatest of all Quebec Liberal orators, and there were many brilliant speakers in the federal and provincial Liberal parties (and powerful speakers among the opponents too, led by Duplessis and Houde). Cardin spoke with great eloquence of the absolute virtue of the Allied cause, enumerated the concessions he and Lapointe had made to reconcile the perspectives of French and English Canadians, but he could not accept the revocation of the guaranties against conscription, which he considered a "betrayal" of Quebec. It was a great speech, the more so because it avoided blowing up the bridges with King and St. Laurent, and the prime minister "sought to lead the applause where he referred to his own and Lapointe's part in campaigns."[53] St. Laurent gave a comprehensive and outstanding reply on June 16 that established him at once, in what was almost a maiden speech on a vital subject, as a fully worthy successor to Laurier and Lapointe. He spoke compellingly for the special interest of French Canada, while expressing his readiness "to deploy whatever effort and sacrifice might ultimately prove necessary to Canada's contribution to victory over the universal enemies of civilization as all Canadians con-strue and cherish it." King credited him with a "service to the Government, to his province, and to the country which is beyond words."[54] Bill 80 was adopted on July 7, by a majority of 104, which meant that Liberals alone carried the measure by 30; King had warned his colleagues before the vote that if the government required opposi-tion votes to prevail, he would resign. The excruciating exchange of minutiae with Ralston over his resignation, which was eventually ten-dered in writing, continued, but the resignation was neither forced nor accepted by King. Journalist and historian Bruce Hutchison claims that if Ralston had insisted on resigning, Macdonald, Ilsley, and Howe would have gone too and brought down the government.[55] Though it was certainly tense, it is not clear from King's diaries that matters were that precarious. Final reading was carried on July 23 by 96 votes, though only two French Quebec private members spoke for the bill, and forty-five Quebec Liberals, led by Cardin, voted against. The House rose on August 1. There was no move to introduce conscription for overseas service. Like the pilot of a bullet-riddled aircraft with sputtering engines and pieces of the fuselage falling off, King had brought the country through three years of war.

Ralston had imperiled the country. John Diefenbaker, when he finally got into government nearly fifteen years later, had no more under-standing of the rights of the French than did Ralston in 1942 to 1944. The generals weren't demanding conscription, and the English-Canadian politicians, Liberal and Conservative, were blasé about the consequences for the country. But the French were a founding race too, and if the English were going to use their demographic superiority to impose their conception of the war on the French, breaking the promise of the gov-ernment all Canada had reelected in 1940, there was no point to Confederation for Quebec. And there would be no party to uphold their rights, despite the federal government's support of the anti-conscription stance of Lapointe, Cardin, Charles Gavan Power, Raoul Dandurand, Godbout, and Bouchard in 1939. The principle of the double majority had been established by Baldwin and LaFontaine and reinforced and effectively institutionalized by John A. Macdonald and Cartier. On an issue so fundamental as conscription for overseas service, both founding societies would have to approve. Conscription can only be imposed where a majority favour it, and if a majority of the French opposed, the imposition of an English overall majority would destroy the nature of the country. Borden did not understand, but Laurier saved the country by accepting electoral defeat in order to preserve productive dissent, and King was acceptable because he was an English Canadian who followed Laurier, coming back to Canada from the cozy comforts of the Rockefellers to sacrifice himself in personal electoral defeat in 1917 for Sir Wilfrid in opposition to conscription. By the narrowest margin, and by dint of his extraordinary genius at political manoeuvre, King kept the country functioning in the Second World War. Confederation had only survived the world wars because of the Liberals under Laurier and King. If the Liberals had stampeded in 1942, there would have been no federal party Quebec could live with.

A federal by-election in Outremont, a prosperous section of Montreal, on November 30, 1942, became a virtual second plebiscite in miniature on government war policy. The deputy defence minister, General Léo Richer LaFlèche, whom King was going to name minister of war services, ran as the Liberal candidate in a normally safe constituency, and the nationalists ran the energetic young lawyer and future mayor of Montreal Jean Drapeau against him. There was a great deal of fiery oratory, and many stars in the firmament of Quebec public life campaigned for Drapeau, including André Laurendeau, Daniel Johnson, and Pierre Trudeau (who rode around on a motorcycle wearing a German army helmet). LaFlèche was supported by the Liberals, federal and provincial, the Conservatives, and, explicitly, by Cardinal Villeneuve himself. Drapeau's campaign manager, Marc Carrière, made a Camillien Houde–like statement that he was ignoring his registration notice under the mobilization legislation, and was led away to detention on November 20 by two Mounties and replaced by, of all people, the Jew-baiting labour agitator and former monk Michel Chartrand. LaFlèche could hardly fail to win with such massive support, and he did, by 12,000 to 7,000, but there was a good deal of political tinder around.

King was given "fresh heart and hope" in October when Mitchell Hepburn resigned as premier of Ontario. At year-end, he congratulated himself on the departure from Canada of Bennett, from public life of Meighen, and from Queen's Park, in Ontario, of Hepburn.[56]

* * *

The war proceeded well in 1942, though, as was inevitable, the Japanese offensive in the Pacific made great strides for several months. General Douglas MacArthur conducted a very skilful retreat in the Bataan Peninsula in the Philippines and defeated the Japanese invaders in January, causing them to pause to regroup and bring in reinforcements for a whole month. Roosevelt eventually ordered MacArthur out of the Philippines, as he wished to retain him as theatre commander for the southern and western Pacific. The remaining garrison of 11,500 finally surrendered the rocky island of Corregidor in Manila Bay in May, a very respectable fight, unlike the utter debacle of the British in Malaya and Singapore, where numerically inferior Japanese forces achieved the abject surrender on February 15 of sixty-four thousand British troops at what had been billed as the impregnable fortress of Singapore.

On April 18, the Japanese were dumbfounded when Tokyo and several other cities were lightly bombed by sixteen B-25 bombers launched from the aircraft carrier *Hornet*. The planes went on to land in China. This was the famous raid of Colonel Doolittle, a little like Churchill's cheeky bomber raids on Berlin in August 1940.

On May 4, U.S. carrier forces, which had been absent from Pearl Harbor when it was attacked, more than held their own with the Japanese at the Battle of the Coral Sea, and a month later the United States won one of the decisive naval battles of world history at Midway, sinking four Japanese aircraft carriers to the loss of only one of its own. MacArthur had taken up his command of the Southwest Pacific at Darwin, Australia, and began by jettisoning the Australian plan of defending the country in its vast and barren heart. He announced that the defence of Australia would be conducted in New Guinea and the Solomon Islands. Skirmishing shortly began there that led to an American and Allied naval victory in the Battle of the Solomon Islands and to the prolonged and decisive struggle for the jungle island of Guadalcanal, which continued through the summer and autumn of 1942.

In Africa, a new British high command prepared a defence in depth west of Cairo, after the thirty-three-thousand-man garrison of the fortress of Tobruk ignominiously surrendered, again to numerically inferior investing forces, of Erwin Rommel, on June 21, 1942, as Churchill was sitting in Roosevelt's office explaining to him and the U.S. Army chief of staff, General George C. Marshall, that Tobruk would certainly be held. Roosevelt handed on the message that came in without comment, except to ask, "What can we do to help?" He and Marshall sent three hundred tanks on fast ships around the Cape, and they made a difference.[57] The new British Eighth Army commander, General Bernard L. Montgomery, prepared a massive counterstroke to fall in November.

The strategic disagreements between the British and Americans over objectives in Europe continued apace, and finally it was agreed between Churchill and Roosevelt to conduct Anglo-American landings in Morocco and Algeria and take those territories away from the Vichy regime; try to force Germany to invade the part of France that was still unoccupied; put a rod on the neutralist backs of Franco and Salazar; destabilize Mussolini; land in Rommel's rear to coordinate with Montgomery's counterattack in Egypt; and facilitate increased quantities of supplies to the Soviet Union through the Mediterranean. Churchill went to Moscow on August 12 for, as he called it, "the raw task" of telling Stalin that there would be no landings in Western Europe in 1942. Stalin claimed to be taking ten thousand casualties a day fighting the Germans, who were proceeding to the southeast in pursuit of the Caucasian oilfields and had arrived at the Volga at Stalingrad. He asked scornfully of Churchill: "Why are you so afraid of the Germans? Armies have to be blooded in battle." The two leaders had a stormy session at times, but it ended in a rather jovial drinking bout and the mission was a considerable diplomatic triumph for Churchill, given the legendary prickliness and brusqueness of his host.[58]

On August 19, a miniature cross-Channel amphibious invasion of France occurred at Dieppe, carried out by five thousand Canadians. It was a disaster, for which Canada had the British, and particularly the special operations director, Admiral Louis Mountbatten, to thank. Close to 3,700 men were killed, wounded, or captured, a 74 per cent casualty level, and nothing useful was achieved, though an Anglo-Canadian myth was then propagated that the raid had been invaluable in planning a real invasion and that much was learned about landing-craft design and German defence techniques. It is as likely that the British were using Canadians to illustrate the validity of Churchill and his senior military staff's fear of becoming heavily engaged with proverbially war-adept Germans in the blood-soaked region of northeastern France where nearly a million Commonwealth troops had died in the last war.

In September and October 1942, the German Sixth Army and the Soviet defenders were locked in deadly struggle in and around Stalingrad. The Germans poured fifteen divisions right into the rubble of the city. It became the greatest land battle in the history of the world, surpassing even Verdun. By November, there were two million men engaged, perhaps 60 per cent of them Russians. There were twenty-five thousand artillery pieces and about two thousand aircraft about evenly divided, and fifteen hundred tanks, about nine hundred of them Russian. Ultimately, the battle took the lives of a million people, with another million wounded, a majority of the casualties among the Russian defenders. As the Germans committed more resources to the remains of the city, the Russians built the flanks, which were protected by Germany's Romanian allies, and a giant pincers was prepared.

Everything came to a head in November 1942. On November 4, Montgomery launched his great attack on Rommel at El Alamein and had pushed the Germans and Italians out of Egypt by November 12. At the other end of North Africa, General Dwight D. Eisenhower, former understudy to General MacArthur in the Philippines, commanded the Operation Torch landings at Casablanca, Oran, and Algiers, and the Vichy forces quickly came over to the Allies. And Germany invaded unoccupied France as the Allies had hoped, bringing the feeble and dishonourable pretence of any sovereignty residing in Pétain and Laval to a suitably inglorious end.* Most of what was left of the French fleet scuttled itself at Toulon on November 27, in what de Gaulle accurately described as "the most pitiful and sterile suicide imaginable."[60] The Americans decisively won the naval battle of

---

* King had endured considerable criticism for maintaining his diplomatic representation (under Pierre Dupuy) in Vichy, but only did so in response to a request from U.S. secretary of state, Cordell Hull, to provide cover for the American mission there, under Roosevelt's World War I crony, Admiral William D. Leahy.[59] The distinguished General Georges P. Vanier, King's minister to France, 1939–1940, was minister to Free France and the French Resistance, 1942–1944, and to the restored French government, 1944–1953. In a typically thoughtful gesture, King personally visited the Vichy representative to Canada, Rene Ristel Lueber, whom he had allowed to remain in Canada, on Christmas Day, 1942. (*Mackenzie King Record*, p. 429).

Guadalcanal on November 12 to 15 and began a great two-year push to the northwest back toward the Philippines under MacArthur, and westward across the Central Pacific under Admiral Chester W. Nimitz. And on November 19, the long-prepared Russian pincers was triggered at Stalingrad, where the trap snapped shut on the German flanks and Hitler would not hear of a breakout retreat. Over three hundred thousand Axis soldiers were doomed, as were the Afrika Korps and the Japanese assault forces against Australia in Guadalcanal. The tide had turned decisively, just a year after Pearl Harbor.

3. Years of Liberation, 1943–1944

Canada did its part and did it well, but it was a country of 11.5 million people, a third of whom did not wish to participate actively in the war. Canada provided about 2 per cent of the forty million armed servicemen represented by the Big Three: Roosevelt and Stalin as commanders-in-chief in their countries, and Churchill as principal first minister of the chief of state of the Commonwealth. The 3,700 Canadian casualties and prisoners at Dieppe may be compared with the disposable manpower involved, and the toleration of casualties implied, in the Soviet casualty level of 1.2 million at Stalingrad, the 15,000 mainly British casualties at El Alamein (of their 200,000 men engaged, against 30,000 Axis casualties out of 110,000 engaged), and the 15,000 American casualties at Guadalcanal (of 60,000 of their men, against 32,000 casualties out of 40,000 Japanese trying to seize and hold that island). There was no excuse for the Canadians to have been used as cannon fodder in the nonsensical Dieppe operation, where their courage was disserved by British strategic errors. But this, and the loss of nearly 2,000 men at Hong Kong, were Canada's two main sources of casualties in 1942, and King was right when he tried to reason with Ralston and Macdonald that they should stop their absurd fuming over the status of Quebec, which could break up the country – the only threat to the existence of Canada there was, even at the high tide of the greatest war in history – and focus on using Canada's own forces more effectively. Obviously, the British could not be relied upon exclusively to deploy them. The performance of Montgomery and the theatre commander, Sir Harold

Alexander, at El Alamein, though they had heavy advantages in numbers and supplies, largely redeemed the disasters in Singapore and Tobruk, but the British services were uneven: the Royal Air Force was superb, as good as any, even the German; the Royal Navy, though not infallible, discharged its immense task very bravely and effectively; but the British Army had some serious lapses.

On the naval front, as Roosevelt's immense armaments program proceeded, the U.S. Navy achieved astonishing proportions: at the end of the war, thirty fleet carriers, seventy escort aircraft carriers, and twenty-five battleships. When Nimitz's entire Pacific Fleet sailed in the last months of the war (when the Atlantic Fleet had largely been transferred to the Pacific), it took 400,000 men to sea and moved in a formation 200 miles square. By then, the Germans had sunk the Russian navy, the Americans had sunk the Japanese navy, the British had sunk the German navy and sunk or accepted the surrender of the Italian navy, and the French navy had been largely sunk by its erstwhile British ally or scuttled. The Royal Navy made good its considerable losses and was still the largest navy in the Atlantic and Mediterranean. Angus L. Macdonald (whose slogan in his sixteen years as premier of Nova Scotia was "All's well with Angus L.") resented and despised King and was grumpy throughout the war, but as navy minister he built the Royal Canadian Navy from 11 ships and 3,000 men in 1940 to 400 ships and 96,000 men in 1945. While a specialist anti-submarine force, it was exceptionally efficient and indispensable to Allied victory, and, at the end, the third navy in the world in effective size.

The Royal Canadian Air Force, which had been founded from Canadian units of the RAF in 1924, grew between 1939 and 1945 from about 7,000 people and 29 front-line aircraft to 215,000 (including 15,000 women) and about 1,250 aircraft, and was the fourth Allied air force, after only the Big Three (though, as in other areas, the gap was considerable; the U.S. Army Air Force had 125,000 aircraft of all types). The Canadian Army, at 500,000, was also the third largest of the Western Allies in 1944, though there were only about 140,000 trigger-pullers. Training and supplying and administering these forces required more manpower than the fighting they did.

Canada's economic growth naturally rose in tandem with its military capability. The country's gross national product rose between 1939 and 1945 from $5.6 billion to $11.9 billion; and household income rose from $731 to almost $1,000. These trends moved sharply higher through most of the postwar twentieth century. C.D. Howe took over as a virtual dictator of the economy as minister of munitions and supply, as was established by the National Resources Mobilization Act, and he exercised his role with what was universally conceded to be extreme efficiency and competence. There was no British or American example to follow, as Britain was not a resource economy and the United States was, at first, a peacetime economy. By 1944, more than $1.5 billion had been invested in war production, which could be (and was), after hostilities had ceased, converted to peacetime industrial production. "An entire new series of industries, from tanks and ships to optical glass and from artificial rubber to radar equipment, came into being."[61] The country's industrial production more than doubled in five years. Canada provided most of the uranium for the atomic project, and almost all the nickel for the Allies. Electric power production increased by 50 per cent, largely to enable an immense increase of output in the aluminum industry to build aircraft. Canada produced a third of the Allies' aluminum, three-quarters of its asbestos, and large quantities of base metals. It was the fourth industrial economy in the war-smashed world in 1945, and, as it utilized just a third of its production for its own needs, Canada was surpassed only by the United States as the world's greatest exporter of munitions and equipment. Its war plants produced more than $10 billion of goods.

Farm income increased by 40 per cent in response to official encouragement of mixed farming, coarser grains, and livestock. Canada never rationed meat during the war, which made it a popular stop for American vacationers and international missions. There were wage and price controls that were observed more faithfully than they normally would be in deference to the international war emergency, and unemployment of work-eligible people evaporated completely. High taxes could be justified both to wage the war and to fight demand-inflation. But although there were huge revenue increases, borrowing for the war was about $12 billion. British investment in Canada was repatriated, over $1 billion, to pay for British imports from Canada, supplemented first by a $700 million loan, and then by an outright gift to Britain in 1942 of $1 billion for acquisition of Canadian exports. Canada effectively conducted its own Lend-Lease program, advancing $1.8 billion of goods and loans for the acquisition of Canadian goods to Britain and other Allies directly. In the end, Canada advanced $4 billion of aid in this way, a remarkable sum that tracks well to the $48.2 billion net Lend-Lease advances of the United States.

Canada's entire war production of over $20 billion also tracked that of the United States. Churchill had been right when he recalled, on the day of Pearl Harbor, a comment of Sir Edward Grey from the previous world war that the United States was "like a gigantic boiler. Once the fire is lighted under it, there is no limit to the power it can generate."[62] On January 6, 1942, Roosevelt had received one of the greatest ovations he had ever had from Congress when he told it that in 1943 the United States would produce the astounding totals of 125,000 aircraft, 10 million tons of shipping, and 75,000 tanks, and added, "These figures will give the Japanese and the Nazis a little idea of just what they accomplished in the attack at Pearl Harbor." Hitler, when advised of these production goals, said, "They can in no way be accurate."[63] All the goals were exceeded, and while it was only to scale, Canada replicated the achievement, and had, out of a population of 11.5 million, over one million volunteers in the armed forces, compared to 13 million members of the armed forces of the United States (in a population of 130 million), technically draftees, though millions had volunteered. Canada had become an important ally, as well as a brave one.

A special concern was the Battle of the Atlantic, conducted by the German submarine forces, which at times threatened to strangle the British. It first became gravely serious in 1941, when losses of merchant shipping peaked, at 687,000 tons, in April of that year. This was reduced to 121,000 in July, a tolerable rate, by assigning more destroyers to convoys, by extending the American sea and air patrol zones, and by adding more and longer-range patrol aircraft from Newfoundland and Iceland. In Britain, there were constant problems of allocation of airplanes between Bomber Command and Coastal Command, and of escort ships between convoys and other tasks. The crisis flared again in 1942, as the United States was not immediately as aware of the danger. The rate at which ships were lost fluctuated according to the state of British decryption of German naval codes and the level of cover and convoy protection, and to the number and increasing sophistication of German submarines. In the end, in early 1943, the Allies closed the "air gap" with adapted Liberator bombers that provided air cover for the entire crossing of the merchant convoys, and with the success of the combined destroyer, frigate, and corvette building programs of the British, Canadians, and Americans to protect them. Canada had two hundred of these anti-submarine vessels and played a key role in this battle, which in the course of the war caused the sinking of 3,500 Allied merchant vessels and 175 warships, with the loss of 73,000 sailors, while the Germans lost 783 submarines and 30,000 sailors.

The war proceeded through the early months of 1943 as it had ended 1942, with the Germans in retreat in Russia and Africa, and the Americans rolling the Japanese back in New Guinea and the Central Pacific islands. It was to be a year of conferences. Roosevelt had had some intimates to a private screening of the about-to-be very famous film *Casablanca*, starring two of the strongest supporters of Hollywood for Roosevelt, Humphrey Bogart and Claude Raines, as well as Ingrid Bergman and others. The collection of scoundrels and sharpers in French North Africa caused Roosevelt to say that he was about to attend a conference in Casablanca with Churchill and the French, and he thought that the film was quite lifelike in its portrayal of some of those among whom he was about to venture. For a time, the Anglo-Americans had been negotiating with the French factions led by Admiral Jean-François Darlan, Pétain's former premier; General Henri Giraud, a traditional French Republican soldier; and General de Gaulle. Churchill's chief of the Imperial General Staff, General Alan Brooke, summed it up: "Darlan has high intelligence but no integrity; Giraud has high integrity but low intelligence; de Gaulle has high integrity and intelligence but an impossible and dictatorial personality."[64] The lives of the British and Americans were made simpler by the assassination of Darlan by a French monarchist (ninety-four years after the overthrow of the last non-Bonaparte monarch), and Churchill and Roosevelt soon realized that Giraud could not possibly be represented as having the stature to lead France.

The Casablanca conference confirmed that when the Germans were flung out of Africa completely, invasions of Sicily and Italy would follow, but that the Italian campaign would not prevent or defer a cross-Channel invasion of France, which would be launched in May 1944. This did not convince Roosevelt and General Marshall however, and with good reason, that the British could be relied upon to stick to that timetable, given their extreme misgivings about fighting the Germans in northern France and Flanders. The conference was from January 14 to 24, and Churchill commented on the rather unspontaneous photograph taken of him with Roosevelt, Giraud, and de Gaulle (whom Churchill threatened to stop supporting financially unless he attended the conference, as de Gaulle objected to being convened by foreigners on what he considered to be French soil): "The picture of this event cannot be viewed, even in the setting of these tragic times, without a laugh."[65] At Casablanca, it was also publicly announced by Roosevelt that the conferees would require the "unconditional surrender" of their enemies, a statement motivated in part by criticism for the dalliance with the slippery Darlan. The British claimed for a time that they had had no notice of this, but it was not the truth. It was also claimed that this position prolonged the war, but the treatment of Italy later in 1943 showed that there could be conditions for surrender if the existing regimes were replaced with less objectionable leaders, a clear incitement to assassination and rebellion, not an unreasonable war aim, and almost a successful one in Germany in 1944.

The German Sixth Army of 300,000 men, terribly afflicted by combat, hunger, and the elements, surrendered at Stalingrad on February 2, 1943. It was now clear that Germany could not win in Russia. For no obvious reason, but having convinced himself that he was forestalling an invasion of Italy and propping up Mussolini, Hitler kept pouring first-rate troops into Tunisia, where they could not possibly survive against the Anglo-Americans under Eisenhower and Alexander, and Montgomery and George Patton. After heavy casualties for three more months, the German and Italian army in Tunisia surrendered to the Allies on May 13, another 250,000 Axis troops bagged by the Allies, a total combined loss of casualties and prisoners in Stalingrad and Tunisia of 750,000 Axis soldiers, mainly German.

There was still no conscription for overseas service in Canada, and there had been no numerically significant Canadian losses since Dieppe, where 3,700, while tragic and needless in that case, wasn't a backbreaker for an army of 500,000. Canadian troops joined with Americans to clear the Japanese out of a couple of the Aleutian Islands in mid-year, but found the Japanese had abandoned the island assigned to Canada, where the NRMA soldiers (conscripted under the National Resources Mobilization Act) in the Aleutians then had a vigorous debate with the Finance Department about whether they could be taxed on their paltry pay packets from Canada while in the United States.

There was another immense conference of the senior Anglo-American command at Williamsburg, Virginia, from May 12 to 25, 1943. It was a radically different command structure than in the Great War. Then, Russia had been much less important, and had collapsed in 1917; the Americans had entered the war late; and the main front was in France, where the French had the largest army, and they commanded. Canada was part of the British group, and the British stressed cooperation with the dominions. Now, the British and Americans provided the great majority of the forces in Western and Southern Europe; the Russians ran the Eastern Front; and the Americans determined the Pacific War, except for Burma, which was a British gig. The Americans were sending troops to Europe until they should have a majority of forces in the theatre, at which point they would be able to force the landings on northern France on the reluctant British. There was not much for Canada to do but await the call to Italy and France. The war would be won by whichever force, the Western Allies or the Russians, occupied Germany, France, and Italy, it being assumed that Japan would be in the American column, come what may. There was a discussion about China at Williamsburg, as Roosevelt was convinced that both China and India were starting into a cyclical upturn to become great powers again. The American commander in China, General Joseph Stilwell, described the president of China, Chiang Kai-shek, to general agreement, as "a vacillating, tricky, undependable old scoundrel who never keeps his word."[66]

In another of the greatest battles in world history, the Germans tried and failed to launch a third Russian summer offensive at Kursk from July 4 to August 23. It was the third consecutive military disaster for Hitler, after Stalingrad and Tunisia. Hitler, unusually, followed the obvious course and delayed for six weeks, bringing in new tanks, while the Russians built defences back 250 kilometres, ten times the width of the Maginot Line. The Germans attacked with 800,000 men, 3,000 tanks, 10,000 artillery pieces, and 2,000 aircraft, against 1.9 million Russians with 5,000 tanks, 25,000 artillery pieces, and 3,000 aircraft.

The Russians repulsed the attack, stopped the German offensive, and went on the offensive themselves, but the Germans inflicted 1.04 million Russian casualties while taking 257,000 themselves, and knocked out 8,000 tanks and 3,600 aircraft while losing 1,040 tanks and 840 aircraft themselves. They were remarkably adept, natural warriors. As de Gaulle said when he toured the Stalingrad battlefield the following year, "The Germans on the Volga, magnificent! What a great people."

The British, Americans, and Canadians invaded Sicily on July 10, 1943, in the greatest amphibious operation in history to that time. Eisenhower was the theatre commander, Alexander the operational commander, and Montgomery and Patton the battlefield army commanders. The Allies landed 160,000 men, including one Canadian infantry division and a tank brigade, with 600 tanks, to meet 40,000 Germans and 230,000 Italians. The British, desperate to keep pace with the Americans, refused to refer to the Canadians in their offical communique, in order to pretend that Canadian forces were effectively British. King urgently telephoned Roosevelt to secure publicity for Canada, and he was happy to comply and ordered Eisenhower to refer generously to the Canadian contingent, which he did.[67] The fall of Messina to Patton on August 17 ended resistance on the island. The Allies had taken 22,000 casualties to 10,000 German and about 30,000 Italian, plus 100,000 Italian prisoners, as the Mussolini regime disintegrated. On July 25, King Victor Emmanuel III dismissed Mussolini after twenty-one years of smarting under his dictatorship and named Marshal Pietro Badoglio, a slippery political operator of the Darlan variety, as prime minister. Badoglio, having long been a fascist grandee, ordered the dissolution of the Fascist Party, and he began at once to negotiate a change of sides to the Allies in the war.

The first Quebec Conference took place at that city between August 11 and 24, 1943, between Churchill and Roosevelt and their military chiefs. There survives a rather irritating correspondence about whether to invite King to the conference. Churchill professed to be the conference host, as the Citadel in Quebec is the summer residence of the governor general of Canada, which he claimed, wrongly, to be British property, and he invited Roosevelt to stay with him there. Roosevelt went through his usual refrain about King being a great "friend," almost invariably a kiss of death in his parlance, but said he worried about the impact on Brazil, Mexico, and China of including King, as if the Latin American countries were making a fraction of the contribution to the war effort Canada was, or as if China – though suffering huge casualties and rather ineffectually absorbing large numbers of Japanese troops – was as important to the defeat of Germany as Canada was, and as if Quebec were not in Canada. Churchill waffled on about the impact of inviting Canada on the other Commonwealth countries. The fact is, neither Churchill nor Roosevelt could enter Canada if King did not choose to admit them at the border, and that such an exchange took place at all indicates that King should have given Canadian views more national definition in discussions with them. De Gaulle would not have allowed them to enter his country unless he was the host. That would not be appropriate, but Canada was the third Western Ally and should not have had to endure one minute of uncertainty on this score. Eventually, it was agreed that Canada would attend the plenary meetings and King would officially be the host, but the principal discussions would be in smaller Anglo-American groups, especially between the two leaders. King accepted this as protective to his dignity and presentation of his role to his countrymen, factors more important to him than actually participating in making urgent decisions. It is easy to criticize King, who was very deferential to Churchill and Roosevelt, and it would not have been appropriate or acceptable to most Canadians to be as obstreperous an ally as de Gaulle was, but King could certainly have pushed matters a lot further with the senior Allies if he had possessed a fraction of the capacity to rouse and stir his countrymen as Churchill and Roosevelt (and de Gaulle even clandestinely) possessed.

The conference confirmed the Trident Conference formula that the Italian landings would take place but would not delay the cross-Channel landings. The operation would be code named Overlord. Matters of force levels between the two campaigns, and a third one in southern France, would be determined later, on a basis of professional soldierly evaluation. As at Casablanca, the Americans didn't believe their balky British allies but were recording the agreements until they had the greater military strength in Europe and could force the issue. The Americans, now that the Battle of the Atlantic had been won, would be sending huge numbers of invasion forces for Operation

Overlord to Britain. General Marshall emphasized that President Roosevelt understood the urgency of the Western Allies taking Berlin. The eccentric British guerrilla leader General Orde Wingate was introduced by Churchill and quickly became the Americans' favourite British general because of his swashbuckling combativity. The presentational highlight in Quebec was Admiral Louis Mountbatten – cousin of King Edward VIII and King George VI and a Churchill protégé and architect of the Dieppe debacle, whom Churchill had just appointed Burma theatre commander – showing his plan for stationary aircraft carriers made of specially treated blocks of ice. He demonstrated this by firing a revolver at untreated and treated ice blocks. The untreated block of ice was reduced to shards and chips, but his bullet ricocheted off the treated block, and it was fortuitous that it did not strike any of the conferees. Junior officers outside were afraid that disputes between the senior service chiefs had reached the point of exchange of gunfire. (Roosevelt and Churchill were not present.)

Roosevelt went on to Ottawa and spoke to 150,000 people on Parliament Hill (half the population of the capital area). He referred to King as "that wise and good and gallant gentleman . . . My old friend, your course and mine have run so closely and affectionately during these many long years, that this meeting adds another link to the chain." As Bruce Hutchinson commented, "Roosevelt was more popular in Canada than King could ever be: his praise was valuable to a politician who, at the moment, needed all the help he could get."[68]

The Allies invaded Italy in September, the British and Canadians across the Strait of Messina on September 3, and the Americans, under General Mark Clark, at Salerno, thirty miles south of Naples, on September 9. King Victor Emmanuel and Badoglio surrendered to the Allies on September 8, and the Italian navy, including four battleships – after the flagship was sunk by German air attacks, killing 1,350 sailors, including the fleet commander – sailed to Malta and surrendered to the British. Churchill ordered that the Italians be treated with the utmost courtesy and cordiality and that it all be filmed to be shown to Italians and contrasted with the arrogance of the Germans. (Churchill, a mighty but gracious warrior, loved Italy, though he hated Mussolini, and was always as magnanimous in victory as he was fierce in combat.) The Germans

seized Rome on September 10, and the king and Badoglio fled to
Brindisi. German paratroopers sprang Mussolini on September 12, and
on September 15 he purported to set up a fascist republic in the north of
Italy with his capital at Salò as the Germans swiftly occupied Italy down
to where the Allies had advanced a little north of Naples. On October
13, Victor Emmanuel and Badoglio declared war on Germany, making
Italy the only country in the war to be a co-belligerent, at war, at different times, with and against both sides.

The year of conferences reached its climax with the Tehran
Conference between Roosevelt, Churchill, and Stalin, from November 27
to December 7. It followed a somewhat absurd meeting between the
American and British leaders at Cairo with Chiang Kai-shek and his
Western educated, Christian wife, sister-in-law of the leader of China's
1911 Revolution, Sun Yat-sen, and a member of the wealthy and influential Soong family. On the way to the conferences on the powerful
new battleship *Iowa*, Roosevelt tore a map of Germany out of a *National
Geographic* magazine in the admiral's wardroom and marked out the
postwar zones of Allied occupation he favoured, if any had to be
agreed. He objected to a demarcation of postwar zones in Germany,
because he thought that once Allied landings in Western Europe were
successful and the Allies were across the Rhine, the Germans would
fight like tigers in the east but surrender quickly in the west in order to
be in the hands of the powers who would observe the Geneva
Conventions for prisoners and the civilian population. This proved
substantially accurate, but on the magazine map where he designated
the zones, he had all three Allied zones meeting in Berlin, a pretty
optimistic scenario given that the Allied landings in Northern Europe
were more than six months away and the Russians were closing in on
the Polish border.

A great presentation was put on for the Chinese in Cairo, at the end
of which, in the words of Alan Brooke, British chief of the Imperial
General Staff, "a ghastly silence" ensued. The Chinese had no comment at all. Chiang spoke in the political meetings, but then his wife
translated, and Roosevelt and Churchill were never sure whose words
they were really hearing. Mme Chiang had an elegant, silk-clad, feline
appearance, and a slit in her long skirt revealed a shapely pair of legs.
She was understood to have had an affair with Roosevelt's late opponent

Wendell Willkie. The Cairo meeting had its diversions, but as a substantive conference it was a mere prelude to the first trilateral meeting with the marshal-premier of the Soviet Union, whom Churchill described, not without admiration, as "the great revolutionary and military chief."

The American legation at Tehran was located out of town, while the Soviet and British embassies were together downtown. For security reasons, Roosevelt was advised by his own people to accept the invitation to stay at one of the other two embassies, and he chose the Russian, ostensibly because it was bigger, and because he had not met Stalin and did not want to encourage the impression of lockstep Anglo-American collusion, but really because he wanted to lobby Stalin privately to help him force Churchill into the cross-Channel landings he favoured, rather than the charge up the Adriatic, or even a wild enfilade via Norway that Churchill proposed, as, despite previous promises at Casablanca, Williamsburg, and Quebec, he was still not eager to re-enter northern France. What now occurred was one of the great masterpieces of modern diplomacy, executed with consummate skill by Roosevelt. Shortly after Roosevelt arrived on November 28, Stalin asked to visit him, and after a few pleasantries Roosevelt asked Stalin his preference between Western Allied landings in northern France or the Adriatic, and Stalin was emphatic for France.

Roosevelt suspected that there had already been contact between Germany and Russia over a separate peace, and as Stalin confirmed a few days later, there had been, earlier that year at Stockholm, at German instigation. Roosevelt, as the only chief of state of the three of them (the president of the Soviet Union was Stalin's old cat's paw, Mikhail Kalinin, and Churchill was King George VI's first minister), chaired the meetings, and after summaries of the different theatres, the next day, he asked Stalin to express his preference between the alternatives the British and Americans were considering. Stalin opted strongly, and in militarily learned terms, for Operation Overlord, supplemented some weeks later by landings in southern France. Churchill was blindsided by this invocation of Soviet preferences, and he tried to promote the value of bringing Turkey into the war and increasing activity in the Balkans. Stalin wasn't hearing any of it and said the Turks would never be helpful and the Balkans were rugged country and a long way from Berlin. Churchill was startled and even slightly offended by the abrupt end run in what he took to be a long-playing game of attrition and passive resistance to American enthusiasm for the cross-Channel operation. The British suspected that Stalin favoured the plan only because he thought the Anglo-Americans would distract the Germans but be thrown into the sea by them, as the Germans had done to the British before, making it easier for Russia to advance farther into Western Europe. Roosevelt suspected the same thing, but unlike the British, he was confident that Allied air and armour superiority would prevail and turn it into a war of swift movement which the West would win. (Again, he was correct.) Roosevelt also correctly assumed that his rooms had been bugged by Stalin and spoke to his colleagues appropriately. Thus, Roosevelt recruited Stalin to do what ultimately disserved the Soviet leader as America's great postwar rival, over the mistaken opposition of America's great ally. This was what saved most of Germany, and possibly, given the strength of the French and Italian communist parties, those countries as well, from Soviet or Soviet-backed takeovers. Immediately after Tehran, Churchill and Roosevelt met with Kemal Atatürk's successor as president of Turkey, Ismet Inönü, but Turkey declined to join the war, and Inönü made it clear that he had no interest in fighting the Germans. When Churchill mentioned that Inönü had kissed him when they parted, Anthony Eden, his foreign secretary, said, "That's all we got out of him."[69] Roosevelt went on to Tunisia and Sicily, and with Churchill's full concurrence he appointed General Dwight D. Eisenhower commander of Operation Overlord.

As a first stage in reorganizing the frontiers of Europe, it was agreed to move the western Soviet borders 250 miles into Poland, and to compensate Poland with 250 miles of Eastern Germany, but the agreement was kept absolutely secret, ostensibly to avoid agitating Polish American voters as the United States entered an election year. Roosevelt secured support for his proposed international organization, called the United Nations, which he intended as a method of disguising predominant American control in the postwar world by dressing it in international collegiality, and as a method of easing his isolationist countrymen into the world on the theory that it was a gentler place now than they had thought in the prolonged period of American withdrawal. In their communique at the end of the Teheran Conference, the Big Three proclaimed themselves "friends in fact, in spirit, and in purpose." This was a serious liberty which conformed with Churchill's assertion, in the most famous line of the conference, in another context, that "the truth deserves a bodyguard of lies." Stalin better described their relations when he later told the Yugoslav communist leader Milovan Djilas that "Churchill would pick my pocket for a kopek; Roosevelt only dips in his hand for larger coins."[70]

Canada's most interesting soldier, General Andrew G.L. McNaughton (1887–1966), was sent home in December 1943 in involuntary retirement as commander of the Canadian Army, ostensibly for health reasons, but in fact because he objected to breaking up the army of 125,000 that he had highly trained and prepared for the supreme battle in France, and which the political leadership wished to reduce in order to become more involved in the war in Italy; and because he was insufficiently subservient to the capable but overbearing British Army group commander for Commonwealth forces, General Montgomery; and because he did not join defence minister J.L. Ralston's endless incantation for conscription. McNaughton was an original and intellectual general. He had been a chemistry professor at McGill University at the outbreak of the First World War, joined the army and rose quickly, and invented a technique for calibrating guns behind the lines and moving them forward precisely targeted from the opening of fire (Chapter 5). He became commander of the army in 1929 and concentrated on armour and advanced technology warfare, and in the depression commanded some of R.B. Bennett's camps for the amelioration of the condition of the unemployed. McNaughton determined that the French Canadians and the Prairies should each have a regiment that was part of the permanent army, the Royal 22nd (the Van Doos) and the Princess Patricia's Light Infantry. He proved to have an un-Canadian flare for the striking phrase. He was featured on the cover of *Life* magazine in 1939, and in 1940 he made the arresting statement that the Canadian Army was "a dagger pointed at Berlin." Churchill wanted to send him on a private mission to Stalin in 1942, but Ralston in his jealousy and antagonism managed to incite the cautious old woman in King, a trait that was never hard to rouse, and King killed the mission.[71] McNaughton objected to sending a division and a brigade of tanks to join the Sicily landings, not just to save casualties but because he wanted the maximum force in what would become the principal Western European theatre. He was overruled by Ralston, who sent a second division to Italy, after the 1st Canadian Division under General Guy Simonds had distinguished itself in Sicily, taken 562 dead, and captured Messina. Mackenzie King had convinced himself that Italy would produce fewer casualties than France, after the contrast between the rates of success and casualties at Dieppe and in Sicily. By the time the second Canadian division started up the Italian peninsula, it was facing Germans, not Italians, and it suffered almost 1,400 dead, taking the village of Ortona, near Naples, alone. The undersecretary of state, Norman Robertson, was advised by the Soviet military attaché in Ottawa, Colonel Nikolai Zabotin, that McNaughton's technical study of improved precision in artillery fire was a classic text read in Soviet military academies with Charles de Gaulle's pioneering texts on mechanized warfare.[72] McNaughton was a soldier of great merit, but he was caught in a double political vortex: he did not join Ralston's call for conscription, and he resisted the British ambition to perpetuate and amplify Mediterranean activities, which he regarded as a sideshow and a cynical and rather diffident British effort to protect its threadbare empire in the Middle East and the Indian subcontinent, while going through the motions for the benefit of the Russians, who were taking over 90 per cent of the casualties fighting the Germans. McNaughton agreed with the Americans that this course risked prolonging the war and eroding political support at home, and that it increased the risk of either a separate peace between Hitler and Stalin or a much larger Russian bite out of Western Europe, possibly including Germany and France, if the landings in northern France were not made earlier than the British wished. McNaughton was popular with Churchill as a scientific and bold and original general with dash and flare; popular with Roosevelt for his support of the French, rather than the Italian, avenue to Berlin; and popular with King for keeping the conscription pressure down. But he was sandbagged by Brooke, the chief of the Imperial General Staff, for his anti-Mediterranean views, supplemented by Ralston for his anti-conscription views. They seized on alleged confusion in a military exercise (called Spartan) to claim that McNaughton had weakened under the strain of the burdens he had been carrying and was not up to commanding the Canadian Army in action. King should have ignored the British and retained McNaughton, kept his army in

England, saved casualties, and dismissed Ralston, but the political threat of the second conscription crisis in 1944 was greater and more immediate than these command issues in the army in Europe. King had a more complicated plan, and as usual outsmarted everyone with a combined military and political shuffle that was up to the highest standards of his creative chicanery. He acquiesced in the retirement of McNaughton but made it clear that McNaughton returned to Canada in the odour of political sanctity. Harry Crerar, a less flamboyant man, replaced McNaughton, but McNaughton was right: Italy was a comparative waste of Canadian resources.[73]

Mackenize King gave one of the most impressive speeches of his career, to the British Parliament on May 11, 1944, confirming the Allied war goals of world peace and the universal pursuit of equitably distributed prosperity, "the glory and the dream – are they not being realized at this very hour?" Yes and no.

Rome had fallen to the Americans and Canadians on June 5, and they were greeted as liberators, as they were throughout Italy, and blessed by Pius XII, an honour he had not given Axis soldiers.

As 1944 unfolded, the Russians moved westward toward Poland and Hungary and Bulgaria, over their devastated western constituent republics, against fierce and ingenious German resistance; the Americans advanced – island-hopping and stranding Japanese garrisons where they could because of increasing naval superiority – northwest from the Solomon Islands toward the Philippines and westwards in the Central Pacific toward the home islands of Japan; and the British, Americans, and Canadians moved slowly up the Italian peninsula, through rugged terrain where the advantage was to the defender, encountering the usual courage and determination of the German army. Churchill had sold Italy as the "soft underbelly of Europe," even producing a drawing of a crocodile and its relatively vulnerable stomach for Stalin when he visited him in August 1942. But that was on the supposition that it would be defended by Italians. Nothing defended by Germans was taken easily, but the Allies were advancing on all fronts, and everyone, on both sides, awaited the landings in France.

D-Day was on June 6, 1944. Eisenhower, as supreme Allied commander, had three British service deputies: Montgomery was the battlefield commander; Air Chief Marshal Sir Trafford Leigh-Mallory was air commander; and Admiral Bertram Ramsay, who had evacuated the British, French, and Canadians from Dunkirk four years and one week earlier, brought the British, Canadians, and Americans back at Normandy. It was the greatest military operation in history, as 5,000 ships and 12,000 airplanes were involved and seven divisions were landed by sea and three by air, 132,000 fighting troops in one day. The landings were on five beaches, Juno Beach for the Canadian division; Gold and Sword for the three British divisions; and Omaha and Utah for the three American divisions; plus one British and two American airborne divisions, and a Canadian paratroop brigade. Within three weeks, more than a million men, 172,000 vehicles, and over 600,000 tons of supplies had been landed. Within three months, the Allies had landed over two million men and nearly 3.5 million tons of supplies at the Normandy beachheads. Stalin, whether he had expected the landings to succeed or not, sponta- neously issued a statement at the end of June declaring that "the history of war does not know of another undertaking comparable to it for breadth of conception, grandeur of scale and mastery of execution."[74] This was nothing but the truth, and high praise from one to whom the praise of others did not come easily or often. There were only four Canadian divisions on the Western Front, but General Eisenhower generously recognized them as one of the seven distinct armies advancing toward Germany, although the French First Army had ten divisions; the British Sixth Army fourteen divisions; and the U.S. First, Third, Ninth and Thirteenth armies from fourteen to twenty divisions each.

It was no longer possible to pretend that Charles de Gaulle did not represent France, and Eisenhower reminded Churchill and Roosevelt that it would be helpful to secure for his armies the active assistance of the one Frenchman who could be of general use to him. Churchill and de Gaulle had quarrelled so violently on the eve of D-Day that Churchill had shouted down the telephone to an aide that de Gaulle could not be allowed to re-enter France and was to be deported to Algiers, if necessary – and in a magnificent Churchillian flourish – "in chains."[75] De Gaulle was annoyed that Eisenhower's statement made no distinction between France as a liberated country continuing the fight and a conquered country, and was becoming seriously exasperated at the failure of his allies to recognize him as the head of the French people. It was clear from his return to France a few days after the initial landing, and from his progress inland, that he was the repository of France's hopes for a national renaissance. He was finally invited to Washington in early July and generously received by Roosevelt at the White House, and they patched up much of their previous lack of rapport.

He travelled on to, as he described it, "the beloved and courageous country of Canada."[76] Of King, de Gaulle wrote, "It was with pleasure that I again saw this worthy man, so strong in his simplicity."[77] (He was not as simple as de Gaulle imagined.) De Gaulle praised the Canadian war effort, military and industrial, the more so "because the country included two coexisting peoples not at all united, that the conflict was a remote one, and that none of the national interests was directly in question."[78] King and St. Laurent liked and respected de Gaulle, and there were none of the abrasions that had afflicted his relations in London and Washington. But King did not attempt to make any sort of common cause with France as a fellow striver for greater recognition from senior allies. De Gaulle's talents at self-promotion, and his genius at advancing the French interest, if King had assisted it more directly, rather than offering his usual good offices with Churchill and Roosevelt, who were not going to be moved by anything King said on this subject, could have emboldened Canada to make itself less taken for granted by its senior allies, with whom it had conducted an intricate roundel now for nearly two hundred years. De Gaulle's was a successful visit, but to some extent, for Canada, a lost opportunity also.

Paris was liberated on August 25, and the following day millions of Parisians lined the Champs-Élysées as Charles de Gaulle led a parade of French officialdom, whatever their political leanings in the previous four years, down the great boulevard. He began at once the propagation of the myths that France had never left the war and had participated importantly in its own liberation. The supreme Allied commander, General Eisenhower, rated the French Resistance as worth a division, but by August 25 he had over eighty divisions. Eisenhower had organized a continuous front from the Channel coast to Switzerland, after the southern invasion of Americans, British, and Free French forces landed near Marseilles and proceeded up the Rhône. McNaughton's desire to hold the whole Canadian effort for the French campaign, rather than the less promising and important Italian sideshow, was militarily and politically sensible. Italy was a flank wound to Germany, a sore, where France was the main onslaught to win the war and the peace by securing France and Germany for the West. The First Canadian Army, under Field Marshal Montgomery's command in the northern army group, had the mission of clearing territory along the coast, and it opened the important port of Antwerp to Allied shipping, and the Canadian Army advanced into the Netherlands, where German flooding of the dykes caused considerable inconvenience. It was a terribly difficult and very obstructed route of march.

4. Year of Victory, 1944–1945

In Quebec, everything was heating up to the provincial election. Duplessis was confined for much of 1942 to an oxygen tent as his drinking caught up to his diabetes. Premier Godbout visited him in hospital, as did Cardinal Villeneuve, and both urged upon him the merits of moderated drinking. He renounced drink completely and returned to active leadership of his party in February 1943. In the spring of 1944, Godbout announced the expropriation by Hydro-Quebec of the Montreal Light, Heat and Power Company. This had been the property of the late and long-serving president of the Royal Bank of Canada, Sir Herbert Holt. (The announcement of Holt's death at a Montreal Royals baseball team game at Delorimier Stadium on September 21, 1941, brought a standing ovation.[79])

Bouchard retired as vice premier and as a member of the Quebec Legislative Assembly after nearly thirty years and was named first president of Hydro-Quebec in deference to his long championship of the cause of publicly owned power, and was named to the Senate. One of the leaders of Quebec's outnumbered anti-clerical faction, he used his maiden speech in the Senate on June 21, 1944, to attack the parochialism and anti-English biases of the clergy. He lay about him with a vengeance of decades, accusing the clergy of portraying the English as "cloven-footed, horned" savages and of miseducating the youth of Quebec. He attacked the former apostolic visitor and a number of other notables, including Duplessis, who accused him of "treason," as well as slander. His remarks were rather well-received by the English-speaking senators, but on June 23 he was fired by Godbout as president of Hydro-Quebec. Two days later, Villeneuve, speaking at a Eucharistic Congress in Bouchard's city of Saint-Hyacinthe to seventy-five thousand people, said, "History has its rights. It was necessary to have a shadow in this splendid picture which your city offers of an admirable spiritual tradition beside which trickles, sometimes observably, sometimes latently, a current of anti-clericalism." He considered "a solemn protest" as his "duty. Events demand it, you yourselves wish it." He described Bouchard's Senate speech as "a ghastly diatribe; unjust, injurious, ill-considered, unfounded, unintelligent and perfidious, [inspired by] corrosive fanaticism excusable only as the product of the grossest ignorance or of congenital madness." He promised to assure that "the episcopate does not become confused with the movements that our insulter," whom he did not name, "has so dishonestly attached to us, the better to hurl his venom." Bouchard was philosophical and claimed a kinship with the cardinal because the fathers of both of them were hat-makers. It was an epochal and fiercely defined schism between Quebec's greatest episcopal leader since Taschereau, if not Laval, and the greatest elected secularist in its history, until twenty-five years later.[80]

This set the atmosphere for a wildly vituperative election campaign that was already underway when Godbout, with no time left to delay, dissolved the Assembly on June 28 for elections on August 8. The nationalist Bloc Populaire ran as the Pétainist party, even as the forces of liberation advanced from Normandy to Paris. The Liberals were the party that identified with the pro-British French, the traditional moderate Republicans; and Duplessis's Union Nationale was more closely akin to the Gaullists, nationalistic and somewhat authoritarian but anti-fascist and unreservedly pro-Allied. The Bloc leader was the talented writer André Laurendeau, still only twenty-eight, supported by the seventy-six-year-old Henri Bourassa, who was slightly affronted by colourful federal Liberal MP Jean-François Pouliot calling him "an old fuddy-duddy on the verge of death." Godbout endured more philosophically the prominent Bloc orator and lawyer Jean Martineau's description of the premier as "an utter imbecile" to great applause from thirty thousand people in Montreal, where Bourassa and Laurendeau spoke after him. Godbout's meetings were often disrupted, and even by Quebec standards the polemical flourishes were amusing. Godbout called the Bloc "a wretched band of separatists," and said that "it is not when the national edifice is loaded with dynamite that one struts about, blazing torches in hand." Duplessis asked the voters to "crucify the traitors . . . the marionettes and Charlie McCarthys who have sabotaged our liberties," and referred to King frequently as a "little Hitler."[81] This was too much even for the Bloc, and did not make for agreeable reading in Laurier House. Duplessis gradually gained ground and made the centre in such a battle a position of comparative strength. Godbout pointed out that there was no conscription and that the war was being won and was a matter of pride. Duplessis agreed but claimed to have held the first referendum on conscription in 1939 and virtually took credit for forcing the federal government to eschew conscription. Both leaders vilified the Bloc as Nazis. Duplessis's final message to his candidates claimed that "the life and survival of our people and our beloved province" was at stake and that Godbout had provided a government of Quebec "not by Quebec and for Quebec but . . . by Ottawa and for Ottawa." In a phrase coined two generations before and popularized a generation later by the separatists, he said, "We have the right and the will to be masters in our own house" (*maîtres chez nous*).[82] To the English, he preached tolerance and quoted approvingly from the social manifesto of the British Beveridge Report (the blueprint for the British Labour Party's proposed health-care and enhanced welfare reform). Cardinal Villeneuve and the episcopate made it clear that either Godbout or Duplessis would be perfectly acceptable but that the Bloc were misguided hotheads; for Bourassa, the star of the Eucharistic Congress of 1910, it was a strange and complete turn. On August 8, by the narrowest of margins, Quebec voters rendered what would prove a fateful result: Duplessis's Union Nationale won forty-eight constituencies to thirty-seven Liberal, four Bloc Populaire, and two others; and the Liberals narrowly won the popular vote, with 37 per cent, to 36 per cent Union Nationale, 15 per cent Bloc, and the rest scattered (Social Credit, Communist, CCF, and outright quacks). Duplessis won about 50 per cent of the French Quebec vote, to 30 per cent Liberal and 20 per cent Bloc. He and Godbout were eloquent and conciliatory on election night.

The fears King had expressed in his diary about Duplessis were unfounded in patriotic terms. Duplessis welcomed Churchill and Roosevelt to the second Quebec Conference, and Churchill attended one of his cabinet meetings and spoke to the Legislative Assembly, where he was received with profound respect. Duplessis happily became head of the Victory Bond drive for Quebec and told the province that as attorney general he would enforce all federal laws designed to assist the war effort.

Where matters would change decisively, if gradually, was that Duplessis would also insist on autonomy for Quebec and exercise of the full extent of the province's concurrent fiscal and other powers under the British North America Act. He was anti-separatist but would be the strongest advocate to date for Quebec's jurisdictional prerogatives, and would unleash a force that would ultimately threaten the country as a federal state, not because that was his wish, but because the federal government was so slow to recognize the implications of the issues he raised.

In an informal moment at the Tehran Conference, Roosevelt had warned Churchill that at the end of the war, which had followed hard on the depression, if he did not offer the British people more than continuation of the Empire and of effectively the same stratification of British society that had long obtained, there would be a danger of losing the postwar election despite his immense achievements as war leader. Roosevelt had already presented his G.I. Bill, the last version of the New Deal, that would be harvested after he died, by which returning servicemen would be entitled to a free year of higher education for every year served in the armed forces, and to low-interest loans to buy a farm or small business. King had inserted in the Throne Speech of the governor general, the Earl of Athlone, on January 27, 1944, that Canada's postwar goals were collective security and general prosperity abroad, and social security and a reasonable general level of welfare at home, and in furtherance of this he presented his family allowance plan, which, after extensive debate and a good deal of grumbling about subsidization of Quebec's high birth rate, was passed unanimously at the end of July.

When Churchill and Roosevelt met at Quebec for the second time, from September 11 to 16, 1944, there was strategic agreement on everything, but Roosevelt felt obliged to agree to the demarcation of spheres of occupation in postwar Germany that the British and Russians proposed. This gave the three powers approximately equal shares of

Germany, but left Berlin in the Soviet zone, with the city divided between all three powers and with three highway links from West Berlin to West Germany. The committee that devised the demarcation – the European Advisory Commission, chaired by the third-ranking figure in the British foreign office, Sir William Strang, and the American and Soviet ambassadors in London, John G. Winant and Feodor Gousev – was kept completely in the dark about the Polish-Soviet and Polish-German border changes agreed at Tehran, so the Soviet zone of Germany was largely in Poland. As eight to ten million Germans would move west on foot or in oxcarts ahead of the Red Army, these measures confirmed Germany, always ambiguous whether it was an eastward- or westward-facing country, as almost wholly in the camp of the West. This, the disposition of Germany, was the supreme determinant of who would win the war. The western position was shaping up very positively, where, four years before, Germany, Japan, and Italy were hostile to the democracies and the Soviet Union was loosely allied to Germany, which had conquered France, and in the interim the Soviet Union had borne the brunt of the struggle to subdue Germany.

From August 1, for two months, and throughout the Quebec Conference, the Soviet Red Army, which had arrived in late July at the opposite side of the Vistula River from Warsaw, remained there while the Polish underground rose up in Warsaw to assault the Germans and assist the Soviet liberation of the city. Stalin, in one of his more note-worthy acts of cynicism, in a career built altogether on little else, waited passively while the Germans killed the Polish resisters and Roosevelt and Churchill bombarded him with requests to aid the Poles or at least to allow British and American aircraft to drop assistance to them and then land at Soviet airfields. Stalin allowed this only for one day. It was a chilling foretaste of the impending fate of Eastern Europe. The Warsaw Uprising took the lives of 30,000 Polish resisters, about 175,000 Varsovian civilians, inflicted nearly 30,000 casualties on the Nazis, and led to the expulsion of 700,000 people from the city, which was largely reduced to rubble and ashes.

At Quebec, Roosevelt had his treasury secretary, Henry Morgenthau, explain to the British his plan for the pastoralization of Germany. The whole idea was nonsense, of course, but the British liked the thought of the elimination of German industrial competition, and Roosevelt thought that next to atomic threats – if the new weapon, which would not be tested for another ten months, worked – a remilitarized Germany was the main card he had to play to persuade Stalin to evacuate Eastern Europe, as Germany and the United States were the only countries Stalin feared.

At the end of the Quebec Conference, King took the occasion of addressing the Reform Club (Liberal Party militants) at the Château Frontenac and declared that the voluntary system was working in the armed forces. Angus L. Macdonald, the conscriptionist navy minister, "like an excitable schoolgirl had run to find Ralston to blurt the news about King's wholly honest anti-conscription indiscretion."[83] Crerar, who had replaced McNaughton as Canadian Army commander, continued McNaughton's policy that although the Canadian Army's six divisions were taking their share of casualties as they advanced in Belgium and Italy, the voluntary system was functioning and conscription was unnecessary. However, Ralston, who was almost demented in his desire for conscription, returned from Europe in October and declared that while the current position was sustainable, senior military staff believed that conscripts would be necessary in a few months. Ralston had no sensitivity to his chief's political problems, neither his no-conscription pledge nor the concerns of Quebec, which was a third of the population and about 40 per cent of King's electoral support. And fifty-five months into his mandate and with victory in Europe in sight, the prime minister was not going to put his government and party at risk. King, whose antennae for self-preservation were notoriously acute, after twenty-five years as Liberal leader, eighteen of them as prime minister, suspected that a larger conspiracy was about than that represented by the Nova Scotians Ralston, Macdonald, and Ilsley. He suspected them and Thomas Crerar of Alberta, and even Howe, men who opposed his family allowance as an undesirable move to the left, and others, of trying to stage a putsch. There were a number of strained interviews with Ralston and difficult cabinet meetings. King had McNaughton in the wings and still had Ralston's resignation as defence minister in his desk drawer from two years before. At one point, King poked the senior ministers and asked them, each in the presence of it all, if they could form a government. None could, none was interested, and most were offended by the question. There were 120,000 soldiers available in Canada and nearly 50,000 draftees for home service, among whom overseas recruits could be found in adequate numbers. The Allies were almost at the Rhine: given the political complexities, the conscription debate made no sense except in emotional (or racist) terms.

At the cabinet meeting on November 1, the issues were all aired again. Ralston confirmed his resignation. King had uttered paroxysms of admiration and comprehension of Ralston's position for many weeks and now he said little for an hour, and then referred to Ralston's resignation letter two years before, now confirmed, and said he had no choice but to accept it. Ralston slowly arose, said he would confirm his resignation in writing, shook hands with all the ministers, King last, and left the cabinet room.[84] At eleven the next morning Ralston's resignation and McNaughton's replacement of him were announced. Ralston might have been able to split off enough Liberals to form a government with the Conservatives, but King could have forced a dissolution for a terribly divisive election. Ralston was inflexible, but never irresponsible or discreditably ambitious. Nothing moved until, on November 22, McNaughton informed King that the Army Council would resign if the Army in Europe did not receive reinforcements. King confided in St. Laurent who objected that Canada was not a Latin American banana republic subject to a putsch, and that they must "fight." King asked, "With our bare hands?" His government could not survive such a drastic step. McNaughton had lost control of his fellow officers. There was no alternative but to send some of the draftees for home service. They would not be numerous and it would take months to get them to the front, which was moving east every day. (And two American divisions were being added to Eisenhower's armies every week.)[85]

On November 27, King opened what would be a confidence debate with one of the greatest orations of his career, lasting three hours, announcing that sixteen thousand National Resources Mobilization Act (NRMA) volunteers would be sent overseas. The associate minister of national defence for air, Charles Gavan Power, who had taken the anti-conscription pledge with Lapointe, Cardin, and Dandurand in 1939, very quietly retired on November 22, in principle but without rancour or ulterior motive, and wishing only to keep faith with his pledge but not harm King or the government.

The confidence vote came at about 1 a.m. on December 8, 1944, and the government won 143 to 73, with even 19 Quebec MPs voting to send the volunteers overseas. King returned home at almost 3 a.m. and massaged a lock of his mother's hair in pious thanks at his deliverance.[86] He had weathered the crisis and achieved what was even by his Houdini-like standards a breathtaking escape. Instead of siding with McNaughton over Ralston the year before, he had allowed Ralston, on behalf of the conscriptionists in Canada and the British Mediterraneanists, especially Brooke and Montgomery, to remove McNaughton, had bought a year of stability with Ralston, then invoked a two-year-old resignation letter (though updated) to dispose of him, and had stabilized a post-Ralston cabinet at once with the appointment of McNaughton to replace him. He had held the line for Quebec but had the country's most famous general vouch for his anti-conscription policy to persuade English Canada. He had then voted to send overseas sixteen thousand NRMA personnel drafted for domestic service, to avoid an officers' revolt, but he took his time actually sending them, without implying that there would be more, which appeased the conscriptionists without unduly frightening the anti-conscriptionists. King, though irritated, was unshaken when the traditionally Liberal district of Grey North was opened up for McNaughton in the by-election of February 5, 1945, only for McNaughton to be defeated, with 7,330 votes for the Progressive Conservative Party (as the Conservatives now styled themselves) to McNaughton's 6,091 and 3,100 for the CCF. King blamed it on a rush of Toronto Tory spending, treachery by local Hepburn Liberals, bigotry by the Orange Lodge because Mrs. McNaughton was a Roman Catholic, and conscriptionist and francophobic irrationalism. The thought that he might have found a more suitable constituency never entered King's mind, though he was frequently self-critical in matters not having to do with political judgment. He effectively ignored the result, as the House would be prorogued soon and a general election was imminent. The Conservatives had become the Progressive Conservatives after electing the Progressive premier of Manitoba, John Bracken, their leader, thus changing the name from National Government, which conspicuously failed to click in 1940. Bracken did not immediately seek a seat in the House.

* * *

While all this was happening, Churchill had visited Moscow and on his own authority made a spheres-of-influence agreement with Stalin that left Greece to the West, divided Yugoslavia evenly, and conceded Hungary, Romania, and Bulgaria to the Russians. Except perhaps for Hungary, the movement of the armies was going to accomplish this anyway, but Roosevelt did not want to legitimize Soviet occupation of any of these countries. Czechoslovakia wasn't mentioned. Franklin D. Roosevelt was re-elected to a fourth term as president, with Harry S. Truman of Missouri as vice president, over Governor Thomas E. Dewey of New York, 54 per cent to 46 per cent (his majority reduced by a vote of Republicans and Southern Democrats to exclude most members of the armed forces from voting, because the Republicans knew most would vote for the commander-in-chief, and the Southern Democrats were afraid of adding to the voter rolls a million African-American servicemen whom they had largely excluded from voting at home). Roosevelt hinted clearly that civil rights was an idea whose time was coming.

On December 16, 1944, Hitler launched what would prove to be his last throw in the war as his enemies closed in on him. Taking advantage of poor winter weather to evade Allied air superiority, he massed five hundred thousand men, about twenty-five divisions, and they erupted out of the Ardennes in an attempted replication of the great success there of 1940. The plan was to overrun Allied supply stores and use them, especially tank fuel, to proceed all the way to the coast at Antwerp and roll back the Allied offensive. Allied intelligence had some warning of an attack, and Eisenhower had very prudently pulled supplies back. The Germans achieved tactical surprise and advanced about fifty miles in the first week and surrounded the famous American 101st Airborne Division in the Belgian fortress city of Bastogne. General George S. Patton's Third Army, in a remarkable recovery, crashed into the southern flank of the Germans on Christmas Day and relieved Bastogne the following day. Montgomery, reinforced by the American Ninth Army, temporarily allocated to him by Eisenhower, attacked in strength from the north on January 2, and the Allied line had regained its original position by January 21. Germany had taken about 120,000 casualties to 90,000 Allied, 77,000 of them Americans. Germany lost about a third of its air force, which was now down to approximately three thousand planes, after the weather lifted at Christmas. The Germans, as always, fought bravely and with ingenuity, but they were heavily outnumbered and out-gunned, and the senior Allied commanders, Eisenhower, Patton, Omar Bradley, and Montgomery, all performed admirably. The Canadians, to the north, were not directly involved. Hitler would not be able to continue in the war for more than a few more months. The Allies were unstoppable on every front, and the battle now was to bring most of Europe as well as Japan into the West and not allow the Russian bear too far into Europe.

Churchill, Roosevelt, and Stalin met for the second time, at Yalta, in the Crimea, for a week starting on February 4. The conference has been much criticized, but the Western leaders got everything they sought; the problems arose in subsequent Soviet non-compliance. Until it was known whether atomic weapons would actually work, Roosevelt was beseeched by his service chiefs to get the Russians to take a share of what were expected to be a million casualties subduing the home islands of Japan. Stalin pledged to enter the Pacific War within three months of the end of the European War, and all was agreed for the setting up of the United Nations at San Francisco even before either theatre of war was pacified. The conference declarations on Poland and on liberated Europe pledged democratic government and free elections with, in Poland, stipulation of "universal suffrage and secret ballot." France would be recognized as a fourth power on the Allied Control Commission and would be given a part of the British occupation zone in Germany.

The conference ended cordially and the protagonists returned to direct their final offensives to secure the unconditional surrenders of Germany and of Japan. Eisenhower's armies prorupted into the Ruhr valley on February 23, attacked at a number of points across the Rhine in late March, and completed Eisenhower's double envelopment of the Ruhr by April 18, capturing 325,000 German prisoners. Roosevelt had been correct that once the Germans saw they were defeated, they would surrender in the west but continue to fight with their usual tenacity in the east to avoid capture by vengeful Russians at the end of the Russo-German war, which saw more than six million prisoners of war and many millions of civilians murdered. Roosevelt had been correct to resist a demarcation of spheres of occupation in Germany but was out-numbered by Stalin and by Churchill, who was afraid that with much the smallest number of forces in Germany of the Big Three, Great

Britain would have an inordinately small zone. Canada was not involved in all this and was only sketchily informed of any of it. With six divisions and two armoured brigades engaged in the northwest and Italy combined, Canada's contribution was well below the summit consultation threshold but did add significantly to Churchill's status. De Gaulle, who eventually clambered up to the Big Three to make it the Big Four (after it ceased to meet or function), wrote King in October 1944 that "he realized he owed the freedom of France in large part to Canadians."[87] Conscription was finally fading as an issue when on April 3 the cabinet agreed with a silent nodding of heads that there would be no conscription for the Japanese war.

Franklin D. Roosevelt died on April 12, 1945, aged only sixty-three, and was generally hailed as a gigantic and benign figure of modern world history. More than two million people stood beside the railway track to see his funeral train pass on its way from his winter home in Georgia, where he died, to Washington and on to Hyde Park. King, who had enjoyed an excellent, if uneven, relationship with him, mourned the deceased president and attended the funeral. On the same day, he determined to dissolve Parliament and lead the Liberal Party into a general election for the seventh time. The date was fixed for June 11, the same day on which Ontario would vote.

Mussolini was summarily executed by Italian partisans on April 28, after being taken off a German army truck disguised in a German army uniform as he fled Italy. His corpse and that of his mistress, Clara Petacci, were hung upside down in a service station in Milan and mutilated, as were the corpses of several of his senior collaborators, who were first made to watch *Il Duce's* final humiliation for a while before they themselves were executed (to popular acclaim), hung upside down, and their corpses too were mutilated. Anxious to avoid an undignified fate, Hitler and his wife of several days, Eva Braun, committed suicide by poison and pistol fire on April 30 and had their corpses burned outside the Führerbunker as the Red Army approached to within a few hundred yards. Germany surrendered unconditionally to the Allies on May 8. King's only reflection in his diary on the deaths of Mussolini and Hitler, both of whom impressed him when he met them, was that that left Stalin and himself as the only national leaders of major combatants at the start of the war who were still in place, and "I have, of course, led my party longer than Stalin has his."[88]

The San Francisco Conference to establish the United Nations opened on April 25 and continued to June 25. King led the Canadian delegation of Louis St. Laurent, CCF leader Major James (M.J.) Coldwell, and a strong group of civil servants and diplomats, including future senior politicians Lester B. Pearson and Jack Pickersgill. On his arrival, King attended a meeting of the Commonwealth delegations chaired by Eden, where Eden shared a message just received from Churchill that Himmler, the chief of the Gestapo, had offered surrender in the West but that Churchill had advised that there would be no separate arrangements from the Russians.[89] King was suffering from a cold, which was aggravated by the San Francisco climate, and he spoke little at the opening sessions of the conference, but when the European war ended, he addressed Canadians, as did St. Laurent in French, in remarks carried also in the United States and by shortwave transmission to Great Britain and all fighting fronts. He had the benefit also of a very generous and gracious message from Churchill praising the Canadian war effort, and King personally. His last act before leaving San Francisco was an extensive conversation with Edward Stettinius, the secretary of state (Cordell Hull had retired in the autumn of 1944 for health reasons after nearly three terms, like his chief the longest-serving holder of his position in U.S. history). King responded to Stettinius's urging that he come back for the closing of the conference, which was then expected at the end of May, with reflections on the fact that "one of the greatest assets I had in the public life of Canada had been my friendship with President Roosevelt. It would be very helpful to me to have the public see that I was carrying on that relationship with President Truman." Despite the terrible inconvenience, "It might nevertheless be the most important step I could take in the campaign to win popular approval and to have the nation realize the influence that I have and the position in which I am held by the Government of the United States." King was rarely so forthright, even in his diary, on matters of rank political opportunism. He meant "perceived influence," as there is no evidence that he altered the intended conduct of Roosevelt a jot, but he was always amenable and they got on well, though Roosevelt found him an odd person, hardly an inaccurate judgment.[90] King left California on May 14 and went to Prince Albert, Saskatchewan, via Vancouver and Edmonton, to open his campaign for re-election, personally and as leader of the government. He delighted in the company of "these simple, direct, humble, honest, and genuine folk."[91]

On receiving a note from Sidney Smith, principal of University College at the University of Toronto (and later secretary of state for external affairs), inviting him to the fiftieth anniversary celebration of his graduation, but adding that, if that were not possible, all in attendance "will be felicitating the most distinguished graduate of the institution," King "almost broke down . . . thinking first of the joy these words would have brought to my father, but even more how little truth, in reality, there was in them, whatever there might be to appearances because of position. I have not measured up to my job as I should have and would have, had I gone about it more in earnest from the start."[92] King always rejected the criticism of others but was often self-critical to a fault. On May 24, he gave a nationally broadcast speech from Winnipeg in which he called for a distinctive Canadian flag. The reception to the idea was cool, and it did not move again for nearly twenty years. Most of King's election speeches were mixtures "of gentle nationalism, attachment to King and Crown, rejection of 'special interests,' pleas for national unity, hints of new social welfare programmes, and pride in the government's war record."[93] President Truman's invitation to King to visit Washington in the first week of June was impossible to accept, but King did seek "permission to have word of the invitation made public."[94] Truman replied happily that he knew something about elections and agreed at once.

The Liberals could not replicate their tremendous victories of 1935 and 1940, and on June 11, 1945, the government lost 59 MPs but still won 118 seats, and lost 11.5 per cent of the popular vote but retained 39.8 per cent. The Progressive Conservatives moved up from 39 to 67 MPs and yet lost 2.8 per cent of the vote to come in at 27.6 per cent. The CCF rose from 8.3 per cent to 15.6 per cent, and from 8 to 28 MPs. And Social Credit moved from 2.5 to 4 per cent of the national vote, and from 10 to 13 MPs. Mackenzie King was defeated in Prince Albert (by the "simple, direct, humble, honest and genuine folk" he revered in his diary), but he had suffered that fate before with equanimity, in 1911, 1917, and 1925.

More disappointing was the defeat again of McNaughton, still being punished by the misguided conscriptionism of much of English Canada (as his leader was). But King had clearly been re-elected, as he could certainly bring a number of independents and, if necessary, the CCF with him on divisions. He was re-elected personally in Glengarry, Ontario, on August 6, the fifth constituency in the third province he had represented.

The Potsdam Conference opened on July 16, with Truman the new-comer, not known to either Churchill or Stalin. Eisenhower had opposed continuing to entice the Soviet Union into the Japanese war and had also opposed using the atomic bomb on the Japanese, as he acknowledged that Russia would take what it wanted but felt the Japanese were already defeated and they could be starved or conventionally bombed into surrender. While Truman was touring the ruins of Berlin (though he declined to visit Hitler's bunker to avoid the semblance of "gloating"), the first atomic test at Alamogordo, New Mexico, was a success, producing a gigantic fireball and a "light not of this world."[95] Truman and war secretary Henry Stimson described it to Churchill the next day, who called it "the second coming in wrath."[96] At the July 21 conference session, Truman and Churchill refused to recognize Stalin's puppet governments in Romania, Hungary, and Bulgaria, or even the neutralist regime of Finland, until the Yalta pledges to democratic government were adhered to; Roosevelt had already held back his $6.5-billion aid package for the Soviet Union pending that compliance, and Truman added that there would be no discussion of reparations either until that matter was resolved. The success of the atomic test had greatly strengthened his hand, and he enjoyed full support from Churchill. The leaders went at the same points again on July 24, after Truman and Churchill had agreed between them that the atomic bomb would be dropped on Japan within two weeks if that country did not surrender, and that the likeliest target was the city of Hiroshima, with a population of about one hundred thousand, the southern headquarters for Japan's home defence forces. The differences of perception became clear. Stalin said, "If a government is not fascist, it is democratic."[97] Churchill, supported by Truman, was having none of it, and contrasted Italy, a free society with a free press, with Romania, where the British embassy was like a prison. "All fairy tales," said Stalin. At the end of that session, Truman casually walked around the table and said to Stalin and his interpreter that the United States had "a new weapon of unusual destructive force." Stalin expressed the hope that it would be used on Japan and showed no curiosity and did not raise the matter again at the conference. He was already working on a similar weapon and being fed information on the atomic program by the scientist Klaus Fuchs, who was at the test centre in New Mexico. That evening, Stalin ordered acceleration of his own nuclear program,[98] Canada having provided the uranium for the atomic bomb. King was kept reasonably current on the state of development and the approach of the bomb's debut. When Japan rejected the Allied ultimatum to surrender that emanated from the Potsdam Conference on July 27, King wrote in his diary, "I feel that we are approaching a moment of terror to mankind, for it means that under the stress of war, men have at last not only found but created the Frankenstein which conceivably could destroy the human race. It will rest with those in authority to decide how it can later be brought to serve instead of destroy mankind."[99]

The extent of King's political achievement at home was emphasized when Winston Churchill was summoned back from the Potsdam Conference to hand over the government to Clement Attlee, leader of the Labour Party, who had severely defeated Churchill's Conservatives in the general election. As Roosevelt had warned at Tehran, it was not a referendum on Churchill's war leadership, which won very wide support and gratitude. There had not been an election since 1935, and the Conservatives carried the can for appeasement and had entered into the election with no vision of social reform or the transformation of the Empire. Mackenzie King wrote in his diary, "I am personally very sorry for Churchill. I would like to have seen him continue his coalition until the Japanese war was over and then drop out altogether. I think he has made a mistake in running again. My own belief is that a man of Truman's stamp is much nearer giving the kind of example which the people want. Back of it all of course is the hatred of the mass of the people for Toryism and the knowledge that Churchill is a Tory at heart though he has broad Liberal sympathies in a way, but it is the old Whig style of Liberalism. Then, too, people do not like any man to become a

God. The higher a man rises on all counts, the more humble-minded he should become." He also thought it a mistake for Churchill's son, Randolph, and son-in-law Duncan Sandys also to stand as MPs in the same election. Then King's Low Church Canadian envy, though not without its intuitive grasp of envious electoralism, crept in: "I do feel that there has been far too much expenditure of public money on these great gatherings; too much emphasis on the sort of Big Three business," by which of course King meant that he was grumpy not to have been invited. "The press in the States were against Roosevelt because he lent himself to drastic extravagances. His infirmity, though, kept him in touch with the people. What above everything else is at the back of this is the feeling of the people that if this war is to mean anything it has to mean a social revolution and that the great body of the people are going to have a larger share of their own lives." (In fact, Roosevelt had the support of the great majority of the media and saw the coming socioeconomic changes more clearly even than King, but he knew, and his electors appreciated, that the chief of state and government in the United States had the trappings of a monarch, especially when he was a natural aristocrat, as Roosevelt was.[*] King, the first minister of an overseas monarch and at the head of a self-conscious and politically ambiguous country, was self-effacing, tactically and because of his indistinct public personality, but perceptive withal, and took his own remarkable political longevity as a greater confirmation of his virtue and prescience than it was, though those qualities were not lacking.[100])

And King could not fail to "confess" to himself that "this morning when I heard the news [of Churchill's defeat], there came over me at once a sense of greater responsibility which is now mine. I am the only one who really was intimate with both Churchill and Roosevelt throughout the war. My position, internationally, will be heightened as a consequence. Also, the victory in Canada strengthens that position." This was all true, as far as it went, but the world seemed to recognize that while King spent a lot of time with Churchill and Roosevelt, it was not because he had a lot of influence on either of them, as Jan Smuts

---

[*] King envied Roosevelt's mastery of the Washington press, who recited, every time King appeared before them: "William Lyon Mackenzie King never tells us a Goddamned thing." (Conversation with David Brinkley.)

had on Churchill, but because they both found him an amenable companion who represented a useful and admirable country. Yet, this was
a great advance on Robert Borden, who scarcely knew President
Wilson, and though he was often with Lloyd George, it was only as
part of the charade of the Imperial War Cabinet. Laurier and
Macdonald, who were not in power during great wars, were well
regarded by the foreign leaders they met but never had occasion to
spend much time with them. Canada and King had progressed a long
way, if not as far as King liked to pretend. But he was still there, and
Churchill and Roosevelt weren't.

Churchill himself said (speaking from his bath) to his doctor, John
Wilson, "If the people want Clem Attlee, let them have him. That's why
we fought and won the war." And Stalin said, as Churchill abruptly
departed the summit conference, "Democracy must be a wretched system to replace a great man like Churchill with someone like Attlee."[101]
(Attlee was a principled retired major but a rather colourless man, especially in comparison to Churchill.) De Gaulle drew a slightly different
conclusion: "Winston Churchill lost neither his glory nor his popularity
thereby; merely the adherence he had won as guide and symbol of the
nation in peril. His nature, identified with a magnificent enterprise, his
countenance etched by the fires and frosts of great events, were no longer adequate to the era of mediocrity. . . . Learning that England had
asked her captain to leave the command to which she had called him
when the tempest fell, I foresaw the moment when I would relinquish
the helm of France, of my own accord, as I had taken it."[102] This is what
de Gaulle did, six months later, as France chose to return to a regime of
fragmented parties and a weak state. De Gaulle returned to his property
at Colombey-les-deux-Églises, in Champagne, 180 kilometres east of
Paris, and waited for twelve years for the Fourth Republic to flounder
to an end. Churchill and de Gaulle would be back, but of the leaders of
the democratic combatants, the indistinct but imperishable William
Lyon Mackenzie King was the only one to proceed in uninterrupted
incumbency into, through, and out of the Second World War, back
again in 1945, as he had been in 1935, as he had been in 1925.

There was now a race between the American release of the atomic
bomb on Japan, which was warned that there was a new weapon which

would be used if it did not surrender, and the Soviet rush to war with Japan, which led to possibly the worst week in the military history of any great power: the Japanese rejected the surrender demand and the United States dropped an atomic bomb on Hiroshima on August 6, killing one hundred thousand people and injuring sixty thousand; the Soviet Union, which had been asked by Japan to mediate peace with the Western powers, declared war instead and invaded Manchuria with a million men on August 8; the Americans, not receiving any interest from Japan in giving up the war, dropped a second atomic bomb, on Nagasaki on August 9, killing seventy thousand people and injuring about fifty thousand; and on August 10, Emperor Hirohito told the nation by radio that "events have not gone altogether as we would have wished" and asked his subjects to "think the unthinkable and endure the unendurable." Japan agreed to surrender on sole condition of retention of the emperor as a constitutional monarch, and Truman accepted these terms on behalf of the warring powers. Hostilities ended on August 13, and Japan submitted to military occupation by the United States and disarmed entirely. The surrender occurred on the U.S. battleship *Missouri* (sister of the *Iowa*) in Tokyo Bay on September 2, six years and one day after the Second World War began. The theatre commanders, General MacArthur and Admiral Nimitz, received the surrender, along with representatives of their allies. (Colonel Lawrence Moore Cosgrave was the unexceptionable representative for Canada, yet one dismissed by the acidulous American General Joseph Stilwell in his memoirs as "an elderly masher of the gigolo type."[103]) MacArthur was declared and was submissively accepted as military governor of the Japanese empire, where he exercised absolute authority with great liberality and success and became a revered figure to the Japanese. Thus, with Japan, there passed into the hands of the West the fourth great strategic prize of the war, after France, Germany, and Italy (where Roosevelt had refused the Soviet Union any position on the control commission). Considering how badly it had begun, the war ended very positively for the West.

Approximately 70 million people had died in the Second World War, 24 million in military roles, including nearly 6 million prisoners of war, and 46 million civilians. More than 100 million were injured, including serious war-related illnesses. The Soviet Union suffered 9.5 million military deaths and 14 million civilian; China 3.5 million military deaths and 12 million civilian; Germany 5.5 million military deaths and 2 million civilian; Japan 2.1 million military deaths and 750,000 civilian; Poland 5.5 million civilian deaths; and there were approximately 500,000 military and civilian deaths combined in each of the United Kingdom, France, and Italy. The United States suffered 322,000 dead and 700,000 injured. Canada suffered 45,000 dead and about 55,000 injured.

The United States emerged from the war as the possessor of half the entire economic product of the world and of a nuclear monopoly; as the founder and host, in New York, of the United Nations Organization; and as by far the most powerful and esteemed nationality in the world by almost any measurement. Its strategic management and quality of civilian and military leadership, under Roosevelt, Truman, Marshall, Eisenhower, MacArthur, Nimitz, and many others, had been of unsurpassable distinction. Canada had again distinguished itself, was in from the beginning as a disinterested and courageous fighter for international law and the cause of freedom throughout the world, and had had a brilliant war in all respects, except that she was even more overshadowed by the United States at the end of the war than at the beginning and Great Britain had slipped – by attrition and despite its heroic war effort and the inspirational leadership of Churchill – as a pole of influence for Canada to cling to in distinction from the United States. Any fear of physical absorption of Canada by the United States had long disappeared, and the internal stresses in Canada had been managed skilfully and were not threatening as the war ended. But the raison d'être of Canada as an independent country, if the French fact was not a federalizing but rather a divisive force, was still vague. William Lyon Mackenzie King, the master of self-serving but constructive ambiguity, was not the leader to solve this problem. But he was not finished yet.

5. Mackenzie King VII: The Start of the Cold War and the Resumption of Federal-Provincial Discord, 1945–1948

As the end of war loomed, King reconvened the Federal-Provincial Conference (they were still called Dominion-Provincial Conferences for a while) in August 1945 to try to start a process for permanent implementation of as much as he could of the recommendations of the Rowell-Sirois Commission. He had persuaded Adélard Godbout of Quebec, but not Ontario's Mitchell Hepburn, to "rent" Quebec's concurrent right to direct taxes to the federal government in exchange for federal grants to assist with provincial spending requirements in health and education, and sought to extend these arrangements. To King, it was perfectly natural and efficient and assisted in the goal of equality in services provided to Canadians in every province. It was among the many contradictions of King's personality that while he was a devious and cynical political operator, he was almost incapable of imagining that anyone could have a radically different notion of the purpose and nature of Canadian federalism to his own. John A. Macdonald, having gone through all the tortuosities of putting Confederation together, knew that there was a sizeable faction in Quebec that opposed Confederation and would like to secede from it, and an even larger one that only entered it as the lesser of evils because Quebec was not capable of functioning as an independent country in 1867 and could not be assured even of being allowed to attempt such a project in peace. Confederation was then a more desirable formula for Quebec than running the risk of being cultur- ally swamped and absorbed into the immense English-speaking sea of Americans and other Canadians. Laurier fought those battles as a young lawyer and newspaper editor, and contended with Honoré Mercier and Henri Bourassa for the loyalties and confidence of the French Quebec intelligentsia and electorate. Although King spoke elemental French, he did not really understand the province. He did understand that for Canada to survive and to function, the French had to be rallied, and Canada had to be made to work for them, both finan- cially and emotionally. He could assure the first, and did, but he relied on Lapointe and then St. Laurent to deliver the votes and the moral commitment of the people of Quebec. He always seemed to think that any provincial leader who disagreed with his vision of federalism was just an insincere rabble-rouser (and some were) and had little compre- hension of the fact that many Québécois didn't believe in Canada at all. (He was, however, correct that most of them, whatever the strength of their reservations, could be bought, fiscally, if their cultural pride was not directly affronted.)

The intergovernmental meeting of August 1945 reassured King to the extent that Duplessis was not the pyrotechnic and even bumptious figure he had been when he met the Rowell-Sirois commissioners on their tour in Quebec, or exchanged fire with King during Duplessis's liquor-sodden alliance with Hepburn. Duplessis was older, wiser, a tee-totaler, and had the inner strength of the reformed alcoholic and the sense of purpose of a man reborn, having spent many months in an oxygen tent and narrowly regained his former office. To some extent, the exchange over the next twelve years between Duplessis and St. Laurent would resemble those between George-Étienne Cartier and Antoine-Aimé Dorion, and Laurier's with Mercier and Bourassa. But Duplessis and St. Laurent weren't competing directly for the same voters, and Quebec voted heavily for both, four elections in a row. Duplessis, who like many educated French enjoyed puns and was quick with them, had the formula that neither the Saint-Maurice nor the St. Lawrence over-flowed its banks into the other, a fluvial displacement of him and St. Laurent that worked in French. His exchanges with St. Laurent were always very civilized and were learned disagreements on constitutional law. Duplessis was anti-separatist and thought Canada was a good deal for Quebec. He was pro-Canadian, pro-American, and pro-British, and his threats never went beyond double taxation: Quebec would impose its own personal and corporate income taxes, as it had a right to do, and if the federal government did not give Quebec taxpayers a credit for that tax in assessing federal tax on Quebeckers, the voters of that province could decide which jurisdiction had it right.

The 1945 meeting was just an opener, with an agreement to recon-vene in April 1946 with substantive proposals then. It did have an amus-ing start, as Duplessis's large official car broke down on the road on the Quebec side of the Ottawa River about twenty miles from Hull. He and his delegation walked up a farmer's long driveway and asked to use his telephone. As the farmer didn't have a telephone, Duplessis asked if he could engage him to drive them to Ottawa in his car. The premier was completely undismayed by the deteriorated condition of the farmer's ancient jalopy, and two of his colleagues had to sit on the knees of two others. When they turned in to the driveway of the Château Laurier, Duplessis told the farmer to pull up right in front of a CBC news camera filming the arrival of the premiers, and then leapt out, brandishing his cane, and said to the astonishment of onlookers, "Look, we are the Quebec delegation. This is the only car we have. We are poor, as you can see. That is why we want our rightful share of the taxes."[104] It was a made-over Duplessis, not the man King remembered and had tried to forget, but a much more formidable and durable one.

Charles de Gaulle made his second visit to Canada starting on August 28, 1945. De Gaulle was "particularly friendly," King wrote in his diary.[105] De Gaulle began what would be a refrain for the remaining twenty-five years of his career: the Americans and British had given away too much at Yalta and Potsdam. This was rubbish in fact, as Truman and Churchill and Attlee demanded that Stalin abide by his promises about withdrawing from the Eastern European countries and assisting in their establishment as democracies. It was part of the myth de Gaulle would confect, that France was the defender of Europe and European democracy and that the Anglo-Saxons could not be relied upon to do it. He was sympathetic to Churchill for his defeat at the polls, and liked the British, as a European democracy, much more than the Russians, whom he distrusted, and the Americans, whose prosperity and power he resented. King wrote, "I was surprised too to find that he still had a little feeling against Roosevelt. I sought to dispel that but there is something in the U.S. relation to France that I do not yet comprehend. He spoke nicely about President Truman but did not seem to be enthusiastic about the States. He seemed to feel that both the U.S. and Russia were too conscious of their power and determined to manage everything."[106] He thought constitutional arrangements in France would be favourable to his wishes for a strong executive. (They weren't, in the event, for many years, until de Gaulle was invited to write them himself.) King explained to de Gaulle that he had flown the Red Ensign over Parliament in his honour as a wartime ally, as that was the flag of the Canadian armed forces. King told de Gaulle of his "feeling now toward the big Five much as France had felt toward the big Four," (China was also a member). He was clear that Canada did not imagine it had any authority over matters that did not concern it, but that where "we were expected to assume responsibility, we should be given fullest powers . . . not merely consultation. . . . I did not think the post-war settlement should follow the pattern of what had been done during the war itself. I spoke of Canada having made a very great contribution."[107]

A few months later, in January 1946, King received a visit from General and Mrs. Dwight D. Eisenhower, and was immensely impressed with Eisenhower. In a dinner he tendered to the Eisenhowers, King quoted verbatim from an address he had given in the same place twenty-five years before in honour of Marshal Foch, the analogous figure from that war. As an encore, in responding to generous words of Eisenhower's at a Canadian Club luncheon, King informed him that one of the larger mountains in the Canadian Rockies had been officially renamed Mount Eisenhower and gave him a certificate to that effect. King found the general a man of such gracious manners, high intelligence, and great charm that he sought him out for extensive conversation. They discussed Churchill, and Eisenhower spoke of his great admiration for Churchill but said he thought him too concerned always to get his way, and said how difficult it had been to dissuade him about his proposed invasion of Southern Europe up the Adriatic and through Slovenia. King showed his limitations as a military strategist by saying Churchill deserved great credit for deferring the D-Day landings as long as he did. Eisenhower diplomatically did not comment, as Churchill had wished to delay it longer, and delays, beyond a certain point, caused increased Soviet penetration of Eastern Europe.[108]

In some respects, the Cold War began in Canada and, almost unbelievably, the ineffable man for all seasons, Mackenzie King, was one of the first protagonists. On the morning of September 6, King was greeted as he arrived at his office by two senior external affairs officials, who advised him of the defection to Canada of a twenty-six-year-old cipher clerk, Igor Gouzenko, from the Soviet embassy with wads of secret documents indicating that a massive espionage operation was being conducted in the West by the Soviet Union. He was a member of the foreign military intelligence directorate of the Red Army and risked the lives of his wife, six months pregnant, and his two-year-old child. Gouzenko bounced around in a chronically distressed state for two days between the Ottawa Journal, the Justice Department, and the Ottawa municipal police, until the RCMP deduced that his apartment had been broken into and he was placed in protective custody, where he remained for most of the rest of his life. (He died in 1982, aged sixty-three.) The operation Gouzenko was part of was designed to accelerate Soviet development of an atomic bomb (he defected a month after the detonations at Hiroshima and Nagasaki), though the material he had obtained was not especially sensitive. But it revealed a widespread communist plot that had seduced the cooperation of about fifteen Canadians including the one Labour Progressive (communist) MP, Fred Rose. The matter was so sensitive that King opened a special secret diary to describe the story as it unfolded. After natural initial skepticism, he quickly concluded that Gouzenko was "a true world patriot" who had been won over to the West by his exposure to Canadian democracy. When he met him in July 1946, King was impressed by Gouzenko as being "clean-cut" and by his "keen intellect . . . manliness, courage, and standing for right." This was not unjustified praise.

King consulted William Stephenson, known as Intrepid, the Winnipeg-born British intelligence chief, and Stephenson dissuaded him from raising the issue directly with the Russians. A secret order-in-council reimposed part of the War Measures Act, which had expired. A British nuclear physicist who had been working at the National Research Council, Professor Alan Nunn May, was detained, and he was later charged, convicted, and imprisoned. King, sinking his teeth into the issue, saw himself as being "singled out as an instrument on the part of unseen forces to bring about the exposure that has now taken place. There has never been anything in the world's history more complete than what we will reveal of the Russian method to control the continent."[109] He determined that he had to go in person to advise President Truman and Prime Minister Attlee of what was afoot. He arranged it in style, as befits a five-term leader of a recently victorious power, intending to travel on his own railway car to Washington before boarding the great liner *Queen Mary* to Britain. He flew to Washington instead when he learned that it would cost three hundred dollars to transfer his private railway car from Grand Central Station to Penn Station. The minister in Washington, Lester Pearson, humorously wrote Ottawa that he had arranged for a storm to be held up over Washington until after King had landed, for the temperature to come down to a comfortable level, and for the autumn rollback of the clocks to give the prime minister another hour's sleep.[110]

In Washington, the director of the FBI, J. Edgar Hoover, who had directed the bureau almost as long as King had led the Canadian

Liberal Party, and would soldier on in that role for another quarter-century, was at first cautious, but after the defection of Elizabeth Bentley in the United States, he urged King to arrest everyone Gouzenko had implicated and considered the Canadian prime minister "spineless" for waiting until the Americans and British were ready to make arrests also.[111] As usual, it is not difficult to make fun of King's habitual caution, but his desire not to go out into the world alone on this as a Judas goat for Canada's senior allies is understandable.

King was concerned about such an explosive matter leading to a political polarization, with good reason, as it soon emerged. He struck a secret Royal Commission of two Supreme Court justices, Robert Taschereau (son of the former premier of Quebec) and Roy Kellock of Ontario, who recommended detention of all who were implicated. Given King's cavalier disregard for the Japanese Canadians who were rounded up without any due process at all during the war, his concern now for the rights of suspects, though admirable, was bizarre. Hoover tried to force King's hand by leaking the story through columnist Drew Pearson, but King, like a majestic hen waiting for her eggs to crack open spontaneously beneath her, refused to be ruffled. The first arrests were in February 1946, although for months before it occurred the arrest of Professor May was repeatedly discussed, even in conversations between the Canadian and British prime ministers and in exchanges of both with President Truman. King's visit to Britain was more a get-acquainted meeting with the new Labour government than an urgent discussion of an impending Cold War. King George VI professed not to be aware of whether Stalin was alive or dead, and King had a convivial luncheon at the Soviet embassy with Ambassador Gousev. Attlee advised him that the British would be happy to have Newfoundland join Canada but did not wish it taken over by the United States. The new government was well disposed to the United States, and King was impressed by Attlee's negative attitude toward the Russians, whom, King wrote in his diary, Atlee described as "ideological imperialists. They were out for power and they were using their ideologies with the masses to secure that end. The masses themselves did not realize the significance of it all."[112] King had an impressive tour of the British establishment, including repeated visits with Attlee and his family, Churchill, senior ministers and shadow ministers, and figures of the past like Queen Mary and Mrs. Neville Chamberlain. In one of the more animated moments of his discussions with the royal family, Princess Elizabeth, then nineteen, said she would have been happy to have shot Hitler herself.[113] Churchill and Eden were more cordial than ever, and King found Attlee a delightful man. It must be said that King and Canada clearly possessed a status in the world that vastly exceeded any it had had before. The British, French, and Americans were not entirely convinced of Canadian sovereignty, and there is some reason to believe, on reading the memoirs of their statesmen of the time, that they never fully appreciated King for the formidable talent that he was and didn't much consider how he had managed to be so successful. But the country and its leader had earned and gained great respect and had gone far in the world over the course of King's long inning at the head of the government.

On February 9, 1946, Stalin, who gave a real public speech only once every two or three years, declared publicly that communism and capitalism were incompatible and that another world war was certain. In initiating the Cold War, he committed a strategic blunder that was surpassed in the twentieth century only by the Japanese attack on Pearl Harbor and by Wilhelm II's recourse in 1917 to submarine warfare against American merchant shipping. All three catastrophic mistakes grossly underestimated the power of the United States and the hazards of provoking it. Clever though Stalin was (unlike Wilhelm and the Second World War Japanese leadership), he didn't realize how much stronger he would have been if he had facilitated the Americans' accomplishment of their ambition to withdraw from Europe and return to a semi-isolated and overwhelmingly civilian existence. On February 22, right after Stalin's speech, senior foreign service official George F. Kennan filed the famous "long telegram" (of eight thousand words) from Moscow, declaring the irreconcilability of the United States and the Soviet Union and stating that the Russians were neurotically suffused with feelings of inferiority and under the Communists were "committed fanatically" to the impossibility of "peaceful coexistence" and to a desire to disrupt the domestic tranquility and destroy the international standing and credibility of the United States.

On March 6, 1946, Winston Churchill acted on an invitation from Truman to speak at Westminster College, in Fulton, Missouri, where he famously stated that "from Stettin in the Baltic to Trieste in the Adriatic, an iron curtain has descended across the continent. Behind that line lie all the capitals of the ancient states of Central and Eastern Europe. Warsaw, Berlin, Prague, Vienna, Budapest, Belgrade, Bucharest, and Sofia, all these famous cities and the populations around them lie in what I must call the Soviet sphere and all are subject [to] . . . control from Moscow."[114] He explained that the Soviets did not want war; they wanted victory without war. King listened to the speech on the radio and telephoned Churchill and Truman and warmly congratulated them. In his diary, he described the speech as the "most courageous speech I have ever listened to. . . . I confess I personally believe that as regards Russia the rest of the world is not in a very different position than other countries in Europe were when Hitler had made up his mind to aim at the conquest of Europe." Churchill asked him to write Attlee, as he was concerned that Attlee not think he, Churchill, had put a foot wrong in foreign policy with his remarks. King was happy to do so, and did. He also spoke to Truman and congratulated him on arranging such an occasion. It must be said that Truman was concerned about how provocative the speech might be considered, and offered to send the battleship *Missouri* to collect Stalin and bring him to America, and convey him, as he had Churchill, in Roosevelt's old railway car, the *Ferdinand Magellan*, to Fulton to give his perspective. Truman later accepted the praise he earned for sponsoring the address, and it says a great deal for King's standing with the leaders of the world that Churchill asked him to intervene with his own country's prime minister as he did. It also shows how clear-headed King was politically so soon after the war. There were still plenty of vocal advocates of open-ended accommodation of Stalin.[115]

King settled very comfortably into the Gouzenko affair and was something of a pioneering Cold Warrior. He conceived the Russian conduct as an assault upon Christianity: "It can be honestly said that few more courageous acts have ever been performed by leaders of the government than my own in the Russian intrigue against the Christian world and the manner in which I have fearlessly taken up and have begun to expose the whole of it."[116] Of course, this was his usual self-serving hyperbole, but was still not entirely undeserved praise. Less creditable was King's interpretation of these events as an act of Jewish insidiousness. King harked back to Goldwin Smith, a mentor, though he became an annexationist, who denounced Jews as "poison in the veins of a community." King did, however, as he had ten years before, write in his diary in 1946 of the unfairness of prejudices against a whole people, religious group, or nationality. But the frequent recurrence of Jewish defendants in the ensuing investigations and prosecutions in the Gouzenko affair fed his anti-Semitic tendencies, as well as his natural paranoia. He even began to doubt the loyalty of his long-serving valet and chauffeur, Robert Lay: "He has openly confessed his sympathy with the Reds." The Taschereau-Kellock Commission recommended that all those named by Gouzenko be charged with violation of the Official Secrets Act, and in the next three years sixteen people were, and nine were convicted. It was a commendable display of due process compared to the witch hunts and virtual show trials in the United States. Still, M.J. Coldwell, the leader of the CCF, and a fair swath of editorial opinion, accused the government of abusing the civil rights of the accused. Somewhat typically of King's desire always to be placatory, at least to the powerful, King sent a message of enduring friendship to Stalin, which elicited no reply at all.[117]

The Federal-Provincial Conference of April 1946 saw the different perspectives on the actual and desirable powers of the two levels of government revealed more clearly than they had been before. For the mainly English-speaking provinces, it was strictly a jurisdictional matter, and the premiers tended to seek greater prerogatives because they wanted more power for themselves. In general, the federal government had a greater call on the loyalty of the voters and taxpayers of those provinces, who identified themselves much more strongly by nationality than by province. As Quebec was the only French-speaking jurisdiction in North America above the level of a municipality, its position was quite different. Apart from whatever reservations Quebeckers still had about Confederation, and however there lingered, even latently, a desire for their own country, there was with all the French Québécois a concern to have in their own hands the powers to assure the survival of the French culture. It had been no small achievement to survive for 340 years since Champlain founded Quebec, and they were more convinced than ever of their right and duty to survive culturally. Some politicians played on this susceptibility, but almost all Québécois genuinely felt it. This, in the hands of so skilful a barrister as Maurice Duplessis, led to an elaborate constitutional argument for maximum decentralization that Duplessis the extremely astute politician (he lasted as long as party leader and won as many elections as King) put in simple and powerful terms to his electors. King was not prepared for this kind of an exchange; he never had really understood the particular concerns of Quebec, though he certainly recognized their existence and, unlike Borden, Meighen, Bennett, and the other leaders of the Conservative Party between Macdonald and Brian Mulroney, the need both to accommodate and even co-opt them. But he left it to Lapointe and St. Laurent to speak for him at any emotional level to his French-speaking compatriots. And where Lapointe was a hardball politician who moved up over many years in Laurier's shadow, St. Laurent was brought in on the eve of his sixtieth birthday as a political leader of the government in Quebec, never having considered a political career in his life.

Duplessis had advantages of formation and temperament, and King was now seventy-two and very tired. Duplessis, just turning fifty-six, was in his prime. These were the protagonists, and Duplessis set it up to advocate greater provincial powers as a dutiful believer in Canada and made it impossible for the Liberals to smear him as an extremist as they had in 1939, when he was pilloried as a Nazi-sympathizer. Duplessis knew that as long as he made his arguments as a respectable believer in Canada (which he sincerely was, unlike a number of his successors as premier of Quebec), the other provincial leaders, as long as they made the federalist obeisances their electors required, would support, for their own jurisdictionally venal reasons, greater powers to tax and spend for themselves. Laurier and Borden had had one Federal-Provincial Conference each. King had one and then rolled out Rowell-Sirois to use the depression as a way of reducing the provinces almost to municipalities. He had plenty of warning of what was coming, but was startled at the force of Duplessis's argument and the suavity and legal reconditeness with which it was advanced.

Essentially, Duplessis made the argument that the provinces had contracted with each other to create the federal government and could not have their agreed rights removed unilaterally by that government, even with the approval of a majority of the provinces; that all Quebec sought was the free exercise of the rights granted to it and the other provinces in 1867 by their own agreement, nothing more or less, with complete liberty to other provinces to make whatever arrangements they wished with the federal government. "The British North America Act gave the provinces exclusive power to legislate in excessively important matters, notably education, municipal institutions, public works in the province, hospitals, asylums, charitable institutions, the administration of justice, and generally everything touching on property and civil rights. To meet these expenses, the provinces were accorded natural resources, public lands, forests, mines and minerals, hydraulic and hydroelectric power, and as a source of revenue, direct taxes."[118] The federal proposals had revived Rowell-Sirois and suggested a complete provincial vacation of taxes on personal and corporate income, capital, and successions, in exchange for a grant based on the gross national product. Duplessis pointed out that the British North America Act had accorded the provinces "an incontestable right of priority" (which could certainly be contested, but not that the provinces had at least a concurrent right), and that in the last eighteen months of the Second World War the federal government had raised $450 million from personal and corporate income taxes alone in Quebec, which was more than five times the revenues of the province from all other sources combined. He considered the proposals on succession duties, an institution of the civil law that the federal government did not touch for the first seventy-five years of Confederation (as it had not touched income taxes for fifty years), to be unconstitutional.

Duplessis gave a very detailed analysis of the federal proposals that left little doubt that the objective of them was to take over the direct governance of every important policy area and the revenue sources to fund them, and reduce the provinces to identikit ministates whose officials would play house on a shoestring budget. The provincial insufficiency of revenue to deal with their obligations in the 1930s was, under the federal proposals, to be dealt with by ceding the spending obligation and the areas of shared revenue rights entirely to the federal government. Duplessis's proposal was to leave the spending obligations where they were, but for the provinces to repossess their full participation in the shared taxing jurisdictions. To a substantial extent, the problem in the 1930s had been addressed by King's constitutional amendment granting the federal government the right to establish and fund an unemployment insurance system. As between the two approaches in the postwar context, Ottawa could not possibly bring Quebec along with its plan, given Quebec's need to retain control of the institutions, especially education, which assured the flourishing of the French fact in North America, and Macdonald and Laurier (both of whom Duplessis frequently quoted) had done their best, sometimes unsuccessfully, to protect French rights outside Quebec. The inability of Quebec to repose full confidence in what would almost be a unitary state with a two-thirds non-French cultural majority in Canada was not unreasonable, and King and St. Laurent could not call Duplessis an extremist for seeking the letter of what Macdonald, Cartier, Brown, Taché, Galt, Mowat, McGee, Tilley, Tupper, and the other members of the Grand Coalition of 1864 to 1867 had agreed. His argument could not fail to tempt the other premiers, especially in the fiscally stronger provinces.

The Quebec nationalists, who had reviled Duplessis as an Uncle Tom, unanimously supported him. André Laurendeau for the Bloc Populaire, the seventy-eight-year-old Henri Bourassa in *Le Devoir*, and, through an authorized spokesman, Cardinal Villeneuve, all endorsed his position. (Writing with the cardinal's approval in *Le Droit*, Camille L'Heureux called Duplessis's presentation "a masterpiece. It is a magnificent and a solid document of a great democrat, of a real statesman, of a true Canadian animated by the spirit of the Fathers of Confederation, of a leader of national stature. It is useless, in fact, to have rights guaranteed by a constitution, if this constitution does not accord at the same time the full capacity to exercise them.")[119] King and his finance minister, James Ilsley, had not thought it through, and they were both too tired and gone in years to take on Duplessis, who was now unbeatable in Quebec.

The federal government could have made a deal on the basis Duplessis proposed, which was a legitimate update of the 1867 arrangements. The failure to do it would haunt the country for a long time. Duplessis was a conservative as well as a Quebec nationalist; most of those who came after him in Quebec were just provincial nationalists. King wrote in his diary that Duplessis "made a fool speech . . . it was in the nature of an appeal to the masses . . . name should be Duplicity. A most asinine kind of speech – all attempt to have it appear that the Dominion was for centralization."[120] (It was, and King apparently sincerely did not realize it.) When he returned to the Quebec railway station from Ottawa, thousands greeted the premier, led by his eighty-eight-year-old leader in the Legislative Council, the distinguished historian Sir Thomas Chapais (who had been the leader of the opposition in the Council throughout the long Liberal reign of 1897 to 1936 and again in the recent Godbout term from 1939 to 1944. He was one of four people who were simultaneously a senator and a Quebec legislative councillor).

King spent much of the spring, starting as soon as the conference with the provinces had ended, in London, and had his now customary liver-busting round of sumptuous lunches and dinners. The king was very interested in the Gouzenko affair; Averill Harriman was very negative about the Russians, especially foreign affairs minister Vyacheslav Molotov, though he thought Stalin too was completely unreliable. Churchill's heart was breaking as Attlee consented to the breakup of the Empire: India was going, with Egypt and Palestine not far behind. King tried to buck him up with comments on the value of self-government. King greatly liked field marshals Harold Alexander and Bernard Montgomery, though they did not like each other. King saw in Montgomery the grandson of the biographer of Christ, Dean Farrar, and admired his asceticism; Montgomery did not wish to stay with Alexander, the new governor general of Canada, when he came to Canada. King repeatedly urged Churchill to retire from the party leadership and focus on writing and Fulton-like speeches. Churchill, though seventy-one, still thought he could lead his party to victory in a general election, which was one of the few things he had not achieved in his career (and he did, though after King was dead). King, who had accomplished that feat six times (including 1925) was everywhere feted as a timeless and admired political leader. While in London, he passed Macdonald as the longest-serving Canadian prime minister (though this did not include Sir John's time as premier of the Province of Canada).

The Cold War became progressively more rigid and preoccupying. The main peace conference took place in Paris from July to October 1946. (De Gaulle had resigned and the French changed governments every few months for the next twelve years.) King conveniently convinced himself that "Canada would expect me to go," as he was the senior world leader and one of the few who had led his country through the war.[121] He was not especially active at the conference, which broke down over the Russian objection to anything more than an observer role for anyone except themselves and the Americans, British, and French. King took little part and was edgy and unreasonable to his staff. On August 6, he listened to Molotov's remarks and concluded that Molotov's "whole performance throughout the day was one akin to that of Duplessis; no sincerity in it at all."[122] King was losing his touch to make that sort of comparison, though Duplessis's verbal excesses were still occasionally inexplicable. King loved hobnobbing intimately with the world's most powerful statesmen, but the righteous Protestant was always appalled by the opulence and grandiosity of these events, one of the reflexes that kept him close to Canadians, a country without glitz or any toleration of glitz. He wrote on August 9, "The social life of the kind one sees in a great capital is something which terrifies me. I thank God for not having been drawn into that whirlpool of suspicion, vanity, deception."[123] He had an innocuous but cordial reunion with Molotov.

On August 22 (after visiting Canadian war sites in Normandy*), he went to Nuremberg and watched some of the proceedings against the accused Nazi war criminals. His descriptions of some of the defendants are interesting. "Streicher and a few of the others looked more like real criminals [than did Göring and Ribbentrop]. It was terrible to think that that particular group of men were seeking to exterminate groups of men, women, and children – burn bodies. . . . The world had known nothing like it in all of its history. If there ever was a real exhibition of what hell can be and must be," that must be it. They looked into the cells of the prisoners, and Rudolf Hess was in his. "When I looked in,

---

* He was conducted around the Normandy sites by his future literary executor, Colonel C.P. Stacey, who found his French "excruciatingly bad," and King personally "most affable," but thought his conversation banal, like "any old gentleman in the back of a Toronto streetcar."[124]

his eyes suddenly blazed up as though he recognized me. . . . They were like coals of fire. He himself is like a man dying of consumption. A hideous, pathetic, figure. I shall never forget the look in his face."[125] King was as impressed by General Georges-Philéas Vanier as ambassador to France (he had been ambassador to Free France) as he was censorious of Vincent Massey, whom King considered, to the end, a self-serving toady, snob, and low careerist. (Massey was some of that, but was also very effective at the different positions he held.) Despite lecturing his entourage on their hotel bills, King returned, as was now his agreeable custom, on the Queen Mary.

Dean Acheson, the U.S. undersecretary of state, came to visit King, and he found him impressive. Acheson (whose mother was a Gooderham from Toronto) was a very capable foreign policy expert and would be a distinguished secretary of state. King was overly impressed with James Byrnes, the current secretary of state, whom Truman was about to dismiss, and showed again that he was starting to lose his touch when he concluded on September 21, 1946, that former vice president Henry Wallace, an even more eccentric mystic than King himself and a fellow-traveller of Stalin and Molotov to boot, "has the popular end of the current controversy."[126] (Truman had fired Wallace, and Wallace was accusing him of fomenting difficulties with the Soviet Union.) King's interpretation was explicable only by a decline in his political acuity and instinct. He was starting to slip and had publicly confirmed that he would not seek re-election.

The peace conference reconvened in New York in November and December, and Italy, Hungary, Bulgaria, Finland, and Romania, all made their peace with Russia and each other. King returned at the end of August and finally faced the fact that he was on the way out. He relinquished external affairs to St. Laurent, while Ilsley took justice and left finance to Douglas Abbott, a capable English Quebecker. Brooke Claxton became defence minister and Paul Martin, an able and bilingual Franco-Ontarian, took over the constitutionally sensitive field of health and welfare. The promotion of St. Laurent comported a rise in status for Lester Pearson also, as undersecretary, and King "was struck by his fine face and appearance. There was a light from within which shone through his countenance."[127] King probably had some premonition by now that St. Laurent and Pearson would lead the Liberal

Party after him (ultimately with fourteen years as prime minister between them).

On February 21, 1947, Attlee cabled Truman that Britain could no longer afford to conduct the defence of Greece against internal communist subversion supported by Stalin (in contravention of his spheres-of-influence agreement with Churchill in Moscow in October 1944) and was withdrawing the forty thousand British troops in Greece. Truman secured at least partial bipartisan support, addressed an emergency session of Congress on March 12, and asked for $400 million of emergency aid to Greece and Turkey. He warned that failure to act at once would imperil Europe, the Middle East, and all of Asia. He enunciated what became known as the Truman Doctrine, a policy of containing Soviet expansion by assisting countries that were resisting its aggression, whether overt or by subversion. At the Moscow foreign ministers' conference in March and April 1947, General George C. Marshall, who had replaced King's friend James Byrnes as secretary of state, and Ernest Bevin, now Britain's foreign affairs minister, failed to make any progress over Germany, from which Molotov and Stalin proposed to extract $10 billion in reparations. Beyond that, the Soviet leaders seemed to seek as much chaos and misery as possible. Marshall became convinced that it would be impossible to achieve any agreement with Stalin, and after stops in Berlin and Paris and discussions with experts, he ordered preparation of a report, by a group chaired by George Kennan (who had composed the Long Telegram), to recommend measures for the reinforcement of non-communist Europe.

Marshall spoke to the American people on April 28 and said, "The patient is sinking while the doctors deliberate," in reference to Congress. On June 5, after extensive discussion with Truman, Acheson, Kennan, Charles Bohlen (head of the State Department's Russian desk and Roosevelt and Truman's interpreter with Stalin), and others, Marshall revealed at a commencement address at Harvard University what became known as the Marshall Plan for combatting, as Marshall said, "hunger, poverty, desperation, and chaos" in Europe. He eschewed any animosity to anyone, but it was clear enough that it was an anti-Soviet defensive move. Marshall called upon the countries of Europe, including Eastern Europe, and the Soviet Union itself, to define their own needs and uses for assistance and work out a plan of economic and social recovery which the United States was largely prepared to fund. Marshall said, "The whole world's future hangs on proper judgment, hangs on the realization by the American people of what can best be done, or what must be done."[128] King's initial reaction was relief that the Americans might be giving the Europeans enough resources for Britain and Western Europe to increase their customary levels of imports from Canada, which would enable Canada to alleviate its negative balance of payments with the United States. King had little early recognition of the visionary and generous nature of what Marshall and Truman proposed. In December, the Canadian government did announce that it would assist the Marshall Plan with a parallel program of credits for the Europeans to buy Canadian commodities when feasible; $706 million worth of food and raw materials and some finished goods were sold to the United States for shipment to Europe under the Marshall Plan, and generous loans were made by Canada to Europe to facilitate these purchases.

On June 10 to 12, President and Mrs. Truman visited Ottawa and were present on Parliament Hill when portraits were unveiled in the Centre Block rotunda of Sir Robert Borden, who had died in 1937, and Mackenzie King. It was a fine occasion, and Governor General Alexander spoke eloquently of the two wartime leaders. King concluded, in his diary, "If anyone would have me believe that there was not behind all this a plan that was being worked out by invisible forces representing Divine Providence, and something of the inevitable Justice, I should tell him that he lacked ordinary intelligence. To speak of this as coincidence is just perfect nonsense. It is evidence of a moral order based on Righteousness and Justice which in the end rules the world and determines the final issues."[129] (Sometimes an unveiling is just an unveiling, even when so distinguishedly attended.) The conversations of the two leaders were very cordial, and Truman's address to Parliament well-composed and well-received. But King did not feel he had such an intimate rapport with Truman as he had had with Roosevelt. (He didn't really with Roosevelt either, but Roosevelt enjoyed enfolding the susceptible in his vast charm and power, and Truman was a much more direct, uncomplicated personality.)

A conference was hastily organized in Paris between the Americans and the prospective recipients of their assistance in Europe. Molotov quickly stormed out of the conference, denouncing what was officially called the European Recovery Program as a "vicious American scheme for using dollars to buy" influence in Europe. All the satellite countries were pressured into declining to participate: Poland, Romania, Bulgaria, Hungary, Czechoslovakia, and Yugoslavia, as well as the U.S.S.R. and the Soviet zone of Germany. This was another disastrous blunder by Stalin; in pulling out and attacking the U.S. plan, he assured its passage by the Republican-led Congress and painted Soviet communism as a retrograde, dictatorial empire of brute force and economic stagnation against the Western forces of democracy and economic growth. When the international game evolved from war-making, chicanery, and sub-version and turned to the rights and welfare of the war-weary masses of the world, Stalin's heavy-handed treachery and authoritarianism were no match for the tough but unaffected generosity of Truman and the other surviving members of the team assembled by Roosevelt (with whom, inevitably, King's spiritualists now claimed he was in contact, along with Laurier, Gladstone, and the others). On September 18, 1947, Andrei Vyshinsky, Soviet deputy foreign minister and former chief prosecutor at Stalin's show trials in the 1930s, where he executed his principal colleagues, denounced the United States in the UN Security Council as "warmongers," and on October 5 Moscow announced the creation of the Cominform (Communist Information Bureau), the suc-cessor to the Comintern (Communist International), which Stalin had theoretically discontinued in 1943 as a sop to Roosevelt and Churchill, who wearied of its revolutionary incitements to their peoples, especially in the British colonial empire.

Despite their differences on almost everything else, on November 29, 1947, the United States and the Soviet Union pushed through at the United Nations a resolution approving the partition of the Palestine Mandate into predominantly Jewish and Arab areas, and Britain announced it would withdraw its fifty thousand soldiers there over the following six months.

King returned to Europe in the autumn of 1947, chiefly for the wedding of Princess Elizabeth to the nephew of Earl Mountbatten. En route in New York, after dinner with Mr. and Mrs. John D.

Rockefeller, he was "horrified" to discover that his suite on the *Queen Elizabeth* would cost $2,200. He was prepared to move to steerage to avoid such a thing, and an accompanying Canadian National Railway executive was able to arrange with the New York manager of Cunard to give the Canadian government King's sitting room at no charge. "There certainly was a providence looking over me, to have saved this situation," King wrote in his diary. "It would be a tragic business where, after all the years I have been in public life, the nation left with the impression that I really cared for luxury and extravagance."[130] (King was deeply upset that his cook at Laurier House, Mrs. Gooch, who was in his party, lost her steamer trunk and went to great trouble to help her retrieve it. It eventually caught up with them in Paris. To the end, he remained a strange amalgam of self-indulgent and self-conscious introversion, unfeigned modesty and humility, and touching generosity of spirit.)

He brought with him, over his arm, the mink coat Canada gave the princess as a wedding gift and presented it to her. He was amused that King George VI had the same concerns about Princess Elizabeth and her husband coming to Canada as King George V had expressed to him more than twenty years before about his sons, the future George VI and Edward VIII, making the same trip. He received the Order of Merit, an exalted honour, as a direct gift from the king, and had his usual tour of the palaces and great houses of London and the inner shires. He returned almost convinced by the stern conviction of Churchill, who was in paroxysms about the demise of the Empire, and Bevin and others, that a third world war could break out at any moment. This was nonsense, given America's arsenal of atomic weapons. King retuned to Ottawa in early December and had an extensive talk with Governor General (Field Marshal, Viscount) Alexander, who was expecting war in six months, not two weeks as King suggested. They agreed that, on consideration, Truman and Marshall doubtless had the determination to threaten atomic attack and Stalin would "climb down." King was afraid of chemical and bacteriological war. The division of India and Pakistan was already going badly, and King was advised to expect a good deal of Arab-Jewish violence in the partitioning of Palestine. It was a grim time, not in the least reminiscent of the false euphoria that engulfed the world after the First

World War, but now the United States was engaged in global affairs, and the prospects were, in fact, infinitely more promising than they had been a generation before, when Mackenzie King was already in his current position but no other government leader in the world was, not even Stalin.[131]

In late December, King intervened in cabinet to overrule St. Laurent's proposal that Canada agree to serve on the United Nations Temporary Commission on Korea. King took the view that Canada knew nothing of the Far East, had no capacity to influence events there, and should have nothing to do with it, and his view prevailed. Over the New Year, King and Pearson, with St. Laurent less involved, cooked up a plan for telling Truman and Marshall that Canada was concerned about the extent of American interference in the Far East. It was an asinine initiative that was about to be overwhelmed by events. The United States governed Japan and the Communists were now clearly winning the Chinese civil war and had fomented revolts in Malaya and Vietnam. King and Pearson were dreaming and had a fatuous vision of placating Asian communism. Once Pearson went to the United States to make representations, as King and St. Laurent agreed he should, he quickly grasped the American view of the gravity of events in the Far East and of their determination not to have communist powers sweep up defenceless countries as Stalin had in Eastern Europe. On receiving a cable from Pearson from New York, King was incited to write that the episode "has considerably shaken my faith in Pearson's judgment. . . . Much too ready to be influenced by American opinion."[132] A month before, King had come back from London announcing that a third world war was about to break out in two weeks, heralded by Soviet attacks with chemical weapons; he was not a natural source for such criticism.

On January 7, 1948, St. Laurent went to Laurier House for dinner, and he and King repaired to the prime minister's library for a discussion afterwards. St. Laurent told King that if this impasse was not resolved, he and Ilsley, the justice minister, would have to resign. King did not understand this, and eventually they worked out a compromise in which St. Laurent would tell the House that the UN commission on Korea, which Canada would join, could only act, as far as Canada was concerned, over the whole Korean Peninsula, which assured that it would be inactive. This cooled things out, but it was increasingly clear how crotchety and eccentric King was becoming. For good measure, St. Laurent told King his fears of imminent war were, he thought, unfounded, and that he did not expect there would be another world war for at least fifty years, if ever. Canada had been elected as a temporary member of the UN Security Council, and King appointed General McNaughton as the country's representative. King had favoured McNaughton as governor general but felt he had to defer to the appointment of so eminent a candidate as Field Marshal Viscount Alexander. (Field Marshal Montgomery, when visiting King, had expressed the greatest respect and liking for McNaughton and professed a desire to see him again. Given his role in McNaughton's removal, this was disingenuous.)

6. Mackenzie King VIII: Twilight, 1948–1949

On January 20, 1948, King announced to a Liberal Party dinner at the Château Frontenac that he would retire and was calling for a leadership convention in approximately six months. He received a tremendous ovation at several points in his remarks of over an hour, especially when he said that he was more thoroughly at the head of a united party and government than ever. His had been an astonishing feat of political survival and accomplishment.

King was very concerned about the Middle East, as was Pearson, but both entertained unrealistic hopes for a conciliatory solution, King even citing *Industry and Humanity* again, which had no possible applicability to such an area of permanent crisis. Britain had effectively promised Palestine as a homeland for the Jews without compromising the rights of the Arabs, which was a chimera, an impossibility whose cynicism is mitigated only by the desperate times of 1917, when Balfour made his very consequential Declaration. The United States – although Marshall and some others did not agree with Truman, and Truman himself took his time coming to the conclusion – was prepared to use force to partition the territory, as the only solution resided in some division of Palestine between Jews and Arabs. King and Pearson, with St. Laurent again skirting the issue for a time, tried to devise a method of not implying a willingness to provide forces without having a direct breach with the United States. St. Laurent again got the government through without serious disagreement by supporting a Belgian resolution to encourage the permanent Security Council members to pursue conciliation, and, if the American resolution to enforce a partition came to a vote, to abstain.

On February 25, 1948, a *coup d'état* in Prague installed the communists, and on March 10, Jan Masaryk, the Czech foreign minister and son of the founder of the country, leapt or was pushed from a window and died. (King at first considered this a suicide, and, as he had known Masaryk, he wondered at the implications of Masaryk, John G. Winant, who was the former U.S. ambassador in London, and former Japanese ambassador to France, K. Kato, all committing suicide. "All three were real personal friends, and three of the best men I have known. What an age we are living in!" They were very distinguishable cases, and only Winant's was the result of a conventional depression.[133])

On March 17, Truman addressed Congress and called the Soviet Union a menace to all Europe and to world peace and asked for immediate passage of the Marshall Plan and reinstitution of conscription. The Italian election on April 18 was a fierce contest between the leftist coalition led by the Communist Party and their leader, Palmiro Togliatti, and the Christian Democrats led by Premier Alcide De Gasperi. There was considerable pre-electoral violence in northern Italy, heavy intervention by the Roman Catholic Church, and massive financing from abroad, specifically the CIA and the Soviet Union. Pope Pius XII effectively declared a Communist vote an act of self-excommunication. The popular formulation was "When you vote, God sees you but Stalin doesn't." The Christian Democrats won, 48.5 per cent to 31 per cent, and the democratic socialists who provided about a third of the leftist vote, flaked off and made their peace with the government. On May 14, the United States recognized the State of Israel, which was immediately attacked by its Arab neighbours who refused to abide by the United Nations partition. Despite being heavily outnumbered, the Jews prevailed and Israel expanded considerably beyond what was initially designated as its borders.

On June 11, 1948, Republican senator Arthur Vandenberg presented a resolution which was quickly adopted by the U.S. Senate authorizing military alliances with regional collective security groups in further-ance of the United Nations Charter. On June 23, the Western Allied powers enacted currency reforms in West Berlin, contrary to the Soviet ambition to circulate its own currency throughout the city. The next day, Stalin abruptly closed the land access from West Germany to West Berlin, and the United States, with the full cooperation of Great Britain and France, began the air supply of the 2.1 million residents of West Berlin. Truman made it clear that any interception of Allied aircraft would be an act of war and ostentatiously moved two squadrons of B-29s and escorting aircraft to West Germany, which were assumed to be ready to launch an atomic attack on the Soviet Union. This was in fact a ruse, as the planes were not equipped to carry atomic bombs, but the Russians never discovered that.

This was another disastrous blunder by Stalin, seeming to break his undertakings, threaten war, and strangle the prostrate city of Berlin, in which there were no military targets. And he failed; he was clearly afraid of the power of the United States, and after 321 days he abandoned the blockade and reopened land traffic to West Berlin from West Germany. Henceforth, the Western Allied objective was to resuscitate Germany as a great industrial power and as a military ally, precisely what Stalin had feared. This sudden escalation of the Cold War did not lead to a great deal of consultation with Canada and swiftly brushed past the King-Pearson formula of equivocal and con-ciliatory noises and avoidance of seeming to fall in too quickly behind the United States. King did have some claim to being one of the cre-ators of the Western Alliance, as the arrangements he had made with Roosevelt in the 1930s and during the war were cited by him and the Americans as the forerunner for what became the North Atlantic Treaty Organization.

In the face of these events, King pulled in behind Attlee and Truman and was steadily advising his cabinet, caucus, and Parliament of the gravity of the international situation. Tempered only by his con-cern that Pearson was capable of immersing Canada in international crises imprudently, King scrambled to the front line of the Cold Warriors again, the position he had held at the outset with the Gouzenko affair almost three years before. On March 19, he wrote in his diary, "It is truly appalling how far the Russians have been permitted and have been able to get ahead in the four years since the war [it was only three years]. I cannot but have the feeling that the United States with its fiddling and fussing and interfering in everything and affording them the platform they have had, has been responsible, as was the League of Nations, for enabling the situation to develop to the point where it has. A perfectly appalling menace."[134] Again, complaints of fiddling and fussing from Mackenzie King were bizarre. He did continue to support British temporizing in Palestine over the American preparedness to force a division, but events took care of that. He also claimed to have been vindicated in Korea, but subsequent events would indicate that the entire debate – which had caused St. Laurent, the clear heir apparent to the headship of the government, to raise the possibility of resignation – completely missed the point of what was happening in Korea.

King and Truman met at a convocation ceremony in Virginia on April 1, 1948, and had a very satisfactory talk. King was always pretty co-operative when consulted by U.S. leaders, and his instincts and loyalties in world affairs were impeccable, as long as he wasn't gulled by wicked people, as he had been briefly by Hitler, or suddenly asked to deal with a very complicated problem like the Middle East. King even had second thoughts about buying a British aircraft carrier, which would be renamed *Magnificent*. "What Canada wants with the largest aircraft carrier afloat under a title like that, I don't know." (The United States had thirty aircraft carriers that were larger, and the British eleven, and even Australia had two sister ships.) King had no notion of what a navy could do for national pride. When Canada received her first cruiser, from the Royal Navy, she was not for a time renamed but continued as HMCS *Uganda* "after the protectorate."[135] On April 17, Paul-Henri Spaak, Belgian foreign minister and one of the leaders of the movement for European cooperation, came to Ottawa and to Laurier House, and King had a very agreeable and informative talk with him. Spaak was concerned but more cool-headed than King, and was confident that Stalin could be deterred by the Americans. There was endless debate and discussion in cabinet about the international tensions, and King occasionally met with the three opposition leaders, John Bracken of the Progressive Conservatives, M.J. Coldwell of the

CCF, and Solon Low of Social Credit, and they were generally supportive. King was reassured to find from St. Laurent and his other French-Canadian ministers that there would be no hesitation from Quebec in the event of a threat of hostilities, that any dispute with the Soviet Union could be fairly presented as a confrontation with communism, and that Quebec would exceed all parts of the country in the vigour of its response, spurred on by the Roman Catholic Church in full battle cry, from Pius XII down. (Villeneuve had died in 1947, and his authority would not be replicated in Quebec until the elevation of Paul-Émile Léger, a close protégé of Pius XII, as cardinal-archbishop of Montreal in 1952.)

King's declining days as prime minister were irritated by a false effort to blame him for negligence in sending the Canadian battalions to Hong Kong shortly before the Japanese attack there in December 1941. The matter was resolved in King's favour by documents tendered to the British House of Commons in response to questions there, but not before King referred to the former Conservative House leader Gordon Graydon, in an unusual association, as being "at best . . . of the calibre of a basketball fan."[136] On April 20, 1948, King surpassed Sir Robert Walpole's record as the longest-serving prime minster in the history of Britain or any of the Commonwealth countries but felt "terrible depression and sadness,"[137] though the testimonials to him in the House were generous. On July 22, Newfoundland voted 52.3 per cent to 47.7 in favour of joining Canada as opposed to the resumption of responsible government. The cabinet agreed that the majority was adequate and proceeded. It was one of the last of King's innumerable successes in office: Sir John A. Macdonald had joined four provinces and added three, Sir Wilfrid Laurier added two more, and King completed the country (though it was under his successor that Newfoundland actually joined Canada).

On July 19, John Bracken announced his retirement as Progressive Conservative leader. King wrote in his diary, "I confess it made me feel quite sad. Bracken's life as leader has really been a tragedy. He should never have left Manitoba. Was never fit for leadership in Ottawa. Has been a failure in every way, but to have him not merely kicked around by his own party but suffering from what may be an incurable disease, made one feel a profound sympathy." He correctly thought Ontario premier George Drew "the most likely person to be chosen leader, simply because he has a dominating way with him. . . . He has an arrogant manner, worse than either Meighen or Bennett, and has a more bitter tongue than Meighen. This helped to destroy these men and the party. Having that type of man as an opponent has been the best asset I have had. . . . I could not stand having Drew as an opponent . . . perpetual antagonism."[138] He congratulated himself, as was his custom, on his good judgment in retiring at the approach of the eighth Conservative leader he would face (counting Meighen twice).

Less welcome news for King came from Quebec on July 28. In 1942, Duplessis had allowed the "rental" by Godbout for five years of Quebec's powers over direct taxes to Ottawa, to lapse in 1947. He had embarked on a program of rural electrification, and by his policy of generous legislation to protect workers and raise their wages, but placing comparative restraints on labour unions, he had attracted a good deal of investment to Quebec, and the province was flourishing. By maintaining clerical personnel in the schools and hospitals at lower wages than would be paid to secular people, and were paid in the other provinces, he avoided debt, reduced taxes, and devoted most of the budget to what would today be called infrastructure: schools, hospitals, universities, roads, as well as advanced social programs, including work accident insurance and daycare. There is no question that the heavy roads and public works budgets generated unusually large financial contributions to the governing Union Nationale, though, despite perfervid efforts by current and subsequent opponents to find it, there has never been any evidence that contracts were inflated in amount at the taxpayers' expense to the benefit of the party treasury. Duplessis perfected the techniques of Quebec premiers Taschereau and Gouin, but did not lower them ethically. Duplessis's nationalist policies were a combination of demanding the letter of the British North America Act's division of taxing and spending powers and jurisdiction, as he had at the Federal-Provincial Conference in April 1946 – a tactically brilliant approach that gratified the nationalists by repulsing centralization and upholding Quebec's rights, and impressed the conservatives by adhering rigorously to the constitution – and tokenistic gestures. He renamed Spencer Wood, the home of the lieutenant-governor, Bois de Coulonge, and, more importantly, he gave Quebec the now familiar blue-and-white fleur-de-lys flag, a politically reward-ing symbol of Quebec's distinct identity.

The 1948 Quebec election was the usual rock 'em, sock 'em affair. Adélard Godbout kicked off on June 13 with the warning that the re-election of Duplessis would give Quebec "a dictatorship of the same calibre as that which existed in Germany with Hitler and which exists at present with Stalin in Russia."[139] Duplessis replied on June 20 that there were communists in Quebec, as the publication of their slender newspaper *Le Combat*, and the election in Montreal of convicted spy Fred Rose as federal MP, proved. The two leaders were scraping the barrel, accusing each other of fronting fascist and communist elements. Duplessis left it to his provincial secretary, Omer Côté, to accuse his opponent in Montreal Saint-Jacques, Roger Ouimet (Ernest Lapointe's son-in-law), of being a communist and to declare that "the Liberal Party is the party of war and conscription, of concentration camps, and of shameful immigration, and the Union Nationale is the party of schools, peace, order, and prosperity."[140]

Montreal mayor Camillien Houde and Maurice Duplessis, estranged since 1931, when Duplessis replaced Houde as provincial Opposition leader, had a grand reconciliation and held an immense joint assembly at Montreal's Marché Saint-Jacques on July 22. Duplessis gave an aggressive recitation of his usual themes, confin-ing the red smear to mere insinuations of Liberal lassitude, and Houde followed by taking up St. Laurent's claim in response to a recent parliamentary question that Quebec's Liberal French-speaking MPs, not Section 133 of the British North America Act, would protect the rights of French-speaking people in Canada. Houde rhetorically wondered which of these MPs could be so relied upon, and went through the Montreal area Liberal members of Parliament, asking, "Is it . . . ?" before naming each of the faceless Liberal backbenchers in turn, ending with Azellus Denis, the veteran MP for Saint-Denis, whom Houde called the "symbol of Liberal mediocrity." At each name, the huge audience, and the whole province by radio, became more infected with the spirit of the mayor's merrymaking. Houde carried on in this vein for half an hour and the crowd was reduced to a near-delirium of laughter.[141] Duplessis was determined to recover the nationalists and restore the two-party system in Quebec, which he had helped shatter fifteen years before by prying the Action Libérale Nationale (ALN) loose from the Liberals, and he did. In the intervening years, the ALN, Franc Parti, Bloc Populaire, Créditistes (the Quebec wing of the Social Credit Party), and CCF had all had some sort of deputation in Quebec.

On July 28, 1948, Duplessis's Union Nationale took eighty-four constituencies to eight for the Liberals, the worst defeat that party has ever suffered in Quebec, and took 53 per cent of the vote to 36 per cent Liberal and 10 per cent Créditiste. Godbout was defeated in his own district and King appointed him to the Senate, where he rejoined Bouchard. (He could have been succeeding King as prime minister had he accepted the succession to Lapointe when it was offered in 1941.) The distinguished representative of the wealthy Montreal district of Westmount, George C. Marler, spent election day golfing at his summer home at Métis on the Lower St. Lawrence and dozed off, expecting to awaken in the new government, and instead found out that he was the acting leader of the Opposition. King recorded in his diary his belief that Duplessis had won because of the attempt to centralize taxes in the federal-provincial discussions (which, as has been recorded, he entirely approved at the time and did not see, and nor did St. Laurent, the political hazards of it) and because of postwar inflation and the failure of his finance ministers, Ilsley and Abbott, to reduce taxes as well as cancelling war debt (which he also approved each year), and because, "most important of all, the organization Duplessis had built up based on moneys derived from liquor licence sources and the immense amount of money used by his government, his promises, patronage, etc. – straight corruption."[142] (King did not require any lessons from Duplessis or anyone else about how incumbent political parties financed themselves.) He wrote that "unfairly trying to concentrate too many of the taxes in federal hands, the unwillingness to make concessions to the provinces . . . handed over the Liberal ground on provincial rights to Duplessis" and Drew. King was typically oblivious to the fact that he had only himself to blame for that.

About ten years later, Duplessis said to his cabinet, "The nationalists in Quebec are a ten-pound fish on a five-pound line; you have to reel them in slowly and let them out slowly. I shut them up for ten years with the flag of Quebec; I'll shut them up for another ten years by opening an office in Paris and official relations with the French – we couldn't do it. in the Fourth Republic but we can with de Gaulle; and for ten years after that with a World's Fair in Montreal. After that, you will be on your own. Someone will take my place but you will not replace me."[143] The failure to make a durable constitutional and fiscal arrangement with Duplessis between 1944 and 1959, when it could have been done, has been a heavy burden on Canada since. Duplessis's successors either died before they could pursue a durable arrangement (Paul Sauvé and Daniel Johnson Sr.), or weren't strong enough politically to attempt one, or have been separatists who did not want an agreement.

The National Liberal Convention opened in the Ottawa Coliseum on August 5, 1948; voting was August 7. King had pushed various people to announce their candidacy and then withdraw in favour of St. Laurent. He didn't like James (Jimmy) Gardiner, who in his nomination speech made much of his friendship with King. "I took that with a grain of salt," wrote King, thinking Gardiner was prepared to join a cabal with Mitchell Hepburn and Charles Gavan Power, who was the third candidate. The vote, on the only ballot, was St. Laurent 843, Gardiner 323, Power 56. King had received a thunderous ovation when he addressed the convention the day before, especially for his favourite line: "I have the confidence of the Liberal Party in greater measure than I have ever possessed it."[144] After St. Laurent's election, King gave a rather moving reminiscence of how, on the way back from Lapointe's funeral, Power had told him that St. Laurent was definitely the man for the succession. This did not imply that King was in any hurry actually to hand over the premiership to his chosen and ratified successor. He went for a holiday in Maine with John D. Rockefeller and was still considering remaining as president of the Privy Council, to "help" the new prime minister.

On August 23, King received Earl Mountbatten, former viceroy of India, who told him and Alexander that "no words could describe the hate which the people of India had of Britain."[145] King made his last overseas visit, arriving at Cherbourg on the *Queen Mary* on September 20 and travelling to Paris by train with General Vanier, his ambassador. He had excellent conversations with the French and then in London with the British leaders, and everyone, including King, was more robust and reassured than they had been a year before. American leadership in the West was clearly effective and appreciated. King found Jawaharlal Nehru, the new Indian prime minister, "reminded me a little of Sir Wilfrid Laurier in his fine, sensitive way of speaking, using his hands, etc."[146] King came down with influenza and fatigue and asked that St. Laurent come and take his place at the Commonwealth Conference, and he did so. King was taking advice from Churchill's rather eccentric and indiscreet doctor, Lord Moran, formerly Charles Wilson, who diagnosed his problem as heart strain. King received a stream of the most exalted visitors in his suite in the Dorchester Hotel (named after Britain's greatest governor of Canada), and St. Laurent would explain to him at the end of each day the goings-on at the conference. King George VI himself arrived on October 21 and had a very cordial chat with his longest-serving prime minister. The king had told Nehru and the Pakistani leader, Muhammad Ali Jinnah, to meet and compose their differences. King, like the ghost of the conference, reached the apogee of his social prestige in London as visitors, telephone calls, and messages poured in to his hotel suite: the queen, Lady Astor, Mrs. Chamberlain, Mrs. Churchill, Rockefeller, culminating in a visit from Winston Churchill on October 29.

Churchill and King reminisced, and King ceremoniously asked him one question: "I asked if, during the time I had been in office, he had ever asked for anything that it was possible for our government to do which we had not done or if I had failed him in anything. He instantly said: 'You have never failed. You were helpful always. There was nothing that you did not do that could be done.' . . . I referred to his great services to the World and to freedom . . . and I said, 'God bless you,' as he was leaving. He came to my bedside and his eyes filled up with tears. . . . He was restraining feelings of emotion. We could not have had a pleasanter talk together."[147] Distinguished journalist Bruce Hutchison claims that King said he asked Churchill to kiss him,* and that Churchill did, but there is no record of it in his diary.[148]

---

* King also claimed to have kissed Roosevelt at their last meeting, on March 20, 1945. "I bent over and kissed him on the cheek. He turned it toward me for the purpose." This must be read with caution. (Conrad Black, *Franklin Delano Roosevelt*, p. 1094.)

Pearson arrived, and King thought he "had a fine intellectual and spiritual look. One could feel he had been participating in a campaign, which gave him a commanding look."[149] Pearson was now MP for the Ontario riding of Algoma East, and was about to be secretary of state for external affairs, and King was bringing the premier of Manitoba, Stuart Sinclair Garson, in as justice minister (the seventh provincial premier he had elevated to the federal ministry). Mackenzie King left London the next day and returned to Ottawa via New York on the *Queen Elizabeth*. (He was now almost a frequent passenger on the two great Cunard Queens.) King learned with delight in mid-Atlantic that Truman had been re-elected, an upset, as King feared that, with the Republicans, government by big business and "a certain jingoism" would have prevailed.

King was back in Ottawa on November 7 and took to his bed, where he received the governor general. He had arranged his resignation for Monday, November 15, and agreed with St. Laurent on the elevation of Robert Henry Winters to the cabinet from Nova Scotia. (Winters would be the runner-up contender for the Liberal leadership, and the post of prime minister, to succeed Pearson nearly twenty years later.) King attended upon the governor general at the appointed hour to tender his resignation and began a cascade of minor ceremonies as he withdrew from his great office, broadening down to addresses to office and household staff. He professed relief and happiness, but it is almost certain that his illness in Paris and London and its recurrences over the next twenty months were at least in part a psychosomatic response to giving up the position to which he had in every sense been wedded for decades, and to the pursuit of it for decades before that. He soldiered grimly into retirement.

William Lyon Mackenzie King would live on quietly for eighteen months. He died on July 22, 1950, aged seventy-six, following a heart attack, at his country home at Kingsmere. Many thousands filed past his casket in the Parliament Buildings, and he had a state funeral at St. Andrew's Presbyterian Church in Ottawa, which he had attended quite faithfully for decades. He was buried with his parents in Mount Pleasant Cemetery in Toronto, where wreaths from followers and admirers still frequently appear on anniversaries.

The evaluation of King is a challenge; it is easier to record what and who he was not. No one – the voters, his colleagues, other states-men – really knew what to make of him, and his acute insecurities forced him to invest excessive and contrived satisfaction in awards and deferences and ovations in the absence of a certainty of his own greatness or believably spontaneous attestations to it. The day he died, his long-time close colleagues Norman Robertson and Jack Pickersgill were unmoved. Robertson said, "I never saw a touch of greatness in him." Pickersgill felt no sadness. He was never a galva-nizing or bold leader, nor a great orator. But he was always there, and it was assumed that he was there (at the head of Canada) because he was extremely competent. It must be said that he was. He won five terms as prime minister, drew one election, and lost one, and served longer in that office than any holder of an analogous position in a serious democratic country in history. He was never involved in a really serious scandal, unlike Macdonald, as the Beauharnois affair did not personally implicate him, and Lapointe and Cardin prevented him from cracking down as hard as he would have liked in the Customs scandal of the 1920s. He never made an administrative error on the scale of Laurier's commitment to the Grand Trunk Railway, nor a political error on the scale of Macdonald's hanging of Riel or Laurier's approach to separate education in the new provinces of Saskatchewan and Alberta.

The most striking version of the dismissive case against King was made by the author of the Regina Manifesto and dean of law of McGill University, Francis Reginald (F.R.) Scott, who largely abandoned his attachments to the left in later years and had no particular aptitudes as a judge of political men and events, but was a perceptive and waspish observer. In a poem called "W.L.M.K." Scott wrote,

> How shall we speak of Canada,
> Mackenzie King dead?
> The Mother's boy in the lonely room
> With his dog, his medium and his ruins?
>
> He blunted us.

We had no shape
Because he never took sides,
And no sides
Because he never allowed them to take shape.

He skilfully avoided what was wrong
Without saying what was right,
And never let his on the one hand
Know what his on the other hand was doing.

The height of his ambition
Was to pile a Parliamentary Committee on a
        Royal Commission,
To have "conscription if necessary
But not necessarily conscription,"
To let Parliament decide—
Later.

Postpone, postpone, abstain.

Only one thread was certain:
After World War I
Business as usual,
After World War II
Orderly decontrol.
Always he led us back to where we were before.

He seemed to be in the centre
Because we had no centre,
No vision
To pierce the smoke-screen of his politics.

Truly he will be remembered
Wherever men honour ingenuity,
Ambiguity, inactivity, and political longevity.

> Let us raise up a temple
> To the cult of mediocrity,
> Do nothing by halves
> Which can be done by quarters.[150]

This was a witty sendup and there is much truth in it. But it doesn't explain King's success and gives no credit to his accomplishments. The fact that he was as successful politically as he was despite not being a gregarious and charming rascal as Macdonald was, nor an august and mellifluous bicultural tribune as Laurier was, must be counted as adding to his achievement in imposing himself on events so improbably and for so long. Unlike those men, who generally enjoyed the loyalty and affection of their colleagues and much of the public, but who allowed the quality of their cabinets gradually to run down, King maintained and renewed his cabinets, and his government was more talented after twenty years in office than in the early years. He did not have the magnificent vision of Macdonald, which led to a unique Confederation and the almost miraculously ambitious railway, and he did not have and personify, as Laurier did, the ideal of a bicultural country. But again, the fact that he was not particularly a visionary or an inspirational leader, or even an evidently courageous one, makes him something of an anti-hero. Thus his success, which surpassed Laurier's and came close to Macdonald's (who served twenty-eight years as prime minister of Canada and premier or co-premier of the Province of Canada, and won nine of eleven general elections and did found the country, though he didn't have to govern in the Great Depression or through a world war), enlarges rather than diminishes King's stature. The country never really warmed to him, and he lost in his own constituency four times while serving thirty-three years in Parliament, against Macdonald's loss of his constituency once in forty-seven years as a legislator, and never in forty-eight years for Laurier.

King has been much reviled for surrendering economic sovereignty to the United States. Prominent journalist Charles Lynch noted the centenary of his birth in 1974 by denouncing him as "a compromiser, an appeaser, a sort of fat Neville Chamberlain, with guile," responsible for transferring us "from the bosom of the British Mother onto the bony lap of the American Uncle."[151]

In fact, in the desperate year of 1940, King's initiative and Roosevelt's broad-mindedness vastly strengthened the prospects of embattled Britain and the security of Canada and its postwar prosperity. The task of assuring Canadian independence of the United States was something that was rightly put over to a less fraught era, when the survival of democratic government in the world would not be under mortal threat from an unholy alliance of Nazism, communism, and imperialist Japan.

Between 1937 and 1956, the share of Canadian exports that went to Britain declined from 40 per cent to 17 per cent, but that was because of American wealth and proximity and British economic decline.[152] The alternative wasn't more exports to Britain, it was Canadian economic stagnation. Canada's domestic market is too small to be autarkic; the country must deal with its problems as they arise and did so very effectively throughout King's long tenure as prime minister.

Above all, King understood the essential thread of Canadian history, the necessity of keeping the double majority of French and English Canadians together, and of balancing British and American influences while steadily enhancing the strength and independence of Canada. This was what began with Champlain's faith in a viable French entity in the northern part of the Americas, evolved into Carleton's vision of an Anglo-French colony, then Baldwin and LaFontaine's goal of an autonomous Anglo-French jurisdiction, and Macdonald's of a transcontinental, bicultural country autonomous of and allied to the British and Americans. Like Macdonald and Laurier, King understood and was fundamentally loyal to and protective of that vision of Canada, in its past and its future, and he led the country a very long way forward and left it in safe hands that directed it for most of the twenty years following his retirement.

He took over a country that didn't have authority over its own halibut fisheries and left one in close cooperation with the United Kingdom and the United States at the highest levels. While he was a less formidable as well as a less important statesman than Winston Churchill and Franklin D. Roosevelt, and he did not have the influence on or intimacy with them that he tried to imply to his electors, he was also never altogether overawed by them. It is true that he was somewhat snowed by Hitler at their one meeting, but so, to a degree, were many people; .

Hitler was a satanically cunning man, and King was quickly disabused. He was also quick to see the great merit in people such as de Gaulle and Eisenhower and Truman before their greatness was generally recognized, and to identify undiscovered talent, such as St. Laurent, Howe, and Pearson. He was very devious, unlike Macdonald, who was merely an expert with a ruse when conditions required or commended one, and he was rather bigoted toward Jews and non-whites, but violently disgusted by barbarism such as even Mussolini's police exhibited, not to mention the atrocities of the Third Reich. He sincerely espoused and advanced the cause of the disadvantaged and those of modest means, but was never hostile or envious toward the highly successful. No one will ever know or have a reliable insight into the full psychological story behind his lack of romantic success and his ancestor worship and spiritualism. But they are not strictly relevant to his accomplishments. He was cautious to a fault, but never terminally so, was never impetuous, and steadily broadened and deepened Canadian life and union for a whole generation.

His mastery of the war effort was his greatest achievement, and he was, undoubtedly, and despite his quirks, a great prime minister. The continuity of purpose: the pursuit of French-English conciliation, the balancing of British and American influences, and the growth of Canadian sovereignty and importance in the world that had motivated and been successfully pursued by Macdonald, Laurier, and King had been the constant themes of the governance of the country for almost a century. Macdonald was the Conservative leader from 1856 to 1891, and Laurier and King between them led the Liberal Party from 1887 to 1948, ninety-six years between the three, only four overlapping, and sixty-five of them at the head of government and the rest at the head of the official Opposition. Of course, there had been eight other prime ministers in the other twenty-seven years of the ninety-two. But in the same period, from 1856 to 1948, Great Britain had seventeen prime ministers leading twenty-nine separate governments and the United States had nineteen presidents and twenty administrations. The stability, continuity, and dexterity provided by John A. Macdonald, Wilfrid Laurier, and William Lyon Mackenzie King had brought Canada from a semi-autonomous congeries of disconnected colonies which need not have been more than a bargaining chip between the British and Americans, to one of the world's twelve or so most important countries. The position of Canada still had many ambiguities, as the personality of its recently retired prime minister reflected and amplified, but it was a remarkable achievement by three consecutive leaders, who performed a feat of continuous national leadership unequalled by contemporaries in any other country.

PART III

Realm:

1949–2014

Louis S. St. Laurent (1882–1973) and Maurice L. Duplessis (1890–1959). St. Laurent, minister of Justice or External Affairs 1942–1948, and prime minister of Canada 1948–1957, was an elegant and distinguished and altogether capable successor to Wilfrid Laurier and Ernest Lapointe. Duplessis was Quebec's longest serving party leader (1931–1959) and premier (1936–1939, 1944–1959). Though controversial and much denigrated by historians, his time was one of unprecedented economic growth, rising prosperity, and investment in schools, universities, social services, public works, and highways. An anti-separatist decentralizer, he was portrayed by St. Laurent and the Liberals as a reactionary when they should have made durable constitutional arrangements with him. (The other person whose hands are in the photograph was Ontario premier Leslie Frost.)

St. Laurent and Duplessis, Canada as a Middle Power, and Quebec in Pursuit of Autonomy, 1949–1966

1. Louis S. St. Laurent: Canada's Distinguished Uncle, 1949–1950

After thirty years in which the unfathomable Mackenzie King had faced a procession of Conservative leaders who never achieved great popularity or a lengthy incumbency, Louis Stephen St. Laurent was received with much enthusiasm. While he was not flamboyant, he was distinguished, straightforward, decisive, equable, had a large and attractive family, a French Canadian who was half Irish, spoke English without a trace of a French accent, had only entered public life as a duty and continued in it on the same basis, and had no motive except to serve the overarching national interest. In his person, he was conciliatory without being for a moment weak or insipid. He was a figure of moral authority, but of an avuncular and professional kind, not in the overbearing, domineering way of Arthur Meighen or R.B. Bennett; there was not at the outset of his career as prime minister, nor at any time afterward, anything substantial that any serious person could say against him. He was particularly friendly with C.D. Howe, who had grown into a unique status almost of a general manager of the Canadian economy, and with Lester Pearson, who had been his understudy in external affairs and whom he, with King, had promoted, and both expected to be the next Liberal leader.

George Drew had become the Progressive Conservative leader on October 2, 1948, and there was some concern that he could make inroads with the Liberals in Ontario, but his former status as an arch-conscriptionist and opponent of family allowances as a shabby payoff to Quebec could, Liberal strategists felt, backfire even in English Canada opposite such a moderate and reputable representative of French Canada as the new prime minister. St. Laurent had made a good impression substituting for King at the Commonwealth Conference in London, as he spoke strongly for solidarity in defence and European political cooperation and a North Atlantic defence community. He also became friendly with the Indian prime minister, Jawaharlal Nehru, and upheld the right of India to be a republic yet remain in the Commonwealth, and for the right of all member countries to choose whomever they wished as their chiefs of state. The British monarch became so by virtue of a British dynastic process and those countries of primarily British origin could logically share that monarch with the United Kingdom. St. Laurent and others felt that there was no reason to purport to require all Commonwealth countries to do so, as long as the British sovereign was recognized also as the head of the Commonwealth, if not the chief of state of each member state of the Commonwealth. At this remove, this seems a footling distinction in an organization of uncertain importance, but as the Commonwealth then consisted of Britain and the so-called White Dominions, and India was a very important but new country starting out in the world and rethinking its British connection almost 200 years after the time of Clive of India and 150 years after Warren Hastings, it was an important subject on which St. Laurent spoke clearly and effectively. He appeared, as his biographer Dale Thomson put it, to have the "rather unusual combination of Gallic warmth and Anglo-Saxon reserve, of idealism and common sense,"[1] and was a good deal clearer and more forthright than Mackenzie King, whose elliptical formulations had been familiar at these meetings for nearly thirty years and were not missed (though he himself was not underestimated for his qualities). At his first cabinet session as prime minister, St. Laurent took a cigarette out of his silver case and fitted it into his cigarette holder. Most of the ministers were smokers who had abstained in deference to King's disapproval of tobacco and were relieved to be able to indulge themselves.[2]

The first parliamentary session of the new prime minister opened on January 26, 1949. St. Laurent and Drew, facing each other, were a more stylish and vigorous duo than had been King, looking his seventy-four years, and the infirm John Bracken (who did not have a terminal illness as King had feared and lived on, out of politics, until 1969, when he died aged eighty-five). King beamed happily on proceedings from the end of the Treasury Bench rather than from one of the party leaders' chairs he had occupied since 1919. The Throne Speech was a commendable pre-electoral basket. It included ratification of membership in the North Atlantic Treaty Organization; the terms of Newfoundland's entry into Confederation; the St. Lawrence Seaway, at last to admit ocean-going ships to the Great Lakes; a trans-Canada highway; the extension of family allowances; and a royal commission on the arts and letters and science (the Massey Commission).

St. Laurent made a brief visit to President Truman on February 11 to seek his support in the St. Lawrence Seaway project, and Truman promised to do what he could. St. Laurent proposed broadening NATO into economic areas, but Truman was almost exclusively focused on the military alliance. In speaking in favour of adherence to NATO, St. Laurent said the democracies must be armed with over-whelming deterrent force, but not only military force. "It must be economic; it must be moral."[3] Parliament ratified NATO on March 28 with minimal debate and only two dissenting votes (from isolationist Quebec independents). St. Laurent welcomed Newfoundland to the country by radio on March 31, telling that province it was joining "a good country" where Newfoundland's distinctive personality would be welcomed and not threatened.[4] It was on a tour to the West in the spring of 1949 that St. Laurent jocularly said in Saskatchewan, where Tommy Douglas and the Co-operative Commonwealth Federation (CCF) formed the government, that socialists were "Liberals in a hurry." This was an aside that would lead to controversy.

The House was dissolved for new elections on June 25. The campaign was strenuous physically, but quite jovial; the Conservatives, having little to criticize in the government's record, accused it of being arrogant, centralizing, and socialistic. Efforts were made to sell Drew as a provincial autonomist in Quebec, and Douglas Abbott, the finance minister, had cut taxes following the electoral disaster sustained by the Liberals in that province. It was another smashing Liberal victory, with 191 MPs and 49.2 per cent of the popular vote (up from 117 MPs and 39.8 per cent in 1945) to 41 MPs and 29.7 per cent of the vote for the Progressive Conservatives (an increase of 2.1 per cent but a loss of 24 MPs). The CCF were down to 13 MPs on 13.4 per cent of the vote (from 28 MPs and 15.3 per cent), and Social Credit was down to 10 MPs and 2.3 per cent of the vote (from 13 MPs and 4.1 per cent). St. Laurent and Drew, as well as the CCF and Social Credit leaders, M.J. Coldwell and Solon Low, were all re-elected personally.

Given the proportions of the government's election victory, George Drew did the gracious thing and did not move for a vote of no confidence following the Throne Speech. Debate arose over the issue of abolishing appeals from the Supreme Court of Canada to the Judicial Committee of the Privy Council. Duplessis in particular, while unenthused by appeals to England, would prefer that appeals went almost anywhere but to a court entirely appointed by the federal government, given the likelihood of jurisdictional disputes. St. Laurent moved for matters of strictly federal jurisdiction to be appealed no farther than the Supreme Court of Canada, but there was an absence of an early consensus on what to do when the provinces were involved. At every opportunity, Duplessis went through his well-worn refrain about the British North America Act being a "pact" between the founding provinces that created the federal government and retained certain parental rights. St. Laurent even wheeled out the standard and, other than in the most tense instances, somewhat hackneyed rallying cry of the French nationalists from the days of Papineau to the present, that patriation of the process of constitutional amendment would make Canadians "masters in our own house." Criminal appeals to the Judicial Committee of the Privy Council had been abolished in 1931 with the Statute of Westminster, but civil appeals were finally abolished in 1949. A number of the committee decisions had been very odd and had limited federal authority excessively, and it was generally recognized that British jurists were too far removed from the issues they would be judging and that any such process had become an affront to Canadian sovereignty.

India's Prime Minister Nehru came to Ottawa from Washington in the autumn of 1949, and addressed Parliament on October 24. He had been anti-American ever since he had found American boys at Britain's exclusive Harrow School too aggressive, and American equivocation over the Kashmir dispute with Pakistan, and its insistence on the evils of communism, irritated him. (Successive American presidents of both parties, for their part, publicly disliked Nehru and his daughter, Indira Gandhi, who was later also prime minister of India.) St. Laurent and Pearson were more impressed than was justified with Nehru and his ostentatious faith in non-aligned foreign policy (as between the American and Soviet blocs), and with his espousal of socialism in domestic policy. Most non-alignment was just hypocrisy, and Indian socialism led to oceanic dysfunction and corruption and impenetrable economic stagnation.

By this time, it was well-known, and in some cases had been publicly stated by St. Laurent, that he favoured dropping "Dominion" from Canadian statutes, having a Canadian governor general, exchanging ambassadors with the Vatican, recognizing the new Communist regime in China (as Mao Tse-tung and Chou En-lai had won the Chinese civil war in October 1949, and Chiang Kai-shek decamped to Taiwan, where the U.S. Seventh Fleet protected him). But St. Laurent was also averse to fragmentation of opinion, and his experience during the Second World War with Canada's fissiparous political tendencies made him cautious about putting any pressure on the still-precarious fault lines of Canadian cultural and religious divisions. St. Laurent called a Federal-Provincial Conference for discussion of a formula for amending the British North America Act in Canada. It was an amicable session, and Duplessis referred courteously to St. Laurent personally but accused the federal government of "playing hide and seek" by not making specific proposals. St. Laurent was a former head of the Canadian Bar, as Duplessis was of the Bar of Quebec, and they had known each other well professionally for many years and always signed their letters to each other, no matter how trenchant their jurisdictional disagreements,

"*Salutations confraternelles*" in professional fellowship. The whole amending and appeals question was referred to a committee of attorneys general for later discussion.

Pearson returned from a Commonwealth foreign ministers' meeting in Colombo, Ceylon, later in January 1950 suffused with a desire to participate in what was called the Colombo Plan for Cooperative Economic Development in South and Southeast Asia, and also for recognition of the Communist regime in China. Chester Ronning, an old Asia hand of the foreign service, son of Lutheran missionaries born in China, and former leader of the CCF in Alberta (where he was steamrollered by Social Credit), was chosen to open the diplomatic mission to the Maoist government. He had fairly predictably upbeat views of East Asian communism, but when St. Laurent learned that neither the British, nor even the Indians, had found the Chinese very receptive, St. Laurent decided to go slow, and Ronning went on a diplomatic posting to Norway instead, though he later had extended tours in East Asia.

Eventually, the parliamentary session got round to considering an official residence for the prime minister, and St. Laurent typically insisted that the occupant pay five thousand dollars annually as rent. This was so Canadian and modest that Parliament eventually balked, and the subject could only be debated whenever St. Laurent was out of Ottawa, as he refused to take any part in such discussions.

These very domestic, almost bucolic, matters were interrupted by the outbreak of war in the Korean Peninsula, as North Korea attacked and invaded the South across the thirty-eighth parallel on June 25. The demarcation between North and South Korea had been decreed by two middle officers in the Pentagon one night in the summer of 1945, one of them then Colonel Dean Rusk, a future secretary of state. The South had two-thirds of Korea's population and a rather larger area than the North. The demarcation was required to advise Japanese armed forces in Korea (a country Japan had occupied since 1895) whether to surrender to Soviet or to American authorities in Korea, as it was not going to be possible to exclude Stalin from Korea at the end of the war as he had been excluded from Japan and Western Europe. (The U.S.S.R. had a short border with North Korea.) It was recounted in Chapter 7 how Mackenzie King had remonstrated with St. Laurent and Pearson and declined to sit on the United Nations Temporary Commission on Korea. He had objected to the partition of Korea, but he had no idea of the political realities there and did recognize South Korea as an independent country when it was established under American auspices. St. Laurent and Pearson immediately began calling for an international police force, but this was fatuous in the circumstances, as North Korea had attacked with an army of over ten divisions and the only possible source of successful resistance was the United States.

It was at first assumed that the Soviet Union was behind the attack, out of anger at having been kept out of Japan, and that it was exploiting the omission by Dean Acheson, General Marshall's successor as secretary of state, of South Korea as a territory within the American defence perimeter in a speech Acheson gave to the National Press Club in Washington on January 12, 1950. Truman remembered the weakness of the West over Axis aggression in Manchuria and Ethiopia in the 1930s, when he had been a senator, and he said, of the collective security system, "In this first big test, we just can't let them down." Eisenhower, who was setting up the NATO military command in Paris, said, "We'll have a dozen Koreas if we don't take a firm stand." St. Laurent and Pearson hurled themselves into the battle for a United Nations fig leaf to cover what was clearly going to be a U.S. operation if what Pearson plainly labelled in Parliament on June 26 "an act of unprovoked aggression" by North Korea was not to succeed. By blind luck and a matter of minutes, this at least was accomplished. The UN Security Council condemned North Korean aggression, taking advantage of a Soviet boycott over retention of the Chinese chair by the Chinese Nationalist Party of Chiang Kai-shek, and the abstention of Yugoslavia, whose communist leader, Marshal Josip Broz Tito, had broken with Stalin. The U.S. government let allied governments know on June 27 that the United States would provide military support to the South, and Pearson lobbied the Americans to do so within a UN framework, no matter how transparent a cover it was. There was nothing wrong with this particularly, except that it was based on Pearson and St. Laurent's conviction that this would somehow diminish the possibilities of a general war in the theatre with China and the Soviet Union. Pearson also asked the Truman administration not to speak of a worldwide communist strategy. The military governor of Japan and American commander in East Asia, General Douglas MacArthur, went to South

Korea and began air and sea intervention in support of the South as soon as Truman made his announcement at midday on June 27, and the Security Council, with the Soviets still absent on their ill-considered boycott, asked for American intervention in South Korea, which was already afoot. Pearson correctly told the House on June 28 that while the U.S. intervention was unilaterally undertaken, it was entirely in accord with the United Nations Charter and was retroactively approved by the Security Council. This may have made the lives of St. Laurent and Pearson and a few other people in other governments easier, but it had no impact on the decision of the issue, which would now be a straight test of military muscle and command ability. MacArthur moved four divisions from Japan to South Korea and was appointed United Nations commander in Korea. On the last day of the parliamentary session, June 30, St. Laurent, having confidentially briefed the other party leaders, Drew, Coldwell, and Low, and secured their support, dispatched some destroyers to Korean waters and announced that Canada would participate in the United Nations police action to defeat aggression. There was no dissent in the House.

Pearson and St. Laurent still were flustered that a very strenuous American response could bring in China, as if it were not involved already, and as if a defensive action could be conducted successfully if governed by fear of offending the Chinese Communists. The North Koreans were well-equipped with Soviet T-34 tanks and they outnumbered the South Koreans, even reinforced by four American divisions, by three to one. In the monsoon season, with teeming rains and temperatures steadily above 100 degrees Fahrenheit, MacArthur and his officers conducted a tenacious rear-guard action and gave up only one hundred miles in July as they made an orderly retreat toward Pusan at the southern end of the Korean Peninsula, and Truman poured in six more American divisions and reinforced Pusan. The Americans exploited their great air superiority, though the heavy cloud and intense precipitation mitigated it. MacArthur's local commander, General Walton Walker, ordered his forces to "stand or die" at Pusan, and promised there would be no retreat and no surrender: "No Dunkirk and no Bataan." MacArthur spent August preparing his counterstroke.

In Canada, St. Laurent's difficulties were compounded by the country's first ever nation-wide railway strike. St. Laurent and the transport minister, Lionel Chevrier, did their best to avoid and then stop the strike, but when mediation failed and the strike began, St. Laurent summoned Parliament and after six days a compulsory back-to-work law was adopted and the strikers obeyed it. St. Laurent and Chevrier handled the emergency capably and with what most of public opinion considered a good balance of concern for the parties and assertion of the national interest. The settlement was reasonably generous for the employees but quite affordable for the companies, who would pass on the increased cost to the public as the economy continued to unwind from ten years of depression and six years of wartime controls.

General MacArthur launched one of the great strategic strokes of modern warfare on September 15 with an amphibious landing in the middle of the Korean Peninsula at Inchon, near the South Korean capital of Seoul. MacArthur had to land his men in a one-hour window at high tide straight onto the seawall, as there were no beaches and thirty-foot tides. In sixty-five minutes, he disembarked 70,000 men from 262 ships while Walker broke out of Pusan. Seoul was recaptured in ten days and the peninsula cut in two and the thirty-eighth parallel restored. Almost the entire North Korean army of nearly 200,000 men was captured or killed or broken up and scattered within two weeks. Rarely in the history of war had there been such a quick turn in so large a combat. For good measure, Truman fired the erratic Defence secretary, Louis A. Johnson, and brought back from retirement one more time as his replacement General George Marshall. With Marshall in the Pentagon, Eisenhower in command of NATO in Paris, and MacArthur of the UN in Seoul and Tokyo, the U.S. was deploying military commanders of the very highest calibre. It is little wonder that a war mentality arose. But this was preventive action. The United States had followed Roosevelt's exhortation to "be wary of those who with sounding brass and a tinkling cymbal preach the 'ism' of appeasement."*

Canada's defence minister, Brooke Claxton, called for fifteen thousand volunteers to ensure sufficient forces to provide a brigade of five thousand men for Korea. There was much talk of conscription, but this was nonsense; there was no need to consider any such step. There were some nostalgic moments: some of the English-language media

---

* State of the Union message, January 6, 1941.

considered a brigade too little, and Pierre Laporte, who would go on to great and tragic fame in 1970, accused St. Laurent of deceiving the country and asked, "Are we to return to Mr. King's lies?"[5] (He had King to thank for the fact that he wasn't conscripted, drilled, and packed off to France to face the Wehrmacht under the orders of an Orange Lodge sergeant from the backwoods of Presbyterian Ontario, as the majority of Canadians would have wished.)

As these debates continued in Canada, MacArthur quickly rolled up both coasts of North Korea and the United Nations and President Truman with his Joint Chiefs of Staff redefined the mission statement of his forces from protection of South Korea and resurrection of the thirty-eighth parallel to complete destruction of North Korean forces and the invasion of North Korea. UN forces crossed the thirty-eighth parallel in great strength going north on October 9, and MacArthur and Truman had their famous meeting at Wake Island on October 15, which was entirely convivial. MacArthur reported military intelligence estimates that there were 125,000 Red Chinese north of the Yalu River, the boundary between North Korea and China, and that the Soviets had about 1,000 military aircraft in Siberia, but he doubted that they would coordinate well or that the Russians would want anything to do with a direct showdown with the United States. The frequently invoked fear was that the Americans would "unleash" Chiang Kai-shek on a return to the mainland in the event of a Chinese-American duel in Korea. MacArthur confirmed at Wake Island that his mission now was to unite Korea and prepare it for countrywide elections. At that point, most of the Chinese forces that he had identified as being north of the Yalu had in fact infiltrated into North Korea. Canada had not dissented on the restatement of MacArthur's instructions – all were united in seeking the end of the war by an outright victory over the communists in Korea.

On November 28, the Chinese went over to the attack with at least 150,000 soldiers that had already infiltrated well into the North and with perhaps 100,000 more across the Yalu, although MacArthur had, with Truman's approval, blown the bridges across the river on the Korean side. MacArthur had been badly failed by U.S. military intelligence, which at that time had no ability to judge the dangers of guerrilla warfare, but he responded with recommendations of counter-escalation, particularly a blockade of China, the use of Chinese Nationalist forces in Korea, and the conventional bombing of China's rudimentary industrial heartland in Manchuria. On November 30, Truman, in response to a press question, did not rule out use of atomic weapons. Most influential opinion – including Truman, Marshall, Eisenhower, Acheson, the Joint Chiefs (chaired by General Omar N. Bradley); younger foreign policy experts, including George Kennan, Charles Bohlen, and Paul Nitze; and all of America's allies except South Korea and Nationalist China – favoured rolling back MacArthur's mission to assuring South Korea at the thirty-eighth parallel. This was done, as there was a general fear that a war with China could be an endless morass that would play into Stalin's hands. All agreed that atomic weapons were out of the question. The alternative view was held by many Republicans and Southern Democrats, including the leading Republican foreign policy expert John Foster Dulles and the rising young congressional star from California – just elected to the Senate over actress Helen Gahagan Douglas by 700,000 votes – Richard Nixon. Their view, and MacArthur's, was that it was morally wrong and tactically hazardous to ask a conscript army to risk the lives of its soldiers for anything less than outright victory in the national interest. They all felt that at this point Red China was extremely vulnerable and could be taught a salutary cautionary lesson in its infancy, that Stalin would not lift a finger to assist Mao, and that what promised to be a terrible long-term nuisance of a Kimist communist regime in North Korea could be easily disposed of, if dealt with now.

The Chinese intervention revealed the extreme feebleness of the Western Alliance apart from the United States. Clement Attlee became so alarmed about Truman's reference to atomic weapons that he bustled over to Washington to offer to negotiate with China the peaceful departure of the United States from Korea. Truman replied that he did not think it would come to such a choice but that he would prefer to be defeated militarily than to avail himself of such an offer. The truth was that the British were terrified of Chinese pressure on Hong Kong and of increased Chinese assistance to the communist guerrillas in Malaya. They were of no use as allies at all, apart from the high quality of their token forces in Korea, when they eventually got there. As the Canadian brigade would not start arriving until February 1951, and would never represent more than between 1 and 2 per cent of the United Nations forces in Korea, it was a bit nervy of Pearson and St. Laurent to make such energetic representations as they did to Truman, but he received them good-naturedly. Attlee came on to Ottawa after visiting Truman, and he and St. Laurent were generally in agreement. Their position was complicated by their desire to stay in lock-step with Nehru, now a very influential member of the Commonwealth leadership, who disapproved of the North Korean invasion of the South, but also disapproved of MacArthur's advance into the North, which Attlee, St. Laurent, and Pearson had heartily endorsed but now abandoned in double-quick time once there was overt Chinese resistance to it.

MacArthur was right in most respects, and time would reveal the dangers of sending a conscript army to East Asia for an objective less than victory and not obviously required by the national interest. This was the weakness of the whole peacekeeping and international police action mode of activity. The communist enemy would approach it as total war, and any response less vigorous than that was unlikely to be successful, and peacekeeping and police actions aren't really war and aren't an effective reply to war. This was the first step in the often thankless task the Americans would assume of protecting the perimeter of the West, a service regarded with real enthusiasm only by those at the point where that perimeter was from time to time being probed or breached. People like Attlee and St. Laurent and Pearson were civilized and well-disposed and full of good intentions, and not without courage if they could be persuaded that courage was called for, but they were unsteady supporters when the adversary was of the nature and moral vacuity of Stalin, Mao, Ho Chi Minh, the Kims, and even some of their successors. As half-Canadian Dean Acheson put it, Canadian foreign policy officials were usually "arm-flapping moralists."

Chou En-lai confirmed to Richard Nixon when he visited China in 1972 that Stalin would not have done anything to help China in Korea, and China could not have sustained for long the sort of counter-blow MacArthur favoured. It is as clear now as ever how much the world would have been spared if North Korea had been, in Churchill's phrase about Bolshevism in 1917, "strangled in its cradle." But MacArthur made his views public, which was not acceptable, and he left Truman little alternative than to remove him, though he need not have dismissed him as governor of Japan, where all agreed his performance had been brilliant. The effect was to end ingloriously the careers of both men, a distinguished president and a brilliant general, and their entourages with them, including General Marshall and Secretary Acheson. They were all at or near normal retirement age, but it should have ended more decorously. Truman, almost panicky for once, removed MacArthur at a press conference at 1 a.m. on April 11, 1951, and replaced him with Walker's successor as field commander in Korea, former paratroop general Matthew B. Ridgway, who had already stabilized the front generally at the thirty-eighth parallel. (Walker had died in a road accident.) Here the fighting continued for over two years, until the new U.S. president, General Dwight D. Eisenhower, let it be known through diplomatic channels in India that if the Chinese did not become serious about negotiating a permanent ceasefire, he would use atomic weapons on them. Truman could have done this but chose not to. The tactic worked; South Korea survived and became an immense economic and political success story. But when MacArthur famously told Congress a few days after his dismissal, in one of the most memorable addresses ever delivered at the U.S. Capitol, that "in war there is no substitute for victory," he spoke nothing but the truth, and the implications of it would haunt the United States for a long time. As Charles de Gaulle remarked at the time, MacArthur was "a general whose boldness was feared after full advantage had been taken of it."[6]

As would long be its habit, the Canadian external affairs squirearchy, generally the followers of O.D. Skelton, affected to have been sober and sensible, constructive, mature, and vindicated in Korea, but in fact their haverings were innocuous and not overly relevant. The Canadian military contingent, as always, fought with distinction. A total of 29,000 Canadians served in the Korean War, including naval and air forces, and 516 died and 1,042 were wounded. The Korean War as a whole resulted in the deaths of 53,000 Americans, 170,000 South Korean military, and 750,000 South Korean civilians; and 300,000 North Korean military, 750,000 North Korean civilians, and 400,000 Chinese. The injured numbered 93,000 Americans and 680,000 South Koreans; and about 1,100,000 North Koreans and 500,000 Chinese. It was a nasty and bloody war (about 5 million casualties), and MacArthur, though there were some risks, would probably have ended it two years before it did end, at a saving of over a million lives and a million injuries (including the great majority of the Canadian casualties), and the world would have been spared the pestilential irritation of the Kimist totalitarians who have psychotically misgoverned the North Korean hermit state ever since.

2. The St. Laurent Regency, 1950–1953

The federal and provincial heads of government were back in conference on September 25, 1950, to discuss amending the Constitution. It was protracted and amicable, as further decades of these meetings – which Duplessis sarcastically called "circonférences," because they went around in circles – would be: the Canadian penchant for endless good-faith negotiation. Much the same atmosphere would prevail when the premiers were back in December to hear federal proposals for a new tax-rental system, though with a 50 per cent greater payout to the provinces. St. Laurent had been a member of the Rowell-Sirois Commission, and his infatuation with the replacement of concurrent federal-provincial taxing by a completely federalized system with formula-based bloc payments to the provinces did not die soon or easily. Because, assumedly, St. Laurent himself was so bilingual and had mixed ascendants, he did not share the concern of the majority of Québécois that the funding sources for the institutions and bulwarks of French Quebec, especially education and social services and the administration of the law, particularly the civil law unique to Quebec, be kept in the hands of a majority-French government; that is, Quebec. This exchange of taxing rights for bloc payments from Ottawa was never going to fly in Quebec, and Adélard Godbout had only agreed to it in 1942 because there was a war raging, and Ernest Lapointe and Arthur Cardin and Charles Gavan Power, with King's blessing, had put him across in the 1939 election. In this area, as in much of Quebec nationalistic questions, St. Laurent, unlike Lapointe and Wilfrid Laurier, had a cloth ear. Duplessis did not, but he was courteous and diplomatic at this meeting and to everyone's astonishment raised no objection to a federal pension scheme.

St. Laurent attended a Commonwealth prime ministers' meeting in London in January 1951, where the thorny matter of Kashmir was avoided in deference to Nehru, despite the ardent desire of the Pakistani prime minister, Liaquat Ali Khan, to discuss it. There was agreement on a basis of cooperation between the Commonwealth countries (still a manageable group of nine), and support was expressed for a peace treaty with Japan, the inevitable call for a negotiated peace in Korea, and increased economic cooperation, which in practice meant more aid for India and British exploration of economic solidarity with the Western Europeans. St. Laurent continued to France for a two-day state visit to Paris, where he was fêted by the president of the republic, Vincent Auriol, by Premier René Pleven, and by foreign minister Robert Schuman, three redoubtable journeymen of the Third and Fourth Republics. He laid a wreath at the Arc de Triomphe and attended a high mass celebrated by the cardinal-archbishop of Paris and primate of France at Notre Dame. St. Laurent did not enjoy these excursions as King had. He generally made a better impression, as a more elegant, better dressed, and more articulate and sociable man, entirely bilingual, and direct and never orotund in his remarks. King was eventually seen as a wily but enigmatic survivor but somewhat laboured conversationalist, where St. Laurent was a reserved but affable man, who was interestingly forthcoming in conversation, if rigorously moderate in his views. Both were quintessential Canadians, strong in their moderation but concealing a more complicated country than Canada was seen from afar to be.

It was agreed at the prime ministers' meeting that not only were republics such as India acceptable in what was now simply the Commonwealth of Nations, and the British monarch was recognized as the "head of the Commonwealth," the British sovereign would also be the monarch of whatever countries sought that arrangement. King George VI became king of "the United Kingdom of Great Britain and Northern Ireland, of Canada, and of other realms and territories." In 1952, Elizabeth II was proclaimed – and in 1953 was crowned – queen of the Kingdom of Canada. Dominion lapsed and John Macdonald's ambition of eighty-five years before that Canada be a kingdom, which was deferred because of American republican and hegemonic sensibilities, was fulfilled.

On his return to Canada, St. Laurent prepared to proceed unilaterally on the St. Lawrence Seaway and reasoned that Canadian nationalism would be quite adequate to absorb the entire cost of the project, which would in any case redeem its cost in increased toll revenues and electric power sales. There was also much enthusiasm for a great power project on the South Saskatchewan River. There was a good deal of completely unnecessary talk yet of conscription for Korea, and the Social Credit leader, Solon Low, even moved such a bill, though only for home defence. Not even Colonel George Drew could chin himself on this, and it was voted down by all the other three parties. A Department of Defence Production was set up, and it was added to C.D. Howe's other capacities.

In March 1951, a dispute arose in the cabinet about the right given to Britain in 1946 to buy Canadian wheat at below the world price, which it did, out of a $1.25 billion loan Canada had made Great Britain at the uneconomic rate of 2 per cent. James Gardiner, the minister of agriculture, had gone out on the limb of Commonwealth solidarity with Britain in explaining to farmers why Britain was paying below the market price for their wheat. In 1951, the British decided to leave $65 million of the available wheat unbought, and Gardiner proposed to bring pressure on the British to complete, but Howe, who was responsible for wheat sales, as he was for most other economic and commercial activities of the federal government, objected that it should be taken as business as usual but remembered the next time Britain wanted anything from Canada. St. Laurent agreed with Howe that there would be no pleading with Britain, but he agreed to let Gardiner go to Britain to try to explain to the British the unfairness of their action. Gardiner did so, without success, and then asked St. Laurent and Howe that the $65 million be paid rateably to farmers to compensate them for the reduced revenues they had received over the last five years. Howe objected, but St. Laurent agreed; it was the smart political move, and was a good object lesson to all of them on how much repayment any country could expect, even from its closest ally, which already owed it much, in tangible *ex gratia* goodwill.

The pension changes and legislation went through without demurral in Ottawa or the provinces. The Conservatives did succeed in baiting the somewhat domineering Howe into making some replies that did not play well in partisan debate in the country over the next few years. In a debate over the ratification of some trade agreements, veteran Conservative MP Howard Green said that he was not sure that the government would not do away with Commonwealth preference entirely, "if it thought it could get away with it." Howe retorted, "Who would stop us? Don't take yourselves too seriously." Green reminded Howe that he was "not yet the dictator of the country." In July 1951, an Opposition MP was questioning administrative costs in the new Department of Defence Production, and Howe said that in an annual budget of more than one billion dollars, "three million dollars is not exorbitant." This entered into the current lore of the country as "What's a million?" a question Howe never publicly put. One of the Conservative orators who started bandying "What's a million?" about was John Diefenbaker, of Prince Albert, Saskatchewan, who invoked it as he described a scene, derived entirely from his imagination, of Communist Chinese sailors on ships bought from Canadians by a Hong Kong financier but not entirely paid for and still Canadian-registered – something which did occur – singing "O Canada" (which Diefenbaker imagined), but, he asked, "What's a million?"[7], tying Howe's supposed complacency about waste to anti-communist fervour. It became a tedious but occasionally amusing refrain, and Diefenbaker was a rather shameless employer of such techniques and would remain so through a turbulent career that would extend for almost another thirty years. St. Laurent doubled the defence budget in three years, to about two billion dollars in 1952, nearly half the federal budget, to assure that Canada pulled its weight in NATO and Korea.[8]

The Massey Commission, chaired by Vincent Massey and the politically hyperactive Dominican priest Georges-Henri Lévesque, dean of social sciences at Laval University and adversary of the Duplessis government, presented its report in early 1951. It proposed the complete domination of broadcasting and television by the Canadian Broadcasting Corporation, heavily supplemented in funding, with independent licences only for scattered low wattage radio broadcasting as alternatives to the CBC. It also proposed direct federal government assistance for universities; the creation of a generously endowed Canada Council for promotion of the arts; a national library; and a new National Gallery building, several specific museums, and more generous funding and greater definition for the National Archives and the National Film Board. The concept of aid to arts and sciences generally was a good one, but Massey and Lévesque's faith in the CBC was exaggerated, and try-ing to leave network broadcasting and telecasting exclusively to the public sector was a bad idea. Lévesque as co-chair had been the choice of Massey and St. Laurent jointly, and Duplessis rightly saw it as a declaration of war on him, given the many public differences he had with Lévesque. (Duplessis once told eminent British journalist Malcolm Muggeridge that the key to governing Quebec was to keep "the Dominicans and Jesuits quarrelling with each other."* He promoted the University of Montreal's School of Industrial Relations, headed by Jesuit Émile Bouvier, as a rival to Lévesque's Laval faculty.)

The Liberal policy biases led to unnecessary frictions. Canadian culture had struggled to define itself in the shadow of the United States, and there were a number of symphony orchestras, ballet companies, the Stratford Shakespearean Festival, and some competent writers and painters, but few of them received any recognition outside Canada. Massey claimed to be "laying the spiritual foundations of Canada," a typically grandiloquent personal mission statement. Most of the recommendations were useful, but Massey and Lévesque would have done better calling for an opera house and a national arts centre (both of which required decades for the country to build) than plunging into a partisan jurisdictional war with Duplessis which they could not (and did not) win.

St. Laurent was again pressing the St. Lawrence Seaway in Washington in late September 1951, but the government there was rather immobilized following the Truman-MacArthur dispute, and was in the midst of the anti-communist campaigns of Senator Joseph R. McCarthy and others and congressional witch hunts in what President Truman called the "red herring" of unearthing domestic communists.

St. Laurent returned from the United States to welcome Princess Elizabeth and Prince Philip on their first trip to Canada, where they made a very good impression, and for the opening of Parliament. The establishment of a St. Lawrence Seaway Commission was announced, as well as a committee to investigate the advisability of the South Saskatchewan hydro project, and the beginning of implementation of Vincent Massey's ambitious program for promotion of the arts. The year ended amid a vigorous debate over legislating against retail price

---

* Muggeridge wrote this in several places, but also confirmed it to the author (with amusing elaborations on Duplessis, whom Muggeridge considered the most capable Canadian political leader he had met).

fixing, which Drew had tried to provoke the government into trying to end by enforcing closure, but St. Laurent, having taken the debate, thought better of such a controversial measure, and the bill was adopted in January 1952.

The National Conference of Canadian Universities had recommended federal aid to universities, as had the Massey Commission, but this was bound to be a delicate issue, especially with Duplessis, as it was indisputably a provincial jurisdiction. In a development that replicated his acquiescence in a federal pension scheme, Duplessis agreed, but for one year only. Duplessis had attacked the measure when it was proposed in November as "a dangerous usurpation," and he said that the "problems of the universities cannot be solved by intrusions, even gilded ones." But in the New Year, he agreed to allow the grants, which were fifty cents per capita for the whole population, or seven million dollars, about 30 per cent of that for Quebec. Duplessis had proposed that 5 per cent of the personal income tax be conceded to the provinces instead, as it was a concurrent jurisdiction where there was no concurrence in practice, but St. Laurent produced a piously ceremonious response worthy of King that such payments to the provinces were illegal, as if all the governments involved could not change the law if they wished. Duplessis, looking forward to another election in the spring of 1952, let it pass. The federal Liberal, Ontario Conservative, and Quebec Union Nationale governments were all solidly and immovably in place. So was Ernest Manning's Social Credit government in Alberta, which was about to win a fifth term, the first two having been won by William Aberhart; and Tommy Douglas's CCF government in Saskatchewan, which was about to win a third consecutive term. And so would be W.A.C. Bennett's Social Credit in British Columbia, about to start a twenty-year incumbency, and Joey Smallwood's Liberals in Newfoundland, three years into a twenty-three-year tenure. The federal official Opposition was not really effective, but Duplessis, and Drew's successor as the Conservative premier in Toronto, Leslie Frost, were very strong and were the real opposition to the federal government.

The seventy-seven-year-old Winston Churchill had led his Conservative Party to victory in Great Britain in October 1951 – his first successful election as party leader in fifty-two years in Parliament and after eleven years as Conservative leader. After a few months as Defence minister in addition to prime minister, he requested the return to Great Britain to take over Defence of his favourite field marshal, Viscount Alexander, who had had a very successful term as governor general of Canada. As an indication of the high regard in which he held Alexander, St. Laurent convened the entire Privy Council of Canada in a farewell ceremony. The last British governor general had perhaps been the very most successful since Elgin, or even Carleton, who had departed 156 years before. St. Laurent nominated Vincent Massey to replace Alexander, and be the first Canadian holder of the office, a choice that was received positively throughout Canada, even by Le Devoir.*

As Alexander departed, King George VI, a popular and dutiful monarch who had not sought the throne but had it thrust upon him, died, at fifty-six. He was widely mourned, but his daughter took the throne as an instantly popular queen, a youthful twenty-five-year-old to lead the British monarchy as Queen Elizabeth II into a new, and in some respects diminished, era.

Duplessis returned to his electors on July 16, after a typically strenuous campaign in which his opponents were led by the former federal MP for Joliette, Georges-Émile Lapalme. Duplessis referred indiscriminately, and in a deliberately and humorously confusing way, to both Godbout and George Marler, the acting leader, as well as Lapalme, as the leader of the Opposition, disparaged Lapalme as a nonentity parachuted in from the Liberal backbenches of Ottawa and a follower of the excitable and communist-backed Iranian politician, Premier Mohammad Mossadegh (based on a couple of Lapalme's unguarded comments). Duplessis had fainted in his bathroom while injecting himself with insulin for his diabetes, incurring a fractured hip, and campaigned with a cast on his torso, but he maintained a very heavy schedule. Lapalme accused Duplessis of running a Gestapo and of selling out Quebec's natural resources to Americans at risible prices, including the immense iron ore projects of northern Quebec, on which

---

* The newspaper's publisher emeritus, Henri Bourassa, Papineau's grandson, was about to follow William Lyon Mackenzie's grandson into eternity, which he did on August 31, 1952, on the eve of his eighty-fourth birthday, practically silent for the last eight years after his defeat by Duplessis in the 1944 Quebec election. Le Devoir was now owned by the Archdiocese of Montreal, directed by the forty-eight-year-old Paul-Émile Cardinal Léger, possibly Quebec's all-time greatest and most generally admired religious leader.

St. Laurent had publicly congratulated him. On election eve, Duplessis spoke to fifty thousand of his constituents and neighbours in Trois-Rivières, only a block away from his opponent, the mayor of the city, J.-A. Mongrain. The mayor had a sound amplification system, and the wind was blowing toward Duplessis as Mongrain made the sort of wild allegations that no sane person would make in a debate. Duplessis quieted his audience, and while Mongrain's followers were applaud-ing, Duplessis replied in hilarious terms to his opponent's excesses, which the mayor had uttered under the mistaken impression that he was entirely among friends. These Quebec elections were always a bit boisterous but were also good entertainment. Duplessis ran on pros-perity, low taxes, massive education and public-works spending, and his autonomist but anti-separatist promotion of Quebec's interest. Duplessis won, sixty-nine constituencies to twenty-three, and 51 per cent of the vote to 46 per cent Liberal, but with about a three-to-two lead among the French-speaking population. It was a respectable per-formance by Lapalme, certainly, but a solid win to bring Duplessis even with Sir Lomer Gouin and Louis-Alexandre Taschereau as the only four-term premiers in Quebec history.

All Canada was growing and prospering, and as the concerns about another world war settled down and postwar prosperity took hold, elec-torates were pretty content. One of the Liberals' election slogans in 1953 would be "For the Best Years of Your Life, Vote Liberal" – Duplessis's, in the campaign just ended, was "Let Duplessis Continue" – and there was much less of the red-baiting and fascistic allegations back and forth. The federal government endured some embarrassment over misappropriation and extravagance at the army camp at Petawawa, Ontario, and St. Laurent referred it all to independent investigation, amid claims of officers' horses being on the payroll and so forth. Montreal accountant George Currie, appointed to look into it, found a good deal to criticize but no sign of misconduct by anyone near any elected officials. St. Laurent received great credit from all sides when he personally mediated a settlement between railway management and employees in January 1953. He announced the arrangements to the House of Commons and typically did not refer to his own role, but both sides, at a news conference, spoke in the most respectful terms of his chairmanship of the discussions. St. Laurent was very effective, even if he was unexciting. And he had none of the foibles or absurdities of his predecessor, though neither was he remotely as motivated and tenacious and crafty a politician. Both were men for their times.

So was Maurice Duplessis. When he declined to accept the federal grants for universities, the Liberals instantly smelled political rewards and cited this as evidence of Duplessis's neo-separatist constitutional Neanderthalism. Duplessis explained that he was taking the step because none of his previously stated objections had been met. He matched the federal grants and won the political argument with his own voters. He believed that the provinces had been exploited by the federal government in that the reward for their thriftiness in forgoing several concurrent direct tax fields had been to have the federal government invade the same fields and then redistribute crumbs while glorifying itself in its fiscal generosity. To his own voters, he said the federal government was like "a pickpocket who steals your watch, gives you back the chain, and calls it a gift." Duplessis's reasoning was in fact supported by most constitutional experts, including even future Quebec federal Liberal leader Pierre Trudeau. To his opponents, the university grants controversy was yet another proof of Duplessis's mulish, misanthropic, and opportunistic anti-Canadianism. To him and his followers, the disagreement was rather an illustration of the jurisdictional greed, insensitivity, bad faith, and political and constitutional meddlesomeness of the federal Liberals. Neither was altogether mistaken nor altogether accurate, but a test was coming before the voters of Quebec.

The voters of Canada would be consulted first. Douglas Abbott's pre-electoral budget reduced personal income taxes by $237 million and cut federal expenditures by $361 million, and Howe announced a twenty-cent per bushel increase in the price of wheat and improved sales prospects internationally.

St. Laurent went to Washington on May 7, 1953, for his first meeting with General Eisenhower as president. The new administration, the first Republican one in twenty years, after five terms of Roosevelt and Truman, had some protectionist leanings, but Eisenhower was on the record as favouring the St. Lawrence Seaway project. The two men had known each other very cordially for some years and were somewhat similar, as being slightly elderly for their positions, not career politicians, and very respected men of unquestioned integrity and high achievements prior to entering public life, world-historic achievements in Eisenhower's case. Their conversations were upbeat and informal, and Eisenhower indicated that he would not be displeasing to Canada but needed time to work things out in his new position.

St. Laurent returned briefly before departing to the coronation of the new queen, very aptly on the great liner *Queen Elizabeth*, the world's largest ship at 83,000 tons. St. Laurent and his wife arrived in London on May 26 and spent two weeks in the capital, and were very respectfully received by the royal family, Prime Minister Churchill, and other dignitaries. The Commonwealth prime ministers were prominently seated at the coronation in Westminster Abbey on June 2, beside the monarch. At a meeting in the Dorchester Hotel, St. Laurent, Smallwood, and senior civil servant Jack Pickersgill agreed that Pickersgill would seek election from Newfoundland and enter the cabinet at once. There was a brief Commonwealth prime ministers' conference and St. Laurent reported on the new U.S. administration, though Churchill and Eisenhower had been close friends and collaborators in world-shaking events for ten years. Then he returned by airplane to Canada, leaving his family to travel by ship (Mme St. Laurent said she would not fly "until I have wings of my own"), and after a cabinet meeting on June 12 dissolved Parliament for elections on August 10. The Liberal slogan would be "Don't Stop Canada's Progress – Vote St. Laurent."

St. Laurent ran on the fact and promise of "good government." Drew had an energetic program of tax reductions, new fiscal arrangements with the provinces, a national health insurance plan, and an outright ban on communist activity and organizations. It ran the gamut from the moist fringes of the CCF almost to the pallid Canadian equivalent of the McCarthyite right. St. Laurent won general admiration for refusing to pander, declining to do more than continue to study the South Saskatchewan hydro project, and deferring an exchange of embassies with the Vatican and the adoption of a distinct Canadian flag. On election day, St. Laurent won the Liberals' fifth consecutive term, and seventh of the last eight full terms, electing 169 MPs on 48.4 per cent of the vote, down from 191 MPs on 49.1 per cent of the vote in 1949. The Progressive Conservatives came in with 51 seats and 31 per cent of the vote, up from 41 MPs and 29.7 per cent; and for the CCF and Social

Credit respectively, 23 MPs and 15 per cent (in 1949, 13 seats and 10 per cent), and 11 MPs and 5.4 per cent (in 1949, 13 seats and 4.1 per cent). It was good government and they were good times.

3. The St. Laurent–Duplessis Duel, 1953–1956

St. Laurent reinforced and somewhat rejuvenated his government in the months following his re-election. In addition to Jack Pickersgill's arrival in the cabinet, Jean Lesage of Quebec City became the minister of natural resources, and Robert Winters, another able young minister, moved to public works. A few months later, three of St. Laurent's most capable ministers told the prime minister of their desire to withdraw: finance minister Douglas Abbott wished to go to the Supreme Court and did so, replacing Chief Justice Thibaudeau Rinfret (though not as chief justice); defence minister Brooke Claxton wished a simpler and quieter life; and transport minister Lionel Chevrier wished to head up the St. Lawrence Seaway Commission, then being established, and St. Laurent agreed. They were all a serious and premature loss to the government. St. Laurent and Howe were older men. The prime minister did not try to prevail upon them to remain, as King would have done, but replaced them with Walter Harris at finance, Ralph Campney at defence, and George Marler, formerly acting leader of the Opposition in Quebec, at transport. Roch Pinard became secretary of state. They were all capable. Even after nearly twenty years of government, the federal Liberals still had profound ministerial reserves.

President Eisenhower paid St. Laurent and Massey a state visit in November 1953 and declared construction of the St. Lawrence Seaway to be "inevitable and certain," and referred approvingly to the joint ministerial committee that had been set up to deal with trade and economic issues and to prevent those issues from becoming too contentious. St. Laurent stoked up what was emerging as almost the ideology of being a middle power, and praised American influence in the world, declaring the two countries to be the proof that "a great power and a lesser one can work in harmony without the smaller being submerged." To someone born in 1882 (just two days after Franklin D. Roosevelt) near the U.S.-Canada border, welcoming the American president in alliance and cordiality was an act that still contained a measure of relief and gratitude that the United States was no longer a physical threat to Canada. It was still a tense international atmosphere, though less so since the death of Stalin in March 1953 and his replacement by an uneasy grouping of his politburo survivors, who agreed quickly on the removal of Stalin's long-time assistant, Alexander Poskrebyshev, and on the execution of his police minister, Lavrenti Beria, but not on much else after that, until a succession of purges (though bloodless ones) concentrated power in the hands of the succeeding Communist Party chairman, Nikita S. Khrushchev (only the third holder of that office, after Lenin and Stalin). The red scare was receding in the United States, and congressional forces led by future presidents Richard Nixon, the vice president, and Democratic Senate leader Lyndon Johnson organized the censure of witch-hunting and red-baiting Senator Joseph McCarthy.

In this atmosphere, there was general solidarity in Canada behind American leadership, which was clearly indispensable. Eisenhower arranged the ceasefire in Korea on July 27, 1953, and it has generally held since. The hysteria about a communist sweep in Europe had declined as Marshall Plan aid and the reconstruction activities of the Western European countries began to bootstrap those peoples back into prosperity and to exceed pre-war living standards, and as conditions stabilized around most of the perimeter of China. The pro-British faction was clearly winning the battle with the communists in Malaya, Japan was flourishing, and the only raw trouble spot was Indochina, where the French – unlike the British in Malaya, which had been promised its independence – were fighting a colonial war. The rule of thumb gradually emerged that where the nationalists and communists were on the same side, they could not be resisted, but where the nationalists were anti-communist, they could, with help, prevail. It was a Western World led by wise, distinguished, elderly men: Eisenhower, Churchill, West Germany's Konrad Adenauer, St. Laurent. There were profusions of bomb shelters in every American city and a good deal of attention to communist infiltration and Third World War scenarios in films and on television, but it was peace and prosperity in a traditional environment. *Father Knows Best* was a popular television program, misbehaving children were confidently but benignly spanked at home and school, and most people in North America went to church every week. It was self-assured and righteous order, and there was steady progress. The generation that had been frightened in the Great Depression and led to victory by great commanders in a just war now worked hard and optimistically and raised their families in a confident, Godly, patriotic capitalism, and the public mood was more upbeat than at any time since the 1920s and more sanely optimistic than at any time since before the lights went out in 1914 with the First World War. In these circumstances, Canadians were pleased to accept American leadership, enjoy the British connection, and celebrate the bountiful growth, domestic peace, and polite international recognition Canada had earned and was enjoying.

A middle power on good terms with the ideologically compatible great powers was a good way station on the national trail, but it was not the destination. Canada was completely overshadowed by the United States, and Quebec was uneasy about being less than sovereign in a country where it was a minority and, while certainly not mistreated, naturally felt somewhat restricted in what it could aspire to achieve. In the idyll of the relatively secure 1950s, there was a certain false complacency, and as time passed, the gentlemanly competence of Louis St. Laurent was bound to fall somewhat behind the zeitgeist – that, as many rightly feared, could lead to impetuosity and wrong turnings as it evolved.

So serene was the re-elected government that St. Laurent biographer Dale Thomson described the prime minister's decision to go on a tour to Europe and South and East Asia in early 1954 as "sensational."[9] It was thought an ambitious undertaking and an unprecedented showing of the Canadian flag, almost a Canadian equivalent of President Theodore Roosevelt painting the U.S. naval fleet white and sending it round the world forty-seven years before. In keeping with what the Canadian external affairs ministry and all the industrious acolytes of O.D. Skelton, led by Lester B. Pearson, considered to be something of a Canadian mission, St. Laurent thought he would have a go at reconciling the American-led, anti-communist West with Canada's Commonwealth associate India and its Third World neutralism. Nehru was the undisputed leader of India (Gandhi having been assassinated in 1948) and carved out a role of detached censoriousness toward the West, though he was something of an anglophile because of his schooling and professional formation in England. Churchill, who had despised and imprisoned him, with the jaunty eloquence of upper class British flattery, now called the beaming Nehru "the light of Asia." Nehru conceived of the United States as an overbearing and unsubtle country (a perception many Canadians could understand, even if they were less aggrieved by it), and he considered communism a legitimate doctrine for generalization of wealth rather than a belligerent and subversive assault on human freedom and respectable intellectual and cultural traditions. Nehru and St. Laurent had got on well when they met at Commonwealth conferences, and Nehru urged St. Laurent to return his visit to Canada of 1949.

In Commonwealth matters, St. Laurent had been a champion of the role of world-bridge, as opposed to the last watch of the old British notion of united action under British leadership, and on this basis he was happy to go to India and to add stops on the way and beyond. It seemed to the hopeful Canadians that a ripe subject for interpretation to the uncomprehending, such as Nehru, was the new American administration, some of whose members, especially John Foster Dulles, now secretary of state, appeared very avid Cold Warriors. The Republicans had accused Roosevelt and Truman of being soft on the "commies" and this worried many less accustomed than Canadians are to the excesses of American political oratory. There was a degree of self-delusion in this, as Eisenhower was a much more cunning operator than was generally appreciated. With his "more bang for the buck" emphasis on nuclear weapons, and the Republican Party's bunk about the "liberation" and "roll-back" in Europe, Eisenhower quickly ended the Korean War, sent Nixon, who had already shown considerable aptitude for foreign policy, to tell Chiang Kai-shek and Syngman Rhee, president of South Korea, not to reactivate recent conflicts with the communists, and to urge Japan's Emperor Hirohito to rearm, just a decade after Nixon had earned battle stars at Guadalcanal and Bougainville. And Eisenhower unveiled an imaginative plan for the internationalization and demilitarization of atomic science. He was the smiling, golfing, avuncular president of whom the nation said "I like Ike," and he was also the five-star general who had won every battle and been victorious in every theatre, successfully conducted the greatest military operation in world history, and received the unconditional surrender of Nazi Germany in the West. And he had coordinated policy with military coalition partners perhaps more satisfactorily than anyone ever, liberated the western Nazi death camps and had them photographed to ensure that the world was not taken in by Holocaust deniers, governed West Germany well, set up NATO very effectively, and had a good start as president. The fancied Canadian role of middleman between Eisenhower and Nehru was chimerical, but neither discreditably motivated nor a bad ambition in itself.

Louis St. Laurent departed Ottawa on his world tour on February 4, 1954, and began in London with a pleasant luncheon with Winston Churchill, who gave him a travel advisory for the elderly statesman: as it was bound to be exhausting, don't walk when it was possible to ride, don't stand when it was possible to sit, don't sit when it was possible to lie down, and never miss an opportunity to visit a washroom, as you never know when the next opportunity will occur.[10] St. Laurent went on to Paris and Bonn, where he had excellent discussions with Chancellor Adenauer and celebrated the complete reconstruction of German-Canadian relations. Adenauer, who was born in 1875 (a few months after Churchill, but eight years before his Canadian visitor and fifteen years before Eisenhower) and was known in Germany as *Der Alte* (the Old Man), had performed probably the greatest single act of statesmanship in the postwar world in rejecting Stalin's offer of German reunification in exchange for German neutrality between the Soviet and American blocs, and carrying West German opinion with him. He said that Germany had lacked allies since Bismarck's time, that it had them now, and would keep them and gain reunification with them. It was an epochal decision, and Canada, though still in the second rank, was at the front of the second rank of Western nations and was part of the great geopolitical equation in her own right. St. Laurent went on to Rome, where an indisposition prevented a reception by Pope Pius XII, but he was received in the pope's name by a future successor, pro-secretary of state, Giovanni Battista Cardinal Montini, later Pope Paul VI.

St. Laurent continued on to Karachi, Pakistan, and was welcomed by Prime Minister Muhammad Ali Bogra, a former high commissioner in Ottawa. He visited universities and went up the Khyber Pass; it was a fine goodwill visit, and he diplomatically dodged all questions about the Kashmir dispute with India and the armament of Pakistan by the United States, which was clearly designed to deter the Soviet Union but which Nehru was interpreting as a hostile act toward his country. Throughout this part of the visit, he trotted out an ingratiating refrain about how much the West owed the East and how Canada's $25 million annual contribution to the Colombo Plan was a mere down payment on retiring that indebtedness. India was the real target of the journey, and St. Laurent was very cordially received by Nehru and addressed a joint session of the Indian Parliament on February 23, a distinct honour for Canada and its leader. He pulled no punches in his defence of the United States and strongly debunked his host's theory that NATO was a manifestation of American "neo-imperialism"; it was, St. Laurent said in his address, an entirely defensive alliance completely compatible with the United Nations Charter, as well as the nucleus of greater Western unity in the higher interests of the whole world. He said, "As we see it, the readiness of the United States to assume the responsibilities of a major power has been of very great benefit to the free world. We who live alongside that great and dynamic nation know from our own long experience that the United States is the most unselfish country ever to play this role and that it has no other ambition than to live and let others live in mutually helpful intercourse. . . . Does anyone really believe that the United States could bring about aggressive or provocative collective action by the countries associated with it?"[11] It was an important statement much reported in the world, and gratefully so in the United States. At a state dinner tendered to St. Laurent, Nehru praised him as one who had made the "deep impress . . . of a man of high integrity, of high purpose, and of high endeavour." That this was true was attested to by the fact that Nehru – who was well-travelled in the sanctimony of India's long pursuit of independence and disliked contradiction more even than most heads of government – spoke as he did of his guest despite St. Laurent's unequivocal contradiction of several of his cherished foreign policy attitudes. Prodded by aggressive press questions, St. Laurent dismissed the suggestion, often made by Nehru, that U.S. arms sales to Pakistan were a provocation of India, and finally closed the discussion by saying, "You are free to criticize the United States government. I am not going to do so."[12] He was much closer to Nehru on the subject of relations with China and said that eventually recognition would have to be extended to whomever actually governed that country. This led to a good deal of intercontinental toing and froing as the American and other governments wondered if St. Laurent was contemplating recognition. He made it clear that he was not proposing recognition of Mao's regime at once. For the first few days, while the pleasantries were amply observed in public, the two prime ministers did not have a frank exchange, causing one Canadian diplomat to say that "these two men haven't got anything to say to each other after all."[13] But after their daughters pushed them, they did have a more free-wheeling discussion after the Canadian party visited the Taj Mahal. There was no dramatic agreement, but at least there was greater mutual comprehension. The fact was that Nehru was a Harrow and Cambridge snob at the head not only of "the ancient and exotic culture and allure of the Subcontinent" but also of what Gandhi called "the 100,000 dung-heaps of India." Nehru attempted to lay claim to a moral superiority that transcended the poverty and dysfunctionalism of his country. And the West, especially the British and their closest affiliates, so badly wanted an independent India to succeed that they overlooked a good deal of hypocrisy and humbug from Nehru and his daughter, Indira Gandhi, when she became the leader of India. (Between them, they led the Indian government for thirty-two of its first thirty-seven years, from 1947 to 1964, 1966 to 1977, and 1980 to 1984.) They were the authors of economic stagnation that made the condition of India's hundreds of millions of terribly poor even more desperate, and a delusional foreign policy based on the friendship of China until it humbled and defeated India and on Soviet benignity and the moral and practical equivalence of the Soviet Union and the West until the U.S.S.R. disintegrated.

St. Laurent went on to Ceylon, Indonesia, the Philippines, and South Korea, where St. Laurent visited the troops. He had done the same in West Germany, but South Korea was still a war zone, the first St. Laurent had seen. There was a temperature variance of 80 degrees Fahrenheit between Indonesia and Korea, which may have contributed to the seventy-two-year-old leader's dysentery, which descended upon him later in Japan. Conscientious in all things, he concealed his condition, compounded by a sleepless night, and had a ceremonious carriage ride to the Imperial Palace in Tokyo and a conversation with Emperor Hirohito, followed by a meeting with Japan's distinguished (Roman Catholic) premier, Shigeru Yoshida, a protégé of MacArthur, and another of the world's eminent senior statesmen (he was seventy-six). St. Laurent visited with the crews of three Canadian destroyers in Tokyo Bay, spoke to the Japan-Canada Society, and returned to Ottawa via Honolulu and

San Francisco, arriving on the evening of March 9 and bestowing on Jeanne, his wife of forty-six years, not just a prolonged kiss but a floral lei he had brought with him from Hawaii. He was welcomed back with great enthusiasm, and George Drew was among those who came to the airport to greet him. The next day, the Speaker of the House, Louis-René Beaudoin, said that the heavy applause of the legislators indicated "the genuine sentiments of admiration and affection felt in all parts of the House for the prime minister."[14] Drew again was among the leading greeters, and his most severe allegation against his official adversary now was that the government was promoting "socialism with a silk hat," a charge the accused good-naturedly accepted. It was in some ways the height of his time as leader of the country. He had made a good impression everywhere and carried the senior official presence of Canada to places it had never been before. The domestic media followed him and reported on the dignity of his person and purpose and the high regard in which he was evidently held wherever he went. But he was exhausted, and slightly gutted by tropical ailments, and never regained the stamina he had shown in making this ambitious tour.

The prime minister returned to find that Maurice Duplessis had finally gone to war fiscally. Ottawa had conducted what Duplessis called "the war of the separate ententes" by negotiating new tax-rental arrangements with the other nine provinces. Quebec was now isolated, and ten years after Duplessis's return to office in 1944, no positive advances had been made in any of the fiscal policy directions he had been urging ever since then. There had been no federal allowance for the concurrent provincial right to levy direct taxes; the federal government levied the tax as heavily as anyone thought the traffic should bear, leaving only a deduction of 5 per cent of the federal tax for the province – that is, a tax of about 2 per cent. There had been absolutely no progress in ten years of discussions about defining taxing powers, simplifying collection methods, or reducing taxes in general. Duplessis determined to force the issue – by double taxation. Quebec would legislate a provincial income tax, and if the federal government did not credit it against federal income tax, Quebec's voters could determine which government was responsible for their escalated tax rate. Duplessis, who knew the people a good deal better than any Quebec Liberal, federal or provincial, was confident that the present 95–5 division of taxes could be shown to be unjust and that the federal government had availed itself of temporary national emergencies to perpetuate a state of fiscal hegemony by a scheme of bribes, alarms, and what Duplessis called "temporarily permanent arrangements."

Through the summer, a verbal war stoked up between the sides in what promised to be the greatest heavyweight constitutional bout the country had seen, at least since the fracases about separate schools. Duplessis accused the federal government of trying to reduce Quebec to a "trusteeship . . . an auxiliary government," appropriate for "drunks, imbeciles, and people incapable of looking after themselves." But Quebec, he said, was "dependent on no one." St. Laurent replied, in an impromptu address on the Cunard liner *Saxonia* in Montreal harbour in September, that only "behind the Iron Curtain and in Quebec" was there a lack of "enthusiasm" at the "growth and development of Canada," because it "means the increasing influence of the federal government." Two weeks later, in opening the new Liberal headquarters in Quebec (the Reform Club; the Union Nationale's was the Renaissance Club), he astounded his listeners by holding forth for two hours. St. Laurent avowed his faith that Providence sent Montcalm and Wolfe "to create a situation where the descendants of the two great races would find themselves together on this northern part of the American continent." This was fine, but less easily digestible was his assertion that "Quebec is a province like the others." He pointedly distinguished between "true provincial autonomy and autonomy as a blind to prevent discussion of provincial affairs."[15] And he ridiculed any suggestion that French-language or Roman Catholic schools could be endangered if they were maintained by federal rather than provincial funding. This was an assertion that was historically vulnerable, and it was political dynamite. Duplessis knew this political combat zone intimately. St. Laurent complained about Quebec not participating in the Trans-Canada Highway, and urged it upon the Quebec government, even though, he sarcastically allowed, the bids to pave the road would have to go to tender, and not just be determined in a cooked deal between the contractor and the Union Nationale. While he was at it, he accused Duplessis, in effect, of being a know-nothing and a supporter of ignorance for his abstention from the federal plan of assistance to universities. This was all a bit thick, as Duplessis had completed a highway in complete conformity with federal standards, at the province's expense, between the Trans-Canada terminal points on Quebec's borders with Ontario and New Brunswick, and the universities had been paid by the provincial government while the federal grants accumulated, which were, when St. Laurent's successor came to office, dispersed with only the slightest modification of the federal grant terms to the province's universities, which thus benefited from double payment, as Duplessis had promised. St. Laurent's attack on Duplessis's patronage system was also cheeky, given that the taxpayers didn't suffer any loss from it and the Liberals were hardly immune to the charge of doling out official business to their friends.

Observers confidently awaited Duplessis's reply; he could not endure an assault like this in silence. He responded in a much-announced speech at a bridge opening at Valleyfield broadcast province-wide on September 26, 1954. He accused St. Laurent of wanting to return to the days of "the English governors." All the provinces would be alike, and centralization would eventually deliver Quebec into the hands of a socialist government that English Canadians could conceivably elect but French Canadians would not. He found it "painful and distressing" that a Quebecker could seriously claim that the provinces were identical and that the protection of the rights of the French could safely be left entirely to the non-French. Quebec, he said, "would never exchange the invigorating air of our province for a federal oxygen tent, our rights as our own masters for the role and title of a pensioner, a ward." He wondered what could have possessed St. Laurent to "lose his self-control to the point of disowning his race and his province," and went on to complain that St. Laurent distributed 17 per cent of tax revenue to help the poorer provinces without allowing Quebec to exercise partially a concurrent jurisdiction to build schools and hospitals in Quebec "and calls it a Canadian policy."[16] He reiterated his willingness to meet with St. Laurent for negotiations without preconditions, and suggested Montreal, as the midpoint between Ottawa and Quebec and a city in the jurisdiction of both governments. He repeated his traditional formula: "Cooperation always; assimilation never." St. Laurent, of course, was not suggesting assimilation, but he showed a serious absence of political judgment to imagine that the Québécois would believe the federal government could durably protect Quebec's French life and culture as well and vigilantly as Quebec itself could.

The two leaders met nine days later in the Windsor Hotel in Montreal, amid a heavy press cordon. As always, the exchange was completely cordial. St. Laurent in effect conceded that he would have to credit the Quebec income tax and recognize the concurrent jurisdiction, but required that Duplessis cease his unfounded claim that direct taxes were a provincial priority. If Ottawa would renounce exclusivity in direct taxes, Quebec would renounce priority. Duplessis made the point that while Quebec was officially imposing a 15 per cent tax on the federal tax, it had so many exemptions, it was really 10 per cent. He would cut it to 10 percent and pledge to confine the spending to which the revenue would be dedicated exclusively to uncontested provincial spending responsibilities. St. Laurent, like all federal Liberals at the time, was passionately committed to the theory that all provinces had to be treated exactly the same and that anything else was a step down the slippery slope to national disintegration, but it was agreed that, structured as described, the same arrangements could be made available to all the provinces by the federal government. There would be a 10 per cent abatement of the federal personal income tax, but to avoid inflicting the requirement of two tax returns, it was agreed that Ottawa would collect the tax and pass on the 10 per cent provincial share to the provinces. Both leaders confirmed to the press that the meeting had been very cordial and constructive but that details would have to be worked out and nothing would be said about the nature of a compromise until a precise agreement had been reached.

St. Laurent's initial communications to the other premiers was rather laborious and even pedantic, and he was at pains to write that Duplessis had requested the meeting and that he, St. Laurent, had attended out of "duty." There were a great many meetings of technical committees, and finally, on January 6, 1956, St. Laurent wrote the premiers with a comprehensive federal proposal that had built a virtuous work of imagination on the necessity of compromise initially imposed by Duplessis. The federal government would make equalization payments to the provinces in order to assure to every province a return per capita from personal income taxes, corporate income taxes, and succession duties equal to the per capita average of the return to these sources from the two wealthiest provinces. The federal government also offered a tax-rental formula that assured a comparable return, averaged over two years, that provided a hedge against sharp reductions in revenue.

All in all, it was a very creditable proposal, if unconscionably tardy. It increased Quebec's revenues, got around insistence on identical treatment of the provinces while officially adhering to that view, and inserted greater flexibility in the tax-rental/autonomy choice, all through the altruistic and politically saleable device of the equalization grant.

This concept had the further advantage to the federal government of reinforcing the material value of federalism in seven provinces, as Ontario, Alberta, and British Columbia would be funding the grants to the other provinces. St. Laurent further wrote Duplessis on February 18, 1956, promising that there would be no federal government attempt to limit pre-tax provincial natural resources royalties (one of the problems that arose in the university grants controversy) and raising the deductibility ceiling on a large number of lesser taxes and fees. St. Laurent was back a month later offering stabilization payments to assure 95 per cent of the average of the two previous years from the provincial revenue sources that were the subject of the discussions. He emphasized that this was as far as he could go. Duplessis put all this through the Legislature amid general congratulations from all areas of Quebec opinion for having achieved a very constructive breakthrough. Despite all the name-calling, in both directions, Duplessis had demonstrated that he wanted an agreement and not unending acrimony, and St. Laurent ultimately showed considerable imagination and flexibility. At the height of the debate, Liberal Quebec legislator René Hamel, a future Quebec attorney general, asked if Duplessis was courting or considering a separatist, secessionist option. Duplessis replied that he would only consider such a thing if the rest of Canada thought Quebec a burden to the country, and that he would entertain it reluctantly.[17] If St. Laurent had struck while the iron was hot, he could have resolved all Canada's future constitutional problems with Duplessis, the last Quebec premier who was enough of a nationalist to deliver the province to a permanent federal accord and who had the following and political agility to hold the line with the Quebec voters. By trying to portray Duplessis as a constitutional dog in the manger, the federal Liberals, and the federalists generally, embarked on a roller-coaster ride that would imperil the future of the country.

* * *

By this time, the French had been defeated in Indochina as they attempted to defend a valley at Dien Bien Phu, in Northern Vietnam, in a guerrilla-infested area where their opponents held the surrounding hills. Eisenhower, when shown the French military plans, cautioned that it did not appear to him to be sensible, and as conditions worsened, the French asked for more and more aircraft and munitions and ultimately for an atomic attack on the Viet Minh communists. Eisenhower warned the French that while he could advance some supplies, he could not become directly supportive of a military effort to suppress Indochinese or Vietnamese independence. The French did not pay much attention and instead tried to broker their presumed ability to veto West German entry into NATO against American support in Indochina. Eisenhower was not having it. Both the chairman of the American Joint Chiefs of Staff, Admiral Arthur Radford, and Vice President Nixon, who were hawks on Indochina, were authorized by Eisenhower to ask Churchill if he would join in a move to help the French, conditional on French recognition of Indochinese independence, but Churchill declined. The Geneva Conference, intended to resolve the conflict, opened on April 26, 1954. Dien Bien Phu, with three thousand French soldiers and ten thousand pro-French Vietnamese, fell to the communist guerrillas on May 7. The French government of Joseph Laniel fell on June 12, a very routine event in the Fourth Republic (as de Gaulle had predicted), and Pierre Mendès-France was inducted as premier with a mandate to end the war, which he pledged to do by July 20. Sensing that a complete sellout was in the offing, Eisenhower reduced American participation to that of observer status only at Geneva.

Mendès-France and even Churchill and Anthony Eden were ambiguous about the European Defence Community (EDC) (the European members of NATO, which was the way for West Germany to join the Alliance). This was the only avenue for the rearmament of Germany, but Churchill and Eden arrived in Washington in late June 1954, and Eisenhower offered them a deal: more atomic bombs to strengthen their deterrent force in their bomber fleet in exchange for support of the EDC and acceptance of the likely Geneva Conference agreement, which was independence for all components of Indochina, Viet Minh withdrawal from Laos and Cambodia, and division of

Vietnam into two countries at the seventeenth parallel. The British were still wavering, but on July 21 the conference in Geneva ended as Eisenhower had foreseen, and it was agreed that there would be a pan-Vietnam election in two years on the issue of reunification. Of course, this was the merest face-saver for France, as Ho Chi Minh would take 100 per cent of the Northern vote and a substantial share of the Southern as well. China's Chou En-lai told Mendès-France that he could deliver Ho Chi Minh if the French prime minister could deliver Eisenhower. The two feats of persuasion were not comparable. Dulles was in Geneva, and when informed in his bath that Chou En-lai had offered normalization of relations and immediate release of all Korean War prisoners, Dulles, on his own authority alone, declined. He famously refused to shake hands with Chou, something that still ran-kled eighteen years later when President Nixon arrived in Beijing and completed the handshake. The Joint Chiefs of Staff and Southern Democrats were suggesting staying out of Vietnam but using atomic weapons on Ho Chi Minh, which Eisenhower dismissed as insane. But to warm up the French and Germans, he had Lyndon Johnson and Nixon put through the Senate a measure authorizing the president to "restore sovereignty to Germany and enable her to contribute to the maintenance of peace and security." On Geneva, the United States had no need to sign but said it would not obstruct the performance of the terms. The American position was that a Vietnam reunification would require the support of both Vietnams separately, and Dulles immedi-ately set about, on an initial suggestion of Nixon's from the year before, recruiting members for a South East Asia Treaty Organization (SEATO), modelled on NATO, and South Vietnam was a founding member. In conferring durable legitimacy on that country, Eisenhower was pulling the pin on a long-fused grenade.

The French National Assembly rejected the EDC on August 30. Eisenhower immediately convened a NATO meeting and rammed through the admission of West Germany as a fully sovereign and effec-tively forgiven state. The French, having been soundly trounced by the Vietnamese communists, had kicked the Americans in the shins despite sound American advice and tangible help on how to avoid the fiasco, and had been rewarded by being given a public thrashing by the Americans for trying to blackball Germany. And the Nazi pariah and rubble heap of nine years earlier was parachuted into the Western Alliance and seated farther up the table than France. Churchill and Eden took note and accepted Eisenhower's offer made in Washington. All this seemed largely to escape the Canadian leaders, who were still somewhat susceptible to Nehru's affected pieties about American crudeness. West Germany formally joined NATO in April 1955 after Eisenhower and Adenauer had agreed that the West German army would not exceed twelve divisions.

A new front opened on September 3, 1954, when China started shelling the tiny offshore islands of Quemoy and Matsu, in the Formosa Strait, which instantly became household words throughout the world. The nearer of the islands is closer to the Chinese mainland than Staten Island is to Manhattan. Chiang had stuffed them with soldiers and used them as jumping-off points for the harassment of the Communist Chinese and coastal shipping. Chiang claimed that the islands were essential to the security of Taiwan, which the Joint Chiefs of Staff considered to be nonsense, but they could not be defended without the assistance of the United States. The Joint Chiefs called upon the president on holiday in Denver with his in-laws on September 12 and asked him for the third time in six months to authorize the use of nuclear weapons on the Chinese and the deployment of American forces to Quemoy and Matsu, but the world was fortunate to have an American president who knew how to deal with high-ranking officers, and Eisenhower summarily refused. In December, Eisenhower signed a mutual defence treaty with Chiang Kai-shek's Nationalist China, by which an attack on either was an attack on both, but confined the definition of Nationalist China to the island of Taiwan and the Pescadores Islands, and Chiang formally committed not to reinitiate war with Mao. At the beginning of 1955, Eisenhower asked Congress to authorize any degree of force he thought necessary to defend Taiwan, the Pescadores Islands, and "closely related localities." It was a sign of the nation's well-placed confidence in him that the Formosa Resolution passed Congress – in the Senate 83–3, and in the House of Representatives 403–3 – although it was specifically understood that this included recourse to nuclear weapons. Churchill and Eden, and presumably St. Laurent and Pearson, with whom they discussed these things, told

Eisenhower and Dulles that they should negotiate the handover of Quemoy and Matsu for a guaranty by China not to attack Taiwan. Eisenhower dismissed this as "more wishful than realistic." The fact is that none of America's allies except the frontline states like West Germany and South Korea had any real idea of how to deal with the communist powers now. Chou En-lai gave a conciliatory speech in Bandung, Indonesia, on April 23, 1955, Eisenhower replied in the same spirit, and the shelling of the islands was reduced then stopped altogether in May. It was a great victory for Eisenhower, who had chosen a testing place where he could afford to lose and American prestige was not really engaged.

In late January 1955, St. Laurent and Pearson had flown to a Commonwealth prime ministers' meeting in London, which would be Churchill's last. He was eighty and had announced his retirement, but he still dominated proceedings and gave his view that nuclear weapons (the hydrogen bomb was infinitely more powerful than the atomic bomb), would now, by the horror at the idea of them being used, ensure the peace. "Safety might be the child of terror and life the twin of annihilation," as he put it with his usual gifted articulation. Nehru, with his usual anti-Western gloom, preferred the baleful thought that terror would be permanent and probably unlimited (unless, of course, humanitarian moralists like himself were heeded). He advanced his customary theory that recognition of the People's Republic of China would reduce tensions. Everyone was eager to play the Americans' hand for them, but at least Churchill and St. Laurent and Adenauer and a few of the others knew their places, unlike Nehru and many of the French.

After the Formosa Strait episode, Eisenhower let it be known that he would consider a peace treaty with Austria leading to the evacuation of that country by the Soviets as a sufficient demonstration of their seriousness to justify a summit meeting if the Soviet Union desired one. This was done, and the Big Four, including France, met in Geneva starting on July 18, 1955. Anthony Eden, who had just succeeded Churchill, and Mendès-France's successor, Edgar Faure, led the British and French delegations, while the Soviet Union sent a patchwork of Kremlin factions led by Nikita Khrushchev, Nikolai Bulganin, Vyacheslav Molotov, and Marshal Georgi Zhukov. They were divided and ill at ease. (Khrushchev purged the other three within a couple of years.) Eisenhower began what proved to be the de-escalation of the Cold War with his Open Skies proposal by which each side would allow aerial inspection and reconnaissance from the other. The Russians were confused and suspicious and rejected the proposal without serious explanation. The conference was a minor success in ambiance even if it did not accomplish much, and it was the first such meeting since Potsdam ten years before. The fact was that beneath his syntactically challenged and affable manner, Eisenhower had moved with consummate skill to equip the West with the fearful might of a rearmed Germany while ending the Korean War, which his predecessor had failed to do in two years, and he had stayed out of Vietnam while possibly salvaging half the country. He and Chou En-lai were the smart players in this high-stakes game, and Eisenhower was in no need of advice on how to defend Western interests and avoid war from the venerable Churchill, and even less so from the earnest Pearson, and less still from the rose-fondling posturer in New Delhi. The West was in capable hands.

In an exchange of notes in 1955, the United States and Canada agreed a series of radar detection lines. The Pinetree Line, close to the U.S.-Canada border, was just coming into operation. Canada opened up the Mid-Canada Line at about the fifty-fifth parallel, but it was agreed that a more elaborate Distant Early Warning (DEW) Line, already built across Alaska, was needed in the Arctic to provide early detection of intruders for interception and early retaliation. This led to some debate in Canada, but it was eventually agreed that the United States would pay for it and it would be manned jointly. As it was an entirely defensive system, it was a politically manageable issue, and it was a further step in a process of joint continental defence that originated in King and Roosevelt's time nearly twenty years before.

In Quebec in 1956, the entire opposition formed an electoral coalition to challenge Duplessis, the Créditistes being nominated as official Liberals in a number of districts. Réal Caouette, who would go on to national fame as a federal candidate, as well as old nationalist René Chaloult, and *Le Devoir* parliamentary reporter Pierre Laporte, all ran as Liberals. Several federal Liberal ministers intervened to help Lapalme, including Jean Lesage; Ernest Lapointe's son, Hugues; and Roch Pinard. Duplessis's campaign was the usual rather hilarious affair, and very lavishly financed, reflecting the tangible benefits of a long incumbency. But the Liberals were well sponsored by their federal big brothers and enjoyed the support of most of the television media, especially Radio-Canada, the French service of the CBC. (René Lévesque was their most prominent commentator and was ostentatiously hostile to Duplessis.) When Lapointe and Pinard joined Lapalme in accusing Duplessis of being insufficiently protective of Quebec's farmers against Ontario margarine, Duplessis was ready: the federal Liberals had admitted to Canada and its unsuspecting breakfast tables 500,000 dozen "communist eggs" from Poland. This unlikely charge had Lesage and the others scrambling around for two weeks. Taking advantage of his rural electrification program, which had been very successful, Duplessis po-facedly announced, "A vote for the Union Nationale is a vote for electricity; a vote for the Liberals is a vote for the oil lamp." In the end, Duplessis ran on his record of low taxes, a balanced budget, huge construction projects, public works, job creation, school and university construction, social programs, almost no unemployment, peace and tranquility, and a firm establishment of the jurisdiction of Quebec. And he ran on his own personality, which captured the humour, the combativity, and the bourgeois solidity of French Quebec. He made no compromise with the coalition of his opponents and their criticism of his authoritarianism.

On June 20, 1956, he was decisively re-elected to an unprecedented, and since unequalled, fifth term as premier of Quebec, and won 73 out of 92 constituencies and 52 per cent of the vote to 45 per cent Liberal. He won more than 60 per cent of the French-speaking Québécois vote and almost all the constituencies, urban and rural, that did not have substantial numbers of non-French. It was a tremendous victory, though Duplessis, like St. Laurent, was tiring after a long career of meticulous micromanagement of almost everything in Quebec. He did not really believe in cabinet government and was known to everyone, friend and foe, in Quebec as Le Chef. Of his colleagues, only Paul Sauvé, son of R.B. Bennett's postmaster general, as the minister of Youth, had any autonomy. This was the time to make permanent constitutional arrangements for taxing, spending, all jurisdictional frictions, and amendment. Both Duplessis and St. Laurent could deliver their jurisdictions, Quebec and the whole country, to an agreement. No such

opportunity would come again in the intervening years, and this window, as the age and now slightly fatigued appearance of both men made
clear, would not be open indefinitely.

4. The Pipeline Debate and the Suez and Hungarian Crises, 1956–1957

In the early 1950s, enthusiasm gradually grew for the transmission by
pipeline of Alberta's recently discovered natural gas to Central Canada.
In 1951, Parliament granted a licence to Trans-Canada Pipelines, a subsidiary of an American company, to build such a pipeline entirely in
Canada. A Canadian company, Western Pipe Lines, backed by Alberta
premier Ernest Manning, sought authority to build a pipeline that
would transmit natural gas to Regina and Winnipeg and then connect
to U.S. gas distribution systems in Minnesota. The Consumers' Gas
Company of Toronto, assembled by a group of mainly Conservative
financiers, sought distribution rights for Ontario. The Alberta government would not allow exports from Alberta until all the needs of that
province were supplied, but in late 1953 it declared that an exportable
surplus existed, and C.D. Howe, a great and visionary builder in all
things, organized an amalgamation of the Trans-Canada and Western
companies and concepts. In 1954 and 1955, necessary permits were
obtained and an agreement for distribution in the United States was
achieved. The total cost of the project was estimated to be $350 million,
and its viability was still dependent on a permit from the U.S. Federal
Power Commission. Canadian lenders and underwriters would not
proceed until contracts were in place to assure the success of the project, and buyers would not contract until they were sure that the project
would get off the ground. In January 1956, the company asked for a
federal government guaranty of a loan of $275 million. Howe was in
favour, but the finance minister, Walter Harris, on advice of officials,
while agreeing on the project's prospects, wanted the U.S. Federal
Power Commission approval in hand and did not wish to guaranty at
4 per cent, as it could ultimately damage Canadian bond sales. Harris
recommended an application to the Industrial Development Bank
(IDB), a subsidiary of the Bank of Canada, which suggested that

$105 million be raised by a sale of common stock and the remainder through the sale of first mortgage bonds. The IDB was prepared to buy $35 million of the stock as convertible debentures yielding 6 per cent, and for a fee would be prepared to buy further if necessary. They also demanded what amounted to control of the board of the company, which was not acceptable to the Gulf Oil Company of Canada – a subsidiary of the American company of the same name – which was supplying most of the natural gas from Alberta.

Trans-Canada had already ordered the steel required for the line when the negotiations collapsed. On March 8, 1956, Clinton Murchison, a renowned Texas oilman, and one of the principals in the Trans-Canada consortium, telephoned Howe and said that if the IDB would raise its investment to $70 million, he and his associates would guaranty all disbursements by the company with full repayment within five years. A stenographer took down the proposal and Howe gave it directly to St. Laurent, who declined, in deference to the views of government officials and what he considered the political risks of going so far out on a limb for foreign investors. The company announced that construction would not proceed because the government of Canada would not produce an arrangement to assist, at no risk to itself, the financing of the project on a basis that did not transfer control of the project and the company to government appointees. This was correct and was admirably fearless, and it smoked out Howe, who was disappointed at the recession of what he had conceived as his last great public/private sector project and doubly irritated that it was interpreted as a putsch by Harris against him in the battle for the heart and mind of St. Laurent. Eventually, in the summer of 1956, Howe came up with a plan by which the federal and Ontario governments would construct the most expensive and least profitable part of the pipeline, through Northern Ontario, and would sell it on to Trans-Canada Pipelines later at an unfixed price.

In the summer and autumn of 1955 there had been a prolonged and acrimonious debate over renewal of the Defence Production Act, and a tired St. Laurent was induced to say a few things that, added to some of Howe's reflections, assisted the opposition agitation that, after twenty years in government, the St. Laurent–Howe Liberals were getting a little out of touch. St. Laurent referred to renewals three years later with the proviso "if we are still here in three years." They were small but telltale signs. The prime minister's elder son and law partner had had a coronary, which distressed his father and assisted in making him seem old. He was seventy-four in 1956. In fact, it was still hard to fault the government on its performance; the country was prosperous, respected in the world, and a relatively generous state where immigrants eagerly arrived every year in considerable numbers, and the federal-provincial scene had even, finally, been addressed in a somewhat imaginative way. The principal ministers were all demonstrably competent, so all that was left to the opposing political parties was to present St. Laurent as benign but geriatric, and the others, led by Howe and Gardiner, as arrogant and authoritarian. The pipeline debate was shaping up as a donnybrook, and the government would have to be careful to appear to be observing the parliamentary niceties.

Howe moved the incorporation of the Northern Ontario Pipe Line Crown Corporation on March 15, 1956. Premier Manning and Ontario's Premier Frost strongly supported the measure, which was carefully designed to bring natural gas to Central and Eastern Canada at good prices in a way that the governments could assist while entirely recovering their investment promptly without impinging on return to private sector investors or raising prices to the consumers. The measure had been adopted unanimously by the Ontario Legislature, which approved investing $35 million, and was adopted almost unanimously in Alberta's Legislature also. Though the majority of founding shareholders was American, the majority of shares overall would be held in Canada, and the majority of officers and directors were assured to be Canadian. Drew spoke immediately after Howe and accused the government of selling out the Canadian national interest to Americans and demanded that the deal be Canadianized, if need be, by public sector ownership with eventual privatization to Canadians. He stirred the Liberals with mordant comments about "vacuous faces opposite," and was followed by M.J. Coldwell for the CCF, who was less provoking but called for straight public ownership. Social Credit, whose leading espouser was Premier Manning, supported the government. Calgary oilman Frank McMahon proposed an all-Canadian alternative to Howe, and although he marked his letter "personal and confidential," he also gave it to the Opposition. Howe felt obliged to deny having received such an offer, and when Howe found out what had been done, McMahon's offer was withdrawn. Howe persuaded the cabinet that to get the project started that summer and to deliver natural gas from Alberta to Eastern Canada on a timetable that would be effective for the financing arrangements, the debate would have to be conducted fairly expeditiously, and that it might be necessary to enforce closure of the debate. The most protracted and unruly debate in the history of the federal Parliament ensued, after Howe announced that the government would advance up to 90 per cent of the cost of constructing the pipeline west of Winnipeg and would receive a pledge of all its assets in return and an option on the company's shares, with full repayment, at 5 per cent interest, in less than a year.

The unparliamentary allegations and shenanigans were a disgrace. Drew, Diefenbaker, Toronto MP Donald Fleming, British Columbia MP Davie Fulton, Coldwell and his chief proceduralist, Stanley Knowles, and several other opposition MPs accused the government of heinous crimes, dictatorship, imposition of the guillotine, emulation of Hitler, degradation of Parliament, cowardice, and so forth, all to achieve what Fulton called a "treaty of surrender to the United States." Howe introduced the prospect of closure on May 9, after stating, with some reason, that "it is obvious that some honourable members prefer to obstruct this motion rather than debate it." Drew made some particularly tasteless remarks aspersing Howe as someone whose loyalty to Canada was suspect because he was born in the United States (though he had been a Canadian citizen since 1914). Howe gamely defended himself and his bill, but St. Laurent was rather passive as the stormy debate unfolded. Many sessions went well into the night, a few almost to daybreak. The Speaker of the House of Commons, Louis-René Beaudoin, almost suffered a nervous breakdown in the midst of the debate, ruling mistakenly and then invoking questionable prerogatives to reverse himself and guide the debate through to conclusion within a few hours of its target date of June 5. At one point, Fleming was expelled from the House for refusing to resume his chair, and Diefenbaker histrionically called out "Farewell John Hampden" (parliamentary dissident of Cromwellian times) as Fleming was led away and Hamilton Conservative MP Ellen Fairclough draped over Fleming's desk a Union Jack that she had borrowed earlier in the day from House staff for what she claimed would be "a party." There were daily scenes of astonishing indignity, at one point Drew and Coldwell shaking their fists at the Speaker as Drew denounced the proceedings as "a complete farce" and Coldwell as "an abomination, an outrageous thing."[18]

As St. Laurent biographer Dale Thomson observed, "Although the government was certainly guilty of disrespect for Parliament in imposing a deadline before the pipeline debate had properly begun, and in applying the closure rule on various clauses of the bill before at least a minimum of debate had taken place on them," the charges against the Speaker, and against the ministry for supposedly dictating to the Speaker, were not justified.[19] On the proposed last day, President Achmad Sukarno of Indonesia, of all people, a corrupt, communist-tainted, buffoonish dictator, was in the gallery as part of a state visit, and observed some of the parliamentary juvenilism, undoubtedly confirming him in his disregard for democracy. The Liberals got their pipeline bill through, and it was a good and well-conceived bill, but they had suffered considerable loss of public esteem in the terrible unseemliness of the debate, though all parties except Social Credit had participated in the degradation of Parliament. Howe's magnificent achievements as a great builder and manager of the country were temporarily tarnished with the charges of dictatorship, and St. Laurent appeared relatively ineffective and diffident through most of the stormy passage. It was a very unedifying episode, compounded by the tactical errors of the House leader, finance minister Harris, and the formerly highly regarded Speaker, Beaudoin, who had to be persuaded by the prime minister not to throw in the towel and resign after a further controversy about a private letter he sent to a journalist at the Montreal newspaper *La Patrie*. St. Laurent was back in top form when he returned from an uneventful Commonwealth Conference and closed out the session on July 11, saying that the Opposition had tried to usurp the position of the government and that it was their conduct that was unconstitutional: "It is not by accident that [my] party has been in office for twenty-one years and plans to continue in office for several years longer."[20]

The autumn of 1956 was one of the most fraught of the entire Cold War, as crises blew up almost simultaneously in the Middle East and Central Europe. Eden had visited Eisenhower in January 1956 and was already very preoccupied with Britain's position in the Middle East, because of oil and the Suez Canal (which Britain had controlled since the 1870s), and reminded Eisenhower of the 1950 Tripartite Declaration between their countries and France that effectively forbade arms sales into the region. This was nonsense, of course, as the Russians would supply the Arabs happily, and the French were supplying Israel and were heavily involved in dealing with a nasty guerrilla war in what was officially the French province of Algeria. Eden proposed that in the Middle East, Britain take the lead and that the United States should join the Baghdad Pact, which linked Turkey, Iraq, Iran, and Pakistan, which he wished to upgrade as a military alliance and use to block Russia's way to the south, somewhat as an extension of NATO. In a final outburst of mad colonial egotism, the British imagined themselves to be dab hands at the complexities of the Middle East and fully capable of leading such an alliance, undaunted by the terrible mess they had made of the partitions of both Palestine and the old British Indian empire. Unfortunately, this delusional notion of their gift for managing Middle Eastern affairs was approximately matched by the equivalent American figment that the Muslims disliked the British and French more than they disliked the Americans, whom they would welcome as the original anti-colonial revolutionaries. It was one of the great fantasies of the American self-image, which started with Roosevelt's nonsense that the Americans would be better received than the British when they invaded Morocco and Algeria in 1942, and that Stalin would take the Western message better from him and his officials than from Churchill and his. The Russians and the Arabs regarded the Americans and the British as interchangeable scoundrels and swindlers, and the Americans would have done themselves a favour by adopting the view of the British (apart from a few hopeless romantics like T.E. Lawrence and Wilfrid Scawen Blunt) that the Arabs were essentially a gang of nomads, pickpockets, and camel thieves. The problem was aggravated by Israeli hatred of Britain because of their not unfounded view that, in blocking Jewish emigration to Palestine, the British had inadvertently been partly responsible for the deaths of hundreds of thousands of Jews killed by the Nazis and their collaborators during the Second World War. The Canadians had a slightly different version of naïveté; they didn't claim to know anything about the Arabs but thought that good old fair play would work and reproached both the British neo-colonialism and the American pretense to plain New World can-dour. Canada favoured good-faith negotiations, like those between Quebec and Ottawa, as if the Arabs really wanted an arrangement with the Israelis that would accept the legitimacy of that country and end their ability to distract the Arab masses with the red herring of Israel, which they portrayed as an insolent, domineering Jewish pres-ence in their midst sustained, as the Arabs would have it, by the insidi-ous philo-Semitism of the Americans. Everyone knew it was a politically unpromising area, but all the parties except Israel seemed to have exces-sive hopes about their ability to manage the Middle East.

Eisenhower recognized that the key was keeping Middle East oil flowing to Western Europe and was suitably wary of Egyptian president Gamal Abdel Nasser's disposition to stir up the Arab masses and draw the Soviets into the region. He started to try to promote Saudi Arabia as an alternative to Egypt as a power in the Arab world, but the House of Saud was a feudal clan of oil-rich nomads and had no mass appeal among the Arabs. As Nasser became a Soviet arms recipient on a steadily larger scale, Eisenhower tried unwisely to bring him to heel by absurd and demeaning measures such as cancelling CARE (Cooperative for Assistance and Relief Everywhere) aid to Egypt and threatening to with-draw financial support for the Aswan Dam, a humanitarian project designed to increase Egyptian agricultural and hydroelectric produc-tion. He did cancel the commitment to finance the dam on July 19. Britain had withdrawn its eighty-thousand-man army force from Egypt, leaving the Suez Canal a sitting duck for Nasser, but the British assumed that Nasser would not know how to operate it. Both the British and American governments should have realized that the Russians would be happy to build Nasser's dam and help him operate the canal, and they were both making up their policy very erratically as they went along.

Nasser seized the Suez Canal on July 26 and took over its operations without difficulty. Eden was apoplectic and threatened military action, which Eisenhower considered an over-hasty recourse in pursuit of quasi-colonial objectives. He sent veteran diplomat Robert Murphy to London and Paris to warn the British and French not to encourage an Israeli involvement and to propose a conference of maritime nations. Eisenhower had irrational fears that the crisis might lead to a cessation of oil supplies to Western Europe, which was out of the question, as Iran, the Saudis, and the Gulf states would have nothing to do with such a thing, and the Arabs had no grievance against most Europeans. Eisenhower feared that oil and gasoline might have to be rationed in the United States to keep the lights on in London and Paris, and that the Panamanians might be spooked by the Egyptians. (Again, this was a fatuous concern, as the United States had created the country of Panama and purported to lease the Canal Zone permanently, and had a very adequate military force around the canal to squash any delusions of liberation by Panama.) As deft as Eisenhower had been with Germany and even Korea, and up to a point Indochina, he was rather inept with Egypt, though still a masterly statesman compared with the escapade in complete lunacy that Eden was cooking up. In a typical time-wasting, cooling-off move, the maritime conference of twenty-two countries that Dulles proposed as a Suez Canal Users' Association meeting took place in August and produced an 18–4 vote for internationalization of the canal, and veteran Australian Prime Minister Robert Menzies was delegated to try to sell this to Nasser. He attempted to do so on September 2, but the idea was nonsense: the "users" had no standing to say who would own the canal and Nasser would not hear of it. He would guaranty access to all countries (except Israel) and reasonable tolls, but that was all. Eisenhower told Eden to keep calm and that Nasser could be worn down and undermined over time, and Dulles was still giving lip service to having Nasser forced to "disgorge his theft." But Eden was hyperactive and irrational and Eisenhower and Dulles were just dispensing bromides and palliatives. The British pilots on the canal abandoned their posts on September 14 and were immediately replaced, without difficulty, by Egyptians.

The Canadian House of Commons had met on July 28 when St. Laurent and Pearson received from Eden the first hint that Britain was considering military action. Progressive Conservative foreign policy spokesman John Diefenbaker starkly warned the government that his party was solidly behind the British, come what may. Pearson responded to him, agreeing that the seizure of the canal was "to be condemned . . . [as] a violation of an international convention," and said that Canada was consulting closely with countries more directly concerned with the problems raised by the canal. Diefenbaker compared Nasser with Hitler and Mussolini, but Nehru and other Asian and African governments were sympathetic to Nasser. (Gandhi had been somewhat sympathetic to

Hitler too, unaware that Hitler had urged Eden to shoot him and Nehru.) St. Laurent and Pearson were more sympathetic to Britain than the United States was, but they felt that any recourse to force had to be under the aegis of the United Nations, which was still taken somewhat seriously as a legitimizing organization. All this was delusional: Nasser had the canal, and the British and French could seize it back, with or without the Israelis, but had no ability to hold it indefinitely. Diefenbaker demanded that Canada attend Dulles's conference, despite Pearson's explanation that since Canada did not use the canal it had not been invited.

Dulles and Murphy told the Canadian ambassador in Washington, Arnold Heeney, on August 4 that the British and French were threatening to go to war. Australia and New Zealand were supporting drastic action by the United Kingdom and France; Nehru and Pakistan and Ceylon favoured Nasser, and Canada held the neutral balance in the Commonwealth, as it did to some extent between the British and Americans, except that both those powers were going to do what they thought best with little consideration of Canada, a peripheral player whose only possible influence would be at the United Nations.

On September 3, the Canadian high commissioner in London, Norman Robertson, told senior members of the British government that Canada understood Britain's position and agreed that the Suez Canal must not be dependent on the whims of any one country but that Canada would not support a premature recourse to force. At the NATO meeting in Paris a few days later, British foreign secretary Selwyn Lloyd told Pearson that Israel might intervene. Pearson said that Israel wouldn't solve the problem; it would unite the Arabs behind Nasser.[21]

Pearson wanted to move it to the United Nations, but Dulles refused (certainly under orders from his president) and objected to Britain and France trying to manoeuvre the UN into approving severe measures against Egypt. This was a bit rich given the large contribution the Americans had made to the problem by doing a U-turn on Aswan and pushing Nasser into the arms of the Russians. Pearson was trying to get the Western Big Three singing at least partially from the same song sheet. Britain and France ignored the Americans and on September 23 asked for UN discussion of the seizure of the canal by Egypt. On September 21, Canada had agreed to sell Israel twenty-four warplanes, and France had secretly been supplying Israel with tanks and aircraft all year. Joint staff talks took place between the British, French, and Israelis, and a military plan was agreed on October 3 between the three powers. The UN Security Council was immobilized by the Soviet Union, which vetoed a proposal that Suez Canal tolls be paid to a users' association. On October 8, Eisenhower, trying to diffuse and confuse as only he knew how, urged the State Department to make "any proposal" to distract Nasser and announced that the United States would not countenance the use of force but that it was building at once sixty-thousand-ton tankers that would reduce British and French dependence on oil coming through the Suez Canal and reduce toll revenues in the canal. On October 16, Eden was back in Paris and agreed with the French and Israeli governments to proceed with the seizure of the canal. The final touches were added to the plan, and an agreement signed on October 24: the Israelis were to attack Egypt on November 1, and Britain and France would then intervene as peacemakers and require both sides to withdraw from the canal and occupy the canal zone; Israel would take the Sinai and the Anglo-French force that would operate and protect the canal would be supplied via Israel. Israel's occupation of the Sinai and access to the canal for its ships was an understandable incentive. The French didn't care if the scheme was exposed as a scam; they wanted only to kick the Arabs hard and send a message to the Algerian guerrillas. The Americans were ineffectual and part of the problem and not of any solution. But Eden, and future prime ministers Harold Macmillan and Alec Douglas-Home, and senior officials like Rab Butler, Eden's senior minister, had all taken leave of their senses and could not seriously have thought that even domestic British opinion would support such a mad enterprise.

On October 29, Israeli paratroopers were dropped twenty-five miles from the Suez Canal, and on October 30, Britain and France issued an ultimatum to Israel and Egypt to withdraw ten miles on either side from the canal within twelve hours. Canada learned of this from the British as it happened, with the usual breezy assertion that Britain hoped it could count on Canadian support, although Pearson and Robertson had made it clear that Canadian support would not be forthcoming. It was the same British assumption that Canada was a tail to the British kite as had existed at the time of the South African War, and St. Laurent found it very annoying. St. Laurent and Pearson, with a divided cabinet and Parliament, set about designing a position that would hold an adequate level of public support. Eisenhower, who was up for re-election five days later, summoned the British chargé, in the absence of the ambassador, and reminded him that the United States had pledged in 1950 to uphold any party in the Middle East that was the victim of aggression. The British and French position was that they were the victims of aggression by Nasser and that Nasser was clearly addressing the canal takeover partly at the Americans for having withdrawn their support for the Aswan project, and the British, French, and Israeli governments did not believe the implicit threat by Eisenhower. The British told the United States it considered the 1950 agreement a dead letter. The U.S. government publicly stated that it thought otherwise and that Egypt was the wronged party.

Very little of what was happening made any sense. The British and Americans, instead of behaving like allies, were behaving almost like adversaries. The motives of everyone else were understandable, including Canada, which had no standing except to champion international organizations, the traditional recourse of secondary powers, bolstered in this case by Canada's fervent desire to prevent a schism in the Western ranks. St. Laurent was, by some measurements, the French-speaking world's most respected incumbent statesman, given the revolving-door governments in France, but France and Israel just wanted to kick the Arabs. Britain was having a *beau geste* moment of Kiplingesque nostalgia, and all the West was hiding behind a misplaced conviction that the other countries wouldn't dare follow through on their threats: Britain, France, and Israel wouldn't dare go to war without consulting with the Americans; and the Americans wouldn't dare desert their greatest allies. No one was leading, except, in his troublesome way, Nasser. And in the midst of it, as the Russians were salivating at the prospect of sowing mayhem in the Middle East, their own brutal usurpation of control of Eastern Europe started to crumble.

Following the release of Khrushchev's address denouncing Stalin at the Twentieth Congress of the Communist Party in February 1956, riots erupted in Poland in June and the puppet satellite regime was thrown out and replaced by former leader Wladyslaw Gomulka, whom the Soviets had forced out as a Titoist in 1948, when Tito was seceding from the Soviet Bloc, and who was in prison awaiting execution when Stalin miraculously died in 1953, whereupon he was released. On October 22, the disturbances spread to Hungary, and the following day the premier the Soviets had fired as a loyalty risk to them, Imre Nagy, was recalled. While Nagy promised democratization and a rising standard of living, the Soviets dispatched units from their occupation forces in Hungary to Budapest to "maintain order." All Hungary erupted, with spontaneous uprisings and freedom fighters throwing Molotov cocktails to blow the treads off Soviet tanks (as Molotov himself accompanied Khrushchev to Warsaw and approved an arrangement with Gomulka whereby he would support Soviet foreign policy but experiment somewhat in domestic policy). Nagy announced Hungary's withdrawal from the Warsaw Pact and its neutrality in the Cold War, while the Soviet ambassador in Budapest, Yuri Andropov (a subsequent chairman of the Soviet Communist Party), claimed to be negotiating the withdrawal of the Soviet occupation forces. Eisenhower doubted the sincerity of the Russians but could not resist smug self-congratulations in his inner circle on the swift disintegration of the Eastern Bloc in response to all the Republican electioneering drivel about "liberation" and "roll-back." Nagy was an innocent, and Eisenhower did nothing to deter the Soviet Union from reimposing its will in Eastern Europe. The United States had been encouraging Eastern Europe to revolt on Radio Free Europe and Voice of America for ten years, and they appeared to be reaping the harvest, just as the West headed, very conveniently for the Russians, over the cliff into ludicrous disarray, because of an infelicitous joint outbreak of counter-historical British stupidity and American delusion in the Middle East.

Parallel to the American misjudgments of the Middle East was another intelligence failure almost as complete as that which did not detect the clandestine Red Chinese invasion of Korea. The Grand Alliance of Roosevelt and Churchill had deteriorated to the point where Eden would not allow American intelligence flights over the Soviet Bloc to originate in the United Kingdom (so much for Eisenhower's imaginative Open Skies proposal of the previous year). And those flights, which now took off from Germany, detected an Israeli forces buildup which was judged to presage an invasion of Jordan, but neither aerial reconnaissance nor fervent efforts by the United States to crack the codes of the British, French, and Israelis (three of America's closest allies) discovered the extent of the buildup of an Anglo-French invasion force on Cyprus. A tragicomedy of errors was afoot. The Americans were stuck on the theory that the Anglo-French expected them to save their chestnuts again, as, according to the American version, they had done in both world wars. All three of the colluding powers underestimated the extent of Eisenhower's hostility, but all they wanted was for the United States to remain on the sidelines while they knocked the stuffing out of Nasser. Given the abrupt American cancellation of aid to the Aswan Dam, it was eccentric for the United States to wax so protective of Nasser, who identified the United States as an enemy as odious as the other three in his ferocious tirades to the Arab world. On October 30, the founding premier of Israel, David Ben-Gurion, sharply rejected Eisenhower's warnings not to advance and wrote that "Israel's survival is at stake."

Instead of seeing it as a challenge to wind down the violence in the Middle East, pressure Russia without blowing up Europe, and find common ground with the countries that would be its principal allies again after all the dust settled, the American government, ever oblivious to its own role in starting the unfolding debacle, was driven by affronted *amour-propre*. On October 30, the U.S. ambassador to the United Nations, Henry Cabot Lodge Jr. (grandson of Woodrow Wilson's nemesis and at the UN as a consolation prize for losing his Senate seat in Massachusetts to the swiftly rising John F. Kennedy), introduced a resolution at the Security Council asking for Israel to withdraw to the previous border. To enable the British and French to support the resolution, the British ambassador, the very articulate Sir Pierson Dixon, asked for it to be broadened to include criticism of Egyptian conduct. Lodge rejected this, and both Britain and France vetoed the resolution, which Lodge, Dulles, and Eisenhower should have known would happen. Australia and Belgium, out of loyalty to Britain and France respectively, abstained, and the Soviet Union and five other countries voted with the Americans. Later that day, the British and French also vetoed a Soviet resolution, on which the United States abstained. On October 31, the Canadian cabinet met to consider the reply to Eden that St. Laurent and Pearson had prepared, as the RAF dropped warning leaflets on Port Said at the north end of the canal and events generally bustled past the distant and providentially disconnected Canadians.

Eden won a confidence motion 270–218, which was uncomfortably close enough for this risky a move and came after a powerful address by Hugh Gaitskell, Clement Attlee's successor as Opposition and Labour Party leader, denouncing the move as insane and uncivilized.

St. Laurent's message to Eden was the best balance that could be struck between the desire of most Canadians to support the British (St. Laurent had told some of his more anglophile ministers that they were "just talking with your blood"[22]) and the correct judgment of the Canadian leaders that the tripartite military action was mad and illegal. St. Laurent conveyed his regret that Britain had plunged ahead without consultation. He expressed understanding of Britain's circumstances and motives for acting, but stated that Canada was unable to support the action and was suspending any military assistance to Israel (including the just-approved sale of the twenty-four fighter planes). While emphasizing relations with the United Kingdom and the importance to Britain of the Suez Canal, St. Laurent expressed particular concern about Britain's departure from the spirit and charter of the United Nations; about the severe stresses being placed on Commonwealth unity (Nehru had condemned the three attacking powers, as expected); and about the strain being placed on Anglo-American relations, which, St. Laurent wrote, were more important to Canada than anything except the survival of Canada itself. He purported to write with regret but with the candour that profound friendship required. The only dissenting minister was the formidable and long-serving agriculture minister, James G. Gardiner, who said the Middle East was no concern of Canada's and it should duck the whole issue.

Eden was disconcerted by the message and, with the usual failure of the British to have any sensitivity for the Canadian perspective, surprised by it. There were slightly farcical scenes even in Ottawa in keeping with the trajectory of events in the world, as reporters were allowed to fill the corridors between the Prime Minister's Office and the Privy Council Office, where the cabinet met, and grilled St. Laurent and his colleagues at intimate range as they went into and out of meetings. At one point, an exasperated St. Laurent disappeared into the Cabinet Room and then reappeared, saying to the news-hungry media, "It's too bad you can't come in and tell us what to do, but we're the ones who have the responsibility."[23] At the November 1 cabinet meeting,

Pearson reported that he had telephoned London and Washington to ask if they would support a proposal for a UN force, but both had replied that while that might be part of an eventual solution, it would not be appropriate now (as the invasion of Egypt was getting into full swing). Pearson told the cabinet that he would do what he could to avoid the British and French being condemned by the General Assembly and to promote the re-establishment of order by an international police force. He went at once to New York and the UN and urged Dulles to slow down and allow time for compromises that would put less strain on the Western Alliance. Dulles was now engaged in an inexplicable race with the Russians to masquerade as the more friendly to Egypt and the more outraged by the aggressions of America's three allies, and the Soviets were uninhibited in their histrionics by the discomforts of their own jackbooted occupation of Eastern Europe.

Dulles told Pearson that their three allies had "damaged the whole cause of freedom by placing us in an inferior position morally to the communists. We could be having a showdown right now over this Hungary situation but for their actions."[24] Like almost everything all the protagonists said, this was half true and half false. The Americans could have all the showdown they wished over Hungary, but they had no stomach for it. They had no forces engaged in the Middle East, and if they had moved light forces into Hungary when Nagy requested it, as he shortly would, and offered the neutralization of a substantial part of Europe to the Russians, it might have been effective, at the least in wrong-footing the Russians. Eisenhower and Dulles preferred to claim that the Anglo-French-Israeli action, the absurdity of which was not at issue, prevented the United States from acting strongly in Central Europe, which, in fact, they had no disposition to do, as Eisenhower acknowledged in his memoirs.[25]

Lodge alit on the idea of a UN force at about the same time Pearson did, and wrote up a resolution for him, which he said Pearson should move, as the Indians and others, as well as the Soviet Bloc, would reject it if they knew it came from the United States. Pearson had heard on November 1 from Norman Robertson in London, after conversations Robertson had had with senior British and French officials, that a police action of adequate size would be welcomed by London and Paris, as would Canada's role in leading it.[26]

Pearson had been working on a plan that would incorporate a large part of the British and French forces into a UN force, cleverly bringing them under the same tent as the Americans and enabling them to claim success and minimize damage to the alliance. He reported to the cabinet in Ottawa on the afternoon of November 2 and then returned to New York. Eden finally started to return to his senses and called St. Laurent on November 3 to enthuse about a UN force that would enable British and French troops to "continue our operations against Egypt under the United Nations flag."[27] St. Laurent couldn't offer much hope that that would be acceptable but would see what could be done. Eden revealed a fallback position of handing over the Anglo-French position to the UN when their initial targets had been achieved. Their conversation started stiffly but progressed well and constituted the beginning of productive resumption of contact between the British, French, and Israeli governments on one side and Washington on the other. By being the only government representatives that made sense, kept calm, and showed some imagination, St. Laurent and especially Pearson seriously distinguished themselves and advanced Canada's diplomatic status to a position it had not held before. While Pearson did most of the thinking, St. Laurent collaborated usefully, gave Pearson the necessary support, and kept in line a fractious cabinet that could easily have been stampeded by the Victorian pyrotechnics of Diefenbaker and others. Pearson told St. Laurent that the best that might be done was to add some British and French forces, as they were "immediately available," to the rudimentary United Nations Truce Supervision Organization headed by Canadian General E.L.M. Burns, and then add a permanent force of troops made up from other countries, including a Canadian contingent.

There was now a circle of coordinators communicating by telephone: St. Laurent keeping the cabinet in line, speaking with Pearson in New York – who was working with Lodge and Dulles, the Indians, and the UN secretary general, Dag Hammarskjöld – and Robertson in London – who was dealing directly with senior officials of the Foreign Office and Quai d'Orsay, which was represented in London by senior career diplomat Ambassador Jean Chauvel (who was well along in a fantastic career that spanned the world and lasted nearly sixty years). It was this group that beat a path through the tenebrous thickets created by the blunders and outrages of many governments (mainly of the traditional great powers) simultaneously. Robertson arranged a delay in British main force landings until after the vote on the Lodge-Pearson resolution on the night of November 3. Pearson was not able to persuade India to join him in moving it, but Norway and Colombia (countries even less directly involved than Canada and as inoffensive as Canada to the protagonists) did join him in a resolution urging Hammarskjöld to produce a plan within forty-eight hours for the "setting up of an emergency UN force to secure and supervise the cessation of hostilities." Lodge was now speaking for America, and in more emollient vocabulary than that of the irascible and sanctimonious Dulles. Eden told Robertson that Britain would hold for the forty-eight-hour deadline, and the Indians obtained from Nasser approval of Canadian, American, and Scandinavian troops in Egypt as a truce force. Pearson made a deal with a nineteen-nation Afro-Asian bloc that produced a resolution calling for a ceasefire within twelve hours. The resolutions were voted concurrently at 2 a.m., November 4. Pearson's passed 57 to 0, with the United States for, and Britain, France, Israel, Egypt, Australia, New Zealand, and the Soviet Bloc abstaining; and the Afro-Asian bloc resolution passed 59–5, with Canada in favour, in accord with Pearson's arrangement, and twelve abstentions. Canada and Pearson were much congratulated at the UN and in world capitals, but the eighty-two-year-old Arthur Meighen spoke for many Canadians when he claimed to have vomited on reading the terms of the resolution. (It was his standard reaction all his adult life to almost any Canadian derogation from the British position, apart from the matter of relations with Japan in 1922. Chapter 6.)

In Hungary, 80 per cent of the army of that country had deserted to form an ad hoc patriotic and anti-communist force, and after ten days of insincere negotiations while they prepared their counter-blow and disorder largely continued all over Hungary, the Soviet Union invaded Hungary with seventeen divisions, including some other Warsaw Pact countries, and seized the Hungarian negotiators. Nagy finally asked for the intervention of the world community, with Soviet tanks less than a mile away from him, and from no one in particular, but claiming now to have responded to the exhortations of Radio Free Europe. The reoccupation was almost complete within a day, and Nagy was captured, tried secretly, and executed in 1958. (On the thirty-first anniversary of his interment in a prison cemetery, face down, and with hands tied by barbed wire, he was reinterred before a crowd of over one hundred thousand in a place of honour.) There were about two hundred thousand Hungarian refugees, and on a per capita basis, Canada and Australia were much more generous in receiving them than the United States was, despite the best efforts of Vice President Nixon, who visited the Hungarian border with Austria and lobbied Eisenhower and House Speaker Sam Rayburn to admit more than the usual quota of twenty-one thousand.[28]

The British finally landed on November 5 at the north end of the Suez Canal, and Soviet Premier Bulganin, in the name of the divided politburo, ignoring his own country's monstrous aggression against the defenceless Hungarians, threatened war on Britain and France. Bulganin proposed joint Soviet-American military intervention in the Middle East. Preposterous as it was, it shook Eisenhower out of his recent piqued torpor. He ignored the joint military suggestion but responded at once that the Unites States would consider any Soviet military action against Britain or France to be an attack on the United States itself and that it would be replied to immediately and with maximum force. There was no more talk from the Kremlin about attacking Britain and France.

Eden could have deferred – that is, cancelled – the attack and claimed that he had accomplished his objectives, but in failing to do so, he threw away the last chance to appear as if he actually knew what he was doing. A run began on the British pound, and Britain's request for a loan from the United States drew the reply that it could be done, conditional on a ceasefire by midnight on November 6. Eden privately declared himself to be "cornered" and declined the appeal of the French to continue for another day to strengthen their position. (Events had come full circle since Churchill and Eden were asking the French to fight on in 1940.) Eden accepted the U.S. deadline; he was finished, his health broken and his career over, but the crisis ended. When Eden called Eisenhower on November 6 to say that he would meet the deadline and asked how the election looked, Eisenhower said, "I don't give a damn about the election; I guess it will be all right."[29] Eisenhower was easily re-elected on November 6, with 57.4 per cent of the vote compared with 42 per cent for his urbane opponent, whom he had also defeated in 1952, former Illinois governor Adlai E. Stevenson. Eisenhower telephoned St. Laurent and was unstinting in his praise of St. Laurent and Pearson. "You did a magnificent job, and we admire it," he said.[30] It was nothing but the truth. St. Laurent sent a conciliatory message to Nehru, who was considering seceding from the Commonwealth, and Eisenhower continued an oil embargo on Britain and France until their forces were out of Egypt. He had already told his ambassador in London, Winthrop Aldrich (brother-in-law of Mackenzie King's friend John D. Rockefeller Jr.), to scheme with Chancellor of the Exchequer Harold Macmillan (whose conduct in the whole affair was not completely disinterested) and government parliamentary leader Rab Butler, as he rightly assumed that Eden was finished and that one of them would be the next leader of the United Kingdom, with whom it would be necessary to rebuild relations.

While it had been a very effective performance by St. Laurent and Pearson, it was given a mixed reception by Canadians. A Gallup poll right after the crisis subsided found 43 per cent of Canadians supported the British and their allies, 40 per cent opposed, and only 17 per cent were undecided, and a majority of English-speaking Canadians felt their government had let Britain down. In parliamentary questioning in late November, St. Laurent said, in a somewhat unguarded moment, that "the era when the supermen of Europe could govern the whole world is coming close to an end."[31] This was, in the circumstances, a very reasonable comment, but it led to further allegations that Canada had rolled over for the United States and betrayed the British and French. It also began a gradual overcommitment of Canada to the whole nebulous notion of peacekeeping; when you have war, peacekeepers can't function, and when there is peace, they are not needed. But it became an inexpensive way to pretend to be maintaining a useful military, and an irreproachable way always to be on the right side orally, until fiascos in Bosnia and Somalia exposed the whole procedure as problematical.

Nehru and his daughter, Indira Gandhi, visited Ottawa in December, and St. Laurent claimed that the Canadian winter was merely his revenge on the teeming heat he had experienced when visiting India in 1954. They had their customary exchange on the need for defensive alliances and even the utility in some respect of nuclear weapons. Nehru trotted out his usual pieties about the virtue of poverty-stricken, chronically corrupt India for eschewing these insidious props of Western misrule. It was all part of St. Laurent's personal campaign to keep the Commonwealth together and relevant in the world. In the same spirit of hosing down the hot embers of recent conflagrations, he had a cordial visit with President Eisenhower in Georgia earlier in the month. (It was a golfing visit, despite the fact that St. Laurent conceded to the media that he had not yet broken 100, when playing by the rules.)

In April 1957, there would occur a tragic illustration of the frictions between America at the height of the Cold War and Canada as it discreetly followed its only slightly divergent path. Career diplomat Herbert Norman, Canada's ambassador to Egypt, whom the Americans had long suspected of being a communist sympathizer, because of university connections he had with the far left, and even of being a Soviet agent, was referred to again in deliberations of the U.S. Senate Subcommittee on Internal Security and committed suicide by leaping from the roof of the Swedish embassy in Cairo. He was a protégé of Pearson, and it was a terrible and unjust fate for a talented foreign service official which gave rise to a good deal of resentment and of conspiracy theories on the right and left. Norman was only forty-seven. Canadians have generally ascribed Norman's death to what Pearson later described as "the black madness of the witch-hunt."[32]

In December 1956 – George Drew having retired for reasons of health and of internecine squabbling – the redoubtable, combative, but erratic John Diefenbaker, four-term MP from Prince Albert, was elected leader of the Opposition. He and St. Laurent had got on reasonably well; St. Laurent respected his barristerial talents but doubted his judgment and whether he possessed the worldly exposure the office needed. He was thirteen years younger than St. Laurent but had served two years longer in the House of Commons.

5. The Tempestuous Interlude of John Diefenbaker, 1957–1962

After nearly five full terms, the government was a melange of talented younger ministers and a leading group that was now elderly. St. Laurent would be seventy-five in February 1957; C.D. Howe would be seventy-one in January; and Jimmy Gardiner had just turned seventy-three. They had all been very strong ministers, probably Mackenzie King's three most brilliant recruits, but they had served between them a total of nearly sixty years in the senior positions of the government, and bruising events like the pipeline debate and the Suez Crisis encouraged the voters to think a change was required, especially as even the courtly and modest St. Laurent, perhaps to counter the insecurities of aging, lost few opportunities to state that the government would be in office for some time yet. St. Laurent observed his eighth anniversary as prime minister in November 1956, and he should have deferred the next election to the autumn of 1957, or even the spring of 1958, and prepared to hand over to a new leader. He, Howe, and Gardiner should have all gone together in 1957 and some more new blood been injected. St. Laurent had been remiss in not recruiting new talent from Quebec. Jean Lesage was capable, but Georges-Émile Lapalme, having been twice defeated by Duplessis, was retiring as Quebec Liberal leader, and it was assumed that Lesage would succeed him. Douglas Abbott and even Brooke Claxton should have been considered for a return to government, though it is possible that neither would have been interested. It was a very accomplished and talented government, but long in the saddle, very complacent, and facing an opponent much more adept at stirring up underdog sentiment and the wrath and ambitions of the average person than any previous Conservative leader had been since John A. Macdonald. Even Robert Borden had been no great popular standard-bearer – a solid Maritimes lawyer who exuded practical Protestant Imperial values and integrity, but no particular man of the people. The others had either been bullhorns like Meighen and Bennett, and even Drew, or inadequately distinct personalities like Robert Manion and John Bracken. Party leaders could only be indistinct in the public mind if they were extremely tactically astute, like King, who extended the frontiers both of indistinctness and of tactical cunning.

In the 1957 session, Diefenbaker opened his career as Opposition leader, a role in which he would excel, with the allegation that the government was full of "resolute inaction" in almost all fields. St. Laurent jauntily responded, welcoming the new leader, the seventh his party had faced since they were last out of government, and referred with typical graciousness and thoughtfulness to Drew and to the just retired Sir Anthony Eden. Walter Harris brought down a tight money budget on March 15, showing admirable Liberal disregard for the political exigencies, the mark of a regime confident of its electoral invulnerability. St. Laurent spoke about attending the Commonwealth Conference in late June and wrote to the new Ghanaian leader, Kwame Nkrumah, that he was looking forward to meeting him. Parliament was dissolved for elections on June 10, 1957. Many Senate seats were left unfilled, though St. Laurent did appoint the thirty-three-year-old Paul Hellyer as the first Toronto cabinet minister in his government, as associate minister of national defence.

The prime minister embarked by rail on a cross-Canada tour determined not to make any election promises for the purpose of generating votes. He had a rather lacklustre campaign opening in Winnipeg, though he managed some good lines about the pipeline debate being "as long as the pipeline itself and as full of another kind of natural gas."[33] He gave a laborious speech in Victoria on foreign policy, prepared by external affairs officials, and in Saskatoon, people were invited to bring their own lunch and watch him being served a proper luncheon before he spoke. There was still no decision on the South Saskatchewan hydro-electric project six years after deliberations on it began. The campaign continued in this subdued, aged, bumbling way, almost lifelessly, while Diefenbaker – who had been a maverick in his own party and an unsuccessful challenger to Bracken and to Drew – had an air of missionary fulfilment, as if he were reaching the summit of a steep mountain he had been climbing a long time. His oratory was sometimes cleverly sarcastic (taking a few Liberal words and misusing them – "the supermen," Canada being "allied with Russia against Britain at the United Nations" – ending punchy sentences "and Howe!" and so forth) and sometimes invoked Canada's future in an almost mystical incantation. It was fervent, witty, and effective, but not altogether substantial. St. Laurent's windup in Toronto's Maple Leaf Gardens was a terrible failure: when an adolescent advanced up some steps toward St. Laurent holding a picture of him and then tore it up, one of the party executive pushed the teenager back, and he fell down the steps and lay unconscious on the floor as the prime minister, gape-mouthed, stared at this unscheduled divertissement and the vast stadium was silent.

On June 10, the Progressive Conservatives gained 61 MPs and 7.8 per cent of the vote to win 112 seats with 38.5 per cent. The Liberals lost 64 MPs and dropped 7.8 per cent of the vote to win 105 seats with 40.5 per cent. The CCF gained 2 MPs for a total of 25, but dropped 0.6 per cent of the vote to 10.6; and Social Credit gained 4 MPs for a total of 19 and gained 1.1 per cent of the popular vote to hold 6.6. All four party leaders were re-elected, but C.D. Howe and Walter Harris and several other ministers were defeated. St. Laurent said to one of his defeated colleagues, "They just got tired of having us around." He was popular and respected and the government was thought competent, but they had taken the country for granted. Of the nearly 8 per cent the Liberals lost in the overall popular vote, post-election polls showed almost 40 per cent of that was because of the pipeline debate, over 25 per cent of it was because of Harris's skinflint pension increase, and 30 per cent of it was just because of a desire for a change, which is always a danger with a government twenty years in office, even if it goes to greater lengths to renovate itself than this one had. The support of Ontario's Leslie Frost and Quebec's Maurice Duplessis had helped Diefenbaker; Frost had appeared publicly with him, and this helped raise the Tory numbers by almost 10 per cent in Ontario, and while Duplessis had been more circumspect, he had committed his organization in several areas and provided the margin for success in seven or eight constituencies, including the defeat of Hugues Lapointe, son of his old nemesis. If Duplessis had sat on his hands and those eight Liberals had been re-elected, St. Laurent would tenuously have won the election and retired in favour of a new Liberal leader, who could probably have won a confidence vote in Parliament.

Jimmy Gardiner had been re-elected, and he led the cabinet faction that wanted to meet the House; he did not believe the smaller parties would support the Tories, and he well remembered King's successful shenanigans against Meighen in 1925. The Liberals had narrowly led the popular vote, and Gardiner believed that the country just wanted to send the Liberals a warning but not actually make a change. Even at this late date, the Liberals found it inconceivable that the country would want to change governments. The government King had built was nowhere stronger than in the conviction of entitlement to govern riveted in his and his colleagues' minds. St. Laurent, ever the man of duty, had never wanted office just to hold it, and while he had hung on too long, he certainly would not fail to do the honourable thing. After a couple of days of consideration, he was determined to tender the government's resignation, and he told Diefenbaker that they should wait for the military vote (which gave the Liberals another MP) and then resign at the Progressive Conservative leader's convenience. Both men were entirely courteous and generous in their comments, privately and publicly.

Louis S. St. Laurent had undoubtedly been a very successful, competent, and distinguished prime minister, surpassed in achievement only by Macdonald, Laurier, and King, all of whom were professional politicians who served much longer in that office. In St. Laurent's nearly nine years in office, the country received efficient, imaginative, scandal-free government, made immense economic progress, and achieved unprecedented feats of diplomatic success and important progress in federal-provincial relations. In his person and by his nature, St. Laurent understood how Canada functioned and must be governed. In their way, he and Pearson had taken the 180-year-old Canadian challenge of maintaining the goodwill of the British and Americans, which for more than a century had been a matter of life and death to the concept of Canada, to a new level of constructive association appropriate to an established country, if still not a large factor in world affairs. The country wanted a change, but few could have imagined that better government would result. The great Liberal era that began in the depression of 1935 ended on June 17, 1957.

After receiving a visit from Lester B. Pearson and the newly re-elected Lionel Chevrier at his summer home at St. Patrick, Quebec (only a few hundred yards from the summer home of John A. Macdonald), St. Laurent announced his retirement as Liberal leader on September 4. Parliament opened on October 11, and in the Throne Speech, read in person by the queen, the new government promised all the measures that St. Laurent and Harris had declined to undertake from frugality and aversion to political opportunism: the South Saskatchewan power project and some other regional initiatives bundled together as a National Development Plan; cash advances on farm-stored grain; and the larger old-age pension that even Harris had decided in mid-campaign should be accorded. In August 1957, Diefenbaker signed the North American Air Defense Agreement (NORAD), which committed the United States to the defence of Canada but also foresaw the establishment of some American service personnel in Canada. Canadians had not enjoyed having Americans in Canada building the Alaska Highway during the war, and were not enthused about having American bases in the country, but it was a small price to pay to have the level of security that only the complete guaranty of the United States could provide.

The Liberal convention was held from January 14 to 16, 1958, in the Ottawa Coliseum, and while it was not as transparent a fix as St. Laurent's elevation by the departing Mackenzie King ten years before, Pearson was the clear favourite over Paul Martin, particularly as he had just been awarded the Nobel Prize for Peace for his services during the Suez Crisis. He won the convention with 1,074 votes to 305 for Martin. Jean Lesage delivered most of the Quebec delegates to the Protestant Pearson over the half-French, Roman Catholic Martin.

On the advice of Jack Pickersgill, the witty and clever jack-in-the-box who had served King and St. Laurent and now looked (physically) like a young Hermann Göring, Pearson, on succeeding St. Laurent as Liberal leader, gave a fighting speech in his opening gambit as leader of the parliamentary Opposition and instead of moving for a vote of no confidence said that an election would not be in the national interest and that Diefenbaker should simply resign and advise the governor general to invite Pearson to form a government. This was in keeping with the Liberal notion of entitlement to office and their assumption that the public would have thought better of the change to the Conservatives by now. Diefenbaker delivered a savage reply full of well-turned sarcasm and dissolved Parliament for an election on March 31. The new government had looked perfectly adequate in its few months in office, and Pearson had had a very rocky start. The government had spread some money around, and it was going to be practically impossible to deny Diefenbaker a fair try at governing. As Pickersgill said, "We are the party of government; the Conservatives are like the mumps, you get them once in your life."[34] Pearson had a difficult campaign, and the country was infatuated with his opponent; he hoped at best to retain one hundred MPs, and was assuming retention of a majority of Quebec's seventy-five MPs.

Maurice Duplessis had other ideas. He had waited nearly twenty years for revenge on the Liberals for their intervention against him in 1939, the one real defeat of his entire career, and with St. Laurent going, now was the time. Quebec didn't know Pearson, and the Liberals were in the most parlous condition they had endured in the history of the party. Edward Blake at least had had the Mowat government in Ontario to help him in the 1880s. The Liberals had not faced a serious challenge in Quebec from the Conservatives since Macdonald's time. Duplessis personally selected fifty of Quebec's federal constituencies for a major organizational effort and authorized $15,000 for each of them, the startling total of $750,000 coming from the well-heeled Union Nationale Caisse Electorale. As the fund was secret, the Liberals had no real idea what was happening, though they could not fail to detect the Union Nationale organizers and activists busy in the province for the first time in a federal election. Even in 1930, the Liberals had won forty seats to twenty-four Conservative in Quebec, and while Bourassa had clipped some votes from Sir Wilfrid Laurier, in 1911 the Liberals had carried the great majority of Quebec MPs. Duplessis's principal organizers, Joseph-Damase Bégin, Édouard Masson, and Daniel Johnson (a future premier and widely referred to as the son Duplessis never had), fanned out across the province. Duplessis chose some of the candidates, including Yvon Tassé in Quebec East, the constituency being vacated by St. Laurent, which had been held continuously for eighty years, through twenty-six consecutive general elections and by-elections, by Laurier, Lapointe, and St. Laurent. The former prime minister had won the district by seventeen thousand votes in 1957, and his successor to run in the riding this year was his former aide Maurice Lamontagne. Duplessis awakened Tassé at home late one evening by telephone and convinced him that it was not a prank only when Tassé saw Duplessis's well-known car, a very large Cadillac limousine with his flag on the fender and licence plate number 1, at his front door that the premier had sent to collect him. Tassé was an architect of schools, and he was in no position to decline the premier's draft to this candidacy and dutifully went to his nominating meeting.

This was the last election in which Duplessis took a direct part and was in some respects the most gratifying of all: the Progressive Conservatives carried all fifty of the constituencies Duplessis had targeted, including Tassé's victory over Lamontagne and the defeat of St. Laurent's son Jean-Paul in Témiscouata. (It was too late for their fathers, but this win, and Hugues Lapointe's defeat the year before, afforded Duplessis some of the pleasures of vengeance.) Even George Marler, the former acting leader of the provincial Opposition, who survived Duplessis's tremendous landslide in 1948, went down in the Liberal stronghold of Westmount; Marler could not escape the premier anywhere. Duplessis had now settled the oldest and most painful scores of his long career with his Liberal adversaries.

In his memoirs, Diefenbaker completely avoids reference to the assistance of the Union Nationale in either the 1957 or 1958 election, apart from saying that Johnson personally was helpful. He would have the reader believe that he alone was the author of his success in Quebec, and it may be that he never knew the proportions of Duplessis's assistance. In the other provinces, it was unambiguously his victory, and in the country it was a mighty sweep from coast to coast and unmistakeably a vote for Diefenbaker. He would have had a safe majority without one Quebec member of Parliament. He took 53.7 per cent of the total vote (up from 38.5 per cent in 1957 and 30.7 in 1953) and the party won an unheard of 208 seats, up from 111 at dissolution. The Liberals dropped to only 48 MPs, down from 104 at dissolution, and their share of the popular vote fell from 40.5 per cent to 33.4. The CCF only declined in percentage of voters from 10.6 to 9.5, but it lost 17 of its 25 MPs; and Social Credit, which had had 19 MPs, was wiped out, losing more than 70 per cent of its votes, descending from 6.6 per cent of the countrywide total to just 2 per cent.

John George Diefenbaker (1895–1979) was as different to his predecessor as it was conceivable for someone elevated to the same office to be. Where Louis St. Laurent had been uninterested in politics other than as an informed citizen until being called upon when he was almost sixty in wartime by the prime minister, never lost an election personally, never wished to hold the office just for the sake of having it, and accepted a very narrow and ambiguous defeat with timeless Roman Catholic resignation tinged by slight moroseness, John Diefenbaker lost five elections at all three levels of government before being elected to Parliament at age forty-five, only eighteen months younger than King was when he became prime minister, was twice badly defeated running for party leader, and, once at the head of his party, clung to it with demonic tenacity, pulling the house down around him. That he felt an outsider is understandable; he was from rural Saskatchewan and did not attend such famous universities as King and Pearson did, nor join such exalted law firms as St. Laurent. German names were not vote-winners during and after Canada's wars with Germany, and he was, at the best of times, an idiosyncratic public speaker. He was a slightly unusual-looking man, with prominent teeth and jowls, an extensive topknot of matted, half-curly hair, and flashing eyes. He had a jerky, abrupt delivery when speaking, but had perfect timing, great wit, a fine ear for the absurd and the incongruous, and a possessed quality, earnest and even fanatical, that commanded attention and, among an irreducible group of followers, adherence. He was absolutely sincere and admirable in his championship of all underdogs – the poor, the disadvantaged, the accused, the infirm, the outcast – and his attitude to non-whites and religious minorities was as distinguished as King's was contemptible. (There was nothing wrong with St. Laurent or Pearson on these matters, but they had not suffered any such indignities themselves and were not especially preoccupied with it, apart from St. Laurent's natural concern for the status of French Canadians.) John Diefenbaker was an astonishing phenomenon: he caught the Liberals just before the governing party was going to change leaders and engage in generational renovation, caught the moment and enough of the public fancy, and reversed decades of unkind personal adversity and emerged as the supreme one-time electoral champion of Canadian history.

Some sensed that it would be a disaster; Canadians who weren't Liberals – from Conservative Quebec nationalists like Duplessis to Western populists tempted by Social Credit to Old Tories grumbling in Canadian Legion branches across Canada and in their clubs and offices on and near Bay Street in Toronto – all got on board but were never likely to stay on board. It had, from the start to the end, a great deal of drama, and Diefenbaker, being the demiurge he was, having torqued up to this moment for more than fifty years (he formed the determination to be prime minister at age six), stretched the drama out to the end of his days, at eighty-four years, thirteen consecutive personal general election victories and forty years in Parliament. It was decade after decade of unrelieved contentiousness, conducted with a singular combination of egalitarian fervour, unaffected if often implausible righteousness, great originality, and more than a trace of irrationalism. It had drama, but not always high drama: tragedy, comedy, farce, vaudeville, and a bit of a magic show. No one knew what they were getting with John Diefenbaker, and few who voted for him got what they expected.

The Diefenbaker government produced a plan to build roads into the North and make the region and its resources more accessible. It was a somewhat visionary idea that was a good long-term measure for developing the vast area, though it did not produce an early population increase. He was also concerned about the sale of natural resources and large parts of the economy generally, to Americans, and about excessive concentration of trade with the United States, and he revived the old notion from earlier times of Commonwealth free trade. In October 1958, Diefenbaker embarked on an even more ambitious world tour than had St. Laurent four years before. He started with Dag Hammarskjöld in New York and went on to meet with Britain's prime minister, Harold Macmillan, and then to Paris for an extensive discussion with Charles de Gaulle, who had returned at last, the indispensable man to extract France from the morass in Algeria. He was still in the Hôtel Matignon, the prime minister's residence, as the last premier of the Fourth Republic. He was composing the new constitution, which he would shortly put to a vote, in which he would heal the monarchic/republican schism that had rent France for 170 years by creating an elective monarchy and calling it a republic, and in which he would be elected president. De Gaulle was promoting a triumvirate of principal NATO states: the United States, the United Kingdom, and France. His point was that everything was being integrated into an American command structure and NATO was becoming less an alliance than an agency of American foreign and defence policy, and he wanted to ensure that France could not be drawn into war without knowing anything of the causes, nor be the launching place for nuclear weapons over which it had no control. Diefenbaker could normally be counted on to be in some sympathy with these views, but once again, as with King during the war, an opportunity was lost to make common cause with the most formidable of the world's statesmen, now that Roosevelt and Churchill had passed from the scene. They discussed trade matters, and de Gaulle replied to Diefenbaker's concerns about European Economic Community (EEC) protectionism with knowledgeable questions as to why Diefenbaker was promoting Commonwealth protectionism. Diefenbaker claims[35] that de Gaulle told him he need not be concerned about Britain joining the EEC, because they would not get in. *"Ils ne passeront pas"* (as Diefenbaker remarked, a quote from Marshal Pétain at Verdun). He asked de Gaulle if he could tell Macmillan that, de Gaulle agreed, and Macmillan said Diefenbaker must have misunderstood the general. This is all a bit far-fetched, and only four years later did de Gaulle veto British entry. De Gaulle invited Diefenbaker to take the salute at Verdun on Remembrance Day, which Diefenbaker did, as de Gaulle, who was wounded and captured there, did not wish to attend himself. It was a high honour for Canada and its leader, and though their relations were not as intimate as Diefenbaker claims, they seem to have had a cordial and rather loquacious exchange. De Gaulle gives a significantly different summary of his relations with Diefenbaker in his memoirs, ignoring this visit, focusing on his own trip to Ottawa two years later, and concentrating on the divisions between Quebec and the English-speaking parts of the country. (Diefenbaker blames de Gaulle's provocative conduct in his 1967 visit to Canada on Pearson, and the whole spirit of his memoirs is vindictive, rancorous, and a constant strain on credulity, but they are an interesting insight into his teeming personality.)

Both de Gaulle and West German chancellor Konrad Adenauer, whom Diefenbaker soon visited, told Diefenbaker of their desire to achieve a rapprochement between their countries. Adenauer joked that he, Diefenbaker, and Eisenhower could excite suspicion on ethnic grounds, and the two agreed with each other and not with de Gaulle on the overarching importance of America's leadership of NATO. Diefenbaker had an informative visit in Brussels with General Lauris

Norstad, the NATO commander, and then with the Italian government, which was unenthused by de Gaulle's triumvirate idea, and with
Pope John XXIII. He went on to Pakistan and India after the now customary Canadian visit to the Khyber Pass. Nehru wanted Diefenbaker's
impressions of the new Pakistani leader, Marshal Ayub Khan, and was,
as always, deeply skeptical about almost everything in the West, especially the conditionality of American aid to India. Diefenbaker continued to Ceylon, Malaya, Singapore, Jakarta, Australia, and New Zealand.

C.D. Howe had been aware that the projected next-generation
Canadian fighter plane, the Avro Arrow, could be a giant white elephant, and on March 20, 1959, Diefenbaker announced that the entire
project was being shut down. A.V. Roe Canada was the third largest
industrial concern in the country, with more than thirty thousand
employees working directly on this project or in feeder occupations,
including almost all the more sophisticated aerospace engineers and
technicians in Canada, and the company had already provided Canada
a good fighter with the CF-100. There was great competition among
countries – and in the case of the United States within its aerospace
industry – to put the next-generation supersonic fighter into production, and there were certainly problems with the range, cost, and fuel
economy of the Arrow. But there were various methods of collaborating
with other manufacturer/buyer countries, and discussions with British,
French, and American programs, having reached an advanced stage,
began to collapse, in part because the A.V. Roe management had left it
late to pursue partnerships and developed a credibility gap, in part also
because the Canadian government had allowed concerns to arise about
whether the project would proceed at all. The shutdown of the Arrow
was defensible, but not the shutdown of the entire industry. The whole
project should have been taken in hand by one of the country's leading
industrialists (Howe himself, who was underemployed, would have
been ideal, and it would have been a brilliant political move as well),
and the shutdown of the fuselage aspect should have been exchanged
for the foreign assured purchase of the Orenda Engine or some such
trade-off. Instead, Canada lost its entire jet engine industry and has
never revived it, and it ceased to make warplanes, unlike Sweden, Israel,
and several other smaller countries, and took a giant step backwards in

the country's advanced industrial and foreign exchange earning potential. A.V. Roe was a British-controlled company, and given its dependence on Canadian government support, the government could have patriated the company while it was sorting out the Arrow and made it a win-double for the country. St. Laurent and Howe and Pearson might have thought in these terms, but no such thoughts would ever have occurred to Diefenbaker, who had never had any connection with industry or commerce.

Maurice Duplessis died on September 7, 1959, of a stroke in the executive guesthouse of the Iron Ore Company in Shefferville in northern Quebec, a region he was personally responsible for developing, in a county now named after him. The rabidly hostile *Le Devoir*, through the elegant reflections of its editor, André Laurendeau, Henri Bourassa's chosen successor and former leader of the Bloc Populaire, summarized the significance of the event fairly: "The man who has just died has dominated the public life of Quebec for a whole generation. He was loved, hated, respected, and always controversial; but his mastery, though passionately combated, has been incontestable over the past quarter of a century. . . . His achievements are still debated. It is incontestable that they have indelibly marked the province. . . . Now [his career] is over, just as it seemed at its zenith. Maurice Duplessis will never have known the bitterness of an ultimate defeat or of a long illness. He has fallen like a soldier."[36] He had been the premier or leader of the Opposition for a total of twenty-eight years, and was scarcely buried – after an immense funeral where the honorary pallbearers included Diefenbaker and Duplessis's five immediate successors as premier of Quebec – when a dense mythology enshrouded his memory to the effect that his had been a dark age in the province's history. The immediate secret to his popularity was precisely his success at modernizing Quebec. Electricity, which only 15 per cent of rural homes enjoyed in 1944, had been extended to 97 per cent of those homes by 1959. Unions were not strong or officially favoured, but contrary to all the rubbish about "cheap labour," industrial wages and safety rules improved more quickly in Quebec than elsewhere in Canada. Construction of roads, hospitals, schools, autoroutes, and universities unrecognizably changed the face and nature of a province where in

1944 only the most important roads were ploughed and passable in the winter. Duplessis's system was intricate and little understood, weaving industry, sociology, and politics closely together.

Duplessis undoubtedly played a role in forcing the departure of the archbishop of Montreal, Joseph Charbonneau, in 1950, after the archbishop had criticized Duplessis's handling of the miners' strike at Asbestos, Quebec. In that famous but much misunderstood affair, Duplessis made a generous award to the workers but cracked down on the international and Catholic unions for inciting violence and seizing control of the mining town. As the international unions were the enemies of the Catholic trade unions (and he kept them quarrelling, as he did the Jesuits and the Dominicans), Duplessis considered it inappropriate for an archbishop to be championing a coalition of the secular, American-dominated, international, and the anti-Catholic unions, and intolerable for Charbonneau publicly to attack him as hostile to labour. He was supportive of labour but hostile to those whom he considered to be the troublemakers in the labour movement. Through the 1950s, Duplessis exploited the low-paid, non-union, and highly motivated clerical personnel in the school and health-care systems to keep the provincial government's wage costs low and focus the budget on tax cuts, deficit reduction, and massive roads and public-works projects. A benign cycle occurred: capital poured in, including on great projects linked to the iron ore and aluminum industries on the north shore of the St. Lawrence and at Lac Saint-Jean; jobs, disposable income, consumer spending, profits, saving, and investment soared, and the Union Nationale, in the Quebec tradition, did not go unrewarded for its patronage.

To some extent, Duplessis was perpetuating a priest-ridden society, but he also accelerated the inevitable start of secularization. He transposed the hierarchy of Church and State in the province; Charbonneau was sent packing only three years after the death of Cardinal Villeneuve. One of Duplessis's famous utterances was "The bishops eat from my hand." The extensive footnote below summarizes the progress of Quebec in this era.* These statistics are recounted so lengthily because they are

---

* From 1941 to 1961, the number of members of religious orders per 100,000 people declined from 1,002 to 860. While this was happening, from 1944 to 1959 gross manufacturing

the product of exhaustive and meticulous analysis, and because they completely destroy the conventional and received wisdom that Duplessis retarded Quebec and that his successors liberated it. This is one of the

production rose from $3.2 billion to $7.4 billion; manufacturing production per worker rose from $6,600 to $16,000 (in Ontario, from $7,500 to $19,400); and average pay rose from $1,500 to $3,800 (in Ontario, from $1,750 to $4,250). Rates of production increase in primary and secondary industry combined were about 8.5 per cent annually in both provinces throughout Duplessis's last four terms. From 1944 to 1959, Quebec hydroelectric production rose from 5.85 million horsepower to 11.26 million (in Ontario, with a state-owned system using the province's credit, it rose from 2.67 million to 7.79 million). Deposits in the province's Church-connected cooperative savings banks, caisses populaires, rose from $99 million in 1944 to $576 million in 1959. From 1944 to 1959, the number of motor vehicles in Quebec increased from 219,000 to 1,122,000 (in Ontario, from 684,000 to 1,978,000). Paved road mileage in Quebec rose in the period from 22,700 to 41,400 (in Ontario, from 56,400 to 68,300), and the Abitibi, Lac Saint-Jean, Mattagami, and Gaspé regions, and both shores of the Lower St. Lawrence, were connected to Quebec City, Montreal, and Ontario for the first time on seriously accessible roads. More than 4,100 schools were built in the period, giving Quebec 8,281 schools for 1,000,959 students and 41,084 teachers by 1959 (Ontario had 7,542 schools, 1,249,673 students, and 43,586 teachers). From 1944 to 1959, the number of enrollees in Quebec's night schools, trade schools, and craft, technical, and specialized schools increased from 20,400 to 48,500; enrolment at graduate business schools doubled, at fine arts schools tripled, and at polytechnic colleges quintupled. University faculty members increased from 1,522 for 23,493 students to 7,281 for 64,119 students in 1959. University bursaries multiplied eightfold, and Quebec, despite having only 80 per cent of Ontario's population, had several thousand more university students. The number of hospital beds increased from 22,000 in 1944 to 54,476 in 1959 (in Ontario, from 31,000 to 56,512, a smaller per capita number than in Quebec). From 1944 to 1959, the percentage of Quebec families with refrigerators, automobiles, and their own bathroom increased by, respectively, 23 per cent, 22 per cent, and 54 per cent, so that 92 per cent had a refrigerator, 57 per cent an automobile, and 80 per cent a bathroom. Quebec's infant mortality rate descended in this time from 175 per cent of Ontario's to 130 per cent. The life expectancy of Quebeckers increased from more than four years less than that of Ontarians in 1944 to within ten months of that of Ontarians in 1959. The number of deaths per hospital admissions declined in the period from parity with Ontario to 25 per cent fewer than in Ontario in 1959. Between 1944 and 1959, secondary school enrolment of teenagers in Quebec increased from 28 per cent to 68 per cent, or from 40 per cent of Ontario's level to almost 80 per cent. The student population as a percentage of the total population rose in the 1950s in Quebec, the United States, and Ontario, respectively, by 23.4 per cent, 12.6 per cent, and 15.1 per cent. Most tellingly, per capita personal income, despite the higher birthrate and larger families in Quebec, rose between 1944 and 1959, as a percentage of Ontario's, from 65 per cent to 87 per cent. (For future contrast, the suicide rate in Quebec rose between 1960 and 1980 from 5 per 100,000 to 17, and expenses of the province as a percentage of gross provincial product rose from 3 per cent in 1944 to only 5 per cent in 1959, to 25 per cent in 1980.)[37]

great frauds of Canadian history and one of the fundamental falsehoods underpinning the lengthy Quebec flirtation with independence. Duplessis was an economic and jurisdictional modernizer, his nationalism tempered by his conservatism. Diefenbaker, though he never understood anything about relations between Ottawa and Quebec and had no one to advise him, was more accommodating than the federal Liberals. He increased the provincial concurrence in the personal income tax from 10 per cent to 13 per cent, installed simultaneous translation in the House of Commons, inaugurated bilingual federal government cheques – a step St. Laurent and his finance ministers had considered too expensive – and appointed the first French-Canadian governor general, the universally respected General Georges-Philéas Vanier. This was the extent of it. Diefenbaker had not the faintest clue of the implications of the existence of two founding races. He thought he was doing the French Canadians a favour by saying they were like everyone else. Because of his own background, he thought hyphenated Canadians should not exist and that French Canadians were no different to German or Italian Canadians, all of which distinctions were outworn and reprehensible. In terms of understanding how the country had always worked, the (Progressive) Conservatives had not learned anything: if the French were just another ethnic group, they had no standing other than bilingual banknotes and postage stamps and parliamentary debates and more MPs than other groups.

St. Laurent, and to a lesser extent Diefenbaker, had the chance to negotiate seriously with Quebec toward permanent changes in the British North America Act and a division of concurrent taxing jurisdictions that reflected the arrangements of 1867, and not a concurrence, extracted by threat of double taxation after seventy years, of 10 per cent, conceded with infinite reluctance by St. Laurent to Duplessis, and then of 13 per cent more graciously agreed by Diefenbaker. The best, though not the last, opportunity closed with the death of Duplessis. The Liberals confected and laid down the myth of Duplessis's unmitigated rascality and cynicism, and there was enough truth to this to satisfy the uncurious and unrigorous. But his departure almost ruined them too. The argument St. Laurent had invoked in favour of equivalence for all the provinces was a poor one, and it had become a federal Liberal truism: "Quebec is a province like the others." In some respects yes, but ultimately not. This was a position that would be demolished completely by two of St. Laurent's ministers, Lester Pearson and Jean Lesage, when, in the next decade, they would accede to even higher offices, and St. Laurent would observe it, blinking in silent disbelief, from his prolonged retirement.

Duplessis had the immense dexterity to persuade the conservatives and nationalists to vote together. He had it arranged for Paul Sauvé to follow him and for Daniel Johnson to follow Sauvé, as they could both manage the same feat (and Johnson did in the 1966 election). But he could not foresee that they would both die in office, as he did, but at the ages of fifty-two and fifty-three, dropping the nationalist torch from the dead hand of the sensible right, to be taken up by the left. The results of these transformations would shake the country profoundly.

An inkling of what impended certainly came to the Machiavellian mind of Charles de Gaulle when he visited Canada in 1960. Beneath the gracious welcome he received and the prosperity of the host country, he said, "It was impossible to disguise from me the mortgages on its structure and condition."[38] He noted that the French and English, "two communities radically different, accommodated each other more or less well by need to inhabit the same geographic space," and a process of the attachment of "a part of the French-Canadian upper class to practice the system. But it was clear that this was a compromise between resignations, not at all national unity." Diefenbaker, "whose intentions were certainly very estimable," according to de Gaulle, relied on France to assist Canada in resisting the overwhelming American influence, even as he espoused nuclear disarmament, not, as de Gaulle noted, with his usual subtle asperity, from the perspective of renouncing anything himself, but in calling upon others to do so. De Gaulle claimed to ask himself, as he departed, if it were not as two states, cooperating "freely and by choice in two versions of independence in order to safeguard them, that one day Canada would erase the injustice that had scarred it, and would organize itself in conformity with its own realities and would be able to remain Canadian." He would be back to test his theories, and of course they were largely self-serving French narcissism and imposture. The severance of Quebec from Canada would just create a weak French Canada and deliver most or all of the country into total dependence on the United States. The British defeat of the French at the Plains of Abraham was not an injustice; Britain ruled the waves, and no victorious power could have been more just than was Guy Carleton, and the victory was necessary to preserve anything of Canada, and especially French Canada, as only the British could protect Canada from absorption and cultural assimilation by the Americans.

De Gaulle, a patriotic French nationalist, saw only what he wanted to see and rationalized a fabricated history as only the French can. But the failure of the Canadian political system to retain fidelity to the founding principle of French-English cooperation and federal-provincial concurrence created vulnerabilities that this very astute statesman could not fail to notice, and that this seeker of the extension of French influence, even in mischief and duplicity at the expense of an historic friend of France, could not resist the temptation to try to exploit.

Duplessis had inaugurated concurrence in tax policy as a fact and brought Quebec into the modern world, with a state no longer under the tutelage of the Church, vested with the instances of a modern people, and armed with the potential for constitutional autonomy. And France was now led by one of the great statesmen of its history, ambitious to retrieve what he could of lost French influence. He was more formidable than any French leader who had dabbled in Quebec since Richelieu, and Duplessis's successors would be more manipulable than he was. It would be an increasingly combustible condition, of the hazards of which Diefenbaker and Pearson were happily unaware as a startling reveille approached.

John Diefenbaker was the supreme example of the man who not only caught history at a miraculously favourable turn and seized the hour opportunistically, but who also suddenly found himself in a position of great importance where he had a conviction of a lifetime that he belonged but little idea what to do with it. His term was frittered away in half measures. After his initial program of belt-loosening, which included an imaginative and successful "winter works" program to alleviate unemployment, there was no program. He did pass, in 1960, a Bill of Rights, which he saw to it got into the hands of almost all schoolchildren in the country in a fine parchment facsimile with antique script and his signature. Of course, its practical importance was limited, as the federal Parliament had little authority in matters of property and civil rights, but it was important symbolically and at least helped to focus attention on the subject of individual liberties, an area where the prime minister had a long and admirable record of service and advocacy. And his bill is much more eloquently composed than previous or subsequent texts addressing the same or similar subjects in Canada, and could be usefully inserted into a preamble to a fully agreed Constitution if one is ever achieved.

Diefenbaker's finance minister, Donald Fleming, was an old-time Toronto Tory who believed in a balanced budget and tight money, and he was continuously discountenanced by his chief's enthusiasm for giveaways. Deficits accumulated, and with them higher interest rates and rising inflation. Canada had to be careful of budget and trade deficits to maintain its currency and avoid spikes of interest and loss of confidence in currency markets, but Diefenbaker was not accustomed to thinking in such terms, and his finance minister was not strong enough to stand up to him, as Walter Harris, C.D. Howe, Douglas Abbott, or James Ilsley would have done (though King and St. Laurent were relatively literate financially compared with most of their successors). Problems gradually arose, and the governor of the Bank of Canada, James Coyne, attempted in 1960 and 1961 to deal with them by tightening credit and encouraging reduced borrowing. He apparently thought he was doing as the government wished, as he was certainly following the line Fleming commended. Fleming and Diefenbaker had always said that the central bank was entirely independent, in the manner of elected leaders who wanted to lay the responsibility for painful corrective measures off on unelected and non-political officials. But suddenly and inexplicably, Fleming changed course and concluded that Coyne was exceeding his authority and trying to sandbag the government and that he must go. The government requested amendment of the Bank of Canada Act on June 23, 1961, to enable the position of governor to become vacant. Coyne would have retired if Diefenbaker had not insinuated that he was a crook, because he had requested and accepted an increase of his pension to twenty-five thousand dollars (compared with an absurd three thousand dollars for Louis St. Laurent). Always quick to impute the worst of motives to anyone with whom he was at odds, Diefenbaker publicly called Coyne a man who "sat, knew, listened, and took." There was no excuse for uttering such an outrageous slander, and no need for the immense fracas that ensued, one that the government, in public relations terms, could not win.

The Liberal Party strategists saw the potential to embarrass the government, though they were not in sympathy with Coyne's views. The Liberals were a big-spending party at this point, under the influence of Walter Gordon, a leading chartered accountant and public policy expert who had a somewhat Mephistophelean influence on Pearson. But party managers immediately saw that the Coyne Affair, as it was soon known, could turn into almost a Canadian Truman-MacArthur episode. The bill to remove Coyne passed the House of Commons on the huge majority the Progressive Conservatives enjoyed there, but the Senate Banking Committee held public hearings where Coyne, quiet, articulate, and knowledgeable, made a very good impression as a consistent public servant carrying out the statutory requirement of the Bank of Canada to control credit and influence the money supply in the national interest as best it could interpret that. Coyne also thought he was carrying out the often publicly expressed wishes of the minister of finance and the prime minister. The Senate rejected the government's bill and at that point, having made his case and debunked any suggestion of corruption on his own part, Coyne resigned on July 13, 1961. He was succeeded by the deputy governor, Louis Rasminsky, but he didn't much change the Bank of Canada's policy in the areas that had caused the split.

A great controversy in Saskatchewan, which would influence Canada more than any other development in that province's history, was well underway. The issue was state assured universal medical care, and it would culminate the following summer in the so-called Saskatoon Agreement. It followed a twenty-three-day doctors' strike, and spared the doctors the indignity of becoming government employees but constrained them as to what they could charge. Their receivables were guaranteed by the government, but everyone was entitled to be treated in hospitals at the province's expense. There was initially a user fee for those who could afford it, and Premier Tommy Douglas had declared that the object was to establish a floor but not a cap for the quality of medical service. None could foresee what a fetish and totem this issue would become.

* * *

In preparation for the now imminent election, Fleming completed his reversal of field and cut taxes by $130 million and posted an estimated deficit for 1962 of an immense $745 million. The response was a flight from the Canadian dollar that caused Fleming abruptly to jettison Canada's long and prideful dollar worth a little more than the American dollar and to try to peg its value at 92.5 U.S. cents. Despite chirpy government efforts to portray this as a brilliant plan to give Canadian exporters a competitive edge, everyone saw it for the outright inflation that it was.

By this time, Canadian foreign policy was becoming quite complicated. Diefenbaker brought to this subject a set of attitudes; he early proposed a serious Commonwealth free trade plan, but when the British agreed, he folded under the realities of the trade relationship with the United States. British prime minister Harold Macmillan regarded him as "a mountebank."[39] Diefenbaker led a tremendous assault on South Africa's apartheid policies segregating blacks and other non-white groups, and pushed through, with the support of African, Caribbean, and Asian member states, such fierce condemnations of the South African racial laws that South Africa withdrew from the Commonwealth in 1961. Diefenbaker had grave reservations about British plans to join the European Economic Community, and in some respects his concerns were well-founded, but not for the reasons that he held them. If he had made serious proposals about enhanced preferences between the more developed Commonwealth countries, he might have been more successful, or at least somewhat prophetic, given the problems the European project eventually encountered. If he had been more supportive of some of de Gaulle's initiatives in NATO, or even had sought an improved trade relationship directly with the EEC, he might at least have gained some credit for the spirit and originality of his views. But Canada just gestured and postured; it couldn't go far with the neutrals like Nehru and Nasser or relations with the United States would have deteriorated dangerously. And most of the declared neutrals, including Nehru, Nasser, and Sukarno were really pro-Soviet charlatans. Apart from the two superpowers and a few of the neutrals, no country had any influence anywhere, except China, Gaullist France, and the United

Kingdom, and it was limited in all cases. All Canada could do was try to come up with some original ideas, and that would not have been impossible, given how sclerotic world affairs were at the height of the Cold War. Diefenbaker tried to show his independence of the United States by selling wheat to Communist China and maintaining trade and touristic relations with Castro's (as of 1959) Cuba (and showing no solicitude for the victims of Castro's dictatorship, which was a good deal more severe than the corrupt despotism that had preceded it). But where it all started to come terribly unstuck, and in both major parties, was in North American air defence.

6. The Disintegration of the Diefenbaker Government, 1962–1963

In 1958, Diefenbaker's minister of defence, Victoria Cross–winning veteran George Pearkes, had agreed to rearm Canadian forces in NATO and NORAD with nuclear weapons. Canada could easily have become a nuclear-capable military power, as it had the scientific capability and was the premier supplier of uranium to the early atomic development programs. By the late 1950s, the world was frozen hard in the Cold War, and yet the Commonwealth was trying to maintain some solidarity with Nehru, who was touting the benefits of disarmament. In these circumstances logically inexplicable notions flowered of unilateral disarmament as a rational tactic for the encouragement of peace. Professedly idealistic youth, singing songs lamenting the violences of war, joined hands with the mothers of military-age sons and the veterans of terrible far-off wars, all decrying nuclear deterrence and often the concept of defence itself. Diefenbaker and even Pearson, of the First World War generation, were strangely susceptible to this sort of appeal, and the ranks of their partisans were infested with such people. In all except the nuclear countries (which now included France and soon China), it was a temptation to engage in such nostrums as a method of trying to assert influence where there was no real ability to do so. Canada was of no military relevance to anyone; its territory was, but the United States had assumed the defence of that territory in 1938, with Roosevelt's address at Kingston, and retained it. Agitating for nuclear disarmament was a method of acting on idealistic, envious, and even spiteful impulses; the problem with it was that it was not sensible, was an irritant to the defensive nuclear powers, and a service to the Soviet Union, where no such dissent was tolerated. The argument arose that acceptance of nuclear bombs or warheads by Canada would be complicity in, and an expansion of, the Damaclean nuclear threat.

Diefenbaker's first external affairs secretary, the president of the University of Toronto, Sidney Smith, was not successful in that role, and died in office. He was replaced by veteran British Columbia MP Howard Green. The undersecretary was the durable Norman Robertson, former clerk of the Privy Council and minister to Washington and high commissioner in London. First Robertson and then Green succumbed to the virus of unilateral disarmament, Robertson, as often happens in the parliamentary system, where the deputy ministers have much greater job security than the ministers and tend to lead them, being the chief agent of this change. In Robertson's case, it is likely that his frustration at the absence of Canadian influence anywhere, and what he, as an old Liberal, would regard as the appalling brinkmanship of the Cold War rhetoric of Dulles and the conservative Republicans and Southern Democrats who controlled most of the U.S. congressional committees, caused him to recoil when he regained the righteous pastoral somnolence of Ottawa after his tours in Washington and London. With Green, there was more of a susceptibility to the evangelical quest for goodness and purity of method as well as motive. John Diefenbaker, resentful of the United States and a fervent Baptist, was vulnerable to approaches on both counts. Pearson wasn't, but he was vulnerable to the views of Robertson, his old friend and soulmate from the days of O.D. Skelton, and the Liberal Party always had a left wing entirely capable of buying into such an idyllic *Weltanschauung*.

Pearkes had retired as defence minister in 1960 and been named lieutenant-governor of British Columbia. He was replaced by Douglas Harkness, another much-decorated officer, an artillery colonel from the Second World War. Diefenbaker deferred the deployment of nuclear warheads and told the United States that domestic public opinion had to be prepared. John F. Kennedy narrowly defeated Richard Nixon in the presidential election of 1960. (In fact, Nixon won the popular vote if the Democratic votes cast for an independent southern segregationist candidate in Alabama are allocated properly, and may well have won the election, but he generously declined Eisenhower's urgings to challenge the election, as he thought it would immobilize the government in the thick of the Cold War.) Diefenbaker was five years younger than Eisenhower, who became a world-historic figure when Diefenbaker was still a freshman MP, and Eisenhower was from Kansas and a Protestant background and had been twice elected president when Diefenbaker became prime minister. He was a man Diefenbaker was bound to treat respectfully (as had even Stalin). Kennedy was twenty years younger, and of Irish Boston/Hollywood and speculation-tainted big money backgrounds, which were equally part of America but very difficult for Diefenbaker to identify with or even understand. Suddenly, everything was youthful image-making and affected, smiling, touch-football-playing dynamism, energy, and American pushiness, and John Diefenbaker, as his own political horizon narrowed, found it confusing, unnerving, and irksome.

In May 1961, Kennedy made what was now the routine early visit to Ottawa of a new American president, and it seemed to be cordial enough, but Kennedy left behind a memorandum of points to raise with his host. These were unexceptionable: that Canada join the Organization of American States and cooperate with the American Alliance for Progress in assisting non-communist developing countries in Latin America, but the paper invited the president to "push" Diefenbaker on these points. This was precisely the sort of expression that inflamed Diefenbaker's inborn tendencies to convenient paranoia. Instead of returning the document, he put it in his "vault," as he breathlessly later identified the depository for such incendiary state papers as he imagined this to be, as if "push" meant advancing Patton tanks across the international Peace, Rainbow, and Ambassador bridges into Canada, and not just, as it did mean, asking Canada's support in a normal diplomatic way. The Kennedy administration quickly came to regard Diefenbaker as a kook filled with a neurotic animus who could not possibly be representative of public opinion in such a sensible place as Canada. A year later, Diefenbaker was scandalized to see Kennedy entertaining Pearson to dinner at the White House and took it as a personal affront, even though the dinner was for Nobel Prize winners. He threatened the U.S. ambassador,

Livingston Merchant, with the publication of Kennedy's memorandum, and Merchant was told to advise Diefenbaker that there had been no official report of the matter, thus, in diplomatese, preserving the ability to make direct contact between the two leaders. Canadian-American relations had suddenly sunk to their lowest depths since the Alaskan boundary affair of sixty years before (in which the Canadians were blameless).

Pearkes and Harkness both considered that Canada was committed to accepting nuclear warheads under a dual-national fire control system; that is, the high command of both countries would have to approve use of the weapons. The Arrow had been replaced by Bomarc anti-aircraft missiles, which had to have small nuclear warheads, and in order to be aerodynamic, pending the fitting of the approved warheads, would have to have sand in their nose cones. It was an increasingly ludicrous state of affairs, as Harkness became steadily more concerned and annoyed at the indecision of the prime minister and the cabinet in the face of Howard Green's passionate argument that Canada would be increasing the chances of "global suicide" if it honoured its NORAD commitments. This was how matters stood when Diefenbaker dissolved the House of Commons for new elections, which were held on June 18, 1962.

Given the Progressive Conservatives' huge majority, it was unlikely that the Liberals could come all the way back, but it was clear that Diefenbaker's Conservatives had seriously disappointed the freakishly large torrent of supporters it had attracted in 1958. In Quebec, Duplessis's chosen and much admired successor, Paul Sauvé, had portentously announced that "désormais" (henceforth) changes impended, and much was expected, but he died after 118 days as premier, at the beginning of 1960, and was succeeded by the unfeasible labour minister, Antonio Barrette. Barrette was not of the stature or acuity required to keep Duplessis and Sauvé's conservative-nationalist coalition together, and Jean Lesage led the Liberals to victory in July. But it was a Quebec Liberal Party unlike Godbout's and had attracted many of the more ardent – that is, not conservative – nationalists, including popular Radio-Canada news commentator René Lévesque. In fact, désormais, Quebec-Ottawa relations were going to become infinitely more complicated, and as a starter Diefenbaker could be confident of the disappearance of most of his Quebec caucus. On the night, Diefenbaker's Progressive Conservatives lost 92 MPs and 16.4 per cent of the popular vote, but still had 116 MPs and 37.2 per cent of the vote. The Liberals rose from 48 MPs and 33.4 per cent of the vote to 99 MPs and 37 per cent. The CCF had renamed themselves the New Democratic Party, and their leader was former Saskatchewan premier Tommy Douglas. The new party raised the previous CCF vote from 9.5 per cent to 13.6 and the parliamentary deputation from 8 to 19.

But the greatest shock of all was that in the vacuum in Quebec created by the decline of the Union Nationale after the sudden death in office of two leaders and the victory of Quebec Liberals not at all dominated by Ottawa for the first time since Taschereau, Réal Caouette's Créditistes took twenty-six Quebec MPs, and Social Credit jumped from 2.6 per cent of the popular vote to 11.6 per cent, and from no MPs to 30, and for the first time became the principal party of the unofficial opposition. The Social Credit leader was Robert Thompson of Red Deer, an articulate Albertan Manningite, but Caouette really held the whip in the unofficial opposition. Douglas was defeated in his own district in Regina and successfully sought entry to the federal House in a by-election in Burnaby, British Columbia.

The country was entering uncharted waters with an unstable government riven by internecine disagreements, an unsteady official Opposition officially committed to a more radical reform program than the country wished for or knew how to implement, and without having recovered its former Quebec base. The federal Quebec Liberal leader was a distinguished but far from a new face, Lionel Chevrier, a former Franco-Ontarian MP from Cornwall. Douglas was a reasonable man of the social democratic left, but Caouette was one of the greatest wild cards of Canadian history, a powerful orator of rustic French-Canadian inflection, but a sort of Poujadist of visceral petit bourgeois and traditional tastes who was effectively incomprehensible in most policy areas.

In an odd way, Diefenbaker strengthened his government. George Nowlan replaced the much-browbeaten Donald Fleming as finance minister, who was knocked down to justice, bumping Davie Fulton to public works. The capable Wallace McCutcheon, a member of the control group of the influential holding company Argus Corporation, headed by King's and Howe's friend E.P. Taylor, came in as a minister without portfolio to assist in economic matters. Harkness was proving a more effective defence minister than Pearkes, and his replacement as agriculture minister, Alvin Hamilton, a more effective holder of that office than Harkness had been. Apart from Diefenbaker and Green, it was a fairly competent government, given that it was a party that had been out of office for twenty-two years, but Diefenbaker misread the election result. He was now in transition from a prime minister to a tenacious and strangely inspired leader of the Opposition, convinced that he had been discommoded by "sinister forces and powerful interests," specifically the United States government, Liberal Party quislings, Toronto high finance, and ethnic and sectarian bigots who objected to his attempted de-hyphenization of Canadianism (and he effectively included the French Canadians as another ethnic minority more than a co-founding, co-equal race, which, of course, is not how they regard themselves).

In April 1961, Kennedy had authorized a hare-brained plan for the liberation of Cuba from Castro's communist and Soviet-supported government of Cuba by fifteen hundred refugees armed by the CIA and supported by inadequate numbers of aircraft known to be inferior to those provided to Cuba and its twenty-five-thousand-man army by the Soviet Union. The Cubans smashed the invasion, and all but about two hundred of the invaders were captured or killed. Kennedy and Khrushchev, now installed as the undisputed Soviet strongman, met in Vienna in May 1961, and Kennedy and his entourage felt that Kennedy had not been adequately strong in rebutting Khrushchev's very aggressive threats and bluster. In August, Khrushchev began construction of the wall separating East and West Berlin, officially the Anti-Fascist Defence Barrier, to stop the flow of 3.5 million East Germans who had fled to the West through the practically undivided city of Berlin. The next phase of escalation of the Cold War was on October 16, 1962, when Kennedy learned from aerial reconnaissance that there were offensive Soviet missile launchers in Cuba. Kennedy was faced with the stern choice of removing the launchers and missiles by force, though that might lead to a direct exchange of fire with the

Soviet Union, possibly escalating to Germany and to atomic weapons, or proposing an exchange for a withdrawal, or simply acquiescing in this dramatic change to the correlation of forces in the Americas, where the United States had long been accustomed to the complete absence of any serious challenge within the hemisphere. The last was not a serious option. About a third of Kennedy's National Security Council advocated an invasion, but Kennedy doubted the CIA assurance that there were no nuclear warheads already in Cuba, was concerned about direct combat with Soviet forces, even though the United States certainly could crush anything in Cuba, and feared a Soviet response in Germany, where atomic weapons would have to be resorted to to counteract Soviet conventional military superiority. The rest of the National Security Council divided between various versions of offering a quid pro quo to Khrushchev to desist.

America's allies, as in Korea and most phases of the Cold War, were largely irresolute and full of peevish misgivings. Kennedy sent former secretary of state Dean Acheson to brief de Gaulle, who declined to look at aerial photographs and said he had always accepted the word of Roosevelt, Truman, and Eisenhower in matters of such gravity and had no hesitation in doing so with Kennedy and that he would inform the Soviet ambassador of France's complete solidarity with any course the U.S. president laid down.* Diefenbaker, unlike Macmillan and some other allied leaders, was not consulted at all. Kennedy addressed the United States on the crisis on October 22, announcing the imposition of a complete sea quarantine on Cuba. On October 28, Khrushchev undertook to remove the Soviet missiles and have that verified by United Nations inspectors. In return, Kennedy guaranteed that Cuba would not be invaded and secretly added that NATO missiles in Greece and Turkey would be removed (contrary to the wishes of those countries). The crisis ended and was generally judged a victory for Kennedy. It was in the sense that subsequent information revealed that, unknown to the

---

* He summoned the ambassador, stated that France and the principal Western powers were fully aware of the Soviet treachery and that France entirely supported President Kennedy. The ambassador said this probably meant war, and de Gaulle replied, "I doubt it, but if so, we will perish together. Good day, Ambassador." De Gaulle was a refreshing contrast to Macmillan's waffling, and his response buttressed his argument that he was always a reliable ally in a crisis, even if his conduct to the "Anglo-Saxons" was normally that of an enemy.

CIA – which was no more efficient at finding out what was happening under its own nose in Cuba than it had been at detecting the Anglo-French preparations for the invasion of Egypt in 1956 or the Chinese infiltration of North Korea in 1950 – there were two whole Soviet divisions in Cuba and short-range missiles with atomic warheads already in the country (though not warheads for the intermediate range missiles). The short-range missiles and warheads would have been available to repel an invasion and to blast southern Florida. But it was not a success in the sense that at the start of the crisis there had been NATO missiles in Greece and Turkey and no Soviet missiles in Cuba and no assurance that the United States would not invade Cuba, and at the end of it there were no NATO missiles in Greece and Turkey, a guaranty of no U.S. invasion of Cuba, and still no Soviet missiles in Cuba. Discerning observers, including Charles de Gaulle and Richard Nixon, considered it an American strategic defeat.

In Ottawa, Harkness was outraged at Diefenbaker's refusal to support the American quarantine and put Canadian forces on a higher state of alert at the most tense period of the standoff. Diefenbaker allowed Howard Green to be the chief advocate of this quasi-neutralist policy, which did not reflect Canadian public opinion at all, until four days after Kennedy's October 22 address, and too late to be counted as a serious ally, when the prime minister came round to the view of Harkness and most of his colleagues and endorsed the naval quarantine. But the defence minister now had grave misgivings about whether he belonged in such a vacillating and unreliable government. He soon required that Green be overruled and that the Bomarc atomic warheads be accepted by Canada under the dual-national fire control system so that the $700 million spent replacing the Arrow with otherwise useless missiles was not completely wasted. (In that scenario, the money would certainly have been better spent in the Canadian aerospace industry on the Arrow, whether it was a commercial success or not.) Diefenbaker's official pronouncements to this point were to the effect that nuclear weapons would be acquired if needed, but the suddenness of the Cuba crisis showed what piffle that was, and the divisions within the cabinet grew deeper each week.

On January 3, 1963, the retiring forces commander of NATO, General Lauris Norstad, gave a press conference in Ottawa and confirmed that of course Canada had committed formally to the acceptance of nuclear weapons, though on a joint authority for use of them in action. Though apparently a routine assertion by the general, it flatly contradicted Diefenbaker, who had been claiming the decision had not been irrevocably made (contrary to the beliefs of Pearkes and Harkness, who had been admirably restrained in their public comments). At this convenient moment, in the highest Kingsian tradition, which did not come naturally to him, Mike Pearson announced a *volte-face* and declared that a Liberal government would accept and deploy nuclear weapons in accord with the country's alliance undertakings. In some respects, this was a return to the ancient Liberal Party proximity to the United States as practised by Sir Wilfrid and King. In others, it was naked opportunism, as the Liberal Party strategists knew well in the gossipy hothouse of Ottawa how precarious the ministry had become after all Diefenbaker's convoluted waffling and procrastinating.

Diefenbaker got a confidence vote from his own party executive and invited himself to a meeting in Nassau, in the Bahamas, between Kennedy and Macmillan, and confected a survival strategy that was the most astonishing contortion of facts this very eccentric leader had yet conjured from his verdant imagination and playbook-in-progress. He informed Parliament on his return on January 25 that the Western World had survived the last few perilous years because it had been "directed by God." He purported to deduce from his meeting with the American and British leaders that there had been a "change in the views of NATO" by which Canada's acquisition of atomic warheads had "been placed in doubt." He claimed that "more nuclear arms will add nothing to our defence" but that negotiations continued between Canada and the United States "in case of need."[40] It was a spectacular improvisation but it certainly would not work; it was too ambiguous to resolve his cabinet problems and too spurious a misinterpretation of the Bahamas discussions not to motivate the Europeans to demand clarifications and be authoritatively contradicted by the Americans and British. It was, in fact, not an altogether sane speech, even without considering Diefenbaker's divinations of the role of Providence.

Harkness hopefully declared, to remove doubt, that his chief intended to assure everyone that Canada would honour its commitments. The following day, Diefenbaker stated that his speech required no elaboration, adding to the necessity of it being explained. The European NATO allies obviously needed to know if there was any truth to Diefenbaker's interpretation of the declining utility of nuclear weapons; either he was misreading the Bahamian proceedings or Kennedy and Macmillan were, on their own authority, changing the course of the whole alliance. Obviously, the first had to be the case, but the Europeans, as the frontline states in the Cold War, had to be reassured. Without consulting President Kennedy or the secretary of state, Dean Rusk, in a considerable foray into insubordination, State Department officials issued a statement that the Nassau agreements, which had already been published (and would prove controversial for other reasons as the British took up the Polaris missile-launching submarine, which was not offered to the French, in replacement of the Skybolt missile), raised "no question of the appropriateness of nuclear weapons for Canadian forces in fulfilling their NATO or NORAD obligations." The statement further announced, even more grievously assaulting Diefenbaker's credibility, that "the Canadian government has not yet proposed any arrangement sufficiently practical to contribute effectively to North American defense." Rusk later regretted if the statement caused "offense" but did not retract it.

Drama swiftly gave way to farce as Diefenbaker imagined that he could ride American official arrogance to domestic political victory. He tried to convert the entire issue to a national refusal to be dictated to by the United States, which was only asking for the performance of defence obligations freely entered into by Canada and of which Canada was the chief beneficiary, as the United States was providing almost all the real defence capability for the whole continent. Diefenbaker recalled the Canadian ambassador from Washington "for consultations" and fiercely rejected the role of "satellite," a tendentious choice of words given that it was the usual description of the Soviet-occupied states of Eastern Europe. Harkness was determined to resign unless his leader was overridden by the cabinet. The associate minister of national defence, Pierre Sévigny, another decorated and seriously wounded veteran, was also disaffected, as were several other ministers, including the photogenic and hyperactive trade and commerce minister, George Hees. The whole government was on the verge of collapse.

The rebels milled noisily about, and Diefenbaker called a cabinet meeting at his residence on February 3, declared the existence of a "nest of traitors," and demanded a unanimous pledge of loyalty. Harkness calmly stated that the cabinet, parliamentary party, and the whole country had lost confidence in the prime minister and that he would resign rather than give the pledge requested. Green intervened and stabilized things briefly with an impassioned plea for loyalty to the chief in the face of an anticipated Liberal non-confidence motion, for which there was no indication yet of the required Social Credit and NDP support to force an election. Pearson made his motion in Parliament the next day as the news of Harkness's resignation circulated. Robert Thompson's own preference was for the government to continue, an anti-American election to be avoided, and for the government to address the country's deepening currency problems (though the economy was reviving) and produce a budget. But Premier Manning urged him to help pull the plug on Diefenbaker, whom Manning, an astute political judge at this point, after twenty years in power in Alberta, regarded as a menace to the Western Alliance. Thompson proposed an even more forceful censure of the government than had Pearson, and after a mélange of stirring and ineffective speeches, including an impressive reply by a beleaguered but unbowed prime minister, the House voted no confidence in an incumbent government for the first time since the Pacific Scandal brought down Macdonald in 1872.

The vote was 142 to 111. The caucus, where Diefenbaker was stronger than he was with the cabinet, met before the cabinet, and George Hees spoke poorly for the rebels, having confected a foolish plan to offer Diefenbaker the post of chief justice (which was not vacant). Senator Grattan O'Leary, formerly long-time editor of the *Ottawa Journal* and no great admirer of his chief, was repelled by the cowardice of rebellion at this stage and rallied the MPs and senators, though he felt Diefenbaker was incompetent and would be defeated in the coming election. Hees and the other waverers rallied briefly, the election was fixed for April 8, but Hees and Sévigny resigned on February 8 and Fleming, Fulton, and Ernest Halpenny* announced that they would not seek re-election.

---

* Secretary of State of Canada and MP for London, Ontario.

Like an unstoppable vaudevillian on autocue, a perversely revived Diefenbaker campaigned fiercely against the forces of privilege and special interests and the American stooges who he claimed were responsible for his problems. He could not really run on his record, and the disorganized government had no platform, but its fervent leader, half aged underdog pugilist and half King Lear, did what he did best and fought like a rabid tiger against a reluctant adversary, Pearson, all of whose instincts were to civility and compromise. As the campaign unfolded, the U.S. government again obligingly blundered, when Defense Secretary Robert McNamara (whose penchant for costly errors would later prove tragically extensive) allowed that the only real use of the Bomarcs was to be a decoy toward themselves and away from populated areas. This was nonsense, as they certainly had the ability to take down a lot of unwelcome aircraft with nuclear detonations at high altitudes. But Diefenbaker seized it as some sort of vindication of his own change of policy, which was now in complete exposure as unfathomably absurd, from the death of the Arrow to his own confirmation that the Bomarcs he had signed on for were militarily worthless as well as immoral (though neither was the case other than with their sand warheads).

Of course, it availed only to confuse some people, and what had become a carnival government ended on election night. The Progressive Conservatives declined from 37.2 per cent of the popular vote and 116 MPs in 1962 to 32.7 per cent and 95 MPs. The Liberals rose from 37 per cent and 99 MPs to 41.5 per cent and 128 MPs. Social Credit raised its vote, entirely in Quebec, from 11.6 per cent of the Canadian total to 11.9 per cent, but lost 6 Quebec MPs and declined from 30 to 24 seats. The NDP declined slightly, from 13.6 per cent of voters to 13.2 per cent, and from 19 to 17 MPs. Lester Bowles Pearson would be prime minister, as Mackenzie King and Louis St. Laurent had foretold fifteen years before.

John Diefenbaker was not a successful prime minister; he was a jumble of attitudes but had little in the way of policy, was a disorganized administrator, and was inconsistent, indecisive, and not infrequently irrational. But he was very formidable: a deadly campaigner, an idiosyncratic but often galvanizing public speaker, a brilliant parliamentarian, and a man of many fine qualities. He was absolutely honest financially, a passionate supporter of the average and the underprivileged and disadvantaged person, a fierce opponent of any racial or religious or socioeconomic discrimination, and while much criticized, as Pierre Laporte wrote of Maurice Duplessis, "Once in his presence, few could find voice for their grievances."[41] He was the first leader of Canada since Champlain, a third of a millennium before, who seriously cared for and respected the native people. His career was far from over; he would continue as probably the most capable and damaging leader of the Opposition in the country's history, and would carry on long after that as dean and master of the House of Commons and the ghost of past victories of the Conservative Party. He did not really have the remotest idea of what was necessary to make Canadian federalism work, of some of the regional forces that had to be managed, especially in Quebec, of the need for a double majority, French and English, on certain issues, or of the sensitivities of dealing with the Americans and British to Canada's advantage. In fact, considering that Borden was re-elected as head of a coalition in 1917, Diefenbaker was the only elected prime minister ever re-elected who did not understand how to attract heavy support in Ontario and Quebec. But he was a very considerable political figure, and unlike any other Canadian prime minister, in this as in many other respects, and despite the shambles of his government, his greatest days were ahead of him.

Lester B. "Mike" Pearson (1897–1972) was, as we have already seen him, a congenial, urbane, and emollient man, rooted altogether in the traditions of Skelton's foreign service, and though now a seven-term MP, with his slight lisp and bow tie, he was no more a politician in manner and appearance than at heart and lacked the instincts of combat on the hustings and for legislative manoeuvre for popular appeal. The Liberals had promised "Sixty days of decision," a distinctive Canadian flag at last, and a comprehensive national health-care policy and pension regime with applicability throughout the country ("portable pensions with leather handles," as Diefenbaker said, with the same gift for associative words with which he habitually referred to Liberal pollster Peter Regenstreif as "Peter Ribbentrop"). The Liberals came in masquerading as a Kennedyesque new wave, but at sixty-six Pearson was only two years younger than Diefenbaker, and while he and a few of his colleagues were seasoned King-St. Laurent veterans, most were untried. Paul Martin and Lionel Chevrier were back, at external affairs and justice, and Jack Pickersgill as secretary of state and a memorably able and colourful leader of the House. Paul Hellyer was at defence, and Howe's old deputy, Mitchell Sharp, very competent at trade and commerce. The new faces from Quebec were led by Guy Favreau and Maurice Lamontagne, intelligent men but completely inexperienced to aspire to the mantles of Lapointe, Cardin, and St. Laurent. Chevrier was an esteemed stopgap, and none of them had any hold on Quebec public opinion. The star of the new team, upon whom all eyes were fixed, was the party platform and campaign chairman and minister of finance, eminent accountant and public policy advocate Walter L. Gordon. It was an intelligent and accomplished front bench, but not exactly dynamic, quite accident-prone, and overconfident opposite an opponent they thought they had vanquished but who was pawing the ground and snorting fire and had already rung the bell for the rematch.

7. The Creative Agony of the Pearson Government, 1963–1966

The new government had initially thought of promising one hundred days of decision, but as that period of time is best known for the events that culminated in the Battle of Waterloo, Walter Gordon shrunk it to a more sonorous and action-packed sixty days. (Ninety days might have produced better results.) Pearson had successful visits to Harold Macmillan and John F. Kennedy at Hyannis Port, and relations with both countries were quickly back to normal. This was Pearson's strongest suit. He reversed Diefenbaker's hostility to the European Economic Community and Britain's participation in it, perhaps rather too selflessly and over-influenced by his predilection to trust such supranational institutions. And he confirmed to Kennedy that Canada would accept atomic warheads in its NATO and NORAD forces. This aroused severe criticism in leftist circles, including the dilettantish Montreal writer and well-to-do inheritor Pierre Elliott Trudeau, who wrote in (and co-founded) the liberal monthly Cité Libre of Pearson, "He had nothing to lose except his honour. He lost it."[42] In fact, it was the promised, contracted, necessary, and wise course. Former defence ministers Pearkes and Harkness, rugged old officers to the end, each lived on to the age of ninety-six and were fully vindicated, and the acceptance of atomic warheads was one of Pearson's best decisions as prime minister and most astute political moves.

There were other steps that fulfilled some of the expectations raised by the fanfare about a decisive new government getting off to a fast start. Territorial waters were extended to twelve miles offshore, which pleased the fishermen. A number of new agencies were established or announced that were going to attack regional economic disparities, and the Economic Council of Canada revealed the contemporary infatuation with government planning, but it would have moments of constructive relevance. And, announced shortly after the sixtieth day, but planned from the start of the new government, the Royal Commission on Bilingualism and Biculturalism was established. It would be co-chaired by university chairman and former head of the CBC, Davidson Dunton, and *Le Devoir* editor and former politician André Laurendeau. An outline pension scheme for the country was revealed, there was important progress on a shared use by Canada and the United States of the power and water resources of the Columbia River, where the Americans and British Columbia had conflicting ambitions, and five maritime unions were placed in trusteeship as a first step to end a good deal of violence in the maritime unions of the Great Lakes.

But on day fifty-three, June 13, 1963, Walter Gordon presented his budget and the wheels came off the new government in all directions. Gordon had told his deputy minister, Kenneth Taylor, that he would be departing finance but didn't make the change right away. His officials were hostile to much of what he wanted to do, especially in using the tax system to discourage greater American control of the Canadian private sector. Gordon was a Toronto gentleman from an old family, soft-spoken and courteous, head of the large accounting firm Clarkson Gordon, and a considerable intellectual in his fields of industrial and economic policy. He was an old friend of Pearson and had a blank cheque in the approval of the *Toronto Star*. But he was not by nature a combative person, and he was venturing into policy areas where, to be successful, he would have to be as close to a rabble-rouser as so genteel, prosperous, and calm a country as Canada could accept. That was not Walter Gordon's style. He was closer to Diefenbaker's reservations about the United States – though not for the same reason of umbilical attachment to Britain and the monarchy – than he was to the traditional Liberal Party affection for America. And he was closer to the NDP's nationalism than was Pearson; though Pearson was closer to the NDP's socialist ambitions than was Gordon, a wealthy Bay Street capitalist after all, if a pretty theoretical one. He was rushing into a hazardous area without the support of his department, and without anything more than the superficial solidarity of his leader and colleagues. Gordon set out to reduce the deficit and clean up the fiscal mess left by Diefenbaker (against the wishes of Diefenbaker's finance ministers, Fleming and Nowlan) and start on a very tentative program of economic nationalism. In this, he was the victim of the previous government's disastrous imbroglio over defence issues, and the Canadian public was in no mood for more strained relations with the United States. In the circumstances, he should not have been overly ambitious in this budget and should have prepared his reforms very carefully, should have thoroughly prepared opinion, and led a united department and cabinet in his next budget. Instead, Gordon had over-imbibed the nectar of Pearsonian reform and even radicalism (which was rarely even rhetorical, much less real) and hurtled into a high-explosive minefield in a chronically anti-controversial country. He would pay the price for centuries of Canadian passivity opposite the Americans, rippled only every few decades by reciprocity and atomic weapons.

He had brought in four helpers in preparing the budget: Geoff Conway, a Canadian at Harvard; Martin O'Connell and David Stanley of Toronto financial firms; and Rod Anderson from Gordon's own accounting firm. They all took oaths of secrecy, which they honoured, and were unpaid by the government. The budget raised revenues in part by ending the suspension on the sales tax on building materials. Since Gordon was trying to stimulate economic activity, there were better ways to achieve the same end. The budget also altered the tax code in ways that Gordon, as an accountant, had long felt were appropriate (expense and executive automobile allowances, and so on; tokens, but probably not bad politics). It would spread some money around less favoured regions through accelerated depreciation allowances, but most controversially it proposed to alter the non-resident dividend tax and encouraged foreign-owned companies to sell some of their interests to Canadians, up to at least 25 per cent, raised the tax rate on the dividends of those that did not, and imposed a 30 per cent foreign takeover tax (a bit steep in the circumstances).

It was a well- and sensibly intended group of objectives, but a bold stroke for Canadians and over-hastily formulated. Pearson assured him of his full support, but Pearson was a diplomat, an even less reliable source of expressions of solidarity than politicians, some of whose mores he also, of course, had acquired (unlike Louis St. Laurent, a man of principle always). A few days before the budget speech, Pearson and Gordon had lunch with the governor of the Bank of Canada, Louis Rasminsky, who was afraid of currency destabilization and possible American retaliation for Gordon's very gentle and incremental measures, but Pearson told Gordon to stick to his guns.

Since the civil service, when peeved, is hugely indiscreet, Douglas Fisher, the NDP member for Port Arthur, Ontario, who had defeated C.D. Howe in 1957, put questions to Gordon in the House of Commons on June 14 about his reliance on outsiders, and Gordon answered somewhat coyly. He was not an experienced parliamentarian, was a shy man personally, and did not take a crash course on the parliamentary ropes from Pickersgill, Martin, and Chevrier, who could have warned him how to steer somewhat clear of Diefenbaker, who was deadly when dealing with a distressed parliamentary opponent. The Opposition tore into Gordon, and there were allegations of budget leaks, a serious matter in the parliamentary system. Gordon's colleagues started waffling, and he probably became the victim of the envy of long-time Liberal MPs who resented the newcomer's prominence. At a meeting at the prime minister's country home at Harrington Lake, near Ottawa, everyone deserted Gordon except Lamontagne, health and welfare minister Judy LaMarsh, and the agriculture minister, Harry Hays, of Calgary (though Mitchell Sharp had spoken effectively for him in the House on June 24).

Gordon agreed to bring in the building materials tax changes gradually and to soften the 25 per cent Canadian ownership requirement to a believable expression of preparedness to comply, but once his retreat began, the assault on him was amplified, and Pearson declined to make any serious effort to save his colleague, to whom he owed a great deal and whom he had urged to go forward and pledged to support. Pearson was looking for a peacekeeping force to stand between himself and Diefenbaker, who was now in full cry, though he started late. Future nationalists, including University of Toronto NDP professor Mel Watkins and Quebec cabinet minister Eric Kierans, former head of the Montreal Stock Exchange, attacked Gordon, which was particularly disgraceful in light of their future policy advocacy. Apart from the incongruity of imposing taxes on building materials when trying to stimulate the economy, the only real problem was the 30 per cent tax on foreign acquisitions of Canadian companies. This meant there would be no such acquisitions, and that would decapitate the Canadian corporate transactional business; 10 per cent would have been quite sufficient, with exonerations for those who kept a substantial Canadian ownership level and gave it some board representation. Basically, Gordon was correct, but his tepid country did not honour him, then or subsequently. The charges of budget leaks were never proved or even made generally believable (although the home of one of Gordon's assistant deputy ministers was ransacked by burglars, who left the text of the speech all over the floor but paid no attention to it).[43]

Walter Gordon withdrew the entire budget a few days later. It was a shocking fiasco, and quite unnecessary, and it revealed Pearson's weaknesses in their most unflattering aspects. His better qualities were in evidence when he declined Gordon's offer to resign, though only after tentatively offering finance to Sharp and Sharp's trade and commerce portfolio to Lamontagne.[44] But Gordon was a wounded figure hereafter, and was shabbily treated by everyone, including Liberal historians such as Michael Bliss, John English, and Bruce Hutchison (the latter two slavering Pearson apologists, though generally fairly reliable in other respects).* Parliament eventually adjourned for the summer, but any sense of having delivered the responsibility to govern to a smooth professional team, as the country remembered from King and St. Laurent and impetuously dispensed with in 1957, had lasted only fifty-three days, if that, and would not be reintroduced in Pearson's time. There was always a sense that it was all a bit too

---

* Michael Bliss, *Right Honourable Men: The Descent of Canadian Politics from Macdonald to Mulroney*, Toronto, 1994; John English, *The Life of Lester Pearson*, vol. II, *The Worldly Years, 1949–1972*, Toronto, 1992; Bruce Hutchison, *Mr. Prime Minister: 1867–1964*, Toronto, 1964.

much for him, that there was a slight unsynchronized delay between when the Liberal Party apparat came up with one of its often astute but sometimes sleazy or silly brainwaves and when it would click in Pearson's mind, and there was the fear that it wasn't really him who was running the government.*

Pearson was a man of exceptional qualities, and his government would accomplish some important achievements. Above all, he recognized that Quebec was a time bomb that had to be addressed, and though he had no idea how to address it, he knew to reach for people who could. He was not at all an unworthy occupant of the office, but the country had gone from a man of great but often misdirected and terribly erratic strength in Diefenbaker to a man of insufficient strength in support of generally good but not confident judgment in Pearson. King and St. Laurent had been right for forty years, seven of them together: the consummate manoeuvrer and the distinguished and principled chairman. Diefenbaker was an aberration, and Pearson was an improvement, but *pas un chef*, not someone in whom the country – though it liked him and would wish to believe in him – could repose the level of confidence a leader must earn and keep to be fully effective.

The government drifted. Judy LaMarsh ran into problems with her own officials trying to confect a national pension plan and then was straight-armed by the provinces. Pearson intervened and practised his legitimately celebrated diplomatic talents on the issue, but LaMarsh felt betrayed by her leader.[46] Chevrier, though admirable and capable, was not the man to lead the federal Liberals in Quebec. He had first been elected in 1935 and was not really a Québécois, and in late 1963 he went to London, succeeding George Drew as high commissioner. The designated Quebec leader of the federal Liberals would be Guy Favreau, who had been Fulton's deputy minister of justice and succeeded to that portfolio on Chevrier's departure. He had only just been elected in 1963, and the burden that was to fall on him was as great and sudden as that assumed by St. Laurent when he

---

* There was also an unseemly self-consciousness about a man of so many attainments. In his memoirs, he wrote of his meeting with General Douglas MacArthur in Tokyo in January 1950: "I felt that I ought to fall down and worship, but I do not very readily fall down and worship," etc. This was a peculiar recollection twenty years later.[45]

entered King's government at the start of 1942. He started well and received considerable credit for his role in the Fulton-Favreau formula for amending the Constitution, which would patriate it completely and provided for unanimous approval of amendments that affected provincial matters but only two-thirds of the provinces representing a majority of Canadians for other matters. Skirmishing arose over Quebec's demands, which some English Canadians claimed would emasculate the federal government, and Tommy Douglas for the federal NDP objected to any "entrenchment" of property and civil rights, partly because of his party's wealth-redistributive ambitions, and partly because he feared that such a step would produce constitutional sclerosis.

Jean Lesage claimed he was just trying to enable Quebec to play its full role in Confederation. Lesage had been re-elected in Quebec in 1962 with the public takeover by the provincial government of practically all the electric power it did not already own in the province, but he was already having difficulty balancing the nationalist and federalist tendencies within his own party. Pearson, though he did not know much about Quebec, recognized a flammable set of conditions that would have to be dealt with diplomatically, and in this case his talents were needed, and would be useful. Lesage had allowed himself to be carried along on the wave of modernization, and the secularization of the schools deprived the religious orders of a large number of their members: many of the teaching and paramedical personnel in the province exchanged holy orders for public service unions and performed the same tasks as before but at much greater expense to the taxpayers, and the union bosses were a good deal harder to deal with than the bishops had been (all of which Duplessis had predicted). One person was killed in a separatist bomb blast in a Montreal army recruiting office in April 1963, the first fatality from that cause. No one could see where it would end. As early as 1964, progressive English-Canadian Quebec-watchers were having serious doubts about where Quebec was going and at what pace, as, for the first time, discussion of the separation and independence of Quebec arose and became quite widespread and intense.

In the spring of 1964, there was a Federal-Provincial Conference in Quebec City, which was a shambles. Lesage demanded the funding of Quebec's own pension plan and objected to the federal government's plan for student assistance. The meeting, which attracted a good many separatist demonstrators, broke up without any agreement. Federal forestry minister Maurice Sauvé and senior policy advisor Tom Kent urged upon Pearson a back-channel comeback to Lesage as they feared that the strains on the country could be irreversible. Pearson authorized their return with a proposal for a division of direct taxes much more generous to the province of Quebec, and Lesage agreed. All the pious and dogmatic humbug that King and St. Laurent had addressed to Duplessis about the subordinate role of provinces and Quebec being "a province like the others" went up the chimney with the velocity of a skyrocket. Judy LaMarsh was kept in the dark as the pension plan she had designed was scrapped and the chief responsibility of her department was negotiated away from under her by, or in the name of, the prime minister whom she served. LaMarsh had to be dissuaded by Kent from resigning as she smashed the framed photograph of Pearson on her desk.[47] Following this arrangement, Quebec would have 50 per cent of direct taxes, not the 10 per cent for which Duplessis had to threaten double taxation to extract from St. Laurent in 1954, raised to 13 per cent with Diefenbaker. What Duplessis the Union Nationale troublemaker had politely but persistently asked for, Lesage the Liberal modernizer would abruptly take. And what St. Laurent the Liberal defender of Canadian federal and national integrity attempted to withhold, Pearson the Liberal saviour of Canada would gladly give away, in the higher interest of Canada (and of the Liberal Party).

As the respected Ontario premier John Robarts (who succeeded Leslie Frost at a provincial Conservative convention in 1961) told the author, "Jean Lesage just bulldozed Mike Pearson."[48] The fact is that Lesage was essentially correct, but Duplessis would have settled for slightly less ten years before and would have thrown in permanent adherence to a domestic amending formula. Pearson had also been right in his arrangements with Lesage, but he should have extracted more for them. As it was, he could not even get Lesage to hold to the Fulton-Favreau formula, though it was very close to what was ultimately agreed, fifteen years later. All Lesage agreed to was a new division of taxing powers that was not assured to be permanent and with no guaranties that Quebec would not be back asking for more jurisdiction and threatening to secede if it didn't get it, which of course is what happened.

While this drama was unfolding, Pearson acted on his promise to endow the country with a new flag and rather bravely unveiled a version of it at a legion hall in his Ontario constituency of Algoma East on May 1, 1964. It was indifferently received by that audience, and was a divisive issue in public opinion. The appropriate legislation was presented on June 15. The acerbic Pierre Trudeau, unaware of how imminent his destiny as a federal Liberal was, wrote that Quebec did not give "a tinker's damn about the flag."[49] On September 10, after stormy parliamentary debate, the issue went to a committee of fifteen, which chose a single red maple leaf in a white field with red borders on either side, the flag of Canada the world now knows, over what was presumed to be Pearson's choice, which had three maple leaves between two blue borders. With Pearson and Diefenbaker flinging insults at each other, and after a closure motion moved by Léon Balcer, Progressive Conservative member for Trois-Rivières (and Duplessis's nephew), who was disgusted at the antics of his own leader, the flag was approved in a free vote, 163 to 78, at 2:15 a.m. on December 15, 1964. It was in fact one of the great moments of Pearson's eventful career; it was his issue, and he had bulled it through. As the struggle with Quebec approached a critical stage, it would only have made the federal position more difficult with two unilingual English-speaking leaders, both past the normal retirement age (though not for Canadian prime ministers), debating, through interpreters, with the Quebec nationalists under a red ensign. It is a distinctive and a distinguished flag.

The Royal Commission on Bilingualism and Biculturalism, also known as the Laurendeau-Dunton Commission, issued a preliminary report in February 1965 stating that "Canada is passing through the greatest crisis in its history."[50] On a Florida holiday, Pearson met Lesage and invited him to come to Ottawa and be the federal leader of the Quebec Liberals and presumed successor to him, as King had offered Godbout in 1941. Lesage declined because he could not leave Quebec and it was impossible to tell where the province was going. He told Pearson he had "a rampaging bear by the tail."[51] In career terms, Lesage's decision was as fatefully mistaken as Godbout's, and his political future would not be much more successful. Like Godbout, Lesage drank too much (but so did Macdonald and Churchill). Lesage was a much more effective premier than Godbout, a more formidable and worldly man, and was very bilingual. He was a serious barrister where Godbout, though a capable orator, was an apple farmer from Frelighsburg.

By this time, justice minister Guy Favreau had run into trouble. Drug dealer Lucien Rivard had tried to bribe a lawyer to persuade prison officials to release him, and Favreau had not consulted his own officials before determining not to prosecute Raymond Denis, who had allegedly assisted Rivard. There was also a peripheral involvement of the prime minister's parliamentary secretary, Guy Rouleau, and Favreau had not mentioned this to Pearson. Favreau had shown a spectacular lack of judgment, and in the autumn of 1964 Diefenbaker massacred him with questions, ably seconded by Yukon Conservative MP Erik Nielsen. Finally, to get the Opposition off his back, Favreau called for a royal commission (the Dorion Inquiry) to look into the Rivard affair, and it criticized the minister's judgment, requiring his resignation and the end of his brief tenure as heir to Lapointe and St. Laurent. He continued as president of the Privy Council and was named a Superior Court judge in 1967, but he died a broken man in July that year, aged fifty, a decent and capable person thrust into a very exacting position for which he was not qualified by reliability of judgment, and where he was abandoned by his patron. Pearson had not lifted a finger to help him and told Parliament that Favreau had not mentioned the Rivard affair until late November 1965, when, as he later acknowledged, it had been September 2. Pearson appeared weak and shifty, and was not conducting himself and his high office in a way calculated to inspire confidence, affection, or loyalty.

In November 1964, Maurice Lamontagne, secretary of state, and René Tremblay, the minister of immigration, were accused of accepting furniture they had not paid for from a bankrupt company. There were no allegations that Lamontagne had done any favours for anyone and it wasn't really a scandal, but Pearson and his entourage by this time were in a state of panic, being tormented by Diefenbaker and his most virulent fellow-assailants. Lamontagne continued through 1965 but was finished, and the balance of his formerly promising career was an anti-climax. He went to the Senate and died in 1983, aged sixty-five. (Walter Gordon appointed him a director of his prosperous company, Canadian Corporate Management, where he suggested uncommercial initiatives such as seasonally reported earnings; that is, averaged according to management estimates of the next quarters.[52]) René Tremblay had ordered some furniture from the same company, but it wasn't delivered and so he did not pay for it, until it was delivered. He had committed absolutely no impropriety, as even Nielsen acknowledged, but Pearson put him over the side anyway. Pearson named him as postmaster general, then dropped him, and he died in 1968, aged forty-five, having done nothing except carry the weight of the cowardice of his leader. A more serious legal problem was the ten-thousand-dollar bribe Yvon Dupuis was accused of taking for assisting in a racetrack licence application. He was fired as minister without portfolio by Pearson in January 1965 (having been appointed as a reward for his strenuous campaign against the Créditistes in 1963). He was acquitted in 1968, and was elected leader of the provincial Créditistes in 1973, but retired after being defeated personally in the Quebec election of that year. He lived on into his upper eighties, being a less sensitive man to aspersions than the tragic Favreau, Lamontagne, and Tremblay, who did not lack integrity, only judgment and support from where they had every right to expect it.

The Pearson government was in disarray and demoralized. For many years, Diefenbaker would convulse audiences in delight with such gambits as, "It was a warm evening, like this one, when the Liberals sent Rivard out to water the ice rink in his prison." (Having failed to bribe his way out of prison, he had used a garden hose to escape over the wall. His legal problems ended after another stint of prison in the United States, and he lived on peacefully for nearly thirty years and died in 2002 at eighty-seven, a resourceful hood who became something of a folk figure.)

Despite all its problems and excursions, Pearson's government did have an activist program, and it gradually put it through. Paul Hellyer unified the armed forces and gave them a common uniform. It was billed as a magnificent reform that would produce astonishing efficiencies. In fact, it proved a disaster, was unpopular in the forces, and caused public confusion. Hellyer was a competent and energetic man, and would eventually be the only person to be a serious contender for the leadership of both major parties, but he did not always have the highest quality judgment. (He attached more credence than he should have, especially given his position, to theories of intergalactic visitors.) The Auto Pact was signed, integrating the automobile fabrication activities of the United States and Canada in a way that proved quite satisfactory for Canada as an exporter and employer of auto workers. Clearly major initiatives were planned on the whole national unity and biculturalism front, and there was an air of slightly disorderly but still somewhat invigorating renovation abroad.

The Toronto group that effectively ran the Liberal Party organization under Walter Gordon and Keith Davey, who would direct eight Liberal federal campaigns, convinced Pearson that all the problems he had had, with ministers being torn down by Diefenbaker and all his policy initiatives so contested, were the result of having a minority government and that what was needed was a return to the polls and the strong mandate of a parliamentary majority. This was deemed to be quite achievable against such a raving and obstructive antiquarian as Diefenbaker. Pearson's heart wasn't really in it, but he allowed himself to be persuaded, and in early September the House was dissolved for a general election on November 8, 1965. It was a lacklustre campaign, as the Liberals could not really convince even themselves that the addition of the five MPs necessary for a majority, since the government had not had even a remotely close call on a confidence vote, was anything to become excited about. But John Diefenbaker, now seventy and with his many and oft-caricatured mannerisms more pronounced than ever, was in his glory. At this sort of campaigning he was dangerous and had the irresistible charm of the underdog.

But it was at this point that Pearson showed he was in the chain of Canadian leaders who had the intuitive genius of a sure instinct for the country's survival, starting with the fundamental requirement of a French-English double majority on key issues that had existed since the Quebec Act rallied the French Canadians and the American Revolution drove enough British subjects into Canada to make it a loyalist country. If it were just the English asserting their majority in the country on a vital issue, such as Confederation itself, Canada would eventually crack up. Pearson had had a glimpse of what was coming in Quebec, and he knew that the federal government was not equipped to deal with it. New leadership from French Quebec had to be found, and it was. Quebec union leader Jean Marchand, of the Confederation of National Trade Unions, *La Presse* editor Gérard Pelletier, and the waspy but elegant and completely bilingual Pierre Elliott Trudeau were all recruited as candidates (the last two to safe Montreal constituencies; Marchand had a battle with the Créditistes in Quebec City). This time, there would be no false starts as there had been with Favreau and Lamontagne.

It was not a serious election, but it did produce the personnel upgrade that would see the country through the next twenty very difficult years. On election night, the Liberals did not gain their majority, though they crept up on it, from 128 MPs to 131, now just two seats short of a majority, while their share of total vote declined slightly, from 41.5 to 40.7 per cent. The Progressive Conservatives gained 4 MPs, increasing from 93 to 97, as their share of the vote also declined slightly, from 32.7 to 32.4 per cent. The NDP had a relatively good election, going from 13.2 per cent to 17.9 per cent and from 17 to 24 MPs. Social Credit finally split, between Caouette's Créditistes, confined to Quebec, and Robert Thompson's Social Credit Party. They had been a pantomime horse before but now were just regional splinter parties. Caouette took 4.7 per cent of the total vote and 9 Quebec MPs, and Thompson took 3.7 per cent of the total vote, similar to the totals Solon Low had obtained, and 5 MPs. Their combined total declined, from 19 to 14 MPs and from 11.9 to 8.4 per cent.

Trudeau, Marchand, and Pelletier were elected and came forward quickly, Marchand straight into government as minister of citizenship and immigration and Trudeau as parliamentary assistant to the prime minister. Walter Gordon, having advised the election, did the honourable thing, as was entirely in character, and resigned from the cabinet.* He remained in Parliament for three years but was a spent force, a gentle, thoughtful, and somewhat prescient man, who by rushing toward his moment of maximum impact, misjudged and missed it, and he could not regain his balance. He deserves to be remembered as an

---

* He remained as an MP and returned as president of the Privy Council in 1967–1968.

admirable ornament, a prophet of integrity lacking the political gifts needed to govern. His place as minister of finance was taken by the capable Mitchell Sharp. And in the eyes of the Toronto business community, who had been disappointed by Gordon's reconnaissance on the left, another important addition – returning after an absence of eight years, and now from Toronto – was Robert Winters, one of the bright young men of the St. Laurent government, who had been president of Rio Algom Mines and took Sharp's place at trade and commerce. It was a decisive changing of the guard in Quebec and Toronto; the future, at least in terms of personalities, was becoming clearer. Pearson's first impulse was to resign with Gordon, but his colleagues wouldn't hear of it. The show must go on; there was one more round of the Pearson-Diefenbaker combat to go, but behind that discordant, unserious circus, great drama was approaching.

Lester Pearson had been persuaded into making an apparently mistaken decision in calling an election but did the right thing for the wrong reasons. In pressing for it, Walter Gordon ended his career in failure but unknowingly created the circumstances for national renewal. The co-chairs of the Royal Commission on Bilingualism and Biculturalism, André Laurendeau and Davidson Dunton, were correct that an immense crisis was at hand in Quebec. Pearson sensed this, knew there was no one in Ottawa to handle it, and had his doubts that Lesage could hold the province much longer either. Trudeau, forty-six, had been a flippant, underemployed poseur, driving around Montreal on his motorcycle in a German army outfit during the war, promoting miscellaneous labour causes, nuclear disarmament, and even opposing Pearson's Maple Leaf flag, but he was a very intelligent, very tough, completely bilingual, and very articulate federalist. Jean Marchand had long been associated with a fairly irresponsible labour confederation, but he too was a strong federalist. Gérard Pelletier was a frequently annoying editorial writer, overburdened with affectations of cultural distinction, but he was a powerful federalist advocate also, and was esteemed, as the others were, in the now largely separatist Quebec media. These were new men of great style and presentational flair and rigour, not grey lawyers that the nationalists could dismiss as *vendus*.

Pearson did not know them and did not personally recruit them, but he demanded the rounding up of such people, as well as a massive strengthening of the French-Canadian section of the senior federal civil service. In a misconceived election call, he preserved the mystical golden thread of Canadian national development: Quebec would send to Ottawa people who could sell an intensified bicultural federalism to the proverbial two solitudes that composed the country. They had their limitations and would make many mistakes, but Trudeau and the others, some already in place, like Maurice and Jeanne Sauvé, John Turner, and Jean Chrétien, were the people who would save the country. An essentially superfluous election would regenerate Canada and enable the Liberal Party to elevate a leader of even more unlikely provenance than Pearson, St. Laurent, and King. The magic of imperceptible, inexorable Canadian maturation was about to rise to its greatest challenge, as the golden thread would be spun out toward a new millennium.

Pierre Elliott Trudeau (1919–2000), prime minister of Canada 1968–1979,
1980–1984, and René Lévesque (1920–1985), prominent television journalist and
Liberal provincial cabinet minister before founding the independentist Parti
Québécois in 1967, leader of the opposition 1973–1976 and premier of Quebec
1976–1984. They dominated the federalist-separatist debate in Quebec for nearly
twenty years. Trudeau regarded secessionism as verging on treason and attacked it
with a severity and fervour unprecedented in Canadian history; Trudeau won their
intense struggle, though the battle continued on for another fifteen years.

CHAPTER 9

Trudeau, Lévesque, and the Quebec Crisis, 1966–2000

1. Canada-France-Quebec Relations, Charles de Gaulle, and the Victory of Daniel Johnson, 1966–1967

In the new year, John Diefenbaker's assault on Lester Pearson's Quebec ministers began again as it came to light that the justice minister, Lucien Cardin, told a television reporter that George Victor Spencer, a postal clerk suspected of being a Soviet agent, would not be indicted but would be subject to RCMP surveillance for the rest of his life. (This wasn't as open-ended a matter as it seemed, as he was terminally ill.) Diefenbaker opened up on this, and he and Tommy Douglas's replacement as NDP leader, David Lewis, demanded an inquiry, as Spencer had not had a chance to defend himself. There was some sympathy for Spencer on the Liberal benches, and Pearson recognized that he might lose a confidence vote on this obscure issue, despite having just been re-elected. He too sympathized with Spencer, and he agreed to an inquiry. By an accidental wiring error, some Conservative MPs could listen in to the Liberal caucus room, and they learned how concerned the government was. Cardin, on March 4, taunted by Diefenbaker, shouted back, "What about Monsignor?" Diefenbaker pressed on, and Cardin was on the verge of resignation; Pearson had lost control of the government again. A number of Quebec ministers, including Jean Marchand, were prepared to resign also. As Ernest Lapointe and Arthur Cardin (no relation to Lucien) had done in the case of Jacques Bureau during the customs scandal forty years before, the French-Canadian ministers locked arms together. By a narrow margin, Lucien Cardin resolved to remain, and the crisis passed, but "Monsignor," who proved to be the call girl Gerda Munsinger, who had had a relationship with one of Diefenbaker's ministers, whose name Cardin had mispronounced and whom he mistakenly believed was dead, became a subject of curiosity to Pearson, and he acted, in conversation with Diefenbaker, as if she were an ace up the government's sleeve. Cardin babbled garrulously to the press about the "late Olga Monsignor," as he called the live Gerda Munsinger, on March 10. This created a tremendous buzz, and an enterprising *Toronto Star* reporter, Robert Reguly, found Frau Munsinger working in a Munich bar. She quickly revealed that her chief contact in the Conservative government had been Pierre Sévigny, Diefenbaker's associate minister of national defence. A Royal Commission chaired by Chief Justice Wishart Spence was established, and while it vastly entertained Canadians, and lightly criticized Diefenbaker and Davie Fulton for insufficient vigilance, it found no security breach. In a sense, Cardin had at least held his own with Diefenbaker, unlike Guy Favreau, Maurice Lamontagne, and René Tremblay. It was a very shabby business, and Parliament plumbed rare depths of absurd and unruly debate.

Canada's relations with the United States were strained through most of the Pearson term after a good start with Kennedy. The U.S. president for all but the first seven months was the flamboyant but rather crude Texan veteran of Congress Lyndon B. Johnson, fabled leader of the Senate who had succeeded on the assassination of President John F. Kennedy on November 22, 1963. Pearson had kept somewhat in touch with what was happening in Vietnam, partly through Canada's role on the practically irrelevant International Control Commission, and partly through his many diplomatic contacts in the United States and other countries. All Pearson's information was that the condition of South Vietnam was eroding quickly, and in a speech at Temple University in Philadelphia on April 2, 1965, just two weeks after Johnson had begun to commit U.S. ground forces to combat in South Vietnam, Pearson publicly suggested there be a pause in bombing. (The use of ground forces in South Vietnam was against the advice of President Truman, President Eisenhower, and General MacArthur, all of whom regarded the country as porous and not worth the cost of rescuing it from an advanced communist insurgency heavily supported by the Soviet Union and China.) Johnson was incensed and raved at Pearson at the presidential retreat at Camp David. In their previous meeting, at the LBJ Ranch in Texas, Pearson had been offended by Johnson's coarseness and bellicosity, and by mannerisms such as interrupting his driving tour of the estate to urinate at the roadside. (By contrast, Britain's Yorkshire prime minister Harold Wilson and West Germany's Bavarian chancellor, Ludwig Erhard, found Johnson's informality refreshing.) Paul Martin had threatened to resign if Pearson gave the speech in Philadelphia, but he did not. The Canadian perspective was correct in that the United States was embarking on an unpromising endeavour, but it was mistaken in so far as it imagined that there were any alternatives to fighting it out successfully or abandoning Indochina completely. Johnson had asked for Canadian good offices in carrying messages of threats and rewards to Hanoi, in North Vietnam, in 1964, and Canadian diplomat Blair Seaborn did so, but reported that Hanoi had no interest in negotiating. Martin, as part of his ramp-up to the succession to Pearson, sent Chester Ronning, the leftist son of missionaries in China and severe critic of U.S. policy, on a fact-finding mission to Hanoi, despite Pearson's realistic pessimism that much would come of it, and nothing did.

If the United States had been serious about Indochina, it should have made the fight as soon as the French conceded the colonial issue, when it would have had serious allies and before Ho Chi Minh had turned the North into a robotic warrior state. Eisenhower judged it not worth such an effort but fatefully guaranteed South Vietnam, on the theory that it could be protected. Johnson made war in increments, raising and lowering the level of bombing and ignoring the advice of MacArthur and Eisenhower that if he was going to fight the war, he would have to cut the Ho Chi Minh Trail in Laos and stop the flow of North Vietnamese soldiers and supplies to the South. He never did, and Ho just kept feeding the slaughter, oblivious to his casualties. Johnson came for a few hours to the world's fair site in Montreal in June 1967, and he and Pearson never met again after that.

Pearson determined to implement completely the bilingualism recommendations for the federal civil service of the Royal Commission on Bilingualism and Biculturalism, which would not fully report until 1969 but was releasing key parts of its report sequentially.

Relations between Ottawa and Quebec had been bubbling for some time. In his 1960 visit, Charles de Gaulle had noted the incongruity between French and English Canada, which was, if anything, accentuated when Diefenbaker visited him and assured him that all such concerns would be resolved eventually by bilingualism, attempting to underline his point by speaking in French and doing so "with great difficulty" (as de Gaulle neutrally commented while commending the Canadian leader's motives). It could be reasonably inferred that what Diefenbaker meant was that eventually the French Canadians and a somewhat increased number of English Canadians would be bilingual. As the decade passed, and especially after de Gaulle's rather ambitious efforts to revive a triumvirate – like that of Clemenceau, Wilson, and Lloyd George – with the Americans and British at the head of the Western Alliance was declined, and he had made his peace in Algeria, and France had become a nuclear power with a stable government and currency, de Gaulle reverted to his chosen method for gaining for France the status he believed his country, or at least he personally, deserved. As when he had, from a position of great dependency, defied Churchill and Roosevelt between 1941 and 1944, he now set out to convince the "Anglo-Saxons," as he habitually described them (the Americans and the British), that they underestimated France and him.

De Gaulle's was a difficult position. He knew better than anyone what a terrible humiliation France had endured in 1940, which made his action more heroic when, as he wrote, he "assumed France" and brought with him to London in his little airplane "the honour of France," as Churchill put it, in 1940. He wished to be the co-leader of Western Europe, but that would require Britain to uncouple somewhat from

America and join him in that endeavour. France could not compete with the United States for the favour of the British. However upstaged the British might be by the Americans, whatever their affection for France as a beautiful and rich neighbouring country that had mastered the arts of civilization, the power of the United States and its indispensability for the defence of the West were beyond challenge. De Gaulle sought from the Americans a status for France equivalent to what Britain enjoyed, but France had not really measured up as an ally. Apart from the contrast in its contributions to Allied victory in the Second World War, pre-Gaullist France had blundered catastrophically in Indochina while the British showed great agility in exiting Malaya and defeating the communists there, and, though uneasy about it, had not hindered the entry of Germany into NATO, which France had tried to block.

The Americans, seconded by the British and Canadians and the French themselves, had achieved the liberation of France in 1944, and starting on the day that Eisenhower had arranged for Free French units to appear to be clearing the Germans from Paris, de Gaulle, for commendable (and anti-communist) reasons, had propagated the myth that France had never left the war and had largely accomplished its own liberation. Though always generous personally to those who had led the Allies, especially Churchill and Eisenhower, de Gaulle had followed the example of the Habsburgs from the previous century and "astounded the world by [his] ingratitude."

The dreadful failure of Suez had demonstrated that it was impossible to resurrect the Anglo-French Entente Cordiale; Eisenhower and Kennedy and Macmillan had rejected a retrieval of the Grand Alliance of 1917 to 1919, de Gaulle turned seventy-five in 1965 (when he was re-elected to a second seven-year term as president), and time was running out. Where Eisenhower had been pushing a unified NATO military under U.S. command, Kennedy had tried a Multilateral Force, which would, effectively, have placed Americans in charge of British and French nuclear weapons. Outrageous though de Gaulle's conduct sometimes became, his impatience with the American inability to grasp that the Europeans, in their gratitude for liberation and the Marshall Plan, did not all want to become satellites of the United States, was understandable. Ironically, if de Gaulle had been a little more careful politically and taken better care of himself so that he served to the end of his second term, he could have got something close to the alliance he sought with the Anglo-Americans, under the Euro-integrationist Edward Heath and the sophisticated pro-Gaullist, and personal friend, Richard Nixon. But de Gaulle left office just after Nixon's inauguration in 1969 and died shortly after Heath's election in 1970.

As he saw the sands running out, de Gaulle donned his Joan of Arc outfit from the Casablanca Conference (as Roosevelt described him) and made his historic rapprochement with Konrad Adenauer's West Germany; threw his weight behind the Arabs in their conflict with Israel; barred the United Kingdom from the European Economic Community; exchanged ambassadors with China; denounced the American involvement in Indochina; set himself at the head of a great swath of Third World and Eurocentric, and even Latin American, opinion, as well as the "community" of former French colonial puppet states he had created in Africa; and tantalized the Russians with the thought of splintering the West if they truckled with adequate fervour to Paris.

All the while, de Gaulle retained the ultimate default position of French adherence to the Western Alliance, as he demonstrated in rallying instantly and unconditionally to Eisenhower at the summit conference in Paris in 1960, which Khrushchev broke up over the U-2 espionage plane affair, and in the Cuban missile crisis in 1962. He emphasized this by leading the foreign mourners at the mighty state funerals of John F. Kennedy in 1963, Winston Churchill in 1965, Konrad Adenauer in 1966, and Dwight D. Eisenhower in 1969. His foreign policy was ultimately an artistic aggregation of confidence tricks, and it was a personal confection from his own frustrations at the shortcomings of France in 1940 and its shortsightedness in not following his advice in 1945, and his having to wait until 1958 for the Fourth Republic to flounder to an end. He was an unbidden and extraordinary source for a blow to Canadian unity. It was outrageous and mistaken, but in the autumn of his days, Charles de Gaulle, a leader of the stature of Churchill and Roosevelt, and the great outsider, in his quest for methods of tormenting his allies and liberators, embraced a romantic vision of a resurrected New France in Quebec.

Quebec had opened an agency-general in Paris in 1961. (Duplessis had promised this in his last year, as he approved of de Gaulle but was contemptuous of the ephemeral regimes of the Fourth Republic, having outlasted as premier of Quebec in his second term the entire twelve years of that republic, which saw twenty-one French governments.) Pearson and Martin had visited Paris starting on January 15, 1964. De Gaulle received them cordially, and it was agreed that there would be regular consultations between the two governments. De Gaulle had referred sarcastically to the Commonwealth as a British "caravan" when he vetoed British entry into the European Economic Community in 1963. He had already begun courting Quebec, an eagerly willing recipient of such overtures. Jules Léger, a career diplomat and brother of the cardinal archbishop of Montreal, was named Canadian ambassador to France in 1964, succeeding Pierre Dupuy, whom de Gaulle had not forgiven for being the Canadian representative Mackenzie King had assigned to Vichy in 1940, after he appointed General Georges Vanier, the current governor general, to represent Canada to the Free French. When Léger presented his letters of credence to de Gaulle, the president of France sarcastically read aloud that accreditation was requested by "Her Majesty Queen Elizabeth II."

There were already a number of problems in France-Canada relations, and Pearson, for an accomplished diplomat, and especially one who had first become acquainted with de Gaulle in London during the war and had always recognized his qualities, had been very insensitive. Whatever the competing merits, much would have been accomplished if Air Canada (as Pearson renamed Trans-Canada Airlines) had bought the French manufactured Caravelle airliner instead of American competitors. He could also have been more astute in his NATO policy and would have lost nothing by supporting the French rejection of the Multilateral Force project; it was a foolish idea and the British opposed it also, though Macmillan allowed de Gaulle to make most of the running. (This was the issue that led to the Nassau meeting Diefenbaker crashed in 1963, when the Skybolt missile was scuttled but it was agreed that the United States would help Britain, but not France, and enable it to take the Polaris submarine. The "Anglo-Saxons" brought a considerable amount of de Gaulle's wrath down on themselves.) Martin and Pearson even had an amateurish stab at appeasement. On December 13, 1964, Martin announced that Canada was opposed to any NATO policy that was unacceptable to France, and on February 10, 1965, Pearson gave a speech in Ottawa in which he said that perhaps NATO should pursue somewhat different goals in Europe and North America. This was a nonsensical concept, considering that the United States provided 85 per cent of the muscle for the entire alliance, and it was an ad hoc, slapdash effort, not part of a coherent effort to head de Gaulle off from wholesale meddling and mischief-making in Quebec, which Pearson and Martin could reasonably have assumed by now was a possibility.

Most important, and probably decisive in the shattering of France-Canada relations that was afoot, was Pearson's decision not to meet French terms for the acquisition of Canadian uranium, though it came from Pearson's own constituency of Algoma East and the industry gave his voters employment. This was one of the biggest blunders of Pearson's career, and despite his many successes he was very fallible in certain areas. Having promised the sale of uranium to France in his visit of 1964 to Paris, in 1965 he decided that Canada's membership in the International Atomic Energy Agency and its status as a signatory of the Test Ban Treaty required that Canada be assured that its uranium was only destined for civil purposes. This was considered by de Gaulle, with some reason, to be provocative, both as a change of terms and as a different basis from that on which uranium was sold to the United States and the United Kingdom. Pearson naïvely thought he could address the issue by applying, henceforth, the same standards to sales of uranium to Great Britain. He had not, even at this late date of June 1965, the remotest idea with what or whom he was dealing.

In February 1965, Quebec and France had signed a cultural entente. Education minister Paul Gérin-Lajoie and Premier Jean Lesage's assistant for intergovernmental affairs, Claude Morin, went to Paris without a word to Ottawa and purported to have the authority to sign international agreements in provincial areas of jurisdiction. In the summer of 1965, an *accord cadre* was signed between Quebec and Paris that would permit agreements on specific subjects of provincial concern, and Lesage showed a reasonable concern for federal sensibilities. Paul Martin, as external affairs secretary, was relatively relaxed, but Pearson, whose diplomatic antennae were more experienced and sensitive, partly because he had worked under O.D. Skelton and Mackenzie King in the 1920s and 1930s as Canada gradually assumed complete autonomy of Britain in a long series of gradual steps, was uneasy.

The conventional wisdom in the Quebec and English media was

that Jean Lesage and his Liberals had freed Quebec from the priest-ridden, patronage-sodden, semi-feudal Huey Long political slapstick farce of the Great Darkness where Duplessis had imprisoned it while the world passed it by, and that out of gratitude the province would keep them in power for a long time (the Quebec Liberals had had thirty-nine uninterrupted years in office prior to Duplessis). But in the Quebec election of June 5, 1966, held on a Sunday in emulation of France, Daniel Johnson led the Union Nationale to a narrow victory, with fifty-six members of the Legislative Assembly to fifty Liberals and two independents, although Lesage won the popular vote, 47 to 41 per cent, because of the customary heavy Liberal majority among the non-French. For the first time, there was an appreciable outright separatist vote, 9 per cent between two parties, 6 per cent for the larger Rassemblement pour l'Indépendance Nationale, led by Pierre Bourgault. As usual, the Pearson government was caught absolutely flat-footed by Quebec events, and no one had any idea if Johnson would continue Lesage's policies of striking up closer relations with de Gaulle. Duplessis's formula had been to get the conservatives and nationalists to vote together and the Liberals were trying to take the nationalist card away from the Union Nationale. Johnson ran against the tax increases and deficits that Lesage had run up as he secularized everything and handed a blank cheque to the public sector unions, and against increased electricity costs that the complete state takeover of electricity in 1962 was supposed to have prevented. But he also revived the traditional claim of his party that only the Union Nationale could deal for Quebec because the Quebec Liberals were bound hand and foot to the federal Liberal Party (the last five Quebec Liberal leaders, including acting leaders, had all been federal MPs or senators at one point: Adélard Godbout, Télesphore-Damien Bouchard, George Marler, Georges-Émile Lapalme, and Lesage). Johnson was an intimate protégé and emulator of Duplessis and the most assiduous disciple of the techniques of Le Chef. Duplessis had saved his career after Johnson's wife was involved with a lover who shot and wounded her and then killed himself. Johnson had few of Duplessis's bad qualities and most of his good qualities, except, like Paul Sauvé, he was not as physically robust as Duplessis was. He did not lose much time picking up relations with de Gaulle where Lesage had left them. He was not a separatist but believed in as much autonomy as possible for Quebec

without losing the economic benefits of Confederation, and he saw the
potential utility of the interventions of the man who was then, on the
entire world stage, rivalled in prestige and stature only by Mao Tse-
tung. Johnson was a Quebec leader of great dexterity, and he was more
than ready to take advantage of the general's patronage. Both men got
more than they bargained for.

General Vanier, an old friend of de Gaulle's, as a wounded and
heroic veteran of Vimy, and as a diplomat and passionate supporter of
Free France, offered to visit de Gaulle as Paris-Ottawa relations tensed,
but the French leader, though "touched," did not accept that, as governor general of Canada, Vanier was a chief of state and he would not
accept him with the honours of one. Pearson was outraged and the idea
was scrapped. The conditions of de Gaulle's visit to Canada in 1967
became the subject of intense and prolonged controversy. He was coming ostensibly to celebrate the centenary of Confederation and visit the
Expo 67 world's fair at Montreal that Duplessis had envisioned, the last
part of his trifecta of placatory gestures to Quebec's nationalists (after
the Quebec flag and the agency-general in Paris). It was customary to
invite the chief of state of every country that was represented at the fair.
In addition, Johnson invited de Gaulle to Quebec in his own capacity
as leader of the provincial government, which came as a revelation to
Ottawa, as did many other quasi-diplomatic rendezvous arranged
between Quebec and French officials. It eventually became known to
Ottawa, first as a rumour, that de Gaulle intended to come to Canada
by ship. This would enable him to land at Quebec rather than the federal capital and should have been more disquieting to Ottawa than it
was. Officially, de Gaulle came by ship (the cruiser *Colbert*, named
after Jean Talon's patron) in order to stop at Saint-Pierre and Miquelon
and show his thanks to those islands for rallying to him in 1941. Of
course, this was spurious, as he could have taken a small plane there
and back from Quebec or could have returned to France by ship and
stopped there. Pearson and Martin blundered again when they agreed
that de Gaulle would come first to Quebec, then Montreal, and then
Ottawa, thinking in their conventional parameters that the visitor
would be careful not to be too provocative if his trip was to end in the
federal capital, though he had already evinced no interest in going to
English Canada at all.

If Pearson and his advisers had thought it through and understood Quebec better, much less France, it would have been possible to work around the personalities and ambitions involved. Johnson, whom the Liberals at both echelons had completely discounted as a yokel whistling in a political graveyard, was a stronger premier than Lesage and less prone to be propelled forward by the nationalists. De Gaulle himself was now winging it on a romantic *mission civilisatrice* according to which he was a virtual Richelieu bringing succour to a fragment of ancient French settlers abandoned by *la mère patrie*, who, though in many ways more advanced a society than France, "spoke the language of Molière's peasants in their farmyards."[1] (This was unmitigated rubbish. They did not speak like seventeenth-century peasants, and it is particularly irritating to read de Gaulle's biographer Jean Lacouture describe Johnson's French in these terms. Like an educated Canadian or American speaking English, Johnson had a Canadian accent but a refined and acoustically unexceptionable one, like most leading Quebeckers.) De Gaulle's emissary Gilbert Pérol claimed to have been frostily received in Ottawa[2] and warning signals multiplied: de Gaulle boycotted the observations of the fiftieth anniversary of the Canadian victory at Vimy in April 1917, having failed to send an appropriate representative to the funeral of Vanier at the end of 1966. These were churlish and contemptible actions, but still Pearson and Martin had no idea what might happen, though they were certainly concerned. Publicly, as the centennial year got under way, all was peaceful as a mill pond. Pearson met Johnson, and Martin called on de Gaulle, both in April 1967, and Martin again saw de Gaulle on June 14, just a month before the visit. Though both sessions were cordial, neither Johnson nor de Gaulle shed any light on what was coming. Johnson did say, as Lesage had been in the habit of doing, that he had to tread carefully because of the nationalists in his own party. Fundamentally, Pearson and Martin just did not believe that the leader of a friendly country, which owed Canada as much as Canada owed it, and for a debt incurred much more recently, could do very nasty things to such a well-intentioned and unoffending country. It was the price of serving so long in the ever-protective shadow of the Anglo-Americans. This time, unlike thirty years before, the world, in Roosevelt's phrase, "would stand idly by" and Canada would have to sort it out for itself.

Finally, on the splendid morning of July 23, 1967, came the man and the moment. The graceful cruiser *Colbert* eased up to the main pier at Wolfe's Cove in Quebec, and de Gaulle, in his general's uniform and cap, emerged to be greeted by the new governor general, Roland Michener (a Conservative and former Speaker of the House of Commons), and by Premier Johnson. De Gaulle and Michener reviewed an honour guard of the Royal 22nd Regiment in its guardsmen's uniforms with bearskin busbies, and the opening speeches were emollient and appropriate. The Quebec City part of the visit was fine, including a trip to the splendid basilica twenty miles downriver at Sainte-Anne-de-Beaupré, and on July 24, on another beautiful summer day, de Gaulle and Johnson drove in an open car the 120 miles along the north shore of the St. Lawrence from Quebec to Montreal, with several stops, including at Trois-Rivières. The highway, which was built by Taschereau and Duplessis, was claimed for the purpose of the visit to be the Chemin du Roy originally constructed by Louis xv, had fleurs-de-lys painted on it every few hundred feet, and the province's school buses were used to bring in crowds from across Quebec to line the entire route. Johnson had pulled out all the stops, and there were perhaps a million people all along the roadsides. The two men, de Gaulle seventy-six years old, stood almost the entire distance to acknowledge the crowds.* In general, the Québécois have never liked the French, felt they were abandoned by them and owed them nothing, and have been keenly aware of the French tendency to disparage them as unlettered and almost incomprehensible corn-cobbers. But Charles de Gaulle was different; he was a giant of history who had resurrected France, raised up the French fact in the world, and brought it out from the shadow of the Anglo-Saxons, made France one of the world's great powers again, and spoke French with such clarity and erudition that he made all French-speaking people proud of their culture.†

As the motorcade crossed Le Gardeur Bridge at Repentigny onto

---

* At a brief stop at Louiseville, one of six along the route, a school choir serenaded a bemused de Gaulle with an improvised ditty punctuated by the refrain: "This general, this general, he's golden."[3]

† The author had a very modest position in the lower entourage of Premier Johnson that summer and observed that many, even higher-ups in the premier's office, raised the quality of their spoken French to coincide with the arrival of their distinguished visitor.

Montréal Island, there were dense crowds, more than five hundred thousand as de Gaulle and Johnson drove through streets jammed with cheering onlookers to Montreal City Hall in Place Jacques-Cartier. The square was filled with applauding spectators right to the Champ de Mars. Many of the people present held separatist placards and shouted the separatist slogan "Vive le Québec libre." Undeterred by Montreal Mayor Jean Drapeau's statement that there was not a microphone on the balcony of City Hall, de Gaulle requested the installation of one and proceeded to it about five minutes after his arrival. The world was watching; for French Canada, after centuries of obscurity, their hour had come at last. No one, and certainly not Johnson or Drapeau, as they explained to me later, had any idea what a blockbuster was about to be detonated.

It was one of the most dramatic moments in Canadian history. In his powerful voice and piercingly eloquent articulation, the greatest Frenchman since Napoleon said,

> My heart is filled with immense emotion in seeing before me the French city of Montreal. In the name of the old country, in the name of France, I salute you with all my heart. I am going to confide to you a secret that you must not repeat: this evening, and all along the route I travelled today . . . with my friend Johnson [considerable applause], I found myself in an atmosphere like that of the Liberation. Beyond that, I noted what an immense effort of progress, of development, and, as a result of it, of emancipation you are accomplishing, and it is here, in Montreal, that I must say this, because if there is a city in the whole world that is outstanding for its successes in modernization, it is yours. And in saying it is your city, I permit myself to add that it is also ours. That is what I have come here to tell you this evening, and I must also tell you that I will take unforgettable memories away from this immense gathering in Montreal. All France knows, sees, and hears what is happening here, and I can tell you that it will learn from it. Vive Montréal! Vive le Québec! Vive le Québec libre!" (An uproar interrupted the sequence.) "Vive le Canada Français! Vive la France!"

It was an unspeakable outrage. The crowd was almost delirious, but in France opinion was largely hostile after the speech and there was a widespread feeling that the general had gone too far. This was an unprecedented insult to a friendly and distinguished country where he was an invited and honoured guest. International opinion, which has never taken Quebec independence very seriously, was nonplussed, and despite de Gaulle's effusions of the balcony, France never cared much about Quebec, going back to Henry IV. Nor were the Québécois as susceptible as de Gaulle imagined; the nationalists were flattered and excited, and Johnson got some impetus for constitutional changes, but no one but a few loopies wanted to liberate Quebec from the economic arrangements it had as a recipient of Canadian transfer payments. There were generous and naïve people who thought de Gaulle had got carried away, as Tommy Douglas said, kindly man as he always was, "at the end of a gruelling day." There were those who recommended a gentle reaction and to let the incident pass. This was Paul Martin's view, but he was not blameless in allowing matters to get to this extremity. It was also what French foreign minister Maurice Couve de Murville recommended, but his advice could hardly be credited, De Gaulle had insulted Canada and opened a domestic sore that almost everyone had been assiduously trying to ignore. De Gaulle himself, and his entourage, left no doubt of his premeditated intention to break up the Canadian federation.[4] De Gaulle spent the night at the French consulate in Westmount (in the very bowels of Anglo-Montreal, which was 40 per cent of the "French city of Montreal" and had probably 60 per cent of its money), and the next day toured the Expo 67 World's Fair site.

By now, as Pearson had feared, the Quebec position was slipping and events in that province threatened to get out of control. Strong French-Canadian federalists had been packed into the highest reaches of government, and new policies were already being devised to carry the fight back against the separatists for the heart and mind of Quebec. Pierre Trudeau (justice minister since April 4), Marchand (whom de Gaulle had declined to receive in Paris, unlike the least member of Johnson's government)[5], Marc Lalonde, Jean Beetz, and Martin's undersecretary of state for external affairs, Marcel Cadieux, were all hardline federalists who could argue the case in French, and they called for radical measures. Pearson would have been within his rights to expel de Gaulle, but he didn't go that far. Following a cabinet meeting on July 25, Pearson issued a statement that referred to the pleasure of all Canadians that General de Gaulle was welcomed to Quebec but pronounced his remarks "unacceptable." Pearson said that all Canadians were free, all provinces were free, and no Canadians were in need of liberation, and mentioned the heavy sacrifices Canadians were proud to have made in assisting in the liberation of France. Pearson spoke of Canada's "friendship with the French people" and purported to look forward to discussing these matters with de Gaulle later in the week.

It was obvious that no such discussions would take place, and de Gaulle abruptly announced that he would return to France the following day (on his aircraft, which had come ostensibly to take him to Ottawa and home). He did this after a morning ceremony at the University of Montreal, where the chancellor, Paul-Émile Cardinal Léger, one of the few people, Canadian or otherwise, whose French was approximately as sonorous and refined as de Gaulle's, gave a cautious address that conspicuously failed to pander to the Quebec nationalists, and a luncheon tendered the departing leader on Île Sainte-Hélène by the City of Montreal. Mayor Drapeau and the formidable metropolitan chairman, Lucien Saulnier were the hosts. Drapeau spoke, in his distinctly Quebec accent that flattens vowels, but with great force, of how the Québécois had had to hang their culture on the barn door for centuries but had persevered and welcomed the return of French interest in them. De Gaulle departed, and Governor General Michener cancelled his official dinner and distributed the fine food that had been prepared for it to underprivileged children in the Ottawa area.

Canada was shaken by the incident. Most English Canadians thought Pearson had responded sensibly and condemned de Gaulle. Most French Canadians were favourable to de Gaulle as a person and thought their anglophone compatriots had overreacted. Drapeau's comments were much admired by all, and Johnson had done well. The outspoken federalists ran ahead of the outright separatists, but the province was shifting in a large zone between constitutional options. It must be said that if Mackenzie King had acted on his call to French Canada to stand in for stricken France in 1940 and been more tangibly supportive of Free France (though his attitude was much preferable to that of Churchill and Roosevelt toward de Gaulle), and if Diefenbaker and

Pearson had had any idea of how to make common cause with some of de Gaulle's reservations about American leadership of the Alliance, and especially if Pearson had not been such a priggish scold about the sale of uranium, even de Gaulle would not have behaved so egregiously. In terms de Gaulle had himself employed in the greatest crisis of modern French history, by the light of the Gaullist thunderbolt, Canadian Confederation was revealed in a state of unsuspected infirmity.

2. The Twilight of Pearson and Diefenbaker and the Dawn of the Trudeau Era, 1967–1968

In Quebec, the ground began to tremble. René Lévesque, a great public figure in Quebec for decades because of his television newsmagazine program *Point de mire*, and a nationalist of the middle left – who was generally assumed to be a separatist but had always said he was not one, though he could become one – once deprived of the perquisites of the government after Lesage's defeat, left the Liberal Party and founded the Mouvement Souveraineté-Association (the Sovereignty-Association Movement), which was, as its name implied, a somewhat hazy effort to imagine that Quebec could both eat and retain its constitutional cake: become an independent country while retaining all the benefits of being part of Canada. It was an astute approach, as it slid into independence as gently and gradually as possible, like a turtle into water, as Lesage and Johnson's constitutional adviser, Claude Morin, had already told Marcel Cadieux was the plan. These nationalists of the moderate to medium far left had infiltrated the conventional wisdom of the new waves of Quebeckers educated in the social sciences, thanks to Duplessis's great expansion of education, and their antlike movements were everywhere, even under strong provincial leaders of more traditional views; Lesage was the nephew and protégé of one of Lapointe and St. Laurent's principal organizers and had been a cabinet protégé of St. Laurent and Pearson's, and Johnson, as Duplessis's understudy, was neither a leftist nor a separatist. Where Duplessis had said that Quebec would only depart Canada if English Canada wished that it go, and Lesage had said that he was anti-separatist but that the separatists could prevail if his demands were not met, Johnson wrote a book entitled *Equality or Independence*, meaning that Quebec would seek independence if it was not a fully equal entity to English Canada, and Lévesque was now calling for independence but with a connection retained. The Rassemblement pour l'Indépendance Nationale leader, Pierre Bourgault, was calling for outright independence and the devil take Canada, so the whole range of options was on offer on the nationalist side before the federalists had advanced beyond the complacent assumption that it was all a matter of concurrent taxation. (Johnson's sons, Daniel and Pierre-Marc, would personify their father's options: Daniel as Liberal premier of the province and Pierre-Marc as Lévesque's successor as the separatist premier.)

The federal Progressive Conservatives had finally recognized that they simply could not go on with John Diefenbaker as leader, that he was a somewhat splendid anachronism but not a man for this era, and a review of the leadership was successfully promoted by the party chairman, Toronto advertising executive Dalton Camp. The principal candidates to succeed Diefenbaker were the provincial premiers Robert Stanfield of Nova Scotia and Dufferin "Duff" Roblin of Manitoba, as well as holdovers from the Diefenbaker wars Davie Fulton of British Columbia, George Hees, and Donald Fleming, and Senator Wallace McCutcheon of Toronto. It was suspected that John Diefenbaker might also seek to resume the leadership. Roblin and Fulton were the closest the Conservatives had to a bilingual candidate, and Camp had pushed across the slogan "Two Nations," by which he meant two cultures, but which, in common English parlance, sounded perilously like a schismatic approach to the Quebec issue, which the president of France had thoughtfully brought to the attention of the country with a passion that had not been seen since the conscription crises, if then. (Even in the world wars, Quebec nationalists were only threatening non-compliance, not secession, and especially not secession when English Canada had a large army that could be despatched in response to a constitutional crisis.) At the Progressive Conservative convention in Toronto in the first week of September 1967, Diefenbaker did enter the lists at the last moment, but came fifth, after Stanfield, Roblin, Fulton, and Hees, and it quickly came down to a runoff between Stanfield and Roblin, which Stanfield won, fairly narrowly. It was a good convention, and the party emerged in a rather united condition and looked as if it might be able to defeat the Liberals, if Pearson remained as leader. But Pearson still had three years to run in his mandate, was seventy, and, especially with Diefenbaker (to whom Pearson publicly sent a gracious message) departing, he was unlikely to lead another election.

In the autumn of 1967, the respected Ontario premier John P. Robarts, successor to George Drew and Leslie Frost, called a Confederation of Tomorrow conference of all the provincial premiers. Johnson, on the heels of his spectacular hosting of Charles de Gaulle, was at his suave and courtly best, scrupulously polite and charming, and electrified the televised conference and millions of viewers with a summary of what Quebec sought. He left no doubt that Quebec could be permanently happy in Canada. He sought explicit priority in many shared jurisdictions and the tax sources to pay for them, but sought nothing from the other provinces or the federal government for the status of French in the country as a whole. He put his views with tact and cogency and exquisite courtesy and concluded, "For decades, my predecessors, M. Taschereau, M. Duplessis, M. Lesage, and I have been asked: 'What does Quebec want?' This is what Quebec wants, and it wants a Canada that is comfortable with it. What does Canada want? I ask you: *Que veut le Canada?*" It was as successful as Duplessis's tremendous exposition of Quebec's constitutional goals at the Federal-Provincial Conference of 1946 (which King later claimed reminded him of Molotov – Chapter 7).

Quebec's renunciation of its Catholic past was now well along, the first stage in the shattering of the nationalist-conservative alliance Duplessis had built and Johnson had salvaged. Johnson said to intimates that the 1966 election was like Duplessis's of 1944 – very close, and won by the Union Nationale despite a larger Liberal popular vote – but that the next election would replicate Duplessis's mighty sweep of 1948. Now the nationalists thought, logically in some respects, more and more ambitiously, and had been steadily less impressed by the Diefenbaker-Pearson circus that for nearly a decade had been the government of their ostensible country. As Johnson was making his final charge to resurrect the Duplessis coalition, the province was in full evolution. Duplessis had warned Cardinal Léger of the Church's hold on the people: "Squeeze a fish hard enough and it will get away." Léger replied that it was Duplessis who was the chief author of the process,[6] Both men wanted some level of modernization and secularization, but the rural bishops wouldn't hear of it. Léger had received some votes in the papal conclave of 1958, partly in respect for Léger's intimacy with Pius XII – the late pope's mother's amethyst and diamonds formed his cardinalitial ring given by the pontiff – and partly because de Gaulle urged the French cardinals to try to elect a French-speaking pope. He was a very astute, contemporary, and popular leader of the Church, but for personal motives he retired as archbishop of Montreal in 1967, though only sixty-three, and departed for the Cameroons, where he launched a successful foundation and hospital for the treatment of leprosy and other illnesses and disabilities.

Johnson commanded the majority in the province and was convinced that he could make the centre a position of strength and keep both Lesage and Lévesque on the shoulders. And Pearson had raised the numbers and quality of federal Quebec ministers and senior civil servants to the highest point in history, and on December 14, 1967, at the end of the centennial year – which had been an immense and joyous success apart from the single, loud, discordant Gaullist note – he announced that he would retire as prime minister and Liberal leader. Pierre Trudeau soon emerged as the favourite to succeed him, as now, above all other times, the Liberals wished to retain their practice of alternating French with English leaders, and Marchand declined the prospect. The crisis was rising, and the federal Liberals were responding with a new Laurier as Quebec came under the steady and artful influence of a modernized Duplessis. The forces both men would deploy and seek to lead surged and spilled beyond any previous parameters. Centuries of pent-up French ambition were oozing or rushing forward, and the federalists too, after decades of almost comatose complacency, were rising and bracing themselves. An epic contest for the adherence of Quebec and the continuity and character of the country was already underway.

Pearson had announced in the Federal-Provincial Conference of 1965 that Ottawa would pay half the cost of a medical-care plan that covered doctors and hospitals, that would be universal and administered by the provinces, and would be seen as the first step to covering all related matters, including dentistry and drugs. After the usual disputes within the cabinet, where Mitchell Sharp led the faction that wished to go slow because of the costs and the currently rising deficit, it was agreed to defer the date of implementation from the day of the centenary of Confederation, July 1, 1967, for one year. Pearson's government also adopted a generous program of regional economic assistance, which in fact was largely directed at Quebec as a preliminary effort, in effect, to buy votes for federalism. Pearson called his last Federal-Provincial Conference for February 5 to 7, 1968, and Trudeau, as justice minister, carried the message for the federal government. He was effectively replying to Johnson's brilliant advocacy of the previous autumn at Robarts's Confederation of Tomorrow conference of the provincial premiers when Johnson ended by asking what Canada wanted. Trudeau served notice that he was opposed to any further devolution of authority to provinces, and he attacked the entire concentration on jurisdiction and evoked the whole matter to a determination and charter of the rights of citizens, which, he said, was vastly more important than scrapping between jurisdictions over their prerogatives. It was a brilliant tactic that caught Quebec off guard, and many English Canadians and even some French-Canadian federalists were delighted to see Trudeau more than hold his own with the cunning and articulate Johnson, in what became, despite Pearson's attempts at asserting a halcyon influence, a rather sharp exchange between them. In the eyes of those inclined to credulity, Trudeau made Johnson and the others look like wolves devouring their prey when they should all be assuring the inalienable rights of all the people. It would not placate the hard-core separatists, but they were not going to be placated, and it uplifted or constructively confused almost everyone else.

As the Quebec delegates to the April Liberal convention lined up solidly behind Trudeau, he emerged as the favourite; followed by Robert Winters as the candidate of the pro-business, C.D. Howe wing; the thirty-eight-year-old minister of consumer and corporate affairs, John Turner; the runner-up from the previous convention a decade before, Paul Martin; and the defence minister, Paul Hellyer. Trudeau, as justice minister, had amended the Criminal Code to liberalize treatment of sex between consenting same-sex adults, famously stating that there was "no place for the state in the bedrooms of the nation." He also liberalized divorce rules, which had been dealt with from Quebec in the

House of Commons because of the hostility of the Roman Catholic Church to the concept of divorce. This facilitated his campaign as an advocate of individual liberties rather than someone preoccupied with the concentration of jurisdictional powers. Just before the convention, Mitchell Sharp folded his candidacy in favour of Trudeau in exchange for the promise of the ministry of external affairs.* On the eve of the leadership vote, April 5, 1968, Trudeau gave a clear hint of the astuteness he would bring to the defence of the federalist cause by concluding his address to the convention: *"Maîtres chez nous, mais pour tout le Canada."* ("Masters in our own house, but our house is all Canada.") Trudeau thus staked out his position as the ultra-federalist, but also the chief civil libertarian, and he espoused the entire emerging program of the Laurendeau-Dunton Commission (the Royal Commission on Bilingualism and Biculturalism) of access to federal government services, broadcasting, television, and labelling in both languages throughout the country. There were many who hoped that this formula – the entrenchment of human rights and official bilingualism from sea to sea – would calm the issue. Anyone who knew the Quebec nationalists knew otherwise. As Pearson handed over, his party gave him a puppy he had previously said he did not want, but which he accepted when for public relations reasons the organizers insisted.

On April 6, 1968, Joseph Philippe Pierre Yves Elliott Trudeau (1919–2000), forty-eight, became leader of the Liberal Party and two weeks later the fifteenth prime minister of Canada. Showing how completely Charles de Gaulle dissented from and underestimated the Canadian tradition of pulling French and English interests together when sorely tested, he wrote his ambassador in Ottawa on April 10: "We have no concession or even courtesy to extend to M. Trudeau, who is an enemy of the French fact in Canada." De Gaulle didn't understand the complexities of the issue, and Trudeau was about to sweep the country, especially Quebec, while the general's own domestic tranquility blew up. He soon dissolved Parliament for new elections on June 25, the day after the national holiday of French Canada, Saint-Jean-Baptiste

---

* Walter Gordon supported Trudeau but declined to join his cabinet or to seek reelection to Parliament, thus possibly losing an opportunity to end his public career on a note of high achievement. The hour of the moderate nationalist had struck. The author got to know Walter Gordon ten years later and he denied any regret at having retired when he did.

Day. In the campaign, he represented the Conservatives as having folded before the demands of the Quebec nationalists with their endorsement of two nations (a spurious charge), and Robert Stanfield, though an earnest seeker and practitioner of French-English conciliation, was anomalous in claiming to wish to do more for Quebec than the French-Canadian Trudeau. A million people, as usual, lined the streets of Montreal for the Saint-Jean-Baptiste Parade, where the reviewing stand was in front of the Bibliothèque Nationale du Québec on Sherbrooke Street East at Parc La Fontaine. On this night, the separatists, led by Pierre Bourgault (who had folded his Rassemblement pour l'Indépendance Nationale into Lévesque's new Parti Québécois), organized a considerable demonstration, and Drapeau had not deployed an adequate number of police to deal with it at the outset. The reviewing stand was raked with stones, bottles, and other projectiles, and the crowd charged the stand, whence all the dignitaries fled except Trudeau, until the police had beaten the demonstrators back. This image, of Trudeau alone facing the rock-throwing mob, was extremely helpful on election eve and was representative of his flinty confidence and determination, and the following day he was rewarded with the first Liberal majority since 1953.

The election result (with 1965 results in brackets) was: Liberals, 154 MPs and 45.4 per cent of the vote (128 MPs and 40.2 per cent); Progressive Conservatives, 72 MPs and 31.4 per cent (97 MPs and 32.4 per cent); NDP, 22 MPs and 17 per cent (22 MPs and 18 per cent); Ralliement Créditistes, 14 MPs and 4.4 per cent (9 MPs and 4.6 per cent). Paul Martin and Robert Winters had not sought re-election. Nor, of course, had Pearson, but John Diefenbaker was re-elected to his tenth consecutive term and would soldier on as in the past, and for more than another decade. This was at least the merciful end of the hair-raising decade in which Pearson bustled about giving pep rallies, steadily renovating the Liberal ranks and doing useful things interspersed with committing frightful mistakes, striving earnestly and rather intelligently for good and sensible reform government but constantly having the ceiling plaster brought down around his shoulders by the ear-rattling and dangerous antics of the bejowelled prairie madman in the attic.

Lester Bowles Pearson had been an innovative and even important prime minister, and while he backed away from Walter Gordon's curbs on foreign ownership, and went slowly, he did resolve the defence debacle Diefenbaker had created; bring a national health-care system forward; launch official bilingualism seriously; give the country a flag it soon came to like and certainly needed; start the process of regional economic equality, an essential arm against the rising separatist tide; and, above all, bring in the cadres of credible French-Canadian federalists who could alone hold the line in the sudden crisis of Quebec's orientation. It was all almost too much for him, but not quite. He had been, in the end, a convivial and purposeful leader, with few illusions of his own frailties. He was the weakest individual in the chain from Baldwin and LaFontaine who had intuitively understood what Canada could be and how to keep the project going. He and all his friends in the Skelton foreign service and in like-minded American circles to whom he was the right type of Canadian – altruistic, soft-spoken, bright, and companionable in his bow tie and personal and national self-deprecation – all the Norman Robertsons (Dean Acheson's "arm-flapping moralists") and their American appreciators, such as pundits Walter Lippmann and Scotty Reston of *The New York Times*, shared a fluid combination of idealism, toughness, and naïveté. Pearson had a limited aptitude for exercising authority, diluted by an excessive rationalization of compromise, but, gripping the controls and holding on grimly, he piloted the country through heavy turbulence and earned its gratitude. He lived on for four years and died at the end of 1972, aged seventy-five, and was buried near his external affairs friends Hume Wrong and Norman Robertson at Saint-Pierre-de-Wakefield in the scenic Gatineau Hills of Quebec, near Ottawa.

The country settled happily into a new regime during the summer, but on September 28, 1968, a few hours before opening the magnificent Manic 5 hydroelectric dam on the Manicouagan River – a mile long and 660 feet high at the top of its graceful vaulted arches, one of the great symbols of the new Quebec – Daniel Johnson died. He was fifty-three, and his demise continued the scourge of Union Nationale leaders who died in office, precedented by Duplessis and Paul Sauvé. (Manic 5 was renamed the Daniel Johnson Dam.) Daniel Johnson had been an outstanding premier who showed great promise. Jean-Jacques Bertrand, the vice premier and minister of education and of justice, an elegant, sensible, and well-respected but not a galvanizing man, succeeded him, but he was not sufficiently agile to fight off René Lévesque from the nationalist bloc that his party had held since Duplessis founded it in 1935. Johnson had pledged the formula of every schoolchild "being able to participate fully in Quebec life" by learning French but with parents having the choice between French and English as the language of instruction. Bertrand promised to enact this formula. With the death of Johnson, the nationalist torch, which had been carried by the right under Bourassa, Duplessis, and Johnson, passed now to the left and Lévesque. The Union Nationale was likely to come apart, and a separatist party was probably going to emerge as the alternative governing party to the Liberals. The Roman Catholic Church was in full retreat as a social influence. Contraception cut down the French-Canadian birth rate, and the stylishly miniskirted young women of Quebec and their highly motivated suitors enjoyed themselves with no less abandon than the rest of the youth of the West. There was little that was conservative or defensive left socially or politically in the zeitgeist of contemporary Quebec.

The departure of Lévesque from the Liberals and of Léger, Quebec's greatest ecclesiastic from Quebec, and the death of Johnson put the province and the country in uncharted waters. Trudeau and Maurice Couve de Murville had quite a cordial conversation at the Citadelle of Quebec following Johnson's funeral, where Couve represented the French president. He was now de Gaulle's prime minister, following the tumultuous events in France in the previous May, when de Gaulle put down a prolonged general strike by waiting until the French bourgeoisie instinctively became frightened at the prospect of actually suffering economic loss and he then called for new elections, threatening to use the army if there was any attempt to prevent them from taking place. (At the climax, on May 30, a crowd of half a million marched up the Champs-Élysées shouting that de Gaulle must go. He spoke for five minutes, calling the election and leaving no doubt that he would not yield other than democratically, and three-quarters of a million marched back down the Champs-Élysées demanding he remain, doubtless including a large contingent of the earlier crowd.) De Gaulle won a crushing victory at the polls, declaring himself to be the "real revolutionary," for, among other attainments, "beginning the liberation of the French of Canada." His triumph over the communists and anarchists was a vital victory for the whole West, as the United States was terribly distracted by the endless guerrilla war in Vietnam. It was in some respects de Gaulle's greatest victory of all, but he was clearly slightly delusional to present such moonshine as his antics in Quebec as indicative of his revolutionary credentials. These credentials were genuine, impressive, and positive, but they were based on his foresight in advocating air and mechanized warfare in the 1930s, his intrepid resistance to the Nazis in the Second World War, and his creation of the Fifth Republic; they had nothing to do with Canada. Quebec was fleetingly noticed in the world, and the flamboyant Trudeau got more international attention than had any previous Canadian politician. Under unprecedented internal pressure, Canada was coming out of itself. The contest between Trudeau and Lévesque promised to be intense. All knew the future of the country was at stake.

3. Trudeau's First Term and the October Crisis and Its Aftermath, 1968–1973

For a time, it was serene. Trudeau enjoyed a honeymoon, and his elegant and stylish confidence and perfect bilingualism conveyed to English Canada the impression that all would now be in the safe hands of a leader who knew Quebec well and had apparently determined to give Quebec what it wanted without denuding federalism, and had even got Quebec to vote for him against Stanfield's incomprehensible incantations about "two nations." Quebec itself was being led, unprovokingly, by Jean-Jacques Bertrand, publicly a good deal more unambiguously federalist than Johnson. Trudeau journeyed to Washington in April 1969 for the funeral of General and President Dwight D. Eisenhower. He had no connection with Eisenhower, a figure of a bygone era; he went (as he acknowledged to the author some years later) to make the acquaintance, in neutral territory, of Charles de Gaulle, who came to honour his wartime comrade and the commander of the armies of France's liberation. They did not get much beyond a handshake, but it didn't matter, because a few weeks later, in the most improbable end imaginable to his astounding career, Charles de Gaulle abruptly resigned and returned to his home in eastern France after his government narrowly lost a referendum on an obscure question of regional government and university organization. It was the general's effort to address the current demand for participatory democracy, but the country was tired of his threats to resign if at any point he was not sustained on every issue. It was a ludicrous ending to a brilliant career, but his departure made matters slightly easier for Canada, as his successor, former prime minister Georges Pompidou, had no interest in stirring matters up in Quebec and had no grievance with the "Anglo-Saxons" generally. De Gaulle died at his home at Colombey-les-Deux-Églises in November 1970, two weeks short of his eightieth birthday, while reaching for the television listings, and his wife moved to a convent, carrying her belongings in one suitcase. Pompidou announced to the world: "General de Gaulle is dead; France is a widow." There were huge silent demonstrations of respect in his memory throughout France, and virtually every prominent leader in the world – including the presidents of the United States (now Richard Nixon) and the Soviet Union and the Duke of Edinburgh and five British prime ministers attended a memorial service in Notre-Dame – but no one prominent from Canada or Quebec. De Gaulle banned everyone except family, friends, neighbours, the aldermen of Colombey, and comrades of Free France and the Resistance from attending his funeral in his parish church. He was the last of the great leaders of the Second World War, and his time had predeceased him. Fortunately, he had not brought his presidential memoirs up to 1967, but his recollection in print of his 1960 visit to Canada was irritating enough reading to a Canadian federalist.

From the start, Trudeau pushed a more ambitious and costly social policy, regional economic equality, and – an emphasis he had already made in Pearson's last Federal-Provincial Conference – individual liberties taking precedence over arguments about jurisdiction. He was advocating what amounted to a residual powers clause that attributed unallocated powers to the people and ring-fenced the individual against government intrusions, and his first step in doing so had been in his revisions to the Criminal Code emancipating homosexuals from legal repression. As he had also promised, he pushed an equal official status for both languages and genuine official biculturalism in federal government services and in federal television and broadcasting throughout the country. He was from the start rather nationalistic by Canadian standards, and he set out to rally Canadians to a more assertive and independent position and to debunk the cant of Quebec nationalists that Canada was merely an excrescence of the Anglo-Americans, a bit of flimsy, pseudo-national scaffolding to anesthetize Quebec while continuing to languish as a satellite of the masters in Washington and London.

It was never clear to what extent Trudeau was acting on his rationalist, though Roman Catholic, faith in the perfectibility of man and the rule of enlightened authority, and to what extent he was invoking intellectually presentable, or at least defensible, positions in support of what was soon identifiable as an onslaught on every material and philosophical front against separatism. The distinction is, in any case, academic, or at least should be confined to another book, one focused directly on Trudeau and the composition of Trudeau's views. For whatever combination of belief and tactical selection, he replaced the Pearsonian flexibility on concurrent jurisdictions and federal-provincial coexistence with a stone wall: the federal government would cede no powers and accept no special or different status for Quebec or any other province. His predecessor had barely sauntered off into the sunset, hands in his pockets and the Liberal Party's presented puppy wagging its tail behind him, before it became clear to all that Canadian federalism was personified now by a new man with a policy and nature that had never been seen before in the country's leading political office. The Quebec nationalists had always seen federalism as led by English-Canadian manoeuvrers like Macdonald and King, or by French Canadians dazzled and acculturated by the English-speaking world, such as Laurier, Lapointe, and St. Laurent, or even indifferent English gentlemen like Borden, or conciliatory, somewhat weak men like Pearson, but never had they seen or dreamt of someone who would stand arms akimbo on top of the constitutional mound and tell them in impeccable French that they were fools and charlatans and that he would crush them and would enjoy doing it. Because Bertrand was not a confrontational leader of the province, and Lesage, who often was, announced his retirement as Quebec Liberal leader in 1969 – to be replaced by the thirty-six-year-old technocrat Robert Bourassa, who was not of a nature, nor in any position, to become too demonstrative – Trudeau's new era was not much contested for a time. René Lévesque was just founding his party and only had a couple of members, including himself, in the National Assembly of Quebec, as Bertrand renamed the Legislative Assembly.

* * *

In the early months of his government, Trudeau didn't do anything that caught the public's imagination or justified the high expectations of him for new government. There was a good deal of the self-important sloganeering and imposed ambiance of change and modernization that starkly new regimes almost always exude. A great many new senior civil servants were attracted, a great many of them French, and portentous new titles, many borrowed from the unique grandiosity of French statism, were bandied about. There was a lot of official talk of "participation" and scientific government with efficiency criteria rigorously applied, but it was all posturing and nonsense, even if reasonably earnest, at least at first, and nothing of consequence came of it. But silently Trudeau was stoking up the regional and social economic transfers, which in practice was a trickle of benefits to Saskatchewan, Manitoba, and the Atlantic provinces, but a torrent of money into Quebec from Ontario, Alberta, and British Columbia. It was vote-buying on a mighty scale, but not old-fashioned patronage ("unusually large post offices in remote Quebec centres," as Jack Pickersgill once answered the author's question about how to sustain a Liberal minority government – he was referring to arrangements with the Créditistes).

The Quebec election of April 29, 1970, signalled the beginning of a sea change in the province. Jean-Jacques Bertrand, a profoundly decent man but a political journeyman now out of touch with the evolving Quebec (the son-in-law of one of Duplessis's early backers, Louis A. Giroux), suffered not only a severe loss of his nationalist base to Lévesque's Parti Québécois (PQ) but a chunk of rural conservatives to the Créditistes, who returned as a provincial party for the first time since Duplessis battered them into insensibility in 1952. Robert Bourassa's Liberals won 45 per cent of the vote, down from 47 in 1966, but rose from 50 to 72 constituencies, as the Union Nationale descended from 41 to 20 per cent and from 56 to 17 members. Lévesque's PQ took 23 per cent of the vote and 7 members (Lévesque was not one of them), and the Créditistes took 11 per cent of the vote and 12 seats. It was a massive mandate for Bourassa, but the Péquiste (this was the agreed adjective in reference to the PQ) threat could now finally be seen vividly.

The rule of thumb was that the Quebec electorate was divided into five approximately equal blocs: (1) the outright French-speaking, *rouge*, federalists and (2) the non-French, and these two groups were practically en bloc Liberal; (3) the conservative *bleus*, still Union Nationale, (4) the nationalists, now PQ, and (5) the floating vote. The Liberals should have been able to pick up most of the *bleus*, but the growth of the 9 per cent separatist vote in 1966 to 24 per cent was startling. Even though the sovereignty-association flim-flam muddied the waters slightly, the goal of the PQ was an independent republic, and that was the burden of all their interminable and repetitive oratory and polemics about "liberated counties," self-determination, and so forth. Quebec was headed to a rendezvous with the silent aspiration of the centuries when, as Drapeau had said to de Gaulle, the *habitants* had hung their culture on the barnyard door.

Bourassa had promised "100,000 jobs" and was soon running a young, lookalike (except for a few Lesage holdovers such as labour minister Pierre Laporte), and rather clichéd government, and was not presuming to argue much with Trudeau, when the political climate changed dramatically with the abduction from his Montreal home of the British trade commissioner in Montreal, James Cross, on the morning of October 5, 1970, by four young men of what they called the Liberation Cell of the Front de Libération du Québec (FLQ). The cell declared that Cross would be executed unless seven demands were met, including the payment of half a million dollars in gold and the release of twenty-three designated political prisoners who had been convicted of complicity in bombing incidents (one of which resulted in a fatality in 1963). The police were only able to identify and release the name of one of the kidnappers, Jacques Lanctôt. The Canadian and Quebec governments rejected the demands but did engage in negotiations and made the concession of having the FLQ's extremely inflammatory manifesto read on the French-language national news. In a considerable feat of self-control, Radio-Canada's chief newsreader, Gaétan Montreuil, expressionlessly read the manifesto's attacks on business and finance, references to Québécois as "a society of terrorized slaves . . . jeered at and repressed on [their] own territory," and its description of Trudeau as a "*tapette*" ("faggot" – he was at this point a bachelor, but had had many relationships with women*).

---

* The rumour of bisexuality has never entirely perished but is scarcely relevant and was, in the circumstances, extremely provocative.

Negotiations and investigations continued, and the FLQ said that the threat on the life of Cross had been "temporarily suspended" on October 8 (and they secured the medicine he needed for his blood pressure), but they set a "final deadline" for 6 p.m. on October 10. Bourassa, in a display of normalcy, had gone to a pre-scheduled series of meetings in New York, and the Quebec minister of justice, Jérôme Choquette, announced that he would reply at 5:30 p.m. on that day. He revealed to Mitchell Sharp, acting prime minister, his plan to release five of the prisoners and the promise of a "ministry of social peace." Sharp was very unhappy with this and eventually told Choquette, after consultations, that this would cause the federal government to "dissociate" itself from the Quebec government. Trudeau spoke to Bourassa, who prevailed on Choquette to hold the line as Trudeau, Sharp, and the federal justice minister, John Turner, had asked. By the time of Choquette's speech, the stakes had already been raised sharply by the abduction on October 10 of labour minister Laporte, effectively the second most important figure in Bourassa's government, while he was playing touch football with his nephew outside his house in the South Shore suburb of Saint-Lambert. These kidnappers described themselves as the Chenier Cell of the FLQ. René Lévesque and the editor of Le Devoir, Claude Ryan, urged the release of some prisoners in exchange for the release of the two captives. (Trudeau later dismissed this in an adaptation of Lord Acton's maxim that originated with writer Kildare Dobbs: "Lack of power corrupts and absolute lack of power corrupts absolutely.") There was some public support for the FLQ and a rally of three thousand students, unionists, and other militants took place at the Paul Sauvé Arena on October 15. Both Trudeau and Bourassa had concluded that there could be no further indulgence of the FLQ and that drastic measures would have to be taken. The only instrument at hand was the War Measures Act, dating from 1914, a draconian statute to deal with war, invasion, or real or apprehended insurrection, which had only been invoked during the two world wars. (Its provisions had stampeded Duplessis into his catastrophic election call in 1939.)

While the FLQ sympathizers were fulminating at the Paul Sauvé Arena, the federal cabinet voted to impose the War Measures Act, which took effect and was publicly declared at 4 a.m. on October 16.

Almost five hundred suspects of potentially seditious behaviour were rounded up for interrogation and subject to detention for up to ninety days. Habeas corpus was suspended, political rallies were banned, and membership in the FLQ was declared to be a criminal offence. Trudeau announced all this in a temperately worded and presented statement in both languages on all radio and television stations. He said, "These measures are as offensive to me as I am sure they are to you" and pledged that all issues would be resolved "in the calm atmosphere of Canadian court rooms." It was an excellent message perfectly delivered.

On October 17, the FLQ directed police to the Canadian Forces air base at Saint-Hubert, where Laporte's body was found in the trunk of a Chevrolet; he had been strangled to death by his own gold neck chain. This was revealed on October 18. Trudeau again spoke very appropriately, of the deceased and of the monstrous crime that had occurred, and stated that "the FLQ has sown the seeds of its own destruction."[7] There was a massive state funeral at Notre-Dame Basilica in Place d'Armes amid immense security, including tanks. All surviving members of the National Assembly, Trudeau, and all of Quebec's political leadership at all levels attended. The rest of October and November passed as police combed the Montreal area and searched for the culprits and the Liberation Cell. They found them on December 2 on Rue des Récollets in North Montreal. Safe conduct to Cuba was arranged for the Liberation Cell in exchange for the release of Cross, unharmed. Two members of the Chenier Cell, Francis Simard and Bernard Lortie, were soon arrested, and the other two, Paul and Jacques Rose, were arrested in a farmhouse south of Montreal. The Laporte murderers were sentenced to eight years, twenty years, and, in two cases, life in prison. The Liberation Cell was not happy in Cuba and moved on to France, and after eight or nine years three of them returned to Quebec and each served less than two years in prison. Terrorism never caught on in Quebec again. Trudeau handled the crisis with great tactical skill and strength of character, which was universally admired in Canada and gained him much respect in the world. He took direct charge of the response, and while some of his reflections to the press – including a gratuitous reference to "weak-kneed bleeding hearts," as if the civil rights concerns that were raised were mere cowardice – were excessive, he earned a status as a single combat warrior.

Only a few of the nearly five hundred people arrested under the War Measures Act were prosecuted, and just a handful were convicted of trivial offences. Huff and puff as they might from time to time, French Canadians were not much more motivated to armed revolt than other Canadians were, and even most separatists were just as opposed to kidnapping and murder as less politically energetic Canadians were. It must be added that the performance of the police was more farcical than, if not as lethal as, that of the revolutionaries. They stormed into the home of poet Gérald Godin and the chansonnière Pauline Julien, a gaminish and very vocal separatist (of the Édith Piaf café school, but with a less husky voice, longer hair, and an overbite) but far from a terrorist, flicked on the lights, and said, "Put your clothes on, Pauline Julien, you're coming with us." (The couple was released after eight days without charges.) So absurd was the list of insurrectionist suspects devised by the Montreal and provincial police that Gérard Pelletier's son had great difficulty dissuading the police from continuing for more than two hours to ransack his father's home in Montreal looking for FLQ literature, although Pelletier was the secretary of state of Canada and had entered Parliament in 1965 with Trudeau and Marchand to promote federalism in Quebec, and had, albeit reluctantly, voted with the cabinet to impose the War Measures Act the day before.[8] Not at all comical but equally indicative of official ineptitude, the soldier assigned to protect the finance minister, Edgar Benson, accidentally killed himself with his own rifle, and Trudeau had to start day one of the War Measures regime comforting the minister.[9]

The initial briefing to the cabinet by the RCMP lasted two hours on October 19, and it was obvious even to the most unworldly of them that the police had not the remotest idea what they were doing. The ministers were shocked by the amateurism and ignorance of the federal police. The best that can be said is that they demonstrated what foreign territory this kind of activity was in Canada. It was not until the release in March 1979 of the Royal Commission report of Alberta justice David McDonald that the public got a serious glimpse of what a shambles the whole affair had really been. What came principally to light was that the prime minister had ordered not just a definitive rooting out of terrorists and political lawlessness, but – in a pioneering initiative that went well beyond anything Duplessis had ever attempted – an official, surreptitious, and in fact illegal attack on separatism. Trudeau sincerely believed that separatism was not far from sedition, even though Lévesque never encouraged violence. Lévesque did, however, leave no one in any doubt that he sympathized with the "frustrations" that propelled people to violence. He was very slow to criticize the FLQ until Laporte, with whom he had served in the senior Quebec media and then in Lesage's government, was murdered, and he routinely explained away bombings as understandable if lamentable. But it was un-Canadian and a severe breach of precedented powers for the federal government to conduct a lengthy harassment of a political movement that was operating within the law and was, by the time the Royal Commission report was released, the duly elected government of Quebec.

The international climate was one of Che Guevara, the Chinese Cultural Revolution, the Chicago Seven, the Baader-Meinhof Gang in West Germany, Daniel Cohn-Bendit and the student and general strike in France, Tariq Ali and others in Britain – but Guevara was caught and summarily executed in Bolivia, the Cultural Revolution was a disaster, most of the Baader-Meinhof Gang committed suicide in custody, and the others were all surmounted and routed by legitimate recourse to the weight of democratic opinion backed by law enforcement, by Nixon with his silent majority, de Gaulle, and others, and there was no need or justification for Trudeau to go to the extremes he did. Between December 1970 and July 1975, the Disruptive Tactics section of the Montreal RCMP broke into the office of the Toronto left-wing group Praxis; stole documents and committed arson; circulated a fraudulent FLQ communique urging violence that the RCMP had in fact composed; recruited FLQ informers by what was admitted to be "force and pressure"; urged cabinet to blackball twenty-one civil servants as members of "non-parliamentary opposition," though nothing more serious than voting NDP was actually found against any of them; burned down a barn in rural Quebec that belonged to an unoffending person to prevent a meeting of the FLQ with the American black radical organization the Black Panthers; broke into the office of the left-wing Agence de Presse Libre du Québec in Montreal and stole two hundred files; broke into the so-called Permanence Nationale of the Parti Québécois and stole the entire computerized PQ membership list; and screened federal government job applicants to weed out separatist sympathizers.

This is all a bit tawdry by Canadian standards, but it is still pretty tame compared with the heavy-handed antics of other countries, such as the American police simply murdering Black Panthers in their home in the dead of night in Chicago in December 1969. Trudeau spread money around Quebec with a figurative steamroller, but the licence the separatists felt they had to use federal government grants for their own anti-federal purposes was annoying. The whole affair was made more distasteful because Canadians, French and English, so overwhelmingly support the police whatever they do. Polling showed 85 per cent were in favour of the use of the War Measures Act, and a heavy majority in both cultural parts of Canada favoured continuation of the War Measures regime long after the crisis had passed. This was because the powers were so little abused; reaction would certainly have been different if the federal police and the army had been routinely shooting demonstrators or torturing those whom they interrogated. And there was a good deal of inflammatory and violent rhetoric from the more militant secessionists. On balance, given that the breakup of the country was under discussion, it was all fairly civilized. And Trudeau was sincere and passionate in his view that it was his task to maintain the integrity of the federal state, and he was not under any illusions about how disdainful of the traditional concepts of individual rights many of the extreme Quebec nationalists were. It is the nature of even relatively restrained revolutions that the originators are the Kerenskys and the Mirabeaus and matters move to the left and the more inflexible in method (unless it is not a social revolution but, like the American Revolution, the displacement of a foreign bourgeoisie by a local one). On balance, Trudeau was impressive and intellectually rigorous, and his concerns about where separatism could lead, though they caused him to authorize some actions that are not defensible, were far from unfounded. At least the federal police ceased to be Keystone Kops improvisers and developed a limited aptitude for internal security matters. The proof that Trudeau did not stifle democracy is the partial success of Lévesque's party in the subsequent twenty-five years.

In June 1971, in Victoria, Trudeau and the premiers came tantalizingly close to agreeing on a formula for amending the Constitution, succeeding that of Davie Fulton and Guy Favreau, and permitting the completion of its patriation to Canada. To block any amendment,

Ontario and Quebec would have a full veto and British Columbia in effect a half-veto, and the other provinces would have to provide a basic majority. This was concerted on a moonlight cruise, where the host, long-serving B.C. premier W.A.C. Bennett, banned alcohol, but some of the official entourages brought their own and an atmosphere of jocular horse-trading ensued. The provinces would also have some say in the nomination of Supreme Court judges, and Trudeau would have his Charter of Rights and Freedoms, the agreed status of the English and French languages, and a recognition of the durable distribution of constitutional powers. All was agreed, but in subsequent weeks Robert Bourassa's capable and influential health minister, Claude Castonguay, and his insidious intergovernmental deputy minister, Claude Morin, as well as the editor of Le Devoir, Claude Ryan, now an advocate of special status for Quebec, all persuaded Bourassa he could not proceed without control of social policy. Trudeau should have conceded social policy on the cruise, as he did it a couple of years later anyway, and it was quite clearly a provincial domain. This agreement would probably have been reopened later, but it would have been an important milestone and spared the country immense friction and official tortuosity that has continued ever since.

There really wasn't much else to show for Trudeau's first term as prime minister other than the steadily increasing flow of money to Quebec, with a trickle to other have-not provinces, and the dramatic episode of October 1970. There was an endless number of white papers and committees and commissions and internal reforms, and Michael Pitfield, the clerk of the Privy Council, devised new ministries, such as Urban Affairs and Science and Technology, but the ministries were ineffectual, ephemeral, and a waste of money, and none of the rest of it amounted to anything, as is almost always the case with such enterprises. Trudeau and his inner entourage had that blasé flippancy of people who have never really done anything but are swept by an esoteric tide of events into positions of great influence, confirming them in their overconfidence that all they need do where others have failed is to implement the conventional wisdom of decades, as if this were a revelation that has been vouchsafed to them alone. Trudeau is frequently billed by his supporters as a philosopher king, but he had a very unoriginal mind. He had a good knowledge of French and English literature from a solid education in the humanities, but his claims to being a lawyer and an economist were tenuous. His father was a wealthy man who had died when Pierre was not yet an adult and left him comfortably off for life. Pierre Trudeau was a traditional French bourgeois tightwad, and it killed him to spend anything. He had a simplistic and contrarian view of almost everything but was a devout Roman Catholic – though he had objected to Cardinal Villeneuve's enthusiasm for the war effort in the Second World War and was a secularizer in the Duplessis and Lesage years. His answer to everything was to throw public sector money at it with the cavalier disregard for the origins of that money of someone who has never had to earn much himself. Trudeau entered politics to make his federalist arguments at his leisure and had to be persuaded by Jean Marchand to accept to be Lester Pearson's parliamentary assistant, as he did not wish to alter his rather relaxed and self-indulgent style of living. He only gradually came to see the potential to succeed Pearson when his legal reforms won him the favour of the Liberals' reform wing, and his resistance to Daniel Johnson's call for increased provincial rights brought him to the front of the federalist column at a decisive time. The Liberals alternated French and English leaders, Marchand did not speak English well and as a labour leader was an unlikely choice (and wasn't interested anyway), and Pearson, aged seventy, accident-prone and exhausted after flying by the seat of his pants through such heavy weather that the plane was shuddering, had to retire. The music stopped and all eyes were on Trudeau. But what very few commentators or even Trudeau biographers have remotely grasped is that nothing counted except the battle with the separatists, and in this one area Trudeau was in some ways perfect.

Trudeau had practised law desultorily, and as a professor he gave one lecture a week on civil liberties. His doctoral thesis was uncompleted, not only because he was not overly motivated, much less driven by economic necessity, but because the subject of his thesis, the relationship between communism and Christianity, was a thin topic, derived chiefly from the lethargic doctoral candidate's wishful fantasies: a sophomore's conjuration for a graduate's opus. There has never in fact been much of a communist-Christian relationship to explore, apart from a few Liberation theologians who were later essentially defrocked as heretics by Pope John Paul II. But once again, the erratically bouncing football of Canadian public life – the unpredictable series of shifts and changes that was necessary to turn New France into a quiescent British colony, Upper Canada from a wilderness into a haven for loyal fugitives from the American Revolution, and the string of detrital settlements along the U.S. border into a country, and to hold the country together through a sequence of crises managed by people who intuitively understood how to round up an adequate consensus of French and English opinion – providentially put the right man in as head of the government now. Even Pierre Trudeau's constitutional policy was doubtful for a federalist: it was needlessly inflexible, and there was no reason to resist any provincial initiative to add a cubit to its stature in areas that were clearly of provincial interest and acknowledged to be shared jurisdictions by Macdonald, Cartier, Brown, and the other founders. Trudeau's admirers have turned themselves inside out trying to claim the success of his economic policies by normal criteria, and his detractors have been reduced to paroxysmal frustration debunking him by the same criteria. His constitutional changes and foreign policy initiatives have elicited the same intense combat. These controversies have almost all missed the point, which was that the only real purpose of any of it was to conserve the country and confuse or suborn or overpower the separatists, and it is by that criterion that they must be judged. It was horribly extravagant to deluge the ostensibly disadvantaged provinces with transfer payments from the richest parts of the country. The whole constitutional approach based on individual rights above all other things went far beyond its alleged objective, turned the country's judges into hyperactive social tinkerers, and reduced much of society to over-litigious bedlam. And his truckling to communists and the Third World, his nonsense with the Club of Rome think tank in opposition to economic growth, like the ludicrous North-South fad, scarcely capable of being recalled at all, in which Trudeau invested such dilettantish interest (as most of the rest of us blinked in disbelief), none of any of it amounted to anything except to cut the Quebec separatists off at the knees.

Trudeau showed that the federal government would defend its position, if need be, with martial law, tanks, and dirty tricks; that Canada was a huge material benefit to Quebeckers; that French was a fact throughout the country, however sketchy in most of it. (He told a complainer about bilingual cornflakes boxes to "turn the box around.") He was a genius in a specialized way that was what the country needed. And his over-respectful attention to Fidel Castro and Soviet puppets like Nicolae Ceauşescu of Romania and Erich Honecker of East Germany was inane but it made the point that Canada was not a lackey of Washington, much less London (and was not more inane than the foreign policy perceptions of a large number of French Canadians). Trudeau did not care a rap what *Le Devoir*, or Radio-Canada, or the Société Saint-Jean-Baptiste at the Monument-National on Boulevard Saint-Laurent (with its unilingual Jewish landlord), or all the *bien pensants* thought of anything. And his pugnacity, his courage, as well as his style – his elegant wardrobe and panache – were admired in Quebec, as they were elsewhere. He was simplistic and even reactionary, but he was a star, was never caught short in debate, and had a bitchy hauteur that was always entertaining and hard not to respect. He was the man of this difficult hour.

The Quebec nationalists like Lévesque had grown from fiery youth to apparent maturity with the notion that the federalist opposition was headed by a composite of the obfuscatory Mackenzie King, the avuncular but detached St. Laurent, the incoherent scourge of hyphenated Canadianism Diefenbaker, and the amiable, accident-prone Pearson, all of them conciliatory to some extent and capable of being gradually moved. Suddenly in their path was a very tough French-Canadian prime minister who was entirely bicultural, had mysteriously developed almost a constitutional religion on the avoidance of further concessions to Quebec, had great flair and enjoyed combat as much as his predecessors had been averse to it, and was prepared to throw all his opponents into prison if they gave him any pretext to do it. (One day, he encountered the half-mad ex-monk and union leader Michel Chartrand in the halls of Parliament, and Chartrand, who had worked with Marchand at the Confédération des Syndicats Nationaux, mocked Trudeau's security escort. Trudeau replied that he didn't need any security with Chartrand and would be happy to settle the differences between them right there. Chartrand declined.) This was not the whey-faced deferential Pearsonism the Quebec nationalists had had in mind as *le vrai visage* of their ancient federalist foe, and Trudeau completely intimidated them.

If Trudeau was unreasonable, and he often was, it must be remembered that his opponents were wolves in sheep's clothing. They masqueraded as civilized respecters of minority rights and all the democratic niceties, but from their restrictive language laws, which were a long sequence of infringements of freedom of expression, through their confiscatory taxes – designed to push out the non-French, finance their self-directed ministerial largesse, and, in changing Quebec's demographics by driving out the minorities, compensate for the province's collapsed birth rate, itself in part a peevish act of rebellion against its priest-ridden past – they were not moderate. There were frequent incitements of ethnic antagonisms, and most of the nationalist leaders were not the *grosses batteries* they presented themselves as, but rather were seedy and contemptible hypocrites. The independence of Quebec can be advocated in a way that is not culturally or morally offensive, and it certainly has an understandable allure, but so does the flowering of a bilingual Canada. The Quebec nationalists could never accept a contest of competing visions; they would only propagate their own vision on the back of a savage defamation of the alternative. They could never compete fairly and could never admit the cost of what they were proposing; it was always *étapisme*, step by step, as one of their leaders, Jacques Parizeau, put it, "tearing the Canadian flag inch by inch until it was easier to tear it completely than mend it." Trudeau, in his sometimes outrageous way, had courage, and he had integrity. Most of his opponents of whom the same can be said were not people of stature in their movement.

Even with Lévesque, it did not take much to elicit a torrent of resentment and vindictiveness, and the further down in the separatist ranks one descended, the harder it was and the less frequently it was attempted to disguise these sentiments behind a pall of elaborate sophistry and prevarication. Trudeau was inflexible, but the separatists were dishonest. Pearson had seen the danger and started to produce his defence, and the Laurendeau-Dunton Commission had recommended in its report in 1969 that English and French be declared formally and in all respects co-equal official languages; that Ontario and New Brunswick become officially bilingual provinces; that bilingual districts be established throughout the country wherever there was a French or English minority of 10 per cent or more of the population; that Ottawa become a bilingual city; and that wherever numbers made it possible, parents should have the right to choose between French and English as the language of instruction of their children (this was the position Daniel Johnson had taken in the last press conference of his life, and which Jean-Jacques Bertrand had entrenched in Quebec in Bill 23, enacted over stormy nationalist protests in 1969). The Royal Commission had found that French Canadians were disproportionately infrequent holders of high positions in the public and private sectors and that their standard of living was lower than that of all other groups except Italian Canadians and native people, though this substantially reflected the condition of French minorities outside Quebec. The exceptionally capable justice minister, John Turner, sold the new Official Languages Act (1969) to the provincial premiers with great tact and enacted and implemented it. If St. Laurent had commissioned this analysis and led national opinion as Pearson had – if it had all been done a decade earlier – matters would have been settled. It was at this point that the nationalist establishment of Quebec betrayed its *bonne ententiste* allies in English Canada.

Always, up to this time, the nationalists of Quebec had said that all they sought was equality with the English. Dr. Philippe Hamel, the leader of the Action Libérale Nationale, which Duplessis had subsumed into his Conservative Party of Quebec to form the Union Nationale in 1935, said, "Conquer us with goodwill, my English friends; you are surely capable of it and you will be astonished by the easy victory that awaits you."[10] All three federal political parties supported the recommendations of the Laurendeau-Dunton Commission, and millions of English-Canadian schoolchildren all over Canada began studying French relatively intensively. It was a powerful shift based altogether on goodwill and the recognition that it was an asset to have both these formidable and vital cultures, in Lord Durham's phrase, "in the bosom of a single state." The great Expo 67 in Montreal, a project in whose success Duplessis, Lesage, Johnson, Drapeau, Saulnier, Diefenbaker, and Pearson had all shared, helped create this new mood, so long in coming, which coincided with the decline of the British connection and the American imbroglio in Vietnam and widespread racial conflict there.

At the prospect of this long-sought consummation of centuries of isolation and insecurity of the French Canadians, who had made the compromises Jean Drapeau had so graphically described to Charles de Gaulle to the general approval of the whole country, the nationalists suddenly veered 180 degrees and declared that bilingualism was, unbelievably, a means to the accomplishment of the most hoary and ancient bugbear of all, assimilation. André Laurendeau (former leader of the Bloc Populaire and Henri Bourassa's chosen successor) and Trudeau, Marchand, Pelletier, and all the promoters of French-English harmony – from Pearson and Davidson Dunton to F.R. Scott (author of the Regina Manifesto, former leader of the Quebec CCF, and dean of law at McGill, who supported imposition of the War Measures Act) – were all, in the minds of the Quebec nationalists, involved in a conspiracy, some doubtless unwittingly, to deracinate the French Canadians and kill them with kindness through the promotion of the notorious evil of bilingualism, for which Quebec had been clamouring for 150 years. English Canada, having been lured to the matrimonial altar and abandoned there, gradually lapsed back into a less sentimental attitude toward its francophone compatriots. Such an abrupt *volte-face*, such a policy betrayal, did not justify the RCMP's burning of barns or stealing the Parti Québécois's membership list, but it did legitimize Pierre Trudeau's contempt for the treachery and moral bankruptcy of most of his separatist opposition.

These Quebec nationalists do not deserve most of the pelagic deluge of tears that many among the gullible English-Canadian left have shed for them. Trudeau was not only at the head of the forces of pan-Canadianism and national renewal, and of traditional emancipation of the French Canadians, he was the leader of the forces of cultural tolerance, mutual respect, and political good faith. He was right; the separatists were morally wrong in their tactics, even if it were possible to have some sympathy for the desirability of an independent French Quebec, but Trudeau was the high road and the brave *chef*. Lévesque had some sense of moderation, if not a surplus of integrity, but most of Trudeau's separatist enemies were weasels and charlatans, and the issue was so quickly polarized, there was for a long time little room in the discussion for well-meaning federal alternatives like Robert Stanfield, or even an ambiguous front man like Robert Bourassa. The young Quebec premier was trying to carve out a nationalist role where retention of participation in Canada was justified almost exclusively on economic grounds, but he was a colourless Quebec Mackenzie King, a technocrat lacking robustness (though he was a very intelligent and charming man personally, and ultimately an important premier). It was coming down to a bare-knuckle fight between Trudeau and Lévesque, and there wasn't much room in the ring for anyone else, and certainly not for a referee.

In straight legislative terms, one of Trudeau's most important measures was his Opportunities for Youth program, announced in 1971. By this means, the federal government simply opened a spigot of money for young people for any apparently respectable purpose. His government also raised the old-age pension and guaranteed income supplement and indexed it to the cost of living. There were new amendments to the Criminal Code and related statutes, and there were rather lethargic efforts to upgrade the prison system to emphasize job training and other methods of rehabilitating inmates. He revised unemployment insurance, by increased payments, effectively changing it from insurance against unemployment to an embryonic guaranteed income plan. The labour minister, Bryce Mackasey, had built in a scheme that would be affordable if unemployment did not go above 5 per cent, but it would be increasingly costly if it rose above that point, and the cabinet did not realize at first that it was a time bomb. In the meantime, it was popular with recipients. And there was a more pallid form of tax reform than Pearson's finance minister, Walter Gordon, had sought, but about a million modest income earners were exonerated from federal income taxes, which were reduced for about 4.7 million people and increased for about 1.3 million higher income earners. It all complimented the regional economic programs in making life more comfortable in the working and rural districts of Quebec and other places, *grace au gouvernement federal*, and the basic political arithmetic made a nice equation.

Foreign policy initiatives were also designed to make Trudeau appear an independent world figure, and Canada exchanged embassies with the People's Republic of China before China was admitted to the United Nations or President Nixon made his spectacular visit to Mao Tse-tung and Chou En-lai in 1972. Trudeau made a state visit to the Soviet Union and extended Canadian territorial waters in the Arctic. But he did not comment on the Vietnam War, as Pearson had, and his relations with President Nixon were not strained. He was impressed by Nixon's evident knowledge of international affairs and many successes, especially in relations with China and the Soviet Union. Nixon and his chief foreign policy colleague, Dr. Henry Kissinger, considered Trudeau "more intelligent than Canadian leaders usually are, but a rather frivolous personality."[11] On principal issues, both Nixon and Kissinger told the author that Trudeau never bothered them, but Kissinger said they viewed with mild curiosity "his fascination with the lesser communists," referring largely to Castro. Nixon said Trudeau was "a poseur, but a smart one, and always very agreeable when we met."[12]

Unemployment had crept up, as had inflation, when Trudeau announced on September 1, 1972, that there would be an election on October 30. He promised to take the "high road" and have a "dialogue" with the country. The Liberal slogan was "The Land Is Strong," and it was a bland and self-satisfied campaign. Trudeau frequently campaigned with Margaret, his wife of less than two years, the beautiful daughter of a St. Laurent government minister from Vancouver, James Sinclair. She was twenty-nine years his junior, a flower child, but a campaign plus point. It was almost as if 1957 had never happened, and the Liberal campaign leadership was imbued with the conviction of its invincibility, though in fact the government's record was undistinguished, apart from Trudeau's handling of the October Crisis. Stanfield had worked hard to learn French and repair the divisions in the Progressive Conservative Party, and he recruited many good candidates, including the runner-up to Bourassa in the contest to succeed Jean Lesage as Quebec Liberal leader, former judge Claude Wagner. (The late Pierre Laporte had come third, but the contest was largely rigged by Trudeau and Marchand, who wanted Lesage out and were concerned at how independent Wagner would be, though he was an unambiguous federalist.) The Liberals were calling for a return to restrictions on foreign acquisitions of Canadian businesses, and the Conservatives were calling for tighter budgeting and even a possibility of wage and price controls to stop inflation. Almost all the government ministers went right through the term and sought re-election. (Only Paul Hellyer and Eric Kierans had retired, mainly because of personality problems with Trudeau.) The results on October 30 were a surprise (1968 results in brackets): the Liberals emerged with 109 MPs and 38.4 per cent of the vote (previously, 155 MPs and 45.4 per cent); Progressive Conservatives, 107 MPs and 35 per cent (72 MPs and 31.4 per cent); NDP, 31 MPs and 18 per cent (22 MPs and 17 per cent); and the Créditistes, 15 MPs and 7.6 per cent (14 MPs and 5.3 per cent). Trudeau had carried 58 out of 75 MPs in Quebec (the only Progressive Conservatives elected were Claude Wagner and Heward Grafftey in voting percentage terms), but he did more poorly in the other provinces combined than Pearson had in the debacle of 1958.

On the face of it, Trudeau had been defeated, but his was still the largest party in votes and MPs, and he was not the sort of person to conclude over-hastily that he had been rejected. After a few days' suspense (during which President Richard Nixon was re-elected by the greatest plurality in American history, over eighteen million votes), Trudeau determined to meet the House. It was not 1957, it was 1925, and Trudeau proved impressively swift on the uptake in determining how to move from being the idol of yesteryear to the scrambler of the moment. Stanfield, a craggy, principled, and rather guileless man, facilitated Trudeau's adaptation of Mackenzie King the survivor, and even somewhat resembled John Bracken, though Stanfield was considerably more effective. Trudeau's public position was that the people had expressed dissatisfaction with aspects of the government, which he would change, but that he still had more support than anyone else. He announced in advance that the government would only consider itself obliged to resign if it lost a designated confidence vote and he set out to assure himself of the support of the NDP. Stanfield would qualify as a Red Tory, but he was not going to win a foot race to the left with the former long-time CCF-NDP supporter Pierre Trudeau. This was where the country stood when Parliament met in January 1973.

4. The Renovated Pierre Trudeau, 1973–1977

Even before Parliament met, Trudeau had had the grace of post-electoral conversion that comes from intimations of political mortality. He announced a reduction in immigration, an area where there were hints of backlash, a crackdown on slackers who weren't really trying to find work while claiming benefits, and an end to family allowances to people whose incomes were above a certain floor. The deadline for twenty-five thousand civil servants to become bilingual would also be extended (in practice, becoming bilingual meant unilingual English-speakers acquiring a working knowledge of French, a serious challenge for most people and a heavy burden to place on their career prospects, and so regarded by many voters). Trudeau's Throne Speech on January 4, 1973, affected a partial humility that he deployed for a time, promising to "correct those areas in our administration where we had been incompetent, or where we had appeared to be incompetent . . . without in any way turning our back on our Liberal principles," and so on.[13] In particular, there was the sacred Liberal principle, chiselled in stone by Mackenzie King, to cling to office. As Trudeau said to an interviewer, "I'm that particular type of person who doesn't like being kicked out."[14]

A new Trudeau swiftly emerged: chastened, but also determined not to be misunderstood as arrogant or detached when he was really concerned with the long-term view. Keith Davey, the chief organizer the Liberals could never dispense with for long, was summoned back. In Liberal mythology, rednecks and an anti-French backlash were blamed for the poor election result, but Trudeau quickly transformed this to an update of the Liberal claim since Laurier's time that only the Liberals could hold the country together. He read in Parliament a Vancouver editorial that was rather blatantly anti-French, and when the House responded in uproar, as he had hoped, he played it like a violin: They do not react when I criticize separatism in Quebec, to the point of imposing martial law and suppressing seditious activity; why do they object when I urge reciprocal respect for both official languages? The subtext was clear: only Trudeau could keep Quebec in Canada and he would not apologize for saving the country. To the *bonne ententistes*, he was the personification of the concept; to the federalists who wanted to sleep at night secure that Canada would be there in the morning, he could be entrusted with that sacred cause; and to the French Canadians, he would end the attempted assimilation of the French outside Quebec, had spread the French fact throughout the country, and had opened the federalist wallet in Quebec while Québécois ruled in Ottawa. But all sensibilities entertained by adequately numerous blocs of voters would be addressed. He had been insufficiently respectful of the queen – this would be addressed by Her Majesty making two visits to her Realm of Canada in 1973, a first, and Trudeau was her constant companion, as was Margaret Trudeau, whose demure curtsies emphasized Trudeau's monarchical appreciativeness without the prime minister himself engaging in exaggerated physical deferences. And Margaret, a young mother, highlighted a new, family oriented Trudeau and pulled the positive attention that beautiful young women with ivory skin, Chiclet smiles, dressed tastefully but with exiguous brevity, revealing them to be ample, callipygian, and possessed of well-toned thighs and calves, always receive.

Also as always, cash was the annealing balm of political renascence: there were 20 per cent spending increases in 1973 and 1974, though Mackasey's wheeze on behalf of the unemployed was unearthed and he was moved to immigration with instructions to make a public display of being choosier about who was admitted to the country. John Turner became finance minister after the election. His first budget indexed income taxes, stealing outright one of Stanfield's promises. It was an innovative step that was much emulated in the world; Trudeau and Turner took all the credit for it, and Stanfield's role was forgotten. Marc Lalonde, Trudeau's iron-fisted lieutenant for thankless and raw tasks, as health and welfare minister was given two billion dollars for pensioners and parents. The philosopher king had become the bountiful, compassionate cynic, harvesting votes with the electors' public credit. Trudeau appeased the West with a Western Economic Opportunities Conference, which he chaired in Calgary.

But international events intruded on the oil industry. Following the Arab–Israeli Yom Kippur War in October 1973, in which President Nixon effectively supplied Israel a new air force in the midst of the conflict, after the Egyptians had successfully crossed the Suez Canal and breached the Bar-Lev Line, and the Israelis under Ariel Sharon had surrounded an Egyptian army in the south, Nixon and Kissinger brokered an important peace that led eventually to a comprehensive settlement between Israel and Egypt. But in the short term it led to an Arab oil embargo, a constriction in the world oil supply, and severe spikes in the price of oil. Trudeau and several of his advisers devised a new energy program that would take complete form only later but started with a single, subsidized national oil price, a national petroleum company to demonstrate that Canada was not just a branch-plant country, and export taxes on oil. In the same philosophical line, he created the Foreign Investment Review Agency to apply the test of "significant benefit" to Canada for the approval of foreign takeovers. It was an innovative program and sensibly nationalistic while avoiding the self-inflicted wounds of Walter Gordon's initial run at it a decade before. And Trudeau preserved his liberal credentials by extending for five years the suspension of the death penalty, which signalled that it would not be brought back, though public opinion favoured it.

By mid-1973, polls were showing that most Canadians thought they were dealing with a new and humbler Trudeau. It was a brilliant performance, and Trudeau's puckish love of farce and imposture were well-served. Soon, he was lampooning the Progressive Conservatives for their disloyalty to the great John Diefenbaker after the reproof of the 1962 election: "The party fell apart. . . . The leader was being slowly murdered by his ministers. . . . Thank God that is not the kind of dissent we see in the Liberal Party."[15] Trudeau had his foibles, but he could more justly have thanked the Almighty for the fact that he had not made such an unutterable shambles of defence policy, nuclear weapons, and alliance obligations as Diefenbaker had. The old chief nodded and smiled benignly at some of Trudeau's invocations of him. Trudeau accused Stanfield of being "power-hungry" (as if there were ever a political party leader in any country who was not), and even more scurrilously, he accused the NDP of "sham and hypocrisy" as the NDP leader, David Lewis, secretly met with Trudeau's agile House leader, Allan MacEachen – and as a sop to the NDP, Trudeau brought in an ineffective Food Prices Review Board and an anti-profiteering law that was just window dressing, as nothing would ever fit the definitions in it. There was another tax cut for low- and middle-income earners and federal subsidies for milk and bread to cushion the public from inflation without discountenancing the agricultural producers. Lewis was effectively suborned, receiving legislation in exchange for support, and Stanfield was unable to attract public and media attention to the outright cynicism of Trudeau's vote-buying.

Trudeau successfully chaired a Commonwealth Conference in Ottawa in the summer of 1973 and had a portentous state visit to China in October, where the leaders of the People's Republic, including Mao Tse-tung and Chou En-lai, now almost a quarter-century at the head of that immense country and people, received him as a serious figure.

In Quebec, Robert Bourassa called a snap election in October 1973 to gain approval of a huge hydroelectric power complex he planned for the rivers flowing into James Bay, and the trend of recent elections was maintained. Bourassa's Liberals jumped from 45.4 per cent of the vote and 72 members of the National Assembly, to 54.6 per cent and 102 members. Polarization continued, as the Union Nationale – now led by Gabriel Loubier, a former scrap metal dealer from Bellechasse and Johnson and Bertrand's minister of fish and game – was wiped out, with 5 per cent of the vote and no one elected; and the Créditistes – now led by the ineffable Yvon Dupuis, who last appeared in this narrative as a victim of Diefenbaker's destruction of ill-advised Pearson ministers from Quebec – descended to 10 per cent of the vote and only 2 legislators. But the Parti Québécois, though it lost 1 member of the National Assembly, to hold only 6, jumped from 23 to 30 per cent of the vote. The overtly separatist vote had increased from 9 per cent in 1966, to 23 in 1970, to 30. Bourassa clearly had all the traditional Liberals, all the non-French, and a big chunk of the old Conservatives and the floating vote, but floating votes, by their nature, are unreliable. It was a good result for the federalists, but the Péquistes were happy to be the official Opposition. All three opposition leaders were defeated personally. Loubier and Dupuis would not be heard from again politically, but Lévesque was still rising.

The federal Conservatives were knocked off stride by the division in their own large caucus when Trudeau, for tactical purposes opposite the Quebec nationalists and the Conservative Western rednecks, reintroduced for renewed ratification, quite unnecessarily, the principles of official bilingualism. Diefenbaker and sixteen others broke official ranks, and in the disorder, Stanfield – in another fatal blunder for which the Canadian federal Conservatives were conspicuously well-known, from conscription in 1917 through all the clangorous misjudgments of Meighen, Bennett, Manion, Bracken, Drew, and Diefenbaker, and for another decade yet – declared that, if elected, his government would freeze wages and prices. Davey's polling showed that concern for national unity had subsided and that the country was very preoccupied by inflation, which was approaching 8 per cent in the aftermath of the oil price spike in early 1974. Trudeau was goading Stanfield and Lewis to bring down his government, as his polls showed him the pre-eminent figure in the regard of the country, and he was promising strong action against inflation, starting with his oil and energy program, and was soon frightening the country with hair-raising invocations of what Stanfield's wage and price freeze would do to it. Trudeau accused the NDP of "hanging on to us like seagulls on a fishing vessel, claiming that they are really steering the ship."[16] In May 1974, Turner, proving very competent as finance minister, produced a budget that continued the government's official generosity but ignored some specific demands of the NDP. Since 1867, elected minority governments had only twice been defeated in confidence votes: the Meighen-Byng bungling of the 1925 to 1926 Parliament (Chapter 6), and Diefenbaker's fumbling his government in the defence debacle of 1963 (Chapter 8). This was different: in the highest (or lowest, depending on one's perspective) tradition of Kingsian Liberalism, Trudeau, Davey, and the Liberal inner circle had baited a trap, and Stanfield and Lewis took the bait and defeated the government.

The election was on July 8. Trudeau campaigned with great energy as the wronged incumbent who wished to remain on the job and was the victim of opposition opportunism. "Zap, you're frozen!" was his answer to Stanfield's wage and price freeze. He would control energy prices with a nationalistic but not socialistic response, would control food prices with subsidies, and jawbone with labour and industry. He would lead, the country would be reasonable, and he would deal with it, as, it was implied, he had dealt with the shenanigans in Quebec. The other parties never got untracked, couldn't get off their back feet, and were not plausible alternatives. The whole, swift regeneration of his standing was Trudeau's third great achievement, next to taking control of the great Liberal governing party in the first place – less than three years after he had been an underemployed rich playboy NDP quasi-academic – and his authoritative handling of the October Crisis, but the greatest achievements were yet to come. On July 8, 1974, Canada elected (1972 results in brackets):141 Liberals with 43.2 per cent of the popular vote (109 MPs and 38.4 per cent); 95 Progressive Conservatives with 35.5 per cent (107 MPs and 35 per cent); 16 NDP with 15.4 per cent (31 MPs and 18 per cent); and 11 Créditistes with 5.1 per cent (15 MPs and 7.6 per cent). Leonard Jones, the former mayor of Moncton, New Brunswick, was elected as an independent; Stanfield had refused to endorse him because of his opposition to official bilingualism (although Moncton has a large French population).*

At this great watershed in his career, Trudeau went into one of his inexplicable torpors and determined to govern quietly, clear up a backlog, consult his ministers, whom he could not have imagined would be a very fecund source of innovative suggestions, and observe his compatriots in contemplative mode. As always for people in roles where activity is expected, this was a serious tactical error. In Quebec, Bourassa had taken advantage of his sweeping victory to try to move his government to a more nationalistic stance to head off the rise of the Parti Québécois. There was a good deal of agitation in Quebec that the French-speaking percentage of the population was in decline and that the French language was under threat, if not from the forces of bilingualism, from acculturation, erosion, and the post-Catholic birth rate. Bourassa to this point had embraced the Johnson-Bertrand formula that all schoolchildren in Quebec would learn to speak French but that the language of instruction would be whichever of the official languages the parents chose. He now presented, through his education minister, Dr. François Cloutier, a former television psychiatrist, Bill 22, which declared French to be the sole official language of Quebec, and determined that the English-language section of the public education system would be accessible only to the children of those parents who already lived in Quebec when the child was born. Immigrants to Quebec would be subject to language aptitude tests, at preschool ages, to determine, according to arbitrary criteria, where they would go to school. Commercial signs would have to be either in both languages, with the French characters larger than those in any other language, or, in stores, in French only, and these matters were to be enforced by the Office de la Langue Française. This gave rise to the so-called language police, who in time became one of Quebec's greatest tourist attractions.

This severely embittered the non-French Quebeckers, a fifth of the population, and more than a fifth in terms of economic activity, who had given all they had for the Liberal Party, provincially and federally.

---

* Réal Caouette, one MP short of official party status for the Créditistes, offered Jones membership in his party despite his views, as Jones did not oppose minority language education, but Jones declined to prop up Caouette's status.

Trudeau and his federal Liberal MPs completely ignored the issue. C.M. ("Bud") Drury, the senior English federal minister from Montreal, who lived in Ottawa and no longer had a home in Quebec, breezily referred to "the celebrated" Bill 22. Drury was unilingual but, though a capable minister, who defeated Arthur Meighen's very able (and bilingual) grandson Michael Meighen in Westmount in 1972 and 1974, could not bring himself to utter a single word in support of the English-speaking majority of his constituents from across the Ottawa River. It was exquisitely ironic in a way: Bourassa, the unfrightening technocrat parachuted into the Liberal leadership by Trudeau, after all his leader's histrionics about individual rights, produced the most egregious official oppression of freedom of expression in Canadian history, throwing acid in the face of the most unquestioning constituency the Liberals had. What was intended as an act of opportunism would prove an act of suicide. The only way to deal with the Quebec nationalists' last refuge of the necessity to persecute cultural minorities because of the alleged feebleness and decline in numbers of French Quebec was to stand tall and denounce this as the defeatist fraud that it was. Trudeau and Bourassa had just been re-elected, but they were negligently squandering their strength, fragmenting their coalition, feeding the enemy, and reducing their own arguments, which the people had endorsed, to piffle and claptrap. They would reap what they sowed.

The first year after the July 1974 election victory was wasted. As inflation worsened, the federal government didn't do anything. John Turner prepared three alternatives: seek consensus, impose the pay and price controls Trudeau had promised to avoid and had ridiculed, or take fiscal and monetary measures, which essentially meant taxing inflationary wage and revenue gains and ensuring an absence of growth in the money supply. The first was rubbish and the face to be put on doing nothing, though market forces would take care of it eventually; controls were bound to cause terrible credibility problems, given the hay made of them in the last election campaign; and the last was at least potentially imaginative. By now, most inflation was of the cost-push variety, largely in heavy wage settlements, which are easier to deal with than internationally driven commodity price increases. Turner had innovated by indexing benefits, and this afforded an opportunity for more innovation. It could have had the effect of controls and been an amorphous, incomprehensible program, such as Nixon had imposed in the United States in August 1971, that at least altered the psychology of the public. And economics is half psychology and half Grade 3 arithmetic. While the government dithered, there were minor errors, including abstention at the United Nations on the issue of whether to hear from the Palestine Liberation Organization. There were no votes in Canada for Yasser Arafat at this point, and no indication that the PLO had relinquished any of its terrorist methods. There were signs, after three elections and seven years of Trudeau and twelve years and five elections with the Liberals, that the country was getting tired of the Liberals, as normally happens with the governing party, and they weren't helping themselves by showing any sign of renovation.

On the contrary, John Turner, the logical successor to Trudeau, after a consistently strong showing in successive cabinet positions, abruptly resigned on September 10, and his portfolio was awarded to the capable Donald Stovel Macdonald. Turner was now the Liberal leader in waiting, like Georges Pompidou after the événements of 1968, in, as de Gaulle put it, *"la réserve de la République."* On October 13, 1975, at the end of the Thanksgiving weekend, Trudeau astonished the country by announcing the imposition of controls on wages and prices. Public reaction was understandably negative, and the government drifted into 1976, its condition rendered less buoyant by Trudeau's distracted public musings that the economic system "wasn't working" and that there was need for a "new society."[17] It was back to the pompous idiocy of Trudeau the lazy academic commentator, wallowing in his inheritance and complaining of the shortcomings of the world, and his electors in particular, while he did not do what he was elected to do, and instead did what he promised not to do. When challenged and insulted, Trudeau's mental and physical agility showed, and the tenor of his voice became sharper and his articulation elegantly hard-hitting. But when Trudeau was not fighting the separatists or for his political life, though always a rewarding conversationalist in person, he tended to be a platitudinous time-warp 1950s leftie, with an irritatingly nasalized and condescending method of self-expression. The country knew his moods well by now, and this was the least attractive one.

* * *

The Progressive Conservatives had a lively leadership convention, starting on February 22, 1976, in Ottawa. The front-runner was Claude Wagner, who had been elected as a Conservative MP for Saint-Hyacinthe, Quebec, in 1972 and 1974, and had been Jean Lesage's minister of justice in Quebec, where he was popular as a law-and-order attorney general. As he considered, with some reason, that the leadership had been stolen from him by the Liberal establishment and given to Bourassa in 1970, he accepted reappointment by Jean-Jacques Bertrand to the bench just before Bertrand dissolved the National Assembly for the 1970 provincial election. Lured back to politics as leader of the Progressive Conservatives in Quebec by Stanfield and others, he was a logical choice: as bilingual as Trudeau and a formidable public speaker in both languages. The Conservatives had never had a French-Canadian leader, or even one who could speak French properly, and – apart from the mighty gift of fifty MPs from Maurice Duplessis in 1958 – had not come close to carrying Quebec in a federal election since Sir John Macdonald's last election, in the all-time heavyweight match of Canadian history, against Wilfrid Laurier in 1891 (Chapter 4).

There was another Quebec candidate: Brian Mulroney, a thirty-six-year-old labour lawyer who had enjoyed extensive publicity for his role on the Cliche Commission, appointed by Bourassa to investigate elements of the Quebec labour movement in 1974. He had been an insider in the thin Quebec ranks of his party for about a decade and had helped to swing a number of Fulton delegates to Stanfield on the last ballot of the 1967 convention. He had helped attract Wagner to the Conservatives in 1972, and though he had never run for elective office, he was a presentable and popular candidate, articulate, bilingual, and a loyal party regular in difficult times. The rationale for choosing a leader who could shake the Liberal stranglehold on Quebec and join usefully in the Quebec discussion, which, though semi-dormant, was clearly going to heat up again, was obvious.

Paul Hellyer, the veteran Liberal minister of the St. Laurent, Pearson, and Trudeau governments, not only crossed the aisle and ran as a candidate for the Progressive Conservative leadership, he chastised the Red Tories in his candidate's speech to the convention for being too much like the Liberals whose company he had departed. He was the only person in history to be a serious candidate for the leadership of both major political parties. There were a number of other candidates, particularly Red Tories Joe Clark of Alberta and Flora MacDonald of Kingston, Ontario.

The oratorical star, apart from Wagner, was eighty-year-old John Diefenbaker, now in his twelfth consecutive parliamentary term, who delighted and convulsed the convention with his usual witticisms and scurrilous embellishments about the shortcomings of the Liberals, including the claim that Trudeau had said in his visit to Moscow that Canada was militarily afraid of the United States. (Trudeau was fundamentally closer at heart to the Soviet Union than to the United States, a country he never understood well, and he took his sons to the Siberian industrial city of Norilsk and claimed that Soviet planning was a success story, but he was not exactly anti-American and did not say exactly what Diefenbaker imputed to him.) It didn't really matter; people would forgive Diefenbaker almost anything now, and he was the last person who had led his party to victory since R.B. Bennett in 1930, before many of the delegates and some of the candidates were born.

Wagner led for three ballots, but Mulroney divided the Quebec vote with him. There were reservations about an unelected candidate, and one whose business connections enabled him to run such a rich campaign as Mulroney's. Wagner had his baggage, and bigotry was part of it. Flora MacDonald withdrew in favour of Clark, and he began moving up as the alternative to the Quebeckers, passing Mulroney on the third ballot to go to a final runoff with Wagner. There was now a distinct lack of rapport between Mulroney and Wagner, and Wagner had prevented Mulroney's selection even as a delegate, a churlish act that cost him now. Joe Clark (b. 1939) was elected leader of the Opposition, with 1,187 ballots to Wagner's 1,122. The Progressive Conservatives had chosen an unprepossessing leader, just thirty-six years old, though one who would enjoy considerable attainments. He was an improbable figure to put up against a man of Trudeau's stature and would not do anything for his party with French Canadians, though his grasp of the language was somewhat better than Stanfield's. Robert Stanfield had been one of the more distinguished of the long list of unsuccessful leaders of his party; he had made the PCs over as a sensible, well-organized, centrist party with a large and reasonably talented caucus. He was universally respected as an intelligent and honest, but unexciting, man, and was long remembered in Nova Scotia as an outstanding premier. Mulroney would be back, but he declined to run for Parliament at this point. Wagner did not get on well with Clark, though he spoke very graciously at the end of the convention. He accepted appointment to the Senate by Trudeau in 1978 but died of cancer the next year, aged only fifty-four, one of the unusual and meteoric figures of Canadian public affairs, a General Boulanger figure to some (a bold-seeming man who was yet rather hesitant), but a compelling public and private personality. His son, Richard Wagner, was appointed a justice of the Supreme Court of Canada in 2012.

The Liberals were confident, and their standing in the polls recovered somewhat as inflation weakened, as it was bound to do under the ministrations of Trudeau's new Anti-Inflation Board. (All these vast agglomerations of controls were more show and fanfare than actual administration. As President Nixon, who had modelled his Pay Board and related parts of the U.S. anti-inflation apparatus on some of Roosevelt's New Deal agencies, told the author, "They just baffle and scare people and slow things down. They don't really do anything, and you can't keep them for long, any more than FDR did." Or Nixon, or Trudeau.) The state oil company Petro-Canada was established, the death penalty was abolished, and Trudeau had a moderately successful trip to Latin America, an area Canada had completely ignored, for decades not even acting on repeated requests by the United States and others to join the Organization of American States (OAS), where, it was said, Canada's chair had been waiting for it since the organization was set up by President Truman in 1948. Trudeau had finally taken Canada into the OAS in 1972.

The country and its government were treading water rather lethargically when Robert Bourassa called an election in Quebec for November 15, 1976, just three years into his current mandate. It was never obvious why he called the election, as there had been a number of scandals that had besmirched the government. The 1976 Summer Olympics in Montreal, another achievement of Mayor Jean Drapeau but not efficiently administered, had hobbled the city and province with an onerous deficit and in its costly aftermath had been almost as deflating to Quebec's morale as the world's fair of nine years before had been exhilarating. But Bourassa had not imagined that the Quebec cultural minority could desert the Liberals in serious numbers and did not understand that the Parti Québécois was capable of running as a straight good-government reform party and consign independence to a referendum to be held in due course under firmly democratic principles. It was assumed at first that the government would be re-elected, but by the end of the campaign it was clear that Bourassa was in difficulty. That did not prepare the country for the thunderclap produced by the voters of Quebec on election day. The Liberals collapsed from 55 per cent of the vote three years before to 34 per cent, suffering wholesale desertions of the non-French to the Union Nationale under Rodrigue Biron. In a final appearance in Quebec history, the Union Nationale jumped from 5 to 18.2 per cent of the vote, and the Créditistes faded from 10 per cent in 1973 to 4.6 per cent. The Parti Québécois jumped from 30 per cent in 1973 (up from 23 per cent in 1970) to 41.4 per cent. The 110 places in the National Assembly were divided as follows: PQ, 71 seats (up from 6); Liberals, 26 (down from 102); Union Nationale 11 (having had no seats); and Créditistes, 1 (down from 2). It was not the case that all the Péquiste voters were automatically for the independence of Quebec, and almost all the other party votes could be assumed to be, at this point, anti-separatist, but the PQ had more than quadrupled the ostensibly independentist vote in ten years, and the trajectory was extremely worrisome to federalists.

The tactic of *étapisme*, gradualism, was clever; Quebec was advancing on independence and secession in almost imperceptible increments. An issue that Canada had assumed was quiescent, if not over, suddenly was spectacularly alive, and while Lévesque spoke soberly on election night, he left no doubt that he would make an all-out drive for a "yes" vote in a referendum in the current term on a question that would lead, however circuitously, to Quebec as an independent and sovereign republic. The nine-hundred-pound gorilla that had been slumbering, albeit sometimes loudly, in the Canadian house since Papineau's time was on its feet, lurching about, and rearranging furniture noisily and unpredictably. As always when under direct challenge, Trudeau responded strongly. He congratulated Lévesque and made it clear that he looked forward to the debate and considered that the new Quebec government was boxed between a commitment to a referendum and the impossibility of winning a referendum on any question that amounted to a proposition to secede from Canada.

Bourassa was defeated in his own district and was completely discredited. His career was mistakenly assumed to be over.

5. Trudeau, Lévesque, and Clark, 1977–1980

In the spirit of crisis that now obtained in Canada, boredom and annoyance with Trudeau suddenly evaporated and with it the idea of disposing of him to bring in Joe Clark to deal with René Lévesque and his powerful coterie (many of whom spoke English with an educated English accent, such as Jacques Parizeau and Jacques-Yvan Morin; "By Jove!" was one of Parizeau's frequent openers, even in French). In January 1977, in Quebec City, Trudeau gave one of the greatest speeches of his career, calling for a referendum in Quebec soon and a question that would be clear and resolve matters once and for all. He emphasized that the burden was on those who would dispense with Canada as it had evolved to justify such a radical course, as it was a successful and admired country that had pursued social and cultural justice with success and would persevere to do better. He could not have imagined that Lévesque would respond as he requested. The whole Péquiste tactic was to defer the referendum, putting it behind good government, and in the name of social democracy squeeze the English and Jewish minorities, who had a relatively high standard of living, always in the intellectually impeccable cause of equity and fairness, and ultimately produce an anodyne question that would not frighten the voters but that Lévesque could use to escalate demands to outright independence.

It was going to be a long and intricate process, and as Lévesque had just got to the controls of government, he would have a honeymoon. Trudeau was well past any such indulgence, and some of his bad brainwaves were coming back to haunt him now. He had squandered billions through his friend Jean-Pierre Goyer, minister of supply and services, on a new airport for Montreal near the Ontario border. Premier Bertrand had warned that it was not a good location, and Trudeau publicly said Bertrand was "off his rocker." It was clear by the late 1970s that Trudeau and Goyer's airport at Mirabel was a disaster that no one used and from which only the serried ranks of the patronage-fed friends of the federal Liberal Party profited. (It was not without its ironies that Montreal's traditional airport was eventually named after Trudeau, as Toronto's, Quebec City's, and Halifax's airports were named after, respectively, Pearson, Lesage, and Stanfield.)

Lévesque attended his first Federal-Provincial Conference in many years in mid-December 1976, was greeted coolly but civilly by Trudeau, and the conference droned on as they always do, with much fewer fireworks than when Trudeau and Johnson had crossed swords in 1968. Lévesque told the Economic Club of New York on January 25, 1977, that Quebec's decision was irreversible and as inevitable as the American Revolution. None of the Americans believed a word of it, and it betrayed Lévesque's tendency as a journalist to oversimplify and to vulgarize complicated points. This was his strength and his weakness. As editor of a news magazine program in the 1950s in Quebec, he introduced much of French Canada to the world, but everything, no matter how complicated, was packaged up and summarized by him in thirty minutes. And that, essentially, was his vision, the simplistic, impatient, impulsive, and unrigorous reflexes of a journalist, but a very skilful journalist. He combined his talents at condensed reporting with the natural charm and frankness of the corner-store merchant, leaning on the counter beside his cash register and chatting with the neighbours about the events and personalities of the day. He knew the people and was an energetic and persuasive man, personally very considerate, often amusing, and never pompous. He was a bundle of nerves, twitching and smoking constantly, and was a tightly wound spring but never overtly racist. He was one of Quebec's all-time greatest public leaders, and enjoys with Honoré Mercier and Maurice Duplessis the distinction of being one of the only people who ever founded a Quebec political party and led it to victory, though he did not have the administrative talent or quality of political judgment or personal self-discipline of Duplessis. He was a remarkable man, but not exactly a great man. Trudeau was more worldly and formidable, more confident and intellectually rigorous. Lévesque was all emotion; Trudeau was all reason to a fault, leading him to irrational and sadistic attachments to abstract principles as only French Cartesians or theologians can be, to the point of nonsensical conclusions sometimes. The prophet of fire was contending with the prophet of ice. Napoleon said that "God is on the side of the heavy battalions." The heavy battalions were with Trudeau, but a gripping contest was developing.

Lévesque was going to defer his referendum and try to prepare the public with normal government, and Trudeau had adopted some techniques, which his federalist successors would follow, that were open to question. Because of the immense scale of transfer payments to Quebec (and tokenistically to the other provinces with below-average income levels), Trudeau and succeeding federal prime ministers have never revealed their full extent, saying, as Trudeau put it, "You can't put a price tag on Confederation." The fear was of an English-Canadian backlash, but it allowed the separatist orators and publicists to claim that Quebec was a net loser in Confederation. The people ultimately seemed to know better, but the argument could have been won, and the English Canadians could have accepted that it was a price worth paying. Also, Trudeau did not try to pre-empt Lévesque with his own law requiring a clear referendum question. He knew Lévesque was going to present a vague question and did nothing to make it more difficult for him to do so. Through 1977 and into 1978, Trudeau pre-pared opinion throughout Canada very calmly and won wide admiration for the conciliatory sobriety and eloquence with which he presented the alternatives. Enthusiasm for official biculturalism rose vertiginously in English Canada; far from recoiling at what might have been perceived as the ingratitude and bellicosity of Quebec, English Canada seemed to have a revelation of its fondness for a bicultural, transcontinental confederation, precisely the grand vision of Macdonald and Laurier, suitably updated.

Trudeau countered Lévesque's appearance at the Economic Club of New York with a far more successful address to a vastly more important audience: a joint session of the United States Congress, on February 22, 1977. He told the American legislators that the separation of Quebec would be "a crime against the history of mankind," and his speech was much admired in the United States as well as Canada. Trudeau got on splendidly with President Jimmy Carter. He never liked strong American presidents but was very impressed with Carter's pre-occupation with details and legalities and his reluctance to use America's great power in any forceful way. He could not fail to be impressed by Nixon's knowledge of the world and his legendary status as one of the most famous people in the world for decades, but he did not have the relaxed relationship with him that he did with Carter. He had a perfectly civil but only very passing relationship with President Gerald Ford. He would deeply resent Ronald Reagan's subsequent success, his popularity, and his technique of approaching issues that almost completely ignored Trudeau's (and Carter's) laboriously unimaginative micro-inspection. Reagan was a man of the fears of the Great Depression, the dreams fulfilled of Hollywood, the just war, the favours of the rich, and the adulation of the masses of America. Trudeau never understood any of it.

The battle lines were drawn more sharply on April 27, 1977, with Bill 1, which Lévesque called the Charter of the French Language. English would no longer be used in debates in the National Assembly, nor in Quebec courts, other than by individuals, and all companies with fifty employees or more would have to apply for and qualify for certificates of francization as a condition of continuing in business, making French the sole language of the workplace. All children, apart from those of Quebec-born English-speaking parents, would have to enrol in French schools. This was the complete reversal of the Johnson-Bertrand policy of eight years before, and a sharp escalation even of Bourassa's repressive measures of three years before. It was, and was declared to be, an outright assault on a bilingual Quebec.

Trudeau, who had not raised a peep over Bourassa's preparatory outrage of Bill 22, finally picked up the gauntlet and described the new bill as a "retrograde" assault on individual liberties and reviled the Parti Québécois's independence as a reversion "to the Dark Ages . . . to tribalism." Bingo! Finally, we were getting down to the real point. Lévesque's culture minister, Camille Laurin – another psychiatrist, like François Cloutier – agreed that it was "ethnocentric" and made the point that all nations were. (Of course, they aren't, but Laurin, like the PQ generally, was not one to be too much inconvenienced by the facts.) Bill 1 was somewhat reformulated as Bill 101 and was undoubtedly popular in Quebec. As always with these measures restricting the cultural rights of the non-French, the second goal was to drive out the English and others, who would put their houses and offices up for sale or occupancy at knock-down rates and increase the chances of nationalist victories in elections and plebiscites. Trudeau noted the popularity of the legislation and declined to disavow it, though its constitutionality was contested. He temporized that he did not wish tactically to play into Lévesque's hands on a side issue, albeit a vital one. Trudeau was advised by his entourage, especially Keith Davey and his astute and charming principal secretary, Jim Coutts, to go to the country and arm himself with a mandate to fight separation, but his marriage was collapsing and he didn't feel up to it.

Lévesque, for his part, was now facing the consequences of thousands of executive positions streaming out of the province and large numbers of less prominent people quietly leaving with them. By late 1977, unemployment climbed to 10 per cent, and the euphoria of the post-election honeymoon was wearing off. But so was Trudeau's surge in rediscovered national appreciation after the Quebec election. In this sense, Lévesque's tactic of seeming unfrightening was working, and English Canadians outside Quebec were no longer so alarmed by him. In a gesture to the old Quebec nationalists, Lévesque dusted off the statue of Maurice Duplessis that Paul Sauvé had commissioned, and which had been in the basement of the provincial police building on Parthenais Street in Montreal for over fifteen years, making Le Chef's successors appear ridiculous by seeming to be afraid of his statue. He unveiled it on the grounds of the National Assembly, declaring that while he had opposed Duplessis, all must recognize his immense services to Quebec through five terms as premier. Unveiling statues was the most civilized form of coalition-building, and the next best remembrance to having airports named after departed leaders. Thirty-five years later, statues of Lévesque and (Robert) Bourassa would flank Duplessis beside the National Assembly.

Claude Ryan announced his candidacy for the Quebec Liberal leadership in January 1978. Austere and monastic, but fearless, highly intellectual, and a courteous gentleman, without vanity and incorruptible in every sense, he would be a very formidable opponent. He had often seemed as much a separatist as Lévesque but was more careful to keep his distance from militant nationalists and favoured a special status for the province whose terms were changeable but somewhat on the lines advocated by Duplessis, Lesage, and Johnson. In June 1978, Trudeau published the federal government's updated constitutional position in the White Paper "A Time for Action," and then in Bill C-60, which included the elevation of the governor general to a co-equal status with the queen by making him or her the "First Citizen," who would open and dissolve Parliament personally and not in the name of the monarch. Trudeau and Lalonde, who was now his minister in this area, proposed to dispense with the Senate and replace it with a House of the Federation, half of whose members would be chosen by provincial legislatures to assure their interests in the federal government, and the provinces would have some say in the appointment of Supreme Court justices and the heads of some regulatory agencies. It was an imaginative series of proposals for which Trudeau received inadequately serious credit and attention. He reiterated something close to the Victoria formula for amending the Constitution, and said that only after that was agreed – and he required completion of it by July 1, 1979, or he would proceed unilaterally – would he discuss distribution of powers with the provinces. All ten premiers had their own meeting in Regina in August 1978 and unanimously determined that unless Trudeau put the distribution of powers first on the agenda, they would not discuss any of it. The premiers were back to the game they had first been taught by Duplessis, unctuously claiming to be committed federalists, waiting until Quebec had shaken something loose from Ottawa, and then saying that they had to have it too. But now, Lévesque, despite his secessionist ambitions, had persuaded them to act pre-emptively: they were all going to demand concessions together, even though it was just *étapisme* for Lévesque on the road to secession. Trudeau had been outmanoeuvred in allowing the premiers to be lured so far into Lévesque's camp.

Trudeau came back and astounded the premiers at a First Ministers' Conference, as they were now called, on October 21, 1978, at Ottawa, when he offered concurrent movement: if the premiers would agree to his points, he was prepared to move at once to concede jurisdiction in a number of areas, including family law and some communications regulations. Even Lévesque said, "Something is happening at last." All that happened, however, was that the joint committee to which the whole package was referred agreed on the handover of family law entirely to the provinces. The premiers, under Lévesque's disingenuous and Mephistophelean influence, had overplayed their hand. If they had accepted Trudeau's proposals, they would have added much more to their jurisdictions than was subsequently on offer. By dragging their feet, they forced a wait for a new federal election and Lévesque's referendum, which, by the beginning of 1979, had to be held within the next two years. Trudeau, as he said, found it "depressing and distressing" that the premiers as a group, and not just Quebec's separatist leader, would, for increased powers for themselves, retard a charter of rights for all Canadians and a patriated power of constitutional amendment. If Trudeau had not wasted the year after the Quebec election treading water amid his marital problems, he could have required action on his proposals and, failing action, have gone to the voters at high tide in 1977 and surely been re-elected on that issue at that time.

As it was, 1979 had dawned, the federal Parliament would have to be dissolved within a few months, and the economy had deteriorated, with double-digit interest rates and stagflation. The federal government's Task Force on Canadian Unity, chaired by former Ontario premier John Robarts and former Liberal federal minister Jean-Luc Pepin, reported out, criticizing Trudeau rather gratuitously and calling for a "distinctive" but not "special" status for Quebec with a general devolution to all provinces of increased powers. Trudeau was taken to task in the report for failure to recognize Canada's "duality and regionalism." The report was relatively well written, stylistically, by the standards of these things, but it was rather strange coming from two men who had spent their public careers claiming to be unreconstructed federalists. Lévesque and Trudeau both praised the report, though Lalonde was outwardly hostile.

Trudeau had run out the clock; unemployment was over 8 per cent, the dollar had fallen to the mid-80s in U.S. cents, the annual deficit was 25 per cent of federal revenues, there was a substantial trade deficit, and Trudeau's giveaways to buy votes, especially in Quebec to gain favour for federalism, were straining the treasury. The country was tired of him. Joe Clark was no one's idea of a galvanizing leader, but after sixteen years of the Liberals even a semi-plausible change would work. Lévesque lay low as his Péquistes simulated a secular equivalent of prayer for a Clark victory. Trudeau called the election for May 22, 1979, after a flourish of expense reductions and promised layoffs in the civil service, which was generally dismissed as a deathbed conversion that was too little too late and insufficiently penitent. (It was all of that.) For good measure, his estranged and flaky wife produced a keyhole-opening memoir in April called *Beyond Reason*, detailing some of her somewhat flagrant promiscuity, including with U.S. senator and surviving womanizer-in-chief of his family, Ted Kennedy. This didn't seem to change things politically, and most people had some sympathy with Trudeau, who retained custody of the couple's three sons. Trudeau won the all-candidates' debate, but Clark held his corner adequately, and, in the circumstances, the country – in the fickle, reflexive, peevish way of electorates that are not permanently addressed by a self-renewing leader like Franklin D. Roosevelt – was afflicted by an infelicitous combination of anger at the economy, ennui, resentment of Trudeau's hauteur, and briefly induced and renewed complacency about Quebec. They thought they could take the plunge. Trudeau was respected, but it was time to put him in his place. Clark was roughly treated by cartoonists, was still often referred to, after a *Toronto Star* headline from 1976, as "Joe Who?" and had lost his luggage on an overseas trip, but he was incidental; he wasn't Trudeau and needed only to clear the low hurdle of not being completely unsuitable. He cleared that; he was unspectacular but competent. Canadians were tired of their leader's churlishness and answered with churlishness of their own. On May 22, Canada strained its fortune but did not quite shatter it. The result of the election was (with 1974 results in brackets): Progressive Conservatives, 136 MPs and 35.9 per cent of the vote (95 MPs and 35.5 per cent); Liberals, 114 MPs and 40.1 per cent (141 MPs and 43.2 per cent); NDP, 26 MPs and 17.9 per cent (16 MPs and 15.4 per cent); Créditistes, 6 MPs and 4.6 per cent (11 MPs and 5.1 per cent). The Liberals led the popular vote by nearly five hundred thousand, and the Progressive Conservatives were seven seats short of a majority in an expanded House; it was not a very convincing mandate, and it wasn't really intended to be a mandate for Clark but a rap on the knuckles for his chief opponent.

The English-Canadian voters had made their point and instantly regretted it. Trudeau was gracious and philosophical, handed over at once, and wished his successor well. Clark too was gracious and began well. But there was something odd and not believable about this whole turn of events. It was as if the country had wanted to send Trudeau a message that he was dispensable and it was tired of his condescensions but wanted him to continue as prime minister, and it instantly resented Joe Clark for not being as formidable a leader as Trudeau was, even though the country knew that when it made the change. This was the season of multiple simultaneous choice: English Canada would dismiss Trudeau but still have him, and French Canada would have sovereignty and exchange embassies with the world and remain in association with Canada. It was a fantasy world that would quickly be reconciled to the facts.*

Trudeau had no interest at all in being leader of the Opposition. While Clark assembled his government and enjoyed a honeymoon of sorts, Trudeau went on a camping holiday in the Northwest Territories, and then to China and Tibet; he had always been an inveterate traveller, even when it was much less fashionable and comfortable. Clark was well-liked and appreciated for his courtesy and personal thoughtfulness, not his predecessor's strongest suits. The redoubtable John Crosbie of Newfoundland was the finance minister and Flora MacDonald the secretary of state for external affairs. Former senior merchant banker Michael Wilson was minister of international trade. Most of the cabinet were competent, and they were fresh faces after the Liberals, who had been clinging to the ministerial furniture since the time of Khrushchev, Kennedy, Pope John XXIII, and Harold Macmillan, and we were now in the era of Thatcher, John Paul II, and (almost) Reagan. But Clark was awkward on television, and he was only forty and didn't appear to be like a prime minister, though he did seem an estimable person who had come a long way by perseverance and the breaks. By October, polls showed the Liberals ahead and that, if there were an election, they would win. Clark, showing his inexperience and his background as a political insider and careerist, had little sense of the country or of his own vulnerability.

It was untimely, though not exactly premature, that at this point – in the midst of a tumultuous time he would have enjoyed, and further

---

* The author sensed the unreality of it and wrote Trudeau, quoting Cardinal Villeneuve's letter to Duplessis after the 1939 Quebec election: "Who is to say that the future does not reserve to you a return to office, and you would come back to it with the strength that adversity alone can give." He replied at once that "of all the roles I have ever played, none has been more delightful than my Duplessis to your Villeneuve." (This is cited only to illustrate the suspensive quality of the election result, even to me as no more than a somewhat informed and well-acquainted member of the public.)

confused – John Diefenbaker died, on August 16, a month short of eighty-four, and in his thirteenth consecutive term and fortieth year in Parliament. Clark, Trudeau, Stanfield, Lewis, and Tommy Douglas eulogized him generously.

Trudeau told an Ottawa constituency association on October 30, "We've got to throw the government out as soon as we can." But as he saw the polls, he assumed the NDP and Créditistes would not evict the government, and on November 21 he announced that he would retire as Liberal leader. Trudeau encouraged Donald Macdonald to run to succeed him, as he regarded Turner as disloyal. His political obituaries in English Canada were generally unflattering; they, like most of posterity to date, had no ability to evaluate the difference he had wrought in the Quebec equation. A Liberal leadership convention was fixed for Winnipeg on March 28. It would not be held; bombshells began falling like confetti.

Lévesque finally revealed the wording of the referendum question in early December. It would ask the voters of Quebec:

> The Government of Quebec has made public its proposal to negotiate a new agreement with the rest of Canada, based on the equality of nations; this agreement would enable Quebec to acquire the exclusive power to make its laws, levy its taxes and establish relations abroad – in other words, sovereignty – and at the same time to maintain with Canada an economic association including a common currency; any change in political status resulting from these negotiations will only be implemented with popular approval through another referendum; on these terms, do you give the Government of Quebec the mandate to negotiate the proposed agreement between Quebec and Canada?

It gave new breadth and meaning to the concept of *étapisme*. The voters were asked to allow Lévesque to try to negotiate the joys of independence while retaining the benefits of Confederation, with the obligation to bring anything agreed upon back to another referendum, or, if nothing could be agreed upon, to come back for an explicit secession vote. It was essentially a fraud, but with the federal Liberal Party going through a leadership change and the provincial Liberals being regrouped by Claude Ryan, who was about to release his own paper on constitutional change, and with a long time to prepare for the vote, it landed softly. The first polls showed the "no" vote about 10 points ahead of the "yes" vote, but a fierce campaign impended, and Trudeau let it be known that he would enter it as a private citizen.

The propensity of the other premiers to hide behind the skirts of Quebec while agitating for more was much in evidence. Newfoundland, as prosperity (from off-shore oil) hove into view for the first time in four hundred years, was now refusing jobs on offshore oil rigs to non-Newfoundlanders, and Alberta demanded a doubling of its oil revenues from Eastern Canada with no increase in volume of sales. Canada was already very decentralized without any devolution in Quebec, and Trudeau had only been gone for less than six months. Clark declared that he would govern "as if we had a majority." This was commendably purposeful, but in practice, with the polls where they were and so much in flux, it was impetuous.

On December 3, Gallup reported the Liberals leading the Progressive Conservatives by nearly 20 points. On December 10, John Turner announced he would not seek the succession to Trudeau; he knew Trudeau would put all his influence behind Macdonald, who would have the advantage of the support of the incumbent equivalent to that of St. Laurent over Gardiner in 1948, Pearson over Martin in 1958, and Trudeau over Winters in 1968 (chapters 7 and 8). On December 11, John Crosbie delivered the government's budget, his party's first since Donald Fleming's pre-electoral effort in 1962. In keeping with the Clark position that there would be no compromise due to the Conservatives' minority status, Crosbie introduced tax increases of nearly four billion dollars to cut the deficit in half within four years and, in particular, an eighteen-cent per gallon gasoline tax. Allan MacEachen, the Liberals' House leader and a very agile parliamentarian, told the Liberal caucus on December 12, after Trudeau had said the party had to fight the budget, that an all-out fight had to be waged against it. It was resolved to support a routine NDP motion against the budget. Trudeau casually eschewed any interest in rescinding his retirement.

MacEachen had already had the chief Opposition whip, Charles Turner, tell all Liberal caucus members to be present for the vote, and Lalonde, presumably at Trudeau's behest, routed two of the Quebec MPs out of their hospital beds to get them there, on the evening of December 13. MacEachen cancelled all vote pairing, except Serge Joyal's with Conservative Alvin Hamilton, who was in hospital. The numbers were tight: 136 Conservatives and 5 Créditistes, where the Liberals and NDP had 140, less one on each side for Hamilton and Joyal. But Flora MacDonald was on official business in Europe and Conservative MP Lloyd Crouse was on holiday in the South Pacific. If MacDonald could be got back and the Créditistes stayed in line and Joyal kept the pair, the vote would be 139–139 and the government would win, because the Speaker, James Jerome, though a Liberal, had researched the issue and discovered that the unbroken precedent was for the Speaker to sustain the government where, as in a budget, the issue would be revisited. Jerome told MacEachen when asked that he would honour the precedent. At this late point, the Progressive Conservatives showed their naïveté, and the only person in the entire Clark entourage who had the faintest idea of the danger they were in was Clark's capable legislative aide Nancy Jamieson, who warned a 9 a.m. strategy session that "I don't think we have the numbers." Apart from other factors, the Créditistes were wobbling, and the Liberals were in a position to make their lives easy or difficult electorally in Quebec. It was suddenly very serious, and by the time Flora MacDonald, who had been advised the night before by Clark's office that there was no need for her to return for the vote, was asked to return, all the flights westward across the Atlantic had departed, and no one thought to charter one, if there was even still time for that. The Clark inner circle still thought the Liberals were bluffing, and did not move to defer the vote as the Liberals would have done had the roles been reversed. They could probably still have done this on a snap procedural vote.

The Liberal faction that wanted Trudeau out, or especially wanted Donald Macdonald in (including Macdonald), was urging caution. But Trudeau smelt the blood of his enemies, and the whips were laid on with the vintage discipline of the party that had governed for forty-seven of the last fifty-eight years. The Créditistes, who had been in decline since the death of Caouette in 1976, abstained, Joyal honoured his pairing with Hamilton, and Flora MacDonald was not present; at 10:21 p.m. on December 13, the government was defeated 139 to 133, with the five abstentions. The prime minister called an election for February 18. But the game was over; the Liberals had a huge lead in the polls, and having sent Trudeau the message, the voters would now bring him back for an encore, and English Canada would unleash him on a Lévesque who, though well-travelled in Quebec politics, would still learn some painful lessons in the vagaries of transcontinental, bicultural politics. The magic thread held: just when it seemed that Lévesque might, with his two-referendum approach, smoke his spurious referendum question past Joe Clark and try to exploit Claude Ryan's muddled thoughts of special status, which he was about to present in his "Beige Paper," Trudeau reappeared like a Transylvanian vampire to terrorize the separatists. The predestined leader of the federalists would lead them in the referendum campaign after all.

There was a flurry of consultation within Liberal ranks, and many of the caucus members would have preferred someone other than Trudeau, but, again, not everyone grasped the tide of events and the legitimacy of continuity. Allan MacEachen did, and said it was unthinkable that anyone would lead the party but the leader it had, or that a new leader could be fairly chosen in the middle of a campaign. The party chairman, Alasdair Graham, had devised a system of regional conventions with ballots placed in sealed boxes that would all be opened together one month before the election. Trudeau seriously considered not coming back. But it was nonsense; of course he had to do it one more time. It was his apotheosis; he entered public life to promote a new federalism of bicultural equality; he was armed with public support reinforced by the satisfaction of the country that it was not being taken for granted; and his hour had come. It was so right artistically, it had to be right politically.

The election campaign was an anti-climax as the Conservatives complained about an unnecessary election, the NDP, now led by the amiable Oshawa MP Ed Broadbent, railed against a "harsh" budget, and the Liberals dismissed the Conservatives as incompetent skinflints with no support in Quebec and no ability to deal with Lévesque. On February 18, Trudeau welcomed Canada "to the eighties." The results (with 1979 results in brackets) were: Liberals, 147 MPs and 44.5 per cent of the vote (114 MPs and 40.1 per cent); Progressive Conservatives, 103 MPs and 32.5 per cent (136 MPs and 35.9 per cent); NDP, 32 MPs and 19.8 per cent (26 MPs and 17.9 per cent); Créditistes (who gained nothing for abstaining) elected no MPs and had only 1.7 per cent of the total vote (5 MPs elected and 4.6 per cent), and the picturesque aberration that began with Réal Caouette in 1962 was over. The Liberals took 74 out of 75 MPs from Quebec as they donned their battle armour for the referendum. Looking beyond the referendum, there were ominous portents, as the Liberals took only two MPs west of Manitoba. But for now, all was in place for the climax of the Trudeau era.

The referendum debate started early, as Lévesque put his enabling bill through the National Assembly and won the public debate with Ryan, who, though very intelligent, was always complicated in his exposition of anything, while Lévesque had never lost his old journalist's knack of packaging even the most complicated and passionately argued issues in simple terms. Trudeau missed his opportunity to legislate that no referendary result in any province would be taken seriously unless it was a clear question and was voted by a substantial majority. He was stuck with Lévesque's disingenuous insinuation of a question. Lévesque set referendum day for May 20. Trudeau entered the public argument on April 15 in the Throne Speech debate and gave a series of speeches at intervals. He sent the bare-knuckle bruiser Jean Chrétien, the eight-term MP from Shawinigan, Quebec, to be Ryan's co-leader of the "no" forces, though he himself was the real leader. Chrétien had for years argued the federalist case and the anti-Créditiste position unfailingly in the great circle of Quebec from Abitibi through the Lac-Saint-Jean area into the Lower North Shore and the Gaspé, where the urbane Trudeau-Marchand-Pelletier-Lalonde group rarely ventured, much less Ryan. In his opening blast, Trudeau began by ridiculing the referendum question and said on April 15 that association was out of the question, as the nine premiers of the other provinces had said they wouldn't have it, and that sovereignty was also impossible, as he had just won a heavy mandate, a thundering landslide in Quebec, to exercise sovereignty in Quebec and elsewhere.

On May 2, he told the Montreal Chamber of Commerce that the original separatists such as Pierre Bourgault had been honest men and independentists and that Lévesque and his colleagues were cowards and charlatans (in so many words), as they presented "a conditional and ambiguous question." On May 9, in Quebec City, he said that courage was with the "no" side, to stay in Canada and exact what "we" needed, not to barricade ourselves "within our walls." These were direct, hard blows against the PQ's chicanery and they stung Lévesque, who blew up on May 12 and played the race card: "Trudeau is naturally for the no, his middle name is English."[18] It was a sign that Lévesque had lost his judgment. Three days later, Trudeau replied at the Paul Sauvé Arena with one of the greatest speeches of his career. The crowd chanted "Ell-i-ott" for seven minutes before he began. Trudeau pointed out that the Elliotts had come to Quebec two hundred years before and that he was no less Québécois than Lévesque's ministers Pierre-Marc Johnson, Louis O'Neill, and Robert Burns, all French Canadian, and that this was the sort of division Quebec and Canada could never accept. He put it straight up to English Canada that a "no" vote would not be seen as an affirmation that everything was fine as it was; a negative referendum vote would lead to a new constitution in which Quebec would truly and fully participate.

On May 20, 1980, the "no" side won, 2,187,991 (59.56 per cent) to 1,485,852 (40.44 per cent), with an 85.6 per cent turnout. It was a solid victory for Trudeau and the federalists. Admittedly, almost half the French-speaking Quebeckers had voted "yes," but they had voted to authorize the government of Quebec to negotiate more powers for the province and then come back for another referendum, not to secede. More than half the French-speaking Quebeckers, and almost all the non-French, had not even voted for that, though their ranks were clearly expanded by Trudeau's promise to strengthen Confederation and reform the Constitution. It broke the momentum of the nationalist rise, as even on this soft question Lévesque had polled a smaller percentage than his party had won at the polls in 1976. The PQ claimed that it had carried the youth and so the future belonged to it, but young people tend to become more conservative as they grow older. Lévesque spoke of federalism having won "a reprieve," but it was a wan and sobered premier who spoke at the much-frequented Paul Sauvé Arena just five days after Trudeau had been there defending his mother's Scottish ancestry. Lévesque conceded graciously, as Trudeau accepted victory with exemplary taste and moderation. Joe Clark gave Trudeau great credit and had said in Shawinigan during the referendum campaign that "the Canada M. Lévesque wants to secede from no longer exists."[19] Trudeau said on May 21 in the House of Commons that he would begin at once a drive to constitutional reform. All the premiers, including Lévesque, came to Ottawa on June 9 for a preliminary conference, and a plenary conference to try to resolve the major issues was set for September 8 to 12. Trudeau made it clear that he considered the entire allocation of powers to be open and not just a discussion of what federal concessions there would be to the provinces. He was prepared to hold a national referendum if he could not secure agreement with the premiers. Having come this far and gone to the brink, he was not going to allow the opportunity for constructive change to slip away again.

6. Trudeau's Legacy: A Canadian Constitution at Last, 1980–1984

The September 8 opening of the First Ministers' Conference was rocky, as Newfoundland's abrasive Brian Peckford said his views conformed more closely to those of Lévesque than of Trudeau. This misjudged the mood of the country, as Trudeau had defeated Lévesque in the referendum and most Canadians felt that it was Trudeau's role and duty now to produce his promised constitutional reform and that he should be encouraged to do that. Trudeau again threatened, as he had intermittently since 1976, to hold a national referendum on patriation and go to London without any provincial accompaniment. If he was rebuffed there, he would consult the country on a unilateral declaration of sovereignty. When Manitoba's premier, Sterling Lyon, a tough, red-haired Conservative, said that if Trudeau did such a thing he would "tear up the country," Trudeau retorted that if the country was "torn apart because we bring back from Britain our own constitution after 115 years of Confederation and after more than fifty years of fruitless discussions, and because we ask for a Canadian charter of rights and most of you already have provincial charters, then the country deserves to be torn up."[20] He had the momentum and he had a mandate, in the post-referendum ambiance, to settle these issues, and, as he later wrote, "The time had come for Canada to choose to be or not to be."[21]

Trudeau's proposed charter would restrict the ability of provinces to infringe minority language rights, but to gain NDP support for it, he did concede further authority to the provinces over natural resources and allowed his charter protection of property rights to lapse. Trudeau's amending proposal was unanimity for two years, followed by the requirement of the Victoria amending formula for the approval of either five provinces representing more than half the population – but with the right for a province to opt out of an amendment in provincial areas, with compensation where applicable – or eight provinces with 80 per cent of the population, with a referendum to choose between those two alternatives. Premiers William Davis of Ontario and Richard Hatfield of New Brunswick agreed with Trudeau, but the Western premiers were virtually up in arms. Lévesque was playing it cagily, saying the great issue was now the economy ("People don't eat constitutions"[22]). There was no progress toward an agreement, and as soon as the First Ministers' Conference ended, Trudeau sent a ministerial delegation to London to begin discussions with the government of that country, now in the firm hands of Margaret Thatcher, for the passage to Canada of its Constitution.

The next step in the federal-provincial tug-of-war came on October 28, 1980, with Trudeau and energy minister Marc Lalonde's National Energy Program (NEP), a draconian assault on oil-rich Alberta. International events in the 1970s, following the Yom Kippur War of 1973 and the Arab boycott of most of the West, had spiked oil prices and conferred on Alberta economic muscle it had not had before. Trudeau objected to what he considered an inadequate share of the profits from that industry for the federal government and also saw the opportunity to emphasize the value of federalism in Eastern Canada by providing cheap oil in the areas which incidentally elected almost all of his MPs while slapping down the obdurately unappreciative Albertans. The NEP was unveiled with the budget, which foresaw a four-year, 25 per cent reduction of the federal deficit essentially by seizing a surcharge on oil production and prices. The NEP produced a blended price for Canadian oil averaging domestic and foreign oil and assuring what was assumed to be a rising price but not more than 85 per cent of the lower of imported oil or the U.S. price, and this subsidized price would be financed by a Petroleum Compensation Charge on refiners. The price of natural gas would rise less quickly than the oil price but would be subject to a new federal tax. There would also be a new 8 per cent petroleum and gas revenue tax on net, pre-royalty, operating gas and oil revenues, and depletion allowances were to be phased out and replaced by direct incentive payments designed to encourage exploration by Canadian companies on Canadian territory. The federal government share of production income would rise over three years from 10 per cent to 36 per cent, and the provincial share and producers' share would descend from 45 per cent each to, respectively, 36 and 28 per cent. There would be incentives offered to producers to encourage conservation and alternative energy sources, including extension of the natural gas distribution network through Quebec and the Atlantic provinces and a Canadian ownership levy to assist in gaining 50 per cent Canadian ownership of the industry by 1990.

The case could be made that the federal government was entitled to more than 10 per cent of the revenues of this industry, but this was not the way to make the case, and it was an outright declaration of war on Alberta and on the private sector of the oil industry, including the domestically controlled part of that sector. Given the delicate negotiations under way constitutionally, it was an astonishingly blunt instrument to apply to this subject, and one that was, as events would reveal, based on completely mistaken pricing assumptions. Alberta's formidable Progressive Conservative premier, Peter Lougheed (who ended the thirty-six-year Social Credit rule of his province in 1971), responded by reducing shipments to the East by 180,000 barrels a day, forcing the importation of more expensive foreign oil. Trudeau began a series of retreats with an agreement on September 1, 1981, by which Canada would go, over five years, to 75 per cent of the world oil price; the federal export tax on natural gas was eliminated; and, in the 1982 budget, the division of revenue between the federal government, provincial governments, and the industry went to 26, 37, and 37 per cent, respectively. The declared objectives of the NEP were defensible, but the extreme assault on Alberta as a punishment for good fortune and sensible government was an outrage. In 1983, Alberta had only one-fifth the national average in income growth, while unemployment almost tripled from 1981 to 1984, rising from 3.8 to 11.1 per cent, and in the same period business capital expenditures declined by 30 per cent.[23] No aspect of the ill-considered and abusively imposed program survived the next change of government.

On April 13, 1981, promising not to hold another referendum in the next term, Lévesque and the Parti Québécois were re-elected as the two-party system was effectively restored in Quebec. In a National Assembly expanded to 122 constituencies, Lévesque's Parti Québécois took 80 members (a gain of 9) on 49.3 per cent of the vote (up from 41.4 per cent). Claude Ryan's Liberal's had 42 elected legislators (a gain of 16) on 46.1 per cent of the vote (up by 12.3 per cent). The Union Nationale's leader, Rodrigue Biron, had defected to the PQ, and former federal MP Roch La Salle led the party to complete extinction and only 4 per cent of the vote. In the sharply formulated debate over the future of Quebec and Canada, there was no longer room for a middle ground between seekers of sovereignty and adherents to Confederation, beyond the sovereigntists' claims to "association" and the federalists' to "special status." Having clearly voted "no" in the referendum, Quebec seemed to be signalling that it did not wish to be seen as surrendering to the federalists. With the parties only three points apart in the popular vote, either side could easily win the next election, and there was no mandate to rock the boat constitutionally or to subscribe to whatever Trudeau might propose.

Just three days after the Quebec election, Lévesque joined with all the other premiers except Davis and Hatfield in what became known as the Gang of Eight to make a serious constitutional proposal to rebut Trudeau's claim, which he had been bellowing from the height of the parliamentary Peace Tower since 1976, that the provinces were trying to hold hostage any progress in bringing the Constitution to Canada and amending it in Canada so as to win a massive concession of federal powers. They proposed patriation of the British North America (BNA) Act to be the Constitution of Canada, without a charter of rights, and with amendment by agreement of at least seven provinces with at least 50 per cent of the total population, and with the right of individual provinces to opt out of amendments that reduced or infringed provincial powers. Quebec gave up its veto, a significant concession by Lévesque, though somewhat a symbolic one, given the right to opt out and Lévesque's continued professed determination to secede and renegotiate an association with Canada anyway. Trudeau rather sharply dismissed this proposal – though not without some insight into Lévesque's tactics – as amounting to the gradual disintegration of Canada, adding, with his characteristic talent at expressive derision, "A confederation of shopping centres is not my kind of Canada."[24] In fact, it would not have been a bad proposal if it had envisioned a consolidation and extension of provincial charters into Trudeau's long sought federal charter of rights.

Quebec, Manitoba, and Newfoundland all challenged the federal plan to patriate the Constitution without reference to the provinces, and the issue eventually went to the Supreme Court of Canada in 1981. The high court ruled that the proposed federal action did affect provincial rights and powers and that convention required substantial provincial consent, but that there was no legal prohibition against the federal Parliament asking Westminster to amend the BNA Act without the consent of the provinces. Like much else in Canadian federal affairs, it was ambiguous and was seen by all as a cautionary signal, and Trudeau pledged to give conciliation and negotiation one more try.

The federal and provincial leaders met on November 2. There was no progress, and as the conference seemed destined to break up, Trudeau suggested that patriation be agreed, because no one could possibly object to that, with two years allowed to sort out other differences, failing which the whole issue could be put to a referendum. He turned to Lévesque and said that Lévesque was the great plebiscitary democrat. "You can't be opposed to a referendum, or are you opposed to taking me on?" Trudeau asked. Lévesque took the bait and agreed spontaneously. Trudeau hailed it as a Quebec-Ottawa alliance and said, "The cat is among the pigeons." He spoke with authority; he was the cat. The seven other members of the fractured Gang of Eight were not prepared to fight a referendum on Trudeau's charter, and Lévesque retracted his acceptance. In the greatest day of his long career, Jean Chrétien persuaded Trudeau not to adjourn the conference and navigated between the disconcerted provincial delegations. With Ontario and Saskatchewan and Newfoundland officials, he produced a proposal that would give Trudeau his charter but with a right of provinces to nullify federal judicial interpretations that infringed their prerogatives. The amending formula of seven provinces with 50 per cent of the population was accepted, so there would be no veto for Quebec or Ontario, nor any compensation for provinces that opted out of federal programs in areas of provincial jurisdiction. (Lévesque had demanded compensation for opting out, and Trudeau had endorsed vetoes for Ontario and Quebec.) It was a considerable feat of swift negotiation by Chrétien.

Trudeau declined the proposal because of the provincial nullification right, which became known as the "notwithstanding clause," but Premier Davis telephoned him at 10:30 that evening and said that Ontario could not support the federal appeal to the British Parliament without this compromise. Trudeau feared that matters could plod on indefinitely until his term came to an end. He knew he could not drag this through another election, and was under no illusions about his ability to come back from yet another appointment with the voters for a fifth term. It was now or never, this or nothing, and he took the deal after layering in a five-year sunset on invocations of the notwithstanding clause and an exclusion for cultural minority rights. (Chrétien later prevailed upon Trudeau to agree to compensation when Quebec opted out in matters of education and culture – a posthumous win for Duplessis on the university grants issue, from three of his most vocal young adversaries, Trudeau, Lévesque, and Chrétien – and provincial control over immigrants' access to minority education in Quebec.)

This dramatic turn of events came as a shocking blow to Lévesque, who called it, in a reference to Hitler's massacre of some of his own SA Brownshirts in 1934, "the night of the long knives" and refused Trudeau's invitation to make it unanimous. Trudeau rather ungraciously blamed Chrétien for the notwithstanding clause, rather than crediting him with the redemption of his long battle for constitutional patriation, an amending formula, and a Canadian Charter of Rights and Freedoms. It was to Chrétien's further credit that he was saddened by the isolation of his native province, and at the end he and his provincial analogues as justice minister, Roy Romanow of Saskatchewan (NDP) and Roy McMurtry of Ontario (Progressive Conservative), earned Canada's gratitude for producing a decision and delivering the country from another round in the interminable constitutional charade. Their agreement was not complete, of course, but it was progress, and not just in constitutional terms.

Lévesque pleaded with his former colleagues in the Gang of Eight to "please give me back my right of veto" (though he didn't really need it with the notwithstanding clause). He does not deserve more than the nostalgic and comradely sympathy that Chrétien extended to him; he was not bargaining in good faith, and he was sleeping soundly in the complacent assurance of having helped derail yet another attempt to make Canada work when the deal was struck and it suddenly did work, as it always has, at the last and least probable extremity of events. The whole separatist game of *étapisme*, and of pretending to play the English-Canadian role of good-faith negotiation when they were just going through the motions and running out the clock, was discreditable. Queen Elizabeth proclaimed the new Constitution Act on April 17, 1982, on Parliament Hill in an elaborate public ceremony.

Lévesque limped out of Ottawa speaking darkly of the "incalculable consequences" of what he represented as the betrayal of Quebec. Canada was no longer risibly, in the eyes of its domestic and foreign skeptics, dependent on any other country even formally for ratification of its constitutional development, and Lévesque's effort to move like a fox among the sheep of the other premiers had been debunked. Trudeau had won, and it was a great victory for the country and the substantial fulfilment of what he had been recruited to federal politics and elevated to the headship of his party and the government to do. But it was his parting trumpet. The balance of his term was an anti-climax, as he devoted his last two years to the faddish hobby horses of his prolonged and comfortably idle youth.

In medical care, originally a provincial field, the Pearson government had put up half the funding to assist the provinces in adopting universal health-care systems. As these became steadily more expensive to operate, the federal share declined to less than a quarter of the total, but in 1984 Trudeau advised his health minister, Monique Bégin, to ignore the wishes of the provinces and doctors and ban extra billing, which then amounted to about $100 million a year. The result was that each year for about five years, Canada lost to emigration (almost all to the United States) more than half as many doctors as it graduated, which only made health care scarcer and more expensive. Canadians inexplicably became so preoccupied with health care that they convinced themselves that it was superior to the American system (and therefore likely the best in the world), and thus it became a raison d'être of the country as independent vis-à-vis the United States. It was superior to the American system in that it took better care of the lowest-earning 30 per cent of the population. But for the other 70 per cent, it was an inferior system, and was, in any case, a ludicrous explanation for the country's existence. By implacably and inflexibly opposing private medicine, Trudeau was abusing the federal government's position as a junior jurisdictional and financial partner in medical care and ensuring the increasing rationing of medical care in the unworthy names of uniformity of service and universality of benefit. By means-testing out those not in need of financial assistance and allowing private medicine to use hospital facilities out of hours and to bill opted-out patients, the progressive deterioration of the health-care system would have been avoided. Trudeau's influence in this area was negative.

Trudeau's last flourishes in foreign affairs were trendy nonsense: a "North–South" dialogue, as if there were the slightest legitimacy to examining development issues in that light; and a personal peace initiative, a completely fatuous enterprise. His peace initiative was unveiled on October 27, 1983, and consisted of proposals for a comprehensive ban on nuclear tests and the testing of high-altitude weapons, a five-nation conference on arms control, and a mechanism for enhancing consultations between NATO and the Warsaw Pact countries. As the sun set on his regime, Trudeau trundled himself around to the five original nuclear powers (Israel did not test or acknowledge that it possessed nuclear weapons) and to eighteen other capitals, including such epicentres of geopolitical influence as East Berlin and Bucharest, and made no headway at all. He had reduced military personnel by 20 per cent and military expenses as a percentage of GDP by 50 per cent. His plan was dismissed in Washington by a prominent commentator with the words "He doesn't have enough country for his ambitions,"[25] The ban on high-altitude weapons was directed against President Reagan's Strategic Defense Initiative (SDI), an entirely defensive, non-nuclear, space-based anti-missile defence system using laser technology. This was the project which, more than any other single policy or event, ended the Cold War satisfactorily and ushered in an era of increased international nuclear security and arms reductions, at least among the major powers.

Since Trudeau saw no moral distinction between the Soviet Union and the United States, wore Canada's founding and consistent Western Alliance status lightly, professed to believe that Roosevelt and Churchill had legitimized Soviet occupation of Eastern Europe (when in fact Stalin pledged democracy and independence for those countries), and developed the most exaggerated admiration for Fidel Castro and his retrograde totalitarian despotism in Cuba, it was not surprising that his peace initiative was a woolly neutralist proposal to talk up the status quo of mutually assured destruction and confer a completely unearned influence on third parties to the superpower rivalry. It was a sophomoric effort to give himself some imagined standing as a semi-neutralist. When Trudeau visited Cuba in 1976, Castro dragooned a crowd of 250,000 to cheer him, and Trudeau praised the new Siberian city of Norilsk, although it was built by victims of the Soviet Gulag and is one of the most polluted cities in the world. Trudeau had no sympathy for Soviet dissidents, and referred to Andrei Sakharov and Anatoly Sharansky as "hooligans." He happily gave Castro landing rights in Newfoundland in the transportation of Cuban soldiers to and from the Angolan Civil War, where they were Soviet mercenaries. Reagan's SDI threatened the Soviet Union with the substantial ineffectuality of its entire first-strike threat, and the inadequacy, for strategic purposes, of its consecration of between a third and a half of Soviet GDP to military strength, and began the entire implosion of the U.S.S.R. and of international communism, to Trudeau's astonishment and scarcely muted disappointment.

Trudeau did better with cultural policy, increasing support for the Canada Council by 13 per cent annually for the last decade of his time in office, and building the splendid new National Gallery and the imposing Canadian Museum of Civilization. For the national capital, he was an outstanding and munificent leader, greatly improving the quality of public buildings and cleaning up the tawdry cross-river city of Hull, Quebec. His efforts to regulate television cablecasting, Canadian content in licenced media, and foreign periodicals were not very successful, frequently unjust, and generally gamed by ingenious and politically connected licence-applicants.

Trudeau's economic record was poor. To some extent, he was the victim of macroeconomic events, and some of his heavy deficitory expenses were the result of his ultimately successful war on Quebec separatism, but they do not entirely, or even largely, excuse the fact that from 1968 to 1984 the federal accumulated debt rose from $19.4 to $194.4 billion (25.5 per cent of GDP to 43.2 per cent); unemployment rose from 4.5 per cent to

11.2 per cent; the annual budgetary deficit rose from 0.9 per cent of GDP to 8.3 per cent; and federal spending rose from 17 per cent to 24.2 per cent of an inflation-bloated GDP. Inflation, spurred by 15.5 per cent annual federal spending increases, was the highest among all developed nations over this period, and the Canadian dollar fell 17 per cent against the U.S. dollar, 47 per cent against the Japanese yen, and 68 per cent against the Deutschmark. He did not reduce poverty and as a percentage of the country's population annual immigration was reduced by half between 1968–1984. Like most people who have never run anything more challenging than a two-car funeral, Trudeau assumed that decreeing that things must happen, creating portentously named agencies and commissions in the French manner to accomplish complex tasks, and throwing money at problems would accomplish the desired results, and he left a flabby and top-heavy governmental infestation of superfluous meddlers and authoritarian interlopers irritating an unprecedented number and variety of Canadians at great ongoing cost to the country. Trudeau's Third Option, to promote economic relations with countries other than the United States, was a complete failure.

Trudeau had promised in 1980 when he came back from his briefly declared retirement that he would retire well before the end of another term, if he were elected to one. By the time he had traipsed around the world peddling his stillborn peace initiative, there was not a year to go · in the mandate. He had hung on by his fingernails in 1972 and come back only thanks to Joe Clark's lack of aptitude as a political leader in 1979, but now all indications showed that the country, if given the opportunity, would propel him at great velocity into retirement and posterity by the scruff of the neck and the small of the back. This was doubly the case because Clark had compounded his errors of 1979 and 1980 by calling a leadership vote at a party conference in January 1983 and declaring that he would call for a full leadership convention if he did not secure the support of 70 per cent of the delegates. He received the support of 66.9 per cent of those voting, after a hilarious campaign of competitive stuffing of instant and specially paid Conservative card-carrying members into the convention hall in Winnipeg.*

---

* The author underwrote the journey from northern Quebec of one busload of supporters of a leadership convention.

This would normally be quite enough support to carry on, and Clark was leading Trudeau in the polls, but he was caught by his unwise promise of a 70 per cent threshold, and at the ensuing convention in June, Brian Mulroney, the surviving runner-up from 1976 (as Wagner had died), edged past Clark and was selected leader of the Opposition on the fourth ballot, 1,584 votes to 1,325. The colourful Newfoundlander John Crosbie ran a strong third. Clark was a man of estimable qualities but had not been an effective leader, though he did defeat Trudeau. He remained in public life and would acquit himself with distinction in high office. Brian Mulroney (b. 1939), now forty-four, was the first really bilingual leader in the history of his party and the first to be intimately acquainted with Quebec politically. He had not stood for elective office but had been a respected labour lawyer and royal commissioner and head of a large mining company (Iron Ore Company of Canada), and he was a Progressive Conservative insider with twenty years' experience in the trenches and backrooms. He was young and presentable, was quickly elected in Nova Scotia in a constituency cleared for him, and presented a mortal threat to the Liberals. He was the first conservative to challenge the Liberal federal grip on Quebec since the death of Sir John A. Macdonald in 1891. It was clear after a few weeks in Parliament that he was a capable leader well formed in the Quebec tradition, *un chef.*

In all of the circumstances, Trudeau decided to take his leave, and he announced this decision on February 29, 1984. His was the most uneven performance in office of any Canadian prime minister. By all the traditional criteria of evaluation – quality of fiscal, economic, social, and foreign policy – Pierre Trudeau's record was mediocre, although he possessed great flair and remarkable qualities of leadership, and was often courageous, always formidable, and frequently eloquent and very witty. He was *un chef,* and everyone knew it. More important, the traditional method of evaluation that elevates Macdonald, Laurier, and King to the rank of great prime ministers, and St. Laurent to an only slightly less exalted category, is an unjust yardstick in Trudeau's case. He was called to public life and great public office in a national emergency to take on the task of dealing with a Quebec independentist problem that had been allowed to fester for fifteen years and had achieved very dangerous proportions before it was even dimly perceived by the Pearson government (and its implications were never remotely grasped by John Diefenbaker).

By early 1984, it was clear that the great separatist drive was blunted and in retreat. Robert Bourassa had been re-elected Quebec Liberal leader after the retirement of Claude Ryan and was leading in the polls. René Lévesque was a spent force. The country had a new Constitution with a Charter of Rights and Freedoms, which would have a very mixed impact on Canadian society but demonstrated that federalism was not as sclerotic as its nationalist Quebec critics had represented; the Conservatives had a completely bicultural Quebec leader and the federal government was pouring money into Quebec through the doors and windows while over a million English-Canadian schoolchildren outside Quebec studied French as a second language. French was available in the electronic media, was on packaging, and was used in federal government services everywhere in Canada. Canada had responded to Quebec's concerns constructively, and 60 per cent of Quebeckers had refused even to authorize their provincial government to try to negotiate new arrangements with the federal government.

In the great challenge and purpose of his political career, Trudeau had succeeded where no one else would have. Lévesque would have smeared and fleeced Stanfield and Clark, who could never have been able to bring the fiscal and intellectual artillery to bear on the problem that Trudeau did; nor could Trudeau's rivals for the succession to Pearson in 1968, with the possible exception of John Turner. Robert Winters and the others either knew nothing of the problem or, like Paul Martin, were *vieux jeu*, passé. John Turner knew Quebec well, spoke French fairly well, and would have approached the problem with originality, but it is hard to believe he would have been as fierce a defender of federalism as Trudeau, and he could not have pulled as much support among the Québécois. Trudeau's successors cleaned up the damage he inflicted in fiscal and social policy and foreign relations while retaining the benefit of what he achieved for national unity.

Trudeau had been the man of the longest and most dangerous hour the transcontinental, bicultural, parliamentary confederation has had, and he renovated the country's government and delivered it securely to his successors. He had grasped and conserved the magic thread of a distinctive Canadian state, founded by Champlain, shaped by Carleton, reformed by Baldwin and LaFontaine, brought to maturity by Macdonald and built upon by Laurier and King and Lapointe and St. Laurent and, in his syncopated way, Pearson. He had grasped and preserved the French-English double majority. Even though he rarely had a majority in English Canada, he usually did in Ontario, and in times of maximum tension he led the whole nation with courage, eloquence, and distinction. For all his foibles and lacunae, Pierre Trudeau must rank behind Macdonald, Laurier, and King, as, *sui generis*, one of Canada's great prime ministers.

7. Brian Mulroney and John Turner, 1984–1993

It was almost certain that John Turner would be the leader to succeed Trudeau, and their relations were poor; Turner was discreetly critical, and not unreasonably so, of many of Trudeau's policies, and Trudeau, somewhat unfairly, regarded Turner as insufficiently loyal, and there were allegedly some indiscretions about Margaret Trudeau's antics that aggravated relations. These factors may have contributed to Trudeau's delay until the Liberal Party could not hold a convention and have a new leader in place until the end of June. Jean Chrétien was Turner's chief rival for the leadership and gave it a rousing try, as was his practice, but Turner prevailed on the second ballot and was installed as prime minister on June 30.

This was a triple first for Canada, and in part a success for Trudeau and for the forces of conciliation in English Canada. Until this point, neither the Conservative nor the Liberal party had elevated a bilingual English-speaking Canadian to the leadership, and now both had, and it was the first time both parties had leaders competent to conduct political combat in Quebec since the 1887 to 1891 match-up between the young Laurier and the elderly Macdonald (who, though not bilingual, can be assumed, after nearly twenty-five years of government or joint government with Étienne Taché, George-Étienne Cartier, and other Quebeckers, to have known his way round the traps in Quebec quite well).

It was also a departure into uncharted waters for the federal Liberal Party. The Liberals had governed for sixty-six of the last eighty-eight years with only five leaders, all of whom were from unlikely backgrounds and had not run for the leadership of their party before. Edward Blake overruled Richard Cartwright's leadership advisory committee to make Wilfrid Laurier the Liberal leader in 1887, a bold step in those times of acute secular and cultural divisions (and Blake's greatest service to the country). When Laurier died in 1919, still the party leader, W.L. Mackenzie King, who was thirteen when Laurier took the leadership, was a defeated junior minister resident in the United States and working for Andrew Carnegie and John D. Rockefeller. When King retired the leadership, he passed it to Louis St. Laurent, who had never in nearly sixty years dreamt of entering public life and came straight in as wartime justice minister, Quebec lieutenant, and effectively deputy prime minister. As King left office and St. Laurent entered it, they drafted Lester Pearson, a career foreign service official, to become external affairs minister, and parachuted him into a safe parliamentary district he had never visited before, in Northern Ontario. They foresaw Pearson's succession to St. Laurent. Pearson drafted Trudeau – who, aged forty-six, had never been tempted by elective politics – immediately appointed him parliamentary secretary to the prime minister, and fifteen months later minister of justice, and eleven months after that helped install him as prime minister. Five party leaders in ninety-seven years. The Liberal Party of Canada was rivalled only by the Holy See among major international institutions for their original, unpredictable, and effective method of leadership selection (and, apart from King, made no claim to divine inspiration. The Holy See had had nine popes while the Liberal Party of Canada had just five leaders.) John Turner (b. 1929), a well-respected lawyer and company director who had been a distinguished justice and finance minister, had run third to Trudeau and Robert Winters in the 1968 Liberal leadership convention, and now, in a way the Liberal Party had never operated before, it was his turn. He should have taken advantage of his jump in the polls to recruit some excellent candidates, and he did round up a couple, and install them in the cabinet even without an election, as King had with General Andrew McNaughton. Trudeau had left Turner only a few months to make a mark before Parliament had to be dissolved, but Turner could have presented what would appear to be a new government, criss-crossed the country in July and August, called Parliament for September and put before it a solid program that would make the point that this wasn't just more of the same, and squired both the queen and Pope John Paul II around the country on long-scheduled visits. Turner had also promised, in writing, to make seventeen departing Trudeau patronage appointments, of which the most controversial was that of veteran minister and public appointee Bryce Mackasey as ambassador to Portugal, an arrangement memorably apostrophized by Mulroney as "No whore like an old whore." Turner should have told Trudeau to make his own appointments instead of being concerned that he could lose his majority in the House; he didn't have to call the House and could have won some by-elections. This made him appear to be bound hand and foot to Trudeau, which was anything but the truth. By dodging the bullet, Trudeau began the practice, which would be emulated, of government leaders ducking out at the end of their terms so successors could take the hit for them. It would be frustrating for electors.

Turner dissolved Parliament on July 9 for elections on September 4. It was a terrible mistake; he was rusty and was put on the defensive by Mulroney, and his campaign came apart like a storm-tossed ship. Mulroney was sharper and more aggressive in the debates, and it was clear as the election approached that the country was going to make a clean sweep of the Trudeau era. It was easy for the author, as a close friend for decades (and still) of both the principal party leaders (and they are both among those to whom this book is dedicated), to share in Brian Mulroney's rising tide of approbation and success, but painful to witness the grinding down of so good and capable a man as John Turner by an improvident weight of adversity. On September 4, the NDP won 30 seats and 18.8 per cent of the popular vote, a decline from the previous election of 2 MPs and 1 per cent. But between the two principal parties, the shift was the greatest in the history of Canadian elections up to this point: the Progressive Conservatives jumped from 32.5 to 50.03 per cent of the vote to win the first absolute majority since John Diefenbaker's in 1958, and before that King's in 1940; while the Liberals descended from 44.3 to 28 per cent, their all-time lowest percentage. The Liberals lost 107 MPs from the previous election to hold 40, and the PCs gained 108 to hold 211, the largest Canadian parliamentary caucus ever. Mulroney in Manicouagan, the county where he was born, Broadbent in Oshawa, and Turner in Vancouver Quadra (becoming only the second Canadian prime minister, after King, to represent three different provinces in Parliament*) were all elected personally. The change of government was on September 17. Joe Clark was in external affairs, John Crosbie at trade, and Michael Wilson in finance.

The electoral sea change would be completed less than fifteen months later with the Quebec election of December 2, 1985. René Lévesque saw the writing on the wall and retired as leader of the Parti Québécois on June 20, 1985, exhausted and disappointed, and on October 3 as premier of Quebec, handing over to Daniel Johnson's son Pierre-Marc, a lawyer and a doctor, as Robert Bourassa returned as leader of the Quebec Liberals. Lévesque had advocated not making sovereignty the main subject of the 1985 election and proposed instead the *beau risque* of a constructive engagement with Brian Mulroney, who was showing himself more flexible than Trudeau had been. Lévesque was repudiated by a sizeable section of his own party, and Johnson had even less time than Turner had had to prepare his party for an election. In the election, Bourassa, faithful to his role as a provincial emulator of the imperishable but unexciting Mackenzie King, was defeated personally, running in a constituency named after his former adversary from fifteen years before, the late premier Jean-Jacques Bertrand, but he carried the province to a third term as the Liberal vote rose from 46.1 per cent in 1980 to 56 per cent, and the Liberal members elected to the National Assembly rose from 42 to 99. The Péquiste totals declined from 49.3 per cent and 80 seats to 38.7 per cent and 23 seats. It was a sweet victory for Bourassa, but also for Mulroney and for Trudeau; the momentum of the twenty-year rise of separatism had been shattered and their founder was out of public life and their party divided. René Lévesque died two years later, in 1987, aged sixty-five. The Quebec Liberal Party now held all the old *rouges*, most of the old *bleus*, and almost all the non-French in Quebec.

If Trudeau's legacy was acknowledged in matters of national unity, it was, in other respects, something which required much of Mulroney's first term in office to dismantle. The Foreign Investment Review Agency

---

* King changed constituencies because he was defeated in his previous constituency. Turner changed constituencies because of redistribution and interim retirement. He was undefeated personally in eight elections.

was renamed Investment Canada and given a vastly reduced mandate; the National Energy Program was junked and replaced by accords with the Eastern provinces and Alberta that allowed for the fact that oil prices had declined to pre-1980s levels and that the entire premise of the NEP was false. Ed Clark, the surviving official who was chiefly responsible for it, was fired (although he went on to a very successful career as a senior bank executive).

Mulroney showed great agility holding his caucus together and generating a consensus for some ambitious policy initiatives, given that his party was the usual somewhat ramshackle coalition of a Progressive Conservative Party that had little of the discipline and tradition of power of its chief competitor and was a grouping of elements that did not have an unlimited amount in common with each other, aside from not being Liberals. There were the Toronto financial community, the smaller city and rural Ontario middle class, the Diefenbaker Prairie populists, the Alberta oil and ranching interests, the conservative but patronage-addicted Maritimers, and the resource industry and ecological blocs from British Columbia, and now a large bloc of Quebec nationalists who were spitting hate for Trudeau but had little in common with their fellow Tories in the parliamentary party of the government.

The Liberals, after twenty-one years of government, had a heavy majority in the Senate, and under Allan MacEachen, the parliamentary engineer of the debacle that befell the Clark government, there was a great deal of sophisticated and not easily visible obstruction of the government program. The Mulroney government privatized much of the Crown corporate sector, including Air Canada and Petro-Canada. The huge spending programs of the previous government saddled its successor with heavy obligations, and it was difficult to deal with the deficit, which generally increased in the Mulroney years. There were some spending cuts, but the government drew back from curtailing universality for the more well off after it came under withering attack from the heavy Canadian welfare lobby, which was motivated more by a fantasy about being more caring and compassionate than the United States than by concern for those who would pay more because they were wealthier. If Mulroney and finance minister Michael Wilson (who had a strong background in the securities industry in Toronto) wanted to attack the deficit on the spending side, this was the time and place to do it, by means-testing the beneficiaries of Canada's relatively ample welfare system and concentrating policy on delivering care to those of modest means who needed it and not on the ideological purity of a futile effort to assure equal health care for everyone, a chimera and not even one that is particularly desirable. They eventually seized upon the Goods and Services Tax (GST), midway between a conventional sales tax and a value-added tax, as a revenue earner, but were inviting both fiscal and political turbulence by cutting income taxes in advance of the next election, having announced the GST for after the election and not applying it at a rate sufficient to assure a real reprieve from chronic deficits. These continued to accrue, and ultimately reached the very worrisome total of $42 billion at the end of Mulroney's time, with a total national debt perilously close to 100 per cent of GDP and a dollar that was below 70 U.S. cents. The GST was, however, a brilliant policy initiative that enabled successor regimes of both major parties to rack up a world-leading record of deficit avoidance.

Despite the difficulties, Mulroney was not fiscally unsuccessful; he was digesting an inherited structural deficit, managing through tolerably well, and sweeping away most of the dreadful nonsense of the Trudeau era, such as the failed energy policy, but he was forced to scrimp and save in ways that got in the way of campaign promises and his own policy preferences. Brian Mulroney was a strong Alliance man and knew and admired the United States, the United Kingdom, and Canada's other principal associates in the Western Alliance, and unlike Trudeau got on well with, and was well-liked by, Ronald Reagan and Margaret Thatcher, both of whom were more than happy to see the back of Trudeau, and not because he was in the slightest effective at discountenancing them in policy terms, but because they found it painful to see Canada's leader conducting an absurd rodomontade on the world stage with the Soviet bloc.* Because of severe budgetary shortages, Mulroney had to forgo his expressed desire to strengthen the armed forces. He had planned to restore 60 per cent of the personnel reduction Trudeau had imposed, but the best he could do was to complete the deconstruction of Paul Hellyer's mad plan to impose a single uniform on the forces and to reequip them to some degree.

---

* Both told me so.

Over-fishing, which had gone on for many years, required the temporary shutdown of the cod-fishing industry. The government provided remedial programs but was unpopular throughout the Atlantic provinces for atoning for the excesses of a previous era. The Mulroney government had, if anything, a record of over-compliance in environmental matters, and signed both the biodiversity and global warming conventions, although assumptions about global warming were based on rather slender evidence. Where Reagan had dismissed Trudeau's concerns about acid rain as mere whining and carping, and his advisers told him that official Canadian films on the subject were just propaganda, Mulroney secured a useful agreement from Reagan.

In foreign policy generally, Mulroney was among the most successful leaders Canada has had. He came into office just as Ronald Reagan was swept back into the White House by one of the greatest pluralities in the country's history, carrying forty-nine states against his opponent, former vice president Walter F. Mondale. The American economy was booming, and the Western Alliance was being led by the formidable duo of Reagan and Thatcher, working closely with West German chancellor Helmut Kohl, and in the destabilization of international communism, with the Holy See under the strong and inspiriting leadership of the Polish pontiff John Paul II, a hero of his country's resistance to the German Nazi and the Soviet Communist occupations.

Mulroney was naturally pro-American and had been appalled by Trudeau's efforts to pretend that Canada had any vocation, will, or standing to pretend to occupy any middle ground in the Cold War. He further recognized, in exact contradiction of Trudeau's methods and leanings, that the only way for Canada to maximize its possible influence in the world was to be perceived as having considerable sway with the regime in Washington. He managed this, and developed the closest and most useful relations with Ronald Reagan and George H.W. Bush that any Canadian prime minister has had with any American president. King got on well with, and saw a lot of, Roosevelt, and did get quick agreement to the Hyde Park Declaration, which assured Canada would not be drained of its foreign reserves as a consequence of the Lend-Lease assistance to Britain and the Commonwealth in 1941 (Chapter 7). But King was a less relaxed and persuasive personality than Mulroney, and by the 1980s Canada was a good deal more substantial in the world and Mulroney had the talents of an ingenuous chameleon, in a good cause. And on the other side, the United States was in the front lines in the Cold War as it was not in early 1941, and Ronald Reagan and George Bush Sr. were much less enigmatic and devious personalities than the bonhomous but inscrutable and overpowering Roosevelt. It was soon well-known that, next to Thatcher, Mulroney was the foreign national leader that Reagan liked and respected more than any other, and as American power in the world, under the impulse of Reagan's immense military buildup and surging productivity and gross production boom, crested to its supreme historic point, that was a status that conferred considerable influence on Mulroney and on Canada.

Mulroney parlayed and levered his status with Reagan and Bush, who had been Reagan's vice president and would succeed him as president of the U.S., into a stronger position in the French-speaking world and in the Western Alliance than Canada had had before, either by virtue of indirect Kingsian lobbying, Pearsonian altruistic companionability, or renegadism of either the eccentric Diefenbaker variety or the nettlesome carping and posturing variety of Trudeau. Mulroney was not a blind follower; he opposed Reagan's support of anti-communist guerrillas in Central America, a policy which went awry and caused Reagan significant embarrassment in the Iran-Contra affair but did help bring the democratic rejection of the communist Sandinista regime in Nicaragua. Mulroney also crossed swords with Thatcher over sanctions against the apartheid regime of South Africa. She did "not see how we will make things better by making them worse," Mulroney told the author, but he was more concerned with sending a message to the non-white world of absolute hostility to racism. South African whites eventually jettisoned what Thatcher described as their "evil and repulsive" system of segregation, and it is doubtful that Canada affected the outcome or the timing, but Mulroney was certainly no mere camp follower.

On June 23, 1985, 268 Canadians (out of 329 fatalities) were killed on Air India flight 182 from Montreal to London, which was to fly on to New Delhi. The aircraft was blown up by a time bomb in Irish airspace at 31,000 feet and was the worst terrorist incident of recent times prior to the attacks on the World Trade Center and the Pentagon on

September 11, 2001. The national police and intelligence service, RCMP and CSIS, were both found to have been seriously deficient in ignoring warnings of possible Sikh violence against Indians and Indian interests.

The general attitude of the Mulroney government to human crises abroad and old grievances at home was an altruistic one. Canada responded more generously and effectively than almost any country to the great Ethiopian famine of 1983 to 1985, which killed millions of people. The Mulroney government gave $100 million to Japanese Canadians in an *ex gratia* settlement of the scandalous detention of twenty-three thousand Japanese Canadians in 1942 and the seizure and sale of their property. And it was consistently generous, if not overly successful, in trying to address the particular problems posed by native people in Canada.

As the end of the first Mulroney term approached, the prime minister put his policy and political eggs in three grand projects: the pursuit of free trade with the United States; the partial move from income taxes to consumption taxes as a means of addressing the deficit he had inherited; and an ambitious return to constitutional renewal and attempts to draw Quebec into constitutional arrangements that would end that province's isolation and effectively lay to rest for a long time the issue of its participation in Confederation. Attempting such a program established Mulroney as a leader of unusually large imagination, and the accomplishment of it all would make him a transformative figure.

Robert Bourassa had identified five principal requirements for Quebec to subscribe to the Canadian Constitution. At a 1987 meeting at Meech Lake in the Gatineau Hills near Ottawa, these points were recognized and modified to be recognition of Quebec as a "distinct society"; a constitutional veto for all provinces; resurrection of the right to financial compensation for provinces that opted out of any federal program in an exclusively provincial jurisdiction (Duplessis was still a ghost rider from the university grants imbroglio thirty years before, his position now unanimously endorsed); increased provincial powers in immigration; and provincial participation in the selection of senators and Supreme Court judges by reference to agreed lists of eligible nominees. Because the Meech Lake Accord was changing the Constitution amending formula (in a very unworkable way, as Prince Edward Island could veto a change), it required unanimous consent within three years.

As it was not even six years after the so-called night of the long knives, Meech Lake was premised on a fast-track healing of deep wounds. The Parti Québécois generally was still led by the hard-liners who had opposed Lévesque, and Johnson resigned and was replaced as PQ leader in early 1988 by former finance minister Jacques Parizeau, who opposed Meech Lake as an insufficient devolution for Quebec. The federal Liberals were divided between the Turner group, which supported Meech Lake, and the Trudeau loyalists, who considered it an unjust and unwise concession of authority to the provinces. The NDP supported Meech Lake, but the new Western group, the Reform Party, led by former Alberta premier Ernest Manning's son Preston, opposed it.

There were storm signals, but as the country progressed through an election year, support appeared to be holding, despite Pierre Trudeau's erupting into the accord ratification controversy with a newspaper article on May 27, 1987, entitled, "Say Goodbye to the Dream of One Canada." The former prime minister's views were well-known, and his response to the agreement was predictable, but the severity of his words was a surprise, and, objectively, to most of his admirers a disappointment. Trudeau accused Mulroney of having "sold out" to the provinces, denied that Quebec was any more distinct than many other places in Canada (which is nonsense), and claimed that "the federation was set to last a thousand years." (It wasn't.) "Alas," Trudeau wrote, "only one eventuality hadn't been foreseen: that one day the government of Canada would fall into the hands of a wimp [*"pleutre"*; "wimp" was his translation for the author]. It has now happened." There were problems with the unanimous consent required for amendment, which seemed excessive and impractical to many; and there were legitimate concerns about giving the provinces the level of influence envisioned in the selection of senators and Supreme Court justices, and enhancing the powers of the Senate. But for Trudeau to denounce Mulroney in such disdainful terms over such an important issue (whatever Mulroney's shortcomings, no sane person would call him a wimp, even in relation to Trudeau), and to claim that Quebec was, in St. Laurent's famous words, "a province like the others," and to equate any devolution of powers to the provinces almost with treason, was preposterous. Mulroney replied with harsh reflections on the notwithstanding clause, where Trudeau was certainly vulnerable, and the entire exchange that Trudeau precipitated was, to say the least, unedifying and unseemly. Better in all respects was the almost unheard-of statement of support for the Meech Lake Accord by that most knowledgeable of parties Her Britannic and Canadian Majesty Queen Elizabeth II, on October 23, 1987.

The big election issue was free trade, and here opinion was divided closely, but the opposition was split radically between the Liberals and the NDP. As the free trade issue became steadily hotter, the Progressive Conservatives gained relatively from being the only refuge for free-traders. It was a tough campaign; the Liberals this time were well-organized, and despite Chrétien's skirmishing in the under-growth against Turner, the Liberal leader led a number of polls during the campaign and Conservative advertising focused heavily on his credibility. In general, Turner fought his corner well and held his own in the debates, but the intensification of both the Liberal scare cam-paign on the dangers of free trade and the hedgehog defence the government conducted against non-believers in free trade, including some expansive claims for its benefits and a shabby exploitation of Turner's problems with the followers of Trudeau and Chrétien in his party, gave the Progressive Conservatives an advantage, as the NDP splintered the anti–free trade vote.

On November 21, 1988, the unlikely happened and all three party leaders did well in the general election. Mulroney's Progressive Conservatives lost 7 per cent in the popular vote and 38 MPs from 1984, but were re-elected with 169 constituencies and 43 per cent, and Mulroney became the first leader since St. Laurent to win two straight majorities, and the first Conservative leader since Macdonald to do so (Borden's re-election in 1917 having been at the head of a coalition). John Turner more than doubled his Liberal deputation, from 40 to 83, and raised the Liberal share of the total vote from 28 per cent to 31.9; and Ed Broadbent led the NDP to the best result in its history, raising the number of MPs to 43 with 20.4 per cent of the vote, up from 30 MPs and 18.8 per cent in 1984.

Most significant, Mulroney retained his pre-eminent position in Quebec. Subsequent events would deprive the Progressive Conserva-tives of that position, but the tribal tidal wave of support that the federal Liberals had had from that province – from Laurier's first election as prime minister in 1896 to Trudeau's last in 1980, broken only by the aberrant and mighty intervention of Maurice Duplessis and his Union Nationale war machine in 1958 – was over, and it has not returned. From here on, as long as there are just two other parties, the Conservatives and NDP, the Liberals have faced a more or less level playing field with an upward incline for them as they move west, and they have not enjoyed the easy formula for victory and natural government that resided in a lock on Quebec and the sole ability to say to Ontario and the rest of English Canada that only the Liberals could deliver the French Canadians to federalism (and to the Liberal Party). It had been a good run, and though hackneyed and overplayed at times, there had been some truth to the Liberals' claim regarding Quebec, and Laurier, King, Lapointe, St. Laurent, Pearson, and Trudeau had, on balance, brought the country a very long way forward through many crises over nearly a century. But it was over. Brian Mulroney had permanently changed the electoral equation in Canada, though on a delayed fuse, as it turned out, because internecine strains in his own swiftly assembled electoral coalition of 1984 would contribute to a one-party Liberal Indian summer.

The Supreme Court of Canada declared Quebec's language legislation unconstitutional insofar as it required unilingual commercial signs, and Bourassa invoked the notwithstanding clause and required that English words on commercial signs be not more than half the size of French words. The whole controversy was so picayune and squalid that it seriously alienated opinion in English Canada, and the consensus to resolve the remaining constitutional patriation issues gave way to a consensus not to make any more concessions to Quebec.

Brian Mulroney pressed on into 1989, trying to herd the Meech Lake Accord toward ratification in all the provincial legislatures and to negotiate free trade with the Americans while puzzling through how to get any final agreement past the Senate. The Goods and Services Tax had been adopted and would come into effect in the new year, and resentment at it, inflated by voter amnesia that income tax abatements had been announced as pre-emptive compensation for it, soon was audible. For the re-elected Mulroney, the wheels started to loosen and depart the axles quite soon after his impressive victory at the polls.

Meech Lake came under a steady crossfire of divergent criticism: to Trudeau's allegations of a sellout – taken up incongruously by redneck circles, especially in the West – and Quebec nationalist allegations that it was an inadequate recognition of Quebec's rights as a French country and of their reluctant participation in the whole Canadian idea, was added the populist fatuity that Canada was being remade by "eleven suits behind closed doors," supposedly unrepresentative and arrogant bourgeois fixers acting without authority, though all were elected to do what they were trying to do. Meech Lake became a symbol, a totem, for discontent, as the long deadline for ratification elapsed. Liberals Frank McKenna in New Brunswick and Clyde Wells in Newfoundland (the latter a disciple of Trudeau) won their elections and announced the revocation of their province's ratification of the Meech Lake Accord. This was almost entirely partisan, as they had nothing to complain about, and their role was raised above the marginal level only by the heavy price of unanimous provincial consent that had been laid on the whole project. This was the ultimate playing-out of the long-running game of the nine other provinces posturing as Union Jack– or Maple Leaf–swaddled pan-Canadians while Quebec extracted concessions from Ottawa. Then they instantly became a pudgy-faced children's choir of psalm-singers to the moral imperative of equal treatment of provinces.

It was a tactical mistake for Mulroney to have rallied the collegial backslapping solidarity of the brotherhood of the premiers for gaining approval of the Meech Lake provisions rather than working it out with Quebec and then dealing with the others. It was difficult to proceed in this way, given the power of Ontario and the benign way Davis and McMurtry had played their hand, but the whole ancient and hoary-headed bugbear of federal Liberal Party orthodoxy to the effect that all the provinces are identical jurisdictions makes the entire process submersible. Canada wasn't an agreement between four provinces; it was an agreement between the French- and English-speaking people of what became Canada, and they were initially grouped in four provinces, two of which had French minorities and one of which had an English-speaking minority. The Liberal Identikit fetishism of turning the issue from a one-to-one to a nine-to-one matter of agreement was intellectually unrigorous and tactically dangerous, and Mulroney, as most of the other nine provinces were in his party's hands, and he was building on a process begun by his Liberal predecessors, who had a different political compass, constructed his Meech Lake Accord, with the best and most assiduous will possible, on a foundation of sand.

Mulroney entrusted his final drive to adopt the Meech Lake Accord to the youthful Jean Charest (b. 1958), future Progressive Conservative federal leader and Liberal premier of Quebec, who at twenty-eight, when he was appointed minister of youth in 1986, was the youngest cabinet member in Canadian history. Charest padded around the crumbling edges of the consensus and made some peripheral concessions, but in doing so he broke open the greatest and most dangerous fissures. Lucien Bouchard, a university friend of Mulroney's and his ambassador to Paris, and now the environment minister after a strenuous by-election campaign in Chicoutimi, Quebec, became discouraged with his entire effort as federal official and MP. He resigned from the government and the Progressive Conservative Party and sat as an independent for a time, before setting up the Bloc Québécois with five renegade Conservatives and two renegade Liberals. It was a movement waiting for its time and would not have long to wait.

Another First Ministers' Conference was convened for June 3, 1990, less than three weeks before the expiry of the deadline for ratification of Meech Lake. A new accord was agreed after a week of intensive negotiations, though it was also agreed that there would be a further meeting to "clarify" the agreement, and there was a new commitment to Senate reform by July 1, 1995, including its transformation into an elected chamber and the conferral upon it of increased powers by the House of Commons. It was agreed that if unanimous agreement was not achieved in the time allowed, the Senate would have twenty-four Quebec members, eighteen Ontarians, four from Prince Edward Island, and the other seven provinces would have eight each. Further guaranties were layered in after the latest canvass of the ambitions of the premiers, for gender equality, the right of the territories to participate in naming senators and Supreme Court justices, and further discussions on Aboriginal issues, minority language rights, the admission of new provinces, and a revisitation of amending procedures (though it was hard to imagine how they would go beyond unanimous consent of the provinces, unless native people and sketchily populated territories were to have a veto as well). There was no end to the demands to be satisfied when it had to be unanimous and the deadline loomed.

Mulroney and most of the premiers had done their best, but in the Manitoba Legislature, MLA Elijah Harper raised objections as a native person. It was agreed to give Manitoba three more months, and this could be done because Bourassa had the votes to have the accord re-ratified by the National Assembly. But Clyde Wells and the Conservative Opposition leader in Newfoundland, Thomas Rideout, had pledged a free vote, and it now seemed that this would not be carried. It was absurd that such a measure would be derailed by one legislator in Manitoba and parliamentary niceties among the Newfies, but such was the extended vulnerability of this kind of discussion. The process was just too wide a circuit, and after each completion of the tour of necessary signatories, things had come unstuck and more concessions were needed. For want of a nail, a shoe, a horse, a battle, and the whole project went down. It was not a particularly good agreement anyway. Unanimity for amendment was nonsense; an elected Senate is probably nonsense, as the Commons will not really surrender it any rights and no serious person would go through an election to sit there. A Supreme Court chosen by one level of government from lists of eligible candidates selected by another level has many problems. All the placebos thrown to every conceivable constituency, down to gender rights, were best left to the regular statutes, not constitutional discussions. It was a well-motivated effort and a grand ambition of Mulroney's, but it couldn't fly, and his government was mortally wounded.

Even now, Mulroney fought on and sent out the former language commissioner Keith Spicer to canvass the country on constitutional matters, following which former prime minister Joe Clark, who had served capably as secretary of state for external affairs, became minister of constitutional affairs and helped arrange the Charlottetown Accord, in which all the provinces and territories and native peoples' organizations agreed on a new devolution of powers restricting federal spending powers and rights of reserve or disavowal of provincial legislation. The accord envisaged a "social charter" about Canada's supposedly defining social programs, a "Canada clause" defining the values of the country (a particular playpen for the platitudinous), and the Senate would be reduced in authority, with six senators for each province and one for each territory, but a double majority would be required in matters involving the French language; that is, an overall majority and also a majority among the primarily French-speaking members. This was a sharp turn from Meech Lake, which had an elected Senate of greater authority, and with provincial representation that conferred an enhanced status on Quebec and the smaller provinces.

The Charlottetown Accord could have been adopted by the parties to the negotiations, as all provinces ratified it, all three federal parties supported it, and all the governments of the provinces and their official oppositions, except the Parti Québécois led by Jacques Parizeau, supported it. Quebec, Alberta, and British Columbia had adopted laws requiring approval of constitutional amendments, and against Clark's advice Mulroney put it to a national referendum, which was held on October 26, 1992.

Opposition was led by Pierre Trudeau, who, in a speech delivered at the Montreal Chinese restaurant La Maison du Egg Roll, blasted the accord as the end of Canada; by Jacques Parizeau and the Parti Québécois and Lucien Bouchard and the Bloc Québécois, who were outright separatists and seekers of an independent Quebec; and, on the other side of the ledger, by Preston Manning and his Western-based Reform Party, which opposed bilingualism outside Quebec. Mulroney campaigned hard but rather aggressively, calling opponents of the accord "enemies of Canada," a difficult charge to make against Trudeau, however obstreperous he might be. Bourassa stood by the agreement but had taken to referring to "a uniquely sovereign Quebec in a Canadian common market" and heavily qualified his support of federalism, having invoked the notwithstanding clause and overridden the Supreme Court of Canada to reduce the language rights of the English in Quebec.

The turnout was 71.8 per cent on referendum day, and the country rejected the Charlottetown Accord 54.3 per cent to 45.7. The turnout was highest in Quebec, at 82 per cent, and that province rejected it 56.7 per cent to 43.3. British Columbia rejected it by 68.3 per cent. Newfoundland, Prince Edward Island, New Brunswick, by the barest margin Ontario, and the Northwest Territories, all approved, and all other jurisdictions opposed. It was the end of the line for constitutional agreement for a long time. The false starts and disappointments had revived sovereigntist fortunes in Quebec, and it now seemed likely that there would be another round on the referendum circuit before anything could be attempted.

Mulroney did succeed in completing a Free Trade Agreement with the United States, and by recourse to a special procedure for adding new senators he gained its adoption by the Senate. It was only supported by about half the people, but it was a signal accomplishment, and despite its fierce vocal opposition, the Liberal Party, when it had the opportunity in subsequent years, made no move to abolish or alter it. Nor, despite a frenzied and effective campaign against the perceived evils of the GST, did they roll that back. These were major achievements for Mulroney, but they stand in a better historic light than they did at the time they were put in place. With the departure in high dudgeon of the Quebec nationalists in Mulroney's ranks, there also came a full-scale grassroots revolt in the West, as Preston Manning's Reform Party railed against overindulgence of the Quebec that Parizeau and Bouchard wished to take right out of the country. There were many incidents that annoyed the West, but one of the turning points was the awarding of a fighter plane maintenance contract to a Montreal firm rather than the Winnipeg company that had held it and had been recommended by the Air Force and appeared to have the more competitive bid. It was a thin and ungrateful reward for the government that had dismantled the NEP, but Mulroney's long dalliance with constitutional agreement strained the patience of the voters, who tired of the issue in both directions, the Québécois and the anti-Québécois.

Brian Mulroney, who grasped passionately and knew intimately the dynamics of the French-English issue, had commendably set himself the very high goal of resolving a problem that had been, as Trudeau had said, the subject of fruitless negotiation for fifty years, and which Trudeau himself could not fully resolve, despite having won a clear mandate from the country three times to do so and having decisively won a referendum on the issue. John Turner had brought his party largely back from the brink of the point of no electoral return, but could not endlessly resist the opposition of Trudeau and Chrétien, and he made his gracious exit, an admired and well-liked politician of the highest dedication and integrity, who went in a few weeks in 1984 from being the man of the future to a man of the past, but who yet retained and will always deserve the respect of the country. He was one of the outstanding justice and finance ministers and Opposition leaders in Canada's history, and it is a misfortune that he could not await another election, which he certainly would have won.

He retired in 1990, and was replaced by the man he had defeated in 1984, Jean Chrétien (b. 1934), a veteran of twenty-six years in Parliament and a remarkable variety of cabinet positions, including external affairs, finance, justice, the Treasury Board, and, as it was in the late 1960s, Indian affairs. He was a strong and determined personality and an unalloyed and apparently ordinary man, which included having only a colloquial grasp of both official languages. He could not have been a greater contrast to his former chief, Trudeau, pillar of the bicultural Montreal socio-economic elite. Chrétien was plausibly challenged by Paul Martin Jr., who gave it a good try but was no match for the long history of service and bruising political combat that had been Chrétien's life for thirty years. (He had retired as an MP for most of Turner's time as Liberal leader, from 1985 to 1990.)

Mulroney had led the country with firmness and effectiveness in the Gulf War, and Canada was in combat in the air in assisting the immense alliance led by President George H.W. Bush in the move to expel Iraq's Saddam Hussein from Kuwait, which he had simply seized, in 1990. The war ended after only a few days of fighting, and the Iraqis were completely routed by the overwhelming might of the American-led coalition. Mulroney also showed great agility in transforming an Open Skies meeting in Ottawa in 1990, where the free access to aerial reconnaissance that had first been proposed by President Eisenhower at Geneva in 1955 came to full fruition, and the meeting focused on the smaller group of the two Germanys and the four postwar occupying powers and terms were swiftly agreed for the reunification of Germany. It was effectively the end of the Cold War; it happened in Canada, and Canada's leader played a valuable role in it. It closed admirably the chapter opened by the First Canadian Army's penetration of Germany in the final campaign in the West in 1945.

Buffeted suddenly and harshly by events, Mulroney followed the example of Trudeau and Lévesque and dodged the electoral bullet intended for himself and announced his retirement as Progressive Conservative leader and prime minister in February 1993. Kim Campbell (b. 1947), the defence minister, and Jean Charest, now minister of science and technology, and still startlingly young at thirty-five (Campbell was only forty-three and Mulroney only fifty-three), were the chief contenders to replace him. Manning was vacuuming up votes in the West and Bouchard had gutted Mulroney's Quebec support, so the task ahead of either contender would be a daunting one. Campbell prevailed, was installed as prime minister on June 25 with only a few months left in the term, and soon called an election for October 25. Chrétien's well-organized Liberals, the Trudeau-Turner schism interred in the deep earth of prospective victory, were the clear favourites, facing a severely divided range of regional and sectional parties (from right to left, Reform, Progressive Conservative, NDP, Bloc Québécois; from east to west, Progressive Conservative, Bloc Québécois, NDP, Reform).

On October 25, 1993, there came the most dramatic realignment of political preferences in any single federal election. Back as solid as ever as the most durably successful political party in the Western democratic world were Jean Chrétien's Liberals, who gained 94 MPs and 9.3 per cent of the popular vote from 1988 to win a solid majority with 177 MPs representing 41.2 per cent of the electorate. Their opponents were very radically and conveniently divided: the Bloc Québécois had 54 MPs and 13.5 per cent of the vote (in 1988, 10 MPs); Reform had 52 MPs and 18.7 per cent (in 1988, 1 MP and 2.1 per cent); the NDP fell from 43 MPs and 20.4 per cent of the vote in 1988 to 9 MPs and 6.9 per cent; and the governing Progressive Conservatives lost all but 2 of their seats and fell to 16 per cent after having had 169 MPs in 1988 and 43 per cent. The prime minister was defeated personally, and her next official position was as Chrétien's consul general in Los Angeles. Jean Charest, who was re-elected in Sherbrooke, succeeded Campbell as head of the battered remnant of the Progressive Conservatives.

Thus, the former pieces of the great Mulroney coalition, the Progressive Conservatives, the Bloc Québécois, and Reform combined, had a formidable 48.2 per cent of the vote. It was an absurd state of affairs: the official federal Opposition was a provincial separatist party, and Reform and the Progressive Conservatives would have to compose their differences and re-amalgamate, and when they did, the Bloc Québécois would hold most of the balance of power between the Conservatives and the Liberals, unless the NDP could subsume the Bloc in Quebec.

Brian Mulroney was not popular as he left office, but he had been a capable leader who had repaired all the damage Trudeau had done in the Western Alliance, and importantly repositioned the country in economic and fiscal terms. The share of Canada's GDP generated by trade with the United States increased from 25 to almost 45 per cent, but Canada did compete and did not become a "fifty-first state," and the total gradually receded as China and India, representing nearly 40 per cent of the world's population, became steadily committed to economic growth and became important markets for Canada. Free Trade was a success, and as economic growth returned to Canada, the use of the GST became more evidently a wise move that permitted Canadian income tax rates to subside. Mulroney had grated on his countrymen with what was seen as his hyperbole and his somewhat contrived optimism. And his term ended on an unhappy note, with his record clouded by the fragmentation that afflicted his party for the following decade. His retirement would be disturbed by unsubstantiated reflections on his probity, though his judgment was open to some question (especially in temporarily accepting $300,000 in cash shortly after he retired, which he refunded, from a dubious financial and political adventurer who was ultimately extradited back to a lengthy prison sentence in Germany). But his record in office was impressive.

Brian Mulroney had understood as well as any Canadian leader in history the implications of the English-French double majority, but in trying to complete Trudeau's quest for a new constitution and the reintegration of Quebec into a more bicultural Canada, at least officially, he had gradually stretched the tent of national conciliation farther and tighter, from Quebec nationalists to Western assimilationists, until it tore. Canada was founded as a country of two official languages and founding groups, but the exigencies of constitutional discussion amplified the insidious process of the other provinces piggybacking on concessions made to Quebec because of its special status. And the result, at Meech Lake and Charlottetown, was first a fragile agreement and then an unsatisfactory one. These attempts at constitutional renewal did not deserve Trudeau's strictures, but a constitutional veto for every province will not work, and is not needed where opting out is provided in provincial fields, and the spectacle of the eleven government leaders pandering to women's and native and territorial and welfare rights, and to other groups, is not ultimately credible. These are statutory and not constitutional fields. Trying to reconcile official

French–English equality with the artificial preoccupation of equal treatment of provinces and unofficial segments of society made it an attempt to square a circle. The fundamental rights of founding peoples became confused with the jurisdictional ambitions of transitory and not always very disinterested provincial officials and interest groups. This was the problem that Trudeau so dramatically attacked at Pearson's Federal-Provincial Conference in 1968.

Mulroney was aware that he was taking a chance; it was his version of what Lévesque called the *beau risque* when Lévesque chose to try to make an agreement with Mulroney in 1985. In risking his government and his party for this elusive goal, Mulroney approached in patriotic devotion the service of Laurier when he accepted the division of the Liberal Party and defeat in the 1917 election to avoid the complete isolation of Quebec or the reduction of the Liberals to an exclusively French-Canadian party. When Bourassa affronted the Supreme Court of Canada and the non-French, who provided about 40 per cent of the Quebec Liberals' support, by invoking the notwithstanding clause against the English language in Quebec, he deprived Mulroney of his English majority, as they drew the line at further concessions to a government, a province, and a people that appeared to be accepting pre-emptive concessions from the majority while intensifying the cultural oppression of English-speaking Quebeckers, who technically had less freedom of expression, at least in commercial matters and access to government services, than much smaller French-speaking communities in English-speaking provinces.

The English-speaking minority in Quebec had for 230 years been exercising rights that were now being abridged, and were a large and strong segment of the Quebec population and the local linguistic representatives of 70 per cent of Canadians and 95 per cent of North Americans north of Mexico. The speed and unapologetic brusqueness with which Bourassa invoked the notwithstanding clause did maximum damage to Mulroney's English language support, and the Reform Party in the West and the Liberal Party in Ontario surged in strength. When Mulroney was then unable to deliver Canada to ratification of Meech Lake, the Quebec nationalists deserted the federal Progressive Conservatives for Bouchard, as they had deserted Jean-Jacques Bertrand for Lévesque in 1970. If Mulroney had remained and fought the hopeless battle as

Laurier had in 1917, he would have salvaged more in Quebec and Ontario than Campbell did, but Alberta was going to be a long-term problem. In the violent disintegration of the federal Conservatives that ensued, Mulroney tasted the hemlock offered to those who make the supreme effort for a good and long-sought cause that is not quite attainable.

He, his party, and the country paid a high price for his avoiding the Trudeau policy of demarcated confrontation, and the King policy of creative evasion. He tried, he lost, and he paid for it, but he deserves the credit at least for a brave and imaginative effort to solve a very difficult, long-festering, and dangerous problem by shoring up national unity with durable constitutional arrangements. Though it ended in rancorous schism and rejection, he had been a skilful political leader who had governed with vision and talent, and he was an important, and in most respects a successful, prime minister. He must rank with St. Laurent and a very few others just behind the country's ablest leaders. Brian Mulroney, John Turner, and Joe Clark left Parliament together; all had contributed importantly to Canadian public life and deserved a greater taste of public respect and gratitude than they, for a time, received. Kim Campbell in other circumstances might have been a passable leader, and she too deserved better than the absurdly immense defeat she suffered.

For the time being, Chrétien had a clear sail and his opposition was the Parti Québécois, which seemed to be on the rise again after the effective mutual rejection of Quebec and English Canada. For the PQ, it was an attempt to raise a fallen separatist soufflé; but it might have been possible to capitalize briefly on the anger of disappointment and rejection, the rage of quarrelling spouses, before realities asserted themselves. Where in 1980 the Quebec nationalists had had the sense that they were invincible and on a permanent rise, they were now recoiling from finding that English Canada, contrary to one of the holiest tenets of the separatist canon, had drawn the line and would not retreat, challenging Quebec to be less demanding or see what the exploration of alternatives to continued participation in Canada really entailed. The decades of fire-breathing oratory, dire threats, and vivid dreams were rudely interrupted by a unilingual shout, in English, to put up or shut up. In the Charlottetown process, the entire political class of Canada had been rejected; the love of the jurisdictional carve-up had so entranced the participants that they got away from their popular underpinnings and cantilevered themselves out over an abyss.

Quebec was angry enough to hold a suspenseful referendum, but the separatists did not have the élan, the exaltation of soul, of the original Lévesque movement. The ambiance of Quebec nationalists had been diluted by disillusionment, some of it of a startlingly tawdry nature. The supreme architect of the advance of Quebec separatism for nearly twenty years, under Lesage, Johnson (*père*), and Lévesque, had been Claude Morin, who had retired as intergovernmental affairs minister in 1982. It was revealed in 1992 that he had been in the pay of the RCMP from 1974 to 1977 (most of which time he was out of office). He had been a very articulate and persuasive advocate of the independentist cause, and the revelation that he was a federalist mole of ambiguous views and defective financial probity was a very demoralizing blow to the militant Péquistes. In place of the joy of creative idealism, there was the anger of spite and rejection; it would be much more difficult to sell that as the shining future, especially with this humdrum cast. Bourassa, Parizeau, and Chrétien were *vieux jeu*, and were an unlikely trio to bring this issue back to the boil. Lucien Bouchard, now the leader of the federal Opposition, but more importantly of the separatist avant-garde, was the man to watch. The political ground was shifting underfoot, impairing everyone's balance, yet again.

8. Jean Chrétien and Lucien Bouchard, 1993–2000

Just eleven weeks after the federal electoral watershed of October 26, 1993, Robert Bourassa followed the example of Trudeau, Lévesque, and Mulroney, and made way for someone else to finish his term and take the fall that the electorate appeared to have in mind for his government. Daniel Johnson Jr., Bourassa's head of the Treasury Board, was elected to succeed him, making the Johnsons the only family in Canadian history to provide three provincial premiers. Bourassa had retired for good, and would die of cancer two years later, aged sixty-three. He had never been excessively popular and was not a strong man or an electrifying leader, but he had been an astute and capable premier whose efforts were devoted altogether to political longevity. He was a skilful political whitewater canoeist, and an unusually intelligent and charming man personally, even by the high convivial standards of most French-Canadian politicians.

The first eight months of 1994 were a run-up to a general election in Quebec, and Parizeau made it clear at every opportunity that he would quickly hold a referendum on separation and independence. A great many Quebeckers, and not only the nationalists, were now spoiling for a fight. In Quebec, it was widely felt that the province had made a great many concessions to get a constitutional agreement and had been rebuffed and insulted, and that its language laws were no legitimate concern of any other province. Underlying it was the fear that the ability of Quebec to threaten acute discomfort to the country as a whole was under threat, something that could not be frittered away or allowed to slip from Quebec's hands without a fight. Chrétien was a much less esteemed figure in Quebec than Trudeau, who was universally respected as a leader and a cultured and forceful personality, or Mulroney, who was admired and popular as an English-speaking Quebecker who was completely bilingual and had, as a federalist, done his best for his native province. Chrétien was respected as a tough and plain and unpretentious man, but not as a cultured francophone or as someone who could command respect by his demeanour and intellectual attainments, as Laurier, Lapointe, St. Laurent, Trudeau, and a number of Quebec's premiers had. He was a fierce fighter for federalism, but for an educated man he had an unfeasible accent and vocabulary in French, and his English was not really adequate for the head of a mainly English-speaking country though his malapropisms were often endearing. He was, however, very experienced and determined, capable of great political courage, and was a sly operator who knew the middle and working classes. It was easy, but unwise, to underestimate him.

Quebec voted on September 12, 1994. Polls indicated that Parizeau and the Parti Québécois would win, but not by a wide margin, and it was not clear that enthusiasm for independence had spiked appreciably. The polls were right, though the margin not as narrow as expected (previous election results in brackets): the Parti Québécois had 77 members of the National Assembly on 44.8 per cent of the

vote (29 MNAs and 40.2 per cent); the Liberals had 47 MNAs on
44.4 per cent (92 MNAs and 50 per cent); and Action Démocratique
du Québec, a new party trying the old formula of nationalist but not
separatist, had 1 MNA and 6.5 per cent of the vote. Parizeau had certainly won the election, but it was not clear that Quebec was in any
great hurry to secede, however aggravated it might be by the constitutional roller coaster. Jacques Parizeau, unlike Lévesque, was not an
exciting leader for a movement that had such a heavy requirement
for panache and the *esprit de corps* of self-liberation. He was an academic economist and senior civil servant who spoke English with an
English accent, but unlike Lévesque, the twitching, benighted little
man of the people, Parizeau was a Molièresque haut bourgeois who
refined to new levels of self-importance the perquisites of a minister in
a camel hair overcoat (usually without his arms in the sleeves) being
conveyed in a Citroën DS with Duplessis's flag fluttering on the fender
to a three-martini lunch in a five-star restaurant. Ample, florid, and
luxuriantly moustachioed, Parizeau was an intelligent man but no
great popular tribune, and slightly difficult to take seriously.

For Jean Chrétien, the world had come along very agreeably: after
thirty-one years in Parliament and almost every major cabinet position,
disparaged in early years by the Conservatives as "the guy who drove
the getaway car" (as Dalton Camp put it), frequently condescended to
by Trudeau and his intellectual or at least metropolitan claque, defeated
by Turner, he was now at the head of the most numerous caucus the
Liberals had had, except for St. Laurent in 1949 and King in 1940, and
was facing a clear horizon of certain victory over a pulverized and atom-
ized opposition led by a rag-tag of unserviceable regionalists. There
were three problems: Quebec was angry and unpredictable; the Liberal
platform (the Red Book) had called for abolition of the GST and withdrawal from the Free Trade Agreement with the United States, which
were clearly not good promises to act on; and the deficit built up by
Trudeau, and which Mulroney had been unable to reduce, was a threat
that was causing problems with interest rates, bond sales, and the value
of the dollar. Mulroney had put the emphasis on fighting inflation and
approved Bank of Canada governor John Crow's high interest rate
policy to discourage borrowing and suppress demand. This was damaging to government interest rate costs and tax revenues, and the deficit

ballooned to $42 billion in Mulroney's last year. Having promised to fire Crow in the election campaign, Chrétien did so and replaced him with the more expansionist Gordon Thiessen. Chrétien's convention opponent, Paul Martin, was the minister of finance and proved very capable. After an indecisive 1994 budget that stirred no confidence and appeased no constituencies, Martin, restrained only slightly by Chrétien, imposed a hair-shirted deficit-reduction budget in 1995, promising a $25-billion deficit cut in three years. Every department except Indian and Northern Affairs (one of the eight ministries Chrétien had held personally) was slashed, and $7 billion was sliced out of transfer payments (mainly to Quebec) with no concession of increased taxing jurisdiction. These payments, especially in consideration of health, welfare, and education, would henceforth be block grants that the provinces could prorate and spend as they wished, but it was a straight transfer of spending responsibility to the provinces with no revenue enhancements. (The most frequent provincial response was to lay the same expenses on the municipalities and invite them to raise local taxes to pay for it. It created great pressures on lower levels of government, but they didn't control the money supply, and the effect on interest rates, the federal deficit, and the value of the dollar was uniformly positive. Martin also cut 45,000 civil service jobs, 14 per cent of the total number of federal government employees, the $560-million Crow rate subsidy for the shipping of agricultural produce was eliminated, and he raised gasoline and aviation fuel taxes to bring in $1.3 billion per year. It was heavy going, and a much harsher dose of austerity than what Trudeau and MacEachen and Chrétien had thrown Joe Clark and John Crosbie out for in 1979, but it worked, and it was one of the more courageous state initiatives of recent years, along with Free Trade and the GST.

Apart from ignoring the horrifying Rwanda genocide of 1994, which took nearly a million lives and which the Canadian government was well informed of – and for which Canada would apologize to the Rwandan survivors in 2000 – little happened in Chrétien's first two years and he rather complacently awaited events in Quebec. Before the referendum campaign began, all polls showed that a sovereignty vote would fail. The federal government had no strategy, and Daniel Johnson was not a strong or aggressive Liberal leader within Quebec. Chrétien relied on the completely unqualified public works minister,

Alfonso Gagliano, to advise the cabinet of his desultory polling and lethargic preparations. On June 12, 1995, Parizeau, Bouchard, and Action Démocratique (ADQ) leader Mario Dumont supported and signed an agreement on the desirability of common political and economic institutions with the rest of Canada. The Reform Party's shadow minister for federal-provincial matters, future prime minister Stephen Harper, declared that his party and Western Canada, which his party represented, had no interest in any such arrangements.

Parizeau announced the referendum question on September 7, calling the vote for October 30. The question was "Do you agree that Quebec should become sovereign after having made a formal offer to Canada for a new economic and political partnership within the scope of the bill respecting the future of Quebec and of the agreement signed on June 12, 1995?" The bill and the agreement were the updated successors of Lévesque's wheeze of fifteen years before about sovereignty-association. A "yes" vote was an authorization to work out something better for Quebec, but the sucker punch was that if Ottawa didn't agree to whatever Quebec was offering, the government of Quebec would declare its independence and purport to be independent. Confident that the sovereigntists were going nowhere, Chrétien and his inner circle sat on their hands and had no contingency plans if things heated up. Given what was at stake, it was an attitude of negligent passivity.

Quebec had never, and did not in the future, take to Jean Chrétien with any enthusiasm, and he was not a strong or instinctively well-endowed leader for this kind of battle. It was fairly tranquil for a few weeks, and then the discouragement of the angry "yes" committee in Quebec caused a putsch: Lucien Bouchard was named negotiator-in-chief for Quebec in the event of a victory, which put him in charge of the campaign, and Parizeau was effectively emasculated and sacked.

Lucien Bouchard, Mulroney's university chum, who had broken bitterly with him after Meech Lake, was a brilliant and passionate man who immediately electrified the campaign. He had recently had a near-death encounter with a freakish flesh-eating bacterial infection that cost him the amputation of a leg, and he embarked on the last three weeks of the "yes" campaign across Quebec with a great reservoir of

38. Duplessis campaigning in 1952 with all-time French-Canadian hockey hero Maurice "Rocket" Richard.

39. Eight-term Montreal mayor Camillien Houde (1889–1958) and the popular and electrifying archbishop of Montreal Paul-Émile Cardinal Léger (1904–1991), in 1954.

40. René Lévesque interviewing External Affairs secretary Lester Pearson in Moscow in 1955.

41. U.S. president John F. Kennedy, Governor General Georges-P. Vanier, Prime Minister John Diefenbaker, and Mrs. Kennedy and Mrs. Diefenbaker in front of Rideau Hall in Ottawa in 1961. Kennedy (correctly) could not believe that this erratic leader represented sensible Canadian opinion.

42. Pierre Trudeau, John Turner, Jean Chrétien, and Lester Pearson, 1967. All would be prime ministers and between them they led the federal Liberal Party from 1958 to 2003, thirty of those years as prime minister.

43. Biculturalism Royal Commissioners André Laurendeau, editor of *Le Devoir* and former politician, and university president and former CBC head Davidson Dunton said Canada was facing its greatest crisis.

44. Quebec premier Johnson recruited French president de Gaulle to assist him in his jurisdictional contest with Ottawa. He got more than he bargained for. De Gaulle came to Quebec in 1967 and urged it to secede.

45. Pearson, Trudeau, Paul Martin, and Premier Daniel Johnson at the end of Pearson's last federal-provincial conference, in early 1968, where Trudeau and Johnson clashed sharply. The battle lines between Quebec and Ottawa were drawn and the skirmishing was intensifying.

46. Prime Minister Trudeau, followed by Quebec premier Robert Bourassa (far right), leaving the funeral of Quebec Labour minister Pierre Laporte in October 1970, after the murder of Laporte by the Front de Libération du Quebec.

47. Chinese leader Deng Xiao-ping receives Pierre Trudeau and his young wife, Margaret (behind). Trudeau had long been interested in China and opened relations with the People's Republic in 1971.

48. Fidel Castro greets Margaret and Pierre Trudeau in Havana. Trudeau lavished altogether unjustified attention on secondary Communist leaders, and Fidel responded by whistling out an immense crowd of well-wishers to greet him.

49. British prime minister Margaret Thatcher, U.S. president Ronald Reagan, Brian Mulroney, and West German chancellor Helmut Kohl at a G-7 meeting. Mulroney got on well with all of them and they were all seminal leaders of their countries. Mulroney contributed valuably to the successful end of the Cold War and helped transform an Open Skies summit meeting in Ottawa in 1991 into a meeting between the two Germanys and the four occupying powers to discuss and agree the reunification of Germany.

50. Lucien Bouchard stares skeptically as leader of the federal Opposition at Prime Minister Jean Chrétien in Parliament. Bouchard almost won the 1995 Quebec independence referendum, but Chrétien recovered with the Clarity Act of 1999.

Manoir du Patriotte Papineau,
Montebello, P. Que.

51. Residential progress from Champlain's Habitation: Papineau's seigneurial manor house at Montebello, *La Petite-Nation*, built between 1817 and 1850.

52. Dundurn Castle, built on Burlington Heights by Sir Allan Napier MacNab in 1835. MacNab (1798–1862) led the militia in suppressing Mackenzie's rebellion in 1837. He was a long-serving legislator and led the government with Papineau's old side-kick Augustin Morin. Papineau's home shows the elegance of the more refined seigneurs, where Dundurn Castle shows the taste and means of a politician who said "All my politics are railroads." He was a flamboyant rascal who yet rendered some service in all his roles.

53. Ravenscrag, the home of ship-owner, bank president, and political intriguer Sir Hugh Allan. Built in 1863, it presaged the palaces of the Robber Barons and from here Allan made the arrangements that brought down Macdonald and Cartier over the Pacific Scandal, in 1873.

54. Ever more opulent residences for Canadian titans of industry: In the early twentieth century – Sir Henry Pellatt's Casa Loma in Toronto, 65,000 square feet, completed in 1914, almost evokes Ludwig II of Bavaria.

55. In the early twenty-first century – Paul G. Desmarais' magnificent and secluded palace on tens of thousands of acres north of La Malbaie, Quebec, completed in 2003. This represents 400 years of progress in residential construction from Champlain's Habitation 75 miles away.

public sympathy. He was a committed and strenuous man who knew as well as Lévesque and Duplessis had how to pitch to the underdog pride and pugnacity of the Québécois. He was from an even more remote corner of Quebec than Chrétien was (Chicoutimi, rather than Shawinigan), and he carried an ark of resentments that had some racial overtones, though they were mainly of economic exploitation of the Québécois by English-speaking commerce. (He certainly had no grievance against any individual on ethnic or cultural grounds, and his wife was an American.) But he exploited the resentments of many Quebec Liberals at Chrétien's opposition (in emulation of Trudeau) to Meech Lake, and he took up the cry of Lévesque that Quebec had been betrayed by the Gang of Eight and Trudeau and Chrétien in 1982, even appearing on television with a false cover of *Le Journal de Québec* purporting to show Trudeau and Chrétien laughing at Lévesque in 1981. The headline was "Quebec Betrayed by Its Allies," and Bouchard sharply stated, "Mr. Chrétien, you won't pull the same trick on us twice." It was very effective. Bouchard was a firebrand and an evocative speaker who suddenly enflamed every reservation the Québécois had ever had about their status in Canada, and he was diabolically well-qualified, with a powerful up-country inflection, except with a more sophisticated vocabulary than Chrétien, standing on crutches and speaking of the completion of centuries of hope and sacrifice, yet all of it on a simple question that polls showed many Québécois thought was just a mandate for a better deal. In the "yes" posters, the *o* in "*oui*" was the Canadian dollar coin. Eat the cake, and you will still have it in front of you.

The whole atmosphere was suddenly one of pent-up tension, with extreme resentment requiring resolution on one side, and on the other side a lingering non-confidence that came only very late to a realization of great danger. The tension and antagonism obscured the logical wisdom that no clear-cut outcome was likely.

In the last few days, Chrétien and his entourage, especially his heavy-handed chief assistant, Jean Pelletier, panicked, and Chrétien almost broke down in front of 170 MPs of his caucus on October 25. Where in 1980 there had been unity between Trudeau, Ryan, and Chrétien, and a complete absence of overconfidence, there was now general disunion and mutual disrespect between the federal and provincial Liberal parties, neither of which had the upper hand at its political echelon in Quebec, and the leadership was in a state of terror. There were elements of farce, as there usually are in Quebec votes. On October 26, disc jockey Pierre Brassard telephoned Queen Elizabeth pretending to be Chrétien and asked her to make a speech supporting a "no" vote. She said she would and that he should send a proposed text. (It did not hold the queen up to ridicule; she was sensible and was entitled to take the advice of the prime minister. The London *Daily Mirror* then hired someone to dress up as a red-coated Mountie and enter Brassard's radio studio and arrest him for affronting the sovereign.) On October 27, Bouchard sent a press release to all military installations in Quebec saying that in a few days Quebec would be setting up its own military. Paul Martin gave speeches in the province warning of the cost to Quebec of independence; the defence minister, David Collenette, evacuated RCAF fighter planes from Quebec to ensure that they did not become entangled in any power play by Bouchard. There was a large unity rally of between 50,000 and 150,000 people in Montreal, and Chrétien gave a somewhat fearful but clearly earnest televised address extolling Canada and offering, implausibly at this point, some unspecified concessions to Quebec apart from restoration of its constitutional veto, and urging caution in a series of paragraphs ending with the exhortation "Think of this before going to vote to break it [Canada] up." It wasn't strong, but it was not entirely unpersuasive, and it seemed that the two sides may finally have frightened and aroused some of Quebec's bourgeois susceptibilities. As the campaign ended, all polls showed it was a toss-up.

Ninety-four per cent of Quebeckers voted on October 30. When the votes were counted, it was 2,308,360 "yes" and 2,362,648 "no"; 50.58 per cent for the federalist side to 49.42 for the separatists. It is unlikely that even a modest "yes" victory would have led to more than a few federal concessions and then a serious campaign, bringing back Trudeau, Mulroney, Ryan, and others, massively financed, to prevail upon Quebec to reconsider. Jacques Parizeau imputed the result to English money and the ethnic vote, a statement that he later regretted, and resigned as premier of Quebec. Bouchard was acclaimed as his replacement. Bouchard had raised the soufflé, but he still couldn't win, even against a terribly inept campaign, and shaken from their torpor the federalists finally played their high card. Chrétien treated the victory as if it were a decisive rejection of the separatists, but shifted the argument to the illegitimacy of a razor-thin plurality on a vague question. Here he had the separatists by the windpipe, and had, by the narrowest of margins, again broken their momentum. The day after the referendum, Chrétien told a Toronto Liberal meeting that such a crisis would never happen again.

As if to illustrate that the federalists were not completely free of their propensity to accidents, a fuming separatist, André Dallaire, broke into the prime minister's residence in the middle of the night intending to cut Chrétien's throat but was detected by Aline Chrétien, who awakened her husband after locking their bedroom door. While Dallaire bumbled around looking for the prime minister's bedroom, Chrétien stood in night attire with an Inuit sculpture in his hand as a cosh and waited interminably for the RCMP, whom he had telephoned, to arrive. Dallaire was disarmed, and the episode wasn't publicly taken too seriously, but it added to the indignity of the whole sequence of events.

Chrétien was still in a daze as he set out to give Quebec back its right of veto. He aimed at a constitutional amendment, which under the existing arrangements required seven provinces, and tried to line up six and then snooker Bouchard by inviting him to be the seventh. But Ontario's new Conservative premier, Mike Harris, balked, which would deprive Chrétien of the 50 per cent of the population required, unless Bouchard agreed. He then proposed a regional veto for Ontario, Quebec, the West, and the Atlantic provinces. British Columbia demanded its own veto, and the squabbling of what Duplessis had called for years the "circonférences" started up again. Eventually, Chrétien gave way to British Columbia's demand and the reinstatement of Quebec's veto was made, not in the Constitution, but by the revocable method of a parliamentary resolution, along with a vague statement that Quebec was a "distinct society" and some changes to jurisdiction over labour training. Bouchard dismissed it as tokenistic window dressing, and for once in federal-provincial matters was fairly accurate. There was a good deal of non-confidence in Chrétien at this point, though he had no difficulty holding his heavy parliamentary majority.

Jean Charest, who had replaced Kim Campbell as the leader of the federal Progressive Conservative Party and its caucus of two people, violently criticized Chrétien's inept performance as leader of the federalist forces in Quebec, and Preston Manning, the senior figure in the unofficial opposition, implied that Chrétien had lost his senses and publicly advised the governor general, Ramon Hnatyshyn, to be ready to change prime ministers within the Liberal Party. This was going too far, but it was indicative of the severity of Chrétien's inadequacy in the latter stages of the crisis that arose in the referendum because of his own mismanagement. Such a shambles is unimaginable under most of his recent predecessors. Such counterattack as there was came from some of the native peoples' groups in Quebec, which announced that if Quebec seceded from Canada, they would secede from Quebec and remain in Canada. Chrétien, at least oratorically, took this up, and it was awkward for Bouchard and his colleagues to deal with it. At the start of 1996, Chrétien brought into his cabinet academic Stéphane Dion (b. 1955), a rigorous intellectual federalist (and son of noted academic Léon Dion, who styled himself "a tired federalist"; in that milieu, federalism would take what it could get), and Montreal lawyer Pierre Pettigrew. They weren't Trudeau, Marchand, and Pelletier, but they had sight in a valley of the unseeing.

Everything went quiet, Chrétien had no particular idea what to do, and Bouchard had no more initiatives to take. Martin continued to manage down the deficit, and the principal issue in Ottawa in 1996 was the allegation, in a letter from a Justice Department official to a Swiss analogue, that Brian Mulroney had taken a five-million-dollar bribe in the acquisition of Airbus planes by Air Canada, and requesting the opening up of Mulroney's bank account in Switzerland. Mulroney sued for fifty million dollars for libel and there was a considerable controversy, which in 1997 led to an admission that the Justice Department could not dispute Mulroney's word that he had no bank account in Switzerland and had not accepted one cent in respect of the $1.8 billion Airbus contract. The charge was withdrawn and more than two million dollars was paid to the former prime minister. It was eventually revealed that the RCMP's entire authority for prompting such a letter from the Justice Department to a foreign government was from the rabidly anti-Mulroney *Globe and Mail* reporter Stevie Cameron (who published a book in which Mulroney was censored even for accepting a box of Oreo cookies from an old friend who was the head of the company that manufactured them). Justice minister Allan Rock tried to allege that Mulroney had released the defamatory letter, and Chrétien claimed to know nothing of it. The whole affair was an unmitigated disgrace, and Mulroney, who took congratulatory calls from many world leaders when the charge against him was withdrawn, declined to take a call from Chrétien, and apart from the merest pleasantries when necessary the two have not spoken since. The RCMP continued their investigation for six years before abandoning it, and there was never any official statement of apology to Mulroney. With a fragmented opposition, Canadians soon had reason to appreciate the problems of a one-party state.

In international affairs, Canadian peacekeepers were found to have tortured a Somali to death, whereupon even senior officials had gone to considerable lengths to cover it up; the government made a ludicrous shambles of the GST, which it had pledged to repeal but now retained; and it paid sixty million dollars to a Conservative consortium when it arbitrarily cancelled the contract to privatize Toronto's Pearson Airport. The government simply shut down the three-person commission it had set up to study Somalia in order for Chrétien, for no reason, and with no issue and no program, to hold an election barely halfway through his mandate, an election he could not lose against four squabbling opposition parties. (The government fired General Jean Boyle, chief of the Defence Staff, and considered the Somalia matter closed.)

In August 1996, the Quebec Superior Court had upheld the claim of former separatist Guy Bertrand that the courts had a say in secession. It had been astonishing that Trudeau and Mulroney, and Chrétien himself until Bertrand was sustained, just meekly accepted that a tiny majority on a vague question could tear the country apart, and not even the creative agitation of the native people had moved Chrétien to do more than give a few punchy speeches about it. In September 1996, the issue was referred to the Supreme Court of Canada, and Stéphane Dion predicted that support for independence would plummet when Quebeckers realized that it was not the day at the beach that Lévesque, Parizeau, and Bouchard had held out, and which Trudeau and Chrétien had not really debunked. Daniel Johnson Jr. and the Quebec Liberals were still in favour of federalism by appeasement, but Chrétien was about to have his epiphany, the change of mind that turned him, along with Paul Martin's uncommon talents as a deficit-slicing finance minister (the deficit had been cut by two-thirds, with minimal inflation but still 9.5 per cent unemployment), into an important prime minister.

The country voted in the federal election with a conspicuous lack of enthusiasm, and no possibility of Chrétien's Liberals being defeated, on June 2, 1997. The results (with 1993 results in brackets) were: Liberals, 155 MPs and 38.5 per cent of the vote (177 MPs and 41.2 per cent); Reform, 60 MPs and 19.3 per cent (52 MPs and 18.7 per cent); Bloc Québécois, 44 MPs and 10.7 per cent (54 MPs and 13.5 per cent); NDP, 21 MPs and 11.1 per cent (9 MPs and 6.9 per cent); Progressive Conservatives, 20 MPs and 18.8 per cent (2 MPs and 16 per cent). Chrétien won his own district in Shawinigan (for the tenth time) only by a little more than a thousand votes, after almost coming to blows with his ancient local foe, former PQ minister Yves Duhaime. The new Bloc leader, Gilles Duceppe, was certainly not the vote-harvester Bouchard was, and Manning now would be the leader of the Opposition (and would occupy the official residence, Stornoway, which Bouchard had eschewed in favour of living in Hull). NDP leader Audrey McLaughlin was not as effective as Ed Broadbent or David Lewis or Tommy Douglas, but she had elbowed her way back as an official party, as had Jean Charest, with a 900 per cent increase on Campbell's two MPs. Chrétien had barely won a majority in the House (155 of 301) – the first back-to-back majorities for the Liberals since St. Laurent in 1953 – and he had 101 of the 103 Ontario constituencies. The new Parliament continued to be full of anomalies, but Chrétien was safe now into the new millennium. He was handicapped, however, by the widely held view summarized by distinguished editor Robert Fulford that "deep within the Canadian spirit lies the idea that there is something honest about ignorance and something slick about knowledge."[26]

Nothing seemed to happen anymore; all was quiet, and the deficit and unemployment were declining, inflation was low, and the dollar was rising. Jean Charest retired as federal Progressive Conservative leader and succeeded the rather ineffectual Daniel Johnson Jr. as leader of the Quebec Liberals, making them, even more than the federal Liberals, an umbrella party for all federalists opposite Bouchard's PQ. The 1996 Supreme Court referral on the legality of provincial secession finally came in 1998 in the tradition of the 1981 decision on unilateral patriation: it would not be legal for Quebec to secede unilaterally, but if a substantial majority of Quebeckers voted to secede on a clear question, the rest of the country would be legally obligated to work with the Quebec government toward secession.

Quebec voted in its general election on November 30, 1998, this time with Lucien Bouchard and Jean Charest, as well as the Action Démocratique's Mario Dumont, as the party leaders. There was only the subtlest change from the previous election (1994 results in brackets): PQ, 76 MNAs on 42.9 per cent of the vote (77 MNAs and 44.8); Liberals, 48 MNAs with 43.6 per cent (47 MNAs and 44.4 per cent); and the same 1 MNA, Dumont, for the ADQ, but the vote increased from 6.5 to 11.8 per cent. It was no momentum for Bouchard, as he fell slightly and Charest narrowly won the popular vote. There had been Quebec federal prime ministers for all but eight months of the last thirty years, and while Chrétien and Martin had reduced transfer payments, they still flowed to Quebec in heavy amounts and the referendum-question card trick could not be played again. Pulling out of Canada would be an expensive and embittering business. Canada wasn't making any more concessions and Quebec was too sensible to take the plunge, too frightened by its bourgeois avarice. It was one thing to persecute the English language and ease the non-French out to booming Toronto, but cutting the painter altogether was a worrisome proposition.

Chrétien visited thirty-four national capitals before he got around to Washington, and his aides even asked that the White House not represent the relations as excessively cozy. But he went along with President Bill Clinton and Prime Minister Tony Blair's attack on Serbia when it appeared to be engaging in genocidal attacks on the Bosnian Muslims in 1998. The months slipped quietly by, the deficit gave way to a surplus – a tremendous achievement for Martin and Chrétien – and the country was prosperous. Quebec and the federalists had taken their stances and there were no substantive efforts to bridge the gap, but the public did not care about the amending formula and the exact demarcation of jurisdiction in every concurrent policy area. There was reasonably benign stasis. Chrétien was a fortunate leader, a lucky one, after all the years of struggle against the Créditistes and separatists in the hinterland of the province. But it was at this point – as a minor scandal burbled away in Shawinigan, indicating Chrétien's propensity for the traditions of Quebec patronage – that the recently turned sixty-five-year-old prime minister suddenly, and with his usual fixity of purpose, chose to strike a mighty blow for federalism. It had been a year since the Supreme Court of Canada had declared that for a movement to secede by a province to be taken seriously, it must be by a popular vote on a clear question of secession being approved by a clear majority.

Chrétien had President Clinton to a conference on federalism at Mont-Tremblant, Quebec, in October 1999, and the president closed the conference, where the independentists had had the upper hand. Clinton gave a learned *ex tempore* assertion of the criteria for a just and successful federation and made the assertion that Canada certainly cleared all the hurdles and that secession from it was not justified. With all the force of his personality and the prestige of his great office, Bill Clinton delivered all he had for Chrétien and for Canada. Lucien Bouchard and his entourage were visibly shaken by the implicit silencing of their unceasing carping and whining.

Jean Chrétien, after extensive consultation, presented his Clarity Act in December. It did not stipulate a precise majority required for a successful vote for provincial secession, only the requirement for a clear majority on a clear question. Chrétien doubted that Bouchard and his followers would be able to generate much heat on the issue in the last weeks of the old millennium. He was right; Bouchard fumed impotently when Chrétien's measure was presented in Parliament. But Chrétien did not follow through on the post-1995 referendum threats by the native people and declare that a province was as divisible as the country in the event of a separatist vote, and that anti-separatist counties or regions could, in the event of an adequate province-wide separatist majority, secede from the province and remain in Canada. Charest and the provincial Liberals, as well as the federal Progressive Conservatives – now led again by Joe Clark, who came snorting out of the Albertan sagebrush when Preston Manning started advocating reunification of the parties – opposed Chrétien's Clarity Act, as did the NDP, ever the appeasers of Quebec nationalism, when not actually participating in it. But the official Opposition under Manning threw in wholeheartedly with the government, and the act cleared Parliament with a heavy majority.

This time, Jean Chrétien erased the near-fatal disaster of the referendum of 1995; there was no significant outcry, and the Quebec media,
having predicted a tumultuous uproar, had to admit that Chrétien had
called it right. Even Trudeau had expected a serious controversy, but
he wished Chrétien well and urged him to proceed: "Bon courage," he
said.[27] Bouchard replied with his Bill 99, supported by the craven
Quebec Liberals, stating that Quebec alone would determine the basis
of its achievement of independence, and that a 50-per-cent-plus-one
vote on any question that worked for Quebeckers would justify a unilateral declaration of independence.

But the crisis was finally passing. Bouchard had lost heart in the
great dream, as Lévesque had, and he had no open-minded and original Brian Mulroney with whom to pursue a *beau risque*. He would be
gone, disillusioned, in another year, and the great nationalist fires were
now hissing sparks that did not illuminate the way forward. It was a dead
end: Canada would not back up any farther, and Quebec could not
chin itself on the terrible fiscal and social penalties of trying to make a
credible exit from a gentle country that was not the sort of place that
provoked the revolt or collective withdrawal of large numbers of its citizens. On disguised payments from English Canada, Quebec was able
to operate an overwhelmingly white collar economy and the days of
hanging the culture on the barnyard door had been replaced by an era
where everyone was an academic, a consultant, or part of Quebec's narcissistic media or of the immense Quebec *fonction publique*, the civil
service. Quebec and its ruling elites had all the instances of a sovereign
state except sovereignty. They attended conferences of La Francophonie
and were semi-autonomous in many policy areas, including immigration. They had most of the psychic income of an independent country
but almost none of the risk. And they acted on their frustrations at being
unable to emancipate themselves completely by periodic impositions of
new rules of absurd restrictiveness on the principal language of the
world and of all the rest of North America above the Rio Grande. It was
a self-administered placebo.

Jean Chrétien had almost severed the magic thread, by his complacency and then his nervosity in the referendum campaign of 1995, but
had wobbled through and then scored an immense victory for Canada
when no one was looking: the swift resurrection of public finances and

the sudden fitting out of impenetrable protection against Quebec's constitutional sabre-rattling by legerdemain. It was a brilliant and stealthy coup from a man widely, and often unjustly, thought to be quite limited. It was not exactly a repossession of the double majority, as English Canada could now almost govern without Quebec but could not really impose a hostile majority will on Quebec. The old two Canadas could move forward by mutual consent, or the country as a whole could develop with a substantial ability for a semi-autonomous Quebec to pursue a different policy path within Quebec. But suddenly, so soon after the intense suspense of the 1995 referendum, the long era when Quebec could threaten the viability of the whole country was almost over, as long as Canada would enforce the Clarity Act and the Supreme Court decision that it entrenched.

The old Canadian technique had worked again: endless good-faith "circonférences" until the parties had enough of what they had to have and all but the fanatics lost interest. Almost unbelievably, Canada was a crisis-free, prosperous, and stable country. In the steaming kitchen of Ottawa-Quebec relations, as all was winding down and the principals had departed, a dogged sous-chef had, with the Clarity Act, produced a miraculous sorbet ready for prolonged national delectation. It wasn't complete or perfect, but it liberated the country from a spectre of French-English division which had haunted it for forty years and lurked for two centuries before that. Quebec had won three-quarters of a loaf, but Canada had a four-course meal: the Cold War had ended, and the country was threatened by no one, inside or out, respected by all, and unbound before an unlimited horizon. The prospects were unlike anything Canadians had seen before. Canada entered a new epoch, on the calendar and in its national life, blinking disbelievingly at its unprecedented fortune and vigour. Like a patient convalescing from a severe medical emergency that was passing, Canada was coming out of it, groggy and exhausted, relieved but too enervated to rejoice.

Though the country was solid, its regions were at odds and its political parties fragmented. And as the United States prepared to say farewell to Bill Clinton, a popular (if hyperactively laddish) president, after a decade as the world's only superpower, Canada's self-consciousness opposite the United States was still almost as pronounced as it had been in the times of Macdonald and Laurier. Yet Laurier had been right in a sense: it had been Canada's century after all, not to rise to world leadership, but to master its internal inhibitions and contradictions, and more. For the insecurity generated by its great and dazzling neighbour, even as Canada shed its ancient fears of internal weakness, would also soon be alleviated by events, foreign and domestic, in the opening years of the new millennium.

Stephen Harper (1959–), leader of the federal opposition 2002–2006 and prime minister
of Canada since 2006, and Barack Obama (1961–), U.S. president since 2009. Harper
has departed from the international organizations-based foreign policy of Pearson and
Chrétien, the anti-Americanism of Trudeau, and the pro-Americanism of Mulroney
and taken a strong and independent line against Russian aggression and militant Islam.
By being the least assertive American president in foreign policy since before the U.S.
Civil War, Obama has enabled Canada to play a larger role in the world than ever
before, though Harper has limited his credibility by failure even to maintain Canada's
military capabilities.

CHAPTER 10

A Force in the World at Last, 2000–2014

1. Jean Chrétien's Last Lap, 2000–2003

Like a long-detained hostage for the first time in many years in broad daylight, Canada, emerging from the pale of the separatist threat and more economically robust than ever in its history, eased hesitantly into the new millennium. Symbolically, the fireworks display on Parliament Hill to mark the turn of the millenium, unlike the magnificent spectacles in many other cities (London, Paris, New York, Sydney, Rio de Janeiro), was a fiasco afflicted by broken sequences and misfirings. Jean Chrétien, characteristically, dismissed these as trivial technical problems. They were, and were nothing to be concerned about, but at his moment of greatest service, in a career that had been dedicated altogether to ploughing the often stony fields of federalism in Quebec for nearly forty years, Chrétien's time had passed.

The regime – despite Chrétien's elaborate and relentless schtick of the honest habitant of working-class background (which was an imposture; his was a numerous but professional family in Shawinigan, and he was a well-trained lawyer, though with the tastes and inflection of a French-Canadian *petit bourgeois*) – had become tainted by scandal. Chrétien was in fact a traditional Quebec politician, schooled in the less progressive Maurice Duplessis techniques of handing out patronage and vengeance by unabashedly partisan criteria. In 1998, Pierre Corbeil, the chief fundraiser for sixteen federal Quebec constituencies, including Chrétien's, pleaded guilty to four charges of fraud (influence-peddling).

More serious and closer to Chrétien personally was the Grand-Mère affair, in which an inn and golf club of which Chrétien was a part owner was sold to a controversial local businessman and received a grant of $164,000 from the Transitional Jobs Fund and a loan of $615,000 from the Business Development Bank of Canada, both on questionable criteria, in which the prime minister's entourage played a role. There was also a very murky sale of Chrétien's interest in the properties, where he was left with a balance of sale that was apt to be influenced by the sale of a neighbouring property at a generous price to a Chrétien political supporter who almost simultaneously received from the Canadian International Development Agency a generous contract to strengthen the electricity distribution system of Mali. It was complex and never really plumbed to the depths, and if a scandal not an earth-shaking one, but it did open serious questions of probity that should not arise with a prime minister.

It also made a mockery of the Liberals' sanctimonious attacks on Brian Mulroney, who had his frailties of judgment but never was compromised to this extent or in these amounts. And in January 2000 came the beginning of the long-drawn-out revelations of gross mismanagement, involving some millions of dollars, in thirty-seven separate projects of the Department of Human Resources Development, though these did not lead to any direct benefit to Chrétien himself. The government managed to keep these matters out of proceedings where evidence was taken under oath and in the hands of the dawdling RCMP, and the media, which had been whipped up to considerable hostility against Mulroney, couldn't quite do it all again with

Chrétien. But the public, though it liked Chrétien personally, was tired of it.

Chrétien turned sixty-six in January 2000, and Paul Martin (b. 1938), as the strong man of the government, five years younger than Chrétien and a very respected finance minister, was discernibly anxious to replace his leader. His followers were hyperactive in the parliamentary caucus and the federal Liberal organization. Chrétien felt acutely the absence of the sort of moral and intellectual authority and political popularity that Trudeau had possessed, but they were very different people. Chrétien had been elected to Parliament two years before Trudeau and was brought into government at the same time by Pearson, but as a minister without portfolio. He moved to national revenue when Trudeau succeeded Pearson, and had held Indian affairs and northern development; the Treasury Board; industry, trade and commerce; finance; justice; energy, mines and resources; and then, under John Turner, deputy prime minister and secretary of state for external affairs. Of those people elected prime minister, only Macdonald, Laurier, and ultimately Diefenbaker served as long in Parliament, and none had held as many cabinet positions. He had never been a star as Trudeau and Turner had been, and while he had his loyalists, they tended not to be the strongest players on the Liberal team.

Chrétien had tightened the leader's control over the party at the expense of the constituency associations, and this was not popular with the rank and file. His position was fraying at the edges everywhere. His government had been successful, though fortunate in the disintegration of the opposition, and he was well-liked and thought to be competent if unexciting. Martin was the chief author of the triumph of the balanced budget, though Chrétien had solidly backed him, and his great achievement in the Clarity Act was underappreciated in English Canada, which apart from specialists never really understood what was happening in Quebec or why there were any separatists to begin with.

In Quebec, Chrétien was not regarded as urbane and authoritative enough to be the unquestioned spokesman for French Canada in times of "national" – that is, French Quebec – crises, as Laurier, Gouin, Lapointe, Taschereau, St. Laurent, Duplessis, Lesage, Johnson (*père*), Trudeau, Lévesque, and Bouchard had been. His portrayal of himself as the dutiful foot soldier gradually advancing through the ranks didn't contain, and he did not possess, any of the magic required to be accepted in Quebec as *un chef*. Relations between Chrétien and Martin had never altogether recovered from the bruising leadership battle they conducted in 1990, when Martin attacked Chrétien for his opposition to the Meech Lake Accord and large numbers of Martin supporters screamed "Judas" and other unflattering epithets at him.

There were constant internecine frictions in the governing caucus, which had only a bare parliamentary majority, and there were disaffected sub-groups within the Liberal parliamentary party. Martin spoke English much better than Chrétien did, and, unlike in Trudeau's time, most of the Liberal MPs were from Ontario. At one point, outspoken anti-American MP Carolyn Parrish, who regularly denounced the United States and especially the incoming administration of George W. Bush in vitriolic terms but was a Chrétien loyalist from Mississauga, attacked the Italian-Canadian Liberal MPs as "wimps and shitheads [in the] pasta caucus"[1] and accused them of disloyalty to Chrétien. This led to a strained meeting between the prime minister and the eight MPs involved, all Martin supporters.

Chrétien's elder brother Maurice advised the press that it was time for his brother to retire, and the prime minister's entourage was reduced to suggesting that Maurice Chrétien was senile, which was obviously not the case. There soon followed, at one of the Toronto airport hotels just before an annual party conference, a meeting of Martin and his senior organizers and helpers for the long-expected drive to succeed Chrétien, an occasion that quickly was brought to the prime minister's attention and stirred his always susceptible concerns about loyalty. There was a good deal of jockeying at the party conference, and Martin somewhat upstaged his leader and acknowledged that he hoped to succeed him eventually, but they all got through it, and Chrétien made it clear that he would lead the Liberals in another election. Nothing was happening, the opposition was still fragmented, and Chrétien used these premature elections as reassurance that his position was invulnerable (like Mackenzie King in his latter days, telling the party faithful that he led a more united party than ever).

Chrétien, who had no feel for foreign affairs and had not held that ministry long enough to acquire any knowledge of it, and whose ideas were scarcely developed beyond replication of Trudeau's anti-Americanism, inexplicably embarked on a trip to the Middle East, where he indulged his talent for vigorous, cloth-eared indiscretions. He implied he favoured a Palestinian unilateral declaration of independence, and then denied it and stated his sympathy for Israel's desire to have entire control of the freshwater Sea of Galilee, and then recanted on that position, leaving everyone dissatisfied. "Clueless in Gaza," headlined the *National Post*.

External affairs minister Lloyd Axworthy announced his retirement in the summer to lead a Western provinces think tank. He had devised the Canadian version of "soft power," which was a fraud, as the concept was devised by Clinton national security adviser Joe Nye as a method for the United States to pursue in foreign policy in preference to the "hard power" option Republican presidents generally preferred. With Canada, there was no hard power option, and no one would pay any attention to Canadian entreaties, as they were not backed with anything, economic or military, and would only be of interest to those whose interests they served. It was like Chrétien's passionate interest in United Nations peacekeeping: it satisfied the gullible Canadian soft left that Canada was making an important contribution to the well-being of mankind without following in lockstep behind the United States, while facilitating shrinking defence budgets.

But in fact most of these operations were ineffectual, as in Somalia and the former Yugoslavia, and many were just methods for impoverished United Nations member states to rent out their forces to factions in exchange for hard currency provided both by the UN and the local warring parties, who used the peacekeepers as mercenaries (though Canadian forces were never misused in this way). This was largely what happened in the largest peacekeeping operation, in the Congo. But it was a satisfactory disguise for Chrétien, as it had been for Trudeau, as he starved the Canadian military of money, equipment, and personnel while unctuously pretending to be toiling effectively in the vineyards of peace.

Chrétien, overcoming significant dissent within his party, finally dissolved Parliament for new elections in September 2000, shortly after Pierre Trudeau's funeral (he died at age eighty) and, though this was only incidental, after Fidel Castro advised him to do that following a brief encounter Castro had after Trudeau's funeral with the new

Opposition leader, Stockwell Day.[2] Chrétien was obviously going to win again, but two-thirds of Canadians thought it was time for him to go, and a great many of his own MPs and party organizers were opposed to an election, although his approval rating was still high at about 60 per cent. Everyone who took the trouble to develop an informed opinion saw that it was just a ruse to keep Martin out and himself in a while longer. As only the Liberal Party had any chance of forming a government, the real political action was now within the governing party. But the Liberals were not going to be able to turn this screw much longer.

The Reform Party had renamed itself the Canadian Alliance. (This was their fifth name in sixty years: Conservative, National Government, Progressive Conservative, Reform.) And they had a new leader. Day was the former treasurer of Alberta and a somewhat more pan-Canadian leader than Preston Manning. He was also a rather more contemporary figure in manner and presentation, and came to his first press conference on a jet ski in a wetsuit. This caused Mulroney to refer to "the Reform Party in pantyhose," Joe Clark to call it "the costume party," and newspapers to refer to "Daywatch." Day was a hard-liner on same-sex marriage, gay rights generally, abortion, immigration, crime, programs for native people, welfare, and transfer payments, and was for the return of the death penalty. And although religion did not enter directly into the campaign, the fact that Day was an evangelical Christian and creationist was well-known and did not resonate well in sophisticated urban centres, east and west.

Joe Clark had taken back the Progressive Conservative leadership when Jean Charest departed to become Liberal leader in Quebec, because Clark wanted to block a Reform takeover of his old party, which had been a Red Tory operation federally at least since Robert Stanfield, if not John Diefenbaker though Mulroney generally finessed these issues. But the two parties were clearly going to unite eventually, and the creation of the Canadian Alliance was just preparing the way. Brian Mulroney had dissolved the Liberal stranglehold on the country: its lock on Quebec. Mulroney was not able to hold the same kind of lock on the province for his own party, though he carried Quebec with heavy majorities in two straight elections, and when his party splintered, those constituencies did not revert to the Liberals as they did after the Duplessis aberration of 1958 (despite Créditiste inroads). Reform and the Progressive Conservatives together had about as many votes as the Liberals, and although a balance of power in a minority Parliament was likely to be in the hands of a party of the left, either the NDP or the Bloc Québécois, the clear advantage of the Liberals as the permanent party of government was over as soon as the Canadian Alliance and Progressive Conservatives made a division of constituencies to assist each other in a fusion alternative. Brian Mulroney had not only been the most successful federal Conservative leader since John A. Macdonald, he had taken the essential step to turn the country from a one-and-a-half- to a two-party system in terms of eligibility to form a government by cracking the Liberal lock on Quebec.

The Liberals had a substantial surplus, and Martin produced a well-designed pre-election budget cutting income tax, while Chrétien threw another chunk of money at the ever-more expensive health-care system. There were no issues really, other than the Liberal portrayal of Day as an extremist, especially in being a closet supporter of two-tier health care, and the opposition attacks on the Liberals as complacent and corrupt. (A further series of revelations came out about Grand-Mère, including that Chrétien had lobbied personally for the Business Development Bank's $615,000 loan and that there had been over two million dollars invested by wealthy immigrants in projects of interest to the government as they were granted entry to the country.) It was a lacklustre, and of course rather unsuspenseful, campaign. Alexa McDonough of Nova Scotia was the NDP leader, and next to the doughty Joe Clark she was the best of the campaigners among the party leaders. Day was well-informed but not overly personable; Chrétien was folksy and entertaining but didn't sound any more like a figure of authority than he had in the previous thirty-seven years of his electoral career.

Election day was November 27, 2000. The Liberals won, for the twentieth time in the last twenty-nine elections, with 172 MPs and 40.9 per cent of the vote (1997 result, 155 MPs and 38.5 per cent); the Canadian Alliance had 66 MPs and 25.5 per cent (previously, Reform had 60 MPs and 19.4 per cent); Bloc Québécois, 38 MPs and 10.7 per cent (previously, 44 MPs and 10.7 per cent); Progressive Conservatives, 12 MPs and 12.2 per cent; NDP, 13 MPs and 8.5 per cent (previously, 13 MPs and 11.1 per cent). The turnout, at 62 per cent of eligible voters, was one of the lowest in Canadian history and five points below that of 1997 (which had been no triumph of political virtuosity either). Day had called on Chrétien to hold the election, which mitigated to some extent the country's irritation that it was taking place at all, but all of the party leaders except McDonough were pretty tired, and the gain by the two main parties combined of 8.5 per cent of the vote indicated the trend to a less fragmented electorate.

The Liberals had split almost evenly with the Bloc in Quebec, 37 to 38 MPs, and had narrowly led them in the popular vote, though not among French Quebeckers, confirming the subsidence of the over-heated spirit of the 1995 referendum aftermath.

In January 2001, while Chrétien was in Florida on a golfing holiday, Lucien Bouchard announced his retirement from politics. The much less imposing Bernard Landry (b. 1937) replaced him as premier, and the fire had gone from the separatist cause. Bouchard had been a formidable but volcanic leader who deserted Lévesque to join Mulroney, first as ambassador to France and then in the government, gave his all for Meech Lake, and then turned 180 degrees, wrenched control of the independentist movement from Jacques Parizeau, and almost won the 1995 referendum because of Chrétien's temporary incompetence. But he was not the man for endless perseverance toward a distant goal, and he decamped.

Chrétien would have great difficulty holding his party in place for a full term, and if the Canadian Alliance could just make even a division of constituencies with the PCs, the game would turn dramatically from all the rules that had obtained for living memory. Chrétien had no ideas and no reform plan to renew his government. He had somewhat strengthened his government by bringing in the premier of Newfoundland, Brian Tobin, at trade and commerce and moving the incumbent, John Manley, to external affairs in place of Axworthy. Both were very capable ministers and potential party leaders. But the leader's only policy was to repel boarders and put his party objectors on the rack.

Chrétien had a relatively cordial visit to Washington with the new president, George W. Bush, having had an exceptionally good relationship with Bill Clinton, who was very helpful with his supportive speech in the prelude to the Clarity Act. Chrétien went on to China, where he did help to continue the upward momentum in bilateral trade. But at home, Shawinigate, as the Grand-Mère quagmire was now called, would not go away, and the Alliance skilfully manoeuvred the government into repudiating its own electoral promise of an independent ethics commissioner. Chrétien kept changing his story, claiming endlessly that his interest had been in a blind trust all the time he was prime minister (a falsehood, at least in terms of his knowledge of the progress of the investment) and missing the year when he had raised the matter of his unhonoured balance of sale to his ethics counsellor, Howard Wilson. He was also contradicted by his partners and buyers on important aspects of the story. It was a very shabby business, but eventually, with Wilson steadily upholding Chrétien's version of events, it all just petered out. Chrétien would not give it to a commission of inquiry that could compel sworn evidence, and the RCMP were notoriously incompetent, and Wilson, who as an ethics counsellor was apparently not independent, simply approved the conduct of his employer at every stage.

After the monstrous smear job Chrétien committed against Mulroney, and after all his pretenses to being the honest little man from Shawinigan, it was a startling development for him to be up to his eyeballs in the greatest federal government scandal in Canadian history that reflected personally on a prime minister's probity. John A. Macdonald did not personally benefit from the Pacific Scandal, though his receipt of campaign funds from a claimant of government favours was outrageous. Mackenzie King did not profit a cent from the customs scandal of the 1920s and was not even aware that his hotel bill was being paid in Bermuda (and the amount of four hundred dollars was not material). It was widely suspected that Chrétien was complicit in the false accusation that Mulroney had accepted a five-million-dollar bribe in the award of a contract for civil airliners. The media widely alleged that Shawinigate was of some direct benefit to Chrétien and that the whole subject involved a number of improprieties and a prolonged campaign of dissembling and evasion. He used his parliamentary majority to shut down a serious unearthing of what really happened. But the whole murky and tawdry saga strained his standing in the Liberal Party. League of political roués though it was, it was not beyond embarrassment at such questionable conduct in the country's highest political office.

There was growing restiveness in the cabinet and caucus at Chrétien's heavy-handed repression of any real discussion or collegiality, and Martin advanced steadily in the parliamentary party and the national organization, promising greater consultation and more respect for Parliament and for traditional cabinet government.

Chrétien hosted quite a convivial hemispheric trade conference at Quebec City in early September, and his personal relations with President Bush continued to be good. Canada and the world were horrified on September 11, 2001, by the terrorist suicide attacks on the World Trade Center in New York and the Pentagon, killing thousands of people and bringing down two of the most famous buildings in the world. Canada accepted the landing of hundreds of civil airliners destined for the U.S. which were rerouted to Canada when American airspace was closed, and lodged the passengers and assisted in delivering them by surface to their destinations. For the first time in history, the presidential aircraft flew with a fighter escort in domestic airspace, though there were no further incidents. Chrétien held an open-air memorial service on Parliament Hill attended by about one hundred thousand people and spoke movingly at it. But there was a sentiment in the American administration and among pro-American circles in Canada that Chrétien could have shown greater solidarity with the United States after this extreme provocation, for which Bush had promised vengeance on the night of September 11, declaring that all countries would be divided into those that opposed terrorism in fact and those that did not, and that no distinction would be made between terrorists and countries that tolerated or abetted terrorism.

Bush responded forcefully, and spoke well, at a joint session of Congress and in a special memorial service at the Washington National Cathedral. In the speech before Congress, Bush thanked Australia, Egypt, El Salvador, Germany, Great Britain, even Iran, Israel, Japan, Mexico, Pakistan, and South Korea, but not Canada. On September 29, 2001, Chrétien took the other four party leaders to New York and went with Mayor Rudolph Giuliani to Ground Zero, where the World Trade Center towers had been brought down. All were moved by the carnage and devastation and eloquent in their reflections.

There had been some recriminations about Canada being too easy a jumping-off point for terrorists to enter the United States, and there was much talk in the United States about substantially sealing the Canadian border, an act that would have had very serious consequences

economically for Canada. Manley handled delicate negotiations skilfully. The Americans plunged into Afghanistan, where the terrorist
attacks had been planned and directed, and had vast support from the
United Nations and NATO. Canada joined in, but the United States
did most of the work and chased out the primitive theocratic regime
with only the destabilizing activities of a relatively small number of
special forces.

The terrorist crisis highlighted the government's failure to replace
navy and rescue helicopters that had been in service for forty years.
Pilots called the old machines "ten thousand nuts and bolts flying in
loose formation."[3] Kim Campbell, when Mulroney's defence minister,
had intended to have them replaced, but Chrétien came in and cancelled the contract that had been let, incurring a non-performance
penalty of $500 million. Eventually, the same firm the Conservatives
had retained was rehired, another embarrassment to the government,
but it was used to such toing and froing. Justice minister Anne McLellan
introduced some fierce tightening of security rules in an anti-terrorism
bill, including the usual panoply of pre-emptive measures, among
them preventive detention. It was, in places, a near regularization of
the War Measures Act that Trudeau had imposed thirty-two years
before, but this was meant to be permanent legislation.

All through 2002, the Chrétien government crumbled from within.
There were revelations that public works minister Alfonso Gagliano, who
had been calling the plays for Chrétien in the run-up to the near-death
national experience of the 1995 referendum, was presiding over, to say the
least, a very reckless patronage machine. A whistle-blower who had been
the head of Canada Lands Company, a Crown corporation, furnished
the auditor general, Sheila Fraser, with evidence of favours for friends of
the regime that cost the taxpayers millions of dollars, and Chrétien reluctantly shipped Gagliano off to Denmark as ambassador and conducted
his usual effort to shut the subject down without a proper inquiry. More
seriously, Fraser was starting to turn up evidence of what haemorrhaged
into the "sponsorship scandal," and announced that Public Works had
not implemented any of the reforms proposed in 1996 by external auditors
and had "broken every rule in the book."

Paul Martin's chief rival to succeed Chrétien was Brian Tobin,
trade and commerce minister, who was championing a billion-dollar

program for a national broadband internet network. Martin was preparing a supplementary budget to allow for additional security expenses to assure against terrorist infiltration of the United States from Canada after it had come to light that some of the September 11 terrorists had entered the United States by that route. The U.S. required such measures, and they were agreed as part of the retention of the heavy trading relationship between the countries. Martin was going to add some other betterments to the government's standing, and Chrétien claimed to Tobin that he had asked Martin to include Tobin's preferred program. Martin only included funding for about 10 per cent of it, and Tobin, to Chrétien's surprise, abruptly quit politics for the private sector in central Canada.

Chrétien then determined on a radical cabinet shuffle and dismissed his senior minister and chief loyalist, Herb Gray, the deputy prime minister and a popular figure in the caucus, as former House leader and an emollient figure at the weekly meeting with MPs. He gave Gray no reason and offered him nothing to move on to, and it seemed to most of their colleagues a shabby treatment of a man who was personally well-liked by all factions and had carried water on both shoulders for the Liberal Party through thirty-four years as an MP. As Tobin vanished as a rival to Martin, and Gray (who had replaced Paul Martin Sr. in his constituency in Windsor*) wondered what to do next in his life, defence minister Art Eggleton, a former mayor of Toronto and another well-liked, rather gentle, personality, was revealed as having given a $36,500 contract to a paramour. Eggleton was abruptly dismissed from government on the advice of the same Howard Wilson who supported every limp excuse Chrétien had improvised for recurrent, and much larger, liberties and extravagances, including the early warnings about the sponsorship scandal. It was all designed to show Chrétien's control of the government and the Liberal Party, but it had the effect of driving more MPs and party regulars into the outstretched arms of Paul Martin.

While the government was in disarray, the Canadian Alliance managed an almost effortless ouster of Stockwell Day, who had not been a successful leader, though he had made appreciable gains in the

---

* Between the two, they had held the district for sixty-seven years, ten terms each.

2000 election (adding six MPs to Reform's 1997 total and gaining 6 per cent of the popular vote) and had moved the Alliance up from Reform's parity in popular vote with the Progressive Conservatives to twice that level of support. Day continued as an MP and became the shadow external affairs minister. A substantial political career still awaited him.

The new leader of the Alliance was a much more serious challenger to the trembling Liberal ascendancy: Stephen Harper. Aged forty-three (to Chrétien's sixty-nine and Martin's sixty-four), Harper (b. 1959) was a former Reform MP and then the head of the National Citizens Coalition, a taxpayer and public policy advocacy group, and was a substantial academic economist. He was a very presentable, articulate, and bilingual alternative head of government. With the Bloc holding thirty-eight Quebec MPs, if Harper could unite with the Progressive Conservatives – and he would be much harder for Joe Clark and the others to resist than were the more severely regional and ideological Preston Manning and Stockwell Day – he was a likely winner. The country was singularly unimpressed with the unfolding spectacle of the outright corruption of the Chrétien government and the prime minister's cavalier dismissal of it. In his parliamentary opener as Opposition leader, Harper made the point that he was only four years old when the prime minister entered Parliament, and "I recall turning to my mother, who is here today, and saying, 'Someone has to do something to stop that guy.'"[4]

In 2001, Chrétien had said that those who might wish to succeed him could begin organizing and fundraising for such a purpose, though he had no intention of retiring anytime soon. He now did an about-turn and ordered the immediate cessation of all such activity, and his office tried to exercise a right of censorship over Martin's speeches as they attempted to force him to resign. Martin told the press on May 31, 2002, that he would have to "reflect upon my options," and on June 2 he learned from the radio that Manley had been appointed as his successor as finance minister. The Chrétien camp tried to claim Martin had (petulantly) resigned and had been disloyal, and Martin and his followers claimed he had been fired by a frightened, grasping, superannuated, and even slightly senescent King Lear of a prime minister who was headed for the last round-up with his party and with his countrymen. This was not the mighty Liberal Party of disciplined legions, in good times and bad, of Laurier, King, St. Laurent, Pearson, and Trudeau. That era, like the old electoral map coloured Liberal red across Quebec, was ending.

Chrétien had a fairly successful G8 summit meeting at Kananaskis, Alberta, on June 26 and 27, in a provincial park near Jasper. (Russia, as a courtesy, had been added to the G7 when the Soviet Union collapsed.) Demonstrators had taken to vandalizing the environs of these meetings in protests against globalization, environmental offences, and out of a mixture of esoteric causes and the temptations of mere hooliganism. This was an innovative venue, as Chrétien could receive his guests in tranquility, many miles of bear- , mosquito- , and even wolf- as well as Mountie-infested forest from the nearest agitator. Chrétien proposed an ambitious plan for aid to sub-Saharan Africa in exchange for pledges of clean and democratic government. This was received with some skepticism by his distinguished guests and his own countrymen as a late rally to an unexceptionable cause that he had ignored for nine years as prime minister, and it was sidetracked by President Bush's advocacy of a new Palestinian leadership. The meeting went well, out of sight, and Chrétien claimed a great victory for his African project, which in fact attracted only inconsequential lip service.

Chrétien spent the summer trying to rally support for the upcoming leadership review of the Liberal Party. His staff came up with the idea of requiring letters of absolute loyalty from all the Liberal MPs, but many refused, and some of those who signed publicly announced their retractions. There was a party caucus meeting at Chicoutimi in mid-August, and Chrétien gave a spirited statement of legislative intent, the first that had been heard since before the adoption of the Clarity Act in 1999. He promised an ambitious agenda of reform of policy toward native people, the environment (he swallowed the completely unworkable Kyoto Protocol holus-bolus), additional funding of health care, urban infrastructure, scientific research, and new approaches to eradicating poverty. It was another grab bag of places to spend Martin's surplus, but at least it showed some imagination and a broader approach to government than just firing loyalty risks in the cabinet and intimidating reticent caucus members.

By this time, Martin had control of the caucus (his nominee had been elected caucus leader) and of the party organization, and Chrétien was just somnambulating to the leadership review vote, which he would lose, and if he insisted on a convention he would be defeated, humiliated, and expelled from his position by Martin. The venerable scrapper finally seized the last train that would take him away with any dignity and announced at Chicoutimi that he would retire in eighteen months. This obviated the leadership vote, but there was considerable skepticism that he would be able to hang on for eighteen months with a party and caucus that had clearly determined that he must go and would not hesitate to sack him.

Chrétien pre-recorded an interview for the first anniversary of the September 11, 2001, terrorist attacks on the United States and announced that this occasion was a time "to realize . . . that the Western world is getting too rich in relation to the poor world and necessarily will be looked upon as being arrogant and self-satisfied, greedy and with no limits." This applied to "the Western world, not just the Americans," he thoughtfully reassured viewers. This was not the message most Canadians thought it appropriate to give on the anniversary of suicide attackers smashing hijacked civil airliners into buildings and massacring thousands of innocent civilians.

Chrétien became more eccentric than ever, strongly supporting the Kyoto accord, which bought into the whole, subsequently largely debunked, hysteria about global warming and the redistribution of hundreds of billions of dollars to underdeveloped countries as penance for operating successful economies based on carbon-based energy. He dismissed concerns about his solicitor general, Lawrence MacAulay, directing government funds to a college led by his brother, which even Howard Wilson had a problem with, and which caused another ministerial resignation. And he went down opposing a vote requiring that House committee chairmanships be filled by secret ballot of the committees and not the imposition of the prime minister; fifty-seven Liberal MPs led by Paul Martin deserted the prime minister and passed the Alliance motion over Chrétien and his loyalists. He stubbornly refused even to reprimand one of his more belligerent aides for calling the U.S. president "a moron," which, regardless of the facts, was a violent departure from diplomatic norms, given the relations between the two countries. (The same charge was not infrequently, though at least as unjustly, levelled against Chrétien.)

Chrétien doubled down on the hideously expensive health-care system, which yet produced longer and longer waiting lines, with a $237 billion, five-year spending increase by the federal government (which provided barely 25 per cent of the funding). Manley, in his first budget, unleashed an 11 per cent spending increase, pouring out money for Chrétien's departing programs.

A highlight of Chrétien's extended twilight, and one for which he deserves significant credit, was the Quebec election on April 14, 2003, in which Jean Charest's Liberals, a federalist Liberal-Conservative coalition in fact, defeated Bernard Landry's Parti Québécois with 76 members of the National Assembly to the PQ's 45, and 46 per cent of the vote to 33.2. This reversed the previous election total of 76 PQ members to 48 Liberal, and 42.9 per cent of the vote for the PQ to 43.6 for the Liberals. Mario Dumont's Action Démocratique, still trying to sell a quasi-Duplessist message of being more nationalist than the Liberals but not separatist, raised its share of the vote from 11.8 per cent to 18.2, and its deputation from 1 to 4. This was the end of the Parti Québécois's second tour in government, which Jacques Parizeau had opened in 1993. To win the support of one-third of the voters was the PQ's poorest performance since 1973, and they had lost even the francophone vote, decisively, to Charest, an emollient and likeable figure but far from a mighty federalist standard-bearer like Trudeau or Lesage. Chrétien's government was drawing somewhat undistinguishedly to a close, but he had played an important role in the victory of federalism – behind Trudeau, certainly, but along with Mulroney and ahead of the many others. His lonely decades of fighting off the separatists and the almost occult forces of *créditisme* in the hinterland of the vast province had not been wasted and have not gone unrecognized.

Chrétien declined to join the U.S. invasion of Iraq in 2003, as he considered that it was not lawful under international criteria if it was not supported by the United Nations, and he was unconvinced of the existence of weapons of mass destruction in Iraq. The principal American and allied arguments (including Great Britain and Australia) were that Saddam Hussein, the Iraqi dictator, had ignored seventeen consecutive United Nations Security Council resolutions, had failed to comply in important respects with the ceasefire agreement at the end of the Gulf

War in 1991, and was guilty of crimes against humanity because of his atrocities inflicted on his own people. Chrétien was correct not to enter the war, but not for the reason he gave; it was impossible to foresee that the United States would attempt to transform Iraq instantly into a sophisticated democracy and that it would take temporary responsibility for the governance of the entire country, beginning by dismissing all four hundred thousand members of Saddam's armed forces and police, who would, though unemployed, be free to retire with their weapons and munitions and then rent themselves out, individually and in groups, to the factions in a fierce civil, sectarian, and ethnic war within Iraq. As a sequel, the Americans fired practically the entire civil service, leaving Iraq with no public administration at all above the provincial level. It was, however, the correct decision for Canada all the same, and Chrétien deserves credit for it, even though the Americans and their allies were quite within their rights to dispose of Saddam.

Chrétien rounded out his long career with a stringent campaign-finance reform – which severely restricted acceptable contributions from corporations and unions and increased public contributions to campaigns based on a criterion of previous party electoral perfor-mance; and with a judicially legitimized recognition of same-sex mar-riage rights.

Martin and his supporters were not prepared to tolerate Chrétien going a full eighteen months from his announcement of his retire-ment at Chicoutimi in August 2002, and the prime minister took his leave at the party conference in November 2003. Bono, the lead singer of the rock group U2 and a crusader for the Third World, joked, accu-rately, of Chrétien and Martin that he was "the only subject these two can agree on." Martin was voted leader without significant opposition and succeeded Chrétien as prime minister on December 12, 2003. He won 93 per cent of the convention vote, with almost all the rest going to Sheila Copps (daughter of the former mayor of Hamilton, leader of the so-called Brat Pack of Liberal MPs, and immortalized by Mordecai Richler as "the captain of a women's industrial league bowling team").

One week earlier, the Canadian Alliance and the federal Progressive Conservatives merged to become the Conservative Party of Canada, back to its name in the times of Macdonald, Borden, Meighen, and Bennett. The free Liberal ride was over, as more than 90 per cent of those voting in both parties approved the merger. Joe Clark had unwittingly rendered great service to the Liberals when he fumbled out of government after six months in 1979; had done them great harm when he fumbled out of the leadership of his party in 1982 and lost to Brian Mulroney; had helped them again by maintaining the fractured conservative vote with his return as party leader from 1998 to 2002; but had concluded this astonishing minuet by inadvertently striking the Liberals an almost mortal blow by retiring from the leadership in favour of Peter MacKay. MacKay had pledged to maintain the party, but on the elevation of Stephen Harper over Stockwell Day, and after negotiation on some policy matters, the two leaders agreed on a merger on October 15, 2003. This would prove an epochal event.

It was forty years and eight months since Jean Chrétien had first entered Parliament. (He had retired from Parliament between 1985 and 1990.) He was a sincere and a courageous federalist, in times and places when it was far from fashionable. He deserved better than he received from Pierre Trudeau, whom he served loyally and capably in many positions, including the senior ministries of justice and finance. He rendered immense service by salvaging the constitutional amendment and patriation formula that was agreed by nine provinces and enacted in 1981. As loyal as he was to Trudeau, he had been disloyal to John Turner, though he was not as obligated to be an enthusiastic booster of the man who had defeated him for the succession to Trudeau. And as scheming and underhanded as he was with Turner, he was oppressive and unreasonable to Paul Martin, whom he had defeated in the succession to Turner, and he was ungrateful for Martin's irreplaceable services to the government by his fiscal competence, though Chrétien did support him in difficult policy decisions. Chrétien almost jeopardized the entire country with his bungled management of the 1995 referendum campaign, which was the more inexcusable given that he had worked closely with Trudeau in the brilliantly managed 1980 referendum. His state of panic and near collapse on the eve of the 1995 referendum was a shocking breakdown at one of the decisive moments of Canadian history, but he made up for it, almost miraculously, by his sudden and relatively uncontroversial presentation and adoption of the Clarity Act in the last weeks of the millennium.

Jean Chrétien was generally unimaginative, often small-minded, suspicious, and lumbered with the self-conscious testiness of the outsider and the rough-hewn in a world dominated by more sophisticated people. But he possessed many virtues, including physical and political bravery, perseverance, and a raw cunning based on long experience in the back alleys of political life in a very tough place. Though personable and humorous, he was not very articulate and was rarely eloquent. (When he appeared on television in France, he was rather gratuitously given subtitles, as if his French were incomprehensible; Queen Elizabeth, who is bilingual, found him difficult to understand in either language, though she thought him convivial and diligent.) He would never have enjoyed the success he did if he had not taken over his party when the official Opposition dissolved into fragments, or relinquished it when the Opposition was reassembled. But as Napoleon said of generals, the greatest political leaders are lucky during, if not at the end of, their careers. He was the only Liberal leader never electorally defeated, personally or as party leader, but he was also the only elected prime minister of Canada to be dumped as prime minister by his own party. Where only one party has a chance to govern, politics does not cease, it intensifies, within the governing party.

He intuitively understood both the value of and the need for maintaining the Anglo-French consensus in the country and successfully delivered three decisive reinforcements of the country as a transcontinental, bicultural, federal state: his role in constitutional patriation; the restoration of fiscal solidity beyond any other G8 country; and a probable death blow to the forces of separatism in the requirement for a clear referendum question and a decisive vote, conditions that his distinguished predecessors Pierre Trudeau and Brian Mulroney could have stipulated but did not. In the whole history of the country, only Canada's greatest leaders can claim to have made such a contribution. His limitations were more obvious than those of most of Canada's prominent leaders. The sponsorship scandal would soon blow up spectacularly and taint his government and record, but, withal, Jean Chrétien was an important, and on balance a good and successful, prime minister, who governed sensibly and in a long career earned the respect and gratitude of Canada.

2. Paul Martin and the End of the Liberal Ascendancy, 2003–2006

Paul Martin was prime minister at last, a position that had eluded his father and him a total of three times (in the Liberal conventions of 1958, 1968, and 1990), but he faced a newly united Conservative opposition directed by an attractive, articulate, and bilingual leader who was learning quickly on the job, with a separatist third party as the principal representative from the Liberals' ancient fortress of Quebec, and after eleven years of Liberal government in which the antics of his predecessor had strained the patience of the country and made it susceptible to the allure of change.

Martin had been such a successful finance minister and had so artfully pushed a tenacious incumbent out of the highest office that much was expected of him. In his quest for office, he had engaged a phalanx of polling and policy consultants who had constantly canvassed public tastes and ambitions, and then pitched to them. As prime minister, he was still in the habit of seeking to discover public ambitions and then satisfy them, rather than leading. It was a hazardous technique that was bound to convey an impression of some irresolution.

Chrétien had left behind grenades with the pins pulled: the sponsorship problem was about to blow up with a tremendous report; and Chrétien's campaign-finance reform abruptly shut the wicket on the Liberals' traditional source of funding advantage, as the post-Mulroney Conservatives were an unlikely beneficiary of the largesse of big business. The Liberals had a big lump-sum payment because of their relatively large number of votes, but they couldn't get at the large corporate donations, which, because of Martin's fine performance at finance, they could have attracted.

On February 9, 2004, auditor general Sheila Fraser declared that of $250 million devoted to the sponsorship program – which was designed, through advertising and public relations agencies, to promote events and programs that would demonstrate the benefits of federalism in Quebec – $100 million had vanished. It was a shocking allegation from a serious source. Martin did not pursue the now rather discredited method of the Chrétien government of leaving it to the RCMP and intervening on the fringes of the investigation, but set up a commission of inquiry under Justice John Gomery, who was alleged to be a friend of

Martin's, and, to thicken the plot, chose as his commission counsel former Mulroney chief of staff Bernard Roy. Martin and Chrétien had gone through three years of opposition and nine generally successful years in government together, but Martin had inflicted a unique humiliation on Chrétien, and Chrétien had used his last year as prime minister as best he could to sandbag Martin. In leaving the sponsorship scandal behind, the departing prime minister would blow the Liberal Party to pieces. In probing it as he did, Martin was settling scores both for himself and for Mulroney, but the collateral damage would engulf him. It was like a suicide pact, as Martin and Chrétien took each other down and their party with them.

Having set up the commission, Martin dissolved Parliament for new elections on June 28, 2004. It was a strenuous campaign, in which the Liberals reviled Harper in personal attack ads as an extremist and a "harsh" conservative, and the Conservatives attacked the Liberals as corrupt, too long in office, and cynical, cowardly manipulators. As the Conservatives were an amalgamation of Reform, the Canadian Alliance, and the Progressive Conservatives, they lost some of the old Red Tories to the Liberals and NDP, and some of the true Reform believers sat it out. Martin did well to hold the decline from the Liberals' 40.9 per cent in 2000 to 36.7 in 2004, but they lost 37 MPs, dropping from 172 to 135; while Harper, whose two former parties had 37.7 per cent of the vote in 2000, emerged with just 29.6 per cent, but the combined total of Conservative MPs jumped from 78 to 99. In the confusion, the fallout benefited the third parties: the Bloc Québécois rose from 10.7 per cent to just 12.4 but jumped from 38 MPs to 54; and the NDP rose from 8.5 per cent to 15.7 and from 13 MPs to 19. The Liberal government was 21 seats short of a majority, the first minority since Joe Clark's ill-fated government of 1979, and the balance of power rested with the Bloc. It was going to be difficult, but it was transitional; Harper would get more of his Western Reformers out, and the Bloc could not hold 54 MPs from Quebec indefinitely, though this was a challenge that called for a specialist in tactical parliamentary manoeuvre, which was not Paul Martin's strong suit. Harper, on the other hand – a secretive, not overly companionable loner, a one-time university dropout before becoming an academic economist – was to prove the greatest party leader at parliamentary and election tactics since King. Beneath a presentable and clean-cut and articulate exterior, he was a formidable political operator who revealed nothing of his intricate game plan.

In a First Ministers' Conference from September 13 to 15, 2004, Martin worked out a $41 billion ten-year plan to help pay for the health-care system's endlessly rising costs, but in October, the opposition parties, led by Harper, put through amendments in the guise of reasserting the rights of Parliament over the single will of the leader of the largest party when that party did not have a majority. Paul Martin was reaping what Jean Chrétien had sown. Martin had promised Newfoundland and Nova Scotia all the revenues from offshore oil and gas, after the federal government had retrieved its equalization payments to those provinces. Harper had promised a complete provincial benefit from that source without reclamation of the equalization payments, and the combined opposition votes eventually imposed this on the government, which was forced into a climb-down from an unsustainable position.

Paul Martin and Jean Chrétien both appeared before the Gomery Commission in February 2005. Martin's appearance was uncontroversial, but Chrétien had already moved for the recusal of Gomery for bias, after Gomery had described Chrétien to a journalist as being "small town cheap," and Chrétien concluded his testimony by taking a series of golf balls from his pockets inscribed with the names of U.S. presidents and asking if the American leaders could be so described. It was a strong, but not a conclusive, performance by Chrétien, who argued that the sponsorship affair had been on behalf of Canadian unity and should not be so discredited, as there was no evidence that government officials had pocketed the vanished sums. This breezy approach to vast misappropriations wasn't going to fly, but Chrétien did get himself clear of any suspicion of direct involvement.

On February 24, 2005, the external affairs minister, Pierre Pettigrew, played the nationalist card on the government's behalf and announced that Canada would not participate in the American continental missile defence system, but Martin allowed that he would expect to be consulted before any missiles overflew Canadian air space. This was a vapid position, as Canada had no standing to enforce it, and the missiles would be at very high altitudes and go over the length or breadth of Canada in a few minutes. It all smacked of Diefenbaker's fumbling of the nuclear issue, a pretense to a state of military self-reliance Canada did not possess. More positively, he did put in train the beginning of a defence plan that provided an alternative to leaving the entire defence of Canada explicitly to the United States, which had been the default strategy since the Second World War and even, up to a point, since Roosevelt had pledged to defend Canada from foreign attack at Kingston in 1938. The idea of Canada taking more responsibility for its own defence was an imaginative concept, but it wasn't seriously developed, and Martin and Pettigrew did not present it in a way that attracted much public interest.

The rising tide of outrage over the Gomery Commission revelations kept tremendous pressure on the government. Paul Martin had not imagined that he would be facing the day-by-day battering of his party and his predecessor with a minority in Parliament. The NDP did not in itself have enough MPs to determine the vote, but the Bloc was completely unreliable, and Harper was always enticing them with side deals in the interest of the reassertion of parliamentary democracy – a scam, of course, but an effective cover for his relentless agitation among the unofficial opposition. The NDP made its support for the budget in May 2005 conditional on not making planned corporate tax cuts and instead splashing money around some of the NDP's preferred beneficiaries of public largesse. The three opposition parties intermittently outdid each other in accusations of cynical opportunism, almost all of them well-founded charges.

As a very tight vote on the budget shaped up, Martin and his finance minister, Ralph Goodale, injected a chunk of aid for the persecuted Christians of Darfur, South Sudan, to round up the vote of David Kilgour, a Liberal MP for Edmonton who for the first half of his career in Parliament had been a Conservative and was now threatening to sit as an independent (and was John Turner's brother-in-law, though their relations were tenuous). But this did not budge Kilgour. Reaching into the old King-Pickersgill bag of tricks, Martin attracted Belinda Stronach, daughter of auto parts and racetrack magnate Frank Stronach and a Toronto area Conservative MP, with direct admission to the cabinet as minister of human resources and skills development. She was a glamorous and flamboyant woman who had run second to Harper for the Conservative leadership with a flashy campaign financed by her father, and who was more or less cohabiting with former Conservative leader

Peter MacKay, who had delivered the rump of the old Progressive Conservatives to the Canadian Alliance. Stronach claimed that she was rebelling against the reactionary tendencies of Stephen Harper and fighting for women and the disadvantaged. This explanation was not entirely implausible, given Harper's cold and authoritarian personality. But her critics imputed to her a less disinterested motivation. With the Speaker of the House casting a deciding vote, the Martin government limped through the budget by a single vote (that of the new minister).

Martin spent a precarious summer but soldiered on. In September, he received a visit from Chinese president Hu Jintao, and together they announced a (rather vague but sonorous) "strategic partnership" between the two countries. He also led the creation of the G20, an expanded and multi-continental version of the G8 that included China, India, Brazil, South Africa, Saudi Arabia, and Turkey. (The former exotic rarity of the summit conference was becoming the merest commonplace and an almost continuous, itinerant, process. At Munich, Tehran, Yalta, Postdam, Geneva (1955), and in the subsequent bilateral U.S.-Soviet meetings, they were confined to great powers.) In November, Martin was able to announce – with the premiers, the governments of the territories, and the leaders of the native peoples' and Métis groups – the Kelowna Accord, which pledged the whole country to the elimination of any inequalities between aboriginals and non-aboriginals in health care, housing, education, and employment opportunity.

The Gomery Commission's big shoe dropped with its report on November 1, 2005. Gomery completely cleared Martin and blamed Chrétien as responsible for the conduct of his high-handed chief of staff, Jean Pelletier, who was, the justice wrote, guilty of gross negligence in not imposing any safeguards at all on the expenditure of hundreds of millions of dollars. Paul Martin had served up a full dose of revenge on Jean Chrétien, but Stephen Harper in particular made sure that it was the Liberals, and not just one or another Liberal prime minister, who carried the can for this debacle. There was a court gag order on the findings, but it was completely evaded by bloggers from the United States. NDP leader Jack Layton, playing above his head, given that he only had 19 MPs, stipulated more exigent terms for continued support, which were not agreed, and on November 28, on Harper's motion of non-confidence, the government was defeated 171 to 133, thanks to the Bloc Québécois. The country's fourth general election in just over eight years was called for January 23, 2006.

Inevitably, it was another messy campaign. Harper proceeded on the plan of making a major policy announcement each day, while Martin waited until the new year for a serious re-electoral effort. The Liberals then launched a traditional campaign based on better health care and daycare, tax cuts, and increasing Canadian autonomy in its relations with the United States (which was now mired in an Iraqi civil war and the Bush administration was quite unpopular, at home and elsewhere). The Conservatives held their position in the polls, leading, but not by a wide margin, and the Liberals resorted to attack ads, which had served them in 2004. This time, however, Harper was ready, and the ad campaign backfired.

The Canadian Liberal Party had been the most successful party in the democratic world, having held office for 80 of the 110 years since the rise of Sir Wilfrid Laurier in 1896 (Chapter 4). The great Liberal ascendancy ended on election day 2006. The results (2004 results in brackets) were: Conservatives, 124 MPs and 36.3 per cent of the vote (99 MPs and 29.6 per cent); Liberals, 103 MPs and 30.2 per cent (135 MPs and 36.7 per cent); Bloc Québécois, 51 MPs and 10.5 per cent (54 MPs and 12.7 per cent); NDP, 29 MPs and 17.5 per cent (19 MPs and 15.7 per cent). Harper's position was even more vulnerable than Martin's in parliamentary terms, but he wasn't carrying Chrétien's baggage and the disingenuousness of years, and after four elections in nine years, the opposition could not precipitate a fifth in less than two years; they had to give Stephen Harper a chance. He was forty-six, and was sworn in as prime minister on February 6, 2006.

Paul Martin retired as Liberal leader and from political life. He had been a brilliant finance minister, but only an average prime minister. His government had been hampered from the start by the Chrétien legacy of scandal, arrogance of office, and unhelpful changes to campaign financing rules. Martin had shown a disposition to think differently in defence and strategic terms, and sought to reduce taxes and promote a greater incentive economy, but he was never able to focus on government while the Gomery Commission kept dropping bombshells about previous Liberal transgressions and Stephen Harper played skilfully on the vanity and ambitions of the unofficial opposition leaders. Now, there was no quick fix to restore the Liberals as there had been in the Bennett, Diefenbaker, and Clark interregna: the retrieval of temporarily lost constituencies in Quebec in the first two instances, and of anti-Trudeau votes in Greater Toronto in the case of the Clark aberration (for that was what it was). And Harper had healed the schism with the West that had sunk Mulroney. The government was in the hands of a very agile leader, a less ponderous and pudgy (and more open-minded, though more autocratic) but apparently no less cunning Mackenzie King. Harper had moved to the centre on gay rights, bilingualism, and several social issues, and was an unfrightening figure of the moderate right, facing three left-of-centre parties (though Martin himself was a centrist). He was competent and he was not another Quebecker like all the other prime ministers elected to full terms over the last forty years after Pearson. This was not going to be another brief Conservative interlude, amateurish and eccentric, like that of Diefenbaker or Clark, or a longer and admirably imaginative and perhaps combustibly over-ambitious one, like that of Mulroney. Harper was an intense and overly serious person, whose campaign plane was sarcastically dubbed "Mr. Happy's Flying Circus."[5]

The natural Liberal lock on the federal government was not all that had ended. So had Quebec's hold on government. Quebec's birthrate had collapsed in the post–Roman Catholic era, and hundreds of thousands of Quebeckers had departed, aggravated by restrictive language laws and the cost of socialist government. Quebec's share of the population and of the federal Parliament had fallen from almost a third to less than a quarter, and French Canadians outside Quebec were opposed to Quebec nationalism, so the solidarity of French Canadians was broken. Stephen Harper was passably bilingual, but he could govern almost without Quebec. The dependence of 160 years on the Anglo-French double majority that began with Baldwin and LaFontaine had been strained when the Quebec establishment, having demanded reciprocal biculturalism for three-quarters of a century, attacked it as an attempt to assimilate the French Canadians. Now, a decade after Canada had refused more concessions to Quebec in the rejection of the Meech Lake and Charlottetown accords, Stephen Harper would return the favour, by governing with no animosity or disdain for Quebec, but

independently of it. The country was in uncharted waters, but buoy-
antly so, and with a capable new leader.

3. Stephen Harper and the New Conservative Era, 2006–2014

Harper entered office with a series of strenuously proclaimed promises:
to clean up government with the Federal Accountability Act; reduce
taxes, starting with the Goods and Services Tax; strengthen the justice
system, which essentially meant a straight pitch to law-and-order
hard-liners; provide direct assistance to parents with young children
and to daycare facilities; introduce special funding to remove health-
care waiting lists; and attack the fiscal imbalance, which was a straight
pitch for the decentralizers, as the imbalance referred to was the one
created by the Chrétien and Martin budget-balancing gambit of piling
expenses onto the provinces without any concessions of accompanying
revenue-raising sources. Harper was an authentic conservative who
wanted to strengthen the family, or at least win the hearts and minds of
social conservatives, by strengthening laws against child pornography,
raising the age of sexual consent, and providing choice in education. In
earlier times, he had spoken out in favour of moderate rights of corporal
punishment for parents. He was a low tax decentralizer, champion of
community as well as family values, and a crime-fighter at home, a
hard-liner in foreign policy, and a conservative in a way that Stanfield,
Clark, and Diefenbaker, and even Mulroney, were not. He had long
inveighed against the dangers of Canada being a second-tier northern
socialist country.[6]

He stopped the Liberal practice of "buying change," supplement-
ing payments for provincial priority areas like health care on condition
of conformity to detailed standards imposed by the federal government.
Harper and his finance minister, Jim Flaherty, who had held the same
post in the Mike Harris provincial government of Ontario, considered
any devolution of authority to the provinces, including the simple handing over of block grants for provincial determination of spending
programs, or tax reductions leaving more demand in the hands of the
people, to conform to their plans for decentralization. There was also an
ideological element in the reduction of the Goods and Services Tax:

successor governments would not dare to raise the tax again, and in reducing it Ottawa was distributing its surplus to the people and putting constraints on the Liberal lust for spending increases. He was shrinking the Liberal and NDP "social engineering playground."[7]

Harper undoubtedly won the gratitude of the country by putting a stop to the endless Federal-Provincial Conferences. These over-publicized and verbose photo opportunities in the Government Conference Centre (the old railway station in Ottawa) were always replete with play-acting and only occasionally with any eloquence (and almost never after the departure of Trudeau and the senior Johnson). And they always ended in an acoustically as well as circumstantially strained singing of "O Canada." Harper had the premiers to dinner at his residence once and did not meet them again as a group after that. He made some yardage with Quebec by making a Quebec representative a member of Canada's delegation to UNESCO and by co-opting a Bloc Québécois motion to recognize Quebec as a distinct nation by recog-nizing Quebec pre-emptively as "a nation within a united Canada." It won all-party support. In the second Conservative budget, the main ele-ment was the five-year recalculation of equalization payments, and it was jigged in such a way as to give Quebec – with 24 per cent of the entire population, and French Quebec with about 19 per cent – 46 per cent of the entire increase in transfers. When Premier Jean Charest took advantage of this by cutting Quebec taxes in a close election campaign against Action Démocratique's effort to revive conservative Duplessis non-separatist nationalism, Harper felt that Charest had undercut the provincial argument that the provinces had inadequate resources to deal with their spending responsibilities.

Harper and his entourage had anticipated an early Liberal leader-ship change and probably an early election, but the Liberals were exhausted and divided and took their time, only calling their conven-tion for December 2006. As Martin had won 93 per cent of the votes on the first ballot of the 2003 convention, against Sheila Copps, who had retired from public life, there was no chance to continue with the new and not very successful Liberal practice of elevating the surviving runner-up from the last convention, as Turner had succeeded Trudeau, Chrétien had succeeded Turner, and Martin had succeeded Chrétien. The three main contestants in 2006 were Bob Rae, former NDP premier of Ontario, where he was thrown out very definitively after one term; Chrétien's federal-provincial and then energy minister, the bookish and not very bilingual Stéphane Dion; and former international television commentator and Harvard academic Michael Ignatieff. In a sense, all met the Laurier, King, St. Laurent, Pearson, Trudeau criterion of outsiders, as none had been prominent in the Liberal Party before, and the only one with a lengthy political background was Rae, and that was from another party. Ignatieff was the front-runner, but he made a number of verbal blunders, including a flip-flop that had him accusing Israel of a war crime in Gaza, and he seemed an alarmist about Quebec and rather incomprehensible on the environment (which had been Dion's last priority as minister). In the end, the Liberals were mistrustful of Rae as a party-changer and of Ignatieff as an amateur who had returned from twenty years outside Canada to take the leadership, and Dion came from far back, only 18 per cent on the first ballot, to win. This too was a first for the Liberals: all previous Liberal leaders elected by conventions, from King on, had led all the way.

The Conservatives greeted him with a series of attack ads, an unsportsmanlike innovation. As Dion was running as a cutting edge environmental zealot, Harper installed his energetic loyalist John Baird in the environment ministry with a mandate to steal Dion's thunder. Harper soon unveiled a peppy campaign against greenhouse gases and air pollution, but Dion, who proved to be an owlish wonk lacking tactical leadership aptitudes, waffled on his former affection for a carbon tax. After a tremendous fanfare, the Harper enthusiasm for combatting climate change withered as the evidence supporting the need of such action came under intense re-examination and the political strength of the movement declined. Dion dramatically announced the Green Shift, a poorly thought out imposition of draconian energy emission standards on industry, including a modified cap-and-trade regime, but there would be no tax relief anywhere; the money harvested from industrial carbon users would be re-enlisted in authoritarian Liberal programs. Harper saw an opportunity for an election and began considering how to provoke one, having devoted his energies to enacting a program quickly that a Liberal government could not undo; he was very careful in presenting legislation and laboured under none of the illusions that had caused Joe Clark to govern as if he had a majority, assuring that he only governed for a few months.

On March 26, 2007, Charest limped back into office in Quebec with a minority government, the first in the province's history, as the Liberals, Action Démocratique, and the Parti Québécois split the vote almost equally (previous election results in brackets): Liberals, 48 MNAs and 33.1 per cent of the vote (76 MNAs and 46 per cent); Action Démocratique, 41 MNAs and 30.1 per cent (4 MNAs and 18.2 per cent); PQ, 36 MNAs and 28.4 per cent (45 MNAs and 33.2 per cent). Charest could work with Dumont; the decline of the Parti Québécois, now led by André Boisclair, to 28.4 per cent of the popular vote was taken for a time as indicating that the party could be headed for the ash heap (there to join the Parti National, Conservative Party, Bloc Populaire, Action Libérale Nationale, Union Nationale, and Créditistes).

Dion was suffering serious expressions of concern within his ranks about his competence as leader, and this made the NDP and Bloc Québécois susceptible to the attractions of an election, as they both thought they could feast on the Liberals, even if the Conservatives held their position. Dion, to put some discipline into his party, said that he would lay the whips on for non-confidence motions, so the unofficial opposition could decide whether to have an election or not. This was enough for Harper, who saw the first stages of the economic meltdown of the autumn of 2008, and on September 7 caused the governor general, the rather glamorous Haitian-Canadian Michaëlle Jean, to dissolve Parliament for elections on October 14, 2008.*

It was a nasty campaign, replete with gaffes, minor dirty tricks, and, especially, mocking television advertisements in both directions. The results (2006 results in brackets) were: Conservatives, 143 MPs and 37.6 per cent of the vote (127 MPs and 36.3 per cent); Liberals, 77 MPs and 26.3 per cent (95 MPs and 30.2 per cent); Bloc Québécois, 49 MPs and 10 per cent (51 MPs and 10.5 per cent); NDP, 37 MPs and 18.2 per cent (29 MPs and 17.5 per cent): Greens, no MPs and 6.8 per cent (1 MP and 4.5 per cent). Harper had edged up to within twelve

---

* The position of governor general had become a method of promotion of minorities. Jules Léger was followed by the German-Canadian former Manitoba NDP premier Edward Schreyer; then the first woman to hold the position, the outstanding former Speaker and federal minister Jeanne Sauvé; then the Ukrainian-Canadian Ramon Hnatyshyn, followed by the Acadian Roméo LeBlanc, both journeyman MPs; then the Chinese-Canadian ex-television reporter and provincial agent in Paris Adrienne Clarkson.

MPs of a majority, insulated himself against the economic crisis, which would be the most acute since the 1930s, and left the Liberals at their lowest point ever in the popular vote and again severely divided. Harper was not a stylish political leader like Trudeau or even Mulroney, and he was fortunate in facing the Liberals when they were, unusually, divided under Martin and ineptly led by Dion, but he had shown himself to be purposeful and consistent in policy terms, and very agile as a political tactician.

By the time the election had occurred, the proportions of the world economic crisis were becoming very clear. The U.S. banking system and allied financial institutions, under the original impulse of legislation and regulation by the Clinton administration, unaltered by the George W. Bush administration, had required heavy commitments by the mortgage industry and lending banks to mortgages that did not meet commercial criteria, in the name of increased home ownership. The American insurance industry purported to ensure these instruments in a way that compensated for their relatively high risk, and pieces of these sub-prime mortgages and the insurance on them were packaged together in what were called consolidated debt obligations, certified by the big credit-rating firms Moody's, Standard & Poor's, and Fitch to be of investment grade, and shovelled out by Wall Street onto the world's banking system in the tens of billions of dollars. The yield was high, everyone was selling them and everyone was buying them. Capitalism again showed itself to be as stupid as Lenin had declared it to be when he opined that the "capitalists will sell us the rope we hang them with" in the later explanation of a senior U.S. banker: "When the music's playing, everybody has to dance." They didn't have to, but almost everybody did, albeit in a coalition of idiocy founded and led by the U.S. government. When the music stopped, the U.S. political class locked arms from right to left and blamed it on private sector greed, but the real initial cause was their own quest for a political free lunch of rising family home ownership levels and fattened campaign donations from developers and the corrupt building trades unions at no additional cost to the taxpayers.

Except for Canada and a few other countries, almost all the world's banking systems hit the wall at once, even those nationalities long culturally synonymous with prudent lending: the Swiss and Scots. It was the most complete American public policy disaster since the foreign, social, and economic policy trifecta of the 1920s and early 1930s which included isolationism, Prohibition, slamming the gate on immigration, the immense stock market bubble, raising tariffs and taxes, and shrinking the money supply. President George W. Bush, when inspirational language was required, warned, "The sucker could go down," referring to the fourteen-trillion-dollar economy of the United States. It had come to this, a banal tocsin from the chief executive that mighty America was on the brink of economic ruin just seventeen years after gaining the greatest and most bloodless strategic victory in the history of the nation state with the implosion of the Soviet Union and the collapse of international communism. The world's largest financial corporation, Citigroup, was effectively bankrupt, as were the country's traditionally largest bank and securities firm, Bank of America and Merrill Lynch. Goldman Sachs, long the virtual junior partner of the U.S. Department of the Treasury and the British Exchequer, was revealed as having been selling billions of dollars of worthless real estate–backed securities to its immense client list while short-selling them out the back door for their house account, and had to seek a distressed infusion of capital from investor Warren Buffett. Mighty Deutsche Bank, in the long reign of Helmut Kohl the virtual partner of the German government in industrial ownership and foreign development projects, and connected intimately to the federal chancellor himself, required government assistance. Large parts of the British, Swiss, Australian, Dutch, Japanese, French, Italian, Spanish, and other banking systems would have failed and brought down all the equity holders and compromised the depositors if governments had not created money to invest in them. Canada, where no fully chartered bank had failed since 1923, suffered no such problems. Most of the six large banks endured some losses in the bursting bubble, but well within their officially imposed ratios and not on a scale to impair the stability of any of them. This was the result of a conservative national savings rate and regulatory climate, and the existence of only six large banks in a rich G8 country then of thirty-three million people. The bank executives of Canada themselves were not necessarily made of sterner stuff than those whose institutions went down like nine-pins in most of the rest of the Western world. The Canadian model of collaboration between the private and public sectors was vindicated. This was essentially the model developed to some extent by Jean Talon, and recreated by John Graves

Simcoe, Francis Hincks, Macdonald, Laurier, Clifford Sifton, R.B. Bennett, and C.D. Howe.

The crisis was addressed everywhere by deluges of newly created money irrigating the system in the guise of debt, when much of it was simply money-supply expansion, what was formerly called "printing money" but now sheltered under the gratingly euphemistic rubric of "quantitative easing." The most worrisome aspect of the entire episode was neither the damage nor the reflexive and almost hysterical response to it (starting inevitably with lame invocations of Herbert Hoover's platitudinous falsehood that "the economy is fundamentally sound") but the fact that almost no one except a few short-selling market sharks and academic kooks foresaw the onrushing crisis. Central bankers, lending bankers, merchant bankers, academic economists, financial journalists, industrialists, financiers, treasury officials, no one had any idea of the proportions of the problem. It was relatively insightful for Canada's finance minister, Jim Flaherty, to refer in his 2006 budget to "the risk of a sudden correction in U.S. house prices." What happened went well beyond a sudden correction, as it swept most of the banking system of the West into technical insolvency.

This sudden economic near-death experience from self-inflicted wounds, as well as the chronic American current account deficit of $800 billion annually, starting in the Clinton years, and the miring of almost the entire U.S. conventional military ground forces capability in the Middle East for nearly a decade, severely eroded U.S. prestige. George W. Bush was not internationally respected, culturally or in terms of policy consistency, and the man who threw his shoes at Bush's head in a press conference in Baghdad enjoyed widespread assent, at least in spirit. It was unusual for the person of the U.S. president not to be respected. The president elected to succeed Bush in 2008, Barack Obama, though as an articulate African-American he started out with great goodwill internationally, was a disappointing ally and policy-maker. Colossal budgetary deficits prevailed throughout his term and there was little real economic recovery despite increasing the accumulated federal debt from $10 trillion to $18 trillion in five years, an 80 per cent increase on where it had been in 2009, after 233 years of American independence. And much of the debt wasn't bought at arm's length but by the Federal Reserve, a subsidiary of the U.S. Treasury

Department. It was paid for by specially issued notes, a shell game that would have been illegal in the private sector.

For Canada – which had lived, often precariously, on the edge of the great American project, conditioned to the rise and rise of that astonishing country, which after the U.S. Civil War operated on a scale unlike anything the world had seen or imagined before – these American reversals were especially shocking. The Civil War was a horrible agony, but the United States was led by its greatest statesman to the victory of the Union and the emancipation of the slaves. The Great Depression afflicted America as it did the whole world, but the country quickly elevated another of its greatest leaders, and in the balance of the 1930s Franklin D. Roosevelt was almost the only leader of an important country not to be ashamed of, neither a barbarous dictator like Hitler, Stalin, Mussolini, and the Japanese, nor an appeaser of them like Chamberlain and Daladier. Now, all the worst qualities of the Americans combined to inflict distinct humiliation on America: venal and ignorant politicians; vulgar and imprudent economic consumption; and foreign policy vacillations between over-hasty recourse to force in support of democracy in unpropitious places and a pallid attempt at realistic cynicism, leading to unrequited concessions to Iran and Russia. America's greatest qualities – enterprise, generosity, courage in national policy – were obscured.

All nations have fluctuations of fortunes and quality of governance, and the United States, having seen off its last rivals, at least for a considerable time – Nazi Germany, the Soviet Union, and, in industrial terms, cartelized Japan – took a good time to rest on its oars. For all its history, Canada had been intimidated by the fact that, no matter how well it did, it was always in the shadow of its overpowering neighbour, always overlooked by the world and taken more or less amiably for granted, by the Americans, the British, and, when they condescended to notice at all, even the French, although Canada, never under threat itself, had given its all in solidarity with all of those countries throughout the twentieth century. This sudden plunge of the American superpower into the tenebrous nether region of misgovernment and national absurdity shifted the basis of Canadian national self-esteem from the confected self-consciousness of caring, sharing social programs and moralizing (whether "arm-flapping," in Dean Acheson's phrase, or otherwise), to the higher ground of recognition that it was a better-governed country and a better-functioning society, with less debt and, in many respects, lower taxes than the United States. This fact, and the defeat of the separatists in Quebec, emancipated Canada from much of the diffidence that had hobbled it for all of its history, and, being Canada, this emancipation came slowly and quietly and was not translated into braggadocio or impetuosity, just a more secure national consciousness.

Stephen Harper and Jim Flaherty observed the deepening economic crisis – from which the strengths of the system they directed, and the talent of Paul Martin and Jean Chrétien, were largely responsible for delivering the country – as an opportunity for a lunge for the political jugular. Since Chrétien's time, official federal parties received $1.95 for every vote they gained in the previous general election, to pay their operating costs and reduce their dependence on private and special interest funding. Harper and Flaherty conceived the plan to include in an economic update for November 27, 2008, a number of belt-tightening measures, including freezes on MPs' pay and expenses and the abolition of this political party funding method. Doing this would cost the Conservatives $10 million, or 37 per cent of their income, but it would cost the Liberals $7.7 million (63 per cent), the Bloc Québécois $2.6 million (86 per cent), and the NDP $4.9 million (57 per cent). Harper calculated that this would put immense heat on the Bloc and facilitate a division of its position between the NDP and the Liberals, who would thus be consoled by their own inconveniences, and that it would enable the Conservatives to exploit their advantages in funding. Flaherty's document was rather complacent in tone and implied that the government had already acted preveniently to mitigate the recession, cutting two points off the GST and increasing infrastructure expenses in 2006 and 2007, and that nothing more was required at this point. The budget would remain balanced, but Flaherty prepared opinion for deficit financing should it become necessary because of the extent of the international vulnerability to the errors of other countries. This was not as pompous as it may seem, and Canada was entitled to pat itself on the back a little, though it should have been more bipartisan.

All three parties said they would vote against Flaherty's plan, and the implications of this were immediately obvious. The three opposition party leaders had already started discussion of a coalition between them. Harper's caucus was soon telling him that reaction from the party faithful to Flaherty's message was hostile, not because of the political subsidy's promised demise, but because of its smugness, given the decline of the automobile industry and other consumer spending and the 30 to 40 per cent crack in the stock market, and that Canada should not pretend to be quite so isolated from worldwide trends. The opposition parties would have their first opportunity to vote down the government on December 1, on a supply motion. Harper began to manoeuvre (unlike Clark in 1979) and said the political subsidy would not be in the measure voted on, but the opposition parties could smell blood and said they would vote against the government whatever was at issue. Harper deferred the December vote for a week, promised that there would be a more comprehensive economic package soon, made the usual references to the inappropriateness of another election, and opened fire on the coalition idea as an unholy alliance to usurp the Conservatives and deliver decisive influence to the separatist enemies of Canada in its Parliament. He gathered polemical strength quickly with talk of "backroom deals" conducted by a defeated leader who had already thrown in the towel (as had Trudeau in 1979, but he had led the popular vote, where Dion had been bombed). He concluded: "The opposition has every right to defeat the government, but Stéphane Dion does not have the right to take power without an election."[8] The Conservatives effectively abandoned Flaherty's entire supplementary budget message, and had fortuitously been advised of the dial-in number for a Jack Layton conference call with his NDP caucus on Saturday, November 28. The Conservatives recorded the call and released, almost at once, comments of Layton's that made it clear that discussion of a coalition had begun before Flaherty's message was released, and that Layton was fairly blasé about making common cause with the separatists. Harper was suffering from an acute influenza infection (contracted at an Asian-Pacific meeting in Lima a few days before) and was not impressive in his comments to the House on November 30.

On December 1, the three opposition leaders met the press together and confirmed their intention to form a coalition government in which all three parties would contribute ministers, under Dion as prime minister. Conservative attacks on reliance on separatists to govern federally in a way that caused Layton and Dion to have misrepresented themselves in the recent election started to take hold and echo in the ears of the MPs of the three federalist parties. On December 2, Harper, recovering and revitalized, told the House of Commons that the coalition deal was "a betrayal of the voters of this country." He attacked the three leaders personally and pointed out that when they signed their corrupt and implicitly treasonable arrangement, they could not have the Canadian flag behind them "because one of them does not believe in this country." (In fact, there were Canadian and provincial flags behind them, but that wasn't the point.) The tide was turning. Harper secured from the governor general a prorogation of Parliament until January 26, and the incipient coalition collapsed under the weight of public denigration. Harper had gone into a self-made trap insouciantly, but had recovered well and again profited from the amateurism of his opponents. Of the three opposition leaders, the only one who recognized that the Bloc's presence in a coalition could be a show-stopper was the Bloc leader himself, Gilles Duceppe.

On December 8, Dion announced that he would resign as soon as the Liberal caucus chose his successor, and two days later Michael Ignatieff was chosen as interim leader, a decision that was later ratified, but with less formality than usual in the Liberal Party. Stéphane Dion thus passed into the footnotes of Canadian history as the first federal Liberal leader not to be prime minister since Edward Blake, who had taken his leave 121 years before. Harper clung thereafter to the position that what was available on the political menu was a Conservative minority or a shabby and cynical coalition of his opponents. Having survived narrowly, he gained strength and stature and was more formidable than ever, as was the country he led, as most other advanced countries wallowed in what was called the Great Recession.

Flaherty's next attempt at a budget, for 2009, forecast $60 billion of deficit over two years and essentially contained all that the NDP and Liberals had been claiming to miss in his ill-fated supplementary budget of a few weeks earlier. There were modest tax cuts and a good dollop of stimulus spending. Ignatieff announced the Liberals would support it if the government explained every three months how the money was actually being distributed to the people. The government jubilantly accepted this as facilitating its propaganda effort to demonstrate its munificence in the guise of satisfying the official Opposition's demands.

At the end of March 2009, Ignatieff was rubber-stamped as permanent leader by the Liberals in Vancouver, in a convention highlighted by a very lengthy and soporific farewell to and by Stéphane Dion. The Conservatives greeted the new leader with the now traditional attack ads on television: "He's not in it for Canada. He's just in it for himself. . . . Michael Ignatieff: just visiting." Ignatieff's vague manner of developing issues, throwing out striking positions and then retreating from them and nibbling around the edges, created an air of fecklessness, of dilettantism.

Harper had realized that successful Conservatives usually hold the nationalist card (Disraeli, Macdonald, Salisbury, Churchill, Nixon, Thatcher, Reagan), and he had noticed that while Brian Mulroney increased Canada's influence in the world with his intimacy with President Reagan and the senior President Bush, it had not gone down well with the Canadian voters. Steeped in the self-consciousness of the unequal continental relationship, Canadians had resented what they took as Mulroney's subordinacy, if not (very unjustly) servility, to the American leader. Harper could also not have failed to notice the nose-dive in America's status in the world since the time of President Clinton. He was happy enough not to be cordially called by George W. Bush on the day before Bush handed over to Obama, unlike many other leaders favoured with such a call, and he made no effort to make anything very noteworthy out of President Obama's visit to him in March 2009.

He was the most pro-Israeli prime minister in Canadian history, or at least since John Diefenbaker, whose government was in office when all the Western powers were pro-Israel, before Anwar Sadat made the Arabs more popular and while King Hussein still represented the Palestinians (despite being a Bedouin that most Palestinians viewed with respectful suspicion). In Harper's case, his stance may have had the benefit of taking the electoral, media, and financial support of Canada's Jewish community away from the Liberals, but there is no reason to doubt that it has been a sincere expression of Harper's view and that of his about-to-be foreign minister (the External Affairs Department was finally changed to the Foreign Ministry), John Baird. Essentially, the Government of Canada's view is that the bar to peace is the refusal of the Palestinians and their sponsors to admit the right of Israel to exist as a Jewish state, and that if this were addressed it would be simple to establish a Palestinian state. The Canadians and the

Czechs are effectively the only countries who join Israel in this view, as even the United States has signed on to a version of the need for Israel to stop completely any construction of West Bank settlements to make peace possible. Although Israel made it clear in Sinai and Gaza that it would uproot settlers if it was part of a real peace, the Israelis became understandably tired of land-for-peace scams in which they would trade territory conquered in wars the Arabs had started and lost, in exchange for cease-fires that would not be observed by the other side.

This stance caused Canada to be blocked in its quest for a seat on the United Nations Security Council in 2010, and Ignatieff, as the son and political heir of the Liberal Pearsonian tradition of enthusiasm for international organizations (his father was a distinguished foreign service officer), took issue with this. But Ignatieff was unambiguously rebuffed by Harper, who dug in on the issue and disparaged the United Nations as a centre of hypocrisy and Third World mockery of the West, which founded and maintained the UN. Harper had also been pretty solid on Afghanistan. It was Chrétien who originated Canada's commitment to the war in Afghanistan, and Martin had held it, even after the United States largely decamped to Iraq and left its UN and NATO allies in a severely undermanned position, trying to maintain an imposed peace in the warlord-riven country while the Bush doctrine of democratization was imperfectly implemented by a corrupt, despotic, and ungrateful regime. Canada was left with responsibility for securing Kandahar, a province of over a million people, with a force of one thousand, about six hundred trigger-pullers. Kandahar was the birthplace of the fundamentalist and terrorist Taliban, and it was a wonder, and a testament to its professionalism, that the Canadian contingent wasn't massacred. Obama increased the U.S. commitment to Afghanistan and the Canadians stayed to the end of the allied commitment in 2014. Whatever the succeeding condition of the country, and despite a controversy about detainees, Canada did its part. It was the largest Canadian military mission since Korea, more than fifty years before, and at time of writing, 158 Canadians had died there.

Harper had kept the spectre of coalition government involving separatist collaboration alive since his brush with catastrophe at the end of 2008. One of the areas where he replicated Mackenzie King was in his solitary, obscure tenacity on points that he detected would be durably useful. There is no reason to believe that Stephen Harper is as sanctimonious or mystical as King – and he has a very attractive and vivacious wife and two children, and they appear to be a typical family, and he is an ardent hockey fan – but he is a remote figure who believes in a modern conservative position of limited government as ardently as King believed in his reconciliation of industry and humanity, and who is as determined as King to take decisions of long-term implications when he can and manage political tactics with an almost imperceptible patience and cunning. He is a more media-presentable person, more photogenic and given to more sharply formulated sentences, not as apparently deliberate and indecisive as King. Unlike King, Harper has never been defeated personally and is bilingual. He did not gain the leadership of the Opposition by representing himself (with questionable accuracy as King did) as the rightful successor to a revered leader, but rather had to toil in the coils of internecine opposition politics, with all its frustrations and antagonisms, to weld two fractious parties together, sell a political perspective to the right of Canadian tradition, and endure five years of minority government against leaders who, however unsuccessful, were more accessible to voter affection than were the leaders King mainly faced, the very accomplished but bombastic and infelicitous Arthur Meighen and R.B. Bennett.

If Harper's playing of the separatist card against the opposition in 2008 had been a little like King's response to the Chanak affair in 1922, or even the Byng affair in 1926, in March 2011 he pulled from the hat a vintage Kingsian rabbit, like King acting on J.L. Ralston's two-year-old letter of resignation in 1944. Jim Flaherty presented another budget on March 23, 2011, and on Harper's orders included only about half of what Jack Layton had asked for as a condition of support for the budget, particularly restoration of the ecoEnergy home retrofit program, increases to the guaranteed income supplement and to the Canada Pension Plan, and to allocations for more doctors and nurses for the health-care system. Flaherty told the press and the House that he had accommodated the NDP, as agreed between Harper and Layton, as if to make sure that Layton noticed that he got less than he had been led to expect. (Harper and Flaherty gave him half what he expected for the home retrofits, less than he wanted for the income supplement, and nothing else.) Layton was fighting mad.

On March 25, 2011, the House of Commons Standing Committee on Procedure found that the government was in contempt of the committee because it had failed to answer with adequate precision opposition demands for estimates of the cost of overruns in the F-35 fighter plane program, corporate tax reductions, the G20 summit meeting Harper had hosted the previous year in and near Toronto, and Harper's draconian crime bills. These last were proposed by his grim, oddly moustachioed, and reactionary public security minister, Vic Toews. They feature construction of new prisons and enforcement of more severe sentences and harsher imprisonment conditions despite a declining crime rate, on the theory of "build and they will come"; that is, be hunted out, convicted, and dragged to detention. They include mandatory sentences by which legislators usurp the role of judges, dispensing with any effort to rehabilitate wrongdoers, and treating families who are visiting inmates with gratuitous official pettifogging and segregation. It is contemptible, especially as the chief victims will be native people, most of whom should not be in the prison system.

Harper treated the complaint of contempt of the committee as just another manifestation of the opposition's will to coalesce in mindless obstructionism. Ignatieff had taken the bait; Layton was furious at being short-changed by Flaherty; and Duceppe would not hang back. Harper and his senior colleagues unctuously masqueraded as diligent governors "trying to make minority government and Parliament work," a Joe Clark phrase from the 1979 fiasco (Chapter 9).*

Harper hit the ground running for the May 2 election after Parliament voted the government in contempt of the committee. He claimed that it was a mere foretaste of the arrogance and irresponsibility of the "coalition" that he was facing, and that the country would have to choose between a Conservative government and a ramshackle and morally bankrupt league of tricksters dominated by separatists; that is, traitors. Harper ran a very controlled campaign, claiming to admit all comers to his meetings until stories came out that his security unit was evicting people for pretty spuriously based suspicions of possible

---

* This was the seventh time a government had lost the confidence of the House: Macdonald in 1873 (though he resigned without a vote), King and Meighen in 1926 (Meighen lost the vote), Diefenbaker in 1963, Trudeau (deliberately) in 1974, Clark in 1979, Martin in 2005, and now Harper deliberately.

troublemaking. Ignatieff didn't click with the voters, proving testy and ineffectual in the debates; Duceppe was now a complete anachronism in Quebec, a Bouchardist heirloom in a post-separatist Quebec in a federal election. But Layton was making it in English and French Canada as the most personable of the leaders. Harper could hold his Conservative forces on an ideological leash, but Layton was making serious inroads against the other two opposition parties. All of the three national parties were giving similar messages about helping families; Harper was offering a less Pearsonian and UN-compliant foreign policy; and Layton started to play footsie with the Quebec nationalists as he smelt a breakthrough in that province, where his entirely bilingual persona of *"le bon Jack"* went over well. Provincial workplace laws oppressive to the non-French would, he said, be applied to federal employees in the province, a harbinger of NDP flim-flam to come. Ignatieff started shouting, "Rise up! Rise up, Canada!" at his audiences and in television advertising. This was a bit over the top for Canadians, no matter how bored they were with their politicians. While this was happening, the Bloc leader, Gilles Duceppe, feeling himself squeezed by Layton and the NDP, got closer to the Parti Québécois and called for solidarity from the sovereigntists to hang on to the PQ's full share of the province's vote (about a third, but not in a federal election, where many of the separatists wouldn't bother voting).

The government made an immense effort in constituencies with large numbers of immigrants, where the minister of immigration, Jason Kenney, had already done a great deal of work to assure a good result. The campaign ended amid efforts by the Sun Media chain of English and French tabloid newspapers and its allied cable television stations to hype a story about Jack Layton being found naked in a massage parlour in 1996. On election night, May 2, Stephen Harper raised his party's standing for the fourth consecutive time, an unprecedented record in modern national elections in serious democracies, and won his long-sought majority. The great Liberal Party was in tatters and the Bloc Québécois was virtually exterminated. The results (2008 results in brackets) were: Conservatives, 166 MPs and 39.6 per cent of the vote (143 MPs and 37.6 per cent); Liberals, 34 MPs and 18.9 per cent (77 MPs and 26.3 per cent); NDP, 103 MPs and 30.6 per cent (37 MPs and 18.2 per cent); Bloc Québécois, 4 MPs and 6.04 per cent (49 MPs and 10 per cent); Green, 1 MP and 3.9 per cent (no MPs and 6.8 per cent). Ignatieff and Duceppe were defeated in their own constituencies and announced their retirement from politics on election night. The centre had once again become a position of weakness, as Ignatieff could not slice votes back from Harper, who ran successfully as a moderate and effective conservative just trying to complete his mandate, or from Layton, who ran as a good and an unfrightening progressive. Quebec had finally figured out that the Bloc couldn't do anything for it, but could not chin itself on the vague Ignatieff or the cold Albertan Harper, though all three national English-speaking party leaders were impressively bilingual. Layton now had 57 per cent of his NDP MPs from Quebec, though 64 per cent of his vote had come from other provinces. There were the usual unlikely beneficiaries of such a sudden Quebec tidal wave. The Progressive Conservatives elected there in 1958 had been reasonably plausible, because they had been chosen by Duplessis and his close associates, but one of Mulroney's Quebec caucus elected on the tide in 1984 was the courier delivery man who brought the constituency association nomination instructions from national headquarters and was chosen by the party executives who were the addressees. Layton had some unilingual English MPs from French districts, a couple of teenage students, and a woman who had been in California during the election and was only dimly aware that she had been nominated.

The burning question was whether the Liberals could be revived or would merge with the NDP. But Stephen Harper, if he just lived out his term, would be the sixth-longest serving prime minister (after King, Macdonald, Trudeau, Laurier, and Chrétien) and appeared for the indefinite future to have almost as fragmented an opposition as Chrétien had enjoyed. But his mastery was of his own design; Chrétien's had been the serendipity of perseverance and the errors of opponents.

Jack Layton died of cancer on August 22, 2011, and Harper generously awarded him a state funeral. He was a well-liked man who had led his party to astonishing heights. He was replaced as leader by Thomas Mulcair, MP from Outremont, Quebec, and a former minister in Jean Charest's Liberal Quebec government. Mulcair (b. 1954) was a formidable and hirsute parliamentarian and debater and promised to be a strong leader of the Opposition, if not as personally affable as the always smiling Jack Layton, who was everyone's idea of someone to have a beer with in a tavern. All three of the major opposition leaders in the late election had now vanished from the scene (although Ignatieff's predecessor, Dion, continued as an MP and shadow minister).

Eventually, the Liberals – having flunked at their old system of elevating the previous runner-up to the head of the party (Turner, Chrétien, and Martin) and struck out badly in their effort to revive the unlikely leader from afar with Dion and Ignatieff (and Bob Rae, though the interim leader from 2011 to 2013, declined to run for the leadership) – tried something altogether different: dynastic heredity, with Justin Trudeau, elected Liberal leader in April 2013. He had been an MP since 2008, had not made much impact in the House, and was dogged by suggestions that he might be intellectually thin for the position. But he carried a name that with time was somewhat magic, was a better looking and less combative man than his father, and was less dogmatically fixed in a social-democratic time warp. He didn't have his father's formidable personality and flinty toughness and bitchy genius for repartee, but he didn't have to fight the separatists from such a tight corner either; his father had done that for the country (and won).

Harper opened his new term by engaging a special adviser in Quebec – former MP André Bachand, who had quit in 2004 saying that Harper "has the charisma of a picnic table" – and trying to devise some way to entice Quebeckers, now effectively the only region of the country his tactics had not penetrated. He also ended the marketing monopoly of the Canadian Wheat Board, ended the long-gun registry as a service to farmers and hunters, and gave notice of withdrawal from the Kyoto accord, which had been an insane leap aboard the global warming alarm movement that, if implemented, would move scores of billions of dollars around between countries that did not deserve to be penalized and those that did not deserve to be rewarded, for scientifically false reasons. Only the recipient countries had signed it with any sincerity. (Effectively, successful economies would have to pay huge penalties to primitive countries because of their industrial and vehicular carbon use, and underdeveloped countries, usually despotisms, would receive bonanzas. China, though the greatest polluter, would be a beneficiary, and so would Russia, because it was a much smaller carbon-user than the former Soviet Union. It was nonsense, and almost all the anticipated payout countries balked.)

The *vieux jeu* is still being played out in Quebec. The Parti Québécois came back for the third time in 2012, but with a minority government in a fragmented Assembly, representing only 32 per cent of the vote and with the most improbable premier Quebec has ever had, the unfathomably humdrum Pauline Marois (b. 1949). She reduced the province to wedge politics of the lowest sub-American variety. In the guise of requiring that Muslim women reveal their identities, the government of Quebec, in what was portentously described as a Charter of Values, purported to have the right to dictate the size of religious ornaments people may wear. A mutation of the infamous language police (much sought out by bemused tourists) was envisioned as, effectively, an apparel police, to impose what was really an assault on the religious, specifically Roman Catholic heritage of French Canada. This is a heritage the atheistic separatists, in their ahistorical nihilism, wish to expunge, even as their own fortunes fade. Thomas Mulcair, Jack Layton's successor as federal leader of the Opposition, expanded Layton's mischievous election pitch for the separatist vote in federal elections by explicitly promising to honour Quebec's oppressive language laws in the federal workforce in Quebec, and to gut or repeal Chrétien's Clarity Act. Mulcair tried tentatively to convince English Canada that he was the true federalist, because only by the grovelling appeasement of these restrictive impulses would Quebec's confidence be reinforced sufficiently for it to resist the temptations of independence. Such sophistry usually announces and precedes the collapse of the movement whose tenets it expresses at their most absurd.

And when Premier Marois called an election for April 7, 2014, ostensibly to approve the Charter of Values and catapult her government into a majority on the charter's assumed popularity, the campaign quickly degenerated into a slanging match about separatism and a possible referendum. Marois was decisively defeated, lost her own district in Charlevoix, and brought Parti Québécois support down to 25.5 per cent, almost where it was in its first general election in 1970. Lévesque had lasted nine years as premier. Parizeau, Bouchard, and Bernard Landry also lasted nine years between them, and Marois, in the party's third try, lasted just eighteen months. The new premier, Liberal Philippe Couillard, former health minister in the Charest government, was elected in the usually separatist district of Roberval, although he was the most unambiguously federalist Quebec Liberal leader since Jean Lesage, if not Adélard Godbout. It is possible that Stephen Harper's ability to govern without Quebec, with cold indifference but without antipathy, has contributed to the weakening of Quebec nationalism. This ability will be increased by the attribution of new constituencies, mainly in English Canada, for the 2015 election. Harper skilfully bought Bloc Québécois support for this measure in exchange for tax concessions from Ottawa. The fact that Harper does not always highlight his achievements should not deny him the credit for them.

Two prolonged controversies arose: the reticence of the United States government to approve the Keystone XL crude oil pipeline that would, if built, ultimately move 830,000 barrels a day of tar sands oil from Alberta all the way to the Gulf Coast and eliminate one-half of U.S. oil imports from the Middle East. There was also robust discussion about proposed pipelines from the same source to Kitimat, British Columbia, for shipment by tanker to East Asia. Both projects raised environmental questions and the pipeline to the West Coast also raised the question of the rights of native people. There was tremendous lobbying on all sides as the Obama administration waffled characteristically between the agitation of interest groups. In Canada, an outfit plumped imaginatively for "ethical oil," which meant oil the sale of which did not benefit antagonistic, and especially terrorism-supporting, governments. Harper was commendably firm that he was not going to avoid job creation to please the environmentalists, while promising ecological vigilance.

The other issue that raised its ungainly head concerned Conservative senators who were alleged by Senate committee and RCMP investigations to have abused their expense accounts, and especially in travel allowances. In an odd move, the prime minister's chief of staff, Nigel Wright, a well-to-do and highly regarded alumnus of Bay Street, paid Senator Mike Duffy, a Parliament Hill roué and television veteran of more than thirty years, ninety thousand dollars, with which he repaid what was deemed to be his overstated travel allowance draws as a senator. On its face, this was merely a wealthy friend assisting a journeyman senator to wind down an embarrassment for the government, and the proceeds went to the taxpayers. But a considerable controversy ensued, and Wright resigned a few days after the arrangement was made public, because of Duffy's own indiscretions, at the end of February 2013. Wright was not indicted, and the government appeared to be following the Chrétien formula of leaving it to the snail's pace of the RCMP.

However, charges have been laid against others and sworn evidence will be required, which can scarcely fail to embarrass the government.

The parliamentary press corps does not like Harper's cold and manipulative style, and he enjoys no great reservoir of public sympathy, and after eight years sometimes seems tired, unimaginative, and peevish. The government has not renewed its program with fresh ideas and targets, much less transformative reforms and prestigious new faces, but it is still managing competently. Its law-and-order plans are primitive demagogy for the benefit of voters it could not possibly fail to attract without them. But they are not determining of the government's merits, which, even if it merely sits on its record and runs the departments, has provided good and consistent government and made Canada a much more successful country than the old socialistic, high tax, slow growth nanny state the Liberals loved to create and manage. (The NDP are no longer, as St. Laurent good-naturedly said of its precursor, the CCF, just "Liberals in a hurry.")

Stephen Harper has changed that trajectory, and has retained his standing as the preferred choice to head the government, from respect and not affection or panache. His tactical chicanery is generally a little more artistic than irritating, and he is in many areas, including almost all aspects of foreign policy, a man of firm and well-thought-out beliefs. His speech to the Israeli Knesset on January 20, 2014, was a seminal address that squarely blamed the Arabs for refusing to recognize Israel's right to exist as a Jewish state, even as he increased aid to the Palestinian Authority. He declined to join in the relaxation of sanctions on Iran over its nuclear military program, and sent six CF-18s to Poland to watch Ukraine in April 2014 when that country was threatened by Russian aggression. The effectiveness of his bold and principled foreign policy is undercut by his failure to deliver on his promise to strengthen Canada's defence capability. Canada's only maintenance vessel broke down in the central Pacific in early 2014 and had to be towed by the Navy to Pearl Harbor, where it was decommissioned. Harper passed on opportunities to buy sophisticated helicopter and aircraft carriers from the Netherlands, France, and the United States.

Harper avoids whole categories of issues, including abortion, euthanasia, and the Constitution, and seems unable to focus on the desirability of income tax cuts against very selective sales tax increases in optional spending areas, presumably because of his determination to keep federal revenues low (under 14 per cent of GDP, the lowest figure in more than fifty years), despite the undisputed fact that reducing income taxes on people and corporations and defence spending are the best ways to stimulate economic growth. He has no grasp of joint public–private sector cooperation, and has thus passed on opportunities to help take the country into an ownership position in the automobile industry. (He did join with the Obama administration in the bailouts of General Motors and Chrysler but had no interest in accumulating equity in that industry in Canada.) But he has performed an essential service in giving the country a serious moderate-conservative party fully capable of governing and competing with the orthodoxy of nearly fifty years, only modestly challenged by Mulroney and Chrétien, that taxing and spending were the answer to all public policy issues.

If he does not become a little less of a time-server and placeman and resume his status as an agent of well-considered change, more focused on reform and less on mere longevity for the love of incumbency, the country will quickly tire of him. In mid-2014, he had yet to complete the transition from a conservative guerrilla warrior sabotaging the march of the left, to a creative author of original policy. And although he has governed competently, he is afflicted by a stubborn authoritarianism, inaccessibility, and what Macauley described, in reference to King William III (whom he admired) as "an almost repulsive coldness." Yet, while political predictions are hazardous, barring something completely unforeseeable, however long he lasts, Stephen Harper will likely be an accomplished and capable prime minister.

This chronicle, as a work of non-fiction, must end at the present, and the dessicated and oppressively serious ambiance created by Harper and his regime may seem an anti-climax to a story largely unfolded by colourful personalities in tumultuous circumstances. But panache has often been scarce in Canada, and most of it has come from the French, who have recently focused more on their own province than on their country. But the competence, determination, and, up to a point, the sly tactical agility of Harper, are a large part of the Canadian story too. (Macdonald, King, and Mulroney, who governed between them for nearly sixty years, were not tyros either.) Stephen Harper has been generally successful, and that quality is the largest single component of the history of Canada, a country that has grown steadily, always pursued admirable goals, has never been defeated, and has rarely embarrassed itself.

Reflections and Prospects

This narrative has followed the arrival of Europeans in Canada all the way forward from the bold vision of Champlain. If the war with Britain had not already ended after Champlain's heroic resistance, when the Kirke family seized Quebec in 1629, the whole French effort in Canada, which did not yet have one hundred permanent French residents, would have failed 130 years before the British did take Quebec, and would have been absorbed entirely by British Americans. Champlain resurrected it, and through Jean Talon's importation of adequate numbers of fertile young French women to enracinate the French in an inhospitable place, and the establishment of enough industry, the colony was built into an autonomous community behind the fierce defence of Frontenac and the Vaudreuils. Fortuitously, as France could not possibly maintain such an entity against British control of the high seas indefinitely, Britain gained French Canada as a prize of war after it had become self-sustaining and unburdensome. While they were

lethargically determining what to do with it, the British were motivated by the disaffection of the Americans to guaranty the security of
the French Canadians in exchange for their loyalty, and to encourage
and receive Loyalists from the United States into what became
English Canada, and to make a reasonable effort to protect Canada
from the Americans.

In what would become a remarkably consistent pattern, Canada
tracked the United States with politically lifesaving precision. After debat-
ing Carleton's Quebec Act for four years, the British government and
Parliament took the one step that would gain the loyalty of the French
Canadians, by assuring their religion, language, and civil law. The
French Canadians seized it as their only means to avoid cultural assimilation by the Americans. Despite many historians' underestimation of
Carleton, and his own disappointment with the French Canadians, they
gave him just enough support to repel Benjamin Franklin and the other
American revolutionaries. The arrival of the Loyalists gave the British a
connection that even the Foreign Office, in all its cynicism, had to take
seriously. Thus were in place the cultural and political armament against
fusion with America and the relationship that could protect the vulnerable and ambiguous northern entity as it plodded determinedly toward a
destiny of its own choice and making.

Talented governors and commanders like Carleton, Simcoe,
Brock, Kempt, Gosford, Bagot, Elgin, and Monck assisted in the
assumption of democratic (responsible) government and autonomy.
The crusty and francophobic veterans of the Napoleonic Wars whom
the British sent to rule Canada (the egregious Colborne, Dalhousie,
and so on) helped in the not always complementary task of protecting
Canada and making it seem less appetizing to its neighbour. Brock
gave his life to prevent an American takeover of Upper Canada (which
was, in any case, 80 per cent American immigrants). The British and
Canadians between them had just enough to resist the American
attack in the War of 1812, a war precipitated by Britain's outrages
against the young republic on the oceans, matters in which Canada
was completely blameless.

The same war yet gave some sense of solidarity to the colonists,
and to the British, and the same sense of self-confidence and confirmation for the Canadians opposite the Americans as the Americans

felt opposite the British, as a result of that war. On the other side of the balance of fates, if the War of 1812 had continued another six months, despite Jackson's victory at New Orleans (over Wellington's brother-in-law), Wellington's Peninsular and Waterloo army would have begun arriving in strength, possibly with Field Marshal the Duke at its head, and might have thrust the Canadian border south to the Ohio River, at least for a time. Chicago and other later great cities of the Midwest would, at least initially, have been in Canada, and the correlation of forces would have been narrower between Canada and the United States and between the Northern and Southern U.S. states.

While the United States walked on eggshells toward the noble and terrible climax of the slavery debate, Canada worked out the responsible government question and had to vaporize an immense fog of British delusion about conditions in the North American colonies. The distraction of the United States with its domestic problems provided the half-century needed for Canada to get through its Gilbert and Sullivan rebellions, build serious relations between Lower and Upper Canada, overcome the British colonial nonsense of proconsular autocracy and Durham's evanescent Ruritanian interlude with his fantasy about assimilating the French. The founders of modern Canada had just enough time to set up a country without creating such agitation that the British would be tempted to throw in the towel and just give Canada to the Americans for consideration elsewhere.

Macdonald, Cartier, Brown, and the others had the grand vision of a transcontinental, bicultural, parliamentary confederation, and the British accepted it as the best bet for Canada's survival beside a United States emerging from its Civil War predestined to become a mighty force in the whole world. Laurier, King, Lapointe, St. Laurent, and Howe built steadily, always overshadowed by America, but never failing to keep pace with it. The liabilities of self-consciousness were generally compensated for by the homely virtues of diligence, prudence, and moderation, with all the tedious Canadian pieties that often went with those qualities. Successful though Canada was, it was very indistinct, the winner of the odd Olympic bronze medal and the birthplace of a few famous film actors (including "America's sweetheart," Mary Pickford, as President Ronald Reagan reminded the Canadian Parliament in 1981). Neither the French fact nor the British connection could substitute for or dilute the scarcely blurred similarity between English-speaking Canadians and greatly more numerous Americans from northern U.S. states.

Where Baldwin and LaFontaine made common cause across the cultural divide, and were both driven to represent constituencies of the other province and language by the skulduggery of the colonial authorities, they recognized the need for political movements that had strength among both founding communities. The alternative was an English party and a French party, the breakup of the link between them, and ultimately the absorption of all into the United States.

The post-war secularization of Quebec, and the dilution of the natural conservatism of an almost ultramontane Catholicism, produced a drive for Quebec's independence that competed strenuously with the earlier somewhat resigned French-Canadian acceptance of an officially bicultural country that would protect French Quebec and enable those French Canadians who wanted to learn English and participate in the scale of the entire country's private or public sector to do so. This competing separatist mission was aided for a time by the revival of France to world prominence and aggressive cultural nationalism, under its greatest leader since Napoleon, after a lapse of two centuries in France's presence in Canada's life.

Once again – as Carleton had produced the Quebec Act on the brink of the American Revolution, and Macdonald had launched Confederation as the American Civil War ended, and Laurier self-sacrificingly preserved national unity in the First World War and King did so (without the extreme and unwelcome inconvenience of self-sacrifice) in the Second World War – the indefinable Canadian process that passeth all understanding worked again. It produced a leader in Pierre Trudeau who was mediocre at almost all areas of policy except regaining the upper hand in the struggle for the hearts and minds of the French Canadians while retaining on the greatest national questions (barely) adequate support from the English-speaking Canadians.

Quebec has been tempted by independence but has had to reflect that it would lose hundreds of thousands of people, annual transfer payments of about two thousand dollars per capita, the security of the Canadian fiscal and international cocoon, and would endure potentially severe frictions, possibly including partition negotiating secession.

The prolonged Quebec crisis put tremendous strain on the unity of the country and on its ability to fund the federalist fiscal effort. But the Canadian genius for endless good-faith negotiation while exploiting French Canada's bourgeois avarice and conceding it all the instances of nationality that do not seriously diminish Canadian federalism appears to be producing a satisfactory if, as always, unexciting compromise without much violence or unsustainable inter-regional hostility.

The whole constitutional problem of putting the country completely back together along contemporary lines was aggravated by the irresponsible posturing of many of the premiers of other provinces. They imposed on the traditional requirement of a double majority, in both founding groups, for the adoption of major policy directions the truism, which Liberal federalist dogma supported, that Quebec is, after all, just another province, and whatever jurisdiction it has, all must have. When the Quebec elites suddenly changed their ambitions from official and practical French–English equality to a special status that usually amounted virtually to independence while retaining transfer payments for Quebec, it was bound to exhaust English Canada's disposition to accommodate the province. This was the wall that Brian Mulroney, with the most admirable ambitions, hit when, perhaps at Meech Lake and certainly at Charlottetown, he gave away too much jurisdiction to the claque of provincial scavengers in quest of a unanimity that was achieved by the first ministers but at the expense of the adherence of the public.

A stasis has settled, for a time. Quebec is autonomous in most internal policy, even more than Canada was prior to Confederation, and is fiscally well-upholstered by transfer payments, Danegeld that Canada can justify as a placatory investment, and the federal government has adequate domestic jurisdiction and speaks for the country in the world.

In this ardent flirtation with independence, the French Canadians have lost a good deal of their bargaining power in Canada. Where they were formerly about one-third of the population, if the French Canadians outside Quebec, and the non-French within, both of whom are almost all federalist, are removed from the equation, they are now less than one-fifth. As there is a very large number of French Quebec federalists, the ability of the separatists to blackmail the entire country with the threat to secede is, as the Charlottetown Accord referendum result demonstrated, now very unclear. In this process, the Quebec nationalists have also weakened the argument for continued parity of the two official cultures. In promoting the nationalism of French Quebec over the status of the French in all of Canada, the Quebec nationalist leaders have fractured and enfeebled both the French fact and the stature of Quebec in the country. Trudeau was correct when he said in 1976 that Lévesque and his followers were trapped – that they could not win a vote to secede and would lose their influence on the federal government and in Canada as a whole.

Quebec, the pre-eminent voice in Ottawa for decades, is now almost without influence there and generally in the country. There is now a functioning compromise but not a permanent solution, which must await a new overture from Canada and the boldness for Quebec to take federalism seriously again, after fifty years of ambiguous and opportunistic posturing. This will have to include ceasing to oppress cultural minorities in Quebec. If the independentists ever were successful, they could not really aspire to drag millions of Quebec federalists out of Canada into a severely divided new republic of Quebec, and the new country would probably be a truncated remnant of its present extent. The Clarity Act should have provided for this, and should be amended to deal with secession in any province on the principle that provinces are no less divisible than Canada itself. Unless the federal hand is played by completely incompetent protagonists, however, no provincial majority will seriously aspire to secede.

It has been unavoidable that this lonely and incomprehensible and involutional quest for national distinction is unheroic or even anti-heroic: it does not rest on resonant epigrams or ringing tocsins and resides only in moderation, compromise, and the attrition of negotiation. The fact that it is so difficult to rouse any interest in it or enthusiasm for it does, oddly, make it heroic. It is relatively simple to whip people up with "Give me liberty or give me death!" but the Notwithstanding Clause, pro or con, is more of a challenge for stirring the juices.

The official entity of Canada since Champlain, Frontenac, and Carleton has been guided by an unglamorous talent of constructive compromise attending an occasionally fervent vision of nationhood. It has resolved itself into hard determination when tested. It has required, and received, cautious but skillful navigation, but also bold innovation and execution, to rise from rung to rung up the long and rickety ladder from New France to the world's Group of Seven leading democratic economies.

Mackenzie King was the supreme cautious navigator among Canada's post-colonial leaders, sometimes notoriously so, and Trudeau was perhaps the boldest, though not the most original, helmsman. Macdonald and Laurier best combined the two roles. The earlier three of those benefited from the creative tradition of public–private sector cooperation introduced by Jean Talon and continued by Francis Hincks, Clifford Sifton, and C.D. Howe, which has been allowed to lapse, though R.B. Bennett, Walter Gordon, and even Pierre Trudeau (Petro-Canada) were somewhat disposed to revive it.

There must be a return to great visions and projects, like Macdonald's railway, Laurier's development of the West, King's management of the Second World War, Trudeau's promotion of biculturalism, the creation of the instances of coherent sovereignty of Bennett and Howe – the CBC, the Bank of Canada, Air Canada, the Trans-Canada Highway, and Trans-Canada Pipelines – and bold initiatives like Mulroney's trade, tax, and constitutional reforms.

The second group of prime ministers was also very talented: Louis St. Laurent was very distinguished and clearly successful, though sometimes erring on the side of caution. Lester Pearson and Brian Mulroney were in or near the same high bracket, though Pearson was sometimes insouciant, inconstant, and disorganized, and Mulroney occasionally over-ambitious and sometimes facile. Both had very important accomplishments to their credit. Stephen Harper may legitimately aspire to join this distinguished company. Robert Borden and Jean Chrétien were generally capable stewards of the federal government, though in very different ways and times. John Thompson and Paul Martin were at least average, and showed promise, which might have borne results if they had lasted longer. The first ten of these men, the above-average prime ministers, have governed for almost 85 per cent of Canada's history since Confederation. American presidents reckoned to be above average have governed for only a little more than 50 per cent of its history since 1789, but those presidents include some of the gigantic statesmen of world history, and they raised the bar of average. (The five most prominent colonial governors in Canada, Champlain, Frontenac, the elder Vaudreuil, Beauharnois, and Carleton: plus Macdonald, Laurier, King, Trudeau, and any one of Borden, St. Laurent, Mulroney, or Chrétien, just ten men, governed for a majority of the 403 years between the installation of Champlain and the first election of Harper. Canada has had no aversion to official longevity.)

The rest of the prime ministers were either unsuccessful in that role or served too short a time to allow a clear appraisal. Arthur Meighen, R.B. Bennett, and John Diefenbaker were outstanding men in other ways, and several, including Charles Tupper, Joe Clark, and John Turner, served with distinction in other great offices of state. But not one of Canada's twenty-two prime ministers was catastrophic, or even venal or contemptible; this is, after all, Canada, and it avoids the extremes of genius, ineptitude, and even depravity of some other countries. Now, more than ever, prime minister of Canada is a position that can influence Canadian history and be a positive force in the world, and should attract qualified claimants. The Canadian political system is complicated, but it works tolerably well; 150 years of continuity make it one of the world's ten senior regimes, and it can be gradually fine-tuned to produce better results.

As in most things, in the quality of its governance and the talent of its leaders, Canada has steered between extremes and earned a good second prize in the national lottery of political history. And it has generally failed to recognize its great achievement in performing so strongly under such constraints of regionalism, cultural diversity, and the magnetic distractions and challenges of the American contiguity.

By the 1980s, Canada had become a G7 country (not so much on its merits as because the United States and Japan did not want to be numerically overwhelmed in the group by Europeans) and was well, if not very excitedly, regarded in the world. It was prosperous and civilized and peaceful, yet skilled in war and always in just wars and always victoriously, but it was still overshadowed by the overwhelming American presence. About 19 per cent of Canadians expressed satisfaction at the thought of federal union with the United States as late as 1999.[1]

And then, in the strangest denouement of all in the astronomically improbable sequence of twists and turns in Canadian history, the great United States of America, at the height of its power and raucous majesty, the only truly great power left in the world, suddenly embarked on a long slide into debt, mediocrity, bungled foreign interventions, consumptive fiscal and trade deficits, and, doubtless temporary and certainly reversible, decline. Only a few years after America saw off its last rival, it ceased to be a threat to Canada's sense of self. At least for a time, its inexorable success and genius of showmanship and self-promotion abruptly ended.

And all the while, it has become more difficult for the sad sacks of Canadian anonymity to deplore that the country's imagination is tweaked and lifted only from outside, and especially from America. Correspondingly, it has become much harder for Quebec nationalists to engage in their well-tried and unutterably tiresome practice of dismissing English Canada as an excrescence deposited by the Anglo-Americans on Quebec's doorstep to anesthetize the forces of noble French-Canadian nationhood. In forty years – and some of Trudeau's cultural policies may deserve some credit for this – Canadian television has developed the ability to compete for and hold the attention of Canadians much of the time, although the full panoply of American television, hundreds of channels (mainly of pap), is available. Canadian astronaut Chris Hadfield attracted millions of followers and correspondents as he circled the earth in 2013 and constantly was in touch by social media from his spacecraft. It was reassuring when Alice Munro, whose finely crafted stories set in small and very ordinary Ontario towns have been familiar to Canadians for decades, won the country's first Nobel Prize for Literature (a shameful oversight by the committee that it took so long to select a Canadian recipient). Canada now is a hot contender for world leadership in the Winter Olympics, a Canadian is governor of the Bank of England, and Canadians are numerous in the highest ranks of the entertainment and film industries. The brain drain to the United States that worried concerned Canadians for all their history as an organized society (despite Jean Chrétien's glib assurance that departing doctors and executives would be happily replaced by Haitian taxi drivers) has stopped and even slightly reversed. Canada has become a country frequently and almost always respectfully referred to, all over the world, for its merits if not its spontaneity.

The Free Trade Agreement was good for Canada and the country did compete successfully with the United States. Macdonald was right to oppose economic union in 1891; Laurier could have sold reciprocity in 1911 if he had taken greater care, but Mulroney was right with Free Trade in 1988. And now, as China and India, representing nearly 40 per cent of the population of the world, reach for economic growth and the market for raw materials can no longer be manipulated by importers because of the scale of new demand, Canada's trade flows are reducing the country's integration with the United States (its share of Canada's trade is down by about 20 per cent). General prosperity is flowing usefully in a benign cycle into strengthened and more sophisticated manufacturing exports. On every front, the country is advancing to a higher plane, including its slow progress back toward a two-party system, where each side comes to bat with some regularity.

It is all, in a way, a legitimization. All Canadians, as a group, are becoming less self-conscious, dour, and envious, without metamorphosing into opinionated braggarts or snobs of a kind whose traits they have had plentiful occasion to remark in other (kindred) nationalities. Even after all that has been accomplished and secured, and the unmistakeable reduction to the human, if still very imposing, scale of the United States, Canadian nationalism is not the quiet and inborn confidence of other great nationalities. Even now it tends to be strung between reactive Tory humbug, reflexive leftist envy and sanctimony, and the obtuse inertia that more or less animates the senior central official clerisy. Canadians should already have ceased to describe themselves in diminutive (and largely false) terms such as "punching above our weight," which they haven't done for decades, though they did in the world wars.

In 1940, when France was overrun by Germany, King exhorted Quebec to take up the fallen torch of France, though he did nothing to encourage it in his relations with de Gaulle, and Quebec was not interested. With America's retrenchment after the second Iraq War, no Canadian official has recognized Canada's duty and opportunity, not to replace America – no country could do that – but to fill some of the space that has been vacated. It is as if no one with any authority has recognized how the world and Canada's place in it have changed.

* * *

There is again an opportunity to bring Quebec completely into a renewed Confederation through constitutional renovation and French-English rapprochement. It is a chance for a de-escalation of the brinkmanship of the Meech Lake and Charlottetown rejections, the 1995 referendum, and the Clarity Act. Most of Meech Lake would have to be retrieved, including a federalization of the Senate and the Supreme Court, but not an amendment veto for every province, nor a raft of statutory, but not constitutional, enactments.

What has become the somewhat anachronistic position of governor general will have to be revisited eventually. The occupant of that post will someday have to be the real chief, or at least co-chief, of the Canadian state and not just a stand-in for a non-resident monarch. The post will have to be filled by a less absurd formula than, as it is now, by a monarchist detritus of the worthy, lofty, public service apparat and as a method of recognizing multicultural factions, which it has been since 1989.

Canada's senior civil service is less corrupt than America's, less hidebound than the British, and almost free of the pseudo-Cartesian dirigitis of the French and the European Union. But most of its members are faceless, terminally earnest, have little imagination, and robotically defend the sagging rampart of Canadian national diffidence. They need, at the least, a little fresh air and companions from the terrestrial world, and should not be choosing (and sometimes managing) the person charged with convincing the world that anyone lumbered with the colonial title and status of governor general personifies the Canadian state and people. And the Senate has excavated new depths of public disregard or even embarrassment. This hodgepodge of federal institutions will need to be altered significantly, but not unrecognizably, to adapt to the much more complicated and substantial country that Canada has become since 1867. Because of the complexity of the country and the necessity for compromise, changes as fundamental as these are laborious.

Quebec's premier, the estimable Philippe Couillard, or a successor, will have to be a stronger and more agile federalist than we have had in Quebec since the senior Johnson, to attract that province to the virtues of participating fully, but with full retention of its culture and prerogatives, in the life of the whole country as Canada quickens its progress among the world's great nations. And Canada will need a federal leader with more imagination than Stephen Harper has shown to date, though perhaps less impetuosity than Brian Mulroney bravely showed, to resolve the last of the constitutional impasse. The challenge is to blend satisfactorily the rights of the founding cultures at the federal level with the appropriate jurisdictions of the provinces, and to restore the reciprocity of Canada–Quebec interest in a successful federation. The country has resolved knottier problems.

Canada, by its nature, has avoided the immense dramas of many other prominent countries, as these usually translate into revolutionary or military bloodshed and the passionate and poignant cultural treatment such people and events incite. Canada's way to greatness is not that of nation states defined by sole possession of a rich language and culture, nor the way of the United States, which was able to represent itself as the world's champion of human freedom, a magnet to all. This is a role it partially performed, to the great benefit of many hundreds of millions of people in all parts of the world, as it turned its possession of the temperate centre of a whole continent to a scale of national strength and activity which the world had never before thought possible. Canada will not follow the Spanish, French, British, Germans, Americans, Russians, and Chinese in contending for the sceptre of the world's pre-eminent nation. But it does possess the ability to gain the world's admiring attention, by continuing to build a country all would wish to emulate. It should aspire to be and can become the world's laboratory for sane government and civil society. It has been relatively advanced in the acceptance of immigration of all kinds, and in the treatment of behavioral minorities; less successful in dealing with the problems of native populations; and does run relatively clean governments. Its courts and legal system are in the top rung of liberality and fairness, though it is backsliding as a carceral state, and in Canada as elsewhere lawyers are in danger of becoming more of an exploitive cartel than a learned profession disinterestedly promoting the rule of law.

And there is a vast blank page for sensible Canadian approaches to new notions of taxes, incentives to poverty reduction, alleviation of extreme income disparities, treatment of criminals (there is no excuse for prisons for non-violent people, though all crime must be punished), delivery of social services, and even for the determination of the rights of the unborn and of the apparently incurably ill. Canada is uniquely equipped to lead the world out of what has become, especially in the United States, a sterile and uncivilized shrieking match between left and right, and into the exploration of sensible public policy in a liberal society devoted altogether to individual rights and dignity.

In his 1945 poem "Canada: Case History," distinguished Western Canadian poet Earle Birney wrote,

> His uncle spoils him with candy, of course,
> Yet shouts him down when he talks at table.
> You will note he's got some of his French mother's looks,
> Though he's not so witty and no more stable.
> He's really much more like his father and yet
> If you say so he'll pull a great face.
> He wants to be different from everyone else
> And daydreams of winning the global race.
> Parents unmarried and living abroad,
> Relatives keen to bag the estate,
> Schizophrenia not excluded,
> Will he learn to grow up before it's too late?

Like Frank Scott's poem about Mackenzie King (end of Chapter 7), there was much truth in this, but it was an amusing, though ungenerous, description of Canada at the end of the Second World War, in which the country had made such a distinguished effort in the ultimate just cause. It was, perhaps, a more complicated process to deal with the Americans, British, and French, and their espousers in Canada, than Earle Birney realized. And Canada progressed more quickly out of what he thought to be national adolescence than he seemed to fear it would. That progress has continued these seventy years; we now know that Canada almost certainly has grown up.

Once again, and once more by a narrow margin, the country is passing out of crises: Quebec separatism and American psychological domination. History is almost always a guide, and again the ambitious if often imprecise plans of the builders of this country throughout its history, which have evolved and moved on to ever higher stages, will take Canada to a new summit of national development. Canada always

seemed to survive precariously, almost inexplicably and even accidentally, but this has made its progress more ineluctable, until it finally,
suddenly, has metamorphosed into a strong country.

It advanced in almost imperceptibly small increments: a "gentlemen's agreement" (on a few hundred immigrants) with Japan (in 1907),
a Halibut Treaty (in 1923), the King-Roosevelt defence agreement at
Ogdensburg (in 1940), abolition of appeals to the U.K. Privy Council (in
1949), but it never stopped advancing.

It is the chief contention of this book that for more than four hundred years there has been a continuous thread of genius and determination to create and build and improve an original and distinguished
political society in the northern half of this continent. The thread has
almost snapped many times, but has never been severed. Though
Canada's progress has often seemed to be a freakish sequence of usually
trivial events, only rarely punctuated by anything grand and dramatic,
it has been invincible. The past reveals the future.

Photographic Credits

1. Nasjonalgalleriet, Oslo, Norway/Bridgeman Images; 2. Private Collection/Bridgeman Images; 3. *Champlain on Georgian Bay* by John David Kelly © McCord Museum; 4. Musée des Beaux-Arts, Rouen, France; Giraudon/Bridgeman Images; 5. Library and Archives Canada, MIKAN no. 3919911; 6. Archives de la Manufacture, Sèvres, France; Archives Charmet/Bridgeman Images; 7. Louis XIV, 1638–1715, Library and Archives Canada, C-042278; 8. Colbert, Library and Archives Canada, MIKAN no. 4312672; 9. Talon, Library and Archives Canada, MIKAN no. 2909677; 10. François de Laval, Library and Archives Canada, C-005183; 11. La Vérendrye at the Lake of the Woods, Library and Archives Canada, Acc. No. 1939-60-1, C-006896; 12. Sir Isaac Brock, Library and Archives Canada, Acc. No. 1991-30-1, e010767950, e010767951, C-007760; 13. Hon. Louis Joseph Papineau, politician, Montreal, QC, 1865 / William Notman (1826–1891) © McCord Museum; 14. William Lyon Mackenzie, Library and Archives Canada, C-001991; 15. Lord James Bruce Elgin, Library and Archives Canada, C-003670; 16. Hon. Sir Francis Hincks; William James Topley, Library and Archives Canada, PA-025467; 17. Hon. George Brown, politician, Montreal, QC, 1865; William Notman (1826–1891) © McCord Museum; 18. I-7956, Hon. George-Étienne Cartier, Montreal, QC, 1863; William Notman (1826–1891) © McCord Museum; 19. Montreal 1849, ©McCord Museum; 20. R-A7518, Courtesy of the Saskatchewan Archives Board; 21. Bibliothèque Nationale, Paris, France; Archives Charmet/Bridgeman Images; 22. Private Collection/Peter Newark/American Pictures/Bridgeman Images; 23. Rt. Hon. Robert Borden and Hon. Winston Churchill leaving the Admiralty. Library and Archives Canada / C-002082; 24. Sir Robert Borden speaks to wounded man at Base Hospital. In the background is soldier, James Clifford Hiscott. March, 1915 Canada. Dept. of National Defence/Library and Archives Canada; 25. Rt. Hon. W.L. Mackenzie King and his dog Pat I at Laurier House. Library and Archives Canada / C-087858; 26. Hon. R.B. Bennett and Senator Arthur Meighen. Library and Archives Canada / C-023539; 27. Regina riot. Royal Canadian Mounted Police / Library and Archives Canada / e004666103; 28. Canadian delegates attending the Imperial Conference. Aitken Ltd. / Library and Archives Canada / C-001690; 29. Gar Lunney / National Film Board of Canada. Photothèque / Library and Archives Canada / PA-141113; 30. Lord Tweedsmuir with President Franklin D. Roosevelt. Yousuf Karsh, Yousuf Karsh fonds / Library and Archives Canada, Accession 1987-054; 31. William Lyon Mackenzie King / Library and Archives Canada / C-035115; 32. National Film Board of Canada. Photothèque / Library and Archives Canada / C-016770; 33. Nicholas Morant / Office national du film du Canada. Photothèque / Bibliothèque et Archives Canada / C-022716; 34. National Film Board of Canada. Photothèque / Library and Archives Canada / C-015126; 35. #21993656 – Churchill and Duplessis. Courtesy: *The Gazette* photo archives; 36. National Film Board of Canada. Photothèque / Library and Archives Canada / C-023281; 37. National Film Board of Canada. Photothèque collection / Library and Archives Canada/ C-004047; 38. #21993657 – Richard, Bellemare and Duplessis. Courtesy: *The Gazette* photo archives; 39. Houde and Cardinal Léger. Photo by Davidson, *The Gazette* © 1950; 40. Soviet / Library and Archives Canada / PA-117617; 41. Duncan Cameron/Library and Archives Canada/PA-154665; 42. Duncan Cameron / Library and Archives Canada / PA-117107; 43. Duncan Cameron / Library and Archives Canada / PA-209871; 44. *Toronto Star* via Getty Images; 45. Library and Archives Canada; 46. Beck/*Montreal Star*/Library and Archives Canada/PA-151863; 47. Duncan Cameron/Library and Archives Canada/PA-136978; 48. Duncan Cameron/Library and Archives Canada; 49. Erik Christensen/*Globe and Mail*; 50. The Canadian Press/Tom Hanson; 51. Montebello – Manoir Papineau; courtesy Archives du Quebec; 52. Dundurn Castle; courtesy Hamilton Public Archives; 53. "Ravenscrag", Hugh Montagu Allan's residence, Montreal, QC, 1901 | Wm. Notman & Son © McCord Museum; 54. City of Toronto Archives; 55. Courtesy QMI Agency; Chapter openers: Introduction, Chapters 1–7: Library and Archives Canada; Chapter 8: *Gazette* archives; Chapters 9–10: Canadian Press.

Notes

PRELUDE

1. Robert Bothwell, *The Penguin History of Canada*, Toronto, 2006, p. 18.
2. Edgar McInnis, *Canada: A Political and Social History*, Toronto, 1947, p. 23.
3. David Hackett Fischer, *Champlain's Dream*, New York, 2008, p. 116. (Fischer, as is his admirable custom, provides a plethora of primary sources to support this quotation and these events.)

CHAPTER 1

1. David Buisseret, *Henry IV*, London.
2. James McDermott, *Martin Frobisher: Elizabethan Privateer*, New Haven, 2001.
3. Samuel de Champlain, *The Works of Samuel de Champlain*, 6 vols., Toronto, 1922–1936, reprinted 1971, pp. 1, 63–65.
4. F. Scott Fitzgerald, *The Great Gatsby*, New York, 1925, last two pages, all editions.
5. David Hackett Fischer, *Champlain's Dream*, New York, 2008, p. 147.
6. Ibid., p. 227.
7. Ibid.
8. Champlain, op. cit., vol. III, p. 328.
9. Fischer, op. cit., p. 269.
10. Champlain, op. cit., vol. II, p. 228.
11. Fischer, op. cit., p. 279.
12. Michel de Montaigne, *The Complete Essays*, trans. Donald M. Frame, Stanford, 1957, pp. 122–23.
13. Champlain, op. cit., vol. V, p. 7.
14. Fischer, op. cit., p. 410.
15. Fischer, op. cit., p. 433.
16. Fischer, op. cit., pp. 467–68, 472.
17. Nicolas Denys, *Histoire naturelle des peuples, des animaux, des arbres & plantes de l'Amérique septentrionale, & de ses divers climats*, Paris, 1672; English edition, *The Description and Natural History of the Coasts of North America (Acadia)*, trans. and ed. William F. Ganong, Toronto, 1908, p. 149.
18. A. Leblond de Brumath, *Bishop Laval*, Makers of Canada, London and Toronto, 1926, p. 84.
19. Robert Bothwell, *The Penguin History of Canada*, Toronto, 2006, p. 51.

20. Ibid., p. 48 ("they were shoveled aboard ship").

21. Edgar McInnis, *Canada: A Political and Social History*, Toronto, 1963, p. 52.

22. Anka Muhlstein, *La Salle: Explorer of the North American Frontier*, New York, 1994, p. 76.

23. McInnis, op. cit.

24. McInnis, op. cit., p. 53.

25. Vita Sackville-West, *Daughter of France*, London, 1959, p. 190. She described Frontenac as "an extremely self-satisfied man. . . . He once spread his new breeches and doublets all over [la grande Mademoiselle's] dressing table, greatly to the astonishment of the king's brother" (ibid.).

26. Charles W. Colby, *The Fighting Governor*, Toronto, 1920, p. 12.

27. Ibid., p. 86.

28. Muhlstein, op. cit., p. 76.

29. Ibid., p. 165.

30. Pierre Margry, *Découvertes et établissements des Français dans l'ouest et dans le sud de l'Amérique septentrionale, 1614–1754*, Paris, 1876–1886, vol. III, p. 330.

31. Colby, op. cit., p. 98.

32. Ibid., p. 115.

33. Cited in Colby, ibid., pp. 121–22.

34. Ibid., p. 129.

35. Ibid., p. 130.

36. W.L. Morton, *The Kingdom of Canada*, Toronto, 1963, p. 90.

37. Arthur R.M. Lower, *Colony to Nation* (Toronto, 1977 edition), p. 53.

38. Morton, op. cit., p. 113.

39. Ibid., p.115.

40. Ibid.

41. Morton, ibid.

42. Morton, op. cit., pp. 123–26.

CHAPTER 2

1. Arthur R.M. Lower, *Colony to Nation: A History of Canada*, Toronto, 1977, p. 91.

2. W.L. Morton, *The Kingdom of Canada*, Toronto, 1963, p. 134.

3. Stanley M. Pargellis, *Lord Loudoun in North America*, London, 1933, pp. 136–38.

4. Fred Anderson, *Crucible of War*, New York, 2000, p. 298.

5. Horace Walpole, *Memoirs of the Reign of King George the Second*, vol. III, London, 1846, pp. 229–30.

6. Anderson, op. cit., pp. 492–93.

7. Antony Beevor, *The Fall of Berlin, 1945*, New York, 2002, p. 204.

8. A.G. Bradley, *Lord Dorchester*, Makers of Canada, Toronto, 1926, pp. 24–25.

9. Edmund S. Morgan, *Benjamin Franklin*, New Haven, 2002, pp. 86, 90.

10. Ibid., p. 114.

11. Ibid., p. 163.

12. Conrad Black, *Flight of the Eagle: A Strategic History of the United States*, Toronto, 2013, pp. 46–47.

13. Bradley, op. cit., p. 17.

14. Ibid., pp. 70–71.

15. Ibid.

16. Ibid., p. 72.

17. Edgar McInnis, *Canada: A Political and Social History*, Toronto, 1947, pp. 142–43; Lower, op. cit., p. 76.

18. Black, op. cit., p. 48.

19. Ibid., p. 58.

20. Lower, op. cit., p. 81.

21. Ibid., p. 87.

22. Ibid., p. 143.

23. Ibid., p. 137.

24. Morton, op. cit., pp. 173–74.

25. Ibid., p. 189.

26. Letter to Colonel William Duane, August 4, 1812, in Merrill D. Peterson, *Thomas Jefferson and the New Nation: A Biography*, Norwalk, Connecticut, 1970, p. 932.

27. Ibid.

28. Lady Edgar, *General Brock*, Makers of Canada, Toronto, 1927, p. 251.

29. Lower, op. cit., p. 182.

30. Morton, op. cit., p. 229.

31. Stephen Leacock, *Mackenzie, Baldwin, LaFontaine, Hincks*, Makers of Canada, Toronto, 1926, vol. v, p. 14.

32. Ibid., p. 15.

33. Peter Burroughs, "Sir James Kempt" in *Dictionary of Canadian Biography*, vol. VIII, Toronto, 1976.

34. Morton, op. cit., p. 234.

CHAPTER 3

1. Arthur R.M. Lower, *Colony to Nation: A History of Canada*, Toronto, 1977, p. 200.

2. Stephen Leacock, *Mackenzie, Baldwin, LaFontaine, Hincks*, Makers of Canada, Toronto, 1926, vol. v, pp. 20–21.

3. Ibid., p. 23.

NOTES | 1025

4. Alfred D. De Celles, *Papineau, Cartier*, Makers of Canada, Toronto, 1926, vol. v, p. 86.
5. Leacock, op. cit., p. 33.
6. Lower, op. cit., p. 254.
7. Francis G. Hincks, *Reminiscences of His Public Life*, "Chapter One," Montreal, 1884, cited in Leacock, op. cit., p. 45.
8. Leacock, op. cit., p. 47.
9. Edgar McInnis, *Canada: A Political and Social History*, Toronto, 1947, p. 220; Sir Francis Bond Head, A *Narrative*, London, 1839, pp. 32, 33; "Letter of Joseph Hume to William Lyon Mackenzie, December 5, 1835," Archives of Ontario, Robinson Papers, (A), E.22-3, ii, 10. Leacock and Hincks thought the colonial secretary, Lord Glenelg, confused Head with future governor general Sir Edmund Walker Head. Leacock, op. cit., p. 48.
10. Head, op. cit., pp. 33 et seq.; Leacock, op. cit., p. 49.
11. Head, ibid., p. 71.
12. Ibid.
13. Ibid., p. 53.
14. Leacock, op. cit., p. 55.
15. De Celles, op. cit., p. 99.
16. Ibid., p. 103.
17. Ibid., pp. 114–15.
18. Ibid., p. 127.
19. Ibid., pp. 133–34.
20. Ibid., p. 135.
21. Ibid., p. 140.
22. W.L. Morton, *The Kingdom of Canada*, Toronto, 1963, p. 241.
23. Ibid., p. 242.
24. Leacock, op. cit., p. 73.
25. Morton, op. cit., p. 249.
26. Sir Charles Lucas, *Lord Durham's Report on the Affairs of British North America*, vol. II, Oxford, 1912, pp. 277 et seq.
27. Ibid., pp. 307–8.
28. Ibid.
29. Ibid., McInnis, op. cit., p. 227.
30. Morton, op. cit., p. 253.
31. Lower, op. cit., p. 256.
32. Thompson to Russell, November 18, 1839, in W.P.M. Kennedy, *Documents of the Canadian Constitution*, Oxford, 1918, p. 526.
33. Morton, op. cit., p. 256.
34. Ibid.

35. Leacock, op. cit., p. 114; *Journal of the Legislative Assembly*, Kingston, 1841, vol. I, pp. 64 et seq.

36. Leacock, op. cit., pp. 138–39, "Stanley Letter to Lord Bagot, October 8, 1841."

37. Ibid., p. 151.

38. *Chronicle and Gazette*, Kingston, September 17, 1842.

39. Lower, op. cit., p. 265.

40. Leacock, op. cit., pp. 155–56.

41. Ibid., p. 210.

42. Ibid., p. 219.

43. *Journal of the Legislative Assembly*, Kingston, November 6, 1843.

44. *La Minerve*, November 16, 1843, cited in Leacock, op. cit., p. 206.

45. "Undated letter in Baldwin Archives" (Toronto Public Library, 1845), cited in Leacock, op. cit., pp. 288–89. This was one of the first enunciations of the concept of the "double majority."

46. *La Minerve*, July 1, 1844, cited in Leacock, op. cit., p. 256.

47. Leacock, op. cit., p. 258.

48. Ibid., p. 262.

49. Ibid., p. 281.

50. Ibid., p. 292.

51. Lower, op.cit., p. 264.

52. Ibid., p. 277.

53. Leacock, op. cit., p. 300.

54. Archives of Ontario, Baldwin Papers, (A), E, 6-7, 12, (15).

55. *La Minerve*, January 24, 1849.

56. The *Times*, June 20, 1849, cited in Leacock, op. cit., pp. 351–55.

57. Lower, op. cit., pp. 270–71.

58. William G. Ormsby, "Sir Francis Hincks" in the *Dictionary of Canadian Biography*, vol. XI, Toronto, 1982, p. 412.

59. Ibid., p. 413.

60. Lower, op. cit., p. 280.

61. Donald Creighton, *John A. Macdonald*, vol. I, *The Young Politician*, Toronto, 1952, p. 198.

62. Peter Baskerville, "Sir Allan Napier MacNab" in the *Dictionary of Canadian Biography*, vol. IX, Toronto, 1976, p. 527.

63. Sir A.G. Doughty, ed., *The Elgin–Grey Papers, 1846–1852*, vol. I, Ottawa, 1937, pp. 39–40 ("Elgin to Grey, May 18, 1847"), cited in Creighton, op. cit., pp. 120–21.

64. Daniel Walker Howe, *What Hath God Wrought: The Transformation of America, 1815–1848*, New York, 2007, p. 266; John Hope Franklin and Loren Schweninger, *Runaway Slaves*, New York, 1999, pp. 294–95.

65. Jane Ridley, *Bertie: A Life of Edward VII*, London, 2012, p. 48; Cecil Woodham-Smith, *Queen Victoria*, London, 1972, p. 517.

66. Alastair Sweeny, *George-Étienne Cartier*, Toronto, 1976, p. 127.

67. Sir E.W. Waskin, *Canada and the States: Recollections, 1851 to 1886*, London, 1887, p. 16; Sweeny, op. cit., p. 129.

68. Lower, op. cit., p. 298.

69. R.W. Winks, "Creation of a Myth: 'Canadian' Enlistments in the Northern Armies During the American Civil War," *Canadian Historical Review* 39, no. 1 (March 1958), pp. 24–40; Lower, op. cit., p. 300.

70. Oscar D. Skelton, *The Life and Times of Sir Alexander Tilloch Galt*, Toronto, 1920, pp. 314–16.

71. *Assembly Debates*, April 17, 1861; Sweeny, op. cit., p. 132.

72. R.R. Palmer, ed., *Atlas of World History*, New York, 1957, p. 193.

73. R.G. Trotter, *Canadian Federation*, Toronto, 1924, p. 5.

74. Creighton, op. cit., p. 264.

75. John Lewis, *George Brown*, Makers of Canada, Toronto, 1926, p. 131 ("letter of January, 1858, to Luther Holton").

76. Queen's University, Mackenzie Papers, Brown to Luther Holton, May 29, 1862; Sweeny, op. cit., p. 137.

77. Library and Archives Canada, Newcastle Papers, Monck to Newcastle, August 11, 1862; Sweeny, op. cit., p. 138.

78. Sweeny, op. cit., p. 142.

79. Sweeny, op. cit., pp. 145–46.

80. Library and Archives Canada, Macdonald Papers, vol. 46, pp. 29–38; Creighton, op. cit., p. 374.

81. Library and Archives Canada, George Brown Papers, George Brown to Anne Brown, October 31, 1864; Sweeny, op. cit., p. 150.

82. Public Record Office, 30/22, Russell Papers, vol. 27, minute by Palmerston on Cardwell's draft dispatch to Monck, July 29, 1984; Creighton, op. cit., p. 361.

83. G.E. Buckle, ed., *The Letters of Queen Victoria*, London, 1926, series 2, vol. I, pp. 248–49, Palmerston to the Queen, January 20, 1865; Creighton, op. cit., p. 405.

84. The *Times*, June 22, 1865; Creighton, op. cit., p. 417.

85. Richard Gwyn, *John A: The Man Who Made Us: The Life and Times of John A. Macdonald*, vol. I, 1815–1867, Toronto, 2007, p. 420; (Keith Johnson).

86. Hansard, London, 1867, series 3, vol. 185, p. 576 G; Creighton, op. cit., p. 461.

CHAPTER 4

1. Arthur R.M. Lower, *Colony to Nation: A History of Canada*, Toronto, 1977, p. 316.

2. Donald Creighton, *John A. Macdonald*, Toronto, 1952, vol. II, *The Old Chieftain*, p. 5.

3. Ibid., p. 20.
4. Library and Archives Canada, Macdonald Papers, vol. 539, Allan to Macdonald, April 24, 1869.
5. Ibid., vol. 516; Macdonald to Sir John Rose, January 26, 1870.
6. Sir Joseph Pope, ed., *Correspondence of Sir John Macdonald*, Toronto, undated, Macdonald to Rose, January 21, 1870.
7. Ibid., Macdonald to Carnarvon, April 14, 1870.
8. Creighton, op. cit., p. 67.
9. James D. Richardson, ed., *A Compilation of the Messages and Papers of the Presidents*, Washington, 1897, vol. IX, U.S. Grant, p. 4057.
10. Ibid.
11. William F. Moneypenny and George E. Buckle, *The Life of Benjamin Disraeli, Earl of Beaconsfield*, London, 1929, vol. III, pp. 473–74.
12. Creighton, op. cit., p. 86.
13. Ibid., p. 92.
14. Ibid., p. 97.
15. W.L. Morton, *The Kingdom of Canada*, Toronto, 1963, p. 343.
16. George R. Parkin, *Sir John A. Macdonald*, Makers of Canada, Toronto, 1926, p. 195.
17. Ibid., pp. 189–90.
18. Creighton, op. cit., p. 148.
19. Ibid., p. 149.
20. Ibid., p. 152.
21. Ibid.
22. Ibid., p. 165.
23. Ibid., p. 171.
24. Ibid., p. 186.
25. Ibid., p. 184.
26. E.M. Saunders, *The Life and Letters of the Rt. Hon. Sir Charles Tupper*, Toronto, 1916, vol. I, p. 234.
27. Creighton, op. cit., p. 189.
28. Ibid.
29. *Montreal Gazette*, November 26, 1875.
30. O.D. Skelton, *The Life and Times of Sir Alexander Tilloch Galt*, Toronto, 1920, p. 483; letter of Macdonald to Galt, June 2, 1875.
31. Edgar McInnis, *Canada: A Political and Social History*, Toronto, 1963, p. 363.
32. Creighton, op. cit., p. 228; letters of Dufferin to Carnarvon, April 27 and May 3, 1877.
33. Ibid., pp. 230–31; letter of Dufferin to Carnarvon, May 3, 1877.
34. Pope, op. cit., pp. 329–42; Macdonald to Northcote, May 1, 1878.

35. *House of Commons Debates*, 1878, vol. II, p. 2564.

36. Creighton, op. cit., p. 233.

37. Saunders, op. cit., vol. I, p. 262; letter of Macdonald to Tupper, October 9, 1878.

38. Ibid.

39. Creighton, op. cit., p. 249.

40. Creighton, op. cit., p. 261.

41. Moneypenny and Buckle, op. cit., vol. IV, p. 1349; letter to Lady Bradford, September 2, 1879. Disraeli added that "I think there is a resemblance" (between Macdonald and himself). Disraeli was relieved that Macdonald had "no Yankeeisms except a little sing-song occasionally at the end of a sentence."

42. Pope, op. cit., pp. 240–41; letter of Macdonald to Northcote, May 1, 1878.

43. Creighton, op. cit., p. 277.

44. *House of Commons Debates*, 1880–1881, vol. I, p. 488.

45. Ibid., p. 494.

46. Library and Archives Canada, Macdonald Papers, vol. 128, J.A. Donaldson to Macdonald, January 18, 1881.

47. Creighton, op. cit., p. 334.

48. Library and Archives Canada, Macdonald Papers, vol. 218, Macdonald to Galt, January 7, 1882.

49. Creighton, op. cit., p. 327.

50. Creighton, op. cit., p. 367.

51. Library and Archives Canada, Macdonald Papers, vol. 206, Stephen to Macdonald, February 27, 1884.

52. Ibid., additional vol. I; Macdonald to home, March 26, 1884.

53. Creighton, op. cit., p. 378.

54. Pope, op. cit., pp. 314–15; Macdonald to Aikins, July 28, 1884.

55. McInnis, op. cit., p. 337.

56. Ibid., p. 389.

57. Creighton, op. cit., p. 422; letter of Macdonald to Lansdowne, May 15, 1885.

58. Lower, op. cit., p. 381.

59. O.D. Skelton, *The Day of Sir Wilfrid Laurier*, Chronicles of Canada, vol. 30, p. 99.

60. Creighton, op. cit., p. 510; letter from Macdonald to Lansdowne, September 6, 1888.

61. Ibid., p. 515.

62. *House of Commons Debates*, 1890, p. 745.

63. Creighton, op. cit., p. 558.

64. Joseph Schull, *Laurier: The First Canadian*, Toronto, 1965, pp. 255–56.

65. Lower, op. cit., p. 385.

66. Bruce Hutchison, *Mr. Prime Minister, 1867–1964*, Toronto, 1964, p. 105.
67. Ibid.
68. Lower, op. cit., p. 399.

CHAPTER 5

1. O.D. Skelton, *Life and Letters of Sir Wilfrid Laurier*, Toronto, 1916, vol. II, p. 20.
2. Ibid., p. 40.
3. Ibid., pp. 70–71.
4. Hansard, May 11, 1898.
5. Arthur R.M. Lower, *Colony to Nation: A History of Canada*, Toronto, 1977, p. 422.
6. Conrad Black, *Flight of the Eagle: A Strategic History of the United States*, Toronto, 2013, p. 272.
7. Ibid., p. 273.
8. Daniel Ruddy, *Theodore Roosevelt's History of the United States*, New York, 2010, p. 218.
9. G.T. Denison, *The Struggle for Imperial Unity*, Toronto, 1909, p. 108.
10. Lower, op. cit., p. 411.
11. Joseph Schull, *Laurier: The First Canadian*, Toronto, 1965, p. 338.
12. Statistics Canada Immigration website; Richard B. Morris and Jeffrey B. Morris, eds., *Encyclopedia of American History*, 6th ed., pp. 648–55.
13. Library and Archives Canada, Laurier, 11019–20.
14. Ruddy, op. cit., pp. 170–71.
15. Hansard, July 31, 1899.
16. Schull, op. cit., p. 380.
17. Ibid.
18. Robert Rumilly, *Histoire de la province du Québec*, Montreal, 1977, pp. 121–22.
19. Hansard, March 13, 1900.
20. Robert Laird Borden, *Memoirs*, Toronto, 1938, vol. II, p. 553.
21. Schull, op. cit., p. 398; Hansard, March 12, 1901, p. 1325.
22. Schull, op. cit., p. 399.
23. Rumilly, op. cit., vol. X, pp. 65–66.
24. Henri Bourassa, *Great Britain and Canada*, Montreal, 1901, preface to English edition.
25. Hansard, May 12, 1902, p. 4726.
26. John Buchan, *Lord Minto*, London, 1924, p. 205; Rudyard Kipling, *Something of Myself*, p. 196.
27. Library and Archives Canada, Laurier, 67501–3.
28. Rumilly, op. cit., vol. X, p. 167.

29. Lower, op. cit., p. 432.
30. Hansard, July 30, 1903, pp. 7659–60.
31. Ibid., September 29, 1903, p. 12656.
32. Skelton, op. cit., vol. II, pp. 143–44.
33. Library and Archives Canada, Laurier, 77602.
34. Schull, op. cit., p. 432; John Dafoe, *Clifford Sifton in Relation to His Times*, Toronto, 1931, p. 238.
35. Hansard, June 10, 1904, p. 4606.
36. Library and Archives Canada, Laurier, 93729.
37. Hansard, February 21, 1905, p. 1458.
38. Hansard, March 28, 1905, p. 3284.
39. Hansard, March 26, 1907, p. 5433.
40. Schull, op. cit., p. 463.
41. Hansard, April 3, 1907.
42. Schull, op. cit., pp. 458–60.
43. Rumilly, op. cit, vol. XIII, p. 105.
44. Skelton, op. cit., vol. II, p. 282.
45. Schull, op. cit., p. 479.
46. Hansard, March 29, 1909, p. 3484.
47. Ibid., p. 3512.
48. Ibid.
49. Library and Archives Canada, the Grey Papers, p. 2442.
50. Rumilly, op. cit., vol. XIV, p. 29.
51. Mason Wade, *The French Canadians, 1760–1945*, Toronto, 1955, pp. 565–66.
52. Rumilly, op. cit. vol. XIV, p. 135; *Le Devoir*, January 17, 1910.
53. Rumilly, op. cit., vol. XV, p. 74.
54. Schull, op. cit., p. 506.
55. Rumilly, op. cit., vol. XV, p. 116.
56. Skelton, op. cit., vol. II, p. 337 (my translation).
57. Letter of President Taft to Roosevelt, January 11, 1910; excerpt in Borden, op. cit., vol. I, p. 319.
58. Skelton, op. cit., vol. II, p. 379.
59. Borden, op. cit., vol. I, p. 333n4.
60. Ibid., p. 330.
61. Ibid., p. 353.
62. Ibid., p. 362.
63. Christopher M. Bell, *Churchill and Sea Power*, Oxford, 2013, pp. 22–32; Borden, op. cit., vol. I, pp. 358–65.
64. Lower, op. cit., p. 456; Skelton, op. cit., vol. II, p. 409.
65. Hansard, December 12, 1912, p. 1031.

66. Borden, op. cit., p. 409.
67. Ibid., p. 411.
68. Ibid., p. 420.
69. Ibid., p. 422.
70. Borden, op. cit., pp. 459–60.
71. Ibid., pp. 460–61.
72. Ibid., p. 463.
73. Ibid., p. 465.
74. Ibid., p. 471.
75. Borden, op. cit., vol. II, pp. 612–13.
76. Borden, op. cit., vol. II, p. 696.
77. Ibid., p. 700.
78. Ibid., p. 702.
79. Ibid., p. 705.
80. Ibid., p. 714.
81. Ibid., pp. 726–27.
82. Ibid., p. 746.
83. Lower, op. cit., p. 416.
84. Edgar McInnis, *Canada: A Political and Social History*, Toronto, 1963, p. 413.
85. Borden, op. cit., vol. II, p. 837.
86. Ibid., p. 854.
87. Ibid., p. 869.
88. Ibid., pp. 886–87.
89. Ibid., pp. 889–90.
90. McInnis, op. cit., p. 418.
91. Schull, op. cit., p. 621.
92. Borden, op. cit., vol. II, p. 914.
93. Lower, op. cit., p. 436n22.
94. Borden, op. cit., vol. II, p. 919.
95. Ibid., p. 927.

CHAPTER 6

1. Joseph Schull, *Laurier: The First Canadian*, Toronto, 1965, p. 594.
2. F.A. McGregor, *The Fall and Rise of Mackenzie King*, Toronto, 1962, p. 319.
3. Allan Levine, *King: William Lyon Mackenzie King: A Life Guided by the Hand of Destiny*, Toronto, 2011, p. 110.
4. Robert Laird Borden, *Memoirs*, Toronto, 1938, vol. II, p. 985.
5. Edgar McInnis, *Canada: A Political and Social History*, Toronto, 1963, p. 422.
6. J.L. Granatstein, *How Britain's Weakness Forced Canada into the Arms of the United States*, 1989, p. 17.

7. Borden, op. cit., vol. II, p. 1004.

8. Ibid., p. 1016.

9. Ibid., p. 1027.

10. Roger Graham, *Arthur Meighen: A Biography*, vol. II, *And Fortune Fled*, Toronto, 1963, p. 36. (King claimed the people's control over Parliament had been usurped, as in Russia, but by legislative rather than revolutionary violence.)

11. Ibid., vol. I, *The Door of Opportunity*, p. 299.

12. Ibid., vol. II, p. 38.

13. Ibid., p. 41.

14. Arthur R. M. Lower, *Colony to Nation: A History of Canada*, Toronto, 1977, p. 535.

15. Levine, op. cit., p. 131.

16. Ibid., p. 132.

17. Roy MacLaren, *Commissions High: Canada in London, 1870–1971*, Montreal, 2006, p. 250.

18. Ibid., p. 251.

19. Grace Curzon, *Reminiscences*, London, 1955, pp. 181–82.

20. Robert Rhodes James, *Anthony Eden*, London, 1986, p. 625.

21. Mackenzie King Diary, January 6, 1924.

22. Graham, op. cit., vol. II, p. 343.

23. Mackenzie King Diary, October 30 to November 4, 1925.

24. Ibid., October 31, 1925.

25. Jeffrey Williams, *Byng of Vimy*, London, 1983, p. 323.

26. Ibid., p. 322.

27. Ramsay Cook, "A Canadian Account of the 1926 Imperial Conference," *Journal of Commonwealth Political Studies*, March 1965, p. 65.

28. Mackenzie King Diary, July 4, 1926.

29. Peter B. Waite, "Mr. King and Lady Byng," *The Beaver*, April–May 1997, p. 24.

30. Levine, op. cit., p. 172. (This was the view of Kevin O'Higgins, a young Irish politician, who was assassinated by the IRA just eight months later, aged thirty-five. King remarked of the Irish in his diary on July 11, 1927, "What a strange race.")

31. Vincent Massey, *What's Past Is Prologue*, Toronto, 1963, p. 112.

32. Levine, op. cit., p. 182.

33. Mackenzie King Diary, May 17, 1930.

34. Lower, op. cit., pp. 480–81.

35. Mackenzie King Diary, September 25, 26, 1928.

36. David Dilks, *The Great Dominion: Winston Churchill in Canada, 1900–1954*, Toronto, 2005, p. 101.

37. Lower, op. cit., pp. 494–95.
38. John Thompson and Allen Seager, *Canada 1922–1939: Decades of Discord*, Toronto, 1985, pp. 197–98.
39. Levine, op. cit., p. 199.
40. Peter Oliver, *G. Howard Ferguson: Ontario Tory*, Toronto, 1977, p. 365.
41. Mackenzie King Diary, April 9, 1930.
42. Ibid., July 29, 1930.
43. Ibid., November 2, 1930.
44. Levine, op. cit., p. 203.
45. *House of Commons Debates*, July 30, 1931, 4387–88.
46. Levine, op. cit., p. 206.
47. Ibid., p. 198.
48. Royal Commission on Dominion-Provincial Relations, vol. I, *Canada: 1867–1939*, Ottawa, 1940, p. 144.
49. Levine, op. cit., pp. 214–16.
50. John Boyko, *Bennett: The Rebel Who Challenged and Changed a Nation*, Toronto, 2010, p. 265; Mackenzie King Diary, June 4, 1935.
51. Library and Archives Canada, Bennett Papers, reel 1025, Herridge to Bennett, April 12, 1934.
52. Lower, op. cit., pp. 515–17.
53. Mackenzie King Diary, January 2 and 9, 1935.
54. Library and Archives Canada, Bennett Papers, reel 3144.
55. Hansard, June 7, 1935.
56. R.J. Manion, *Life Is an Adventure*, Toronto, 1936, p. 213.
57. Mackenzie King Diary, October 14, 1935.
58. Conrad Black, *Render Unto Caesar: The Life and Legacy of Maurice Duplessis*, Toronto, 1998, p. 84.
59. Ibid., p. 104.
60. Original letter of Franklin D. Roosevelt to Margaret Suckley, March 8, 1936 (author's collection).
61. Mackenzie King Diary, January 20, 1937.
62. Ibid., June 29, 1937, and memo on meeting with Hitler; James Eayrs, *In Defence of Canada: Appeasement and Rearmament*, Toronto, 1965, pp. 226–31.
63. Ibid.
64. Conrad Black, *Franklin Delano Roosevelt: Champion of Freedom*, New York, 2003, p. 468.
65. Library and Archives Canada, John Buchan Papers, Tweedsmuir to King, July 3, 1937.
66. McInnis, op. cit., p. 474.
67. Mackenzie King Diary, September 24, 1938.

68. Terry Reardon, *Winston Churchill and Mackenzie King: So Similar, So Different*, Toronto, 2012, p. 87; Mackenzie King Diary, September 14, 1938.

69. Black, *Franklin Delano Roosevelt*, op. cit., p. 484.

70. Mackenzie King Diary, November 12, 1938.

71. Ibid., November 24, December 1, December 13, 1938.

72. Black, *Render Unto Caesar*, op. cit., p. 163.

73. Ibid., pp. 163–64.

74. Mackenzie King Diary, June 15, 1939.

75. Ibid., May 20, 1939.

76. Ibid., May 22, 1939.

77. Ibid., September 2, 1939.

78. Ibid., September 4, 1939.

79. Hansard, September 8, 1939.

80. Ibid.

81. Mackenzie King Diary, September 10, 1939.

82. Black, *Render Unto Caesar*, op. cit., pp. 169–85.

83. Mackenzie King Diary, January 25, 1940.

CHAPTER 7

1. Winston S. Churchill, *The Second World War*, vol. I, *The Gathering Storm*, London, 1948, p. 527; Martin Gilbert, *Winston S. Churchill*, vol. VI, *Finest Hour, 1939–1941*, London, 1983, p. 317.

2. Charles de Gaulle, *Complete War Memoirs*, vol. I, *Call to Honour, 1940–1942*, New York, 1955, p. 57.

3. Warren F. Kimball, ed., *Churchill and Roosevelt: The Complete Correspondence*, vol. I, *Alliance Emerging*, Princeton, 1984, p. 40.

4. J.W. Pickersgill, ed., *The Mackenzie King Record*, vol. I, *1939–1944*, Toronto, 1960, p. 118.

5. Ibid., pp. 120–21.

6. Conrad Black, *Franklin Delano Roosevelt: Champion of Freedom*, New York, 2003, p. 554.

7. Allan Levine, *King: William Lyon Mackenzie King: A Life Guided by the Hand of Destiny*, Toronto, 2011, p. 310.

8. Ibid.

9. Black, op. cit., p. 555.

10. Kimball, op. cit., p. 44.

11. Pickersgill, op. cit., p. 124.

12. Gilbert, op. cit., p. 218.

13. De Gaulle, op. cit., pp. 80, 693.

14. Black, op. cit., p. 560.
15. Black, *Render Unto Caesar: The Life and Legacy of Maurice Duplessis*, Toronto, 1998, p. 189.
16. Ibid.
17. Ibid., p. 190.
18. Hansard (U.K.), June 18, 1940, columns 51–61; Gilbert, op. cit., p. 571.
19. Black, *Render Unto Caesar*, op. cit., p. 185.
20. Ibid., p. 191.
21. Ibid., pp, 192–93.
22. Levine, op. cit., p. 314.
23. Mackenzie King Diary, August 22, 1940.
24. Joe Garner, *The Commonwealth Office, 1925–1968*, London, 1978, p. 225.
25. Levine, op. cit., p. 314, Churchill to King, September 12, 1940.
26. Pickersgill, op. cit., p. 140.
27. Black, *Roosevelt*, op. cit., p. 583; Gilbert, op. cit., p. 855.
28. Kimball, op. cit., vol. I, p. 81.
29. Pickersgill, op. cit., pp. 148-149
30. Kimball, op. cit., pp. 84–85; Samuel E. Morrison, *History of US Naval Operations in World War II*, vol. III, *The Rising Sun in the Pacific, 1931–April 1942*, Boston, 1984, p. 139.
31. Pickersgill, op. cit., p. 149.
32. Ibid., p. 153.
33. Black, *Roosevelt*, op. cit., p. 622.
34. Pickersgill, op. cit., p. 193.
35. Author's collection.
36. Charles Ritchie, *The Siren Years: A Canadian Diplomat Abroad, 1937–1945*, Toronto, 1974, pp. 110–111.
37. Mackenzie King Diary, August 19, 1941.
38. David Dilks, *The Great Dominion: Winston Churchill in Canada, 1900–1954*, Toronto, 2005, p. 152.
39. Black, *Roosevelt*, op. cit., p. 685.
40. Ibid., p. 686.
41. Pickersgill, op. cit., p. 297.
42. King Diary, July 14, 15, 1941.
43. Pickersgill, op. cit., p. 289.
44. Ibid.
45. Ibid., p. 291.
46. Ibid., p. 294.
47. Black, *Roosevelt*, op. cit., p. 709.
48. Desmond Morton, *A Military History of Canada*, Toronto, 1985, p. 188.

49. Black, *Render Unto Caesar*, op. cit., p. 204.
50. Black, *Roosevelt*, op. cit., p. 736, Roosevelt to King, April 27, 1942. I wish to thank journalist and historian Lawrence Martin for sending me a copy of this letter.
51. Pickersgill, op. cit., p. 382; Mackenzie King Diary, June 11, 1942.
52. Levine, op. cit., p. 333, attributed to journalist Grant Dexter.
53. Pickersgill, op. cit., p. 381.
54. Ibid., p. 389.
55. Bruce Hutchison, *The Incredible Canadian*, Toronto, 1953, p. 310; Hutchison, *Mr. Prime Minister, 1867–1964*, Toronto, 1964, pp. 270–71.
56. Mackenzie King Diary, December 31, 1942; Pickersgill, op. cit., p. 465.
57. Black, *Roosevelt*, op. cit., pp. 747–48.
58. Ibid., p. 760.
59. Pickersgill, op. cit., pp. 208–12, 422–29; Hutchison, *Incredible Canadian*, op. cit., pp. 316–17.
60. De Gaulle, op. cit., p. 359.
61. Edgar McInnis, *Canada: A Political and Social History*, Toronto, 1963, p. 489.
62. Churchill, op. cit., vol. III, *The Grand Alliance*, pp. 608–9.
63. Black, *Roosevelt*, op. cit., p. 712; Black, *Flight of the Eagle: A Strategic History of the United States*, Toronto, 2013, p. 402.
64. Field Marshal Lord Alanbrooke, *War Diaries, 1939–1945*, London, 2001, p. 363.
65. Churchill, op. cit., vol. III, *The Grand Alliance*, p. 621.
66. Black, *Flight of the Eagle*, op. cit., p. 416.
67. Hutchison, *Incredible Canadian*, op. cit., p. 324.
68. Hutchison, *Incredible Canadian*, op. cit., p. 325.
69. Black, *Roosevelt*, op. cit., p. 889
70. Black, *Roosevelt*, op. cit., p. 865.
71. Pickersgill, op. cit., pp. 419–20.
72. John Swettenham, *McNaughton*, vol. II, 1939–1943, Toronto, 1969, p. 233.
73. Ibid., pp. 343–45.
74. Black, *Roosevelt*, op. cit., p. 948.
75. Ibid., p. 941.
76. De Gaulle, op. cit., p. 571.
77. De Gaulle, op. cit., p. 577.
78. Ibid.
79. Peter C. Newman, *Flame of Power: Intimate Profiles of Canada's Greatest Businessmen*, Toronto, 1959, p. 44.
80. Black, *Render Unto Caesar*, op. cit., pp. 215–16.
81. Ibid., pp. 271–78.
82. Ibid., p. 219.
83. Levine, op. cit., p. 351.

84. Hutchison, *Incredible Canadian*, op. cit., pp. 357–61; Pickersgill, op. cit., vol. II, 1944–1945, pp. 111–28.

85. Hutchison, ibid., pp. 374–75; ibid., Pickersgill, ibid.

86. Levine, op. cit., p. 357.

87. Pickersgill, op. cit., vol. II, p. 151.

88. Ibid., p. 378.

89. Ibid., p. 376.

90. Ibid., pp. 388–89.

91. Ibid., p. 393.

92. Ibid., pp. 389–90.

93. Ibid., p. 396.

94. Ibid., p. 398.

95. Black, *Flight of the Eagle*, op. cit., p. 453.

96. Ibid., p. 455.

97. Ibid.

98. David McCullough, *Truman*, New York, 1991, p. 443.

99. Pickersgill, op. cit., vol. II, pp. 447–48.

100. Pickersgill, op. cit., vol. II, pp. 445–46.

101. Black, *Roosevelt*, op. cit., p. 1128.

102. De Gaulle, op. cit., pp. 900–901.

103. Barbara Tuchman, *Stilwell and the American Experience in China, 1911–45*, New York, 1970, p. 522.

104. Black, *Render Unto Caesar*, op. cit., pp. 488–89.

105. Mackenzie King Diary, August 28, 1945; Pickersgill, op. cit., vol. II, p. 468.

106. Ibid.

107. Ibid., pp. 468–69.

108. Pickersgill, op. cit., vol. III, 1945–1946, pp. 118–22.

109. Levine, op. cit., p. 373.

110. Ibid., p. 374.

111. Ibid.

112. Pickersgill, op. cit., vol. III, p. 71.

113. Ibid., p. 77.

114. Robert J. Donovan, *Conflict and Crisis: The Presidency of Harry S. Truman, 1945–1948*, New York, 1977, p. 191.

115. Pickersgill, op. cit., vol. III, pp. 183–86.

116. Mackenzie King Diary, February 17, 1946.

117. Levine, op. cit., p. 378.

118. Black, *Render Unto Caesar*, op. cit., pp. 312–19.

119. Ibid., pp. 318–19.

120. Pickersgill, op. cit., vol. III, p. 208.

121. Levine, op. cit., p. 382.
122. Pickersgill, op. cit., vol. III, p. 297.
123. Ibid.
124. C.P. Stacey, *A Date with History: Memoirs of a Canadian Historian*, Ottawa, 1985, pp. 183-7.
125. Pickersgill, op. cit., vol. III.
126. Ibid., p. 343; Mackenzie King Diary, September 21, 1946.
127. Pickersgill, op. cit., vol. III, p. 336.
128. Black, *Flight of the Eagle*, op. cit., p. 462.
129. Mackenzie King Diary, June 12, 1947; Pickersgill, op. cit., vol. IV, 1947–1948, p. 47.
130. Pickersgill, op. cit., vol. IV, pp. 93–94.
131. Pickersgill, op. cit., vol. IV, pp. 108–20.
132. Ibid., p. 146.
133. Ibid., p. 165.
134. Ibid., p. 177.
135. Arthur R. M. Lower, *Colony to Nation: A History of Canada*, Toronto, 1977, p. 562.
136. Ibid., p. 243.
137. Ibid., p. 279.
138. Ibid., pp. 137–38.
139. Black, *Render Unto Caesar*, op. cit., p. 253.
140. Ibid., pp. 254–55.
141. Ibid., pp. 255–56.
142. Pickersgill, op. cit., vol. IV, p. 351.
143. Black, *Render Unto Caesar*, op. cit., p. 507.
144. Pickersgill, op. cit., vol. IV, p. 359.
145. Ibid., p. 377.
146. Ibid., p. 404.
147. Ibid., p. 423.
148. Terry Reardon, *Winston Churchill and Mackenzie King: So Similar, So Different*, Toronto, 2012, p. 371.
149. Pickersgill, op. cit., vol. IV, p. 425.
150. Frank R. Scott and A.J.M. Smith, eds., *The Blasted Pine*, Toronto, 1957, pp. 27–28.
151. J.L. Granatstein, *How Britain's Weakness Forced Canada into the Arms of the United States*, Toronto, 1989, p. 7.
152. Ibid., p. 57.

CHAPTER 8

1. Dale Thomson, *Louis St. Laurent*, p. 250.
2. Ibid., p. 251.
3. Edgar McInnis, *Canada: A Political and Social History*, Toronto, 1947, p. 533.
4. Thomson, op. cit, p. 262.
5. *Le Devoir*, September 12, 1950.
6. Conrad Black, *Flight of the Eagle*, p. 486.
7. Thomson, op. cit., p. 315.
8. McInnis, op. cit, p. 533.
9. Thomson, op. cit., p. 357.
10. Thomson, op. cit., p. 361.
11. Thomson, op. cit., p. 364.
12. Ibid., p. 366.
13. Ibid., p. 364.
14. *House of Commons Debates*, March 18, 1954.
15. Thomson, op. cit., p. 378.
16. Thomson, op. cit., pp. 380-81.
17. Black, *Render Unto Caesar*, op. cit., p. 343.
18. *House of Commons Debates*, May 24, 1956, p. 4302; May 25, p. 4365; May 30, p. 4464.
19. Dale Thomson, *Louis St. Laurent*, p. 439.
20. *House of Commons Debates*, July 9, 1956, p. 5852.
21. T. Robertson, *Crisis: The Inside Story of the Suez Conspiracy*, Toronto, 1964, p. 101.
22. Thomson, op. cit., p. 466.
23. *Montreal Star*, November 1, 1956.
24. Thomson, op. cit., p. 472.
25. Black, *Flight of the Eagle*, op. cit., p. 533.
26. Thomson, op. cit., pp. 472-73.
27. T. Robertson, op. cit., p. 200.
28. Conrad Black, *The Invincible Quest*, Toronto, 2006, p. 348.
29. Stephen E. Ambrose, *Eisenhower: Soldier and President*, New York, 1991.
30. Dwight D. Eisenhower, *Waging Peace*, New York, 1965, pp. 92-93.
31. Thomson, op. cit., p. 486.
32. *Great Unsolved Mysteries in Canadian History*. Larry Hannant, *Death of a Diplomat: Herbert Norman and the Cold War*. Internet under Herbert Norman.
33. Thomson, op. cit., p. 505.
34. Conversation with Hon. J.W. Pickersgill, October 1962.
35. John G. Diefenbaker, *One Canada*, vol. II, Toronto, 1975, p. 92.

36. Black, *Render Unto Caesar*, op. cit., pp. 496-97.

37. Vincent Geloso, *Du Grand Rattrapage au Déclin Tranquille, Une Histoire économique et sociale du Québec de 1900 à nos jours*. Éditions Accent Grave, Montreal, 2012, pp. 56, 75, 86, 160, 206; Black, *Render Unto Caesar*, Toronto, 1976, pp. 404-36.

38. Charles de Gaulle, *Memoirs of Hope*, London, 1970, p. 239.

39. Michael Bliss, *Right Honourable Men: The Descent of Canadian Politics from Macdonald to Mulroney*, Toronto, 1994, p. 214.

40. Bruce Hutchison, *Mr. Prime Minister, 1867–1964*, Toronto, 1964, pp. 341-42.

41. Black, *Render Unto Caesar*, op. cit., p. 472.

42. Bliss, op. cit., p. 225.

43. Walter Gordon, *A Political Memoir*, Toronto, 1977, p. 156.

44. Ibid.

45. Lester B. Pearson. *Mike: The Memoirs of the Right Honourable Lester B. Pearson*, vol. II, Toronto, 1973, p. 146.

46. John English, *The Life of Lester B. Pearson*, vol. II, *The Worldly Years, 1949–1972*, Toronto, 1992, p. 287.

47. Ibid.

48. Conversation with the author, June 1977.

49. English, op. cit., p. 291.

50. Ibid., p. 281.

51. Ibid., p. 298.

52. Author's conversation with Walter L. Gordon and with the chief executive officer of Canadian Corporate Management, Valentina N. Stock, 1977.

CHAPTER 9

1. Jean Lacouture, *De Gaulle*, English edition, vol. II. *The Ruler, 1945–1970*, New York and London, 1985, p. 450.

2. Ibid.

3. Jean Lacouture, *De Gaulle*, vol. III, *Le Souverain*, p. 519.

4. Summarized by his principal biographer, Jean Lacouture, in *De Gaulle*, vol. III, *Le Souverain*, pp. 516-34.

5. John English, *The Life of Lester B. Pearson*, vol. II, *The Worldly Years, 1949–1972*, Toronto, 1992, p. 328.

6. Conversation with Paul-Émile Cardinal Léger, August 10, 1971, Yaoundé, Cameroon. (The author was the vice-president of the cardinal's charity, Le Cardinal Léger et ses oeuvres.)

7. Richard Gwyn, *The Northern Magus*, Toronto, 1980, p. 109.

8. Ibid., p. 118.

9.   Ibid., p. 119.
10. Black, *Render Unto Caesar*, p. 205.
11. Author's conversation with Dr. Kissinger, November 23, 2014.
12. Author's conversation with President Nixon, June 23, 1992.
13. George Radwanski, *Trudeau*, Toronto, 1978, p. 275.
14. Gwyn, op. cit., p. 140.
15. Radwanski, op. cit., p. 279.
16. Ibid., p. 282.
17. Ibid., p. 303.
18. Gwyn, op. cit., p. 371.
19. Ibid., p. 374.
20. Pierre E. Trudeau, *Memoirs*, Toronto, 1993, p. 303.
21. Pierre Trudeau and Thomas D. Axworthy, eds., *Towards a Just Society*, Toronto, 1990, p. 421.
22. Bob Plamondon, *The Truth About Trudeau*, Ottawa, 2013, p. 110.
23. Ibid., p. 286.
24. Ibid., p. 110.
25. Ibid., p. 58.
26. Lawrence Martin, *Iron Man: The Defiant Reign of Jean Chrétien*, vol. II, Toronto, 2003, p. 180.
27. Ibid., p. 250.

CHAPTER 10

1.   Lawrence Martin, *Iron Man: The Defiant Reign of Jean Chrétien*, vol. II, Toronto, 2003, p. 260.
2.   Ibid., p. 285.
3.   Ibid., p. 342.
4.   Ibid., p. 364.
5.   Paul Wells, *The Longer I'm Prime Minister: Stephen Harper and Canada, 2006–*, Toronto, 2013, p. 25.
6.   Ibid., p. 68.
7.   Ibid., p. 80.
8.   Ibid., p. 211.

CONCLUSION

1.   Robert Bothwell, *The Penguin History of Canada*, Toronto, 2006, p. 501.

Bibliography

Abella, Irving and Harold Troper. *None Is Too Many* (Lester & Orpen Dennys, 1983).

Abels, Jules. *The Rockefeller Billions* (Macmillan Company, New York, 1965).

Acheson, Dean. *Present at the Creation: My Years in the State Department* (Norton, New York, 1969).

Adams, Eric. *Canada's Newer Constitutional Law and the Idea of Constitutional Rights* (McGill Law Journal 51, 2006).

Adams, Michael. *Fire and Ice: The United States, Canada and the Myth of Converging Values* (Penguin, Toronto, 2003).

Addams, Jane. *Twenty Years at Hull-House* (Macmillan Company, New York, 1910).

Akenson, Donald. *The Irish in Ontario: A Study in Rural History* (McGill-Queen's University Press, Montreal & Kingston, 1999).

Allen, Ralph. *Ordeal by Fire, Canada 1910–1945, Vol. 5* (Doubleday, Toronto, 1961).

Allen, Richard. *The Social Passion: Religion and Social Reform in Canada 1914–1928* (University of Toronto Press, 1972).

———. *A Region of the Mind: Interpreting the Western Canadian Plains* (University of Saskatchewan, 1973).

Alliston Karen, Rick Archbold, Jennifer Glossop, Alison Maclean and Ivon Owen, eds. *Trudeau Albums* (Penguin, Toronto, 2000).

Ambrose, Stephen. *Eisenhower, The President, Vol. 2* (Simon & Schuster, New York, 1984).

Anastakis, Dimitri. *Auto Pact: Creating a Borderless North American Auto Industry* (University of Toronto Press, Toronto, 2005).

Anderson, Fred. *Crucible of War: The Seven Years' War and the Fate of Empire in British North America* (Alfred A. Knopf, New York, 2000).

Andrew, Christopher and Oleg Gordievsky. *KGB: The Inside Story* (HarperCollins, New York, 1990).

——— and David Dilks. *The Missing Dimension: Governments and Intelligence Communities in the Twentieth Century* (Macmillan, London, 1984).

Armstrong, Christopher. *The Politics of Federalism: Ontario's Relations with the Federal Government, 1867–1942* (University of Toronto Press, Toronto, 1981).

Armstrong, Sally. *Mila* (Macmillan, Toronto, 1992).

Avakumovic, Ivan. *Socialism in Canada: A Study of the CCF-NDP in Federal and Provincial Politics* (McClelland & Stewart, Toronto, 1978).

Axworthy, Lloyd. *Navigating a New World: Canada's Global Future* (Vintage, Toronto, 2004).

Axworthy, Thomas S. *Passionate Rationalist Pierre Trudeau and the Transformation of Canada* (Penguin, Toronto, 2004).

——— and Pierre Elliott Trudeau, eds. *Toward a Just Society: The Trudeau Years* (Viking, Markham, 1990).

Azzi, Stephen. *Walter Gordon and the Rise of Canadian Nationalism* (McGill-Queen's University Press, Montreal & Kingston, 1999).

Bain, George. *Gotcha! How the Media Distort the News* (Key Porter Books, Toronto, 1994).

Baker, James A. with Thomas M. DeFrank. *The Politics of Diplomacy* (G.P. Putnam & Sons, New York, 1995).

Baker, William. "The Miners and the Mediator: The 1906 Lethbridge Strike and Mackenzie King" (*Labour/Le Travail* 11 – Spring 1983; 99-118).

———. "The Personal Touch: Mackenzie King, Harriet Reid and the Springhill Strike, 1909–1911" (*Labour/Le Travail* 13 – Spring 1984; 159-176).

———. "A Case Study of Anti-Americanism in English-Speaking Canada: The Election Campaign of 1911" (*Canadian Historical Review* 51:4 – December 1970; 426-449).

Ball, Norman. *Building Canada: A History of Public Works* (University of Toronto Press, Toronto, 1988).

Bangarth, Stephanie. *Voices Raised in Protest: Defending North American Citizens of Japanese Ancestry, 1942–1948* (UBC Press, Vancouver, 2008).

Banting, Keith G. *The Welfare State and Canadian Federalism* (McGill-Queen's University Press, Montreal & Kingston, 1987).

Banting, Keith G. and Richard Simeon, eds. *And No One Cheered: Federalism, Democracy and the Constitution Act* (Methuen, Toronto, 1983).

Barber, Clarence L. and John C.P. McCallum. *Controlling Inflation: Learning from Experience in Canada, Europe and Japan* (Canadian Institute for Economic Policy, 1982, Ottawa).

Barros, James. *No Sense of Evil: Espionage, The Case of Herbert Norman* (Deneau,Toronto, 1986).

Barry, Donald, Mark Dickerson, and James Gaisford. *Toward a North American Community? Canada, the United States and Mexico* (Westview Press, Boulder, 1995).

Bastien, Frédéric. *La Bataille de Londres: Dessous, secrets et coulisses du rapatriement constitutionnel* (Boréal, Montreal, 2013).

Beaverbrook, (Lord) Max Aitken. *Friends: Sixty Years of Intimate Personal Relations with Richard Bedford Bennett* (Heinemann, London, 1959).

Beck, J.M. *Pendulum of Power: Canada's Federal Elections* (Prentice-Hall, Scarborough, 1968).

———. *The Shaping of Canadian Federalism: Central Authority or Provincial Right?* (Copp Clark, Toronto, 1971).

Bedore, Margaret. *The Reading of Mackenzie King* (Ph.D. dissertation, Queen's University, 2008).

Beevor, Antony. *The Fall of Berlin, 1945* (Viking, New York, 2002).

Bell, Stewart. *Cold Terror: How Canada Nurtures and Exports Terrorism Around the World* (Wiley, Toronto, 2004).

Bercuson, David and Holger H. Herwig. *One Christmas in Washington* (Overlook Press, New York, 2005).

Berger, Carl. *The Sense of Power: Studies in the Idea of Canadian Imperialism, 1867–1914* (University of Toronto Press, 1970).

Bernard, Jean-Paul. *Les Rouges: Liberalisme, nationalisme et anti-cléricalisme au milieu du XIXe siècle* (Montreal, Les Presses de l'Université du Quebec, 1971).

Berton, Pierre. *Marching as to War: Canada's Turbulent Years, 1899–1953* (Anchor Canada, Toronto, 2002).

———. *The Last Spike: The Great Railway 1883–1885* (McClelland & Stewart, Toronto, 1971).

———. *The Promised Land: Settling the West 1896–1914* (McClelland & Stewart, Toronto, 1984).

———. *The Great Depression 1929–1939* (McClelland & Stewart, Toronto, 1990).

Betcherman, Lita Rose. *Ernest Lapointe: Mackenzie King's Great Quebec Lieutenant* (University of Toronto Press, Toronto, 2002).

———. "The Customs Scandal of 1926" (*The Beaver* 81:2 – April/May 2001; 14-19).

Biggar, E.B. *Anecdotal Life of Sir John Macdonald* (John Lovell, Montreal, 1891).

Bishop, Morris. *Champlain: The Life of Fortitude* (Alfred A. Knopf, New York, 1948).

Black, Conrad. *Duplessis* (McClelland & Stewart, Toronto, 1977).

———. *A Life in Progress* (Key Porter Books, Toronto, 1993).

———. *Flight of the Eagle: A Strategic History of the United States* (McClelland & Stewart, Toronto, 2013).

———. *Franklin Delano Roosevelt: Champion of Freedom* (Public Affairs, New York, 2003).

———. *The Invincible Quest: The Life of Richard Milhous Nixon* (McClelland & Stewart, Toronto, 2007).

Blackburn, Robert H. "Mackenzie King, William Mulock, James Mavor, and the University of Toronto Students' Revolt of 1895" (*Canadian Historical Review* 69:4 – December 1988; 490-503).

Blais, André, Elizabeth Gidengil, Richard Nadeau and Neil Nevitte. *Anatomy of a Liberal Victory: Making Sense of the Vote in the 2000 Canadian Election* (Broadview Press, Peterborough, 2002).

Bliss, Michael. *Right Honourable Men: The Descent of Canadian Politics from Macdonald to Chrétien* (HarperCollins, Toronto, 2004).

———. "Privatizing the Mind: The Sundering of Canadian History, the Sundering of Canada" (*Journal of Canadian Studies* 26:4. – Winter 1991-92).

Borden, Henry, ed. *Robert Laird Borden: His Memoirs, Vols. 1 and 2* (Macmillan, Toronto, 1938).

Borden, Robert. *Robert Laird Borden: His Memoirs* (Macmillan Company, Toronto, 1938).

———. *Letters to Limbo* (Macmillan Press, Toronto, 1971).

Bordo, Michael, Angela Redish and Ronald Shearer. *Canada's Monetary System in Historical Perspective: Two Faces of the Exchange Rate Regime* (University of Vancouver Press, Vancouver, 1999).

Borins, Sandford. *The Language of the Skies: The Bilingual Air Traffic Control Conflict in Canada* (McGill-Queen's University Press, Montreal & Kingston, 1983).
Bothwell, Robert. *Nucleus* (University of Toronto Press, Toronto, 1988).
———. *Canada and Quebec: One Country, Two Histories* (UBC Press, Vancouver, 1998).
———. *A Penguin History of Canada* (Penguin, Toronto, 2007).
———. *Alliance and Illusion: Canada and the World, 1945–1984* (UBC Press, Vancouver, 2007).
———. *Eldorado: Canada's National Uranium Company* (University of Toronto Press, Toronto, 1984).
———, Drummond, Ian and John English. *Canada, 1900–1945* (University of Toronto Press, Toronto, 1989).
———, Drummond, Ian and John English. *Canada since 1945: Power, Politics, and Provincialism* (University of Toronto Press, Toronto, 1981).
Bothwell, Robert and William Kilbourn. *C.D. Howe: A Biography* (McClelland & Stewart, Toronto, 1979).
——— and Norman Hillmer, eds. *The In-Between Time: Canadian External Policy in the 1930s* (Copp Clark, Toronto, 1975).
Bouchard, Lucien. *On the Record.* Translated by Dominique Clift (Stoddart Publishing, Toronto, 1994).
Bourassa, Henri. *Great Britain and Canada* (Beauchemin, Montreal, 1902).
Bourne, Kenneth. *Britain and the Balance of Power in North America 1815–1908* (University of California Press, Berkeley, 1967).
Bouthillier, Guy and Édouard Cloutier. *Trudeau's Darkest Hour: War Measures in Time of Peace* (Baraka Books, Montreal, 2010).
Bowen, Roger, ed. *E.H. Norman: His Life and Scholarship* (University of Toronto Press, Toronto, 1984).
———. *Innocence Is Not Enough: The Life and Death of Herbert Norman* (Douglas & McIntyre, Vancouver, 1986).
Bowering, George. *Egotists and Autocrats: The Prime Ministers of Canada* (Viking Press, Toronto, 1999).
Boyer, Patrick. *A Passion for Justice: The Legacy of James Chalmers McRuer* (University of Toronto Press for the Osgoode Society for Canadian Legal History, Toronto, 1994).
Boyko, John. *Last Steps to Freedom: The Evolution of Canadian Racism* (J. Gordon Shillingford Publishing, Winnipeg, 1998).
———. *Into the Hurricane: Attacking Socialism and the CCF* (J. Gordon Shillingford Publishing, Winnipeg, 2006).
———. *Bennett: The Rebel Who Challenged and Changed a Nation* (Key Porter Books, Toronto, 2010).
Bracq, J.C. *The Evolution of French Canada* (The Macmillan Company, New York, 1924).
Bradley, A.G. *Lord Dorchester* (Oxford University Press, London, 1926).
Bradwin, Edmund. *The Bunkhouse Man: A Study of Work and Play in the Camps of Canada 1903–1914* (University of Toronto Press, Toronto, 1972).
Brebner, J.B. *The Explorers of North America* (A. & C. Black, London, 1933).
———. *North Atlantic Triangle* (Ryerson Press, Toronto, 1945).
———. *Canada: A Modern History* (University of Michigan Press, Ann Arbor, 1960).
Brennan, Patrick H. *Reporting the Nation's Business: Press-Government Relations during the Liberal Years, 1935–1957* (University of Toronto Press, Toronto, 1994).
Broadfoot, Barry. *Ten Lost Years: Memories of Canadians Who Survived the Depression* (Paper Jacks Ltd., Toronto, 1973).
——— and David R. Facey-Crowther, eds. *The Atlantic Charter* (St. Martin's Press, New York, 1994).
Brodie, J. "The Free Trade Election" (*Studies in Political Economy* 28 – Spring 1989; 175-182).
——— and J. Jenson. *Piercing the Smokescreen: Brokerage Parties and Class Politics in Canadian Parties in Transition: Discourse, Organization and Representation.* Edited by Alain G. Gagnon and A. Brian Tanguay (Nelson Canada, Scarborough, 1989).
———. *Crisis, Challenge and Change: Party and Politics in Canada* (Methuen, Toronto, 1980).
Brodsky, Alyn. *Grover Cleveland: A Study in Character* (Truman Talley Books, New York, 2000).
Brown, G.W. *Canada* (United Nations Series. Berkeley: University of California Press, 1950).
———. *Readings in Canadian History* (J.M. Dent Limited, Toronto, 1940).
Brown, Lorne. *When Freedom Was Lost: The Unemployed, the Agitator and the State* (Black Rose Books, Montreal, 1987).
Brown, Patrick, Robert Chodos and Rae Murphy. *Winners, Losers: The 1976 Tory Leadership Convention* (James Lorimer & Co., Toronto, 1976).

Brown, Robert Craig. *Robert Laird Borden: A Biography: I: 1854–1914* (Macmillan of Canada, 1975).
—— and Ramsay Cook. *Canada 1896–1921: A Nation Transformed* (McClelland & Stewart, Toronto, 1974).
Bryant, Arthur. *The Turn of the Tide: A Study Based on the Diaries and Autobiographical Notes of Field Marshal The Viscount Alanbrooke* (Collins, London, 1957).
Bryden, Penny. *Planners and Politicians: Liberal Politics and Social Policy* (McGill-Queen's University Press, Montreal & Kingston, 1997).
Buck, Tim. *Thirty Years: The Story of the Communist Movement in Canada 1922–1952* (Progress Books, Toronto, 1975).
Buissert, David. *Henry IV* (G. Allen & Unwin, London, 1984).
Bullock, Allison. *William Lyon Mackenzie King: A Very Double Life* (M.A. thesis, Queen's University, 2009).
Bumsted, J.M. *Fur Trade Wars* (Great Plains Publications, Winnipeg, 1999).
Burelle, André. *Pierre Elliott Trudeau: L'Intellectuel et le Politique* (Fides, Montreal, 2005).
Burke, Sara Z. *Seeking the Highest God: Social Service and Gender at the University of Toronto, 1888–1937* (University of Toronto Press, Toronto, 1996).
Burney, Derek. *Getting it Done: A Memoir* (McGill-Queen's University Press, Montreal & Kingston, 2005).
Burpee, L.J. *A Historical Atlas of Canada* (Thomas Nelson & Sons Limited, Toronto, 1927).
Burt, A.L. *The Old Province of Quebec* (University of Minnesota Press, Minneapolis, 1933).
Bush, Barbara. *A Memoir* (Lisa Drew Books, New York, 1994).
——. *Reflections: Life After the White House* (Simon & Schuster, New York, 2003).
Bush, George H.W. and Brent Scowcroft. *A World Transformed* (Alfred A. Knopf, New York, 1998).
Bushnell, Ian. *The Federal Court of Canada: A History, 1875–1992* (University of Toronto Press, Toronto, 1992).
Butler, Richard Austin (Lord). *The Art of the Possible: The Memoirs of Lord Butler* (Hamish Hamilton, London, 1971).
Butler, Rick and Jean-Guy Carrier. *The Trudeau Decade* (Doubleday, Toronto, 1979).
Byers, R.B., ed. *Canadian Annual Review of Politics and Public Affairs, 1984* (University of Toronto Press, Toronto, 1987).
Byng, Evelyn. *Up the Stream of Time* (Macmillan Company, Toronto, 1946).
Cahill, Jack. *John Turner: The Long Run* (McClelland & Stewart, Toronto, 1984).
Calomiris, Charles. "Financial actors in the great Depression" *(Journal of Economic Perspectives 17, No. 2 – Spring 1993; 62).*
Cameau, Pauline and Aldo Santin. *The First Canadians: A Profile of Canada's Native People Today* (James Lorimer & Company, Toronto, 1995).
Camp, Dalton. *Gentlemen, Players and Politicians* (McClelland & Stewart, Toronto, 1970).
Campbell, Kim. *Time and Chance: The Political Memoirs of Canada's First Woman Prime Minister* (Doubleday, Toronto, 1996).
Campbell, Robert Malcolm. *Grand Illusions: The Politics of the Keynesian Experience in Canada, 1945–1975* (Broadview Press, Toronto, 1987).
——. "Post-Mortem on the Free Trade Election" *(Journal of Canadian Studies 24:1 – 1989; 3-4, 163-165).*
Cambridge History of the British Empire, Vol. 6. *Canada and Newfoundland* (Cambridge University Press, Cambridge, 1930).
Canadian Historical Association Annual Reports from 1920
Canadian Historical Association, Historical Booklets (The Association, c/o Public Archives, Ottawa):
    Burt, A.L. *Guy Carleton, Lord Dorchester, 1724–1808*, revised version (No. 5, 1955).
    Fregault, Guy. *Canadian Society in the French Regime* (No. 3, 1954).
    MacNutt, W.S. *The Making of the Maritime Provinces, 1713–1784* (No. 4, 1955).
    Masters, D.C. *Reciprocity, 1846–1911* (No. 12, 1961).
    Morton, W.L. *The West and Confederation, 1857–1871* (No. 9, 1958).
    Ouellet, Fernand. *Louis-Joseph Papineau: A Divided Soul* (No. 11, 1960).
    Rothney, G.O. *Newfoundland: From International Fishery to Canadian Province* (No. 10, 1959).
    Soward, F.H. *The Department of External Affairs and Canadian Autonomy, 1899–1939* (No. 7, 1956).
    Stacey, C.P. *The Undefended Border: The Myth and the Reality* (No. 1, 1953).
    Stanley, G.F.G. *Louis Riel: Patriot or Rebel?* (No. 2, 1954).

Trudel, Marcel, *The Seigneurial Regime* (No. 6, 1960).

Underhill, F.H. *Canadian Political Parties* (No. 8, 1957).

Canadian Historical Review, Vols. I-XLI.

Caplan, Gerald, Michael Kirby and Hugh Segal. *Election: The Issues, the Strategies, the Aftermath* (Prentice-Hall, Scarborough, 1989).

Careless, J.M.S. *Brown of the Globe: Voice of Upper Canada, Vol. 1* (Macmillan Company, Toronto, 1959).

———. *The Union of the Canadas: The Growth of Canadian Institutions 1841–1857* (McClelland & Stewart, Toronto, 1972).

Carisse, Jean-Marc. *Privileged Access with Trudeau, Turner, and Chrétien* (Warwick, Toronto, 2000).

Carlton, David. *Britain and the Suez Crisis* (Basil Blackwell, Oxford, 1988).

Carney, Anne. "Trudeau Unveiled: Growing Up Private with Mama, the Jesuits and the Conscience of the Rich" (*Maclean's*, February, 1972).

Carty, Kenneth and Peter Ward, eds. *National Politics and Community in Canada* (UBC Press, Vancouver, 1986).

Champlain, Samuel de. *The Works of Samuel de Champlain*, 6 vols. (University of Toronto Press, Toronto, 1971).

Chapais, T. *Cours d'Histoire du Canada 1760–1841.*

Charest, Jean. *My Road to Quebec* (Éditions Pierre Tisseyre, St. Laurent, 1998.)

Chernow, Ron. *Titan: The Life of John D. Rockefeller, Sr.* (Random House, New York, 1998).

Chevrier, Lionel. "The Practical Diplomacy of Lester Pearson" (*International Journal* – Winter 1973–74; 127-128).

Chrétien, Jean. *Straight from the Heart* (Seal Books, Toronto, 1986).

———. *My Years as Prime Minister* (Knopf Canada, Toronto, 2007).

Christie, Nancy and Michael Gauvreau. *A Full-Orbed Christianity: The Protestant Churches and Social Welfare in Canada, 1900–1940* (McGill-Queen's University Press, Montreal & Kingston, 1998).

Churchill, Winston S. *Churchill Speaks: Winston S. Churchill in Peace and War: Collected Speeches 1897–1963.* Edited by Robert Rhodes James (Barnes & Noble, New York, 1998).

———. *Closing the Ring, Vol. 5, The Second World War* (Houghton Mifflin, Boston, 1951).

———. *The Gathering Storm, Vol. 1, The Second World War* (Houghton Mifflin, Boston, 1948).

———. *The Grand Alliance, Vol. 3, The Second World War* (Houghton Mifflin, Boston, 1950)

———. *Great Contemporaries* (Thornton Butterworth, London, 1937).

———. *The Hinge of Fate, Vol. 4, The Second World War* (Houghton Mifflin, Boston, 1950).

———. *Their Finest Hour, Vol. 2, The Second World War* (Houghton Mifflin, Boston, 1949).

———. *Triumph and Tragedy, Vol. 6, The Second World* War (Houghton Mifflin, Boston, 1953).

———. *The World Crisis: The Aftermath, 1918–1928* (Charles Scribner's Sons, New York, 1929).

Clark, S.D. *Movements of Political Protest in Canada, 1640–1840* (University of Toronto Press, Toronto, 1959).

Clarke, Harold D. *Absent Mandate: Interpreting Change in Canadian Elections* (Gage Educational, Toronto, 1991).

Clarkson, Stephen. *Charisma and Contradictions: The Legacy of Pierre Elliott Trudeau* (University of Toronto Bulletin, October 16, 2000).

———. *The Big Red Machine: How the Liberal Party Dominates Canadian Politics* (UBC Press, Vancouver, 2005).

———. "Gaullism: Prospect for Canada" (*Canadian Forum* – June 1966; 52).

——— and Christina McCall. *Trudeau and Our Times, Vol 1: The Magnificent Obsession* (McClelland & Stewart, Toronto, 1990).

——— *Trudeau and Our Times, Vol. 2: The Heroic Delusion* (McClelland & Stewart, Toronto, 1994).

Cohen, Andrew. *A Deal Undone: The Making and Breaking of the Meech Lake Accord* (Douglas & McIntyre, Vancouver, 1990).

———. *While Canada Slept: How We Lost Our Place in the World* (McClelland & Stewart, Toronto, 2003).

——— and J.L. Granatstein, eds. *Trudeau's Shadow: The Life and Legacy of Pierre Elliott Trudeau* (Random House, Toronto, 1998).

Cohoe, Margaret M. comp. *Sir John A. Macdonald: A Remembrance to Mark the Centennial of his Death, June 6, 1891* (Kingston Historical Society, Kingston, 1991).

Colby, Charles W. *The Fighting Governor* (Glasgow, Brook, Toronto, 1920).

Coleman, Ronald. *Just Watch Me: Trudeau's Tragic Legacy* (Trafford Publishing, Bloomington, 2003).

Colley, Linda. *Captives: Britain, Empire and the World, 1600–1850* (Pimlico, London, 2003).

Comber, Mary Anne and Robert S. Mayne. *The Newsmongers: How the Media Distort the Political News* (McClelland & Stewart, Toronto, 1986).

Connors, Richard and John M. Law. *The Politics of Energy: The Development and Implementation of the National Energy Program* (Methuen, Toronto, 1985).

Conrad, Margaret. *George Nowlan: Maritime Conservative in National Politics* (University of Toronto Press, Toronto, 1986).

Cook, Ramsay. "J.W. Dafoe at the Imperial Conference, 1923" (*Canadian Historical Reivew* 41:1 – March 1960; 19-40).

——. *The Politics of John W. Dafoe and the Free Press* (University of Toronto Press, Toronto, 1963).

——. *Provincial Autonomy, Minority Rights and the Compact Theory* (Queen's Printer, Ottawa, 1969).

——. "A Canadian Account of the 1926 Imperial Conference" (*Journal of Commonwealth Political Studies* 3:1 – March 1965; 50-63).

——, ed. *The Dafoe-Sifton Correspondence 1919–1927* (Manitoba Record Society, Winnipeg, 1966).

——. "Spiritualism, Science of the Earthly Paradise" (*Canadian Historical Review* 65:1 – March 1984; 4-27).

——. *The Regenerators: Social Criticism in Late Victorian Canada* (University of Toronto Press, Toronto, 1985).

——. *The Teeth of Time: Remembering Pierre Elliott Trudeau* (McGill-Queen's University Press, Montreal & Kingston, 2006).

——. "Not Right, Not Left, But Forward" (*Canadian Forum* – February 1962; 241-2).

——. *The Maple Leaf Forever* (Macmillan, Toronto, 1971).

Cook, Tim. *Shock Troops: Canadians Fighting the Great War, 1917–1918, Vol. 2* (Penguin, Toronto, 2008).

Copps, Sheila. *Nobody's Baby: A Woman's Survival Guide to Politics* (Deneau, Toronto, 1986).

Corbett, David. *Canada's Immigration Policy: A Critique* (University of Toronto Press, Toronto, 1956).

Coulon, Jocelyn. *Soldiers of Diplomacy: The United Nations Peacekeeping and the New World Order* (University of Toronto Press, Toronto, 1998).

Couture, Claude. *Paddling with the Current: Pierre Elliott Trudeau, Étienne Parent, Liberalism, and Nationalism in Canada* (University of Alberta, Edmonton, 1990).

Cowan, Helen I. *British Emigration to British North America: The First Hundred Years* (University of Toronto Press, Toronto, 1961).

Coyne, Deborah. *Unscripted: A Life Devoted to Building a Better Canada* (Canadian Writer's Group, Kindle Edition, 2013).

Craig, Gerald. *Early Travellers in the Canadas, 1791–1867* (Macmillan, Toronto, 1955).

——. *Upper Canada: The Formative Years, 1784–1841* (McClelland & Stewart, Toronto, 1963).

Craven, Paul. *An Impartial Umpire: Industrial Relations and the Canadian State 1900–1911* (University of Toronto Press, Toronto, 1980).

Creighton, D.G. *Dominion of the North* (Macmillan Company of Canada, Toronto, 1957).

——. *Canada's First Century (1867–1967)* (St. Martin's Press, Toronto, 1970).

——. *The Empire of the St. Lawrence* (Macmillan Company of Canada, Toronto, 1956).

——. *John A. Macdonald: The Young Politician* (Macmillan Company of Canada, Toronto, 1952).

——. *The Forked Road: Canada 1939–1957* (McClelland & Stewart, Toronto, 1976).

——. *John A. Macdonald: The Old Chieftain* (Macmillan Company of Canada, Toronto, 1955).

——. *Towards the Discovery of Canada* (Macmillan, Toronto, 1972).

Crosbie, John C. *No Holds Barred: My Life in Politics* (McClelland & Stewart, Toronto, 1997).

Crowley, Brian. *Fearful Symmetry: The Rise and Fall of Canada's Founding Values* (Key Porter Books, Toronto, 2009).

Crowley, Terence. *A Marriage of Minds: Isabel and Oscar Skelton Reinventing Canada* (University of Toronto Press, Toronto, 2003).

Dafoe, J.W. *Laurier: A Study in Canadian Politics* (Thomas Allen, Toronto, 1922).

Dale, Arch. *Five Years of R.B. Bennett* (Winnipeg Free Press, Winnipeg, 1935).

Danson, Barney with Curtis Fahey. *Not Bad for a Sergeant: The Memoirs of Barney Danson* (Dundurn, Toronto, 2002).

Davey, Keith. *The Rainmaker: A Passion for Politics* (Stoddart, Toronto, 1986).

Dawson, R. MacGregor. *Canada in World Affairs: Two Years of War, 1939–1941* (Oxford University Press, Toronto, 1943).

Dawson, R. MacGregor. *William Lyon Mackenzie King, Vol. 1* (University of Toronto Press, Toronto, 1958).

———. *Constitutional Issues in Canada, 1900–1931* (Oxford University Press, London, 1933).

———. *The Conscription Crisis of 1944* (University of Toronto Press, Toronto, 1961).

de Brumath, A. Leblond. *Bishop Laval* (Oxford University Press, London, 1926).

de Celles, Alfred D. *Papineau, Cartier* (Oxford University Press, London, 1926).

de Gaulle, Charles. *Complete War Memoirs* (Simon & Schuster, New York, 1955–1959).

De Kiewiet, C.W. and F.H. Underhill. *The Dufferin-Carnarvon Correspondence, 1874–1878* (Champlain Society, Toronto, 1955).

Delacourt, Susan. *United We Fall: In Search of a New Canada* (Penguin, Toronto, 1994).

Delisle, Esther. *The Traitor and the Jew: Anti-Semitism and the Delirium of Extremist Right-wing Nationalism in French Canada from 1929 to 1939* (Robert Davies, Montreal, 1993).

de Montaigne, Michel. *The Complete Essays*. Translated by Donald M. Frame (Stanford University Press, Stanford, 1957).

Denison, G.T. *The Struggle for Imperial Unity* (Macmillan and Co., London, 1909).

Dent, J.C. *The Last Forty Years: The Union of 1841 to Confederation* (McClelland & Stewart, Toronto, 1972).

Denys, Nicolas. *Histoire naturelle des peuples, des animaux, des arbres & plantes de l'Amérique septentrionale, & de ses divers climats* (Paris, 1672); English edition, *The Description and Natural History of the Coasts of North America (Acadia)*, trans. and ed. William F. Ganong (Praeger, Toronto, 1908).

Desbarats, Peter. *René: A Canadian in Search of a Country* (McClelland & Stewart, Toronto, 1976).

Desrosiers, L.P. *Iroquoisie* (L'Institut d'Histoire de L'Amerique Français, Montreal, 1947).

de Vault, Carole with William Johnson. *The Informer: Confessions of an Ex-Terrorist* (Fleet Books, Toronto, 1982).

Dickason, Olive. *Canada's First Nation: A History of Founding Peoples from Earliest Times* (Oxford University Press, Toronto, 1977).

Diefenbaker, John. *Memoirs of the Right Honourable John G. Diefenbaker: The Crusading Years 1895–1956* (Signet Books, Toronto, 1975).

———. *Memoirs of the Right Honourable John G. Diefenbaker: Years of Achievement 1956–1962* (Signet Books, Toronto, 1976).

———. *One Canada: The Tumultuous Years 1962–1967* (Macmillan, Toronto, 1976).

Dilks, David. *The Great Dominion: Winston Churchill in Canada, 1900–1954* (Thomas Allen, Toronto, 2005).

Dimbleby, David and David Reynolds. *An Ocean Apart: The Relationship between Britain and America in the Twentieth Century* (Random House, New York, 1988).

Dobell, Peter. *Canada's Search for New Roles: Foreign Policy in the Trudeau Era* (Oxford University Press, Toronto, 1972).

Doern, Bruce and Glen Toner. *The Politics of Energy: The Development and Implementation of the National Energy Program* (Methuen, Toronto, 1985).

——— and Brian Tomlin. *Faith and Fear: The Free Trade Story* (Stoddart, Toronto, 1991).

Donaldson, Gordon. *The Prime Ministers of Canada* (Doubleday, Toronto, 1994).

Doughty, A.G. (Sir), ed. *The Elgin-Grey Papers, 1846–1852* (J.O. Patenaude, Ottawa, 1937).

Doyle, Richard J. *Hurly-Burly: A Time at the Globe* (Macmillan, Toronto, 1990).

Drummond, Ian. *Progress without Planning: The Economic History of Ontario* (University of Toronto Press, Toronto, 1987).

Duchaine, Jean-François. *Rapport sur les événements d'octobre 1970* (Ministry of Justice, Quebec, 1981).

Duchesne, Pierre. *Jacques Parizeau, Tome 1, Le Croisé* (Québec-Amérique, Montreal, 2001).

———. *Jacques Parizeau, Tome 2, Le Baron* (Québec-Amérique, Montreal, 2002).

———. *Jacques Parizeau, Tome 3, Le Régent* (Québec-Amérique, Montreal, 2004).

Duffy, Dennis. "Love Among the Ruins: The King of Kingsmere" (*American Review of Canadian Studies* 37:3 – Autumn 2007; 355-396).

Duffy, John. *Fights of Our Lives: Elections, Leadership and the Making of Canada* (HarperCollins, Toronto, 2002).

Dummitt, Christopher. *The Manly Modern: Masculinity in Postwar Canada* (UBC Press, Vancouver, 2007).

Dryden, Jean. "The Mackenzie King Papers: An Odyssey" (*Archivaria* 6 – Summer 1978; 40-69).

Eade, Charles, ed. *Churchill by His Contemporaries* (Hutchinson, London, 1954).

Easterbrook, W.T. and H.G.J. Aitken. *Canadian Economic History* (Macmillan Company, Toronto, 1956).

Eastman, S. Mack. *Church and State in Early Canada* (The University Press, Edinburgh, 1915).

Eayrs, James. *The Art of the Possible: Government and Foreign Policy in Canada* (University of Toronto Press, Toronto, 1961).

———. *In Defence of Canada: Appeasement and Rearmament* (University of Toronto Press, Toronto, 1965).

———. *In Defence of Canada: Peacemaking and Deterrence* (University of Toronto Press, Toronto, 1972).

———. *Northern Approaches: Canada and the Search for Peace* (Macmillan, Toronto, 1971).

Eccles, W.J. *Frontenac: The Courtier Governor* (McClelland & Stewart, Toronto, 1959).

———. *Canada Under Louis XIV* (McClelland & Stewart, Toronto, 1964).

Eckes, Alfred. *Opening America's Markets: U.S. Foreign Trade Policy Since 1776* (University of North Carolina, Chapel Hill, 1995).

Eden, Anthony (Sir). *Full Circle: The Memoirs of Sir Anthony Eden* (Cassel & Company, London, 1960).

Edgar, Matilda Rideout (Lady). *General Brock* (Oxford University Press, London, 1926).

Ehrman, John. *The Younger Pitt: The Years of Acclaim* (Constable, London, 1969).

Ellis, Lewis E. *Reciprocity in 1911: A Study in Canadian-American Relations* (Greenwood Press, New York, 1968).

English, John. *Arthur Meighen* (Fitzhenry & Whiteside, Don Mills, 1977).

———. *The Worldly Years: The Life of Lester Pearson, 1949–1972* (Vintage, Toronto, 1993).

———. *Just Watch Me: The Life of Pierre Elliott Trudeau, 1968–2000* (Knopf Canada, Toronto, 2009).

———. *Citizen of the World: The Life of Pierre Elliott Trudeau* (Knopf Canada, Toronto, 2006).

———. *Shadow of Heaven: The Life of Lester Pearson, Vol. 1: 1897–1948* (Lester & Orpen Dennys, Toronto, 1989).

———. *The Decline of Politics: The Conservatives and the Party System, 1901–1920* (University of Toronto Press, Toronto, 1993).

——— and J.O. Stubbs, eds. *Mackenzie King: Widening the Debate* (Macmillan of Canada, Toronto, 1977).

———, Kenneth McLaughlin and P. Whitney Lackenbauer, eds. *Mackenzie King: Citzenship and Community* (Robin Brass Studio, Toronto, 2002).

——— and Kenneth McLaughlin. *Kitchener: An Illustrated History* (Wilfred Laurier University Press, Waterloo, 1983).

———, Richard Gwyn and P. Whitney Lackenbauer. *The Hidden Pierre Elliott Trudeau: The Faith behind the Politics* (Novalis, Ottawa, 2004).

Enoch, Simon. "Changing the Ideological Fabric? A Brief History of Canadian Neoliberalism" (*State of Nature* 5 – Autumn 2007).

Ermatinger, Edward. *Life of Colonel Talbot and the Talbot Settlements* (Mika Silk Screening, Belleville, 1972).

Errington, Jane. *The Lion, the Eagle, and Upper Canada: A Developing Canadian Ideology* (McGill-Queen's University Press, Montreal & Kingston, 1987).

Esbrey, Joy E. *Knight of the Holy Spirit: A Study of William Lyon Mackenzie King* (University of Toronto Press, Toronto, 1980).

Fairbank, J.K. *Chinabound: A Fifty-Year Memoir* (Harper Colophon, 1983, New York).

Faragher, John M. *A Great and Noble Scheme: The Tragic Story of the Expulsion of the French Acadians from Their American Homeland* (Norton, New York, 2005).

Ferguson, Bruce. Hon. *W.S. Fielding, I: The Mantle of Howe* (Lancelot Press, Windsor, Nova Scotia, 1970).

———. *Hon. W.S. Fielding, I: Mr. Minister of Finance* (Lancelot Press, Windsor, Nova Scotia, 1971).

Ferns, H.S. *Reading from Left to Right: One Man's Political History* (University of Toronto Press, Toronto, 1983).

——— and Bernard Ostry. *The Age of Mackenzie King* (William Heinemann, Toronto, 1955).

Finkel, Alvin. *Our Lives: Canada after 1945* (James Lorimer & Company, Toronto, 1997).

Fischer, David H. *Albion's Seed: Four British Folkways in America* (Oxford University Press, New York, 1989).
——. *Champlain's Dream*. (Simon & Schuster, New York, 2008).
——. *Paul Revere's Ride* (Oxford University Press, New York, 1994).
Fleming, Donald M. *So Very Near: The Political Memoirs of the Hon. Donald M. Fleming, Vol. 2, The Summit Years* (McClelland & Stewart, Toronto, 1985).
Flenley, R. *Essays in Canadian History* (Macmillan Company, Toronto, 1939).
Forsey, Eugene. *Trade Unions in Canada, 1812–1902* (University of Toronto Press, Toronto, 1982).
——. *A Life on the Fringe: The Memoirs of Eugene Forsey* (Oxford University Press, Toronto, 1990).
——. *The Royal Power of Dissolution of Parliament in the British Commonwealth* (Oxford University Press, Toronto, 1943).
——. *Freedom and Order* (McClelland & Stewart, Toronto, 1974).
Forster, Ben. *A Conjunction of Interests: Business, Politics and Tariffs 1825–1879* (University of Toronto Press, Toronto, 1986).
Fosdick, Raymond B. *John D. Rockefeller, Jr.: A Portrait* (Harper & Brothers, New York, 1956).
Foster, Donald and Colin Read. "The Politics of Opportunism: The New Deal Broadcasts" (*Canadian Historical Review* 60, No. 3. 1979).
Fox, Bill. *Spinwars: Politics and New Media* (Key Porter Books, Toronto, 1999).
Franks, C.E.S. *The Parliament of Canada* (University of Toronto Press, Toronto, 1987).
Fraser, Graham. *Sorry, I Don't Speak French: Confronting the Canadian Crisis That Won't Go Away* (McClelland & Stewart, Toronto, 2006).
——. *Playing for Keeps: The Making of the Prime Minister, 1988* (McClelland & Stewart, Toronto, 1989).
Freeman, Linda. *The Ambiguous Champion: Canada and South Africa in the Trudeau and Mulroney Years* (University of Toronto Press, Toronto, 1997).
Frégault, G. *La Civilisation de la Nouvelle-France* (Société des Éditions Pascal, Montreal, 1944).
——. *Histoire de la Nouvelle France* (Fides, Montreal, 1967).
French, G.S. *Parsons and Politics: The Role of Wesleyan Methodists in Upper Canada and the Maritimes from 1780 to 1855* (Ryerson Press, Toronto, 1962).
Friedland, Martin L. *The University of Toronto: A History* (University of Toronto Press, Toronto, 2002).
——. *My Life in Crime and Other Academic Adventures* (University of Toronto Press, Toronto, 2007).
Friesen, Gerald. *The Canadian Prairies: A History* (University of Toronto Press, Toronto, 1984).
Frizzell, Alan, Jon Pammett and Anthony Westell, eds. *The Canadian General Election of 1988* (Carleton University Press, 1989, Ottawa).
Fry, Michael, ed. *Freedom and Change: Essays in Honour of Lester B. Pearson* (McClelland & Stewart, Toronto, 1975).
Fullerton, Douglas. *Graham Tower and His Times* (McClelland & Stewart, Toronto, 1986).
Fullick, Roy and Geoffrey Powell. *Suez: The Double War* (Leo Cooper, London, 1990).
Garner, Joe. *The Commonwealth Office* (Heinemann, London, 1978).
Geloso, Vincent. *Du Grand Rattrapage au Déclin Tranquille, Une Histoire économique et sociale du Québec de 1900 à nos jours.* (Éditions Accent Grave, Montreal, 2012).
Gibson, Frederick W. and Barbara Robertson, eds. *Ottawa at War: The Grant Dexter Memoranda, 1939–1945* (The Manitoba Record Society, Winnipeg, 1994).
Gidney, Catherine. *A Long Eclipse: The Liberal Protestant Establishment and the Canadian University, 1920–1970* (McGill-Queen's University Press, Montreal/Kingston, 2004).
Gilbert, Martin. *Churchill: A Life* (William Heinemann, London, 1991).
——. *Finest Hour: 1939–1941, Vol. 5, Winston S. Churchill* (Heinemann, London, 1984).
——. *Never Despair: 1945–1965, Vol. 8, Winston S. Churchill* (Stoddart, Toronto, 1988).
——. *Road to Victory: 1941–1945, Vol. 7, Winston S. Churchill* (Stoddart, Toronto, 1986).
——. *Winston S. Churchill, 1922–1929, Vol. 5, Winston S. Churchill* (Heinemann, London, 1976).
Gillespie, W. Irwin. *Tax, Borrow and Spend: Financing Federal Spending in Canada 1867–1990* (Carleton University Press, Ottawa, 1991).
Glassford, Larry. *Reaction and Reform: The Politics of the Conservative Party Under R.B. Bennett 1927–1938* (University Press of Toronto, Toronto, 1992).
——. "A Retrenchment – R.B. Bennett Style: The Conservative Record Before the New Deal" (*American Review of Canadian Studies* 19:2 – Summer 1989; 141-157).

Glazebrook, G.P. *Canadian External Relations: An Historical Study to 1914* (Oxford University Press, Toronto, 1942).

———. *A History of Transportation in Canada* (Ryerson Press, Toronto, 1938).

———. *Canada at the Paris Peace Conference* (Oxford University Press, Toronto, 1942).

Godin, Pierre. *Daniel Johnson*, 2 vols. (Éditions de l'Homme, Montreal, 1980).

Goldenberg, Eddie. *The Way It Works: Inside Ottawa* (Douglas Gibson Books, McClelland & Stewart, Toronto, 2006).

Goldfarb, Martin and Thomas Axworthy. *Marching to a Different Drummer: An essay on the Liberals and Conservatives in Convention* (Stoddart, Toronto, 1988).

Goodman, Allan E. *The Last Peace: America's Search for a Negotiated Settlement of the Vietnam War* (Hoover Institution, Palo Alto, 1978).

Goodman, Eddie. *Life of the Party* (Key Porter Books, Toronto, 1988).

Gordon, Philip H. and Jeremy Shapiro. *Allies at War: America, Europe and the Crisis over Iraq* (McGraw-Hill, New York, 2004).

Gordon, Stanley. *R.B. Bennett, MLA 1897–1905: The Years of Apprenticeship* (University of Calgary, Calgary, 1975).

Gordon, Walter. *A Political Memoir* (McClelland & Stewart, Toronto, 1977).

———. *Troubled Canada: The Need for Domestic Policies* (McClelland & Stewart, Toronto, 1961).

Gossage, Patrick. *Close to Charisma: My Years Between the Press and Pierre Elliott Trudeau* (Formac Publishing, Halifax, 1987).

Gotlieb, Allan. *Washington Diaries, 1981–1989* (McClelland & Stewart, Toronto, 2006).

Grabb, Edward and James Curtis. *Regions Apart: The Four Societies of Canada and the United States* (Oxford University Press, Toronto, 2005).

Graham, John R. "William Lyon Mackenzie King, Elizabeth Harvey and Edna: A Prostitute Rescuing Initiative in Late Victorian Toronto" (*The Canadian Journal of Human Sexuality*, 8:1 – Spring 1999; 47-60).

Graham, Roger. *Arthur Meighen: The Door of Opportunity* (Clarke, Irwin & Company, Toronto, 1960).

———. *Arthur Meighen: A Biography* (Clarke, Irwin & Company, Toronto, 1960).

———. *Arthur Meighen: No Surrender, Vol. 3* (Clarke, Irwin & Company, Toronto, 1965).

Graham, Ron. *One-Eyed Kings: Promise and Illusion in Canadian Politics* (Collins, Toronto, 1986).

———. *The French Quarter: The Epic Struggle of a Family – and a Nation Divided* (Macfarlane, Walter & Ross, 1992).

Granatstein, J.L. *Canada's War: The Politics of the Mackenzie King Government (1939–1945)* (Oxford University Press, Toronto, 1975).

———. *Canada: The Years of Uncertainty and Innovation* (McClelland & Stewart, Toronto, 1986).

———. *Canada's Army: Waging War and Keeping the Peace* (University of Toronto Press, Toronto, 2002).

———. *How Britain's Weakness Forced Canada into the Arms of the United States* (University of Toronto Press, Toronto, 1989).

———. *Yankee Go Home? Canadians and Anti-Americanism* (HarperCollins, Toronto, 1996).

———. *Mackenzie King: His Life and World* (McGraw-Hill Ryerson, Toronto, 1977).

———. *The Politics of Survival: The Conservative Party of Canada, 1939–1945* (University of Toronto Press, Toronto, 1967).

———. *The Ottawa Men: The Civil Service Mandarins 1935–1957* (Oxford University Press, Toronto, 1982).

———. *The Generals: The Canadian Army's Senior Commanders in the Second World War* (Stoddart, Toronto, 1993).

——— and Norman Hillmer. *Prime Ministers: Ranking Canada's Leaders* (HarperCollins, Toronto, 1999).

——— and Desmond Morton. *Canada and the Two World Wars* (Key Porter Books, Toronto, 2003).

——— and Robert Bothwell. *Pirouette: Pierre Trudeau and Canadian Foreign Policy* (University of Toronto Press, Toronto, 1989).

——— and David Stafford. *Spy Wars: Espionage and Canada from Gouzenko to Glasnost* (Key Porter Books, Toronto, 1990).

Grant, George. *Lament for a Nation* (McClelland & Stewart, Toronto, 1965).

———. *Technology and Empire: Perspectives on North America* (House of Anansi, Toronto, 1969).

Grant, W.L. *Makers of Canada*, 12 Vols. (Oxford University Press, Toronto, 1926).

Gratton, Michel. *So What Are the Boys Saying?* (McGraw-Hill Ryerson, Toronto, 1987).

Gray, Charlotte. *Sisters in the Wilderness: The Lives of Susanna Moodie and Catharine Parr Traill* (Viking, Toronto, 1999).

———. *Mrs. King: The Life and Times of Isabel Mackenzie King* (Penguin, Toronto, 2008).

———. "Crazy Like a Fox" (*Saturday Night* 112:8 – October 1997; 42-46, 48, 50 and 94).

Gray, James H. *Troublemaker! A Personal History* (Macmillan, Toronto, 1978).

———. *Men Against the Desert* (The Modern Press, Saskatoon, 1967).

———. *The Winter Years: The Depression of the Prairies* (University of Toronto Press, Toronto, 1967).

———. *R.B. Bennett: The Calgary Years* (University of Toronto Press, Toronto, 1991).

Grayson, L.M. and M. Bliss, eds. *The Wretched of Canada* (University of Toronto Press, Toronto, 1971).

Green, Alan G. "Twentieth Century Canadian Economic History" in *The Cambridge Economic History of the United States, Vol. 3, The Twentieth Century* Edited by Stanley L. Engermand and Robert E. Gallman (Cambridge University Press, Cambridge, 2000).

Greenhous, Brereton. "Dieppe Raid" in *The Canadian Encyclopedia* (McClelland & Stewart, Toronto, 2000).

Greer, Allan. *Brève Historie des Peuples de la Nouvelle France* (Boréal, Quebec, 1998).

———. *Peasant, Lord and Merchant: Rural Society in Three Quebec Parishes 1740–1840* (University of Toronto Press, Toronto, 1985).

———. *The Patriots and the People: The Rebellion of 1837 in Rural Lower Canada* (University of Toronto Press, Toronto, 1993).

Groulx, Lionel. *Histoire du Canada français, 4 Vols.* (L'Action Nationale, Montreal, 1951–1952).

———. *Notre Maître le Passé, 3 Vols.* (L'Action Nationale, Quebec, 1922–1944).

———. *Mes Memoires, Vol. 1* (Fides, Montreal, 1970).

Gruending, Dennis, ed. *Great Canadian Speeches* (Fitzhenry & Whiteside, Markham, 2004).

Guillet, Edwin C. *You'll Never Die John A.!* (Macmillan of Canada, Toronto, 1967).

Guttman, Frank M. *The Devil from Saint-Hyacinthe: a Tragic Hero, Senator Télesphore-Damien Bouchard* (iUniverse Inc., New York, 2007).

Gwyn, Richard. *John A: The Man Who Made Us: The Life and Times of John A. Macdonald, 1815–1867* (Random House of Canada, Toronto, 2007).

———. *The Northern Magus: Pierre Trudeau and Canadians* (McClelland & Stewart, Toronto, 1980).

———. *The Shape of Scandal: A Study of a Government in Crisis* (Clarke, Irwin and Company, Toronto, 1965).

Gwyn, Sandra. "Where Are You Mike Pearson, Now That We Need You? Decline and Fall of Canada's Foreign Policy" (*Saturday Night*, 1978).

———. *The Private Capital: Ambition and Love in the Age of Macdonald and Laurier* (McClelland & Stewart, Toronto, 1984).

———. "The Politics of Peace" (*Saturday Night*, May 1984).

Haddow, Rodney. *Poverty Reform in Canada, 1958–1978* (McGill-Queen's University Press, Montreal & Kingston, 1978).

Hall, Trevor. *In Celebration of the Queen's Visit to Canada* (Collins Royal, Toronto, 1984).

Hallahan, Kirk. "W.L. Mackenzie King: Rockefeller's Other Public Relations Counselor in Colorado" (*Public Relations Review* 29:4 – November 2003; 401-414).

Hambly, Daniel. *The 1986 CF-18 Maintenance Contract: A Legitimate Grievance or an Issue of Mis-information?* (M.A. thesis, University of Western Ontario, 2006).

Hamilton, Robert and Dorothy Shields, eds. *The Dictionary of Canadian Quotations and Phrases* (McClelland & Stewart, Toronto, 1979).

Hardy, H. Reginald. *Mackenzie King of Canada* (Oxford University Press, London, 1949).

Harney, Robert F. and Harold Troper. *Immigrants: A Portrait of the Urban Experience, 1890–1930* (Van Nostrand Reinhold, Toronto, 1975).

Harris, R. Cole and John Wartenkin. *Canada Before Confederation* (Oxford University Press, Toronto, 1974).

Hart, Michael. *A Trading Nation* (UBC Press, Vancouver, 2002).

———, Bill Dymond and Colin Robertson. *Decision at Midnight: Inside the Canada-US Free-Trade Negotiations* (UBC Press, Vancouver, 1994).

Havard, G. and C. Vidal. *Histoire de l'Amérique Française* (Flammarion, Paris, 2003).

Hay, Douglas. "Tradition, Judges and Civil Liberties in Canada" (*Osgoode Hall Law Journal*, XLI/2 & 3).

Heeney, Arnold. *The Things that Are Caesar's: Memoirs of a Canadian Public Servant* (University of Toronto Press, Toronto, 1972).

Heinmiller, B. Timothy. "Harmonization through Emulation: Canadian Federalism and Water Export Policy" (*Canadian Public Administration* 46:4 – Winter 2003; 495-513).

Hellyer, Paul. *Damn the Torpedoes: My Fight to Unify Canada's Armed Forces* (McClelland & Stewart, Toronto, 1990).

Henderson, George F. *W.L. Mackenzie King: A Bibliography and Research Guide* (University of Toronto Press, Toronto, 1998).

Henderson, T. Stephen. *Angus L. Macdonald: A Provincial Liberal* (University of Toronto Press, Toronto, 2007).

Hillmer, Norman. *The Foreign Policy that Never Was, 1900–1950* (Canadian External Affairs).

——. "O.D. Skelton and the North American Mind" (*International Journal* – Winter 2004–2005; 93-110).

Hincks, Francis G. *Reminiscences of His Public Life* (W. Drysdale & Co., Montreal, 1884).

Hitsman, J. Mackay. *Safeguarding Canada* (University of Toronto Press, Toronto, 1968).

Hoar, Victor. *The On to Ottawa Trek* (Copp Clark, Toronto, 1970).

Hodgetts, J.E. *Pioneer Public Service, 1841–67* (University of Toronto Press, Toronto, 1955).

Hodgins, Bruce W. *John Sandfield Macdonald 1812–1872* (University of Toronto Press, Toronto, 1971).

Holmes, John W. *The Shaping of Peace: Canada and the Search for World Order 1943–1957* (University of Toronto Press, Toronto, 1979).

Hoogenraad, Maureen. "Mackenzie King in Berlin" (*Archivist* 20:3 – 1994; 19-21).

Horn, Michael. *The Dirty Thirties: Canadians in the Great Depression* (Copp Clark, Toronto, 1972).

Horne, Alistair. *Harold Macmillan: Vol. 1: 1894–1956* (Macmillan, London, 1988).

——. *Harold Macmillan: Vol. 2: 1957–1986* (Macmillan, London, 1988).

Horowitz, Gad. *Canadian Labour in Politics* (University of Toronto Press, Toronto, 1968).

How, Douglas. "One Man's Mackenzie King" (*The Beaver*, 78:5 – October/November 1998; 31-37).

Hoy, Claire. *Margin of Error* (Key Porter Books, Toronto, 1989).

Humphries, Charles W. "Mackenzie King Looks at Two 1911 Elections" (*Ontario History* 56:3 – 1964; 203-206).

Hunt, G.T. *The Wars of the Iroquois* (University of Wisconsin Press, Madison, 1940).

Hustak, Allan. *Peter Lougheed: A Biography* (McClelland & Stewart, Toronto, 1979).

Hutchison, Bruce. *The Far Side of the Street* (Macmillan, Toronto, 1976).

——. *The Incredible Canadian* (Longmans, Green & Company, Toronto, 1952).

——. *Mr. Prime Minister, 1867–1964* (Longmans, Green & Company, Toronto, 1964).

——. *Canada: Tomorrow's Giant* (Longmans, Green & Company, Toronto, 1957).

——. *The Unfinished Country: To Canada with Love and Some Misgivings* (Douglas & McIntyre, Toronto, 1985).

Hyde, Montgomery H. *The Quiet Canadian: The Secret Service Story of Sir William Stephenson* (Hamish Hamilton, London, 1962).

Iglauer, Edith. "Prime Minister/Premier Ministre" (*The New Yorker*, July 5, 1969).

Ignatieff, George. *The Making of a Peacemonger: The Memoirs of George Ignatieff* (Penguin, Markham, 1987).

Innis, H.A. *The Cod Fisheries* (Revised Ed., University of Toronto Press, Toronto, 1954).

——. *The Fur Trade in Canada* (Revised Ed., University of Toronto Press, Toronto, 1956).

——. *Select Documents in Canadian Economic History, 1497–1783* (University of Toronto Press, Toronto, 1929).

——. "Great Britain, the United States, and Canada" in *Essays in Canadian Economic History*. Edited by Mary Quayle Innis, 394-412 (University of Toronto Press, Toronto, 1956).

—— and A.R.M. Lower. *Select Documents in Canadian Economic History, 1783–1885* (University of Toronto Press, Toronto, 1933).

Irving, J.A. *The Philosophy of Social Credit* (University of Toronto Press, Toronto, 1959).

Jackman, Martha. "Canadian Charter Equality at 20: Reflections of a Card-Carrying Member of the Court Party" (*Policy Options* – December 2005 – January 2006).

Jeffrey, Brooke. *Divided Loyalties: The Liberal Party of Canada, 1984–2008* (University of Toronto Press, Toronto, 1956).

Jockel, Joseph. *No Boundaries Upstairs: Canada, the United States and the Origins of the North American Air Defence, 1945–1958* (UBC Press, Vancouver, 1987).

Johnson, Gregory and David A. Lenarcic. "The Decade of Transition: the North Atlantic Triangle During the 1920s" in *The North Atlantic Triangle in a Changing World: Anglo-American-Canadian Relations, 1902–1956*. Edited by Brian McKercher, James Cooper, and Lawrence Aronsen (University of Toronto Press, Toronto, 1996).

Johnson, William. *Stephen Harper and the Future of Canada* (McClelland & Stewart, Toronto, 2005).

Johnston, Donald. *Up the Hill* (Optimum, Montreal, 1986).

Joy, Richard. *Languages in Conflict: The Canadian Experience* (McClelland & Stewart, Canadian Library, Toronto, 1972).

Julien, Claude. *Canada: Europe's Last Chance* (Macmillan, Toronto, 1968).

Kalm, Peter. *Travels in North America, Vol. 2* (Dover, New York, 1964).

Kalman, Harold. *A History of Canadian Architecture, Vol. 1* (Oxford University Press, Toronto, 1994).

Karsh, Yousuf. "The Portraits that Changed My Life" *(Finest Hour: The Journal of Winston Churchill 94 – Spring 1997– 12-14).

Kealey, Gregory S. *Workers and Canadian History* (University of Toronto Press, Toronto, 1995).

Kealey, Linda, Ruth Pieson, Joan Sangster and Veronica Strong-Boag. "Teaching Canadian History in the 1990s: Whose National History Are We Lamenting?" (*Journal of Canadian Studies* 27, No. 2 – Summer 1992).

Keenleyside, Hugh L. *Memoirs: Hammer the Golden Day, Vol. 1* (McClelland & Stewart, Toronto, 1981).

Keirstead, B.S. *Canada in World Affairs, September 1951 to October 1953* (Oxford University Press, Toronto, 1956).

Kellogg, L.P. *The French Regime in Wisconsin and the Northwest* (State Historical Society of Wisconsin, Madison, 1926).

Kennedy, W.P.M. *Statutes, Treaties and Documents of the Canadian Constitution, 1713–1929* (Revised Ed., Oxford University Press, Toronto, 1930).

———. *The Constitution of Canada, 1534–1937* (Second Ed., Oxford University Press, London, 1938).

Kent, Tom. *A Public Purpose* (McGill-Queen's University Press, Montreal & Kingston, 1988).

Kerr, D.G.G. *Sir Edmund Head: A Scholarly Governor* (Toronto University Press, Toronto, 1954).

Kersaudy, François. *Churchill and de Gaulle* (Atheneum, New York, 1983).

Kershaw, Ian. *Fateful Choices: Ten Decisions That Changed the World 1940–1941* (Penguin, New York, 2008).

Keshen, Jeff. *Saints, Sinners and Soldiers: Canada's Second World War* (UBC Press, Vancouver, 2004).

Keyserling, Robert H. "Mackenzie King's Spiritualism and His View of Hitler in 1939" (*Journal of Canadian Studies*, 20:4 – Winter 1985–1986; 26-44).

———. "Agents within the Gates: The search for Nazi Subversives in Canada during World War II" (*Canadian Historical Review* 66:2 – June 1985; 211-239).

Kierans, Eric with Walter Stewart. *Remembering* (Stoddart, Toronto, 2001).

Kilbourn, William. *The Firebrand* (Clarke, Irwin & Company, Toronto, 1956).

Kimmel, David and Daniel J. Robinson. "Sex, Crime, Pathology: Homosexuality and Criminal Code Reform in Canada 1949–1969" (*Canadian Journal of Law and Society* 15:1 – 2001; 147-165).

Kindleberg, Charles Poor. *The World in Depression 1929–1939* (University of California Press, Berkeley, 1986).

King, William Lyon Mackenzie. *The Secret of Heroism* (Fleming H. Revell, New York, 1906).

———. *Industry and Humanity: A Study in the Principles Underlying Industrial Reconstruction* (reprint Toronto, 1973).

———. *Canada and the Fight for Freedom* (Macmillan, Toronto, 1944).

———. *Canada at Britain's Side* (Macmillan, Toronto, 1941).

———. *William Lyon Mackenzie King Papers* (Library and Archives Canada, Ottawa).

Kissinger, Henry. *White House Years* (Little, Brown, Boston, 1979).

Knight, Amy. *How the Cold War Began: The Gouzenko Affair and the Hunt for Soviet Spies* (McClelland & Stewart, Toronto, 2005).

Kolber, Leo with L. Ian MacDonald. *Leo: A Life* (McGill-Queen's University Press, Montreal & Kingston, 2006).

Kolodziej, Edward A. *French International Policy under de Gaulle and Pompidou: The Politics of Grandeur* (Cornell University Press, Ithaca & London, 1974).

Kottman, Richard N. "The Canadian American Trade Agreement of 1935" (*The Journal of American History* 52:2 – September 1965; 275-296).

Lachance, Micheline. *Le prince de l'église: le cardinal Léger*, 2 vols. (Éditions de l'Homme, Montreal, 1982).

Lacouture, Jean. *De Gaulle* (Seuil, Paris, 1984–1986).

Laforest, Guy. *Trudeau and the End of a Canadian Dream.* Translated by Michelle Weinroth and Paul Leduc Brown (McGill-Queen's University Press, Montreal & Kingston, 1995).

LaMarsh, Judy. *Memoirs of a Bird in a Gilded Cage* (Pocket Books, Toronto, 1970).

Lanctot, Gustave. *The History of Canada from its Origins to the Royal Regime* (Harvard University Press, Cambridge, 1963).

LaPierre, Laurier. *Sir Wilfrid Laurier and the Romance of Canada* (Stoddart, Toronto, 1996).

LaPorte, Pierre. *The True Face of Duplessis* (Harvest House, Montreal, 1960).

Laroque, Sylvain. *Gay Marriage: The Story of a Canadian Social Revolution* (James Lorimer & Company, Toronto, 2006).

Lascelles, Alan. *King's Counsellor: Abdication and War: The Diaries of Sir Alan Lascelles.* Edited by Duff Hart-Davis (Weidenfeld & Nicolson, London, 2006).

Laschinger, John and Geoffrey Stevens, eds. *Leaders and Lesser Mortals* (Key Porter Books, Toronto, 1992).

Lash, Joseph P. *Roosevelt and Churchill: The Partnership That Saved the West* (Norton, New York, 1976).

Laskin, Bora. *Peace, Order and Good Government Re-Examined in the Courts and the Canadian Constitution* (McClelland & Stewart, Toronto, 1964).

Lawson, Philip. *The Imperial Challenge: Quebec and Britain in the Age of the American Revolution* (McGill-Queen's University Press, Montreal & Kingston, 1989).

Laxer, James and Robert Laxer. *The Liberal Idea of Canada: Pierre Trudeau and the Question of Canada's Survival* (James Lorimer & Company, Toronto, 1977).

Leacock, Stephen. *Mackenzie, Baldwin, LaFontaine, Hincks* (Oxford University Press, London, 1926).

Lederle, John W. "The Liberal Convention of 1919 and the Selection of Mackenzie King" (*Dalhousie Review* – April 1947; 85-92).

LeSueur, William Dawson. *William Lyon Mackenzie: A Reinterpretation.* Edited and introduction by A.B. McKillop (Macmillan Company, Toronto, 1979).

Lévesque, René. *Option Quebec* (McClelland & Stewart, Montreal, 1968).

———. *Memoirs.* Translated by Philip Stratford (McClelland & Stewart, Toronto, 1986).

Lewis, John. *George Brown* (Oxford University Press, Toronto, 1926).

Levine, Allan. *Scrum Wars: The Prime Ministers and the Media* (Dundurn, Toronto, 1996).

———. *The Devil in Babylon: Fear of Progress and the Birth of Modern Life* (McClelland & Stewart, Toronto, 2005).

———. *King: A Life Guided by the Hand of Destiny* (Biteback Publishing, London, 2012).

Lewy, Guenter. *America in Vietnam* (Oxford Unviersity Press, New York, 1978).

Leyton-Brown, David, ed. *Canadian Annual Review of Politics and Public Affairs, 1988* (University of Toronto Press, Toronto, 1995).

Lind, Jennifer. *Sorry States: Apologies in International Politics* (Cornell University Press, Ithaca, 2010).

Linteau, Paul André, René Durocher, Jean-Claude Robert, and François Ricard. *Histoire du Quebec contemporain, Vol. 2* (Boréal, Montréal, 1989).

Lipset, Seymour Martin. *Continental Divide: The Values and Institutions of the United States and Canada* (Routledge, New York, 1990).

———. *Agrarian Socialism: The Cooperative Commonwealth Federation in Saskatchewan – A Study in Political Sociology* (University of California Press, Berkeley, 1950).

Litt, Paul. "Trudeaumania: Participatory Democracy in the Mass-Mediated Nation" (*Canadian Historical Review* 89:1 – March 2008; 27-53).

———. *Elusive Destiny: The Political Vocation of John Napier Turner* (UBC Press, Vancouver, 2011).

Liversedge, Ronald. *Recollections of the On to Ottawa Trek* (McClelland & Stewart, Toronto, 1973).

Lower, Arthur R.M. *Great Britain's Woodyard: British America and the Timber Trade 1763–1867* (McGill-Queen's University Press, Montreal & Kingston, 1973).

———. *My First Seventy-Five Years* (Macmillan, Toronto, 1967).

———. *Colony to Nation* (Longmans Green, Toronto, 1957).

———. *Canadians in the Making* (Longmans Green, Toronto, 1958).

——. *The North American Assault on the Canadian Forest* (Ryerson Press, Toronto, 1938).

Lucas, Sir Charles. *Lord Durham's Report on the Affairs of British North America* (Clarendon Press, Oxford, 1912).

Lynch, Charles. *Race for the Rose: Election 1984* (Methuen, Toronto, 1984).

MacCulloch, D. *Reformation: Europe's House Divided, 1490–1700* (Allen Lane, London, 2003).

MacDonald, L. Ian. *Mulroney: The Making of the Prime Minister* (McClelland & Stewart, Toronto, 1984).

——. *From Bourassa to Bourassa: Wilderness to Restoration* (Second Ed., McGill-Queen's University Press, Montreal & Kingston, 2002).

——. *Free Trade: Risks and Rewards* (McGill-Queen's University Press, Montreal/Kingston, 2000).

MacFarlane, John. *Ernest Lapointe and Quebec's Influence on Canadian Foreign Policy* (University of Toronto Press, Toronto, 1999).

MacGuigan, Mark. *An Inside Look at External Affairs During the Trudeau Years: The Memoirs of Mark MacGuigan.* Edited by Whitney Lackenbauer (University of Calgary Press, Calgary, 2001).

Mackesy, Piers. *The War for America, 1775–1783* (Harvard University Press, Cambridge, 1964).

Mackey, Frank. *Steamboat Connections: Montreal to Upper Canada 1816–1843* (McGill-Queen's University Press, Montreal & Kingston, 2000).

MacLaren, Roy. *Commissions High: Canada in London 1870–1971* (McGill-Queen's University Press, Montreal, 2006).

——. *Honourable Mentions: The Uncommon Diary of an M.P.* (Deneau, Toronto, 1986).

MacLean, Andrew. *R.B. Bennett* (Excelsior Publishing, Toronto, 1935).

MacLennan, Christopher. *Towards the Charter: Canadians and the Demand for a National Bill of Rights 1929–1960* (McGill-Queen's University Press, Montreal, 2003).

MacLeod, Alex. *The Fearsome Dilemma: Simultaneous Inflation and Unemployment* (Mercury Press, Stratford, 1994).

MacNicoll, John R. *The National Liberal-Conservative Convention* (Southam, Toronto, 1930).

MacNutt, W.S. *Days of Lorne* (Brunswick Press, Fredericton, 1955).

——. *The Atlantic Provinces: The Emergence of Colonial Society, 1712–1857* (McClelland & Stewart, Toronto, 1965).

MacPherson, C.B. *Democracy in Alberta* (University of Toronto Press, Toronto, 1956).

Maddison, Angus. *The World Economy: Historical Statistics* (Organization for Economic Co-operation and Development, Paris, 2003).

Mallory, J.R. "Mackenzie King and the Origins of the Cabinet Secretariat" (*Canadian Public Administration* 19:2, 1976; 254-266).

Malone, Richard S. *A World in Flames, 1944–1945, Vol. 2, A Portrait of War* (Collins, Toronto, 1984).

Manchester, William. *Winston Spencer Churchill, Alone, 1932–1940, Vol. 2, The Last Lion* (Little Brown, Boston, 1988).

——. *Winston Spencer Churchill, Visions of Glory, 1874–1932, Vol. 1, The Last Lion* (Little Brown, Toronto, 1983).

Manion, R.J. *Life Is an Adventure* (Ryerson Press, Toronto, 1936).

Manley, John. "Audacity, Audacity, Still More Audacity: Tim Buck, the Party and the People 1932–1939" (*Labour/Le Travail* 49 – Spring 2002; 9-41).

Mann, W.E. *Poverty and Social Policy in Canada* (Copp Clark, Toronto, 1970).

Manning, Helen Taft. *The Revolt of French Canada, 1800–1835* (Macmillan, Toronto, 1962).

Maple Leaf Sports and Entertainment. *Maple Leaf Gardens: Memories and Dreams, 1931–1999* (MLG, Toronto, 1999).

Margry, Pierre. *Découvertes et établissements des Français dans l'ouest et dans le sud de l'Amérique septentrionale, 1614–1754* (Paris, 1876–1886).

Marr, William L. and Donald G. Paterson. *Canada: An Economic History* (Macmillan, Toronto, 1980).

Marrus, Michael. *Mr. Sam: The Life and Times of Samuel Bronfman* (Viking, Toronto, 1991).

Marshall, P.J., ed. *Oxford History of the British Empire, Vol. 2, The Eighteenth Century* (Oxford University Press, Oxford, 1998).

Marshall, Peter. "The Balfour Formula and the Evolution of the Commonwealth" (*Round Table* 90: 361 – September 2001; 541-553).

Martel, Marcel. *Not This Time: Canadians, Public Policy and the Marijuana Question, 1961–1975* (University of Toronto Press, Toronto, 2006).

Martin, Chester. *Empire and Commonwealth* (Oxford University Press, Toronto, 1929).

———. *Foundations of Canadian Nationhood* (University of Toronto Press, Toronto, 1955).

Martin, Ged. "Mackenzie King, the Medium and the Messages" (*British Journal of Canadian Studies* 4 – 1989; 109-135).

Martin, Joe. "William Lyon Mackenzie King: Canada's First Management Consultant?" (*Business Quarterly* 56:1 – Summer 1991; 31-35).

Martin, Lawrence. *The Myth of Bilateral Bliss, 1867–1982* (Doubleday, Toronto, 1982).

———. *The Presidents and the Prime Ministers: Washington and Ottawa Face to Face* (Doubleday, Toronto, 1982).

———. *Chrétien, Vol. 1, The Will to Win* (Lester, Toronto, 1995).

———. *The Antagonist: Lucien Bouchard and the Politics of Delusion* (Penguin, Toronto, 1998).

———. *Iron Man: The Defiant Reign of Jean Chrétien* (Viking, Toronto, 2003).

Martin, Patrick, Allan Gregg and George Perlin. *Contenders: The Tory Quest for Power* (Prentice-Hall, Scarborough, 1983).

Martin, Paul. *A Very Public Life, Vol. 2, So Many Worlds* (Deneau, Toronto, 1985).

———. *Hell or High Water: My Life In and Out of Politics* (McClelland & Stewart, Toronto, 2008).

Maryse, Robert. *Negotiating NAFTA: Explaining the Outcome in Culture, Textiles, Autos and Pharmaceuticals* (University of Toronto Press, Toronto, 2000).

Maslove, Alan M. and Gene Swimmer. *Wage Controls in Canada, 1975–78: A Study of Public Decision Making* (Institute for Research on Public Policy, Montreal, 1980).

Massey, Vincent. *What's Past Is Prologue* (Macmillan Company, Toronto, 1963).

Masters, D.C. *Canada in World Affairs, 1953–1955* (Oxford University Press, Toronto, 1959).

McCall, Bruce. *Thin Ice: Coming of Age in Canada* (Random House, Toronto, 1997).

McCall-Newman, Christina. *Grits: An Intimate Portrait of the Liberal Party* (Macmillan of Canada, Toronto, 1982).

McCalla, Douglas. *Planting the Province: The Economic History of Upper Canada* (University of Toronto Press, Toronto, 1993).

McClellan, David S. and David C. Acheson. *Among Friends: Personal Letters of Dean Acheson* (Dodd Mead, New York, 1980).

McCreery, Christopher. *The Order of Canada: Its Origins, History and Development* (University of Toronto Press, Toronto, 2005).

McDermott, James. *Martin Frobisher: Elizabethan Privateer* (Yale University Press, New Haven, 2001).

McDowell, Duncan. *Quick to the Frontier: Canada's Royal Bank* (McClelland & Stewart, Toronto, 1993).

McGowan, Mark. *The Waning of the Green: Catholics, the Irish and Identity in Toronto, 1887–1922* (McGill-Queen's University Press, Montreal/Kingston, 1999).

McGregor, F.A. *The Fall and Rise of Mackenzie King* (Macmillan, Toronto, 1962).

McIlwraith, T.F. Edited by E.K. Muller. *North America: The Historical Geography of a Changing Continent* (Rowman & Littlefield, Lanham, 2001).

McIninch, Elizabeth and Arthur Milnes, eds. *Politics of Purpose: 40th Anniversary Edition* (McGill-Queen's University Press, Montreal/Kingston, 2009).

McInnis, Edgar. *Canada: A Political and Social History* (Holt, Rinehart, and Winston, 1947).

———. *The Unguarded Frontier* (Doubleday, Duran & Company, New York, 1942).

McKenty, Neil. *Mitch Hepburn* (McClelland & Stewart, Toronto, 1967).

McLaren, Angus and Arlene Tigar McLaren. *The Bedroom and the State: The Changing Practices and Politics of Contraception and Abortion in Canada, in 1880–1980* (McClelland & Stewart, Toronto, 1986).

McLaughlin, Audrey. *A Woman's Place: My Life and Politics* (Macfarlane, Walter & Ross, Toronto, 1992).

McMillan, Alan D. *Native People and Cultures of Canada: An Anthropological Overview* (Douglas & McIntyre, Vancouver, 1995).

McMullen, Stan. *Anatomy of a Séance: A History of Spirit Communication in Central Canada* (McGill-Queen's University Press, Montreal, 2004).

McNaught, K.W. *A Prophet in Politics* (Oxford University Press, Toronto, 1959).

McRoberts, Kenneth. *Misconceiving Canada: The Struggle for National Unity* (Oxford University Press, Toronto, 1997).

——— and Patrick Monahan, eds. *The Charlottetown Accord, the Referendum and the Future of Canada* (University of Toronto Press, Toronto, 1993).

McTeer, Maureen. *In My Own Name: A Memoir* (Random House, Toronto, 2003).

Meisel, John. "The Boob-Tube Election: Three Aspects of the 1984 Landslide" in *The Canadian House of Commons: Essays in Honour of Norman Ward*. Edited by John C. Courtney, 341-72 (University of Calgary Press, Calgary, 1985).

———. *Working Papers on Canadian Politics* (McGill-Queen's University Press, Montreal & Kingston, 1973).

Meisel, John. *The Canadian General Election of 1957* (University of Toronto Press, Toronto, 1962).

Merchant, Livingston T., ed. *Neighbors Taken for Granted: Canada and the United States* (Praeger, New York, 1966).

Michaud, Nelson and Kim Richard Nossal, eds. *Diplomatic Departures: The Conservative Era in Canadian Foreign Policy, 1984–1993* (UBC Press, Vancouver, 2001).

Miedema, Gary R. *For Canada's Sake: Public Religion, Centennial Celebrations, and the Re-making of Canada in the 1960s* (McGill-Queen's University Press, Montreal & Kingston, 2005).

Milgaard, Joyce with Peter Edwards. *A Mother's Story: My Fight to Free My Son David* (Doubleday, Toronto, 1999).

Miller, Carman. *Canada's Little War: Fighting for the British Empire in Southern Africa, 1899–1902* (James Lorimer & Company, Toronto, 2003).

Miller, J.R. *Skyscrapers Hide the Heavens: A History of Indian-White Relations in Canada* (University of Toronto Press, Toronto, 1989).

Miquelon, Dale. *New France, 1701–1744* (McClelland & Stewart, Toronto, 1987).

Moher, Mark. "The Biography in Politics: Mackenzie King in 1935" (*Canadian Historical Review* 55:2 – June 1974; 239-248).

Moir, John S. *Church and State in Canada West* (University of Toronto Press, Toronto, 1959).

Monahan, Patrick J. *Meech Lake: The Inside Story* (University of Toronto Press, Toronto, 1991).

Moneypenny, William F. and George E. Buckle. *The Life of Benjamin Disraeli, Earl of Beaconsfield* (Peter Davies, London, 1929).

Montgomery, Bernard Law (Viscount). *The Memoirs of Field Marshal Montgomery* (Collins, London, 1958).

Morin, Claude. *Le Pouvoir Québécois en Négociation* (Boréal Express, Montreal, 1972).

Morton, Arthur S. *History of the Canadian West to 1870–1871* (University of Toronto Press, Toronto, 1973).

Morton, Desmond. *A Military History of Canada* (Hurtig Publishers, Edmonton, 1985).

Morton, H.V. *Atlantic Meeting: An Account of Mr. Churchill's Voyage in HMS Prince of Wales, in August 1941 with President Roosevelt Which Resulted in the Atlantic Charter* (Reginald Saunders, Toronto, 1943).

Morton, W.L. *The Kingdom of Canada: A General History from Earliest Times* (McClelland & Stewart, Toronto, 1960).

———. *The Progressive Party in Canada* (University of Toronto Press, Toronto, 1950).

———. *Manitoba: A History* (University of Toronto Press, Toronto, 1957).

———. *The Red River Journal of Alexander Begg* (Champlain Society, Toronto, 1956).

———. *The Critical Years: The Union of British North America, 1857–1873* (McClelland & Stewart, Toronto, 1964).

Muhlstein, Anka. *La Salle: Explorer of the North American Frontier* (Arcade Publishing, New York, 2011).

Muggeridge, John. "Why Trudeau, in 1973, Became a Monarchist" (*Saturday Night*, January 1974).

Mulroney, Brian. *Memoirs 1939–1993* (McClelland & Stewart, Toronto, 2007).

———. *Where I Stand* (McClelland & Stewart, Toronto, 1983).

Munro, W.B. *The Seigneurial System in Canada* (Harvard University Press, Cambridge, 1907).

Murphy, Rae, Robert Chodos and Nick auf der Maur. *Brian Mulroney: The Boy from Baie-Comeau* (James Lorimer & Company, Toronto, 1984).

Murray, Geoffrey. "Glimpses of Suez 1956" (*International Journal* – Winter 1973–74: 46-48).

Murrow, C. *Henri Bourassa and French-Canadian Nationalism: Opposition to Empire* (Harvest House, Montreal, 1968).

Nash, Knowlton. *Kennedy and Diefenbaker: Fear and Loathing across the Undefended Border* (McClelland & Stewart, Toronto, 1990).

Neatby, Hilda. *Quebec: The Revolutionary Age, 1760–1791* (McClelland & Stewart, Toronto, 1966).

Neatby, H. Blair. *W.L.M. King, Vols. I, II, III* (University of Toronto Press, Toronto, 1968–1977).

———. *The Politics of Chaos: Canada in the Thirties* (Macmillan, Toronto, 1972).

Nel, Elizabeth. *Mr. Churchill's Secretary* (Hodder & Stoughton, London, 1960).

Nelles, H.V. *The Politics of Development: Forests, Mines and Hydro-Electric Power in Ontario, 1849–1941* (Macmillan, Toronto, 1974).

———. *The Art of Nation-Building: Pageantry and Spectacle in Quebec's Tercentenary* (University of Toronto Press, Toronto, 1999).

Nemni, Max and Monique. *Young Trudeau, 1919–1944: Son of Quebec, Father of Canada* (McClelland & Stewart, Toronto, 2006).

———. *Trudeau Transformed: The Shaping of a Statesman, 1944–1965.* Translated by George Tombs (McClelland & Stewart, Toronto, 2011).

Neufeld, E.P. *The Financial System of Canada: Its Growth and Development* (Macmillan Company, Toronto, 1973).

New, C.W. *Lord Durham* (Oxford University Press, London, 1929).

Newman, Peter C. *The Canadian Establishment, I: The Great Dynasties* (McClelland & Stewart, Toronto, 1975).

———. *The Canadian Revolution* (Viking, Toronto, 1995).

———. *Flame of Power: Intimate Profiles of Canada's Greatest Businessmen* (Longmans, Green, Toronto, 1959).

———. *Renegade in Power: The Diefenbaker Years* (McClelland & Stewart, Toronto, 1963).

———. *The Secret Mulroney Tapes: Unguarded Confessions of a Prime Minister* (Random House, Toronto, 2005).

———. *The Distemper of Our Times: Canadian Politics in Transition, 1963–1968* (McClelland & Stewart, Toronto, 1990).

———. *A Nation Divided: Canada and the Coming of Pierre Trudeau* (Alfred A. Knopf, New York, 1969).

———. *True North Not Strong and Free* (McClelland & Stewart, Toronto, 2004).

Nichols, Marjorie. *Mark My Words: The Memoirs of a Very Political Reporter* (Douglas & McIntyre, Toronto, 1992).

Nicholson, Murray W. *Woodside and the Victorian Family of John King* (Ottawa National Historic Parks and Sites Branch, Ottawa, 1984).

Nicolson, Harold. *Diaries and Letters, 1939–1945.* Edited by Nigel Nicolson (Collins, London, 1967).

Nicolson, Nigel. *Alex: The Life of Field Marshal Earl Alexander of Tunis* (Weidenfeld & Nicolson, London, 1973).

Niegarth, Kirk. *William Lyon Mackenzie King's 1908 Adventure in Diplomacy: Coming Back a Public Man* (Unpublished paper presented at the Canadian Historical Association Meetings – May 2009).

Nielsen, Erik. *This House Is Not a Home* (Macmillan, Toronto, 1989).

Noel, S.J.R. *Patrons, Clients, Brokers: Ontario Society and Politics, 1791–1896* (University of Toronto Press, Toronto, 1990).

Nolan, Brian. *King's War: Mackenzie King and the Politics of War 1939–1945* (Random House, Toronto, 1988).

Norman, Herbert. *Japan's Emergence as a Modern State: Political and Economic Problems of the Meiji Period* (Institute of Pacific Relations, New York, 1940).

Norrie, Kenneth and Douglas Owram. *A History of the Canadian Economy* (Harcourt Brace Jovanovich, Toronto, 1991).

Nute, G.L. *Caesars of the Wilderness* (Appleton-Century, New York, 1943).

O'Leary, Gratton, ed. *Unrevised and Unrepented: Debating Speeches and Others by the Rt. Hon. Arthur Meighen* (Clarke, Irwin & Company, Toronto, 1949).

O'Leary, Gratton. *Recollections of People, Press and Politics* (McClelland & Stewart, Toronto, 1977).

Oliver, Craig. *Oliver's Twist: The Life and Times of an Unapologetic Newshound* (Viking, Toronto, 2011).

Oliver, Michael. *Social Purpose for Canada* (University of Toronto Press, Toronto, 1961).

Oliver, Peter. *G. Howard Ferguson: Ontario Tory* (University of Toronto Press, Toronto, 1977).

Ormsby, Margaret. *British Columbia: A History* (Macmillan Company, Toronto, 1958).

O'Sullivan, Sean. *Both My Houses: From Politics to Priesthood* (Key Porter Books, Toronto, 1986).

Owen, Frank. *Tempestuous Journey: Lloyd George, His Life and Times* (Hutchinson, London, 1954).

Owram, Douglas. *Promise of Eden: The Canadian Expansionist Movement and the Idea of the West* (University of Toronto Press, Toronto, 1980).

———. *The Government Generation: Canadian Intellectuals and the State, 1900–1945* (University of Toronto Press, Toronto, 1986).

———. *Born at the Right Time: A History of the Baby Boom Generation* (University of Toronto Press, Toronto, 1996).

Pacy, Desmond. *Creative Writing in Canada* (Ryerson Press, Toronto, 1961).

Palmer, Bryan D. *Working-Class Experience: Rethinking the History of Canadian Labour, 1800–1991* (McClelland & Stewart, Toronto, 1992).

Paltiel, K.Z. *Political Party Financing in Canada* (McClelland & Stewart, Toronto, 1970).

Pargellis, Stanley M. *Lord Loudoun in North America* (Oxford University Press, London, 1933).

Park, Julian. *The Culture of Contemporary Canada* (Cornell University Press, Ithaca, 1957).

Parker, Richard. *John Kenneth Galbraith: His Life, His Politics, His Economics* (HarperCollins, Toronto, 2005).

Parkin, George R. *Sir John A. Macdonald* (Oxford University Press, Toronto, 1926).

Parr, Joy. *Domestic Goods: The Material, the Moral and the Economic in the Postwar Years* (University of Toronto Press, Toronto, 1999).

Patry, André. *Le Québec dans le Monde* (Leméac, Montreal, 1980).

Pearson, Lester B. *Mike: The Memoirs of the Rt. Hon. Lester B. Pearson, 3 Vols.* (University of Toronto Press, Toronto, 1972).

———. *Democracy in World Politics* (Saunders, Toronto, 1955).

———. *Words and Occasions* (University of Toronto Press, Toronto, 1970).

Pelletier, Gerard. *The October Crisis.* Translated by Joyce Marshall (McClelland & Stewart, Toronto, 1971).

Penner, Norman. *Canadian Communism: The Stalin Years* (Methuen, Toronto, 1988).

Penniman, Howard, ed. *Canada at the Polls, 1984* (Duke University Press, Durham, 1988).

Penslar, Derek J., Michael R. Marrus and Janice Gross Stein, eds. *Contemporary Antisemitism: Canada and the World* (University of Toronto Press, Toronto, 2005).

Perlin, George. *The Tory Syndrome: Leadership Politics in the Progressive Conservative Party* (McGill-Queen's University Press, Montreal & Kingston, 1980).

Peyrefitte, Alain. *C'était de Gaulle, III* (Fayard, Paris, 1997).

Phillips, Nathan. *Mayor of All the People* (McClelland & Stewart, Toronto, 1967).

Picard, Jean-Claude. *Camille Laurin: L'homme debout* (Boréal, Montreal, 2001).

Pickersgill, J.W. *My Years with Louis St. Laurent: A Political Memoir* (University of Toronto Press, Toronto, 1975).

———. *Seeing Canada Whole: A Memoir* (Fitzhenry & Whiteside, Markham, 1994).

———. *The Road Back, by a Liberal in Opposition* (University of Toronto Press, Toronto, 1986).

——— and Donald Forster. *The Mackenzie King Record, Vols. 3 and 4* (University of Toronto Press, Toronto, 1960).

Pierson, George W. *Tocqueville in America* (Johns Hopkins University, Baltimore, 1996).

Plamondon, Bob. *Blue Thunder: The Truth About the Conservatives from Macdonald to Harper* (Key Porter Books, 2009, Toronto).

———. *The Truth About Trudeau* (Great River Media, Ottawa, 2013).

Plecas, Bob. *Bill Bennett: A Mandarin's View* (Douglas & McIntyre, Vancouver, 2006).

Plumptre, A.F.W. *Three Decades of Decision: Canada and the World Monetary System, 1944–1975* (McClelland & Stewart, Toronto, 1977).

Poitras, Jacques. *The Right Fight: Bernard Lord and the Conservative Dilemma* (Goose Lane Editions, Fredericton, 2004).

Pope, Joseph (Sir), ed. *Correspondence of Sir John Macdonald* (Oxford University Press, Toronto, 1921).

———. *Memoirs of the Right Honourable Sir John A. Macdonald* (Musson Book Co., Toronto, 1894).

Pope, Maurice A. *Soldiers and Politicians* (University of Toronto Press, Toronto, 1962).

Potvin, André, Michel Letourneux and Robert Smith. *L'Anti-Trudeau: Choix de textes.* (Éditions Parti-pris, Montreal, 1972).

Pound, Richard. *Chief Justice W.R. Jackett: By the Law of the Land* (McGill-Queen's University Press, Montreal & Kingston, 1999).

Stikeman Elliott: The First Fifty Years (McGill-Queen's University Press, Montreal & Kingston, 2002).

Powe, B.W. *Mystic Trudeau: The Firs and the Rose* (Thomas Allen, Toronto, 2007).

Prang, Margaret. "The Origins of Public Broadcasting in Canada" (*Canadian Historical Review 46*, No. 1, 1965).

———. *N.W. Rowell: Ontario Nationalist* (University of Toronto Press, Toronto, 1975).

Quinn, Herbert F. *The Union Nationale: A Study in Quebec Nationalism* (University of Toronto Press, Toronto, 1963).

Radwanski, George. *Trudeau* (Macmillan, Toronto, 1978).

Rae, Bob. *From Protest to Power: Personal Reflections on a Life in Politics* (Penguin, Toronto, 1997).

Rasporich, Anthony W., ed. *William Lyon Mackenzie King* (Holt Rinehart & Winston of Canada, Toronto, 1972).

Rea, J.E. *T.A. Crerar: A Political Life* (McGill-Queen's University Press, Montreal & Kingston, 1997).

———. "The Conscription Crisis: What Really Happened?" *(The Beaver* 74:2 – April/May 1994; 10-19).

Reardon, Terry. *Winston Churchill and Mackenzie King: So Similar, So Different* (Dundurn, Toronto, 2012).

Regehr, R.D. *The Beauharnois Scandal* (University of Toronto Press, Toronto, 1990).

Regenstreif, Peter. *The Diefenbaker Interlude: Parties and Voting in Canada* (Longman, Don Mills, 1965).

Reid, Escott. *Radical Mandarin: The Memoirs of Escott Reid* (University of Toronto Press, Toronto, 1989).

———. *Diplomat and Scholar* (McGill-Queen's University Press, Montreal & Kingston, 2004).

———. *Time of Fear and Hope: The Making of the North Atlantic Treaty, 1947–1949* (McClelland & Stewart, Toronto, 1977).

Reynolds, David. *In Command of History: Churchill Fighting and Writing the Second World War* (Allen Lane, London, 2004).

Reynolds, Louise. *Mackenzie King: Friends & Lovers* (Trafford Publishing, Victoria, 2005).

Ricci, Nino. *Extraordinary Canadians: Pierre Elliott Trudeau* (Penguin, Toronto, 2009).

Rich, E.E. *History of the Hudson's Bay Company, 1670–1870*, 2 Vols. (Hudson's Bay Record Society, London, 1958 & 1959).

———. *The Fur Trade and the Northwest, to 1857* (McClelland & Stewart, Toronto, 1967).

Richards, David Adams. *Extraordinary Canadians: Lord Beaverbrook* (Penguin, Toronto, 2008).

Richardson, James D., ed. *A Compilation of the Messages and Papers of the Presidents*, vol. ix, U.S. Grant (Bureau of National Literature, Inc., New York, 1897).

Richler, Mordecai. *The Apprenticeship of Duddy Kravitz* (Deutsch, London, 1959).

———. *St. Urbain's Horseman* (McClelland & Stewart, Toronto, 1971).

———. *Oh Canada! Oh Quebec!: Requiem for a Divided Country* (Viking, Toronto, 1992).

Riddell, W. Craig. *Dealing with Inflation and Unemployment in Canada* (University of Toronto Press, Toronto, 1986).

Ritchie, Charles. *The Siren Years: A Canadian Diplomat Abroad, 1937–1945* (Macmillan, Toronto, 1974).

———. *Diplomatic Passport: More Undiplomatic Diaries, 1946–1962* (Macmillan, Toronto, 1981).

———. *Storm Signals: More Undiplomatic Diaries, 1962–1971* (Macmillan, Toronto, 1983).

Ritchie, Gordon. *Wrestling with the Elephant: The Inside Story of the Canada-US Trade Wars* (Macfarlane, Walter & Ross, Toronto, 1997).

Roazen, Paul. *Canada's King: An Essay in Political Psychology* (Mosaic Press, Oakville, 1998).

Roberts, Andrew. *Eminent Churchillians* (Simon & Schuster, New York, 1994).

———. *Masters and Commanders: The Military Geniuses Who Led the West to Victory in WWII* (Penguin, Toronto, 2009).

Robertson, Barbara. *Wilfrid Laurier: The Great Conciliator* (Oxford University Press, Toronto, 1958).

Robertson, Gordon. *Memoirs of a Very Civil Servant: Mackenzie King to Pierre Trudeau* (University of Toronto Press, Toronto, 2000).

Robertson, Terence. *The Shame and the Glory: Dieppe* (McClelland & Stewart, Toronto, 1962).

———. *Crisis: The Inside Story of the Suez Conspiracy* (McClelland & Stewart, Toronto, 1964).

Robin, Martin. *The Rush for Spoils: The Company Province, B.C. 1871–1933* (McClelland & Stewart, Toronto, 1972).

———. *Pillars of Profit: The Company Province, 1934–1972* (McClelland & Stewart, Toronto, 1973).

Robinson, Basil. *Diefenbaker's World: A Populist in Foreign Affairs* (University of Toronto Press, Toronto, 1989).

Rogers, Norman McLeod. *Mackenzie King* (George N. Morang & Thomas Nelson & Sons 1935 – a revised and extended edition of a biographical sketch by John Lewis, published in 1925).

Romanow, Roy, John Whyte and Howard Leeson. *Canada . . . Notwithstanding* (Carswell, Methuen, Toronto, 1984).

Ronning, Chester. *From the Boxer Rebellion to the People's Republic: A Memoir of China in Revolution* (Pantheon, New York, 1974).

Ross, Douglas. *In the Interest of Peace: Canada and Vietnam 1954–1973* (University of Toronto Press, Toronto, 1984).

Roy, Patricia, J.L. Granatstein, Masako Lino and Hiroko Takamura. *Mutual Hostages: Canadians and Japanese During the Second World War* (University of Toronto Press, Toronto, 1990).

Rumilly, R. *Histoire de la province du Québec* (1940 to 1969 – 41 Vols., various publishers).

Russell, Bob. *Back to Work?: Labour, State and Industrial Relations in Canada* (Nelson Canada, Toronto, 1990).

Russell, Peter. *Constitutional Odyssey: Can Canadians Be a Sovereign People?* (University of Toronto Press, Toronto, 1992).

Rutherford, Paul. "Designing Culture: Reflections on a Post-Modern Project" in *Media, Policy, National Identity and Citizenry in Changing Democratic Societies: The Case of Canada.* Edited by J. Smith, 184-94 (Duke University, Canadian Studies Center, Durham, 1998).

———. *When Television Was Young* (University of Toronto Press, Toronto, 1990).

———. *Weapons of Mass Persuasion: Marketing the War Against Iraq* (University of Toronto Press, Toronto, 2004).

Ryan, William F. *The Clergy and Economic Growth in Quebec, 1896–1914* (Presses de l'Université Laval, Quebec, 1966).

Sackville-West, Vita. *Daughter of France* (London, 1959).

Safarian, A.E. *The Canadian Economy During the Great Depression* (Carleton University Press, Ottawa, 1970).

Sanger, Clyde. *Malcolm MacDonald: Bringing an End to Empire* (McGill-Queen's University Press, Montreal, 1995).

Saunders, E.M. *The Life and Letters of the Rt. Hon. Sir Charles Tupper* (Cassell and Company, Ltd., London and New York, 1916).

Sawatsky, John. *Gouzenko: The Untold Story* (Macmillan, Toronto, 1984).

———. *The Insiders: Government, Business, and the Lobbyists* (McClelland & Stewart, Toronto, 1987).

Saywell, J.T. *The Journal of Lady Aberdeen* (Champlain Society, Toronto, 1960).

———, ed. *Canadian Annual Review of Politics and Public Affairs, 1971* (University of Toronto Press, 1972).

———, ed. *Canadian Annual Review of Politics and Public Affairs, 1973* (University of Toronto Press, 1974).

———. *Just Call Me Mitch: The Life of Mitchell F. Hepburn* (University of Toronto Press, Toronto, 1991).

Schama, Simon. *Rough Crossings: Britain, the Slaves and the American Revolution* (Viking, Toronto, 2006).

Schenkel, Albert F. *The Rich Man and the Kingdom: John D. Rockefeller Jr. and the Protestant Establishment* (Fortress Press, Minneapolis, 1995).

Schull, Joseph. *Laurier: The First Canadian* (Macmillan, Toronto, 1966).

Scott, Frank and Michael Oliver, eds. *Quebec States Her Case* (Macmillan, Toronto, 1966).

Scott, F.R. and A.J.M. Smith, eds. *The Blasted Pine* (Macmillan, Toronto, 1967).

Scott, J. *Sweat and Struggle: Working Class Struggles in Canada, 1789–1899, Vol. 1* (New Star Books, Vancouver, 1974).

Segal, Hugh. *No Surrender: Reflections of a Happy Warrior in the Tory Crusade* (HarperCollins, Toronto, 1996).

Sellar, Robert. *The Tragedy of Quebec* (University of Toronto Press, Toronto, 1973).

Sharp, Mitchell. *Which Reminds Me . . . A Memoir* (University of Toronto Press, Toronto, 1994).

Sharp, Paul F. *Whoop-Up Country: The Canadian-American West, 1865–1885, 2 Vols.* (University of Minnesota Press, Minneapolis, 1955).

Sheppard, Robert and Michael Valpy. *The National Deal: The Fight for a Canadian Constitution* (Fleet, Toronto, 1982).

Shermer, Michael. *Why People Believe Weird Things* (Henry Holt, New York, 2002).

Sherrard, O.A. *Life of Lord Chatham*, 3 vols. (Bodley Head, London, 1955).

Shortt, A. and A.G. Doughty. *Canada and Its Provinces*, 23 Vols. (Glasgow, Brook & Company, Toronto, 1914).

Shuckburgh, Evelyn. *Descent to Suez: Diaries 1951–1956* (Weidenfeld & Nicolson, London, 1986).

Siegfried, André. *The Race Question in Canada* (McClelland & Stewart, Toronto, 1966).

Silver, Arthur. *The French-Canadian Idea of Confederation, 1864–1900* (University of Toronto Press, Toronto, 1997).

Simeon, Richard. *Federal-Provincial Diplomacy: The Making of Recent Policy in Canada* (University of Toronto Press, Toronto, 1972).

Simpson, Jeffrey. *Spoils of Power: The Politics of Patronage* (Collins, Toronto, 1988).
——. *Discipline of Power: The Conservative Interlude and the Liberal Restoration* (University of Toronto Press, Toronto, 1996).
Singer, Barnett. *The Great Depression* (Collier Macmillan, Toronto, 1974).
Skelton, O.D. *The Life and Letters of Sir Wilfrid Laurier, 2 Vols.* (Oxford University Press, Canada, 1941).
——. *The Life and Times of Sir Alexander Tilloch Galt* (Oxford University Press, Toronto, 1920).
Slayton, Philip. *Mighty Judgment: How the Supreme Court Runs Your Life* (Penguin, Toronto, 2011).
Smith, Cynthia M. and Jack McLeod, eds. *Sir John: An Anecdotal Life of John A. Macdonald* (Oxford University Press, Toronto, 1989).
Smith, David. *The Regional Decline of a National Party: Liberals on the Prairies* (University of Toronto Press, Toronto, 1981).
Smith, David E., Peter MacKinnon and John C. Courtney, eds. *After Meech Lake: Lessons for the Future* (Fifth House Publishers, Saskatoon, 1991).
Smith, Denis. *Gentle Patriot: A Political Biography of Walter Gordon* (Hurtig Publishers, Edmonton, 1973).
——. *Rogue Tory: The Life and Legend of John G. Diefenbaker* (Macfarlane, Walter & Ross, Toronto, 1955).
Snider, Norman. *The Changing of the Guard* (Lester Orpen & Dennys, Toronto, 1985).
Snow, Dean. *The Iroquois* (Wiley-Blackwell, Oxford, 1996).
Soderlund, Walter C., E. Donald Briggs, Walter I. Romanow and Ronald H. Wagenberg. *Media and Elections in Canada* (Holt, Rinehart & Winston, Toronto, 1984).
Somerville, David. *Trudeau Revealed by His Actions and Words* (BMG Publishing, Richmond Hill, 1978).
Southam; Nancy, ed. *Pierre: Colleagues and Friends Talk About the Trudeau They Knew* (McClelland & Stewart, Toronto, 2005).
Soward, F.H., J.F. Parkinson, N.A.M. MacKenzie and T.W. MacDermott. *Canada in World Affairs: The Pre-War Years* (Oxford University Press, London, 1941).
Spaulding, William B. "Why Rockefeller Supported Medical Education in Canada: The William Lyon Mackenzie King Connection" (*Canadian Bulletin of Medical History* 10 – 1993; 67-76).
Spencer, Robert A. *Canada in World Affairs: From UN to NATO, 1946–1949* (Oxford University Press, Toronto, 1959).
Spicer, Keith. *Life Sentences: Memoirs of an Incorrigible Canadian* (McClelland & Stewart, Toronto, 2004).
Stacey, C.P. *Canada and the Age of Conflict, Vol. 1, 1867–1921* (Macmillan, Toronto, 1977).
——. *Mackenzie King and the Atlantic Triangle* (Macmillan, Toronto, 1976).
——. *Six Years of War: The Army in Canada, Britain and the Pacific, Vol. 1, Official History of the Canadian Army in the Second World War* (Queen's Printer, Ottawa, 1966).
——. *A Very Double Life* (Macmillan, Toronto, 1976).
——. "The Divine Mission: Mackenzie King and Hitler" (*Canadian Historical Review* 61:4 – 1980; 502-512).
——. *A Date with History: Memoirs of a Canadian Historian* (Deneau, Ottawa, 1985).
Stanley, G.F.G. *The Birth of Western Canada* (University of Toronto Press, Toronto, 1960).
——. *Canada's Soldiers* (Macmillan Company, Toronto, 1960).
——. *Louis Riel* (Ryerson Press, Toronto, 1963).
——. *New France, The Last Phase, 1744–1760* (McClelland & Stewart, Toronto, 1968).
Steed, Judy, ed. *Broadbent: The Pursuit of Power* (Penguin, Markham, 1989).
Steele, Ian K. *Betrayals: Fort William Henry and the "Massacre"* (Oxford University Press, New York, 1990).
Stevens, G.R. *History of the Canadian National Railways* (Macmillan, New York, 1973).
Stevens, Geoffrey. *Stanfield* (McClelland & Stewart, Toronto, 1973).
——. *The Player: The Life and Times of Dalton Camp* (Key Porter Books, Toronto, 2003).
Stevens, Paul. *The 1911 General Election: A Study in Canadian Politics* (Copp Clark, Toronto, 1970).
Stevenson, David. *Cataclysm: The First World War as Political Tragedy* (Basic Books, New York, 2004).
Stevenson, Garth. *Community Besieged: The Anglophone Minority and the Politics of Quebec* (McGill-Queen's University Press, Montreal & Kingston, 1999).
Stevenson, Michael D. *Canada's Greatest Wartime Muddle: National Selective Service and the Mobilization of Human Resources During World War II* (McGill-Queen's University Press, Montreal & Kingston, 2001).

Stewart, Douglas and William Tow. *The Limits of Alliance: NATO Out-of-Area Problems Since 1949* (Johns Hopkins University Press, Baltimore, 1990).

Stewart, Gordon and George Rawlyk. *A People Highly Favoured of God: The Nova Scotia Yankees and the American Revolution* (Toronto, 1972).

Stewart, Sandy. *From Coast to Coast: A Personal History of Radio in Canada* (CBC Enterprises, Toronto, 1985).

Stewart, Walter. *Shrug: Trudeau in Power* (New Press, Toronto, 1971).

Straight, Michael. *After Long Silence* (Collins, London, 1983).

Struthers, James. "Canadian Unemployment Policy in the 1930s" in *Readings in Canadian History: Volume Two.* Edited by R.D. Francis & Donald B. Smith (Nelson Canada, Toronto, 2002).

Stuart, Reginald C. *United States Expansionism and British North America 1775–1871* (University of North Carolina Press, Chapel Hill, 1988).

Stursberg, Peter. *Lester Pearson and the Dream of Unity* (Doubleday, Toronto, 1978).

———. *Lester Pearson and the American Dilemma* (Doubleday, Toronto, 1980).

———. *Diefenbaker: Leadership Gained, 1956–1962* (University of Toronto Press, Toronto, 1975).

———. *Diefenbaker: Leadership Lost, 1962–1967* (University of Toronto Press, Toronto, 1976).

Sullivan, Martin. *Mandate '68: The Year of Pierre Elliott Trudeau* (Doubleday, Toronto, 1968).

Sunahara, Ann Gomer. *The Politics of Racism: The Uprooting of Japanese Canadians During the Second World War* (James Lorimer & Company, Toronto, 1981).

Swainson, Neil A. *Conflict Over the Columbia: The Canadian Background to an Historic Treaty* (McGill-Queen's University Press, Montreal & Kingston, 1979).

Swatsky, John. *Gouzenko: The Untold Story* (Macmillan, Toronto, 1984).

Sweeny, Alistair. *George-Étienne Cartier* (McClelland & Stewart, Toronto, 1976).

Swettenham, John. *McNaughton.* 3 vols. (Ryerson Press, Toronto, 1969).

Swift, Jamie. *Odd Man Out: The Life and Times of Eric Kierans* (Douglas & McIntyre, Toronto, 1988).

Tanner, Marcus. *The Last of the Celts* (Yale University Press, New Haven, 2004).

Tansill, C.C. *Canadian-American Relations, 1875–1911* (Peter Smith, Gloucester, Mass., 1964, a reprint of 1943 edition).

Taras, David. *The Newsmakers* (Nelson Canada, Scarborough, 1990).

Taylor, A.J.P. *Beaverbrook* (Hamish Hamilton, London, 1972).

Taylor, Alan. *American Colonies* (Viking, New York, 2001).

———. *The Divided Ground: Indians, Settlers and the Northern Borderland of the American Revolution* (Alfred A. Knopf, New York, 2006).

Taylor, John H. *Ottawa: An Illustrated History* (James Lorimer & Company, Toronto, 1986).

Tetley, William. *The October Crisis, 1970: An Insider's View* (McGill-Queen's University Press, Montreal & Kingston, 2006).

Thatcher, Margaret. *The Downing Street Years* (HarperCollins, New York, 1993).

Thomas, L.H. *The Struggle for Responsible Government in the North-West Territories 1870–1897* (University Press of Toronto, Toronto, 1956).

Thompson, D.C. *Alexander Mackenzie: Clear Grit* (Macmillan Company, Toronto, 1960).

Thomson, Dale. *Louis St. Laurent: Canadian* (Macmillan, Toronto, 1967).

———. *Vive le Québec Libre* (Deneau, Toronto, 1988).

———. *Jean Lesage and the Quiet Revolution* (Macmillan, Toronto, 1984).

Thompson, John Herd and Allen Seager. *Canada 1922–1939: Decades of Discord* (McClelland & Stewart, Toronto, 1985).

Thordarson, Bruce. *Trudeau and Foreign Policy: A Study in Decision-Making* (Oxford University Press, Toronto, 1972).

Thoreau, Henry David. *A Yankee in Canada* (Ticknor & Fields, Boston, 1866).

Tobin, Brian with John Lawrence Reynolds. *All in Good Time* (Penguin, Toronto, 2002).

Toner, Glen. *The Politics of Energy: The Development and Implementation of the NEP* (Methuen, Toronto, 1985).

Trigger, Bruce & Wilcomb E. Washburn. *The Cambridge History of the Native Peoples of the Americas – Vol. 1, Part 1, North America* (Cambridge University Press, Cambridge, 1996).

Trofimenkoff, Susan M. *The Dream of Nation: A Social and Intellectual History of Quebec* (Gage, Toronto, 1983).

Trotter, R.G. *Canadian Federation* (J.M. Dent & Sons, Toronto, 1924).

Trudel, M. *L'Influence de Voltaire au Canada* (Fides, Montreal, 1945).

———. *Memoirs of a Less Travelled Road: A Historian's Life* (Véhicule Press, Montreal, 2002).

Trudeau, Margaret. *Beyond Reason* (Paddington Press, New York & London, 1979).

Trudeau, P.E. *La Féderalisme et la Société Canadienne Français* (Editions, HMH, Montreal, 1967).

———. *Memoirs* (McClelland & Stewart, Toronto, 1993).

———, Gerard Pelletier, ed. *Against the Current: Selected Writings 1939–1996* (McClelland & Stewart, Toronto, 1996).

———, Thomas Axworthy, eds. *Towards a Just Society* (Viking, Markham, 1990).

Tucker, G.N. *The Commercial Revolution in Canadian History* (Yale University Press, New Haven, 1936).

Tulchinsky, Gerald. *Branching Out: The Transformation of the Canadian Jewish Community* (Stoddart, Toronto, 1998).

Tupper, Charles (Sir). *Recollections of Sixty Years in Canada* (Cassell and Company, Toronto, 1914).

Turner, John. *Politics of Purpose* (McClelland & Stewart, Toronto, 1968).

———. "The Senate of Canada – Political Conundrum" In *Canadian Issues: Essays in Honour of Henry F. Angus*. Edited by Robert M. Clark, 57-80 (University of Toronto Press, Toronto, 1961).

Underhill, Frank. "Concerning Mr. King" (*Canadian Forum* 30 – September 1950; 121-127).

———. *In Search of Canadian Liberalism* (University of Toronto Press, Toronto, 1960).

Vallières, Pierre. *Nègres blancs d'Amérique* (Parti-pris, Montreal, 1968).

Van Dusen, Thomas. *The Chief* (McGraw-Hill, Toronto, 1968).

——— with Susan Code. *Inside the Tent: Forty-Five Years on Parliament Hill* (General Store Publishing House, Burstown, n.d.).

Van Loon, Rick. "Reforming Welfare in Canada" (*Public Policy* 27:4 – Fall, 1979; 469-504).

Vastel, Michel. *The Outsider: The Life of Pierre Elliott Trudeau* (Macmillan, Toronto, 1990).

Veilleux, Gérard. *Les Relations Intergouvernementales au Canada, 1867–1967* (Presses de l'Université du Québec, Montreal, 1971).

Vigod, Bernard L. *Quebec Before Duplessis: The Political Career of Louis-Alexandre Taschereau* (McGill-Queen's University Press, Montreal & Kingston, 1986).

Villa, Brian Loring. *Unauthorized Action: Mountbatten and the Dieppe Raid* (Oxford University Press, Toronto, 1994).

Von Baeyer, Edwina. *Garden of Dreams: Kingsmere and Mackenzie King* (Dundurn, Toronto, 1990).

Wade, Mason. *The French Canadians* (Macmillan Company, Toronto, 1955).

Wagenberg, R.H., W.C. Soderlund, W.I. Romanow and E.D. Briggs. "Note: Campaigns, Images and Polls: Mass Media Coverage of the 1984 Canadian Election" (*Canadian Journal of Political Science* 21:1 – March 1988; 117-129).

Waiser, Bill. *Saskatchewan: A New History* (Fifth House, Calgary, 2005).

———. *All Hell Can't Stop Us: The On to Ottawa Trek and Regina Riot* (Fifth House, Calgary, 2003).

Waite, P.B. *The Life and Times of Confederation, 1864–1867* (University of Toronto Press, Toronto, 1961).

———. *Canada, 1874–1896: Arduous Destiny* (McClelland & Stewart, Toronto, 1971).

———. *Loner: Three Sketches of the Personal Life and Ideas of R.B. Bennett, 1870–1947* (University of Toronto Press, Toronto, 1992).

———. "Mackenzie King and the Italian Lady" (*The Beaver* 75:6 – December 1995/January 1996; 4-10).

———. "Mr. King and Lady Byng" (*The Beaver* 77:2 – April/May 1997; 24-30).

Walker, Michael, ed. *Which Way Ahead? Canada after Wage and Price Control* (Fraser Institute, Vancouver, 1977).

Wallin, Pamela. *Since You Asked* (Random House, Toronto, 1998).

Walpole, Horace. *Memoirs of the Reign of King George the Second* (Colburn, London, 1846).

Walsh, H.H. *The Christian Church in Canada* (Ryerson Press, Toronto, 1956).

Ward, N., ed. *Party Politician: The Memoirs of Chubby Power* (Macmillan Company, Toronto, 1966).

——— and David Smith. *Jimmy Gardiner: Relentless Liberal* (University of Toronto Press, Toronto, 1990).

Ward, W. Peter. *White Canada Forever* (McGill-Queen's University Press, Montreal, 1978).

Wardhaugh, Robert A. *Mackenzie King and the Prairie West* (University of Toronto Press, Toronto, 2000).

Warner, D.F. *The Idea of Continental Union* (University of Kentucky Press, Louisville, 1960).

Waskin, E.W. (Sir). *Canada and the States: Recollections, 1851 to 1886* (Ward, Lock and Co., London, 1887).

Waterfield, Donald. *Continental Waterboy: The Columbia River Controversy* (Clark, Irwin, and Company, Toronto, 1970).

Watkins, Ernest. *R.B. Bennett: A Biography* (Kingswood House, Toronto, 1963).

Watts, George. *The Bank of Canada: Origins and Early History* (Carleton University Press, Ottawa, 1993).

Watts, Ronald L. and Douglas M. Brown, eds. *Options for a New Canada* (University of Toronto Press, Toronto, 1991).

Wearing, J., ed. *The Ballot and Its Message: Voting in Canada* (Copp Clark, Toronto, 1991).

Wearing, Joseph. *The L-Shaped Party: The Liberal Party of Canada, 1958–1980* (McGraw-Hill Ryerson, Toronto, 1981).

Wells, Paul. *The Longer I'm Prime Minister: Stephen Harper and Canada, 2006–* (Random House Canada, Toronto, 2013).

Werth, Barry. *Strained Relations: Canadian Parties and Voters* (McClelland & Stewart, Toronto, 1988).

Westell, Anthony. *Paradox: Trudeau as Prime Minister* (Prentice-Hall, Scarborough, 1972).

Weston, Greg. *Reign of Error* (McGraw-Hill Ryerson, Toronto, 1988).

Wetzler, Scott. *Living with the Passive Aggressive Man* (Simon & Schuster, New York, 1992).

Wheare, K. C. *The Statute of Westminster and Dominion Status* (Oxford University Press, Toronto, 1934).

Whelan, Eugene, with Rick Archbold. *Whelan: The Man in the Green Stetson* (Irwin, Toronto, 1986).

Whitaker, Reginald. "Mackenzie King in the Dominion of the Dead" (*Canadian Forum* 55 – February 1976; 6-11).

———. *The Government Party: Organizing and Financing the Liberal Party of Canada 1930–1958* (University of Toronto Press, Toronto, 1977).

White, Richard. *The Middle Ground: Indians, Empires and Republics in the Great Lakes Region, 1650–1815* (Cambridge University Press, Cambridge, 1991).

Wiegman, Carl. *Trees to News* (McClelland & Stewart, Toronto, 1953).

Wier, Austin. *The Struggle for National Broadcasting in Canada* (McClelland & Stewart, Toronto, 1965).

Wigley, Philip G. *Canada and the Transition to Commonwealth: British-Canadian Relations, 1917–1926* (Cambridge University Press, New York, 1977).

Wilbur, John R.H. *The Bennett New Deal: Fraud or Portent?* (Copp Clark, Toronto, 1968).

———. *H.H. Stevens, 1878–1973.* (University of Toronto Press, Toronto, 1977).

———. *R.B. Bennett as a Reformer* (Canadian Historical Assoc., Historical Papers, 1969. 103-111).

Williams, Jeffrey. *Byng of Vimy* (Secker & Warburg, London, 1983).

Willoughby, William R. *The Joint Organizations of Canada and the United States* (University of Toronto Press, Toronto, 1979).

Wilson, Garrett and Kevin Wilson. *Diefenbaker for the Defence* (James Lorimer and Company, Toronto, 1988).

Wilson, G.E. *The Life of Robert Baldwin* (Ryerson Press, Toronto, 1933).

Wilton, Carol. *Popular Politics and Political Culture in Upper Canada 1800–1850* (McGill-Queen's University Press, Montreal & Kingston, 2000).

Winks, Robin W. *Canada and the United States: The Civil War Years* (Johns Hopkins University Press, Baltimore, 1960).

Winn, Conrad and John McMenemy. *Political Parties in Canada* (McGraw-Hill Ryerson, Toronto, 1976).

Wolf, Morris. "Tim Buck Too" (*Canadian Forum*, December 1991).

Wood, J. David. *Making Ontario: Agricultural and Colonization and Landscape Re-creation Before the Railway* (McGill-Queen's University Press, Montreal & Kingston, 2000).

Wood, Luis Aubrey. *A History of Farmers' Movements in Canada: The Origins and Development of Agrarian Protest 1872–1924* (University of Toronto Press, Toronto, 1975).

Wright, James V. *A History of the Native People of Canada, Vol. II, 1000 BC–AD 500* (Canadian Museum of Civilization, Ottawa, 1999).

Wright, Robert. *Three Nights in Havana: Pierre Trudeau, Fidel Castro, and the Cold War World* (HarperCollins, Toronto, 2007).

Zakuta, Leo. *A Protest Movement Becalmed: A Study of Change in the CCF* (University of Toronto Press, Toronto, 1964).

Zaslow, Morris. *The Northwest Expansion of Canada, 1914–1967* (McClelland & Stewart, Toronto, 1988).

Zinc, Lubor. "The Unpenetrated Problem of Pierre Trudeau" (*National Review*, June 25, 1982).

Index

Notes: A page number in *italic* indicates a photograph, illustration or map.
The lowercase letter *n* following a page number indicates a footnote.

1072 | RISE TO GREATNESS